LAW AND POPULAR CULTURE

CURRENT LEGAL ISSUES 2004

Volume 7

CURRENT LEGAL PUBLICATIONS

Law and Popular Culture

Current Legal Issues 2004

VOLUME 7

Edited by
MICHAEL FREEMAN
Professor of English Law
University College London

UNIVERSITY PRESS

Great Clarendon Street, Oxford OX2 6DP

Oxford University Press is a department of the University of Oxford.
It furthers the University's objective of excellence in research, scholarship,
and education by publishing worldwide in

Oxford New York

Auckland Bangkok Buenos Aires Cape Town Chennai Dar es Salaam Delhi Hong Kong
Istanbul Karachi Kolkata Kuala Lumpur Madrid Melbourne Mexico City
Nairobi São Paulo Shanghai Taipei Tokyo Toronto

Oxford is a registered trade mark of Oxford University Press in the UK and in
certain other countries

Published in the United States
by Oxford University Press Inc., New York

First published 2005

British Library Cataloguing in Publication Data
Data available

Library of Congress Cataloging-in-Publication Data

Law and popular culture / edited by Michael Freeman.
p. cm. — (current legal issues; v. 7)
Includes bibliographical references and index.
ISBN 0–19–927223–9 (hard cover : alk. paper) 1. Culture and law. 2. Law in literature. 3. Popular culture. I. Freeman, Michael D. A. II. Series.
K487. C8L393 2005
340'. 115—dc22

2004028387

ISBN 0–19–927223–9

1 3 5 7 9 10 8 6 4 2

Typeset by Newgen Imaging Systems (P) Ltd., Chennai, India
Printed in Great Britain
on acid-free paper by
Biddles Ltd., King's Lynn

General Editor's Preface

This volume contains the product of UCL's seventh annual international interdisciplinary colloquium held in July 2003. I hope *Law and Popular Culture* will give scholars and students as much pleasure as was enjoyed by those participating in the colloquium.

I convened the colloquium but was able to call on the assistance of many colleagues, to all of whom I am grateful. I was also ably assisted by Lisa Penfold, the Law Faculty's events organizer, and by various secretaries including Alison Compton, Sarah Petrie, and Laura Smith. I am very grateful to Clintons who provided some much-needed financial support for the colloquium.

Future colloquia include Law and Sociology in 2004, Law and Psychology in 2005 and Law and Philosophy in 2006. Further details of these colloquia and the ongoing programme may be sought from Michael Freeman at Bentham House, Endsleigh Gardens, London WC1H 0EG (uctlmdf@ucl.ac.uk).

Michael Freeman

May 2004

Contents

General Editor's Preface v
Table of Cases xi
Table of Statutes xiv

Law in Popular Culture 1
Michael Freeman

PART I: INTRODUCTORY THEMES

Law and Film Studies: Autonomy and Theory 21
Peter Robson

Where the Wild Things *Really* Are: Children's Literature and the Law 47
Desmond Manderson

The Absence of Contradiction and the Contradiction of Absence: Law, Ethics and the Holocaust 71
David M Seymour

PART II: REEL JUSTICE

Law's Enchantment: The Cinematic Jurisprudence of Krzysztof Kieslowski 87
Richard K Sherwin

When Celluloid Lawyers Started to Speak: Exploring Juriscinema's First Golden Age 109
Francis M Nevins

Emergency! Send a TV Show to Rescue Paramedic Services! 130
Paul Bergman

Procedural Unfairness in Real and Film Trials: Why do Audiences Understand Stories Placed in Foreign Legal Systems? 148
Stefan Machura

Military Justice in American Film and Television Drama: Starting Points for Ideological Criticism 160
Matthias Kuzina

Courtroom Sketching: Reflections on History, Law and the Image 173
Lynda Nead

What Movies Can Teach Law Students 183
John Denvir

PART III: THE NOVEL

Popular Fiction and Domestic Law: *East Lynne*, Justice, and the 'Ordeal of the Undecidable' 197
Marlene Tromp

Law's Agent: Cultivated Citizen or Popular Savage? The *Crash* of the Moral Mirror 212
Melanie Williams

Law's Diabolical Romance: Reflections on a New Jurisprudence of the Sublime 226
Leslie J Moran

Re-Imagining the Practice of Law: Popular Twentieth-Century Fiction by American Lawyer/Authors 243
David Ray Papke

The Materiality of Symbols: JG Ballard and Jurisprudence: Law, Image, Reproduction 273
Adam Gearey

L'œuil qui Pense: The Emotive as Grounds for the Pensive in Phenomenological Reflection 291
Claire Valier

PART IV: MUSIC

Doing Time and Doing it in Style 303
Milner S Ball

Why Law Needs Pop: Global Law and Global Music? 316
Thilo Tetzlaff

PART V: CRIME AND PUNISHMENT

Badfellas: Movie Psychos, Popular Culture, and Law 339
Nicole Rafter

Reel Violence: Popular Culture and Concerns about Capital Punishment in Contemporary American Society 358
Roberta M Harding

Public and Private Eyes 375
Lawrence M Friedman

Seeing Blind Spots: Corporate Misconduct in Film and Law 385
Michael Robertson

Repressed Memory Revisited: Popular Culture's Impact on the Law—Psychotherapy Debate 404
Stuart Weinstein

What Law Cannot Give: *From the Queen to the Chief Executive* 425
Anne S Y Cheung

PART VI: LAW, SEXUALITY AND THE POPULAR CULTURE

It's About *This*: Lesbians, Prison, Desire 449
Jenni Millbank

'Juliet and Juliet Would be More My Cup of Tea': Sexuality, Law and Popular Culture 470
Didi Herman

PART VII: HUMAN RIGHTS

Image as Evidence and Mediation: The Experience of the Nuremberg Trials 491
Christian Delage

Film, Culture and Accountability for Human Rights Abuses 504
Carolyn Patty Blum

Science Fiction as a World Tribunal 520
Wai Chee Dimock

PART VIII: SOME OTHER CULTURAL PHENOMENA

Neoliberalism, Shopping Malls and the End of 'Property'? 537
Malcolm Voyce

'Do You Want Fries With That?' The Franchise as a Cultural and Legal Phenomenon 560
Rex J Ahdar

PART IX: LAW, LAWYERING, AND THE POPULAR CULTURE

Legal Negotiation in Popular Culture: What are We Bargaining For? 583
Carrie Menkel-Meadow

Popular Culture and the American Adversarial Ideology 606
Michael Asimow

The Double Meaning of Law: Does it Matter if Film Lawyers are Unethical? 638
Steve Greenfield and Guy Osborn

Adaptation: What Post-Conviction Relief Practitioners in Death Penalty Cases Might Learn From Popular Storytellers about Narrative Persuasion 651
Philip N Meyer

Narrative Determination and the Figure of the Judge 677
David A Black

Index 687

Table of Cases

Armour v Anderson 1994 S.L.T. 1127; 1994 S.C.L.R. 642, IH (1 Div) 26
Australian Competition and Consumer Commission v Simply No-Knead (Franchising) Pty Ltd [2000] FCA 1365 576

Beasley v State 269 Ga 620, 627 (1998). 89
Bilgola Enterprises Ltd v Dymocks Franchise Systems (NSW) Pty Ltd [2000] 3 NZLR 169 572
Bobux Marketing Ltd v Raynor Marketing Ltd [2000] 1 NZLR 506 . . . . 564, 573
Burdine v Johnson, 262 F 3d 336 (5th Cir 2001) 372
Burger King Corp v Weaver 574

Cockrell v Burdine, 535 US 1120 (2002) 372
Cohen v California, 403 US 15, 25 (1971) 312
Commonwealth v Frangipane, 744 NE 2d 25 (Mass 2001) 420
Commonwealth v Graziano, 331 NE 808 (Mass 1975) 89
Commonwealth v Souza, 689 NE 2d 1359 (Mass App Ct 1998); 653 NE 2d 1127 (Mass App Ct 1995) 405

Daubert v Merrell Dow Pharmaceuticals, 509 US 579 (1993) 418, 419, 420
Dillon Holdings Ltd v Stirling Sports Francises Ltd, High Court Invercargill, CP10/00. 564
Doe v McKay, 700 NE 2d 1018, 1024 (Ill 1998) 417
DPP v Whyte Sub Nom Corbin v Whyte (Patrick Thomas); Corbin v Whyte (Pearl Rosemary); DPP v Whyte (Pearl Rosemary) [1972] A.C. 849; [1972] 3 W.L.R. 410; [1972] 3 All E.R. 12; (1973) 57 Cr. App. R. 74; [1972] Crim. L.R. 556; 116 S.J. 583, HL 214
Dymocks Franchise Systems (NSW) Pty Ltd v Bilgola Enterprises Ltd (1998) 8 TCLR 612, 628 . . . . 560, 564, 571, 572
Dymocks Franchise Systems (NSW) Pty Ltd v Todd [2002] UKPC 50; [2002] 2 All E.R. (Comm) 849, PC (NZ) 570, 573, 574

Echevarria v Secretary of Health and Human Services, 685 F2d 751 (2d Cir 1982). 614

Far Horizons Pty Ltd v McDonald's Australia Ltd [2000] VSC 310 . . . . 563, 571
Fitzpatrick v Sterling Housing Association Ltd [2001] 1 A.C. 27; [1999] 3 W.L.R. 1113; [1999] 4 All E.R. 705; [2000] 1 F.L.R. 271; [1999] 2 F.L.R. 1027; [2000] 1 F.C.R. 21; [2000] U.K.H.R.R. 25; 7 B.H.R.C. 200; (2000) 32 H.L.R. 178; [2000] L. & T.R. 44; [2000] Fam. Law 14; [1999] E.G.C.S. 125; (1999) 96(43) L.S.G. 3; [1999] N.P.C. 127; (2000) 79 P. & C.R. D4; Times, November 2, 1999; Independent, November 2, 1999, HL 25
Flanders v Cooper, 706 A 2d 589, 591 (Me 1998) 417
Ford v Garcia, 289 F 3d 1283 (11 Cir 2002). 505
Frye v United States, 293 F 1013 (DC Cir 1923) 418, 419, 420
Furman v Georgia, 408 US 238 (1972). 361, 362, 367, 368

Garret v City of New Berlin, 362 NW 2d 137 (Wis 1985) 416
General Electric Co v Joiner, 522 US 136 (1997). 420

Gillick v West Norfolk and Wisbech AHA [1986] A.C. 112; [1985] 3 W.L.R. 830; [1985] 3 All E.R. 402; [1986] Crim. L.R. 113; (1985) 82 L.S.G. 3531; (1985) 135 N.L.J. 1055; (1985) 129 S.J. 738, HL. 12
Gregg v Georgia, 428 US 153 (1976) 360, 362, 367

Hall v Hebert [1993] 2 S.C.R. 159 51
Harrogate BC v Simpson [1986] 2 F.L.R. 91; (1985) 17 H.L.R. 205; [1985] R.V.R. 10; [1986] Fam. Law 359, CA (Civ Div) 25
HKSAR v Hui Chi Wai, CACC 78/1999 (unreported judgement) 438
Hungerford v Jones, 722 A 2d 478 (NH 1998) 417
Hussain v United Kingdom; Singh v United Kingdom (1996) 22 E.H.R.R. 1; 1 B.H.R.C. 119; Times, February 26, 1996, ECHR 433, 434, 435, 436

Interfoto Picture Library Ltd v Stiletto Visual Programmes Ltd [1989] Q.B. 433; [1988] 2 W.L.R. 615; [1988] 1 All E.R. 348; (1988) 7 Tr. L.R. 187; (1988) 85(9) L.S.G. 45; (1987) 137 N.L.J. 1159; (1988) 132 S.J. 460, CA (Civ Div) 573

JAH v Wadle & Assoc, 589 NW 2d 256 (Iowa 1999) 417
Joseph Burstyn Inc v Wilson 343 US 495 (1952) 126

Kansas v Plaskett, 27 P 3d 890 (Kan 2001) 421
Kumbo Tire Co Ltd v Carmichael, 526 US 137 (1999) 420

Lloyds Bank Plc v Rosset [1991] 1 A.C. 107; [1990] 2 W.L.R. 867; [1990] 1 All E.R. 1111; [1990] 2 F.L.R. 155; (1990) 22 H.L.R. 349; (1990) 60 P. & C.R. 311; (1990) 140 N.L.J. 478, HL 79
Logerquist v Superior Court, 1P 3d 113 (Ariz 2000) 419, 420

Mabo v Queensland (1994) American L. Rev 397 545
McDonald's v Steel, 1997 569
Mutual Film Corp v Industrial Commission of Ohio 236 US 230 (1915) 126

Neffeld v Neffeld 1395 10

O v Wedd [2000] TASSC 74 540

R. v Bourne [1939] 1 K.B. 687 14
R. v Bywaters and Thompson [1922] 174, 175
R. v Calder & Boyars Ltd [1969] 1 Q.B. 151; [1968] 3 W.L.R. 974; [1968] 3 All E.R. 644; (1968) 52 Cr. App. R. 706; 133 J.P. 20; 112 S.J. 688, CA (Crim Div) 214
R. v Humphreys [1995] 4 All E.R. 1008; [1996] Crim. L.R. 431; (1995) 145 N.L.J. 1032; Independent, July 11, 1995, CA (Crim Div) 12
R. v Keegstra [1990] 3 S.C.R. 697, Sup Ct (Can) 322
R. v Perrin (Stephane Laurent) [2002] EWCA Crim 747, CA (Crim Div) 213
R. v R (Rape: Marital Exemption) Sub Nom R. v R (A Husband) [1992] 1 A.C. 599; [1991] 3 W.L.R. 767; [1991] 4 All E.R. 481; (1992) 94 Cr. App. R. 216; (1991) 155 J.P. 989; [1992] 1 F.L.R. 217; [1992] Crim. L.R. 207; [1992] Fam. Law 108; (1991) 155 J.P.N. 752; (1991) 141 N.L.J. 1481; (1991) 135 S.J.L.B. 181; Times, October 24, 1991; Independent, October 24, 1991; Guardian, October 30, 1991, HL 25

R. v Secretary of State for the Home Department Ex p. Venables; R. v Secretary of State for the Home Department Ex p. Thompson [1998] A.C. 407; [1997] 3 W.L.R. 23; [1997] 3 All E.R. 97; [1997] 2 F.L.R. 471; (1997) 9 Admin. L.R. 413; [1997] Fam. Law 789; (1997) 94(34) L.S.G. 27; (1997) 147 N.L.J. 955; Times, June 13, 1997; Independent, June 18, 1997, HL 425, 431, 432, 434, 436, 438, 439
Roe v Wade 410 US 113 (1973). 12, 17
Romagoza v Garcia (2003) 35 U of California Davis L Rev 1213. 504

S v HM Advocate Sub Nom Stallard v HM Advocate; 1989 S.L.T. 469; 1989 S.C.C.R. 248, HCJ Appeal 25
Sawyer v Midelfort, 595 NW 2d 423(Wis 1999) 415, 416, 417, 418
Schuste v Altenberg, 424 NW 2d 159 (Wis 1988) 415, 416
Shahzade v Gregory, 930 F Supp 673, 1996 (D Mass 1996) 405
Stallard v HM Advocate see S v HM Advocate
Standard Chartered PLC v Price Waterhouse, CV 88-34414 (Sup. Ct. Maricopa Co, Ariz, 1989) 88
Steel and Morris v McDonald's Restaurants Ltd [1999] EWCA Civ 1144 569
Stogner v California, 539 US 633 (2003) 411
Strickland v Washington, 466 US 668 (1984) 372

T v United Kingdom (24724/94); V v United Kingdom (24888/94) [2000] 2 All E.R. 1024 (Note); (2000) 30 E.H.R.R. 121; 7 B.H.R.C. 659; 12 Fed. Sent. R. 266; [2000] Crim. L.R. 187; Times, December 17, 1999, ECHR 425, 436, 438, 440
The Estate of Karen Silkwood v Kerr-McGee Inc. (2000) 9 Clinical L. Rev 229–292 663
The State of California v Charles Manson. 671
Thynne v United Kingdom (A/190) Sub Nom Thynne v United Kingdom (11787/85); Wilson v United Kingdom (11978/86); Gunnell v United Kingdom (12009/86) (1991) 13 E.H.R.R. 666; Times, December 10, 1990; Independent, November 2, 1990; Guardian, November 2, 1990, ECHR. 431, 432
Trear v Sills, 82 Cal Rptr 2d 281 at 282 . . . . 417, 418

United States v Bianco No H-90-18 [AHN] [D Conn, July 16, 1991] 89

V v United Kingdom see T v United Kingdom

Wollstonecraft v Shelly (1999)12 Australian Feminist LJ 21. 227

Yau Kwong Man v Secretary for Security HCAL 1595/2001 (unreported judgement) 437

Table of Statutes

Abortion Act 1967 12
Anti-Drug Abuse Act 1988 369
Anti-Terrorism and Effective Death Penalty Act 1996 369

Children Act 1908 . . . . . 431, 435
Children and Young Persons Act 1933 . . . . . 431, 435, 441
Contempt of Court Act 1981
s.8 18
Countryside and Rights of Way Act 2000 . . . . . 542, 559
Criminal Evidence Act 1898 174
Criminal Justice Act 1925 . . . . . 178, 179
s.41 . . . . . 173, 179, 180
Criminal Justice Act 1991
s.34 432
Criminal Justice and Court Services Act 2000 436
Criminal Justice and Public Order Act 1996 212
Criminal Law Amendment Act 1885 226
Criminal Lunatics Act 1800
s.2 431

Emergency Medical Services Act 1973 132
Emergency Services Act 1974 134

Housing (Homeless Persons) Act 1977 . . . . . 17, 22, 131
Human Fertilisation and Embryology Act 1990 12

Infanticide Act 1938
s.1 13

Libel Act 1843
s.3 377

Matrimonial Homes (Family Protection) (Scotland) Act 1981
s.18(1) 25

National Assistance Act 1948 22

Obscene Publications Act 1959 . . . . . 212, 214, 215

Paramedic Act 1970 . . . . . 136, 138, 142

Torture Victim Protection Act. 504
Trade Practices Act 1974
s.51AC 575
s.51AC(1) 576
s.51AE. 575

Violent Crime Control and Law Enforcement Act 1994. 369

Law in Popular Culture

Michael Freeman

Law's engagement with popular culture goes back to the mists of time, to the Old Testament, perhaps beyond. There is much jurisprudence in *Genesis*, as George Fletcher reminds us.[1] 'Adam, Eve, Cain, Abel, the serpent—we could hardly think about good and evil, free will and determinism, crime and punishment without them.'[2] Just as significantly, nor could those to whom these stories were originally addressed. The story of the patriarch, Abraham, remains deeply embedded with today's cultural imagination.[3] His haggling with God over the fate of the cities of Sodom and Gomorrah is a model of legal negotiation.[4] His trial,[5] the 'Akedah'[6] (the attempted sacrifice of Isaac), has fired artists (Mantegna,[7] Rembrandt,[8] Chagall[9] amongst many others), poets (think of war poet Wilfred Owen's savage subversion of the Biblical account,

> But the old man would not do so, but slew his son, -
> And half the seed of Europe, one by one, . . .),[10]

composers (Stravinsky wrote a ballad,[11] Benjamin Britten juxtaposed Owen's lines with those from the Requiem 'quam olim Abrahae promisisti'[12] in his *War*

[1] 'The Jurisprudence of Genesis' (2003) 56 CLP 41–61. See also Ronald R Garet, 'Natural Law and Creation Stories' in J Roland Pennock and John W Chapman (eds), *Religion, Morality and the Law* (New York: 1988) 218–262.

[2] Fletcher, n 1 above, 41.

[3] Note its influence, direct or indirect, in all three 'Abramaic' religions. Jews read the 'Akedah' on Rosh Hashanah and Muslims re-enact the event on the feast of the sacrifice at the end of the *Haj* rituals. For Christians it anticipates the Crucifixion and Genesis 22 is part of Easter week services.

[4] Genesis 18: 22–23. This smacks of 'theological challenge and judicial debate' (*per* Stefan C Reif, *Judaism and Hebrew Prayer* (Cambridge: 1993) 32).

[5] See Carol Delaney, *Abraham on Trial* (Princeton, NJ: 1998). See also David Lee Miller, *Dreams of the Burning Child* (Ithaca: 2003).

[6] Literally 'the binding' [of Isaac]. See further, Shalom Spiegel, *The Last Trial* (New York: 1969). Muslims believe it was Ishmael who was the intended sacrifice, but see Reuven Firestone, *Journeys in Holy Lands: The Evolution of the Abraham-Ishmael Legends in Islamic Exegesis* (Albany, NY: 1990).

[7] Painted about 1490 (it is in the Kunsthistorisches Museum, Vienna).

[8] Painted in 1635 (it is in the Hermitage in St Petersburg).

[9] Painted between 1960 and 1966 (it is in the Musée National Message Biblique Marc Chagall in Nice). Isaac in this painting has been sacrificed, presumably like Jesus. Alice Miller, *The Untouched Key: Tracing Trauma in Creativity and Destructiveness* (New York: 1990) critically examines a number of paintings of the incident.

[10] Genesis 22: 1–14.

[11] *Abraham and Isaac* completed on 3 March 1963 and dedicated to the people of Israel.

[12] Which of old Thou didst promise to Abraham [and his seed].

Requiem,[13] Bob Dylan too wrote a song—'Highway 61 Revisited'—that imagined Abraham questioning God's order[14]). It formed the sub-text for Woody Allen's film *Crimes and Misdemeanors*[15] and for Neil Gordon's novel, *The Sacrifice of Isaac*, about the ambivalent legacy of the Holocaust.[16] And, even if it passed Freud by,[17] it has had enormous influence on later psychoanalysts.[18] But why not, we may ask, on contemporary jurisprudence where there is so much concern with unjust law,[19] civil disobedience,[20] even the 'discretion to disobey'[21]? Or on family law? It raises issues of adult responsibility and care. What are Abraham's obligations toward Isaac? Although Isaac is an adult, Abraham remains his father. To whom does Isaac belong? And where is Sarah?[22] What her absence from the story tells us is obvious from today's perspective, informed as it is with feminist insight. But how would those to whom the story was directed, thousands of years ago, have reacted? Where they would have taken the story literally—as many believers today still do—we, like Kierkegaard perhaps,[23] would see it as a story about the trials of faith and commitment, about trusting powers and purposes that lie beyond human understanding. And this remains relevant as we grapple to understand much beyond our comprehension: on one level disasters such as the Holocaust,[24] but rather more mundanely contemporary issues of life and death.[25] Richard Miller, I note, uses the Abraham-Isaac Midrash to offer insights into the trust we put in the medical profession in paediatric care.[26]

Law's engagement with popular culture reached a crescendo in Ancient Greece.[27] Kitto,[28] paraphrasing Pericles,[29] says of the Greeks that they 'throw open to all our common cultural life, nor do we deny them any instruction or

[13] Commissioned to celebrate the consecration of Coventry Cathedral in May 1962 (the original building having been destroyed by German bombs in 1940—a war crime passed over by Wai Chee Dimock (see p 520 below). I attended the second performance of this.

[14] This was written as a protest to the Vietnam War.

[15] The psychiatrist in this film is Martin Bergman, who subsequently wrote *In The Shadow of Moloch: The Sacrifice of Children and its Impact on Western Religions* (New York: 1992).

[16] New York: 1995. The 'Akedah' had earlier been retold by Thomas Mann in *Joseph and His Brothers* (trans HT Lowe-Porter) (Harmondsworth: 1978) 64–67.

[17] He wrote about Moses instead (see Yosef Hayim Yerushalmi, *Freud's Moses: Judaism Terminable and Interminable* (New Haven, NJ: 1991)).

[18] In particular, Erich Wellisch, *Isaac and Oedipus* (London: 1954), on which see n 5 above, 213–215 (who also considers Georges Devereux, David Bakan, Marie Balmary, Alice Miller and Martin Bergman (referred to at n 15 above)).

[19] See David Dyzenhaus, *Recrafting the Rule of Law: The Limits of Legal Order* (Oxford: 1999).

[20] See, eg, Peter Singer, *Democracy and Disobedience* (Oxford: 1973).

[21] Mortimer R Kadish and Sanford H Kadish, *Discretion to Disobey* (Stanford, California: 1973).

[22] See n 5 above, 22–23. In the Muslim version, it is, of course, not Sarah, but Hagar.

[23] See *Fear and Trembling* (trans by Alastair Hannay) (Harmondsworth: 1985).

[24] Different views of which include Daniel Jonah Goldhagen, *Hitler's Willing Executioners* (New York: 1996) and Götz Aly and Susanne Heim, *Architects of Annihilation* (London: 2002) (first published in German in 1991).

[25] See Michael Freeman, 'A Time To Be Born and A Time To Die' (2003) 56 CLP 603.

[26] See his *Children, Ethics and Modern Medicine* (Bloomington, Indiana: 2003).

[27] See Sir Arthur Pickard-Cambridge, *The Dramatic Festivals of Athens* (Oxford: 1968).

[28] HDF Kitto, *The Greeks* (Harmondsworth: 1951) 74.

[29] His funeral oration.

spectacle'. As Kitto explains, these words are 'almost meaningless until we realize that the drama, tragic and comic, the performance of choral hymns, public recitals of Homer, games, were all necessary and normal parts of "political" life'.[30] The theatre was popular culture, and through it the population was introduced to jurisprudential conflicts like positive law versus natural law, law and equity, rule versus discretion. The debates are reflected in many of the great tragedies. Thus, note the way Hecuba, in Euripedes' play of that name, implores Agamemnon to punish Polymestor, the King of Thrace, who had killed her son, Polydorus. She is a slave and therefore weak, but:

> . . . the gods are strong, and over them
> there stands some absolute, some moral order
> or principle of law more final still.
> Upon this moral law the world depends;
> . . .
> Apply that law to me. For if you flout it now, and those
> who murder in cold blood or defy the gods
> go unpunished, then human justice withers,
> corrupted at its source.[31]

And observe also Agamemnon's response. He prays in aid expediency, pragmatism. The law should reflect public opinion. Posner sees a parallel in the judge of today who concedes the natural justice of a litigant's case whilst deciding against him on the ground that positive law, 'crystallised public opinion', entitles his opponent to judgment.[32]

If Agamemnon was the first legal positivist, Creon (in Sophocles' *Antigone*) has some claim to be the second. When he orders that Polynices should remain unburied—a savage punishment in Greek theology[33]—Antigone, his sister, defies the order and buries her brother. Her trial follows and contains her impassioned assertion of the primacy of divine law in language which has echoed over the millennia. *Antigone* is often performed when a country is in trouble.[34] Anouilh wrote an *Antigone* for occupied Paris in 1944.[35] In Brecht's version, Creon is a Fascist.[36] In Tom Paulin's *The Riot Act*, set in Northern Ireland, Antigone is a freedom fighter and Creon sounds like Ian Paisley.[37] And in Athol Fugard's *The Island*,[38] two prisoners

[30] See n 28 above, 74.

[31] Euripedes, *Hecuba II*, 795–805. *Hecuba* may have resonated also with an audience of Shakespeare's day: note the allusion to the play in *Hamlet*.

[32] *Law and Literature* (Cambridge, Mass: 1998) 95.

[33] It is to be found also in Homer's *Iliad* and in *Hecuba*. On disgust, shame and the law generally see Martha C Nussbaum, *Hiding from Humanity* (Princeton, NJ: 2004).

[34] See George Steiner, *Antigones: How the Antigone Legend has Endured in Western Literature, Art and Thought* (Oxford: 1984).

[35] First published in Paris 1946, in London in English in 1954.

[36] *In Die Antigone Des Sophokles*, written in 1948, and set after the Second World War. It is an adaptation based on Hoelderlin's translation.

[37] See Tom Paulin, *The Riot Act* (London: 1985).

[38] See Athol Fugard: *The Township Plays* (Oxford: 1993). The play was first performed in Cape Town in 1973.

perform *Antigone* in prison to preserve their sanity in the insane conditions of apartheid South Africa.[39]

Perhaps the fullest exploration of justice in Greek literature is in Aeschylus' *Eumenides*. Aeschylus grapples with the notion of 'justice': what it is, how it is to be realized in the sphere of human activity, and what part the gods play in helping men to achieve it. In *Agamemnon* he has had the chorus in the first Choral Ode sing: 'Wealth provides no defence against greed for the man who kicks and obliterates the great altar of Justice'.[40] In *Eumenides* words derived from the root that designates 'justice' (*dik–*) occur with striking frequency.[41] It is frequently used to refer to the state of affairs which parties who believe they are aggrieved wish to have restored. It is but a short step from this to the use of *dikē* with a specific, concrete legal or judicial connotation: 'prosecute at law', 'institute legal proceedings'. And as Podlecki notes,[42] 'it is precisely this field of meaning which enables Aeschylus to bring Justice as an abstract concept or personification into the everyday reality of an Athenian law court'. But how would an Athenian audience have reacted to the trial in the play? As a reflection of contemporary legal practice or as a parody? Or both? Lebeck, I note, makes the point that 'accuracy is an essential ingredient of parody'.[43] Is the trial then a caricature of Athenian procedure, revealing both its strengths and its weaknesses? Orestes' acquittal, we observe, does not depend upon the trial but on divine will. Would the audience to whom the play was originally addressed have been as puzzled by the relationship of justice and injustice as some are today?[44] And how would they have reacted to many of the arguments which seem (to us) quibbling and trivial? One, which has always interested me as a student of parentage,[45] is that which proclaims the male as the true parent:

> The so-called mother is no mother of a child,
> but nurturer of a newly seeded embryo. The
> parent is the one who mounts her . . . [46]

The 'belittlement'[47] of the role of women in procreation makes Agamemnon's wrong (the killing of Iphigenia) seem less serious than Clytemnestra's in killing him and distinguishes parricide and matricide. But I doubt if an Athenian audience would have seized upon the belittlement or seen it as we do through feminist

[39] Could these only be brought to closure by truth and reconciliation? An *Antigone* to take account of this is still awaited. On this more generally, see Martha Minow, *Between Vengeance and Forgiveness* (Boston: 1998).

[40] *Agamemnon*, 381–384.

[41] A point noted by Anthony J Podlecki in his Introduction to Aeschylus: *Eumenides* (Warminster: 1989) 42. Etymology connects this with 'the way' suggesting a common meaning with the Jewish *Halakhah* and Muslim *Sharia*.

[42] See n 41 above, 43.

[43] Anne Lebeck, *The Oresteia—A Study In Language and Structure* (Cambridge, Mass: 1971) 135.

[44] eg, Austin Sarat and Thomas R Kearns, *Justice and Injustice in Law and Legal Theory* (Ann Arbor, Mich: 1996).

[45] Michael Freeman, 'Medically Assisted Reproduction' in I Kennedy and A Grubb (eds), *Principles of Medical Law* (Oxford: 2004) 639.

[46] In the translation by Christopher Collard, *Aeschylus—Oresteia* (Oxford: 2002) 103.

[47] See n 32 above, 65.

spectacles. What would have met the social realities of Aeschylus' Athens, to us today constitutes both palpable nonsense and through this injustice. It is possible, as Podlecki acknowledges, to read the *Eumenides* as 'an anti-feminist tract'.[48] The audience would have been predominantly, if not solely, male. But was Aeschylus feeding his audiences' prejudices or telling them they were misguided to acquiesce in a state of affairs that was so obviously unfair?[49]

There are many engagements of law with popular culture in Shakespeare too.[50] I have always thought it interesting that Shakespeare's most popular character, so popular we are told that a further play was written about him just to please Queen Elizabeth the First,[51] is Falstaff, an armed robber,[52] a debt defaulter, a (would-be) serial adulterer![53] But already in the very early *King Henry VI Part 2* Shakespeare was encouraging what we may think a refreshingly critical attitude to law, lawyers and legality. Into Jack Cade's mouth Shakespeare puts the memorable: 'The first thing we do, let's kill all the lawyers'.[54] The Jack Cade episodes 'comment indirectly on [Shakespeare's] own Tudor audiences'[55]. As Honan explains: 'Parodying inversions of misrule, and of "barring out" when pupils smashed school windows, Cade inverts civilized codes with cheerful blasphemy'.[56]

There are, of course, famous trial scenes in Shakespeare. That in *The Merchant of Venice* is most often commented upon.[57] At the play's heart is a conflict between Tudor common law and the mitigating equity of the Chancery courts. Of course, the drama is a folk tale for no English law permitted anyone to put his life at jeopardy as Antonio had done. How would the 'folk' to whom the play was presented in the late 1590s have reacted? That such a thing was possible outside England? That anything was possible in a society with a Jew-villain like Shylock? It is of course doubtful if any of them would have encountered a Jew but phobia, prejudice and hatred were deeply ingrained.[58] Since usury is at the heart of the play it is worth noting that since 1571 the lending of money at interest had been de facto legal.[59]

48 See n 41 above, 48.

49 See Philip Vellacott, *The Logic of Tragedy: Morals and Integrity in Aeschylus' 'Oresteia'* (Durham, North Carolina: 1984) for the view that he was being elaborately ironic.

50 See Ian Ward, *Shakespeare and Legal Imagination* (London: 1999).

51 The truth of this is debated by HJ Oliver in his Arden edition of *The Merry Wives of Windsor* (London: 1971) xliv–lii.

52 See the Gad's Hill incident in *Henry IV, Part1*.

53 In *The Merry Wives of Windsor*: executed so much more pithily in Verdi's *Falstaff* (there are at least nine operas based on the 'Merry Wives', exceeded only by *The Tempest, Romeo and Juliet, Hamlet, A Midsummer Night's Dream, The Taming of the Shrew* and *The Merchant of Venice*). See, further, Winston Dean, 'Shakespeare and Opera' in Phyllis Hartnoll (ed), *Shakespeare in Music* (London: 1964). In *Falstaff*, of course, the wit is in the music.

54 IV, ii, 86. In Cade's London, literacy is a crime.

55 *Per* Park Honan, *Shakespeare—A Life* (New York: 1999) 140.

56 ibid.

57 See eg Posner, n 32 above, 103–110 and 115–121, and John Denver, 'William Shakespeare and the Jurisprudence of Comedy' (1987) 39 *Stanford L Rev* 825.

58 On the origins of the Jewish political economy see Derek J Penslar, *Shylock's Children* (Berkeley, California: 2001). On Shakespeare's Shylock (and much else) John Gross's *Shylock—Four Hundred Years in the Life of a Legend* (London: 1992) can be recommended. Medieval stereotyping lives on in Mel Gibson's 2004 film *Passion*.

59 The interest rate could not exceed 10%. See, further, Norman Jones, *God and the Moneylenders: Usury and Law in Early Modern England* (Oxford: 1989).

'A reasonable return on a loan was coming to be given a grudging acquiescence'.[60] But in this and much else *The Merchant of Venice* may be a response to, as well as a reflection of, popular beliefs and prejudices.[61] It is an historical document which contains 'history's complexities and ambiguities'.[62]

The trial scene itself has all the rhetoric of what Karl Llewellyn[63] called the 'grand style' (the famous 'quality of mercy' speech[64]) but it ultimately rests on legalism (and as such is Llewellyn's 'formal style' personified). As Lyon puts it: 'The Christians out-Shylock Shylock as the letter of the law defeats the letter of the law in ways oblivious to its spirit and destructive of the human spirit'.[65] Shylock after his degradation is not even allowed an exit line.[66] He is shown no mercy. Indeed, for all its eloquence, Portia's famous speech is irrelevant to the resolution of the dilemma the court confronts. The conflict is apparent too in *Measure for Measure*. When Isabella pleads 'Yet show some pity', Angelo responds 'I show it most of all when I show justice'.[67] Of course, the conflict between justice and mercy is stronger and more central in *Measure for Measure*.

There is much to interest the lawyer in *Measure for Measure*: the obsolescent laws 'Dead to infliction, to themselves are dead; And liberty plucks justice by the nose'.[68] But are laws against fornication enforceable? Or is this just our view? Would a different one have appealed to an early seventeenth century audience?[69] The emphasis is on the 'rule of law'. So when Isabella pleads for her brother's life, Angelo's response is 'It is the law, not I, condemn your brother'.[70] The insights we are offered into matrimonial law are also of interest. Why Shakespeare employed the 'bed-trick' he had already exploited in *All's Well That Ends Well* is marginal to my concerns.[71] But how would a Jacobean audience have reacted?

The play hinges on Claudio's breach of the obsolescent fornication laws. No one doubts that he is guilty.[72] But then the Duke tells Isabella that, in the light of the marriage contract with Marianna that Angelo had broken, it would be fitting to substitute Marianna for Isabella in Angelo's bed. In England (where, of course, the play is set despite its fictional location in Vienna), a marriage contract probably created a valid marriage even if it was not solemnized. That Shakespeare seems to

[60] *Per* Patrick Atiyah, *The Rise and Fall of Freedom of Contract* (Oxford: 1979) 66. By 1625 Francis Bacon in 'On Usury' was seeing it as a necessity and looking to the benefits of the practice.

[61] As argued long ago by EE Stoll, *Shakespeare Studies* (New York: 1927) 255–336. And see James Shapiro, *Shakespeare and the Jews* (New York: 1996).

[62] *Per* John Lyon, *The Merchant of Venice* (Hemel Hempstead: 1988) 28.

[63] *The Common Law Tradition* (Boston: 1960).

[64] Act IV, i, 180–201.

[65] See n 62 above, 107.

[66] Compare the ridiculed Malvolio in *Twelfth Night* who is allowed to retort 'I'll be reveng'd on the whole pack of you' (Act V, i, 364).

[67] Act II, ii, 99–100.

[68] Act I, iii.

[69] But cf Posner, n 32 above, 118 who believes the attempt to outlaw fornication as 'quixotic' in the culture of the play as it would be today.

[70] Act II, ii, 84. Much the same point is made in Herman Melville's *Billy Budd* by Captain Vere.

[71] It could be to turn what would have otherwise been a tragedy into a comedy. On matrimonial law and Shakespeare see Margaret Loftus Ranald, *Shakespeare and Historical Context* (New York: 1987).

[72] Including Claudio himself.

know this is implied by the bed-trick played on Angelo. Even if Shakespeare was aware of the outlawing of informal marriage by the Council of Trent a year before he was born[73]—and this would have affected Vienna, represented in the play as Roman Catholic, and not England—would his audience have appreciated what was going on?[74] It may, of course, be that the two contracts were different—*de futuro* and *de praesenti*—but Shakespeare describes them in virtually identical ways.[75] It is hardly surprising that 'the courts themselves in Shakespeare's day were frequently at a loss to distinguish the two types of betrothal contract'.[76] One of the ironies of the play is that Claudio's sexual relationship with Julietta is the only one undertaken with mutual consent and dignified by mutual love.[77]

My last Shakespearean illustration is *King Lear*. As Posner observes, it is 'not usually considered one of Shakespeare's "legal" plays'.[78] This is surprising given the images of 'nature' and natural law[79] that permeate it, and the fact that it has three trial scenes, one, as in *The Tempest*, a trial of the imagination. Less surprising perhaps because we have left the law/equity debates of *The Merchant of Venice* and *Measure for Measure* for events and debates closer to the last judgment.[80] Of the three trials in *Lear* (the mock trial of Goneril and Regan by Lear, the trial of Gloucester on false charge of treason, and the trial by battle in which Edgar kills Edmund), the first is much the most interesting. The first may be 'an ostensible farce'[81] but from it we learn much about law, justice, authority, and, possibly, Shakespeare. Its radicalism is striking. It has been observed (by Charles Hobday) that 'Lear's ravings often come near to the thought of the egalitarians'.[82] Justice fails because 'those luxurious and voluminous "robes and furr'd gowns hide all"—whether these are the robes and furred gowns of the justices themselves, which hide their taking of bribes, or the robes and furred gowns of the economically privileged, which hide their avarice, and which blind justice to their sins'.[83] The mock trial may be exploited as social or legal protest. But it is more than this. It could also be non-political bawdy and satiric fun. Mock arraignments were part of law students' Christmas revels at the

[73] In 1563.

[74] See, further Margaret Scott, 'Our City's Institutions: Some Further Reflections on the Marriage Contracts in *Measure for Measure*' (1982) 49 *English Legal History* 790.

[75] See I, ii, 138–143 and III, i, 206–209.

[76] *Per* Davis P Harding, 'Elizabethan Betrothals and *Measure for Measure*' (1950) 49 *J of English and Germanic Philology* 139, 149.

[77] See Harriet Hawkins, *Measure for Measure* (Brighton: 1987) 23. Contrast the Duke's 'marriage' of Isabella at the end of the play, which finds echoes in Gilbert and Sullivan's *Trial By Jury* in which the judge says 'I will marry her myself!' (Muriel C Bradbrook has noted the parallel too: see 'The Balance and the Sword in *Measure for Measure*' in *Artist and Society in Shakespeare's England* (Brighton: 1982) 146.)

[78] See n 32 above, 100.

[79] See John F Danby, *Shakespeare's Doctrine of Nature* (London: 1949).

[80] See Act V, iii, 264–265 and Frank Kermode, *Shakespeare's Language* (Harmondsworth: 2000) 184.

[81] See n 32 above, 100.

[82] 'Clouted Shoon and Leather Aprons: Shakespeare and the Egalitarian Tradition' (1979) 23 *Renaissance and Modern Studies* 75. This has led to debates about Shakespeare as proto-Leveller and to all sorts of speculation about why the scene was omitted in the Folio (eg was it censorship?).

[83] As argued by Judy Kronenfeld, *King Lear and the Naked Truth: Rethinking the Language of Religion and Resistance* (Durham, North Carolina: 1998) 204.

Inns of Court 'when they set up miniature kingdoms and chose a monarch in direct imitation of the government at Whitehall'.[84] The mock trial is notable also for its meditation upon corrupt justice. Thus:

> . . . plate sin with gold,
> And the strong lance of justice hurtless breaks;
> Arm it in rags, a pigmy's straw doth pierce it.[85]

There are several related ideas about corrupt justice in Lear's imagined trial of his daughter. He remarks to Gloucester (who by then has had his eyes put out):

> Look with thine ears: see how
> yond justice rails upon yond simple thief. Hark, in
> thine ear: change places, and handy-dandy, which
> is the justice, which is the thief?[86]

And, in lines which could have come from *Measure for Measure*:

> Thou rascal beadle, hold thy bloody hand!
> Why dost thou lash that whore? Strip thine own back;
> Thou hotly lusts to use her in that kind
> For which thou whipp'st her.[87]

Lear rails not only against the 'false justices'—this allows for the possibility that some judges are honest—but goes further, condemning the entire system of justice. He equates the 'images of Authority' with the 'dog's obey'd in office'.[88] He draws parallels between the 'farmer's dog [which] barks at a beggar' and the 'justice [who] rails upon yond simple thief'.[89] He relegates justice to a barking dog, yet promotes the thief to a beggar who is not guilty of theft. Seen as a barking dog that scares a beggar, the 'image of authority' is reduced to a brute animal who terrorizes the weak (in particular innocent beggars). But was this Shakespeare's view when he wrote *King Lear* in the early years of James I? The criticisms of justice and of authority were not new or unique: Shakespeare was on well-trodden ground.[90] But we also find in Shakespeare exhortations to obey authority, most famously Ulysses' speech in *Troilus and Cressida*.[91] This is not the place to explain let alone resolve these contradictions, if they are to be characterized as such. Nor must we read the trial scene with an eye on today's concepts. But it does throw, I believe, light on concerns of an early seventeenth century audience and reflected

[84] *Per* James Sharpe, 'The People and the Law' in Barry Reay (ed), *Popular Culture and Seventeenth Century England* (London: 1985) 261–262. The authorities did not approve of this sort of parody.

[85] Act IV, vi, 163–165.

[86] Act IV, vi, 149–153.

[87] Act IV, vi, 158–161. It emerged in June 2004 that a Crown Court judge in Portsmouth who had presided over child abuse cases was downloading child pornography! And Portsmouth had earlier emerged as a hotbed of intolerance towards paedophiles with mass demonstrations on working class estates.

[88] Act IV, vi, 156–157.

[89] Act IV, vi, 154 and 150.

[90] For illustrations see Kronenfeld, n 83 above, Ch 8.

[91] Act I, iii, 86–137.

movements then current, and latent and not so latent discontents that would see, in the generation after Shakespeare, the civil war.

I have focused thus far on Biblical sources, the Greeks and Shakespeare. If I jump now to more modern times it is not because I do not think the popular culture of the seventeenth or eighteenth centuries does not ooze with images of law, lawyers and legal practice. A study of the law and justice in Ben Jonson[92] or an exploration of matrimonial laws and manners in Restoration comedies[93] or the paintings of William Hogarth[94] would throw much light on the societies for whom these authors and painters produced their works. Nor, given space considerations, will I look at the novels of Dickens—we still take many of our images of nineteenth-century justice from his novels—or at Dostoevsky's *Crime and Punishment* (though is there a better example of interrogation than Porfiry's of Raskolnikov?[95]) or at *Billy Budd*[96] or Kafka's *The Trial* (surely *the* key text for understanding so much about the insecurities of living under totalitarianism).[97] Instead, I will examine, albeit briefly, two socio-legal problems, domestic violence and abortion through examples of popular culture.

When Roddy Doyle's *The Woman Who Walked Into Doors*[98] was published to much acclaim in 1996 it was hailed as the first domestic violence novel.[99] But, as Marlene Tromp (one of the contributors to this volume) has shown in *The Private Rod*,[100] this is far from the case. Her title is taken from Wilkie Collins' *The Woman in White* published in 1860:[101]

> The rod of iron with which he rules her never appears in company—it is a private rod, and is always kept upstairs.

Tromp excludes from her discussion George Eliot's novella 'Janet's Repentance',[102] which is slightly earlier than *The Woman in White*, because, she argues, it is 'complicated by the question of drunkenness, a "moral disease" that was believed to go hand in hand with marital violence'.[103] Domestic violence was emerging as a social

[92] In *Volpone*, for example. See generally, John J Enck, *Jonson and the Comic Truth* (Madison, Wisc: 1957). Note also the satire on marriage in *Epicene*.

[93] On which see Robert D Hume, *The Rakish Stage* (Carbondale, Ill: 1983) Ch 6. Restoration comedy is said to exhibit an 'awareness of the drawbacks and possible pitfalls of matrimony' (at 183).

[94] The series known as 'The Rake's Progress', for example.

[95] *Crime and Punishment.*

[96] On which see Richard Weisberg, *The Failure of the Word: The Protagonist As Lawyer in Modern Fiction* (New Haven, NJ: 1984).

[97] Posner discusses this, see n 32 above, Ch 4.

[98] London: 1996.

[99] But see Jane Smiley's *A Thousand Acres* (New York: 1991) and Fannie Flagg's *Fried Green Tomatoes at The Whistle Stop Café* (New York: 1987). It was not even the first modern domestic violence novel.

[100] Charlottesville: 2000.

[101] London: 1860.

[102] First published in serial form in Blackwood's *Edinburgh Magazine* in 1857 and republished in 1858 in *Scenes of Clerical Life*. It will be noted that in David Lodge's Penguin edition (Harmondsworth: 1973) the heroine's drinking problem is referred to without even mentioning that she is a battered wife. But Rosemary Ashton, *George Eliot—A Life* (London: 1996) refers to the 'remarkably accurate depiction of the psychology of a battered wife' (at 178).

[103] See n 100 above, 252, n 31. But see Sandra Gilbert and Susan Gubar, *The Madwoman in the Attic* (New Haven, NJ: 1979) and Virginia B Morris, *Double Jeopardy: Women who Kill in Victorian Fiction* (Lexington, Kentucky: 1990).

problem for which legal solutions were sought. John Stuart Mill had written of 'a bulldog set at the heels of a wife, blows with a poker, attempted murder by hanging, stabbings, murder in a fit of drunkenness' in *The Sunday Times* in August 1851.[104]

Frances Power Cobbe's pamphlet *Wife Torture in England* was published in 1878 and was instrumental in putting legislation onto the statute book.[105] Each time domestic violence has surfaced,[106] there is feminist questioning of women's role and of patriarchy (the other occasions being the suffrage movement before the First World War[107] and the 1970s[108]).

It is all too easy to overlook the significance of 'Janet's Repentance'. Certainly, when I read it for the first time as an 'A' Level student—*Middlemarch* was then a set text!—I glossed over the domestic violence (though this concept was not yet in common currency[109]). Eliot challenges the hierarchical view of marriage and the ramifications of its physical abuses. And she was writing when there were few challenges to patriarchy,[110] and the so-called 'rule of thumb'[111] was far from dead. Eliot captures the conflicts and tensions that beset battered women then, and now. And she seeks solutions: through the Evangelical Minister she suggests mediation by 'some man of character and experience',[112] through the victim's mother, a man who 'knows the law'[113] and of whom the battering husband is 'afraid' is posited as an answer. But Eliot must have known the law offered no solutions, not even the option of divorce.[114] Even more surprising, at least in the light of present knowledge is 'the absence of any helpful verbal discourse for defining and appraising domestic violence'.[115] None of the middle-class characters admits that the husband in 'Janet's Repentance' beats his wife and only a few hold him accountable.[116]

[104] I quote this in MDA Freeman, *Violence In The Home: A Socio-Legal Study* (Aldershot: 1979) 5. See also Margaret May, 'Violence In The Family: An Historical Perspective' in JP Martin (ed), *Violence and the Family* (Chichester: 1978) 135–168. Another example is JW Kaye, *North British Rev* 25 May 1856, 249–250 who explains that husbands wanted to return home to 'a comfortable arm chair, a singing kettle, a tidied room'.

[105] She discusses the background in her *Autobiography* (London: 1894). The legislation was the Matrimonial Causes Act 1878 (the first 'separation order').

[106] Of course, it is always 'there'. The earliest legal case I have found is *Neffeld v Neffeld* in 1395. RM Helmholz, *Marriage Litigation in Medieval England* (Cambridge: 1974) 105 discusses the case.

[107] See Jill Liddington and Jill Norris, *One Hand Tied Behind Us* (London: 1978).

[108] Erin Pizzey's *Scream Quietly or the Neighbours Will Hear* (Harmondsworth: 1974) was the first graphic portrayal which made a modern audience sit up.

[109] I doubt if it was in use before the early 1970s.

[110] See Sylvia Walby, *Theorizing Patriarchy* (Oxford: 1990), Ch 6.

[111] On which see RE Dobash and RP Dobash, *Violence Against Wives* (New York: 1979).

[112] *Scenes of Clerical Life* (Oxford: 1985) 292.

[113] ibid, 295.

[114] Divorce was introduced in 1858, the same year as *Scenes of Clerical Life* was published.

[115] Noted by Mark Spilka, *Eight Lessons In Love* (Columbia, Missouri: 1997) 35.

[116] And note the silence of Eliot's leading biographer: see Gordon G Haight, *George Eliot: A Biography* (Oxford: 1968).

There are numerous novels and stories after 'Janet's Repentance' which portray domestic violence. Spilka[117] and Tromp[118] offer excellent, and very different, analyses of these. Tromp uses the genre of the Victorian sensation novel, which was particularly popular in the 1860s and 1870s. Novels raised questions about domesticity, the relationships of men and women, and violence against the backdrop of public and parliamentary debate about rights and obligations within and outside marriage. Of *The Woman in White* Tromp notes that it 'took up the tensions represented in the Divorce Act of 1857'. It 're-marks the language of violence in the domestic space, anticipating and casting the frame of later debates'.[119]

The sensation novels 'challenged the solidity and impermeability of the legal and cultural understanding of violence in the home, offering not the pleasing safety of morality in the ranks of the well-to-do, but a wealthy family in strife'.[120] Spilka shows us domestic violence in the writings of Lawrence,[121] Joyce,[122] Hemingway[123] and Steinbeck[124] amongst others. Of these others the most interesting is Isaac Bashevis Singer[125] with an account of domestic violence in a shtetl in Poland in circa 1900. Spilka finds Singer's 'struggles with his own hostilities toward women, his attractions toward violence . . . offers a useful key to the male struggles in our time with abusive propensities'.[126]

The Woman Who Walked Into Doors reflects today's greater sensitivity and deeper understanding of domestic violence. It is narrated by the victim of 17 years of a brutal, now dead, husband. And it is graphic:[127]

> There wasn't one minute when I wasn't afraid . . . waiting for the fist, waiting for the smile. I was brainwashed and brain-dead, a zombie for hours, afraid to think, afraid to stop. . . . I sat at home and waited. I mopped up my own blood. I lost all my friends, and most of my teeth. He gave me a choice, left or right; I chose left and he broke the little finger on my left hand. Because I scorched one of his shirts. Because his egg was too hard. Because the toilet seat was wet. Because because because. He demolished me. He destroyed me. And I never stopped loving him.[128]

The narration answers so many questions posed by those who look for solutions, and not just legal solutions, to domestic violence. Why did she put up with it, why

117 See n 115 above. 118 See n 100 above. 119 ibid, 71. 120 ibid, 72.

121 Spilka concentrates on 'The White Stocking' but equally, perhaps more, interesting is *The Rainbow* where physical abuse/sexual abuse of a child by a young schoolmistress masquerades as legitimate corporal punishment. The novel has two moving-image versions, a 1984 film directed by Ken Russell and a 1989 BBC TV drama (in the latter the caning was extremely violent).

122 'Counterparts' in *Dubliners*, first published in 1914.

123 'The Snows of Kilimanjaro'. See, further, Mark Spilka, 'Hemingway and Lawrence As Abusive Husbands' in *Renewing the Normative D. H. Lawrence: A Personal Progress* (Columbia, Missouri: 1992).

124 'The Murder' in *The Long Valley* (New York: 1948).

125 'The Wife Killer: A Folktale' in *Gimpel The Fool and Other Stories* (New York: 1957).

126 See n 115 above, 10–11. 127 See n 98 above. See eg, 175–176.

128 ibid, 176–177.

stay, why not leave him? 'She didn't exist, she was good for fuckin' nothing',[129] she 'needed him to punish her'.[130] Her family saw nothing. She went to her GP accompanied by her husband and he prescribed valium.[131] She told the A&E that she had fallen down stairs and doctors believed her.[132] She insists she would have 'told them everything . . . if they'd asked',[133] but would she? She is, we discover, full of defence mechanisms.[134] Her sister suggested the police and barring orders but it was 'none of her business'.[135] Instead, she 'ran away in her dreams', 'to twenty years ago', 'to another country'.[136] Eventually she strikes back: she 'wallops'[137] him with a frying pan and throws him out. But is her reaction that of the provoked reasonable man or the battered woman?[138] He is subsequently killed by the police in the course of an armed robbery, but what if she had killed him?[139] What would have been her defences and how would they have been responded to?[140] Would her story have been the same?[141]

Debate about abortion may begin with moral argument,[142] it often proceeds to the interpretation of statistics, but it usually ends with stories. The 14-year-old girl who would not have had an abortion had she been able to tell her mother about her predicament[143]—the law gave her the 'right' to have an abortion because she was 'Gillick competent'.[144] The woman, who would have had an abortion, had she known her child was going to be disabled or that her partner was going to leave her. Perhaps one day, at least in fiction, the story of the aborted foetus who lived.[145] The abortion debate is framed within overlapping narratives of pregnancy and birth. As Judith Wilt explains, one of these is 'abstract, scientific or religious'. Others are 'essentially female'.[146] The law, though more liberal since 1967[147] (1973 in the United States[148]) remains essentially contested. In recent US elections it has been

[129] See n 98 above. See eg, 177 and passim. [130] ibid, 177. [131] ibid, 190.

[132] ibid, 199. [133] ibid, 201. [134] See especially the first paragraph on 188.

[135] ibid, 205 (curiously the only reference to legal remedies, a sign perhaps of their perceived irrelevance to a woman in her position or their general perceived impotence).

[136] ibid, 210, 211. [137] ibid, 216.

[138] See *R v Humphreys* [1995] 4 All ER 1010. In relation to the US see Anne M Coughlin, 'Excusing Conduct' (1994) 82 *California L Rev 1.*

[139] According to Holly Maguigan, 'Battered Women and Self-Defence: Myths and Misconceptions in Current Reform Proposals' (1991) 140 *U of Pennsylvania L Rev* 379–486, 80% of battered women who kill do so in a direct confrontation.

[140] See Susan Edwards, *Women on Trial* (Manchester: 1984). See also Dan M Kahan and Martha Nussbaum, 'Two Conceptions of Emotion in the Criminal Law' (1996) 96 *Columbia L Rev* 269–374.

[141] See Peter Brooks, 'Storytelling Without Fear? Confession in Law and Literature' in Peter Brooks and Paul Gewirtz (eds), *Law's Stories* (New Haven, NJ: 1996) 114–134. See also JM Coetzee, 'Confession and Double Thoughts: Tolstoy, Rousseau, Dostoevsky in *Doubling The Point* (Cambridge, Mass: 1992) 274.

[142] One of the earliest and most famous defences is Judith Jarvis Thomson, 'A Defense of Abortion' (1971) 1 *Philosophy and Public Affairs* 47.

[143] This 'story' got considerable media coverage in May 2004.

[144] See *Gillick v West Norfolk and Wisbech Area Health Authority* [1986] AC 112.

[145] Sensationalized in the *Daily Mail,* 22 June 2004, 1–2. And see Thomas Keneally, *Passenger* (London: 1979). [146] *Abortion, Choice and Contemporary Fiction* (Chicago: 1990) 3.

[147] Abortion Act 1967: liberalized further in 1990 (Human Fertilisation and Embryology Act).

[148] *Roe v Wade* 410 US 113 (1973).

virtually the only issue of legal policy on which votes hinged. In England, as I write, the courts are hearing a challenge to the 'foetal abnormality' ground brought by a young female priest, herself born with a (now corrected) cleft palate.[149]

Where there are early depictions of the maternity dilemma, often after rape,[150] the issue is infanticide rather than abortion. But infanticide did not exist as a separate category of crime until juries' refusals to convict women of murder and thus potentially to condemn them to death led Parliament to create the crime of infanticide in 1938.[151] Tess dies for killing her seducer, not her baby.[152] When pregnant she had cried out to her mother, 'why didn't you warn me? Ladies know what to fend hands against, because they read novels that tell them of these tricks; but I never had the choice of learning in that way, and you did not help me!'[153] I am not sure what novels Tess had in mind. Presumably not *Anna Karenina*,[154] or *The Scarlet Letter*,[155] or *The Heart of Midlothian*[156] or *Adam Bede*.[157] Would it have been those of Jane Austen (look at the hostile attitude to children in *Persuasion*[158] where 'being released from' her sister's child begins the process of becoming reattached to her lover and future husband)? Or the Brontë sisters? Wilt comments that: 'The crowd of foster mothers in the Victorian novel generally signified not only the true state of maternal mortality in the nineteenth century but also the subliminal sense of the whole culture that pregnancy has in it a death as well as life'.[159]

The morality of abortion, its status as a key issue in gender politics, the ways in which a masculine law drove women into the back streets and a medical profession which even today (in Britain at least) acts as gatekeeper and policeman—all are to be found represented in modern fiction. There are so many examples—I can pick out only a couple.

The classic short story about abortion[160]—Ernest Hemingway's 'Hills Like White Elephants'[161] even omits the word. A young American couple are at a railway junction in Spain. He remarks on the 'awfully simple operation'[162] that they are travelling for. 'It's really not anything. It's just to let the air in.'[163] He only wants her but she (speaking for Hemingway) senses that it will change their relationship

[149] See *The Times* 12 April 2004.

[150] As in one of the earliest novels, *Clarissa* by Samuel Richardson, published in 1748.

[151] See Infanticide Act 1938, s 1.

[152] See Thomas Hardy, *Tess of the D'Urbervilles*, first published in 1891.

[153] London: 1954, 106.

[154] Tolstoy's novel was first published in 1878 but it seems unlikely that Hardy would have known it.

[155] Nathaniel Hawthorne, *The Scarlet Letter*, first published in 1850.

[156] First published in 1818.

[157] George Eliot, *Adam Bede*, first published in 1859. Hetty Sorrel is convicted of the murder of her baby but saved from the foot of the gallows by a pardon obtained by her seducer. It is common to say she was convicted of infanticide, but that is anachronistic.

[158] First published in 1818. This is glossed over in all the critical accounts to which I have referred.

[159] See n 146 above, 24.

[160] To Wilt, ibid, 103 it is the classic 'American' short story about abortion.

[161] First published in 1927. I am using *The First Forty-Nine Stories* (London: 1939).

[162] ibid, 250. [163] ibid.

as much as would the birth of their child. She probes: 'And you think then we'll be alright? If I do it you won't worry?'[164] He insists it is her decision: 'I don't want you to do it if you don't want to'.[165] And she is driven to a final outburst: 'would you please please please please please please please stop talking'.[166] An aborted dialogue, symbolic perhaps of their relationship and certainly of their different ways of viewing the pregnancy: for him as an end, for her as the beginning of something else. And we note the station is between the 'dry side' of the valley and the fertile side, banked by hills 'like white elephants'. He remarks he hasn't seen white elephants. 'No you wouldn't have'[167] she replies. She, of course, has, for they are a symbol of her pregnancy.

Margaret Drabble's *The Millstone* was published at the very end of the pre-legal abortion days.[168] I vividly recall reading it as I taught criminal law (and hence the nineteenth century law of abortion) at Leeds University in 1966 and 1967. And I remember the deep impression it made upon me then. The metaphor is drawn from the book of Matthew: 'Whoso shall offend me of these little ones which believe in me, it were the better that a millstone were hanged about his neck, and that he were drowned in the depth of the sea'.[169]

The protagonist of *The Millstone* is a literary scholar enjoying an active but sexless social life when love—itself a 'millstone'—brings pregnancy. Logic dictates an abortion but maternal force inclines her to pregnancy.[170] Initially she was inclined to induce an abortion herself: she half remembers the old wives' prescription of gin and hot baths.[171] It doesn't work. Abortion is still at this time a criminal offence, only not unlawful under the vague defence of *Bourne's* case[172] that it was necessary to save the life or health of the mother.[173] One of the characters in *The Millstone* points to the 'Catch-22' of this that abortion might only be lawful where the mother was mentally unstable but that abortion might destabilize her further. She chooses birth as an 'initiation into reality'.[174] It means learning to live within a human limit.[175] Pregnancy is part of the process of discovery, mirroring the intellectual activity with which she is engaged. The baby has a serious birth defect, a flawed heart that requires a life-threatening operation to correct. She survives. Much of the remainder of the novel is about—or should one say also about—challenging rules, for the hospital rules forbid mothers visiting their infant children. Up to now the mother has been fighting tensions, battling conflicts within

164 First published in 1927. I am using *The First Forty-Nine Stories* (London: 1939), 251.

165 ibid. 166 ibid, 253.

167 ibid, 249. And see Pamela Smiley, 'Gender-Linked Miscommunication in "Hills Like White Elephants" ' in Jackson J Benson (ed), *New Critical Approaches to the Short Stories of Ernest Hemingway* (Durham, NC: 1990) 288–299.

168 London: 1965. Another Drabble novel whose fulcrum is pregnancy and the choice to bear or abort is *The Middle Ground* (London: 1980). 169 Matthew 18:6.

170 Drabble was in her third pregnancy when she wrote *The Millstone*.

171 In a case in 1927, a girl of 13 was prosecuted for attempting to induce an abortion by taking laxative tablets and sitting in a hot bath. 172 *R v Bourne* [1939] 1 KB 687.

173 The judge said there might be a 'duty' to abort to save the 'yet more precious life' of the mother.

174 See n 168 above, 41. 175 ibid, 65.

herself. Now the conflicts are with authority, with hospital middle management, all women. The attitudes they exude are, like the laws of abortion, of another age: ethics within health care barely merited consideration. She wins the right to see her daughter, but only because she enlists the support of a male doctor, a friend of her father. Wilt comments: 'The quality of this life is that mothers can mother only through the influence of men'.[176]

This is the historical context—or a slice of it—for this volume. What follows is not a summary of the papers—they can speak for themselves—but rather a few thoughts, some pointers, some responses.

Only one of the papers explores children's literature: Desmond Manderson on Maurice Sendak's *Where the Wild Things Are*. As Manderson notes, Sendak took children's literature seriously. I fear too few of us do.[177] As a result there are too few examples which examine such literature through law spectacles. Of course, the category itself is far from unproblematic.[178] What is *Harry Potter*? Those I see reading JK Rowling's books on the tube are certainly not children! And if children's literature has been neglected, what of children's comics?[179] There are few better examples of popular culture. And as with children's literature more generally lots of insights into children's concepts of law emerge. Piaget, as is well-known, found that children commonly thought it was naughtier for a child to break ten glasses when doing their best to help than to break one on purpose in a fit of rage.[180] A young child's sense of justice can be similarly crude. S/he may well believe in an expiatory form of justice, where the wrongdoer should be made to suffer a punishment painful in proportion to the offence committed. This can be found in the literature they read which reflects this, and may well reinforce it. Manderson shows how *Where the Wild Things Are* encourages a positivistic model of law with authority not expected to be questioned.[181] Seymour challenges this.[182] The book itself is one of the most striking picture books published in many years. And it divided both critical and lay opinion. Sendak himself said his 'object is never to lie to children'.[183] But what is a 'lie'? Into what category do fantasy and escapism, prime ingredients of adult entertainment, come? As a child I remember being absorbed in Frank Richards[184] and Anthony Buckeridge.[185] On one level these

[176] See n 146 above, 58.

[177] A good recent illustration is Brian Klug's study of 'Peter Pan' in Kathleen Alaimo and Brian Klug, *Children As Equals—Exploring the Rights of Children* (Lanham, Maryland: 2002).

[178] See generally Nicholas Tucker, *The Child and the Book* (Cambridge: 1981).

[179] See George Perry, *The Penguin Book of Comics* (Harmondsworth: 1971). See also n 178 above, Ch 5.

[180] Jean Piaget, *The Moral Judgment of the Child* (London: 1932). But see Peter Bryant, *Perception and Understanding in Young Children: An Experimental Approach* (London: 1974).

[181] Associated particularly with HLA Hart, *The Concept of Law* (Oxford: 1961).

[182] See p 71 below. Seymour is responding to an earlier version of Manderson's paper, but the differences are not material to his argument.

[183] See Maurice Sendak, *Where the Wild Things Are* (London: 1967).

[184] See ES Turner, *Boys Will Be Boys* (London: 1975).

[185] His 'Jennings' stories. On books for girls see Mary Cadogan and Patricia Craig, *You're a Brick, Angela: A New Look At Girls' Fiction from 1840 to 1976* (London: 1976).

authors wrote (harmlessly) about challenges to authority: in Richards' 'Bunter' stories, then extremely popular children's television, the end was always a beating; in Buckeridge's 'Jennings' stories the chief character was invariably good at bungling things so as to bring maximum danger to himself from exasperated teachers. At least children then read. Has anyone considered what impact the absence of reading—its replacement by computer games—has on legal socialization for the current generation of children?[186]

A number of the papers in this book explore aspects of the novel. Papke's account of five US lawyer/story-tellers is fascinating and thought-provoking. What equips lawyers like Erle Stanley Gardner ('Perry Mason'), Scott Turow and John Grisham to write popular fiction? What is it about lawyers and law that sells so well? Are we troubled by the law, excited by it, searching for the 'right answer'?[187] Does it tell us anything about societal change that where once—as in the Perry Mason stories—there was formulaic justice, now it is not uncommon (Turow's *Presumed Innocent* is an example[188]) to find ambiguity rather than closure? Do these examples of popular fiction offer us a view (or views) on fears and expectations about law and lawyers in twentieth-century America?[189] Or do they go beyond this and offer insights into the United States more generally? Why, one may ask, has this cultural phenomenon (Papke calls it 'complex and varied') not taken root so persuasively in other countries such as Britain? I remember devouring the stories of Henry Cecil, a county court judge at Willesden, and he was very popular in the 1950s and 1960s.[190] But is he read today? I doubt it, and no one springs to mind as an obvious successor, though claims may be made for Frances Fyfield.

However, as Gearey shows, a novelist does not have to be concerned with lawyers, courts or 'what has passed until now as the themes of legal philosophy' to engage with jurisprudence. And he argues that JG Ballard does just this. Perhaps any text seen as fundamental, around which society defines itself, can be read in this way. The Bible, the Greek Tragedies, Shakespeare, as I have already argued, can be seen thus. As can other forms of popular culture: Verdi's operas in Risorgimento Italy,[191] Wagner's 'Ring'[192] and his 'Meistersinger'[193] in Bismarck's Germany (and rather more malignly in Hitler's[194]), the Hollywood musical, the

[186] See Elliot Turiel, *The Culture of Morality* (Cambridge: 2002).

[187] cf Ronald Dworkin, *Taking Rights Seriously* (London: 1977). For a contrast with literature see Maria Aristodemou, *Law and Literature* (Oxford: 2000) 230.

[188] New York: 1987. And see Christine Corcos, 'Presuming Innocence: Alan Pakula and Scott Turow Take on the Great American Legal Fiction' (1977) 22 *Oklahoma City U L Rev* 129.

[189] See Mary Ann Glendon, *A Nation Under Lawyers* (New York: 1994).

[190] His best story (and most well-known) was *Sober As A Judge*. As a 14 year old I appeared before him (Judge Leon) to ask for an adjournment—I got it!

[191] The people would chant Verdi's name—it stood for 'Vittorio Emanuelle Re D'Italia'. Many of Verdi's early operas, in particular *Nabucco*, paralleled the Italian peoples' fight for independence. See Mary Jane Phillips-Matz, *Verdi—A Biography* (New York: 1993).

[192] See Deryck Cooke, *I Saw the World End: A Study of Wagner's Ring* (Oxford: 1979).

[193] In particular the paean to 'die heil'ge deutsche Kunst' at the opera's conclusion.

[194] On which see Paul Lawrence Rose, *Revolutionary Antisemitism in Germany From Kant to Wagner* (Princeton, NJ: 1990).

Beatles, the 'Bollywood' film. Even a medium such as a photograph—Valier describes that of a man about to be tried and condemned to death—can 'code' the terror of law. As Douzinas points out, 'the law loves and fears images'.[195] Hence the reluctance in Britain to allow cameras into courtrooms[196] and the development of the stylized courtroom sketch, discussed in Lynda Nead's paper. Are the 'images' then different in countries which allow cameras into courtrooms? And would the trials, both image and discourse, change if the trial were presented as entertainment? Imagine (say) the Jeffrey Archer trial 'staged' in the United States, or as it would have been had it taken place in the United States.

There are several contributions to this volume that focus on novels which at first sight have nothing to do with legal issues and yet which in different ways throw light on aspects of law. Thus Marlene Tromp addresses 'sensation' fiction which questioned not just social policy, but also normality and morality. In terms of popular culture, what is of particular interest is how this genre of literature was received by nineteenth century readers and critics. As Tromp points out, when fiction leaves us 'feeling vexed, unsettled, discomforted—as sensation fiction did its Victorian readers, it may be providing us with a cue for social change'. Put this into a contemporary context and the most likely vehicles of such transformation become the 'soaps'.[197] Certainly, they have been credited with bringing home to a mass population an awareness of any number of social (and therefore potentially legal) problems,[198] much as the television drama *Cathy Come Home* did for homelessness a generation ago.[199]

The contemporary significance particularly for our understanding of jurisprudence, of genres of earlier ages is brought out in Leslie Moran's exploration of the Gothic imagination.[200] His argument is that some recent jurisprudential scholarship, informed by post-structuralist and psychoanalytic thought, engages with themes that are integral to the Gothic imagination. Uncertainties about the nature of power, law, society, family, and sexuality dominate Gothic fiction. This is true also of literature influenced by the Gothic imagination, for example Kafka's work.[201] From Kafka it is not a long way to the Nazi concentration camps[202]—or to Guantanamo Bay. The opacity of the law could not be 'clearer', nor could its hypocrisy or contradictions be more manifest.[203]

The film, of course, is a modern genre. It is a focus of the majority of the papers in this collection. It is not surprising that there should be such a vibrant interest in law

[195] 'The Legality of The Image' (2000) 63 MLR 815.

[196] On which see Martin Dockray, 'Court On Television' (1988) 51 MLR 593.

[197] J. Fiske, *Television Culture* (London: 1987)

[198] One can only speculate what the possible impact of John Irving's *The Cider House Rules* (New York: 1985) would have been on *Roe v Wade*, had it been published earlier.

[199] It led to the passing—albeit 10 years later—of the Housing (Homeless Persons) Act 1977.

[200] See p 226 below.

[201] See C Agamben, *Potentialities: Collected Essays In Philosophy* (Stanford: 1999) Ch 10.

[202] It is not surprising that Kafka's work was banned both by the Nazis and post World War by the Communists. See Nicholas Murray, *Kafka* (London: 2004) 387–388.

[203] See Ronald Dworkin, 'Terror and the Attack on Civil Liberties', *New York Review of Books* 6 November 2003.

and film studies.[204] Themes about subjects concerned with law have had such a pervasive influence in the first century of film making. And many of them are wonderful introductions to law. Is there a better way of introducing jury decision-making than by showing *12 Angry Men*?[205] It may also reinforce myths, for example, as John Denvir points out,[206] of good lawyers and bad legal systems. It also tends to bring out the pathological side of law, with a greater emphasis on dispute resolution, in particular the trial, than on, what Llewellyn called, 'preventive channelling'.[207] Film has, it would seem, emerged as a legitimate element of law studies because it provides 'an apparently credible account of the operation and personnel of the law'.[208] If, as Stewart Macaulay has argued,[209] people derive their knowledge about the law from popular culture, in particular film, then the accuracy of its portrayal must be of concern. Of course, films can show features of the law, such as jury decision-making, from which research is banned.[210] It would not altogether surprise if jury persons acquired an understanding of their role more from films than a judge's instructions. It is probably more complex than this, and so Sherwin[211] and Meyer[212] have argued. They have argued that the form and nature of presentations in trials in the United States increasingly corresponds to the expectations of juries. The 'autonomy' model of law does not work when there is interpretation and mutual dependence. But it is not just juries who may get their understanding of law from films, but the population in general. As Sherwin notes: 'popular legal representations serve as a cultural barometer revealing pressing needs, fantasies, and anxieties, as well as beliefs, hopes and aspirations that are circulating in society'.[213] And they shape the way we understand the role of law in society. This itself may change as a result. Of course, not all films which portray legal issues are set within legal systems with which the audience has familiarity. Do we know if audiences appreciate the differences? And if they do, are films a medium of legal pluralistic awareness? Or do they reinforce stereotypes or foster xenophobia? Machura points out that Nazi propaganda films used conventions of American courtroom dramas to denounce the American legal system.[214]

These are just a few of the themes which emerge in the papers in this volume. Legal *realism* threw light on the legal system in the twentieth century, even if it often exposed the obvious. Legal *reelism*—and other forms of law and popular culture studies—similarly has much to offer to the student of law and society. Our jurisprudence is constantly enriched from new sources and perspectives. This volume takes the pulse of a new and vibrant field. It offers explanations of the past, understandings of the present, and pointers as to the future.

[204] Exemplified by the many books that have been published in recent years including David Black, *Law in Film* (Kansas: 1999), Nicole Rafter, *Shots in the Mirror* (Oxford: 2000), Steve Greenfield, Guy Osborn and Peter Robson, *Film and the Law* (London: 2001).

[205] United Artists, 1957.

[206] See p 183 below.

[207] See Karl Llewellyn and EA Hoebel, *The Cheyenne Way* (Norman, Oklahoma: 1941).

[208] See p 186 below.

[209] 'Images of Law in Everyday Life' (1987) 21 *Law and Society Rev* 185–218.

[210] On problems of researching juries see Contempt of Court Act 1981, s 8.

[211] *When Law Goes Pop: The Vanishing Line Between Law and Popular Culture* (Chicago: 2000).

[212] See p 65 below.

[213] See p 90 below.

[214] See p 148 below.

PART I

INTRODUCTORY THEMES

Law and Film Studies: Autonomy and Theory

Peter Robson

The Questions of Theory and Method

A new focus for academic study has emerged, principally within Law Schools from 1986 onwards, concerned with the relationship between law and popular culture generally, and law and film in particular. Given the extensive amount of books and articles and courses that have emerged during this period it is not fanciful to talk of a discrete area of law and film studies. Discussions on the theoretical and methodological practices appropriate to this area of scholarship have not been at the forefront of the agenda of what has been written in law and film studies in the years from 1986. What unites the writing is that they link in a range of different ways the fields of law and film. This essay seeks to explore the implications for law and film studies of this limited direct engagement with theory and method.

There are similarities between the emergence of law and film studies and that of law and literature. In the early part of the twentieth century we find work lauding the aesthetic quality of writings about lawyers.[1] This work is interesting to read but did not claim to be anything more than a pleasant diversion from the 'real' business of law and lawyering.[2] The field took on a rather different aspect with John Wigmore's more systematic legally-centred list of 100 legal novels[3] updated in the 1970s.[4] Law and literature has since developed a much closer affinity with literary studies.[5] It is a contrast with Gest to read the kinds of work found in the last decade of the twentieth century and into the first decade of the new millennium. Law and literature has come of age in the sense that it is now found as a distinct area of scholarly endeavour within a significant number of Law Schools.[6] It now ranges

[1] J Gest, *The Lawyer in Literature* (London: 1913).

[2] For a modern equivalent see J Wishingrad (ed), *Legal Fictions* (London: 1995).

[3] J Wigmore, 'A List of One Hundred Legal Novels' (1992) 17 *Illinois L Rev* 26.

[4] R Weisberg and K Kretschman Wigmore, ' "Legal Novels" Expanded: a Collaborative Effort,' *New York State Bar Journal*, February 1978, 122.

[5] E Gemette, 'Law and Literature: An Unnecessarily Suspect Class in the Liberal Arts Component of the Law School Curriculum' (1989) 23 *Valparaiso U L Rev* 267.

[6] I Ward, 'The Educative Ambition of Law and Literature' (1993) 13 *Legal Studies* 323; E Gemette, 'Law and Literature: Joining the Class Action' (1995) 29 *Valparaiso U L Rev* 665.

across the links with classical literature,[7] the significance of nineteenth century realist novels,[8] as well as a range of other guises.[9]

There has been a similar shift from comments and use of film references as mere diversions to various extensive and detailed analyses of the precise nature and impact of law films. Many of these early references were confined to classroom illustrations rather than integrated into any fully articulated analysis of law in film. They were intended to highlight particular doctrinal issues of principle or practice. For example, the author has shown, when teaching the law of wills, extracts from *Laughter in Paradise* (1951, Transocean). In this film, the testator is a practical joker who has decided to leave very substantial bequests to his relatives on condition they do something completely against their normal character. His class-prejudiced and snobbish sister, Fay Compton, who maltreats her domestic staff, is required to work satisfactorily as a servant for a minimum period of one month. A philandering cousin is required to marry the first woman he speaks to after the reading of the will. The first lawful bequest and the second challengeable condition[10] contrast with the unlawful conditions attached to two other cousins. Mild-mannered bank clerk, George Cole, is required to rob a bank, and timid writer of pulp fiction, Alistair Sim, must somehow receive and serve a 28 day jail sentence. These and other extracts were used on an ad hoc basis simply to provide entertaining and memorable moments to fix elements of core principles in the course. The nature of the content of available films means that such 'diversionary' didactic techniques have been unsystematic and dependent on the courses taught. For example, in teaching about dubious forms of eviction such as 'winkling',[11] it was possible to show a lightly fictionalized version of the career of Nicolas Van Hoogstraten which neatly highlighted the problems of enforcement in this area in a striking and engaging way (*Sitting Targets*, 1988, BBC).[12] The same went for the official treatment of homeless families. Showing *Cathy Come Home* (1966, BBC) provided, then and now, a highly effective way of drawing attention to the limitations of the pre-1977 administrative and legal framework in student minds.[13] Such opportunities, however, are dependent on chance being limited to the issues encountered in film, which tend towards the violent and exotic rather than the stuff of everyday life.[14]

[7] M Aristodemou, *Law and Literature* (Oxford: 2001).

[8] M Williams, *Literature and Law* (London: 2002).

[9] J Morison and C Bell (eds), *Tall Stories? Reading Law and Literature* (Aldershot: 1996); M Freeman and A Lewis (eds), *Law and Literature* (Oxford: 1999).

[10] On the grounds of being contrary to morality or public policy under Scots law.

[11] D Nelken, *The Limits of the Legal Process* (London: 1983).

[12] This was complemented by a documentary from April 1988 on Hoogstraten as well as showing the video of Carter the Unstoppable Sex Machine performing 'Sheriff Fatman' with its catalogue of his unsavoury landlord practices and references to the leading Rachman figure, Nicolas Van Wotshisface.

[13] The Housing (Homeless Persons) Act 1977 introduced the right for homeless families in priority need to be provided with permanent accommodation—this replaced the right to temporary hostel accommodation available in terms of the National Assistance Act 1948.

[14] L Friedman, 'Law, Lawyers and Popular Culture' (1989) 98 *Yale LJ* 1579 at 1588.

The potential for popular culture in legal situations was highlighted in a rather more systematic way by Chase. In his challenge to the aridity of the doctrinal ideological analysis of critical legal studies he set out an agenda for empirical investigation into a whole range of areas of popular culture. He pointed out that whilst critiquing the political jurisprudence of appellate courts was not wrong, it told only part of the story. Ideology resides in other locations such as popular culture and it is an exploration of how these operate that Chase identified as worthwhile.[15] Similarly, Friedman, proceeding from the starting point that people know little about law and that their information comes second-hand, suggested research in this area as a scholarly priority. In this process the distorted picture from films and television played a crucial role. Although law itself occupied a central role in people's lives, little was known about how people acquire the 'hodge-podge of notions about rights and duties' that the population carry round in their heads.[16]

The early use of film as illustration links with the contributions encountered in the 1993 collection from David Gunn.[17] These essays consisted of the proceedings of a conference of American lawyers on popular culture. There are brief comments on film, literature, women's studies and television in the context of why lawyers should study popular culture. They are a celebration of the role of popular culture in equipping the lawyer with valuable life skills. The style is short and a wide range of fascinating vignettes can be found ranging from the image of District Attorneys[18] to Gilbert and Sullivan at law[19] to the notion of the lawyer as hero.[20] It also acted as a call to examine the potential of popular culture with systematic scholarly rigour. The vast majority of subsequent scholarship has tended to avoid the question of exactly what methodology or theory underpins such work. This, it is suggested, is an issue which needs to be addressed, for the health of law and film studies.

The Relevance of Popular Culture in Law's Construction

The crucial point behind the emergence of film within law studies relates to film's ability to provide an apparently credible account of the operation and personnel of law. Film provides a valuable vehicle for such broader representations and hence has been perceived as crucial in both legal theory and socio-legal studies in relation to the nature of legal phenomena. A number of issues emerge from this broader role.

15 A Chase, 'Towards a Legal Theory of Popular Culture' (1986) *Wisconsin L Rev* 527 at 553–554.

16 Friedman, n 14 above, 1605.

17 D Gunn (ed), *The Lawyer and Popular Culture: Proceedings of a Conference* (Littleton: 1993).

18 J D Bounds, 'Noble Counsellor: "Perry Mason" and Its Impact on the Legal Profession' in Gunn, n 17 above.

19 D Whaley, 'Gilbert and Sullivan at Law' in Gunn, n 17 above.

20 G Clark, 'The Lawyer as Hero' in Gunn, n 17 above.

Accuracy of Representation

One matter is the question of popular culture as the source of knowledge about the operation and nature of institutions. Rather than just providing a reflection of the reality of the life of law, popular culture has a constructive role in the *creation* of law. In a provocative challenge to law and society scholars in 1986 Stewart Macaulay suggested that people increasingly obtained their knowledge about law from popular culture.[21] One problem for lawyers and those involved in socio-legal studies is, of course, the extent to which these representations are inaccurate and lead to a distorted version of the nature of law and the role of various legal actors. The work of Bergman and Asimow provides an important section in the overview of the films the authors selected as the best on the law in the courtroom. They draw attention to the 'sleights of hand' which would not or could not occur in real life in their 'Legal analysis' section on each film. Hence this question of accuracy was at the core of their concerns.[22]

On a slightly different tack popular culture has the potential to shed light on the vexed question of law's 'autonomy'. It has been suggested that the notion of law being autonomous bolsters law's power and authority.[23] Thus, rather than being dependent on shifting trends in political or social thinking, law has been taken as the 'normative voice of reason and authority'. Law is put forward as the embodiment of rationality. This is principally derived from the method of law. Behind the façade of the rule of law and law's splits between fact finding and applying legal principles, law is a practice rather than an intellectual discipline.[24] The contrast is with popular culture which embodies emotion, corporeality, tactility, aestheticism and the spectacular.[25]

'Porous' Law

It would be misleading, though, to talk as though there were two distinct spheres—law on one side and popular culture on the other. For perfectly good political reasons lawyers particularly have maintained the view that law is autonomous. They have done this through the notion of 'legal positivism'. Initially this set of ideas found currency with those struggling against tyrannical regimes that based their injustices and oppression on the vague and variable content of 'natural law'.[26] Conceived as a bulwark against tyranny, legal positivism has, however, proved to be a problem in providing a 'legal' point of attack against oppressive regimes. Law by the legal positivist account is valid if created in the formally

[21] S Macaulay, 'Images of Law in Everyday Life' (1987) 21 *Law and Society Rev* 185–218 at 197–204.

[22] P Bergman and M Asimow, *Reel Justice* (Kansas City: 1996).

[23] M Thornton, 'Law and Popular Culture: Engendering Legal Vertigo' in M Thornton (ed), *Romancing the Tomes* (London: 2002).

[24] P Kahn, *The Cultural Study of Law: Reconstructing Legal Scholarship* (New Haven and London: 1999) 2.

[25] Kahn, ibid, 15.

[26] B Fine, *Democracy and the Rule of Law* (London: 1984).

prescribed way. There is no further standard by which rules can be judged. The pages of jurisprudence are replete with how to avoid the imprecision of natural law formulae and the abject passivity of legal positivism.[27] Neither the prospect of being exposed to whatever the regime in power determines to be law nor relying on such notions as 'the popular will' or the 'national interest' has proved appealing.

During times of accountable democracy, debates on the nature of law and legality may seem less than crucial. Apart, however, from the question of how law is defined, there is the rather more fruitful question of how porous the legal rules are in practice. Critics have pointed to the fact that judges and juries are open to social influences.[28] They do not deliberate in a vacuum. This applies in the way in which the rules of the common law systems are 'refreshed' and adapted to modern circumstances. It is not difficult to illustrate this process in operation—albeit that it occurs in an unsatisfactory, ad hoc and incremental way. The legal rights stemming from the relationship between men and women within marriage have been altered between 1880 and the present in Britain. The formal inequality in the relationship has been altered in piecemeal fashion. The anomalous position of women in relation to conjugal relations was altered by the judiciary when they accepted the proposition that rape within marriage was possible.[29] Their avowed reason for changing was quite explicitly tied to perceived changed social attitudes.

The rights of same sex partners to succeed to private sector tenancies was accepted by the courts in 1999 after being rejected as too 'advanced' some 15 years before.[30] The judiciary were able to clothe their policy decision in the language of precedent and the changing meaning of the nature of the family over the years. This meant that they were able to accept that same sex relationships were now acceptable as coming within that term. At the time of the enunciation of the variable nature of the family the judges had expressed strong antipathy to heterosexual relationships outwith marriage. This major change was achieved through the ability of the judiciary to inform themselves from the changing mores of society as to what kinds of relationships were acceptable in society and worthy of protection. In rejecting the notion of protection in 1985, a judge in the House of Lords indicated to the author that the country was 'not ready' for such a seismic change. By the end of the millennium it was adjudged to have changed.[31]

Finally, a cohabitee in Scotland sought a court order excluding her partner from the matrimonial home.[32] The relevant legislation extended the protection afforded spouses to any man and woman who 'are living with each other as if they were man and wife'.[33] The woman had fled the couple's home. The lower court held that the words of the statute provided protection only to those who were actually

27 M Freeman (ed), *Lloyd's Introduction to Jurisprudence* (7th edn, London: 2001).

28 J Griffith, *The Politics of the Judiciary* (London: 1997).

29 *Stallard v HM Advocate* 1989 SLT 469 (Scotland); *R v R* [1992] 1 AC 599 (England and Wales).

30 *Harrogate BC v Simpson* (1984) 17 HLR 205.

31 *Fitzpatrick v Sterling Housing Association* [2001] 1 AC 27.

32 In terms of the Matrimonial Homes (Family Protection)(Scotland) Act 1981.

33 s 18 (1).

cohabiting. On appeal, it was determined that the legislation should be read in order to provide effective protection to avoid the woman having to risk harm in order to qualify for protection with a court order.[34] These illustrations make clear that legal principles can be adapted to changing social circumstances. One of the indicators and measures of social change is popular cultural representations of legal phenomena. Hence films and their role in this process have been deemed worthy of examination.

Mutual Reflection and Interpenetration

The relationship between law and popular culture also involves mutual reflection and interpenetration. Culture is not simply a set of practices which reflect the reality of official norms of the legal system. This system itself involves a mix of rules, understandings and applications which produce different results at different times. What factors are dominant in any part of the complex process of making rules effective is the very essence of socio-legal studies. A fresh slant has been added to the notion that popular culture forms a source (accurate or not) of knowledge by the work of Meyer[35] and Sherwin.[36] Looking at trial practice in the United States they suggest that the form and nature of presentations increasingly corresponds to jury expectations. These expectations are perceived to be shaped by the forms observed in popular culture, particularly television and film. In confronting gangster Louie Failla's racketeering charges his counsel sought to construct a defence using the 'braggart' model from Mafia movies.[37] Thus the focus on popular culture goes further than simply whether or not media presentations of law are accurate to the nature of the process of mutual interpenetration and how law is actually created and processed.

The Need for Criteria in Delineating the Field of Study

Just as the early illustrative work in teaching about law involved a range of filmic sources, so, in the development of law and film studies, there has been discussion about the boundaries of the material worth examining. The interests of those writing about the interface between law and film are diverse. Much of the early work was related to legal practice teaching. Hence the kinds of film material which would be used were tightly circumscribed to the clearly forensic. Few commentators have devoted extensive consideration to this issue.

[34] *Armour v Anderson* 1994 SLT 1127 at 1131.

[35] P Meyer, 'Desperate for Love: Cinematic Influences Upon A Defendant's Closing Argument to a Jury' (1994) *18 Vermont L Rev* 721; P Meyer, 'Desperate for Love II: Further Reflections on the Interpenetration of Legal and Popular Storytelling in Closing Arguments to a Jury in a Complex Criminal Case' (1996) 30 *U of San Francisco L Rev* 931; P. Meyer, 'Why a Jury Trial is More Like a Movie Than a Novel' in S Machura and P Robson (eds), *Law and Film* (Oxford: 2001).

[36] R Sherwin, *When Law Goes Pop* (Chicago and London: 2000).

[37] Meyer, 'Desperate for Love II' n 35 above.

The professional orientation of the interests of Bergman and Asimow led them to assume that the focus on trial movies was both self-explanatory and unproblematic. Their goal was to provide an overview of the kinds of films on which law teachers might draw.[38] Although not all the films they examine are actually limited to courtroom dramas, this is the principal focus of their work. The reason, they suggested, for the success of such films is a combination of a number of discrete factors. Trial stories work because they provide the drama of one-on-one confrontation and have a built-in suspense factor. They are concerned with the eternally fascinating themes of murder, treachery and sex. They also present controversial legal and moral issues in a palatable form. As far as what constitutes the possible subject matter, the authors focus on 'trial movies'. This focus is emphasized with the scoring system of gavels by which films are assessed for 'the quality, dramatic power, and authenticity of the trial scenes in the movie'.[39]

By way of a different approach we find Denvir's contributors to Legal Reelism[40] opting to illustrate their discussions with reference to films with little ostensible connection to the legal system. These range across a wide range of film genres—westerns, gangster films, foreign classics, contemporary comedies and sex thrillers as well as a couple of films that centre on the trial process. Denvir and his contributors are examining films as legal texts. They are, Denvir explains, 'cultural artifacts open to warring interpretations'.[41] The films are plundered for their meaning/s in relation to various different ideas. For instance, in discussing the different ways in which native Americans have been presented in films, Terry Wilson examines the way in which Hollywood mostly ignored Indians as 'a continuing presence in American life'.[42] Margaret Russell in the same volume looks at the way in which film has taken a stereotypical view of race in Hollywood's treatment of history.[43]

Yet another focus adopted was that of Rafter[44] looking at 'crime films'. This covered films that portray cops, courts, prison or crime itself. Hence the trial movie does not exhaust the field of representations of criminal law with which she is concerned. As she explains, her focus is on the broad impact of crime films in the way that they both reflect our ideas about fundamental social, economic and political issues as well as tending to shape the way we think about these issues. She concludes that these films criticize some aspects of society such as police brutality and prison violence and the legal barriers to justice. She also notes that these films offer solace or resolution by showing triumphs over occupation and brutality. Insofar as Rafter is writing about crime films her canvas is broader than the typical law and film studies syllabus as well as excluding significant material on civil aspects of law. Its focus derives from the sub-discipline of criminology, with the consequent limitations.

Black[45] takes an even more expansive approach, suggesting that going beyond courtroom films to films about law opens up the category not only to detective and

[38] Bergman and Asimow, n 22 above. [39] ibid, xviii.
[40] J Denvir (ed), *Legal Reelism* (Urbana and Chicago: 1996). [41] ibid, xii.
[42] ibid, 222. [43] ibid, 172. [44] N Rafter, *Shots in the Mirror* (Oxford: 2000).
[45] D Black, *Law in Film* (Urbana, Illinois: 1999).

prison films but 'possibly to virtually every commercial fiction film ever made'.[46] Whilst this makes sense in the context of Black's exploration of how both law and film are reflexive, it offers an unacceptable hostage to fortune. It suggests that there are no boundaries to the films which are of potential value in seeking to throw light on how legal phenomena appear in film and how these representations affect the life of formal and informal norms. This seems a step too far. Only by stretching meaning to extraordinary lengths can one squeeze any justice relevance from *Big* (1988, TCF), *About a Boy* (2002, UIP/Universal/Tribeca/Working Title/Kalima) or *About Schmidt* (2002, Entertainment/New Line). Many more examples could be added to illustrate this point.[47]

For the purposes of retaining a link with the study of law it has been suggested that what should be taken as the core of law and film studies is a limited range of films.

> In order to qualify as a law film the following characteristics must be present in some shape or form: the geography of law, the language and dress of law, legal personnel and the authority.[48]

This excludes films where 'justice' is enforced outside of any legal framework, for example, war films, social dramas and family sagas. This means that there are some films that are perhaps not immediately easy to classify but which we would regard as generally outwith the compass of 'law film', such as horror films. Like Black and Rafter, however, it is clear that the focus may be rather broader than the nature and impact of the trial movie. Without some boundaries, however, the practice of analyzing films about law threatens to dissolve into film studies with limited interest to the original legal and social theory audience.

The Range of Activities in Law and Film Studies

Law and film studies now occupies a distinct place in the academy. The nature and development of this emergence of film in legal studies has been described as a 'movement' by Machura.[49] This perhaps suggests a coherence and consistency of approach which seems to be lacking. There are different methods employed. It is possible to identify three principal kinds of academic course in which law and film scholarship has been encountered within Law Schools.

Legal Practice and Legal Studies

The initial interest in Law Schools has been to use films as illustrative of aspects of legal doctrine. As noted, the availability of material for such a purpose is highly

[46] D Black, n. 45 above, 3.

[47] When dealing with this point in oral presentations the author has been wont to produce the lists of current Top Ten films in that particular week and demonstrate that normally only a couple have legal issues.

[48] S Greenfield, G Osborn and P Robson, *Film and the Law* (London: 2001) 24.

[49] S Machura, 'The Law and Film Studies Movement' in P Robson and S Machura (eds), *Law and Film Perspectives* (Oxford: forthcoming).

variable. Lawrence Friedman pointed out that film makers have eschewed the everyday commonplace of law in favour of the dramatic.[50] Most of this product has focused on the criminal law and its processing of social deviance. The area most often encountered is that of murder. This in turn restricts the areas of legal practice which can benefit from a use of filmic inserts.

Course outlines from Schools such as the Golden Gate Law School in San Francisco indicate a principal interest in the ways in which film can shed light on problems within legal practice.[51] The range of issues which have been raised in films covers substantive as well as evidential issues. Thus the distinction between direct and hearsay evidence can be seen in such unlikely locations as *Roxie Hart* (1942, Twentieth Century Fox).[52] Similarly, starting with this film we can see that alternative styles of courtroom delivery can be illustrated. In the films down the years contrasts in approach can be noted in a whole range of films. The possibilities are endless and it would be surprising if this process were to cease given the advances in digitizing technology and the use of sophisticated audio-visual material in teaching.[53]

Legal Theory and Film

An alternative focus has been to use the medium of film to illustrate not examples of principles of the legal system in action but rather elements of theory which have featured in one way or another in film. Thus we find many course providers electing to use Kurosawa's *Rashomon* (1950, Daiei) as a vibrant exemplar of the problems of constructing truth. This pathbreaking film shows events in which a bandit encounters a wealthy couple in a woodland. The husband dies and there is a hearing to investigate the death. We see how the different accounts of the events by the parties appear to be consistent with the physical evidence first encountered by the woodcutter who finds the husband's body.

In a slightly different area of interest we can see how a notion associated with American legal realism, that our ideas stem from our social backgrounds, is a staple feature of filmic law. Thus we might look to such diverse sources as *12 Angry Men* (1957, United Artists) and *Serial Mom* (1994, Guild/Savoy/Polar) to see a jury's reactions to evidence in a trial being strongly influenced by the backgrounds of the members. In *12 Angry Men*, for instance, the social experience of being raised in the ghetto of juror number 5 (Jack Klugman) leads him to come to life and reject the casual racism of juror no 10 (Ed Begley) and reconsider the evidence in this capital case. By contrast, the black comedy *Serial Mom* employs the trope of Kathleen Turner (Beverly Sutphin) playing on the weaknesses of individuals to secure her acquittal on murder charges. One witness recants when she appeals

[50] Friedman, n 14 above, 1588.

[51] Golden Gate Law School Prospectus, 2003—Law 783 Law and Film outline.

[52] The death of the janitor witness to Roxie's innocence and the consequent unavailability of his direct testimony.

[53] The author currently uses PowerPoint with embedded digitized videoclips and DVD clips.

to his sexual peccadillo by 'flashing' him while he is being questioned by the DA. No-one in the courtroom notices this, of course. The evidence of another witness is revealed to be highly suspect when Beverly Sutphin exposes her as a woman who does not recycle her waste. The jury and all in the courtroom, being civic-minded responsible people, react as if the witness had admitted to having coprophiliac tendencies.

The traditional conflict between positivism and natural law approaches to novel criminal issues can be delineated by a range of film material. The test of eternal justice as a criterion rather than humanly created law is well illustrated by the reflections of the judges in both *Judgment at Nuremberg* (1961, United Artists) and *Judgment in Berlin* (1988, Hobo/Bibo TV/January Enterprises/Sheen-Greenblatt) although extensive coverage of the process of judicial decision-making is not a feature of many law films.[54]

Social Theory and Perspectives on Film

Similarly, the ability of film to shed light on debates within social theory can be usefully illustrated. There is ample material in films for those dealing with the relationship between issues such as racism, sexism, ageism and homophobia in society. Gender stereotyping and its effect have featured in a range of films where the second-class treatment of women by the legal system can be highlighted. In *Physical Evidence* (1989, Rank/Columbia) prosecutor Theresa Russell is limited to doing routine low level work rather than taking important cases like murder. Although she challenges this assessment of her abilities, the film finds her following meekly behind the male protagonist. In *Legal Eagles* (1985, Universal/Northern Lights), although portraying a lawyer, Debra Winger (Laura Kelly) takes the traditional role. She has a fixation on an older successful Assistant DA, Robert Redford (Tom Logan). She gazes at him throughout the film with puppy-like devotion, following him as he sleeps with the client, solves the mystery, secures an acquittal and at the finale they end up as marriage and legal partners. They are clearly on their way to a professional and domestic relationship of dominance and subservience. Other portrayals are rather more encouraging (*The Accused* (1988, UIP/Paramount) *Primal Fear* (1996, UIP/Paramount/Rysher).

Changes in attitudes and the role of both ethnic minorities, women and gays can also be demonstrated through the representation in film over the years. The female-free Law School class of Edward G Robinson (Professor John Lindsay) in *I Am the Law* (1939, Columbia) is a contrast with that encountered by Reese Witherspoon (Elle Woods) in *Legally Blonde* (2001, MGM). One of the knowing visual references in the latter film is the way in which in the final courtroom scenario all the protagonists in the case are women—judge, prosecutor, defence counsel, accused and witness. A more realistic kind of transformation of lawyer

[54] Greenfield, Osborn and Robson, n 48 above, 141–160.

protagonists in respect of ethnicity can also be observed, contrasting some of the earlier standard trial movies with contemporary settings—*Anatomy of a Murder* (1959, Columbia), ... *And Justice for All* (1979, Columbia), *The Verdict* (1982, TCF), *Jagged Edge* (1985, Columbia) *Suspect* (1987, Columbia/Tristar)—with more recent offerings from the 1990s—*Philadelphia* (1993, Tristar), *Losing Isaiah* (1995, Paramount) and *Primal Fear* (1996, UIP/Paramount/Rysher). The authority figure of the judge is played by African American women in both *Big Daddy* (1999, Columbia/Out of the Blue) and *Legally Blonde* (2001, MGM) and African American men in *Fighting Justice* (1989, Columbia), *Presumed Innocent* (1990, Warner/Mirage), *The Client* (1994, Warner/Regency/Alcor) and *Bonfire of the Vanities* (1990, Warner). Again the issues which can be enhanced by such material are extensive and only limited by those issues that the cinema has tended to avoid, such as poverty and the struggles between labour and capital. There is remarkably little on these areas in either British or US cinema. Rather than being seen as potential box office failures, such matters have been subject to official as well as industry censorship.[55]

This brief survey indicates that law and film studies operate in a range of academic settings. These employ different methods and varying kinds of filmic evidence. They include individual ad hoc illustration of specific points such as legal points or practical techniques. There are also overviews of developments in film in terms of personnel or content to illustrate changes in social or political perspectives in different eras. This is achieved by contrasting one or more films from one period with those from another. This data speaks for itself and has not been treated as problematic in terms of meaning. There are major variations in the extent of filmic evidence used as the basis for the interpretations which writers have used in this process.[56] As we shall see, this difference in methodology has not been an issue which has been given any prominence in the scholarship of law and film studies. It is a deficiency which needs to be addressed.

The Relationship Between Law and Film Studies and 'Host' Disciplines

Accordingly, the different focus and distinctive criteria of the disciplines which inform law and film studies require to be examined. There are, in the author's view, valid reasons why it is worth locating the questions and focus of law and film studies outwith another domain discipline. These categories, of course, should not be

[55] P Robson, 'Fade to Grey: portraying the ethnic minority experience in British film' (2002) 30 *Intl J of the Sociology of Law* 235 at 255.

[56] Contrast R Sherwin, 'Cape Fear: Law's Inversion and Cathartic Justice' (1996) 30 *U of San Francisco L Rev* 1023 and G Thain, 'Cape Fear' in Machura and Robson, n 35 above, with L Graham and C Maschio, 'A false public sentiment: narrative and visual images of women lawyers in film' (1995–96) 84 *Kentucky LJ* 1027.

fetishized. They are in reality no more than heuristic devices for organizing knowledge into manageable segments for teaching and publishing purposes. That said, nonetheless, there is a danger that, in being a subset of either legal practice, popular culture or film studies, the agenda of these larger enterprises will distort the kinds of inquiries which led scholars to focus on the interface and relationship between law and film in the first place. It is worth addressing these principal areas individually.

Legal Practice Studies

The problem with legal practice studies is that the professionally orientated syllabi have in practice focused on the legal answer to the exclusion of concern with the social function and political impact of the rules. This persistent debate within Law Schools and the legal profession has been the relationship between the perceived conflict between law as a vocational study and as an academic discipline. This theme was played out during the emergence of full-time legal education in Scotland and England in the nineteenth century.[57] The need for legal study to avoid being unreflective training for the profession was recognized in the debates. The result was the requirement for law degrees to contain an obligatory element of theory through the inclusion of jurisprudence. The question of how effectively this balance has been achieved has been one of the reasons behind the rise of socio-legal and critical legal studies. The concentration on the rules at the expense of the politics and social impact of law was instrumental in changing the content of the syllabus in Law Schools.[58]

It was not merely the content that changed from the 1970s. It was also the exclusively doctrine-orientated focus which was challenged. Nonetheless, notwithstanding the emergence of a context for legal rule teaching, the actual focus of much of the work undertaken in Law Schools remains wedded to the professional needs of neophyte lawyers, judging by the content and nature of forms of assessment employed. Hence, the concerns of law and film studies can find themselves strongly harnessed to questions of the effectiveness of legal practice. At bottom the contextualization of legal studies might be seen as little more than 'topping' and 'tailing' of the true purpose of the exercise which is to produce an effective proto-lawyer. The goal is one who can answer the problems brought in by actual clients rather than one who is familiar with the gendered nature of the law or the unequal application of sanctions as between business crime and street offences. In this atmosphere the purpose of looking at film is to enhance technique and identify ways of making lawyers better at being lawyers rather than socio-legal analysis. Whilst these are laudable training outcomes, in this setting the broader questions of how cinema renders the reality of law and the legal system's idiosyncracies becomes of marginal import.

[57] P Robson, *Housing and the Judiciary*, Strathclyde University Doctoral Thesis (Glasgow: 1979) 24–60.

[58] G Osborn, 'Borders and Boundaries: Locating the Law in Film' in Machura and Robson, n 35 above.

Popular Culture

By the same token the concerns of popular culture diverge from what a law and film studies agenda needs to embrace. Just as legal practice sets boundaries centred on the lines of 'is it legal', so the interests of those in popular culture have their own dynamic. Issues such as the nature of popular culture as 'mass culture' or 'people's culture' or an aspect of 'hegemony' are of interest as a general background to the assessment of film's potential to affect public attitudes to law and justice. There is, however, a sense in which these issues of definition are questions whose resolution is not vital to the law and film studies enterprise. That has its own goals which are intimately linked to legal phenomena in a way in which discussions on such issues as whether it is valuable to make a distinction between 'high' and 'low' culture are not. Law and legal phenomena remain the focus, albeit in a wider sense than the professional concerns of legal practice.

Film Studies

Finally the world of film studies is just that. It is a discipline whose concerns are reflexive. David A Black sums up the situation contrasting the audience for legal studies with that of film studies. As he indicates, there is a functional goal in legal scholarship which is missing in the various areas of scholarship that make up film studies. Legal studies, he suggests, has a constant and identifiable 'telos'.[59] The interest of scholars in law and film studies in some of the more arcane areas of film studies is likely to be limited. There is no clear reason why one would expect to find scholarship on graphics and sound of major importance in law and film studies. This is not to deny that this topic might be intrinsically interesting, but within any attempt to construct a coherent area of scholarship some things are beyond the radar. Some areas have potential. For the immediate future their significance is likely to be limited—the technology of film and the distinctive nature of national cinemas spring to mind. How editing and lighting enhance film is an integral part of film studies. It is, however, peripheral to any serious consideration of law and film, at least at this stage in the development of the area. Such topics as the whole range of films are useful background but to dwell in this area leads us to film studies and not to film and law studies.

Whilst the ambit of legal studies is rather less constrained than Black implies, there is nonetheless a contrast between the perceived 'utility' of legal studies and that of film studies. The likelihood of the courts taking into account academic doctrinal analysis is never high but it does exist, particularly since the end of the self-denying ordinance of the courts against citing living writers. By the same token there are instances where the results of socio-legal studies have a place in the day-to-day work of the legal system. Black seems to feel, somewhat pessimistically, that there is no equivalent 'goal' for film studies. Film studies, he indicates, has 'no

[59] Black, n 45 above, 133.

clear-cut relation with an overriding and constant goal'. Whether or not this is so would seem to depend on the way in which film studies is conceived. A significant part of the literature seems replete with the social as well as the technical role of film, both in its production and impact. Nonetheless the danger of academics talking solely to an academic audience is one which seems more likely to occur within film than law and this is a situation which law and film studies would want to avoid.[60] The social impact of film in relation to law must be the goal, not simply an aesthetic or technical analysis of film.

The Themes and Methods Encountered in Law and Film Studies

The relationship between law and film has been discussed in a variety of academic texts in the years from 1986. In the absence of any tradition of academic scholarship and any formally agreed set of concerns the issues covered in this work and methods of analysis have been highly diverse. It is possible, however, to draw up a list of the matters which recur most frequently on which there have been significant contributions and, in some instances, debate.[61] The undernoted are drawn from a survey of English language material.[62] In these early stages much of the work has been taxonomic. The principal methodology employed has been either literary or empirical. The use of a small batch of films or even a single film on which to base comments has been extensive. It dominates the literature. There are, as we have seen, a number of overviews of law films which seek to base their conclusions on rather broader evidence.[63] Which of these methods is more valuable has not been an issue discussed in the literature.

The Image of the Screen Lawyer Over Time

A significant focus for a number of essays has been the different ways in which the image of lawyers has been presented over time. It is an area where there has been some controversy. The basic conflict has been between whether there has been a decline in the quality of the screen image of lawyers. Asimow[64] and Rafter[65] have

[60] These are issues debated at the Law and Society Association annual meeting in June 2003 and at the Association for the Study of Law, Culture and the Humanities Annual Conference, March 2004.

[61] For a full description and analysis see P Robson, 'Theory and Method in Law and Film Studies' in Robson and Machura, n 49 above.

[62] The material which the author has seen in French is limited currently to the 2002 volume from CinemAction, *Justice Sur L'Ecran*. There has been work in German: S Machura and S Ulbricht (eds), *Recht im Film* (1998).

[63] Bergman and Asimow, n 22 above; N Rafter, *Shots in the Mirror* (Oxford: 2000); Greenfield, Osborn and Robson, n 48 above and A Chase, *Movies on Trial: The Legal System on the Silver Screen* (New York: 2002).

[64] M Asimow, 'Bad lawyers in the movies' (2000) 24 *Nova L Rev* 533.

[65] Rafter, n 63 above.

suggested there is evidence of a decline. Asimow points to the increase in the prevalence of 'bad' lawyers as protagonists in law films. In place of Atticus Finch (*To Kill a Mockingbird*, 1962, U-I) and Sir Wilfred Robards (*Witness for the Prosecution*, 1957, United Artists) we have Frank Galvin (*The Verdict*, 1982, Universal) and Dave Kleinfeld (*Carlito's Way*, 1993, TCF). Amanda Bonner (*Adam's Rib*, 1949, MGM) and Paul Biegler (*Anatomy of a Murder*, 1959, Columbia) are replaced by Martin Vail (*Primal Fear*, 1996, UIP/Paramount/Rysher) and Jennifer Haines (*Guilty as Sin*, 1993, Buena Vista/Hollywood). Rafter associates the decline in the moral character of the lawyers with the decline of the genre into excessively reworked themes.

Greenfield,[66] both individually and along with colleagues,[67] has suggested that the matter is rather less clear cut. It is argued that the notion that films contain a single image of the lawyer which is 'good' or 'bad' is too limited. Films tend to include a range of legal protagonists, some of whom are more or less admirable. Individual lawyers themselves tend to contain more depth and character traits than simply being 'good' or 'bad'. In films such as *The Verdict* (1981, TCF/Zanuck Brown), *Primal Fear* (1996, UIP/Paramount/Rysher) and *Erin Brockovich* (2000, Columbia Tristar/Universal/Jersey) the principal lawyers have weaknesses which they overcome. This question of single or multiple 'images' is an issue that continues to divide commentators.

Changing Personnel in the Law Film

There has been a shift in the kinds of lawyers whom we see on the screens. They were once almost exclusively male, white and heterosexual. This was a matter of comment amongst a range of writers. Between 1980 and the end of the millennium the picture had altered. A number of writers have tracked this process both generally,[68] and in relation to gender,[69] ethnicity,[70] and sexuality.[71] The significance of this change has also been discussed.[72]

Contrasting Images of Justice

There has been a good deal of work on the different ways in which justice in the broad sense is portrayed. The clash between lawlessness and emerging notions of civilized

[66] S Greenfield, 'Hero or Villain? Cinematic Lawyers and the Delivery of Justice' in Machura and Robson, n 35 above.

[67] Greenfield, Osborn and Robson, n 48 above.

[68] N Rosenberg, 'Hollywood on Trials: courts and films 1930–1960' (1994) 12 *Law and History Rev* 341.

[69] R Sheffield, 'On Film: A Social History of Women Lawyers in Popular Culture 1930 to 1990' (1993) 14 *Loyola of Los Angeles Entertainment LJ* 7; L Graham and C Maschio, 'A false public sentiment: narrative and visual images of women lawyers in film' (1995–96) 84 *Kentucky LJ* 1027.

[70] R Sheffield, 'A social history of black lawyers in popular culture' (1991) 7 *Focus on Law Studies* 4.

[71] L Moran, 'Heroes and Brothers in Law: the male homosexual as lawyer in popular culture' (1998) 18 *Studies in Law, Politics and Society* 3.

[72] Greenfield, Osborn and Robson, n 48 above.

justice have figured in writings centring on Westerns.[73] Coverage has also included the roster of John Grisham's lawyers.[74] Even more exotic locations have been included such as science fiction,[75] American social issues films,[76] and Nazi courtroom films.[77]

The Portrayal of Substantive Legal Issues

Not surprisingly, given the background of many scholars in professional legal studies, there have been a number of surveys of areas of substantive law. Asimow has looked at the way in which the coverage of divorce in the movies altered between the 1930s and the introduction of the moviemakers' system of self-censorship, the Hays Code, to the 1970s.[78] There have also been comments on environmental law and international law.[79]

The Relationship Between Reality and Filmic Justice

There is a persistent interest in the accuracy of representations of the legal process in films. This is understandable given the way that extracts from film are used to illustrate technical points in professional legal studies. Whether or not it be the rules of evidence or methods of presentation before juries, it is important that the models encountered in such versions of law's practice are not misleading. We see this in *Catch Me If You Can* (2002, Dreamworks/Amblin/Kemp/Splendid) where Frank Abagnale, Jr (Leonardo di Caprio) is upbraided for his forensic style by the judge. The young conman had in fact learned about the law from watching *Perry Mason* in the same way as he learned medical terms from *Dr Kildare* on television.

A somewhat different concern has been the distortion of the truth of events through film adaptation in relation to miscarriage of justice films,[80] as well as the mechanics of the process.[81] On the same tack more recently Moran has examined

[73] F Nevins, 'Man in the middle: unsung classic of the Warren Court' (1996) 30 *U of San Francisco L Rev* 1023.

[74] J Grant, 'Lawyers as Superheroes: The Firm, The Client and The Pelican Brief' (1996) 30 *U of San Francisco L Rev* 1111; P Robson, 'Adapting the Modern Law Novel: Filming John Grisham' in Machura and Robson, n 35 above; K Bartlett, 'Grisham Adaptations and the Legal Thriller' in S Neale (ed), *Genre and Contemporary Hollywood* (London, 2002).

[75] P Joseph and S Carton, 'The Law of the Federation: Images of Law, Lawyers and the Legal System in *Star Trek: The Next Generation*' (1995) 24 *U of Toledo L Rev* 43–85.

[76] M Kuzina, 'The Social Issue Courtroom Drama as an Expression of American Popular Culture' (2001) *J of Law and Society* 79.

[77] P Drexler, 'The German Courtroom Film During the Nazi Period: Ideology, Aesthetics, Historical Context' (2001) *J of Law and Society* 64.

[78] M Asimow, 'Divorce in the Movies: From the Hays Code to Kramer vs Kramer' (2002) XXIV *Legal Studies Forum* 221.

[79] M Schraf and I Robert, 'The Interstellar Relations of the Federation: International Law and *Star Trek: The Next Generation*' (1994) 25 *U of Toledo L Rev* 577; Joseph and Carton, n 75 above.

[80] S Greenfield and G Osborn, 'Pulped Fiction? Cinematic parables of (in)justice' (1996) 30 *U of San Francisco L Rev* 1181.

[81] S Shale, 'The conflicts of law and the character of men: writing *Reversal of Fortune* and *Judgment at Nuremberg*' (1996) 30 *U of San Francisco L Rev* 991.

the ways in which the versions of the Oscar Wilde trials which reached the screen were adaptations of highly selective readings of the original events.[82]

Film Technique in Law Films

In the early years of looking at the representation of law in film there has been a relatively modest amount of work looking at techniques employed. There has been work on a distinctive tranche of films which Rosenberg terms 'law noir'.[83]

Subsequently the filmic conventions used in the area have been examined by Silbey where her close reading of a number of classic courtroom dramas unveils the conventions used by film makers when working in this vein.[84] Bohnke, in his examination of some of the justice cinema of John Ford, has gone beyond the lawyer's concern with narrative and looked at the stylistic elements in this work.[85] Such a focus, while it has been limited in the past, is attracting further attention from outside the Law School.[86]

Adaptation and Law Films

There has been some interest in the implications of the process of adaptation for the kinds of narratives and the way in which there is a flattening of narrative style from the personal to the objective[87] whilst at the same time a heightening of certain critical elements.[88] Again this work is far from extensive. It has covered the work of James Ellroy[89] and John Grisham.[90] It runs the risk of producing material which may be of some interest within literary studies but which adds little to the concerns of law and film studies. Thus, for instance, in his analysis of the film *The Sweet Hereafter* (1997, Electric/Speaking Parts/Alliance/Ego) Sarat[91] does not examine the very different structure and narrative encountered within Russell Banks' original book.

The Development of Theory in Law and Film Studies

Introduction

Whilst noting the failure of scholars to address the issue of method when discussing film, there has also been a limited engagement with what are the

[82] L Moran, 'On realism and the law film: the case of Oscar Wilde' in L Moran et al (eds), *Law's Moving Image* (London: forthcoming).

[83] N Rosenberg, 'Law Noir' in Denvir, n 40 above.

[84] J Silbey, 'Patterns of Courtroom Justice' in Machura and Robson, n 35 above.

[85] M Bohnke, 'Myth and Law in the Films of John Ford' in Machura and Robson, n 35 above.

[86] Moran et al, n 82 above; R Sherwin, *Law's Moving Image* (New York: forthcoming).

[87] Meyer, 'Why a Jury Trial is More Like a Movie Than a Novel', n 35 above.

[88] Robson, n 74 above.

[89] Meyer, 'Why a Jury Trial is More Like a Movie Than a Novel', n 35 above.

[90] Robson, n 74 above; Bartlett, n 74 above.

[91] A Sarat, 'Imagining the Law of the Father: Loss, Dread and Mourning in the Sweet Hereafter' (2000) 34 *Law and Society Rev* 5.

theoretical assumptions underpinning the work. Given the novel nature of the work looking at film and law such an approach is not surprising. In this section a number of distinct approaches are described. The majority eschew discussion of theory. There is a considerable body of work which seeks to identify and classify the kinds of films being examined. There are, in addition, many essays which operate within theoretical frameworks that are not explicitly discussed but which can be inferred from the context in which these works appear. Finally there are a small number of interventions which operate within specific theoretical boundaries.

The Taxonomic Phase

There has been a body of work in which the emphasis has been to identify and classify. This has involved ethnicity and gender. It has also involved using such categories as good and bad lawyers as well as films featuring judges, juries, courts martial and incompetent lawyers.[92] In about half of the work carried out which is referred to by scholars in law and film studies the main emphasis has been to delineate the kinds of materials being drawn on and the links between such films. It would be reasonable to categorize Bergman and Asimow's *Reel Justice* in this way as well as some of the work which has been presented at conferences on such areas as judges, juries and trial movies.[93] It is also a significant element in other work which has analyzed both the 'golden age' of courtroom dramas[94] and the full spectrum of 'law films'.[95]

Implicit Theoretical Frameworks

Socio-legal

The question of how close to reality the representation of law is has an impact on the likely effectiveness of official norms. It is a question of empirical investigation. In the general context of beliefs and behaviour this kind of research about the implementation of societal values has been undertaken on a range of issues. It is not, however, an area which has attracted much attention in law and film studies.

There have been three kinds of approach within this general theoretical framework. Firstly we have statements to the effect that there must be a connection between what people watch and what they believe.[96] There is no specific evidence provided in these writings to substantiate these claims. Given the focus of these writings on the mechanics of the process this means that we need to seek a

[92] For an overview of this work see Greenfield, Osborn and Robson, n 48 above.

[93] P Robson, *The Judge in the Picture*, Law and Society Association Annual Meeting, 1998; P Robson, *Judges in Film: a reappraisal*, Law and Society Association Annual Meeting, 1999; P. Robson, *Courtroom Drama in Film: Subgenre on Trial*, Law and Society Association Annual Meeting, 2003.

[94] T Harris, *Courtroom's Finest Hour in American Cinema* (Metuchen, NJ: 1987).

[95] Greenfield, Osborn and Robson, n 48 above.

[96] Macaulay, n 21 above, 197 et seq; Sherwin, n 36 above, 18.

framework in other work. It is nonetheless a fundamental part of advertising and political lore that media effects exist and the literature is implicit rather than explicit. There is also related work which investigates the extent of exposure of the population to certain kinds of media images. Since work in other areas demonstrates that there is a general media effect such an effect is, not unreasonably, inferred. In Germany work on the effect of media on children has led scholars to assume that the prevalence of lawyers on television must have an impact on how the public perceive issues of law.[97] The formal basis on which the operative assumptions are constructed has been examined in scholarship on the image of lawyers.[98] This latter work on media effects has produced further empirical work.[99]

Legal Practice

The interest of professional legal educators in how law represents the system has as its largely unstated goal the more effective protection of clients' interests. Whilst there are ethical boundaries and standards which must be adhered to by members of the legal profession, the underpinning assumption for those involved in legal education is that the knowledge and skills being learned by students will in due course be put to the service of some group or individuals. With the dominance of the adversarial system within Anglo-American common law jurisprudence, the focus of attention is clear. Most obviously applicable have been the examinations of the nature of the American jury trial by Meyer[100] and Sherwin.[101] Meyer describes the process whereby the effectiveness of addressing a jury is deemed to be enhanced where the lawyers focus their efforts on the narrative structure of the case and fit into the jury/audience's preconceptions of plausible motives and patterns of behaviour. These are demonstrably gained from models found in films and television insofar as Meyer looks at the racketeering charges against Louie Failla. Those dealing with media-orientated audiences such as juries owe it to their clients to fashion the narratives into a pattern which the audience can follow. This was a matter which was acknowledged in the past in relation to novelistic tropes. Both the prosecution and defence, for example, in the notorious Madeline Smith case adopted a narrative which made sense in terms of romantic melodrama.[102] Given the dominance of professional goals within legal education this is a train of scholarship which is unlikely to diminish in importance.

Cultural Zeitgeist

The ways in which law films encapsulate a particular set of social values and perspectives on law is an approach which has been prevalent. Sherwin contrasts the

[97] S Machura and S Ulbrich, 'Law in Film: Globalising the Hollywood Courtroom Drama' (2001) *J of Law and Society* 117.

[98] Asimow, n 64 above.

[99] M Asimow et al, *Law Students' Perceptions of Law* (forthcoming).

[100] Meyer, 'Desperate for Love I and II', n 35 above.

[101] Sherwin, n 36 above.

[102] R Kennedy, 'Legal Sensations: Sexuality, Textuality and Evidence in a Victorian Murder Trial' in M Thornton (ed), *Romancing the Tomes* (London: 2002).

nature and reputation of the legal profession in the 1950s and 1990s.[103] The kind of lawyers found in J Lee Thompson's *Cape Fear* (1961, United Artists/Melville-Talbot) played by the rules, by and large. The situation in which the lawyer protagonist, Sam Bowden finds himself as the victim of Max Cady's revenge stems from the laudable act of simply prosecuting the case. Bowden is a family man with loving wife and daughter and a high professional reputation. In Martin Scorsese's *Cape Fear* (1991, Universal/Amblin/Cappa/Tribeca) there is a clear rationale for Cady's reaction. His lawyer has let him down. He has acted against the canons of his profession. In this version he has been transformed from a decent family man with loving wife into an adulterous cynic. He is willing to ignore the ethical requirement to fully represent his client's interests in favour of the appeal of securing a conviction. He has not become amoral but rather more ambivalent about the value of the rule of law.

Lawyers by the 1990s have been transformed in the public consciousness. No longer enjoying a high public reputation they are much more troubled figures prepared to bend/break the rules. What is altered is not simply the characters in the film but the society in which they operate. After Richard Nixon's ignominious resignation and a series of scandals the lawyer can never again be seen as incorruptible.

Rafter traces the way in which the 'golden era' of lawyers was displaced through the 1980s and 1990s by a very different kind of lawyer.[104] As film makers struggled 'to find fresh ways of depicting the gap between natural and man-made law'[105] the system is routinely depicted as flawed. At the same time a new kind of lawyer emerges alongside the traditional white male. The style, she suggests, involves tokenism towards ethnic minorities and almost always 'inadequate' woman lawyers.

Moran in a slightly different way notes the way in which the changes in society's general attitudes to gay and lesbian issues altered between the making of *Victim* (1961, Rank/Allied Filmakers/Parkway) and *Philadelphia* (1993, Tristar/Clinica Estetico). It is not just the subject matter that has altered, of course. In the first film we are in the era of prosecution for homosexual acts in private. Thirty years later the gay lawyer is not a victim of blackmail but seeking redress for discrimination on account of his sexuality. The themes as well as the tone have altered. The films provide a vivid demonstration of the shift within society on same sex relationships from criminalization to a mix of general tolerance and respect along with fear and loathing.

Gramscian Hegemony

One of the staple features of socio-legal studies has been the examination of how class, ethnicity and gender have an impact on the operation of the system of justice. The investigations in these areas have reported on levels of representation of hitherto minorities in the ranks of jurors, police or judiciary. The assumed

[103] R Sherwin, 'Cape Fear: Law's Inversion and Cathartic Justice' (1996) 30 *U of San Francisco L Rev* 1023.

[104] Rafter, n 63 above.

[105] ibid, 106.

desirable situation is the broad notion of equivalence within the institutions of justice. The courts of the rich and powerful have long been mistrusted. They have not been seen as likely to deliver justice. From the 1982 Scarman Report and the 2002 Equal Opportunities Report on women and men in Britain and public and political life to the 1999 MacPherson Report and the Patten Report,[106] the failure of institutions to command the respect of those for whom they were responsible has been noted in relation to ethnicity, gender and religion.

Just as the reality of institutions is important so too is their image. As noted above, the importance of the image has come into prominence in the past 25 years in Britain from the work of the Birmingham Centre for Contemporary Cultural Studies.[107] Greenfield, Osborn and Robson take as their point of departure the assumption that the images of law and justice reproduced in the media have a potential to impact on the behaviour of the public.[108] When this image is part of a consistent pattern wherein some groups have access to the power of the media then the situation is akin to the earlier Marxist analysis of the ownership of means of production in the Industrial Age. The major theoretical links between the materialist tradition are the work of Gramsci, and Adorno and Horkheimer.[109] As yet these links remain implicit and unacknowledged although work to rectify this has started.[110]

Explicit Theoretical Interventions

Baudrillard and Hyperrealism

The theoretical background which relates to Sherwin's observations about the interpenetration of legal and cultural practice that he draws on and refers to in *When Law Goes Pop* is that of Baudrillard. In talking of the 'vanishing line between law and popular culture' Sherwin utilizes the notion of hyperrealism discussed by Baudrillard.[111] Baudrillard suggests that in modern society the impact of media has been of such a pervasive nature as to blur the gap between what people perceive through their own senses and that which appears through the media. Other writers in this field have not gone this far.

Impact Studies

Little work has been done on the question of seeking to measure the impact of popular culture on the public. One of the first areas to be explored in British socio-legal studies in its expansion of the boundaries of legal study was the question of

[106] *A New Beginning: Policing in Northern Ireland* (September 1999).

[107] D Morley (ed), *Critical Dialogues in Cultural Studies* (London: 1996).

[108] Greenfield, Osborn and Robson, n 48 above.

[109] A Gramsci, 'Hegemony, intellectuals and the state' in J Storey (ed), *Cultural Theory and Popular Culture: a Reader* (Hemel Hempstead: 1998); T Adorno and M Horkheimer, *Dialectic of Enlightenment* (London: 1979).

[110] Robson, n 61 above.

[111] Sherwin, n 36 above.

knowledge and opinion of law. Its impact on how law operated was seen as crucial.[112] In the context of the 'decline of lawyers' debate Asimow has explored the literature on the impact of media images[113] in this context. Machura and Ulbrich refer to German research on the impact of Hollywood on the perceptions of children of the justice system.[114] As they note, the symbols of Anglo-American jurisprudence, the gavel and the wig, are taken by German children to be consonant with their notion of law and justice.

More recently a related area of investigation has been undertaken in Argentina, Australia, England, Germany, Scotland, and the United States. Researchers have investigated the influences on first year law students in their first week of Law School on their understanding of law. These cover family, school, film and television.[115] We were concerned to see if it was possible to identify which elements, if any, of popular culture had penetrated the consciousness of law students before they were immersed into the socialization process of the Law School. The contribution of popular culture seemed to be higher than any other factor such as family background, schooling or personal experience.

Film Studies

Writing in law and film studies has tended to be carried out by lawyers rather than by film scholars. There has, however, been work from outside the legal community. Black examined the nature of narrativity and reflexivity and the different kinds of impact such images of law can produce.[116] His analysis makes the same kind of bifurcation as Asimow[117] and Rafter[118] make between those which are supportive or critical of the legal order. These can be orientated towards consensus or have a critical element. The terms Black uses are reflective and refractive.[119] As indicated this reduction of films and their characters into a simple dichotomy of good/bad; consensus/critical is a useful enough starting point. It needs to be supplemented, however, by a closer reading of films. Many contain a range of characters and incidents. Some of these will be of a predominantly positive nature. All the characters in *Anatomy of a Murder* (1959, Columbia) are acting professionally as are those in *Witness for the Prosecution* (1957, United Artists) and *Primal Fear* (1996, UIP/Paramount/Rysher). On the other hand most of those in . . . *And Justice for All* (1979, Columbia), other than Arthur Kirkland, and *The Rainmaker* (1997, Paramount), other than Rudy Baylor, are driven by a self-seeking agenda. Detailed readings are, however, largely absent.

Within the legal community there has been exploration within this tradition. Bohnke provided an analysis firmly within the tradition of auteur theory in his examination of three films of the director John Ford.[120] He examines *Young Mr Lincoln* (1939, TCF), *The Searchers* (1956, Warner), *The Man Who Shot Liberty*

112 A Podgorecki (ed), *Knowledge and Opinion about Law* (London: 1973).
113 Asimow, n 64 above.
114 Machura and Ulbrich, n 97 above.
115 Asimow et al, n 99 above.
116 Black, n 45 above.
117 Asimow, n 64 above.
118 Rafter, n 63 above.
119 Black, n 45 above, 71.
120 Bohnke, n 85 above.

Valance (1962, Paramount). Silbey focuses on the filmic techniques employed within a range of law films and produces an analysis firmly rooted in film studies. She looks at the way in which law films introduce the serious theme of law with establishing shots of the halls of justice, how they frame their subjects and how they position the audience as additional jurors.[121] Some interesting work has strayed outside traditional socio-legal boundaries and drawn on feminism[122] and psychoanalysis.[123] As indicated the signs are that this will continue to attract further scholarship.[124]

Problems With and Without Theory

It is easy to demonstrate that a range of very different approaches have been utilized in law and film studies scholarship over the years. It is worth looking at reasons why a more rigorous approach to theory and method is required. This involves the factors impeding such a shift of focus from taxonomy and single film analysis as well as reasons for its possible emergence.

Peer Respectability

An important criterion within both the British and the US academy is the respect and recognition of peers. In Britain the system is relatively formal. In the past decade there has been a dual system of assessment of the quality of the publicly funded Universities in Britain. All but one of the 121 Universities in Britain are public. They are rated in terms of their research output and the quality of their teaching. The amount of government funding that they are awarded is partly determined by the grade of research rating which they receive. This assessment is carried out by centrally appointed subject committees of well-respected academics. They rate departments on a seven point scale from outstanding work of international excellence to work which is not even of national excellence.[125] The ratings are based on the perceptions of the subject panel members on the submissions of individual academics. Examples of work were required in each quinquennium between 1986 and 2001. Publication in well-respected peer review journals was indicated as the most likely to be regarded as prestigious. Funding for departments

[121] Silbey, n 84 above.

[122] O Kamir, 'Feminist Law and Film: Imagining Judges and Juries' (2000) 75 *Chicago-Kent L Rev* 899; O Kamir, 'X-Raying Adam's Rib: Multiple Readings of a (Feminist?) Law-Film' (2001) *22 Studies in Law, Politics and Society* 103.

[123] Sarat, n 91 above.

[124] Moran et al, n 86 above; Sherwin, n 86 above.

[125] The seven categories range from: 5*—levels of international excellence in more than half of research submitted; 5—international excellence in up to half of research submitted; 4—national excellence in virtually all research; 3A—national excellence in over two-thirds of research activity; 3B—national excellence in more than half of research; 2—national excellence in up to half of research activity; 1—national excellence in none or virtually none of research activity.

from central government has been based on the number of staff whose work is submitted and the gradings applied to each person's submission.

The search for peer respectability, hence, in modern day Britain brings not merely the massaging of one's ego. Respected work has meant money to the department to support research. The risk of any area of academic study which is regarded as 'lightweight' is obvious. Far safer to stick in an established area. The problem for any new area is the process of establishing academic respectability. Journals are likely to be resistant to new areas which fall outside their traditional coverage. They are, after all, commercially driven. The assessment system has put pressure on them from those working in traditional professionally orientated fields.

If law and film studies is to escape from being dismissed as academic 'fluff' then it must show that it has something to offer within the world of the Law School. It is not enough to be well-regarded in other disciplines. Whilst this is a possible way forward it nonetheless does not seem to secure the kind of recognition required by the RAE system of assessment.

The situation in the United States is rather different. The Law Schools are independent of the process of professional qualification. Their reputations are assessed by the somewhat arcane method of peer reputation. Lists are published every year ranking the Law Schools in general and specialist areas in particular. The basis of this assessment is not explicit but would seem to be strongly driven by professional criteria. The tuition fees that Law Schools are able to charge are determined by the market. Given the possibility of working in the lucrative end of the legal profession, demand permits very expensive annual tuition fees. This provides freedom from formal external constraint. The question of what builds reputation is, however, connected to a range of factors. These would not in theory militate against the existence of non-professional courses. In practice this seems to be the thrust of the courses examined.[126]

Mastering Multiple Disciplines with Debates and Conflicts

A significant, although often unstated, problem for interdisciplinary studies is the mastery of the different sources and approaches. This is somewhat easier to observe with those outside the area of law making assumptions about the domain concerns of those working in the area. Just as there is no resolution as to debates about the nature of law, the function of official norms or the appropriate kind of input for legal education programmes, the same sorts of issues abound in other areas of study. Without being either unduly deferential to formal study programmes or precious about how one achieves a reasonable level of understanding in new areas, the difficulty of cross-disciplinary work is most acute when we look at theory and require to make sense of the controversies within these new fields.

[126] The position on the Continent is rather more problematic. There is a clearer physical separation between the degree taken at the Law School and the professional qualifications obtained at either national or state level than in Britain. The University syllabus is, however, centrally determined in those countries where there has been work in law and film—France, Germany and Spain.

Connection with Mainstream Legal Disciplines

As indicated above, there is a strong professional incentive to remain connected to a well-established discipline. This is how education is organized. Law courses are notorious for being taught within the confines of the Law School rather than being easily available for those in other Faculties. The problem is that the dominant ethos of the Law School is professional legal education. As indicated already, there is a considerable push towards the practical and useful. This has always existed. The balance between professional focus and the socio-legal or critical brands of scholarship is ultimately determined by the marketability of the Law School product. Whilst potential employers may well have a strong preference for the well-rounded broadly educated graduate, the author's student-advising work within Scotland has made it clear that this is not the perception of students. They are almost all strongly focused on meeting an assumed heavily professional employer requirement. This implies that the Law School context will be highly geared to the profession—hence in this climate law and film studies would be infused with practical rather than theoretical goals. This means that the self-referential world of film studies or the theoretical thrust of cultural studies pose problems for the success of the law and film studies enterprise. Despite the increase in the interpenetration between popular culture and legal process noted in American trials, this kind of scholarship runs the risk of becoming marginalized.

The Future

Whilst the foregoing is no more than an argument for a more explicit recognition of the need for clearer signposting of methodological questions in scholarship, there is always the danger that it might be seen as seeking to be prescriptive. This is not the intention nor the expectation. The author's own work has focused previously on both the classification and the question of impact of popular culture. This has been conceived of within a broadly materialist framework. These are the areas that seem to me to be worthwhile exploring in seeking to uncover the way in which law exercises power and who benefits from such an exercise.

There is no reason to suppose that scholars will want to abandon their very different approaches to the field of law and film studies. Although it has been suggested in the previous section that there are some pressures for the area to achieve academic 'respectability', there are also countervailing forces at work.

Academics value the freedom that they have to follow their own instincts and react to any purported orthodoxy. In addition, many of those who have written on law and film are involved principally in other areas. The suggestion that there be an agreed orthodoxy is unlikely to appeal to many of those already working in this area. For those coming into the area, however, a clearer guide as to what is being examined and to what purpose would surely assist in the development of law and film studies as a serious area of scholarship.

There is no professional external pressure other than possibly indirectly. That is to say it does not seem likely that professional bodies will start to require their members to attend courses on lawyers and film. That said, courses orientated to law and film run in the United States have attracted Continuing Professional Development recognition by dint of being offered by approved providers and are planned in Britain for the Scottish legal profession. There is also the experience from France and Portugal. In the former in November 2003 a week-long law and film studies course was offered as part of French judicial training by the Institut des Hautes Etudes sur la Justice (Institute of Advanced Studies on Justice) in partnership with the Ecole Nationale de la Magistrature (National School of Judicature). It was entitled 'L'Image de la Justice dans le Cinema Européen' ('The Image of Justice in European Cinema'). This looks at how lawyers and law systems have been presented in the cinema of France, Germany, Italy and the United Kingdom. In Portugal, lawyers have arranged to undertake professional development work on law and film in 2004 under the auspices of the Catholic University of Portugal.

Thus, despite the threats and dangers which attend this new area of scholarship there are reasons to be cheerful about the future.[127] If the opportunity to debate the issues of methodology and theoretical approach is seized and vigorous debate ensues, then law and film studies may escape the marginalization that threatens any area which is not central to the professional concerns of legal educators.

[127] There is also the question of the role and significance of television. Some of the early work on images of lawyers in popular culture in the 1980s was carried out in relation to television and this continues to be the focus of some work. There is a range of reasons why the area of film has attracted far more attention in the years where there has been a focus on law and popular culture. There is a difficulty of access to television material which certainly affects anyone in Britain, along with the problem of the sheer volume of material. The nature of weekly appearances and the possibility of extensive character and issue development during the runs of these shows requires a rather different kind of reading from 90 minute one-off films which have dominated law and film studies hitherto.

Where the Wild Things *Really* Are: Children's Literature and the Law*

Desmond Manderson[†]

Where the Wild Things Are

The present study takes as its principal concern perhaps the most influential and best known of all books for very young children on the cusp of literacy and, as we will see, the verge of legality. Maurice Sendak's *Where the Wild Things Are* has become a, or even the, classic of children's literature.[1] Since its first publication in 1963, it has gone through innumerable printings, been translated into dozens of languages, received all imaginable plaudits, and been subject to varied scholarly analyses.[2] In the year 2002 alone, there was a major retrospective of Sendak's work, entitled *Where the Wild Things Are*,[3] a video and DVD released,[4] and a film version slated to begin production. For 40 years Sendak's book has been loved for its textual lyricism, its illustrative wit, and its emotional depth. Yet when it first appeared, Sendak's book was not universally praised. So violent and hostile a reaction did it provoke that some libraries even banned it. Sendak recalls:

When that came out, there were psychologists who said, This is a bad book. Any mother who sends their child to bed without dinner is a terrible mother. They objected to that, they

* This essay is a short version of a longer essay entitled 'From Hunger to Love: Myths of the source, interpretation, and constitution of law in children's literature' (2003) 15 *Law & Literature* 87–141.

† Canada Research Chair in Law & Discourse, Faculty of Law and Institute of Comparative Law, McGill University, Montréal. This article had its genesis in an essay written by Ms Ellie Parker for the course *Law & Discourse* which I taught at the University of Sydney Law School 2000–2001. It was her idea to look at the Sendak story through the theoretical perspectives covered in that course, and I am entirely in her debt for the careful research she did for that essay, as well as for the ideas that she stimulated. Although the current essay has changed a great deal in both detail and theoretical focus since then, I am immensely grateful to Ms Parker for all her work and her inspiration. I also wish to thank Nicholas Kasirer, Rod Macdonald, Peter Goodrich, Mark Antaki, Ellie Parker, Olivia Kasirer and William MacNeil, all of whom commented—often with extraordinary care and in great detail—on early drafts. Special gratitude goes also to the government of Canada who have generously funded the Chair I hold, thus allowing me to pursue my research interests in an outstanding working environment.

1 Maurice Sendak, *Where the Wild Things Are* (New York: 1984, 1963). References to the text of the book in this essay will be to this edition by way of in-text citation.

2 See especially, Ellen Spitz, *Inside Picture Books* (New Haven: 1999); Selma Lane, *The Art of Maurice Sendak* (New York: 1993).

3 Skirball Cultural Center, Los Angeles: September 20, 2002—January 5, 2003.

4 *Where the Wild Things Are and Other Maurice Sendak Stories* (New Video Group, 2002).

objected to him being so rude to his mother, they objected to her yelling back at him, they objected to the Wild Things being too scary. They objected to everything. When it was first published it was very novel and different. In fact, [Bruno Bettelheim] said that. He did take that back later in life. He did me a lot of damage at the beginning. Now it's a classic and cult book and showered with praise. And I know it's going to be on my tombstone, I just know it. And of course, I won't care, 'cause I'll be dead.[5]

Although the eponymous monsters were said to be too frightening for young children, it was the fear that Sendak stirred up in adults that lay behind their antipathy. Sendak's story respects children's behaviour, and represents not only their intelligence but their emotional ambivalence. In so doing, like all good literature, *Where the Wild Things Are* transformed the field.[6] On his tombstone I would engrave the following: Maurice Sendak took children, and children's literature, seriously.

Where the Wild Things Are is a book about the emergence of law. It is the story of a little boy named Max who is sent to bed without supper and, like HLA Hart, becomes a King in his dreams. It is also the story of how Max, through the dream, comes to understand something of the necessity of law and our responsibility in relation to it. Finally, it is a story that stages the child's movement from a state of disorder to participation in the human community of law, and therefore (mythologically) helps to constitute a parallel movement in its readership. Yet neither law nor literature sustain themselves as decretals. Their legitimacy stems from their ability to speak with us and through us, not merely *at* us. This is the message of the text, about law, and it is convincing precisely because it is expressed with the openness of literature. By showing compassion to its readership and by acknowledging the listening child's emotional complexity, *Where the Wild Things Are* transcends the status of a pallid primer. The influential best-seller, *Why Johnny Can't Read*, had in the 1950s inaugurated the process of transforming children's literature from 'horrible, stupid, emasculated, pointless, tasteless little readers' into something of actual experiential relevance to the child.[7] *Where the Wild Things Are* exemplifies that transformation. By becoming literature, inviting readers to make their *own* judgments and contributions, it becomes part of the child's life, and so succeeds pedagogically. So too its story transcends the status of an instructional manual on the importance of obedience. By introducing responsibility, inviting the reader to make their *own* judgments and contribution, its ideas, too, become part of the child's life, and so succeeds as law. Like all myths, it works through an alliance of form and content that leads people not merely to be told certain things, but to experience them and work through them in themselves. Myth is the *fusion* of law and literature.

[5] http://www.post-gazette.com/movies/20010810video0810fnp7.asp.

[6] Jacques Derrida, 'Before the Law' in Derek Attridge (ed), *Acts of Literature*, (New York: 1992) 181–220, 215.

[7] Rudolf Franz Flesch, *Why Johnny Can't Read* (1955) discussed and quoted in Louis Menand, 'Cat People', *The New Yorker*, December 23 & 30, 2002, 148.

Before the Law

That night Max wore his wolf suit and made mischief of one kind
and another
his mother called him "WILD THING!" and Max said "I'LL EAT YOU UP!"
so he was sent to bed without eating anything.

That very night in Max's room a forest grew and grew—
and grew until his ceiling hung with vines and the walls became the world all around
and an ocean tumbled by with a private boat for Max & he sailed off through night & day
and in and out of weeks and almost over a year to Where The Wild Things Are.[8]

Where the Wild Things Are dramatizes both (a theory of) childhood and (a theory of) law, and unifies them in narrative form. It treats them both as elements of what the great German sociologist Norbert Elias termed *The Civilizing Process.*[9] Elias argues that civilization is the 'self-consciousness of the West'.[10] It stands, as Mirabeau observed in 1760, equipoised between barbarism and decadence.[11] But Elias focuses on civilization not as a natural gift, nor as the inevitable progression or the eternal condition of a culture, but as a specific mode of affect developed over many centuries. This affect might be characterized by the growth, from the end of the medieval period onwards, of a sense of individualism and privacy, leading to increasing physical and emotional restraint across all aspects of social life. Elias goes straight to the daily experience of people's lives. How do people eat together? Do they sleep in the same room? Do they use cutlery or handkerchiefs or must their hands suffice? What is the intensity of their public emotional state? Elias argued that what we call 'civilized' behaviour is the result of the physical, emotional, and psychological distancing effects inculcated during our upbringing.

> People who ate together in the way customary in the Middle Ages . . . such people stood in a different relationship to one another than we do. And this involves not only the level of clear rational consciousness; their emotional life also had a different structure and character. Their affects were conditioned to forms of relationship and conduct which, by today's standard of conditioning, are embarrassing or at least unattractive.[12]

The civilizing process, which begins merely as a kind of imitation, deepens over time. It operates psychologically through the transformation of restraint into self-constraint, 'partly [in] the form of conscious self-control and partly that of automatic habit'.[13] The outward and bodily openness in relation to others that marked the medieval world becomes, over the course of centuries, transmuted into an

[8] Sendak, n 1 above, 4–19. The book is unpaginated; for the purposes of this essay I have paginated it myself beginning with the title page.

[9] Norbert Elias, *The Civilizing Process*, trans Edmund Jephcott, ed Eric Dunning, Johan Goudsblom and Stephen Mennell (Oxford: 1994, 1939). Originally published in two separate volumes as *The History of Manners* and *State Formation and Civilization* (1939).

[10] ibid, 5.

[11] ibid, 39.

[12] ibid, 60.

[13] ibid, 375.

internal discipline. Fear is likewise displaced inwards, and becomes anxiety—the psychological illness of the civilized.

Elias' contribution to the theorization of childhood is two-fold. In the first place, he recognizes how important the children's primer or textbook of manners is in our attempts to understand the affective world of the past and the development of modern and obsessively refined notions of bodily propriety. Erasmus' *De civilitate morum puerilium (On civility in children)* (1530),[14] which Elias studies with great care, is a pivotal moment, since Erasmus thereby 'gave new sharpness and impetus to the long-established and commonplace word *civilitas*' which became thereafter 'fixed into the consciousness of people with the special sense it received from his treatise'.[15] Coloured though it is by his gentle irony, Erasmus' little work is particularly illuminating both because he took the importance of etiquette in the formation of character seriously, and because his precepts show us at once the corporeal elements at the heart of the civilizing process, and yet how far we have traversed from that time to this:

> It is disgusting to spit out chewed food and put it on your plate. If you happen to have eaten something that cannot be swallowed, you should discreetly turn away and toss it somewhere.[16]

Secondly, Elias insisted that it is through the social and habitual education of children that the civilizing process of the centuries is performatively re-enacted, in miniature, in the course of each and every life. Children must learn very quickly to accept the patterns of control and self-discipline that took our societies many centuries to adopt. They must learn, in a few short years, the privatization of impulse and the shame of the body. Yet this socialization is imperative to the structure of modern law, which depends at every turn upon a basic fabric of autonomy, self-restraint, and distance. It makes possible the intercourse of daily life, and the very freedom that might otherwise undo it. Elias notes, with considerable prescience, how we take for granted the predictability and stability of social relations that this affective restraint affords us, and the complex webs of interaction it thereby permits us to weave in safety. Only place us in a context of renewed and unpredictable external fear, and see how quickly we succumb to extreme and irrational responses.[17] Civilization, in the sense that Elias uses it, must be constantly re-instilled if it is to maintain the *habitus* on which our legal and social structures unhesitatingly depend.

Furthermore, as each generation increasingly re-organizes its social structures on the assumption of just the kind of affective restraint that permits greater personal security and social inter-dependence, society demands at each turn a gradual *intensification* of this discipline. There is a process of amplification at work. Indeed, only by the extended discipline of children can such discipline be learnt.[18]

[14] Erasmus, 'On good manners in boys', trans Brian McGregor, in Erasmus, *Collected Works vol 25*, JK Sowards (ed) (Toronto: 1985, 1530) 269–289.

[15] Elias, n 9 above, 55.

[16] ibid, 283.

[17] ibid, 441.

[18] ibid, 365–400.

No doubt it seems that, on the contrary, children have much more freedom than they used to, say one hundred years ago. Yet that is, as Ariès noted, a change in the theories by which we believe discipline and education can best be instilled. At the same time, it can hardly be doubted that the length of childhood has steadily expanded over the centuries, until now it would hardly be an overstatement to imply that children do not properly grow up and leave the nest until they are 25. Or 30. Or 40. Ariès' theory then is surprisingly Lamarckian, which is to say not genetic but 'socio-genetic': as we stretch like giraffes towards the farthest leaves, we transmit our attenuated necks—so much more agile, so much more fragile—to our offspring, through a process of socialization reproduced in slightly more extended form at each succeeding iteration. Max lies at the farthest end of some 25 generations of socio-genetic evolution. No wonder he finds civilization, at first, a little hard to stomach.

Children's stories then are agents in the transmission of discipline to children, not merely by their immediate instructive power but through their deployment of myth and their capacity not only to narrate the stories of a civilization but to echo and to contribute to the echoes of these myths as they suffuse the child's world. Sendak's story provides a particularly striking example of the operation of subliminal influences that is inherent in myth's process of resonance imaging. Indeed, not only are Sendak's readers unaware of the mythic and historical dimensions which the story evokes and with which it resonates across many centuries, but it is entirely plausible that the author is too. Yet the associations are too clear to be ignored or dismissed. I am drawn to an unusual conclusion—we do not set out to tell myths; myths tell us.

Max begins the story, like all children, as 'a wild thing'. The tropes of his wildness are not hard to find. 'That night', we are first told, 'Max wore his wolf suit (p 4).' The head of the suit looks particularly lupine, with its large whiskers and its great pointy ears that conceal all Max's hair and cheeks (p 5). Now the image of the wolf has for a long time been synonymous with ideas of alienation from human society, and abundant with connotations of uncontrollable animal fury. In *De civilitate morum puerilium*, Erasmus himself cautions his young charge not to set upon dinner with ravening greed. 'That is the behaviour of wolves . . .'[19] Emmanuel Levinas, drawing on the language of Thomas Hobbes, asks us to consider whether 'man is a wolf for man'.[20] To wear the suit of the wolf is to reject all the accoutrements of law and society and return instead to a solitary life of predatory behaviour.

The 'lone wolf' has long been a symbol not just for an outsider to the social order, but precisely for an *outlaw*. An outlaw is a grave threat to community. He is not a barbarian, the enemy at the gates but, far more perilously, the enemy within. And the Latin term was *caput lupinum*: wolf's head;[21] in Anglo-Saxon or Germanic

[19] Erasmus, n 14 above, 282.

[20] Emmanuel Levinas, with Philippe Nemo, *Ethique et Infini* (Paris: 1982) 74–75. Translation mine.

[21] *Hall v Hebert* [1993] 2 SCR 159 *per* McLachlin J (Supreme Court of Canada).

sources, *wulfesheud* or *wargus* and sometimes *werewolf*. All are liminal figures, neither man nor beast but, as Agamben writes, '[he] who dwells paradoxically within both while belonging to neither'.[22] Wild, and a thing. But the wolf's head was not even a legend. It was a legal term with precise legal consequences as far back as (and before) the laws of Edward the Confessor which demand of the outlaw that 'he bears the wolf's head from the day of his expulsion'.[23] So too Bracton[24] writes in the most famous text of thirteenth century jurisprudence, *De Legibus et Consuetudinibus Angliæ*:

> An outlaw also forfeits everything connected with the peace, for from the time he is outlawed he bears the wolf's head, so that he may be slain by anyone with impunity, especially if he resists or takes to flight so that his arrest is difficult.[25]

On the next page, Max is depicted, *caput lupinum*, terrorizing the family dog with a fork (p 7). What is a dog, after all, but a wolf that has been civilized—an inlaw not an outlaw? As for the fork, its role as a harbinger of civilization can scarcely be overstated.[26] Elias notes that the fork enters the West only in the late Middle Ages. Its arrival served the needs of neither practice nor hygiene.[27] Its first recorded use was by a Byzantine Princess who, arriving in Venice at the close of the tenth century, appears to have been adjudged shockingly decadent on account of it.[28] James Giblin quotes a contemporary source:

> Instead of eating with her fingers like other people, the princess cuts up her food into small pieces and eats them by means of little golden forks with two prongs . . . God in his wisdom has provided man with natural forks—his fingers. Therefore it is an insult to Him to substitute artificial metallic forks for them when eating.[29]

Margaret Visser argues that the development of conventions of eating, or etiquette, and in particular the use of cutlery, served to enhance bodily security, since it allowed nobles to leave their knives outside of dining halls—blunter and more specialized implements were provided for dinner guests inside.[30] Yet as Elias insists, the function of the fork is primarily aesthetic. It expresses and in time *produces* a distaste for the bodily production of food; it distances us from it, and from all those who share it with us. The history of European culinary practice may be described as the alienation of alimentation. We do not eat from a common bowl with our fingers any more. We are served on personal platters, and the food travels from plate to mouth by means of dedicated instruments.[31] Touching food directly seems not so much wrong as disgusting, and it is one of the earliest and most fundamental

[22] Giorgio Agamben, *Homo Sacer* (Stanford, 1998) 104–105.

[23] ibid, 105.

[24] Henry Bracton (1210–1268).

[25] Bracton, *De Legibus et Consuetudinibus Angliæ* (Thorne Edition, Vol 2, p 362, lines 12–15), http://supct.law.cornell.edu/bracton/Unframed/English/v2/362.htm.

[26] See James Giblin, *From Hand to Mouth: or How We Invented Knives, Forks, Spoons, and Chopsticks & the Table Manners to Go with Them* (New York: 1987).

[27] Elias, n 9 above, 107.

[28] Peter Robb, *Midnight in Sicily* (London: 1999) 61–67.

[29] Quoted in Giblin, n 26 above.

[30] Margaret Visser, *Much Depends on Dinner* (Toronto: 1987).

[31] Elias, n 9 above, 90–120; and see generally Giblin, n 26 above.

steps in the civilizing of young children to ensure that they *feel* that disgust themselves. To use a fork once seemed decadent; to use one's fingers now seems barbaric. That is the civilizing process in miniature. Max shows himself, however, radically insensible to the proper use of cutlery, instead brandishing the fork as the very weapon that it was intended to abolish, and thereby reminding us once again that in his socio-genesis, he remains very much a denizen of the early Middle Ages.

Finally, on the third page, and as the apogee of this lawlessness, Max threatens to eat his mother (p 8). It is this that allows Sendak's story to resonate most clearly with the stories about the savages of the Cannibal Islands whereto (perhaps) he later travels. The Western myth of cannibalism expresses our profound horror at behaviour that seems at once the ultimate breakdown of the most basic of social contracts and legal norms, and the ultimate in bad, bad manners.[32] It is this scandalous transgression that leads to Max's banishment and sets in train the psychological logic of his awakening.

Outlaw, barbarian, cannibal, Max has most assuredly broken the law. Parents, naturally, have their own and distinct sanctions to apply. Max is 'sent to bed without eating anything' (p 8). Bracton notes likewise it was illegal to feed an outlaw after his expulsion.[33] This is serious punishment indeed for a little boy who has communicated, with his every word and gesture, nothing but a need to be fed. Perhaps one might be led to believe from this that civilization is commensurate with learning obedience. Do what you're told—or suffer the consequences. The story of *Where the Wild Things Are* has been criticized, in the influential work on 'picture books' by Ellen Spitz, for example, for its ethical shallowness in this respect.[34] But this essay will insist that a careful reading of Sendak's work soon problematizes the simplicity of its apparent legal formulations. The text is alive with the tension between authority and desire, and if we are to find a resolution within it, a way of satisfying both, it cannot be solely on the basis that we should do what our betters tell us or, to put it another way, that we should *only follow orders*. There is a more ethically compelling reading available that starts from and is continually aware of the ambiguity of Max's position as he sits alone in his room. A *punishment* for being barbarian? Where is the justice in that?

Max is depicted as experiencing the paradox that sits at the origin of any legal system, and that marks, moreover, the very entry of the child into law and the symbolic order. The child's first encounter with law leaves him or her feeling,

[32] My claim does not relate to any actual or supposed practices of human flesh eating in any community, about which the meaning, nature, and extent is strongly contested. My claim is rather about the way in which a certain image of cannibalism has lodged itself in the Western mind, and the way in which that image is constructed as a fearful archetype of savagery and a test, therefore, of what we might in this context describe as civility. It is a question of the way in which the symbols of cannibalism have been developed and used within this particular culture: Lawrence Goldman, *The Anthropology of Cannibalism* (London: 1999); Reay Tannahill, *Flesh and Blood: a History of the Cannibal Complex* (London: 1996); W Arens, *The Man-Eating Myth: Anthropology & Anthropophagy* (New York: 1979).

[33] Bracton, n 25 above, 361, line 33. I am indebted (yet again) to Peter Goodrich for pointing me in the direction of Bracton.

[34] Spitz, n 2 above.

ironically, the subject of an injustice. Children are 'before the law' in precisely the dual sense that Derrida draws out of Kafka's parable.[35] That is, they are both ignorant of the legal order and yet subject to it. A child is a pre-legal subject and yet the quintessential object of regulation. Their lives are an experience of rules that are learnt only through the process of breaking them. Derrida's point, and he makes it again in 'Force of Law' and elsewhere, is that this structure is inherent in the iterability of language itself.[36] Since interpretation is always a judgment on and after an act, and cannot be entirely pre-determined, there is a sense in which the proper meaning of law is incapable of being understood in advance. Meaning is like the rear-view mirror, judged only retrospectively and from a moment that has passed. In this sense, 'the passage of time and the violence of law form two sides of the same coin'.[37] The force of law, then, contaminates every moment of its expression. While Hans Kelsen, therefore, would insist that only the *Grundnorm*—the first law of a community that establishes the conditions under which it takes place—suffers from this deficiency, Derrida argues that every norm contains within it a tiny fractal *Grundnorm* of its own, some decision or judgment that remains unmandated by the past.

One might take the analysis back, as Derrida does, to the Bible.[38] God mandated that Adam and Eve should not eat of the fruit of the tree of knowledge. But the two 'make mischief of one kind and another' and are duly punished for it. Like Max, they must learn the penalty for disobedience. Yet how ought they to have known what disobedience *was*, let alone its consequences?[39] This question, it seems to me, lies at the heart of the very idea of obedience. It derives, to be sure, from the Latin *audire* meaning to listen, but it implies something rather more than mere comprehension. To obey requires a kind of action in response to or *ob-*, which is to say, 'on account of', our having listened. So to obey is to submit to the decision of another, regardless of our own judgment, and to comply with their instructions. One cannot obey without our obedience manifesting in a mandated course of action (or in this case, of inaction), and on the other hand one cannot disobey without an intention to act otherwise. Disobedience is an act of defiance against authority, just as obedience is an act of conscious submission to it. But Adam and Eve live in a world before such a distinction has been formed. How were they to know the wrongful character of disobedience, which is to say its implications for the authority against which it is set, when they had not yet experienced it—and moreover when the very means by which they could have learnt to distinguish good from evil was prohibited them? It was only by eating the fruit of the tree of knowledge that they *became* aware of the distinction between obedience and disobedience. In which case, there is no sense in which they could appreciate the

[35] Derrida, n 6 above, 185–196; Franz Kafka, 'The Parable of the Law' in *The Trial*, trans Wilma and Edwin Muir (New York: 1956) 303.

[36] Jacques Derrida, 'Force of Law: The Mystical Foundation of Authority' (1990) 11 *Cardozo L Rev* 919.

[37] Richard Beardsworth, *Derrida and the Political* (New York: 1996) 101.

[38] Jacques Derrida, *The Gift of Death*, trans David Wills (Chicago: 1995).

[39] I am grateful to Mark Antaki who has helped clarify my ideas on this point.

meaning or implications of their actions *prior* to their disobedience. They were, in the fullest possible sense of the word, innocent. The punishment of God was a lesson in the meaning of disobedience, but it must itself have been unjust.

This is particularly true, of course, of children, like Max, who discover that they have 'gone too far' *only* by experiencing the punishment for having done so. Indeed, it is precisely the purpose of children's play to learn the boundaries of propriety through a process of trial and error. Children are common lawyers: they provide a constant series of cases and ask for judgment upon them. And they are experimental sociologists whose parents are the rats in their mazes. They play, and in playing they learn the law. This experimentation, this *tasting* of apples, is the means by which the knowledge of good and evil is learnt. But in what sense can we characterize their behaviour as wrongful when it depends only on the distinction between play and mischief that cannot be determined in advance? One might say that Max is being punished for his ignorance of a law impossible to determine. One might go further and suggest that he is being punished for his very efforts to learn the law.

Let us take the poster-boy of modern jurisprudence and that whipping-boy of postmodern jurisprudence, Herbert Lionel Adolphus Hart, as our exemplar. While conceding that *some* laws cannot be properly determined in *some* circumstances, he insists that this problem is only 'penumbral' to the experience of language. On the contrary, law is mainly preoccupied with 'a hard core of settled meaning'[40] that enables all of us, once we become familiar with the words of the rule of law, to modify our actions accordingly. In other words, obedience to law, which is to say acting under instructions without judgment, is largely unproblematic.

> By contrast, to soften the distinction . . . is to suggest that all legal questions are fundamentally like those of the penumbra. It is to assert that there is no central element of actual law to be seen in the core of central meaning which rules have, that there is nothing in the nature of a legal rule inconsistent with *all* questions being open to reconsideration . . .[41]

The notion of obedience and the theory of hard-core meaning are necessarily connected. Obedience requires the following of rules without any reconsideration of them and therefore requires them to have some objective content that can be determined by the law-*giver*, alone and in advance. And Hart's lesson for a child like Max would be this: we expect you to learn the law, and to do so you need only obey the words we tell you. On such an analysis, legal civility would be a function of one's obedience to the pre-determined meaning of articulated norms.

But a hart is no match for a wolf. In evaluating such a theory of legality, one could do much worse than to look at it from the perspective of a child. There are few so literal as a child. They appear therefore well placed to test Hart's contention that words have an unambiguous 'core of central meaning'. Max is being punished

[40] HLA Hart, 'Positivism and the Separation of Law and Morals' (1958) 71 *Harvard L Rev* 593, 614.

[41] ibid, 615.

because he has been judged by his parents to have exemplified a 'core instance' of the prohibited behaviour known as 'mischief'. Clearly the more unambiguously mischievous his actions, the more disobedient his actions, and therefore wrongful. Hart again, *mutatis mutandis*:

If we are to communicate with each other at all and if, as in the most elementary form of law, we are to express our intentions that a certain type of behavior be regulated by rules, then the general words we use—like ['mischief'] in the case I consider—must have some standard instance in which no doubts are felt about its application.[42]

Two elements present themselves as candidates for this unambiguous core of meaning. The first element is his mother's proclamation that he is a 'wild thing!'[43] What was it that justified this declaratory judgment? Was it the wolf suit? The mischief? The fork? For Max, all of these components were simply part of the fantasy world that he had created. Whilst Max was allowed to play, however, it seemed that there were implicit limitations placed on the *types* of games he could play. Yet Max, as a child who is before the law in his understanding of the operation of language and context, is unable properly to decipher the guidelines. Lon Fuller, quoting Ludwig Wittgenstein, offers a similar scenario:

Someone says to me: 'Show the children a game'. I teach them gaming with dice and the other says, 'I did not mean that sort of game'. Must the exclusion of the game with dice have come before his mind when he gave me that order?[44]

The limitations that words embody are penetrable only in light of a context of common purposes and objectives. So much is a familiar argument that Lon Fuller developed, and that critical legal studies later elaborated, precisely in response to Hart.[45] As Derrida notes in 'Force of Law', 'the violence of an injustice has begun when all the members of a community do not share the same idiom throughout'.[46] The study of children demonstrates just how difficult, how cultural, and how important is the ascription of purposes to words as an integral part of learning to make sense of them. It places this problem of interpreting idioms not in terms of some cross-cultural difficulty or some sociological difference, but at the heart of how every single one of us actually learns about law and rules. It is the gradual emergence of children's understanding of their *context*, not those words, which marks their emergence from a state of primitivism. So this is what children first learn about law: that it is something that cannot be properly applied without reference to a purposive context of which they are only gradually aware. Children's mischief is precisely evidence of the importance of, and their ignorance of, a normative context, an understanding of what the laws are *for*. Moreover, their

[42] HLA Hart, 'Positivism and the Separation of Law and Morals' (1958) 71 *Harvard L Rev* 607.

[43] In the following discussion I am indebted to the work on Sendak by Ellie Parker in the course *Law & Discourse* at the University of Sydney.

[44] Lon Fuller, 'Human Purpose and Natural Law' (1956) 53 *J of Philosophy* 697 at 700.

[45] Lon Fuller, 'Positivism and Fidelity to Law' (1958) 71 *Harvard L Rev* 630.

[46] Derrida, n 36 above, 951.

playful literalness, in which their mischief so often consists, demonstrates with considerable clarity the impossibility of arguing otherwise. Children very often act mischievously—either intentionally or otherwise—precisely when they take a rule literally and fail to consider its purpose in a wider context. HLA Hart's theory of language is the experience of *none* of us: not as children, not as parents.

The second element that might serve as the unambiguous core of meaning of the word 'mischief' appears to be his threat to 'eat you up' (p 8). Is this not a standard instance of wrongfulness? Yet even here, or perhaps especially here, the complexity of the process by which contexts determine meanings becomes apparent. Sendak himself recalls the origin of the phrase in his own life.

> I remembered how I detested my Brooklyn relatives as a small child . . . I remember how inept they were at making small talk with children. There you'd be, sitting on a kitchen chair, totally helpless, while they cooed over you and pinched your cheeks. Or they'd lean way over with their bad teeth and hairy noses and say something threatening like, 'You're so cute I could eat you up'. And I knew that if my mother didn't hurry up with the cooking, they probably would. So on one level, at least, you could say that wild things are Jewish relatives.[47]

Sendak's account illuminates just how difficult and contextual is the process by which even simple structures of prescription are developed and stabilized. There is no such thing as a standard instance of the phrase 'I could eat you up'. It is apparently a metonym of affection in one context, and of wickedness in another. Indeed, later on in the story, the monsters that Max visits in his dream proclaim, 'Oh please don't go—we'll eat you up—we love you so!' (p 34), leaving alarmingly unclear whether they mean to speak metaphorically or literally. In those primitive societies in which some version of 'cannibalism' may have been practised, it is typically *both*: a symbolic expression of love through the physical incorporation of parts of the dead into the bodies of the living.[48]

One begins to see that there is a certain traumatic irresolution in the child's earliest encounters with the law. *Obey*. But obey what and how? How is Sendak to know that his relatives did not really intend to eat him up? How is Max to know that mischief-making does not belong to the repertoire of accepted play? And why will no-one tell him these things before—rather than by the very act of—sending him to bed? The regulatory framework in which the child immediately finds themselves, at home, requires not an isomorphic mapping of words onto objects—since that cannot by itself adequately create meaning in the child's world—but rather a subtly complex reflexive equilibrium that children develop only gradually and through suffering. The child's challenge is not simply to accept and obey the commands of a sovereign, but to understand the variable contexts and purposes that give meaning and value to them. This, not Hart's fantasy of primitive cultures, is the concept of law that children learn at first hand. In the first part of the story,

[47] Harry Morton, (ed), *The Art of Maurice Sendak* (Tokyo: 1980) 93.

[48] See especially Goldman, n 32 above; Maggie Kilgour, *From Communion to Cannibalism: An Anatomy of Metaphors of Incorporation* (Princeton, NJ: 1990); Peggy Reeves Sanday, *Divine Hunger: Cannibalism as a Cultural System* (Cambridge: 1986).

Max experiences his relationship to law as a crisis. The question I now pursue is exactly what he learns about law and his relationship to it, that allows him to resolve this crisis; allows him, in other words, to become civilized.

The Civilizing Process

And when he came to the place Where The Wild Things Are
they roared their terrible roars and gnashed their terrible teeth
and rolled their terrible eyes and showed their terrible claws
till Max said "BE STILL!" and tamed them with the magic trick
of staring into all their yellow eyes without blinking once
and they were frightened and called him the most wild thing of all
and made him king of all wild things.
"And now," cried Max, "let the wild rumpus start!"

"Now stop!" Max said and sent the wild things off to bed
without their supper.[49]

Max re-enacts 'the civilizing process' through a dream (pp 10–15). The 'wild things' themselves are encountered only after Max's unconscious has travelled for almost a year over an ocean, to a land of forests, vines, and palm trees (pp 15, 19). Sendak again plays with the inherent instability of language in the experience of a child, taking Max's mother's standard instance—'his mother called him "WILD THING!"' (p 8)—literally. Like something out of Ovid's *Metamorphoses*, the 'wild things' have been transformed from metaphors into beings.[50] But what sort of beings are they? Both in scenery and in characters it appears that we have returned to Jean-Jacques Rousseau,[51] and the imperialist myths of the South Pacific he spawned. Max finds himself in a land of noble savages and cannibal kings (pp 18–21).[52] One might even say that Sendak's images of the wild things, equal parts monstrous and loveable, amount to a finely balanced depiction between the savage and the noble. Nothing could be clearer: a child is a savage and a savage is a child. Erasmus would certainly not have approved. His analysis of civility begins with the body and moreover with the eyes, 'calm, respectful, and steady . . . not darting and rolling, a feature of insanity . . . nor staring like those of idiots'.[53] Max's lack of civility marks him as the king of the wild things (pp 22–23).

[49] Sendak, n 1 above, 20–32.

[50] Ovid, *Metamorphoses*, trans Arthur Golding (Baltimore: 2001); and see also J Hillis Miller, *Versions of Pygmalion* (Cambridge, Mass: 1990).

[51] Jean-Jacques Rousseau, *Discourse on Political Economy and The Social Contract*, trans Christopher Betts (Oxford: 1994); Terry Ellingson, *The Myth of the Noble Savage* (Berkeley: 2001); Maurice Cranston, *The Noble Savage: Jean-Jacques Rousseau, 1754–1762* (Chicago: 1991).

[52] Frank Lestringant, *Cannibals* (Berkeley: 1997); Barbara Creed and Jeanette Hoorn, (eds), *Body Trade: Cannibalism and Colonialism in the Pacific* (Sydney: 2001); Jonathan Lamb, Vanessa Smith and Nicholas Thomas, (eds), *Exploration and Exchange: A South Seas Anthology 1680–1900* (Chicago: 2000).

[53] Erasmus, n 14 above, 274.

At this point, Max's subconscious permits him to take on the role of authority denied to him in the waking world. He is depicted with all the trappings of law-making (p 24). It is an authority that rapidly reproduces the law of the mother. He first permits and indeed participates in a wild rumpus that endures the whole night long (pp 26–31). It resembles nothing so much as the kind of pagan (or savage) religious bacchanalia common to many societies. Yet Max's ambiguous relationship to this community is already a symptom of his modernity and will ultimately lead to his decisive rejection of the wild things. Just like his mother, he sends them off to bed (very late) without their supper (p 32). In Elias' terms, this transition represents the history of the civilizing process: from rumpus to sleep. And of course it is not just a story. Max's dream represents a child's growing up in terms that are embedded in the myths of the history of the West; its multiple layers echo, resonate, and parallel the emergence of civilization from savagery and the emergence of modernity from feudalism.

'Now stop!' Max says (p 32) and reproduces his mother's law, the law of restraint and interdiction. This reproduction of discipline comes with a psychic loss, but a necessary one, if the child is to participate in the modern world. He finds that he cannot join the ecstatic community of the wild things, that he is with them but does not belong with them. In us, the intensity of emotional exchange, the meaning of friendship and the value of passion, have been privatized, 'everything is more subdued, moderate and calculated, and . . . social taboos are built much more deeply into the fabric of our drive-economy as self-restraints'.[54] We have locked up our rumpuses in rooms,[55] and set apart our wildness and our wilderness.[56] Max's recognition of the need for order is nothing but the disciplining of the wild things of his own subconscious, and therefore precisely the internalization of self-restraint that Elias insists *is* 'the civilizing process'. Whilst Max's obedience remains contingent only on the threat of punishment, he remains a barbarian. The internalization of the necessity for restraint indicates his socio-genesis: *Where the Wild Things Are* reproduces in the space of a page many centuries of historical development, and that which would no doubt take 'almost over a year' in the life of a child.

Yet the capriciousness of this volte-face comes as something of a shock to the reader, as no doubt it did to Max when he was its victim. '"Now stop!" Max said and sent the wild things off to bed without their supper.' Neither is Max content to revel in the power of his position. Having reproduced the legal order that first demanded his obedience, he finds himself 'lonely' and dispirited (pp 32–33). I want to take seriously the nature and implications of this emptiness and where it leads Max.

[54] Elias, n 9 above, 168.

[55] The development of the bourgeois home from its origins in sixteenth century Holland is a history of the relentless privatization of public space and specialization of social function. This history forms yet another and highly significant aspect of the physical and quotidian ways in which the West constituted an ever-increasing discipline and self-restraint amongst its members: Witold Rybczynski, *Home: a Short History of an Idea* (New York: 1986).

[56] For a discussion of the history of the changing concept of wilderness over the past two centuries, see Simon Schama, *Landscape and Memory* (New York: 1995).

Jean Piaget[57] continues to be of central importance to the field of educational psychology. Undoubtedly Carol Gilligan is correct to remark upon his somewhat authoritarian treatment of his child informants, and his willingness to entice, demand, and even force their responses into the unyielding matrix of his predetermined categories of moral development.[58] In all this he is distinctly a creature of the nineteenth century: a structuralist, with all the taxonomic effrontery that applies. All the same, Piaget's arguments for the stages by which questions of morality and judgment are developed within children, remain persuasive.[59] Although over-simplified, Piaget's work is constantly inventive and, moreover, founded on a respect for how children learn and an attention to what they say, that remains, even in this day and age, quite radical. Let us look, says Piaget, at a context in which rules really *are* important to children—a game of marbles, for example—and let us observe the way in which their understanding of rules matures.[60] Let us acknowledge, in other words, the idea of play as the origin of law.

Amongst very young children, rules are treated as absolute and inviolable, and obedience to them a sacred duty. As we have seen, however, punishment for something done without intention is at the same time both unfaithful to the notion of yet inherent in the experience of disobedience amongst children. It was just that dilemma in which Max found himself at the beginning of our story. In order to make sense to themselves of the way in which the *fact* of a disobedient act may itself merit punishment, children begin life as moral realists. Even a child of seven or eight may speak of a bridge that collapses as punishing the child who had been forbidden from crossing it; or the scissors that cut them as exacting vengeance on the child that had been barred from using them.[61] A six-year-old may display finely-honed Jesuitical skills in the art of casuistry.

> What happened?—*The bridge cracked.*—Why?—*Because he had eaten the apples.*—If he had not eaten the apples, would he have fallen into the water?—*No.*—Why? *Because the bridge would not have cracked.*[62]

In the animist and literal world of the young child, everything is filled with a consciousness of rules and the will to enforce them. Piaget concludes, 'for since he takes rules literally and thinks of good only in terms of obedience, the child will at first evaluate acts not in accordance with the motive that has prompted them but in terms of their exact conformity' with the rules.[63] This is part of the logic behind Max's abrupt announcement that sends the wild things off to bed without their supper. Max is not expressing his mother's *judgment*, but a fact about the world that inherently applies to wild things. He still understands law as being fundamentally descriptive rather than prescriptive. Going to bed without their supper is just what wild things *do*. Just like Max. As Piaget makes clear, the question of fault or intention is not even relevant at this point.[64] Rules have consequences, and do not embody judgments at all.

[57] (1896–1980). [58] Carol Gilligan, *In a Different Voice* (Cambridge: Mass: 1982).
[59] Jean Piaget, *The Moral Judgment of the Child* (New York: 1997, 1932). [60] ibid, 13–108.
[61] ibid, 252–258. [62] ibid, 253. [63] ibid, 111–112. [64] ibid, 260–270.

At this point, Elias and Piaget part company. For Elias the sociologist, inculcating in children an habitual obedience to external rules of conduct constitutes civilized self-restraint unproblematically. For Piaget the psychologist, nothing could be further from the truth. The externalized and sacred objectivity that parental demands instil *inhibit* self-restraint. While Elias tends to treat physical habits as the natural progenitor of habits of mind, Piaget, for his part, focuses instead on what Hart might call 'the internal perspective' of the *habitué*. Piaget here is particularly critical of the connection between obedience and morality insisted upon by Emile Durkheim.[65] Durkheim's mistake, according to Piaget, lay in reducing morality to 'a body of rules sanctioned by society . . . which we obey because it is authority and for no other reason'.[66] But a civilized relationship to law requires far more than obedience to it, as Elias clearly recognized and as Hart himself affirmed. We need to internalize its demands and the habits of mind it depends upon in order to function: we need to value it and to be able to interpret it *for ourselves*. This step is essential for the development of self restraint and discipline that is the hallmark of modern man. But the nature of language being as ambiguous and slippery as it is, no mere principle of obedience can constitute this figure. Children understand, through their own bodies, that to be able to apply laws themselves, *a priori*, and not just to be a victim of them, *post hoc*, requires a sense of law's justifications, its contexts, and its purposes. Only then, positioned as an interpreter and not just as a recipient of law, can one internalize the restraints and norms of society and treat them as one's *own*, as civility demands. Only then will we move, in the language of Hart, from being an object obliged to follow orders, to a legal subject who feels a genuine sense of obligation to the law.[67]

The problem as Piaget sees it, is that the structure of absolute obedience of a child's early life ill prepares them to take on these added burdens. On the one hand, the idea of obedience demands of the citizen nothing but the conformity of their outward actions: it asks of them no opinions, no judgments, no beliefs. On the other hand, its unilateralism encourages a balancing egotism in the child (or the subject): since they are not expected to think for themselves, they can hardly be expected to think of others. In attaining a bilateral *relationship* to legal rules, then, Piaget sees the unilateral respect that initially underscores absolute parental authority as an obstacle to be overcome. In this, Piaget displays a bracing hostility to the function of parents in the child's attainment of moral knowledge. Autonomy and justice make their way in the lives of children 'at the expense of the adult and not because of him'.[68] Piaget postulates two incommensurable moral orders,[69] the first unilateral and authoritarian, the second based on mutual respect. This latter model teaches the child about the importance of intention and motive, the relationship of justice to equality, and the need to interpret laws in terms of their contexts and purposes. Piaget provides powerful evidence for the emergence of this

[65] ibid, 353–370. [66] ibid, 354–355.
[67] HLA Hart, *The Concept of Law* (Oxford: 1961) 79–88. [68] Piaget, n 54, above, 198.
[69] ibid, 327.

new language from the age of about eight onwards and attributes it to 'the intervention of a new factor'.[70] The supervening factor, according to Piaget, is to be found in the way that children begin to engage with each *other* on terms of reciprocity and equality. The emergence of genuinely co-operative relations, particularly through informal institutions of play, transform the child's comprehension of law, its purposes and its creation, not only enriching the child's understanding but allowing for its internalization. The civilizing process is accomplished, then, by children themselves—despite their parents.

There is much that seems right in this analysis: above all, Piaget shows compassion and respect for children's abilities. But just as Elias (and Durkheim *a fortiori*) assimilates the constraints of obedience to the emergence of co-operation, treating the former as the natural origin of the latter; so Piaget segregates the two, treating the latter as a radical departure from the former. In Piaget the two models of reasoning are utterly heteronomous;[71] one supersedes and indeed 'drives out' and even 'delivers the child'[72] from the other. Is there no relationship between the two then? This hardly seems tenable. A careful analysis must move from the conflation of these modes of legal reasoning on the one hand, or their separation on the other, to their dialectic. And in this regard, *Where The Wild Things Are* proves an instructive text. In the next section I will look at Max's 'return to civility' with this problem in mind. In the prescriptive reading I propose, Max returns home not simply as an obedient child, but, which is more, as a responsible one. The emergence of this newly-responsible legal subject is the crowning feature of the myth of civilization that *The Wild Things* constitutes in its readership.

The Dawning of Responsibility

And Max the king of all wild things was lonely
and wanted to be where someone loved him best of all.
Then all around from far away across the world he smelled good things to eat
so he gave up being king of Where The Wild Things Are.
But the wild things cried, "Oh please don't go—we'll eat you up—we love you so!"
And Max said, "No!"[73]

Let us begin to think about the transition from an authoritarian to a more responsive understanding of law. First, mere obedience to a text—*just do as I say*—leads inexorably to injustice: saying and meaning are two different things. The injustice is both original and continuing. One does not have to be playing with other children in order to become aware of this. Children's sense of unfairness is acute and frequently vociferous. Max experiences this injustice himself, then imagines inflicting it upon others, and is left, perhaps, reflecting on his own capacity for

[70] Piaget, n 54 above, 275. [71] ibid, 110. [72] ibid, 187.
[73] Sendak, n 1 above, 32–34.

violence. In *Where the Wild Things Are*, the inadequacy of mere obedience as a model for law—understood, as I have argued, as mandating actions and behaviour that conform without question to the authoritative demands of another—is scarcely articulated. Nevertheless Max is depicted as lonely and unhappy: neither as the giver nor as the recipient of commands, neither as master nor as slave, is he content. Secondly, the theme of the inadequacy of literal meanings is developed throughout the text, right from the literalization of wildness incipient in the *incipit*. Literalism leads *of its own nature* to an awareness of the necessity for a contextual and purposive reading of texts. Children have particular cause to be aware of the difficulties involved in determining the relevant context of a legal principle. They learn about these problems just by being children; they explore them in the games they play, the mischief they make—and the books they read.

Finally, Max's emptiness leads him to conclude that he 'wanted to be where someone loved him best of all' (p 32). This is the pivotal moment in the book and I will argue that it can be read as suggesting a complex turn in the legal argument of the book. On one level, it portrays obedience as a condition of belonging in which subjugation to absolute parental authority is traded—for love. It is an invitation for Max to return, then, suitably disciplined, to a world that promises to provide him, in return, with love and protection. Ariès argues that the depth of emotional investment in the lives of their children is what leads the modern family to insist so adamantly on their training and awakening.[74] Love and citizenship are correlative. Max must trade in his wolf suit—it is the price of his domestication. As the necessity and the desirability of this change and exchange dawns on Max, he experiences an 'awakening' or *Aufklarüng* of his own. He becomes a legal subject before our very eyes. And not to put too fine a point on it, Sendak's illustration likewise depicts sleeping monsters, and a solemn boy, all lit by the rosy-fingered *dawn* (pp 32–33). The parallels with Elias are unmistakable and convincing. This is a text of legal awakening. It enacts and realizes the child's path to law.

Nevertheless, I do not think that *Where the Wild Things Are* either can or should—since a manner of reading necessarily involves the taking of normative positions[75]—be interpreted as the glorification of obedience, the obeisance to authority, or the commodification of love. Such an approach does no justice to our best relationships either to law or to each other. Max has been offered solidarity and belonging, which is just what he cannot find as a wolf amongst the wild things. But one might initially observe that the idea that obedience needs to be *justified*, in terms of an obligation on the authority figure to provide something in return, already invites the child to evaluate the purpose of laws in determining their meaning.[76] One no longer simply obeys the law 'for no other reason'.[77] The child

[74] Philippe Ariès, *Centuries of Childhood: A Social History of Family Life* (New York: 1962) Part III, 339–410.

[75] See Fuller's elegant deconstruction of Hart's own rejection of the claim in the first two pages of Fuller, n 45 above.

[76] ibid.

[77] Piaget, n 59 above, 355.

is beginning to see that the 'why' of law and the 'what' of law are inextricably connected. This is what Fuller calls its 'external morality' and no system of interpretation can function without it.[78]

Furthermore, the promise of obedience in exchange for love establishes something like a social contract and certainly establishes a relationship which is most assuredly *no longer* unilateral in its structure. Indeed, the text makes the bargain explicit. 'Then all around from far away across the world he smelled good things to eat, *so* he gave up being king of Where The Wild Things Are', Sendak continues (p 33). And when he returns home 'into the night of his very own room' the bargain is consummated and consumed 'where he found his supper waiting for him' (pp 38–39). Once obedience is understood to derive not from the 'command of the sovereign'[79] *qua* sovereign but, conditionally, in terms of the *benefits* it makes possible to a community, destabilizing elements of critique—equality, justice, and participation—have already been injected into our understanding of law. For the love that is offered in return for obedience is already social, is enduringly purposive.

The pact of civilization between parents and their children, forged on a battlefield strewn with tears and tantrums, allows us to see the *transition* between Piaget's two moralities, and not just their disjunction. Again, the transition is necessitated by an instability *inherent* within the orthodox model and not just antagonistic to it. Piaget sees justice as a social and interpretative exercise and finds it only in the community of children *inter se*. But the social and interpretative meaning of justice is already present even in a model of obedience that simply cannot sustain its legitimacy—even to children, especially to children, though it may for a time sustain its power—without the commitment of love. In that sense, therefore, a parent must already be 'a collaborator and not a master'[80] in the social life of their children.

The love for which Max abdicates his crown is not simply a return to a familiar place where everybody is just the same as him. I do not want at this stage to enter upon a taxonomy of love, or the distinctions between *filia, eros*, and *agape* in the literature. But I think it a fair claim that love in its various forms, when it is understood as a positive constitutive force, is built upon the recognition of difference. It is therefore distinguishable from forms of narcissism that merely seek or reproduce sameness. The very word *relationship* is integral to most understandings of love; it implies a connection between two bodies that maintain their distinctness. To say 'you are just like me' is just a way of talking about me.

To develop this idea further, Levinas sharply distinguishes love from hunger, an elemental need which drives *Where the Wild Things Are* from first page till last. Hunger may be characterized as the means by which the 'alterity of nutriments enters into the same'.[81] In other words, eating takes components from the external

[78] Fuller, n 45 above, 638–643.

[79] See John Austin, *The Province of Jurisprudence Determined* (Aldershot: 1998, 1851).

[80] Piaget, n 59 above, 404.

[81] Emmanuel Levinas, *Totality and Infinity*, trans Alphonso Lingis (Pittsburgh: 1969, 1961) 129.

world, and processes them into forms capable of appropriation and use by the body. It destroys the other in order to turn it to selfish use. This is the child's first process of pleasure-seeking, and it is applied to every object that comes within reach: he or she grasps, brings close, and tries to *eat*. 'All enjoyment is in this sense alimentation', Levinas notes.[82] But as Max discovers, the desire to be loved is not simply a kind of hunger. Love involves a gesture outside of oneself, and not just the grasping of things to convert them into *part* of oneself. 'We'll eat you up—we love you so', say the wild things, no doubt in their broad Brooklyn accents, neatly conflating hunger for another with love of them (p 34). But Max and his readers have already understood on some instinctive level that this consumption is an utterly terrifying threat: it is a perversion of love, the impossibility of any enduring community, and it augurs the annihilation of the child. It is nothing but emotional cannibalism. 'And Max said, "No!"' (p 34). Of all Max's exclamatory negations—'be still!', 'now stop!'—this is by far the most courageous and decisive.

To be loved best of all is not then to be cannibalized. It is not only his difference from the wild things but his difference from those who form part of *his own* community that structures the terms of his new-found relationship to others. Once one understands that difference and not sameness is the necessary condition of any enduring relationship within a community, the implications for the legal subject are significant. Jacques Derrida, not only in 'Force of Law' but also in *The Gift of Death*,[83] argues on this basis against the commodification or codification of justice. No system of rules can do justice to justice, since to treat like cases alike according to some pre-set formula, without more, would sacrifice the element of the *judgment* of difference that is equally necessary.

> In short, for a decision to be just and responsible it must in its proper moment, if there is one, be both regulated and without regulation: it must conserve the law and also destroy it or suspend it enough to have to reinvent it in each case, remystify it, at least reinvent it in the reaffirmation and the new and free confirmation of its principle.[84]

A rule can never capture the complex process of judgment that must always be experienced as both bound and unbound, unique and universal. To be responsible is precisely to *respond* to the particularities of a situation, and to make a choice in relation to it. Merely to apply in rote fashion the words of a rule is no exercise of responsibility at all, because it involves no decision at all; it is, in fact, a claim that one's hands are tied. No one would ask a machine or the wind to act *responsibly*. Obedience, then, is the polar opposite of responsibility. The recognition of difference, and the necessity of continually making judgments that attend to that difference, marks the end of the possibility of unquestioning obedience and the true dawn of responsibility.

Indeed, the story itself strongly suggests that obedience without more is a condition of savagery. On one level, the only truly obedient subjects in the story are, ironically, the wild things themselves. They are stilled when told to be still,

[82] ibid, 111. [83] Derrida, n 6 above. [84] Derrida, n 36 above, 961.

rumple when told to rumpus, and sleep when sent to bed (p 32). In all this, they are unlike Max. They are caught in vassalage, tossed between extremes of violence and loyalty—unthinkingly, which is to say irresponsibly.

Ironically, the poverty of obedience contaminates the law-maker who demands it no less than the loyal subjects who provide it. As Piaget insisted, on the evidence of his psychological studies, the relationships of parents and children are, in their unilateralism, defective yet self-sustaining. It is striking how similar his argument is to Hegel's analysis of the relationship of 'master and slave'.[85] The absolute authority of the Master (or, in Piaget, the parent) effectively *relieves* the Slave (or the child) from all responsibility, and permits, subject only to its commands, an utter egotism. Obedience removes the obligation to think, and in particular to think of others. Yet at the same time the Master has only his own desires to realize. He too, need never think, and certainly not of others. Both master and slave, for comparable reasons, find themselves walled up in self-absorption. Perhaps it is significant that as king of the wild things, Max's crown looks a lot like the headdress of his wolf suit, which it almost conceals but does not at any moment displace (pp 24–33). The unquestioning obedience of slaves may be, Hart blithely concedes, 'deplorably sheeplike';[86] while the sovereign whose absolute authority demands it is nothing but a wolf in a suit.

On another level, Max's own obedience to and reproduction of the rules laid down only intensifies his disquiet. Perhaps Max sensed that it was irresponsible of him to send the wild things off to bed without their supper, in obedience to his mother's rule but without the exercise of judgment as to its meaning and purpose. This arbitrary injustice *together with* their unquestioning subservience to it—this mutually sustaining obedience—leads him eventually to think more reflectively on his own difference from the wild things (p 33). So Max wisely decides to return to a community. Not, it must be said, a community in which the problem of judgment is solved because everybody is the same. But a community in which, nevertheless, he will be able to take responsibility.

His new-found responsibility will be manifest not in his simple obedience to the rules laid down, but rather in the growing intelligence of his interpretation of them. Moreover, the dream has told him something about the purposes of the rule that ought to guide his judgements about, for example, the distinction between 'play' and 'mischief'. Those purposes are characterized in *Where the Wild Things Are*, in terms of parental or filial 'love'; hardly a detailed explication in Sendak but nevertheless, in the vocabulary of very young children, a powerful beginning to the interpretative project of a lifetime.

I think that the love of a parent and a child for each other ultimately involves the child (and the parent no less) in the awareness of the importance of a relationship that lies *outside* of him or herself. Understanding what it means to love another human being breaks down the wall of self-sufficient egotism that Piaget argued

[85] Georg Hegel, *Phenomenology of Spirit: Selections*, trans and annotated by Howard Kaintz (University Park, Pa: 1994, 1807) Ch IV.

[86] Hart, n 67 above, 114.

derived from the unilateral authority invested in the parent.[87] The experience of loving another, of being loved by another, will lead Max's readers, and sooner rather than later, to be aware of just this *otherness*, this difference which it seems to me is the necessary condition for the very possibility of love. It is not too much to say that love involves a sacrifice as both its desire and its token. There can be no sacrifice unless we differ from each other, for if we were just the same, what would I be giving up?[88] If we were not different, how could protecting your interests be distinguishable from furthering my own?

Children begin therefore to think about the consideration for differences that their play ought to show; moreover, that consideration becomes the very expression of their love for another. They sacrifice, they give up something for somebody else. Thus we love and thus we show our love. In light of the purposive structure of love that the story introduces, Max's mischief consisted in the lack of consideration he showed for the different needs of others (such as peace and quiet) in his play. Without love—from the perspective of the pure 'enjoyment' of the infant—his mother's rule seemed to impose a constraint which was unjust, incoherent, and therefore ultimately impossible to fulfil. With it—from the perspective of the child's developing community that necessarily includes an appreciation of his difference from others—the rule has suddenly developed both purpose and content. Max can at last make sense of it. Now he can play responsibly.

One might ask if the responsibility that has been awakened in Max is itself a purely unilateral burden. Do not then these reflections require of his parents a more responsible sensitivity to Max's own childhood in *their* obedience to the rules of play they have enacted, so as not to reproduce the injustice under which Max first suffered? Undoubtedly, and the dawning of their own responsibility can be observed in what Max finds on his return: his supper. To conserve the law, they have suspended it.

Conclusion

> *The wild things roared their terrible roars and gnashed their terrible teeth*
> *and rolled their terrible eyes and showed their terrible claws*
> *but Max stepped into his private boat and waved good-bye*
> *and sailed back over a year and in and out of weeks and through a day*
> *and into the night of his very own room*
> *where he found his supper waiting for him*
> *and it was still hot.*[89]

Every aspect and dimension of Sendak's 'parable of the law' maps precisely the odyssey described psychologically by Piaget and sociologically by Elias. But *Where*

87 Piaget, n 59 above, eg 90–94.

88 The argument is developed in many places in recent literature: see Derrida, n 38 above, itself indebted to the work of Emmanuel Levinas discussed below.

89 Sendak, n 1 above, 35–40.

the Wild Things Are must be understood in two additional ways. First, the story confronts a jurisprudential argument—an argument about legal ethics—as to the best way to approach the interpretation of law. The relationship to law that the story develops problematizes rather than merely sustains a lesson in obedience. Instead, it invites children to begin to see themselves as actors in the play of legal interpretation, and to reflect on the purposes and meaning of law and not just on its force. The transition from obedience to responsibility which Sendak portrays therefore moves beyond the synthesis of the two in Elias and the antithesis of the two in Piaget. Whereas Levinas characterizes both these models as ways of remaining mired in stasis,[90] Sendak provides resources that might enable children to grow *as* legal subjects. Max ceases to be wild. But, unlike the wild things, he will not be tamed either.

Secondly, the story confronts a jurisprudential argument—an argument about legal pluralism—as to the best way to approach the sources of law. It is entirely inadequate to think of this as a story about the law, or even as a story that portrays how children think about the law. It is not law 'and' literature. Rather, the story helps form and develop the mental attitudes to law of the children who read it. It does not just illustrate but inaugurates legal subjectivity. It is law *as* literature and literature *as* law, which is to say, myth. *Where the Wild Things Are* is not a legislative instrument; its authority and influence on our habits of thought and life is more profound than that. Ariès calls children's books 'propaganda'[91] but that is too hostile a judgment. Such stories are, in the fullest sense of the word, *constitutional* documents. They are the epics and scriptures that sustain and direct our normative commitments at a formative stage of our development.[92] They provide vital strands in a web of meaning that resonate throughout our lives.

Sendak's *Wild Things* is a myth that traces the emergence of modern subjectivity in a young child and, through its power, works to constitute that subjectivity amongst its readership. It is a parable of civility and legality that sustains and resonates with background myths of savagery and dimly perceived memories of feudalism. It is a *chanson de geste* of modern jurisprudence, a *Bildungsroman* in the dual sense of a novel about *bildung* and a novel that builds. Like all myths, it is neither true nor false, but strands in a complex web that *becomes* true in all those who learn it 'off by heart'. So important are such texts that we need to take them seriously, to think through the many implications of the text and the context of its reception in order properly to asses the relationships to law thus constituted. These relationships are by no means unambiguous; in *Where the Wild Things Are*, for example, there is clearly a tension between obedience and responsibility running right through the book.

[90] Levinas, n 81 above. [91] Ariès, n 74 above, 412.

[92] Of course many of these assumptions about childhood and parental influence might be challenged from the perspective of genetic determinism, given such prominence recently in work, for example, by Judith Rich Harris, *The Nurture Assumption* (New York: 1999) and Steven Pinker, *The Blank Slate* (New York: 2002). Suffice it to say that not only is the argument grossly overstated in these authors, but they simply do not address questions of *value* formation at this level. To attempt to elide this distinction, as Pinker has a tendency to do, is nothing short of crass polemics.

The book does not, of course, offer a regulatory solution or a philosophical resolution to these tensions, but rather an aesthetic and emotional one. Let us dwell for a moment on the love that recalls Max and that Max recalls. It hinges on the trope of hunger that gnaws incessantly at one from first page till last. Sendak describes a movement from hunger to love which, as Emmanuel Levinas points out, is likewise a movement from the enjoyment of consumption to the goodness of non-consumption. Relationships with others require, first and foremost, not the satisfaction of our own needs (narcissism is merely the relationship between a person and their own image) but the desire to preserve, respect and attend to the difference of another.[93] This is 'a non-possession more precious than possession, a hunger that nourishes itself not with bread but with hunger itself'.[94] Such a desire is unquenchable, 'the desired does not satisfy it, but increase it'.[95] Max, no doubt, gets his supper in the end, and it is still hot (p 40). Yet it would appear to have undergone a sea-change in the course of Max's ocean voyage. It is no longer merely the enjoyment of a need fulfilled. As in most cultures, food has become the symbol of a love and not by any means a substitute for it (p 39). It is no longer to be 'eaten up' but on the contrary to be kept constantly replenished. The supper to which Max returns is not just rain but a rainbow: the promise of enduring relationship. One might well say then that Max returns with a greater and more difficult hunger than he began with, for it is now 'the *Other's* hunger—be it of the flesh, or of bread'[96]—or for peace and quiet, one might add—that concerns him. This is what it means to be responsible for another. It is nothing but a matter of 'calling into question my spontaneity'—Max's wildness—by the presence of the Other.[97] The importance of this calling into question, as restraint and as a responsibility to others, was what Max learnt in the course of the book. It would therefore be wrong to say that love is the *exchange object* or *reward* in return for which Max agrees to accept a certain responsibility.[98] On the contrary, responsibility and love are coeval.[99] Each is the condition of possibility of the other.

Max has been enriched by becoming decentred.[100] Just like the experience of a good book or an adventure, and through the medium of the one about the other, he has 'lost himself' and thereby discovered something immeasurably more. This too Sendak manages to convey visually, for Max's private boat was labeled 'MAX' outward bound to the land of the wild things, which is to say as he journeyed inward to face the demons of his own subconscious (p 17). But his boat shows no

[93] Levinas, n 81 above, Section III, 187–219, and Conclusions, 287–305, and for the particular distinction to the concept of need, see in particular 50, 62, 117, 304–305.

[94] ibid, 183.

[95] Emmanuel Levinas, *Le Visage de l'autre*, illustrated by Martin tom Dieck (Paris: 2001), no pagination.

[96] Emmanuel Levinas, *Difficult Freedoms: Essays on Judaism*, trans Séan Hand (Baltimore: 1990, 1963) xiv.

[97] Levinas, n 81 above, 84; n 95 above.

[98] ibid, Section II.

[99] Emmanuel Levinas, *Otherwise Than Being or Beyond Essence*, trans Alphonso Lingis (Pittsburgh: 1981, 1974), 124–25.

[100] Levinas, n 81 above, refers instead to the 'eccentric', or ex-centric subject, which is to say the subject whose centre of gravity is outside himself: 303–305.

such name as he turns for home, which is to say as he journeys outward to be reunited with his family (p 37). Max no longer inhabits a purely egotistical vessel. There is a place for others *in* him: he is 'otherwise than Max'.[101] This is particularly apparent in the final illustration, in which for the first time Max is depicted bareheaded, his headdress pulled off and rumpled round about his neck (p 39). An outlaw, says Bracton, 'is bound to no-one, nor anyone to him'.[102] But Max has at last discarded the *caput lupinum*, and returned home a responsible legal subject.

[101] The reference of course is to *Otherwise Than Being*, n 99 above.
[102] Bracton, n 25 above, 363, line 8.

The Absence of Contradiction and the Contradiction of Absence: Law, Ethics and the Holocaust

*David M Seymour**

Introduction

It may not be too much of an exaggeration to note that the history of critical theory can be characterized by one overarching debate.[1] On the one side, and originating with Kant, is the grounding of critique of modernity upon *absence*. On the other side, and beginning with Hegel, the premise of critique is *contradiction*. Kant's work is structured around the absence of full cognizance of the moral law, whilst for Hegel, ethical life is presented as the reconciliation of contradictory elements already present in the world. In recent years, the terms of the debate have shifted markedly in favour of absence.

An important catalyst for this contemporary imbalance is traceable to the occurrence of what has come to be known as the 'Holocaust'.[2] Confronted with the sheer horror and magnitude of the crimes committed, many critical theorists committed to contradiction lost their confidence and moved, often with regret, to the side of 'absence'. Most emblematic of this despair is Adorno's *Negative Dialectic*, and, in particular his discussion of 'Auschwitz';[3] the inverted commas indicating a concept whose content remains beyond capture; that is, whose content remains absent. In many ways, much contemporary theorizing from the side of absence has offered a radical version of Adorno's pessimistic work. Most notable in this stream are the writings of Lyotard[4] and Agamben.[5]

* With thanks to Alison Diduck, Robert Fine, Michael Freeman and the participants of the Law and Culture Conference (Summer 2003). And thanks to Max whose dinner is always on the table. Whether he eats it or not is, of course, another matter.

[1] For example, see Gillian Rose's discussion of this debate in G Rose, *Hegel Contra Sociology* (London: 1995) esp Ch 1.

[2] The term 'Holocaust' was first used by Elie Wiesel in a review of *The Terezin Requiem* published in the *New York Times*, 27 November 1963. See J Najarian, 'Gnawing at History: the rhetoric of Holocaust denial' (1997) 39 *The Midwest Quarterly* 74 [www.codoh.com/reference/gnawhistory.html].

[3] T W Adorno, *Negative Dialectics* (London: 1996) See, esp, Section III, 'Meditations on Metaphysics'.

[4] See, Jean-François Lyotard, *The Differend: Phrases in Dispute* (Minneapolis: 1988); *Heidegger and "the jews"* C Minneapolis: 1990) and *Political Writings* (London: 1993) Section IV, 'More "jews" '.

[5] Giorgio Agamben, *Remnants of Auschwitz: The Witness and the Archive* (London: 1999).

Alongside this shift of perspective is a radicalization within the tradition of absence itself. Most notable is the hardening of Kant's connection between the trilogy of the absent ground of the moral law, the sublime and the Second Commandment forbidding the representation of the 'Jewish God'[6] into a trilogy in which the holocaust is its absent core. This essay offers an engagement with this development through a discussion of Desmond Manderson's highly original and innovative article, 'From Hunger to Love: Myths of the Source, Interpretation, and Constitution of Law in Children's Literature'.[7]

Drawing on the contrast between legal positivism and legal ethics, Manderson's reading of Maurice Sendak's classic children's story, *Where the Wild Things Are*,[8] offers a thesis that is grounded on the idea of the absence of ethics within modern law. This absence, he argues, is brought about by the dominance (and domination) of a legal positivism that emphasizes obedience to the narrow meaning of the text at the expense of negotiation, responsibility and context. The first section of this essay argues that Manderson undermines his argument through reading positivism too positivistically thereby breaching his own interdiction on ways of reading the law. I argue that this paradox arises from Manderson's appropriation of Adorno's 'immanent critique'[9] in which contradiction is substituted by absence. This first section is organized around the question of whether 'absence' can, like 'contradiction', be treated as *mediating* between legal positivism and legal ethics.

Assuming a negative answer to this question, a further one arises. If ethics is absent from modes of rational cognition, such as positivism, then, by what means can its presence become, first, known, and, second, actualised? The answer to this question returns Manderson to an aestheticization of law; of a 'legal ethics' that can only be intimated but never fully comprehended. I argue, finally, that this aestheticization of law and the nature of its content express the continuing trope of the conflation of ethics, aesthetics and the holocaust and its radical distinction from the trope of positivism, rationality and history; a result that indicates the contradiction of absence that lies buried within the absence of contradiction.

Immanent Critique: The Equivocation of Positivism

Drawing on the work of HLA Hart and Hans Kelsen, Manderson offers an authoritarian and unidimensional picture of legal positivism in which obedience, certainty of meaning and injustice are brought together.

> The notion of obedience and the theory of hard-core meaning are necessarily connected. Obedience requires the following of rules without any reconsideration of them and, therefore, requires them to have some objective content that can be determined by the law-*giver*, alone and in advance. And Hart's lesson for a child like Max would be this: we expect you

[6] I Kant, *Critique of Judgement* (Cambridge: 2000) 156.

[7] (2003) 15 *Law and Literature* 87.

[8] M Sendak (New York: 1991).

[9] Manderson, n 7 above, 119. For a discussion of the notion of 'immanent critique', see n 14 below, 6.

to learn the law, and to do so you would need only obey the words we tell you. On such an analysis, legal civility would be a function of one's obedience to the predetermined meaning of articulated norms.[10]

At the heart of this representation of legal positivism is an emphasis upon the literalness of text and the presumed certainty of meaning at the expense of context and equivocality of meaning. More generally, these attributes contribute to conceiving of legal positivism as an arbitrary exercise of sovereign power into which all subjects are ensnared in an a priori constituted web. As a consequence, legal positivism is implicated in the perpetuation of injustice:

> The child's first encounter with law leaves him or her feeling, ironically, the sense of injustice. Children are 'before the law' in precisely the dual sense that Derrida draws out of Kafka's parable. That is, they are both ignorant of the legal order and yet subject to it. A child is a pre-legal subject and yet the quintessential object of regulation. Their lives are an experience of rules that are learned only through the process of breaking them.[11]

This view of positivism is contrasted with that of legal ethics. Reading the law ethically emphasizes responsibility, equivocation, negotiation, taking into account the context of the words that acknowledge the slippage of meaning that is to be negotiated, respect for difference, honour for the law, in which law which appears as third party, occupying the space between words and between persons:[12]

> A rule can never capture the complex process of judgement that must always be experienced as both bound and unbound, unique and universal. To be responsible is precisely to *respond* to the particularities of a situation and to make a choice in relation to it. Merely to apply in rote fashion the words of a rule is no exercise of responsibility at all, because it involves no decision at all; it is, in fact, to claim that one's hands are tied. No one would ask a machine or the wind to act *responsibly*. Obedience, then, is the polar opposite of responsibility. The recognition of difference, and the continually making judgements that attend to that difference, marks the end of the possibility of unquestioning obedience and the dawn of responsibility.[13]

In characterising positivism as the 'polar opposite' of responsibility and reducing it to a species and justification of an unreflective, 'only obeying orders' obedience, Manderson overstates his case. He does so by elevating positivism's undoubtedly dominatory and authoritarian *tendencies* into its sole content. It is this closed and unequivocal reading of legal positivism that is set in opposition to something claimed (or posited) to exist outside or beyond itself, in this instance, legal ethics. In the discussion, that follows, I argue that this strict bipolar reading of positivism and ethics emanates from Manderson's use of the critical tool of immanent critique, but in which Adorno's insistence upon contradiction is confused with that of absence.

[10] ibid, 109. [11] ibid, 106–107.

[12] On this point, see also, Peter Goodrich, 'Law in the Courts of Love: Andreas Capellus and the Judgment of Love' (1996) 48 *Stanford L Rev* 160. [13] Manderson, n 7 above, 123.

Simon Jarvis identifies three aspects to Adorno's notion of immanent critique.[14] First, identification of internal contradictions within the work itself. Secondly, 'utopian negativity'; and, thirdly, notions of 'the absolute'.

Internal Contradictions

Jarvis explains the idea of internal contradiction as follows:

> 'Immanent' means remaining within. An immanent critique is one which 'remains within' what it criticises. . . . It uses the internal contradictions of a body of work to criticise that work in its own terms. . . . It is interested in what Adorno calls the 'truth-content' of entire works and authorships, which are more than the sum of its parts. . . . it is. . . . to understand the significance of the particular kinds of contradiction present in a given body of work—in particular, to understand what these contradictions tell us about the social experience out of which the work was written.[15]

At the core of this understanding of immanent critique is the idea that in identifying contradictions within the work, one has identified contradictions within the social world. In other words, the text, and its fault lines, expresses and includes within itself its social, political, ethical and cultural context.

There is little doubt that Manderson is correct to identify a particular constellation of contradictions present within the concept of 'law', contradictions that are expressed in the dichotomy of legal positivism and legal ethics. However, Manderson does not bring this logic of immanent critique to bear upon what are for him the now *distinct* notions of positivism and ethics. Instead, the 'relationship' of legal ethics to legal positivism is expressed through the negative language of absences. Legal ethics is presented as that which legal positivism does not contain, as opposed to each possessing elements of the other. This point is evidenced in the manner in which the characteristics of legal positivism and legal ethics are articulated through a series of oppositions rather than that of internal contradictions; a point illustrated through a brief discussion of text and context in the work of Hart and Kelsen.

One of the most relevant contexts of both these thinkers' writings is the rise of counter-liberal social and political tendencies that culminated in the racist totalitarianism of Nazi Germany. This context comes to the surface in Hart's depiction of legal positivism upon which Manderson relies. In his 1958 article for the *Harvard Law Review*, Hart was concerned with the difficult legacy of Nazi totalitarianism and the crimes committed in and under its name. It is a legacy, one needs add, that had remained relatively unexamined until that time and for many decades since.[16]

Correspondingly, it becomes obvious that a significant motivation for Kelsen's development of legal formalism (it is, in fact, questionable whether Kelsen can be

[14] Simon Jarvis, *Adorno: A Critical Introduction* (Cambridge: 1998). [15] ibid, 6.

[16] See R Cotterrell, *The Politics of Jurisprudence: A Critical Introduction to Legal Philosophy* (2nd edn London: 2003) Ch 5. See also, M Stolleis, *Law Under the Swastika: Studies on Legal History in Nazi Germany* (Chicago: 1998); AL Jacobson and B Schlink, *Weimar: A Jurisprudence of Crisis* (Berkeley, California: 2000); *Darker Legacies of Law in Europe: The Shadow of National Socialism and Fascism over Europe and its Legal Traditions* (Oxford: 2003).

called a legal 'positivist'[17]) was to oppose and neutralize contemporaneous theories of law and state founded upon historical and/or organic myths of *volk*. The irony of Kelsen's assertion of the autonomy of law is that it can be interpreted equally convincingly as political as well as legal work. It is in this way that the broader context (including ethics) of Kelsen's formalism attains visibility within the words of his texts. It is precisely this context that comes to be expressed *within* the *Grundnorm* itself in its attempt to distinguish law from its extra legal genesis and thereby ensure a body politic premised on inclusion rather than upon racist exclusion.

Utopian Negativity

This last point leads into the second aspect of immanent critique; utopian negativity.

> Adorno's utopian negativity. . . . works through immanent critique. It cannot provide a blueprint for what the good life would be like, but only examines what our 'damaged' life is like. It hopes to interpret this damaged life with sufficient attention and imagination to allow intimations of a possible, undamaged life to show through.[18]

Following Hegel and Marx, Adorno eschews outlining a future utopia, a future perfect world. Taking Hegel's ironic comment '*Hic* Rhodus, *hic saltus*' ['here is Rhodes, jump here'][19] seriously, Jarvis notes Adorno's insistence that 'the social theorist [can] not pretend that he or she [is] speaking from some place outside society'.[20] Rather than draw up and impose a blueprint for the perfect society upon the world in which the injustice it sought to diffuse is reinstalled, Adorno insists[21] that the elements for the 'good life' are already actualized. In this way, therefore, Adorno is categorical that future freedom is not absent from the world as it is, but is fragmented and diffused throughout it, including, of course, throughout the domain of law. It is also necessary to note that this actuality of a potential utopia from within the confines of a 'damaged life' in which the actual is rational and the rational actual, does *not* rule out of court the exercise of the imagination (of non-instrumental rationality), but is rather dependent upon it.[22]

In the light of these comments, it is clear that both Hart's and Kelsen's work contain a moment of utopian negativity through which a better future can be imagined even if limited in its actualization. This utopianism is that element of political and legal thought which includes the dream of a universal community mediated through the rule of law in which, and through which, each individual is

[17] For a discussion of this point see M Freeman (ed), *Lloyd's Introduction to Jurisprudence* (7th edn, London: 2001).

[18] Jarvis, n 14 above, 9.

[19] GWF Hegel, *Philosophy of Right* (Cambridge: 1991) 21.

[20] Jarvis, n 14 above, 9.

[21] See G Rose, *Judaism and Modernity: Philosophical Essays* (Oxford: 1993) Introduction; G Rose, *Mourning Becomes the Law: Philosophy and Representation* (Cambridge: 1996) Introduction. See also, David Seymour, 'Representation and the Framing of Modernity' (2001) 10 *Griffith L Rev* 259; David Seymour, 'Film and Law: In Search of a Critical Method' in Leslie Moran, Ian Christie, Elena Louzidou, *Law's Moving Image* (London: forthcoming).

[22] On this point see, G Rose, *The Melancholy Science: An Introduction to the Thought of Theodor W. Adorno* (London: 1978) esp Ch 2.

respected as a person regardless of class, creed or the more pernicious category of 'race'; it imagines a community of stability and security in which individuals are able to flourish to their full potential.

The nature of this discussion of the work of positivism's and formalism's modern proponents is not simply to counter Manderson's negative reading with a positive one. Rather, it is the suggestion that Adorno's notion of immanent critique points less to the absence of legal ethics within legal positivism, of context within text, and more to the idea of contradiction within and between them. This suggestion is reinforced through the third attribute of immanent critique discussed by Jarvis: the notion of 'the absolute'.

The Absolute

Manderson's substitution of absence over contradiction emphasizes Walter Benjamin's influence over Adorno.[23] This influence is clear in Adorno's belief in the dominance of abstract exchange-value over the specificities of use-value so that 'anything can be made to stand for absolutely anything else':[24]

> Any person, any object, any relationship can mean absolutely anything else. With this possibility a destructive, but just verdict is passed on the profane world: it is characterised as a world in which the detail is of no importance.[25]

Adorno has shorn this influence of its spiritual and messianic aura. Whereas Benjamin argues that 'without a perspective outside this "context of guilt" or "natural history" '[26] the context cannot be 'interpreted', Adorno insists in remaining within the domain of 'damaged life'. For Adorno, 'the Absolute' is less a deistic figure or intervention form 'beyond' as it is fragments of freedom, of moments of 'utopian negativity', already present in the world. The materiality of this fragmentary nature of 'the Absolute' is evidenced through its existence as an expression of the fragmentary nature of freedom as it exists in a society and social relations organized around the diverse division of labour. For Adorno, therefore, the appearance of 'the absolute', of freedom, of emancipation, cannot be positively thought in theory until it is positively expressed in practice.

In this section it has been argued that the rupture between legal positivism and legal ethics emerges through Manderson breaching his own codes of reading; a code that is made overt in the following:

> My own reading of Sendak is not obedient to the text, but *responsive to its purposes*, just as the concept of law that the text suggests involves the child who reads it in a growing

[23] W Benjamin *The Origin of German Tragic Drama* (London: 1990). See also Rose, n 22 above, 35–42; Jarvis, n 14 above, 10.

[24] See on this point, TW Adorno and Max Horkheimer, *Dialectic of Enlightenment* (London: 1972).

[25] Jarvis, n 14 above, 10.

[26] For a discussion of Benjamin's meaning of the term 'natural history' and Adorno's adaptation of it see Rose, n 22 above, Ch 3 and Max Paddison, *Adorno's Aesthetics of Music* (Cambridge: 1993) Ch 2.

responsibility to the laws and the principles surrounding them, rather than a *mere formal obedience to them.*[27]

Manderson's reading of legal positivism, therefore, takes it at its own face-value, it accepts positivism's own claims and ambitions without being 'responsive to its purposes', purposes inherent within its texts. Manderson, in other words, reads positivism too positivistically.

With absence prioritized over contradiction, an unbridgeable gap cannot but appear between legal positivism and legal ethics, between text and context. It is the consequences of this rupture that are discussed in the following section, and which bring to the fore the intimately connected issue of the aestheticization of 'legal ethics'.

"I'll eat you up": Consumption and Aestheticization

A further dimension of Manderson's thesis in which he discusses Sendak's use of the phrase 'I'll eat you up' compounds the difficulties associated with absence over contradiction. Drawing on the ethical philosophy of Emmanuel Levinas, Manderson offers a distinction between hunger and love, themes he sees as central to the nature of *Where the Wild Things Are*. On the one hand, there is love, which:

> as a positive constitutive force is built upon the recognition of difference. . . . The very word *relationship* is integral to most understandings of love; it implies a connection between two bodies that maintain their distinctness.[28]

On the other hand, there is hunger. In its consumption, hunger is said to absorb the other into the self, an absorption that destroys difference. It represents 'forms of narcissm that merely seek or reproduce sameness':

> To say 'you are just like me' is a way of talking about me. Emmanuel Levinas explained this paradox through the experience of desire. The danger of desire is that it 'tends to bring the object "close enough" to be engulfed' by the self, and, consequently, destroys the sensation of difference that generated the attraction in the first place. Such desire, like a parasite, consumes the host that makes it possible. Love, for Levinas at least, if it is to survive, promises to respect difference and not obliterate it.[29]

This depiction of hunger, desire and consumption as the erasure of difference echoes Adorno and Horkheimer's discussion of the fate of knowledge as the handmaiden of domination. Two facets of this connection are relevant here. First, the idea that what is not of 'use' in the sense of instrumental rationality is denied or expelled; it remains unrecognized. This 'non-rational' aspect remains 'outside' or 'beyond' the world moulded in the image of domination. Secondly, this consumption of object into concept is determined by the universality of exchange; that which remains outside the concept is what is left when all is made equal to everything else—particularity or difference—when all is made the same.

[27] Manderson, n 7 above, 100, emphasis added. [28] ibid, 122. [29] ibid, 122.

It is within this environment that positivism gains its meaning as that which circumscribes the contingency of the world to that of 'brute facts' [30] and invariable laws of nature. Reduced to a series of endless and inflexible repetitions, positivism converts its conceptual representation to 'given[s] before which thought must simply come to a halt. . . . positivism becomes the liquidation of the new, of the possibility that the facts might change'.[31] Positivism's domination manifests itself in its demands to obedience; demands, in other words, that the subject sacrifice its difference and particularity to the world as it is, to a world imbricated in domination and denial. Manderson himself draws a similar connection between legal positivism, consumption and domination,

> 'We'll eat you up—we love you so', say the wild things. . . . neatly conflating hunger for another with love of them (p34). But Max and his readers have already *understood on some instinctive level* that this consumption is an utterly terrifying threat: it is a perversion of love, the impossibility of any enduring community, and it augurs the annihilation of the child.[32]

With the world consumed by the hunger and desire for instrumentality and its expression within positivistic concepts, both within and outside of law, a fundamental problem arises. What space remains that the 'absent-presence' of legal ethics can reach? This is a problem present in the contradiction inherent within Manderson's phrase, 'understood on some instinctive level'. 'From Hunger to Love' points to two such spaces. The first space can be articulated as the 'jurisdiction of legal ethics'; and the second, as the 'jurisprudence of legal ethics'.

The Jurisdiction of Legal Ethics

The jurisdiction of legal ethics draws on the familiar figure of the subject of legal positivism; an isolated monad, autonomous and independent, pursuing its own self-interest through which all others, and the social totality, is seen as a hindrance. This image is given a twist by Manderson in his emphasis upon this subject's absolute separation and subservience to the external sovereignty of the law-giver, a sovereign that imposes its will upon this abject legal subject in such a way that the only obligation that inheres on the latter is that of automatic obedience.

It is precisely in the unrecognized and unacknowledged space that is erased by this positivistic concept of law that Manderson locates the jurisdiction of legal ethics. It is a space in which the sovereignty of law is said to be shared and its meaning negotiated. In it, law does not 'consume' the other, but acknowledges and develops difference and distinctness through that communication and negotiation.

[30] Jarvis, n 14 above, 88.

[31] It is interesting to note that in this account of positivism, Adorno comes perilously close to denying any dialectic between positivism and its 'remains', a problem that he solved, at least to a certain extent, through the triad of notion of identity, non-identity and rational-identity thinking (see Rose, n 22 above, Ch 3).

[32] Manderson, n 7 above, 122.

Manderson argues that it is 'this [notion of law that] is meant by legal discourse: specific, embodied, interpretative practices'.[33]

Manderson explains this point through the illustration of the rituals of bedtime stories in which the parent 'reads to' the child. This account is sensitive especially to questions of power and hierarchy that exist in the parent and child relation, and the way in which such power can be neutralized or shared between the parties.

Manderson argues that the ownership of the reading materials, of the book, is shared between parent and child. This shared ownership manifests itself in the parent's possessing 'the key to the meaning of the book' and the child's physical custody of it. Interestingly, Manderson likens this dual notion of ownership to that of the trust.[34]

> The relationship of divided possession here is surprisingly complex and might well be summed up, both in legal and psychological terms, as a *trust*. The legal institution of the trust divided ownership in much this way, between the one who owns the physical form of something and the one entitled to benefit from the use of it. At the same time, only the social institution of trust between parent and child can reunite its physical form and the beneficial meaning its contains.[35]

The upshot of this equitable relationship is that:

> The child is well aware of the double identity of the book, possessed by both and neither without the other; it gives them a sense of the necessity for co-operation and shared communication. . . . The constructive trust implicit in the act of reading demonstrates that the parent is already a 'collaborator and not a master'.[36]

With this distribution of possession over the unity of ownership, this dissolution of autonomy and isolation, the book and its meaning now become the object of shared conversation and negotiated meaning.

> Since the book itself is external to the direct relationship between parent and child, as if it were a third party, it presents the possibility of an interpretation in which both speaker and listener can participate.[37]

Opened in this way to the contingency of negotiation, the certainty of words claimed by legal positivism is undermined and replaced by meanings that can never be foreclosed.

> [T]he exegesis of the text is typically open-ended in its possibilities. Like Talmudic *mishnah*, the verses of a book like *Where the Wild Things Are* form the framework for a conversation: about the story, about Max's experience of the story, about the child's own and parallel experience.[38]

[33] ibid, 128.

[34] For a less romantic reading of the trust, see R. Cotterrell in W Twining, *Legal Theory and Common Law* (Oxford: 1986) 81–98; and *Lloyd's Bank plc v Rosset* [1991] 1 AC 107. For a discussion of the constructive trust in particular, see A Diduck and F Kaganas, *Family Law, Gender and the State* (Oxford: 1999) 199, 202.

[35] Manderson, n 7 above, 129.

[36] ibid, 129–130.

[37] ibid, 132.

[38] ibid, 130.

Aside from the context of the reading situation and the reader's experience informing the meaning of the text to be negotiated, Manderson is emphatic in noting that:

crucially, the text is not just a description of this cathartic event, but an occasion for the event itself, an invitation to a dialogue about feelings and experiences that both parent and child might share.[39]

Taken together, these factors bring to the fore Manderson's central point: the way in which the sovereign authority of the positivistic text, its purported certainty of meaning and its in-built demand for obedience, is dislodged and supplanted by the openness of meaning brought about through the negotiation and communication of the parties. Informed as it is by their diverse and unique experiences, context informs text. It is this methodology of juridical interpretation that permits one and all to be responsible to, and to assume *responsibility* for, the law.

The sparseness of both text and illustrations implies a secrecy that demands investigation. Like the *Mona Lisa,* a good children's book is inscrutable enough to incite its own supplement. . . . The supplement is called forth by the form, it is the strength of the form. . . . But this approach is anything but a literal analysis of textual facts. This is the exercise of judgement that the child's reading mandates; the judgement that the text alone cannot hope to provide.[40]

It is, in turn, such interpretative strategies that are said to bring the absence of ethics into presence, to make ethics resound in the words of the text itself:

The skill of reading texts allows the unfolding of complex chains of events far into the future and long in the past. Without the ability to represent what is not present, without the capacity, therefore, to project one's ideas into an absence, there can be no morality (the point is a familiar Kantian one).[41]

The Jurisprudence of Legal Ethics

It is through this discussion of 'the jurisprudence of legal ethics' that the fault lines present in Manderson's reading of law come clearly into view.

As with its jurisdiction, the jurisprudence of legal ethics indicates something within the interstices, something 'outside' or 'beyond' the insular hermeneutics of legal positivism. This point is implied through Manderson's conflation of absence and externality. For example, toward the end of 'From Hunger to Love', he states:

a contextual approach has already begun to pry apart the 'strict and complete legalism' of the very young child. The child is beginning to see that the 'why' of law and the 'what' of law are inextricably connected. This is what Fuller calls its 'external morality' and no system of interpretation can function without it.[42]

[39] Manderson, n 7 above, 120. [40] ibid, 131. [41] ibid, 121. [42] ibid, 121.

Similarly, in an insightful comment on Derrida's 'Force of Law', Manderson notes the way in which *all* legal judgments are informed by a moment of externality:

> Whilst Hans Kelsen, therefore, would insist that only the *Grundnorm*—the first law of a community that establishes the conditions under which it takes place—suffers from this deficiency, Derrida argues that every norm contains within it a tiny fractal *Grundnorm* of its own, some decision or judgement that remains unmandated by the past.[43]

This motif of absence as externality continues in Manderson's already noted attempt to externalize the ethical source of law. As custodians and negotiators of meaning of the book, the book now appears as a 'third party' over and above those from whom responsibility toward it is demanded. Paradoxically, whilst the interpreters are empowered through the *praxis* of legal ethics, they are correspondingly *disempowered* from the origination or founding of that source, of that text. The book, in other words, appears as a radicalized image of the positivist law-giver admitting of an even greater distance between authorial, and authoritative, command and subject.

This discussion of the jurisdiction and jurisprudence of legal ethics throws up immediate similarities with the nature of the jurisdiction and jurisprudence of Judaism. Although almost absent in Manderson's article itself, the connections and similarities between the two are indicated in Manderson's advocacy for an interpretative strategy akin to that of 'Talmudic *Mishnah*'.[44] This mode of reading, here equated with an ethics of reading, is alluded to also in the notion of 'supplementing' the bare words of a text. Such supplementing requires that words are pored over and endlessly debated in a spirit of collaboration (which, of course, does not negate hierarchy) leading to its relevance and application within contemporary contexts. What is *not* permitted, or what breaks these rules of interpretation, these rules of ethics, is the calling into question of the foundational status (and its authorship) of the *Torah*, the law itself. Replicating the power of the positivist sovereign, one is not permitted to call into question the text's own *Grundnorm*.

This connection between legal ethics and Judaism is further evidenced by Manderson's reference to the idea that the telling of the story is not just a description of past events, but 'an occasion for the event itself, an invitation to a dialogue about feelings and experiences that both parent and child might share'.[45] This notion of eternal presence replicates the Passover *Seder* edict to recount the story of the Exodus *as if* the participants at the table were themselves present at that event. This similarity between Manderson's ethical reading and the *Seder* is strengthened further by the idea that the narration of the story is such as to encourage questions, dialogue and interpretation. The jurisprudence of legal ethics appears, therefore, as the jurisprudence of Judaism, or, rather, a specifically 'post-holocaust' notion of Judaism; of a 'Judaism without Jews'.

[43] ibid, 107. [44] ibid, 132. [45] ibid, 130.

Ethics as Judaism without Jews: Aestheticizing the Holocaust

In his discussion of Levinas' distinction between hunger and love, Manderson notes that:

> love involves a gesture outside of oneself, and not just the grasping of things to convert them into *part* of oneself. Love is not just fuel; it must be a burning bush, alight but *un*consumed.[46]

Manderson's use of the imagery of the burning bush, as that which burns but does not consume, brings to the fore the place and the meaning of the holocaust implicitly contained within his thinking on legal ethics.

In its literal sense, a holocaust points to something (not necessarily a sacrifice) consumed by fire. Yet, by making reference to the idea of that which is 'alight but unconsumed', Manderson is indicating that something remains after the conflagration; that something is left over once the desire of consumption has satiated itself. For Manderson, that remnant is Judaism; a Judaism, in other words, without Jews that, as noted, becomes the model and meaning of legal ethics.

This notion of legal ethics as a Judaism without Jews returns us to Manderson's discussion of the nature of positivism. As noted, positivism is the conceptualization of a world dominated in the name of instrumental rationality. Although variations remain as to specifics, the Jews came to be conceptualized as that which was surplus to requirements (Adorno[47] and Arendt[48]), as a difference that could not be universalized (Bauman[49]) or as an ethics that remained in 'Europe's' subconscious (Lyotard[50]). They were murdered, in other words, under the name of a concept, a concept of 'the Jews'.

As with all positivistic concepts, this concept of 'the Jews' is said to leave something unacknowledged and unrecognized; a something that continued and continues to be present even when the concept has been eradicated in a holocaust. And, as Manderson and others imply, this remnant is an ethical Judaism, or a Judaism of ethics, a Judaism and an ethics that remain within the interstices of the modern, rational, world.

This connection, or rather sublation, of legal ethics, the holocaust and a Judaism without Jews is brought into closer view through their respective aestheticization. Just as legal ethics presents itself as a Judaism without Jews, so too the holocaust comes to be presented as that which cannot be represented.[51] Concerned as it is with the absences within modernity in general and the absence of ethics in particular,

[46] Manderson, n 7 above, 122 (emphasis in original). [47] See n 24 above.

[48] See, H Arendt, *Origins of Totalitarianism* (New York: 1979).

[49] See Z Bauman, *Modernity and the Holocaust* (Oxford: 1991).

[50] See, *Heidegger and "the jews"* and *Political Writings*, n 4 above.

[51] See Adorno (n 3 above) and Lyotard's radicalization of Adorno's thought in *The Differend* (n 4 above).

the holocaust escapes cognitive representation.[52] In the wake of this failure of representation, an understanding of the holocaust, like the understanding of legal ethics, is replaced by its aestheticization. It becomes the limit of human knowledge and human cognition. In so doing, legal ethics, Judaism without Jews and the holocaust take on the aura of positivism, of 'given events', 'before which thought must simply come to a halt'.

'Outside' or 'beyond' human cognition, the holocaust takes on extra-human dimensions. Like legal ethics and Judaism, it becomes something whose origins are so mysterious[53] that as much as we can negotiate its meaning and speak of it as if we were there, we can never begin to *understand* and so represent it through our critical faculties. Rather, this 'three in one' becomes that which throws these faculties into disarray, a disarray that is said to act as a constant reminder of humanity's own hubris.

It is in this aestheticized form that the holocaust comes to be presented as the absent 'context' of modernity, its instrumentality, its positivism and its concepts. It comes to occupy the void that, since Kant, has been said to haunt the modern world. Taking on the characteristics of the moral law, it shares with it the inability of representation. As something 'sublime' it remains faithful to the prohibition of the second commandment. 'Perhaps sensed' or 'understood on an instinctive level', it becomes the law according to which we must act *as if* we were cognizant of it, and incumbent upon us in living our lives as if it were eternally occurring. And, in a final paradox, the holocaust becomes as much the context for Manderson's legal ethics as I argued it was for both Kelsen's and Hart's positivism.

Conclusion

Manderson's conflation and aesthicization of legal ethics, Judaism without Jews and the holocaust on the one hand, and its radical separation and opposition to legal positivism on the other hand, is, I have argued, the result of his substitution of absence for contradiction in the utilization of Adorno's immanent critique. As a consequence, Manderson is unable to acknowledge or recognize the implication and imbrication of each within the other. In place of contradiction that emphasizes and mediates the ethics of positivism and the positivism of ethics, absence cannot mediate, it can only obliterate.[54]

It is for these reasons that Manderson's thinking offers a series of radical separations and oppositions—those between ethics and positivism, text and context, aesthetics and politics, modernity and Judaism, Jews and Judaism; oppositions

[52] In some instances, it is precisely these 'modern' modes of cognition that are held *responsible* for the Holocaust, see Bauman, n 49 above, and James MacMillan's attempt to bring into being a 'spiritual modernism': 'Unholier Than Thou', *Guardian Review* 11 October 2003.

[53] On this point see Heidegger *and "the jews"*, n 4 above.

[54] See n 26 above.

that Manderson lays at the feet of positivism. This paradox of replication exhausts itself in the fact that in the opposition between positivism and aesthetics, legal ethics, Judaism and the holocaust become imbued with the same characteristics Manderson identified with positivism in general. Removed from the ambit of human activity and human cognition, they confront the world with the power and mystery of a natural force. Outside or beyond the scope of human possibility, they demand of humanity its subjection and adaption, and in this way ethics, like positivism, inverts into domination, and the holocaust into mythology.

PART II

REEL JUSTICE

Law's Enchantment: The Cinematic Jurisprudence of Krzysztof Kieslowski

Richard K Sherwin *

Mythos begets *nomos*. In myth begins the normative universe in which we live.[1] Law emerges to maintain that universe, and to foreclose others.[2] Law polices normative reality through the official stories that it tells, for these are stories whose meanings are backed by the force of the state. But law is not autonomous. There is a two-way street between law and culture. Law's stories are often shaped and informed by popular narratives from the culture at large.[3] This shared process of narrative production, adaptation, and critique attests to law's deep entanglement in the meaning-making function of culture.[4]

* Professor of Law, Director, Visual Persuasion Project, New York Law School.

1 This marks a Vichian take on Robert Cover's seminal essay, 'Nomos and Narrative' in M Minow, M Ryan and A Sarat (eds), *Narrative, Violence & the Law: The Essays of Robert Cover* (Ann Arbor, Mich: 1995) 95–96 ('No set of legal institutions or prescriptions exists apart from the narratives that locate it and give it meaning. For every constitution there is an epic, for each decalogue a scripture. Once understood in the context of the narratives that give it meaning, law becomes not merely a system of rules to be observed but a world in which we live.'). For an example of what is meant by 'the Vichian take', see J Mali, *The Rehabilitation of Myth: Vico's New Science* (Cambridge: 1992) 2–3 (describing the definition of myth in Vico's work as 'true narration', 'the main mode of knowledge in which men have actually constituted their civil world'). For an impressive application of this insight in the context of contemporary legal studies, see Desmond Manderson, 'From Hunger to Love: Myths of the Source, Interpretation, and Constitution of Law in Children's Literature' (2003) 15 *Law & Literature* 53–86. See also S Gourgouris, *Does Literature Think?* (Palo Alto, CA: 2003) xix (noting that 'to ask the question, "Does literature think?" also means to reanimate the mythical power of signification from within an Enlightenment framework against both theological and rationalist transcendentalism'); and G Mazzotta, *The New Map of the World: The Poetic Philosophy of Giambittista Vico* (Princeton, NJ: 1999) 88 ('true history needs poetic fictions—such as those Homer tells—because myths are, paradoxically, truer than facts, and because they are ancient memories or imaginative whorls on the spindle of time') and 138 ('Aeneas's epic journey from fallen Troy to the foundation of a new cultural order and empire brings into focus geopolitics or the politics of territoriality as the flip side of the myths of the Earth').

2 Here we encounter the binary 'law preserving/law destroying' thematic that can be traced to Walter Benjamin and that Robert Cover subsequently adopted. See W Benjamin, 'Critique of Violence' in P Demetz (ed), *Reflections* (New York: 1978) 277–300; Cover, n 1 above, 103–113.

3 See A Amsterdam and J Bruner, *Minding the Law* (Cambridge, MA: 2000).

4 See Mali, n 1 above, 118–119 ('Paradoxically, man becomes free from "the tyranny of self-love" only by becoming a "member of the society of the family, the city, and finally, of mankind" . . . we are all necessarily constrained by the "authoritative horizons" of our social orders, and therefore cannot, and should not try to, free ourselves so imperiously from their traditional values and norms.'). See also J Bruner, *Acts of Meaning* (Cambridge, MA: 1990) (discussing the role of narrative in the construction and distribution of self).

In early times, the engines of cultural production were poems and songs; mythic tales were recited or sung to the community. Later, they were written down and copied, as rapidly as the technology permitted. In our time, to an ever increasing extent, culture's products are projected electronically onto screens—at work, at home, and in other places of cultural (re)creation. Our narrative taste is for sight and sound, preferably served with speed. Law is a part of this visual world, and as a result, today law, too, lives in images.[5]

One may approach the electronic visualization of law from a variety of perspectives. For example, in a pragmatic sense, we might talk about the different ways in which lawyers are now integrating visual images into their practices. Visual evidence at trial includes day-in-the-life videos, digitalized graphics, accident and crime reconstructions as well as long-distance testifying via closed-circuit television.[6] The proliferation of visual surveillance—from police vehicles, security cameras, and amateur videos—has also made its mark inside the courtroom. One need only call to mind the defence's sophisticated digital reconstruction of George Holliday's fortuitously captured images of Los Angeles police officers beating Rodney King.[7] Even legal argument has taken to the screen. In a growing number of trials videos are being used as part of closing argument. In one instance a video replaced oral argument altogether.[8]

Law lives in images. We make sense of reality by drawing upon the stories and storytelling modes that are most familiar to us.[9] And these days, television and film are by far the most popular sources of the stories and story forms that we all know.[10]

[5] Austin Sarat, 'Imagining the Law of the Father' (2000) 34 *Law & Society Rev* 9, 39 ('Today we have law on the books, law in action, and now, law in the image . . . Law lives in images that today saturate our culture and that have a power all their own').

[6] See Richard K Sherwin, 'Law/Media/Culture: Legal Meaning in the Age of Images' (1999–2000) 43 *New York Law School L Rev* 653–654.

[7] See RK Sherwin, *When Law Goes Pop: The Vanishing Line between Law and Popular Culture* (Chicago: 2000) 272 (describing the defence's digital re-orchestration of George Holliday's videotape to persuade jurors that Rodney King's movements 'caused' Los Angeles police offices to strike him with their batons). See also Richard K Sherwin, 'The Narrative Construction of Legal Reality' (1994) 18 *Vermont L Rev* 681, 691.

[8] See *Standard Chartered PLC v Price Waterhouse*, CV 88-34414 (Sup Ct, Maricopa Co, Ariz, 1989).

[9] See, eg, H White, *Tropics of Discourse* (Baltimore, MD: 1978) 60 ('What the historian must bring to his consideration of the record are general notions of the kinds of stories that might be found there, just as he must bring to consideration of the problem of narrative representation some notion of the "pre-generic plot-structure" by which the story he tells is endowed with formal coherency. In other words, the historian must draw upon a fund of culturally provided *mythoi* in order to constitute the facts as figuring a story of a particular kind . . . '); Bruner, n 4 above, 80 ('While we have an "innate" and primitive predisposition to narrative organization that allows us quickly and easily to comprehend and use it, the culture soon equips us through its tool kit and through the traditions of telling and interpreting in which we soon come to participate').

[10] See Gregor Goethals, 'The Electronic Gold Calf' in *Video Icons & Values* (Albany, NY: 1991) 64 ('Television tells stories that are readily identifiable and offer reassurance; they provide something of the elementary, the primary, the fundamental and stable. Without some commonly accepted narratives that articulate the truths and falsehoods, the values and disvalues of a culture, we would find life intolerably disorienting. In this sense, television's entertainment programs may speak to a human need for identity, both individual and social').

It should hardly prove surprising to find trial lawyers importing popular film plots and characters as well as familiar cinematic styles into their courtroom performances. For example, Oliver Stone's *Natural Born Killers* served, in different ways, both the prosecutor and the defence in a recent Georgia murder case.[11] Francis Ford Coppola's malevolent organized crime characters from *The Godfather* have served more than one prosecuting attorney.[12] And in one complex organized crime case a defence attorney skilfully used a humorous and surreal cinematic storytelling style to transform his mafia wannabe client into a harmless buffoon.[13] It was like watching a Quentin Tarantino movie,[14] or a scene from the comedic imagination of Woody Allen.[15]

Popular images of lawyers, criminals and the legal system help people to understand, or think they understand, the reality these images depict. Whether accurate or not, these are the images that people carry around in their heads.[16] When jurors come into court these are the images that they bring with them. For good or for ill, trial lawyers will have to work with, or around, the images that circulate within the popular imagination. And to greater or lesser degrees of self-awareness, they do.[17] Teaching popular legal studies can help to train lawyers to become better storytellers. It can also help litigators not only to discern the narrative strategies that are marshalled against them, but also to cross-examine, deconstruct, and ultimately supplant those narratives with effective stories of their own.[18]

That is the pragmatic payoff of learning more about law in the image. Society's shift to visual literacy is opening up a new professional tool kit for effective lawyering. It is important that contemporary legal practitioners and academics alike study these new tools with care in order to hone their understanding of the craft of law in the digital age. In the years ahead it will become increasingly difficult not to practise law on the screen, whether in court or out.[19]

[11] See, eg, *Beasley v State* 269 Ga 620, 627 (1998).

[12] See, eg, *Commonwealth v Graziano* 331 NE 808 (Mass, 1975); Jeremiah Donovan, 'Some Off-the-Cuff Remarks about Lawyers as Storytellers' (1994) 18 *Vermont L Rev* 751, 753 (referring to prosecution's invocation of images from *The Godfather* in *United States v Bianco* No H-90-18 [AHN] [D Conn, July 16, 1991]).

[13] See Donovan, n 12 above, 759.

[14] See Sherwin, *When Law Goes Pop*, n 7 above, 30–31.

[15] See Philip N Meyer, 'Desperate for Love: Cinematic Influences Upon a Defendant's Closing Argument to a Jury' (1994) 18 *Vermont L Rev* 721.

[16] See Vicki Smith, 'Prototypes in the Courtroom: Lay Representations of Legal Concepts' (1991) 61 *Journal of Personality and Social Psychology* 857; A Ries and J Trout, *Positioning: The Battle for Your Mind* (New York: 1986).

[17] See, eg, Anthony G Amsterdam and Randy Hertz, 'An Analysis of Closing Arguments to a Jury' (1992) 37 *New York Law School L Rev* 55; Neal Feigenson, *Legal Blame: How Jurors Think and Talk About Accidents* (Washington, DC: 2000).

[18] See generally, Marc Galanter, 'An Oil Strike in Hell: Contemporary Legends About the Civil Justice System' (1998) 40 *Arizona L Rev* 725 ('Folklore expresses deep and abiding sentiments and perspectives, and examining it can illuminate our dispositions that are otherwise difficult to fathom . . . My point is how deeply this kind of discourse has penetrated current debate about legal policy').

[19] This includes litigating cases in the mass media. See Sherwin, *When Law Goes Pop*, n 7 above, 141–152 (on the litigation public relations phenomenon). See also J Haggerty, *In the Court of Public Opinion* (Hoboken, NJ: 2003).

From a more scholarly perspective, the emerging popular legal studies movement also has a lot to tell us. The kinds of images that find their way into law films—the stories that are told, the character types that are portrayed—help to inform us about the society we live in. For example, popular legal representations serve as a cultural barometer revealing pressing needs, fantasies, and anxieties, as well as beliefs, hopes and aspirations that are circulating in society. These narrative elements shape and inform the way we understand current legal issues, notorious trial outcomes, and the role of law in society in general.[20]

In prior work,[21] I have discussed in greater detail both the pragmatic (rhetorical) aspect of visual legal representations as well as the contribution they can make to cultural analysis and critique. In this essay, I want to concentrate on a less familiar aspect of popular legal studies. I want to consider film from the perspective of jurisprudence.[22] Film, at its best, like all forms of art, provides a way of understanding significant shifts in modes of knowing and being in the world.[23] In addition to fresh epistemological and ontological insights, film also serves as an important source of normative vision. It can help us to understand the way things are (or how we perceive them to be), how life is lived now, so to speak, and how we might learn to live better, more wisely. This includes the life we live in the law. Thus, in addition to thinking about the practical and pedagogic implications of law's life in images, I submit that we must consider as well how visual representations on the screen affect legal theory. In pursuit of this contention, in what follows I explore what it might mean to take up 'cinematic jurisprudence'.

Film, like literature, has the capacity to 'theorize the conditions of the world from which it emerges and to which it addresses itself'.[24] New digital technologies of visualization, working in tandem with current developments in cultural studies and constructivist theory, have given rise to new issues and concerns, such as the

[20] Sherwin, *When Law Goes Pop*, n 7 above, 73–78.

[21] ibid.

[22] To date the jurisprudence of film has been pursued by only a handful of legal scholars. See Austin Sarat, 'Living in a Copernican Universe: Law and Fatherhood in *A Perfect World*' (1999–2000) 43 *New York Law School L Rev* 843, 847 ('I turn to film because law exists in a world of images whose power is not located primarily in their representation of something exterior to themselves, but instead is found in the image itself'); Norman Rosenberg, '*Young Mr. Lincoln*: The Lawyer as Superhero' (1991) 15 *Legal Studies Forum* 215, 227 (comparing film scenes to legal realist insights of the 1930s); Alison Young, 'Murder in the Eyes of the Law' (1997) 17 *Studies in Law, Politics and Society* 31 (bringing together feminism, psychoanalysis, critical criminology and film theory in an effort to explore 'how cinema is jurisprudence'); and Sherwin, *When Law Goes Pop*, n 7 above, 171–203 (examining *Cape Fear* (1962) (1991), *Twin Peaks*, and other films for insights into popular cultural beliefs about law, lawyers, and the possibility [or impossibility] of approximating truth and justice in the legal system).

[23] See, eg, P Pisters, *The Matrix of Visual Culture* (Palo Alto, CA: 2003) 2 ('it is through the camera that we have come to live in a universe that is metacinematic . . . [W]e come to understand our past, present, and future through a new "camera consciousness" that has entered our perception'); and DN Rodowick, *Reading the Figural, or, Philosophy after the New Media* (Durham, NC: 2001) xii ('The Modern era required a strict separation between plastic space, which organizes representation, and linguistic reference, which excludes it. But in the era of electronic and digital communication, the figural is increasingly defined as a semiotic regime where the world of things is penetrated by discourse, with its ambiguous power to negate and divide or differ, and the independent weight of things congeals into signs that proliferate anonymously in everyday life').

[24] Gourgouris, n1 above, xix.

vanishing line between the virtual and the actual, docudrama and documentary, subjective fantasy and the reality principle.[25] Film affords us the opportunity to assess critically different forms of knowledge.[26] For example, moving images invite us to *feel* our way into knowing. Cinematic insights typically bypass intellectual analysis. We identify and dis-identify with characters, pass judgments on their choices and actions, and instantly react to dramatic situations. Simply stated, film enchants us with its images. It binds us to the screen.

There is something erotic in this bond. Consider the intimacy of sharing one's fantasies and feelings with another. Or, moving from the subjective to the sublime, consider what the Renaissance writer Henry Corbin called 'the manner of theophanic apperception' through which a sublime wisdom reveals itself visibly with such sweetness as to bring forth joy and delight.[27] This is reminiscent of the neo-Platonic musings of other Renaissance thinkers, such as Ficino and Agrippa of Nettesheim, who conceived of light and fascination itself as a force that enters the eyes.[28] Or consider the great Renaissance magician and rhetorician, Giordano Bruno, who wrote extensively about the phantasmic process of moving the soul.[29] Reading Bruno today is eerily akin to reading the most sophisticated public relations manuals. Take, for example, Bruno's reference to the *vinculum vinculorum*, the chain of chains.[30] By this he means the production and manipulation of phantasms and the activation of eros after having won the good faith of the target. No doubt, manipulating eros has always been at the heart of the science and craft of persuasion. Just as it has offered the most reliable formula for cinematic success—for commercial and independent films as well as for political propaganda, public relations, and advertising.

As we all know, normative commitment is never simply a given. Normative yearnings must be met anew in every generation. The meanings that hold a world together must be actively experienced, performed, and thereby re-enacted, at least on occasion, so that the wellsprings of commitment may be refreshed. This elementary need points to the ongoing social function of ritual and drama in the service of enchantment.[31]

[25] See Rodowick, n 23 above, 51 ('"Discourse" is no longer linear and reversible; it is becoming increasingly entropic and dispersed; in the language of computer networking, it is "distributed" communication. Similarly, distinctions between subject and object are no longer clear-cut. This is understood well by those who finance, govern, market, and manage. The philosopher, whose function should be to develop concepts and tools for critical understanding, is panting to catch up').

[26] See, eg, DN Rodowick, *Gilles Deleuze's Time Machine* (Durham, NC: 1997), 5 ('the development of cinema provides a privileged site for comprehending a decisive shift in strategies of signification, understanding and belief that is no less true for aesthetic thinking than it is for philosophical and scientific thinking'); and B Nichols, *Representing Reality* (Bloomington, IN: 1991).

[27] See IP Couliano, *Eros and Magic in the Renaissance* (Chicago: 1987) 18. See also Richard K Sherwin, 'Law's Beatitude: A Post-Nietzschean Account of Legitimacy' (2003) 24 *Cardozo L Rev* 683, 690 (describing Nietzsche's joyous intuition of the eternal recurrence of the same).

[28] Couliano, n 27 above, 30. [29] ibid, 58–59.

[30] ibid, 90–99. See also FA Yates, *Giordano Bruno and the Hermetic Tradition* (Chicago: 1964) 265–266.

[31] See V Turner, *Drama, Fields, and Metaphors* (Ithaca, NY: 1979) 45, 49 (describing *communitas* as a bond uniting people over and above any social bonds or structure and which is particularly apparent at liminal moments of conflict and attempts at resolution).

I use the word enchantment here deliberately to evoke the eros of logos.[32] Enchantment is an admittedly provocative way of thinking and talking about rhetoric, persuasion and belief. Through enchantment desire mixes with healing and persuasion.[33] Enchantment evokes the power to compel and be compelled.[34] It is a strange compulsion, not entirely apprehended or apprehensible by the rational mind. Hence, the historic fear of bewitchment and magic that has dogged rhetoricians, playwrights, poets, and artists from Socrates' generation to our own.[35] Yet, once encountered, how can we not be awed by the power of seduction, of becoming enamoured, of falling under the spell of love or beauty?[36] To enchant is to blend power and delight. It is the Sirens' song, 'crying beauty to bewitch [Odysseus and his men]'.[37] Perhaps it is the same inhuman cry that sings 'beyond the genius of the sea', echoing the 'rage for order' that Wallace Stevens records at Key West.[38] Perhaps it is the same call that Heidegger invokes when he writes of 'the echoing response to the first call of Being'.[39] With these words Heidegger links singing and thinking, the poet's way to truth, art's domain. As Heidegger puts it: 'Beauty is one way in which truth occurs . . . Setting up a world and setting forth the earth, the work [of art] accomplishes this striving.'[40]

Without enchantment and belief the force of law ultimately decays into naked power alone. Then the thrill of control, and the various gratifications (material and otherwise) that control brings unite those who rule.[41] And among the ruled, in place of active commitment, an endemic Hobbesian fear becomes the only means of cohesion society knows: fear of chaos and fear of pain in the face of law's might.[42]

[32] See Gorgias, *Ecomium of Helen*, DM MacDowell (ed), (5th C. BC), 1982); Couliano, n 27 above; J Rajchman, *Truth and Eros* (London: 1991).

[33] See PL Entralgo, *The Therapy of the Word in Classical Antiquity* (New Haven: 1970).

[34] See J Romilly, *Magic and Rhetoric* (Cambridge, MA: 1975) 77 ('sublime speech "does not produce persuasion in the audience, but enchantment and ecstasy . . ." '[quoting from *On the Sublime*]). See also Couliano, n 27 above, 107 (noting that Giordano Bruno concerned himself with the possibility of 'erotic manipulation of the individual and the masses').

[35] See, eg, D Freedberg, *The Power of Images* (Chicago: 1989), 378–428 (on the history of idolatry and iconoclasm). See also P Goodrich, *Oedipus Lex: Psychoanalysis, History, Law* (Berkeley, CA: 1995) 41–107 (tracing the history of antirrhetic, or rhetoric as a form of anti-rhetoric, and of imagery that exists to efface itself in order to repress idolatry, sensuality, and dishonor of the Deity).

[36] See GRF Ferrari, *Listening to the Cicadas: A Study of Plato's Phaedrus* (Cambridge: 1990) 60 (on love as one of the four forms of divine madness).

[37] *Homer's Odyssey* (trans R Fitzgerald), (Durham, NC: 1963) 210.

[38] Wallace Stevens, 'Order at Key West' in *The Palm at the End of the Mind* (New York: 1972) 97.

[39] M Heidegger, *Poetry, Language, Thought* (trans Albert Hofstadter) (New York, 1971) 9.

[40] ibid, 49, 56.

[41] See S Bartsch, *Actors in the Audience* (Cambridge, MA: 1994) 1, 20 ('The atrocities of a Roman emperor corrupted by his power often found both audience and victim in the theatrical and gladiatorial games of the city . . . [W]hen an emperor's audience fails to decode the spectacle before their eyes into reality and then to recode their own response back into the feigned and theatrical, the outcome is death'). E Auerbach, *Mimesis: The Representation of Reality in Western Literature* (Princeton, NJ: 1946) 55 ('Grotesque and sadistic, spectral and superstitious, lusting for power yet constantly trying to conceal the chattering of their teeth—so do we see the men of Ammianus' ruling class and their world').

[42] T Hobbes, *Leviathan* (Herbert W Schneider (ed), [1651], Indianapolis, IN: 1958) 17 ('It is men and arms, not words and promises that makes the force and power of the laws'). Compare HLA Hart's *Concept of Law* (Oxford, 1961) 97–114 (describing the concept of coercive 'obligation' [being motivated

To escape this crude fate law needs normative vision, in the spirit of hope, to impel it to span from the present toward a possible future. In this sense, normative vision is law's life-blood. Without it, the bridge falls. Law ossifies into imperial enforcement.[43]

Theorizing film from the lawyer's perspective, which is after all the perspective of the rhetorician, the one intent on persuading others, cannot avoid difficult ethical issues regarding the authority and deceits of visual communication. I raise these issues because they also lie at the heart of the film that I wish to discuss in this essay. That film is *Red*, the final masterwork of the late Polish filmmaker, Krzysztof Kieslowski. *Red* was released in 1994, and is the last in a trilogy of films called *Blue, White*, and *Red*, the colours of the French flag.

It was Krzysztof Piesiewicz, an attorney, and Kieslowski's longtime collaborator, whose idea it was 'to attempt to return to elementary values destroyed by communism'.[44]

In the *Three Colours* trilogy Kieslowski and Piesiewicz consciously set themselves the task of confronting the core values that constitute the mythical foundation of the European Enlightenment. This effort was undertaken not as a philosophical venture, but rather as a poetic one. Kieslowski's interests lay not so much in abstract ideas as in interior states. As he puts it: 'I think it is time to ponder the actual meaning of everything within [our cultural] tradition . . . [W]here are [these values] located within us, what is our real attitude to them?'[45]

The *Three Colours* trilogy seeks the current, *embodied* meaning of once revolutionary values. What do they mean in the concrete context of a particular life? In Kieslowski's words: 'Blue, liberty; White, equality; Red, fraternity . . . We looked very closely at these three ideas, how they functioned in everyday life, but from an individual's point of view . . .'[46] This emphasis on particularity is crucial. If the values and beliefs at stake here are to have meaning for us today, they must be performed in contexts that we recognize as part of the life we live. Performance actualizes description. But it does more. It also has the capacity to test aspirational values. It can perform utopian possibilities.

In this respect, I contend that Kieslowski's film embodies a vital mythical presence in society. I use the word 'myth' here to refer not to some primitive or antecedent fictional tale of origins, but rather, in its Vichian sense, as an ongoing social and normative force. Mythic narratives perform cultural meanings; law's narratives police them. But law exercises more than a merely regulatory function.

from without] with the internalized viewpoint of 'being obliged' [premised upon affirmative belief]. For his part, Vico was an early, staunch opponent to Hobbes' cynical view of human nature. See Mali, n 1 above, 52.

[43] See Cover, n 1 above, 16 ('The sober imperial mode of world maintenance holds the mirror of critical objectivity to meaning, imposes the discipline of institutional justice upon norms, and places the constraint of peace on the void at which strong bonds cease').

[44] D Stok (ed), *Kieslowski on Kieslowski* (London: 1993), 212.

[45] P Coates, *Lucid Dreams: The Films of Krzysztof Kieslowski* (Wilshire: 1999) 171.

[46] ibid.

It is also constitutive. This is law's poetic, regenerative function. New normative longings may come to displace inherited conventions. As a reconstructive force, law destroys the old identificatory terms in order to make way for new forms of identity and community, coincident with new social visions.

I wish to link the constitutive capacity of law and film to what Richard Rorty has described as the visionary dimension of the American pragmatist tradition. Rorty writes about the 'breakthrough into romance' and the 'poetry of justice'.[47] In some respects, Kieslowski may be said to share an affinity with social visionaries such as John Dewey and Ralph Waldo Emerson. Kieslowski's final film, for example, is imbued with a profoundly ethical vision of contemporary life in community with others under law. Yet, given the deeply tragic sensibility that haunts Kieslowski's work, this affinity is a limited one. Kieslowski is unmistakably a man of our time: meanings are contingent, uncertain, without guarantee, like identity itself. But for chance connections, who knows who we might become? Such is what has come to be known as the postmodern condition.

Whatever else the word 'postmodern' may mean, and there are surely more meanings than we can bear (a sure sign of postmodernity), I offer the following signs of the times:

(a) We have come to realize that we live in webs of meaning that are of our own making; law, as Clifford Geertz has said, is a particular way of imagining the real.[48]

(b) This constructivist insight in combination with new technologies of simulation and mass communication have led to problems; for example, distinguishing between truth and fiction, reality and fantasy, reason and desire has grown increasingly difficult in our time.[49]

(c) This confusion is aided and abetted by a massive proliferation of images; we are so saturated with images that it is difficult enough just to keep up, much less assess what they mean.[50]

(d) The commercial production of images places a premium on audience share, which in turn leads to a heightening of the sensational power of images to draw and maintain their hold upon the viewer's attention.[51]

(e) Sensation, saturation, and speed tend to reduce depth as the viewer rushes along the surface of the screen in an effort to keep up with the flow.[52]

[47] Richard Rorty, 'The Banality of Pragmatism and the Poetry of Justice' (1990) 63 *Southern California L Rev* 1811, 1818.

[48] C Geertz, *Local Knowledge* (New York: 1983) 184.

[49] See Sherwin, *When Law Goes Pop*, n 7 above, 15–39.

[50] See J Baudrillard, *Fatal Strategies* (New York: 1990); JB Twitchell, *Carnival Culture* (New York: 1992) 51 ('What characterizes the condition of culture since World War II is . . . that now we have more signs that point nowhere').

[51] See Sherwin, *When Law Goes Pop*, n 7 above, 37.

[52] P Virilio, *The Aesthetics of Disappearance* (New York: 1991) 35 ('turned causal by its excessive speed, the sensation overtakes the logical order').

(f) Fragmentation, the rush of desire, and the contingent meaning of juxtaposed images tend to destabilize categorization, undercut deliberation, and displace linear causation for the sake of free association among ideas and affects.[53]

In *When Law Goes Pop*, I examine the impact of postmodern conditions on law. In particular, I criticize the predominantly sceptical or disenchanted attitude that characterizes a good deal of recent critical scholarship. I contend that excessive scepticism does law no good.[54] Fortunately, scepticism does not have a lock on postmodern culture. There is another, more affirmative kind of postmodernism.[55] Affirmative postmodernism is postmodern in its understanding of how we construct meaning in everyday life and how self and social reality are built up from the different stories that we tell ourselves and that we share with others in the course of our social and professional practices.[56] It is also postmodern in its recognition of the cognitive habits that help to construct and maintain the diverse micro-identities that comprise the self from one context to another. And it is postmodern in its acceptance of contingency and the disruptive, uncontrollable surge of the irrational both within and without.

Even so, postmodernism need not be sceptical. For example, a postmodern story might convey meaning by making novel connections or juxtapositions in the mind. Thus a narrative may be postmodern in its non-linear use of popular cultural images and symbols, but need not employ these images and symbols in an insular or exclusively self-referential manner. A story might concede the demise of the autonomous modern subject, but still find meaning through the distributed self: an identity comprised of multiple cultural and social constructs shared by others in particular communities. In this postmodern but non-sceptical spirit, one might recognize the irreducibility of truth and justice to any abstract meta-narrative (for example, a system based on axiomatic principles such as fairness, liberty, or some felicific calculus) but still experience the vitality of a discrete truth or a localized, embodied sense of justice.

Abstraction may give way to particularity, contextuality, multiplicity; judgment may turn toward characteristic voices and localized accounts. But localization and contextualization are not fatal to meaning. It remains possible to seek rather than abandon meaning for concepts such as truth and justice—even in the face of contingency, unpredictability, and spontaneity. In this way, human depth remains. Internal forces (such as motivation, intention, and choice) rather than wholly external forces (such as chance or fate) still account for events and provide a basis for meaning and accountability.

Of course to say as much is not to deny the presence of strange irrational forces within and without—forces that can never be fully mastered. Still, the ability to

[53] See Sherwin, *When Law Goes Pop*, n 7 above, 19–25 (on visual literacy and the ascendancy of associative reasoning).

[54] ibid, 186–203.

[55] ibid. See also P Rosenau, *Post-Modernism and the Social Sciences* (Princeton, NJ: 1992) 57–60.

[56] See Bruner, n 4 above, 116, 132–138.

embrace meaning, to say 'yes' to ethical enchantment, remains intact. Indeed, rather than deny the contingency and ultimate fragility of meaning, these now become the very conditions that inform our shared responsibility for meaning's construction, maintenance, and change. By accepting normative constraint in this way, we actively engage in de-liberation, which serves as the counteragent to impulsiveness and irrational manipulation.

The affirmative postmodern viewpoint takes us beyond demystifying critique and the sceptic's stance of perpetual irony by embracing the possibility of enchantment and wisdom. I would even go so far as to say that the affirmative postmodern actor seeks the re-enchantment of ethics and wisdom.[57]

This approach comports with what Richard Rorty and Clifford Geertz, among other postmodern thinkers, refer to as philosophizing without foundations. The goal is not to displace one system, or axiomatic principle, with another. Wisdom remains local, contextual, relational, and contingent. Immanent meanings may be cultivated or seized, a gift of the moment; but they are not guaranteed.[58]

I believe that the sort of ethical postmodern attitude that I have been describing pervades the aesthetic and ethical vision that we find in Kieslowski's *Red*. There is nothing romantic about his view. In many ways it is tragic.[59] But it eschews a temptation that has captivated many critics of postmodern disenchantment. Kieslowski avoids nostalgia. He resists the temptation to envision some unspoiled past, such as the distant age of the Enlightenment whose traditions and values simply await our embrace.[60] Kieslowski understands the limits of postmodern scepticism, but he does not turn his back on the world we know. His challenge, and ours, is to work through, by working with, current cultural conditions. We cannot simply turn away.

The world Kieslowski depicts is familiar to us. Yes, even this Polish director's world, filmed in Geneva, in French, is our world too. It is part of the multi-faceted global culture that is forming around us—in all its fragmented, contingent, and unreasoned glory. It is also a world of law and lawyers and judges. I contend that the ethical vision that it presents helps us to think in new ways about law and justice in postmodern times.

In *Red* Kieslowski tells the stories mainly of three characters: a retired, disenchanted judge named Joseph Kern; a young lawyer named Auguste Bruner, who is about to become a judge himself; and a young woman named Valentine Dussaut, a student and part time model, who fortuitously enters and changes Kern's life, and

[57] See FJ Varela, *Ethical Know-How: Action, Wisdom, and Cognition* (Palo Alto, CA: 1999) 75 ('My presentation is, more than anything, a plea for a re-enchantment of wisdom, understood as non-intentional action. This skillful approach to living . . . opens up openness as authentic caring').

[58] See J-P Sartre, *Nausea* (New York, 1964) 131 ('The essential thing is contingency, I mean that one cannot define existence as necessity. To exist is simply to be there . . .').

[59] See C Segal, *Tragedy and Civilization* (Norman, OK: 1999) 408. ('The tragic poet becomes a kind of culture hero who confronts the darker mysteries of life and by his art, like Oedipus by his god-given power, transmutes the pollutions of an accursed past into blessings for his fellow citizens').

[60] See Richard K Sherwin, 'A Matter of Voice and Plot: Belief and Suspicion in Legal Storytelling' (1988) 87 *Michigan L Rev* 555–557.

perhaps Bruner's as well. Who knows, perhaps the older Kern and the younger Bruner are the same man subject to a different fate. Kieslowski leads us to wonder whether we all lead lives that are contingent upon chance encounters. Perhaps each of us might be different, might become another, unimaginable to us now, this moment, but for some unforeseen event in our lives, an event over which we have no control whatsoever.

Red is at least in part a film about the ramifications of disenchantment and belief. It addresses the perennial question: what basis do we have for affirmation and for wise judgment? Culture is an invaluable guide in this matter. It helps us when we find ourselves wondering, what is there beyond custom and habit to hold our normative universe together?

The normative vision presented here in response is neither instrumental nor deontological. Kieslowski does not speak in terms of individual entitlements, nor does he calculate pleasure and pain. He identifies no system of principles from which we may assess how to relate to or judge others. In Kieslowski's normative universe people learn from chance events, from the immediacy of concrete experience in relation to others, and from critical self-reflection upon that experience. Meaning is an immanent possibility. It hinges on attentiveness to what the lived moment offers. Attentiveness, however, may be blocked by habits of thought, memory, and emotion—habits that are manifest in self-fulfilling patterns of behaviour that tend to reinforce the sameness of lived experience. In this sense we may say that character is fate, the sum of our life history. But our fate is not sealed. The possibility of redemptive change, through chance, openness, trauma, and critical reflection, remains.[61]

We begin with the film's chief metaphor: telephone lines shoot out over land and sea amid a cacophony of overlapping voices. In a flash we are witness to the ongoing process of making and breaking off connections. Immediately, contingency reaches for an embodied form: being in touch, making contact with another, with the one nearby (the 'neighbour'). The tangential coincidence of sharing a common time/space is ramified electronically in a sweeping network of lines mapping interpersonal ties. Community (the domain of the fraternal) is constituted by a network of coincidental tangents, graced by love and bowed by betrayal, as we shall soon see. Epiphanic knowledge (the gift of grace) becomes the regenerative force of culture manifest in love and beauty. But trouble ramifies discord, fuelling narrative development in time, albeit not without the opportunity for momentary grace and contingent union. That is the essence of redemptive possibility that Kieslowski's vision holds out: the possibility of insight, change, and corrective action leading to healing, and the possibility of redemptive justice, amid the inescapable reality of tragic suffering.

[61] S Freud, 'Inhibitions, Symptoms, & Anxiety' in James Strachey (ed. and trans), *The Standard Edition of the Complete Works of Sigmund Freud* (London: 1959) vol xx, 159–160 (on working through neurotic repetition). See also Varela, n 57 above, 30–31.

On what basis, the film leads us to ask, do we enter into relationship with another, and with what transformative effect? From the outset of Kieslowski's film we are introduced to a network of connected, soon-to-be connected, and soon-to-be disconnected lives. Consider: Michel, whom we will never see, always speaks from a distance. We hear his disembodied voice in telephone calls from some foreign land. He never speaks face to face with his girlfriend, Valentine Dussaut. And when he does speak, jealousy, insecurity, and perverse desire fill the air. These are the hallmarks of his troubled relationship with Valentine. His opening words in the first conversation with Valentine are typical of their every exchange, 'First it was busy, then the machine. Are you alone?' 'Is someone there?' Ungrounded suspicion and jealousy are Michel's calling cards. And when at one point he asks Valentine to get into bed, an apparently familiar overture to some kind of phone-sex ritual that has plagued Valentine before, we hear her sadly whisper, 'Ah, it commences'. No doubt about it, the connection between Michel and Valentine is troubled.

Meanwhile, just across the street, unbeknown to Valentine, the young lawyer Auguste Bruner is also on the phone with his girlfriend, Karin. Karin is a 'personal weather reporter'.[62] She plies her trade by telephone. In contrast to Michel's perpetual suspicions about Valentine's faithfulness, Auguste exhibits an open, trusting nature toward Karin. Just the whisper of a kiss into the receiver, he has no doubt that she will know it is him. Who else could it be? Auguste may not realize it now, but Karin will soon betray him by sleeping with another man.

It is the same betrayal that occurred long ago in the life of another, now far older man, the retired judge Joseph Kern. Kern has been disappointed in life and in love. He spends his time now in retirement eavesdropping on his neighbours' telephone conversations. The travails and suffering that he overhears only confirm his philosophy of disenchantment and cynical indifference.

But chance changes everything. Or, at least, such is its power and potential. And it is by chance that Valentine comes into Kern's life. The agent is Kern's stray dog whom Valentine inadvertently strikes with her car.[63] The address inscribed on the injured dog's collar leads her to Kern's home. Kern has placed himself outside the social loop. Alone, unconnected to others, he no longer acts. He simply listens, furtively, to the private sufferings of his neighbours, as their no longer private telephone conversations amply reveal. The lies, the betrayals, the cruelty—here is human nature laid bare. That, at any rate, is how Kern explains his life as Valentine

[62] Ironically, her inability to predict a storm on the English Channel will lead to her own and her new lover's death at sea. By chance, Karin also happens to be one of Kern's neighbours. His eavesdropping upon her conversations with Auguste Bruner leads Kern to conclude that Karin's and Auguste's relationship will not last. ('She is not the one he is looking for', Kern will tell Valentine.)

[63] Arguably, the accident is not entirely fortuitous. Valentine momentarily loses her concentration when a strange sound of electronic interference comes on the car radio. It is the same sound that we hear when Valentine first enters the room that contains Kern's eavesdropping equipment. Could it be that Kern has somehow reached out to Valentine, that he is signalling his need, that his 'interference' with her life course is a call beckoning her into his orbit?

silently listens. To judge, he tells her, is pointless. Nothing changes. Besides, who knows when forgiveness is better than condemnation? Kern then tells an anecdote to explain. Once, 35 years ago, when still a judge, Kern mistakenly acquitted a man. The man, he later learned, was guilty. But upon making his own investigation into the matter many years later, Kern also learned that the man subsequently married, had three children and a grandchild, and was, as Kern puts it, 'living in peace'. 'Deciding what is true and what isn't now seems to me a lack of modesty', Kern concludes. So he contents himself simply with listening. It is like when he was a judge except that now he knows the stories he hears are true. And the futile responsibility of judging has been lifted from his shoulders.

Kern then recounts a story from his life. Over 35 years before a man seduced and ran off with Kern's one and, as it turned out, only love. Years later, the same man came before Kern in court. The roof of a closed market that Kern's rival had been building had collapsed. People were killed. Kern condemned him. 'It was a legal sentence', he tells Valentine. But Kern's tone betrays his doubts. Indeed, it proved to be Kern's last judgment from the bench. After issuing it he asked for early retirement.

But the tale does not end there. Valentine does not share Kern's dismal view of life. Her fresh spirit wafts over his deadened one. Valentine succeeds in re-animating something that had for many years lain dormant within Kern. Old memories of lost love are stirred, perhaps along with the inextinguishable power of love itself. He stopped believing, Kern tells Valentine, but then he adds, 'Maybe you're the woman I never met'. If only their paths had crossed when he was still young, perhaps she could have changed his life. But perhaps she still can.

Consider this exchange between them. Kern has been leading Valentine through the personal travails of his neighbours as their exposed telephone conversations play out, one after the other, on the air inside Kern's cramped living room. 'Ah, next programme, not very interesting', Kern will say. A mother who incessantly calls her daughter, bombarding her with false complaints about ill health and lack of food, lies that now fall on deaf ears. They barely conceal her desperate need for her daughter to come, to ease the terrible suffering of loneliness. 'Next programme', Kern dispassionately intones, as if this conversation and the others that we have heard were no more than a TV soap opera. As Andy Warhol has said, 'once you see emotions from a certain angle you can never think of them as real again'. [64]

This is what it is like when the real collapses into the insular domain of free-floating images. Compassion and sympathy lose their meaning. Judgment becomes impossible. This is what has become of Kern in the face of life's tragic disappointments. The suffering around (and within) him has destroyed his capacity to feel or care about anyone. Without the capacity for sympathy, stories become

[64] See A Warhol, *The Philosophy of Andy Warhol* (San Diego, CA: 1975) 27; Mark Poster, *The Mode of Information* (Chicago: 1990) 63 (describing how TV ads operate as 'floating signifiers' that convey 'desirable or undesirable states of being . . . in a way that optimizes the viewer's attention without arousing critical awareness').

inconsequential, disembodied. They lack weight. That is why Kern can eavesdrop without experiencing moral compunction. He is cut off.

On the other hand, Kieslowski also presents us with the embodiment of authentic connection. This is the connection that emerges between Kern and Valentine. Valentine is repulsed both by Kern's actions and by his cynical philosophy, and she tells him so. When Kern says he cares for nothing, Valentine replies, 'So stop breathing!' 'Good idea', is Kern's nihilistic response. But Kern's long infatuation with loss and death is about to end. In Valentine the breath of life is strong. She radiates innocence, vulnerability, and compassion. 'You are mistaken', she tells Kern. 'People aren't bad. It's not true . . . People may be weak sometimes.' She then rushes in tears from his house. But not before having bestowed a great gift. Her vibrant spirit opens up a redemptive moment for Kern, and he realizes its potential. After she departs he sits down at his desk to compose letters to each of his neighbours in turn. In the letters Kern confesses his immoral and illegal acts of spying. Kern's remembrance of lost love precedes the change. It is against this backdrop that he understands, perhaps for the first time, the real nature of his suffering and of the rage that he has been acting out in his abusive and perverse relations with others. Kern's cynicism is but a defensive shell, protecting him from the pain of unexpressed love.

Inhaling Valentine's breath of life revives Kern's hardened heart. He now repudiates fatalistic passivity and the paralysis of judgment that it brings. In his first act of judgment Kern judges himself. Guilty. Passive voyeurism, the reflection of his deadened spirit, must end. If character is fate now Kern will alter his fate by repudiating the perverse character that he has become. Kern's chance connection with Valentine has stirred memories of youthful love. But Valentine has done more. She has inspired within him love of another sort: the selfless love of *agape*, a form of love that aspires to spiritual or fraternal rather than physical consummation.[65]

Kern's connection to others in the world will now be restored. Rather than passively (and perversely) enjoying the spectacle of human suffering, Kern will actively seek to untangle crossed connections and foster authentic ones. Years of listening to people's stories of suffering and conflict, both on and off the bench, have given him peculiar insight into the mysterious ways of chance and the vicissitudes of human interactions. Like Oedipus at Colonus, whose long years of exile culminate in divine sanctification, or Prospero's fateful enchantments in Shakespeare's *The Tempest*, so too Kern's years of lonely suffering seem to have bestowed upon him not only tragic wisdom, but something more. Something akin to oracular vision, the foresight of a fate god, or perhaps an oracle

[65] See S Zizek, *The Fright of Real Tears* (London, 2001) 161. See also Peter Goodrich, 'Laws of Friendship' (2003) 15 *Law & Literature* 27 (noting that in Aristotle's view, amity 'was a stronger bond of community, and more likely to ensure harmonious co-existence, than any code of laws. Friendship was a prior or first law of community, and without it there could be no justice in the sense of government and law').

of law.[66] Kern will now set in motion ripples of fate that will change Valentine's life, and perhaps young Auguste Bruner's life as well. For it is through Kern's designs that their paths will finally cross. In this way the 'mistake in time' that long deprived Kern of the chance for a fulfilling relationship will be rectified.[67] The elderly Kern may not be able to court the young Valentine himself, but he can reciprocate in a fashion the selfless love and compassion that emanate from her. Kern will now use his knowledge and revived sense of care for others to save the young Auguste Bruner from suffering Kern's fate. No, Bruner need not replicate Kern's disappointment and ensuing cynicism. And it is toward this end, inspired by and expressing Valentine's compassion and selfless kindness, that Kern brings the two together. Seeing their contentment will suffice.

Strange forces have been unleashed. The cherries on the slot machine outside the café near Valentine's apartment building have all lined up, which means—according to the law of the conservation of chance—that a correction is at hand. And so it is. That very day a photo of Valentine's younger brother will appear in the newspaper above a caption announcing an increase in the number of young Swiss heroin users. Another development is also afoot. Karin is about to betray Auguste. And soon thereafter Valentine will come to question her connection with Michel. It is against this backdrop of trauma and flux that Kern sets in motion a chain of events that leads Valentine's and Auguste's paths to cross.

Six separate lives, three relationships: Valentine's faltering connection with the perverse Michel; Auguste's betrayed relationship with the fickle Karin; and Kern's transformative relationship with Valentine. How easily each could become another. Like the way Auguste, a judge by film's end, also spurned in love and in so many other ways Kern's double, seems primed to replicate Kern's disenchanted life. Just as Valentine, caught in Michel's perverse gaze, might never pierce the veil of inauthenticity but for a chance event, a fateful encounter.

Kieslowski has constructed a tightly woven network of relationships that undergoes significant reconfiguration. The nature and meaning of this process of change teaches us about perversion and betrayal in our relation to others and the price to be paid in personal suffering and disenchantment. But another possibility also emerges. By reintroducing the forces of love and kindness into Kern's life Valentine reveals the moment's redemptive potential, and the epiphanic power of grace. And, of course, it is through Kern's reciprocal intervention that Valentine comes into Auguste's life, holding out the promise of a more meaningful, more deeply committed relationship than either had known before.

[66] Throughout the film Kieslowski hints at Kern's unusual abilities, such as his prediction of a sudden change of light, his seeming ability to influence the spin of a coin, and his prediction that Auguste's and Karin's relationship is about to end. Indeed, Kern not only arranges for Valentine and Auguste to meet, but he also seems to foresee Valentine's future. 'Last night I dreamed of you', he tells Valentine. 'You were 40 or 50 years old and you were happy.' 'Will this happen?' Valentine will later ask Kern. 'Yes', he confidently replies. With awe in her voice and face, Valentine says, 'What else do you know? Who are you?' The strangeness of Kern's power points toward the uncanny, a species of enchantment.

[67] See G Andrew, *The Three Colours Trilogy* (London: 1998) 64.

What Kieslowski has done here is to lay out a span of relational norms. They range from the flawed (eros as use and consumption with its attendant features and concomitants: the inauthentic self, the wounded lover) to the authentic (unselfish compassion and authenticating care, as evidenced in the relationship between young Valentine and the elderly Kern). Forces of chance and contingency reign over all. Their central metaphors in the film are the weather report and the slot machine. Kieslowski also uses familiar images to add significance to unstable relationships. For example, Valentine's perverse connection with Michel aptly parallels her part-time work as a model. A successful photo shoot culminates in a 25 by 60 feet wide advertising banner featuring Valentine's face in profile set against a red backdrop. The ad uses her face to sell a popular brand of bubble gum. 'A breath of life', reads the logo. An ironic message, for Valentine does become a breath of life for Kern, though not for her current lover, Michel. Indeed, like Michel's perverse and distant gaze, so too the objectifying gaze of the prospective consumer mocks authentic ('face-to-face') relationships. Here we witness unfulfilled desire being used and used up, like chewing gum perhaps, or like any commodity that we take in and spit out once its use is done. This is how we consume images and objects everyday, for the use value that they offer. The pursuit of self-gratification, trading on a fantasized relationship with the object of one's gaze, serves as an apt model of narcissistic inauthenticity in our relationships with others.[68]

Kieslowski similarly presents us with a spectrum of authentic and deficient relational norms in regard to judging. For example, we witness the deficiency of Kern's judgments in connection with his illicit and cynical eavesdropping on his neighbours. Of his life as a judge, Kern says, 'I never knew if I was on the good side or the bad. Who knows if condemnation is more just than mercy? Whatever we say, sooner or later something will happen, all hell will break loose and there's nothing we can do about it.' He adds, 'Here at least I know where the truth is. My point of view is better than the courtroom.' But what purpose can judgment serve when fate remains inscrutable and resists every human effort to make justice rule? Kern's fatalism induces passivity and cynical indifference. Indeed, even empathy in this dispensation fares no better.

In pure subjectivity the judge who wholly identifies with the fate of the judged becomes forgetful of others. As Kern says, 'I'd do the same if I were them . . . And that goes for everyone I've judged; given their lives I would steal, I'd kill, I'd lie.' Total empathy with the actor's subjective reality prompts a forgiveness that paralyzes judgment. This too is a form of detachment and indifference, a state of disconnection from the sorrow and pain that has befallen others, perhaps as a direct consequence of what the accused has done. Indifference here is yet another sign of what it means to dwell outside the lived experience of human relationships.

[68] The same tempest that brings Auguste Bruner and Valentine together on their trip across the English Channel simultaneously causes Valentine's advertising poster to be taken down. One might say that her inauthentic (commodified) being in the world is now giving way to an authentic (face-to-face) relationship with someone who is, unlike Michel, worthy and capable of love.

Such a life cannot escape the insular world of a particular 'I'. Only here it is the 'I' fused with the other, an 'I' that could not have done otherwise. In short, the inability to take responsibility for judgment or consider the impact of acts or judgments upon others characterizes both fatalistic and wholly empathic judging. Both suffer from the insularity of unchecked narcissism.

By contrast, in wiser forms of judgment responsibility to and for the other becomes central. Consider, for example, Kern's first act of judgment: he turns himself in. The first sign of Kern's redemptive transformation is his taking responsibility for his perverse relationship to others around him. Spurred by Valentine's impassioned and unselfish condemnation of his behaviour Kern is no longer able to experience the suffering of others as a disembodied spectacle—raw material for his personal amusement. Others are no longer commodities, like Valentine's profile, or the TV images that we watch and discard once their value is used up.

Only when Valentine's revivifying spirit leads him to understand the origin and meaning of his perverse relations with others is Kern able to rekindle his own spirit of care and unselfish fellow-feeling. Only then does he take active responsibility for Valentine and her younger brother, as well as for others living around him. Indeed, by reaching out to his younger double, by bringing Auguste Bruner and Valentine together, Kern redeems his own life through another's. What was lost to him may now be gained in Auguste's life. It is the quintessential enactment of *agape*.[69] The shattering of indifference in the awakening of love for the other precedes the possibility of justice and authentic judging. [70] It also marks the birth of community. We are born into, and sustained by, culture; its stories help to define who we are, and guide the range of our choices in community with others. As Mali notes: 'we are all necessarily constrained by the "authoritative horizons" of our social orders . . . complete freedom would be a void in which nothing would be worth doing, nothing would deserve to count for anything'.[71]

In *Red*, the epiphanic awakening of love, of care for another, becomes the pivot point for authentic identity, judgment, and connections with others. And while the elderly Kern cannot consummate his relationship with Valentine, he can set her on a course that will cause her to cross paths with his younger double, Auguste Bruner.

Valentine and Auguste meet on a ferry that tragically capsizes in a storm, but they survive. We see them together at the end of the film. They are shown on

[69] See G Outka, *Agape: An Ethical Analysis* (New Haven, CN: 1972); E Levinas, *Entre Nous Thinking-of-the-Other* (New York: 1998) 105 ('in the relation of the Face, it is asymmetry that is affirmed: at the outset I hardly care what the other is with respect to me . . . he is above all the one I am responsible for').

[70] ibid, 108 ('Justice comes from love . . . Love must always watch over justice'). Levinas and Kieslowski are closely linked in their shared desire to shatter indifference. Compare Levinas ('It is this shattering of indifference . . . that constitutes the ethical event') [ibid, xi] and Kieslowski's co-writer Krzysztof Piesiewicz ('*Red* is a film against indifference') [A Insdorf, *Double Lives, Second Choices The Cinema of Krzysztof Kieslowski* (New York: 1999) 181].

[71] Mali, n 1 above, 119. See also Sherwin, n 27 above, 687 ('In the grip of metaphysical beatitude, sick reason is haunted by an insatiable phantom—a Dybuk, the soul's dark double, product of repressed forces. Dead, yet living, the phantom cries out to us . . . It is the sweetness of eros captured by death. To yield to the call of the undead is to embrace death itself').

a television news report that lets Kern know that they have in fact met. The look on Kern's face—the hint of a smile, the faint trail of a tear—intimates hope, amid tragedy. Perhaps Valentine and Auguste now will be allowed the kind of connection that circumstances in Kern's life did not permit. We are encouraged in this belief by a strange coincidence. The image of Valentine that we see on the news is identical to the image in her larger-than-life advertising banner for chewing gum. The same tempest that caused the ferry to capsize also forced the ad with Valentine's disembodied profile to be taken down. Decommodification, it seems, is the precursor to authentic identity. We see on screen the same image of Valentine, but how different its energy the second time we see it. A staged look of pain now becomes real, embodied—authenticated by lived experience.

In Kieslowski's film, insight comes suddenly, by grace and tragedy; wisdom builds over time in the way we choose to respond to both. Intuitively, we grasp that Valentine, Kern and Auguste, like each one of us, may become another. Each of us is susceptible to tragic or redemptive transformation, in moments, like contingent gifts, of accidental encounters, tangential connections through which one becomes responsible for another, and responds with love or betrayal.

Justice in a world of chance and contingency points to life lived amid forces beyond our control, the vicissitudes of desire, rage, love and compassion. Yet, fraternity is coincident with contingency. Our sympathy widens and our compassion grows in the face of such uncertainty. As Martin Luther King once said, 'Whatever affects one directly affects all indirectly. We are all links in the great chain of humanity.' We are interconnected in ways we can barely begin to fathom. At any moment, each of us might become another—an Other even to ourselves. Such is the source of our shared humanity. It is in this sense that we can understand Kieslowski's words when he says, 'the life of every single person is interesting if you just look at it'.

'Character is fate', said the ancient Greek philosopher Heraclitus. A paradoxical saying. Fate shapes character, but character is also what we make of our fate. In *Red* we learn that both interpretations may be true. But we also come to see that the passive indifference of disenchanted fatalism is a form of death in life, while the immanent call of the redemptive moment, that moment of hope and deliberate change, calls us back to life in a world where wisdom in judgment, while threatened, still remains possible.

Kieslowski's relational vision for law and justice, his ethical universe of authentic ('face-to-face') relationships, models an elementary norm for law. It is a norm that stands apart from the aggregation of individual self-interest as well as claims of systemic rights or entitlements that centre upon the autonomous self.[72] Kieslowski's is an ethical vision inspired by the force of our obligation to the other. The rest follows from this originary, meaning-generating moment. From the contingency

[72] Compare Robert Cover, 'Obligation: A Jewish Jurisprudence of the Social Order' (1988) 5 *Journal of Law & Religion* 65, 70 ('Rights, as an organizing principle, are indifferent to the vanity of varying ends. But mizvoths [obligations] because they so strongly bind and locate the individual must make a strong claim for the substantive content of that which they dictate').

of eventful contacts, from the suffering or grace that they bring, from tragic or redemptive possibility, the life of each one among others takes shape. The birth and development of self, we come to see, are concomitant with our entanglements with others, which is to say, concomitant with the birth and development of community. The work of forging and maintaining identity and community is at once the work of culture—which, in turn, is coincident with the performative enchantment of mythic narrative. The power of myth lies precisely in its poetic (constitutive) function in conjunction with its authoritative claim to (authenticate) truth.

In *Red* Kieslowski conveys an ethos of care and openness toward the other based on the moment's redemptive possibility. In that possibility also lies the power of enchantment and belief—the same mysterious power that impels commitment from within, and that inspires commitment from without. *Red* tells us about the fraternal force, the force of ethical commitment. It signifies responsibility to and for the other. Geoff Andrew's apt summary is worth quoting in full:

> We must reach out to others, through love, compassion and understanding, and we should accept that there are bonds between us which we may not fully comprehend; to recognize our common humanity, our equal worth as individuals with our own special needs, desires, fears and responsibilities, is to accept our 'destiny'. Only by accepting the mysteries of existence for what they are can we proceed towards a greater understanding of ourselves and others unfettered by any notions of ideological or moral absolutes.[73]

Emmanuel Levinas tells us that it is before the Face of the other that we acquire moral consciousness. The Christian tradition speaks of *agape*, through which two people meet in openness and affection, aware of one another's inner lives. And in the Buddhist tradition, we find the word *prajnaparamita*, which means supreme generosity. These overlapping meanings emphasize the supreme value of the other in the creation of an ethical world. I believe that Kieslowski's ethical universe of authentic ('face-to-face') relationships models a legitimating norm for law. That norm is inspired by the force of our obligation to the other. Within it lies the power of enchantment and belief—the same mysterious erotic bond of which Giordano Bruno spoke centuries ago. It is the erotic bond that impels commitment from within, and that inspires commitment from without. This is the fraternal force that *Red* embodies, the bonding force of ethical commitment.

I should like to conclude this meditation on Kieslowski's cinematic jurisprudence with the following words, written by Franz Rosenzweig: '[A]ll turns into black nothingness unless you color the world—yours are the tinges that illuminate it . . . At each moment the future presents to man the gift of being present to himself.'[74] And that is the paradox with which Rosenzweig and Kieslowski leave us. For we are never more present to ourselves than when we steep ourselves in the countenance of the one we happen to meet, face to face.

[73] ibid, 76.

[74] F Rosenzweig, *Understanding the Sick and Healthy* (trans N Glatzer), (Cambridge, MA: 1999) 78–79.

Conclusion

Law is not just on the books, or in the gap between books and practice. It is in people's heads in the form of scripted expectations, popular story forms, and recurrent images. A newly emerging popular legal studies movement embraces, but also takes us beyond, disembodied critical theory. It points toward rich microanalytic studies of highly contextualized, concrete legal practices. Using a multiplicity of disciplines—such as cultural anthropology, cognitive psychology, linguistics, media studies (including advertising and public relations) and rhetoric—legal scholars are assessing more closely the legal meaning-making process, in court and out. In this view, law is both a producer and product of popular culture. One domain informs and shapes the other.

This cultural approach operates within a postmodern framework, but it resists the sceptical strain in postmodern thought and expression. Rather than deny the contingency and ultimate fragility of meaning, these now become the very conditions that inform our shared responsibility for meaning's construction, maintenance, and change. To reconceive our legal system along these affirmative postmodern lines requires that we rethink such core Enlightenment ideals as the abstract universality of rational truth, the stability of the autonomous self, and the presumption of progress that these ideals purportedly guarantee. The priority traditionally assigned to deductive and inductive logic, rationalist agency and calculative reason must also undergo review so that notions of plurality, complexity, contingency, and uncertainty may be more fully and deliberately considered. In this way, the unduly repressive inclinations of the modern rationalist's mindset may be eased, and the non-rational forces that surge within and around us—fate, chance, fury and desire—may be more readily assessed as co-constitutive of self, social and legal reality. This too opens the door to enchantment.[75]

Psuchagogein is the ancient Greek word for 'raising spirits'.[76] It is a word that evokes the eros of *logos*, the mysterious power of language itself. It is this power that claims us in words and images—in poetic utterance, the gift of the Muses.[77] Such words and images instil sorrow and longing, pity and fear, or perhaps joy, pleasure, ecstatic delight in the heart and soul of the one who listens. And here we approach the essence of the rhetorician's art: to move the soul where he wills.

It is the function of art, poetry, and rhetoric alike to make a particular form of truth (and reason and justice) compelling, sufficiently compelling, ultimately, to lead the subject to a specific judgment or course of action in a particular context. It is the particular function of *tragic* poetry and narrative to make the contingency, multiplicity, and complexity of truth and reason compelling. Indeed, it must do so even in the face of the irrational forces that surround us. Tragic wisdom urges us to

[75] See Sherwin, *When Law Goes Pop*, n 7 above, 205–233.

[76] ibid, 222.

[77] ibid, 204 (citing Hesiod on the speech of the Muses).

discern critically the reality- or meaning-making power and technique of rhetoric, but it also compels us to acknowledge the limits of reason and the contingency of truth and meaning. By describing in dramatic detail the effects of forces such as chance and desire on human life, tragic narrative delineates the bounds of rationality. In this way, it invokes a sense of finitude, humility, fear and pity, and in doing so the tragic perspective brings into focus the shifting patterns of meaning and mystery that rationality and irrationality create in dynamic disequilibrium. These patterns constitute the lived realities of truth and reason, and law and justice in our time.

Cultural texts, including film, can provide insight into the ongoing process of world-building. Kieslowski's *Red* is such a film. It teaches ways of living and judging. The normative vision at work here is neither instrumental nor deontological. It emerges neither on the basis of individual entitlements nor some felicific calculus of pleasure and pain. It covets no system of principles from which we may assess how to relate to or judge an other. Kieslowski's film comports with postmodern conditions. In philosophical terms, it is a way of doing theory without foundations. This is what thinkers such as Friedrich Nietzsche, Martin Heidegger and Richard Rorty have urged in their work. We must escape the grip of metanarratives, totalizing systems, and disembodied dogmas. It suggests an affirmative way to address the vital questions that we face under postmodern conditions: Where do we turn for normative guidance in order to nourish and bind belief? How do we sustain meaningful relationships among others within a meaningful normative universe—within the nomos that we inhabit?

Today, whatever else may be said about the possibilities of enchantment and affirmation, its normative impulse cannot escape or supplant postmodern conditions. The more affirmative kind of postmodernism that I have sought to evoke here offers insights into how we construct meaning in everyday life. It is postmodern in its notion of the way self and social reality are built up from the different stories that we tell ourselves and share with others in the course of our social and professional practices. It is also postmodern in its recognition of the cognitive habits that help to construct and maintain the diverse micro-identities that comprise the self from one context to another. And it is postmodern in its recognition of chance, contingency, and the disruptive, uncontrollable surge of irrational forces both from without and from within.

I hope this begins to suggest what it might mean to adopt an affirmative postmodern understanding of the interpenetration of law and culture. The challenge is to integrate critical constructivist insights regarding how the meanings we live by are made and disseminated (*by whom? and with what effect?*) with the human capacity to affirm deep cultural values and beliefs. Only then may we avoid the dangers posed by pervasive disenchantment: whether in the form of detached irony or in the modernist mindset's denial of the 'magic' or mythic enchantment of words and images.

At the core of Kieslowski's ethical vision is a fraternal force, a force of normative commitment. It embodies our responsibility to and for the other. These fateful possibilities for law's future are hardly reducible to rational calculation, or even to rational principles of autonomy or contract-based entitlement. They point instead to a form of ethical enchantment. This normative vision directs us to the eros of thinking and judging that we find in Foucault and Lacan and that harks back to early Greek thought as well. It recalls Bergson's and Levinas's immanentist ontology[78] and the mind's passion to seek meaning and perhaps also wisdom in our lives among others.[79]

Unlike judgments in which the self operates in isolation, disconnected from others, wiser forms of judging make responsibility to and for others its most central feature. This obligation is prior to all contract. And here we may adopt Levinas' crucial correction of Heidegger: it is the call of the other, not the call of Being, to which we owe primary allegiance.[80] This fateful choice marks the elevation of ethics over esthetics.

To live well in the law we need to affirm and commit ourselves to an ethical vision. This requires more than self-gratification in the here and now. In order to plot law's possible future we need ethical enchantment. We need the force of belief and interpersonal commitment. Demystification is not enough to live on.

In the prologue to his *Prometheus Unbound* Shelley gave eloquent expression to this thought when he wrote: 'Until the mind can love, and admire, and trust, and hope, and endure, reasoned principles of moral conduct are seeds cast upon the highway of life which the unconscious passenger tramples into dust'.[81] If we are enchanted with the affirmative ethical vision that postmodern conditions allow, if we learn its cultural texts, including visionary films such as Kieslowski's *Red*, and practise its ethical norms in acts of interpersonal commitment, perhaps we can claim its mythic truth as our own—as one of the stories that bounds (and binds) our lives among others. In the contingent reality of our lives together, self and community are made and remade—not only by the law that polices meaning, but also by the law that inspires hope, graced by epiphanic wisdom, and action conceived at once in the spirit of justice and fraternal love.

[78] See Levinas, n 69 above, xi ('The main intent here is to try to see ethics in relation to the rationality of the knowledge that is immanent in being, and that is primordial in the philosophical tradition of the West').

[79] See Rajchman, n 32 above, 1 ('One of the great questions of ancient philosophy was: What is the eros of thinking? . . . What is the eros of the peculiar sort of truth of which philosophy is the pursuit? . . . It is in order to rediscover such questions that I have turned to the work of . . . Jacques Lacan and Michel Foucault . . . [E]ach of them in different ways re-erotized the activity of philosophical or critical thought for our times').

[80] See Levinas, n 69 above, xi ('The main intent here is to try to see ethics in relation to the rationality of knowledge that is immanent in being, and that is primordial in the philosophical tradition in the West . . . '), and 233 (referring, in a final evocation of Rosenzweig and Heidegger, to the 'obligation toward the other prior to all contract').

[81] *The Complete Poems of Keats and Shelley* (New York: 1978) 228.

When Celluloid Lawyers Started to Speak: Exploring Juriscinema's First Golden Age

Francis M Nevins

I. Introduction

By the criteria of quality, quantity and leitmotifs, those films that take law, lawyers, lawyering and justice as their subjects—a loosely connected assortment which I hereby dub juriscinema—enjoyed the first of three golden ages between the dawn of talkies in the late 1920s and the descent of strict self-censorship upon Hollywood in mid-1934. The films of juriscinema's second golden age, which roughly coincides with the flourishing of the Warren Court, and those of the third, the post- and anti-Warren Court era that still seems to be with us in the early twenty-first century, and also certain individual films that fall between the great ages, have been discussed over the last several years in a spate of essays and even a few books. Until now the films of the first golden age have been neglected.

This neglect is unfortunate but far from unaccountable. Discussion of old movies is difficult to say the least when many of the films are all but inaccessible. The videocassette revolution has facilitated factually reliable discussion of many cinematic subjects but juriscinema of the first golden age is not among them: very few of the important titles in that category have ever been made available on commercial videocassette or DVD. Small wonder then that not a single film from the period is discussed in the leading guide to juriscinema,[1] whose authors restricted themselves by and large to commercially obtainable titles. That most of the films I discuss here are otherwise accessible (at least by those with cable or satellite) is due largely to Turner Classic Movies (TCM), without whose vast resources this essay could never have been written. Films from studios whose back catalogue is not owned by TCM must be discussed on the basis of reference books—an unsatisfactory situation but, thanks mainly to the catalogues published by the American Film Institute, not an impossible one.

[1] Paul Bergman and Michael Asimow, *Reel Justice: The Courtroom Goes to the Movies* (Kansas City: 1996). For commentary on this book, see Francis M Nevins, 'Book Review' (1996) 20 *Legal Studies Forum* 145.

Those catalogues enabled me to identify more than 200 films from juriscinema's first golden age that to one degree or another are law-related. Doing justice to all of them would take a book. Even after excluding all the product of the countless 'poverty row' studios that came and went at a dizzying pace during the early 1930s, plus all the Westerns[2] and all the films set in England or Europe or in any legal environment other than that of the United States at roughly the time a particular film was made, there are so many movies left to consider that space limitations compel me to offer in Section II only a brief overview. Section III deals with the cynically exuberant cycle of 'shyster pictures'—all of whose protagonists were avatars of the same real-world lawyer—and Section IV with *Counsellor at Law* (1933), surely the finest law-related film of its period and one of the finest ever. Finally in Section V, I sketch the impact on juriscinema of the curtain of self-censorship that fell over Hollywood in the summer of 1934.

Understanding certain aspects of the American scene in the last years of silent cinema is a huge help in understanding certain aspects of early talkies. We who have lived through the cultural upheavals of the past few decades tend to think of the 1920s as a dead Puritanical time, but those who lived and were young at the time saw it quite differently: saw the social, political and religious dogmas of previous generations dismissed as 'a farrago of balderdash'[3] and saw freedoms hardly dreamt of in previous decades exploding into life all around them. They read the novels of Theodore Dreiser and Sinclair Lewis and the short stories of Ring Lardner and the essays of HL Mencken, all four of them radical iconoclasts who gleefully debunked everything dear to the conventional American heart. They discarded their parents' inhibitions and joined the sexual revolution with the same enthusiasm that, 40 years later, their own children exhibited in their generation's sexual revolution. The insanity of Prohibition led them to consume whisky at a feverish rate and the corruption of government at every level that followed in Prohibition's wake made them vastly cynical about American political institutions and officeholders—and about lawyers too.

Near the end of that wild decade came the technological breakthrough that permitted sound to be recorded directly on film and with it of course came the first talkies, which naturally reflected the cultural orientation of their time. Add an insatiable hunger for film stories full of dialogue to be captured by the new technology, and it was inevitable that Hollywood would become a sellers' market for plays and short stories and novels and original scenarios that offered oratorical duels (whether in or out of court) between lawyers—in short, for the raw materials of juriscinema.

[2] By far the most interesting law-related Western from the early 1930s is *One Man Law* (Columbia, 1932). For an account of this film, see Francis M Nevins, 'Through the Great Depression on Horseback: Legal Themes in Western Films of the 1930s' in John Denvir (ed), *Legal Reelism: Movies as Legal Texts* (Urbana & Chicago: 1996) 44–69.

[3] This elegant euphemism for an earthier phrase at which most law publishers would look askance I owe to Edmund Wilson, *The Dead Sea Scrolls* (New York: 1969) 281.

II. Early Juriscinema: An Overview

A silent lawyer is a contradiction in terms. This fact alone explains why lawyers acting as lawyers were all but unknown as protagonists of silent movies. Conversely, once all-talking films had irrevocably displaced both the silent cinema and the part-talkie hybrids that were common in the late 1920s, it was a sure bet that moviegoers would see and, more important, hear an abundance of lawyer characters on the screen.

Approaching the subject from behind a Rawlsian veil of ignorance, one might assume that in any film with a significant legal component a protagonist (by which I mean a character played by one of the two actors top-billed in the credits) would be both described as a lawyer and seen performing lawyerly functions. This description certainly fits *Counsellor at Law* and the 'shyster films' to be considered in Section III. It also fits a few other law-related films of the early 1930s.

Lionel Barrymore played such a character in *A Free Soul*[4] and won an Oscar for his performance as a hard-drinking, free-thinking San Francisco criminal lawyer whose passionate courtroom defence of the fiancé (Leslie Howard) of his daughter (Norma Shearer) literally costs him his life. In a lighter vein, *Peach-o-Reno*[5] starred vaudeville comics Bert Wheeler and Robert Woolsey as a pair of zany divorce lawyers in the city that at the time was the marriage dissolution capital of the United States. In a few early talkies the lawyer protagonist is a woman, but that does not mean they would appeal to women lawyers today. In *Ann Carver's Profession*,[6] Fay Wray of *King Kong* fame plays a woman who stumbles into a meteoric legal career while that of her husband (Gene Raymond), a singing college football hero turned architect, stagnates. When the new woman in his life (Claire Dodd) accidentally chokes herself to death while drunk and he is charged with murder, Ann comes to his defence, tells the jury that his troubles are her fault, and announces that after this case she will return to housewifehood.

A film may also be of legal interest if the character described as a lawyer and seen performing lawyerly functions is significant to the story but less than a protagonist. Perhaps the finest example from first-period juriscinema is *An American Tragedy*.[7] The film follows the broad outlines of the Dreiser novel in which dirt-poor but ambitious Clyde Griffiths (Phillip Holmes) rises to become foreman in his rich uncle's shirt factory and, defying plant rules, begins a furtive affair with newly hired worker Roberta Alden (Sylvia Sidney), only to drop her when he meets and

[4] MGM, 1931, directed by Clarence Brown from a screenplay by John Meehan and Becky Gardiner based on Adela Rogers St Johns' 1927 novel and Willard Mack's 1928 stage play of the same name.

[5] RKO, 1931, directed by William A Seiter from a screenplay by Ralph Spence, Tim Whelan and Eddie Welch.

[6] Columbia, 1933, directed by Edward Buzzell from a screenplay by Robert Riskin.

[7] Paramount, 1931, directed by Josef von Sternberg from a screenplay by Samuel Hoffenstein based on Theodore Dreiser's 1925 novel of the same name.

falls for the beautiful and wealthy Sondra Finchley (Frances Dee). Learning that Roberta is pregnant, Clyde devises a plan to take her out on the lake in a canoe and drown her so that her death looks like an accident, but when the two are actually on the water and out of others' sight he changes his mind (or does he?) and agrees to jettison his plans for social advancement and marry her. Roberta, who cannot swim, accidentally overturns the boat. Clyde ignores her screams for help and swims to shore, letting her drown as he had first intended. He is soon arrested and charged with murder, but his uncle's money gifts him with a fine pair of shysters (Emmett Corrigan and Charles Middleton) and the film climaxes at his trial where opposing counsel rant and rave and strut their stuff and almost come to blows in open court before Clyde is convicted and sentenced to death. In the story as Dreiser told it, Clyde is a toad beneath the harrow, victim of a society obsessed by money and status. In Josef von Sternberg's version society is never indicted and Clyde comes across as a cold, calculating opportunist. The film's message—the system works and all is well—so infuriated Dreiser that he sued Paramount, claiming that the distorted movie version of his novel had damaged his literary reputation. He lost.[8]

One also finds in early juriscinema a number of interesting films with a protagonist who is described as a lawyer but is never seen doing a lawyer's work. Most of these films are emotional dramas which, thanks to their female stars and primary appeal to a female audience, are known as 'women's pictures' or 'weepies'. Most of the admirable lawyer characters in first-period juriscinema are found in films of this sort. *Possessed*[9] deals with Marian Martin (Joan Crawford), a small-town girl who goes to New York to better herself and begins a three-year-long affair with wealthy attorney Mark Whitney (Clark Gable) that brings her sophistication, culture and money. She nobly disappears in hopes of saving him political embarrassment when he decides to run for governor, but the opposing candidate makes her a campaign issue anyway. Finally one night at a huge rally she speaks out from the audience, describing Mark as an honourable man who once belonged to her but now belongs to them, then runs out sobbing into the rain. Mark catches up and, as the film ends, commits to her whatever the political fallout.

Juriscinema of all periods is replete with films in which the person described as a lawyer but not invariably seen acting as such is not the protagonist but an important subsidiary character—usually a swine of the first water. The lawyer in *The Furies*[10] murders the husband of the woman he desires and then acts as defence counsel when her childhood sweetheart is charged with the crime. In *As the Devil Commands*[11] the lawyer character kills his wealthy dying cousin, frames the young

[8] For details of the litigation, see WA Swanberg, *Dreiser* (New York: 1965) 369–372, 376–378.

[9] MGM, 1931, directed by Clarence Brown from a screenplay by Lenore Coffee based on Edgar Selwyn's 1920 stage play *The Mirage*.

[10] First National, 1930, directed by Alan Crosland from a screenplay by Forrest Halsey based on Zoe Akins' 1928 stage play of the same name.

[11] Columbia, 1932, directed by Roy William Neill from a screenplay by Jo Swerling based on an original story by Keene Thompson.

doctor (Neil Hamilton) who is caring for the old man, represents the doctor at trial, throws the case, then for ridiculous 'legal' reasons unframes him and plots instead to kill him in a death chamber he has rigged up in his basement, from which the doctor is saved at the last minute by the nurse (Mae Clarke) who loves him. There are easily a dozen more early talkies in which the non-protagonist lawyer character is a fiend but space precludes describing any more.

III. The Fallon Connection: A Smorgasbord of Shysters

William J Fallon is little known or remembered today, but in his last decade of life he typified the legal profession like no other attorney of his time and after his death he figured crucially in several key works of early juriscinema. Getting to know Fallon, however, is not an easy task. The only readily available source of information about him is Gene Fowler's *The Great Mouthpiece*,[12] a book which Fowler himself called a 'life story' of Fallon rather than a biography, and rightly so: it is cast in the mould of what today we call the non-fiction novel, built around real people and places and events but full of incidents and dialogue that clearly do not come intact from real life even when the author seems to be quoting trial transcripts. Unreliable though the book may be, we need to consider it here.

According to *The Great Mouthpiece*, William Joseph Fallon was born on New York City's West 47th Street on 23 January 1886, the son of a well-to-do Irish contractor who moved the family upstate to Mamaroneck in Westchester County when the boy was ten.[13] Gifted with a near-photographic memory that enabled him to read a book in two hours and 'repeat almost word-for-word the entire text. . . ', he graduated from Fordham University in 1906 as valedictorian of his class and with a medal for the highest grade in philosophy.[14] Three years later, after completing Fordham Law School and passing the New York Bar, he went to work in the White Plains office of veteran criminal defence lawyer David Hunt.[15] He married the former Agnes Rafter in 1912 and soon became the father of two daughters.[16] Between 1914 and 1916 he served as an Assistant District Attorney in Westchester County.[17]

Gene Fowler devotes little space to Fallon's time as a prosecutor but, near the end of the book, has him recollect one incident worth our attention. 'I sent a man to prison for life, on a murder-charge. A year later, I found he was innocent. That's what cured me of wanting to prosecute. I got the Governor to pardon the man. But the damage already was done. . .' .[18] Variations of this incident were to figure largely in the movies inspired by Fallon's life.

On 12 January 1918 Fallon 'invaded' New York City.[19] Over the next nine and a half years he devoted his considerable talents to the defence of Manhattan's

[12] New York: 1931. [13] ibid, 23. [14] ibid, 76. [15] ibid, 90.
[16] ibid, 88. [17] ibid, 98. [18] ibid, 350–351. [19] ibid, 133.

wealthiest gangsters, bootleggers, con artists and stock swindlers. 'Fallon's fees were the first tremendous ones to be paid by captains of modern crime-syndicates for legal advice. He became, in fact, a corporation counsel for the underworld. . . . After a few successes, . . . his services were virtually commanded by men powerful in politics and in criminal circles.'[20] 'He became the Great Mouthpiece for the grand dukes of Racketland.'[21]

Fallon's forensic skills included arranging for incriminating evidence to vanish from prosecutors' offices, lying to and baiting trial judges, making honest and truthful witnesses seem perjurers or fools. He was a genius at 'riding over courts and hypnotizing juries . . . '.[22] He 'was completely the actor; the dramatic effect of the moment was all-important to him . . . '.[23] So great was his flair that the theatrical impresario David Belasco once offered to have a play written for him if he would agree to star in it.[24] He was an expert at playing to the media, which in the 1920s meant the many newspapers that were published daily in New York City. 'My clients always are [innocent]. I'd be helpless if they weren't.'[25] In any event very few of them were convicted when he was defending them. 'If [a Fallon client] were not acquitted, he was reasonably sure of incredible delays or a jury disagreement. . . . It seems incredible how many times Fallon accomplished a hung jury by the count of 1 to 11. Hints of jury-bribing began to travel the court-corridors.'[26] In 1924 he was tried in federal court on two counts of bribing a juror named Charles W Rendigs[27] but defended himself with the same vigour and flair and trickiness he sold at top prices to underworld clients and was acquitted.[28] Two years later, when disbarment proceedings were brought against him, he reached into the same bag of tricks and got the charges dismissed.[29] When not twisting judges and prosecutors around his little finger he had affairs with countless Broadway showgirls (keeping his wife and daughters discreetly in the background) and, like thousands of others during Prohibition, drank whisky as if it were water. He died of a gastric haemorrhage and heart attack on 29 April 1927, not long after his 41st birthday and shortly before the silent films of his lifetime were displaced by talkies.

For Gene Fowler, who apparently knew and clearly admired his subject, Fallon was 'this impulsive, vain, brilliant, reckless, gay, tragic fellow'.[30] Most readers of *The Great Mouthpiece* probably saw him as the shyster incarnate; in any event that was how film-makers saw him. He was 'sturdy and handsome. He moved with the grace and sure rhythm of a trained boxer. . . . His erect bearing, his squared shoulders, inflated chest, large head, and the tangle of apricot-colored hair, made him appear six feet two inches, instead of five feet eleven. . . . [He had a] remarkably resonant voice . . . [and] a wit that danced.'[31] This description suggests that the perfect actor to have played Fallon in a movie based on his life would have been Spencer Tracy. Hollywood never made such a film, but the legends of Fallon's

[20] New York: 1931, 145. [21] ibid, 148. [22] ibid, 313. [23] ibid, 239. [24] ibid, 176, 319. [25] ibid, 168. [26] ibid, 163. [27] ibid, 337–340. [28] ibid, 384. [29] ibid, 391–392. [30] ibid, 239. [31] ibid, 139.

exploits at the Bar, some found in Fowler's book and others in more ephemeral sources, literally created the image of the lawyer in half a dozen movies released in the early 1930s. The Fallonesque lawyer of juriscinema, however, is never conspicuously Irish and has not the slightest resemblance to Spencer Tracy, being slender, suave and smooth-voiced and usually sporting a tiny moustache. Unlike their real-world original, Fallon's cinematic avatars invariably reform before the end titles.

The earliest creative work to show the Fallon influence, even to gifting its shyster character with a similar name, was Maurine Watkins' hit stage play *Chicago*, which opened in New York on 30 December 1926, four months before Fallon's death. Roxie Hart (Francine Larrimore), married but promiscuous and desperate for a career in show business, shoots her lover and retains as defence counsel shyster William J 'Billy' Flynn (Edward Ellis), who with help from two cynical newspaper reporters (Charles Bickford and Eda Heinemann) turns her murder trial into a shambles and a farce, generating publicity that leads to a lucrative vaudeville contract for her after her acquittal.[32] Whether Fallon ever saw this play is unknown but, if he had heard anything about its storyline, how could he not have gone? He died several months before the release of the silent movie based on the play. In *Chicago*[33] Roxie (Phyllis Haver) is still represented by Billy Flynn (Robert Edeson), but the film-makers downplay the courtroom scenes—it is a silent movie, remember—and after her acquittal the cinematic Roxie becomes so publicity-mad that eventually her long-suffering husband Amos (Victor Varconi) kicks her out.[34]

The earliest talkie inspired by Fallon is *For The Defense*.[35] Shrewd criminal defence lawyer William Foster (William Powell), whose activities are being investigated by police detective Daly (Thomas Jackson), is emotionally involved with actress Irene Manning (Kay Francis) but refuses to commit to her. To make him jealous Irene starts going out with a wealthy waster named Defoe (Scott Kolk). One night the two are driving back from a drinking party with Irene at the wheel when their car runs over and kills a pedestrian. Defoe takes the blame and is tried for manslaughter with Foster as his defence counsel. The trial is going badly for Foster when Irene confesses that she was to blame for the accident and Foster decides that the only way to get both her and Defoe off the hook is by bribing one of the jurors. At this point the film begins to echo the Rendigs jury-bribery scandal: Foster's scheme works but afterwards Detective Daly looks into the matter, makes the bribe-taker talk and puts Foster under arrest. Irene is about to confess her own guilt to the District Attorney (William B Davidson) when Foster saves her from doing so by pleading guilty and is sentenced to five years in prison. Irene promises to be waiting for him when he gets out.

32 For a brief account of the play, see Gerald Bordman (ed), *The Oxford Companion to American Theatre* (2nd edn, New York: 1992) 140–141.

33 DeMille/Pathé, 1928, directed by Frank Urson from a scenario by Lenore J Coffee.

34 For a discussion of the film, see Jay Robert Nash and Stanley Ralph Ross, *The Motion Picture Guide: Silent Film 1910–1936* (Chicago: 1986) 47.

35 Paramount, 1930, directed by John Cromwell from a screenplay by Oliver HP Garrett based on an original story by Charles Furthman.

April and May of 1932 must have been the perfect spring for moviegoers who thought of lawyers as the men they loved to hate. Within a span of about six weeks three new films sprang up on the nation's screens, each from a different studio, each with different directors and writers and stars, each built around a shyster with roots in William J Fallon. *The Mouthpiece*[36] opens with a sequence that is clearly an intensified version of an incident in Fallon's life: prosecuting attorney Vincent Day (Warren William) obtains a conviction in a murder case, only to discover later—too late to prevent the man's execution—that the defendant was innocent. Ridden with guilt, Day switches sides and soon becomes the city's most prominent and trickiest criminal defence lawyer.

About a third of the way through this film comes a self-contained sequence that for me is the perfect embodiment of early juriscinema's take on lawyers. When auditors begin to go over a bond house's books, cashier Barton (John Wray), who embezzled $90,000 from the firm, comes to Day in desperation, bringing with him a handsome briefcase containing the $40,000 he has not already lost on the market and women. Day calls in Smith (Morgan Wallace), the head of the firm, and inveigles him into accepting partial restitution and agreeing not to file charges.

DAY: Your stock and bond customers—the unfortunate publicity of an embezzlement would naturally affect their confidence in your institution. How much confidence can you afford to lose this year, Mr. Smith?

SMITH: Day, you're an unmitigated scoundrel.

DAY: Thank you! But I find it much nicer than being just an ordinary one.

As negotiations proceed, Smith's blood begins to boil.

SMITH: Day, you're positively the most unmitigated scoundrel in the world.

DAY: It's comforting to know that I'm progressing so rapidly in your esteem.

Day turns over $30,000 in cash, keeping Barton's briefcase for himself, then brings out his client.

SMITH: Don't speak to me! You've lost the right to talk to honest men!

DAY: Don't worry, Barton. You can talk to us.

BARTON: I'm sorry, Mr. Smith.

SMITH: Sorry! You steal $90,000 and you're sorry!

BARTON: But I tried to make restitution.

SMITH: Restitution! A paltry thirty thousand!

BARTON: I restored forty thousand.

SMITH (gesturing at Day): He said thirty thousand.

DAY (smugly): Naturally there was the attorney's fee.

[36] Warner Bros, 1932, directed by James Flood and Elliott Nugent from a screenplay by Joseph Jackson and Earl Baldwin based on Frank L Collins' 1929 stage play of the same name.

SMITH: You—-you took $10,000 for your part in this criminal affair?

DAY: I took $10,000 for my advice as a lawyer. . . . I may be able to be of service to you some day, Mr. Smith.

After Smith has stalked out of the office, Day contemptuously kicks his client out to face the Depression economy penniless.

BARTON: But—you're not—you're not going to keep all of my $10,000, are you, Mr. Day?

DAY: Yours? *You* stole it. *I* earned it.

BARTON: But—but it's all I've got!

DAY: You haven't got it. You *had* it.

BARTON: But I can't get a job now. What can I do?

DAY: Go out and jump in the river, you cheap tinhorn crook. Now get out!

Day's eventual downfall takes the form of a stenographer sent to his firm by an employment agency, and a delightful form it is. Celia Faraday (Sidney Fox) is a teenage sexpot fresh from Kentucky and hopeless at secretarial work. Day not only does not fire her but lures her to his apartment and propositions her. She turns him down on the ground that she is in love with bank messenger Johnny Morris (William Janney). In time Celia comes to despise Day's legal tricks and quits her job in disgust,[37] but Johnny is arrested for bond theft before the couple can relocate to Kentucky and she is forced to come back and beg the lawyer to use his wiles on her fiancé's behalf. Underworld connections tip Day that the real thief was Joe Garland (Jack LaRue), who is arrested at Day's behest after refusing to confess and clear Johnny. Day resolves to give up shystering, but before he can become an honest lawyer Garland gets out on bail and guns him down.

Early in *Attorney for the Defense*[38] comes a scene with marked similarities to the early sequences of *The Mouthpiece* as district attorney William J Burton (Edmund Lowe) is berated by his secretary Ruth Barry (Constance Cummings) for obtaining a murder conviction and death sentence against James Wallace (Dwight Frye) on purely circumstantial evidence. When Wallace is proven innocent shortly after his execution, Burton seeks to make amends by resigning his office and putting Wallace's son Paul (Donald Dillaway) through law school. Years pass and Burton, now a criminal defence attorney with Paul working in his office, launches a civic crusade against gangster Nick Quinn (Bradley Page), who in turn has Val Lorraine (Evelyn Brent), his present paramour and Burton's former mistress, make a play for Paul and get him into trouble that can be used against Burton. The sexual intrigue comes to a head when Val gets Paul drunk and phones Burton to come for him.

[37] As a going-away present Day gives her a cheque for $100 which he was paid, so he says, by the *American Journal of Law* for a recently published article. In order to prove that the gift does not come from his shystering activities he shows her a copy of the article, which we see is entitled 'Contracts and Torts: An Analysis'. As if any journal would publish an article on such a gargantuan topic, written by an attorney whose practice is exclusively criminal, and pay him a then huge sum for it to boot!

[38] Columbia, 1932, directed by Irving Cummings from a screenplay by Jo Swerling.

Burton arrives to find her dead and Paul unable to remember what happened. Still feeling responsible for the wrongful execution of Paul's father, Burton sends the young man home and confesses to the murder himself. Ruth Barry, who has followed Burton into private practice as his secretary, tries but fails to borrow money for his defence, then visits him in jail, tells him she loves him and urges him to defend himself at trial. This is all Burton needs to restore his will to live, and his cross-examination of prosecution witnesses generates enough new evidence to pin Val's murder on Nick Quinn.

State's Attorney[39] was written in part by the author of *The Great Mouthpiece* and clearly betrays the influence of that book: not only is the protagonist a drunk like William J Fallon (and like John Barrymore during filming), but defendants take the Fifth Amendment in the unusual form that Fowler attributes to Fallon: 'I refuse to answer, on the ground that to do so might tend to incriminate or degrade me'.[40] But in the film as a whole, Fallon's career is not so much replicated as flipflopped. Tom Cardigan (John Barrymore), hard-drinking mouthpiece for mob boss Vanny Powers (William 'Stage' Boyd), has no qualms about using his skills on behalf of what Holmes called 'the bad man'.[41] 'The grocer takes your money, doesn't ask any questions. A criminal lawyer doesn't cross-examine his fees.' For a fee of $5,000 from Powers he defends and wins an acquittal for prostitute June Perry (Helen Twelvetrees), then takes her out of Powers' stable and makes her his mistress.

After being wounded by a rival gangster, Powers suggests that Cardigan accept an offer to become First Assistant District Attorney and serve in effect as double agent for the mob. Cardigan refuses. 'Vanny, when I'm with you, I'm with you hook, line and sinker. If I go on the other side, I stay there.' His ambition to be governor soon leads him to switch and he quickly rises to the position of District Attorney, getting convictions via the same kind of tricks with which he had previously got acquittals. 'You know, if I was defending that dame, she'd be free tonight', he remarks after winning a murder case. Although still involved with June, Cardigan starts seeing Lillian Ulrich (Jill Esmond), the bloodthirsty daughter of his political patron (Oscar Apfel). Lillian asks Cardigan to marry her and he agrees, but minutes after the ceremony he realizes he has made a huge mistake and, when he tells June what he has done, she moves out of their love nest. Lillian quickly becomes involved with a tenor (Albert Conti) and an annulment of her marriage is arranged, but June is gone.

Time passes and she comes back into his life. She happens to witness Powers murder Duffy, the rival gangster who wounded him, but is warned that both she and Cardigan will be rubbed out if she tells the truth. Cardigan gets June to leave town and himself leads the police team that arrests the gangster chief. 'It's a great world', remarks Powers' new shyster (C Henry Gordon). 'Duffy's on a slab. You defended him once. Then you defended Powers.' Cardigan replies: 'Yeah. Now

[39] RKO, 1932, directed by George Archainbaud from a screenplay by Gene Fowler and Rowland Brown based on an original story by Louis Stevens.

[40] See n 12 above, 249.

[41] Oliver Wendell Holmes Jr, 'The Path of the Law' (1897) 10 *Harvard L Rev* 457, 459.

I'm going to hang him.' A little later the medical examiner asks: 'Remember the old days, Tom? This would have been an open-and-shut case of self-defense.' Cardigan's response echoes his previous exchange with the new shyster: 'Remember when I used to send to Milwaukee for the eyewitnesses?' In a nutshell, whether a lawyer stands up for A and smears B or vice versa depends on what is in it for the lawyer. This time of course Cardigan cannot use the testimony of the one genuine eyewitness, but at trial June is subpoenaed for the defence: apparently both to support a self-defence claim *and* to testify that Powers was not the shooter! Cardigan waives cross-examination but, when Powers lets out a loud guffaw, he retracts the waiver—'That laugh is going to cost you your neck', he whispers to Powers—and wrings the truth from June on the stand. 'All right', she tells him as she steps down, 'now go ahead and be governor!' That reproach spurs Cardigan to do an about-face. Although the case is not over, he makes an emotional speech to the jury in which he reveals that he and Powers had been in reform school together for burglary, renounces his political ambitions and resigns on the spot. 'I shall return to the defense of those unfortunates who, like myself, were reared in the gutter.' Leaving his assistants to complete the case against Powers, Cardigan walks out of the courthouse with June at his side.

From an attorney's perspective one of the most unsatisfying of the films indebted to Fallon is *Lawyer Man*.[42] As we follow the career of Anton Adam (William Powell) it soon becomes clear that the people who made this picture knew nothing about their subject and could not care less: the simplest legal distinctions are ignored and almost all the lawyer work takes place out of the camera's eye. But it is also an exceptionally lively and funny film, with that quintessential WASP William Powell—hopelessly miscast as an ethnic (né Antonio Adamo?) with roots in Manhattan's Lower East Side—loping and leering and waggling his eyebrows and phallic cigars for all the world like Groucho Marx with a real moustache. Adam wins an offstage acquittal (apparently on a murder charge) for petty hoodlum Izzy Levine (Allen Jenkins) and is offered a partnership by his courtroom adversary, prosperous uptown attorney Granville Bentley (Alan Dinehart). Was Izzy innocent or guilty? By what tactics did Adam prevail? How did a big-shot civil lawyer get to be prosecuting a criminal case? As they say on the Lower East Side, dun't esk! With his secretary Olga Michaels (Joan Blondell) in his wake, Adam moves into a palatial office and begins dating his new partner's sister Barbara (Helen Vinson). In another offstage trial he trounces political boss John Gilmurry (David Landau), who offers him a place in 'the organization' which Adam refuses. Later he is retained by showgirl Virginia St Johns (Claire Dodd) to bring a breach of promise suit against Dr Frank Gresham (Kenneth Thomson), a Gilmurry ally. The torrid letters from her former lover that Virginia leaves with Adam lead him to anticipate a six-figure settlement and a huge fee for himself, but she and Gresham

42 Warner Bros, 1932, directed by William Dieterle from a screenplay by Rian James and James Seymour based on Max Trell's 1932 novel of the same name.

reconcile before the trial begins, and the results of Adam's demand that she not drop the suit are devastating: the Gresham love letters vanish from his office and Adam is indicted for extortion. That trial, which we glimpse for just a few seconds, ends in a hung jury, but Adam's career in the big leagues is ruined and, in a key sequence, he decides to break with Barbara and, in effect, become a Fallon figure.

> Look down there. People. Millions. Every guy for himself. Pushing, shoving, trampling each other, sure. City full of them. Crooked streets and crooks. Fight, cheat, deal from the bottom. Boost the guy that's riding high and kick the guy that's down. That's what it takes to make good here. And that's what I'll give them. When they kick you, kick back, only harder. Sock 'em. If they can't take it, that's their hard luck. They made a shyster out of me. Okay. I'll be the biggest, busiest shyster that ever hit this town. If they want rats, I'll be a rat. The daddy of all rats! I'll show them.

After a period as a shyster that whizzes by in about a minute of screen time, Adam stumbles into and accepts a civil case of some sort against Gilmurry. The issues are not explained and the trial is not shown but, just before the jury returns with a verdict, Adam bluffs the political boss into settling: $20,000 for the client, $10,000 for himself. On his way out of the courthouse Gilmurry asks a juror how much they awarded the plaintiff. 'Oh', the other replies, proving once more that no one involved in this film grasped the simplest legal distinctions, 'we found you not guilty.'

Gilmurry again offers Adam a place in his organization. This time Adam agrees, but only if he is appointed an Assistant District Attorney. Strange appointment! The lettering on his new office door reads Deputy District Attorney, not Assistant, and he is never assigned any cases to prosecute but simply uses his power to pursue the vendetta against Dr Gresham, getting him indicted and convicted for billing the city thousands of dollars for services never performed. Gilmurry retaliates by sending gunmen to kill Adam, who counters by bringing in Izzy Levine as his bodyguard. Finally Gilmurry offers Adam a judgeship if he will lay off, but our hero opts for a rather different career move.

> I'm going back to my own people, where you don't have to be a rat to succeed. . . . A lawyer's job is like a doctor's. That's what it should be. A guide. A helper. A big brother to a lot of poor trampled slobs who can't hold their own against party bosses like you. Not a trickster and a cheat but a counselor and a friend. That's what I was. And that's what I'm going to be again. And that's why I don't want your judgeship or anything else that you've got to offer. I'm finished, washed up, fed up. With you, and your party, and your politics.

The film ends with Adam back in his Lower East Side Eden, poor but happy and with Olga who has always loved him still at his side.

The protagonist of *The Nuisance*[43] is lawyer Phineas 'Joe' Stevens (Lee Tracy), who—with the help of the drunken quack Prescott (Frank Morgan) and a

[43] MGM, 1933, directed by Jack Conway from a screenplay by Bella and Samuel Spewack based on an original story by Chandler Sprague and Howard Emmett Rogers.

professional accident victim (Charles Butterworth) and various paid-off witnesses—makes a nice living out of fraudulent lawsuits against the local streetcar company. Finally company attorney John Calhoun (John Miljan) declares war, hiring Dorothy Mason (Madge Evans) to pose as an accident victim and retain Prescott, whose instructions to her on how to fake various injuries she secretly tapes, while Calhoun himself cosies up to Prescott at his favorite speakeasy and is soon privy to his methods of faking X-rays. Joe discovers that Prescott has spilled the beans and, after a vicious tongue-lashing, the doctor walks in front of a passing auto and kills himself. Ridden by grief and guilt and unaware that Dorothy is part of the plot against him, Joe explains to her that he became a shyster only after the streetcar company used shyster tactics against a genuinely injured client of his. Dorothy refuses to inform further on Joe, with whom she has fallen in love, despite Calhoun's threats to have her charged with perjury. Joe discovers a cheque from the streetcar company in Dorothy's luggage but what he does about it is not revealed until the trial, where Calhoun cross-examines Dorothy and is about to make her tell who was behind the phony accident ring when Joe interrupts: Dorothy cannot be forced to testify against him because he has just married her! After the trial Joe kicks Dorothy out but, when she is arrested for perjury as Calhoun had threatened, stages a harassment campaign against the streetcar company and Calhoun himself until the charges are dropped. The film ends with Dorothy released from jail and Joe promising to become an honest lawyer.

The Women in His Life[44] opens with criminal lawyer Barry Barringer (Otto Kruger)—a hard-drinking womanizer who never got over being deserted by his wife—receiving visits from two potential clients. Doris Worthing (Irene Hervey) begs him to represent her father (Samuel S Hinds), an innocent man charged with murdering his sluttish second wife, and Florence Steele (Irene Franklin), who freely admits that she murdered her husband, asks Barry to get her off. At first Barry accepts the guilty client and rejects the innocent, but when Doris mentions that Florence strongly resembles a modiste she knows, a light bulb goes on in his head and he agrees to represent Worthing too. But after getting Florence acquitted (by bringing the modiste to court and totally confusing the eyewitnesses who identified the defendant) he drops the Worthing case and takes off for a Florida vacation with his girlfriend Catherine Watson (Isabel Jewell). While he is gone, his junior partner Roger McKane (Ben Lyon) develops some leads suggesting that Mrs Worthing was murdered by gangster Tony Perez (C Henry Gordon), with whom she had been having an affair. When Barry returns he sees a photograph of Mrs Worthing and—gasp!—recognizes her as the ex-wife who had dumped him years before. He goes out on a near-fatal drinking binge and, while he is in the hospital, Worthing is found guilty of murder and sentenced to the electric chair. Barry recuperates and resumes work on the case but so ineptly that McKane first knocks him down and then gets him disbarred, after which he opens a so-called legal

[44] MGM, 1933, directed by George B Seitz from a screenplay by F Hugh Herbert.

consulting firm, with a clientele consisting solely of criminals. But eventually he has a change of heart and, minutes before Worthing's execution, tricks Tony Perez into a confession secretly caught on tape. The film ends with Barry readmitted to the Bar and engaged to Catherine while McKane prepares to tie the knot with Doris.

The final film of the first golden age inspired by Fallon's chequered career was *The Defense Rests*.[45] Matthew Mitchell (Jack Holt) is a brilliant shyster with a bottomless bag of legal tricks and a reputation so awesome that newspapers print extras announcing the acquittal of his clients even before the verdicts are in. When Mabel Wilson (Shirley Grey) is tried for the murder of her gambler lover Ballou (J Carrol Naish), Mitchell gets her acquitted by having her testify—tearfully and with much display of her legs—that she shot him in self defence while he was drunk and abusing her. In fact, as Mitchell knows, Mabel is innocent. His assistant Joan Hayes (Jean Arthur), a lawyer herself, is disgusted by his tactics and berates him for legal trickery that has let the real murderer go free, but he defends himself on the ground that he owes no loyalty except to his client. Joan investigates the murder on her own, finds evidence indicating that the real killer was Ballou's partner Gentry (Robert Gleckler), and threatens to have Mitchell arrested for suborning perjury if he does not give up shystering, but he refuses to change his ways. His next client is Cooney (John Wray), a gangster charged with the murder of the four-year-old child he had kidnapped even though the family had paid the ransom. Mitchell accepts a $50,000 retainer, employs his usual shyster tricks at the trial, and is winning the case hands-down when the murdered child's mother (Sarah Padden) commits suicide in his office. Suddenly Mitchell is a changed man. When Joan discovers that his $50,000 retainer came from the ransom money, he resigns as Cooney's lawyer and secretly gives the evidence to the district attorney (Arthur Hohl), who uses it to obtain a guilty verdict. As for the Mabel Wilson case, Mitchell tells Joan to file a subornation of perjury charge against him but Joan, who loves him despite his years of shyster practice, has a better idea: if he marries her, she can never be made to testify against him about anything! The murder of Ballou is taken care of extra-legally when his henchmen rub out Gentry.

IV. The Jewel in the Crown: *Counsellor at Law*

Of all the films discussed in this essay, the only one that deserves to be called a masterpiece is *Counsellor at Law*.[46] All the events take place in a lavish Art Deco suite of law offices high up in the then new Empire State Building, with not a moment of courtroom action so that we are spared the nonsensical trial sequences

[45] Columbia, 1934, directed by Lambert Hillyer from a screenplay by Jo Swerling.

[46] Universal, 1933, directed by William Wyler from a screenplay by Elmer Rice based on his 1931 stage play of the same name.

that make so many law films of the early 1930s laughable to viewers who are attorneys. Instead Wyler and Rice offer a multi-layered and richly nuanced portrait of the private and professional lives of a manic-depressive workaholic attorney—and of the simultaneous crises in each that drive him to the brink of suicide—as well as incisive sketches of the staff, and of the clients and others who have occasion to enter the offices, and of the various ethnic cultures (Jewish, Irish, Italian, German) whose members are bonded by the experience of steerage and the scorn of their common foe the WASP. 'Those guys that came over on the Mayflower don't like to see the boys from Second Avenue sitting in the high places.' The cast is so huge, the pacing so brisk and the interplay among characters and storylines so complex that any viewer whose attention wanders, however briefly, gets lost. Even the people who at first glance seem dispensable—like the blonde receptionist with the glass-shattering voice (Isabel Jewell) and the unbilled walk-on who comes into the suite to shine the partners' shoes—have serious functions to perform in one part of the panoramic story or another.

'The last time I crossed the Atlantic it was in steerage.' That was then. 'People from old families come and think I'm doing them a favor if I accept their retainers.' This is now. George Simon (John Barrymore), senior partner in the New York firm of Simon & Tedesco, has risen from Jewish immigrant origins to great success as an attorney and to social prominence as well, thanks to having married 'one of the Four Hundred', a WASP divorcée (Doris Kenyon) with two teenage children from her first marriage (Richard Quine and Barbara Perry) whom Simon loves as if they were his own even though they may well be the most obnoxious brats ever seen in a movie. '*Our* father lives in Washington', boasts the male half of the detestable duo. '*He's* not *our* father!' But he has resisted total assimilation and welcomes his old mother (Clara Langsner) with open arms when, looking as if she had just stepped off the boat, she visits his plush offices and asks him for a favour. Simon's secretary Rexy Gordon (Bebe Daniels) is constantly being asked out by law clerk Herbert Weinberg (Marvin Kline) and constantly turns him down: not because she is anti-Semitic as Wyler fools us briefly into suspecting, but because she is hopelessly in love with another Jew, her married boss. Simon's partner John Tedesco (Onslow Stevens), who by common consent 'ain't so hot on the legal end', is nevertheless being considered for a judgeship. 'I got a young Harvard boy named Weinberg in here', Simon tells the county clerk (TH Manning) who visits him to discuss the matter. 'He could be John's secretary. And, believe me, he'll hand down opinions that'll give the Court of Appeals an inferiority complex.'

Judging from the variety of its cases and clients, the firm seems to hold itself out as omnicompetent. The curtain rises shortly after Simon has secured an acquittal for Zadorah Chapman (Mayo Methot), who was charged with and almost certainly guilty of her husband's murder. But in the course of a single day we see him handling a breach of promise suit for a gold-digging slut (Thelma Todd), lobbying a US Senator over the phone on behalf of a client, dictating correspondence in a will contest (which his wife pressures him to drop because the party on the other side is a social acquaintance of hers), arbitrarily tripling the fee he charges one of his divorce clients, and making a quick profit in the market from an advance tip on a forthcoming US Supreme Court decision. Like the makers of the films inspired by the career of William J Fallon, Wyler and Rice see the practice of law through unfooled eyes.

But if George Simon is far from an idealized Atticus Finch prototype, neither is he a shyster. Mrs Becker (Malka Kornstein), a woman from the old neighbourhood, prevails upon him to represent her firebrand son Harry (Vincent Sherman), who was clubbed by police and arrested for making a Communist speech in Union Square. Simon arranges with an assistant DA for a guilty plea and a suspended sentence but Harry refuses the deal.

HARRY: I don't want your advice or your help or your friendship. You and I have nothing in common. I'm on one side of the class war and you're on the other.

SIMON: Oh, stop talking like an idiot! Do you think I was born with a silver spoon in my mouth? I began life in the same gutter that you did. Why, you wouldn't have the guts to go through one tenth of what I went through to get where I am! You and your Cossacks and your class wars! Do you think I don't know what it means to sweat and go hungry? Don't come around me with any of that half-baked Communistic bull and expect me to fall for it.

HARRY: . . . How did you get where you are? I'll tell you! By betraying your own class, that's how! Getting in right with bourgeois politicians and crooked corporations that feed on the blood and the sweat of the workers. . . . Sitting here in your Fifth Avenue office with a bootblack at your feet and a lot of white-collar slaves running errands for you. You're a renegade and a cheap prostitute, that's what you are! You and your cars and your country estate and your kept parasite of a wife . . . and her two pampered brats! Comrade Simon of the working classes, who's rolling in wealth and luxury while millions of his brothers starve. You dirty traitor, you! (Spits and stalks out.)

As the film proceeds, all these threads combine with others to push Simon to the brink. On the professional front, he discovers that a kind deed he had performed a few years earlier—setting up a phoney alibi so that small-time criminal Johan Breitstein (John Qualen), who has since gone straight, will not be sent to prison for life—has come to the attention of Grievance Committee bigwig Francis Clark Baird (Elmer H Brown) and may soon lead to his disbarment. 'Don't you know, whenever you give anybody a helping hand, he always turns around and kicks you in the pants?' The crisis forces him to cancel his plans to sail to Europe with his wife, who refuses his anguished plea to stay with him in his hour of need ('Well, isn't that just a little bit selfish, George?') and insists on going alone. Then Simon learns that Harry Becker has died of his injuries. 'In his own eyes he died a hero and a martyr to a cause. That's better than living to be old and ending your days in disgrace.' Then, in a moment of defiance, he cries out: 'Let 'em disbar me! What do I care? I'll spend the rest of my life enjoying myself.' Then after thinking a minute he reverses himself. 'I'd go nuts in six months. How am I going to spend the rest of my life? I'm no golf player and I don't know an ace from a king. I don't even know how to get drunk![47] All I know is work. Take work away from me and what am I?. . . . A living corpse.'

In a desperate bid to salvage his career, Simon sends investigator Charlie MacFadden (J Hammond Dailey) to shadow Baird and find something scandalous in the latter's life. With the help of some offscreen breaking and entering, MacFadden brings back evidence that Baird is supporting a mistress and an illegitimate child, and Simon blackmails the hypocritical WASP into dropping the ethics inquiry. He then begins a mad rush to get to the ship before it sails and join his wife, only to discover that she is not sailing alone but with a companion in the form of suave Roy Darwin (Melvyn Douglas), a man of her own social class to whom Simon had recently lent money. That is what breaks him.

It is night. Simon sits alone in his palatial office suite, then slowly as if in a trance rises and approaches the window and throws it open. For the first time in the film we hear street noises—from dozens of stories below. Simon climbs the sill and is about to jump when the office door opens behind him and Rexy sees him and screams—one of the most intense emotional moments in any movie—and in a fit of manic fury he all but physically attacks her for stopping him. But the moment is past. They sit there in the dark at opposite ends of the office, drained, spent. Suddenly the phone rings. It is the president of a steel company, whose son has just killed his wife. The office lights blaze on and Simon is galvanized into life, flailing about, screaming, chortling with delight and, as the film ends, dashing off with Rexy at his side to save another wealthy guilty client from a murder charge. And we in the audience are delighted to see him recover the will to live.

Almost 30 years after this magnificent film was released, many in my generation were inspired to choose law school by Gregory Peck's performance as Atticus Finch in *To Kill a Mockingbird*. Anyone who would make that choice because of seeing *Counsellor at Law* belongs in an asylum. We can never admire and love George Simon as we love Atticus, but—and in the last analysis this may be more important—we come to understand him as Atticus, seen as he is through an idealized lens, can never be understood.

V. Conclusion: How Censorship Changed Juriscinema

For anyone interested in how and why strict self-censorship came to Hollywood and in what respects the new regime changed movies, the essential book is Thomas Doherty's *Pre-Code Hollywood: Sex, Immorality, and Insurrection in American Cinema, 1930–1934*.[48] The so-called Motion Picture Production Code had been

[47] This line is particularly ironic in view of the fact that John Barrymore was a compulsive alcoholic whose absences from the set and inability to remember lines caused long delays in production. For an account of the filming of *Counsellor at Law*, see Jan Herman, *A Talent for Trouble: The Life of Hollywood's Most Acclaimed Director, William Wyler* (New York: 1995) 114–119.

[48] New York: 1999.

in effect since 1930 but, as Doherty makes clear, was almost completely ignored during the early 1930s and had much the same effect on American films of the period that Prohibition had had on liquor consumption. Then came the reaction. As Doherty puts it: 'After four years of gun-toting gangsters and smart-mouthed convicts, adulterous wives and promiscuous chorines, irreverence from the lower orders and incompetence from above, the immoral and insurrectionist impulses on the Hollywood screen were beaten back by forces dedicated to public restraint and social control'.[49]

The prime mover behind strict enforcement of the Code was the Roman Catholic church, whose leadership 'embarked upon a nationwide crusade to lead parishioners away from Hollywood's temptations'.[50] Late in 1933 the hierarchy formed a National Legion of Decency, whose aim was to clean up 'the pest hole that infects the entire country with its obscene and lascivious moving pictures'.[51] Catholics were made to recite the Legion pledge at Sunday mass. In a 'command binding in all conscience under pain of sin'[52] Cardinal Dougherty of Philadelphia ordered his entire flock to boycott not just 'obscene and lascivious' films but all movies. Other religious groups quickly boarded the bandwagon, and at the same time the FDR administration in Washington began making noises about content regulation for the film industry, which according to the Supreme Court had no rights under the First Amendment.[53] 'The whole world has gotten the idea that Hollywood is Hell's home office. . . . ,' said one theatre manager.[54]

In order to avert both a nationwide religious boycott and the threat of federal censorship, the industry resolved to censor itself, bringing in Joseph I Breen, a prominent Catholic layman, as head of the Production Code Administration. 'I am the Code', Breen announced.[55] Clearly he did not mean to claim plenary power over movies. Just as it is the function of a federal or state administrative agency to interpret and enforce its enabling legislation, Breen's function was to interpret and enforce the Production Code, the 1930 document whose principal drafter was a Jesuit priest and which with its Amendments is reproduced in Appendixes 1–3 of Doherty's book.

Even a casual reading of the Code establishes that its principal targets were the celebration of sexual freedom and the glorification of crime. If Breen and his cohorts ruled that a film dealt improperly or too explicitly with seduction or pre-marital hanky-panky or prostitution or adultery, or that women in the cast were exposing or wiggling the wrong parts of their bodies, they demanded cuts, or the rewriting and reshooting of offending scenes. The kind of 'women's pictures' that were characteristic of the early 1930s were promptly demolished. What the

[49] New York: 1999, 319. [50] ibid, 320. [51] ibid, 320. [52] ibid, 321.

[53] During and for almost 20 years after the first golden age of juriscinema, the leading US Supreme Court case on this subject was *Mutual Film Corp v Industrial Commission of Ohio* 236 US 230 (1915), which had held that movies were not protected under the First Amendment. That decision was not overruled until *Joseph Burstyn Inc v Wilson* 343 US 495 (1952). For a comprehensive overview, see Edward de Grazia and Roger K Newman, *Banned Films: Movies, Censors & the First Amendment* (New York: 1982).

[54] See n 48 above, 325.

[55] ibid, 327.

Code's sexual proscriptions outlawed was the sympathetic portrayal of female characters who enjoyed sex either before or outside of marriage. But, by abolishing one of the most fruitful venues for presenting lawyer characters (always male) who tended to behave more honourably than their counterparts in other film genres, the banning of such films caused a great deal of collateral damage to juriscinema.

The Breen office also demanded cuts and revisions in any film that was deemed to glorify crime and criminals. 'Law . . . shall not be ridiculed, nor shall sympathy be created for its violation.'[56] This and similar provisions of the Code were clearly aimed at banning the classic gangster films of the early 1930s, which probably would have died out anyway once Prohibition was repealed. But they too inflicted much collateral damage on juriscinema, all but outlawing the cycle of pre-1934 films whose lawyer protagonist was modelled on William J Fallon.

Nowhere does the Code say that lawyers may not be ridiculed or portrayed in a negative light. Yet from shortly after the coming of strict Code enforcement until its slow dissolution beginning more than 20 years later, the kinds of films considered in this essay became rare. When such a film was made, it lacked life and bite. Even when a law film from the early 1930s was remade, as many of them were,[57] the remake was almost always a pale imitation of its original. The Code put an end to the first golden age of juriscinema indirectly, by suffocating the unfooled, sexually and intellectually liberated environment that early talkies had imported from the cultural climate of the 1920s. We can see and feel the difference when we consider two films released very shortly after the Code began to be strictly enforced.

The protagonist of *Crime Without Passion*[58] is attorney Lee Gentry (Claude Rains), who defends guilty criminals and uses shyster tactics to get them acquitted and winds up suffering the fate of James M Cain's protagonist in *The Postman Always Rings Twice* (1934). Gentry accidentally shoots fiery-tempered Spanish dancer Carmen Brown (Margo) while trying to break up with her and, convinced that he killed her, pulls out all the stops trying to set up an alibi for himself. Eventually he discovers that Carmen's friend Della (Greta Granstedt) happened to

[56] ibid, 361.

[57] *A Free Soul* was remade as *The Girl Who Had Everything* (MGM, 1953, directed by Richard Thorpe from a screenplay by Art Cohn), starring Elizabeth Taylor, Fernando Lamas and William Powell. The Josef von Sternberg version of Dreiser's *An American Tragedy* was superseded by the Oscar-winning *A Place in the Sun* (Paramount, 1951, directed by George Stevens from a screenplay by Michael Wilson and Harry Brown), starring Montgomery Clift, Elizabeth Taylor and Shelley winters. *State's Attorney* was remade as *Criminal Lawyer* (RKO, 1937, directed by Christy Cabanne from a screenplay by GV Atwater and Thomas Lennon), which starred Lee Tracy, Margot Grahame and Eduardo Ciannelli. *The Nuisance* returned to the screen as *The Chaser* (MGM, 1938, directed by Edwin L Marin from a screenplay by Everett Freeman, Harry Ruskin, and Bella and Samuel Spewack), starring Dennis O'Keefe, Ann Morriss and Lewis Stone. *The Mouthpiece* was remade twice: as *The Man Who Talked Too Much* (Warner Bros, 1940, directed by Vincent Sherman from a screenplay by Walter DeLeon and Earl Baldwin), starring George Brent, Virginia Bruce and Brenda Marshall, and as the much better *Illegal* (Warner Bros, 1955, directed by Lewis Allen from a screenplay by WR Burnett and James R Webb), starring Edward G Robinson, Nina Foch and Hugh Marlowe.

[58] Paramount, 1934, directed by Ben Hecht and Charles MacArthur from their own screenplay based on Ben Hecht's 1933 magazine story 'Caballero of the Law'.

see him under circumstances that destroy his phoney alibi. Then he gets into a fight with Della's boyfriend Eddie White (Stanley Ridges) and shoots him in self-defence but under circumstances that make the act seem like cold-blooded murder. As the police lead him away, Gentry discovers that Carmen is not dead after all. Here is a textbook example of what happened to a film about a lawyer after the Breen office monkeyed with it.[59] The miracle is that, compulsory retribution and all, it is still a fascinating movie.

So too is *The Case of the Howling Dog*,[60] which starred Warren William in the first of a six-film series about lawyer-detective Perry Mason. In Gardner's novel Mason represents Bessie Forbes on the charge that she murdered her husband, who had dumped her for another man's wife. What makes *Howling Dog* unique among the 82 Mason novels is that this time Mason's client is guilty, and he knows it when he gets her acquitted so that she can never be tried again. '... I am not a judge; nor am I a jury. . . . I have never heard the story of Bessie Forbes; nor has any one else. It may have been that anything she did was done in self-defense. . . . But I acted only as her lawyer.'[61] Every moment of the novel is seen from Mason's point of view and nothing happens outside his presence. In the film we witness enough of the murder scene so that we can be certain that Bessie (Mary Astor) did indeed act in self defence. Before strict enforcement of the Code that alteration would not have been necessary.

Several years later, when Maurine Watkins' 1926 stage play *Chicago* was adapted into the movie *Roxie Hart*,[62] the Breen office rejected several versions of the screenplay on the grounds that 'the story seems to be a travesty on the administration of justice and on the courts of this country which would undoubtedly tend to weaken respect for law and order generally'.[63] Wellman finally satisfied the censors with a bowdlerized reworking of the story: Roxie (Ginger Rogers) is still tried for murder with Billy Flynn (Adolphe Menjou) pulling publicity strings and turning the courtroom into a carnival, but it turns out that the murderer is Amos Hart (George Chandler) and that Roxie framed herself in order to garner publicity and launch a career as a dancer.

As Thomas Doherty points out, under the strictly enforced Code 'cinematic space was a patrolled landscape with secure perimeters and well-defined borders'.[64] But the years of strict enforcement were far from a cinematic wasteland: indeed they were precisely the years that saw *Stagecoach* (1939), *The Grapes of Wrath* (1940), *Citizen Kane* (1941), *Casablanca* (1942), all the classics of what Doherty

[59] For excerpts from some of the documents pertaining to the censorship of this film see *The American Film Institute Catalog of Motion Pictures Produced in the United States: Feature Films, 1931–1940* (Berkeley: 1993) 424–425.

[60] Warner Bros, 1934, directed by Alan Crosland from a screenplay by Ben Markson based on Erle Stanley Gardner's 1934 novel of the same name.

[61] Erle Stanley Gardner, *The Case of the Howling Dog* (New York, 1934) 294.

[62] 20th Century Fox, 1942, directed by William A Wellman from a screenplay by Nunnally Johnson.

[63] Quoted in *The American Film Institute Catalog of Motion Pictures Produced in the United States: Feature Films, 1941–1950* (Berkeley: 1999) 2044.

[64] See n 48 above, 1.

calls 'Hollywood's vaunted "golden age" . . . [a]n artistic flowering of incalculable cultural impact. . . . '.[65] 'The fractures of American life, still less the open embrace of sex, did not close up when the Code clamped down. No matter how rigid the body cast, Hollywood cinema is too supple and expressive an art to constrain [sexual energy or social protest]. . . . [I]n the hidden recesses of the cinematic subtext, under the surface of avowed morality and happy endings, Hollywood under the Code is fraught with defiance of Code authority.'[66]

The Code did not put an end to lawyer characters or legal themes in films but it surely ended the first golden age of juriscinema. Between the second half of 1934 and the beginning of the breakdown of censorship 20-odd years later, Hollywood offered relatively few films with a legal component. Most of the post-Code law films were not as rewarding as their counterparts from the early 1930s and even the gems among them, like John Ford's *Young Mr Lincoln* (1939) and Wellman's *Roxie Hart*, were not connected by leitmotifs as so many pre-Code law films were connected by the cultural forces sketched at the beginning of this essay. It was not until the years that coincided with both the breakdown of the Code and the rise of the Warren Court that film-makers launched juriscinema's second golden age. But that, as Scheherazade might have said, is another story.

[65] ibid, 1. [66] ibid, 3.

Emergency! Send a TV Show to Rescue Paramedic Services!

Paul Bergman[1]

Prologue: A fire department crew rushes to the scene of a grisly accident. The crew finds an electrical worker high up in the air, draped over sizzling electrical wires and rendered unconscious by a sudden surge of electricity. As soon as the electricity can be shut off, the intrepid rescuers pull the worker off the wires. They immediately begin to give him oxygen, and rush him to hospital. Standing by at the hospital is a nurse who shouts, 'Cardiac arrest, electrocution!' An emergency room doctor is also at the ready, and he uses a defibrillator and gives the still-unconscious worker an injection in a feverish effort to try to resuscitate him. Alas, despite everyone's heroic efforts, it is too late. The worker is dead. 'If only a paramedic with equipment had been on the scene', remarks the nurse to the doctor, 'this man would have survived.'[2]

* * *

Introduction

Movies, television shows and other forms of popular culture have the potential to lead to formal legal changes. What Peter Robson's contribution to this volume refers to as 'impact studies'[3] examine the extent to which this potential has been realized. This essay is an impact study whose purpose is to demonstrate the influence of a popular 1970s American television series called *Emergency!* on the development of paramedic services. The essay argues that the TV show stimulated popular demand for paramedic services and was largely responsible for the fact that

[1] Thanks to the UCLA School of Law's Dean's Fund for economic support of my research. Special thanks for helping me to locate materials to Jean Cinader, the widow of the late Robert Cinader, who created the show *Emergency!* and was its Executive Producer. I am also very grateful for the research assistance provided by UCLA Law Librarians Linda O'Connor, Laura Cadra and Kevin Gerson as well as UCLA law student James Stein. Finally, thank you to Michael Freeman, University College London, and Clintons for sponsoring the July 2003 Law and Popular Culture Colloquium and to the participants for their many helpful comments on my presentation.

[2] Pilot episode of *Emergency!* (Jack Webb Productions, 1972).

[3] See Peter Robson, p 21 above.

in the short span of a few years nearly every state in America amended its laws so as to allow such services to exist.

Impact studies such as this one are consistent with Lawrence Friedman's argument that a useful social theory of law should attempt to address the mechanism by which social changes or technological inventions produce changes in legal rules and institutions.[4] Friedman posited that popular legal culture, including the attitudes, norms and behaviour of ordinary people, constitutes just such a mechanism.[5] He argued that: 'These elements of legal culture act as an intervening variable between *social* innovation and legal change'.[6]

Nevertheless, demonstrating a link between a work of popular legal culture and specific legal change is likely to be a difficult task. Social orders are vast and amorphous, and individuals' norms, beliefs, customs and desires are multifaceted and often in conflict. Moreover, while works of popular culture can act as a catalyst of attitudinal change, the likely presence of other contributors makes it difficult to isolate popular culture's role in fostering legal change. However, the belief that popular culture can produce legal change is widespread. For example, a 1965 British televised play called *Cathy Come Home* dramatized the plight of homeless people.[7] Many people credit the television show with leading to the creation of Shelter, an English charity that advocates on behalf of the homeless. Shelter in turn pressured the government into enacting the Housing Act of 1977, which extended aid to homeless persons.[8] Yet the difficulty of documenting the connection between works of popular culture and social change means that scholars generally have to be content with assertions that popular culture 'must' in some inchoate way contribute to formal legal developments.[9]

This essay, by contrast, seeks to document the pivotal role of *Emergency!* in producing an array of legal changes that resulted in an explosion in the availability of paramedic services during the time that the TV show aired new episodes. The argument in its strongest form is that laws authorizing paramedics to perform medical procedures that were formerly the exclusive domain of doctors may well not have been enacted but for the influence of *Emergency!* A weaker form of the argument is that while paramedic services would very likely eventually have become legalized, *Emergency!* is largely responsible for such laws spreading like wildfire throughout the United States during the first half of the 1970s.

[4] Lawrence Friedman, 'Law and Popular Culture' (1989) 98 *Yale LJ* 1579, 1583.

[5] ibid, 1583–1584. [6] ibid, 1584 (italics in original).

[7] The television show was directed by Ken Loach and written by Jeremy Sandford.

[8] For a description and analysis of the Housing (Homeless Persons) Act 1977 and its later amendments, see Peter Robson and Mark Poustie, *Homeless People and the Law* (3rd edn, 1994) Ch 2.

[9] See, eg, Melvin Gutterman, ' "Failure to Communicate": The Reel Prison Experience' (2002) 55 *Southern Methodist U L Rev* 1515, 1558. In his essay on prison films, Gutterman states that 'popular films serve as a barometer, and can operate as a catalyst to stimulate us to demand political action'. While Gutterman's assertion contemplates that legal changes may flow from prison films, the essay does not indicate that this has actually occurred.

Emergency Medical Care Prior to *Emergency!*

The 'back story' to the development of paramedic services begins in the 1960s, when research into the number of American lives that could be saved through improvements in emergency care began seeping into the public consciousness. One of the most prominent sources of information was a 1966 report prepared under the auspices of the National Academy of Sciences. The report revealed that in 1965 alone, accidental injuries had killed 107,000 Americans and caused permanent disabilities to another 400,000. The report also concluded that existing emergency equipment and personnel were generally incapable of providing quality emergency care.[10]

Around the same time, other studies demonstrated that lives were being unnecessarily lost to sudden illness. Most of these studies focused on victims of sudden heart attack. One prominent study estimated that if quicker emergency care were available, 'from 5 to 20% of deaths resulting from heart disease—700,000 annually—could be prevented if the public were educated to recognize the symptoms of heart attack and if ambulance attendants were adequately trained to provide immediate emergency treatment'. In sum, 'a minimum of 67,000 deaths could be prevented annually if EMS [Emergency Medical Services] systems . . . were operational nationwide'.[11]

Thus, as the 1960s ended one might have predicted the upgrading of emergency medical services throughout the United States, at least if the federal and state governments were willing to put their money where these reports' mouths were. However, the shape that improvements in EMS would take was uncertain. One possible model that many in the United States initially looked to for guidance had been established by Dr Pantridge and others in Belfast, Northern Ireland in 1968.[12] The Belfast system relied on ambulances staffed with physicians, who could begin immediate treatment of patients needing coronary care on site rather than having to wait for patients to be transported to hospitals. Similar emergency programmes began in a number of American communities.

However, the influence of the Belfast programme in America was short-lived. Part of the reason was that the Belfast system was directed exclusively at coronary problems and did not address other emergency medical situations. Thus, American emergency care experts tended to prefer 'Mobile Intensive Care Units' that could provide emergency care for victims both of accidents and sudden illness. However, the move to Mobile Intensive Care Units revealed a second problem

[10] *Accidental Death and Disability: The Neglected Disease of Modern Society* (National Academy of Sciences and the National Research Council, 1966).

[11] Senate Report No 93-397 on the Emergency Medical Services Act of 1973, 119 *Congressional Record* 2535, 2547 (1973).

[12] See Joe Slotkin and Elliott Salenger MD, 'National Paramedic Survey—Part 1,' *Paramedics International* 17 (Summer 1976).

with the Belfast model for the United States: the country did not have nearly enough doctors to staff fleets of mobile care units.[13] Thus, American communities quickly abandoned the Belfast model.

Perhaps because of the uncertainty concerning an appropriate model to follow, as the decade of the 1970s began, improvements in emergency care were proceeding slowly. A second National Academy of Sciences report in 1972 (the year that *Emergency!* went on the air) described how little progress in the provision of emergency medical services had been made. According to that report,

> Emergency medical service is one of the weakest links in the delivery of health care in the Nation. . . . Few at the site of accidental injury or sudden illness are trained in the fundamentals of (emergency treatment) . . . The majority of ambulances in the United States are . . . inadequate in space and equipment and are manned by individuals with inadequate training to provide essential life support.[14]

Paramedic Services Prior to *Emergency!*

The generally sorry state of emergency medical care in the United States at the end of the 1960s coincided with suggestions for including paramedics in expanded emergency services. In Congress, a number of experts suggested the use of physicians' assistants, or paramedics, who could be trained to perform emergency medical services.[15] Unlike existing ambulance personnel, who could do little more than render basic first aid, the new emergency professionals would be able to undertake such tasks as administering drugs and intravenous fluids and performing cardiac defibrillation.

Such recommendations were given further impetus by the Sixth Bethesda (Maryland) Conference of the American College of Cardiology. The conference, which took place in 1969, was the first major medical conference to envision a role for paramedics.[16] The conference report suggested that 'medical manpower is limited, and many programs will depend heavily on the increased utilization of specially trained paramedical personnel'.[17]

However, the inclusion of paramedic services in upgraded emergency care systems was by no means a 'done deal' at the beginning of the 1970s. The legalization of paramedic services required major changes in legal principles relating to both

[13] ibid, 17; see also, 'Paramedics and the Medical Manpower Shortage: The Case for Statutory Legitimization' (1971) 60 *Georgetown LJ* 157.

[14] *Roles and Resources of Federal Agencies in Support of Comprehensive Emergency Medical Services* (National Research Council of the National Academy of Sciences, 1972).

[15] See 'Hearings on Health Care in America Before the Subcommittee on Executive Reorganization of the Senate Committee on Government Operations', *90th Congress, 2d Session, Part 2* at 487, 923 (1968).

[16] James O Page, *The Paramedics—An Illustrated History of Paramedics in Their First Decade in the U.S.A.* (1980) 20.

[17] 'Bethesda Conference Report', *American Journal of Cardiology* (April 1969).

criminal and civil liability.[18] For example, laws in all states made it a crime for non-physicians to practise medicine without a licence. These laws rendered paramedic services unfeasible, because many of the medical functions that paramedics might have performed constituted the 'practice of medicine'. Paramedics could be criminally prosecuted under these laws even if they had undergone training and could demonstrate expertise in carrying out their paramedic tasks.[19]

Civil liability rules also posed significant challenges for the development of paramedic services. Paramedics could be ordered to pay damages for any harms that patients incurred due to paramedics' negligence. A showing of negligence was likely not to be a significant hurdle for plaintiffs to overcome, however, since in most jurisdictions performing illegal medical procedures constituted 'negligence per se'.[20] Even apart from the 'negligence per se' reasoning, paramedics were likely to be held to the same standard of care as physicians.[21]

The Senate Report on the Emergency Services Act of 1974 summarized the legal challenges facing the development of paramedic services as follows:

> The reported bill directs the Secretary to conduct a study of the legal barriers to the effective delivery of medical care under emergency conditions. . . . The provision of emergency medical services is affected in some states by inflexible laws on licensure, malpractice and liability.[22]

Adding to the need for legal changes that would have to occur if paramedic services were to develop and expand was the opposition of many physicians' and nurses' groups to the paramedic concept. For example, two researchers writing in 1969 surveyed over 1,300 Wisconsin physicians. The researchers asked the physicians whether they would be willing to permit paramedics to perform duties closely related to their medical specialties. The physicians' answers were strongly negative.[23]

The physicians' professional association, the American Medical Association (AMA), counselled delay, that favourite tactic of opponents who might not want to challenge a reform directly. The AMA's position was that more experimentation was needed before legislation authorizing paramedic services was enacted.[24] Individual doctors, however, were not so restrained. For example, one Illinois

[18] See 'Emergency Medical Services at Midpassage', A Report of the Committee on Emergency Medical Services, Assembly of Life Sciences, National Research Council, National Academy of Sciences (1978) 38, 40 (1978).

[19] 'Paramedics and the Medical Manpower Shortage', n 13 above, 159–160. The article also points out that the laws criminalizing paramedic activities also discouraged licensed physicians from employing paramedics because state licensing boards could revoke the licences of doctors who aided unlicensed people to practise medicine. Ibid, 161.

[20] ibid, 162. The 'negligence per se' standard meant that a paramedic could be held liable for performing unauthorized medical procedures even in the absence of evidence that the paramedic was in any way careless.

[21] ibid, 163.

[22] Senate Report No 93-397, n 11 above, 2567.

[23] See Coye and Hansen, 'The "Doctors" Assistants', (1969) 209 *of the American Medical Association* 529, 531.

[24] See 'Of Physician Assistants', (1970) 212 *J of the American Medical Association* 1057.

doctor thought that: 'This whole mobile medical thing is loaded with danger! How would you like it if someone, after only a few weeks of training, took over your husband's job?' Another opined that authorizing paramedics would 'be responsible for bringing socialized medicine to the Midwest'.[25]

Nurses often opposed the legalization of paramedic services because, much more so than for doctors, paramedics presented a potential 'turf' issue for many nurses and nursing groups.[26] Legalization of paramedics created a risk that duties previously regarded as part of nursing would be shifted to paramedics, especially with respect to new medical technology.[27] Thus, a number of nursing associations initially went on record as opposing the legalization of paramedic services.[28]

Even paramedic proponents themselves were divided, at least as to the desirable form of legalization. Some proponents favoured a comprehensive licensing scheme. Other proponents, however, thought that such schemes were too restrictive, and wanted laws that allowed physicians to decide for themselves whether non-physicians were qualified to perform medical services without regard to licensing.[29]

As a result of all these challenges and despite the glimmerings of hope for including paramedics in improved emergency services, the reality was that actual paramedic services were virtually non-existent at the end of the 1960s. As of 1971, only 12 paramedic units were in existence in the entire United States.[30] A number of these operated somewhat clandestinely, in the absence of legislative authority.[31]

As luck would have it, however, two of these 12 paramedic units were based in Los Angeles, the show-business capital of the world. California was the first state to enact a comprehensive law authorizing paramedic services,[32] and Los Angeles' two

[25] Page, n 16 above, 69.

[26] Jan Schwettman was an Illinois woman whose husband's sudden death caused by cardiac arrest moved her to press actively for paramedic services. While the Illinois legislature was considering legalizing paramedic services, Schwettman wrote to a doctor that she 'learned today that the nurses are furious and are planning lobbying action'. Page, n 16 above, 74.

[27] See 'Paramedics and the Medical Manpower Shortage', n 13 above, 180.

[28] See, eg 'Testimony of Rheba de Tornyay, President of the California Nurses Association', in *Hearings on Physicians' Assistants Before the Interim Comm. On Health and Welfare* (Cal Assembly, 1970 Sess 50–55, 1969).

[29] See 'Paramedics and the Medical Manpower Shortage', n 13 above, 182–183.

[30] *Making a Difference: The History of Modern EMS* (JEMS Communications, 1997), videotape documentary narrated by James O Page. Another source indicated that 20 paramedic programmes were 'in various stages of development in 14 locations scattered throughout 11 states' as of 1970. See Kadish and Long, 'The Training of Physicians' Assistants—Status and Issues' (1970) 212 *J of the American Medical Association* 1047, 1049.

[31] See James O Page, *National Study of Paramedic Law and Policy 1975–1976* (Table 1, pp 8–11). For example, paramedic service began in Miami and Jacksonville in Florida in 1967 but express legal authority was not enacted until 1973.

[32] Page, n 31 above, 3. Page was a Battalion Chief with the Los Angeles Fire Department who worked closely with the creators of *Emergency!* At the time he prepared the 1975–76 study, Page was the Executive Director of Lakes Area Emergency Services in Buffalo, NY.

paramedic units operated under the authority of that law, the Wedworth-Townsend Paramedic Act of 1970.[33] Reflecting the uncertain future of paramedic services, Wedworth-Townsend was merely an experimental pilot programme. The law expired automatically two years after its enactment, and it authorized paramedic services only in counties 'with a population of over 6,000,000' people, meaning that the paramedic services that Wedworth-Townsend authorized were limited to Los Angeles County. Despite its rudimentary and hesitant approach, however, the Wedworth-Townsend Paramedic Act provided the impetus for *Emergency!*

Emergency! and the Growth of Paramedic Services

Popular culture's contribution to the development of paramedic services began shortly after the enactment of California's Wedworth-Townsend Paramedic Act. In the words of Los Angeles County Fire Captain Jim Page, who was involved in Los Angeles' earliest paramedic training programmes, '11 May 1971 was a day of great significance to the paramedic concept'.[34] On that date veteran television producer Robert Cinader, working with Jack Webb (of *Dragnet* fame) 'took a meeting'[35] with Captain Page and other Los Angeles County Fire Department officials to discuss the development of a new television series based on the exploits of fire department rescue personnel.

Cinader's initial concept focused on physical rescue situations. Cinader asked Captain Page for help in developing rescue scenarios that could be depicted in a weekly series. Captain Page began collecting story ideas, but soon realized that the focus on physical rescue situations was too limiting: 'There were only so many kinds of cave-ins, building collapses and similar calamities that could be depicted without encountering potentially boring similarities'.[36] As fate would have it, Captain Page was familiar with Los Angeles County's experimental paramedic operations.[37] Moreover, shortly after his initial meeting with Cinader, Captain Page was promoted to the office of Battalion Chief, and as a result had the County's two paramedic units under his command. Battalion Chief Page then suggested to Cinader that the focus of the show be changed from physical rescues to depicting paramedics in action. Cinader was initially cool to the idea, but he quickly became a believer. Cinader became a fixture in the stations that housed the paramedic

[33] Cal Health & Safety Code Sec 1480 et seq. The Wedworth-Townsend Act specified the emergency medical procedures that paramedics were authorized to perform as well as the type of training that paramedics had to undergo in order to receive a licence to perform those services. Ironically, Assemblyman Townsend, one of the state legislators for whom the bill was named, suffered a heart attack at the state capitol in Sacramento in 1973 and died later in a hospital. At the time of his heart attack, the paramedic services which had been authorized by the law that carried his name were not yet available in Sacramento. See Page, n 16 above, 4.

[34] Page, n 16 above, 25.

[35] This is Hollywood lingo for 'met'.

[36] Page, n 16 above, 51.

[37] Los Angeles County's paramedic experiment was conducted under the authority of the Wedworth-Townsend Paramedic Act of 1970.

units, and he accompanied the paramedics on numerous emergency calls.[38] In September of 1971, Webb and Cinader signed a contract with the National Broadcasting Company (NBC) television network to produce a two hour 'world premiere movie' based on the work of the paramedics. The movie, titled *Emergency!*, was first shown in Los Angeles in December 1971 and it aired nationally in February 1972.

In the pre-cable, pre-satellite era when most American television viewers had access to programming only on three national networks and perhaps one or two local stations, *Emergency!* became a very popular series that ran on Saturday nights on NBC. New one hour episodes of *Emergency!* continued to air through 1977. All told, the series consisted of 129 one-hour episodes and six two-hour 'Movies of the Week'. *Emergency!* was often ranked among the ten most-watched shows in the country, and its national audience averaged about 30 million viewers per episode.[39]

The popularity of *Emergency!* coincided with the explosive expansion of paramedic services. As mentioned above, 12 paramedic units (some of dubious legality) were operating in a few states in 1971. In 1974, President Ford signed the Emergency Medical Services Act into law. That law established funds for which local communities could apply for the purposes of establishing or improving their emergency medical services systems. The Senate Report on the Act identified the requirements that applications for funding had to meet for communities to receive funding. Barely two years after *Emergency!* went on the air, paramedic services had moved from a scarce and sometimes illegal resource to a requirement for receiving federal funds:

> The importance of adequate training of the paraprofessional, who in most instances is the first person at the scene of the emergency, cannot be overemphasized. . . . These individuals on the emergency scene . . . are capable of providing lifesaving care and utilizing complex equipment essential to save the patient from death and protect him from serious disability.[40]

With the aid of federal funding, by the end of 1975 (during the first three years that *Emergency!* was on the air), 46 of the 50 American states had enacted laws

[38] Page, n 16 above, 52. Cinader became so knowledgeable about paramedic operations that an article in one of the industry's leading magazines on the quality of LA County paramedic services includes the transcript of an interview with Cinader. See 'Paramedics Interview: The Los Angeles County-Wide Paramedic System', *Paramedics International* at 10 (January/February 1978). Ironically, Cinader's reactions to these experiences reflect both *Emergency!*'s influence in the development of paramedic programmes as well as its negative effects on the Los Angeles County programme: 'The Emergency! TV show has given the Los Angeles program such worldwide recognition that the people involved with the L.A. paramedic program have become rather smug and arrogant about it, having convinced themselves that they have the best of all possible systems'. Ibid, 37.

[39] 'Honoring Emergency Services in Long Beach', *Newsday*, Nassau and Suffolk Edition, 10 May 2000, A–30. Different members of the *Emergency!* cast appeared on at least four covers of *TV Guide*, a popular national weekly magazine that provides programme listings and TV-related articles.

[40] Senate Report No 93-397, n 11 above, 2559.

authorizing paramedic services.[41] By the end of the decade, about one half of all Americans lived within ten minutes of a paramedic unit.[42]

An analysis of *Emergency!*'s influence on the rapid expansion of paramedic services must begin with the acknowledgement of the familiar bromide that 'correlation does not equal causation'. That is, *Emergency!* may not have played an independent role in the development of paramedic services but rather its popularity may have reflected the same interest in paramedic services that produced their spread throughout the country. However, ample evidence supports a conclusion that the TV show was a primary factor that fuelled the legal changes that allowed paramedic services to develop and expand.

One of these factors is the two hour pilot episode of *Emergency!* that aired nationally in February, 1972 and set the tone for the rest of the series. That pilot episode was in essence a two hour plea for the legalization of paramedic services. The show opens with firefighters rushing to the scene of a warehouse fire; the scene is similar to those now shown almost every evening on typical local news programmes across the country. Later in the episode, a Battalion Chief tries to talk Fireman Jim Gage (Randolph Mantooth) into becoming part of a 'special training program' to become a paramedic (the term is at this point so unfamiliar that Gage cannot pronounce it properly). Gage initially refuses: 'I don't want to be an ambulance attendant'. However, Gage is the firefighter who had unsuccessfully tried to save the life of the electrical worker whose death is described in the prologue above. Realizing that the worker would have survived had he been given medical treatment immediately, Gage decides to become trained as a paramedic. He is also partly influenced by Roy DeSoto (Kevin Tighe), a firefighter who has just completed the very first paramedic training course. Roy tells Gage how important paramedics can become, but also warns him that the medical procedures he will be taught might be useless because current law does not allow its use by non-physicians. Roy also tells Gage about a proposed law then pending in the California state legislature that if enacted would allow paramedics to give emergency aid. This law, Roy tells Gage, would be 'the most important advance in emergency medicine in the last 50 years'.[43]

Enactment of the new law is far from certain, however. Dr Brackett (Robert Fuller) is the state's most highly regarded specialist in emergency medicine. The bill's chief sponsor, State Senator Wolski (Jack Kruschen) tells Dr Brackett that his support is crucial if the proposal is to become law. Like many of his real-life counterparts, Dr Brackett is initially quite strongly paramedic-phobic. His nurse (and lover—this is TV, after all) Dixie McCall (Julie London) pleads with him to support the bill but Dr Brackett is adamant: 'I spent 12 years in school and I'm still

[41] Page, n 16 above, 139. [42] *Making a Difference: The History of Modern EMS*, n 30 above.

[43] The legislation alluded to in the show is undoubtedly the 'Wadsworth-Townsend Paramedic Act of 1970', Cal Health and Safety Code Sec 1480, which authorized trained paramedics to give specified medical treatment. The Act was clearly experimental, however, since it was valid for only two years, and only in Los Angeles County.

learning my trade. I'm not putting amateurs out on the street. One paramedic will kill someone, there will be a huge malpractice suit and that will be the end of the program.'

In true melodramatic fashion, the turning point occurs when Gage, Roy and Nurse McCall arrive at the scene of a single-car rollover accident. Their rescue truck is fully loaded with paramedic equipment, but they have no legal authorization to use any of it. The occupants of the car have life-threatening injuries, and a bad situation becomes worse when Nurse McCall is critically hurt in the rescue process. Gage and Roy call in to Dr Brackett and ask for his medical advice. Dr Brackett instructs them to do nothing until medical help arrives. Gage and Roy heroically ignore his instructions: 'To hell with orders'. They render illegal emergency treatment and save everyone's lives.

A few days later, Dr Brackett has had a change of heart, so to speak. He appears before the state Senate committee considering the paramedic bill and testifies passionately in support of passage: 'You are all in danger. If an earthquake or a bomb hits, all an ambulance or fireman can do is cart you off to where a doctor is waiting. I'd like to see everyone treated by a doctor, but people die by the hundreds every year because of the lack of time. This bill will save lives.'

No sooner does the committee hearing end than Dr Brackett is called to a construction site where a large tunnel has collapsed, trapping and injuring hundreds of workers. Gage and Roy are on the scene, and come upon one worker who has suffered cardiac arrest and is near death. Their defibrillator is close at hand, but in the absence of legal authorization they are reluctant to use it. They radio Dr Brackett, who tells them to go ahead, they need to save the man's life. They use the defibrillator and the worker survives. When he arrives, Dr Brackett offers Roy and Gage 'my highest congratulations'. The show concludes with a weary Gage and Roy reading the afternoon paper's headline: 'Paramedic Bill Passes, Governor Signs Bill'.

As this summary suggests, what may be most striking about the pilot episode of *Emergency!* is the salience of legal issues. When Gage signs up for paramedic training, he is advised that existing laws forbid him from using the training he will be given, and that enactment of the pending paramedic legislation would be the 'most important advance in emergency medicine in the last 50 years'. Dr Brackett opposes paramedics in part because an inevitable huge malpractice lawsuit will be the end of the programme. A state legislator is one of the show's key characters. Throughout the show he advises Gage, Roy and Dr. Brackett of the political difficulties that the paramedic authorization bill faces, and the show depicts the legislative process at work as Brackett testifies before a state Senate committee. Finally, the show's final image, the newspaper headline trumpeting the bill's passage, is of the law's triumph. Thus, viewers of *Emergency!*'s pilot episode were certainly made aware not only of the benefits of paramedic services, but also of the scope and nature of the legal changes that had to occur if paramedic services were to exist.

The legal issues depicted in *Emergency!*'s pilot episode accurately reflected the legal reforms that made paramedic services a reality. Most importantly, the new laws that were adopted in one state after another between 1971–1975 insured that the performance of medical procedures by licensed paramedics did not constitute the crime of 'unauthorized practice of medicine'. Medical procedures that these new laws typically authorized paramedics to perform included cardiac defibrillation, intravenous therapy, the administration of drugs and the use of ventilation techniques.[44]

On the civil side, the development of paramedic services also depended on recognition that paramedics should not be judged under the same standards of care applicable to physicians. Thus, many new laws provided immunity from liability for paramedics who carried out their tasks in good faith in emergency circumstances, unless they were grossly negligent.[45]

Especially considering the significant challenges confronting proponents of paramedic services and the paucity of such services as of 1971, the fact that nearly every state in the country had authorized paramedic programmes during the first three years that *Emergency!* was on the air is powerful circumstantial evidence that the show was a primary catalyst in their growth. *Emergency!*'s influence was especially likely to have been strong because the show was a popular one that aired weekly, and the pilot episode stressed the need for paramedics and the legal changes that would have to occur were paramedic services to exist.

Further evidence of *Emergency!*'s influence is provided by fire department officials and others with first-hand knowledge of the development of paramedic services. Foremost among these experts is Chief James O Page. Chief Page was the LA County fire official who helped design the county's earliest paramedic services and worked with Cinader in creating the TV show. Thereafter, Chief Page set up North Carolina's state-wide emergency medical services programme,[46] and helped to draft the Model State Emergency Medical Services Statute. In addition, Chief Page has written a book and prepared a videotape detailing the history of paramedic services and has studied paramedics as a fire department official and an attorney for more than 30 years.[47] Thus, Page is uniquely qualified to assess the role of the TV show in furthering the legalization of paramedic programmes. Chief Page summarizes *Emergency!*'s role thus:

> While Congress and the states were debating how best to attack the problems of accidental death and disability, a form of public education was about to be introduced to America and the world on entertainment television. . . . When the world premiere of 'Emergency!' first broadcast in December of 1971, there were 12 paramedic rescue units in the entire country. Ten years later, more than half of all Americans were within 10 minutes of a paramedic. That simply would not have happened without the impact of 'Emergency!' All of a sudden,

[44] 'Emergency Medical Services at Midpassage', n 18 above, 41.

[45] ibid, 43; James E George, *Law and Emergency Care* (1980) 60.

[46] Page, n 16 above, 139.

[47] For example, while the Executive Director of the Lakes Area Emergency Medical Services, Page prepared the *National Study of Paramedic Law and Policy, 1975–1976*.

a whole generation of kids announced that they wanted to be paramedics when they grew up.[48]

Of course, a legitimate question is whether the fact that Chief Page helped to create *Emergency!* may have led him to overestimate the show's influence. However, many others who had no involvement with the TV show echo Page's views. For example, the Editor/Publisher of one of the largest magazines for paramedic professionals wrote that: 'This TV show resulted in widespread public acceptance of the paramedic program . . . throughout the world'.[49] An article in *Newsweek* discussing the emerging specialty of emergency medicine noted that 'the television series "Emergency!" helped create a national demand for such services'.[50]

Similarly, a Dallas Fire Chief had this to say:

I think that this show has had significant impact on Emergency Medical Services, and paramedics in general across the country. I don't think that the fact that it is based on the Los Angeles County Fire Department paramedic system detracted in any way . . . I think personally that the 'Emergency!' TV program probably has done more for paramedics throughout the country than any other one item.[51]

Further support for *Emergency!*'s influence on paramedic programmes comes from an Arizona fire department official:

It was not until after the popular series 'Emergency!' in 1972, however, that most fire departments initiated emergency medical services. The show greatly influenced the public, which then demanded the service.[52]

Missouri fire department officials Brandes and Zaitz said much the same thing at festivities celebrating 20 years of paramedic services in that state. They had remained paramedics during the entire 20 years, and 'insisted that a popular television drama of that era had played just as big a role (as pressure from the federal government). The show, "Emergency!," featured tales of professionally trained paramedics in Los Angeles. The people here who watched it could see what other places had—and could compare it with what we had.'[53]

Of course, in addition to the accounts of paramedic professionals, the legislative history of statutes legalizing paramedic services (including statements of legislators and testimony presented to legislators) would provide additional evidence of

[48] *Making a Difference: The History of Modern EMS*, n 30 above. Chief Page reiterated this opinion during a personal telephone conversation with the author on 13 November 2002.

[49] Ron Simmons, *Paramedics International* 11 (January/February 1978).

[50] 'It's an Emergency!', *Newsweek*, 21 November 1977, 105.

[51] 'Dallas Paramedics System', Interview with Division Chief Bill Roberts, *Paramedics International* 37 (Fall 1977). According to Chief Roberts, the TV show's popularization of paramedic services was a mixed blessing: 'I guess that the only negative thing that comes to mind is as a result of the TV show is the fact that, with a lot of people watching it, some of the ridiculous calls that the TV paramedics have to respond to are similar to some of the calls that we get called out on'.

[52] Gary Morris, '15 Years of Paramedic Engines', *Fire Chief* 41 (May 1993).

[53] 'Old Guard—Six Paramedics Mark 20th Anniversary, to be Honored at Event', *St. Louis Post-Dispatch*, 9 January 1995, 18.

Emergency!'s impact on the legislation that legitimated and expanded paramedic services. One such piece of evidence consists of a September 1972 letter from United States Senator Alan Cranston to Jack Webb, whose company produced the TV show. After describing legislation that he had introduced authorizing paramedic services, Cranston wrote as follows:

> Jack, your 'Emergency!' series fired the public imagination and was the harbinger of a medical idea whose time, I believe, has come . . . 'Emergency!' has dramatized the potential of the paramedic. I hope the House of Representatives and the President will now follow the lead of 100 Senators—and Jack Webb. Thank you for the good work, Jack. And congratulations to you and all the people connected with 'Emergency!'[54]

Legislative history at the state level is notoriously difficult to locate, especially when statutes are as old as 30 years. Nevertheless, brief snippets from hearings held by the California state assembly's Health Committee suggest that awareness of the TV show may have helped prompt the re-enactment in 1972 of the state's path-breaking Wedworth-Townsend Paramedic Act. During a hearing that took place in Los Angeles, Assemblyman Richard Hayden stated as follows:

> I don't listen to television very much but I did see one broadcast on this emergency program which fascinated me a little bit, primarily because Larry Townsend [another assemblyman on the Health Committee] told me about the program one day up in Sacramento. But what are the liability aspects when a paramedic goes beyond his instructions. It so happens that that particular program was based on that.[55]

At another point during that same hearing, a paramedic explains medical procedures to the committee members and indicates that 'underneath this unit is the defibrillator which is used quite a bit on the show "Emergency!" '[56]

As time has passed, *Emergency!* continues to be recognized as a primary influence on the development of paramedic programmes.[57] For example, in the year 2000, the president of the American College of Emergency Physicians recognized 'the significant role the TV series "Emergency!" played in raising public awareness of emergency care and promoting the early history and development of modern EMS'.[58] That same year, another story noted that: 'In the early 1970's, the NBC television series "Emergency!" changed the face of emergency services around the world, inspiring thousands of people to become firefighters and emergency

[54] The language quoted in the text was taken from the following website in April 2003: http://www.emergencyfans.com/basement/articles/abouttheproduction.htm.

[55] 'Interim Hearing on Emergency Medical Services', Assembly Committee on Health, 11 October 1972, 23. Assemblyman Hayden referred to an episode of *Emergency!* entitled 'Decision'. The episode first aired on 16 September 1972, and one of its plot lines depicted Roy treating an injured man without medical supervision, causing the man's personal physician to attack the paramedic programme.

[56] ibid, 59.

[57] As of the year 2000, *Emergency!* was 'still running on the TV Land cable channel and draws a million viewers a day, five days a week'. See 'Honoring Emergency Services in Long Beach', *Newsday*, Nassau and Suffolk Edition, 10 May 2000, A-30; ' "Emergency!" Star Draws a Crowd of Faithful Fans', *Chicago Sun-Times*, 7 May 2000, 27 ('The show is credited with creating demand for on-site medical treatment').

[58] Statement of Dr Michael Rapp, *Dayton Daily News*, 12 May 2000.

medical providers, and creating an enhanced awareness of the need for advanced on-site emergency care.'[59] Another indication of the programme's contribution to paramedic services is that in the year 2000, a fully restored 'Engine 51', the paramedic vehicle created for the TV show and featured in all of its episodes, became part of the Smithsonian American History Museum in Washington, DC.

Of course, legalization of paramedic services across the country would have been useless without a cadre of qualified paramedics. And in addition to influencing the development of paramedic services, *Emergency!* created in many viewers the desire to become paramedics. For example, one long term paramedic stated that: 'About the age of 16 or 17 I got my first exposure to "Emergency!" and Johnny and Roy popping by cars and saving lives and really at that moment I knew I was hooked'.[60]

Looking backwards from the year 2000, Long Beach Deputy Fire Commissioner Scott Kamins tells much the same story:

> I remember watching that show [*Emergency!*] when I was 10 years old, and it is definitely what pushed me into fire services. There were hardly any emergency service units in local fire departments back then in the early 1970's, and it was this show that made people want to have such teams in their community while at the same time making it an attractive career path.[61]

Kamins' thoughts are echoed by Tim Stokes, the Commander of Chicago's Fire Department, who stated that *Emergency!* was filled with:

> excitement and adrenaline. That all got me motivated. I think I failed health in high school, but I graduated at the top of my class in paramedic school.[62]

Finally, a reporter who interviewed a number of firefighters who spent a busy fire season in 2002 responding to a string of wildland fires in California noted that: 'For some, the compulsion to fight fires started with TV's "Emergency!" They wanted to be Johnny Gage or Roy DeSoto, rushing on Rescue Squad 51 to Rampart General.' One firefighter who was interviewed for the story stated that, 'I was one of those kids who grew up watching "Emergency!" I know that sounds trite, but I looked at that and said, "That's the coolest thing ever." I liked Johnny Gage, because he was always playing with people.'[63]

A cross-country promotional tour may have been the final event that cemented *Emergency!*'s influence on the rapid growth of paramedic services. After *Emergency!*'s initial season on the air, 'there were still thousands of communities where the "Emergency!" TV series was perceived as mere Hollywood fantasy—a

[59] 'Emergency! Fest to Kick Off National EMS Week and Celebrate Groundbreaking TV Show; May 15th Event Expected to Draw Thousands from Across North America', PR Newswire Association, 2 May 2000.

[60] Statement of AJ Heightman in *Making a Difference: The History of Modern EMS*, n 30 above.

[61] 'Honoring Emergency Services in Long Beach', n 57 above.

[62] ' "Emergency!" Star Draws a Crowd of Faithful Fans', n 57 above.

[63] 'Diary of a Fire Season: A Season in Purgatory', *Los Angeles Times Magazine*, 15 December 2002, 21.

medical version of "Star Trek." '[64] However, the next season of the show was to feature a new 'Engine 51' of the type that the Los Angeles Fire Department had just purchased. Instead of shipping the TV show's new 'Engine 51' across the country from New York to Universal Studios in Hollywood by rail or truck, a combination of actors from the show and actual paramedics drove it on a cross-country tour. Stop after stop resulted in large crowds who came to see the actors and the demonstrations of paramedic techniques. Coverage by newspapers and on television stations furthered the tour's impact. Engine 51's arrival at Universal Studios in Hollywood 'ended a most unusual chapter in the history of the paramedic concept . . . The big red truck had served as the backdrop for an important message that was delivered to millions throughout the nation.'[65]

Accounting for *Emergency!*'s Influence

This paper has argued that *Emergency!* was a primary catalyst for the explosive development of paramedic programmes in the early 1970s. Obviously, for the show to have had this impact a number of other factors had to be present as well. For example:

- Medical technology had to have advanced to the stage that trained professionals could use mobile equipment to render treatment that had previously been within the exclusive domain of doctors.
- The federal government as well as state and local governments had to be willing to provide the funding to train and hire paramedics and the equipment necessary for them to do the job.
- A pool of potential paramedics was available. In this instance, many of the first paramedics had served as medics in the Army during the Vietnam War.[66]

Crucial as such factors may have been, paramedic programmes may not have developed, at least in anything like the rapid time frame in which they did, without the existence of *Emergency!* The TV show 'helped convince the public that they are entitled to the highest levels of emergency medical aid technologically available.'[67] This section of the paper speculates on the processes that might account for the TV show's extraordinary influence.

In his essay suggesting that popular culture can lead to legal change, Lawrence Friedman remarked that a social theory of law ought to address the question of how social forces affect the legal system, and that popular legal culture was a mechanism

[64] Page, n 16 above, 135. [65] ibid, 137.

[66] See 'Paramedics and the Medical Manpower Shortage: The Case for Statutory Legitimization' (1971) 60 *Georgetown LJ* 157, 158, n 9 ('Most physician assistant programs are designed for trainees with medical backgrounds from among discharged medical corpsmen of the Armed Forces, registered nurses, and students in allied or other health professions').

[67] Byron Toma, 'The Decline of Emergency Medical Services Coordination in California: Why Cities Are at War With Counties Over Illusory Ambulance Monopolies' (1994) 23 *Southwestern UL Rev* 285, 287.

capable of producing legal change.[68] But what elements are needed if that mechanism is to work? Why did *Emergency!* have such a demonstrable effect on the legal system while most other works of popular culture are valuable chiefly for *reflecting* popular attitudes towards law, lawyers and the legal system?

Friedman's essay does not provide a schema that might suggest answers to these more specific types of questions. However, Malcolm Gladwell's book, *The Tipping Point*,[69] does suggest possible answers. For Gladwell, tipping points are 'mysterious changes that mark everyday life'.[70] These changes typically happen not gradually, but at one dramatic moment.[71] Gladwell identifies three possible agents of change: the Law of the Few, the Stickiness Factor and the Power of Context.[72] Evaluating *Emergency!* according to these three factors helps to suggest specific elements that allowed the show to exercise such a powerful influence on the legal system.

The 'Law of the Few' means that major social changes are typically produced by a small number of people whose sociability, energy and knowledge allow them to exert great influence on their peers.[73] Gladwell refers to such people as 'connectors', because they regularly come into contact with many different kinds of people.[74] Most of us have to 'rely on them [connectors] to give us access to opportunities and worlds to which we both belong'.[75]

Emergency!'s Gage and Roy appear to qualify as connectors as Gladwell uses the term. They came into electronic contact with about 30 million people a week, performed daring rescues and were trained paramedics, giving them a special kind of knowledge and ability that few people were even aware of in the early 1970s. Moreover they were firefighters, an occupation that has always enjoyed high prestige.[76] That so many paramedics attribute their career choice to watching Gage's and Roy's weekly exploits testifies to their success as connectors.[77]

[68] See Lawrence Friedman, 'Law, Lawyers, and Popular Culture' (1989) 98 *Yale LJ* 1579, 1583–1584.

[69] Malcolm Gladwell, *The Tipping Point—How Little Things Can Make a Big Difference* (2000). The references in this essay are to the Back Bay paperback edition published in 2002.

[70] ibid, 7.

[71] ibid, 9. What Gladwell means by 'one dramatic moment' seems to be a definable and relatively short period of time rather than literally a single moment in time. For instance, one of his examples of a tipping point is that New York's murder rate fell by two-thirds over a period of five years. Ibid, 7. By this measure, the dramatic growth of paramedic services in the early to mid 1970s clearly qualifies as a 'tipping point'.

[72] ibid, 29.

[73] ibid, 21.

[74] ibid, 46.

[75] ibid, 54.

[76] For example, a 1968 public opinion poll conducted by the Opinion Research Corporation indicated that about half of all American adults believed that firefighters were underpaid. See *Westlaw Document 17-04-54-728.doc.* Moreover, a 1978 resolution of the US House of Representatives (Public Law 95-463) designated 7 October 1979 as 'Firefighters' Memorial Sunday', citing the 'courageous firefighters [who] have protected the lives and dreams of their neighbors from the ravages of fire since the beginning of civilization' and noting that 'numerous churches and many denominations have indicated a desire to participate in a designated memorial Sunday honoring these consecrated firefighters for their ultimate sacrifices'. Firefighters continue to enjoy high prestige. A Gallup Poll conducted at the end of 2001 (after the bombings of the World Trade Center on 11 September 2001) indicated that Americans ranked firefighters first among all professionals for 'honesty and ethics'. See http://www.gallup.com/subscription/?m+f&c_id-10916 (website visited on 22 July 2003).

[77] An unusual measure of Gage's influence as a 'connector' is that 'Gage' became an extremely popular first name in the early 1990s, bestowed on their babies by mothers who had watched *Emergency!* 20 years earlier. See 'Professor Tracks Where Babies' Names Come From', *Omaha World Herald*, 24 March 1997, 1.

The 'Stickiness Factor' refers to messages that are so memorable that they spur those who hear it to action.[78] Interestingly for purposes of this essay, a television show, in this case the children's programme *Sesame Street*, is one of Gladwell's primary examples of how to create a 'sticky message'.[79] According to Gladwell, *Sesame Street* demonstrates that 'if you paid careful attention to the structure and format of your material, you could dramatically enhance stickiness'.[80]

Of course, the factors that may have made *Emergency!* sticky enough to stimulate the explosive growth of paramedic services must be different from those that have allowed the lessons of *Sesame Street* to stick in the minds of pre-school age children. However, one common factor is that both appear to have been *designed* to be sticky. *Emergency!*'s pilot episode, for example, plays almost as a primer on the need for paramedic services, the types of emergency aid that paramedics would be able to render when permitted to do so, and the need for legislative action to allow paramedic services to operate. These same messages found their way into later episodes of *Emergency!* and likely increased the series' 'stickiness'.[81]

Gladwell's description of a social science experiment designed by Leventhal in the 1960s may also suggest why *Emergency!*'s message may have been sticky. In the experiment, college students were much more likely to get tetanus shots when the messages they were given about the dangers of tetanus included information on where and when tetanus shots were available on campus. By contrast, few students got tetanus shots in response to messages that focused only on the dangers of tetanus, even when they were presented in gory detail.[82] What made the messages sticky, according to Gladwell, was information that told the students 'how to fit the tetanus stuff into their lives'; the information changed 'an abstract lesson in medical risk' into 'a practical and personal piece of medical advice'. In much the same way, *Emergency!* combined abstract information about the need for paramedic services with practical illustrations of how to bring about the legal changes that could make the services possible. Perhaps the latter element was the key to *Emergency!*'s stickiness.

A final element tending to explain *Emergency!*'s stickiness emerges from Gladwell's discussion of a second children's television show called *Blue's Crews*. He considers *Blue's Crews* to be even stickier than *Sesame Street*, because *Blue's Crews* has a narrative structure that grows out of children's own experiences.[83] *Emergency!*

[78] Gladwell, n 69 above, 92.

[79] *Sesame Street* is a long-running television show that aims at increasing the reading, mathematical and social skills of pre-school age children. Featuring a mix of live performers and puppets, the show focuses on such basic skills as letter sounds and counting.

[80] Gladwell, n 69 above, 110.

[81] For example, an episode called 'Problem' (aka 'Decision') first aired on 16 September 1972, during the show's second season. During this episode, Roy defends the role of paramedics to an angry doctor whose patient Roy has just saved from death. Also during the second season, a show called 'Trainee' first aired on 11 November 1972. In this episode, Roy stresses the importance of paramedic training to a new trainee who once served in Vietnam, after the trainee attempts a procedure that would have killed a victim if Roy had not intervened.

[82] Gladwell, n 69 above, 96–98.

[83] ibid, 121.

may have been sticky for much the same kind of reason. Nearly everyone who watched *Emergency!* had personal or vicarious experiences concerning coronary and traumatic emergencies, and the show's messages about the critical importance of immediate medical care were consistent with their own experiences.

The 'Power of Context' is the third factor that Gladwell associates with the development of tipping points. The Power of Context refers to circumstances in the environment that produce social changes, and such changes can be brought about by 'tinkering with the smallest details of the immediate environment'.[84] Moreover, big social changes are typically the result of 'many small movements' moving in the same direction rather than one single movement.[85]

As with Gladwell's first two factors, the context in which *Emergency!* arose may help to explain its ability to stimulate the development of paramedic services. As depicted in the TV show, huge benefits would flow from making a small environmental change. That is, the technology that made emergency medical care rapid and mobile was already in existence. Moreover, non-physicians had already been trained to use the technology successfully, and training programmes were already in place to provide cadres of additional technicians. The only missing piece was legislation authorizing paramedics to function, but such legislation had already been drafted and all that was needed was to get it passed and signed. The paramedic future apparently required only a small environmental change.

Finally, that change did not have to occur all at once, on a national scale. The tipping point with respect to paramedic services came about through legislative changes in individual states. For example, Hawaii, Illinois, Oklahoma, and Wisconsin formally authorized paramedic services in 1972. Alaska, Georgia, Idaho, Indiana, Minnesota, New Jersey, Oregon, Texas and Virginia followed suit in 1973, and so forth.[86] Thus, just as Gladwell would have predicted, *Emergency!* stimulated the national development of paramedic services one state at a time.

Conclusion

As Chief Jim Page acknowledges, 'The precise impact of the television program [*Emergency!*] . . . will never be known'. However, perhaps every reader of this paper knows of at least one relative or close friend who has needed and been promptly attended to by a paramedic. May this paper help such readers remember that a TV show may deserve much of the credit for the paramedic's existence.

[84] ibid, 146. [85] ibid, 192. [86] See Page, n 31 above, Table 1.

Procedural Unfairness in Real and Film Trials: Why Do Audiences Understand Stories Placed in Foreign Legal Systems?

Stefan Machura

Introduction

The American movie *Hart's War* (2002) provides a striking example of the self-reference of film. The German commander of a Second World War prison camp asks the American POWs whether they are going to hold a trial just like in their American movies. In this scene, *Hart's War* plays with the twenty-first century audience's memory of earlier films. However, a member of the film team with an excellent grasp of film history might have known that American courtroom scenes did in fact appear on German screens in the days of Nazi rule. In 1939, for example, the Nazi propaganda film *Sensationsprozess Casilla* used conventions of American courtroom dramas to denounce the American legal system and society.[1] Hollywood courtroom dramas are sold worldwide, and they apparently influence the cinema of other countries. European films almost invariably fall back on the popular storylines of their American counterparts.[2] That is to say, films react to prior films. These form the main reference, not the actual law which provides just elements to be used by the film artists. To formulate it in Niklas Luhmann's terms, law films belong to the system of art and not to the system of law.[3]

However, it has to be explained what factors contribute to the universal success of American cinema. This article tries to figure out one reason for this. Regardless of strong differences between national legal systems, law films from one country are usually sufficiently understood by audiences almost everywhere. Part of the explanation for this may be that people, at least throughout the Western world,

[1] For a discussion of this film, see P Drexler, 'The German Courtroom Film During the Nazi Period: Ideology, Aesthetics, Historical Context' in S Machura and P Robson (eds), *Law and Film* (Oxford: 2001) 64, 75–76.

[2] S Machura and S Ulbrich, 'Law in Film: Globalizing the Hollywood Courtroom Drama' in Machura and Robson, n 1 above, 117.

[3] ibid, compare N Luhmann, *Die Kunst der Gesellschaft* (Frankfurt: 1997) for a systems analysis of art.

share similar criteria for procedural fairness or unfairness.[4] This article combines perspectives from two distinct camps of scholarship.

(1) The law and cinema movement started to develop in the 1980s.[5] Experts on law and—to a lesser degree—film scholars engaged in hermeneutical analyses of such cultural representations of law. They frequently encountered films in which neither justice in terms of outcomes nor fairness in terms of the process leading to a legal decision are realized.

(2) Distributive justice and procedural fairness are basic terms in social justice research. This field of scholarly interest opened up after John Rawls' book *A Theory of Justice* became widely known.[6] Rawls was interested in how the founding principles of a just society can be detected. Fair procedures might lead to fair principles. The philosopher's interest, however, was not in investigating existing procedures. It was not until later that the pioneering publication *Procedural Justice* by John Thibaut and Laurens Walker laid the foundation for empirical research into the criteria and consequences of people's perception of fairness.[7] This kind of research is mainly quantitative and social psychologists have a leading role. Its basic distinction is between procedural justice (hereafter: fairness) and distributive justice.

This article argues that fairness is of prime importance in films about law. Legal institutions, their procedures and their representatives, whether real[8] or fictional, are evaluated according to basic standards of fairness. In legal films, deviations from these criteria create suspense and attract viewers. Typical film plots reinforce the social norms of fairness.

Fairness and Unfairness—Main Topics in Law Films

Both film audiences and film makers share a fascination for fairness in legal procedures, its endangered nature and the overcoming of prejudice, forged evidence, ignorance, or illicit intervention from outside. Recently, more than six million people watched the German TV film *Für immer verloren* (2003, *Forever Lost*). This drama depicts the suffering of the innocent mother-of-three Sabine at the hands of

[4] By 'Western world', I mean cultures and groups which share principally the following assumptions: separation of courts, politics and religion, human rights, rule of law and democracy. Also, one must add, at least some exposure to the Jewish-Greek-Christian cultural heritage. Other factors contributing to an understanding of law films from other countries are of course: (1) Viewers have almost certainly seen law films before with similar situations. (2) Movie lawyers give rudimentary explanation of their actions. (3) Most people are somehow familiar with the setting of courts and have some understanding of the social roles at a court.

[5] For a selected bibliography see S Machura and P Robson, 'Law and Film: Introduction' in Machura and Robson, n 1 above.

[6] J Rawls, *A Theory of Justice* (Cambridge, Mass: 1971).

[7] J Thibaut and L Walker, *Procedural Justice* (Hillsdale, NJ: 1975).

[8] By 'real' I do not venture to declare films as something of a lesser reality than actual legal proceedings. They are better understood as another type of reality.

the Turkish justice system.[9] Öcelit, her Turkish prosecutor, is obsessed by the idea of seeing her punished for smuggling drugs and having her in prison within his reach. He even goes so far as to ignore a statement given by Sabine's husband about the real perpetrator. The prosecutor elicits an argument against Sabine from her husband's testimony. Rumour has it that the Turkish embassy in Germany had been concerned about the country's image.[10] The Turkish newspaper *Milliyet*, which is much read among immigrant workers, even called for a boycott of the TV station.[11] Other examples of unfairness in films are easily found. In a number of films on Nazi Germany, judges and prosecutors are depicted as the biased representatives of a dictatorial regime. French and Italian movies typically show how a righteous judge finds himself isolated in a corrupt apparatus. The American movies *. . . And Justice For All* (1979) and *The Star Chamber* (1983) deal with forms of conspiracy among judges. Frank Galvin, the protagonist of *The Verdict* (1982), has to fight a biased judge as well as a demonic defence lawyer in order finally to win his civil suit with the help of the jury. Movies such as *Erin Brockovich* (2000) and *A Civil Action* (1998) dramatize the disparity between small plaintiff lawyers on the one hand and powerful law firms representing big business on the other. Fairness and unfairness appear in different forms over and over again in law films.

In 2003, the American Film Institute declared lawyer figure Atticus Finch from *To Kill a Mockingbird* the most outstanding popular hero in film history.[12] As readers most certainly know, this movie criticizes blatant discrimination against black Americans. An innocent young black finds himself in a hopeless situation when he is accused of an alleged rape of a white woman. Finch fails to win his case before an ignorant racist Southern jury. However, his character appears even better. Audiences tend to measure lawyers and legal institutions by general ideas of what they should be like in a rule of law environment. Finch comes close to the ideal, despite losing for his client in the end. That legal process and lawyers are legitimized by lawyer films was affirmed by Greenfield and Osborn.[13] The films show '. . . good people working within a fair system or, at least, a system that delivers justice in some shape or form'.[14] There are films on miscarriages of justice, but:

> The beauty of these films is that they do not disturb our faith in the law; the failings are those of individuals, normally police officers, who are shown as corrupt. The ideal of law is shown as subverted by individual or even communal dishonesty.[15]

Part of an explanation for the popularity of heroic lawyers like Atticus Finch or righteous detectives like Oberinspektor 'Derrick' (1973–1998) can be explained

[9] http://www.liljan98.de/mmws/walter/arbeit/verloren.html, visited 27 June 2003.

[10] Alexander Bartl, 'Dabei wollte sie nur schnell ein Souvenir kaufen', *Frankfurter Allgemeine Zeitung*, 28 April 2003.

[11] http://www.milliyet.com.tr/2002/10/29/guncel/gun02.html, visited 3 July 2003.

[12] http://www.afi.com/tv/pdf/handv100.pdf, visited 27 June 2003.

[13] Steve Greenfield and Guy Osborn, 'Where Cultures Collide: The Characterisation of Law and Lawyers in Film' (1995) 23 *Intl J of the Sociology of Law* 107, 120.

[14] S Greenfield, G Osborn, and P Robson, *Film and the Law* (London: 2001) 27.

[15] ibid.

by uneasy feelings towards the legal system.[16] Fatal decisions can always occur, partly because of flawed procedures, partly because of the wrong people in public functions.

Social Criteria for Fairness

Social justice researchers have identified criteria for fairness which are valid for almost all people in the Western world. Almost without exception, they are applied by workers in Hong Kong as well as by juvenile prisoners in Germany,[17] by American defendants as well as by Russian lay judges.[18] What constitutes fair procedures? Gerald Leventhal has identified six criteria.[19] Procedures appear to be unfair if they are not consistently applied to all cases and people. Furthermore, onlookers focus on the decision-maker's bias or absence of bias. They observe whether all relevant information is gathered before a decision is reached. Parties should have the opportunity to present their position (or should be represented in the process). There must be an opportunity to correct a decision and the proceedings should comply with social morality. Social psychologists Tom Tyler and E Allan Lind argue that fairness is of prime importance in interpersonal relations and that institutions and their representatives are mainly judged by criteria of procedural fairness.[20] A substantial body of research literature supports this assumption.[21] People are used to a 'fairness heuristic' in their dealings with various kinds of authorities.[22] They learn about the quality of their relation with an authority from the way they are treated. The individual performing a powerful role stands for the institution, for example the judge for the justice system.

[16] The German TV series *Derrick* is carefully constructed around the figure of a police inspector who never fails to comply with the strictest rules of correctness and accuracy. This also makes the series popular in countries like Russia, where the audience experiences their national police as unreliable and often brutal.

[17] TR Tyler, EA Lind and Yuen J Huo, 'The Relational Model of Authority: Social Categorization and Social Orientation Effects on the Psychology of Legitimacy', *American Bar Foundation Working Paper Series* (Chicago, 1995) no 9504 for the study on workers; Volkmar Haller and Stefan Machura, 'Procedural Justice at German Courts as Seen by Defendants and Juvenile Prisoners' (1995) 8 *Social Justice Research* 197.

[18] Tom R Tyler, 'Perceived Injustice in Defendants' Evaluations of their Courtroom Experience' (1984) 18 *Law and Society Rev* 51; Stefan Machura, 'Fairness, Justice and Legitimacy: Experiences of People's Judges in South Russia' (2003) 25 *Law and Policy* 123.

[19] GS Leventhal, 'What Should Be Done With Equity Theory?' in KJ Gergen, MS Greenberg and R H Willis (eds), *Social Exchange: Advances in Theory and Research* (New York: 1980) IX, 27.

[20] TR Tyler and EA Lind, 'A Relational Model of Authority in Groups' in M Zanna (ed), *Advances in Experimental Social Psychology* (New York: 1992) XXV, 115; TR Tyler and EA Lind, *Procedural Justice* in J Sanders and VL Hamilton (eds), *Handbook of Justice Research in Law* (New York: 2001) 65.

[21] For overviews: Stefan Machura, 'Introduction: Procedural Justice, Law and Policy' (1998) 20 *Law and Policy* 1; S Machura, *Fairneß und Legitimität* (Baden-Baden: 2001) 81–87.

[22] E Allan Lind, Carol T Kulik, Maureen Ambrose, and Maria V de Vera Park, 'Individual and Corporate Dispute Resolution: Using Procedural Fairness as a Decision Heuristic' (1993) 38 *Administrative Science Q* 224, 226.

This combines easily with a major cinematic feature. The medium of film depends strongly on personalization. So do films on lawyers, judges or public prosecutors, on paralegals and other staff of the legal system. Films as a combination of moving images, montage and sound direct the audience's attention away from the abstract legal rule to the individual case. Anthony Chase explicitly welcomes this and sees the emergence of a 'cinematic jurisprudence'.[23] The new jurisprudence should be more in conformity with the needs of the people. A certain sceptical attitude towards this development might be advisable, since there are multiple ways in which legal scholars may react.

Human suffering can be effectively expressed in films. A masterpiece such as *To Kill a Mockingbird* speaks out against racial discrimination. Even overtly commercial films such as *Für immer verloren* may call for social reform. But not only are the parties a centre of attention, viewers are also interested in the person of the decision-maker.[24] Judges, public prosecutors and lawyers are subject to a character test. Such constellations are essential to the drama as a form of art. In real and in fictional trials people observe the quality of the procedures and the integrity of the personnel. Social scientific research shows that the individual in power stands for the institution, the state, or even society. It is likely that recipients employ this heuristic when interpreting film characters. Therefore, criteria for fairness which are found in studies of legal institutions should be important for an audience's evaluation of filmic portrayals.

Social criteria for the fairness of judges have been studied in the United States,[25] in Germany and Russia.[26] Initially, it was not clear whether the Russians employed criteria similar to the other nationalities mentioned. A location at the eastern border of Europe was chosen for a test: lay judges in the South Russian province of Rostov on Don.[27] At the time of the study, Russian lay assessors at local courts (raionnyi courts)

[23] A Chase, *Movies on Trial. The Legal System on the Silver Screen* (New York: 2002) 30.

[24] A personalization may be a common characteristic of all sorts of visual legal communication: Klaus F Röhl and Stefan Ulbrich, 'Visuelle Rechtskommunikation' (2000) 21 *Zeitschrift für Rechtssoziologie* 355, 381–382.

[25] eg Tyler, n 18 above; TR Tyler, *Why People Obey the Law* (New Haven: 1990).

[26] Haller and Machura, n 17 above; Machura, *Fairneß*, n 21 above; Machura, n 18 above; S Machura in collaboration with D Donskow and O Litvinova, *Ehrenamtliche Richter in Südrussland* (Munster: 2003).

[27] The respondents were people's assessors who decided cases in 11 raionnyi courts, ie county or town district courts. Eight of the courts in the sample are located in Rostov on Don. Three other courts (Asowski, Neklinowski, Mjasnikowski) are located in the countryside near Rostov. The court of the harbour town Taganrog was also included in the sample. Between May and December 2001, court clerks distributed envelopes with questionnaires to the people's judges when they arrived in court. The clerks later collected the envelopes. All in all, 400 questionnaires were distributed to the courts in the sample: 160 to the eight Rostov courts, 180 to the three country courts, and 60 to Taganrog. The return rates (overall 37%) were very uneven from court to court. The return rate in Rostov was 66%, a highly acceptable rate. In Taganrog, the return rate was 18% and at the three country courts it was 17%. Most likely, the response rate calculated not with the questionnaires distributed to the court clerks but with the questionnaires actually offered to serving people's judges would be higher. From the 147 returned questionnaires, 72% came from Rostov courts, 18% from Taganrog and 17% from the country courts.

Table 1. Criteria for the fairness of the presiding judge to parties and defendants, perceptions of Russian lay assessors

		Answers in percent, 5 ranks						Other reactions, in percent		Spearman-Rho
		1	*2*	*3*	*4*	*5*		don't know	no answer	
Tried to be just to the parties	very	74	19	1	—	—	no	1	5	.40***
Weighed arguments in favour and against parties equally carefully	yes	82	12	1	—	—	no	1	5	.33***
Considered the evidence	yes	83	10	1	—	—	no	1	5	.27**
Gave parties opportunity to state their views	yes	81	12	1	—	—	no	2	4	.45***
Took time for deliberation#	very	29	26	18	12	1	not at all	4	10	.26**
Gathered enough evidence	yes	82	10	2	—	1	no	3	3	.35***
Protected the parties' rights	very	83	7	1	1	—	no	2	7	.27**
Neutrality#	very	80	6	2	1	1	no	3	7	.40***
Tried to clear up the causes	very	76	18	1	—	—	no	1	4	.45***
Honesty and correctness to the parties#	very	78	8	3	1	1	no	1	8	.43***
Tried not to annoy parties before the verdict	yes	74	11	3	1	3	no	2	7	.37***

$127 \leq n \leq 134$, ** $p < .01$ *** $p < .001$

#Items originally formulated negatively.

Spearman-Rho indicates correlation with the overall evaluation 'fairness of presiding judge to parties'. Percentages may not add up to 100 because of rounding.
Median underlined.

Source: Stefan Machura, 'Fairness, Justice and Legitimacy: Experiences of People's Judges in South Russia' (2003) 25 *Law and Policy* 123; S Machura in collaboration with D Donskow and O Litvinova, *Ehrenamtliche Richter in Südrussland* (Munster: 2003) 78.

were selected randomly to serve for 14 days as judges. The panel of judges consisted of two 'people's assessors' and the presiding professional judge. The presiding judge dominated the trial ('inquisitorial procedure'). Table 1 lists specific criteria for the behaviour of presiding judges towards parties. These criteria were significantly related to a general evaluation of the presiding judges' fairness to defendants in prior US and German studies.[28] Table 1 shows that these factors were correlated individually to how Russian lay assessors perceived the fairness of the presiding judge to the parties. When

[28] Tyler, n 18 above; Tyler, *Why People*, n 25 above; Machura, *Fairneß*, n 21 above, 104 and 219–220.

all these criteria are combined to an index variable,[29] it is significantly related to how the respondents evaluated the fairness of the presiding judge to the parties in the trials (Spearman-Rho = 46, $p < .001$, $n = 99$) and to how they perceived the fairness of the trials (Spearman-Rho = .41, $p < .001$, $n = 103$). The aspects in Table 1 can be traced back to four of the six fairness criteria of Leventhal—fair procedures are earmarked by unbiased decision makers who carefully gather the relevant information. The parties should have the opportunity to present their positions and the proceedings should comply with social morality.[30]

Previously, Leventhal, Thibaut and Walker had emphasized the opportunity for parties to state their view as the main criteria for procedural justice.[31] Later research questioned this particular assumption. Regarding law films it is interesting that parties usually have a good opportunity to state their view. This pattern is due to dramatic reasons and has its roots in film history. According to Nevins, law became a major topic with the replacement of silent movies by talkies.[32] Film makers used legal disputes to incorporate powerful speeches into their movies.

More on the level of the legal system, the rules governing legal procedures should be fair and there should be sufficient opportunity to appeal against a court decision. Rules governing trials are made by the legislator. They are applied, distorted, or supplemented at the local level. Appeals are provided by the general court system but are in fact also influenced by the stance of the judges. The evaluation of the fairness of courts is related to how procedural rules are perceived. In the Russian study, the respondents were asked for their opinion on the fairness of Russian courts to citizens. A statistical analysis (a logit model) showed two significant factors ($p < .001$, $N = 134$, $R^2 = .46$) accounting for perceived fairness of national courts to citizens. This variable was found to be related to how fair the lay assessors evaluated the treatment of the parties to be in the proceedings in which they served as lay judges (Beta = .46). And it was related to the perceived fairness of the procedural rules (Beta = .34).[33] Another aspect of fairness was highlighted by a study on German lay assessors at the court of Frankfurt. Here, the perceived correctability of court decisions contributed to the opinion on how fairly German courts are treating citizens.[34] Interestingly, Russian lay assessors were more sceptical than their German colleagues about the chance to appeal a court decision, reflecting a general public view in this country.[35] Correctability forms one of Leventhal's fairness criteria.[36]

[29] For the index 'fairness of the presiding judge to parties' a reliability test has been performed with Cronbach's alpha = .7667, n=103.

[30] Leventhal, n 19 above.

[31] Thibaut and Walker, n 7 above; John Thibaut and Lawrence Walker, 'A Theory of Procedure' (1978) 66 *California L Rev* 541.

[32] FM Nevins 'Through the Great Depression on Horseback' in J Denvir (ed), *Legal Reelism* (Urbana: 1996) 44, 45.

[33] Machura, n 18 above; Machura, Donskow and Litvinova, n 26 above, 64.

[34] Machura, *Fairneß*, n 21 above, 267.

[35] ibid, 266 for German respondents; Machura, n 18 above and Machura, Donskow and Litvinova, n 26 above, 61–62 for the Russian study.

[36] Leventhal, n 19 above.

Aspects of Fairness and Unfairness in Law Films

It seems more likely than not that such fairness criteria are relevant wherever people encounter legal authorities in reality as well as on the screen. There are plenty of examples of unfair judges in fictional films. For instance, the refusal to listen properly to the defendant's version is impressively depicted in John Ford's *Prisoner of Shark Island* (1936), where the defendants are generally treated as if they were worthless human beings. In this film, the US Secretary of War instructs his officer judges in person about the political nature of the impending trial. In Yves Boisset's *L'affaire Dreyfus* (1995), an officer messenger enters the tribunal's deliberation room and delivers the war minister's 'moral order' to read a secret dossier against Dreyfus. Also, French military authorities faked evidence and even sheltered the actual traitor. Judge Fleming in . . . *And Justice for All* (1979) and Judge Crusius in the German movie *Ein Richter in Angst* (1995, *A Judge in Fear*) are in the habit of rendering harsh verdicts out of prejudice, of depriving defendants and lawyers of their procedural rights and of submitting everyone lower on the social hierarchy to their dictatorial rule. Both films then show that behind the judges' straight law and order façade there is an ugly character that is capable of committing the most awful crimes.

For dramatic reasons, law films usually contrast a good with a bad figure.[37] Nicole Rafter wrote that a 'justice figure' and an 'injustice figure' are pitted against each other in films.

> Courtroom films usually include an injustice figure, the person responsible for creating or maintaining the gap between justice and man-made law. Most courtroom films also include a justice figure, a hero who tries to move man-made law ever closer to the ideal until it matches the justice template.[38]

For instance, in *Young Mr Lincoln* (1939) the later US President faces an outrageously zealous prosecutor. Paralegal *Erin Brockovich* (2000), rookie lawyer Rudy Baylor of *The Rainmaker* (1979) and numerous colleagues fight for the rights of their clients. Arguably, such fairness criteria as mentioned above also apply to lawyers. As a study on the evaluation of American lawyers by former clients concluded:

> . . . lawyers are perceived to have treated their clients with respect, to have been willing to talk about their problems in context, to have been responsive and supportive, to have listened to their views and taken them into consideration.[39]

Sometimes films expose an unfair treatment of clients by their attorneys. In the British film *Eight O'Clock Walk* (1953), the defendant's American wife Jill contacts

[37] Machura and Ulbrich, n 2 above, 124–125.

[38] N Rafter, *Shots in the Mirror. Crime Films and Society* (Oxford: 2000) 94.

[39] WLF Felstiner, B Petit, EA Lind and N Olson, 'The Effect of Lawyer Gender on Client Perception of Lawyer Behaviour' in U Schultz and G Shaw (eds), *Women in the World's Legal Profession* (Oxford: 2003) 23, 27–28.

lawyers to seek help.[40] But the legal professionals do not appear engaged in the case. What is worse, the defending barrister refuses to see her and her husband in prison, because he wants to preserve an 'objective view' on the case. Jill's opinion is that this:

> Means they are not even interested, I suppose it's because we are not paying anything. . . . Doctors—see you, talk to you, give you help. Lawyers—they stay on the outside and make you stay there, too.

One of the old English rules—as depicted by the movie—demanded that the barrister must not talk to the defendant. For if the defendant pleads not guilty but confesses to the barrister, the latter will be in an awkward situation. Being American Jill expects a lawyer to fight for the client searching for favourable evidence, as numerous Hollywood movie lawyers do in accordance with the role of the American lawyer in criminal trials. Finally she finds a young lawyer who discovers the real murderer.

The betrayal of clients also appears in movies. Sometimes films rectify the negation of rules by lawyers. *Cape Fear* (1991) is a significant example. Lawyer Sam Bowden withheld evidence in favour of his client. As Mike Nevins noted:

> . . . what precipitates the nightmare events is the attorney betraying professional ethics in order to keep his sociopath client from going free, Scorsese's film joins the roster of movies which radically condemn the legal system by hinging on acts which are justified dramatically, morally, indeed every way in the world except under the law.[41]

In lawyer films, rules are often broken for the sake of 'higher' values.[42] This scheme is used as a device to dramatize. But the film makers take pains carefully to construct a situation which calls for extraordinary measures. By this, they certify for the existence of fairness rules.

The good judge embodies the principle of fairness regardless of the person in front of his bench, like Judge Priest in John Ford's *The Sun Shines Bright* (1953).

> The judge is a Southern Democrat whose morning routine is to have a reveille recalling his days as a bugler in the Civil War in the Kentucky regiment. His political opponent, Horace Maydew, is standing in the upcoming election as judge. He is the local public prosecutor and a member of the Republican Party.[43]

Of course, this is the scene of an American comedy. One case involves the accusation of vagrancy. The viewer may think that Confederate veteran Judge Priest is going to sentence the accused young black banjoist oddly named US Grant Woodford. Investigating the case, Priest asks Woodford to play his banjo. To Priest's disapproval and to Maydew's delight, he chooses the Union marching

[40] Hal Erickson for Jill's nationality (http://www.blockbuster.com/bb/movie/details/0,7286, VID-V++++90333,00.ht., visited 18 November 2002).

[41] Francis M Nevins, 'Cape Fear Dead Ahead: Transforming a Thrice-Told Tale of Lawyers and Law' (2000) 24 *Legal Studies Forum* 611, 641.

[42] Greenfield and Osborn, n 13 above.

[43] Greenfield, Osborn and Robson, n 14 above, 152.

anthem, 'Yankee Doodle'. Immediately, Woodford's uncle intervenes anxiously and advises him to change to the Confederate's song, and the locals frenetically fall in with Priest playing his bugle. Having won Priest's benevolence, Woodford is not sentenced, but is sent out of court to look for paid work on the cotton fields.

Fairness criteria also apply to prosecutors who represent the public. As in the cases of the judges Fleming and Crusius, the following examples of prosecutors reinforce the pattern that corrupt and unfair individuals epitomize wrongs in the legal system. In *Anwalt Abel—Ein Richter in Angst* (1995), Crusius is the main suspect for the murder of a prostitute. Everyone in the local court and among the lawyers feels malicious joy which is reinforced when it turns out that Crusius has hidden a homosexual partnership with a dancer. But this is nothing compared to the zealousness of Crusius's prosecutor, Staatsanwalt Reuss. Some time ago, the self-righteous judge spoiled the prosecutor's further career with a complaint. Now Reuss's revenge even goes so far as to conceal evidence which is in favour of Crusius. During the trial he uses every opportunity to expose Crusius's most secret feelings to the audience. Eventually Reuss is withdrawn from the trial and replaced by his superior. Director Fred Breinersdorfer, who is a lawyer himself, wanted to criticize homophobia, careerism and authoritarianism in the German courts.

Rosen für den Staatsanwalt (1959, *Roses for the Prosecutor*) opens with scenes of a drumhead court martial. Kriegsgerichtsrat (military prosecutor) Dr Wilhelm Schramm asks for the death penalty in a theft case involving the soldier Rudi Kleinschmitt and two bars of chocolate. He even warns the judges how eagerly the Nazi authority follows the application of the strictest rules. An Allied air raid eventually saves the defendant from execution, so that he encounters Dr Schramm again in the 1950s. Schramm has continued his career and is now elevated to the function of an Oberstaatsanwalt (senior prosecutor). He fears that his past might be uncovered and plots to drive Kleinschmitt out of town. Finally, Kleinschmitt is in court with Dr Schramm as his prosecutor, again due to his appetite for the same bars of chocolate. In his plea, Schramm has a momentary lapse of reason and calls for the death penalty as he did before. The film's topic, namely the inclusion of Nazis in the ranks of West German state officials, proved very provocative in the 1950s, when many wanted to forgive and forget.

Director Wolfgang Staudte only managed to get the film made by turning the original, grim political script into a comedy. However, it may be said that this even contributed to the critical impact of the film. When some 'good' state-employed lawyers also have to appear, due to pressure on the film makers, it does not destroy the movie's message. The morally corrupt individual personifies major shortcomings of the legal system. As if to prove this, the East German film poster for this movie depicts Schramm in Second World War uniform behind Schramm in the prosecutor's robe. The character stands for the alleged continuity of the fascist system in the West, which is reflective of the East German spirit of the times. In comparison, the West German film poster opts for the funny side of the story.

These examples demonstrate that the view on fairness can be very broad and may question the system in general. In the procedural justice scholars' camp, Morton Deutsch formulated the most comprehensive approach:

Under the general heading of procedural justice, I would include such processes as decision-making procedures, the assignment of personnel to roles in the decision-making and distribution process, the styling and timing of the distribution, the rules or criteria employed to represent the distributive values, and the measurement procedures used to implement the criteria.[44]

Such a comprehensive view on fairness is indeed suggested by a subgenre of the courtroom drama: court-martial films.[45] Films on military justice usually juxtapose principles of individual fairness and the rule of law on the one hand and strict military codes of conduct and the subjugation of the individual to the interests of the institution on the other hand. Abuses of power in the pursuit of political objectives and personal interests of high-ranking officials abound in court-martial pictures. Some truly anti-military films such as *Paths of Glory* (1957) or *King and Country* (1964), or perhaps *Breaker Morant* (1980) may serve as examples. Under some codes of court-martial procedures, a high commanding officer selects the judges from the officers of his unit. Legal regulations are easily replaced by convenient and traditional considerations of the military. Verdicts are measured less by some standard of individual justice but rather by the supreme goal of securing discipline. Punishment is often harsh, sometimes carried out in the most cruel manner and in a humiliating setting.

Films on Unfairness as an Educational Device

Since fairness and unfairness in fictional films allude to the reality in trials, mediation or negotiation, the popular media can also be used for educational purposes. Many law and film scholars, law professors and other academics stress the importance of films as a means of education.[46] Greenfield and colleagues formulated that it would be a 'tragic waste' to confine legal films to the narrow role of another sort

[44] M Deutsch, 'Justice. Why We Need a New Moral Philosophy' in BB Bunker and JZ Rubin (eds), *Conflict, Cooperation, and Justice* (San Francisco: 1995) 371, 374–375.

[45] On court-martial films as a sub-genre of the courtroom drama: Greenfield, Osborn, and Robson, n 14 above, 41–49; M Kuzina 'Die amerikanische Militärjustiz im Film: The Caine Mutiny Court-Martial' in S Machura and S Ulbrich (eds), *Recht im Film* (Baden-Baden: 2002) 126, 142–148. Relating courts-martial to war films also: M Kuzina, 'Das Kriegsgerichtsverfahren als Filmsujet: US-amerikanische Erzählmuster' in S. Machura and R. Voight (eds), *Krieg im Film* (Muester, 2005).

[46] eg, SN Gatson, *'Its About Law' Accessible Teaching Sources for Law and Society*. Paper presented at the Annual Meeting of the Law and Society Association, Toronto, 1–4 June 1995; L Stuesser, in GF Hess and S Friedland (eds), *Techniques for Teaching Law* (Durham, NC: 1999) 100; Solomon F Fulero, Edith Greene, Valerie Hans, Michael T Nietzel, Mark A Small, and Lawrence S Wrightsman, 'Undergraduate Education in Legal Psychology' (1999) 23 *Law and Human Behavior* 137, 144; FM Nevins, 'Using Fiction and Film as Law School Tools' in S Machura and S Ulbrich (eds), *Recht—Gesellschaft—Kommunikation. Festschrift für Klaus F. Röhl* (Baden-Baden: 2003) 175.

of traditional legal teaching material.[47] Since they often deal with moral or social issues, legal films may contribute to a general education of students. Skills that may be furthered are 'viewing and listening, teamwork, presentation and research'.[48] More than that, if, as the present article argues, people share basic criteria for fairness, films may direct law students' attention to the dualism of fair and unfair structures and corresponding behaviour.[49] In a similar way, the pointed depiction of unfairness in films may also inform lawyers or judges about illicit behaviour or about the needs of the people they daily encounter.[50] Law films can be a powerful teaching instrument in the hands of scholars who are familiar with patterns of fairness and unfairness in the legal world.

But there is still more to legal films, in which the morality of the parties and of the people holding legal authority is regularly questioned. Where are the moral limits of human behaviour? What is the essence of justice? How well are legal institutions and legal professions working? Who has been entrusted with power? These topics appear over and over again in fictional films and TV series. Ideally, the conscience of the audience is sharpened. On rare occasions society looks at its own shortcomings and injustices.

[47] Greenfield, Osborn and Robson, n 14 above, 6.

[48] ibid, 8.

[49] Two examples may illustrate this. The author has used the degradation scene from Yves Boisset's *L'affaire Dreyfus* (1995) as an example for Garfinkel's concept of a 'degradation ceremony': Harold Garfinkel, 'Conditions of successful degradation ceremonies' (1956) 61 *American J of Sociology* 420–424. To exemplify bias, the author discusses the pre-trial negotiation scene in the judge's chamber from *The Verdict*.

[50] There are examples of the training of judges. In a psychological experiment, judges have been made more sensitive to the defendant's view of a trial by reading phrases reflecting harsh treatment: Anne-Marie Tausch, Inghard Langer, 'Soziales Verhalten von Richtern gegenüber Angeklagten; Merkmale, Auswirkungen sowie Änderungen durch ein Selbst-Training' (1971) 3 *Zeitschrift für Entwicklungspsychologie und pädagogische Psychologie* 283.

Military Justice in American Film and Television Drama: Starting Points for Ideological Criticism

Matthias Kuzina

Cinematic Depictions of Military Justice

The term military justice conjures up notions of rigidity, prejudice, even command influence, not to speak of cover-ups and political justice. In the immediate aftermath of My Lai, a book title led people to believe that 'military justice is to justice as military music is to music'.[1] Nowadays, court-martial procedures (as distinct from practices) are quite transparent and hence well-known to a wider public. The Uniform Code of Military Justice (UCMJ), which was enacted by Congress in 1950, can be obtained through the World-Wide Web.[2] Likewise, the Manual for Courts-Martial (MCM) and the 2002 Amendments to the MCM are easily accessible for everyone interested in the intricacies of military justice.[3] The paragraphs set out the rules, but say nothing at all about military justice in actual practice, for example how military courts for members of the armed forces handle the principles of equal justice under law. Critics may argue that a disciplinary system which is not necessarily open to public scrutiny is incapable of delivering justice impartially. Civil libertarian John Swomley, for instance, expresses concern about the military's deprivation of human rights in recent years.[4]

As an essentially internal matter, military justice has inspired novelists, dramatists and film makers to formulate their own vision of the dispensation of justice behind closed doors. The emergence of the court-martial drama roughly corresponds with the genesis of legal films in America. Considering the data given in the subject

[1] R Sherrill, *Military Justice is to Justice as Military Music is to Music* (New York: 1970). See n 8 below for information on My Lai.

[2] See www.au.af.mil/au/awc/awcgate/ucmj.htm.

[3] See www.jag.navy.mil/documents/mcm2000.pdf and www.whitehouse.gov/news/releases/2002/04/20020412-4.html respectively.

[4] Swomley gives a brief account of what happened to conscientious objector Yolanda Huet-Vaugn, a medical doctor and reservist who refused to become involved in military action in the 1991 Gulf War. Swomley, who was present throughout her trial, describes the prosecutorial process as a 'judicial farce' since the court seemed to be prejudiced against the defendant. The defence even brought up the subject of the legitimacy of this military engagement. See John M Swomley, 'WATCH ON THE RIGHT: An Example of Military Justice' (2002) 62.2 *The Humanist* (available at http://www.FindArticles.com).

indexes of the *American Film Institute* catalogue, it can be seen that the earliest military courtroom dramas date back to the end of the nineteenth century.[5] The court-martial was a topic in 34 American movies from 1931 to 1940.[6] Contemporary movies include *Dangerous Evidence: The Lori Jackson Story* (1999), *Rules of Engagement* (2000), *One Kill* (2000), *Hart's War* (2002) and *High Crimes* (2002). Generally speaking, court-martial films tend to oscillate between the traditional generic categories of courtroom dramas and war films. If the court-martial drama is defined in terms of its central dramatic focus, the adversarial system of American justice, it may conveniently be described as a subgenre of the courtroom film. The universal appeal of court-martial dramas resulted in British films like *King and Country* (1964), Australian films like *Breaker Morant* (1979) and German films like *Kriegsgericht* (1959). Some of them share certain affinities with crime films. Court-martial dramas are usually rich in dialogue scenes, sometimes exhibiting expressions of the message movie, addressing problems of moral concern, or simply offering pure entertainment. More than ordinary courtroom dramas, they probe into the legalistic background of the judiciary in such a way as to give some insight into the politicized nature of the system of military justice.[7]

Fictional cinematic representations and the media coverage of specific trials such as the notorious court-martial of William L Calley are often balanced with factual and scholarly accounts on these subjects.[8] While it is difficult to conjecture which domain has gained an advantage over the other in shaping the public's perception of the system of military justice, differential critical stances in both domains can be easily deduced from the texture of the artistic or academic achievement. *The Caine Mutiny* (1954) and *A Few Good Men* (1992), two memorable American films within the court-martial genre, bear the influence of a military mentality. Kelly's article on the film version of Humphrey Cobb's *Paths of Glory* and Belknap's book on the Calley case, on the other hand, take on a more appropriate reflexive focus.[9] Stanley Kramer's *Paths of Glory* (1957), which is set during World War I, is indeed one of the most forceful indictments of drumhead courts-martial ever projected on a screen. This prominent film example underlines the concept of 'military justice' as an oxymoron—of justice, as it is conceived of in

[5] *American Film Institute Catalog of Motion Pictures Produced in the United States; A: Film Beginnings, 1893–1910* (Metuchen, NJ: 1995).

[6] *American Film Institute Catalog of Motion Pictures Produced in the United States; F3: Feature Films, 1931–1940* (Berkeley: 1993).

[7] S Greenfield, G Osborn and P Robson, *Film and the Law* (London: 2001) 49.

[8] See, eg, MR Belknap, *The Vietnam War on Trial: The My Lai Massacre and the Court-Martial of Lieutenant Calley* (Lawrence, Kans: 2002). Belknap's bibliographical essay alone is 14 pages long. The court-martial of Lt Calley, who was convicted of killing 22 Vietnamese civilians in My Lai, became an international cause célèbre. Belknap points out that his court-martial 'took place in a . . . courtroom . . . decorated in patriotic red, white, and blue. The judge sat between an American flag and one emblazoned with the infantry's "Follow Me" motto.' (Ibid, 145.)

[9] See Andrew Kelly, 'The Brutality of Military Incompetence: *Paths of Glory*' (1993) 13.2 *Historical Journal of Film, Radio and Television* 215–227.

the civilian world, being totally incompatible with the requirements of the military in wartime. The majority of Hollywood court-martial dramas, however, highlight the due process of law, the legal principle that the United States is proud of. That is to say, the institutional justice system depicted in court-martial dramas is not necessarily more biased than the corresponding system presented in civilian Hollywood courtrooms.

The Caine Mutiny (1954) and *The Court-Martial of Billy Mitchell* (1955) mark the court-martial drama's coming-of-age in the United States at the time when the American courtroom film reached its first apogee. With Gary Cooper cast as the officer charged with insubordination and 'conduct of a nature to bring discredit upon the military service', but who was to become a hero of the US Air Force, *Billy Mitchell* is as elaborated as a trial movie could possibly be in the 1950s. The movie depicts Mitchell as a visionary who does not fit into the hierarchical system of command and obedience, but who is, paradoxically, completely at home in the military. Biographer James J Cooke points out that the historical figure was 'certainly not the Gary Cooperesque saint of the 1955 movie'.[10] The movie circumvented the political dimension of Mitchell's crusade for air-power.[11] It ultimately tries to legitimize authoritarian rule through a patriotic stance. Cooke admits that the movie was 'great propaganda' when America's rise to global power was under way.[12] The post-Civil War southwest also proved to be the perfect setting for a court-martial drama. *Sergeant Rutledge* (1959), directed by John Ford and starring Woody Strode as the cavalryman on trial for rape and murder, stigmatizes racial bigotry when the US Army was segregated and black units were led by white officers. *Judgment at Nuremberg* (1961), with Spencer Tracy as the chief judge, is a fictionalized, yet compelling account of the 1946 war crimes trial in which a few members of Hitler's judiciary were brought to justice.[13] Although the movie could not come up to the cultural critics' expectations, it is perhaps the most important American contribution to the courtroom genre so far. In the words of Alan Mintz, who comments on *Judgment at Nuremberg* from a Jewish perspective, the film includes 'an implicit story about the majesty of American justice—as well as its vulnerabilities—as a moral yardstick for understanding human affairs'.[14] Gottfried Reinhardt's 1961 film *Town Without Pity* is a seminal work destined to remain in the shadow of *Judgment of Nuremberg* and other courtroom classics. It poses the problem of fair administration of justice in a gang rape case, when the Army and other authorities press for the death penalty. The film highlights the defence counsel's legal manœuvres to save the lives of the accused GIs, when American justice is considered by some as an instrument of revenge. Recent commercial films focus on equally controversial issues. *Rules of Engagement* (2000),

[10] JJ Cooke, *Billy Mitchell* (Boulder and London: 2002) x. [11] ibid, 284. [12] ibid, 5.

[13] Abby Mann adapted the screenplay for Stanley Kramer's film from his own television play broadcast in 1959 as part of the Playhouse 90 series.

[14] A Mintz, *Popular Culture and the Shaping of Holocaust Memory in America* (Seattle and London: 2001) 91.

for instance, is about what happens if the rules of engagement (the debatable precepts of military conduct) cancel out the law of war (the Geneva Convention and other principles of civilized conduct).

The Legacy of *The Caine Mutiny*

When Edward Dmytryk adapted Herman Wouk's Pulitzer Prize winning novel *The Caine Mutiny* for the screen, he created a precursor of the modern court-martial drama. Steve Maryk's court-martial for 'conduct to the prejudice of good order and discipline' was designated as 'one of the most famous trials in American fiction'.[15] In 1951, when major Hollywood studios asked the Navy Department for possible assistance in a film project, it refused to cooperate. A mutiny had no place in Naval history, nor was the characterization of Lieutenant Commander Philip Francis Queeg as a lunatic deemed adequate.[16] It was producer Stanley Kramer whom the Navy finally seemed to trust, but the script had to be re-written to meet the demands of the military—the achievement of a positive image. And a positive image it was: in contrast to the novel, Captain Queeg (Humphrey Bogart) emerges as a war hero, a victim of combat fatigue, who concomitantly becomes a tragic figure with sympathetic traits. His breakdown in the witness stand represents one of the most intriguing courtroom scenes ever. After his acquittal, Maryk's attorney accuses the 'mutineers' of having refused loyalty to their captain. But what is more: the movie stresses the glory of the Navy and its personnel—apart from the opportunist (Tom Keefer) who dares write a critical novel. As the embodiment of an intellectual, the reserve officer does not live up to the patriotic self-image of the Navy. Suid comments: 'naval officers were enthusiastic about the way Kramer had handled the story when they saw the finished film at a Pentagon screening in January 1954'.[17] The film is actually dedicated to the US Navy. It falls short of a recruiting movie.

The image of *The Caine Mutiny* court-martial reverberated through many decades, and its attraction for the viewer is still unabated. It is the US Navy that exercises a tremendous fascination for film makers and audiences alike. Because of its special aura, the US Marine Corps is also extremely popular. In Rob Reiner's *A Few Good Men* (1991), based on Aaron Sorkin's Broadway play, two Marines are accused of murdering a fellow soldier. The film's overwhelming box-office success is down to celebrity casting and the specific tone of the movie, which conveys views of military romanticism, views that far surpass any critical implication. There is the stunning performance of the US Marine Corps Colour Guard in the opening sequence: 'With pomp and circumstance, Rob Reiner sucks us into

[15] JL Breen, *Novel Verdicts: A Guide to Courtroom Fiction* (Metuchen, NJ and London: 1984) 201.

[16] LH Suid, *Guts and Glory: The Making of the American Military Image in Film* (2nd edn, Lexington, Kentucky: 2002) 152.

[17] ibid, 157.

the rigid and controlled world of the fourth and most mythologised branch of the US Armed Forces', says Rod Lurie.[18] The principal characters are from both the Navy and the Marines. The rivalry between a Navy defence attorney (Tom Cruise as Lt Dan Kaffee) and a Marine prosecuting attorney (Kevin Bacon as Capt Jack Ross) diminishes when Kaffee as the Navy hero confronts a decorated Marine officer: Colonel Jessep (Jack Nicholson), whose rank empowers him to subjugate anyone who interferes with his own selfish interests, and who considers himself above the law, functions as Kaffee's real adversary. Jessep is a character reminiscent of Queeg. 'Honour' (the Marine code of honour and discipline, that is), the codes of 'unit', 'corps', 'God', 'country' and 'loyalty' (to the commander) amount to a confused value system the Marines are attracted to. The story entails the perversion of a military ideal—maintaining discipline at any cost. When Kaffee decides to put Jessep on the witness stand, the courtroom showdown unfolds. In real life, the Marine Public Affairs Office was dissatisfied with this script.[19] Again, it was the officers—the Marine Corps characters—the military were unconfident with. The public relations officers were also fussy about the small number of Marine characters in the film. Finally, when the military judge was made a Marine colonel rather than a Navy captain, they gave their formal blessing to the script. While the courtroom sequence in *The Caine Mutiny* evinces a certain profundity, its counterpart in *A Few Good Men* expresses superficiality.

Depictions of Military Justice in Television Series and TV Movies

According to its level of international fandom, Donald Bellisario's long-running television series *J.A.G.* (1995–) must be superior to any conceivable military TV drama in terms of its audience captivation. The main characters are Navy Judge Advocate General lawyers pursuing criminal investigations. Unfortunately, the quality of a TV series is prone to be inversely proportional to the number of formulaic episodes produced. A series allows greater character development, but this is only rarely made use of in mainstream television. As a highly patriotic series integrating soap opera-like storylines, elements of crime drama and military drama—suggesting grandeur of the Navy —, *J.A.G.* might fulfil recruitment purposes. It comes close to an epitome of a hybridized genre.[20] An overtly reactionary view is conveyed in 'King of the Fleas', an uninspired 1997 episode directed by Tony Wharmby and written by Dana Coen. It draws attention to what happened to a deserter: Roscoe Martin (Kevin Conway) portrays a Vietnam

[18] Rod Lurie, 'Toy Soldiers' (1993) 44 *Empire* 60.

[19] Suid, n 16 above, 597–598.

[20] See G Turner, 'Genre, Hybridity and Mutation' in G Creeber (ed), *The Television Genre Book* (London: 2001), 6.

veteran and former POW who has actually suffered 30 years of anguish in a wheelchair. His late confession, which takes place in a courtroom setting in the final sequence of the episode, happens to be the result of an informal interrogation in lieu of regular court-martial procedures. In an unintentionally funny scene, the male protagonist's father—a fighter pilot missing in action—is characterized as a tough fellow. Broadly, the film touches on a popular American concept of the enemy: in the prelude to the story, Roscoe kills a Vietnamese civilian who turns out to have been a sadistic war criminal. When the plot is unravelled, the episode takes a revisionist view of the Vietnam experience: it seems as if the film makers somehow seek to distort the roles of perpetrator and victim.

Sporadically, legal questions were dealt with in Gene Roddenberry's *Star Trek* and its successors.[21] *Star Trek: The Next Generation* vaguely projects the military judicial system into the twenty-fourth century, thereby maintaining its imaginative plausibility. In the episode entitled 'The Measure of a Man' (1989), an improvised court-martial has to adjudicate on whether an android officer with human character traits should be treated as the property of Star Fleet and thus be at the mercy of military technocracy. An eager scientist wants to pull him apart and tamper with his positronic brain in order to be able to clone him. The object, or rather, being that is shown as evidence is Lt Commander Data (Brent Spiner), already an audience favourite at the time of screening, but whose popularity ran to unprecedented heights in the development of the series, in the course of which he assimilates truly human qualities. The ensuing legal proceeding is not only a derivative of the present adversarial system, but it is compatible with the ideal of fairness, since basic human rights are hardly ever abandoned on board the *USS Enterprise* under the auspices of Captain Jean-Luc Picard. Data's legal status is quickly clarified in accordance with the rule of law (by today's standards). Instead of declaring him legally incapable, the court decides in favour of his personality rights.

In the 1970s, military justice was discovered as a handy subject for dramatic stories in movies made for television and has been utilized right up to the present. Such movies as *The Trial of Chaplain Jensen* (1975) and *The Court-Martial of George Armstrong Custer* (1977) belong to the lesser known artefacts of popular culture. They did not receive much critical acclaim. The latter is adapted from Douglas C Jones' novel, in which the prosecution figures way above the defence.[22] Custer is court-martialled on the hypothetical basis of his survival. The court tries to recapitulate the events of Custer's Last Stand, ie the defeat of his troops at the

[21] See P Joseph and S Carton, 'Perry Mason in Space: A Call for More Inventive Lawyers in Television Science Fiction Series' in MT Wolff and DF Mallett (eds), *Imaginative Futures: Proceedings of the 1993 Science Fiction Research Association Conference* (San Bernardino, Cal: 1995) 307–317; PR Joseph, 'Science Fiction' in RM Jarvis and PR Joseph (eds), *Prime Time Law: Fictional Television as Legal Narrative* (Durham, NC: 1998), 155–166.

[22] See D C Jones, *The Court-Martial of George Armstrong Custer* (New York: 1976) 57–179 and 195–278.

Little Bighorn on 25 June 1876. Is Custer guilty of criminal neglect? The film shows a rather balanced court-martial, in which the adversaries are permitted to be equals, and ends with Custer's acquittal.

Based on Wouk's stage play of the same name, Robert Altman's *The Caine Mutiny Court-Martial* (1988) bears little dramatic resemblance to its famous predecessor. So meticulously detailed is its depiction of the legal process and the formality of judicial proceedings that it can be regarded as a genuine trial film. This TV adaptation opens with the defence attorney telling the accused that he would rather be prosecuting than defending him. Later on, the president of the court is worried about an adequate defence, but this fear proves unfounded. Lt Barney Greenwald (Eric Bogosian) is eager enough to win the case, only to denounce the 'mutineers' because of their supposed disloyalty and to implant the idea that Captain Queeg is a misunderstood hero. The ending forms an antithesis to the preceding story of Queeg's psychopathology, thereby echoing the post-trial anticlimax of Dmytryk's *The Caine Mutiny*.

Dangerous Evidence: The Lori Jackson Story (1999) by Sturla Gunnarsson pays homage to the civil-rights activist involved in the Lindsey Scott case, but it is also a gripping drama about the inconsistencies of military justice. The cable TV movie is an outgrowth of the vogue for fact-based dramas. It follows the book of the same name by Ellis A Cohen. A black Marine corporal named Scott (Richard Yearwood) is charged with raping and stabbing a woman on Quantico Marine Base. What follows is the re-enactment of his trials. The narrative projects two stories, Scott's victimization (as a result of the arrogance of military authority) and Jackson's struggle for objective justice. As a corollary of her determination in getting Scott freed from prison, her family encounters public hate. Prior to the first court-martial sequence, Scott mentions the dubious outcome of the obligatory Article 32 hearing. What could the thorough and impartial investigation required by Article 32, UCMJ, have been like? Despite insufficient evidence to justify criminal proceedings against Scott, he faces general court-martial. The movie leaves the question unanswered, but blames his superiors, the NIS (Naval Investigative Service) and the first defence attorney named Ervan Kuhnke. The proposition 'innocent until proven guilty' is ultimately reversed in the film. According to Article 51, UCMJ, the accused must be presumed to be innocent until his guilt is established beyond reasonable doubt. Otherwise the doubt must be resolved in favour of the accused and he must be acquitted. The Court of Military Appeals, which convenes in the last third of the film, does not include an all-white, all-male panel of officers assigned as judges to the court (this was the make-up of the general court-martial), and the president of the court is black. To sum up: the film formulates an honest appeal to assure the defendant compliance with the rule of law. Because of the film's structure along two different storylines, however, one has the impression that *Dangerous Evidence* uses the military as a backdrop to the melodramatic story of Lori Jackson's private life.

Images of Lawyers in Court-Martial Dramas

First of all, there is the idealized image of the military lawyer. Lt Commander Harmon 'Harm' Rabb, Jr (David James Elliot) from the cast of the CBS series *J.A.G.* approximates to the clichéd image of the all-American hero in uniform. Dan Kaffee, the lead defence attorney from *A Few Good Men*, fits into the same category: he is the plea-bargaining compromiser turned courtroom tactician. In terms of his career as an actor, Cruise's military alter ego evolved from *Top Gun*'s sensationally popular 'Maverick' to *A Few Good Men*'s more sober Dan Kaffee: 'In fact, with Tom Cruise again playing a successful military hero, the film undoubtedly benefited the Marines, the Navy, and the military as a whole simply by showing that the services could attract the best and the brightest to honorable duty for their nation'.[23] Catherine Bell as Major Sarah 'Mac' MacKenzie, another JAG lawyer, finds a counterpart in the good-looking Lt Cmdr JoAnne Galloway (Demi Moore) as a young naval lawyer in Dan Kaffee's defence team. Female lawyers are under-represented in any area of military legal drama. They frequently conform to stereotypical images of the military woman.[24] Less spectacular male characters include John Leino (Jeff Clark) as Scott's competent defence counsel in the post-trial DuBay hearing in *Dangerous Evidence*, Allan Jacobson (Brian Keith), Custer's shrewd defender in *The Court-Martial of George Armstrong Custer*, and Frank R Reid (Ralph Ballamy), the civilian attorney who represents Billy Mitchell with a professional touch. Colonel Tad Lawson (Richard Widmark), the righteous US prosecutor in *Judgment at Nuremberg*, lacks the charisma of his opponent: because of his relentless cross-examination tactic, Maximilian Schell steals the show as chief counsel for the defence named Hans Rolfe. Interestingly, the TV drama mini-series *Nuremberg* (2000) by Yves Simoneau renders the defence in this recreation of the international military tribunal virtually impotent and thereby deprives the justice system of its supposed adversarial quality.

The negative image of the prosecutor in film is reinforced by *Assault at West Point: The Court-Martial of Johnson Whittaker* (1993), which dramatizes the nineteenth century military system's susceptibility to political justice. This television movie tells the story of a black military cadet who is beaten unconscious by racist fellow cadets and then tried by court-martial. Since the military is only interested in protecting the academy's reputation, the court finds Whittaker guilty of faking his own assault, ie of mutilating himself. Whittaker is represented by two civilian

[23] Suid, n 16 above, 601.

[24] The implementation of gender issues is a recent phenomenon. *She Stood Alone* (1995), which does not include a trial scene, is one of the first military TV dramas to pay special attention to the question of how women fit into the male-dominated military system. Courtroom procedures interweave with unoriginal characteristics of the thriller in *High Crimes* (2002), with Claire Kubik (Ashley Judd) as a civil criminal lawyer.

attorneys: Richard Greener (Samuel L Jackson), a black graduate from Harvard, is forced to play second fiddle to Daniel Chamberlain (Sam Waterston), a former governor of South Carolina. With respect to the adequate defence, Greener is irreconcilably at odds with Chamberlain. That is, Greener's liberal views are contrasted with Chamberlain's rather dishonest ethos. Asa Bird Gardiner (John Glover), the racist prosecuting attorney, embodies the morally corrupt lawyer in *Assault at West Point*. Captain Shattuck (Carleton Young), the racist trial judge advocate in *Sergeant Rutledge*, does not differ from that image at all. Unable to inquire into the Lindsey Scott case, Ervan E Kuhnke (Peter MacNeill) cannot protect his client's interests in *Dangerous Evidence*. Kuhnke combines an incredible slackness with complacency, thereby furthering an image that is likely to bring the legal profession into disrepute. As far as issue-oriented films are concerned, there is no distinctive lawyer-bashing since negative representations are still balanced with favourable portrayals of lawyers.[25] Fact based dramas often feature attorneys who combine legal expertise with social involvement.

A few court-martial dramas characterize lawyers as ambiguous figures: Sergeant Rutledge is defended by his commanding officer, Lt Tom Cantrell (Jeffrey Hunter), who beats the truth out of the final witness. Rod Steiger as army prosecutor and brilliant cross-examiner Allan Gullion destroys Mitchell in the witness stand and, further, expounds his view on freedom of speech in the military. He succeeds in making Mitchell appear an unstable person. Quite frequently in legal films, lawyers experience a conflict of interest. Major Steve Garrett (Kirk Douglas), the appointed defender and protagonist of *Town Without Pity*, faces a moral crisis. In order to save his clients (four GIs accused of raping a German girl) from the death penalty, he impugns the victim's reputation. The devastating cross examination, ie the re-victimization of the girl, is the dramatic focus of the movie. Public sentiment eventually drives her to suicide.

As a curiosity of military legal drama, the *Star Trek: TNG* episode described above features would-be lawyers without legal training. In his role as legal counsel in Data's trial, Captain Picard (played by Shakespearean actor Patrick Stewart) brings his commitment to humanity to bear on the court. With rhetorical eloquence, he thereby upholds true justice, which is evocative of Colonel Dax's courageous defence of the accused soldiers in *Paths of Glory*. The official who prosecutes the case is also represented by a layman, Commander William T Riker (Jonathan Frakes). To complicate matters, Riker must act against his will, but he is clever enough never to let emotions interfere with his professional duty:[26] the obligation to expose his friend Data as an exhibit, a thing that can be turned off at will. Captain Phillipa Louvois, the judge in 'The Measure of a Man', is too marginal a character to be of particular interest here. She is no match for the authoritative presence of Picard.

[25] See Michael Asimow, 'Bad Lawyers in the Movies' (2000) 24 *Nova L Rev* 577.

[26] Major Asa B Gardiner (Ken Howard), the prosecutor in *The Court-Martial of George Armstrong Custer*, suffers a similar fate.

The Resuscitation of Classical Formulae

In order to heighten the dramatic interest of court-martial films, screenwriters resort to familiar, well-established character configurations, storylines and motifs.

(1) *The David and Goliath courtroom battle.* This conflict usually comes down to the individual's (vain) fight against the system. In films about true cases, the defence attorney typically represents a client who is threatened with being outmatched by institutions of power—the authority of the court and of the military command, at times even the political elite. Thus Lindsey Scott (*Dangerous Evidence*) and Johnson Whittaker (*Assault at West Point*) are victims of military justice. Leitch points out that films on non-criminal law are equally suggestive of authoritarianism: 'Since the constant implication is that any system with so much power must be corrupt or unfair, lawyer films use the very power of the law as an argument against its unquestioned moral authority'.[27] Granted that many court-martial dramas do not fall into the category of the lawyer film, the inflexibility of law in fictional court-martial settings often remains an obstacle to gaining justice, even an obstacle to guaranteeing a fair trial. The rule that David trumps Goliath is broken in such films as *Assault at West Point* as an example of a historical court-martial film and *She Stood Alone* (1995), a dramatization of the Tailhook scandal of the early 1990s.

(2) *The accusation of an innocent person (in a system of authoritarian rule).* This formula has figured prominently in film culture to entertain the viewer and to build up tension. It is the historical reality of the court-martial as an agent of the executive authority that laid the foundation for this formula. As long as the investigation, the selection of trial jurors and other judicial duties are the prerogative of the military commander, there is little prospect of justice—this is the statement expressed in a number of movies. Billy Budd's fate is a case in point. The accusation of an innocent is especially effective when he or she embodies a heroic character. The apotheosis of the black protagonist in *Sergeant Rutledge* comes to mind when considering this formula.

(3) *The dubious role of the psychologist as an expert witness.* The doctor's role is likely to conform to the popular film image of a quack showing psychological aberrations himself. Over the years, film makers have cultivated the image of the headshrinker: 'American movies frequently portray psychiatrists as eccentric or weird on the assumption that one must be a bit crazy oneself to become a psychiatrist'.[28] While

[27] T Leitch, *Crime Films* (Cambridge: 2002) 245. Leitch argues that '[e]ven when they present value systems in collision, Hollywood courtroom dramas end by appealing to allegedly universal moral norms that have less to do with transcendental authority, historical tradition, or the legal precedents of particular social orders than with a surprisingly simple ideology of Hollywood entertainment. The unbroken rule is that David trumps Goliath; the underdogs always have moral right on their side. Hence the few are always more justified than the many, the poor than the rich, the lower class than the upper class, the powerless than the powerful, the individual than the system.' (Ibid, 250–251.)

[28] K Gabbard and GO Gabbard, *Psychiatry and the Cinema* (Chicago and London: 1987) 18.

the character of young Navy psychiatrist Dr Bird (played by Ken Michels) in *The Caine Mutiny Court-Martial* is arrogance personified, Dr Beard's (Brad Greenquist) contempt for the accused in *Assault at West Point* can only be described as utterly grotesque. Bird's eccentricity, not to mention his disrespect for the court, gives the film greater dramatic appeal. Beard is an even more one-dimensional figure.

(4) *The construction of a capital case, ie a case in which the accused can face the death penalty.* This is one of the more blatant means to keep the viewer in suspense, especially if the accused is deprived of due process or if the letter of the law is rigorously applied to make an example of the accused. *The Execution of Private Slovik* (1974), a television movie based on William Bradford Huie's factual novel on a case from the close of World War II, is about the military system's cynical disregard for human life: Martin Sheen plays Eddie Slovik, the one American soldier shot for desertion since the Civil War, when thousands who were court-martialled for that offence were given prison sentences. Due to 'a series of military and bureaucratic foul-ups', Slovik's execution cannot be avoided.[29] *Man in the Middle* (1963) features an officer on trial for his life. Unlike Slovik, Lieutenant Charles Winston (Keenan Wynn) murders a British sergeant in cold blood. The American defender (Robert Mitchum as Lt Col. Barney Adams), whose commanding general makes no secret of his determination to hang the culprit, proves at the court-martial that his client is a psychopath not legally responsible for his crime. In opting for his obligation to Winston, Adams sacrifices himself.[30] Traditionally, a general courts-martial panel consists of not less than five members, whereas in civilian justice—and in almost every feature film—, 12 jurors are common. A recent amendment to the UCMJ states that in capital cases, a 12-member courts-martial panel is required.[31]

(5) *The 'truth-is-stranger-than-fiction' formula.* This formula is usually more than a dramatic convenience, since it may adopt the characteristic of a metaphor for ideological critique. No one should expect a movie to portray the military justice system or even the finer points of military justice accurately. Basically, films try to contrast the ideal of the rule of law with the rule of a particular group—certain circles that may exert influence on court-martials. A prolific director of legal dramas, Stanley Kramer also produced *The Court-Martial of Lt. Calley* (1975), a political trial in reality.[32] True cases are also dramatized in *The Court-Martial of Jackie Robinson* (1990, about racially discriminatory laws), in *Serving in Silence: The Margarethe Cammermeyer Story* (1995, about the subjugation of women in a patriarchal system of the military) and *Dangerous Evidence* (see above). Authentic stories in which military law is used to make a political point are almost exclusively represented in television drama.

[29] F McAdams, *The American War Film: History and Hollywood* (Westport and London: 2002) 188.

[30] On Barney Adams as a powerful derivative of the Atticus Finch ideal see Francis M Nevins, '*Man in the Middle*: Unsung Classic of the Warren Court' (1996) 30 *U of San Francisco L Rev* 1097–1110.

[31] This provision applies in respect of offences committed after 31 December 2002.

[32] See Belknap, n 8 above, 3.

(6) *The violation of the individual's right to due process.* The emphasis on the injustices of the justice system figures as one of the most pertinent formulae made use of in film. Court-martial dramas are often characterized by an anti-establishment stance. Is justice too precious to be left to the military? An expert in military law states that 'the military enjoys infinitely more rights than a civilian defendant'.[33] In the words of Robert Sherrill, '[o]ne favored military method of conditioning a man into docility is to make trial and punishment not only arbitrary but unpredictable'.[34] As previously noted, *Assault at West Point* offers a scathing portrait of military injustice. The military command in *Man in the Middle* attempts to maintain a facade of due process.

(7) *The patriotic strain exposed.* It is not unusual for American film makers to make concessions to the Department of Defence to obtain approval.[35] *The Caine Mutiny* and *Rules of Engagement* received full cooperation from the military. In avoiding critical thought, affirming patriotism and advocating the justification of power (in an ideological sense), popular court-martial dramas do not express libertarian attitudes. The entertainment media perpetuate the resurgence of chauvinistic values in accord with the public need. Whether films that depict the armed services unfavourably have an effect on audiences is open to question. A truly pacifist statement has hardly ever been successfully embedded in a court-martial drama. As the paradigm of an antiwar movie, *Paths of Glory* is an exceptional case likely to entail positive consequences. It highlights the corruption of the military system along with the implications of an erosion of moral standards and therefore remains an outstanding achievement of the large screen. The same disposition holds true for *The Execution of Private Slovik* on the small screen. However inconsistent with a demonstration of the real nature of the bureaucrats' complicity in genocidal crimes, *Judgment at Nuremberg* brings the Nazi perversion of justice and the question of German responsibility to public awareness. Moreover, it takes a critical look on US post-war policy, which means that a just punishment of the crimes of Nazism almost falls victim to the dictates of the Cold War. As Mintz puts it, '[a]lthough they sit in judgment, the Americans are themselves not beyond judgment. The exercise of justice is everywhere and always exposed to the pressures of [political] expediency'.[36]

War films are in no way immune to ideological thought. In *The Caine Mutiny*, even a paranoid Captain has good facets. Despite his courtroom breakdown, a transfiguration takes place: the movie attempts to retrieve Queeg's honour by showing other officers in an even more unfavourable light. It salvages his pride through a fundamentally patriotic approach. Deflaux states: 'Si la glorification de

[33] MJ Davidson, *A Guide to Military Criminal Law* (Annapolis: 1999) 53.

[34] Sherrill, n 1 above, 63. In Yves Boisset's *Le pantalon* (1996), which is about the actual historical Lucien Bersot case, several of the formulae mentioned before are integrated.

[35] McAdams, n 29 above, throughout. In *Guts and Glory*, n 16 above, Suid explores the symbiotic relationship between the motion picture industry and the American military.

[36] Mintz, n 14 above, 91.

la puissance américaine présente un tour plus pudique que dans une oeuvre purement propagandiste du temps de guerre, il est néanmoins certain que l'orgueil national est ici source d'un lyrisme délibéré et melliflue'.[37] Patriotic movies are widely appreciated in the United States but viewed suspiciously outside the Anglo-American world: instead of maturing into a culturally more respectable form, the war film genre is now likely to be subject to propagandistic regression.[38] There is a clash between what is politically desirable—antiwar films to supplement today's critical discourse—and what is economically unavoidable. Films imbued with humanistic values do not pay at the box-office. The film industry incessantly resorts to patriotic stories and, in the case of *Rules of Engagement*, even to xenophobic imagery.[39] That might be detrimental to legal culture in the long run.

[37] P Deflaux, 'Le réflexe conservateur: *The Caine Mutiny*' in D Royot (ed), *Hollywood: Réflexions sur l'écran* (Aix-en-Provence: 1984) 98.

[38] M Strübel, 'Kriegsfilm und Antikriegsfilm: Ein filmgeschichtlicher Abriss aus der Sichtweise der internationalen Politik' in M Strübel (ed), *Film und Krieg: Die Inszenierung von Politik zwischen Apologetik und Apokalypse* (Opladen: 2002) 68.

[39] See Michael Asimow and Khaled Abou El Fadl, 'The Military Justice Movie That Can't Cut It–Rules of Engagement', *Picturing Justice: The On-line Journal of Law and Popular Culture,* www.usfca.edu/pj/military.htm

Courtroom Sketching: Reflections on History, Law and the Image[1]

Lynda Nead

Courtrooms generate an abundance of visual images. From the architecture of the building to the ornamentation of the court, the space is a visual articulation of the symbolic meanings of the law. Dress and gesture express power and deference and constitute an additional register of visual semantics. But the courtroom is a site of *re*presentation as well as presentation and it is this question of how the courtroom and the trial may be *shown* which is the subject of this article. The representation of the courtroom offers a striking instance of the interface between law and the image, and more particularly between visual technologies and the law. The last century has seen extraordinary changes in the modes of visual reproduction. Photographic technologies have become faster and more instantaneous and, in turn, have yielded to the revolution of electronic imaging. In spite of these immense changes, however, English trials are represented in the media by the courtroom sketch. The fact that in the twenty-first century, the law is represented through such an anachronistic medium is testimony to a much longer and uneasy relationship between law and the image. In his work on the legality of the image, Costas Douzinas has written: 'The law loves and fears images, it both prohibits them and organizes its own operation in a highly spectacular and visual manner'.[2] The courtroom sketch tests this assertion and gives it historical specificity. The sketch is a visual manifestation of law's oscillation between the desire to show and the need to regulate that visual display; of its need to be pictorially represented and the corresponding requirement to police that representation. These are images which are charged with meanings; not simply those that relate to the particular cases concerned, but those that belong to the ongoing relationship between history, law and the image.

Photography and sketching in court and the publication of such photographs or sketches have been prohibited in English law since 1925.[3] So other than the small

[1] My thanks to Steve Connor, Lindsay Farmer, Frank Mort, Matthew Weait for their comments on earlier drafts of this article. I am most grateful to Siân Frances, courtroom artist, for giving up her time to discuss her work with me. The research and writing of this article was undertaken during my Leverhulme Major Research Fellowship. I would like to thank the Leverhulme Trust for their generous support. A version of this paper was published in (2002) 3 *Visual Culture in Britain* 119–141.

[2] Costas Douzinas, 'The Legality of the Image' (2000) 63 MLR 815.

[3] Criminal Justice Act 1925, s 41.

numbers of people who actually attend court, the majority of the public attains a visual impression of a trial while it is being heard through the pictorial mnemonics of the courtroom artist. We can all, surely, recall the look of a courtroom sketch; its composition, style and context, for it is one of the most highly conventionalized forms within contemporary visual media. Courtroom art condenses major criminal trials into generic, gently anachronistic images which are then reproduced in newspapers and broadcast on television. The faces of fraudsters, murderers and hijackers are known to us through the hasty notations of the courtroom artist, made not on the spot but from memory. This paper is the story of the courtroom sketch; of how the 'eyes of the press' were removed from the camera lens and replaced by the conventions of the courtroom artist.

R v Bywaters and Thompson [1922]

By the first decades of the twentieth century major criminal trials had become cultural spectacles and a form of popular entertainment.[4] Tickets were issued for seats in the limited public areas of the courtroom and in especially notorious cases admission to the court became part of a nefarious economy with people queuing for tickets in order to sell them on at a substantial profit. But it was only a tiny minority who experienced the live drama of a trial within the court; mass audiences were created by the press, who transformed promising legal cases into sensational news. From the end of the nineteenth century major trials were reported in detail and often occupied several pages of the daily and Sunday papers during the period of the trial. Newspapers deployed their full battery of journalistic devices—photographic spreads, banner headlines and hectic prose—which had been developed since the 1880s, to draw their readers into compelling narratives of desire, betrayal and violence. Here were all the familiar subjects of Victorian melodrama, with the added frisson of real life. Trials provided the raw materials for character and plot; the villains and the victims, the crimes and the punishments, which the newspapers spun into stories that bound the nation together in the early years of the twentieth century.

Following the passing of the Criminal Evidence Act in 1898 which allowed the accused to give evidence on their own behalf, the cross-examination of the accused became the centrepiece of the criminal trial. The procedure of the trial seemed fortuitously to meet the general temporal requirements of the press. Lapses of interest and dramatic lacunae could be excised and the narrative of the case reshaped in order to create a continuous pitch of emotional interest. The progress of the trial could be unfolded day by day, issue by issue, punctuated by strategic highpoints

[4] On the cultural significance of major trials at the end of the nineteenth century see Nancy Erber and George Robb, 'Introduction', in George Robb and Nancy Erber (eds), *Disorder in the Courts: Trials and Sexual Conflict at the Turn of the Century* (London: 1999) 1–11. For a good analysis of one murder trial from this period see Julie English Early, 'A New Man for a New Century: Dr Crippen and the Principles of Masculinity', in Robb and Erber, ibid, 209–230.

such as the arrival of key witnesses, the testimony of the defendant, and the climax of the verdict and sentence. Shorn of the legal niceties and intervals of the courtroom itself, the trial offered newspaper editors a complete, self-contained narrative module; in other words, a perfect story.

By the 1920s, anyone who was involved in a major trial was considered fair game by the news and picture editors. Witnesses, defendants, members of the jury, counsel, judges, as well as their relatives, might find themselves the target of a press photographer and on the front page of a mass circulation paper the following day. Inevitably, murder trials offered the press and the public the most provocative story lines. Defendants in these cases faced the death penalty and, prompted by the papers, verdicts often resulted in public demonstrations and petitions to the Home Secretary.

At all stages of trial reporting women played a central part in the dramatic potential of the case and its ability to capture the public imagination and win newspaper sales. As victim, women conformed to a familiar enough image of passive object of what was commonly proved to be male violence; but as the accused, they presented a far more fascinating opportunity for a public examination of the nature of modern femininity and the pathology of female violence. The trial in 1922 of Frederick Bywaters and Edith Thompson for the murder of Edith's husband Percy, had all the elements necessary for the creation of a big newspaper story; there was an adulterous affair, a handsome young lover, an adoring older woman and, most extraordinarily of all, the evidence of a cache of love letters, written by Edith to Frederick, which were shown to the jury, read aloud in the court, reported in the papers and provided the public with a tawdry and explicit true-life tale of crime and passion.[5]

This was a photogenic story; the case hung on the relationship between the two defendants and called out for revealing and lifelike portraits. Their appearance before and during the case, as well as their demeanour in the courtroom were reported in detail, in pictures and in words, and scrutinized for signs of innocence or guilt. The newspapers then were obsessed with the case, but it remains a notorious instance of press coverage of criminal trials before the 1925 statutory prohibition of photography and sketching in the courtroom.

In October 1922, Percy and Edith Thompson were returning to their home following a theatre visit in London when a man leapt out of the darkness and fatally attacked Percy with a knife.[6] Within days, both Edith Thompson and Frederick Bywaters had been charged with murder.[7] Bywaters admitted to lying in wait for

[5] The enduring popular interest in this case is suggested by the novels based on it, see Fryniwyd Marsh Tennyson Jesse, *A Pin to See the Peepshow* (London and Toronto: 1934) and Jill Dawson, *Fred and Edie* (London: 2000).

[6] Accounts of the case are given in Travers Humphreys, *A Book of Trials* (Melbourne, London and Toronto: 1953) 147–155; Robin Odell, *Landmarks in 20th Century Murder* (London: 1995) 122–126; Jean Graham Hall and Gordon D Smith, *R. v. Bywaters and Thompson* (Chichester: 1997).

[7] See the *Daily Sketch*, 7 October 1922, 1; *News of the World*, 8 October 1922, 5. A transcript of the trial and related papers are kept at the National Archives, London: DRIM 1/206/5; HO 144/2685; PCOM 8/22; PCOM 8/436.

the Thompsons but claimed that he had never intended to kill Percy. The notoriety of the case, however, rested largely on the case against Edith Thompson. Although she had been accompanying her husband, she had not actually struck a blow and so the question was whether she was guilty of aiding and abetting the crime by inciting Bywaters to murder. Both were found guilty and sentenced to death. A public petition was presented to the Home Secretary requesting that Edith's sentence be commuted to one of life imprisonment, but no reprieve was given and Thompson was hanged along with Bywaters.

The trial at the Old Bailey in December 1922 aroused unprecedented public interest, reaching a climax in the cross-examination of Edith Thompson, during which lengthy extracts from her letters to Bywaters were read out in the court. The forlorn melodrama of Thompson's life and letters was reconstructed during the trial and then recreated in the newspapers like instalments of a cheap novel. The trial, law itself, was utterly caught up in this tapestry of public drama and popular fantasy. The courtroom could not extract itself from the irresistible production of sensational news reporting nor could it sustain its image as a discrete and pure space for the exercise of justice, but was drawn into a world of petit bourgeois sexual fantasy and transgression symbolised by Edith Thompson and magnified through the mass readerships of the early-twentieth-century popular press.

Through their reporting of trials such as Bywaters and Thompson, the newspapers brought the public into the courtroom; they penetrated its enclosed and rarefied space and opened it up to the mass audiences which had been created by the modern press. Each reader had to feel implicated and involved in the progress of the case; they had to feel, through the agency of the paper, part of the live action that was taking place in and around the courtroom.

Of those who made up the modern public for sensational murder trials, one group was of particular interest to the press and was singled out for comment. It was the women, of all ages and different classes, who were defined as the most voracious consumers of murder. Women queued overnight; they scrambled for admission; and packed into the courtroom. And amongst the witnesses were a waitress and the manageress of a teashop, whose photographs shared the front pages with those of the judge, counsel and defendants. The many women caught up in the trial—as defendant, witnesses, onlookers and newspapers readers—seemed indistinguishable. The *Daily Graphic* juxtaposed a photograph of Edith Thompson and two details of women in the crowd, with the caption: 'Among the crowd are to be seen many women in furs and young girls of the age at which the present generation is, as a rule, chiefly interested in the dramas of the film'. Fashion and fiction united these women and, in excess, had brought about Edith Thompson's downfall. These were sensation-loving women, but the questions raised by the trial were, did these women murder and were they fit to vote and fit to judge innocence and guilt?[8]

[8] Women over 31 years of age were first given the vote immediately after World War I, in 1919.

Among the many distinctive features of the case, was the fact that the jury included one woman. The first female juror was sworn in at an Old Bailey trial in January 1921 and their appearance in court still excited special comment. Photographs of the entire jury in the Bywaters and Thompson case were printed with impunity,[9] but the woman juror was picked out by the press. The *Daily Sketch* showed her on her way into the Old Bailey[10] and the *Illustrated London News* was one of a number of papers to show her returning with the rest of the jury from a Sunday service at St Paul's Cathedral. In her formal attire of furs and black hat, there was little to differentiate the jurist from Edith Thompson or the morbid voyeurs in the public gallery. But these sartorial similarities were precisely the point; the press had turned murder trials into spectacles that compromised respectability and judgment. Modernity had disturbed the certainties of the courtroom.

Bywaters and Thompson showed how far the courtroom had been infiltrated by modern mass culture and the extent to which it was consumed through the narrative structures of theatre, film and photography. By the 1920s, it seemed as though newspaper and photographic technologies had been moving inexorably towards turning the criminal trial into the perfect tabloid story.

Photographs for the Papers

Two histories of modernity converge in the visual cultures of the English courtroom; firstly, the development of the adversarial trial, and second the rise of the mass circulation press.

The mass circulations of the daily newspapers arose chiefly out of the introduction into news reporting of the direct reproduction of photographic images. By the 1890s newspapers were reproducing images printed from half-tone blocks and in 1904 the *Daily Mirror* became the first newspaper in the world to be illustrated exclusively by photographs.[11] The illustrated front page, with its dramatic photographs and bold headlines, became the tabloid papers' chief weapon in the race for mass circulation. And it was effective; in 1912 the *Daily Mirror* became the first paper to reach a circulation of one million.

By the second decade of the twentieth century, photography dominated the output of the popular papers and the press photographer had emerged as a new hero of modern life. Editorial staffs commonly included picture editors, and news agencies were joined by specialist picture agencies. This was the world of the press

[9] See the *Daily Mirror*, 9 December 1922, 1 and 11 December 1922, 1. Also the *Daily Graphic*, 11 December 1922, 1.

[10] See also the *Daily Graphic*, 9 December 1922, 1.

[11] On the early history of news photography see Ken Baynes (ed), *Scoop, Scandal and Strife: A Study of Photography in Papers* (London: 1971); Ian Jeffrey, *Photography: A Concise History* (London: 1981) esp 242–244; Beaumont Newhall, *The History of Photography from 1839 to the Present* (London: 1982) 251–252; Petr Tausk, *A Short History of Press Photography* (Prague: 1988).

photographer who, working either freelance or for particular papers, was creating the modern pictorial journalism of the twentieth century.

The potential of the courtroom as a source of sensational news images was understood from the beginning. There is no reliable documentation of the first appearance of a news camera at a trial, but what is clear is that by the early-1920s still photography of court proceedings was commonplace in the nation's mass circulation papers.[12] John Everard, a press photographer and author of *Photographs for the Papers: How to Take and Place Them* (1923), advised the novice photographer:

> Photographers with a desire for sensationalism will find plenty to do in following up criminal cases. A certain section of the daily press and week-end (Sunday) papers make a special feature of such reproductions. In the provinces there is also a large market for photographs of murder scenes and sensational pictures.[13]

Photography in the courtroom was not a straightforward matter, however. If it became intrusive, it could be seen to interfere with the course of justice and to constitute a contempt of court and a judge could choose to prohibit photography throughout a trial. Everard sensed a change in attitude towards press photographers and predicted legal intervention: '. . . the time may come when photographing without permission where private individuals are concerned will be made an indictable offence'.[14] But in the ambiguous situation of the early-1920s, the cunning veteran press photographer could always find ways of sneaking a camera into the courtroom and taking a photograph.[15] Once taken, the photograph could be published with impunity since before the 1925 Act there was no statutory prohibition of either photography in the courtroom or its publication.

This was the peculiar nature of the relationship between the law and the press in the years immediately leading up to the framing and passing of the Criminal Justice Act. Within a couple of decades of their creation, the popular newspapers had successfully secured mass readerships and press photography had emerged as the key player in the look and presentation of the modern news. Women and the working classes; the uncritical romance readers and cinema-goers were the new consumers of the law. Melodrama had contaminated justice, and justice had been reduced to little more than a source of popular entertainment. At its most bathetic, trial by jury itself had become nothing more than a trope for an advert for indigestion salts.

[12] For an outstanding discussion of the history of courtroom photography in the context of recent debates on televized court proceedings see Marjorie Cohn and David Dow, *Cameras in the Courtroom: Television and the Pursuit of Justice* (Jefferson, NC and London: 1998).

[13] John Everard, *Photographs for the Papers: How to Take and Place Them* (London: 1923) 19.

[14] ibid, 26. See also '[Photographs taken in court] frequently come very near contempt of court', 42–43.

[15] Reminiscing on his career as a press photographer in these years, William Turner recalled the tactics used in the courtroom to avoid detection. Experienced photographers would get to know the 'geography' of individual courtrooms and would change their positions throughout the trial to avoid being noticed by officials. He describes other tricks such as resting his small, hand-held camera on the seat beside him and photographing the accused in a murder trial. William R Turner, *Eyes of the Press* (London: 1935) 208. See also 205 and 217.

To many Members of Parliament and peers it seemed that the press had turned the great legal and moral narratives of the age into a profit-driven circus. Courtroom photography was not an isolated phenomenon, but was part of a sensational, popular discourse surrounding major criminal trials. It was time to separate the conduct of the court from modern mass media; the camera had to be banished from the courtroom and its environs. Against the background of the fragmented politics and rapidly-changing governments of Britain in the early-1920s, action was finally taken. In 1923 the Conservative Government introduced a Criminal Justice bill; it was unsuccessful, but the following year Ramsay Macdonald's Labour Government took over the legislation, adding a clause prohibiting court photography.[16] In 1925, following the sudden collapse of the Labour Government, another Conservative Government reintroduced the Criminal Justice bill, including the section concerning courtroom photography, and the notoriously puritanical Home Secretary, Sir William Joynson-Hicks, took the issue back to Parliament.

The Criminal Justice Act 1925

The 1925 Criminal Justice Act created two separate offences: the making of an image of the courtroom and its publication.[17] Furthermore, the prohibition covered both images made in the courtroom itself and those made in the precincts of the building in which the court was held.

Section 41 of the 1925 Act was the product of the historical development of the popular press. Photography had transformed the new journalism and had created the modern tabloid, a compelling combination of nineteenth-century sensation and twentieth-century photographic technologies. In certain respects, government had taken some time to react; photography had, after all, been a staple of the mass circulation press for a number of years. In other ways, however, the politicians had timed it just right. Camera technology was on the brink of further revolutionary change. Within a couple of years they would become smaller, faster and more adaptable; the perfect instrument of the determined and ambitious press photographer. Newsreel cameras would also move further centre stage and access to the courtrooms would be a question not only of the still but also of the moving image. It can come as no surprise, therefore, that this was the moment for the passing of

[16] On the history of the Criminal Justice bill see EJ Hayward, *The Criminal Justice Act, 1925 (Annotated), Together with Rules, Orders and Forms* (London: 1926) ix; (1925) 89 JP 136 *Manchester Guardian*, 21 November 1925, 7.

[17] For commentaries on the Act see Albert Lieck and ACL Morrison, *The Criminal Justice Act, 1925, with Explanatory Notes* (London: 1926); RE Otter and GB McClure, *The Criminal Justice Act 1925 with Notes* (London: 1926). For more recent discussion see Geoffrey Robertson and Andrew GL Nicol, *Media Law: The Rights of Journalists, Broadcasters and Publishers* (London: 1984) 212–213; CJ Miller, *Contempt of Court* (2nd edn, Oxford: 1990) 128–132; Nigel Lowe and Brenda Sufrin, *The Law of Contempt* (3rd edn, London: Dublin and Edinburgh: 1996) 24–27.

s 41 and, at the time of writing, the clause remains the prevailing law in England and Wales on the matter of photographing and sketching in court.

The Art of the Courtroom Sketch

We all know what a courtroom sketch looks like; we can visualize its style and picture its treatment of individuals and settings. The courtroom sketch is highly generic; it obeys rules and conventions that subordinate the particular details of individual cases and identities within general categories of types and location. There is a universal quality about the courtroom sketch.[18] The viewpoint is everywhere and nowhere: from the dock, the judge's bench, the public gallery. The specificity of the viewpoint ultimately matters less than the general impression of presence within the courtroom. The portraits are a curious synthesis of nobody in particular and potent or notorious individuals. Identities slip in and out of vision; faces resemble people we know, or feel we should know, but features dissolve and are forgotten. The identities of individual artists obey the same cognitive logic and become submerged within a generic category of 'courtroom artist'. The sketch declares its status as 'an artist's impression', but we have no idea who the artist is. We are aware, at some level, that there must be technical differences and individual styles, but they cannot be captured and melt into an homogeneous look and feel. This is a singularly styleless style in which distinctive elements add up to a lack of distinction.

To look at a sketch depicting a dramatic highpoint in the trial narrative—the summing up, the sentencing etc—is to feel oneself to be already familiar with the scene. But what we take to be an understanding of the situation, is in fact a grasp of the signs and orthodoxies of the image. Courtroom dramas on film and television provide a lexicon of the legal process which can be mobilized by the viewer of the courtroom sketch. The sketch is a cipher for these other fictional representations. We recognize the conventions of the courtroom sketch and its referents and conflate this recognition with a knowledge of that which is represented. We are present at the trial only by virtue of the courtroom sketch; but the sketch does not have the unmediated presence of the camera. We are aware of its artifice and of the agency of the artist; we are conscious of the act of portrayal. The courtroom sketch acknowledges its own madeness, perhaps, in part, because it appears to show not the scene itself but the impression made on a viewer by the scene: 'This is how I saw it'.

There is, then, a remoteness about the courtroom sketch which is a sign of the gap between the actual trial and its representation. In her outstanding study,

[18] Wendy Lesser uses the term 'Everyman' quality in her description of Howard Brodie's drawings of the execution of Aaron Mitchell in 1967, see *Pictures at an Execution* (Cambridge, Mass and London: 1993) 166. Lesser's insightful observations on the portrayal of murder in the United States offer invaluable ways of understanding courtroom sketches.

Pictures at an Execution, Wendy Lesser argues that the portrayal of murder is always, necessarily, a reflection on the nature of representation itself. She writes:

> To portray murder . . . is to acknowledge the distance between the Act of murder and its rendering. The murder story is always in part about this distance. This is also true of murder trials . . . the trial is just a rough sketch of what happened, an incomplete and inadequate portrayal, not the thing itself.[19]

I am drawn to Lesser's metaphor of the trial as a sketch of the crime; an evocation of 'the thing itself' which draws us further and further into the world of representations. In these terms, the courtroom sketch is a second-order evocation; a rough sketch of the trial and confirmation of the distance between the actual administration of justice and its representations.

The artist can take written notes during the trial but must leave the courtroom to make the sketch. The image is thus made outside the sitting of the court and is not part of the legal process of the trial. It has a particular temporality. It does not belong to the time of the court; it is not a record or evidence of the trial, but is retrospective and remembered. The courtroom sketch is thus *of* the trial but is not *a part* of the trial; it does not infiltrate the hermetically-sealed world of the courtroom as the camera would do, but maintains and strengthens the essential borderline between the inside and the outside of the legal process. The sketch is thus a testimony to the partial and incomplete nature of portrayal and to law's regulation of the visual image. The hasty notations; the sketchy outlines and roughly filled-in blocks of colour; the unfinished edges which dissolve before the frame, remind us of what must be imagined and of the gulf between image and event.

The rights of the press and of the public to see and to know, and the protection of individual privacy and the decorum of the courts defined the terms of the political debate in 1925 and continue to structure it today. The camera may seem to promise unmediated access to the courtrooms and to open up the law to the scrutiny of the public, but there is a political danger in this liberalization of which the history of press photography and the mechanics of courtroom sketching remind us. Drawn by the photographic image into the conventions of mass cultural consumption, the events of a trial are all too easily and uncritically processed into the familiar narratives of sensation. What may initially, therefore, be defended in the name of public information and accountability, might end up as simply more material for voyeuristic gratification. In this context, there is a helpful moment of critical distance between the courtroom sketch and the event that it represents. It is an interval which acknowledges that what we see is representation—made and composed—rather than a transparent transmission of the whole truth. At the end of 2000, the Labour Government announced that during a second term of office it would introduce legislation to allow television cameras into courtrooms and in 2004 a pilot scheme was introduced allowing filming in the

[19] ibid, 131–132.

Court of Appeal. But let us not forget the insights offered by the courtroom sketch. Its foregrounding of artifice and its distance from the moment of the trial, are a constant reminder of the role of representation and ritual at all levels of the legal system. The law is a complex and discrete discourse. Broadcasting its dramatic highlights and personalities will not necessarily assist in opening up the legal field to informed public scrutiny.

What Movies Can Teach Law Students

John Denvir

Each year more law schools add a law and film course to their curriculums. Maybe it is time to ask exactly what these courses provide students that they would otherwise miss. First, I would say that movies, contrary to the conventional wisdom, give law students a positive image of the lawyer. The typical 'lawyer' film depicts the lawyer as a hero. The protagonist is usually a criminal defence lawyer defending an innocent defendant. It is the legal system that is the villain, and the plot usually revolves around the attempts of the 'good' lawyer to wrench justice from the 'bad' system. Of course, there are some negative portrayals of lawyers in films, but even these are consistent with the hero thesis in a larger sense. Bad lawyers are those who have aligned themselves with the corrupt system instead of challenging it.

But I think there is another message that study of movies provides for law students: the practice of law is fraught with ethical consequence. Every day movie lawyers are confronted with the choice of fighting for justice or permitting the unjust system to prevail. To me this 'popular' image of the practice of law is especially valuable because it subverts the 'professional' image of the lawyer as a technically proficient craftsman that students imbibe in their other courses. My point is not to defend the accuracy of the hyper-moralistic popular image of the lawyer, but to insist on its importance as an antidote to the amoral image so dominant in the rest of the law school curriculum.

But first I would like to back up my reading of the popular image of the lawyer by discussion of six 'lawyer' films, three of which depict lawyer heroes and three depict lawyer villains. I will then contrast this rather Manichean popular image of the lawyer with the professional image of lawyers implicit in the academic discourse prevalent in law schools. Finally I will attempt to how law students might negotiate in their choice of a legal career the tensions the conflicting images create.

Heroes and Villains

Young Mr. Lincoln

I must admit that I had always remembered John Ford's *Young Mr. Lincoln* (1939) as a sentimental paean to the majesty of the law. I guess I was thinking of an early scene in which Lincoln (Henry Fonda) is given an old copy of Blackstone's *Commentaries* that he fondles reverently like Moses receiving the Ten Commandments. Yet soon we find young lawyer Lincoln subverting law's majesty with typical lawyerly chicanery in a search for justice. Ford gives us three examples in quick succession of Lincoln flouting a formalistic conception of law to achieve concrete justice.

One of Lincoln's first cases involves dispute about a small amount of money. Abe first outlines a common sense settlement that would avoid litigation and then playfully, but meaningfully, threatens both parties with physical violence if they do not agree to the deal. Abe does not seem to have much time for law as rational discourse. We next see Lincoln as the judge of the pie contest at the county fair. Here Ford has Lincoln burlesque the job of judging. First, Abe tastes the peach pie and likes it; then he tastes the apple pie and thinks he likes that even more. But then he feels it his duty as judge to give the peach pie one more taste, and on it goes. I think here we can see two messages. First, the judge does not want the contest to end before he has had his fill of the evidence. Secondly, judges rely on taste as much as rules and procedures. After consuming the pie, lawyer Lincoln moves on to participate in a 'tug of war'. He finds himself on the weaker side so Honest Abe cleverly rescues victory from defeat by hitching his side's end of the rope to a passing wagon heading in the opposite direction. It appears sometimes the end does justify the means.

Of course, the central scene in the movie is Lincoln's famous cross-examination of a hostile witness in a murder trial. Lincoln first artfully lures the witness into agreeing that he could identify Lincoln's client as the murderer because the moon shone so bright the night of the murder and then blithely destroys the witness's credibility by brandishing the Farmer's Almanac to prove that there was no moon the night of the murder. This, of course, is an example of admirable lawyerly trickery—saving an innocent man from the blind justice of the law. But once Lincoln has destroyed the credibility of the witness, he proceeds to bully him in the best Perry Mason fashion to confess that he himself committed the murder. Substantive justice is done here only because Lincoln pays little attention to the niceties of legal procedure.

Within the structure of the film, the hero must save society from two evils. The first is the evil of mob violence that presents itself in the form of a lynch mob screaming for his clients' blood. This scene is usually interpreted as an homage to the rule of law, but actually, it is not law that saved the potential lynching victims, but Abe's personal courage to face down the mob. The second evil Lincoln must combat is the law of homicide in the State of Illinois that seems to require the execution of both Lincoln's clients even though at best only one of them committed a murder. The hero lawyer is forced to do battle with an unjust legal system. We will see this same theme repeated time and again in the movies that follow.

True Believer

It is hard to think of a lawyer less like Abraham Lincoln than Eddie Dodd, the protagonist of *True Believer* (1989). When we first meet Dodd (James Woods) he is a drug lawyer, using the intricacies of the law to keep drug dealers on the streets. This professional image does not appeal to Dodd's young associate, Roger Barron (Robert Downey Jr), who has come to work for Dodd because of his former reputation in the civil rights area.

Barron accuses Dodd of 'selling out' by defending clients he knows are guilty because they can pay high fees. Dodd first accuses the neophyte lawyer of naïveté. He rejects the argument that criminal defence lawyers are there to protect the innocent defendant with the quick retort, 'They're all guilty'. But the young idealist Barron also rejects Dodd's rationalization that his real clients are not sleazy drug lords, but the constitutional protections against unlawful searches and seizures.

Finally Dodd comes up with a justification that makes sense to Barron, himself, and the audience. Dodd's reason appears in the form of a mother asking him to help her son. The mother is a Korean immigrant whose son is serving a life sentence for a gang murder and who is now accused of a second murder in a prison gang fight. The audience already knows her son; the opening shots of the film had shown him in preparation for the prison fight, taping knives to his hands to transform himself into a lethal bird of prey. It had never occurred to us at that time that he could be somebody's baby boy.

Dodd's professional cynicism dissolves at the sight of how incarceration has transformed a young boy into a killing machine. He decides that no matter what the boy has done, he has been in prison long enough. He uses his professional skills to help the young man. And since movies like to improve on real life, we are not too surprised to find out that Dodd's client is not guilty after all. His first conviction was the product of a police frame-up, and his prison homicide turns out to be a case of self-defence.

But one senses that Dodd's response would have been no different if his client had been guilty—and no less heroic. Here the lawyer's quest for justice transcends guilt and innocence in the individual case to confront the injustice of the larger legal system. Most Americans only know about the world of crime from the images that appear on movie and television screens. Hollywood likes to show us evil geniuses played by the likes of Anthony Hopkins. These projections of our darkest fantasies work on the dramatic level, but experts tell us that crime on the street is a more prosaic matter. You do not have to jettison the concept of free will to concede that most denizens of our prisons are not psychopathic geniuses like Hannibal Lector, but losers who have been given the wrong end of the social stick from birth and it is to the credit of the criminal defence Bar that its members defend them to the best of their ability without regard to guilt or innocence.

. . . And Justice For All

The most baroque illustration of how a defence lawyer's commitment to justice requires him to take up a stance against the law is found in *. . . And Justice for All* (1979). The film begins like the orthodox 'good' defence lawyer movies we have been discussing. Al Pacino plays Arthur Kirkland, an idealistic criminal defence lawyer, trying to snatch his innocent client from the clutches of the criminal justice system. He fails when a 'law and order' judge played by John Forsythe refuses, on the basis of a technicality, to accept evidence that proves the client's innocence. Infuriated by this insensitivity to the claims of justice, Kirkland takes a punch at the judge which lands him in jail for contempt of court.

As he tells his grandfather, Arthur Kirkland very much wants to be a 'good' lawyer, but is not quite sure what that means within the context of contemporary American society. He soon finds out when the 'law and order' judge is himself accused of raping a young woman and asks Kirkland to defend him. When Kirkland initially rejects the case, the judge assures him that he is innocent and even suggests that if he takes the case the judge might intervene to free Kirkland's innocent client.

But in preparing the case, Kirkland comes across evidence that proves the judge is guilty. Now Kirkland is concretely confronted with the issue of what it means to be a 'good' lawyer. Should he follow the professional ethic and give his client the zealous defence the law demands of a defence counsel? To do this will require that he demolish the innocent victim on cross-examination, creating an image of her that he knows is false. Or should he choose truth and justice over professional duty and turn on his client?

The final scene of the movie shows Kirkland making his opening statement to the jury. I think it one of the classic film discussions about the connection between law and justice. Kirkland talks about law and its promise of 'justice for all'; he also talks about the incentives the legal system gives to lawyers to work for victory instead of justice. He then lays out the strength of his case for acquittal; after all, it is just the word of the alleged victim against that of a well-respected judge. 'Why would she lie?' Kirkand muses. Was it jealousy, greed or any of the other myriad reasons that lead witnesses to perjure themselves? He concludes there is no obvious reason why the victim lied for the simple reason that she did not lie. His client did rape and violently beat this young woman, and since the legal system seems incapable of seeing justice done, defence counsel will do it himself. He ends his argument with the cry that the jury put his client in jail where he cannot do any more harm. One assumes a mistrial will be declared.

. . . *And Justice For All* provides a nightmare vision of the law. The judge who is not a rapist is a gun-toting manic-depressive who contemplates suicide every morning before ascending the bench. All the defendants but one are innocent, yet all the innocent defendants are found by the law to be guilty. The one guilty client is found to be innocent and goes out to commit another murder.

The film is hardly an objective portrayal of the legal system, but it does raise vividly an issue that audiences seem to take very seriously—the lawyer's relationship to justice in an unjust legal system. Like *Young Mr. Lincoln* and *True Believer*, the movie's message is clear; a 'good' lawyer must always choose justice over law.

The Verdict

But not all movie lawyers are 'good'. And the lawyer villains are just as instructive about popular conceptions of law and justice as their hero counterparts.[1] Usually, 'villain' lawyers work in large firms defending the anti-social activities of corporate interests. My two personal favourite villain lawyers are Ed Concannon (James Mason) in *The Verdict* and Jerome Facher (Robert Duvall) in *A Civil Action*.

Concannon is a 'bad' lawyer only in a moral sense. He is a superb legal technician with a keen insight into human psychology. We are not surprised that he has risen to the top of his profession in the tort defence Bar. We first see him meet a small squadron of associates in a conference room in his law firm. The room is part college seminar room complete with blackboard and part Renaissance palace with an ornate fireplace in front of which a uniformed African-American butler serves coffee. This setting perfectly reflects the mixture of intellect and privilege that the contemporary large American law firm likes to project. And Concannon's message to his minions is clear: their professional purpose is to win and to win decisively. To Concannon the fact that the plaintiff is a young mother entombed in an iron lung because of a medical foul-up at his client's hospital is just an obstacle to victory that must be overcome.

Later in the film we see how victory is achieved. There is a talented preparation for trial testimony of the stuffed shirt doctor where Concannon first destroys his client's story and then rebuilds it according to a script that will appeal to the jury. We also see him cleverly discredit the plaintiff's expert witness and persuasively argue arcane procedural points to keep out damaging evidence. His technical performance is indeed superb. But Concannon goes even further, stationing his own personal spy in the enemy camp to keep him informed of the plaintiff's strategy. I doubt that corporate litigators go this far. But that is just dramatic hyperbole, Concannon's real failure is choosing money over justice as his goal in practising law. Screenwriter David Mamet (the son of a lawyer) gives us a riveting scene where Concannon articulates his theory of the practice of law. Simply stated, it is all about winning because that is what clients pay for. And then Concannon lists the 'perks' that winning subsidizes. It is winning that pays for the fancy office, the stylish clothes, the single malt whisky, and even the pro bono work the firm performs. Winning even finances the luxury of philosophical chats about the ethics of legal practice. I imagine that Concannon might also mention the high salaries that law teachers command and even conferences on hip topics like law and popular culture. Concannon makes clear that the pursuit of justice and the pursuit of money often take divergent paths.

A Civil Action

Ed Concannon is corrupted by his love of wealth, but this vice does not explain the professional actions of Jerome Facher, one of the corporate defence lawyers in

[1] I would like to recommend Michael Asimow's excellent essay 'Bad Lawyers in the Movies' (2000) 24 *Nova L Rev* 533.

A Civil Action (1998). Facher displayes no special interest in money. Despite his partnership in a blue blood Boston law firm, he wears inexpensive suits and carries a well-worn brief case. No connoisseur of single malt scotch, Facher seems happiest at a table in his firm's law library eating homemade sandwiches and listening to a baseball game on radio. Facher likes to win for the sport of it. He is the quintessential legal craftsman, using all the technicalities of the law to protect his client with no concern about the justice of the result. We have no doubt he would be no more or less interested and just as efficient if assigned the other side of the case. For Facher, the game is the thing and winning is the game.

In *A Civil Action* Facher's opponent is Jan Schlichtmann (John Travolta), a flashy trial lawyer who is attempting to sue two large corporations for the deaths that have resulted from the pollution of drinking water in a small Massachusetts town. Facher takes the depositions of the plaintiffs who appear to be honest working people who have been devastated by deaths caused by the poisoned water. The primary lesson Facher draws from this encounter is that these witnesses must never be allowed to testify before a jury. He then sells the judge a procedural plan that accomplishes exactly this goal. The judge sends the technical question of negligence to the jury before allowing the plaintiffs to testify to damages, thereby insulating the jury from the real world effects of his clients' actions. He is successful and his client is exonerated. He has won the game. Facher incarnates the lawyer as cynic. When Schlichtmann tells him the jury will find out the truth, Facher chillingly replies, 'The Truth? I thought we were talking about a court of law.' For Facher, law is a war with no connection to truth or justice.

Despite this cynicism Duvall's Facher comes across as unassuming and almost likeable. He announces at one settlement conference that he has just been given a Chair at Harvard Law School, only to explain that the 'chair' is made of wood and is a gift from students in his trial practice course. At Harvard he teaches not the grand principles of legal theory but the legal craftsman's skills of quietly disrupting an opponent's case. Facher is what we sometimes call a 'lawyer's lawyer', a fact which should give all members of the profession pause.

Dirty Harry

William T Rothko (Joseph Sommer), the District Attorney who stymies Clint Eastwood's efforts in Don Siegel's *Dirty Harry* (1971) represents another type of 'bad' lawyer altogether. If Concannon represents corruption by greed and Facher represents the lawyer as cynical technician, Rothko is best described as the overburdened bureaucrat. But he shares with Concannon and Facher the same essential vice—he has given up on law as the agent of justice.

Harry Callahan (Clint Eastwood), the maverick San Francisco police detective, has finally brought to justice a vicious psychopath who has been terrorizing the Bay Area's women. Callahan is called to the District Attorney's office after the killer's arrest expecting an expression of gratitude. Instead Rothko informs him that the defendant will be set free because Callahan has not followed all the technical rules the US Supreme Court has laid down for the arrest of alleged wrongdoers. Rothko reminds Callahan that 'the defendant has rights', but the audience instinctively feels he is not talking about rights, but rules that must slavishly be followed irrespective of context. Callahan replies that he is more interested in the rights of the women the defendant has already killed and the others he will kill when released. Rothko is unmoved; Callahan has not obeyed the law, a comment to which Harry replies 'the law is crazy'. Harry leaves vowing to bring the defendant to justice in his own violent way, a promise he later keeps to the audience's delight.

We see here the same face-off between law and justice that we have noted in all the other films discussed. In movies, the hero chooses justice; the villain hides behind law. Some lawyers are heroes; others are villains. And when lawyers choose law over justice, the hero role devolves on vigilantes like Dirty Harry Callahan. The message of films like *Dirty Harry* is that if the law is ineffective in achieving justice, the public is willing to delegate the job to a charismatic man of righteous violence.[2]

Legal Technicians

We can see that these movies provide us with a clear model of the 'good' lawyer; he or she is an idealist who skilfully forces the legal system to yield justice to an underdog client. Law is always subservient to the search for justice. 'Bad' lawyers are those who get their priorities confused, abandoning the search for justice in favour of other rewards such as money, winning, or bureaucratic routine. We must admit that this 'popular' image of lawyering is extremely simplistic. Its Manichean image of the lawyer ignores a good deal of reality. For instance, it ignores the fact that most lawsuits have little to do with justice in any strong sense; they are just disputes about money between organizations neither of which can claim any morally privileged status. So too, it is silly to suppose that criminal defence counsel and plaintiff tort lawyers are always on the side of justice. We know that some criminal defendants like OJ Simpson are guilty and use their expensive lawyers to obstruct the quest for justice, and not every tort suit is meritorious, or even filed in good faith. 'Lawyer' films are much more interested in drama than truth, and factual accuracy is often quickly discarded for dramatic effect.

But I think it would be unfortunate if we dismissed this 'popular' view of lawyers. No doubt it has its distortions, but it may provide an effective counterweight to another myth about lawyering taught in our law schools, one I call the 'professional' model of lawyering. The professional model includes assumptions that are just as problematic as those in the popular model.

[2] See R Slotkin, *Gunfighter Nation: The Myth of the Frontier in Twentieth-Century America* (New York 1992).

The popular model highlights the human desire for a 'just' result. The professional model is less interested in just results than allegedly fair procedures. It assumes that procedural justice will yield substantive justice, but this assumption ignores the fact that the legal resources needed to work the system are not allocated on a basis even approaching equality. Procedural justice might yield justice in a society in which all citizens had equal access to the top-flight lawyers, but this necessary condition is clearly not present in even our most wealthy societies. Jan Schlichtmann and his clients are frustrated in *A Civil Action* not because Facher has a better case but because he has a larger bank roll.

A second element of the professional model is related to this procedural bias; it holds that we must put our faith in procedures because there are simply no substantively 'right' answers in difficult cases, only arguments that favour plaintiff or defendant. Convincing law students of the truth of the 'no truth' thesis seems to be one of the major goals of the first year law school curriculum. Students must abandon 'fuzzy' thinking and accept that truth and justice are chimeras. One law student put it thus:

> 'I made certain *naïve* emotional and political arguments before law that I no longer buy into. Part of me feels, well, there are certain things that are just right and wrong and then there's another part of me that says, well, wait a minute, things aren't that simple in the real world and you really can't go around making silly emotional arguments about what's right and wrong.'[3]

The fact that the truth is sometimes difficult to determine does not mean that there is no truth, nor does it mean that all resolutions of a dispute have an equal claim to the adjective 'just'. The primary goal of legal procedures should be to design systems which allow the true facts to emerge in complicated situations. My recollection is that Socrates was fighting the Sophists who believed there was no truth to be found, but now the Socratic method is usually employed to bolster these same Sophist conclusions.

Worse yet, students are led to believe that their earlier faith in 'emotional arguments' is a sign of intellectual immaturity and that adoption of the value-free professional model is a form of personal progress. I would suggest that (to use the facts in *A Civil Action* as an example) whether or not the defendant corporations polluted the water that the plaintiffs drank is a factual question to which a true answer can be found. And if true, the related question of whether and how much compensation the plaintiffs should receive from the defendant corporations is a question of justice as well as law. And finally, acknowledging an emotional dimension to the assignment of proper legal responsibility to the defendants for their actions is not a sign of intellectual immaturity; instead it is evidence of a richer humanity. At least that is what movies suggest.

[3] Quoted in R Granfield, *Making Elite Lawyers: Visions of Law at Harvard and Beyond* (New York 1992) 80.

A third element of the professional model is its definition of 'good' and 'bad' lawyering solely in terms of craft skills. Since law is a series of preset procedures in which plaintiff and defendant wage a form of warfare, and since there is no right answer to the issues they contest, a good lawyer is not a hero who obtains justice, but rather an expert who works the procedures to yield a result favourable to his client. He or she is not a moralist like Eddie Dodd or Jan Schlichtmann, but a skilled technician like Jerome Facher. The professional model pictures lawyers operating in a morally flattened universe in which craft values dominate. It is at least ironic that we should refer to Facher who cleverly blocks the plaintiffs' attempts to tell their stories to the jury as the 'good' lawyer and Schlichtmann who ruins his career in an attempt to see that they are heard the 'bad' lawyer, but that is how the professional model rates them.

What Movies Can Teach Law Students

So, to return to this essay's title, what can movies teach law students? Certainly they do not provide a realistic description of the day-to-day activities of the average American lawyer. Movie lawyers have little time for mundane legal tasks such as answering interrogatories. And we must admit that the hero/villain theme that runs through these movies does not reflect fairly the complexity of what might be called the ethical dilemmas of the legal practice. Life seldom presents the clear choices between good and evil which movies prefer. But still I would claim that movies can teach law students much of value that is too often underplayed in the law school curriculum.

The first lesson is that justice counts. The very quantity of 'law' films demonstrates that the human appetite for justice is just as strong as our appetites for power and sex. And while justice is not the only human value involved in the practice of law, it is an important one. And once we expand our notion of the ethical life beyond the narrow canons of lawyerly ethics to include the importance of living a life in which the pursuit of justice is one important component, we find that the practice of law is fraught with ethical consequence.

I think the experience of Jan Schlichtmann, Jerome Facher's opponent in *A Civil Action*, is a good example of this fact. Schlichtmann comes into the case thinking his goal is a simple one—to get as large a fee as possible with as little risk as possible. Yet slowly he discovers he wants more; he wants to see justice done even though it is not exactly clear what that concept means in this context. He finds himself in a quandary. If he 'takes the money and runs' as he originally planned, he is no more than the 'ambulance chaser' big firm lawyers like Facher think him. But if he proceeds with the case, he puts his clients, his partners, and himself at financial risk. It is not easy to balance these conflicting considerations, especially since they do not calibrate on the same measure. Jerome Facher leads a simpler life from a moral perspective, but that is not necessarily to his credit.

A second lesson law students can learn from movies is the need to question the moral status of the status quo. Time and again, movies show us that the law and its appointed guardians are often the enemies of justice not its guardians. To mention just two of the most egregious examples of evil hiding behind legal office, we can note the prosecutor in *True Believer* who frames an innocent man to conceal his own involvement in a murder and the judge in . . . *And Justice For All* who believes his professional status affords him immunity for the violent rape of a young woman. Once again let us not confuse drama with fact. Prosecutors are not murderers and judges are not rapists. None of these plot devices have much connection with reality as at least I understand it, but metaphorically they teach us that good lawyers never take anything for granted, especially the claims of the powerful to represent justice. If 'fuzzy' thinking is one intellectual limitation in the entering law student that law school attacks, moral and political naïveté should be another. We raise our children to trust institutions and perhaps that is a virtue on a personal level, but it is a professional vice. Lawyers have to delve beyond appearances to find the true facts, and movies teach us that reality is often more complex and less just than the powerful would like us to believe.

A third lesson would be the importance of choosing your employers well. Once you take a client, a lawyer has an ethical duty zealously to promote the client's interests, but there is no duty to accept any client except in the rare instance where other competent counsel is unavailable. The law school culture tells students that 'good' lawyers work for 'good' firms and the 'best' firms are large corporate firms. The fact that these firms earn their income from representing corporate clients is an ethically neutral factor according to the professional model.

But movies tell a different story. Corporate firms represent their clients' interests and these interests are often in conflict with the ethical values of many law students. To simplify but not distort, large corporations tend to believe that the best of worlds is one in which government interferes the least in the corporate drive for profit. This tenet translates into reading environmental laws, work safety laws, and civil rights laws as narrowly as possible. Of course, there is nothing unethical in that, but it does cause a moral cognitive dissonance in young lawyers who happen to believe personally in broad readings of these same laws. Law students would do well to listen to Ed Concannon's description of corporate law practice. It is all about winning. Corporations pay lawyers big money to win with no interest in how winning reflects or conflicts with the personal values of the individual lawyer. That is the bargain and corporations expect it to be honoured. While corporate firms might like to present themselves as public interest organizations while wooing summer interns, the reality is they are committed to protecting their clients' bottom lines, not the public interest. It is best that law students know this elementary fact coming in.

Finally, I think that the best 'lawyer' movies teach law students not only that moral decisions are an important part of a lawyer's life, but also that often it is difficult to know what is the ethically correct concrete decision. Just as Arthur

Kirkland warned us, it is difficult to know how to be a 'good' lawyer in both the craft and ethical senses of the word. Here I think Jan Schlichtmann is again a very valuable model for law school study, perhaps because the movie character is drawn from real life. Jan wants so much. He wants to win. Winning is not everything, but winning is important. Clients do not come to lawyers to lose. He wants money. Money is not everything, but money is important too. He wants the respect of his peers like Facher. And he should. Let's face it; Facher is a helluva lawyer. And like Abe Lincoln, Eddie Dodd, and Arthur Kirkland, (and even Harry Callahan), he wants to see justice done.

Schlichtmann can be an inspiration to law students not because he is a hero; in many senses he is not a hero at all. I certainly would not care to be his law partner. Schlichtmann is important as a model because he shows us how a lawyer slowly comes to question where professional success really resides. He teaches us that the life of a lawyer is much more than just a game to be won. And he also teaches us that exactly what constitutes that 'more' is difficult to determine.

PART III

THE NOVEL

Popular Fiction and Domestic Law: *East Lynne*, Justice, and the 'Ordeal of the Undecidable'

Marlene Tromp

'Sensationalism is the crying literary vice of our times', remarked one Victorian critic, for we have lost '[q]uiet pictures of common every-day life.'[1] Indeed, it is in part this loss that makes sensation especially effective at critiquing domestic law. While lawyers, lawmakers, and criminals populate most Victorian sensation fiction, the trial scenes are not the primary way in which the appeals for justice in these novels are made. In fact, if we read them through the lens of postmodern theory, we discover what may be even more effective ways in which this fiction gestures towards justice for women: the very sensational elements that made them seem far afield from carefully ordered courtrooms and Parliamentary debates—their scandalous plot lines, such as bigamy, murder, assumed identities, fraud; their transgressive heroines; and their unresolvable mysteries.

These disruptive qualities may have given this arguably female-dominated genre[2] another way to speak to the law—famously characterized in *Bleak House* as pervasive, powerful, impenetrable, and exclusively managed by men[3]—particularly in regards to gender concerns. As Paula Jean Reiter points out, good

[1] 'Recent Novels: Their Moral and Religious Teaching' (1866) 27 *London Quarterly Rev* 103.

[2] Many authors who wrote in the genre were women and the leading characters were often female as well.

[3] As Dickens writes: 'The raw afternoon is rawest, and the dense fog is densest, and the muddy streets are muddiest near that leaden-headed old obstruction, appropriate ornament for the threshold of a leaden-headed old corporation, Temple Bar. And hard by Temple Bar, in Lincoln's Inn Hall, at the very heart of the fog, sits the Lord High Chancellor in his High Court of Chancery. Never can there come fog too thick, never can there come mud and mire too deep, to assort with the groping and floundering condition which this High Court of Chancery, most pestilent of hoary sinners, holds this day in the sight of heaven and earth. On such an afternoon, if ever, the Lord High Chancellor ought to be sitting here—as here he is . . . outwardly directing his contemplation to the lantern in the roof, where he can see nothing but fog. On such an afternoon some score of members of the High Court of Chancery bar ought to be—as here they are—mistily engaged in one of the ten thousand stages of an endless cause, tripping one another up on slippery precedents, groping knee-deep in technicalities, running their goat-hair and horsehair warded heads against walls of words and making a pretence of equity with serious faces, as players might' (London, 1853; Penguin edn, Nicola Bradbury, (ed), New York: 1996) 14.

Victorian women, in general, and wives, especially, could not speak to or for the law.[4] Their husbands (and the lawyers, who stood metaphorically in this role) were to represent them before the law. Though these dualisms were never entirely stable—a fact that makes my claim about sensation fiction possible—they represent the pervasive pattern.[5] Under these conditions, what happened if the marriage was unhappy or the husband was not good? To whom would the wife turn and how could she speak in a system that did not grant her voice? As Drucilla Cornell notes in her discussion of Carole Pateman: 'Implicit in [the] idea of the [social] contract is that what men do with women is considered "private" and, thus, not to be regulated by the state'.[6] The binaries that secure this social contract (man/wife, public/private, active/passive)[7] may be upset, however, 'irritated' as Cornell would have it,[8] by disruptive representations. When this occurs, the seemingly closed legal system may be disrupted as well. I argue that fiction, particularly sensation novels, supplies the irritation that Cornell suggests may help generate cultural and legal change. Charles Dickens's metaphors of legal fog, mud, and undecidability point to the ways this genre may have created a kind of gendered justice-making, a model of interpreting this fiction that turns Dickens's critique on its head. While it is not unusual to read realist, high culture literature or traditional legal fiction[9] as narrative forms that engaged in conversation with the law, sensation fiction's cultural concerns have often been described as a compromised critique or even as ultimately repressive.[10] I have argued elsewhere that sensation fiction did indeed engage with the law, and in fact altered the understanding of the real.[11] In this essay I will explain why sensation is a particularly theoretically apposite model for seeking justice, especially as those issues emerge from realms that were less legally accessible, like the non-economic aspects of the relationship

[4] 'Husbands, Wives, and Lawyers: Gender Roles and Professional Representation in Trollope and the Adelaide Bartlett Case' (1998) 25 *College Literature* 43.

[5] Drucilla Cornell makes a persuasive argument about the way in which anti-woman structures in the law persist in spite of activism and a certain kind of cultural awareness about gendered bias in 'The Philosophy of the Limit: Systems Theory and Feminist Legal Reform' in Drucilla Cornell, Michel Rosenfeld and David Gray Carlson (eds), *Deconstruction and the Possibility of Justice* (New York: 1992).

[6] Cornell, n 5 above, 73.

[7] Helene Cixous explores these binaries and their social implications at length in 'The Laugh of the Medusa' in Elaine Marks and Isabelle de Courtivron (eds), *New French Feminisms* (New York: 1981).

[8] Cornell, n 5 above, 83.

[9] Certainly, these forms bleed together. Wilkie Collins, a sensation novelist, also wrote *The Moonstone*, a novel regarded by many to be the first proper detective novel. I am particularly interested in fiction in which the focus is less legal transgressions and more the violation of social codes that simultaneously suggest the justice of such violation.

[10] Anne Cvetkovich, for example, argues that sensation fiction reduces political action to affect (*Mixed Feelings* (New Brunswick, NJ: 1992)), and Elaine Showalter, in her early discussion of *Lady Audley's Secret* argues that whatever critique of social codes Lady Audley offered, her 'unfeminine assertiveness must ultimately be defined as madness' in order to mitigate the threat that it implies ('Desperate Remedies' (1976) 49 *Victorian Newsletter* 5).

[11] In *The Private Rod* I contend that the pervasive that private, domestic concerns should remain untouched by the state preserved a husband's right to batter his wife, even in the middle and upper classes where such violence was thought not to exist. Sensation fiction rendered visible both the violence and the state practices.

between husband and wife. Even when these tales resort to the law as a means of restoring order and the letter of the law is strictly observed, as in Wilkie Collins's *The Woman in White* (1859), the text often simultaneously undermines claims of legal justice.[12] Moreover, the conversation between this fiction and the law occurs not only in the novels' explicit critiques of legal insufficiencies (as in Collins's *Man and Wife* (1870)[13]), but also, and perhaps more pressingly, in the narrative moments where they are the most sensational, undecidable, and erratic.

The theoretical framework for such an exploration begins at the distinction between justice and the law. While we attempt to institutionalize justice in our legal codes, several things prevent the law from being just. First, our own cultural blind spots, tensions, and contradictions emerge as pressure points that harm those who fall outside the norms that produce our laws. As Eloise A Buker has argued in her feminist study of the law: 'Normative values and equality based on similar treatment [create] inequality for those who are in any way considered "different"'.[14] In nineteenth-century English law, as many critics have argued, that meant women, the poor, non-white people, and those who engaged in non-heteronormative relationships, to name but a few. Second, when the law 'acts', it remains static. It cannot be a living text that shapes itself to respond to individual situations,[15] and, further, when legal evolution does occur, it is a complex process that can be protracted by political negotiation—sometimes even long after the need for reform has been widely acknowledged. Though these features provide safeguards against caprice, they also make the law painfully unresponsive to cultural change and place it in the service of the status quo. Finally, in spite of these gaps and its inelasticity, the law is totalizing:[16] it is *intended* to be stable and to eschew exceptions. There are no dispensations for 'outsiders'. If one does not fit the profile of the person for whom the law is written—either as a victim or perpetrator—one may be unprotected when the law ought to serve as a shield or named guilty when that claim is unfounded.

[12] While Marian Halcombe argues that the 'murder will out' and Percival's significant forgery is discovered, freeing Laura to marry Walter, the law has not only been incapable (in protecting Laura or discovering Percival's fraud, for example), but is insufficient. Whether Sir Percival had made a forgery or not, he was a cruel and violent husband who remained beyond the reach of the courts and Laura's earnest expression of her desires prior to her marriage fail to secure her happiness—both of which are clearly unjust. In sensation fiction, we often find portraits of the law failing because of its rigidities, not its murkiness, as Dickens suggested.

[13] In this novel, the unevenness of Scottish and English marriage laws and the lack of recourse for wives as victims of marital violence are central concerns.

[14] Eloise A Buker, *Talking Feminist Politics* (New York: 1999) 191.

[15] Though it is true that some judicial decisions involve the interpretation of a judge, which gives the administration of the law some flexibility and causes the codes to shift, the judge must also rely on precedent and is bound by the limits of the law.

[16] Derrida notes that the law 'seems always to suppose the generality of the rule, a norm or a universal imperative' ('The "Mystical Foundation of Authority" ' in Cornell et al, n 5 above, 17) and Michel Foucault's central criticism of totalizing structures was that they were inevitably unjust (see especially *Discipline and Punish* (trans Alan Sheridan, New York: 1975) and *The History of Sexuality* (trans Robert Hurley, New York: 1978)).

Let me offer some contemporary examples. A woman who had recently emigrated from East Asia to the United States left home to buy groceries while her graduate-student husband was away. She 'safely' locked her two children behind her apartment door, as she had done for years at home. When a neighbour saw her leave without them, he reported her to the police. That day, she was arrested for child abuse, and her children were removed from her care. The tensions generated here are more than those of cultural difference. Whether or not we agree with her child care practices, the exercise of the law in this case was clearly not simply about justice. Instead, it exposes a blindness to the highly-gendered nature of childcare and domestic labour. No one complained, for example, that the husband, who had been in the United States for many years, had taken no responsibility for the children. Instead, while such practices were sanctioned by both parents, only the mother was arrested. Conversely, in child abuse cases in which the father or a male custodian harms the children, the mother is often also legally punished for failing to protect her children. These patterns point to the ways in which we hold mothers almost exclusively responsible for the well-being of their children, in spite of the fact that both parents are named legal guardians.[17] Furthermore, it privatizes a father's behaviour in the home—he is not responsible for a mother's abusive child care—but places a mother's conduct under constant legal scrutiny.

In another case, a woman whose former boyfriend was a prominent local businessman called the police when he broke into her house, kidnapped her dog, and arrived at her door with photographs of the animal. She had already been to court to seek legal redress for a letter in which he had threatened to kill her. His attorney had complained to the judge—not that the man was innocent—but that a finding against the man would harm his business. The police apparently agreed that this man's public work provided a safeguard against the law and refused to arrest him in spite of physical proof and his willing admission that he had violated the court's mandate. Instead, they explicitly told the victim that an important business man must have better things to do besides harass an ex-girlfriend—a remarkable refusal to acknowledge the material evidence. Whatever he had done to make her feel threatened (he never, in the end, seriously injured the woman or her dog physically) seemed a private matter to police and even to the court that had legally constrained his contact with her, particularly given his social status outside the home. They determined the conflict between them was best resolved without further legal action. While they did not live together and virtually all of his threats had been made in public, it was not the physical space in which these behaviours occurred that made them inaccessible to the law, but the more abstract space

[17] This phenomenon also has the effect of denying male guardians custody of children should a couple separate. This practice, however, often dovetails the expectations and wishes of both parents, and while allowing a mother more access to her children, usually significantly reduces her standard of living and fails adequately to compensate her financially for her care of the children. Nor is this a 'natural' pattern. Mary Lyndon Shanley has pointed to the ways in which child custody evolved from a male right to a virtual female privilege in *Feminism, Marriage, and the Law in Victorian England* (Princeton: 1989).

between the two people—their 'private' relationship—that made the police and courts reluctant to intervene unless and until he did visible, public harm.

A third case illustrates the potential outcomes of such a legal and social phenomenon and leads us to the broader social analysis. A woman living on a university campus called the police because her ex-husband, against whom the courts had issued a protective injunction, was driving up and down the road in front of her university apartment with a gun pointed out his truck window at her. The university police refused to act because he was on city property, and the city police refused to act because she was on university property. While it is hard to imagine a robbery or stranger assault in which the police would be utterly paralyzed by such a fragile physical boundary, in this case, as in the previous one, the most significant boundary was the 'private' one between husband and wife, and the police held their peace. The ex-husband shot the complainant between the hairs of that advantageous gap in the law and law enforcement later that week.[18] While everyone was shocked and saddened by this event, it is not uncommon, nor are those I described earlier—and this is a telling point. Countless women have been harassed and even murdered by their partners or ex-partners, in spite of lodging complaint after complaint with law enforcement and the courts and following all the proper legal procedures to secure their own safety. If we do value women's lives, we clearly value other things more—like ensuring that men have the right to do as they wish in the private sphere, even if it harms a woman.[19]

Each of these cases has its own complications, and none of them suggests that we should not have law or that the law consistently fails to protect people or prosecute perpetrators. Rather, they emphasize the way that the law may sanction stereotyped gender roles in the form of gendered expectations and the public/private divide[20] and render insignificant women's rights, a phenomenon that can (most literally, in some cases) limit women's lives. While we claim to offer women equal protection under the law, the law chafes against this impulse when it enters the home and it is a *man's* behaviour that requires scrutiny. We must take special care to root out the ways in which the law fails to guarantee women's safety and autonomy in the domestic space. While we need the law, we must consistently work to eliminate its violence, exclusion, and prejudice: the reasons that Jacques Derrida suggests we must deconstruct the law.[21] He remarks: 'Every time that something comes to pass or turns out well, every time that we placidly apply a good rule to a particular case, to a correctly subsumed example, according to a

[18] The first case took place in 1993 at the University of Florida in Gainesville, Florida, where I served on the planning committee of a feminist activist group. The latter two occurred in 1987 and 1992, respectively, during my tenure as a hotline volunteer and President of the Board of Directors of the SAFE house, a shelter and counselling centre, in the state of Wyoming for victims of domestic violence, sexual assault, and incest.

[19] Alice Abel Kemp makes a similar argument about the alleged 'sanctity' of motherhood in 'Poverty and Welfare for Women' in Jo Freeman (ed), *Women: A Feminist Perspective* (Mountain View, Cal: 1995).

[20] Drucilla Cornell notes that the same is true of 'mommy tracks' in law firms (ibid).

[21] *Specters of Marx* (trans Peggy Kamuf, New York: 1994) 30.

determinant judgment, we can be sure that law (*droit*) may find itself accounted for, but certainly not justice. Law (*droit*) is not justice. Law is the element of calculation, and it is just that there be law, but justice is incalculable . . . the decision between the just and unjust is never insured by a rule.'[22] The law is constructed, built with all the tensions I have described, but justice is undeconstructable; it is a fluid and mobile ideal.[23] Indeed, if we attempt to speak definitively to justice, to pin it down, we are again trapped in the limitations of that moment and of our own blind spots—a tremendously ironic difficulty and one that makes postmodern theory difficult for some.[24]

We might, then, ask, where we can find justice, if not in the law and how can we create legal change? Derrida suggests that 'justice is an experience of the impossible. A will, a desire, a demand for justice whose structure wouldn't be an experience of aporia would have no chance to be what it is, namely, a call for justice.'[25] In other words, it is in the space that remains beyond the ordering of culture—in the endlessly perplexing, interpretable and undecidable—that the call for justice most potently emerges. For this reason I have chosen to turn to fiction, with its limitless possibilities for reading. Further, I am particularly interested in fiction that deals with a domestic space, and not just those narratives that address legalities directly. While Anne Humphreys points to the flood of fictional narratives that considered what women might do in the wake of a divorce when divorce was becoming a legal possibility, we rarely explore the way that fiction may have actually shaped the law by creating a kind of social discomfort, an 'ordeal of undecidability' in which we might poignantly feel the lack of justice in the current legal framework. Certainly, realist and domestic fiction engaged in legal critique and dramatized the tension of the domestic space. Humphreys, for example, argues that: 'In many [divorce] novels, whose whole point is to call for redress for women's inequality under the marriage law, this contradiction [between a desire to maintain sympathy for the unhappy party and the unresolvability of the situation under current legal structures] can destabilize the narrative and open a fissure through which new types of narrative structures and closures are tried, not always successfully'.[26] These new plots,

22 Derrida, n 16 above, 16.

23 '[I]f', as Derrida says, 'such a thing exists' (n 16 above, 14).

24 William B Turner explores this tension as it applies to questions of gender and sexuality in *A Genealogy of Queer Theory*. While he acknowledges the impulse in the gay community to unite under a banner of stable biological determinism and authenticity (ie, 'we are born gay, cannot control it, and, therefore, deserve the same rights as others born with "disabilities" such as femaleness or a non-white racial identity'), he argues that it would be more politically efficacious to take up a Foucaultian stance, which would resist such a monolithic stance for identity—one which could, ultimately, produce more repression than it resists (by, for example, suggesting the abortion of foetuses with the 'gay gene'). He argues instead that we must engage in perpetual critique of the rhetorical structures of the culture that allow for oppression and recognize, with Foucault, that 'the moral implications of any exercise of power will remain always ambiguous and labile, requiring an attitude of perpetual suspicion and critique' (176). Similarly, a merely static law cannot respond to the shifting concerns of a population and, indeed, as Foucault has argued, the law may institutionalize repressive, disciplinary structures.

25 Derrida, n 16 above, 16.

26 Anne Humphreys, 'Breaking Apart: the early Victorian divorce novel' in Nicola Diane Thompson (ed), *Victorian Women Writers and the Woman Question* (New York: 1999) 46.

of which she sees two—the Jane Eyre plot and Caroline Norton plot[27]—critically examined traditional modes of operation in the culture.

As Valerie Sanders argues, even novels by seemingly antifeminist women such as Charlotte Yonge, Eliza Lynne Linton, Mrs Humphrey Ward, and Margaret Oliphant, 'bec[a]me a troubled site of struggle, a place where the meaning of marriage [was] repeatedly contested'.[28] Sanders reads the work of Oliphant as key 'in the deromanticizing of marriage in preparation for Ibsen and the New Woman of the 1880s and 1890s'.[29] Sensation fiction, however, went farther, offering a greater, more disturbing range of possibilities than the Jane Eyre/Caroline Norton plots. If domestic novels were undermining normative notions of marriage through their conflicted representation—in spite of what Nancy Armstrong has persuasively identified as their largely ideologically normalizing and disciplinary function for women[30]—how much more so were the vexed narratives of sensation fiction that made the villain the sympathetic heroine?[31]

Sensation novels made this shift in part because they disrupted the boundary between the interior feminine, domestic (and psychological) space and the external, masculine, public, and political space. Whereas the public space, by virtue of its avowedly political and evolving character was perceived as amendable, the domestic space was conceived of as pure, naturalized, and unlegislatable, as was the feminine. By consistently focusing on the domestic as the source of the problem and drawing the domestic and private into the public eye, sensation novelists called into question more than simply social policy, but normality and morality. Other novelists, like Dickens,[32] maintained the critics' affection when they '[spoke] to specifically removable evils' in the public space, like the problematic poor laws in *Oliver Twist*.[33] Dickens's critiques of the law did not turn provocatively to what was considered unlegislatable. One critic noted: 'Fagin and the Dodger, Bill Sykes and Nancy, were admirable subjects for legislation'.[34] Moreover, when Dickens turned to the domestic, he presented 'beautiful pictures of scenes from family life . . . put[ting them] together in a natural, logical plot restrained in its use of incident and deliberate effects'.[35] Despite what critics regarded

[27] Caroline Norton was separated from her husband, but he continued and was well within his legal rights, to seize the money she earned even after their separation and to prevent her from seeing her children. She made a public case of his cruelty, essentially demanding that the state step in as a surrogate husband/father when an individual man failed to do his duty by his family. In *Jane Eyre*, of course, Jane must wait to marry Rochester until his mad, but legal, wife Bertha perishes in a fire.

[28] Valerie Sanders, 'Marriage and the antifeminist woman novelist' in *Victorian Women Writers and the Woman Question* (New York: 1999), 25.

[29] ibid, 35.

[30] See *Desire and Domestic Fiction* (New York and Oxford 1987).

[31] We might be reminded here of Jean Rhys's rewriting of *Jane Eyre*'s Bertha Mason in *Wide Sargasso Sea* and Gayatri Chakravorty Spivak's reading of both texts ('Three Women's Texts and a Critique of Imperialism' in Robyn R Warhol and Diane Price Herndl (eds) *Feminisms* (New Brunswick, NJ: 1991).

[32] Dickens, of course, is noted to have included many sensational incidents in his fiction. However, he was not conceived of as a sensation novelist, in the Victorian period or now, an issue to which I will return below.

[33] Benito Perez Galdos, 'Carlos Dickens' *La Nacion* 9(1968) in Michael Hollington (ed), *Charles Dickens: Critical Assessments*, vol. 1(Mountfield, Sussex, 1995), 450–454, 224.

[34] 'Sensation Novels' (1863) 3 *Medical Critic and Psychological J* 513, quoted in Andrew Maunder, (ed), *East Lynne* (Toronto, 2000) 723.

[35] Benito Perez Galdos, 224.

as his ignorance about many of the issues he tackled, it was generally believed he addressed them ethically and 'observed,' as one reviewer indicated, 'conventional rules' of propriety.[36] Compare a review of Dickens, for example, in 1862, just as sensation fiction was making a critical name for itself:[37] 'Mr. Dickens merits much praise for the tone of healthful morality that pervades all his tales . . . [for he never] places his characters in those questionable circumstances where the lie between right and wrong is nearly obliterated, a [serious] fault, which has greatly injured some of our recent novels'.[38]

Sensation novelists, however, were perceived as blurring the very line that Dickens maintained: these novels 'depreciate[d] custom' and 'weaken[ed] established rules of right and wrong'.[39] They presented a style 'in which right and wrong was muddled up together into a sort of neutral tint, the author, and consequently, the reader, taking no trouble to distinguish them'.[40] Significant to my analysis is the precise way in which this critic indicated that sensation novelists had failed morally. They rendered indistinct the line between 'right and wrong'; they erred in depicting women and men outside their proper roles and marriage as a less than blissful state. This, the author suggests, 'produce[s] a blurred and blotted vision of life, which . . . is either infinitely sad or infinitely harmful'.[41] Perhaps this vision of life was harmful because it undermined the social acceptance of norms with its critique. Since sensation novelists 'reduce[d] marriage to a temporary connection' and 'show[ed] the inconveniences of matrimony',[42] they challenged both the value and the privacy of that state. One reviewer said of a popular sensation novel: 'The purport of the volume is as a contribution to the sad subject [of divorce]. . . . We perceive that even the poetical justice which we expect to find in works of fiction is too coarse and rough to be able to adjust properly degrees of guilt and punishment.'[43] To locate the central conflict of the novel in the domestic space and to suggest, somehow, that this might not be related simply to an amendable statute or policy—worse, to make propriety itself difficult to determine—was to earn the designation of 'unscrupulous' or 'morally depraved'. These sensational narratives were not perceived as social analysis, like Dickens's novels had been. They assailed the very terms of normality, and, thus, were immoral. Entry into the domestic sphere was appropriate, if, as Nancy Armstrong indicates, the narrative modelled 'a set of mental processes that guaranteed domesticity'.[44] Sensation fiction failed to domesticate.

This pattern is evidenced by the contrasting way in which Dickens, and two sensation novelists, Mary Elizabeth Braddon and Ellen Wood, depicted the

[36] Walter Bagehot, 'Charles Dickens' (1858) 7 *National Review* 458.

[37] Jonathon Loesberg argues that this happens quite literally through the identification of the sub-genre by the critics.

[38] Anon. Review of the Collected Works of Charles Dickens, *British Quarterly Review*, 1 Jan 1862 in Hollington, n.33 above, 135–139.

[39] 'Our Female Sensation Novelists' (1863) 78 *Living Age* 365, 369.

[40] On Novels and Novel-Makers (1881) *22 Good Words* 322–327.

[41] ibid, 325.

[42] Henry Longeville Mansel, 'Sensational Novels' (1863) 113 *London Quarterly Rev* 257.

[43] Review of *East Lynne*, *Literary Gazette*, 19 October 1861, 370, quoted in Maunder, n 34 above, 710.

[44] Robyn R Warhol and Diane Price Herndl (eds), 'The Rise of the Domestic Woman' in *Feminisms* (New York: 1999) 907.

prevailing figure of the domestic space, the 'angel in the house'. The remarks of their reviewers indicate that their evaluation had less to do with the quality of their 'realism' or the inherent quality of their writing, than their adherence to notions about gendered identity. In an article entitled 'The Genius of Dickens', Edwin P Whipple notes that Dickens's oversentimentalized heroines:

> are all models of self-devoted, all-enduring, all-sacrificing affection, in respect to both sentiment and principle. Illustrating as they do the heroines of tenderness. . . . It may be that they are too perfect to be altogether real; but still . . . their reality, if questioned by the head, is accepted undoubtingly by the heart. . . . [T]he fact that they are domesticated by so many thousands of firesides shows that they are not the airy nothings of sentimentalizing benevolence, but have in them the substance of humanity.[45]

His unrealistic women characters are acceptable because he does not disturb idealized notions of womanhood and the domestic space. He 'has a distinct and conscious moral aim which inspires and dominates over the narrative' and this 'paints reality' in spite of its 'idealization'.[46] Though the critics admitted that his characters were 'profoundly unreal', and that he 'has been least successful in the portraiture of his heroines',[47] this was not wielded against him in the critiques. Alternatively, Margaret Oliphant reserves a special place for the heroine of Wood's *East Lynne* in her sweeping condemnation of the sensation novel, remarking: 'From first to last, it is in [the fallen heroine] alone in whom the reader feels any interest. . . . The Magdalen . . . who is only moderately interesting while she is good, becomes, as soon as she is a Magdalen, doubly a heroine . . . This is dangerous and foolish work, as well as false, both to Art and Nature.'[48] Braddon suffered similar critiques, her supposed 'lack of realism' often being offered as the reason for her condemnation. Her 'personages were not like living beings. . . . [Braddon] should have known that a woman cannot fill [the parts] into which she places them.' Her female characters are 'unnatural', and by virtue of that fact, 'grave ethical errors'. These flaws render her novels 'the most noxious book[s] of modern times'.[49]

Female characters and, presumably, female writing, should have been directed by her naturalized gender role. One essayist meditating on the question of novel writing argued that the women novelists must encourage 'mutual comprehension[,] mutual understanding of each other. . . . not the spirit of discontent. . . . From all participation in such may Heaven keep women, and especially the women of England!'[50] This lament suggests that sensation novels disruptively generated dissent, not simply in their tales, but in the real lives of women readers as well. Furthermore, many critics urged that all novelists must write from their knowledge of the world. For women novelists, this posed a special

45 Edwin P Whipple, 'The Genius of Dickens' (1867) 10 *Atlantic Monthly* 222.

46 George Stott, 'Charles Dickens' in 'Charles Dickens: Critical Assessments' (1995) 10 *Contemporary Rev* 235.

47 ibid, 153.

48 Margaret Oliphant, 'Sensation Novels', *Blackwoods Edinburgh Magazine*, 1 May 1862, 567.

49 W Fraser Rae, 'Sensation Novelists: Miss Braddon' (1865) 43 *North British Rev* 96.

50 'Lady Novelists of Great Britain' (1853) 15 *Living Age* 476.

bind. Separate spheres ideology, whether practised in fact or not, mandated that a woman did not enter the political and social realm, and this, thus, denied them knowledge of it. Therefore a woman novelist could not 'fetch up material from haunts into which a Dickens or a Bulwer may penetrate'.[51] Nor could she write about 'the odd and disreputable members of society whom every man must mix with more or less. . . . Her delicacy binds her to a double reserve, unless, indeed, she have the shameless assurance to unsex herself.'[52] While writers like Dickens depicted women, even fine ladies, who fell, abandoned children, and led false lives—we might think of Dedlock, not Audley—these women were most often returned to the fold of the faithful or died invisibly; sensation heroines did not go down quietly and furthermore, added new sins to their list of crimes—but not unsympathetically, and that tension offers a new look at justice.

The discomfort the Victorian readers felt with sensation fiction is key to reading it as potentially transformative in terms of Derrida's argument. When the tale leaves us feeling vexed, unsettled, discomfited—as sensation fiction did its Victorian readers—it may be providing us with a cue for social change. It is for this reason that I turn to one of the most anxiety-producing novels of the day, Ellen Wood's *East Lynne* (1860). Not only was *East Lynne* one of the three novels for which the sensation genre was named,[53] it was '*the* best-selling novel of nineteenth-century England'.[54] While we might find similar patterns of social critique in much 'low-brow' and transgressive fiction—from other Victorian sensation novels to contemporary science fiction, the latter of which is discussed in other essays in this volume—I chose *East Lynne* both because of its wide readership and because it embodies the sensational and transgressive elements I have described. Each of the novel's most significant moments seem vexed by underlying sensational and gendered tensions. For example, following the birth of her first child, the heroine Lady Isabel addresses an astonishing plea to her devoted lawyer-husband: 'Oh, Archibald! Archibald! Don't marry her! I could not rest in my grave.'[55] While her husband stands by astounded, the reader has already sensed that, somehow, he will do the very thing that Isabel fears the most. Indeed, Archibald marries the offending 'other woman', and—worse yet—while Lady Isabel is still alive to witness their caresses. The disruption that makes these events possible also transforms this Earl's daughter into a shamed and disfigured governess: the schism between justice and the law for women. Not only is the law in this novel 'prone to unpredictable errors and abuses',[56] those abuses render us (and clearly did the Victorians) sympathetic to the law-breaking Lady Isabel and uncomfortable with the cultural context in which such social crimes—not just

[51] 'Lady Novelists of Great Britain' (1853) 15 *Living Age* 471.

[52] 'Contemporary Literature: Novelists' (1879) 125 *Blackwoods* 325.

[53] The other two were Braddon's *Lady Audley's Secret* and Collins's *The Woman in White*.

[54] Susan Balee, 'Correcting the Historical Context: the Real Publication Dates of *East Lynne*' (1993) 26 *Victorian Periodicals Rev* 143.

[55] ibid, 229.

[56] Brian McCuskey, 'The Kitchen Police: Servant Surveillance and Middle-Class Transgression' [2000] *Victorian Literature and Culture* 368.

legal ones—are possible. Though the tale depicts a cowardly murder perpetrated by an unpunished aristocratic man, an innocent man accused, and a noble man betrayed, these injustices are legally resolved by the novel's end. However, for a genteel woman—silenced, deceived, and abandoned—and her bastard child, tragic accidents, physical disfigurement, emotional torment, and death are the significant conclusions. Overtly, the text condemns Lady Isabel for discarding her home, husband, and children, repeatedly describing the suffering she so liberally endures as fitting for her crime—'the cross she . . . *must* bear'.[57] However, many of the narrative's most conflicted and conflicting moments revolve around questions of gender justice for Lady Isabel, a thread of the narrative that emerges just as powerfully as her condemnation.[58] This tension, in fact, is the lynchpin of the novel's call for justice.

The way in which *East Lynne* offers an agonizing read—to both Victorian and contemporary readers—explains how. It opens with a heroine anyone could love: a kind and beautiful Earl's daughter, who is unspoiled by her title and privilege. Lady Isabel, generous in spirit and practice, engineers a benefit concert for a poor piano tuner in the first scenes of the novel. Nearly everyone with whom she comes in contact benefits from her kindness, but nearly everyone injures her in return—though the novel rarely points up this pattern overtly. Her spendthrift father, in spite of his £60,000 a year, squanders his fortune, accumulates massive debts, and leaves his teenage daughter with no money and no one to care for her at his early death. Her uncle, who inherits her father's lands and title, takes her in, but her vain and jealous aunt abuses her while he is away—even resorting to physical violence. Ultimately, a wealthy middle-class lawyer proposes to Lady Isabel, and her aunt unceremoniously hands the girl over to him in spite of the difference in their rank and training. While an honourable and decent man, Archibald Carlyle works for a living and virtually abandons his young wife with nothing to occupy her but the cruelties of his sister, a penny-pinching spinster who insists that Lady Isabel is an inappropriate expense for the household. In spite of this keen-eyed lawyer's claims that his 'chief object in life now is [Isabel's] happiness',[59] he fails to see that she 'was in a state of galling subjection in her own home'[60]—no better than the untenable situation in her uncle's home that justified the unorthodox proposal with which he seemed to rescue her.

While an ordinary Victorian novel might end with a resolution to the conflicts in the home and a moralistic comment on middle-class virtues or Christian values, things only become more complicated. Archibald engages in secret business dealings with Barbara Hare, a woman who has inappropriately confessed her love for him after his marriage (and whom all the town and all the servants believe

[57] Ellen Wood, *East Lynne* (Ontario, Canada: 2000) 468.

[58] Indeed, even one contemporary critic argued that this metaphor of Lady Isabel's cross, because of the primary referent in Christ, suggests her purity—something which made this Victorian reviewer uncomfortable with the metaphor. It is precisely this tension and the injustice of the sentence that I wish to explore.

[59] Wood, n 57 above, 195.

[60] ibid, 216.

is angling for him—as one says, 'if anything happened to my lady, Miss Barbara, as sure as fate, would step into her shoes').[61] Though he is working to assist Barbara's fugitive brother who has been wrongly accused of murder, Archibald tells only his sister and Isabel's uncle the reason for his strange behaviour, leaving his wife with no way to interpret his secret assignations with Barbara. Lady Isabel, already wounded by Archibald's benign neglect, discovers a tryst between Barbara and her husband after he stands his young wife up for a dinner party. In this moment of grief and humiliation, she falls prey to an unscrupulous man who assures her that Archibald has betrayed her and that he, instead, will care for her.

The story does not abandon Isabel with sad hints at the travails and punishment of the fallen woman or offer the shocking truth of a long-past crime at the end of a suffering woman's life as a Dickens novel might. Instead, we closely follow her and her seducer, Francis Levison, who we discover late in the novel has committed the murder of which Barbara Hare's brother stands accused and who abandons Isabel before the birth of their child. Left again with nothing and no one to care for her, Isabel and her bastard son are involved in a train accident, which kills her child and horribly disfigures her. Believing in her imminent death, she dispatches a farewell note to her uncle, which morally frees her husband—who had immediately divorced her—to marry the faithful Barbara Hare. Longing desperately for her lost children and husband, and unrecognizable as a result her physical and emotional suffering, Isabel returns in disguise to serve as a governess to her own children, and is forced to witness both the loving exchanges between her former husband and her rival and the consumptive death of her son. She dies, grief-stricken, a servant in her own household.

The narrative relentlessly pursues Isabel and the ballooning horrors of her situation, and it is for this reason that this tragic novel and its sensational peers gesture toward justice.[62] Through its interrogation of the extremity and complexity of Isabel's sad life, the novel effectively points up the tensions in a law that convicts her and finds those around her innocent. In a culture that valued a woman's fidelity above most else, the narrative still calls for more just treatment of the dishonoured Isabel, and thus of women and wives in general. While Lady Isabel's reckless fall from grace is openly condemned by the narrator, we are simultaneously encouraged to sympathize with the extraordinary and complicated circumstances that mitigate her crime. Her husband is clearly complicit in her choices and it is through his blindness to her pain and his unwillingness to hear not only her daily concerns,[63] but her pleas and those of others not to admit the depraved Francis Levison to their home that helps create the tragic situation.

Further, while one might be forced to admit that Barbara Hare, the true and faithful second wife, seems a more likely heroine, she is not favourably depicted in

[61] Wood, n 57 above, 228.

[62] As Archibald himself says, 'justice and law are sometimes opposed to each other' (318), but it is not merely this claim that makes the novel resonant on these issues.

[63] She begs Archibald to stay with her when he leaves her alone to recover her health in the vicinity of Francis Levison, but he refuses and 'she felt that it [her wish] would not be listened to' (263).

much of the novel. In our introduction to her, she is impatiently snappishness with her universally-beloved and meek mother. And even when Isabel has been fully debased and Barbara elevated to the lady of the household, the latter's coldness towards Isabel's gentle-hearted and sickly boy, along with her chilly assertion that she 'was never fond of being troubled with children'[64] make her seem, ironically, the heartless usurper *and* the good wife. Meanwhile, Isabel remains in our sympathies in spite of her transgressions—a phenomenon that is not simply the experience of the modern, feminist-minded reader. Victorian critical opinion united with *John Bull* in calling Barbara 'disagreeable',[65] and the *Literary Gazette* 'confess[ed] that of the two wives [their] sympathies rather [went] with the first'.[66] Margaret Oliphant's angry critique condemned the novel for making Isabel so attractive and Barbara a character whom we 'should like to bundle to the door and be rid of anyhow'.[67] Even the novel's Mrs Hare, Barbara's conservative and delicate mother, says of Isabel after her daughter's marriage to Archibald: 'I loved [Isabel when she was Archibald's wife], and I cannot help loving her still. Others blamed, but I pitied her. They were well matched: he, so good and noble; she, so lovely and endearing.'[68]

It is not only the critique of Barbara, who *should* claim our affection, that complicates a reading of the narrative, however. The slippage between Barbara and Isabel haunts the novel.[69] They are both 'Mrs Carlyle', Archibald's wife, and mistress of East Lynne, and they both long for someone improperly and outside the bounds of marriage. If Isabel had feelings for Francis Levison that were too warm, feelings that made her vulnerable to his seduction and lies, there was '*one* [who] was hidden in [Barbara's] heart, filling up every crevice, one who had no right there'[70]—and Barbara's desire is precisely what, in justice, Isabel fears and what shapes future events, though Archibald continually dismisses his first wife's concerns. Indeed, if we were to miss such subtle parallels, the two women become shadows of one another when Isabel witnesses the very same scene of love between Barbara and Archibald at the piano that Barbara had seen years before: 'So, once had stolen, so, once had peered the unhappy Barbara, to hear this self-same song. *She* had been his wife then; she had received his kisses when it was over. Their positions were reversed.'[71] Another reversal occurs in the novel's final moments when Barbara learns that Lady Isabel had lived in their home disguised. In spite of Barbara's seeming moral superiority, she responds precisely as Isabel had years

[64] Ellen Wood, n 57 above, 464. [65] Review of *East Lynne, John Bull*, 4 May 1861, 284.

[66] Quoted in Maunder, n 34 above, 710. [67] Oliphant, n 48 above, 567.

[68] Wood, n 57 above, 487.

[69] Even at the sentence level, the narrator slips between Barbara and Isabel. After Isabel's return as Madame Vine, the governess, the narrator describes one of Archibald's homecomings with the words: 'In the sanguine moments of realization or of hope, some dark shadow will step in to mar the brightness. Barbara stood in the drawing room window watching for him. Not in her was the dark shadow' (495). Though the disavowal follows the naming of Barbara, and we are, presumably, to read Isabel as the dark shadow, the strange placement and sentence structure shift their positions in this clearly painful moment for Isabel, and Barbara is the blight on Isabel's happiness.

[70] Wood, n 57 above, 285. [71] ibid, 490.

earlier to Barbara's presence in the Carlyle's home: she asks her husband, 'has she taken your love from me?'[72] While we might wish to separate the two wives into good and bad, or even likeable and not, they insistently slide together, making the sinner difficult to identify.

The novel, in fact, is painfully undecided about Isabel, and this indecision emerges in the courtroom scenes, in spite of the ease with which the court acts on Levison's guilt. The novel's justice system, we are told, is askew and even calculates offences outside the norm: 'things were not conducted with the regularity of the law. The law there was often a dead letter. . . . [E]vidence was advanced that was inadmissible—at least that would have been inadmissible in a more orthodox court.'[73] As Victorian readers recognized, this novel and others like it demonstrated 'an impatience of old restraints, and craving for some fundamental changes in the working of society'; it shifted the terms of justice. Here, in the courtroom of this narrative, we can hear the story—wild and impossible as it is—of not just Sir Francis Levison's crimes, but of Isabel's injuries. Brian McCuskey's claim that the law in *East Lynne* is 'prone to unpredictable errors and abuses'[74] suggests why. We are led across the register of Isabel's sins and the narrator's condemnations to Isabel's innocence and the narrator's sympathy—in part because the law is vexed as well. Both positions are present themselves with force because the novel embodies the tensions of the period, and, when read through Derridean theory, offer a response, a challenge for change. As Jonathan Loesberg notes, much sensation fiction is 'almost deliberately thematically indeterminate'.[75] *East Lynne*, he points out, can be read as simultaneously subversive and conventional, citing both Elaine Showalter's championing of Wood's sympathy with Isabel's 'sexual boredom' and Jeanne B Elliot's argument that Isabel adheres to the 'most rigid of Victorian sexual stereotypes'.[76]

Derrida argues that deconstruction is not merely 'the oscillation or tension between two significations'—like a universal morality and a situational ethics or between Isabel's status as a feminist heroine and social villainess—but is the obligation:

> to give itself up to the impossible decision, while taking account of law and rules. A decision that did not go through the ordeal of the undecidable would not be a free decision, it would only be the programmable application or unfolding of a calculable process. It might be legal; it would not be just. . . . And once the ordeal of the undecidable is past (if that is possible), the decision has again followed a rule or given itself a rule, invented it or reinvented it, reaffirmed it, it is no longer *presently* just, fully just.[77]

Isabel's guilt and innocence, fully undecidable, full of pain and suffering, can provide the prodding of justice. Nicola Diane Thompson puts it succinctly when she discusses Victorian women's fiction, 'The lives and fictions of Victorian

[72] Wood, n 57 above, 690. [73] ibid, 601. [74] McCuskey, n 56 above, 368.

[75] Jonathan Loesberg, 'The Idealogy of Narrative Form in Sensation Fiction' (1986) 13 *Representations* 116. [76] ibid, 136 note.

[77] Derrida, n 16 above, 24.

women writers reveal endlessly contradictory perspectives on the woman question.'[78] In those moments that are not resolved as a traditional Victorian narrative might resolve them—cleanly, teleologically, normatively—fiction provides us with a call for justice for fallen women and for mistreated wives. Fiction is, to be sure, irresolvable, infinitely interpretable—how could we, otherwise, continue to return to Shakespeare's or Woolf's most compelling moments again with each generation? Sometimes Isabel *is* the heroine, sometimes the villainess. J Hillis Miller goes even farther when he says, 'literature lays down the law',[79] but he also acknowledges that the tale's 'effects are always unreadable before the fact' of their entry into the social context. While I am not suggesting that Wood planned to write a feminist liberation novel in taking up the most private, domestic issues of the day, she reimagined justice. The tensions that called to her (and clearly to others, in order to make this the best selling novel of the period) spoke to the concerns of many even as (and, in part, because) they raised the ire of some critics. In this way, her work engaged in conversation with the law.[80]

It is precisely this kind of figuring and refiguring for which Derrida calls. He challenges us as scholars, lawmakers, citizens to apply pressure to the law, to continually recast it, to compel change. The Victorians did, and we continue to do so. If the three cases I discussed earlier in the essay—the mother perhaps too eagerly brought before the law and the two men who seemed to escape it—create in us discomfort, if they seem almost unbelievable, unjust, even sensational, then we must look at them even more carefully. They are not simple cases. They are not easy tales of people—from the victims to the police—failing to follow the rules. They are vexed sites of cultural tension. Derrida's injunction to find justice in the undecidable is not a call for social paralysis. We should not avoid making legal rulings or critiquing the law. Instead, we should never stop critiquing it. We should remain mobile. And when we address the kinds of injustices that produced the problems I cited in the three cases above, we should seek the others that certainly lie buried in them as well.

[78] Nicola Diane Thompson, 'Responding to the woman question; rereading noncanonical Victorian women novelists' in *Victorian Women Writers and the Woman Question* (New York: 1999) 3.

[79] J Hillis Miller, 'Laying Down the Law in Literature' in *Deconstruction and the Possibility of Justice* (New York: 1992) 324.

[80] I have made such an argument about the body of sensation fiction in *The Private Rod.*

Law's Agent: Cultivated Citizen or Popular Savage? The *Crash* of the Moral Mirror

Melanie Williams

> Is this harnessing of our innate perversity conceivably of benefit to us? Is there some deviant logic unfolding more powerful than that provided by reason?
>
> JG Ballard, Introduction to *Crash*[1]

This quotation from the text of *Crash* by JG Ballard poses a crucial but unacknowledged question facing secular liberalism: to what extent can, or should society unleash, explore and experiment with the 'pathological' aspects of human interest in the *unmediated* context that is 'mass' culture? Despite passing media comment regarding the banal combination of sex and violence which forms the everyday diet of popular culture, the diet itself has become staple. Already subject to little scrutiny, the sex-violence *nexus*—the intimate linkage of the two factors—is queried even less. Though the text of *Crash* has an erotic, violent, even 'pornographic'[2] content, the text disturbs rather than facilitates the process of erotic 'consumption' *simpliciter* , providing a consciously disruptive perspective upon elements of human culture and nature, elements of crucial importance to the law but remaining curiously unexamined. Furthermore, the movement from text to film, from word to image, creates an additional aspect to the variables confronting self understanding in this age of rapid cultural change, with its emphasis upon consumption of the visual.

At present our culture tends to proceed on the premise that the autonomy of adulthood corresponds to a developed, discriminatory power over stimuli

[1] JG Ballard, *Crash*, first published in 1973. All references are to the 1995 (London) edition. A brief chronology of events and facts relevant to this paper may be of use at this point. The film version of *Crash* appeared in 1996, though lobbyists were still working to have it banned in 1998. Bernard Williams' *Shame and Necessity* (n 34 below) was first published in 1993, though the lectures upon which the book is based were first delivered in 1989. The Report of the Committee on Obscenity and Film Censorship appeared in 1979. The Obscene Publications Act dates from 1959, with electronic transmission of pornographic material now covered in the Criminal Justice and Public Order Act 1996.

[2] 'There is no settled definition of pornography either in the United Kingdom itself or especially in a multi-national environment such as the Internet where cultural, moral and legal variations all around the world make it difficult to define "pornographic content" in a global society'—Y Akdeniz, 'The Regulation of Pornography and Child Pornography on the Internet' (1997) 1 *J of Information, Law and Technology* 2.

encountered, both by accident and design. Any argument that material might be potentially 'harmful' or 'altering'—either in terms of direct or oblique effects—tends to collapse under the weight of a presumption in favour of what is termed 'freedom'—that unless direct change can be *proved*, suppression of information is potentially and *actually* more harmful than exposition. It is a complex argument at the heart of the laws of censorship and of how we determine the 'pornographic' as opposed to 'erotic'.

Crash is a story—originally a novel, later a film—tracking the erotic potential and social consequences of a consumer-led culture, in which the potential intimacy between sexual and violent impulses, specifically, the car crash as an erotic stimulus, is fostered. The importance of this text will be discussed later; for the moment, it creates a useful introductory reminder of the varied and growing popular culture impacting upon, and producing insights for, formal institutional cultures. Recent case law demonstrates the process of logic to which law has traditionally subscribed when dealing with such issues of freedom and moral character. The juristic process exhibits symptoms of an hermeneutic trap, an underlying stasis deriving from the image of mankind allowed to the law by current culture. Law must subscribe to, and protect, notions of autonomy, of rights, of individual judgment and personal freedom, notions nourished by a loosely hypothesized average legal subject, oddly separated from community in terms of the journey from right and responsibility, yet modelled as thoroughly integrated in terms of conscience.

The case of *R v Stephane Laurent Perrin* (2002)[3] demonstrates the difficulty. The case reviewed the legality of an internet site advertising its pornographic wares by way of a 'preview' available free of charge to anyone with access to the internet.[4] The facts clearly indicated that a rejection of the appellant's case would be appropriate since the preview could be accessed by anyone, including children.[5] The risk to children rather overshadowed the residual question raised in the case—of how we might understand such 'harm' in relation to adults—though it was acknowledged obliquely, as an issue of relevance. Discussion considered jurisdictional issues in the light of the global availability of internet sites—a key consideration in terms, not just of the internet, but of a great deal of popular media. The central legal—and moral—questions however focused upon understanding the implications of

[3] *R v Stephane Laurent Perrin* (2002) WL 347127 [CA (Crim Div)], (2002) EWCA Crim 747, No: 2000/6463/Y2. All references use Westlaw pagination.

[4] The notional 'screening' process derived from access available only by entering credit card details (proving a traceable, positive act on the part of the user, a traceable identity, and accession to adulthood denoted by such financial status) was therefore absent, thus creating a possibility that 'vulnerable' and 'young' people might view the preview, which involved scenes of coprophilia and fellatio. Given this risk, the outcome of the case was relatively predictable, with the website perpetrator failing in his appeal against conviction.

[5] There is a clear juristic awareness that protection of children from harm is a paramount—and separate—concern from possible 'harm' posed to adults by the availability of pornographic materials. As the article by Adkeniz (n 2 above, 1) makes clear, 'the regulation of *harmful* content such as pornography and regulation of *illegal* content such as child pornography . . . are issues different in nature and should not be confused' (italics added).

English domestic law—the 'tendency' to 'deprave and corrupt' as cited in the Obscene Publications Act 1959, and those of Articles 7 (requiring that the conduct in question be demonstrably proscribed by law) and 10 (the right to freedom of expression) of the European Convention on Human Rights. The case thus manifests an interesting tension between morally grounded prohibitions, the assertion of civil liberties 'rights' to freedom and the formal positivist expectation of certainty in maintaining the rule of law. The Court concluded that Article 10 provides for State proscription of activities that threaten the interests of democratic society, and that, in this case such concerns outweighed the notional assertion of freedom within it. Given the risk to children posed by the site, this outcome seems unavoidable. The broad normative question, raised by juristic consideration of material tending to deprave and corrupt in relation to the *general* population however, remains largely unexplored. In reviewing precedent, it was acknowledged that a 'risk' of corruption to only a small proportion of the population did not necessarily justify the risk.[6] Even when understanding of the risk quotient was expressed—as later case law suggests it should be—in terms of a 'significant risk', it was acknowledged that the magnitude of such 'significance' would remain proportional to the circumstances in question; in other words, a risk might be significant *even if* the 'pool' of persons likely to be affected proved relatively small.[7] The Court was reminded[8] of a *ratio* derived from the House of Lords to the effect that the Obscene Publications Act 'was not merely concerned with the once and for all corruption of the wholly innocent, it equally protected the less innocent from further corruption and the addict from feeding or increasing his addiction'. Later,[9] the Court cited the observation made by Salmon LJ (in the 1968 *Last Exit to Brooklyn* case):[10] 'The Legislature can hardly have contemplated that a book which tended to corrupt and deprave the average reader or majority of those likely to read it could be justified as being for the public good on any ground . . . What is a significant proportion is a matter entirely for the jury to decide.'

The present case conceded that the concern to refrain from an overly 'draconian' interpretation of statutory constraints in the case of a book already in circulation (where, 'if the word "persons" was given the widest possible meaning, injustice might [have been] done to the defendant because, as Salmon LJ said "there are individuals who may be corrupted by almost anything"') differed where a web page was concerned.[11] Furthermore, Lord Wilberforce[12] was quoted stating: 'the tendency to deprave and corrupt is not to be estimated in relation to some assumed standard of purity of some reasonable average man. It is the likely reader. And to apply different tests to teenagers, members of men's clubs or men in various occupations or localities would be a matter of common sense.'

[6] WL 347127:4, especially when that proportion may include children.
[7] ibid.
[8] WL 347127:5.
[9] WL 347127:9
[10] *R v Calder and Boyars Ltd* (1968) 52 Cr App R 706.
[11] WL 347127:9. As already noted, the case rightly drew this conclusion bearing in mind the increased risk to children posed by the internet, and indeed the 'interactive' nature of the medium poses great challenges to the law in relation to different groups and categories of harm.
[12] In *DPP v Whyte* [1972] AC 849, quoted at WL 347127:10.

The play of logic, cautioning against invocation of notions of the 'average' and the 'reasonable' and acknowledging the difficulty posed by such concepts—of an *empirically* ascertainable core which yet eludes proportionality arguments beyond those of the most general kind—demonstrates the hermeneutic paralysis gripping the field. In part this is due to juristic concern to produce a *ratio* sufficiently flexible to be of use to the infinitely variable cases to come. Yet additional unease is detectable, a shrinking from the task, rendered by something less tangible than conscientious unwillingness to produce a censorious normative ruling on matters of taste.

Though the concepts giving rise to the Obscene Publications Act now have a substantial history, heavily debated in the popular and legal domains,[13] resistance to real examination of the image reflected back at humanity through the refractory mirror that is popular appetite seems almost perverse in itself. Jurisdictional issues, the variability of proportionality arguments, the tension between matters of corruptibility, freedom, certainty and the rule of law are all in themselves matters both of fact and value, the formal and the substantive. When elucidation of what is meant by a 'tendency to deprave and corrupt' remains patently unexplored, the concentration upon these more practical aspects of the problem simply compounds the state of paralysis. Expounding upon the statutory provision, the implicit *aura* of the case law exhibits a commitment to the maintenance of an invisible bulwark against corruption. Yet 'corruption' itself, though given the weight of proportionality arguments, is never discussed. Is it simply the lessening, by degree, of formerly held moral certitude? A loss, of a never-to-be-defined innocence? An individual, leading imperceptibly to collective, decline? Certainly, such miasmic concerns seem to underpin the play of arguments, whilst at the same time undermining them, since the role of law—and the rule of law—must avoid overt forays into censorious *leading* positions. And the more 'solidly' legal ground—of demonstrating a direct link between controlling 'deviant' tendencies and thus inhibiting activities proscribed by the criminal law—is hotly disputed and empirically debatable.[14] Though case law faces a direct confrontation between socially deviant and criminalized behaviour, juristic debate is muted by consciousness of its uncertain 'supporting' role in the constant reinvention of cultures. Even where practical

[13] Though there has been a rich history of landmark cases on censorship English law, an interesting phenomenon in itself is the relative *lack* of published academic discussion of censorship, certainly in Britain, from the 1970s to the present day (though occasional texts arose, eg D Tribe, *Questions of Censorship* (London: 1973). Recent texts include J Lewis, *Hollywood v hard core: how the struggle over censorship saved the modern film industry* (New York and London: 2000); Y Akdeniz, C Walker and D Wall, *The Internet, Law and Society* (London: 2000). For a comprehensive and useful review of current law and debate concerning the specific issues raised by the availability of pornography on the internet, see Akdeniz, n 2 above. Tangentially of course, the 'Hart-Devlin Debate' produced a fruitful series of exchanges in relation to putative links between perceived deviations from public morality and tangible, and less tangible harms to society. The millennium seems to herald a revival of the debate; such revival may be for a multitude of reasons. The tendency of lobbying groups to identify themselves either with the 'Civil Liberties' tag, or with 'Family Protection' can be predictably misleading, given the 'bandwagon' nature of popular debating polemic.

[14] See discussion and references to various materials on this topic in 'The Year 2000—The Empty City' in M Williams, *Empty Justice, One Hundred Years of Law, Literature and Philosophy* (London: 2002) esp 10–16.

outcomes are inevitable in terms of mediating excesses, such outcomes cannot be traced by tracking a developing juristic rationale.

Crash has been discussed by academics and others largely in terms of ongoing debates upon pornography and erotica, and much of the critical appraisal remains somewhat superficial because conducted at this level of 'appetites' without more searching enquiry as to what this implies. One recent book, *The Crash Controversy: Censorship Campaigns and Film Reception*,[15] undertakes an *empirical* study of audience responses to the film and thus might seem to promise tangible material for the notionally empirical 'proportionality' and 'reasonable' vs 'average' case law discussions. The book provides statistical analysis of questionnaire answers, with tabulated outcomes in terms of 'positive' and 'negative' reactions. The study asserts a neutrality of stance in relation to research findings. It surveys the film's link to social and legal debates regarding censorship and recognizes the difficulty of the terrain in the task of empiricism—the popular preconceptions, institutional assertions, the sensational and the mundane.

Yet, perhaps not surprisingly, the overall composition of the study—undertaken by senior academics within film and media scholarship—cannot but betray a predilection for particular views. The researchers portray themselves as social scientists in search of big game—chapters are headed 'One Big Controversy, Several Large Research Tasks', 'Reviewing the Press', 'Expecting the Worst', 'Talking about Sex', 'The Shape of Positive Responses', 'Four Men's Positive Responses to *Crash*'. Despite boldly framed assertions concerning the role of the study in exploring the unexplored, of its embedded critique of the popular and the political, the text fails to transcend the level of prosaic and pruriently anecdotal. Those who responded 'positively' to the film (that is, 'liked' or 'enjoyed' it) are labelled 'Positives' for the purposes of the study, whilst those reacting with reserve or hostility are the 'Negatives', with 'neutrals' in between. The resultant critique is simplistic in the extreme:

> Centrally, we learned that there were only small differences in *what* people found memorable; the differences were in how they *evaluated* these. But the evaluations were complicated. While the Negatives were almost uniformly hostile to the kinds of characters in the film, the Positives were mixed—suggesting that positivity does not have to mean simple *liking*. More detailed comparison of the most frequently mentioned items showed that for the Negatives these were (absence of effective) storyline, and their (hostile) reponses to characters; while for Positives they were general aesthetic appreciation of the film, along with a positive recognition of its themes linking cars, bodies and sex. The quantitative information on cinema and video-viewing habits supported the general notion that those with greater cinematic 'literacy' were generally more likely to be favourable to *Crash*—but the association was not very strong . . .[16]

This philosophically, rationally and empirically flimsy 'finding'—that discerning people will respond favourably to the film—is corroborated by researcher conjecture

[15] M Barker, J Arthurs and R Harindranath, *The Crash Controversy: Censorship Campaigns and Film Reception* (London: 2001).

[16] ibid, 164.

concerning the likely impact of the popular press, particularly the contribution of the *Daily Mail* to the debate.[17] The location of the *Daily Mail* as an assumed 'universal' promotes the linkages forged by the text—conjecturally locating 'negatives' or *proto*-negatives as probable *Mail* readers, with 'positives' as 'anti'-*Mail* and therefore liberal, freethinking and enlightened individuals:

> . . . there was a strong tendency for those with positive orientations to *Crash* to engage in talk about their prior orientation to the film. This was more true of those who *liked* the film than of those who *approved* of it. We believe this arises mainly from the discrepancy [between] the nervousness induced in many viewers by the *Mail's* campaign, and their realisation that they enjoyed the film. Those most strongly registering approval were more suspicious, we suspect, of the *Mail*, therefore less fearful in advance of the film. There was a smaller, but still noticeable tendency for Negatives, and especially Disapprovers, to want to talk about intended/implied audiences—which fits well with our perception that those who disapprove a film such as *Crash* will tend to work with a 'figure' of some other audience who might be affected by it . . . Positives were considerably more keen to speak their minds on censorship than Negatives . . .
>
> A more puzzling finding was that Likers and Approvers were much more likely to want to talk about characters; while in the opposite direction it was especially the Disapprovers who avoided such talk. These tendencies are sufficiently strong to provoke some speculation. Might it be that the Disapprovers tended to be so strongly hostile to the film *per se* that they declined to discuss the characters as such, since to do so would be to allow their fictional status and the defences that that might introduce?
>
> To us, though, the most striking tendency came with Modality Talk, that is, with talk concerning the relations between the film and the filmic world, and the world beyond the film . . . to our surprise, in both cases it emerged that Positivity was strongly associated with a propensity to such talk . . . What is interesting about this . . . was that the Disapprovers of *Crash* are evidently the least likely to want to discuss it in modality terms. This is surprising, and counter-intuitive. One might expect that those who reject the film on moral grounds might have been expected to want to raise questions of censorship, and of the possible impact of the film on the world, or to worry about a breakdown of the fiction/reality boundary. None of these appears to have been the case. Instead it is the Positives who want to talk about modal issues . . .[18]

What is 'counter-intuitive' for the researchers, 'true' and 'more' true is not necessarily grounded in universals as the language suggests. The broad message of the research—supported by the nomenclature, is that 'Positives' emerge as free-thinking individuals, open to experience and more reflective. They are prepared to look 'beyond' the erotic and talk about 'characters' and are clearly enlightened intellectuals engaged

[17] The *Daily Mail* did in fact pursue a campaign against 'moral corruption' centring upon films such as *Crash* and this campaign would form an understandable feature of the popular topography for the researchers. The location of the *Mail* in the midst of *empirical* findings rather oversimplifies the possible role played by such media however, despite the *Mail's* clear associations with certain polemical positions. For a succinct discussion of the *Mail* campaign, and its attempts to influence the British Board of Film Classification, see 'They know what's good for you' at http://film.guardian.co.uk/censorship/news/0,11729,661823,00.html. For a note on the current position, see C Munro, 'Not the last picture show' [2003] PL 2

[18] Barker et al, n 15 above, 171.

with the scientific media discourse that is 'Modality Talk'.[19] Yet the research does not consider the host of issues which such assumptions might ignore. Aside from the clear predisposition of the researchers towards those responding as 'Positives', what does it really mean, to be 'a' Positive? The research simply mirrors the same ethically distorted simplicity satirized in Huxley's *Brave New World*. Does 'liking' the film—even to the extent of thinking about characters and entering into Modality Talk—necessarily tell us anything about the issues underlying the censorship and civil liberties debate? We are meant to be persuaded that the research produces incontrovertible evidence of the innate moral superiority of audiences who 'like' films on the edge of the censorship debate—that they are more empathic (talk Modally and of characters), more intellectually discursive—that the real 'deviants' are those who 'disliked' the film. Given the controversial nature of the themes in the film, there is little reason to believe that such questionnaire responses are at all reliable. Without further, perhaps more sensitively situated research, individuals in such circumstances are just as likely to give the response which corresponds to their 'workaday' view of themselves.[20] They may be motivated to respond in a particular way by a host of concerns, some of them repressive of 'true' responses, some mimicking imagined 'ideal' responses and so on. Even straight admissions that the film was enjoyed for the erotic idea of the sex-violence collision, may be vouchsafed for reasons not entirely appreciated by the respondent herself.[21] Indeed, this 'critical mass' neatly demonstrates that the film *Crash* can be identified *with* pornography/erotica, or with compounding an impoverished and prejudicial critique of it. Certainly the film version of *Crash*, by its very nature as a predominantly visual, rather than textual medium, tends to lose the problematizing aspect. Two qualities arguably make the *text* more challenging, quite apart from the demand for greater intellectual engagement posed by textual as opposed to visual material. Firstly, Ballard's prose *anatomizes* the sexuality/violence/machinery problematic literally 'warts and all' and second, he attempts, albeit in a somewhat hazy fashion, to explore what this might mean. At times one might wonder whether this is simply 'dressing up' an essentially prurient text. Rather, it seems an early prototype in Ballard's developing work, where, with some temerity, he deploys the anatomical, the physical, to critique the

[19] Whilst it would not be suggested that any member of the sample audience was either insincere, or had 'criminal', 'deviant' or any other socially disapproved tendencies, it is well known that paedophiles for example are highly skilled in 'emotive' sensitivities, taking great interest in characters, personalities, motivations and so on. Such ability or interest in itself does not 'prove' anything.

[20] Empirical findings are clearly fraught with difficulties even in the most rigorous study; how much more so when the human mind is the object of that study, and more so again when the mind is asked to report *on itself*—as David Hume is quick to point out.

[21] Though the newly established convention 'herself' is used at this juncture perhaps advisedly, its widespread adoption in legal debate is, it might be argued, questionable. Emerging feminine cultures in the West, of boldly 'defiant' behaviour may be in part a reaction to former inhibitory factors and indeed, this entire field is the subject of sociological and socio-legal study in itself, an issue about which the researchers in the study seem blissfully unaware. In short, the recorded reactions of female and male respondents cannot be read as simple indicators.

metaphysical.[22] It may be said that this can assist with a process of 'forensic' legal theory—with tracking every fragment of evidence bearing upon human nature. When law, with its brother religion, could simply demonize many practices and interests as the pursuits of an 'unnatural' and 'deviant' minority, the task of law seemed simple—to identify these few and continue to protect the many. Present case law reflects a new-found caution, yet remains powerless to advance a consequent rationale. Ballard too recognizes that traditional notions of deviance present far too simple a picture—that we are all more or less implicated in such questions.[23] If the law once believed itself to be dealing with a social profile dominated by a somewhat mummified 'reasonable man', it might now question its model of human nature, in view of the vast access to forceful material. In the absence of religion this brave new world takes on more particular significance. Though society itself may fulfil the role of an authoritative and judgmental parent, current culture is hostile to such figuring, for understandable reasons. The 'paternalistic' community or State conflicts with the 'autonomous' individual. Indeed, both the authoritative and the nurturing aspects of parenting are absent—the benevolence of society lies in its willingness to *tolerate* the ongoing, unfolding human experiment. And this is Ballard's point. Where is it taking us? When Ballard asks: 'Can the writer leave out anything he prefers not to understand, including his own motives, prejudices and psychopathology?'[24]—the question is just as relevant to the jurist. Aware of the shortcomings and doubtful quasi-mystical origins of the reasonable man—the approved legal agent—the jurist may well adopt Ballard's assertion about the writer:

> His role is that of the scientist, whether on safari or in his laboratory, faced with an unknown terrain or subject. All he can do is to devise various hypotheses and test them against the facts.[25]

As Ballard points out, *Crash* is not simply situated, but *constituted* by a moral vacuum, a vacuum which resonates strongly with our own consumer culture. Indeed, addressing questions of *what* sort of creatures we are, so that society and law can consider what *kind* of constraints or debate should be put in place, demands a dispassionate objectivity which law, as the creature of culture, seems no more equipped to produce than any other social institution.

With the movement from text to film, additional 'unknowns' arise in the impact of the medium upon the human psyche. The Williams Committee on Obscenity and Film Censorship[26] adopted a minimalist approach in its recommendations

[22] For a discussion of the ethical implications of Ballard's more recent work, see M Williams, n 14 above.

[23] 'Throughout *Crash* I have used the car not only as a sexual image, but as a total metaphor for man's life in today's society. As such the novel has a political role quite apart from its sexual content, but I would still like to think that *Crash* is the first pornographic novel based on technology. In a sense, pornography is the most political form of fiction, dealing with how we use and exploit each other, in the most urgent and ruthless way'—JG Ballard, Introduction to *Crash*.

[24] ibid.

[25] ibid.

[26] *Report of the Committee on Obscenity and Film Censorship*, Cmnd 7772 (London, 1979).

regarding legal constraints, bearing in mind the largely uncontrollable material viewed in 'private' clubs and venues on the one hand, and the underlying principle that law should be concerned with preventing exploitation of minors, or representations of physical harm in the production of film, on the other. Subsequent adaptations of law aimed at extending some control over the Pandora's box of internet material, maintain this philosophy.[27] The emphasis is still upon the maximization of freedoms alongside minimalist constraint, adopting a neutral, 'holding' position in the exponentially unfolding social experiment that is our cultural life. In considering the movement from text to film, JG Ballard himself appears to apprehend little alteration in the response of the reader, indeed, he has said of the film that he would be disturbed to think that an audience might set out deliberately to imitate, or re-create the film scenario 'in reality'.[28] Given the location of the film and text of *Crash*, on the margins of popular culture, the risk of imitatory response may be minimized by dint of a less than 'mass' audience. In addition, the researchers in *The Crash Controversy* study would seem to believe that the film's 'art-house' location in the aesthetics of film render it somehow beyond the reach of ethical enquiry and indeed, an analogous rationale of permissible aesthetics of appetite seem to underlie the web market in pornographic imagery. Yet this dogged blindness to the philosophical implications of the film yields the deepest irony, as Ballard himself clearly appreciates in the very creation of *Crash*. The issue is not, whether the film 'is' obscene, rather it is how the text and images, the 'collision' of ideas and values in the film provoke questions about ourselves which simple 'shoot 'em up' films, or sexually explicit websites, leave dormant.

Consider the following thought-experiment.[29] Suppose in observing spider monkeys in a compound, we 'discovered' that the 'collision' of sensory stimuli, for example the smell of the herb lovage at the edge of the compound, caused a uniform side-stimulus in a number (perhaps a large number) of individual monkeys—say, a tingling in the left hand—but it had simply never been noted before. We would want to know why, what 'pathways' neuro-chemically, were responsible. Suppose also that we found a number of the creatures began to *seek* the sensation, as opposed to stumbling upon it. Now suppose that we also found that the tingling was accompanied, in a smaller sample of individuals, by a desire to relieve the tingling by pressing the affected hand hard on the face of a neighbouring spider

[27] See Akdeniz, n 2 above.

[28] 'People ask me how I would feel if young men, after seeing the movie, went and crashed their cars into other people, and of course, if this did happen, it would be a tragedy. But it hasn't happened anywhere in the world where it's been shown and its highly unlikely to happen, because the sort of kids who go to see . . . non-stop, end-to-end violence are not going to be able to read a film like *Crash* . . . '—Ballard, quoted interview, http://www.finelinefeatures.com/crash/cmp/ballard-interview.html.

[29] The production of a practical ethics analogy at this point seemed appropriate, and the felt need to do so is illustrative of the intransigent, fixed location of different discourses. The choice of lovage is made to minimize reader response to a more commonplace herb ('mint never has that effect on *me*'), so distracting from the model. The choice of spider monkeys is similarly less directly traceable to instantly anthropomorphic identification than, say, chimpanzees, though still sufficiently analogous.

monkey. Indeed, for some of those individuals, relief from the tingling could only be found *by* pressing hard on the face of another monkey. Pressing the hand on a cloth, a doll or some other similar object would not bring relief. The neuro-sensory synaptic circuit could not complete.[30]

Now suppose that, added to this already bizarre series of circumstances, a behaviour pattern began to emerge amongst the *non-participating* members of the community. Spider monkeys normally engaged in tasks in other parts of the community began to drift towards the lovage-smelling spectacle, either to witness the visibly intoxicating inhalation-tingling sensation, or to observe the peripheral inhalation-tingling-relief-by-face-pressing scenario. At some point, 'outside' observers would have to log an alteration, not only in community activity, but also in evolving appetites for stimuli. At the very least, the change in community behaviour would have 'knock-on' implications for the investment in, or viability of, other potential activities. Even if only a small group formed the participant/audience population, this would be the case. There would be implications for the 'shaping' of the community and of individuals within it. The reader may well feel her intelligence is somewhat insulted by this crude analogy between monkeys and ourselves, and in mitigation it must be pleaded that it is simply an attempt to move the debate beyond the improbable neutrality assumed by jurists and researchers alike. The belief that the Cartesian split in human nature is *so* effective as to entirely divide ourselves from the world of stimuli assaulting us from every side, is naïve in the extreme.[31] Not only does it disregard the inter-personal dynamics of evolving selves and concomitant links to community practices, it also disregards the first lessons of Aristotelian ethics—that our behaviours *shape* ourselves, and that social organization holds responsibility for that shaping.[32] This is not to say that any social or legal presumption should favour inhibitory or pre-emptive proscription. Indeed, the eccentric excesses now pouring from the internet, as well as the particular scenes depicted in *Crash*, pose a rather more complex question, poorly explored by popular debate, by committees or by case law. The creation and fostering of appetites, driven by market forces, provides fascinating potential insights into ourselves—holding a veritable hall of mirrors to our understanding of human nature. But as we discover such facts about ourselves, what do we do with the information? At present, we are rather strongly located within the passive compound audience and indeed the notion of scaling the fence may take the thought experiment beyond viable realms of possibility. But we seem incapable

[30] For an introductory discussion, see J Bickle, P Mandik, 'The Philosophy of Neuroscience' in Edward N Zalta (ed), *The Stanford Encyclopedia of Philosophy* (Winter 2002), http://plato.stanford.edu/archives.win2002/entries/neuroscience/.

[31] For a brief history of Cartesian dualism, see Robert H Wozniak, 'Mind and Body: Rene Descartes to William James', at http://serendip.brynmawr.edu/Mind/Descartes.html.

[32] An excellent critique of understandings of Aristotelian Ethics, and especially of the relation between law and moral education as expounded in Aristotle's *Nicomachean Ethics*, can be found by Lester H Hunt, 'On Improving People by Political Means' in Hugh LaFollette (ed), *Ethics in Practice* (Oxford: 2002).

of even planning an outbreak, preferring instead to groom ourselves whilst sitting back on the haunches of our ethical selves, willing only to see the mirror image best satisfying a regal vanity of all encompassing power, over our selves and our world.

The vocabulary of ethics seems quaint and singularly irrelevant to the world of *Crash*, where disability is simply another course in the widening and jaded erotic diet, where the character Vaughan:

> . . . unfolded for me all his obsessions with the mysterious eroticism of wounds . . . dreamed of ambassadorial limousines crashing into jack-knifing butane tankers, of taxis filled with celebrating children colliding head-on below the bright display windows of deserted supermarkets. He dreamed of alienated brothers and sisters, by chance meeting each other on collision courses on the access roads of petrochemical plants, their unconscious incest made explicit in this colliding metal, in the haemorrhages of their brain tissue flowering beneath the aluminised compression chambers and reaction vessels . . . [33]

Just how far we have strayed from the allegedly 'known' conceptual territory of law and ethics becomes apparent when such prose from *Crash* is juxtaposed with a text concerned with moral valuations. To be sure, traditional moral philosophy, steeped in the lessons of classical thought, is directly relevant to us. The great classical philosophers dealt with the profound questions of human existence which have not, despite appearances, altered in essence. In particular, they recognized that questions of individual freedom were intimately linked to those of moral, social and legal organization. But making those insights work for us now is a challenge—indeed, there is a danger that moral philosophy, alongside its co-worker, law, may operate in a sealed unit of rationality far removed from the pressing subject matter of its discourse. Consider an essay entitled 'Shame and Autonomy'[34] by Bernard Williams himself, the Chairman of the Committee on Censorship and Pornography. The very words examined therein—'shame' and 'guilt'—seem quaint and singularly irrelevant to the world of *Crash*. Williams's critique of the minutiae of Homeric and Kantian notions of shame and guilt may seem otiose and obsolescent, a raindrop against a deluge. But Williams does point up concepts which, by their very deliberate impoverishment in *Crash*, help to clarify the points Ballard pursues. Asking himself 'what is involved in shame itself', Williams replies:

> The basic experience connected with shame (aidos) is that of being seen, inappropriately, by the wrong condition. It is straightforwardly connected with nakedness, particularly in sexual connections . . . a further step is taken when the motive is fear of shame at what people will say about one's actions . . . The reaction in Homer to someone who has done something that shame should have prevented is nemesis, . . . defined as a reaction [such as indignation] . . . depending on what particular violation of aidos it is a reaction to. As Redfield has put it, aidos and nemesis are a reflexive pair . . . People can feel indignation or other forms of anger when honour is violated, in their own case or somebody else's. These are shared sentiments with similar objects, and they serve to bind people together in a community of feeling . . .[35]

[33] Ballard, *Crash*, 12–13.
[34] B Williams, 'Shame and Autonomy' in *Shame and Necessity* (California and London: 1994).
[35] ibid, 78–80.

Now shame at nakedness, even shame at what people will say about one's actions, are both apparently irrelevant scruples in the world of *Crash*: the community works upon an entirely different logic. And that is Ballard's point. We live in a surreal world where the obscene jostles with the mundane, where personal tragedy is another unit of consumption:

> I looked round at the crowd. A considerable number of children were present, many lifted on their parents' shoulders to give them a better view . . . None of the spectators showed any signs of alarm. They looked down at the scene with the calm and studied interest of intelligent buyers at a leading bloodstock sale . . .[36]

This deadening community is quite clearly a crucible for the more stylized and specialized proclivities or activities of particular groups, and within such groups, what Bernard Williams calls the community of *feeling*, in which shame would be a shared product, becomes a community of *appetite*. Shame and nemesis will be inverted—the root of indignation will lie in *feeling* shame. As Williams explains:

> Even if shame and its motivations always involve in some way or other an idea of a gaze of another, it is important that for many of its operations the imagined gaze of an imagined other will do . . . He might think that it was shameful to do it, not just to be seen doing it, and in that case an imagined watcher could be enough to trigger the reaction of shame.[37]

For the figures in *Crash*, the immediate and extended 'community' of watchers and imagined watchers *endorse* the aberrant behaviour. This should be a concern for the law both in terms of understanding the growth of clearly 'deviant' communities—especially in the age of the internet—and in grasping the broader role of legal and other institutions in relation to the freedom and regulation of the legal subject.

Now this seems to be veering towards an hypothesis concerning the need for increased regulation of individuals 'adrift' in this moral void. But then one simply becomes enmeshed in the old polarized arguments—between freedom and censorship and so on. Ballard's approach strives to maintain a critical neutrality in relation to the uncertain journey of modern life. In so doing, he draws the debate away from conventional concerns, highlighting instead the *experimental* nature of the journey, the questions about ourselves left unanswered by the reciprocity of a doubtful shame culture. He is prepared to take risks with conventional assumptions about harm, recognizing that we cannot understand the full implications—for good or bad—of our present emerging selves. It would be difficult for a legal theorist to find himself asking the question posed by this anthropologically orientated writer—'Is this harnessing of our innate perversity conceivably of benefit to us? Is there some deviant logic unfolding more powerful that that provided by reason?' For some, the question may offend in its apparent disregard for a world of normative value. Yet perhaps Ballard is after all a moralist crying: this is how we *really* are, all of us, more or less. The old myths have perpetrated as much harm as good, being merely cosmetic. Let us look full-square at the subject and without making condemnatory judgments, but with the cool eye of the scientist,

[36] Ballard, *Crash*, 155. [37] Williams, n 34 above, 82.

have a keener sense of the factors weighing in the equation. Without truth, there can be no ethics . . .

In discussing shame, Bernard Williams concludes that *aidos*:

> Cannot merely mean 'shame', but must cover something like guilt as well . . . The idea of reparation is prominent in Homer, and the need for it, for gestures that compensate and heal, must surely be recognised in any society if the notion of holding oneself responsible is to have any content . . . In the Greek world there was room, too, for forgiveness. It is often thought that forgiveness speaks more effectively to guilt than to shame: if the people who have been wronged forgive me, then perhaps the case is withdrawn from the internal judge . . .[38]

Somehow in this new Godless world of heartless externalities, it seems meet that the subject—for example the narrator in *Crash*—has as much compassion for his own disturbed and disturbing consciousness as for that of his fellow beings. The 'internal judge' is held in abeyance, whilst reparation, healing and forgiveness (to use Williams' terms) are liabilities flowing as justly *towards* the damaged subject as from him: his wounds are deeper than skin, his need endless, his vulnerability in the face of the machine acute. The legalistic relation of guilt and reparation loses clarity when all participants in the drama are not agents atop of the world, but linked orphans inching sideways on an existential precipice. Moreover, not guilt, but 'only shame', says Williams, can help one:

> . . . to understand one's relation to happenings or to rebuild the self that has done these things and the world in which that self has to live. Only shame can do that, because it embodies conceptions of what one is and of how one is related to others . . .[39]

—but this presupposes a sense of self and belonging ripe for such embodiment. Shame in the 'robust' context of *Crash* seems a somewhat superfluous and prudish emotion. It is after all through a surfeit of such scruples, a surface of respectability, that repressive and corrupt cultures are maintained. Yet Williams's analysis assists in understanding its potential relevance. Bereft of 'a conception of what one is and how one is related to others', one is deprived of the healing power of shame, or at least something akin to it. The difficulty lies in the realization that the self same presumption of an ethical world ever-present, instantly accessed and deployed, underpins legal philosophy and doctrine just as surely as it forms the classical philosophy in the mouth of Williams. That such 'brakes' might be neutralized, in the pleasure dome that is our culture, leaves the law in an ethically discursive limbo. It would be unthinkable simply to invoke an 'anthropological' discourse in its place—to suggest that on our mother's or our father's side we are descended from the apes.[40] Yet we do need to consider how the gap, between the *discourse* of reasonableness and responsible free will, and the *course* of unmediated appetites—whether lovage-,

[38] Williams, n 34 above, 90–91. [39] ibid, 94.

[40] Bishop Wilberforce was provoked by Darwin's Theory of Evolution to ask Julian Huxley 'whether it was on his mother's side, or his father's side that he was descended from the apes?' Few people now share the Bishop's scepticism of evolutionary theory, though institutional human imagery is resistant to deriving implications from human location in the chain of primates, let alone in the chain of biological being. The Bishop's identity as primate remained, of course, purely ecclesiastical.

Hollywood-, or brave new web-scented—is taking us. In short, we are neurochemical selves as well as selves with an ethical capability. The sensory self interacts with the ethical self. Empirical corroboration that the sex-violence nexus produces 'positive' response tells us no more than a fleeting visitor to the zoo might divine from a notice declaring the lovage-smelling propensities of the monkeys: just another exotic fact on the way to the ice-cream vendor. And remember that we are not secure in such a role of passing super-species. We understand little of how the reciprocity of values—the dynamic between individual and community—has faltered or failed. Williams' assertion that: 'the internalised other . . . still has some independent identity . . . it is not just a screen for one's own ethical ideas, but is the locus of some genuine social expectations . . . '[41] is dependent upon an entrenched reciprocity between individual and community, whereas Ballard perceives his world and ours as systematically alienating, in the cathection of sensibility, where a:

> coming autogeddon . . . conjunctions between elbow and chromium window sill, vulva and instrument binnacle, summed up the possibilities of a new logic created by these multiplying artefacts, the codes of a new marriage of sensation and possibility . . .[42] The destruction of this motor car and its occupants seemed, in turn to sanction the sexual penetration . . . both were conceptualised acts abstracted from all feeling, carrying any ideas or emotions with which we cared to freight them . . .[43]

How would Williams respond to the world of *Crash*? It is a world of as yet unmeasured possibilities for good and ill, stripped of the old cultures and old judgments. It is a world where individuals understand that autonomy is both blunted and sharpened by mortality, and their claim upon the fragments of selfhood frail yet all the keener. For Williams, any such world of greater social heterogeneity must predicate not only the existence of a more discriminatory internalized other, but one which is the locus of 'genuine social expectations'—suggesting not just a responsible subject, but a responsible, reciprocal community. And, Williams suggests:

> If a charge of social heteronomy is to stick at a more interesting level, its claim will have to be that even this abstracted, improved neighbour lodged in one's inner life represents a compromise of genuine autonomy . . .[44]

It is not the primary work of the law to effect such compromise, but that of the social compact underpinning it. As with current culture, the agents of *Crash* are drunk with possibility. That unbridled possibility leads both to new horizons and to chaos is clear, but who will determine which course prevails? *Crash* simply poses this question. Law, and legal argumentation, can make a useful contribution to the debate, as a source of development in the search for our own identifiers where, at its best, it forces refinement of the contest in ideas and values. The conundrum of whether we might all be described as cultivated citizen or popular savage is perhaps best informed by reflecting upon popular appetites, through the fragmented mirror to ourselves that is *Crash*.

[41] Williams, n 34 above, 98. [42] Ballard, *Crash*, 106. [43] ibid, 129.
[44] Williams, n 34 above, 99.

Law's Diabolical Romance: Reflections on a New Jurisprudence of the Sublime

Leslie J Moran

Introduction

The phrase, 'diabolical romance', found in the title of this article, is a term that refers to the Gothic, which is associated with a collection of novels that date from the late eighteenth and early nineteenth centuries. The Gothic is also more generally used to name a literary genre commonly associated with popular rather than high culture. 'Diabolical romance' is a phrase that draws attention to the connection between the Gothic and the romantic tradition in general and differentiates it from that other dimension of the romantic tradition, the pastoral romance. The 'diabolical' highlights particular romantic preoccupations (settings, devices and events), characterized as pertaining to the darker, the negative and the underside of life. The general objective of my engagement with 'diabolical romance' is to explore the complex interface between law and the Gothic. However, it is not my intention to pursue this objective by way of 'the Gothic' as a reference to a particular popular literary grouping of authors or texts or a visual mode of cultural production (such as is found in architecture or film) confined to a particular era. My interest lies more with 'the Gothic imagination' rather than 'the Gothic'. The phrase 'Gothic imagination' suggests something less specific than a set of common thematic characteristics that are confined to a grouping of particular texts or authors, and something that is more general in its significance and in its operation. My approach to the Gothic echoes Peter Brooks' approach to genre, explored in his work on melodrama. He describes melodrama as' . . . less a genre more an imaginative mode'.[1] Brooks goes on to explain that the melodramatic imagination is a '(fictional) system for making sense of experience, as a semantic field of force'.[2] His approach brings together ideas about the origins of melodrama (in literature) and

[1] P Brooks, *The Melodramatic Imagination*, (New Haven: 1995) vii.

[2] Brooks, n 1 above, xii. Judith Walkowitz's *City of Dreadful Delight* provides an example of an attempt to realize Brooks's idea of the melodramatic imagination as a more general cultural intelligibility through an analysis of English Victorian campaigns relating to female sexuality. A few asides are made in that study to the significance of the Gothic fairy tale in relation to the enactment of the Criminal Law Amendment Act 1885. However they remain undeveloped in that study. See JR Walkowitz, *City of Dreadful Delight: Narratives of Danger in Late Victorian London* (London: 1992).

the effects of melodrama as an imaginative mode, and the shift from 'genre' to 'imagination' draws attention to the significance and diffusion of melodrama across the wider culture. The phrase 'Gothic imagination' signifies my adoption of this approach to 'genre' albeit in a different context, the Gothic. It is an approach already recognized by many scholars of the Gothic. Fred Botting suggests the Gothic is a mode of writing that exceeds genre and categories and is restricted neither to a literary school nor to a historical period. Gothic features are diffused across texts and historical periods.[3] Bayer-Berenbaum describes the Gothic as a particular 'philosophy'.[4] Karen Halttunen, writing about changing representations of murder in early nineteenth century America gallows sermons, explains the Gothic in terms of a 'mental and emotional strateg[y] employed within a given historical culture . . .'.[5] The phrase 'the Gothic imagination' captures this emphasis upon the wider cultural and political significance of the Gothic as a particular mode of intelligibility.

My resort to the phrase, 'the Gothic imagination', is important in another way as it signifies a departure from the study of law as represented in Gothic literature. This is not to suggest that law is absent from that literature.[6] Themes of law within that literature have ranged from the domestic legal tradition in general, the English common law, to a more specific focus on a wide range of locations within law's institutional topography. Of particular prominence are crime and criminality, dungeons and prisons, gaolers, lawyers and detectives, the trial process, monarchy and sovereignty, contracts, wills and an obsession with evidence.[7] In these various contexts the law appears as the archaic and the dark, a vestigial shadow that haunts the legal and social order of the enlightenment and of modernity characterized by rationalism and neo-classicism. William MacNeil's work on nineteenth century literature is a good example of work by a legal scholar that explores legal themes in texts that fall within the canon of Gothic literature.[8] My departure from this approach is not to suggest that this work is of no interest or importance. My work is connected with and draws upon such matters.

However, my interest in the interface between law and the Gothic imagination has a different focus. I am not so much concerned with the Gothic as a popular literature of law but more concerned with law as a source of the Gothic imagination and with the operation of the Gothic imagination within law and legal scholarship.

[3] F Botting, *Gothic* (London: 1996) 14.

[4] L Bayer Barenbaum, *The Gothic Imagination* (London: 1982) 12.

[5] K Halttunen, *Murder Most Foul: the Killer and the American Gothic Imagination* (Cambridge, Mass: 1998) 2.

[6] David Punter's work offers an example of a Gothic literary scholar exploring legal themes in Gothic literature. He suggests that within true Gothic literature themes of law have a particular importance. See D Punter, *Gothic Pathologies: The Text, The Body and The Law* (Basingstoke: 1998).

[7] For a summary of law themes within that literature see LJ Moran, 'Law and the Gothic Imagination' in F Botting (ed), *The Gothic* (Woodbridge: 2001) 89.

[8] See W MacNeil, 'The Monstrous Body of the Law: Wollstonecraft v Shelly' (1999) 12 *Australian Feminist LJ* 21; W MacNeil, 'Beyond Governmentality: Retribution, Distributive and Deconstructive Justice in "Great Expectations" ' (1999) 13 *Australian Feminist LJ* 98.

I have written elsewhere about the jurisprudence of spectrality and monstrosity, of legal techniques of ghost writing and the doppleganger effect (the double) in law. These were all explored in relation to the crime of buggery from the seventeenth century to the present and in the context of the eighteenth and nineteenth century jurisprudence of robbery.[9] Work by Peter Hutchings on nineteenth century criminology, criminal law and criminal justice,[10] provides another example of scholarship that explores similar themes in a more general context.[11] His scholarship on Bentham and spectres is exemplary in this respect.[12] Over against Bentham's utilitarian reformist vision of law informed by scientific rationalism, Hutchings explores the ways in which, for Bentham, the English common law (in particular judge-made law and legal fictions) takes on the form of a ruin and a ghostly labyrinthine presence. These aspects of common law haunt Bentham and his rationalist project, threatening to corrupt and ultimately destroy law's reason and the will to reform by way of codification.

In this article my concern is not so much with the significance of the Gothic imagination in the distant past of law but with its contemporary significance and more specifically with its operation in some contemporary jurisprudential writings. My argument is that a body of recent jurisprudential scholarship, which has been particularly informed by post structuralist and psychoanalytic thought, evidences an engagement with themes that are integral to the Gothic imagination. Central to this insight and argument is the sublime. The sublime, I want to argue, is a key theme of this jurisprudence, and it is this engagement with the sublime which provides the link to the Gothic imagination. Before turning my attention to this Gothic jurisprudence, by way of introduction I want to say a little more about the sublime and its place within the Gothic imagination.

The Sublime and the Gothic Imagination

Fred Botting, in his book *Gothic*[13] suggests that the sublime occupies a pivotal role in the Gothic. The sublime is not so much a term that refers to a single unchanging concept but a reference to a variety of historical and theoretical accounts. Its roots lie in the first century writings of the Greek scholar Longinus. It is, in the context of this article, neither possible nor necessary to map the whole of the history

[9] Moran, n 7 above.

[10] PJ Hutchings, *The Criminal Spectre in Law, Literature and Aesthetics: Incriminating Subjects* (London, 2000).

[11] Hutchings does not specifically use the concept of the Gothic in his writings.

[12] PJ Hutchings, 'Spectacularizing Crime: Ghost writing the Law' (1999) 10(1) *Law and Critique* 27. It is perhaps ironic that the aesthetics of the new Courts of Justice in the Strand, London was the Gothic, albeit a 'muscular Gothic', see DB Brownlee, *The Law Courts: The Architecture of George Edmund Street* (Cambridge, Mass: 1984).

[13] Botting, n 3 above. David Morris describes the place of the sublime within that Gothic genre in the following terms: as, 'a vital and integral part . . . not merely an incidental, ornamental, scenic prop'. D B Morris, 'Gothic Sublimity' (1984-5) XVI (2) Winter, *New Literary History* 299, 300.

and conceptual terrain of the sublime.[14] First, I want to draw out some aspects of both past and present engagements with the sublime. I will then outline some of the main characteristics of the sublime as it appears within the Gothic imagination. In that context the Romantic sublime, with its roots in eighteenth century philosophy and aesthetics, has particular significance.[15]

Various scholars offer an insight into the different traditions and categorizations of the sublime. In *Ruin the sacred truths*, Harold Bloom[16] offers the following taxonomy of traditions of the sublime: Hebraic Christian sublime; Homeric sublime; daemonic sublime; natural sublime. This taxonomy combines both a range of cultural influences (Jewish, Christian as well as Greek thought) and different historical concerns (the daemonic and natural sublime have particular importance in the eighteenth century though they are not unique to that period). It also draws attention to a connection between the sublime and religion, theology and metaphysics. This is important in various ways. Jan Rosiek notes that the sublime has a close affinity with matters of good and evil and more specifically with matters of the sacred, the divine, and the supersensory (the metaphysical).[17] Key features of the sublime are a concern with emotion and affect (more specifically terror, fear, horror, excess, awe) and with the connection between, on the one hand, terror and repulsion, and on the other hand, fascination and attraction. All connect the sublime to ideas of the divine (the numinous) and the sacred. The sublime, Roseik suggests, can be understood as a theoretic construct that aestheticizes the sacred and sacralizes aesthetics. More specifically by reference to the work of Lacoue-Labarthe, Rosiek suggests that the eighteenth century scholarship on the sublime[18] transforms the meta-physical tradition of the sublime into a different tradition of the ethico-aesthetic. Through this eighteenth century scholarship the sublime is made a theoretic construct in which ideas more associated with the pre-modernity are re-figured for modernity.

I want to refer to another somewhat different taxonomy offered by Rosiek. He draws distinctions between '[t]he religio-literary' which gives some priority to the sublime understood by way of a connection to rhetoric, and the ethico-anaesthetic sublime, particularly associated with Kant,[19] in which the sublime is connected with a moral project about representation.[20] The latter has particular significance in two important ways. First, Kant's study of the sublime together with Edmund Burke's

[14] A useful introduction to the history and diversity of the sublime is to be found in J Rosiek, *Maintaining The Sublime: Heidegger and Adorno* (Bern: 2000). On Kant see also JF Lyotard, *Lessons on the analytic of the sublime* (trans E Rattenberg, Stanford: 1994).

[15] Morris, n 13 above.

[16] H Bloom, *Ruin The Sacred Truths: Poetry And Belief From The Bible To The Present* (Cambridge, Mass: 1989).

[17] Rosiek, n 14 above. See esp 'The religio-literary translation of the metaphysical'.

[18] Particularly those found in the work of Kant, see E Kant, '*Book II, Analytic of the Sublime*' in *The Critique of Judgement* (trans James Creed Meredith, Oxford: OUP, 1978).

[19] Kant, n 18 above.

[20] Weiskel suggests that the Romantic sublime is particularly concerned with hermeneutics. See T Weiskel, *The Romantic Sublime: Studies in the Structure and Psychology of Transcendence* (Baltimore: 1976).

writings on the sublime,[21] were an important influence on eighteenth century authors who founded the Gothic as a literary genre. Secondly, the Kantian idea of the sublime is at the heart of what Jean-Luc Nancy has described as the 'fashion of the sublime' in much late twentieth century scholarship.[22] The sublime, Nancy explains, has become central to the 'philosophy *of* aesthetics and philosophy *in* aesthetics, for the thought of art and for the art of thought'.[23]

I want to highlight a number of themes within the Kantian tradition of the sublime. In the *Analytic of the Sublime*, Kant explains the sublime and the emotional intensities associated with the sublime (pain, fear, terror, awe) in terms of an experience of the 'supersensible'. This is an experience associated with the mind[24] and not something that has its origins in found objects such as nature (which is in sharp contrast to beauty).[25] As Kant explains: 'For the beautiful in nature we must seek a ground external to ourselves, but for the sublime one merely in ourselves . . . '.[26] More specifically the sublime, for Kant, is ' . . . a disposition of soul evoked by a particular representation engaging the attention of the reflective judgement, and not in the Object, that is to be called sublime'.[27]

A second important dimension of the Kantian sublime is concerned with terror, fear, horror, awe and the distinctions and connections between fear/horror and terror and pain and pleasures, associated with the sublime. Fear may both immobilize and transport. The former, Kant suggests, has little to do with the sublime. He explains: 'One who is in a state of fear can no more play the part of a judge of the sublime of nature than one captivated by inclination and appetite can of the beautiful'.[28] Thus: 'We must see ourselves safe in order to feel this soul-stirring delight'.[29] As Kant illustrates in the following extract:

> The idea of sublimity of that Being which inspires deep respect in us, not by the mere display of its might in nature, but more by the faculty which is planted in us of estimating that might without fear, and of regarding our estate as exalted above it.[30]

Here terror and fear in relation to the sublime are associated with an ontological experience of revelation and insight arising out of reflection and of elevation and transformation not with a crushing immobility, confinement or constraint. Kant offers an example of this distinction in the following observation:

> The man that is actually in a state of fear, finding in himself good reason to be so, because he is conscious of offending with his evil disposition against a might directed by a will at once irresistible and just, is far from being in a frame of mind for admiring divine greatness,

[21] E Burke, *A Philosophical Enquiry Into The Origin Of Our Ideas Of The Sublime And The Beautiful* (London: 1958).

[22] JL Nancy, 'The sublime offering' in JF Courtine et al (eds), *Of the sublime: Presence in Question* (trans JS Librett, Albany 1993) 25.

[23] Nancy, n 22 above.

[24] Kant, n 18 above, 103.

[25] ibid, 98.

[26] In part Kant is responding to the association between the sublime and nature. Rather than the sublime being in nature, Kant's focus is on the very attitude of mind that introduces sublimity into the representation of nature. See Kant, n 18 above, 93.

[27] ibid, 98.

[28] ibid, 110.

[29] ibid, 112.

[30] ibid, 114.

for which a temper of calm reflection and a quiet free judgement are required. Only when he becomes conscious of having a disposition that is upright and acceptable to God, do those operatives of might serve to stir within him the idea of the sublimity of this Being, so far as he recognizes the existence in himself of a sublimity of disposition consonant with His will, and is thus raised above the dread of such operations of nature, in which he no longer sees God pouring forth the vials of the wrath.[31]

Thus the distinction between immobilizing fear and uplifting terror produces for Kant a contrast between respectively subordination and subservience on the one hand and 'a religion consisting of the good life' on the other.

Terror, fear, horror and awe are matters at the heart of the themes of reflective judgment in the Kantian sublime. They also play a central role within the Gothic imagination. In the Gothic, reflective judgment is located in relation to transgression and excess, which are attributed with negative values in contrast with the positive values associated with the status quo. At the same time those positive social values, virtue and propriety, are not only closely associated with the negative but called into question and both enforced and transformed by that proximity. Scholars of the Gothic draw attention to the importance of the function of fear and horror in the Gothic imagination in relation to Kant's idea of the good life rather than in terms of immobilizing subordination.

I want to highlight two aspects of the contemporary engagement with the Kantian sublime that have particular significance in relation to the jurisprudential writings I will engage with later. One context in which the sublime has returned as an important theme is in the context of work on representation and its limits, be it by way of reflections on the avant garde and painting in particular[32] or in relation to texts in general.[33] Here the sublime is the void, the infinity, the awesome nothingness against which boundaries and borders of current meanings and the possibility of meaning are both made and enforced, transgressed and transcended. This echoes Kant's position that the sublime is 'the mere capacity of thinking which evidences a faculty of mind transcending every standard of sense'.[34] Lyotard connects the emotional intensities associated with the sublime (pain, fear, terror, awe) that are experienced in the context of these limits/boundaries of meaning with a series of privations. Terrors associated with darkness, solitude, silence, emptiness and death are respectively connected to privations of light, others, language, objects, and life. These conjunctions occur in the context of various experiences such as facing the challenge of a strange and novel situation or being confronted by the radical differences of another human subject. They take the form of sudden jolting, violent shocks, vertiginous moments, intense anxieties, states of confusion, and quixotic temporal ecstasies to name a few.[35] A second context in which the emotional economy of the sublime has gained contemporary

[31] ibid, 113–114.

[32] JF Lyotard, 'The sublime and the avant garde' in A Benjamin (ed), *The Lyotard Reader* (Oxford: 1989) 196.

[33] See Rosiek, n 14 above, 'The sublime in contemporary theory'.

[34] Kant, n 18 above, 98.

[35] Lyotard, n 32 above, 204.

significance is in the context of ethical questions that arise in encounters with 'the other' which is understood as absolute difference.[36] The ethical demand is made in and through this encounter with 'the other' as one whose difference is irreducible, which cannot be reduced to the same, the subject that is already imagined and thereby already delimited.[37] Both contemporary contexts draw attention to the way the current 'fashion of the sublime' draws heavily upon an aesthetics that puts into play ideas of excess, limitlessness, formlessness, the absolute, infinity, magnificence and awful power.

The relationship between the sublime and the Gothic is explained by Botting in the following terms: the Gothic 'signified a trend towards an aesthetics based on feeling and emotion . . . associated primarily with the sublime'.[38] In its emphasis upon feeling and emotion the Gothic imagination might well be described as a sensational intelligibility.[39] The sublime plays a key role in producing the Gothic imagination as an intelligibility that foregrounds passion, excitement, fear, horror, terror and awe emotions as intense and extreme (hyperbolic) emotions/sensations. Second, the sublime, as that which lies beyond and that which threatens boundaries and borders, informs what Botting has described as the 'stock features', which provide the principal embodiments and evocations of the cultural anxieties that the Gothic imagination highlights and gives form to. These stock features are multiple and changing over time. The descent into confusion and the threat of formlessness is invoked by tortuous, repetitive, labyrinthine, fragmented narratives which are in stark contrast to the solid linearity of prose. There is a preoccupation with horrible images and life threatening pursuits, a recurrence of spectres, monsters, demons, corpses, skeletons and, in the eighteenth century, evil aristocrats, all of whom run in parallel, haunting and infecting the figures who personify respectability, good order, the norm. In the nineteenth century the Gothic imagination began to speak to cultural anxieties associated with new locations, the urban rather than the rural, and reflecting the increasing importance of science. A whole new cast of Gothic characters and geographies, embodying and locating these cultural anxieties, arose. These included the more frequent appearance of scientists unleashing the monstrous inventions born in their diabiolical laboratories, to a persistent preoccupation with madmen and criminals who were to be found in the dark, dank, squalid, labyrinthine streets of London's East End. A new preoccupation emerged with families and family members with dark secrets; evil fathers and husbands now haunted the respectable cosy homes of emerging suburbia south of

[36] For an exploration of these themes in the work of Lyotard see GE Aylesworth, 'Lyotard, Gadamer and the relation between ethics and aesthetics' in HJ Silverman (ed), *Lyotard: Philosophy, Politics and the Sublime* (London: 2002) 84.

[37] The writings of Emmanuel Levinas have been particularly important in this respect. For example see E Levinas, *Otherwise Than Being Or Beyond Essence* (trans A Lingis, London: 1991). For a general introduction see E Levinas, *The Levinas Reader* (S Hand (ed), Oxford: 1989).

[38] Botting, n 3 above, 3.

[39] In part it is this focus on the emotions that led the Gothic to be a genre associated with low and popular culture rather than high culture.

the river Thames.[40] In various ways these figures and places embody and evoke the many 'uncertainties about the nature of power, law, society, family and sexuality'[41] that dominate Gothic fiction.

Before I turn my attention to contemporary jurisprudence I want to make one more general comment about the Gothic imagination. I want to reflect briefly on the changing embodiments and evocations of the Gothic produced in and through the Gothic imagination. Their form and mobility draw attention to an important dimension of the Gothic; its historical, social and political dimension. The particular historical context of the rise and consolidation of the Gothic imagination by way of a distinctive literary genre, is eighteenth century English modernity. Furniss argues that the eighteenth century writings on the sublime, particularly those of Edmund Burke, connect those writings to the emergence of a gendered (masculine)[42] bourgeois subject and the rise of the middle class.[43] But as Bayer-Barenbaum[44] and others have noted, its significance is not limited to that particular historical or political moment. Gothic scholars have suggested that as an imaginative mode and philosophical schema the Gothic is an effect of and response to many dimensions of modernity. More specifically it arises in the context of the transformations brought about by a modernity dominated by the Enlightenment's obsession with the scientific and the rational and an aesthetics associated with Greco-Roman classicism. The Gothic, Botting explains, '. . . is fascinated by the objects and practices that are constructed as negative, irrational, immoral and fantastic'[45] within a project of modernity. Through the Gothic, modernity is experienced not only as the end of tradition (the dead weight of the past), the loss of the divine and the sacred (the metaphysical), as organizing principles of moral truth and social order but also as their return. The unreason and the irrational that are banished in and through modernity return to haunt and disturb. The connection between the Gothic imagination and modernity also offers some insight into the persistence of the Gothic imagination through the nineteenth century and its revival in the late twentieth century. The socio-political context of contemporary resort to Gothic themes, the postmodern, might be characterized as a response to 'an escalating anxiety regarding modernity'[46] such as is to be found in the growing body of scholarship on fear[47] and in the sociological writings of scholars such as

[40] On the geographies of the Victorian gothic see R Mighall, *A Geography of Victorian Gothic Fiction: Mapping History's Nightmares* (Oxford: 1999).

[41] Botting, n 3 above, 5.

[42] For other scholarship on gender and the gothic see T Castle, *The Apparitional Lesbian* (New York: 1993); P Palmer, *Lesbian Gothic: Transgressive Fictions* (London: 1999); C Hendershot, *The Animal Within: Masculinity and the Gothic* (Ann Arbor: 1998).

[43] T Furniss, *Edmund Burke's Aesthetic Ideology: Language, gender and political economy in revolution* (Cambridge: 1993).

[44] Bayer-Barenbaum, n 4 above, 12.

[45] Botting, n 3 above, 2.

[46] Botting, n 3 above, 169.

[47] See, eg, M Davis, *Ecology of Fear* (London: 1998); N Ellin (ed), *Architecture of Fear* (Princeton: 1997); F Furedi, *Culture of Fear* (London: 2002); B Glassner, *The Culture of Fear: Why Americans are Afraid of the Wrong Things* (New York: 1999); C Hale, 'Fear of Crime: a review of the literature' (1996) 14 *Intl Rev of Victimology* 79–150.

Giddens,[48] Bauman,[49] Beck,[50] and Young[51] to name but a few. The Gothic is an intelligibility, which addresses the challenges of new uncertainties, new developments, new technologies of communication giving rise to dramatic changes in and through the project of modernity.[52]

A Gothic Jurisprudence

Now I want to turn my attention to a selection of jurisprudential writings of various contemporary legal scholars; in particular, to a group of writers whose work is informed by post structuralism. I want to argue that at the end of the millennium a Gothic jurisprudence has emerged in anglophone legal scholarship. I begin by highlighting various aspects of this post structural jurisprudence which point towards a Gothic sensibility in these writings. Thereafter I explore the place of the sublime within this work in more detail focusing particular attention upon textual aspects of the sublime.[53]

One aspect of the Gothic imagination that has gained importance in this contemporary jurisprudential writing is found in a return to the sacred and in a re-evaluation and a recuperation of the iconography of the religious in law.[54] One example is to be found in Peter Goodrich's work that draws parallels between the rituals of the Eucharist and legal rituals.[55] It is also a theme present in his more recent work that poses the problem of representation of law by way of the struggle over representation in the emergence of the Protestant church in northern Europe; iconoclasm.[56] For Goodrich iconoclasm is at work in the characterization and elevation of the written text and in the denial of the significance of other modes of representation in law. Iconoclasm also draws attention to the problem of meaning in the text; a meaning that is always contingent, limited, bounded over against the awesome void of all other possible meanings. Iconoclasm provides a link between the text, the sacred and the sublime. The supreme example of the sublime, for Kant, is the 'altogether negative' which connotes 'the unbounded'. In turn the

[48] A Giddens, *The Consequences of Modernity* (Polity Press: 1990).

[49] Z Bauman, *Modernity and Ambivalence* (Polity Press: 1991).

[50] U Beck, *Risk Society* (London: 1992).

[51] J Young, *The Exclusive Society* (London: 1999).

[52] Botting, n 3 above, 165.

[53] The other context in which recent jurisprudential writings have encountered and engaged with the sublime is in relation to ethics. Here much of the work is informed by the writings of Levinas. See, eg, C Douzinas and R Warrington, *Justice Miscarried: Ethics, aesthetics and the law* (London: 1994) and M Diamantides, *The Ethics of Suffering: Modern Law, Philosophy And Medicine* (Aldershot: 2000).

[54] See, eg, J Butler and A Gearey (eds), *Law and the Sacred* (2000) 5 (1) *Law, Text, Culture.*

[55] P Goodrich, *Languages of Law* (London: 1990). See also C Douzinas, R Warrington and S McVeigh, *Postmodern Jurisprudence* (London: 1991).

[56] P Goodrich, 'The Iconography of Nothing; Blank Spaces and the Representation of Law in Edward VI and the Pope' in C Douzinas and L Nead (eds), *Law and the Image: The Authority of Art and the Aesthetics of Law* (Chicago and London: 1999); C Douzinas, 'Prosopon and Antiprosopon: Prolegomena for a Legal Iconology' in Douzinas and Nead, ibid.

Judaic prohibition of representations of God is the best example of this. Kant explains:

> Perhaps there is no more sublime passage in the Jewish Law than the commandment: Thou shalt not make unto thee any graven image, or any likeness of any thing that is in heaven or on earth, or under the earth, etc. This commandment can alone explain the enthusiasm which the Jewish people, in their moral period, felt for their religion when comparing themselves with others, or the pride inspired by Mohammedanism. The very same holds good of our representation of the moral law and of our native capacity for morality. The fear that, if we divest this representation of everything that can commend it to the senses, it will thereupon be attended only with a cold and lifeless approbation and not with any moving force or emotion, is wholly unwarranted. The very reverse is true.[57]

The jurisprudential encounter with the prohibition of images of law in the context of the policing of boundaries of possibility of representation and meanings of law itself installs an idea of the sublime not only within legal scholarship and legal practice but also within critical scholarship of law.

An engagement with the work of a continental jurisprudential scholar, Pierre Legendre, is also of importance here. Legendre explores the relation between the sacred and the secular through a study of the emergence of the civilian legal tradition in the context of a culture dominated by the Catholic Church. The blurb on the inside of Goodrich's collection and translation of Legendre's work draws out its particular significance. His work, Goodrich explains, will introduce us to the law as 'delirium' and 'passion'.[58] These terms point to Legendre as a scholar whose study of the sacred in the secular institutions of law might offer us a sensationalist jurisprudence and a jurisprudence which will speak of that which is denied and repressed within jurisprudence as a project of the enlightenment with its rationalist preoccupations.

The references to Legendre in jurisprudential scholarship also point to another aspect of the turn to the Gothic imagination; an engagement with psychoanalysis. Lacan, in particular, has come to achieve a certain prominence in Anglo-American legal scholarship. Evidence of this is to be found, for example, in the writings of Caudill,[59] Cornell,[60] Douzinas and Warrington,[61] Felman[62] and Goodrich.[63] But how does this engagement with psychoanalysis work to connect this jurisprudential scholarship to the Gothic imagination? Recent critical scholars of both

[57] Kant, n 18 above, 127.

[58] P Legendre, *Law and the Unconscious: A Legendre Reader* (P Goodrich, A Pottage and A Schutz (trans), P Goodrich (ed), Basingstoke: 1997).

[59] D Caudill, 'Freud and Critical Legal Studies: Contours of a Radical Socio-Legal Psychoanalysis' (1991) 66 *Indiana L Rev* 651; D Caudill, 'Lacan and Legal Language: Meanings in Gaps, Gaps in the meaning' (1992) 3 *Law and Critique* 165; D Caudill, 'Name of the Father and the Logic of Psychosis: Lacan's Law and Ours' (1993) 4 *Legal Studies Forum* 421; D Caudill, *Lacan and the Subject of Law, Towards a Psychoanalysis of Critical Legal Theory* (New Jersey: 1997).

[60] See, eg, D Cornell, *Philosophy of the Limit* (London: 1992).

[61] Douzinas and Warrington, n 53 above.

[62] S Felman, *The Juridical Unconscious: Trials And Traumas In The Twentieth Century* (Harvard: 2002).

[63] P Goodrich, *Oedipus Lex: Psychoanalysis, History, Law* (Berkeley: 1995).

melodrama[64] and the Gothic[65] have noted that psychoanalysis takes on cultural and historically specific forms, in particular those of melodrama and the Gothic. Brooks notes that there is a 'convergence in the concerns of melodrama and psychoanalysis'[66] which he suggests requires that we think of psychoanalysis as 'a kind of modern melodrama'.[67] In the context of the Gothic, Mighall reflects on the resort to psychoanalysis in order to read Gothic texts. He draws attention to the way in which the psychoanalytic model 'actually mirrors many of the basic rhetorical and ideational properties of [the Gothic] . . . '.[68] For Mighall, this suggests that psychoanalysis is not so much a critical tool, which might be used to offer new insights into the figures, themes and underlying concerns of Gothic fiction, but already an expression of the Gothic imagination itself. My argument is not that contemporary jurisprudential resort to psychoanalysis presupposes the very thing that it seeks to explain (the Gothic). I want to suggest that through a reading of law by way of psychoanalysis, law in general and jurisprudence in particular is being analysed and formed by way of a Gothic imaginary, already naturalized in the tropes of psychoanalysis. In its application to law psychoanalysis offers an analysis infused with a Gothic sensibility helping to forge a Gothic jurisprudence.

These various themes come together in some of the work of Peter Goodrich. In both *Oedipus Lex*[69] and *Law in the Courts of Love*[70] the object of analysis is the power of the image. For Goodrich the image is important as it is the means whereby '[t]he memory of Law—as custom and tradition, as precedent and antiquity . . . '[71] is (re)produced. Goodrich's object of analysis and critique is English scholarship and legal practice that celebrates rule, reason and logic of the status quo. In juxtaposition to this he offers an engagement with that which is repressed, rendered vestigial, made other to this status quo; the dark side. 'Oedipus Lex', he explains:

> . . . concerns the politics of recuperation, of recovery of the traumas that law cannot consider, of recollection of the repressed and failed images, figures, texts, and thoughts prohibited by the prose of doctrine, by the language of judgment, by the protocols of a wisdom without desire.[72]

[64] Brooks, n 1 above. [65] Mighall, n 40 above. [66] Brooks, n 1 above, xi.

[67] ibid, x. [68] Mighall, n 40 above, 249. [69] Goodrich, n 63 above.

[70] P Goodrich, *Law in the Courts of Love: Literature and Other Minor Jurisprudences* (London: 1996).

[71] ibid, 96.

[72] Goodrich, n 63 above, x. Writing in *Gothic Pathologies: The Text, The Body and The Law*, literary scholar David Punter (1998) offers an instance of this intelligibility at work in the following reflection on law in similar terms. 'What' he asks, 'is the law?'. He answers as follows: 'We may hazard an initial answer: it is the mass, specific to a particular society, of the supposedly unhaunted textual materials, which it knows. In other words, the law is the imposition of certainty, the rhetorical summation of the absence, or the loss of doubt; which means in turn that the law is a purified abstract whole, perfected according to the processes of taboo, which can find no purchase on the doubled, creviced, folded world of the real, by which it in turn is destined to be haunted. The law is thus there to will away the body; where the law is, bodies cannot exist or plead. Similarly, the law can have no cognisance of ghosts; it can exist and function only on a radically thinned terrain, where the deeps and crests of imaginary geographies have no being; it takes its sights along a single trajectory, and in doing so it seeks to exile haunting, seeks to find a pure line of explanation.' (2–3) For Punter law appears to be represented

Here Goodrich's jurisprudence draws upon a poetics of spectres (the repressed), ruins (failed images), the enduring sites of violent shocks (traumas) and emotions (desire). Thereby he writes a jurisprudence that seeks to offer an encounter with the other side of the legal establishment, which is for him a pre-requisite for Justice. In this scheme of things 'Justice' is ' . . . both blindness and insight, both rage and reconciliation'.[73] This characterization of Justice as a conflation of opposites, as sensation (passion and desire) rather than reason, echoes some of the hyperbolic attributes of the infinite and the abyss closely associated with the sublime.

A Jurisprudence of the Sublime

One source of contemporary jurisprudential engagements with the sublime has its origins in the writings of Kafka and Derrida. Kafka's influence has been promoted in legal scholarship by way of Derrida's work on his short story 'Before the law'.[74] Derrida's analysis of Kafka's short story that'. . . condenses the whole of "The Trail" in the scene of "Before the Law" '[75] offers a Gothic jurisprudence.[76] Central to this conclusion is Derrida's reading of the theme of the nature of law found in Kafka's text. Derrida, I want to argue, offers an analysis of law and justice according to the logic of the sublime.

Much of the analysis focuses upon boundaries. Derrida's starting point is the relation between the gatekeeper/door/castle and the one at the door, before the castle, in front of and facing the gatekeeper, the countryman. By way of these two characters and their different positions a series of binary oppositions is set in motion; of city and country, of nurture and nature, of dark and light.[77] These oppositions conjoin with other binaries that have a more obvious juridical focus; in the relation between positive law and the natural or moral law. At the same time these binaries appear to be internal to positive law. They are given expression

as little more than code/rule, reason and logic. Yet, he suggests in this very image an image of the other of reason/the mind, the body, which connotes unreason, passion and emotion. While their return threatens to destroy, the terror of that which returns offers the possibility of new sensations, new insights, new social orders.

[73] P Goodrich, 'Justice and the Trauma of Law: A Response to George Pavlich' (1998) 18 *Studies in Law, Politics and Society* 278.

[74] J Derrida, 'Before the Law' in D Attridge (ed), *Acts of Literature* (London: 1992) 181. Agamben has also written about the significance of Kafka's writings, see G Agamben, *Potentialities: Collected Essays in Philosophy* (Stanford, 1999) Ch 10. Derrida's other major text on law is J Derrida, 'Force of Law: The Mystical Foundation of Authority' in D Cornell et al (eds), *Deconstruction and the Possibility of Justice* (London: 1992). It also tells a tale of law according to various Gothic tropes; of ruins and spectres. Here the law as sublime takes the form of an originary violence.

[75] Derrida, 'Before the Law', n 74 above, 209.

[76] Some scholars have noted the mediaeval Gothic iconography (particularly that of the Last Judgment) in Kafka's two texts that are most pertinent to law; 'The Trial' and 'The Castle'. See, V M Hyde, 'From the Last Judgment to Kafka's World: A Study of Gothic Iconography' in GR Thompson (ed), *The Gothic Imagination: Essays in Dark Romanticism* (Pullman: 1974) 128.

[77] Derrida, 'Before the Law', n 74 above, 195.

in the countryman's expectations that '. . . the Law, he thinks, should surely be accessible at all times and to everyone'.[78] Here law is clear, transparent, logical, the fullness of meaning and the transparency of meaning in contrast to another side of law; of opacity, confusion, unknowability, knowable only to specialists—lawyers, gatekeepers.

In Kafka's tale the opacity of the law is that which returns to confound the countryman's assumption and expectation of transparency. The tale tells of his experience of the return of this repressed image. I want to argue that Kafka's tale and Derrida's reading of it goes beyond this. The nature of that beyond might be examined by way of a return to the gatekeeper. As the one who represents the law, the gatekeeper might be expected to know the law. However, Kafka's tale suggests otherwise. The gatekeeper only knows of other gatekeepers who regress endlessly into the distance and who at each portal are more powerful. The law remains unknown to them. The succession of gatekeepers are an anthropomorphized form of the law as labyrinth, a common figure of disorientation found in the Gothic. At the same time that law is that which is lost or deferred (absent) in the experience of the labyrinth, the law is also that which lies beyond both the anthropomorphic figures of gatekeeper and countryman. Here law is also a third term to the binary structure.

It is law as the third term, which Derrida describes as 'the law of the law',[79] I want to suggest, that connects this law of the law (Justice) to the sublime.[80] Derrida explains this law as that which 'exclude[s] all historicity and empirical narrativity',[81] '. . . it must be without history, genesis, or any possible privation'.[82] It is invisibility, silence, discontinuity, the inaccessible, the impossible an absolute. It is 'obscene and unpresentable',[83] an infinity and an excess that violates all boundaries, puzzles and paralyzes[84] a locus that is a non locus of terror.[85] As such it does not merely mirror attributes of law's dark underside (evil other) which are set up over against the countryman's expectations of law as knowledge, reason, logic, knowability, transparency (the good). The third term is characterized in hyperbolic terms as a founding supra evil, an evil beyond good and evil, out of which all other binaries, narratives, histories flow. Here law is represented according to the aesthetics of excess associated with the sublime. Derrida, following Kafka, offers an instance of the story of the nature of law (Justice) as a diabolical or dark romance.

Costas Douzinas and Ronnie Warrington's *Justice Miscarried: Ethics, Aesthetics and the Law*[86] offers an extended study which echoes and draws upon this aesthetics of excess in the characterization and analysis of Justice. Justice is associated with 'suddenness', 'awesome overpowering'[87] and an 'inestimable force'.[88] It is figured in hyperbolic terms, as 'excess', and in the negative, which is figured in various ways as 'the unsayable', 'a silence' as an 'impossible necessity, an 'insubstantial

[78] Derrida, 'Before the Law', n 74 above, 183. [79] ibid, 205. [80] ibid, 190.
[81] ibid, 190. [82] ibid, 191. [83] ibid, 205. [84] ibid, 196. [85] ibid, 203.
[86] Douzinas and Warrington, n 53 above. [87] ibid, 86. [88] ibid, 91.

substance'.[89] It is an 'aporia', which generates an ethical call. Characterized in this way Justice is intimately connected to Kant's quintessential example of the sublime, the Judaic prohibition on representations of God. Their analysis of *Antigone's* Dike[90] is of particular significance as it is through a reading of Sophocles' play that their characterization of Justice emerges. This is subsequently applied in various contexts, for example in relation to texuality and meaning and in the context of a number of case studies focusing on UK legal judgments relating to asylum. The following extract is taken from their analysis of *Antigone*:

> But the law of the law, destiny, is unknown. We can never know destiny but we must follow it, like Antigone. Fate comes as the other, the dying/dead other who asks us to save or bury him. The force of the 'must' is the force that the most remote and different from self imposes on self. Death as the other of life; the stranger who is left outside the wall of Thebes to be devoured by the dogs; the force of *eros* as the total transcendence of the world projected by and revolving around self . . . Could we not argue then that (unknown) fate is the good (or God?). It stands before the law and it infuses it both with opposition to Justice and with the superiority of Justice over Law. It is also destiny as the force of the multiplicity of Being (gods as others) that propels the law into being.[91]

Here 'destiny' and 'fate' are metaphors for the void that is Justice. 'Death' has a similar significance. As Douzinas and Warrington explain, 'death' is a 'register of destiny [that] put[s] into operation its unwritten and universal law'.[92] 'Death' is also important in another way. Within the Burkean tradition of the sublime the terror at the heart of that aesthetics is the apprehension of death. 'Death' is the extreme (hyperbolic) event, that also figures the exaggerated emotion and excess of feeling which, Morris argues, 'is the law for Gothic'.[93] Gothic writers, he explains, 'invest death and dying with new prominence and new terrors'.[94]

A final example of an engagement with the sublime is to be found in the work of Giorgio Agamben. I want to explore the influence of the sublime within his work *Homo Sacer*.[95] His resort to an aesthetics of the sublime appears in a different topographical context from that outlined above; of sovereignty and its institutions. In *Homo Sacer* Agamben locates characteristics that Derrida associates with law as the sublime in the practices and metaphor of the concentration camp. For example law institutionalised in the camp is law without (human) origin. He explains this by reference to a quote from Deils, the head of the Gestapo: 'Neither an order nor an instruction exists from the origin of the camps: they were not instituted; one day they were there . . . '.[96] Here law is an origin without origins. Other associations between law and the sublime are reinforced and reinscribed in Agamben's repeated assertion that the law of the camp is law as exception. It is characterized in his description of this law as a 'zone of indistinction', which he describes as 'totalitarian'.[97] Its particular force is

89 All in ibid, 202–203. 90 ibid, Ch 2. 91 ibid, 92. 92 ibid, 91.
93 Morris, n 13 above, 303. 94 ibid, 308.
95 G Agamben, *Homo Sacer: Sovereign Power and Bare Life* (trans Daniel Heller-Roazen, Stanford: 1998).
96 ibid, 169. 97 ibid, 170.

described in various ways. It is a supremely destructive force. Law is here a force that destroys the sense of 'subjective right and juridical protection'.[98] It collapses distinctions: between law and fact; rule and exception; between law making and the administration of law; between law's production and its application;[99] between legality and illegality; inside and outside; between exception and rule; between licit and illicit. Under this law right and wrong become impossible distinctions, '. . . no act committed against them could appear any longer as a crime'.[100] Law is also to be understood as a supremely creative force. It makes 'everything . . . truly . . . possible'.[101]

The institutionalization of this logic of law as an awesome terrifying power in the Nationalist Socialist concentration camp is for Agamben closely associated with Schmitt's jurisprudence. Agamben suggests that Schmitt's jurisprudence is 'unwittingly Kafkaesque'.[102] He illustrates the point by reference to an extract from Schmitt's chapter, 'State Movement, People'. Here the Kafkaesque is in Schmitt's association between law and unreason. Law's corruption is to be found in the 'indeterminate' nature of juridical concepts that in turn give rise to 'juridical uncertainty'. The opacity of the law and the loss of direction is, in the extract from Schmitt offered by Agamben, not characterized by way of the structure of the labyrinth but is explained by way of an aqueous metaphor; we are condemned '. . . to a shoreless sea'.[103] The corrupting force of 'indeterminate' judicial concepts infects the alternative vision, of law as rule and reason. Schmitt concludes that this alternative is nothing more than 'superstition' and an archaic trace of the 'senseless' in law.

These themes are given particular concrete significance by Agamben in the context of the indeterminacy of the 'National Socialist notion of race'.[104] The indeterminacy of 'race' is the point of rupture that is the sign of the corruption of the legal body that opens the way for the terror of law. Agamben's particular concern is the potential for the transformation of the exceptional, the sublime violence of law, to become the normal. The camp is an institutional metaphor that seeks to mark that transformation. Set up as a form of law that is an exception and an exceptional response, through the camp, 'the state of exception . . . is realised normally'.[105]

For Agamben the camp is not just the institutionalization of an aberration in a particular historical moment. It has wider significance: ' . . . the birth of the camp in our time appears as an event that decisively signals the political space of modernity itself'.[106] It arises in the context of the 'rupture of the old *nomos*'.[107] The camp is endemic to the political system of the modern nation state. But it is hidden. It is always ready to assume new forms: 'we must learn to recognize [it] in all its metamorphoses'.[108]

[98] G Agamben, n. 95 above, 170. [99] ibid, 173. [100] ibid, 171.
[101] ibid, 171. [102] ibid, 172.
[103] On the uses of aqueous metaphors in relation to the rise of Nazi Germany see K Theweleit, *Male Fantasies* (trans S Conway, E Carter and C Turner, Cambridge: 1987) Vol 1.
[104] Agamben, n 95 above,172. On the theme of race see also P Lacoue-Labarthe and JL Nancy, 'The Nazi Myth' (trans B Holmes) (1990) 16 *Critical Inquiry* 291.
[105] Agamben, n 95 above, 170. [106] ibid, 174. [107] ibid, 175. [108] ibid, 175.

Like Schmitt, whom he criticizes, Agamben, in his characterization of law in terms of the sublime, appears to be 'unwittingly Kafkaesque'. Like Schmitt, he writes a jurisprudence of sovereignty according to Gothic themes. He puts into full play the nightmare vision of the sensational jurisprudence that Derrida perhaps more benignly writes in his reflections on Kafka. For a different politics from Schmitt, Agamben produces the legal order according to the same logic of a diabolical romance.

The contrast between the sublime as it appears and informs Agamben's work with its appearance in the other jurisprudential writings discussed above draws attention to the way the sublime may work within both conservative and progressive contexts.[109] Rolando Gaete in his essay, 'Desecration, Law and Evil',[110] warns of the dangers of focusing merely on the progressive characterizations of the sublime and of the need to take them seriously. He argues for the need to take more seriously the conservative, fascistic and totalitarian manifestations and warns of the difficulties this may generate pointing to a resistance to taking 'the sacred' and 'evil' seriously in 'our techno-scientific civilisation'.[111] He highlights Kant's classical analysis of the sublime as the heart of the problem. Kant's analysis of the sublime, he suggests, offers an aesthetics that 'not only transgresses limits but makes them impossible'.[112] Like Agamben, for Gaete, Hitler's Germany provides the example of a regime which deployed transgression to devastating effects.[113] He also connects these dangers to the romantic tradition and the Gothic. The sublime of Hitler and the Nazi regime in general, Gaete suggests, 'might seduce romantic temperaments attracted to the gothic, ready to glimpse into the abyss and experience the fascination and repulsion of horror'.[114] While Gaete's concerns and his call to take the sacred and evil more seriously are welcome and timely warnings, his characterization of the problems and difficulties mentioned here are problematic.

His reference to 'romantic temperaments' is welcome not in order to advocate an abandonment of the romantic tradition (as he seems to suggest) but in order to highlight the continuing significance of the romantic tradition, which is largely unspoken and unrecognized. A recognition of the continuing importance of the romantic tradition and a more critical engagement with it is, I would argue, a prerequisite for an understanding not only of the problems and dangers that might be associated with the sublime but also with its more progressive aspects. In turn Gaete's reference to the Gothic is welcome but not helpful. It appears only to be dismissed all too quickly. In doing so, I would suggest, Gaete misses an opportunity to engage with an intelligibility (the Gothic) that will enable the study (and critique) of the operation of the sacred and of evil in contemporary society. As has

[109] Furniss, n 43 above, 20.

[110] R Gaete, 'Desecration, Law and Evil' in Butler and Gearey, n 54 above, 377.

[111] ibid, 378. [112] ibid, 389.

[113] This is not a theme unique to these authors nor is it one limited to associations with Nazi Germany. It has also been considered in relation to Stalinism. See, eg, P Lacoue-Labarthe, *Heidegger, Art and Politics* (trans C Turner, Oxford: 1990) and Lacoue-Labarthe and Nancy, n 104 above.

[114] Gaete, n 110 above, 379.

already been noted, by way of the sublime ideas more associated with the pre-modernity, in this instance the sacred, the divine, evil, are re-figured for modernity. It is the sublime which provides the core at the heart of the Gothic imagination. Rather than dismiss the Gothic, I would suggest that it needs to be taken more seriously. It is not only an intelligibility through which the sacred and evil are understood and experienced in contemporary society but it also offers a vehicle through which to develop an analysis and critique of the sacred and evil. While his reference to the Gothic echoes his important insights into the contemporary significance and political effects of the sublime, his crude and one dimensional understanding of the Gothic is a reflection of the failure to take the Gothic seriously. Finally, Gaete's concerns need to be treated with caution for another reason; he seems to ignore the importance of terror as a force associated with a transcendence, liberation and freedom that calls the ethical into being within the romantic tradition. The challenge will be to keep both the progressive and conservative dimensions of the sublime in the frame of analysis.

The analysis offered here, of contemporary jurisprudential writings, seeks to draw attention to the continuing, and I would suggest, growing importance of key themes within the romantic and more specifically the diabolical romance tradition. The resort to and importance of the sublime within this scholarship is rarely acknowledged. The engagement of this work in a romantic tradition would appear to be frequently unwitting. The Gothic, I would suggest, provides a means of understanding the aesthetic turn in jurisprudence and the particular poetics of this body of work. It also draws attention to its cultural sources and its diverse, complex and contradictory political history. In doing so it also offers an opportunity for critique.

Re-Imagining the Practice of Law: Popular Twentieth-Century Fiction by American Lawyer/Authors

David Ray Papke[*]

This article examines the lives and fiction of five twentieth-century American lawyer/authors—Melville Davisson Post, Arthur Train, Erle Stanley Gardner, Scott Turow, and John Grisham. All had severe reservations about law, lawyers, and legal practice, and, with the exception of Turow, all eventually left the legal profession and devoted themselves to literary and pop cultural pursuits. However, while they abandoned the practice of law, the practice of law did not depart from the authors' creative work. Their large bodies of fiction are replete with portrayals of lawyers and narratives of legal cases.

These stories and novels became the most popular law-related fiction of the authors' eras. Immense numbers of readers took up the works and found their stock characters and formulas engaging and satisfying. Law-related fiction by Post, Train, Gardner, Turow, and Grisham proffered stories about lawyers and legal practice that readers wanted to hear. Indeed, these works of fiction count among the most successful examples of American pop culture in the twentieth century.

What were the reasons why and the conditions under which Post, Train, Gardner, Turow, and Grisham developed their creative practices? What were the dominant features of the resulting works, and why did the works appeal to readers? Answers to these questions will suggest the diverse ways lawyer/authors have re-imagined the practice of law in their fiction and also the manner in which fiction by and about lawyers might appeal to American readers.

Melville Davisson Post

Melville Davisson Post was a popular writer of detective and mystery stories in the first decades of the twentieth century. His stories appeared in the era's most popular magazines, were collected in numerous hard-cover volumes, and even struck some

* The author thanks Professors Christine Corcos, Mary Mitchell and Steve Pepper for insightful critiques of earlier drafts of this article and law student Jane Jacobs for valuable research assistance.

as comparable to the stories of Edgar Allan Poe.[1] Post continued to write until his death in 1930, but of particular interest for purposes at hand are Post's early stories concerning the fictional attorney Randolph Mason. Post seems in the stories to be uneasy and even fearful regarding legal practice and thought, and as Post developed his Randolph Mason series, he also determined to leave the legal profession once and for all. The Mason stories themselves, meanwhile, struck a chord with the public. Readers found Mason's command of the curious, mysterious law fascinating.

Post hailed from West Virginia. His mother's family, the Davissons, were among the earliest white settlers in what became the Clarksburg area, and one of Post's ancestors served as a major on the patriots' side in the Revolutionary War. Post's own parents were well-to-do farmers and members of the rural elite, and Melville was their first son and second of their five children. Post began his education at Raccoon Run, the local elementary school, but then switched to the private Buckhannon Academy. He earned his bachelor's and law degrees from the University of West Virginia, and he began practising law at the age of only 23. Family wealth and his own income enabled Post and his wife to live more than comfortably. Post had a passion for polo, and he also enjoyed summer vacations in Newport, Rhode Island, and Bar Harbor, Maine.

During his twenties Post practised law primarily in Wheeling, the bustling Ohio River town in which he had a partnership with John A Howard. The men represented both criminal defendants and corporations, and the Post papers show substantial billing to the Wheeling Bridge and Terminal Railway Company during 1896–98.[2] Post and Howard also turned to that venerable staple of general practitioners of earlier years: debt collection. This pursuit seemed not to harm Post's reputation. He was active in the Democratic Party, became an influential presidential elector, and even served on one occasion as the secretary of the United States Electoral College.

Post's consciousness during this period seems very much that of the young, eager lawyer. He corresponded regularly with WML Coplin, a cousin and a member of the Jefferson Medical College faculty in Philadelphia, and the bantering in their letters is frequently that of the self-conscious lawyer and the self-conscious doctor. In an 1897 letter Coplin playfully tries to convince Post to join him and a Dr. Harris on a trip to Italy: 'Now as a lawyer, you might possibly want to spend some time in Northern Italy and study the methods in vogue with the Brigands there, or might desire to investigate the methods of homocide in vogue in Cicily [sic] . . . .'[3] Post joins the fun, taking more delight than offence from the slings and arrows of his era's lawyer jokes. In an 1898 letter he writes to Coplin, 'I cannot

[1] 'It is even said of him that, with one exception—Edgar Allen Poe—he is the world's greatest writer of mystery stories.' Ethel Clark Lewis, 'West Virginia's Most Noted Writer' (1930) *West Virginia Rev* 81.

[2] West Virginia University Archives and Manuscripts, *Post Family Collection; Legal Papers, 1864–1915* [*Post Family Collection*].

[3] West Virginia University Archives and Manuscripts, *Melville Davisson Post Collection* [*Post Collection*]; Correspondence; letter from WML Coplin, 6 December 1897.

understand how it could under any circumstances be possible that a Professor in a medical college should require the services of a skilled liar'.[4] In an undated letter thanking Coplin and Harris, 'Samaritans of Philadelphia', for dinner, Post quips: 'It isn't every member of my profession who has a dinner nouadays [sic]. . . .'.[5]

While being well paid and to some extent delighting in being a lawyer, Post began during this period to write stories about the fictional lawyer named Randolph Mason. GP Putnam's Sons, a highly respected New York concern, published the first seven of these stories in 1896 as *The Strange Schemes of Randolph Mason*.[6] When these first stories sold well, Post and Putnam's rushed into print a second set of stories titled *The Man of Last Resort; or, The Clients of Randolph Mason*.[7] Post later remembered the first of the two collections addressing 'the inadequacies of the criminal law' and the second 'dealing with the defects of the civil law. . . .'.[8] But this difference was clearer in Post's mind than in his texts themselves. More so than anything else, the character Randolph Mason, a fictional attorney, is the most distinctive feature of the stories.

Surprisingly, Mason does not emerge a sympathetic character with whom the reader might identify or as a hero deserving admiration. He is instead an exceptionally resourceful, somewhat frightening figure. Mason comes from Virginia and is in his middle forties. He is tall and broad across the shoulders and has a high forehead. His hair is brown with streaks of gray, and beneath heavy, almost bushy eyebrows, his eyes are a 'restless inky black'.[9] Looking at the face of Randolph Mason from above, 'the expression in repose was crafty and cynical; viewed from below upward, it was savage and vindictive, almost brutal. . . .'[10]

We know from 'The Animus Furandi', a story in the first collection, that Mason had earlier lost a fortune in France, but with the help of Courtlandt Parks—his short, bald, and loyal secretary—Mason is attempting to put both his practice and battered psyche back together in New York City. Perhaps not surprisingly, Mason's fictional practice resembles the actual one of Melville Davisson Post. Mason specializes in criminal defence work and corporate representation, and he also tries frequently to resolve debt-related problems. Mason 'found holes in the law through which his clients escaped, holes that by the profession at large were not suspected to exist, and that frequently astonished the judges'.[11] This ability, in fact, is what 'caught the attention of great corporations. They tested him and found in him learning and unlimited resources. He pointed out methods by which they could evade obnoxious statutes, by which they could comply with the apparent letter of the law and yet violate its spirit'.[12]

How might one justify this type of practice? Mason sees himself rising to two challenges. The first is the system itself. He delights in the well-executed manœuvre, the

[4] ibid, letter to WML Coplin, 4 October 1898.
[5] ibid, undated letter to WML Coplin and Henry F Harris.
[6] Melville Davisson Post, *The Strange Schemes of Randolph Mason* (New York: 1896).
[7] Melville Davisson Post, *The Man of Last Resort; or, The Clients of Randolph Mason* (New York: 1897).
[8] *Post Collection*, n 3 above, letter to Virgil A Lewis, 20 February 1899.
[9] Post, 'The Corpus Delicti' in *Strange Schemes*, n 6 above, 21. [10] ibid. [11] ibid, 16.
[12] ibid, 16–17.

perfectly guided and defended crime, and the skilful use of flawed laws and legal procedures. Beat the system. Win the game. Secondly, Mason perceives virtually mythic nemeses, opposing forces larger than life. Individual clients might be weaklings, 'making puny efforts to escape from Fate's trap, or seeking to slip from under some gin set by his fellows. . . . What miserable puppets men are!'[13] However, 'in these problems one pits himself against mysterious intelligence of Chance,—against the dread cunning and the fatal patience of Destiny. Ah! These are worthy foemen. The steel grates when one crosses swords with such mighty forces'.[14]

'The Corpus Delicti', Post's first and to this day best-known story, nicely illustrates Mason's approach to practice. The client, one Richard Warren, loves and hopes to marry a beautiful socialite, but his Mexican mistress refuses to let go of him and also threatens to reveal Warren's tawdry past. Insisting first that his directions be followed to the letter, Mason tells Warren how to kill his former mistress in a way which cannot lead to a successful murder prosecution. Following orders, the disguised Warren stabs the mistress and then uses acid to dissolve her corpse in a bathtub. At trial, Mason obtains a directed verdict of not guilty by pointing out that no one had witnessed the murder and no corpse had been found. Circumstantial evidence was everywhere, but a direct showing of the fundamental elements of the crime, the 'corpus delicti', is required before the case could go to the jury.[15] Spectators in the courtroom are aghast. 'They had heard always of the boasted completeness of the law which magistrates from time immemorial had labored to perfect, and now when the skilful villain sought to evade it, they saw how weak a thing it was.'[16]

Underscore the way Mason not only defends his client at trial but also develops the criminal plan in the first place. 'Remember', Mason says to Warren in 'The Corpus Delicti', 'that you are only the hand, and the hand does not think'.[17] In other stories as well Mason helps his clients design the 'perfect crime'—one that cannot be successfully prosecuted. In 'The Sheriff of Gullmore', for example, Mason devises a scheme through which a corrupt sheriff pushes his pilfering of county funds onto his successor,[18] and in 'The Animus Furandi' Mason advises a client how to pull off a robbery in order to save his son from impending embezzlement charges.[19]

Mason has obviously violated professional canons in devising and promoting criminal conduct even if the charges can be beaten. But Mason rationalizes his work by pointing to the amorality of the law. When, in 'The Grazier', Mason actually encounters a client who will not follow his advice on moral grounds, Mason huffs at the client:

> Moral wrong! A name used to frighten fools. There is no such thing. The law lays down the only standard by which the acts of the citizen are to be ignored. What the law permits is

[13] Post, 'The Error of William Van Broom' in *Strange Schemes*, n 6 above, 149. [14] ibid.

[15] In support of the fictional directed verdict, Post sends readers to real-life law. 'See Lord Hales Rule, Russell on Crimes. For law in New York see 18th N.Y. Reports, page 179; also N.Y. Reports 49, page 137.' Post, 'The Corpus Delicti' in *Strange Schemes*, n 6 above, 11. [16] ibid.

[17] ibid, 39. [18] Post, 'The Sheriff of Gullmore' in *Strange Schemes*, n 6 above, 199.

[19] Post, 'The Ammius Furandi' in *Strange Schemes*, n 6 above, 249.

right, else it would prohibit it. What the law prohibits is wrong, because it punishes it. This is the only lawful measure, the only measure bearing the stamp and sanction of the State. All others are spurious, counterfeit, and void. The word moral is a pure metaphysical symbol possessing no more intrinsic virtue than the radical sign.[20]

Shaking his head at Mason's crafty legal manœuvring, a judge at the end of 'The Men of the Jimmy' says: 'this is not a matter of sentiment; it is not even a matter of morality; it is not even a matter of right. It is purely and simply a matter of law. . . . '.[21]

Post could have defended his chief character by saying that it was just fiction after all, that he was only trying to create something interesting for his readers. And to some extent, he makes an effort to do this. 'Strange tales', he says in the introduction of *The Strange Schemes of Randolph Mason*, relieve the 'tedium vitae'.[22] More specifically, readers love puzzles, mysteries, and detective stories. Post immodestly claims he has added to the genre, creating a distinct variety of the tale in which 'the "punishing" power of the State might be baffled'.[23]

But while Post is thinking in literary terms and trying to carve a place for himself in an emerging genre, he is also projecting through the Randolph Mason stories his own growing uncertainty and distaste for the practice of law. In real life, Post wavered in his practice and then left it completely. In 1901 he dissolved his partnership with John A. Howard in Wheeling and formed a new partnership with John T McGraw in Grafton, West Virginia.[24] He remained unhappy, and his health declined. He complained to his father that his 'stomach has gone back to its old habits inspite of all I can do. I am rather discouraged with hoping to get along with it in an office.'[25] Even more ominously, Post composed a distraught and melancholy tale titled 'The Story of a Suicide'.[26]

Finally, Post suffered some sort of nervous breakdown. 'As a result of labor incident to his practice', Howard later explained, 'Mr. Post's health was broken down. . . .'.[27] In keeping with doctor's orders, Post travelled to Brides de Bains in the South of France to recover. When he returned, having toured the English countryside and becoming fond of hunt club attire, Post determined completely to abandon the practice of law and devote himself to a writing career.[28]

Readers were oblivious to Post's career changes, and the subsequent Randolph Mason stories were as popular as the prior ones. The final stories appeared first in *Pearson's Magazine*, a popular English magazine, which had launched an American edition in 1899.[29] The stories started to appear at the beginning of 1907, continued

[20] Post, 'The Grazier' in *Man of Last Resort*, n 7 above, 252–253.

[21] Post, 'The Man of the Jimmy' in *Strange Schemes*, n 6 above, 204.

[22] Post, '*Strange Schemes*' n 6 above, 1. [23] ibid, 4.

[24] Francis W Nevins, 'From Darwinian to Biblical Lawyering: The Stories of Melville Davisson Post' (1994) 18 *Legal Studies Forum* 177, 178.

[25] *Post Family Collection*, n 2 above, Personal Correspondence, 1850–99; letter to Father; no date but on 'McGraw and Post, Attorneys at Law, Grafton, W. Va.' stationery.

[26] Charles A Norton, *Melville Davisson Post: Man of Many Mysteries* (Bowling Green, Ohio: 1973) 25.

[27] Quoted ibid, 29. [28] ibid, 29.

[29] Frank Luther Mott, *A History of American Magazines* (New York: 1957) Vol IV, 228.

at rate of one per month for 18 months, and were collected in *The Corrector of Destinies; Being Tales of Randolph Mason as Recalled by His Private Secretary Courtlandt Parks.*[30]

Mason at this stage has developed a greater interest in righting wrongs, and more of his clients are deserving souls.[31] Yet Mason himself has hardly become a warm and congenial practitioner. His 'lean, sinewy, protruding jaw is almost a menace',[32] and he still abrasively uses his knowledge of law's curious intricacies to devise plans for his clients. Mason tells one client, 'You will remember to do exactly as I say; do you understand that?'[33] When the client is so foolish as to ask for further explanation, Mason snaps back: 'It is sufficient that I know'.[34] Devoted readers, of course, also got to know how law worked its curious magic. This apparently was engaging early in the century. Much more so than today, law had a 'believe-it-or-not' quality to it.

Arthur Train

Well before Melville Davisson Post passed away, the author Arthur Train had replaced him as the leading American lawyer turned writer. Train's lawyer character Ephraim Tutt appeared regularly in the *Saturday Evening Post* and in a raft of collections during the 1920s and 1930s. Tutt's practice of law and his attitude toward practice differed significantly from what Train himself had been able to muster as an actual practitioner. Train's idealized portrayals, the author acknowledged, were what he had hoped for as an attorney. A large reading public delighted in Train's re-imagining of what the practice of law might be like.

Like Post before him, Train hailed from a comfortable and well established family. His father was a Civil War veteran, a prominent lawyer, and Attorney General of Massachusetts from 1872–79. Train reported in *My Day in Court*, a 1939 memoir, that as a boy he met and stood in awe before the great New England literati of the era—Emerson, Holmes, Lowell, and Longfellow—and during his days as a student Train dreamed of becoming a writer.[35] However, within the Back Bay elite to which his family belonged, 'the writing of fiction was looked upon as, at best, a frivolous and even a rather scandalous vocation'.[36] After receiving his bachelor's degree from Harvard College, Train, the good soldier of his family's values, enlisted at the Harvard Law School and then, several months after his law school graduation, trooped off to Manhattan to pursue his legal career.

During the next 20 years Train had a variety of legal positions, but none of them were personally satisfying. While at the firm of Robinson, Biddle & Ward, his

[30] Melville Davisson Post, *The Corrector of Destinies; Being Tales of Randolph Mason as Recalled by his Private Secretary Courtlandt Parks* (New York: 1908).

[31] *Pearson's Magazine* even announced in promotional materials that the newest Mason stories would be more appealing to readers because Mason would be a champion of justice rather than the tutor of criminals. Nevins, n 24 above, 189.

[32] Post, 'My Friend at Bridge' in *Corrector of Destinies*, n 30 above, 10.

[33] ibid, 17.

[34] ibid.

[35] Arthur Train, *My Day in Court* (New York: 1939) 5.

[36] ibid, 6.

gloomy, isolated office made him feel as if he was 'imprisoned at the bottom of a well'.[37] In a seven-year stint as an assistant district attorney he perceived 'an atmosphere of suspicion and inertia, engendered by conscious incompetence'.[38] Pursuing a solo practice at 32 Nassau Street, he festered at his desk, irritated at his 'combination stenographer-office boy-telephone operator-bookkeeper and process server', who before answering Train's call button 'would with exasperating deliberation arise, take a comb and brush and carefully arrange his curly golden hair'.[39] In a partnership with George H Olney, a fellow scion of Boston's Back Bay elite whose father had been United States Attorney General during the Pullman Strike and later Secretary of State,[40] Train was professionally and personally frustrated. 'I rapidly became more and more discouraged at the piecemeal jobs that were thrown my way', Train said, 'and which were, I thought, far less than my ability deserved'.[41]

If there was anything that kept Train going as a lawyer, it was his sense that legal practice provided him with material for his writing. Throughout his two decades as a practitioner he wrote on a part-time basis, publishing short stories and serials in popular magazines, a book providing an insider's look at the criminal justice system, and even a study of the mafia.[42] The Criminal Courts Building and the Tombs, Train thought, were 'as depressing an environment as could be found anywhere and yet it was richer than Golconda in the rich gold of experience. A daily succession of melodramas was enacted before my eyes, in which every human passion was laid bare. . . . Every case was a tragedy; every trial a detective story'.[43] Private practice, Train concluded, 'offered as much dramatic material for fiction as had the criminal courts'.[44]

Yet the sense of having an opportunity to find material was ultimately not enough to sustain Train as a lawyer. In 1921, he was happy to retire his shingle:

> I left the bar with some forebodings but no qualms. For over twenty years, in company with a miserable minority of the fifteen thousand other lawyers in the City of New York, I had lived upon the crimes and weaknesses, economic disasters, and sexual entanglements of my fellow men, until I had learned to look upon any one not involved, or at least involvable, in legal complications, much as does the medico to whom a sound and healthy human being seems a total loss. I have neither remorse nor regrets that I no longer earn my living out of the misfortunes or difficulties of others.[45]

Train's sense of having escaped the legal profession was important to him, and *My Day in Court* reads almost as a tale of liberation, with the parts of Train's adult life labelled in order 'Prosecutor', 'Lawyer', and 'Writer'. He suggests there is virtually no one else who had made the switch from lawyer to writer. He boasts that a 'large

[37] ibid, 7. [38] ibid, 13. [39] ibid, 254.

[40] David Ray Papke, *The Pullman Case: The Clash of Labor and Capital in Industrial America* (Lawrence, Kansas: 1999) 30. [41] Train, n 35 above, 261.

[42] Arthur Train, *The Prisoner at the Bar* (New York: 1906); *Courts, Criminals and the Camorra* (New York: 1911). [43] Train, n 35 above, 12.

[44] ibid, 336. [45] ibid, 368.

number of lawyers' among his readers have asked 'for advice as to whether they had better shut their desks and embark upon a career of art',[46] but he warns that this is best not attempted. Even though Train himself gathered ideas and published a great deal while practising law, in general 'the practice of law ceases to be an aid and tends to become a detriment—even a menace—to the writer'.[47] Train had been so unhappy as a lawyer that he would not even grant that experience as a lawyer could be a leg up on doing something else.

Dozens of magazine stories, serials, and novels flowed from Train's pen after he left the profession completely,[48] but especially relevant for purposes at hand were Train's Mr Tutt stories. Train published the first Tutt tale in the *Saturday Evening Post* in 1919, and a total of 86 appeared between then and Train's death in 1945. The *Post's* readers loved the tales, and almost all of the stories were collected in volumes such as *Tutt and Mr. Tutt*; *Tut, Tut, Mr. Tutt*; and *When Tutt Meets Tutt*.[49] Tutt's popularity even led Train to edit a Tutt 'case book' and write a mock Tutt autobiography.[50]

The fictional Ephraim Tutt is the head of a small Manhattan law firm, Tutt & Tutt, where tea is served every afternoon at 5:00. Tutt had first made his name in legal circles with a successful lawsuit against the Comers Hotel, which had negligently served a dead mouse in an order of kidney stew.[51] Tall and ungainly with a passing resemblance to Abraham Lincoln, Tutt has a passion for cheap cigars and a preference for manners and dress suggesting a past generation, 'the suggestion being accentuated by a slight pedantry of diction a trifle out of character with the rushing age in which he saw fit to practice his time-honored profession'.[52] Samuel Tutt, Ephraim Tutt's partner, shares the hero's surname but is unrelated. He hails from Bangor, Maine, and not only his short, chubby stature but also his frenetic mannerisms are comic. When Ephraim Tutt originally asked Samuel Tutt why he was seeking to join the firm, the latter replied, 'I feel I should be associated with a good name'.[53]

The Tutts get along superbly well as a sort of Mutt and Jeff of the Manhattan Bar, with Ephraim Tutt always in the superior position to Samuel. They are knowledgeable about the law, but unlike the fictional Randolph Mason they are not fascinated by the formal law in and of itself. They master the discipline without

[46] Train, n 35 above, 369.

[47] ibid, 358. Lawyers, Train thought, were trained to elicit 'fact' as opposed to 'truth'. For writers, by contrast, the recital of fact does not suffice. 'The writer must make use of simile, analogy, metaphor—every artifice at his command to get the truth—*his* truth—across to the reader'. Ibid, 359.

[48] Train provides a thorough bibliography of his publications up till 1939 in *My Day in Court*, n 35 above. A fine bibliographical essay regarding Train's Ephraim Tutt fiction is Francis M Nevins, 'Mr. Tutt's Jurisprudential Journey: The Stories of Arthur Train' (1995) 19 *Legal Studies Forum* 455.

[49] Arthur Train, *Tutt and Mr. Tutt* (New York: 1922), *Tut, Tut! Mr. Tutt* (New York: 1923), and *When Tutt Meets Tutt* (New York: 1927).

[50] Arthur Train, *Mr. Tutt's Case Book* (New York: 1936) and *Yankee Lawyer: The Autobiography of Ephraim Tutt* (New York: 1943).

[51] Train, 'Wile Versus Guile' in *Tutt and Mr. Tutt*, n 49 above, 186–190.

[52] Train, 'The Human Element' in *Tutt and Mr. Tutt*, n 49 above, 3.

[53] ibid, 5.

being walled in by it. 'Both Tutts enjoyed the law as a science and delighted in it as a craft, joyfully uniting science and craft in a scientific craftiness. . . . They loved their profession for its own sake, apart from the fact that they earned their living by it; but they cared for it rather upon its pragmatic than upon its academic side.'[54]

In addition to the two Tutts, five others hang their hats at Tutt & Tutt. Ezra Scraggs is an elderly scrivener and 'unsuccessful teetotaler', who copies documents in a wire cage in the outer office.[55] Willie Toothaker is a freckled orphan, who is the firm's office boy, and Miss Sondheim is a charming, sometimes flirtatious 'stenog'. Bonnie Doon is a 'runner' for the firm, hustling clients in the criminal courts and at accidents. He is sometimes charged with distasteful tasks and always buoyed by his 'wise guy' attitude. Last but not least, Minerva Wiggin is chief clerk and resident conscience.[56] 'Because she drew her grey hair straight back from her low forehead and tied it in a knob on the back of her head, wore paper cuffs and a black dress, she looked nearer to fifty than forty-one, which she was.'[57] She has a law degree but seems not to conduct herself as a practitioner.

Along with Ephraim and Samuel Tutt, the firm's staff members obviously have amusing names and characteristics. They are caricatures as much as characters. But this is less a literary flaw than a feature of the popular fiction that appeared in the *Saturday Evening Post* and elsewhere in the 1920s. Train was a masterful pop cultural writer.

The imaginative origins of the Ephraim Tutt character reside within Train's frustrations as a practising lawyer. While in practice, the bored and uninspired Train began to imagine 'a sort of protagonist of real Justice, a human character endowed with these seemingly necessary attributes,—an "ideal lawyer", like Schopenhauer's "ideal tree" '.[58] When Train tried a case, he imagined this ideal lawyer standing beside the defendant with his hand on his shoulder. 'It was with this ghostly presence that I struggled, as Jacob wrestled with the Angel.'[59] When Train began to write his Tutt stories, the ideal lawyer took the more concrete form of Ephraim Tutt, 'a sort of "father-in-law" of the ignorant, helpless, and underprivileged—a voluntary defender of those unjustly accused of crime'.[60] In the story 'The Liberty of Jail' Train describes Tutt as 'an avenging jack-in-the-box',[61] an apt metaphor for the way he rose in defence of those who needed him.

Tutt's practice is both similar to and different from that of Randolph Mason. The two most popular fictional lawyers of the early twentieth century were both

[54] Train, 'The Liberty of the Jail' in *Tut! Tut! Mr. Tutt*, n 49 above, 91.

[55] Train, 'Samuel and Delilah' in *Tutt and Mr. Tutt*, n 49 above, 108. Many years earlier while Tutt was a police court practitioner, he paid a fine for the drunken Scraggs and offered him a position in the firm. Tutt then became a life-long source of stability for Scraggs. Train, 'The Cloak of St. Martin' in *Tut, Tut! Mr. Tutt*, n 49 above, 275–276.

[56] Miss Wiggin has a 'clear moral vision' and 'uncompromising attitude toward anything but the highest standards'. Whenever Tutt 'played too close to the line he carefully did so without her knowledge'. Train, 'Hocus-Pocus' in *Tut, Tut! Mr. Tutt*, n 49 above, 150.

[57] Train, 'Samuel and Delilah' in *Tutt and Mr. Tutt*, n 49 above, 112.

[58] Train, n 35 above, 115. [59] ibid. [60] ibid.

[61] Train, 'The Liberty of the Jail' in *Tut, Tut! Mr. Tutt*, n 49 above, 88.

superb litigators and able to command specialized and technical aspects of the law. Both also have meaningful cases and win all of the time. But with the exception of the very earliest stories Tutt is always on the side of truth, fairness, and justice. Mason, by contrast, expends most of his effort on behalf of people without moral or even meritorious claims. It is only the later Mason of *The Corrector of Destinies* who represents the truthful and deserving.

More so than Post, Train's dissatisfaction with practice derives from his inability to perceive himself as a servant of justice. During his 20 years of practice Train felt himself distanced from justice. Train was frustrated not to be on the side of the right and the good. He wrote proudly in his memoirs of imagining a lawyer who stood for justice, and in the Tutt stories Ephraim Tutt is the concrete embodiment of that ideal lawyer.

The legendary evidence scholar John Henry Wigmore came close to grasping this in the introduction he wrote for *Mr. Tutt's Case Book*,[62] an essay which in and of itself is less surprising in light of Wigmore's demonstrated fascination with the interrelationship of law and literature.[63] In lumbering prose which seems even heavier given its proximity to Train's light and breezy writing, Wigmore argued that the Tutt stories 'give a realistic expression to the contrast that has so long been the theme of philosophers and jurists, namely, the relation of Law and Justice,—in particular, the contrast between the rule of law that forms the ostensible issue in the litigation and the merits of the parties where all the circumstances are considered,—in short, the justice of the case'.[64] 'Every juristic writer', Wigmore continued, 'has had his chapter on this antinomy.'[65] The Tutt stories, Wigmore suggests, are Train's exploration of the law/justice antinomy, and they illustrate the collision of law and justice for the layman.[66]

What Wigmore fails to say is that any time law and justice collide, any time strict adherence to legal form gets in the way of justice, Tutt opts for the latter. In 'Hocus-Pocus', for example, the rules regarding proving a will stymie Tutt's efforts on behalf of a loving, devoted, adopted daughter named Lucy Ayman. Tutt has in his hands a memorandum regarding the will which would suffice were it not excluded as a privileged communication. The solution? Office boy Willie Toothaker with Tutt's approval surreptitiously places the memorandum in the deceased's desk. When found in that location—recall the title of the story—the memorandum can be used to prove the will.[67]

Train realized what was missing in his practice and that if he added this missing element to a fictional practice, he could have something special.

> Were I asked to furnish an explanation for the affection in which Mr. Tutt is held by many, I should say it was due to the general impression that the laws of man, like those of nature,

[62] John H Wigmore, 'Introduction: A Salutation to Mr. Tutt's Case Book' in *Mr. Tutt's Case Book*, n 50 above, vii–viii.

[63] See John H Wigmore, 'A List of Legal Novels' (1922) 17 *Illinois L Rev* 26, originally (1908) 2 *Illinois L Rev* 574.

[64] Wigmore, n 62 above, viii.

[65] ibid.

[66] ibid.

[67] Train, 'Hocus-Pocus' in *Tut, Tutt! Mr. Tutt*, n 49 above, 153–154.

often work deep hardship. We do the best we can by applying legal rules-of-thumb based on the doctrine of averages, which we hope in the long run make for justice. But the law rarely, if ever, does exact justice in any individual case, and its so-called 'protection' is often available only to the wealthy.[68]

Tutt, although a lawyer, does deliver justice. According to Train: 'He is the Quixote who tries to make things what they ought to be in this world of things as they are. . . .'.[69] During the interwar years many delighted in a fictional lawyer who could take them to a fantasyland of fairness and justice.

Erle Stanley Gardner

Erle Stanley Gardner found greater popular and commercial success than any other twentieth-century American lawyer/author, but his flight from the legal profession and subsequent fiction are less intriguing than the comparable flights and fiction of Melville Davisson Post and Arthur Train. Although quite genuine, Gardner's reasons for leaving the legal profession lack sustained reflection, especially with regard to law and legal practice. Perry Mason, Gardner's fabled lawyer character, meanwhile, is neither an alter ego nor a self-conscious fictional projection of the ideal lawyer. In essence, Gardner was able to earn much more as a writer of popular fiction than he could as a lawyer. Wealth gave him the freedom and lifestyle he liked, and for decades the Perry Mason character was his biggest money-maker.

Gardner was born in 1889 in Massachusetts, the son of a civil engineer. Gardner's family moved to California while he was a boy, and although Gardner sometimes accompanied his father to exotic locales such as the Klondike, he spent most of his boyhood in the Golden State. His older brother attended Stanford University, but the family was not wealthy enough to send a second son to such an expensive school. Furthermore, young Erle was not sure he even wanted a university education. He thought he might simply apprentice in a law office and enter the profession via that route. Instead, he decided at the last second to attend the Valparaiso Law School in Indiana, a bachelor's degree not necessarily being required for law school in early twentieth-century America. Later, Gardner said of his days at Valparaiso, 'I learned more law there in a period of three or four weeks than I ever learned anywhere in anything like the same amount of time'.[70] However, Gardner had no opportunity to build on his learning. After a dormitory row in Gardner's first semester, university officials tossed him out of school.

After the fiasco at Valparaiso, Gardner resurrected his original plan. He returned to California and read law in various lawyers' offices. He took and passed the state

[68] Train, *Mr. Tutt's Case Book*, n 50 above, xii. [69] ibid.

[70] Quoted in Dorothy B Hughes, *Erle Stanley Gardner: The Case of the Real Perry Mason* (New York: 1978) 47.

bar exam, and he was formally admitted to the bar at the age of only 21. The only stumbling block was not the law, which seemed to come easily to Gardner, but rather his fondness for boxing. He had been in a boxing match the night before the swearing in ceremony, and Gardner joked that he was the only man formally to become a California lawyer with two black eyes.[71]

Gardner practised in various office and partnership arrangements primarily in Oxnard—a rough town full of brothels and violence—and in the nearby and more respectable county seat of Ventura. Gardner's practice was low in prestige and largely uninspiring for Gardner himself. He picked up clients and earned small fees in the local Chinese community, but one of the reasons he had Chinese clients is that other lawyers did not want them.[72] Hustling to make a go of it as a lawyer, Gardner wrote to his father, 'I am terribly busy. I have clients of all classes except the upper and middle classes.'[73]

While trying to build his practice and make ends meet, Gardner began to write and submit articles and stories to various publications. He composed jokes and skits, and 'Nellie's Naughty Nightie' might charitably be labelled his first literary work.[74] Published in *Breezy Stories*, the tale concerned the proverbial travelling salesman. A Pullman porter, thinking that a forgotten nightie belonged to the salesman, placed it in his suitcase. When the salesman's wife discovered it, the salesman found himself in big trouble. Ho, ho. Gardner received $15 for the story and considered himself well compensated.[75]

More sales followed, but Gardner's successes as a writer were hard-earned and slow in coming. In 1921, Gardner's first year of writing he earned $974, and in 1922, with many late nights pecking at the typewriter and literally bloody index fingers to prove it, Gardner earned only $3,436.[76] What is more, Gardner's law partners thought his writing efforts were distracting him from his legal work, and they exerted pressure on him to concentrate on just his practice.[77]

In Gardner's own mind, his chief weakness as a writer was plotting, and he doggedly worked to eliminate the weakness. He launched a careful study of other authors' plots, even maintaining for himself a 'fault book' of plotting do's and don't's.[78] He also used a curious device called 'The Plot Genie' developed by Wycliff A Hill.[79] The device had two cardboard wheels attached back-to-back listing settings, character types, and actions.[80] Unlike the post-modern deconstructionist, who might be intrigued by the genie for other reasons, Gardner could spin the wheels and come up with plot ideas.

[71] Quoted in n. 70 above, 50.

[72] ibid, 53.

[73] Quoted in Charles W Morton, 'The World of Erle Stanley Gardner', *Atlantic Monthly*, January 1967, 81.

[74] Hughes, n 70 above, 75.

[75] ibid.

[76] Francis L and Roberta B Fugate, *Secrets of the World's Best-Selling Writer: The Story Telling Techniques of Erle Stanley Gardner* (New York: 1980) 32.

[77] ibid, 34.

[78] ibid, 31.

[79] J Dennis Bounds, *Perry Mason: The Authorship and Reproduction of a Popular Hero* (Westport, Connecticut: 1996) 33.

[80] ibid.

The device was probably not the key, but eventually Gardner learned to write sharp and shaped stories. By 1925 he had become a mainstay under various pen names in the 'pulps', cheap fiction periodicals so-named because of the inexpensive brownish wood-pulp paper on which they were printed.[81] In 1926, Gardner had 97 sales, mostly to *Black Mask* and *Top Notch*.[82]

What led Gardner to write? Why did he begin during the 1920s to put aside his legal career for one as an author? His thoughts on the matter lack the introspective depth of Melville Davisson Post and Arthur Train, both of whom wrestled with what it meant to be a lawyer. 'I was a small-time lawyer in a small town, and I couldn't see any future in it', Gardner said. 'When my third year of writing stories brought me in $28,000, I saw that there was work that I liked, and I could take it with me and live the way I wanted to live anywhere in the world'.[83] Gardner was easily bored and hated routine work. In 1925 he said in a letter to Robert Hardy, his first agent: 'What I am working for is to get myself sufficiently established in the literary game so I can quit law entirely'.[84] Using capitals to emphasize the point, Gardner declared, 'I DO NOT LIKE OFFICE LAW, and I cannot stand the confinement of an office'.[85] Even writing itself had no magical attraction. 'I took up writing', he said, 'not because I felt any interior urge, but because I wanted some way to make a living where I could be out of doors a large portion of the day time, and be a master of my own time. . . .'.[86]

Gardner's stories from the 1920s did not for the most part feature lawyers and legal themes. Characters whose fictional exploits he recounted more than once included but are not limited to western heroes such as Black Barr, The Old Walrus, and Fish Mouth McGinnis; 'good badmen' such as Lester Leith, Sidney Zoom, and Senor Arnaz de Lobo; and various scam artists including El Paisano and Ed Migrane, The Headache.[87] Nobody ever said stories in the pulps were fine literature, and Gardner gravitated to the genres and kinds of characters he thought were marketable. He wanted to leave the legal profession, but he was not using his stories to expel the demons or project idealized versions of legal work.

Ironically, though, it was Gardner's background as a lawyer that enabled him once and for all to leave the legal profession. In 1932 and early 1933 Gardner wrote two short novels with lawyers at the heart of them, novels he hoped would appear as serials in respected magazines or perhaps on their own as books. The lawyers had originally been named Ed Stark and Sam Keene, but when editors at William Morrow and Company saw a possible series in the making, Gardner blended the characters into one and gave his new hero the name 'Perry Mason'.[88] In March of 1933 Perry Mason made his debut in *The Case of the Velvet Claws*, immediately attracted readers, and quickly appeared again in *The Case of the Sulky Girl*.[89]

[81] Gardner looked back at his days writing for the 'pulps' in Erle Stanley Gardner, 'Getting Away with Murder', *Atlantic*, January 1965, 72.

[82] Fugate and Fugate, n 76 above, 91.

[83] Quoted in Morton, n 73 above, 81.

[84] Quoted in Fugate and Fugate, n 76 above, 33.

[85] ibid.

[86] ibid.

[87] Francis M Nevins, 'Samurai at Law: The World of Erle Stanley Gardner' (2000) 24 *Legal Studies Forum* 43, 48.

[88] Bounds, n 79 above, 39.

[89] Erle Stanley Gardner, *The Case of the Velvet Claws* (New York: 1933); Erle Stanley Gardner, *The Case of the Sulky Girl* (New York: 1933).

The popularity of the Mason stories prompted Gardner to abandon legal practice,[90] and if he had any lingering doubts about being able to support himself as a writer, they must have disappeared when Pocket Books and other publishers paid to reissue the earliest Perry Mason novels with fancier covers and more elaborate advertising. The *Saturday Evening Post* also bought the serial rights for several new novels,[91] and the *Post* was at the time the nation's most popular magazine. In the first third of the twentieth century it had published a veritable who's who of American fiction writers: Willa Cather, Theodore Dreiser, William Faulkner, F Scott Fitzgerald, Sinclair Lewis, Jack London, Booth Tarkington, Edith Wharton.[92] With a circulation that exceeded three million a week as of 1937,[93] the *Post* was able to pay authors of serials between $50,000 and $100,000—huge amounts in 1930s America.[94]

The success of the Perry Mason novels did not lead Gardner immediately to sever ties with the pulps,[95] and he also launched and sustained for years completely new fiction series.[96] But the Mason series was obviously Gardner's greatest success. By the end of the 1930s he had published 15 Perry Mason novels, and almost all of them were best-sellers. When Frank Luther Mott compiled a list in 1947 of novels with sales equal to at least one per cent of the United States population at the time of their publication, he listed seven Perry Mason novels from the 1930s.[97] Since only 19 novels from that decade appeared on Mott's list,[98] it could be argued that Erle Stanley Gardner was the nation's single most popular author during the Great Depression.

Popular biographers and other lionizers liked ultimately to lump Gardner and Mason together, to act as if the latter was the fictional version of the former.[99] Yet Gardner is perhaps better seen as someone who worked extremely well within the pop culture industry. He stumbled onto a lawyer character, and he listened to editors who urged him both to stick with Perry Mason and to make him less abrasive, physically imposing, and—in detective fiction terms—less 'hard-boiled'.[100] As the 1930s went on, Gardner also heeded editors' advice to create and use a regular stable of secondary characters. Loyal secretary Della Street and resourceful detective Paul Drake were on board from the beginning, and before long, Lieutenant Tragg and frequently foiled prosecutor Hamilton 'Ham' Burger also became regulars.

[90] Hughes, n 70 above, 107. [91] Bounds, n 79 above, 171.

[92] Mott, n 29 above, 704. [93] ibid, 696. [94] ibid, 698.

[95] Fugate and Fugate, n 76 above, 38. [96] See Nevins, n 87 above, 62.

[97] Frank Luther Mott, *Golden Multitudes: The Story of Best Sellers in the United States* (New York: 1947), 311–314. [98] ibid.

[99] See, eg, Fugate and Fugate, n 76 above, 13 or the caption under the first photo of Gardner in Bounds, n 79 above.

[100] Bounds, n 79 above, 39; Hughes, n 70 above, 22, 24, 95. In the earliest novels Perry Mason had been a chain-smoker with a bottle of whiskey in his desk. He punched out a reporter and roughly pushed around various butlers, shysters and even a client. His 'creed', Mason tells detective Paul Drake, is simple: 'I take people who are in trouble, and I get them out of trouble'. Gardner, *The Case of the Velvet Claws*, n 89 above, 182.

Burger and his assistant prosecutors in fact became Mason's special nemeses, particularly in the hearings and trials in the novels. Like Melville Davisson Post and Arthur Train before him,[101] Gardner had developed a distaste for the occupational narrow-mindedness of prosecuting attorneys. Gardner and his handlers appreciated the appeal of defeating a DA who wants to convict at all cost. 'The D.A. always howls to high heaven about the crooked criminal lawyers who manipulate the facts', Mason tells Drake in *The Case of the Sulky Girl.* 'But whenever the D.A. uncovers any evidence that gives the defendant a break, you can bet something happens to it'.[102] In the novel's concluding trial or preliminary hearing, Mason not only exonerated his client and identified the guilty partner but also trounced and embarrassed the prosecutor.[103] Gardner had to be convinced to conjure up such trials (and the subsequent office wrap-up),[104] but Mason's courtroom prowess as much as his loyalty to clients became part of the series' formula.[105]

Gardner perhaps caused panic among his publishers and editors when after 35 novels he announced he had 'skimmed the cream' from the series' characters and thought it was time to move on to something else,[106] but the series continued, ultimately growing to 82 in number. Gardner had long since abandoned his 'Plot Genie', but in the 1950s he maintained a notebook with plot synopses in order to guard against inadvertently using a plot from an earlier novel![107] Gardner also stopped his two-fingered typing and came to rely instead on dictation. Several loyal secretaries followed him around his sprawling California ranch and recorded virtually his every word. Gardner was fond of saying, 'I'm no writer',[108]and he described himself as a 'prose industrialist' commanding a 'fiction factory'.[109]

Beyond his Perry Mason novels in and of themselves, Gardner supervised or at least contributed to a long-running Perry Mason radio drama with 3,221 episodes; seven Perry Mason motion pictures from Warner Brothers; the Perry Mason television series which ran on CBS from 1957–66; and assorted Perry Mason stage plays, boxed games and comic books.[110] Perry Mason even survived Gardner. After the latter's death in 1970, *The New Perry Mason* starring Monte Markham had a short run on CBS, and Raymond Burr reprised his Mason portrayal in two dozen original made-for-television movies premiering between 1985 and 1994.[111]

[101] Train offered a word of warning for those becoming prosecutors: 'The danger to a young lawyer who out of desire for public service seeks an appointment as an assistant district attorney, is that in the passion of the case the conviction and punishment of some—to him—obviously guilty criminal may seem more important at the moment than the strict preservation of his own integrity or the unwavering maintenance of the principles of justice'. Train, 'The Bloodhound' in *Tut, Tut! Mr. Tutt*, n 49 above, 6.

[102] Gardner, *The Case of the Sulky Girl*, n 89 above, 139.

[103] Gardner's very first novel, *The Case of the Velvet Claws*, did not contain an extended courtroom scene.

[104] Bounds, n 79 above, 36.

[105] Hughes, n 70 above, 25.

[106] Morton, n 73 above, 83.

[107] Fugate and Fugate, n 76 above, 119.

[108] Quoted in Hughes, n 70 above, 27.

[109] ibid; Fugate and Fugate, n 76 above, 110, 115.

[110] Bounds provides a full listing of Mason artifacts in his book's appendix. Bounds, n 79 above, 111.

[111] ibid.

The huge popularity of Perry Mason is a crude indicator of fantasies regarding the lawyer in the middle decades of the twentieth century. Americans imagined a hard-working and independent lawyer, who was committed to his clients and to obtaining justice, especially skilful in the courtroom, and not driven by financial gain.[112] Perry Mason epitomized that ideal.

Scott Turow

While in a sense Arthur Train received the mantle of America's most popular lawyer/author from Melville Davisson Post and then passed it to Erle Stanley Gardner, no one clearly received the mantle from Gardner. Part of the reason is that the era of American popular fiction in which Post, Train, and Gardner had thrived came to an end. Lawyers wishing to publish law-related fiction could no longer turn to large-circulation popular magazines or inexpensive paperback publishers. The market for a series of tales recounting the exploits of a single fictional lawyer dried up. Only the emergence of blockbuster fiction in the last quarter of the twentieth century provided lawyer/authors with an opportunity to achieve fame and fortune comparable to Gardner's. Scott Turow was the first lawyer/author to publish a blockbuster legal novel.

Born in 1949, Turow grew up in a well-to-do Chicago family. He graduated with high honours from Amherst College and as a young man was active in civil rights work, participated in Vietnam War protests, and worked for George McGovern's ill-fated 1972 Presidential campaign.[113] After marrying and working for three years as a writing teacher at Stanford, he signed a contract with GP Putnam's Sons for a book about attending law school.[114] He then enrolled at the Harvard Law School, and *One L*, an account of his first year, appeared during his third year.[115]

While Melville Davisson Post, Arthur Train, and Erle Stanley Gardner all practised for some time before losing faith in the profession, Turow became disenchanted with the profession while still a student. Law school, Turow argued, was absolutely crucial in how lawyers approached their work and saw their world. It was a type of boot camp or trial, and even though he himself had experienced only the rarefied Harvard Law School, Turow was convinced all American lawyers had through law school 'survived a similar initiation'.[116] Law school and especially the

[112] I explored the characteristics of the fantasized pop cultural lawyer in interwar America in 'Lawyer Fiction in The Saturday Evening Post' (2001) 13 *Cardozo Studies in Law and Literature* 207.

[113] Scott Turow, *One L* (New York: 1977) 102.

[114] See http://www.bookmagazine.com/archive/issue 6/turow.shtml.

[115] When the book appeared, a Harvard Law School professor recognized the version of himself and called a press conference to explain why the portrayal made him furious. Ibid.

[116] Turow, n 113 above, 295. Reviewer Steve Pepper wonders if *One L* provides a truly representative picture of American legal education. The pressure and ugly competitiveness may be more pronounced at elite law schools than at the more numerous non-elite schools. Steve Pepper, 'Book Review' (1977) 31 *Arkansas L Rev* 529, 537.

first year of law school are 'something of a grand tradition'.[117] Law school involved staggering amounts of work and provided those never-to-be-forgotten classroom humiliations, moot court arguments, bewildering examinations, and desperate quests for law review membership.[118] Even more importantly, law students 'develop the habits of mind and world perspective' that will stay with them throughout their careers.[119] During the first year, Turow continued, 'many law students come to feel, sometimes with deep regret, that they are becoming persons strangely different from the ones who arrived at law school in the fall'.[120]

Who were law students becoming? To begin with, given the consuming nature of the legal study, law students began to talk only about the law and to see everything in legal terms. Turow recounts how he began to use legalistic arguments in disagreements with his wife,[121] a development perhaps not unrelated to the couple's declining sex life.[122] Turow was also struck by the increasing harshness and competitiveness of the lawyers-in-the-making, a tendency evident in their laughter over one another's classroom mistakes and their approach to examinations and grades.[123] Law school, Turow thought, gave students the 'ineradicable impression that it is somehow characteristically "legal" to be heartless, to be brutal'.[124] They could 'carry that attitude with them into the execution of their professional tasks'.[125] 'Legal thinking is nasty', Turow tells a classmate in a moment of insight. 'Thinking like a lawyer involved being suspicious and distrustful'.[126]

On top of all this, Turow argued, lawyers in the making increasingly manifested a 'seeking after sureness and definition, a desire to subdue the random element, to leave nothing to chance. . .'.[127] The lawyer's 'war against ambiguity and uncertainty' made him or her 'less a person'.[128]

> Not even the law can abolish the fundamental unclearness of many human situations, but in the law schools there is precious little effort made to address the degree to which human choice is arbitrary. Too much of what goes on around the law school and in the legal classroom seeks to tutor students in strategies for avoiding, for ignoring, for somehow subverting the unquantifiable, the inexact, the emotionally charged, those things which still pass in my mind under the label 'human'.[129]

This dehumanizing, Turow thought, was especially unfortunate because 'the law, like any other field, is little more than the people who live it. . .'.[130]

Turow's critique of legal education and the lawyer's mind-set did not stop him from finishing law school. He may have fancied himself a child of the politicized, countercultural 1960s, but he was a man of the late-1970s—ambitious and self-interested. The dust jacket photo on *One L*, taken by his long-suffering wife and no doubt approved by the author, hardly suggests the tortured champion of humane

[117] Turow, n 113 above, 295.

[118] Turow himself felt cheated when his grades were too low for law review. 'My sense of jealousy and denial left me dizzy for a day'. Ibid, 299.

[119] ibid, 10.

[120] ibid.

[121] ibid, 92.

[122] ibid, 141.

[123] ibid, 54.

[124] ibid, 296.

[125] ibid.

[126] ibid, 93.

[127] ibid, 297.

[128] ibid.

[129] ibid.

[130] ibid, 11.

and humanistic values. Moustached, small-shouldered, and smirking, Turow looks almost belligerent.

After law school Turow returned to his native Chicago. He worked for eight years as an Assistant US Attorney, prosecuting a number of cases involving corrupt local judges and, at the same time, publishing careful law review expositions of criminal procedure from a prosecutor's perspective.[131] Perhaps Turow's publications were part of a long-range plan to seek a position as a law professor. However, when Turow eventually left the US Attorney's office, he moved not to academia but to a lucrative private practice. He also in 1987 published *Presumed Innocent*.[132]

The novel concerns the prosecution of prosecutor Rusty Sabich for the alleged murder of Carolyn Polhemus, another prosecutor and a woman with whom Sabich was infatuated and extramaritally involved. The first half of the novel is rich in gritty criminal investigating and office politics, and the second half features a tense, dramatic murder trial, revolving more around what might be presented as evidence than the gradual revelation of supposed facts. Prosecutors are present at every turn, and the corrupt, confused, and conniving lot must have left Turow's former colleagues at the US Attorney's office wondering about his sources of inspiration. In the end an unscrupulous judge dismisses the case against Sabich, but Turow hardly invites his readers, unlike the readers of the Perry Mason novels, to rest easy knowing the courts are reliable sources of justice. In an article critiquing both the novel and the cinematic version of it, Christine Alice Corcos writes:

> We obtain no public resolution, no 'truth'. . . . Rather, along with Rusty, we obtain a private resolution—we learn 'truth' in a way that leaves permanently unresolved the basic questions that the system is designed to answer.[133]

This ambiguity seemed to bother neither the reading public nor the producers and marketers of popular culture. The publishing house of Farrar, Straus & Giroux paid Turow $200,000, the most it had ever paid for a first novel.[134] Farrar was rewarded for its investment when in the second half of 1987 and then into 1988 the novel sat at or near the top of the *New York Times* best-seller list, ultimately selling 700,000 copies. Paperback rights sold for over $1 million, and the paperback edition of the novel darted to the top of the paperback best-seller list.[135] By 1991 six million consumers had purchased the paperback.[136] Hollywood producers then bid eagerly against one another for movie rights, and United Artists and

[131] Don K Webb and Scott F Turow, 'The Prosecutor's Function in Sentencing' (1982) 13 *Loyola U of Chicago LJ* 64; Scott F Turow, 'RICO Forfeiture in Practice: A Prosecutorial Perspective' (1983) 52 *U of Cincinnati L Rev* 404, and 'What's Wrong with Bribery' (1985) 4 *Business Ethics* 249.

[132] Turow, *Presumed Innocent* (New York: 1987).

[133] Christine Alice Corcos, 'Presuming Innocence: Alan Pakula and Scott Turow Take on the Great American Legal Fiction' (1997) 22 *Oklahoma City U L Rev* 129, 133.

[134] David Ray Papke, 'The Advocate's Malaise: Contemporary American Lawyer Novels' (1988) 38 *J of Legal Education* 413, 417.

[135] ibid.

[136] John Grisham, 'The Rise of the Legal Thriller: Why Lawyers are Throwing the Books at Us', *New York Times Book Review*, 18 October 1992, 33.

Sydney Pollack prevailed by offering $1 million.[137] The legal thriller genre now had 'its first superstar'.[138]

Turow's success was one example of larger developments in the writing and reading of American fiction. In the opinion of historian Michael Oriard, the 'golden age of American popular fiction' had ended in the 1950s.[139] Fiction gradually disappeared from large-circulation magazines, and television, of course, came to be the chief source of narrative entertainment. Book publishing hardly ceased, but against the backdrop of industry concentration, publishers avidly sought those particular books which could generate huge sales and profits and, in effect, carry whole lines of less successful books. 'The big-company, big-book era' had begun.[140] 'The resulting "blockbuster complex" meant that a handful of popular novels sold more spectacularly than ever before but then disappeared from the readers' consciousness as new blockbusters appeared'.[141] 'Certain books were now encountered as cultural phenomena rather than more simply as literary narratives for personal pleasure'.[142] For better or worse, Turow's *Presumed Innocent* was such a phenomenon.

In the years since, Turow has published a large law-related novel approximately every three years. His works are *Burden of Proof* (1990), *Pleading Guilty* (1993), *The Laws of Our Fathers* (1996), *Personal Injuries* (1999), and *Reversible Errors* (2002). All have been best-sellers in both hard-cover and paperback, and Turow's web-site claims that his work has sold over 20 million copies and been translated into over 20 foreign languages.[143] Erle Stanley Gardner's title as America's all-time best-selling author seems safe, but Turow is obviously a master of the popular literature marketplace. Indeed, 'Scott Turow' has become marketable along with the individual. Between his first and most recent novel, the author's name as it appears on the book's cover and spine has grown larger than the novel's title in the same places. Furthermore, all of the Warner Books paperback editions of the novels are in a uniform format with distinctive raised letters on the front.

None of this is to deny, meanwhile, that Turow's novels are engaging. The setting is largely Kindle County, a fictional Midwestern metropolis. Euro-American ethnicity plays a large role in Kindle County's three adjacent cities, as do race and class. Like the fictional Yoknapatawpha County, the setting for 14 novels and many stories by William Faulkner,[144] Turow's Kindle County acquires more texture and depth each time the author and reader revisit it. Turow's characterization in particular is strong, and introspective narrators and characters frequently explore both their own and others' psychological make-up. The characters are fully drawn and more two-dimensional than those in popular law-related fiction by Melville Davisson Post, Arthur Train and Erle Stanley Gardner.

137 Papke, n 134 above, 417. 138 Grisham, n 136 above, 33.

139 Michael Oriard, 'Popular Literature' in *Encyclopedia of American Social History*, Vol III (New York: 1993) 1728.

140 Thomas Whiteside, *The Blockbuster Complex: Conglomerates, Show Business, and Book Publishing* (Middletown, Connecticut: 1980) 104. 141 Oriard, n 139 above, 1740.

142 ibid. 143 See http://www.scottturow.com.html.

144 James D Hart, *The Concise Oxford Companion to American Literature* (1986) 454.

Of particular interest in the context at hand are Turow's portrayals of lawyers. He says at the beginning of *Personal Injuries*, '[t]his is a lawyer's story',[145] but to a significant extent all of his novels are lawyers' stories. Turow features lawyer characters from the major branches of the profession, and, indeed, he often uses lawyer narrators to tell the lawyers' stories. In general, an heroic practitioner resembling either Ephraim Tutt or Perry Mason is hard to find, and Turow's literary portrait of the profession often approaches an indictment.

As already noted, prosecutors take their lumps in *Presumed Innocent*, Turow's first novel, and the pounding continues in selected sections of the later novels as well. Like Arthur Train before him, Turow worked for a lengthy period as a prosecutor, but this seems only to have increased the distrust and dislike both authors feel for their former colleagues. Turow's Stan Sennett, for example, served for years as a district attorney in Kindle County and then became the area's US Attorney; he plays a major role in several of the novels. Speaking through attorney Sandy Stern, Turow says in *Burden of Proof*, 'Sennett was the kind of grim bureaucrat, a person of strong discipline and limited vision and courage, who seemed to turn up too often in prosecutors' offices'.[146] 'Military strategists will tell you about replication', George Mason, the attorney/narrator of *Personal Injuries*, observes, 'an inviolate principle which says that organizations which oppose each other tend, over time, to become alike.'[147] It comes as no surprise, therefore, when prosecutors become lawbreakers.

If prosecutors' offices seem disagreeable places, Turow's corporate law firms are not any better. They receive a blistering literary critique in *Pleading Guilty*. Kindle County's Gage & Griswell is a 130-member firm, which we are invited to contemplate through the narrative of partner Mack Malloy. 'G&G's reception area', Turow tells us snidely, had oaken bookcases 'filled with dozens of antique books, bought by the gross, to lend the proper air'.[148] The offices are decorated 'in the manner of an English hunting lodge'.[149] The infamous Management Oversight Committee 'over the years has created more subcommittees than either House of Congress, each one empowered with dominance over some minor region of law firm life'.[150] Exploitation of the staff and junior associates is standard, and ambition and intrigue lurk around every corner. Most of Malloy's fellow partners 'are men and women with fancy degrees—Harvard, Yale, and Easton—intellectuals for a few minutes in their lives, the types who keep *The New York Review of Books* in business, reading all those carping articles to put themselves to sleep'.[151]

Anyone seeking legal careers outside the institutional settings of district attorneys' offices and corporate firms in Turow's fictional world is forewarned that smaller partnerships, especially those of personal injury lawyers, are just as phony

145 Turow, *Personal Injuries* (New York: 1999) 3.
146 Turow, *The Burden of Proof* (New York: 1990) 263.
147 Turow, *Personal Injuries*, n 145 above, 383–384.
148 Turow, *Pleading Guilty* (New York: 1993) 125.
149 ibid, 126.
150 ibid, 286.
151 ibid, 20.

and unethical. In *Personal Injuries*, partners Morton Dinnerstein and Robbie Feaver have become millionaires pursuing tort claims largely against insurance companies. When push comes to shove, Dinnerstein secretly turns on Feaver, while Feaver, the centrepiece of the novel, has faked his law school graduation, cheated on his dying wife, routinely bribed the Kindle County judiciary, and developed the ability to weep on cue during intake meetings with potential personal injury clients. Nothing excites Dinnerstein and Feaver more than the prospect of signing up a new client. When they learned of a possibility: 'They reached a state of high alert, as if they'd smelled gunpowder on the air'.[152] Personal injury work, Turow tells us, has a 'grim alchemy', one 'in which misfortune was turned into gold'.[153]

Might we at least hope that the best of the prosecutors, corporate attorneys, and personal injury lawyers can rise to the top, that the proverbial cream of the Bar might become judges? Unfortunately, Turow's judges are likely to be men and women whose personal weaknesses led them to the bench, which in turn made them even worse. Moira Winchell in *The Burden of Proof*, for example, was the first woman in the district named to the federal bench. But alas: 'Facing the manifold burdens of life as a federal judge—crowded dockets, churlish lawyers, middling pay, and almost unlimited power—some people did not respond well. They came to the bench thrilled by the acclaim of their peers and became, in a short period of time, as temperamental as Caligula. Moira Winchell was one of them—snappish, sarcastic, even, at moments, downright mean'.[154] Sonny Klonsky, herself a Kindle County judge, says in *The Laws of Our Fathers*: 'There's no other job I know of that more reliably reveals the shortcomings of personality than being a judge. The pettish grow even more short-tempered; the silently injured can become power-mad or abusive'.[155] And, then too, in Turow's view, judges are routinely tempted by bribes and favours, and many are unable to resist. In *Reversible Errors* the Honorable Gillian Sullivan accepts bribes in part to service a worsening drug-addiction. In *Personal Injuries* the previously mentioned Robbie Feaver, himself facing a federal prosecution, agrees to go undercover to ensnare corrupt judges. The catch is sizable: six of Kindle County's most prominent judges exchange their robes for prison clothes.[156]

To some extent, Turow himself is apologetic about his portrait of the legal profession and tends to retreat behind the 'it's-only-fiction' fortification. In an introductory note for *Pleading Guilty*, he thanks his colleagues at the actual Chicago firm of Sonnenschein, Nath & Rosenthal for 'unflagging support in a variety of circumstances which have occasionally surprised us all'.[157] Gage & Griswell, the fictional firm he reduces to well deserved rubble in the novel, neither resembles Sonnenschein, Nath & Rosenthal nor 'shares its atmosphere of

152 Turow, *Personal Injuries*, n 145 above, 108.

153 ibid, 109.

154 Turow, *The Burden of Proof*, n 146 above, 250.

155 Turow, *The Laws of Our Fathers* (New York: 1996) 80.

156 Turow, *Personal Injuries*, n 145 above, 397.

157 Turow, *Pleading Guilty*, n 148 above.

sustained decency'.[158] In *Personal Injuries* Turow thanks several Chicago personal injury lawyers for taking the time to reflect on their practices but underscores that none of them bears 'the remotest resemblance to Robbie',[159] that is, the duplicitous Robbie Feaver.

If Turow admires any of his fictional lawyers, they tend to be lawyers who have learned some of the lessons Turow himself learned in law school. Turow does not like the nasty and aggressive lawyer, and he wants lawyers who are introspective and aware of the human condition. His preferred lawyers are flawed human beings who recognize their own limitations and also the limitations on what law, legal institutions, and even reason in general can accomplish.

Turow's favourite fictional lawyer is probably Alejandro 'Sandy' Stern, who first appears as Rusty Sabich's lawyer in *Presumed Innocent*, is the protagonist in *Burden of Proof*, and makes at least a brief appearance in each of Turow's other novels. An Argentine Jew by birth, Stern as a youth immigrated to the United States with his mother and sister in 1947. Although feeling out of place every step of the way, he graduated from prestigious Easton Law School. He then began his legal career hustling criminal cases in and around the courthouse, and he worked so hard for one stretch that he lost close touch with his family. Hearing repeatedly that his father was at trial, Stern's young son Peter was confused: 'I couldn't figure out what a trial was. I thought it was a place you went. Another city'.[160] Although Stern was invited to become an Assistant US Attorney, the idea of being a prosecutor, federal or otherwise, did not appeal to him.

> Oh, he did not hate prosecutors. He had gotten over that early in his career. He admired at times the incandescent zeal of these young people as they attempted to smite evil for the sake of life on the straight and narrow. But that was not his role, not his calling. He was Sandy Stern—a proud apologist for deviation. No person Argentine by birth, a Jew alive to hear of the Holocaust could march in the jackboots of authority without intense self-doubt. . . . [161]

As a result of the Sabich case and others, Stern eventually developed a high-toned and quite lucrative specialty in white-collar criminal defence. Stern reconnected with his family, even bringing a daughter into his small firm. In *Reversible Errors*, Turow's most recent novel, he describes Stern as 'the dignified dean of the criminal defence bar in Kindle County'.[162] 'The rushing about, the telephone calls, the small breaks of light in the tangle of egos and rules. Mr. Alejandro Stern adored the practice of law'.[163] Yet adoration was not blind:

> Some spoke of the nobility of the law. Stern did not believe in that. Too much of the grubby boneshop, the odor of the abattoir, emanated from every courtroom he had entered. It was often a nasty business. But the law, at least, sought to govern misfortune, the slights and injuries of our social existence that were otherwise wholly random. The law's object was to

[158] Turow, *Pleading Guilty*, n 148 above.
[159] Turow, *Personal Injuries*, n 145 above, 403.
[160] Turow, *The Burden of Proof*, n 146 above, 29.
[161] ibid, 145.
[162] Turow, *Reversible Errors* (New York: 2002), 247.
[163] ibid, 463.

let the seas engulf only those who had been selected for drowning on an orderly basis. In human affairs, reason would never fully triumph, but there was no better cause to champion.[164]

Turow's sense of the appealing lawyer, in short, is quite different from that of Arthur Train and Erle Stanley Gardner. Outnumbered by the profession's unappealing majority, his favoured lawyers do not represent only the innocent and always win at trial; they might not be criminal defence lawyers or even litigators. However, they do understand that perfect justice is unavailable through the law and that reason neither conquers nor explains all. Weary professionals in a post-modern world, these lawyers find a way to carry on. Living in the same era as Turow and his fictional lawyers, thousands of loyal readers find in Turow's conflicted lawyers the kind of protagonists whose partially successful searches for contentment and meaning parallel their own.

John Grisham

While Scott Turow published the first 'blockbuster' legal novel, his contemporary John Grisham has surpassed Turow in number of novels and total sales. Indeed, during the 1990s Grisham's novels about lawyers and legal cases sold well over 60 million copies, the highest figure for any American author in the period.[165] Plagued by large organizations, monied interests, and nefarious schemes, Grisham's lawyer protagonists muster the courage to fight back. But in the end they are inclined, just like Grisham himself, to wash their hands of the legal profession.

Born on 8 February, 1955 in Jonesboro, Arkansas, Grisham was the son of a construction worker and grew up in a humble home. As a boy, he dreamed of being a professional baseball player, but he instead studied to be an accountant at Mississippi State University. After graduating from college, he enrolled in law school at Ole Miss in Oxford, Mississippi.

Was law school an inspiration? Did it prompt thoughtful reflections on what a life in the law might entail? Hardly. Grisham lacked the type of introspectiveness and sensitivity which led Turow to write a law school memoir. Grisham appears to have been a cynical law student more interested in the next party than in the current reading assignment. Later in life he peppered his fiction with shallow criticisms of legal education. Virtually none of his fictional lawyers has kind words to say about law school. Rudy Baylor, who at the beginning of *The Rainmaker* (1995) finished his final semester at the Memphis State Law School, might be allowed to speak for the other disenchanted law school graduates. Baylor cynically dubs his Elder Law course 'Geezer Law' and says his other courses are 'equally as worthless'.[166] Almost all of his professors 'are teaching because they can't function

[164] ibid, 220. [165] http://www.randomhouse.com/features/grisham/author.html.
[166] John Grisham, *The Rainmaker* (New York: 1995) 30.

in the real world'.[167] Overall, Baylor thinks: 'Law school is nothing but three years of wasted stress'.[168]

Wounded but still standing, Grisham himself finished his march through the impractical wasteland of legal education in 1981 and began practising in Southaven, Mississippi—a sizable, if provincial town not far from Memphis. His practice was modest, and to the extent he specialized, it was in personal injury work and criminal defence. He also served two terms in the state's House of Representatives, but his practice seems to have been a much more powerful experience than were his political activities.

For some sense of how Grisham saw himself and his practice, one might contemplate the fictional lawyer Jake Brigance in Grisham's novel *A Time to Kill* (1988). 'There's a lot of autobiography in this book', Grisham wrote in a preface to a later edition.[169] The character Brigance seems to share Grisham's low opinion of legal education: 'He hated law school—every law student with any sense hated law school. . . .'.[170] In addition, Grisham says:

> Jake and I are the same age. . . . Much of what he says and does is what I think I would say and do under the circumstances. We both drive Saabs. . . . We've both lost sleep over clients and vomited in courthouse rest rooms.[171]

In their fictional and actual practices Brigance and Grisham, respectively, are examples of what Grisham calls a 'street lawyer'.[172] The latter represents little people and not banks, insurance companies, and big corporations. Neither the fictional Brigance nor the real-life Grisham delighted in the work of being a lawyer, but both wear the mantle of 'street lawyer' proudly.

Although he had never taken a writing course or harboured dreams of being a writer,[173] Grisham began writing during his spare time as a practitioner. When he finished *A Time to Kill*, the novel was rejected by 28 agents and editors before Wynwood Press agreed to publish 5,000 copies.[174] By contrast, his second novel, *The Firm* (1991), was a huge commercial success. Paramount Pictures bought the movie rights before it was published, and Grisham was suddenly free to leave his practice behind, an option he hastily exercised. Even a successful return to the courtroom in 1996 was not enough to rekindle his interest. Honouring a prior commitment, he represented the family of a railroad worker who had been crushed between two cars and won a jury award of $683,500.[175] 'When I left the

[167] John Grisham, *The Rainmaker,* n 166, 60. Thomas Callahan, a law professor with a drinking problem in *The Pelican Brief,* embodies Grisham's sense of legal academics. Callahan lasted only two years in private practice. As a law professor, Callahan 'slept late, worked five hours a day, wrote an occasional article, and for the most part enjoyed himself immensely'. Grisham, *The Pelican Brief* (New York: 1992) 74.

[168] ibid, 27.

[169] Grisham, *A Time to Kill* (New York: 1992) xi.

[170] ibid, 285.

[171] ibid, xi.

[172] ibid.

[173] Grisham, 1992 Mississippi State University Summer Commencement Address, available at http://library.msstate.edu/grisham_home/best_plans.html.

[174] Bob Minzesheimer, 'Grisham's New Book Takes a Literary Turn', *USA Today*, 6 February 2001, 2A. Grisham himself bought 1,000 copies and attempted to peddle them to independent bookstores from the trunk of his car. Ibid.

[175] See http://www.randomhouse.com/features/grisham/about.html.

courtroom that day', Grisham recalls, 'I said "Never Again," and I meant it'.[176] He still annually renews his Mississippi licence, but he boasted in a 2000 interview, 'I have yet to miss practicing law'.[177]

Since the publication of *The Firm*, Grisham's accomplishments have been extraordinary. The novel was *the* bestselling novel of 1991,[178] and a new novel has sprung from Grisham's computer every year since. Works such as *The Pelican Brief* (1992) and *The Client* (1993) reached number one on the *New York Times* bestseller list,[179] and *The Partner* (1997) had the largest initial printing in United States publishing history until the publication of *Harry Potter and the Goblet of Fire* (2000).[180] *The Summons* (2002) was the biggest selling book of 2002, when he sold 2.6 million copies.[181] Hollywood has made six of Grisham's legal novels into movies, and *The Client* inspired a short-lived television series of the same name. Grisham's popularity has even resulted in the republication of *A Time to Kill*, his first novel and the only work which did not quickly become a bestseller.

Critics often enjoy Grisham's novels less than the reading public does.[182] While critics routinely praise his fast-paced plots, they often 'dismiss his characterization as simplistic and some of his writing as clunky'.[183] The criticism seems to roll off Grisham's back, and he suggested critics are 'biased against popular fiction . . . holding it against me because I'm not Faulkner'.[184] 'I try to write commercial fiction of high quality—no attempt at literature here—just good books that people enjoy reading', he adds. 'The libraries are already filled with great literature. There's no room for me.'[185]

Paranoia is present in much of Grisham's fiction. Readers share the major characters' foreboding, their growing sense that something is wrong. Frequently, it turns out, greedy businesses, groups, or institutional menaces are conspiring or perhaps even secretly in control. The historian Richard Hofstadter wrote in the late 1960s of the way a paranoia of this sort has often manifested itself among average Americans.[186] The anti-Masonic and anti-Catholic movements of the nineteenth century are examples. In his own era Hofstadter witnessed McCarthyism's paranoia about a Communist underground, and in the present, members of the militia movement suspect the federal government of a far-reaching and liberty-denying plot.[187] Grisham's fiction reflects this cultural rhythm, and his paranoia may in fact be one of the reasons for his great popularity.

176 See http://www.chat.yahoo.com/c/events/transcripts/special/020300.

177 ibid.

178 See n 175 above.

179 ibid.

180 'Potter Book Sets Printing Record', *Indianapolis Star*, 8 July 2001, A16.

181 Phil Kloer, ' "Harry Potter" Comes Under Academic Scrutiny', *Milwaukee Journal Sentinel*, 21 April 2003, 6B.

182 Columnist Dave Barry quipped that there must be a Federal Aviation Administration rule that all passengers boarding airplanes must carry a Grisham novel. See Mary Beth Pringle, *John Grisham: A Critical Companion* (Westport, Connecticut: 1997) 6.

183 Minzesheimer, n 174 above, 2A.

184 ibid.

185 ibid.

186 See Richard Hofstadter, *The Paranoid Style in American Politics and Other Essays* (New York: 1966) 10–14.

187 See David Ray Papke, *Heretics in the Temple: Americans Who Reject the Nation's Legal Faith* (New York: 1998) 136–142.

To be sure, Grisham's conspiring groups and menacing institutions change from novel to novel. In *A Time to Kill* the Ku Klux Klan is able to intimidate witnesses and jurors, burn down the home of which Jake Brigance is so proud, and strip and brutalize Ellen Roark, the law student who altruistically assists Brigance in a murder case. In *The Firm* the Morolto crime family of Chicago runs a large money-laundering operation and pulls the strings in more ways than one can count. In *The Pelican Brief* an oil and gas tycoon named Victor Mattiece can arrange the murder of not one but two United States Supreme Court Justices. In *The Rainmaker* (1995) the Great Benefit Insurance Company preys on the poor and uninformed and then systematically denies their claims. In *The Street Lawyer* (1998) RiverOaks, a large developer, tosses out the Washington, DC poor and more generally gets whatever it wants. In *The Brethren* (2000) disabled CIA Director Teddy Maynard, in terrible pain in his wheelchair, can arrange the release of federal prisoners, eliminate those who might squeal, and hand-pick the next President. And in *The King of Torts* (2003) a multi-national pharmaceutical company is using unsuspecting human subjects and then spending millions to cover it up.

These Grisham villains as well as others constitute a kind of collective evil, a nightmarish vision of forces controlling and manipulating the American public. Furthermore, the villains do not so much violate the law as they seek and successfully arrange to have skilled and high-priced legal professionals help them get around the law. The large law firm, in particular, emerges as part of the conspiracy. Grisham's fictional Memphis, for example, is the home of both Bendini, Lambert & Locke, which represents the Mafia and lures unsuspecting young lawyers into its web, and Tinley, Britt, defender of Great Benefit Life and 'the largest, stuffiest, most prestigious and wealthiest firm in the state'.[188] In Grisham's Washington, DC, meanwhile, elite firms include the likes of White & Blazevich, 'one of those lily-white silk-stocking outfits filled with Ivy Leaguers and long names that ended in numerals',[189] as well as Drake & Sweeney, muscular champion of the developers and heartless contributor to homelessness. With 800 lawyers, the latter is the fifth largest firm in the country.[190] At the beginning of *The Street Lawyer* a homeless man takes nine lawyers hostage in one of Drake & Sweeney's elegant conference rooms, and the reader can delight as the captor forces the snivelling lawyers to reveal not only their outrageous salaries but also the piddling charitable contributions listed on their tax returns.[191]

Commonly a lawyer or perhaps a law student is able at the end of a Grisham novel to defeat and topple the force of evil and its supporting large law firm. Intrigued by this type of denouement, one commentator has characterized three of Grisham's victorious legal figures—attorney Mitch Deere in *The Firm*, attorney Reggie Love in *The Client*, and law student Darby Shaw in *The Pelican Brief*—as

188 Grisham, *The Rainmaker*, n 166 above, 281.

189 Grisham, *The Pelican Brief*, n 167 above, 281.

190 Grisham, *The Street Lawyer* (New York: 1998) 373.

191 ibid, 14–21.

'superheroes'.[192] More generally, there is a populist dimension to these fictional struggles. Individuals, often from humble backgrounds, defeat the embodiments of greed, wealth and power. Little people triumph over big people. Terry K Diggs compares Grisham's heroes to the appealing outsiders in many of Frank Capra's films from the 1930s and 1940s.[193]

For example, Rudy Baylor, the son of a jobless alcoholic, had to wait tables, deliver pizzas, and struggle to pay his rent during college. At the beginning of *The Rainmaker*, Baylor is finishing law school at Memphis State and contemplating bankruptcy. By the end of the novel, he has won $50 million (the largest jury award in fictional Tennessee history) in a plaintiff's action against Great Benefit Insurance and its stable of Ivy League lawyers from Memphis' largest firm. It is little wonder Baylor invokes the 'theme of David versus Goliath' when he argues before the jury.[194]

Grisham's crusading populists, it should be added, are not necessarily noble from the start. They are themselves often cynical and fundamentally self-interested, but in the course of battling evil forces they undergo a type of moral awakening. A case in point is Michael Brock, a workaholic antitrust lawyer in *The Street Lawyer*. After being part of the previously mentioned hostage-taking at Drake & Sweeney and seeing a sniper shoot off the head of the hostage-taker, Brock is told by an obtuse supervising partner that he should feel free to take a day off.[195] Brock discovers his firm's tawdry involvement in the evictions of poor people, and he becomes enamoured with the work of Mordecai Green and others in a legal clinic for the homeless. Brock has regained a moral life, and he even inspires the senior partner at his former firm to require that all lawyers in the firm do pro bono work. Legal ethics scholar Carrie Menkel-Meadow acknowledges how unrealistic *The Street Lawyer's* conclusion is, but she nevertheless cites the work as a novel willing 'to dramatize the work of the lawyer seeking social justice'.[196]

But alas, if Brock becomes a moral lawyer with a purpose, he is not the typical lawyer protagonist in Grisham's fiction. His 'Davids' may triumph over sinister 'Goliaths', but his characters are not like the later Randolph Mason or like Ephraim Tutt and Perry Mason. Grisham's protagonists do not rise up time and again to protect the innocent and the worthy. Indeed, they do not even reappear as do certain of the lawyers and judges in Scott Turow's fictional Kindle County. The reason, simply, is that after prevailing in their struggles against the Mob, environmentally insensitive oil and gas interests, corrupt insurance companies, the CIA, and assorted corporate law firms, Grisham's lawyers want to wash their hands of legal practice. They want to escape the legal profession.

192 Judith Grant, 'Lawyers as Superheroes: "The Firm," "The Client" and "The Pelican Brief" (1996) 30 *San Francisco L Rev* 1111.

193 Terry K Diggs, 'Through a Glass Darkly', *American Bar Association Journal*, October 1996, 73.

194 Grisham, *The Rainmaker*, n 166 above, 450.

195 Grisham, *The Street Lawyer*, n 190 above, 29.

196 Carrie Menkel-Meadow, 'The Sense and Sensibilities of Lawyers: Lawyering in Literature, Narratives, Film and Television, and Ethical Choices Regarding Career and Craft' (1999) 31 *McGeorge L Rev* 2, 16.

The escapes, of course, are as dramatic and unbelievable as the novels' overall plots. (Grisham is correct when he says he is not the author of 'great literature'.) Mitch McDeere in *The Firm* ends up on a Caribbean island with his wife Abby at his side and $8 million in a secret bank account. 'The truth is', he tells Abby, 'I never wanted to be a lawyer anyway.'[197] Darby Shaw, the law student who solved the murder of two Supreme Court Justices in *The Pelican Brief*, finds a cosy room in St Thomas and vows to 'read nothing about law until she was fifty.'[198] Rudy Baylor in *The Rainmaker* and Kelly, the woman he rescued from an abusive husband, leave Memphis for a college town in the West, where he hopes to become a high school history teacher. 'I will not under any circumstances', Rudy tells Kelly as she rests her head on his shoulder, 'have anything whatsoever to do with the law. . . . I will never voluntarily set foot in another courtroom.'[199] If any of Grisham's lawyers sees his escape go awry, it is Patrick Lanigan in *The Partner*. After getting his raft of federal and state charges dropped, divorcing his cheating wife, and sending millions of dollars to Eva Miranda, his stunning Brazilian lover, Lanigan eagerly abandons the practice of law and journeys to the South of France. But alas, Eva fails to appear, breaking Lanigan's heart and leaving him almost penniless.[200]

Why are these lawyers and law students so eager to engineer their escapes from the legal profession? For Grisham's most developed lawyer protagonists, long and traumatic experiences help explain the eagerness to abandon the law. But Grisham also suggests that the longing for escape is pervasive in the profession. When early in *The Partner* Patrick Lanigan is brought back to Mississippi to stand trial, friends from the local bar lionize him for having run off to South American with millions of dollars which were not his own. 'Escape was a common, usually unspoken, dream of many small-town lawyers trapped in an overcrowded, boring profession where expectations were too high.'[201] Despite their high salaries and well-upholstered offices, lawyers in the large urban firms also dream of escape. Lamar Quinn, a 32-year-old lawyer in Bendini, Lambert & Locke, levels with Mitch McDeere, his new associate:

> This business works on you. When you were in law school you had some noble idea of what a lawyer should be. A champion of individual rights; a defender of the Constitution; a guardian of the oppressed; an advocate for your client's principles. Then after you practice for six months you realize you're nothing but hired guns.[202]

Lest there be any doubt, this is John Grisham talking. He admitted in an Internet chat his special fondness for Patrick Lanigan. 'We all dream of escaping',

[197] Grisham, *The Firm* (New York: 1991) 501.

[198] Grisham, *The Pelican Brief*, n 167 above, 433.

[199] Grisham, *The Rainmaker*, n 166 above, 598.

[200] In responding to an Internet question about the novel's ending, Grisham admitted a sensitivity to the criticism that his work was too predictable. 'So with *The Partner*, I chose the unpredictable'. See n 176 above.

[201] Grisham, *The Partner* (New York: 1997) 175.

[202] Grisham, *The Firm*, n 197 above, 68–69.

Grisham said.[203] In another context, Grisham announced that the most satisfying part of law practice was: 'Getting out of it'.[204] He himself escaped the legal profession by writing of fictional lawyers who themselves escape the profession. Intriguingly, readers who are not lawyers also relate to Grisham's theme. Grisham arouses a sympathetic response with tales of individual lawyers who triumph over menacing forces and then leave the practice of law.

Conclusion

Throughout the twentieth century, lawyer/authors have published fiction about lawyers and legal themes. The most popular of these authors—Melville Davisson Post, Arthur Train, Erle Stanley Gardner, Scott Turow, and John Grisham—were unhappy as lawyers. Turow continues to work part-time in a large Chicago law firm, but the others abandoned the legal profession completely once their writing careers blossomed. Yet despite their reservations about practising law and despite their career switches, the authors continued to tell stories featuring lawyers and legal themes that engaged large numbers of readers.

The particular reasons the lawyer/authors abandoned legal work are suggestive of what might be alienating about the legal profession. Post had a respected and financially remunerative practice, but the stressfulness of a lawyer's life seems simply to have been too much for him. Life as gentleman writer in hunt club attire offered more peace and tranquility. For Train and Gardner, respectively, the denial of moral integrity and personal independence were the most troubling aspects of practising law. Train longed for a type of practice truly connected to truth, fairness, and especially justice. Gardner hated confinement in a low-budget law office and his inability to be the master of his own time. A product of another era, Turow became alienated while still in law school and has never recanted his argument in *One L* that legal thought is unduly confident and fundamentally dehumanizing. For Grisham, losing sleep over clients and vomiting in courthouses are the things he remembers of his Mississippi practice, and he saw leaving the law as an 'escape', almost as if the Bar was some kind of prison.

The lawyer/authors may be especially sensitive men, and they cannot be made to speak for the entire legal profession. However, in each instance the lawyer/author re-imagined what he had observed about law, lawyers, legal thinking into popular fiction about legal practice. Some of the fiction is in short-story form, and some is novelistic. Some of the fiction is in itself critical of lawyers and their narrow-mindedness, while some presents heroic lawyers who serve deserving clients and fight for justice. All of it was and still is remarkably popular.

[203] See n 176 above.

[204] The Book Report Interview with John Grisham, available at http://www.capitolabookcafe.com/andrea/grisinto.html.

While readers of course turned to the fiction for different reasons, the works can be seen as a row of windows on Americans' fears and hopes regarding lawyers in the course of the twentieth century. Post's fictional attorney Randolph Mason commanded the curious, mysterious law, and readers could learn about the law as Mason pursued his unethical causes. Train and Gardner created heroic lawyers in the person of Ephraim Tutt and Perry Mason. The two would probably not have cared for one another had they met at some fictional Bar association meeting, but readers admired the characters' representation of the worthy and their ability to see that justice was done. Against a backdrop of deepening doubt and cynicism, Turow and Grisham during the final decades of the twentieth century provided large stables of lawyers who are more protagonists than they are heroes. Readers liked Turow's ruminations through his lawyer characters on the existential disappointments of legal practice and contemporary life. Grisham's lawyers, who are haunted by menacing forces and then defeat them only to leave practice, resonated with even larger numbers of readers, readers who themselves felt menaced and estranged.

The collective picture reveals the conditions that might direct one from legal practice to writing and also a large variety of pop cultural forms, themes, and content. Popular American fiction by and about lawyers in the twentieth century is a complex and varied cultural phenomenon. When we contemplate the lives of the lawyer/authors and critically read large amounts of their fiction, we are reminded of the roles lawyers play in American life, the conflicts and pressures of their professional work, and the range of ways tales of lawyers can engage readers and provide them with meaning. We have, in short, a powerful illustration of the legalistic character of American culture.

The Materiality of Symbols: JG Ballard and Jurisprudence: Law, Image, Reproduction

Adam Gearey

This is The Way, Step Inside

Popular culture challenges our jurisprudence to think law's reproduction in the age of the simulacra and the spectacle. Ballard's role as a cult figure of popular culture, an inspiration for songs from Joy Division to David Bowie, suggests that this issue is not just a concern of academic philosophy, but part of the popular imagination, particularly when it is linked to questions of identity and alienation. But we need to be more precise. This is not an argument that Ballard's work concerns itself with lawyers, court procedure or what has passed until now as the themes of legal philosophy. There is an engagement at a much deeper level. To make sense of Ballard's jurisprudence, law must be seen as a fundamental text[1] that is transmittable, that can be passed on and inherited; a text around which a society defines itself. In the past, the great works of mythology and religion fulfilled this function. Have we come to the end of this order? What are the consequences for law now that we have entered the post modern, the order of the image? Ballard takes this issue seriously. His writings could be seen as providing a contemporary mythology of

[1] The notion of the law as text is drawn from the work of Pierre Legendre; although, in the present essay, Legendre is read through Guy Debord. A useful introduction to the notion of the text is *L'Empire De la Vérité* (Paris, 1983) 35–39. The text represents a universal structure that may or may not take the form of the written word. In whatever form it takes the text relates to an idea of the dogmatic communication of messages that are predicated upon reference back to the fundamental truth of the foundational reference. The transmission of the text is the 'dissemination' of a discourse that for the society in question has the status of truth. To engage with the text is to accept its hold, to submit to a 'pre-existent' embodiment of the truth. The text itself bestows on the interpreter the authority to interpret and thus carry forward the function of reference. In other words, the truth of the text is largely a notion of the conditions of its own remembrance, perpetuation and continued dissemination. Law is exemplary of the text. It is tentatively suggested in this essay that the society of the spectacle is wound up with the logic of the text, see Guy Debord, *The Society of the Spectacle* (Detroit, 1983). Ballard's *The Atrocity Exhibition* provides a kind of mediating point. The spectacle is not entirely visual, although this is perhaps the primary mode of its self representation. One might understand the spectacle as the reproduction of a particular economic order, dedicated to its own perpetuation: 'the spectacle is capital to such a degree of accumulation that it becomes an image' (34). As such, the spectacle represents an insight of Marx taken to an extreme. We have created an order that alienates us; we work to perpetuate our own alienation; as Debord puts it: 'Separated from his product, man himself produces all the details of his world with ever increasing power, and thus finds himself ever more separate from his world' (33).

the law, or, as we shall see, a jurisprudence of the image. Our core concern will be the way in which his texts re-articulate the central question: how does the law communicate and reproduce itself and the social? After examining the appearance of these ideas in legal and social thought we will concentrate on Ballard's disturbing text, *The Atrocity Exhibition*. We are perhaps returning to what jurisprudence always was: a study of the means and affects of transmission.

We need to stress a particularly important feature of this argument. A contemporary mythology of law must confront the image and the society of the spectacle. It might seem that the order of the image is the 'end' of certain concerns that have always founded and sustained the social. This would appear to be a contradiction of the central thesis of this paper; that the text is about transmission and the sustenance of social order. This seeming contradiction can be resolved only by raising it to a higher level. We need to ask how we can continue to make sense of these fundamental terms within the order of the image.

How to write about Ballard? It would be wrong to impose on Ballard's texts a logic that is not their own. The claim that Ballard is writing a kind of jurisprudence clearly necessitates a certain rigour. This demand will be honoured. However, for a writer so concerned with the derangement of sense, or the vision that comes out of derangement and psychosis, it would be wrong to believe that conventional scholarship can provide the correct approach. At the same time, a complete disruption of the conventions of journal articles would not be helpful. The argument will proceed in such a way as to develop the main thesis, but to allow a certain degree of digression and interruption. This essay is then, something of a hybrid; a conjunction of social and literary theory, science fiction, psychoanalysis and jurisprudence. This admixture will at least hint at the strange and terrible experience of reading *The Atrocity Exhibition*.

Jurisprudence as Legal Theory

Our first step is to make clear a peculiar understanding of jurisprudence. What can jurisprudence learn from popular culture; or, more precisely, what can legal theory learn from the theory of popular culture? It may be the case that a formal jurisprudence can learn nothing about the nature of law from popular culture. Something could be said about law's location in culture, but a strict postivism, for example, would see this question as meaningless. Jurisprudence is an examination of the nature of law. It cannot learn anything from other fields, especially from one as distant as popular culture. A less strict approach might relish the observations on law drawn from popular culture, but would consider this a distraction from the more serious business of defining and understanding legal operations. It is necessary, then, to insist on a particular understanding of jurisprudence: jurisprudence as legal theory. This conjunction suggests that jurisprudence should be seen as inseparable from other theoretical endeavours. However, it will not be suggested that jurisprudence as legal theory simply lines up alongside other forms of cultural theory, offering yet another interpretation of the social world to an increasingly rich and varied pattern. Jurisprudence may have to learn from the techniques of theoretical inquiry, but it must not abandon the insight that it offers into the construction of the social world. The thesis of this article will be that theoretical jurisprudence identifies a key, if not definitional aspect of the social; it lays bare an operating code. Law is essential to social reproduction. One might even suggest that the law is now what remains of the original summoning into being and definition of community. This abstract and general thesis must now be more usefully defined.

Law as Mediology: The Becoming Material of Symbolic Forms

As far as the western tradition is concerned, law has always fulfilled a certain function. It is only of late, however, that scholars of legal theory have begun to understand the ancient provenance of their field. This beginning, although something of a false start, was the turn to the study of law as ideology in the mid to late seventies. This approach, associated with critical legal studies, allowed a revision of the Marxist distinction between base and superstructure. Law had always been seen as an element of the superstructure of the state, secondary to the economic base. Positing law as ideology effectively raised the importance of the former, as it became central to an account of the reproduction of the social. This may have enabled new ways of thinking but its Marxist framework also proved restrictive. An emphasis on the nature of power as state power, or class power, was too limiting. Furthermore, the understanding of law as ideology contained in itself a fundamental misunderstanding. Ideology was opposed to scientific knowledge. Scientific knowledge, an understanding of real relations, could be obtained through Marxist theory and practice. Theoretical work proceeded on the basis that there was a strict opposition of science and ideology. This was a fundamental error, as both science and ideology are more properly understood as rival 'forms of organization'.[2] The whole approach could be recast as a concern with the communication of messages, and the cohering of certain groups around a diversity of positions.

It is not simply the case that Marxist scholarship was wrong; rather Marxist insights need to be rethought. Consider the following claim: '[q]uestions that were once said to be ideological we would today say are symbolic or cultural'.[3] To determine the operation of ideology, and to be able to speak of law as an ideology, we thus need to extend our study into the field of symbolism and culture. Underlying both these terms, and suggesting itself as the true 'object' of study, is a notion of transmission. Constituting the social is a fundamental text that allows both the

[2] Regis Debray, *Media Manifestos* (trans Eric Rauth, London: 1996) 4. [3] ibid, 4.

foundation and transmission of an essential truth. This can be shown through any anthropological study of a 'primitive' society. The text is frequently one that is held to be sacred and brings together a foundational story and a law code. There are also certain guardians of this text; a class of priests who preserve its meaning and develop techniques for both preserving its purity and updating its reach into the changing social world.

We are thus, for the moment, primarily concerned with the description of a structural function and the different material forms that this function takes. In our 'post modern' times, the text and its preservation are clearly radically different from the sacred text of the primitive society. It is at this point that we inherit the distinction between the primitive and the modern, the simple and the sophisticated that is such an important issue for conventional jurisprudence. This boundary cannot be forgotten or wished away; it must be re-inscribed. The present analysis would assert a fundamental similarity between supposedly primitive and modern or even post modern societies. Both primitive and modern forms of social organization are founded on a text. Again risking banality through intense compression, it might be suggested that, for us, the fundamental text is human rights. This is the fundamental 'ideology' of our times. It is a mode of organization that appears to determine every aspect of social being from the issue of legal sex through to the justification for waging war. The other key point is that this fundamental text will take, has to take, certain material and institutional forms; and these forms are different for different social formations. It is in this sense that we can deploy, as a form of shorthand, the notion of law as mediology.

Law as mediology is a regard to the essential way that fundamental social meanings are articulated through various media. Put slightly differently, it is the study of how 'an abstract symbol can produce a concrete effect'.[4] This can again be usefully explained by reference to the original religious codes that thoroughly understood this function. In Christian theology, the messenger carries the word. Thus, the truth demands both a messiah and a text that is the witnessing and record of that messiah and his truth. The truth cannot stand outside of these institutional forms. In turn, the truth becomes the foundation of the ecclesia, the community of those who believe. Truth's institutionalization is not an abstract operation. The crucifixion is the truth as marked out on the broken body of the messiah; the truth is witnessed in blood and pain as well as the marks on the page of the Gospel. In the broadest sense, the truth writes itself on the body of the believer as she kneels to pray, does penance, and takes part in Holy Communion. Elaborating the operation of this particular machinery would require an account of the various techniques whereby a truth is memorialized. Memorialization is not just the perpetuation of a memory of a text, but the creation of the institutional and physical forms that the text becomes. To switch registers momentarily, ideology describes a way of organizing a community; putting in place a set of institutions, beliefs and practices.

[4] ibid, 5.

It is now necessary to be more precise about the way that different regimes of symbols can be organized. This can provide us with a typology of the text and a sense of its development through different technologies. Indeed, mediology describes something broader than those institutions that merely transmit messages; it also carries the meaning of the bringing together of different procedures or techniques. These can be grouped underneath the general heading of the mediasphere.[5] We could sketch a broad historical movement between three stages: from logosphere, through graphosphere to videosphere. As with all ideal types these terms are not sealed categories, but tendencies that overlap and coexist alongside each other. Indeed, all three spheres could exist at any one time. As far as the relevance of these categories to law is concerned, the following transition could be pointed out. The logosphere could be associated with Weber's notion of charismatic authority; the graphosphere describes the era in which law becomes the written record. Law is now bound up, to a problematic extent, with the spectacular nature of the contemporary. Law is contained in electronic archives; law is becoming virtual. Law is part of the videosphere.

The logosphere, as the most primitive stage, represents a historical moment where the transmission of a message is primarily through the word and the memory of that word. This can be made a little more historically compelling, even in this summary form, by considering a pre-historical period that archaeology still considers to be a time without writing. Pre-history obviously leaves its monuments, but these are not in a form that would be associated with writing as such. Think of Silbury Hill or Avebury. Such huge testaments to cultural effort possessed a meaning for those who built them, and a meaning that was deemed to be worthy of preservation. We could thus slightly mutate this category to suggest that the logosphere can be seen as a period where the memory of cultural worth is transmitted, but not formally through any system that could be equated with writing. The age of writing could be seen as stretching from the handwritten script, the manuscript, through to Gutenberg and the printing press. With the graphosphere arises the possibility of the record and the archive; and the forms of social organization that can now be more accurately described, taxed and controlled. The videosphere is the age of the electronic archive, the recorded voice and audiovisual technologies.

This typology of the organization of symbols is useful. We could see it as relevant to a history of writing, or a history of law as writing.[6] To make sense of this claim,

[5] ibid, 26.

[6] See Peter Goodrich, *Language of Law* (London: 1990). See also Gilles Deleuze and Felix Guattari, *Anti-Oedipus: capitalism and schizophrenia* (trans Robert Hurley, Mark Seem and Helen R Lane, New York: 1977). Deleuze and Guattari's history of writing begins with the primitive. Law is seen as debt, inscribing legality in the economy of desire. Debt creates alliance and allows, if one follows Nietzsche, an account of memory, and hence also of the subject who belongs to a family and a tribe, who is initiated into a community that defines itself through exclusivity. This is indeed a reading, albeit a partial one, of ancient law. As a matter of ethnographic and anthropological enquiry, there is an interruption of the primitive community, not in all places, but to an extent that we can talk of a general

we would have to focus on the interrelations between various forms of communication and legal forms. This is a difficult endeavour and can only be sketched out within the confines of this paper. A second critical issue, and one that can also only be touched upon here, is the evolutionary underpinnings of the move from logosphere to videosphere. A simple model of evolution is simply too crude to describe historical patterns; but, for the moment, we might suggest that the notion of the different spheres is merely a retrospective understanding of the development of law from a contemporary viewpoint. We also need to emphasize that the different spheres can exist together within a single period. There could also be different relationships of priority between the different spheres. For instance, contemporary law would be marked by the increasing dominance of the videosphere in relation to the logosphere and the graphosphere. In contrast, the legal forms of the last century were marked almost exclusively by the logosphere and the graphosphere. Our focus here, however, is on the videosphere.

In turning to the videosphere, we might suggest that this represents not the end of law, but the fact that law is now implicated in and inseparable from an order of images. It goes without saying that understanding tele-technologies is an essential task for jurisprudence, for a revision or reclassification of the fundamental notions of law and legal argument. However, perhaps what it forces on the entire endeavour is an awareness that jurisprudence, or jurisprudence practised and thought in a certain way, was always concerned with something spectral; a spectral jurisdiction that, bizarrely, makes jurisprudence that study of the reproduction of law's material culture. Elaborating this line of argument, though, returns to the persistent themes of legal and social theory: how does one live the law, live ethically, within the order of the image?

Mediology and Grammatology

The essential function of the text is the composition of the social. Crudely, this could be seen as the provision of fundamental social structures and relationships. These can be speculatively described as existing in the line of development that reaches from the logosphere, through the graphosphere to the contemporary videosphere. The videosphere is the age of the electronic archive, the recorded voice and audiovisual technologies. We are concerned, then, with a moment of transmission and its material supports; a moment when the way in which law is

pattern that needs to be explained. This can be represented as the barbarian despotic machine, and is associated with the earlier writing of Empire, Assyrian cuneiform script, for instance. The despot 'breaks up' the alliances that held together the primitive socius; he also places himself as a representative of the divine on earth, forcing a conjunction of people, land and deity. An administrative structure is imposed on a pre-existing rural community and extracts, through tributes, the surplus value of production whilst making itself seem the true cause of this production. This history could be further traced in capitalist methods of control.

practised, perpetuated and understood is reinvented. The key scenes in this transformation all relate to American trials: Rodney King, OJ Simpson, Bush v Gore. These cases represent the emergence of the trial as a televisual spectacle. Of course, there had been dramatic and fictional representations of court processes, but what marks these cases is 'a new form of visibility'.[7] Law is transformed. The form of the media impacts on the techniques of law to the extent that it has to submit to the operations of a media network that finds it difficult to accept the forms of legal argument developed in relative independence from wider culture forms and demands:

> The law became instantaneous, and the public presence of the law is taken out of the exclusive and solemn or learned hands of the lawyers and passed down, as with the Supreme Court judgment in Bush v Gore, to waiting reporters who would read and interpret it live on camera.[8]

This might represent a complete reversal of legal techniques. Systems of precedent depend on the weight of past instances that are applied to the present case. Instantaneous communications suggest that one is less able to deploy arcane vocabularies and to justify the resolution of present disputes by the regurgitation of past instances. The visual media demands instant and justifiable decisions and sound bites. But, perhaps most importantly, the effect of the law becomes essential to the dissemination of the legal decision. One can see, instantaneously, the effect of a verdict on the accused or the jubilation of winning a case. Law was always linked up with its effects, but now, and most visibly in the public eye, law is seen to be its effects. One might suggest that this is a visible politics, where law's impact on the social is impossible to disguise. Thus, televisual trials stage the fundamental traumas of the American body politic. With OJ Simpson, the issue was race and gender; Rodney King displayed in most brutal terms the racism of American institutions; Bush v Gore the near paralysis of a democratic culture.

It is as if we need a new poetics of the object to read law's inhabitation of the videosphere. Mediology is thus a regard to the essential way that fundamental social meanings are articulated through the image. What are the consequences of this movement; this becoming virtual of the law? We will see that for Ballard, it means a thorough questioning of what it means to be human. The old certainties, the old foundations are crumbling. Is there a genealogy for these ideas in other areas of recent jurisprudence? How can we further our examination of the videosphere? It could be suggested that this takes us to those scholars of law and literature who have interrogated Ballard's texts and wider issues of ethics and interpretation.

[7] Peter Goodrich, 'Europe in America: Grammatology, Legal Studies, and the Politics of Transmission' (2002) 102 *Columbia L Rev* 2075. See also Richard Sherwin, *When Law Goes Pop* (Chicago 2000), especially the notion of a 'jurisprudence of appearances'.

[8] Goodrich, n 7 above, 2075.

Dreams of Structures

The following quotation opens Aristodemou's *Law and Literature*. It could be read as a response to the videosphere:

> We live in a world ruled by fictions of every kind—mass merchandising, advertising, politics conducted as a branch of advertising, the pre-empting of any original response to experience by the television screen. We live inside an enormous novel. It is now less and less necessary for the writer to invent the fictional content of his novel. The fiction is already there. The writer's task is to invent reality.[9]

For Aristodemou, Ballard's fiction is a key text for the definition of a new law and literature scholarship. Literary jurisprudence must address the simulacra; the order of the image, where reality has been replaced by the image, or rather, by the network of signifiers where signs no longer relate to an external referent but to each other. Her work moves out from the observation that law and literature are both sign systems that invent a reality that remain chaotic and beyond our grasp. It is in this movement that she both discovers and reinvents the idea of the fundamental social text. Whereas law is founded on a belief in the necessity of its constructions, literature is better disposed to an understanding of its own contingency, its own fictional nature. Literature, in some senses, replaces the law. Literature, like the dream, is a rebus that offers itself to our interpretation as the very mystery of interpretation itself. We may be within the order of images but we cannot abdicate a responsibility of interpretation, even if our interpretations are bound to be contingent and fragmentary. Indeed, we cannot but help to be interpreters, even if we now must interpret the society of the spectacle in the way that we would read a novel.

'Ms. Williams, It appears your texts have taken on a life of their own!'

Ballard's work prompts similar questions in the work of Melanie Williams.[10] Williams is concerned with a notion of character, of the human as agent. Williams is concerned with an emptiness that is double: emptiness is the void, but it is the void that demands articulation. Emptiness is both despair and hope. We are caught up in a persistent, uncertain search for what is both necessary and impossible. In Ballard's fictional worlds the mask of civility appears to conceal a creature of lust and appetite. How should we respond to these inherent failures of 'human nature'? Williams' work communicates with the broader concerns developed thus far; it

[9] Maria Aristodemou, *Law and Literature Journeys from her to eternity* (Oxford: 2000).
[10] Melanie Williams, *One Hundred Years of Law, Literature and Philosophy* (London: 2002).

also broadens the agenda. When we turn to Ballard's text, we will allow our reading to be guided by the themes developed above. However, before we can read the text itself there is a final issue of importance; the experimental nature of Ballard's writing.

El Hombre Invisible

The narrative of *The Atrocity Exhibition* can be seen as an expression in a 'popular cultural form' of stylistic experiments that can be traced to Joyce's *Ulysses*, as mediated by William S Burroughs. The disappearance of the narrator, and the appearance, in his place, of the text, might mark a particular feature of the graphosphere. Although this is important, it will not organize our analysis.[11] Our primary concern must be with how Ballard's text operates. Ballard's experiments in style return to the theme of the text as transmission. However, this needs to be placed in context:

> It was the subject matter of those stories that defined the way in which they were written . . . I once said those condensed novels, as I called them, are like ordinary novels, with the unimportant pieces left out. But its more than that—when you get the important pieces together, really together, not separated by great masses of 'he said' and 'she said' . . . —the great tide of conventional narrative—it achieves critical mass as it were, it begins to ignite and you get more unexpected and previously totally unrelated things, events, elements of the narration, ideas that in themselves begin to generate new matter . . . the crossovers become very unusual.[12]

Ballard's suggestion is, first of all, that style follows content. This would beg the question of the author's perception of the content of this work:

> What The Atrocity Exhibition was about was the way that the media landscape has created something very close to a gigantic art gallery with a lot of very lurid paintings on exhibition—that was in the 60's—and the way in which psychopathic strains which are normally either ignored or suppressed were beginning to use the media landscape to express and reveal themselves . . . Its still going on, but one saw it in particular in the 70's with the TV coverage of the Vietnam war, and the reduction of all events to pure sensation.[13]

So, the style of these fictions is meant to capture something of the kaleidoscopic media spectacle that exploded in the sixties. Events have been reduced to 'pure sensation'. The main point is that this leads to a 'death of affect' or a disassociation of

[11] This is the peculiar phenomenon where the author who desires to efface himself from his work becomes celebrated as the disappearing man. Perhaps graphic authority becomes reinvented as the authority of the image of the author; his media presence. Ballard's shopping basket was featured in a Sunday paper. It contained wine, gin and meat.

[12] James Goddard and David Pringle (eds), *JG Ballard, The First Twenty Years* (Middlesex: 1976) 29–30. One of the most essential work of criticism on Ballard is Roger Luckhurst, *The Angle Between Two Walls; the Fiction of J. G. Ballard* (Liverpool: 1997).

[13] *NME*, 22 October 1983, 29.

sensibility as representations of wars and atrocities appear to be interchangeable with advertisements for soap powder. This is, to some extent, a typical science fiction theme: a warning against the rise of science and the loss of the human soul. We can see that it is conjoined with what would now be called a typically post modern concern with the media-scape and the collapse of meta narratives. The concern with the death of affect is a kind of pre-runner for the debates about the effects of the simulacrum, or the relativizing tendencies of post modern thinking. Indeed, this would add to the thesis that science fiction was the first post modernism.[14] If this is so, there are clearly some interesting connections between science fiction and those forms of legal thought that take their prompting from post modernism and post structuralism, but this is not our primary concern. The passage above can be related back to our previous comments on the politics of the image. Ballard is linking a style, a way of writing to a content, a message. The image has flattened out social reality. This may be the most modern return of the ancient theme of the fallen world. Where in this veil of tears, in this alienation, are we to find ourselves, our true being? How are we to live? Within the order of images, there appears no way to judge between atrocity and advertising. The point of *The Atrocity Exhibition* is to push this logic to its extreme. Is there a redemption from violence through violence? Could this make for a responsibility? Again, these essential questions recur. But, we must not run ahead of ourselves. We must stick with questions of style, before addressing issues of form. There is more to the writing of the fictions of *The Atrocity Exhibition* than the removal of narrative linkage!

Cut-Up/ Fold In: 'I can tell you nothing you do not know, I can show you nothing you have not seen.'

Ballard's 'experiments' with narrative can be directly related to Burroughs' own use of various experimental techniques. Drawn from dada, surrealism and psycho-analysis, these techniques bring to writing a concern with the manifestation of the image and its interpretation. Burroughs introduces his own reflections on the cut up method with a story about Tristan Tzara, 'the man from nowhere'.[15] One night in performance, Tzara claimed that he would make a poem by pulling words at random out of a hat. The audience was so enraged by this attack on their artistic sensibilities that they wrecked the theatre. It is as if the audience appreciated that an attack on the notion of poetry was an attack on the supporting humanistic structures. Rather than being the expression of genius, poetry becomes mechanical, no more than random connections. More importantly, from Burroughs' own

[14] See the work of Eric Rabkin, in particular 'What Was Science Fiction?' in Marleen Barr (ed), *Envisioning the Future: Science Fiction and the Next Millennium* (Wesleyan University Press, 2003) and 'Science Fiction and the Future of Criticism' (2004) 119 PMLA 457.

[15] William Burroughs, 'The Cut-Up Method of Brion Gysin' in John Calder (ed), *The William Burroughs Reader* (London: 1982) 268.

perspective, cut up technique was reborn by the artist Brion Gysin. Gysin experimented with the possibilities offered by tape recording, producing cut ups of his own voice. Cut up becomes a way of reinventing writing by connecting it with practices that are primarily associated with the visual arts and cinema. The collage is a cut up and a re-composition. Consider a tracking shot by a camera. It cuts up parts of observable reality and recomposes them in the linearity of the film. The individual frames remove from the flow of reality lives and objects that are then captured as images on film.

Cut up, as practised by Burroughs, could thus be seen as an attempt to make writing filmic. The consequences of the cut up technique in writing, though, are perhaps more radical than those in painting or film. The 'literary' practitioner of cut up is making a claim about the nature of writing itself. Burroughs' choice of exemplary texts to cut up is instructive: Rimbaud and Shakespeare. Through cut up these major literary figures are re-authored; one might even say democratized. The effect of this may even be to reduce literary writing to a technique that anyone can use; indeed, for Burroughs, '[c]ut- ups are for everyone'.[16] As opposed to abstraction or philosophical obfuscation, the cut up is immediate, a practice. It allows texts to be opened to 'extension and variation'. Rimbaud's derangement of the senses makes utter sense in the theory and practice of the cut up: words become rearranged, adjectives attached to different nouns, language deranged and confused.[17]

Ballard's Videosphere

Through cut up, writing is seen as closer to any form of physical production; a set of ways for doing things for achieving an end. It thus returns to the notion of affect and the videosphere; writing as film. So—what does it mean to have entered a time when the logic of the image, the ability of the image to achieve a material effect is increasingly the way in which the text operates? It would appear that we are about to enter the atrocity exhibition; the site where reproduction of the social operates through the image. Can we make any sense of this vast spectacle?

The End of Interpretation

Apocalypse, from the Greek, has the root meaning of uncovering, but, via its use in *The New Testament*, takes the sense of revelation. It is, then, a word associated with

[16] Burroughs, n 15 above, 269.

[17] In a slightly different account of the cut up method, it appears unconsciously in the composition of the *Naked Lunch*. Its advent is fortuitous, as much a reflection on the difficult process of writing/editing, than a properly theorized borrowing from the dadaists or the surrealists. During the composition of the *Naked Lunch*, Burroughs was living in a Paris hotel, and trying to kick his junk habit. His book existed as fragments, scattered around the room, and indeed around the various cities of the world in which he had lived. Writing new sections of the book took place at the same time as old sections were either discovered or re-discovered; the book's manuscript became inseparable from other notes and materials lying around.

the visual register: with things and wonders seen. Why is it offered as the first word of *The Atrocity Exhibition*: how can it help us to read this most disturbing and problematic of texts? This first paragraph forefronts the scene of interpretation. Catherine Austin, one of the protagonists, is described viewing paintings of world cataclysm. They are the 'codes of insoluble dreams, the keys to a nightmare in which she had begun to play a more willing and calculated role'.[18] Note two things. The most central is that the order of the active viewer of the passive image has been reversed. The viewer has somehow been co-opted by the image, and plays a role in its logic. To extend the other metaphor: the dream creates the dreamer. Because there is no analyst who can work out the logic of the dream, the dream code is insoluble. What is available, what may allow us to approach the order of the image, is suggested by the fragments that these pictures bring together: 'Eniwetok and Luna Park, Freud and Elizabeth Taylor'.[19] What could possibly connect this diverse catalogue? Eniwetok is a test site for the atomic bomb. Luna Park is a Paris funfair, inspiration for the surrealists; Elizabeth Taylor, the celebrated actress. The catalogue thus mixes popular culture and 'high' culture, science, war and the media. Tentatively, we might suggest that the conjunction here suggests a particular form of specifically visual culture; and, a code or a logic that lies behind it—that can connect together the seemingly random. The paragraph is itself brought to a conclusion by a demand that the reader engage in a hermeneutic endeavour; just as Catherine Austin must—prompted by Dr Nathan: 'What do you think of them? I see that there's War in Hell.' Here Catherine Austin, as the namesake of one of the fathers of jurisprudence, declares the end of a certain order of interpretation. If there is a code, a code that law as the fundamental text represents, it has become so entangled with the image as to make law fundamentally part of the atrocity exhibition. Other central supports of the law are realigned.

The End of Character/the End of Memory

These early paragraphs of *The Atrocity Exhibition* set up an attack on the novelistic conventions of character. One would expect to be privy to the inner thoughts of the character, and to know, through conventions set up by the novelist, when each individual 'voice' was speaking. Moreover, one would expect the characters' voices to be distinguishable from that of the narrator's voice. Delineations of character would also presuppose a sense of the characters' context; their time and place, and that most bourgeois of concerns, their status, determinable partly through their relationship with other characters, and their location in a familiar social setting.

These novelistic conventions associate the novel very strongly with the law. Indeed, the coming of age of the novel is roughly contemporary with the settling of the foundational notions of contemporary law. Thus, one might like to see at least structural or ideological linkages between notions such as mens rea, actus reus

[18] JG Ballard, *The Atrocity Exhibition* (St Albans: 1970) 7. [19] ibid, 7.

and causation and certain features of the novel. This is because both forms are concerned with the explanation of action, and with rendering a believable account of events. To move away from the settled modes of narrative and the foundational terms character, is to suggest that a shift in novelistic practice may be the token of the need for the law to develop new concepts that could match the novel's depiction of social reality.

Narrative in *The Atrocity Exhibition* rewards our expectations in some ways and frustrates them in others. We are aware, first of all, that we are in some institution, possibly a psychiatric hospital, but, as the story develops, we seem to move inexplicably from a shabby hotel in Earls Court, to London Zoo and then to some deserted weapons range at an undisclosed location. In some ways this shifting of location identifies Ballard's work with the picaresque, and there is a continuing sense, confirmed by the novel *Crash*, that this is a major trope in his work. For our purposes, though, it can be related to an unsettling of Aristotelian plot certainties that correspond with certain substantive concerns that we will elaborate presently. How does character work against this disturbing background?

Character coheres only to dissipate. This is one of the assaults on novelistic and legal certainty and can be traced at a number of levels. A site of this breakdown is the failure of memory. Memory is one of the key components of the novel, relating to the development of personality and manners. The novel takes as one of its primary concerns the growth of character. In the hands of, say, Henry James, the concern with memory becomes a sophisticated location of the individual soul in the context of social mores, the past and the future. In *The Atrocity Exhibition*, memory, if it exists at all, is memory of trauma, or a failure to make links between the past and the present.

Let us consider the character Talbot. There are fragments in Talbot's memory: incidents from the Second World War; images that may be from his own past, or from films he might have seen. He sees himself walking though a desolate and war torn landscape to a hut where he finds some 'psychological tests'. Although 'he had no means of checking' the tests, 'the answers seemed to establish an identity'.[20] But this identity seems to come to nothing more than an empty Coke bottle and some old documents.

The failure of memory can be linked to the erasure of other traits of character. The mysterious figure of the bomber pilot appears and disappears throughout the book. When his body is found washed ashore on a French beach,[21] it leaves us no clearer about who he might have been. We are given a number of options; there are references to him in a journal on psychiatric illness; he appears in the trailer for a television series that was never made, *Lieutenant 70* and in the sleeve notes of a band called The Him. Rather than the coherence of character, then, we find false leads, alternative stories, rumours and gossip. This is perhaps taken to an extreme in the shadowy figures that accompany the pilot: Kline, Coma and Xero. One of

[20] ibid, 32. [21] ibid, 91.

them, it is not clear which, speaks with the recorded voice of a doll. Talbot is able to hear Coma talk to Kline, but he is never able to remember what they say to each other.[22] Xero's shadow remains when he passes, but is itself a 'cryptic formula'. Ballard's notes refer to them as 'shadows' or projections from Talbot's unconscious. Their meaning appears to escape even the author: they 'materialized', but then 'exited and never returned'.[23]

It would appear that the image demands a new notion of character. Rather than a node or a locus of personality, an inner essence, character has become externalized; a set of traumas where one is linked to wider networks or codes of time and place. We can study this process further: the image enters the very place where we think that we are most ourselves.

The End of the Human: Internalization of the Image: Dis-association and Alienation

Talbot, Tallis, Trabert, Talbert

There are the shifts of the character that begins as Travis, and becomes, in sequence, Talbot, Tallis, Trabert and Talbert. These appear to be metamorphoses of an individual character, a fragmentation of personality through psychosis. Talbot's degeneration is presented as a relationship with images, or rather, the way in which images play out internal emotional processes. The image appears first of all, as something external; merely an object for a spectator. Thus, Talbot is described as seeing Catherine Austin's 'naked body' as a 'bizarre exhibit, its anatomy a junction of sterile cleft and flaccid mons'.[24] Perhaps the most extended engagement with this phenomenon is the fragment entitled 'The Summer Cannibals'.

The leitmotif of the book is figured in the opening image: a woman watching a man through a 'dust covered windscreen'.[25] The characters are un-named, 'he' and 'she', although one of them may be one of Talbot's personae, and 'she' could be Catherine Austin. Perhaps, though, it is essential that they remain un-named; they have disappeared from even the tokens of their own identity. 'He' seems distracted, wandering around 'as if following an invisible contour inside his head'. Human association is not about communication, but alienation, separateness; at best a kind of terminal state where one dies to become something else. Hence the setting of the story in a deserted resort, presumably somewhere on the Spanish coast; a limnic zone where Europe ends and Africa begins; a place bleached by the sun; a place of ash and sand. Bodies tend to become insubstantial. Stepping from the shower, 'her' body becomes 'pink meniscus'.[26] The relationship between the characters is marked by boredom or distraction. Intercourse is an 'elaborate game' or 'some perverse pleasure of his own'.[27] She figures to him as a cipher. To the extent

[22] JG Ballard, *The Atrocity Exhibition* (St Albans: 1970), 31. [23] ibid, 30–31.
[24] JG Ballard, *The Atrocity Exhibition with author's annotation* (London: 1993) 14.
[25] Ballard, *The Atrocity Exhibition*, n 18 above, 65. [26] ibid, 66. [27] ibid, 67.

that she is meaningful it is because she can become an analogy or an algebra that makes her something else: '[p]erhaps an obscene version of her body would form a more significant geometry, an anatomy of triggers?' This obscene version is finally figured as a series of conjunctures of her body with car parts; for example: '(1) the conjunction of aluminised gutter trim with the volumes of her thighs'[28] or '(2) the just and rake of her pubis as she moved into the driving seat'.[29] These positions are numbered because this is an attempt to write pornography as if it were a cockpit drill. The suggestion at the end of the story is that this new obsession has brought the characters closer together. Still distracted in each other's company, she seems to appreciate the erotic potential of her flesh and the hot metal of the car—'deliberately' leaning against the vehicle as he passes her. The concluding image presents her studying images of automobile accidents, with 'her hand in his lap'.[30]

So, this appears to be a dialectical process. It is precisely this externality that appears to connect with some inner meaning: '[t]he concrete landscape of underpass and overpass mediated a more real presence, the geometry of a neural interval, the identity latent within his own musculature'.[31] To understand this strange dialectic, we need to concentrate on the body and the image. We have already been told that the human body itself is the atrocity exhibition, and so it seems to hold a clue to the meaning of this text. The body is experienced as image, as externality, at the same time that the image is internalized, linked to our sexuality as the most intimate expression of the self. Could this peculiar exchange be related to the order of the image?

Rather like the classic Freudian dreamer, Ballard's characters experience the body as disassociation, as fragments:

> His room was filled with grotesque magazine photographs: the obsessive geometry of the underpass, like fragments of her own body; X-rays of unborn children; a series of genital deformations; a hundred close-ups of hands.[32]

Despite the clearly disturbing quality of these images, the juxtaposition of the organic with the inorganic, the diseased and the pathological with the mundane, they appear to gesture beyond themselves. They have been collected together as their conjunction appears to represent something that cannot be articulated. It is precisely this sense of connection that runs obsessively through the image of the car crash, the auto disaster:

> After the police had left they walked for an hour amongst the cars, staring through the steam at the bodies propped up against the fractured windshields. Here he would find his alternate death, the mimetized disasters of Vietnam and the Congo recapitulated in the contours of these broken fenders and radiator assemblies.[33]

This is very detached, objective writing. As far as the narrative is concerned, this scene is experienced from Talbot's viewpoint. Any sympathy for the victim, any

[28] ibid, 69. [29] ibid, 70. [30] ibid, 72. [31] ibid, 14. [32] ibid, 15.
[33] ibid, 17.

sense of tragedy is lacking. But there is also a quality to this writing that is wilfully and disturbingly literary, and this is because the crash is primarily a metaphor. The destruction that can be directly witnessed, the bodies at which one can peer through the steam, represent a wider catastrophe.

Erotics and the Image

The crash is a metaphor, but it is also a reproduction, a re-creation or 'recapitulation' of what was first experienced as an image, a representation of the wars in the Congo and Vietnam. At this point in the narrative, then, the logic of the image is such that the psychotic Talbot can re-experience the image of destruction through the witnessing of the aftermath of an auto-disaster. Essential to the order of the image is this switching between the image as representation, and the image as material affect. The later half of the text is almost exclusively an analysis of this way in which the disaster, the atrocity becomes image again:

> The latent sexual content of the automobile crash. Numerous studies have been conducted to assess the latent sexual appeal of public figures who have achieved subsequent notoriety as auto-crash fatalities, e.g. James Dean, Jayne Mansfield, Albert Camus. Stimulated newsreels of politicians, film stars and TV celebrities were shown to panels of (a) suburban housewives, (b) terminal patients, (c) filling station personnel. Sequences showing auto-crash victims brought about a marked acceleration of pulse and respiratory rates. Many volunteers became convinced that the fatalities were still living, and later used one or other of the crash victims as a private focus of arousal during intercourse with a domestic partner.[34]

The effect of this passage is achieved by playing off the scientific objectivity of the prose and the description of a rigorous experiment with the bizarre nature of the thesis that dead celebrities are sexually arousing. The image is a form of resurrection; or, to be precise, a resurrection as fantasy. In this way the dead become mediated by the image, become material affects that are experienced erotically. Rather than shock us, this does no more than reveal a truth known for centuries: the image, the icon has an affect that communicates with what could either be described as the soul, or that which in contemporary terms makes us most ourselves: our sexuality. Ballard has uncovered the erotics of the image, and the religious associations are not lost on *The Atrocity Exhibition*. Perhaps we need to move to the next phase, the next abomination.

The Crucifixion as Car Crash

The Atrocity Exhibition is rooted in Judaeo-Christian religious imagery, and with mythology in general. In its broadest sense, the Christian moment figures in a genealogy of the image that runs through the entire text. References to classical

[34] Ballard, *The Atrocity Exhibition*, n 18 above, 108.

mythology suggest that this is a self-conscious attempt to write a history of the image. In the first fiction, Catherine Austin is described as 'Eurydice in a used car lot'. The reference is to the descent into the underworld. Likewise, the references to the Styx refer to transitions between life and death. The Christian myth is seen as a re-treatment of this ancient concern with death and rebirth. These myths are completed by the order of the image:

> The planes of their lives interlocked at oblique angles, fragments of personal myths fusing with the deities of the commercial cosmologies.[35]

The interlocking of myths suggests that the role of religion has been taken by the order of the image; or, rather, the society of the spectacle is the most recent working through of the social effects of the image. But Ballard's reading, cleverly, stays at the level of the image, as opposed to attempting to make reference to any order that stands outside this spectacle (there is nothing outside the spectacle anyway). The only possible critique of the order, it may even be impossible to describe it as such, is to take the logic of the image to the ultimate conclusion; to affirm the myth of the resurrection or the new life as a life lived amongst images. This is the theme to which the title 'You and Me and the Continuum' alludes. The continuum is the ongoing society of the spectacle; you and me are only to the extent that we take our identity and our sense of self in an order of images. This is why Talbot, in a final transformation, becomes a kind of Christ figure, or an 'Ur-Christ of the communications landscape'.[36]

The Jurisprudence of the Image

Talbot's becoming Christ is the most difficult moment in *The Atrocity Exhibition*. It accords with one of the logics of the spectacle suggested by Debord, where the most modern is the most archaic.[37] How can we read it? It could represent the final point of his psychosis, the final death of coherent meaning, or it might suggest that this is, in some ways, the moment that the spectacle realizes itself by returning to the most fundamental of images. Talbot becomes his own icon; his own imago dei. It is as if the atrocity exhibition, the spectacle, has become complete by producing a total order where the theological is a fundamental part of the reproduction of the order of the image. Just as the believer identifies with Christ as a means of redemption and salvation, Talbot has become one with the spectacle itself. He has become the image. This is the dramatic summation, where the text and the spectacle become one.

Can we protest? The image has become the ruination of everyday life; the stream of images is now detached from a reality that cannot be re-established. It is as if we have become spectators on something that 'unfolds' as to its own logic—or 'the

[35] ibid, 18. [36] ibid, 17. [37] Debord, n 1 above, 4.

autonomous movement of the non living'.[38] Is there an authentic, non-mediated moment? Ballard's mythology would suggest otherwise: we cannot, through any notion of struggle or opposition, transcend this order. The issue is how do we live our flesh as image; which is to say that we are only just beginning to understand that we need a jurisprudence of the spectacle.

[38] Debord, n 1 above, 3.

L'œuil qui pense: The Emotive as Grounds for the Pensive in Phenomenological Reflection

Claire Valier

C'est l'intime qui veut parler en moi, faire entendre son cri, face à la généralité, à la science.[1]

Roland Barthes, in *La Chambre Claire*, wrote of the photographic image as a memento mori, provoking thoughts about time, death and mortality. 'Memento': this term functions linguistically as an imperative, issuing a command to remember. Considered in this way, the photograph appears to be memorial and commanding. 'L'œuil qui pense' is an invitation to reflect upon that viewing event in which there occurs a sense of being moved to mortal thoughts. The analysis addresses the photograph as a phenomenon, that is, as an experienced object. It is focused on the act of looking at one particular photograph, that of a young prisoner, who was executed soon after the picture was taken. Within this viewing experience, there may arise a sense of felt responsibility. The paper explores the introspective thinking engendered in the encounter with the image. It makes a contribution to that tradition in which the thinking of mortality is a privileged trope for the study of ethics in law.[2] At the same time, it is offered as a contribution to phenomenology, in particular in refutation of the charge of solipsism.

Tied up with the apprehension of this image is a reflexive encounter which is peculiarly compelling. It is not however didactic for photography is, as Barthes seeks to show, pensive rather than instructive. It makes you think. Consider the following statement:

Au fond la Photographie est subversive, non lorsqu'elle effrai, révulse ou même stigmatise, mais lorsqu'elle est *pensive*.[3]

It is not photographs that make the viewer fearful or disgusted which are subversive, or so Barthes says. He instead writes about those photographs that elicit a thoughtful attitude in the spectator. His essay looks into those photographs in

[1] R Barthes, 'Longtemps je me suis couché de bonne heure', in *Le bruissement de la langue* (Paris: 1978/1984) 320.

[2] For instances of this kind of study, see the essays by Douzinas, Diamantides, Gearey and Goodrich in D Manderson, *Courting Death. The Law of Mortality* (London: 1999).

[3] R Barthes, *La Chambre Claire. Note sur la photographie* (Paris: 1980) 65.

which 'something happens' when he views, and thinks of, them. In trying to make sense of this 'something' and the mental process of its happening, Barthes addresses himself to the poignancy with which the photographs strike him. It is possible to read his essay as a pithy demonstration of the idea that in the arresting image, the emotive grounds the pensive. There is also arguably the inchoate notion that the poignancy which gives pause to thought may prompt ethical engagement. The anterior future with which the image of a condemned man confronts the viewer is moving. Barthes considers that in looking at deathbound photographs such as this, he is moved to feel pity. If this is the point at which *La Chambre Claire* arrives, it is also the point at which the essay draws to a close. The potential for pensive spectatorship to be a species of ethical encounter is hence quite speculative, and calls for further elaboration. This paper will make the case that viewing the image of the condemned prisoner can give rise to a sense of responsibility.

The Pensive and the Poignant

Photography, or so Barthes says, is subversive only when it is pensive, when it makes the viewer thoughtful. Photography, this drawing with light, is subversive insofar as the encounter with the image is an experience in which one becomes occupied in thought. Moreover, subversive photography is pensive in its power to elicit states in the viewer of melancholy and worried concern.[4] In this way, one thinks of the sorrowfully thoughtful, the mournfully serious. To explore this pensiveness, Barthes follows the precept in phenomenology of the binding of affected subject and affective object. He takes his own consciousness, and particularly the bodily dimension of this consciousness, as the measure of the object. In this connection, he asks himself: 'Qu'est-ce que mon corps sait de la Photographie'.[5] This question leads Barthes to expand upon the event of being moved by certain photographs. During the course of his reflections, he comes to 'see' that pensiveness, this being thoughtful, does not signify the contemplative, in which the viewer drifts lost in his or her own thoughts. Rather than solipsistic abandonment, the thoughtful signifies a being-preoccupied-with. This being full of thought is one of being concerned about, being worried about, or caring about, the other.

Barthes advises that he set out to explore photography not as a question or theme for analysis, but as a wound. In explanation of this approach he says 'je vois, je sens, donc je remarque, je regarde et je pense'.[6] Here a thought process of seeing, feeling, and hence noticing, looking concernedly, and thinking, unfolds. Barthes muses on those photographs that give him to feel emotion, that are especially meaningful for him, photographs indeed that he says he loves. In this connection

[4] Benjamin wrote of pensiveness as eminently characteristic of the mournful. W Benjamin, *Ursprung des deutsches Trauerspiels* (Berlin: 1928).

[5] Barthes, n 3 above, 22.

[6] ibid, 42.

he speaks of the photograph of one now dead as that which is bruising. He depicts the sense of temporality that unfolds in this viewing experience as something uncanny. Rather than being just troubling, unfamiliar and strange, it is wounding. Indeed Barthes chooses the word *déchirant* (heartrending, harrowing, lacerating) to convey the intensity of this feeling. The book moves through a series of speculations upon photographs that moved Barthes, in that, through temporal disjunction, they ruptured his body into feeling.

Remember the resounding words of Heidegger, 'time produces itself only insofar as man is . . . time fashions itself into a time only as a human, historical being-there'.[7] The essay of Barthes places into question the 'is' and the 'being-there' upon which this important proposition depends. *La Chambre Claire* advances the idea that in photography everything has already happened, will always have already happened. Barthes describes the anterior future that confronts us in a photograph, this future that is already a past. This permits him to offer a vivid sense of photography as spectral and elegiac. Barthes' words draw upon the analysis of imagination and the given-in-its-absence presented by Sartre in *L'imaginaire* (1940). In that text, Sartre writes of his experience in trying to recall the face of an absent friend. He takes a portrait photograph of this friend, Pierre, from a drawer, and thinks about the way in which it enables him to envision (make a mental image of) the man's face. Sartre emphasizes that the imagination of Pierre is a bodily one, an envisaging of his flesh and bone physicality. It is aimed at the Pierre that I can see, touch and hear, although at one and the same time I am also thinking that I cannot really touch him. Looking at the photograph, or so Sartre says, is not to consider it as an image of Pierre. Instead, within the imaginative attitude, in which I represent to myself my friend, he is attained directly. The attention is not directed toward an image, but at an object. The scene depicted in the image is no more than a way for Pierre to appear to me as absent. Hence the picture delivers Pierre, although Pierre is not here. He is thus presented as absent. For Barthes, as for Sartre, there is the notion of absent presence, or the spectral. This corresponds with the movement of a thought that is introspective, a looking inward. The photograph, as analyzed by Barthes the spectator, seems to provoke mortal thoughts. We can note Barthes' description of this provocation in the following passage: 'Je suis le repère de toute photographie . . . pourquoi est-ce que je vis *ici et maintenant*'.[8] I am the reference point, the marker, of every photograph, Barthes says. Being brought back to myself in this way, I am led to question my location, my existence. Viewing images of those now dead engenders a challenging confrontation with one's own mortality.

Pierre, the absent friend of Sartre, is now in Berlin. He is not really here, for he is living in a city some distance away. He is elsewhere. Sartre does consider the case of historical portraits, for which it is known that the person pictured is now deceased. These lead him to comment that the imaginative relationship between

7 M Heidegger, *An Introduction to Metaphysics* (New York: 1953/1961) 71.

8 Barthes, n 3 above, 131.

the portrait and the referent is nothing short of magical.[9] Barthes' text is devoted to the experience of looking at photographs of those no longer alive. They are not here because they are not anywhere, for these are photographs of those now dead. He emphasizes that in looking at the photograph the spectator does not only posit the absence of the object. What comes across more poignantly is that the object once existed, right there where it is seen in the image. The photograph is, for him, a matter of reference, of the powerful sense of the 'that has been'. Nevertheless, this referentiality is nuanced with a pathos that sounds the note of loss and desire. Pathos and melancholy are, for Barthes, the effects of the spectralization of people and things resulting from the photograph's temporality. *La Chambre Claire* hence has as much to say about grief and pain as about absence. If the photograph is spectral, photography is also, as Susan Sontag put it, 'an elegiac art'.[10] The instant it is taken, the moment chronicled by the photographer has passed. Photography, then, inherently memorializes its subjects. According to Sontag, the photographed subject is, merely by being photographed, touched by pathos. Because the camera produces mementoes of that which has passed away, it provokes thoughts of absence, loss, and desire. In place of the magical, Barthes will come to speak of the irrational, and of being crazed with grief.

Pathos, this experience of suffering, which may arouse pity as well as sorrow, brings us to consider the poignant. To convey the notion of that arresting detail in the photograph which, somewhat ineffably, stings, cuts, pierces and wounds the spectator, Barthes turns to the Latin word 'punctum'. This is what he says:

> Un mot existe en latin pour designer cette blessure, cette piqûre, cette marque faite par un instrument pointu; ce mot m'irait d'autant mieux qu'il renvoie aussi à l'idée de ponctuation et que les photos dont je parle sont en effet comme ponctuées, parfois même mouchetées, de ces points sensibles; précisément, ces marques, ces blessures sont des points.[11]

The punctum is the point, the distinguishing detail that jumps out at you. As point, the punctum has the senses of prick, mark and the moment. Barthes says that the punctum is both triggered and something that the spectator adds. As a supplement it is both an addition and what is already there. Also as a supplement, a one too many, the punctum is that which my intellection cannot absorb. It is, for

[9] J-P Sartre, *L'Imaginaire. Psychologie phénoménologique de l'imagination* (Paris, 1940) 38. Similarly, Maurice Merleau-Ponty, in *L'Œil et l'Esprit* called the relationship between time, vision and imagination in the experience of looking at an old painting 'magical'. He writes: 'Le sourire d'un monarque mort depuis tant d'années, dont parlait la *Nausée*, et qui continue de se produire et de se reproduire à la surface d'une toile, c'est trop peu de dire qu'il y est en image ou en essence: il y est lui-même en ce qu'il eut de plus vivant, dès que je regarde le tableau. L' "instant du monde" que Cézanne voulait peindre et qui est depuis longtemps passé, ses toiles continuent de nous le jeter, et sa montagne Saint-Victoire se fait et se refait d'un bout à l'autre du monde, autrement, mais non moins énergiquement que dans la roche dure au-dessus d'Aix. Essence et existence, imaginaire et reel, visible et invisible, la peinture brouille toutes nos categories en déployant son univers onirique d'essences charnelles, de resemblances efficacies, de significations muettes' (M Merleau-Ponty, *L'Œuil et l'Esprit* (Paris: 1964) 35). To the viewer of the painting, or so Merleau-Ponty says, the smile of the king appears not as an image, but 'as itself'.

[10] S Sontag, *On Photography* (London: 1978) 15.

[11] Barthes, n 3. above, 49.

this reason, a blind spot, a momentary opening out onto an ineffable beyond. Here the title of the book, *La Chambre Claire*, comes into play, with the significations of *claire* as light, transparent and lucid. With the punctum there is a mere glimpse of the clair-obscur, a glimpse in the twilight. Pointedly, this is not a book that assumes the transparency of experience. It ultimately disallows any such notion, by infusing the notion of appearance with that of the apparition, or spectre.[12]

What is it that for Barthes makes the image of the prisoner a *photo pointée*, a photograph, that is, from which affect breaks through? Barthes identifies the noeme, which one might call the intentional object of the thinking eye, as the 'this was', as time. He does so when writing about the image of the prisoner. The anterior future, he says, wounds because in it death resides in the future perfect. The photograph tells of a death in the future, yet this is a death that has also already taken place. 'He is dead and he is going to die': the photograph is an image of Lewis Powell, who was executed as a conspirator in the assassination of Abraham Lincoln.[13] For Barthes this phrase, 'he is going to die', evokes the punctum of the photograph, that inexpressible something that arises from the image, pierces and wounds. 'This will be . . . this has been', he adds, explaining that the anterior future declares both that this youth is going to die and that he is already dead. There is, with this photograph, something like what Barthes called the 'impossible performative', the 'I am dead', spoken by Valdemar in Poe's tale.[14] So Barthes, like Benjamin before him, writes of the haunting character of the photograph, and he shudders at its ghostliness. The photograph, according to Barthes, brings the return of the departed. Yet while photography has the power to open a punctum to the realm of the dead, at the same time, the past that the photograph represents cannot be recaptured. While it seems to offer a 'certificate of presence', this is always and only retrospective. So if we ascribe to the photograph a power of testimony, it is as a witness to that which is no more.

Gone Mad for Pity's Sake

Through Barthes' thoughts on photography, he comes to see his introspections as reverberations, as echoes of the other. He begins to envisage his experience of being a pensive spectator as a looking into oneself at the intimations of this other. These reverberations emanate out from the anterior future of the photographic image. They flow out from the 'this was', this 'wound', this emotive affectedness which prompts him to introspection. Looking into himself, he senses the reverberations

12 Arguably, Barthes' notion of experience can support the notion of a punctured, ruptured subject (see M Jay, 'Roland Barthes and the Tricks of Experience' (2001) 14(2) *Yale J of Criticism* 469–476).

13 Powell's alias, 'Paine', was misspelled in the court records and newspaper reports as 'Payne'. After his execution, the authorities were able to verify his identity as Lewis Thornton Powell, aged 21, from Florida. The photograph is held in the collection at the Library of Congress.

14 R Barthes, 'Analyse textuelle d'un conte d'Edgar Poe' in *L'Aventure Sémiologique* (Paris: 1985) 354.

of this lost other. In *A Lover's Discourse*, Barthes defined reverberation (*retentissement*) as the fundamental mode of amorous subjectivity, with the embodied and memorial echoes of images and words, in which 'time is jerked forward . . . and back'.[15] He described the temporality of waiting as integral to, if not definitive of, the existential experience of the lover. In phenomenological terms, the time of this waiting, the time of desire, is the time of both absence and presence, of presence as a memory only. The lover waits, and endures absence and expectation, in a time of suspense flooded with memorial echoes of the beloved. The discourse of the other's absence, Barthes tell us, engenders an unbearable kind of present, in which the lover is 'wedged between two tenses . . . you have gone (which I lament), you are here (since I am addressing you)'.[16] More poignantly perhaps, in *La Chambre Claire* photography figures a present that is past, but one that is continually emanating from out of death.

Looking into the eyes of the photographed subject, he senses a powerful link coming into play. He insists that the photograph is, quite literally, an emanation of the referent, an emanation of past reality. Barthes opens his essay by recalling his astonishment when, looking at a photograph of Jérôme, brother of Napoleon, he suddenly realizes, 'I am looking at eyes that looked at the Emperor'. There is here a certain relay of gazes. Moreover, this is an almost tangible link, for, as Barthes describes it, the gaze of the viewer is seemingly touched by the body of the photographed subject. Light, like an umbilical cord, links the photographed thing to the spectator's gaze:

> La lumière, quoique impalpable, est bien ici un milieu charnel, une peau que je partage avec celui ou celle qui a été photographié.[17]

Light is a carnal medium, fleshly, sensual. It makes of the gaze (*le regard*) a caress. Or rather, Barthes writes of our carnal imagination when viewing these photographs. He is evoking the seemingly reciprocal encounter of the one photographed and the spectator, as an embrace or passionate engagement. The one who looks with that 'eye who thinks', as an I who thinks, is touched by the emanations, and also reaches out to touch.

Barthes writes that he came to realize during the course of his reflections that there is a link between photography, madness and the pangs of love (*la souffrance d'amour*). He then adds that actually this feeling is something broader than love (as eros), and is better described as pity. Pity is the sentiment of affliction that one experiences for the pains and sufferings of others. It is a feeling for the other. Collecting together all of the wounding photographs he writes:

> A travers chacune d'elles, infailliblement, je passais outré l'irréalité de la chose représentée, j'entrais follement dans le spectacle, dans l'image, entournant de mes bras ce qui est mort, ce qui va mourir.[18]

[15] R Barthes, *A Lover's Discourse. Fragments* (London: 1977/2002) 200. [16] ibid, 15.
[17] Barthes, n 3. above,126–127. [18] ibid, 179.

To convey the movement of passing beyond, the transcendence that opens out in the viewing experience, Barthes says that he entered crazily into the spectacle, going into the image, and encircling in his arms what is dead, what is going to die. This is the limit description of the temporal ekstasis experienced in the encounter with the photographic image. This ekstasis is the state of affect directed at what does not exist, but certainly did exist. This is a desperate embrace, because it is a reaching out toward the ungraspable. A notion of the amorous text as that which makes a transcendence of egotism had already been indicated in 'Longtemps je me suis couché de bonne heure'. In this lecture, Barthes rehabilitates pathos as a force of reading. He mentions two literary scenes of mourning, which lead him to allude to a love that is pity or compassion. *La Chambre Claire* can be seen, then, as an amorous text, a lacerating explosion of tenderness. In this lecture, Barthes emphasized that a text of this kind would be nondidactic, by working through the truth of affects rather than the truth of ideas.[19] The pensiveness that arises from the poignant, this introspection, is hence a looking inward that moves out toward the other.

According to Barthes, the ghostly touch of the condamné makes of the gaze a caress. Yet, as Derrida points out, it is a caress that cannot be returned.[20] He interprets Barthes' text to mean that images are haunting because they make almost visible that which nevertheless is intangible. The visible body represented in the image is not visible in flesh and blood. So the spectre looks out at me, and it touches me, but I cannot return this touch. Derrida adds that neither can I meet the gaze of this other who looks out of the picture at me, whereas I am in his sight. I can never exchange a glance with him. I can never look him in the eye, yet the spectre *regards* me (he watches me and he is of concern to me). This non-reciprocal look addresses to me an injunction or command, but the obligation is one I cannot fulfil because of this absence of the other. We look at the dead, reduced to images, and we are looked at by them, but there is no symmetry of gazes, and no possibility of recuperation. So Derrida sees a glimmer of responsibility written there in *La Chambre Claire*. This is an ethics that arises from the poignant.

From Pity to Responsibility

At first Barthes believes that the punctum is amoral, writing: 'Le punctum ne fait pas acception de morale ou de bon goût'.[21] The punctum, he tells us, has no preference, no care, for morality or good taste. The punctum is indifferent towards moral or aesthetic categories, or so he says. Nevertheless, by the end of *La Chambre Claire*

[19] In the words of Barthes, 'puisque son écriture est médiate (il ne presente les idées, les sentiments que par des intermediaries), le Roman, donc, ne fait pas pression sur l'autre (le lecteur); son instance est la vérité des affects, non celle des idées: il n'est donc jamais arrogant, terroriste: selon la typologie nietzschéenne, il se place du côté de l'Art, non de la Prêtrise' (Barthes, 1 above, 324–325).

[20] J Derrida, *Echographies de la Télévision. Entretiens Filmés* (Paris: 1996).

[21] Barthes, n 3 above, 74.

Barthes has come to realize that pity is what is moving in him, as he put it, when he enters into the image. Pity, a feeling for the plight of the other, an affliction for the pains and the suffering of the other, does come across to the reader. What is also perhaps inchoate in Barthes' essay is some sense of responsibility. At one point, he remarks that in looking at the photograph of a man who was 'born a slave', the noeme, the 'that has been', is particularly intense. The power of photography as a certificate of presence that Barthes has wanted to emphasize, he sees as striking in this image. He writes that the photograph certifies that slavery has existed, and not so long ago or so far away. The pensive spectator sees that slavery is not so far from his time, his place, not so far from him. As testimony to a scandal, the image of one who was 'born a slave' might give rise to a sense of moral outrage, rather than of pity. If this photograph, as Barthes says, makes him 'see' slavery as something not so distant from him, this implies some sense of taking responsibility. What, then, of the violence emanating out from the photograph of the prisoner, soon to be executed? What sense of moral outrage might it evoke? What of the responsibility to which one might be moved in looking at it?

Barthes shudders at the anterior future enacted by the photograph of Powell. Faced with the representation of this departed being, he is moved. He shudders at the prospect of imminent death and the retrospective knowledge of it. Like the Milton of 'Lycidas' he is struck by the memory of one who met an untimely death, by the death of one so young, by a death which comes too soon. One might say that in a photograph of a prisoner who was executed, the seemingly paradoxical sense of temporality of which Barthes writes is heightened. Yet something is missing in the text of Barthes, and later that of Derrida. What seems an integral aspect of looking at, being affected by, and thinking about, this image, is thoughts concerning the penal significance of this death. It is a terrible death which is foretold in the photograph of Powell. Barthes and Derrida do not reflect upon the fact that the person looking out from this image is to be, and has been, *condemned to* death, *put to* death. Looking at the photograph of Powell we are not only remembering a death; we are remembering a killing. This death of which the photograph speaks was an ignominious and a violent one. Moreover, it is a death that was imposed in the name of the moral, as the ultimate in moral denunciation.

A future that is already a past . . . For Barthes, the photograph bespeaks a certain horror, for as the living image of a dead thing it certifies that the corpse is alive, as corpse. There is then, in addition to the impossible performative, 'I am dead', the corpse's accusative, 'You killed me', the speaking of an injustice, and a speaking that demands a response from the viewer. My punctum, that which in the photograph makes me shudder, is not, with Barthes, the realization that 'he is going to die', but rather, that 'they are going to kill him'. Perhaps this punctum strikes out at me from the glimpse of the shackled wrists, immobilized by the somewhat incongruously named 'lily irons'. Although Barthes writes that the image of Powell shows him in the death cell, the young man has not yet been tried. Nevertheless, he is already bound for the gallows. He is in custody, a prisoner held aboard a ship, and in the photograph he is seated on the deck, leaning back against the gun turret. During his stay on board the ship, Powell was confined in the chain locker, alone and in the dark. After a few days, an order came to fit canvas hoods over the detained suspects. These were painful to wear, muted the detainees and shrouded them in total darkness. Blind and mute, the hooding foreshadows the absolute silence and darkness of the grave. The photograph of Powell in *La Chambre Claire* codes that terror of law which renders the convict incommunicado. Like many nineteenth century convicts, Powell gave an alias and did not want his photograph taken. Sullen and silent, he vigorously shook his head each time Gardner removed the lens cap, resulting in a blurred and unrecognizable image. The enraged guard struck him. The surviving images bear the mark of this coercion. Powell has not yet been condemned to death, but he is only days away from the execution. He seems already marked by the *condemnare*, with the *damnum* of penalty, as also of damnation and the irredeemable.

The punctum here is a full stop, at the limit of punctuation, a deadly sentence without possibility of reply. The punctuated image of the condemned man is an arresting image insofar as its referentiality, its 'that has been', attests to the certainty of the end to life decided upon and executed by the state. This imposed deadline has been identified by both Dostoevsky and Derrida as the inherent 'cruelty' of the death sentence.[22] Perhaps the responsibility arising from the encounter with this image is also moved by sadness at the deadly moral vision within which the young assassin was framed. The case of Powell was, assuredly, framed in emotional and moral terms, and these were not those of the tender feelings. The most famous instance might be Herman Melville's 'The Martyr'. This poem, 'indicative of the Passion of the people', linked mourning for Lincoln with righteous retribution.[23] The pensive spectator, as a responsive viewer, makes an ethical recoil against the irresponsibilities of capital punishment. Such a recoil is a jolt away from its deadly temporality, fixated on past crimes and killing the future. In this way, ethical engagement is prompted by the spectacle of one of the ultimate failures of the ethical. Barthes wrote of the temporality of waiting as central to amorous subjectivity. Here there is the temporality of belatedness. The photograph certifies that 'this has been'; so the pensive spectator, however moved, arrives on the scene too late to intervene.

[22] F Dostoyevsky, *The Idiot* (Harmondsworth: 1868/1955) 47–48; J Derrida, *Without Alibi* (Stanford: 2002).

[23] 'There is sobbing of the strong
And a pall upon the land;
But the People in their weeping
Bare the iron hand
Beware the People weeping
When they bare the iron hand'

(H Melville, 'The Martyr' in *Selected Poems of Herman Melville* (Carbondale: 1865/1964) 42).

Conclusion: Introspection and Encounter

La Chambre Claire is a text which opens out onto the ethical. Despite the argument of Roughley, it does not embody an affective phenomenology that is solipsistic, and hence meaningless to others.[24] The charge that the text is meaningful only to its author is unconvincing. Barthes' essay works through metonymy, through the resonance of the text in me. Barthes said that metonymy asks: 'De quoi ceci, que j'énonce, peut-il être suivi? Que peut engendrer l'épisode que je raconte?'[25] What can follow, he says, what can be engendered by this that I am saying, this tale that I am telling? Barthes writes about his own viewing encounters as this experiencing subject of the thinking eye/I, this pensive spectator. In doing so he evokes, he calls to mind in the reader, the affect of poignancy, and the way in which the poignant might be said to be stirred by loss. His essay calls the reader to see, feel, look concernedly, and think, in short, to read the text as a pensive spectator. The reader of *La Chambre Claire* must think philosophically. He or she must take the time to dwell introspectively on the arresting image, to respond to the image as that which makes you stop and think. The text leaves open the question of the ethical, and in doing so points the reader to take it forward. The solipsistic thinker however would likely be unconcerned about any but him- or herself. He or she would be irresponsible toward the fate of the other, uncaring and unresponsive. Such a reading of *La Chambre Claire* is unsupportable. As an amorous text it moves beyond amour-propre, provoking the pensive spectator to envisage the viewing event as an encounter.

[24] N Roughley, 'The Post-Poststructuralist Attitude: Remarks on the Affective Phenomenology of Roland Barthes's *Camera Lucida*' (1994) 24 *New Formations* 108–121.

[25] Barthes, n 1 above, 314–315.

PART IV

MUSIC

Doing Time and Doing It in Style

Milner S Ball

My subject here is three forms of music by, for, or about the imprisoned. My larger, background concern is prison's image in popular culture, a concern first prompted by pants rather than by music.

My son-in-law teaches in the lower grades of a Georgia public school. Most of his students are African-Americans. The boys sometimes arrive for class wearing baggy, beltless pants. Inevitably, the pants slide down, and, when an unacceptable length of cleavage comes into view, he requires the offender to snap on a pair of the suspenders that he keeps at hand and that students view as a shaming device. My son-in-law believes and others confirm that the style comes from prison where, in certain cases, inmates are forbidden to wear belts with their pants and laces in their shoes.[1]

The style has currency among white students at the University of Georgia. I recently saw an undergraduate on his way to the Main Library pause to examine his beltless pants. He found them unfashionably high and gave them a downward tug, to mid-thigh. But then he had to turn back from the library. His legs were too restricted to mount the entrance stairs.

The clothing as well as the style is in fashion. One company, Prison Blues, offers a full line of prison clothes. And prison design, too, is popular. One hot item is, remarkably, the prison toilet—stainless steel, all one part, no lid, no fold-down seat—offered by Acorn Engineering in what they describe as their 'Neo-Metro collection of repurposed prison fixtures in response to popular demand'.[2] Paul Wright, a prisoner and the editor of Prison Legal News, objects that such 'commodification of prisons . . . has contributed to normalizing the abnormal'.[3]

A white undergraduate's attempt to make a cool fashion statement with beltless pants trivializes prison and in doing so hides its violence, but otherwise the style has little consequence for the wearer. The black children in my son-in-law's class present a different, more complex case. They may only be having some fun with their falling pants. But they may also be rehearsing an assumed future of crime and

[1] For confirmation, see, eg, Andrew Octopus, 'Off the Wall' (16 August 2002) 1 www.altrap.com/articles 1; Paul Wright, 'The Cultural Commodification of Prisons' (2000) 27 *Social Justice* 15, 18.

[2] 'In the Modern World' (June 2003) *Dwell* 28, 30. See also www.neo_metro.com/toilets.htm.

[3] Wright, 'Cultural Commodification', n 1 above, 16.

punishment—making imprisonment normal in the non-trivializing sense that it is what they and others expect will happen to them. Last year, when America's prison population first rose above two million, some 12 per cent of all African-American men between the ages of 20 and 34 were incarcerated. It is calculated that 28 per cent of African-American men will be incarcerated at some point in their lives.[4] If prisoners become popular role models and imprisonment a normal rite of passage, statistics may translate into the world of black schoolboys as anticipation, a self-fulfilling expectation encouraged by popular culture.

Gangsta Rap is an animating element in that culture. I would not argue that music and verse cause crime or that they warrant governmental censorship. However, they do have effects, whether measurable or immeasurable. What follows is a description of three forms of prison music and their function. Prison Songs enabled prisoners to survive. Outlaw Country enhances entertainer image and sales but also provides some representative voice to the imprisoned. Gangsta Rap markets an image, sells recordings, and gives expression to survival and death on the streets as well as in prison, but in some of it there is scant distance between the art and the crime that is its subject.

Prison Songs

By Prison Songs I do not mean excerpts from *Fidelio*. I mean outdoor songs of the kind that black prisoners sang on southern prison farms and that were recorded in the field by John and Alan Lomax beginning in the 1930s.[5] Those farms were a continuation of slavery by other means. The work was long, steamy, hot, and hard, and prisoners were 'humiliated, bullied, beat, often tortured, and sometimes murdered'.[6] But they sang. They sang together to endure.

The music they developed was confined to prison. Prisoners who were released left the songs behind and did not sing them outside. Prison songs never emerged in popular culture.[7] An early scene in the recent hit film *O Brother, Where Art Thou* portrays a southern chain gang accompanied by a Lomax-recorded Prison Song on

[4] Fox Butterfield, 'Prison Rates Among Blacks Reach a Peak Report Finds', *New York Times*, 7 April 2003, 11, col 5.

[5] For an account of the recordings and the songs, see Alan Lomax, *The Land Where the Blues Began* (New York: 1993) 256–313. Selections of the recordings are available on compact discs: *Prison Songs*, 2 vols. (Cambridge, Mass: 1997) (The Alan Lomax Collection) (Rounder CD 1714–15). Commentary on and transcriptions of Prison Songs by a subsequent field recorder are to be found in Bruce Jackson, *Wake Up Dead Man* (with a New Preface, Athens, Ga: 1999) (includes a selected Prison Song discography).

[6] Lomax, *The Land*, n 5 above, 257. See also David Oshinsky, *Worse Than Slavery: Parchman Farm and the Ordeal of Jim Crow Justice* (New York: 1996).

[7] Alan Lomax persuaded Doc Reese, long after he had served his prison term, gone to school and become a preacher, to assemble some of his old buddies for the Newport Folk Festival, where, Lomax reports, they presented their 'work chants to an astonished youth audience that had come to hear Bob Dylan and the Kingston Trio'. Lomax, *The Land*, n 5 above, 287. He also says that, after one of his

the soundtrack. The film rendered the chain gang comic and quickened the popularity of other 'roots' music it features, but it did not make Prison Songs either funny or popular. The stark beauty and raw power of that music still bears the forbidding marks of its original context's brutality.

Men brought songs with them when they entered the prison farms—levee hollers, work songs, blues, and the like—and these became material for development inside. Each prison farm's music had a distinctive style influenced by its particular store of imported music, its array of long-term residents with varying abilities in performance, and its own conditions of work. In general the fundamental subject of the songs was enduring hell, but the particular topics ran from women and sex, to travel and flight, to despair, to coded commentary on the guards.[8]

Prison Songs ended with racial desegregation. The songs had their matrix in the rhythms and movements of the black prisoners, and white prisoners did not sing with them. When the scholar Bruce Jackson asked why, a black prisoner explained: 'The way they work, they works a lot different. The way we do it, we do it by time. We have a steady rock.'[9]

A prisoner's 'holler' was his own and functioned as a 'personal musical signature'.[10] It was sung solo, and others paid their respects by not joining in or interrupting. Hollers had developed in the construction of massive levees along the Mississippi River where men worked with mules and wheelbarrows in conditions scarcely less horrific than those of prison.[11] A holler was an individual's wailing appeal to the heavens or an expression of hurt and weariness or an entertainment of co-workers.[12]

About communal Prison Songs, Lomax remarks that 'the old comforting, healing, communal spirit of African singing cooled the souls of the toiling, sweating prisoners and made them, as long as the singing lasted, consolingly and powerfully one'.[13] Community structure was part condition for and part product of the singing. Work squads chose their song leaders,[14] the complex forms of the music provided participation for all, and the tempo set the pace for the joint labour.

Jackson points out that group labour done with communal singing was protective for if all worked in chorus no individual could be singled out and 'punished simply because he was weaker than his fellows'. And, as he also notes, the singing

recordings was released, it was used without attribution to orchestrate an Alvin Ailey dance titled *Work Song Ballet*. Ibid, 272. There was some limited commerce in Prison Songs in the repertoire of popular black performers like Paul Robeson and Harry Belafonte. See Jackson, *Wake Up*, n 5 above, xix–xx.

[8] See Jackson, *Wake Up*, n 5 above, 37–39; Lomax, *The Land*, n 5 above, 263–267, 277.

[9] Jackson, *Wake Up*, n 5 above, 18.

[10] Lomax, *The Land*, n 5 above, 232.

[11] ibid, 212.

[12] Two recordings of hollers are available on compact disc: 'Hollers', *Prison Songs*, n 5 above, Vol II, No 11.

[13] Lomax, *The Land*, n 5 above, 258.

[14] A prisoner explained to Lomax that 'it take the man with the most understandin . . . [M]aybe he ain't got no voice for singin, but he's been cooperating with the peoples so long an been on the job so long, till he know just exactly how it should go.' Ibid, 262–263.

constituted a resisting claim by the prisoners: it was distinctively *their* music and put 'the work into the worker's framework rather than the guards'.[15]

Chopping weeds with hoes called for one type of song. Men formed a long line across a field and moved forward at the same pace. The chosen leader needed a strong tenor voice that would carry over the distance. There was less at stake in leading because the work was uniform and non-hazardous, but the beat of the music had to accommodate both the rhythm of raising and lowering long-handled hoes and the long hours of unbroken, repetitive work—'if you're flatweeding, you're liable to flatweed from here to yonder—all day long'.[16]

Lomax describes a particular flat-weeding song as 'composed of many intertwined parts improvised by the singers joining and leaving the chorus as they pleased, stroking in tones, part phrases, and harmonies just where they were needed to round out the blend'. And in the same song 'the leader and chorus parts overlapped rhythmically as the chorus came in under the leader and replaced him until he was ready with his next line. He, in his turn, overlapped with the chorus, as they held their last notes, thus creating moments of polyrhythm.'[17]

More complex music and dance were involved when several men using sharp, double-bladed axes brought down a single large tree. A crew of four, for example, would make two cuts on opposite sides of the tree. The two men standing at 12 and 6 o'clock would strike the opposite cuts at the same time with righthanded blows, followed by the two standing at 3 and 9 o'clock striking lefthanded. 'You take four . . . around a tree', one prisoner explained, 'they'll sing it down, they'll sing it down in harmony, they'll sing and cut. . . .'[18]

One such song Lomax recorded, 'Early in the Mornin', employs tricky syncopation, word-splitting, and improvised rhythmic breaks opposed to the main beat, with the whole organized, he says, on 'a vertical model' that allows simultaneous parts and space for all contributions and interjections. It is, he adds, a style 'difficult for Europeans . . . to perform or even to perceive'.[19]

Prison songs were nurturing expressions of prisoners' humanity. Those who sang them, Lomax says, 'looked death in the face everyday, suffered degradation far more painful than death, and created songs of matchless power to keep their hearts alive'.[20] Blues, too, was sung in southern prisons, notably by the great guitar master and blues man, Huddie Ledbetter, better known as Lead Belly, the prison name bestowed on him in tribute to his endurance in field labour. He sang his way out. He walked free when his song 'Governor Pat Neff', written around 1924, won from the Texas governor a commutation of 23 years from his sentence for murder

[15] Jackson, *Wake Up*, n 5 above, 30.

[16] ibid, 25 (quoting an unnamed prisoner).

[17] Lomax, *The Land*, n 5 above, 260. A recording of the example, 'O Rosie', is available on *Prison Songs*, n 5 above, Vol II, No 10.

[18] Jackson, *Wake Up*, n 5 above, 26 (quoting an unnamed prisoner).

[19] Lomax, *The Land*, n 5 above, 269. Lomax provides a transcription of the song, 'Early in the Mornin', with helpful commentary at ibid, 268–272, and his recording of the song is to be found at *Prison Songs*, n 5 above, Vol I, No 13.

[20] Lomax, *The Land*, n 5 above, 285.

and assault.[21] Prison Songs never gained release for anyone who sang them. They never became popular. And they never made prison appealing.

Outlaw Country

Country Music has many sources, including levee hollers, jazz, gospel, western swing, and the ballads and lullabies of England and Scotland; and it comes in a variety of forms from bluegrass and folk to honky tonk and the Nashville Sound. At heart it is, in Nicholas Dawidoff's description, 'simply worded, string-driven, melodic music concerned with subjects that are both quotidian and universal: faith, love, family, work, heartbreak, pleasure, sin, joy, and suffering'.[22] The Country star Emmylou Harris says it 'deals with issues that everyone from a blue-collar worker to a Yale literature professor experiences'.[23]

Country Music's first records were cut in the early 1920s,[24] and its centre of gravity was long located in the Grand Ole Opry, broadcast live on Saturday nights from the Ryman Auditorium in Nashville, Tennessee. Hank Williams became its first superstar at the age of 25, and he died of a drug overdose in 1953 at the age of 29 on the back seat of a Cadillac, in the middle of the night, in transit from one gig to another. Rock and Roll drained away much of Country Music's audience and money, and in response the industry went easy listening with the Nashville Sound that changed Country's character. It removed the twang, hard edges, and distinctiveness and produced what came to be known as 'ear candy'. It also recaptured some of the lost market share.

Jimmie Rodgers, who was born in 1897 and died in 1933, is the generally acknowledged father of Country. It is said that his adoring audience found in him 'someone who thought what they thought, felt what they felt, and sang about the common person honestly and beautifully'.[25] This identification with common people continues to be a singular mark of Country's stars for whom fans are, as the *New York Times* recently noted, 'like extended family'.[26]

[21] See, Kip Lornell, 'Lead Belly's Life', (liner notes) 1, 3 in Lead Belly, *Gwine Dig A Hole To Put the Devil In* (Cambridge, Mass: 1991) (Recorded by John and Alan Lomax) (Rounder CD 1045).

[22] Nicholas Dawidoff, *In the Country of Country* (New York: 1997) 310.

[23] ibid, 288.

[24] Dawidoff gives 1923 as the date of the first record's production. Ibid, 12. David Vinopal gives the first record's date as 1922 in 'Beginnings: Hillbilly, Old-Time, and String-Band Music' in V Bogdanov, C Woodstra and ST Erlewhine (eds), *All Music Guide [AMG]* (4th edn, San Franscisco: 2001) 701.

[25] David Vinopal, 'Jimmie Rodgers,' in *AMG*, n 24 above, 700.

[26] '[U]nlike rock and rap celebrities, [country stars] tend to bring their fans into their personal lives, to introduce them to their wives and children, and even to let them into their homes.' Neil Strauss, 'The Pop Life: Lord, They Hate To See Her Go', *New York Times*, 21 May 2003, B3, col 4 (about the funeral of June Carter Cash, wife of Johnny Cash and member of the legendary, old-time music family, the Carter Family. Johnny Cash died four months later.) This devotion to the common person has led country performers to think of Bruce Springsteen as a fellow practitioner of the art. Dawidoff, n 22 above, 310–311. His music is 'country', Emmylou Harris says, 'even if it doesn't have a pedal steel guitar'. Ibid, 289.

The commoner character of the music and the musicians helps to explain Country's feeling for prisoners. Country's first big hit was 'Prisoner's Song' in 1924.[27] Then, beginning in the 1970s, artists like Johnny Cash, Merle Haggard, Willy Nelson, and Waylon Jennings were identified as 'Outlaw Country' as much for their opposition to the Nashville Sound as for their personae, their alcohol-and-drug-laced lifestyle, and the fact that some of them had been incarcerated, an asset among fans who love prodigal sons and losers.

Cash, a major influence in Country from his early recordings in the mid-1950s until near the end of his life in September, 2003, was one of the 'Outlaws' who had been jailed—in his case, seven one-night stays for episodes arising out of his drug addictions.[28] Haggard is another. He escaped incarceration 17 times before his twenty-first birthday but was at last held for two years and nine months in San Quentin, a maximum security prison.[29] Both men thrived on voices with character and lived-in faces.[30]

In contrast to Prison Songs, Outlaw Country's prison music is not done by prisoners in prison to make life inside endurable. It is characteristically done by outsiders looking in, or by former insiders looking back in. The conditions of modern imprisonment are not conducive to inmate song, especially not to group singing in the prisons that emphasize isolation and punishment and those where labour tends to be individual and machine-driven.[31]

Some prisons allow instruments, bands and gospel choruses. Merle Haggard reports that his prison allowed an evening music hour in the cells. 'More than half of the convicts . . . were like me', he says, 'they wanted to be musicians. And during that hour, you could hear saxophones, guitars, banjos, and verbal fights and misunderstandings, along with several instruments I couldn't define.'[32] The music done inside by insiders during music hour was a cacophonous time of everyone-for-himself with each making whatever noise he wished. Perhaps only the American composer Charles Ives could have loved it.

Outlaw Country adopts the voice of the prisoner, and, when its stars take their road shows into prison, it can also affirm prisoners' personhood, inspire them and offer some hope of rehabilitation[33]—even if only indirectly. Haggard was an

[27] Vinopal, 'Beginnings', n 24 above, 701.

[28] Johnny Cash, *Man in Black* (Grand Rapids: 1975) 130.

[29] Dawidoff, *In the Country*, n 22 above, 249; Merle Haggard and Tom Carter, *Merle Haggard's My House of Memories* (New York: 1999).

[30] 'It takes a dark side to sing about people whose lives are blasted by misery, gin, and faithlessness with the kind of pathos you hear in the voices of Johnny Cash . . . and Merle Haggard.' Dawidoff, *In the Country*, n 22 above, 196.

[31] For recent, critical examination of the role of Christian theology in the history of this emphasis in penology, see Muriel Schmid, '"The Eye of God": Religious Beliefs and Punishment in Early Nineteenth-Century Prison Reform' (2003) 59 *Theology Today* 546.

[32] Haggard, *My House*, n 29 above, 126.

[33] In an explanatory statement to accompany a recording from one of his prison concerts, Johnny Cash writes, apparently addressing first the prisoners and then the reader: 'You know you're here to stay, and for some reason, you'd like to stay alive—and not rot. . . . So . . . I have brought my show to Folsom [Prison]. Prisoners are the greatest audience an entertainer can perform for. We bring them a

inmate at San Quentin when Cash did a concert there in 1958. Cash was in bad shape and bad voice.[34] Haggard says the rough performance convinced him that 'I could do whatever he was doing. . . . It gave everybody the feeling that if they could learn to play *Folsom Prison Blues* maybe they could stay out of prison.'[35] Outlaw Country concerts are a hit with prisoners. When one Country show was scheduled on a bill that included a stripper act, the audience paid the great tribute of 'digging that bad old country music more than the naked girls'.[36]

Prisoners are not the audience producers have in mind when the concerts are recorded. Prisoners and the background prison noises—clanging doors and individual prisoners summoned by number and called away—ornament the 'reality' performance and validate the image of the Outlaw performer. Prison is a big seller outside. Two of Cash's most popular albums are prison concerts, one in Folsom and the other in San Quentin. (Such successes caused the 'Live At . . .' phenomenon to spread—even to England which offers several such albums, including—is it not wonderful?—*Live at Chelmsford Top Security Prison* by The Sex Pistols, released in 1990.)

The highly-charged atmosphere of *Johnny Cash at Folsom Prison* rides on the gravity of the voice[37] and the plain, essential components of Country: a narrative line, an uncomplicated progression of chords, a straightforward string band, and the rhythm driven by plucking the bass string of a guitar with the thumb or a pick, and then strumming the chord down and up—also known as *Boom*-chick-a, *Boom*-chick-a.[38] Cash had by then adopted the wardrobe and signature role of the Man in Black—'for perpetual mourning and perpetual sympathy with humanity's suffering'[39]—and there is in the Folsom performance something of his contemplation of 'the darkest, most violent human impulses with realism and remorse' and of his difficult 'struggle against sin'.[40]

Trains and their lonesome whistles make frequent runs through Country songs as they do through the old Prison Songs, and a train opens the featured track on the

ray of sunshine in their dungeon and they're not ashamed to respond ...' Johnny Cash, 'Folsom Prison Blues' in *Songs of Johnny Cash* (New York: 1970) 226, 227. BB King, the great blues musician who also has a *Live at San Quentin* album (Santa Monica, 1990; remastered 2001), is co-founder with the lawyer F Lee Bailey of The Foundation for the Advancement of Inmate Rehabilitation and Recreation.

[34] Cash's father was present at another of his prison concerts when he was in better performing condition. Cash said he was 'proud that he could see me do a totally sober concert'. Cash, *Man in Black*, n 28 above, 158. Sobriety had been a great rarity for Cash.

[35] Merle Haggard (liner notes), in Johnny Cash, *Johnny Cash at San Quentin* (New York, 2000; originally recorded 1969) 6–7 (referring to a 1958 concert).

[36] Haggard, *My House*, n 29 above, 141.

[37] 'It was the voice that compelled attention from the start . . . the unimpeachable integrity and originality of its sound—but it was the conviction *behind* the voice that allowed Johnny Cash to create a body of work as ambitious in its scope as it was homespun in its sound.' Peter Guralnick, 'Everyman, With a Voice', *New York Times*, 14 September 2003, 11, col 2 (Op-Ed).

[38] See Happy Traum, 'Picking with Johnny Cash' in Johnny Cash, *Songs of Johnny Cash* (New York: 1970) 230–231.

[39] Jon Pareles, 'The Line Cash Walked', *New York Times*, 13 September 2003, A17, col 1 (Arts & Ideas).

[40] ibid, A22.

Folsom album, 'Folsom Prison Blues', that, 'with its bare-bones realism, . . . distilled the sepulchral grimness that often seemed to engulf Mr. Cash':[41] 'I hear a train a comin; it's rollin' 'round the bend . . .'[42]

A later line of the song is: 'I shot a man in Reno, just to watch him die'. Cash's in-your-face-attitude, together with the chillingly enthusiastic response the line draws from the Folsom audience cuts through any locomotive melancholy. Steve Earle, a kind of Country Outlaw of the second generation, says about Cash at Folsom: 'He was BADASS. He wore a lot of black and he sang about murder and dope and adultery and ghosts. He had genuine attitude.'[43] Attitude is prominent, too, in the recording of the San Quentin performance.[44] If there is fellow-feeling, shared misery, and joint rage artfully expressed in Cash's attitude, it is not constitutive of community as the old Prison Songs were.

Merle Haggard has an album titled *Prison*. It is one of four in a collection of his work that includes albums entitled *Drinkin'*, *Hurtin'*, and *Cheatin'*. An advertisement urges: 'Collect all four and enjoy the pain'.[45] Dawidoff observes that 'melancholy music makes Haggard very happy'.[46] One of the *Prison* album's songs is 'Sing Me Back Home'. It is the plea of a prisoner on being led to his execution: 'Sing me back home with a song I used to hear . . . Sing me back home before I die.'[47] The pain in the song is not tragic, but it can be heard with melancholic pleasure. (I plead guilty. I have for years taken pleasure from Cash and Haggard and their prison music.) For Haggard, the pleasure does not necessarily put a false face on prison because it did him some good. It was, he said, 'as beneficial to me as the army is for some people. I was twenty and full of piss and vinegar, with no intention of doing anything right. . . . God . . . threw me in prison I think to slow me down.'[48] Dawidoff says that Haggard's 'years in prison, like so many of his other experiences, turned out to be so much research'.[49] I know of no country musician who, like Lead Belly, sang his way out of prison, but Merle Haggard's music did win him a pardon long after he had served his time from then Governor Ronald Reagan of California.[50]

But some prisons are modern versions of the hellishness of the old southern prison farms. In his book *A Place to Stand*, the poet Jimmy Santiago Baca provides an unblinking account of the chaos and brutality that accompanied his own imprisonment.[51] In these instances, the popular, pleasurable voice Outlaw Country creates, like stylish prison wear and high design toilets, lends prison a misleading cachet.

[41] Stephen Holden, 'Johnny Cash, Country Music Bedrock, Dies at 71', *New York Times*, 13 September 2003, 1, col 2.

[42] The recording can be found at Johnny Cash, 'Folsom Prison Blues', *Johnny Cash at Folsom Prison*, No 1 (New York, 1999; originally recorded 1968).

[43] Steve Earle, in ibid, (liner notes), 15.

[44] A good example is to be heard at Johnny Cash, 'San Quentin', n 35 above, No 8.

[45] Merle Haggard, *Prison* (Nashville, 2001; digitally remastered) (album cover).

[46] Dawidoff, *In the Country*, n 22 above, 252.

[47] Haggard, *Prison*, n 45 above, No 2.

[48] Haggard, *My House*, n 29 above, 126.

[49] Dawidoff, *In the Country*, n 22 above, 257.

[50] Haggard, *My House*, n 29 above, 146.

[51] Jimmy Santiago Baca, A *Place to Stand* (New York: 2001).

Steve Earle belongs to the generation that follows Cash and Haggard. He was nurtured by their music and, like them, had personal experience of incarceration when a drug addiction led to his arrest and sentencing for heroin possession. Earle has taken a turn toward the non-melancholic. His 2002 album *Jerusalem* presents a series of sharp-eyed reflections on contemporary American society. In his song 'The Truth' prison is both subject for protest and material for larger critique. A little of the old *Boom*-chick-a can still be made out underneath a prominent, raw, penetrating banjo, but the listener takes no melancholic pleasure from the reflections of the prisoner who speaks:

> [I]t doesn't matter what you do
> 'Til you gaze in the mirror with an eye that's true
> And admit that what scares you is the me in you.[52]

The song is a departure from Outlaw Country's basic prison repertoire. It does not popularize imprisonment. It is the voice of political dissent.

Gangsta Rap

The art and culture we know as hip-hop—the sneakers, sweatshirts and baggy pants, the breakdancing, the graffiti, and the rhymes and rhythms of rap—began in the early 1970s in the dances and block parties of the South Bronx, New York. Perhaps these were 'celebrations of survival' reflecting 'what the people wanted and needed—escape'.[53] Perhaps hip-hop was an invasion rather than an escape, an invasion fought with boom boxes and graffiti on subways, sidewalks, and walls in a 'a defiant act signalling African-American and Latino youth's reclamation of public space'.[54] Perhaps the action was something else altogether: 'hip-hoppers joined pleasure and rage while turning the details of their difficult lives into craft and capital'.[55]

In any event hip-hop soon had purchase among young people in urban centres across the nation—Miami, Atlanta, Houston, and California. And then it broke through the boundaries of location, class, race and ethnicity. Now, according to a recent *New York Times* report, 'hip-hop is the dominant youth culture of the land . . .'.[56] That may understate the case. A more recent and more enthusiastic *New York Times* piece floridly proposes: 'The history of style in the later 20th Century . . . is substantially the history of hip-hop whose effects on the aural texture of contemporary life are more than matched by its influence on how, at a

[52] Steve Earle, *Jerusalem* (New York: 2002) No 7.

[53] Jeff Chang, 'Stakes Is High', *The Nation*, 13/20 January 2003, 17.

[54] William Eric Perkins, 'Preface' in William Eric Perkins, *Droppin' Science* (Philadelphia: 1996) vii.

[55] Michael Eric Dyson, *Between God and Gansta Rap* (Oxford: 1996) 177.

[56] Frank Rich, 'Tupac's Revenge on Bennett', *New York Times*, 18 May 2003, 1, col 2, and 22, col 6 (Arts and Leisure).

certain cultural moment, people around the globe decided they wanted to be seen'.[57] The latter article points out that hip-hop, including 'prison-style jumpsuits', now reigns on the runways and in the audiences of Parisian and Milanese couture houses.[58] All the hype may portend a forthcoming end to hip-hop's season.

Rap has its own, independent share in hip-hop's present dominance of the scene. 'Rap', it is reported, 'is now a $1.6 billion engine that drives the entire music industry and flexes its muscle across all entertainment platforms.'[59] Rap may wind down with hip-hop.[60] Post 9/11 needs have awarded sales success to country and religious music, especially 'Christian Music', which, according to one report, 'is the only format that has increased sales in the past year'.[61] Whatever its future, Rap's roots may reach deep into a sustaining past of African-American music and tales and of African call-and-response chants.[62]

Gangsta Rap is a subcategory of rap. One of my students carefully instructed me that 'most rap is not gangsta rap. Most rap is simply story telling and imagination. Some people rap about their experience in an extremely oppressed neighborhood and how they got out. Many rap about the status that rap music has given them, but this is not gangsta rap.'[63]

Gangsta Rap originated in the gang life of Los Angeles and was typified first by the group NWA and then by Tupac Shakur, Dr Dre, and Snoop Doggy Dogg. It is expressive of rage, misogyny, and other violence, including violence involving police and violence in internecine struggles between rival rappers. The warning label on the cover of Gansta Rap albums—'explicit lyrics'—is a frail effort at description of what lies within. The lyrics have been the subject of congressional hearings and moral crusades. One crusader, William Bennett, referred to them as 'the filth, sewage and mindless bloodletting of the popular entertainment industry'.[64]

In the Vietnam-era case of *Cohen v California*, in which the Supreme Court of the United States found that the phrase 'fuck the draft' printed on a young man's jacket was constitutionally protected speech, Justice John Marshall Harlan calmly observed: 'One man's vulgarity is another man's lyric'.[65] One challenge to discernment of the lyric in Gangsta Rap's vulgarity—in addition to the mysogny and other violence—is the use of the 'N-word'. It is generally spelled and pronounced in Gangsta with an ending 'a' or 'ah' (Nigga) as compared to the racial slur ending

[57] Guy Trebay, 'Taking Hip-Hop Seriously', *New York Times*, 20 May 2003, C14, col 1 (Fashion).

[58] ibid.

[59] Chang, 'Stakes is High', n 53 above, 17.

[60] Another *New York Times* article says that 'by 2003, rap music was a globe-spanning, middle-aged, multi-billion-dollar concatenation of thick-tongued rhythms, thuggish boasts and overproduced rap-R & B fusion.' David Samuels, 'The Vanished Writing on the Subway Wall', *New York Times*, 11 May 2003, Section 2, 17 col 1 (Arts & Leisure). (The *Times* responds to Rap, as it does to Hip-Hop, with a certain excitement of its normally reserved writing style.)

[61] Lauren Dandler, 'Holy Rock "N" Rollers', *The Nation*, 13/20 January, 2003.

[62] See, eg, Robin Kelley, 'kickin' reality, kickin' ballistic: gansta rap and postindustrial los angeles', in Perkins, *Droppin' Science*, n 54 above, 117, 119; Perkins, 'the rap attack: an introduction', ibid, 1.

[63] Kevin Gooch, e-mail of 6 March 2003.

[64] Quoted in Rich, 'Tupac's Revenge,' n 56 above, 1.

[65] 403 US 15, 25 (1971).

'er'. There are unresolved tensions in use of the word.[66] Does it exploit or embrace a vicious stereotype, extend it or give it a new context? Is it an expression of self-hatred or of black pride? Is it a simple, black neighbourhood term? Some of my black students use the word but heartily endorse my not doing so: it is not for a white Southerner but is for them and for rappers to use.[67] In 'Live at the O.M.N.I.', for example, an Atlanta group, Goodie Mob, delivers, over a typical, machine-driven beat, the lines: 'One Million Niggaz Inside . . . / You can't break me even though you try/ One Million Niggaz Inside.'[68]

The 'inside' is a reference to imprisonment. Crime and prison are prominent on the surface of Gangsta. The albums sport showy production labels like Death Row and Murder, Inc, and a gangster image is as important to rappers' authenticity and success as it is to Outlaw Country's. Some rappers are 'studio gangstas' only, and, as Robin Kelley says, much of the violence in the lyrics is nothing more than boasting in which the imagery may be metaphor aimed at competitor rappers.[69] Rappers' competitive battles with each other are sometimes fought on mix tapes like those of DJ Kay Slay's and are sold on the streets and the web.[70]

To some degree, certainly in original Gangsta, the violence in the lyrics is not metaphorical. It is an account of neighbourhood happenings and is delivered with what has been described as 'prophetic rage' at the conditions there.[71] A track from Ice Cube's album*AmeriKKKa's Most Wanted* opens with an excerpt of NBC TV news reader Tom Brokaw introducing a story about Los Angeles as having become, after a year of 453 murders, 'the gang capital of the nation'.[72] Another Ice Cube number on that album, 'Drive By', features the sound of a car, a car radio, gun-loading, and a drive-by shooting.[73]

In the same artist's '24 Wit an L'—24 years old with a life sentence—the reference is not to a prison farm or a penitentiary but to the comparably oppressive streets of a Los Angeles ghetto. A young man feels permanently sentenced to his neighbourhood: 'L.A. is like a jail cell/And I got 24 wit an L./"Get in that cell, nigger."'[74]

Violence, crime and prison may be boasts or metaphors or descriptions of the neighbourhood, but they are also facts of Gangsta Rap itself. Rappers' battles are fought on the streets as well as on the mix tapes. Tupac Shakur was murdered in 1996, and the following year, Biggie Small, a rival rapper suspected of involvement,

66 See Randall Kennedy, *Nigger: The Strange Career of a Troublesome Word* (New York: 2002).

67 The Gangsta Rapper Ice Cube made the same point: 'Look, when we call each other nigger it means no harm . . . But if a white person uses it, it's something different, it's a racist word.' Kelley, 'kickin reality', n 54 above, 156, n 54.

68 Goodie Mob, 'Live at the Omni', *Soul Food* (Atlanta, 1995), No 11.

69 Kelley, 'kickin' reality', n 54 above, 121.

70 Lola Ogunnaike, 'Hip-Hop's One-Man Ministry of Insults', *New York Times*, 4 May 2003, Section 2, p1 (Arts & Leisure).

71 Dyson, *God and Rap*, n 55 above, 16.

72 Ice Cube, 'Endangered Species (Tales from the Darkside)' (featuring Chuck D), *AmeriKKKa's Most Wanted* (Hollywood, 2003; 1990), No 17.

73 ibid, 'The Drive-By', No 12.

74 Ice Cube, '24 Wit an L', *Bootlegs And B Sides* (Hollywood, 1994).

was himself killed. 50 Cent has survived nine gunshot wounds and one stabbing. The New York police established a special six-person squad, the 'hip-hop cops', in the wake of a rapper's trial. The squad is presently attempting to solve the 2002 murder of DJ Jam Master Jam. And ties between the industry and the drug trade are under investigation.[75] One Gangsta Rapper describes his vocation as 'getting paid and staying alive'.[76]

Crime and prison are a reality close to rappers, and their treatment of these subjects is diverse and complex. Some Gangsta is aimed at deterring young men from becoming criminals and prisoners. This is certainly the purpose of the album *Lifer's Group* done by men serving life sentences in New Jersey's Rahway Prison.[77] And the album *No More Prisons* by various rappers—among them the distinguished professor Cornell West, then of Harvard, now of Princeton—is devoted to advancing a moratorium on prison construction.[78]

Some Gangsta Rap provides sympathetic portraits of black inmates 'as real human beings trying to survive inhuman conditions'.[79] Some, like Ice Cube's afterword to his *AmeriKKKa's Most Wanted*, is a protest against what rappers view as a conspiratorial continuation of slavery-like bondage.[80] Similarly, in 'The Tower', Ice T, while not excusing the violence prisoners do to each other, indicts prison administration use of inmate conflict—especially racial conflict—as an instrument of institutional control. In addition to its dark music, 'The Tower' includes background voices that are or affect those of real inmates, and the rapper adopts the voice of a new inmate rolling into prison in a grey bus: 'So I studied the inmates/To see who had the power:/The Whites? The Blacks? Or just the gun tower.'[81]

Gangsta Rap can thus bear witness against oppression experienced in prison and on ghetto streets, but as a dominant force in pop culture it can also attract listeners for whom prison is, as Robin Kelley says of the ghetto, 'a place of adventure, unbridled violence, and erotic fantasy, or an imaginary alternative to suburban boredom'.[82] Paul Wright reports that prisons are available as tourist attractions and as sites for parties and weekend 'prison experiences' (men only).[83] In the suburbs, prison as popular commodity may cause political blindness to penal reality but inflict no other harm.

In the ghetto, among men facing a 28 per cent probability of doing time, Gangsta Rap may be the source of some fun, or of some means of expression of felt

[75] Simon Houpt, 'The Jiggy's Up', *The Globe and Mail*, 30 January 2003, Globe Review, Section R, p R1, col 6; Michael Wilson and Lynette Holloway, 'Inquiry into Rap Label Asks, Is "Gangsta" More Than a Genre', *New York Times*, 26 January 2003, New York Report, 20, col 4.

[76] Dyson, *God and Rap*, n 55 above, 162.

[77] Lifer's Group in New Jersey's Rahway Prison, *Lifer's Group* (Hollywood, 1991; originally released 1990).

[78] Cornel West, 'Inspiration', *No More Prisons* (New York, 1999), No 13.

[79] Kelley, 'kickin reality', n 54 above, 135.

[80] Ice Cube, 'I gotta Say What Up!!!', *AmeriKKKa's Most Wanted*, n 72 above, No 23.

[81] Ice T, 'The Tower', *O.G. Original Gangster* (New York, 1991), No 23.

[82] Kelley, 'kickin' reality', n 54 above, 122.

[83] Wright, 'Cultural Commodification,' n 1 above, 17.

rage, or of some strength for resistance. The risk is that popular culture's embrace of Gangsta Rap may sanction crime and prison in a way that helps to predestine both as the future for some youngsters. The Gangsta Rappers Chuck D and Public Enemy themselves protest their genre's 'socially sanctioned desire for self-destruction' and insist that 'the real beneficiaries of gangsta rap are the denizens of the racist New World Order'.[84]

Conclusion

Prison Songs never became popular. They were a rich form of insiders' music that had no outside effect. Outlaw Country enters prison to entertain inmates and sometimes leaves prison with hit recordings for the popular market. Gangsta Rap shares with Prison Songs a capacity for contributing to endurance and with Outlaw Country a capacity for turning prison into popular entertainment, but is there more in what Gangsta Rap is and does?

Crime and imprisonment have sorrowful appeal in Outlaw Country, and Johnny Cash's 'Folsom Prison Blues' has been identified as a forerunner of Gangsta Rap. But there is a distinction between the two. A *New York Times* obituary for Cash noted that 'the sinners that Mr. Cash sang about, unlike those in most gangsta raps, were usually plagued by guilt and seeking God's forgiveness. His tales may have been grim, but they were not nihilistic.'[85] The question for me is whether the nihilistic role crime and imprisonment play in Gangsta's subject matter and its stars' life-and-performance-styles exert gravitational pull on some members of its audience. My hope is that my son-in-law's students are practising resistance while having fun mooning the world.

[84] Dyson, *God and Rap*, n 55 above, 169.

[85] Holden, 'Johnny Cash', n 41 above, 1.

Why Law Needs Pop: Global Law and Global Music?

Thilo Tetzlaff

I. 'Do not forget about the so-called popular' (Leopold Mozart)

When I first started to read one of the primary books on law and popular culture, namely Richard Sherwin's *Why Law Goes Pop* back in 2000, I was mainly focused on what Sherwin was about to define as Pop. This expectation almost naturally had to be disappointed, for obviously Sherwin was not giving anything like a definition. Wisely. I am not trying to argue that a definition in the narrow sense of that word would be really helpful. However, I assume that some remarks on what Pop means or should mean in general and with respect to law can be useful. This is especially true considering that the importance and number of objects qualified as Pop seem to be growing rapidly. Comparing the usual plain hints we can get from encyclopaedias, telling us that the term has been first used to describe arts that did not intend to be high art, such as in Pop art or Pop music with today's usage of the word, it seems that there is always a slightly derogative connotation implied.

Historically, 'Pop' does not seem to be a phenomenon of the 20th century. Around 1750 Diderot started his 'philosophie populaire', which was intended to be understood by everyone.[1] So accessibility and availability are key elements in the structure of popular culture. As the title of this introduction indicates, already with the invention of transforming music into notations the wish to cross social boundaries and to make it available for all classes appeared. One of the main functions of law in this context was to keep class boundaries alive. A police regulation in Nuremberg maintained: 'At wedding ceremonies no servant should dance and act in the round dances of citizens' (14th century).[2] The concept of musical entertainment was for the upper class only and servants were excluded. Only when Alois Senefelder developed a special technology to print notations in 1796, was the idea of 'Music for the Public' initiated. 'The masses stand in notes up to the head' was the title of the *Neue Zeitschrift für Musik* in 1835.[3]

I would like to thank Dr M Connor (Valskog) for her helpful hints concerning language and style and Prof Ko Hasegawa (Hokkaido) for extensive discussions and inspiration.

[1] Peter Wicke, *Von Mozart zu Madonna* (Leipzig: 2001) 7.

[2] John Schikowski, *Geschichte des Tanzes* (Berlin: 1926) 56.

[3] *Neue Zeitschrift für Musik*, II, (39) 1835, 107.

This invention kick-started the music business. In the beginning, however, bureaucracy intended to control upcoming entrepreneurs. The Royal Bavarian Minister of State demanded that musicians who could not qualify through outstanding musical achievements should have a certificate of good conduct and the number of musicians in a family was limited to one.[4] Music as entertainment became a daily companion of ordinary people, but was always suspected of uncontrollable social and erotic powers. Subsequently, Pop music always had to find ways to satisfy people's expectations without losing too much ground with public authorities.

So, when we are looking for Pop and Pop culture this description of the emerging popularity of music already gives us a first hint: it is about music being available for people who stand outside a narrow social class and who are not related to the apparatus of a state. Second, in spite of its—at first glance—entertaining goals, Pop culture contains the potential for social criticism, especially through the means of parody.[5] To verify this thesis, we should keep in mind that more explicit lyrics do not lead us to classical political propositions directly, but that this is a process of correlating symbols which need to be analyzed (II).

This analysis will guide us to form two main theses:

- Pop culture is a way of expressing statements important to civil societies;
- Pop culture shows a path between local identities and global networks.

Since I have been addressing the first thesis, a few more remarks about the second are required. The investigation of the border-crossing potential of popular cultures brings us back to other elements of Pop. Sherwin describes Pop as being based on associative logic.[6] The reason for this development is supposed to be the fact that texts that qualify as Pop do not rely significantly on the written word, but on visual effects, which is especially obvious in the context of advertisements. This might even be seen as one of the main systematic characteristics of Pop, namely its visual qualities.[7] To be more precise, we should talk about an iconographic dimension of Pop culture. This is so, because focusing on visual images and ignoring the other senses has been a common policy of Western culture ever since Aristotelian times.[8]

Contrary to traditional Western culture, which has suffered from a close link between logic and written words (graphocentrism),[9] the multimedia age promises to cross the epistemological boundaries of the logocentric tradition.[10] Through

[4] Irmgard Keldany-Mohr, *Unterhaltungsmusik als soziokulturelles Phänomen des 19.* Jahrhunderts (Regensburg: 1977) 99.

[5] Wicke, n 1 above 33.

[6] Richard K Sherwin, *When Law Goes Pop* (Chicago: 2000) 20.

[7] ibid, 144.

[8] Aristoteles, *Peri Psyches*, book 8, Chs 5–12; Anthony Synnot, *The Body Social: Symbolism, Self and Society* (London: 1993) 132, 270; Constance Classen, *Worlds of Sense: Exploring the Senses in History and Across Cultures* (London: 1993) 2.

[9] Jacques Derrida, *Of Grammatology* (Baltimore and London: 1976) 6, in his version of a criticsm of graphocentrism.

[10] David N Rodowick, *Reading the Figural, or, Philosophy after the New Media* (Durham and London: 2001) 79.

this it reaches out and touches other local cultures, which may not share these traditions, but may still share globally transmitted icons. Because the symbols of Pop culture do not fully stem from a particular traditional cultural context, they are fitted with increased transferral skills. 'Globalism' is in legal terms often understood as a form of metaphysical universalism. However, the fact is that these global symbols afford an increased sophistication in media literacy skills. Applying an enhanced analysis to some pieces of international Pop culture will show that a Madonna song performed in Islamabad is not a form of post-colonial oppression, but a quite complicated form of global cross-cultural dialogue.

Even though we are dealing with Pop culture in general and even though there are significant differences between the phenomenon of Pop culture, Pop literature and Pop music, most of the examples used here will be drawn from Pop music. One of the reasons is that music has some reflective effects, especially on law.[11] Second, I want to show that some elements of Pop culture, like music, movies and so on, can be connected on a rather schematic basis, so that in the form of cross-references an enriched and unified analysis can be performed (II 1.). This meets with another prerequisite of law in Pop times: enchantment. In contrast to Posner, for example, and going beyond Sherwin's Dionysian approach, I would like to stress that this magic is intrinsic to legal understanding (II 1).

'What images do we share?' asks Sherwin at the end of his book.[12] The main questions in this paper will be about the 'we' in this question. In a world as it is—and this is not meant to be a purely empiric item—*who* can shares images and sound and in *which* way do 'we' share them? If globalism is meant to be something different than a menace to inferior societies, it needs to find a way between the extremes of universalizing particular interests and anti-discoursive procedures.[13] However, before we reach this programmatic passage we have to walk through the maze of law and Pop.

II. Cross-references

1. A Journey to the Amazon

As everybody knows, if one orders a book from one of the online bookstores one will always be confronted with a display telling you 'People who ordered this book, also ordered . . .'. This information is not only narrowed to books, but is also meant to give you advice about music, movies, games and so on. It always made me wonder why readers being fond of Kafka's *The Castle* devote themselves to Bruce

[11] Thilo Tetzlaff, 'The Sound of Law' in G Kreuzbauer, S Augeneder (eds), *Der juristische Streit*, ARSP-Beiheft 68 (Stuttgart: 2004) 288.

[12] Sherwin, n 6 above, 264.

[13] Jürgen Habermas, 'Vom pragmatischen, ethischen und moralischem Gebrauch der praktischen Vernunft' in Jürgen Habermas (ed), *Erläuterungen zur Diskursethik* (Frankfurt: 1991) 12. Jürgen Habermas, 'Eine genealogische Betrachtung zum kognitiven Gehalt des Sollens' in Jürgen Habermas (ed), *Die Einbeziehung des Anderen* (Frankfurt: 1996) 60.

Springsteen, but this is not what we should discuss here. Of relevance, however, is what the most familiar music to recent publications in law would be. What is the deeper link between a law book about freedom of speech and Robbie Williams' *Swing When You're Winning*? Since I do not intend to discuss this merely on the basis of my personal taste, I have scanned quite a number of law publications in ten law departments (seven in the UK, three in Germany). To reach full empirical validity the number should be increased. Therefore I am going to take the recent publications of a typical law department (University College London). This brings us to the following scheme:

Author	Publication	Music	Movie
Barendt, E	*Introduction to Constitutional Law*	*Escapology* (R Williams); *Be Not Nobody* (V Carlton); *Come Away with Me* (N Jones)	*Men in Black II*; *Road to Perdition*; *We Were Soldiers*; *Monsters Inc*
Barendt, E	*Freedom of Speech*	*Swing when you're winning* (R Williams); *Collection* (T Chapman)	*Crouching Tiger, Hidden Dragon*; *Moulin Rouge*
Dennis, I	*Law of Evidence*	*8 Mile* (Eminem); *Heathen Chemistry* (Oasis); *Hail to the Thief* (Radiohead)	*The Godfather Trilogy*; *Matrix*
Dworkin, R	*Law's Empire*	*Escape* (Enrique Iglesias); *Come Away with Me* (N Jones)	*The Godfather Trilogy*; *Six Feet Under*; *Bowling for Columbine*
Dworkin, R	*Sovereign Virtue*	*Come Away with Me* (N Jones); *On the Beach* (N Young); *Led Zeppelin II*	The *Indiana Jones* Trilogy; *Back to the Future*; *Forrest Gump*
Dworkin, R	*Taking Rights Seriously*	*Come Away with Me* (N Jones); *Escape* (Enrique Iglesias)	*Doctor Strangelove*; *Bowling for Columbine*
Freeman, M	*Introduction to Jurisprudence*	*Escape* (Enrique Iglesias); *Blue Train* (J Coltraine)	*Spiderman*; *Bowling for Columbine*; *Moulin Rouge*
Markesinis, B	*Tort Law*	*Justified* (J Timberlake); *Nu Flow* (Big Bravaz)	*The Godfather Trilogy*; *Harry Potter and the Philosopher's Stone*; *8 Mile*
Pettet, B	*Company Law*	*Morning Glory* (Oasis); *Escapology* (R Williams)	*Harry Potter and the Philosopher's Stone*; *Bridget Jones's Diarys*; *Moulin Rouge*

Even though I cannot discuss all references found here, the above table tries to list hits that are either rather peculiar with a certain person (for example, the link between Ronald Dworkin and Norah Jones) or for law books in general (for example, a preference for movies with mafia settings). The three movies most often connected to legal publications are:

- *The Godfather Trilogy*
- *Moulin Rouge*
- *Bowling for Columbine*

On the basis of the data of a one-faculty research things are less clear in Pop music. There seems to be a certain affinity to Robbie Williams' music. The same is true of a typical German law faculty (Munich), so that his music can be expected to have closer links with legal thinking. A ranking of most appearances with publications in the different areas of law would contain in the top three positions:

- Robbie Williams
- Enrique Iglesias
- Eminem

As already indicated, as many law faculties as possible should be scanned in this way to identify certain types of Pop music which are qualified by an especially close relationship to certain areas of law. Usually the publications require a certain age to form a data pool which is big enough to relate other items to it relevantly. So there is a variety of publications which do not provide any further information about the preferences of their readers.

2. Evaluation of Relations

After counting the relations between legal publications and Pop music and movies we should now ask about the content of the connections. What makes Michael Freeman's *Lloyd's Introduction to Jurisprudence* a desirable item to those who like Enrique Iglesias? We should begin with the links between jurisprudence and cross-cultural Pop music, before we continue with Robbie Williams' album *Swing When You're Winning*, which seems to be important for quite a few consumers of legal texts.

a) Jurisprudence and Latin Pop

Another connection that derives from the above scheme is the one between jurisprudence and Enrique Iglesias, whom I choose to take here as a prototype for Latin Pop. Even though we are beyond the peak popularity of this specific style, I assume it is worth dealing with it, because it can be considered one example for forming a cross-culture music style. What has been starting with some still rather clumsy variations of ethno-pop has been arriving at a two-direction motorway: Western Pop music receives impulses from Africa, South America and India

(Punjabi MC), other cultures implement Western Pop music into their traditional sound system, as with the winning song of the Eurovision Song Contest. A song quite typical of blended Turk Pop style (Sertab Erener's 'Everyway that I can', 2003) won over a number of national Pop songs.

I would emphasize that what might seem on a first glance as a domination of Western music has become a multicultural project. A spirit of foreign music styles is appreciated by audiences all over the world.[14] Law traditionally has problems crossing boundaries that easily. Public International Law is suffering from a crisis and not only due to the politicians who try to marginalize it.[15] But this should not hide the increasing interest in foreign legal systems. European Law faces the most difficult task, namely trying to unify what has to be unified for practical reasons, but also maintaining some specific legal traditions.[16] What is true of so-called black letter law has never been true of the theoretical analysis. Even though I would suspect many theoretical comments made being based on one legal system only, there is a general wish to approach law independently from national specifics.

Jurisprudence on the other hand means to understand how law works in different times and cultural contexts without restricting it to these very circumstances. Some aspects of universalizing certain values turned out to be inappropriate,[17] but the project is still very much alive.[18] The specific function of jurisprudence in this area is to analyze the juridical practice and use the essence of it to form a concept of law. Enrique Iglesias, in order to be successful as a Pop singer, has a quite similar task. He had to find the characteristics of Latin American music and then to blend them with a Pop sound which still retains recognizable elements of his Latin sources. The point is not to be as authentic as possible, but to be as acceptable as possible. This appeals to the ideal of tolerance which has always been a fundamental for any transcendental kind of legal philosophy.

Pop culture today therefore demands a degree of reflection from the audience, for example, of different cultures, that in the early 20th century not even more educated people could achieve.[19] As a mass phenomenon this is quite different from the Chinoise artefacts rich noblemen used to equip their environment. This is something that jurisprudence, with a few other legal disciplines, still has to promote in legal research. What might seem plausible at first glance—that legal research should be as 'national' as the legal system—is not plausible at all in jurisprudence. And if we consider EU law, which is a syncretistic version of

[14] Winfried Fluck, 'Aesthetics and Cultural Studies' in Emory Elliott, Louis F Caton, J Rhyne (eds), *Aesthetics in a Multicultural Age* (Oxford: 2002) 87.

[15] Marcus Krajewski, 'Selbstverteidigung gegen bewaffnete Angriffe nicht-staatlicher Organisationen' (2002) 40 *Archiv des Völkerrechts* 186.

[16] Patrick Glenn, *Legal Traditions of the World* (Oxford: 2000) 123.

[17] John Rawls, *Political Liberalism* (New York: 1993) 284.

[18] Charles Jones, *Global Justice* (Oxford: 2001) 109.

[19] Bazon Brock, 'Popart und Popkultur' in *Meyer's Enzyklopädisches Wörterbuch*, Bd 19 (Mannheim: 1977).

national legal systems, it becomes completely implausible, as outdated as the national music concept.

b) Freedom of Speech and Swing

Since this section is dedicated to swing music, we should recall what the spirit of swing is. Swing is a form of ensemble music with a dense, rhythm-driven sound (almost always using a hard driving 'Riff' against which the melody could be played).[20] This is more of a definition. The idea is, though, a contrast between the individual, usually an instrument-playing band leader, and the ensemble. More fundamentally it is a music style according to the theme of freedom of thought and style, protected against a uniformity of a group. In this context it also became a symbol of resistance in Nazi Germany, as shown in the Disney movie '*Swing Kids*' (1993).

In particular, the swing we are talking about now is presented by a person, who as a member of a boy group that only the older generation will remember (Take That), stood for a commodity type of singer. Boy groups since Take That have been a part of a Pop music product that is almost a symbol for synthetic exchangeability. Yet Robbie Williams has more and more become an artist who excels in presenting quite authentic ideas and performing them, disregarding the mainstream policies. Even though 'Come Undone' (2003) is not part of the album I am addressing here, it is a good example. Similarly swing music is like the background for what is executed in many of his songs, namely to use music as a means of personal expression. So Robbie Williams turning back to swing music after a while is no surprise.

Freedom of speech is trying to find a similar way of protecting the individual expression against a censoring executive power or even the public opinion.[21] 'The danger of suppression of free speech . . . is a worse evil by far than the toleration on occasion of publications that could legitimately be proscribed.'[22] The limits set up for free speech in different countries have been opening more space for most kinds of artistic expression.[23] Popular music, especially dance music, has been regulated by state authorities, as mentioned above, because of concerns for moral deflation. But the number of cases bringing Pop music in the courtroom is not very high and groups with 'unsexy' names like 'Citizens for Safety and Environment' have been trying to stop Ozzy Osbourne and Marilyn Manson without any success.[24] Swing has been leading this path, so the fact that one of the entertainers profiting from this process dedicates an album to swing is quite consistent.

[20] Frank Tirro, *Jazz* (2nd edn, New York: 1993) 85, 241; this contrast between individualism and ensemble in riff techniques is discussed for techno music by Ian Hoy, 'Rave Culture', http://tomorrowtoday.biz/generations/xpaper1006.htm (visited 29 September 2003).

[21] Eric Barendt, *Freedom of Speech* (Oxford: 1987) 118, 83.

[22] ibid, 302.

[23] ibid, 269; an exception might be the 'hate speech' decision (*R v Keegstra* [1990] 3 SCR 697) of the Canadian Supreme Court.

[24] *Seattle Times*, 27 February 2003.

3. Carry on the Journey

a) Movies

Since we agreed on visual effects being one typical aspect of Pop culture, let us follow this line a little further. One of the movies quite often named as linked to law books is *Moulin Rouge*. I am choosing the example in spite of *The Godfather Trilogy* having more listings, because *Moulin Rouge* works with some obvious concepts of visualization itself. Besides it is also part of a trilogy, the so-called Red Curtain trilogy, which additionally consists of *Strictly Ballroom* (1992) and William Shakespeare's *Romeo and Juliet* (1996).

Tackling ethics, which I tend to take as the more general approach to law, not only from an ethically unembodied side, but also taking into consideration by which means of expression and impression ethical rules are brought to us, has become quite 'fashionable'.[25] 'Fashionable' I say, but this is rarely a matter of mere fashion. But ethics as a philosophical discipline has often been lacking concreteness and particularity.[26] Images should not only be treated as an illustration of thoughts. As Sherwin pointed out correctly: 'Multiple ways of seeing . . . self and social reality are so valuable'.[27] Seeing in this context should not be treated as metaphorical speech, because the professions of law are together all working on story reconstruction, comprehension and telling.[28] Movies turned out to be a quite effective way of doing so. Generally speaking the organisation of 20th and 21st century culture is relying on images and signs which are anti-chronological and in a way anti-historical.[29] The Movement-Image and the Time-Image of cinematic narration have been affecting any kind of narration, because they allow the formation of ambiguous, undeciphered and undialectical images.

How does this relate to the legal discourse? Sherwin's major explanation model has been to talk about the transformation of law into a commodity by becoming part of the visual complex.[30] This is, with the deepest respect, a quite American way of explaining the visual impact on law. The *Flashdance* law is not all you can expect from the movies.[31] So far I have refrained from giving many examples, and indeed the inductive elaboration of theses is what I have in mind here. However, we should take a brief look at *Moulin Rouge*, since it seems to be part of an ethical-legal discourse. In this film the life in Paris is contrasted with that inside the micro-cosmos of the Moulin Rouge. In spite of strict ethical rules the Moulin Rouge tries to be an oasis of libertinage. The movie refers to the legal formation of ethical rules; when the character Christian, played by Ewan McGregor, first enters the Moulin Rouge

[25] Burton F Porter, *Philosophy through Film and Fiction* (New Jersey: 2004).

[26] Christopher Falzon, *Philosophy goes to the Movies* (New York: 2002) 3.

[27] Sherwin, n 6 above, 241.

[28] David A Black, *Law in Film* (Urbana and Chicago: 1999) 57.

[29] Rodowick, n 10 above, 174.

[30] Sherwin, n 6 above, 142.

[31] Robert Laurence, 'Last Night While You Prepared for Class I Went to See Light of Day: A Film Review and a Message to My First-Year Property Students, Annotated for my Colleagues'(1989) 39 *J of Legal Education* 89.

he does so by naming the virtues of truth, justice and love. This is so, because they form his personal value system which is going to be reshuffled in the following scenes. Interestingly, this leads to a debate whether it is a conservative movie promoting traditional values under the disguise of artistry.

I hold for a moment with the quite interesting combination of musical and cineastic elements and would further stress that both allow a teleological understanding which leads law to its own *telos*.[32] Teleology has always been a key structure of legal thinking, but learning about the limitations and functions of teleological legal thinking is one of the biggest advantages of the cinematic techniques identified above. Methodologically, films establish narrations which can be categorized in terms of genre, style and so on. To do something similar with law requires bringing the individual narrations of legal texts into the daylight.[33] Even if it is almost certain that we cannot approach law as a part of film studies, the dissatisfaction with current legal methodology[34] should be reason enough to appreciate quite sensitive films which point out societal weaknesses, for example *In the Name of the Father* (1993).

b) Music

According to Sherwin another important feature is a non-linear stream of thought. This is when a musical stream of thought, which has always been seen as non-linear, kicks in. Since we have been dealing with Robbie Williams already, we should have a closer look on one of his songs, a duet with Nicole Kidman titled 'Somethin' Stupid' (2001). The first remarkable point is the technique of a remake or cover version, here of Nancy and Frank Sinatra (1967). Even though we tend to concentrate on the presumably new aspects of Pop culture, one of the quite fundamental strategies used is to sculpture symbols of experiences.[35] As I tried to indicate with my introductory remarks, many ways of making things Pop therefore are not so new at all.

It is important to stress the underlining principles for another reason. Because Pop culture is also a youth culture, performers are usually quite young. It has been said about Pop literature that this is an important reason why it does not incorporate personal memories that much, but forms encyclopaedic lists.[36] Given this fact it is obvious why it is difficult to form a Pop music canon. Critics have been raising eyebrows about this way of producing literature, but in Pop music this is widely accepted. The idea is to draw attention to certain facets of an artefact. Legislation uses this strategy, for example, when labour law started to lighten certain aspects of

[32] Black, n 28 above, 135.

[33] This means first to accept that there is individuality in law at law, see Pierre Schlag, 'The Problem of the Subject' in Dennis M Patterson, *Postmodernism and Law* (Dartmouth: 1994) 1643.

[34] Ulfried Neumann, 'Juristische Methodenlehre und Theorie der juristischen Argumentation' (2001) 32 *Rechtstheorie* 240.

[35] No wonder that Sherwin in his constructive part (n 6 above, 228) returns to Gorgian Sophists. More positively: Volker Boehme-Neßler, 'Recht als Theater?' in *Zeitschrift für Rechtspolitik* (2003) 128.

[36] Moritz Baßler, *Der deutsche Pop-Roman* (München: 2002) 94.

civil law contracts. Actually most of the impressions Sherwin gives about elements of Pop culture in the courtroom can be seen as methods of drawing the attention to something different than what the previous narration was stressing.[37] The defendant's lawyer will wish to emphasize other aspects of a case from those that the jury already knows from the prosecution.

Another idea behind remakes in Pop music is to keep certain traditions alive, because they are worth it. Pop music professionals hope to process sounds that are already known to the next generation by adapting them to the sound (techno etc) of their successors. It is clear that law, which is full of traditions, in theory and in practice, has difficulties in coping with the heartbeat of modern times. When people think that the legal routine, to use Burroughs' term, is a matter of distraction, it is time to think of ways to keep law in touch with what people think today. The German Civil Law Code contains rather detailed regulations on bees (ss 961–964), but it took more than three decades of discussion to implement a minimal appendix on the legal status of animals (s 90a). This is an example of how it should not be. Legislators are often suspected of legal activism by the academic community, but to make law Popular, there is indeed a need to 'bring law back in'.

c) Movies

Ethical thinking is one of the key elements of many movies. *Crimes and Misdemeanors* discusses the question of why we should be moral at all, and Plato's Gyges story gives an ontological outline of ethics.[38] Plato talks about imprisoned handcuffed cavemen who can see the world only as projections against a wall; thus he could be named as the inventor of modern cinematic technology.[39] Taking the insights from this parable, two major ways of understanding the visual legal aspects can be reconstructed. One is looking for visual elements in the legal procedures, no matter whether these are obvious or sublime; the other way of understanding this project would be to see the legal procedures in general as a form of visualizing justice.

Naturally the more interesting approach is the second one. The starting point is legal and cinematic narratives. David Black was right in trying to make these terms more adaptable.[40] Leaving aside his suggestions for more precise terms, Black continues by suggesting that there is a closer connection of law and power than between law and narrative as part of a power regime. To me these suggestions fail to make plausible how power manages to work at all if we do not think of vis absoluta. The 'pleasure in narrative and power in law' distinction[41] forces law into a role which restricts it to power execution. But does not law retain a certain difference to this power? Film as well as law has a choice to follow certain powers or to undermine

[37] Sherwin, n 6 above 126, 206.
[38] Falzon, n 26 above, 86.
[39] Ian Jarvie, *Philosophy of the Film* (London: 1987) 48.
[40] Black, n 28 above, 13.
[41] ibid, 40.

them by quite sophisticated means. Black himself touches this matter when discussing the differences between art house cinema and 'normal movies'.

Since the goal is to understand popular culture, this is the place to discuss popular movies. There are two major aspects to consider. One is the way how more or less traditional film making affected the modes of narration even in literature. These effects have been mostly concentrated on the pragmatic level.[42] In contrast to this approach, Pop culture in the digital age goes further and changes the modes of language on the semantic and even syntactic levels.[43] Second, the idealistic structure of movie presentation I reminded of a few paragraphs earlier when mentioning Plato's ontology, remains, despite the severe changes in movie productions, quite important. The speculations in the process of truth-finding in visualizations are a reservoir for highlighting certain aspects and neglecting others, which is the idea of forming facts into a plot. Sherwin describes this in his analysis of the question of TV cameras in the courtroom. Earlier the storytelling-movement produced similar reconstructions, for example of the 'Miranda' warnings.[44]

4. A Global Constitution of Pop

Law is being urged into a universal constitutional framework.[45] This can be said in spite of the most recent threats, which substantially reshuffled this framework. A global constitutional dimension nevertheless remains relevant, especially if we do not have a universal legal world order in mind, but the form of organizing international relations and the overlapping of concepts of law. Speaking in terms of system theory there is a certain pressure on local legal entities to adapt themselves to this international legal system.[46] Before we link this demand with the inspiration of Pop culture we should analyze it a little more carefully.

Why is popular culture especially dedicated to a global extension? Part of the answer is that Pop culture, and this is referring to the second meaning of 'Pop' in this context, has some knowledge of how to bring special effects in structures that have not previously been used to this.[47] Since we are focusing here on Pop culture through the looking glass of artistic expression, two remarks seem to be necessary: the globalisation of Pop culture took place 'long before Al Gore invented the internet'[48] and could be found as local events claimed some universal importance.

[42] Wallace Martin, *Recent Theories of Narrative* (Ithaca: 1986) 15; David Barry, 'Strategy Retold: Towards a Narrative View of Strategic Discourse' (1997) 22 *Academy of Management Rev* 436.

[43] David N Rodowick, 'Reading the Figural' (1990) 24 *Camera Obscura* 10: elaborated Rodowick, n 10 above.

[44] Peter Brooks, 'Storytelling Without Fear?' in Peter Brooks and Paul Gerwitz (eds), *Law's Stories* (Yale: 1996), 114.

[45] Philip Allott, 'The Emerging Universal System' (2001) 3 *International Law Forum du droit international* 12.

[46] Wolfram Hertel, *Supranationalität als Verfassungsprinzip* (Berlin: 1999) 61.

[47] Thomas Jung, 'Alles nur Pop?' in Thomas Jung, *Osloer Beiträge zur Germanistik* 32 (Frankfurt: 2002) 146.

[48] Eddy von Mueller, 'Pop culture goes global', at www.atlanta.creativeloafing.com/2000-10-07/flicks_feature.html (visited 3 June 2003).

The Olympic Games are a good example. They developed from a sports competition between Greek tribes into a global movement, not only of sportsmanship, but of a certain way of recognising achievements from all over the world. Pop cultures continue to allow these local interferences by fitting them into a more widely understood cross-cultural context (which is the more downsized term for 'global' here). Second, the event of a political state with all its deficits depends on the quality of its media presentation. This is most comprehensively argued for in Paul Cantor's *Gilligan Unbound*, where he insists that not only morons are influenced by Pop culture.[49] On the contrary, by becoming an important factor of socialization for everyone, the media presentation also becomes important for any kind of institution including the state.

Moreover the concept of global constitutionalism should bear as few implications as possible of any further terms of human rights or democracy concepts. Constitution in this sense means to define areas which should remain normally unchanged during the life of an institution. Only in finding out which areas could be relevant, may there be some dispute. Understanding constitution in this way it is almost natural that the focus is on institutional and organizational matters. The organizations we talk about here, are more or less agreed on internationally; which is quite surprising thinking of the different tradition and principles that lie behind these entities. These can be legal cultures, but also cultural traditions.[50] In spite of some previous critical remarks, I would consider that the ideal of democracy has been known in institutions and procedures far beyond its actual scope. So even if they are not actually alive in a certain society they are still in use as a means of justification or contrastive construction.

However, if this were the only function of a global approach to democratic constitutionalisation, it would have more similarities with utopia than with having a basis in human society. To what extent a model of democracy can be globalized depends ultimately on the characteristics of such a model. One of the problems with some of the previous suggestions has been that they have been very much linked with the national state and have tried simply to extend the range of national democratic systems.[51] But this is like hoping the whole world might fall for a certain kind of local music, Scottish bagpipes for example. But Pop music teaches us that even a democratic extension comes at a high cost.[52] An example is the globalization of the rule of law.[53] Encouraging this process often implies reshaping the socio-economic circumstances in societies. The result then is a blend of some classic elements mixed with local traditions.

[49] Paul Cantor, *Gilligan Unbound: Pop Culture in the Age of Globalization* (Lanham, Maryland: 2001).

[50] Discussion of the European Union in Hendrik Zahle, *EU og den Danske grundlov* (Copenhagen: 1998), Chs 1 and 2.

[51] Martin Shaw, *Theory of the Global State* (Cambridge: 2000) Ch 1, suggesting an interpretation as a transitional period.

[52] Daniel Bell, *East Meets West* (Princeton: 2000) 116.

[53] Maxwell Chibundu, 'Globalizing the Rule of Law' (1999) 79, *Indiana J of Global Legal Studies* 7; Kanishka C Jayasuriya, 'Globalisation, Sovereignty, and the Rule of Law: From political to Economic Constitutionalism' (2001) 8(4) *Constellations* 442.

Quite often these are perceived as weak hybrids and not, as in Pop music, as a progressive style.

The prime reason for this is the suspicion that the concept of a restricted application of the rule of law is motivated by darker political positions. This suspicion however assumes that a Western shaped rule of law has a deeper legitimacy. This could be an empiric approach, but only one based on a minor part of European history. Additionally there is a danger of a lack of enforcement, if the legal system does not incorporate cultural traditions. This would be a major deficit, especially when it comes to something as essential as the rule of law.[54] So it might be an option either to transplant a rule of law without any power of enforcement or to embroider it on existing systems of sanctioning norms.[55]

If Pop music manages to communicate new listening skills to modern global audiences, the receptive process of listening is made compatible with those of a number of other people from quite different cultural backgrounds.[56] Music has always been interpreted as a border-crossing part of culture, because it is not strictly linked to national languages.[57] But only in the age of global distribution of Pop music, when a song can actually be heard simultaneously in Arkansas and Nairobi, does this promise of understanding without boundaries achieve real influence in people's lives. This has become possible because music has found institutions other than the local concert hall which was the natural place to consume music for a long time.[58]

Accordingly this development can be understood as the institutionalization of a certain way of music consumption. Institutionalization then is precisely what could underpin those fragments of a global constitution.[59] But how can this be without a global society backing those institutions? Nevertheless this question implies a certain perspective on what these institutions and their society should be like, namely those we became familiar with in the history of the nation state. Yet, there is some evidence that these structures are not helpful as soon as it comes to institutions that have to work outside the frame of the nation state. Hence there is a shift in the perception of a global society as well, which is more than an aggregation of national societies. The next section will elaborate why the concept of civil society suits much better in multi-national environments.

[54] Adama Dieng (ed), 'Mondialisation, human rights, and the rule of law' (1999) 61 *International Commission of Jurists: The Review* 127.

[55] BC Smith, 'Local Government and the Transition to Democracy' (1998) 18 *Public Administration and Development* 85.

[56] Maria Shelton, 'Whitney is Every Woman? Cultural Politics and the Pop Star' (1995) 36 *Camera Obscura* 135.

[57] Veit Erlmann, 'Tradition, Popular Culture and Social Transformation' in MP Baumann (ed), *Traditional Music and Cultural Policy* (Wilhelmshaven: 1991) 123. The first World Music Exhibition in Berlin (1994) used the slogan 'The art to be local worldwide' to express this idea.

[58] Edward Said, *Musical Elaborations* (New York: 1991) 13.

[59] For the European Union: Frank Schimmelpfennig, 'Liberal Norms and the Eastern Enlargement of the European Union: A Case for Sociological Institutionalism' in (1998) 27 *Österreichische Zeitschrift für Politikwissenschaft* 459.

III. Global Law and Global Pop

1. Pop Culture and Civil Society

a) Political Action and Civil Society

Pop culture stands for a particular relation to privacy. Whereas the performance of classical music is usually linked to the event of a concert,[60] Pop music surrounds us in often very private moments. To make this thesis more plausible, we should first explain the charm of private activities in contrast to the more and more problematic sphere of politics. Traditionally the fora of legitimating discourses can be divided into state, society, and contract.[61] In this triangle society is qualified as a form of private ordering, external to the state, but also external to strict market behaviour.[62] Even in the crudest market economy there are goods that are organized other than by market logics.[63]

Civil society, a concept based on the ancient idea of a 'societas civilis', which has been re-imported during the transformation period of the East European states,[64] has become a crystallization point of recent democracy theory. It has also initiated some new reflections about the idea of public politics: the dilemma of classical sovereignty is a swing between hyperactive politicians and passive citizens. The concept of civil society tries to communicate a space of action in which the frustration of people is lowered by a part-time engagement.[65] The recent MTV clips under the headline of 'War is not the answer', which opposed the war against Iraq, might indicate something different, so that some additional remarks are necessary (2). Here we should concentrate on the implications of civil society concepts for Pop cultures as non-etatistic cultures.

Civil society from the perspective of entertainment markets is sometimes discredited as scornful consumer's sovereignty,[66] but this tends to ignore the autonomous decisions of listeners as well as the specific function of music.[67] Since ultimately the Pop market offers only absolutely superfluous goods, the chance (which would elsewhere be restricted) to make a deliberate choice becomes available. But in fact consumer sovereignty in the civil society has multiple functions. The classical function, of course, is the influence on economic transfers.[68] But, additionally, consumers can concentrate their budgets

[60] Said, n 58 above, 13.

[61] Peer Zumbansen, *Ordnungsmuster im modernen Wohlfahrtsstaat* (Baden-Baden: 2000) 93.

[62] Udo Di Fabio, 'Verwaltung und Verwaltungsrecht zwischen gesellschaftlicher Selbstregulierung und staatlicher Steuerung' (1997) 56 VVDStRL 235.

[63] Michael Walzer, *Spheres of Justice* (1983) 134.

[64] Jean L Cohen and Andrew Arato, *Civil Society and Political Theory* (Cambridge: 1992) 17.

[65] Michael Walzer, *Zivile Gesellschaft und amerikanische Demokratie* (Berlin: 1992) 64.

[66] Peter Drexl, *Die wirtschaftliche Selbstbestimmung des Verbrauchers* (Tübingen: 1998) 91.

[67] Tetzlaff, n 11 above.

[68] Ulrich K Beck, *Macht und Gegenmacht im globalen Zeitalter* (Frankfurt: 2002) 58, 114.

on common goal activities, which are embedded into the modern communication and information society.[69]

Pop culture is a part of the entertainment market, but one should not forget its enormous creative potential. Even if buying Eminem's latest album is not per se a critical act, it can be taken as sponsoring a certain form of activism. In certain places, putting aside the option of emigration, voice is the only way to achieve influence at all. And since the single voice's weight can be neglected, citizens are forced to look for methods of mass articulation.[70] Proceduralistic theories tend to turn the formal part of this into a concept of legitimization. But this fails to deal with the content of people's opinions and beliefs. A theory of civil society, therefore, has to watch out for the reservations of non-etatistic expressions. One of them is definitely the cyber community, which allows some kind of temporary emigration,[71] another is Pop culture.

Pop cultures in particular consist of many civil institutions gaining autonomy; many democracy theories still drape themselves around political civil rights without forming a perspective on the field of cultural DIY autonomy.[72] In a global context the experiences of civil society activities have to be associated with non-etatistic institutions, because so far the international community does not have any, as has been proved by past incidents. Civil society has often been reconstructed as part of a non-instrumental rationality, a perspective based on a Hegelian tradition.[73] Pop culture would be excluded from this, because it relies on people's tastes as criteria of success on the market. But the hypothesis that civil society structures need to stand on grounds of non-instrumental rationality is highly questionable. I do not intend to argue for the anti-thesis here in detail. It should be pointed out, however, that a concept of responsibility as part of the civil society opens floodgates to an approach that does not demand civil societies to take over the state, but to search for other forms of action.

The main tool for this is the wording of impressive goals that gain public attention, since these actions naturally lack the execution force of state entities. These goals have to compete with empty messages (such as mere product commercials) as well as with the actions of other non-profit organizations, so they need to grab the public attention. For example, one of the fathers of the concept of Pop literature, Leslie A Fiedler, got this attention by publishing his paper 'Cross the border, close the gap' (1968) not in a literary journal but in the *Playboy*.[74] In this context the idea that law could be autopoietic in a way that draws clear lines between the legal

[69] David Lewis, *The Soul of the New Consumer* (2000) 23.

[70] Gralf-Peter Calliess, 'Das Zivilrecht der Zivilgesellschaft' in C Joerges and G Teubner (eds), *Rechtsverfassungsrecht* (Baden-Baden: 2003) 9.

[71] David G Post, 'Anarchy, State, and the Internet' (1995) *Journal of Online Law*, art 3 (www.temple.edu/lawschool/dpost/Anarchy.html).

[72] Jürgen Maier, 'Transparenz oder Lobby hinter den Kulissen? Zum Einfluss privater Akteure in der Klimapolitik' in Tanja Brühl et al (eds), *Die Privatisierung der Weltpolitik* (Bonn: 2001) 282.

[73] Calliess, n 70 above, 22.

[74] Thomas Jung, 'Vom Pop International zur Tristesse Royal' in Jung (ed), *Alles nur Pop?* (2002) 35.

system and its environment seems to be problematic. To be fair, it must be added that probably nobody would put it this way today.[75]

It would be too strong a statement to say that every law needs Pop elements to be successful at all, but in the areas on which I have just focused, law is only one candidate for the attention of public opinion and action. The question 'what does Pop do to literature' can be answered by saying that, in contrast to some interpretations, Pop is a project of some consequence still related to the values of modernity.[76] Although these values might be criticized, the 'Concept of Law' seems almost affectionately based on them. Thus this perspective on Pop elements in law might be easier to digest. If we focus on the ideals of the early seventies which started to question the eternity of law and to reconstruct legal happenings instead,[77] for example in affirmative action programmes, Pop law is only continuing these thoughts. This refers especially to parliament and government and should be extended to the forensic practice in the next chapter.

b) Pop Culture and Privacy

At first glance one could think that Pop and privacy are irreconcilable with each other. Pop is characterized as loud, annoying, obvious, whereas privacy remains within the decency of four walls. On the other hand, Pop culture is often synchronized with a certain withdrawal from a political public forum. Its narrations usually spin around a quite dominating ego.[78] The function of this narrative technique seems to refute what has been said so far about sophistication of narration due to an audiovisual regime. A quite plausible explanation of this phenomenon is the suggestion that the ego works as an archive which is needed to form those encyclopaedic lists that are necessary to uncover the patterns of Pop culture. Novelists Bret Easton Ellis and Nick Hornby deliver quite typical examples verifying this idea.[79] In Ellis' *Less Than Zero* (1985) the hero Clay constantly refers to song titles, but also works himself through a number of street and brand names. In Nick Hornby's *High Fidelity* (1995) these lists are even more prominent, because they are created as charts in a second hand record store ('OK guy, best five pop songs about death'). The concentration on this kind of listings and archives is often constructed against the narrative stream of the story. The identities of the character are therefore defined by symbols of popular culture, rather than by private opinions and attitudes.

On the other hand, civil societies in a globalized world are directed to find a sphere of privacy, so that they can repress the state.[80] The idea is a political statement

[75] That is why Niklas Luhmann, *Das Recht der Gesellschaft* (Frankfurt: 1995) 64, has reconsidered his conception of an autopoietic legal system.

[76] Peter Zima, *Moderne. Postmoderne* (Tübingen, Basel: 1997) 252.

[77] Wendy Schoener, 'Non-Governmental Organizations and Global Activism: Legal and Informal Approaches' (1997) 4 *Global Legal Studies J* 537.

[78] Dirk Frank, *Popliteratur* (Stuttgart: 2003) 158.

[79] Baßler, n 36 above, 186.

[80] Calliess, n 70 above, 11.

through non-political expression. This strategy is chosen because of some dissatisfaction with the current models of representation.[81] Trying to become elected in a parliamentary body is not what politics is about. The traditional construction of political debate is that of a market place or a debate forum, but even though there is still space for political demonstrations on the street, for example in the form of techno demos,[82] the internet and a commodity culture based on private consumption create space for a private political sphere. The discussions about a 'critical pop culture' during the annual Popup-fair in Leipzig have been trying to make these political statements more obvious;[83] special genres in Pop cultures (such as hip hop) have been giving voices to marginal social groups.[84]

Pop music can be a matter of shared emotions, but, by means of a wide range of home entertainment facilities, also allows what has been described as 'cocooning'. This implies the danger of mixing private affairs with political opinions. In other areas this process is said to create a quite different corporate culture.[85] What can definitely be said is that Pop cultures draw different lines between private and public. It has been quite common to see rights as natural candidates when it comes to trying to separate private from public. Rights lay a legal frame around privacy which might set borders that are not in harmony with the new understanding of private life and public activities. Still, it is difficult to see how an idea of *natural* rights can adapt to privacy problems in digital times.

Law obviously has a choice: it can either maintain the previous structures or it can try to follow new models of privacy. The first, it has been argued, would be in the interest of law's integrity,[86] the second would be on behalf of law's credibility. Even though I am not advocating a position of a zero-distance between law and popular privacy models, I would think that law has to be alongside an appropriate reality.[87] Legislation does consider stimulus from outside, as has been shown especially in the field of consumer law,[88] so the task is more on behalf of jurisdiction and administration. To find out which images we share is essential for an appropriate legal understanding, but if we keep a line between Pop and law in the construction of us and our environment, I would expect it to become more difficult for justice.[89]

The same problem more or less applies to the ethical foundation of law in general. As Robert W Pittman, 'creator' of MTV, stated, the way of processing information in any kind of discourse has been changed by the audio-visual regime, either by cultural, ethical or aesthetical norms.[90] The consequence of that is: no

[81] Michael Zürn, *Regieren jenseits des Nationalstaates* (Frankfurt: 1998) 347, stressing the aspect of globalization in this context; empirical analysis: Michael Steed, 'The Constituency' in V Bogdanor (ed), *Representatives of the People?* (Hants: 1985).

[82] Thilo Tetzlaff, 'Versammlungsrecht und Loveparade' [2003] *Verwaltungsrundschau* 196.

[83] http://www.anarchie.de/main-25597.html (visited on 4 June 2003).

[84] Liesbet Van Zoonen, 'Popular Culture as Political Communication' (2000) 7 *The Public* 14.

[85] Gertrud Höhler, *Die Sinn-Macher* (3rd edn, München: 2002) 229.

[86] Sherwin, n 6 above, 141.

[87] Similar, but still sceptical: ibid, 243.

[88] Drexl, n 66 above, 69.

[89] This view differs from Sherwin, n 6 above, 263.

[90] Quoted in Rodowick, n 10 above, 107.

matter which ethical theory law might follow, it has to adapt to the changes, because processing information is a core part of any theory. Any consensus, to take consensus-based theories for example, needs to rely on an informed consent.

2. Pop Culture and Global Communication

What has been said so far was dealing with the supposedly contrasting spheres of the private and the public. But the argument here probably needs a stronger thesis, which takes into consideration particular legal aspects. The master of law, politics, turned into elements of popular cultures in various countries.[91] Leaving aside the discussion whether this is undermining the viability of democracy in the long run[92] and is a symptom of a corrupted political cast, it can at least be taken as a hint that in spite of the somewhat antagonistic roots of politics and popular culture, both have become complementary, rather than oppositional, resources of political communication.[93] Political knowledge in general has not decreased at all in spite of the weakening power of traditional ways of accessing political information through the media.[94]

Media indeed are not completely neutral to the information they are expected to transmit. Political communication when using popular culture elements usually harnesses audio-visual effects. This is a new feature in politics which was thought to be qualified by the power of argument only. This is a rather idealistic perception bearing in mind that there are several prerequisites to making an argument at least a topic in the discourse.[95] Law seems to oppose this process because there is a certain resistance to individuality which is typical for pop culture. However, this statement actually contains two assumptions which should be doubted. First, it is assumed that Pop culture artefacts do not intend to be part of a socio-political discourse. Second, it seems to imply that law needs to keep an anti-individual approach. Both assumptions need to be criticized. It seems to be accepted meanwhile[96] that there are important clusters of a cultural public sphere in addition to the political public sphere.[97] Putting the focus on the latter, this is more and more considered to be a misconception emphasizing the oral and written discourse too heavily and neglecting the audio-visual

[91] Liesbet Van Zoonen, 'Popular Culture as Political Communication' (2000) 7 *The Public* 6.

[92] Neil Postman, *Amusing Ourselves to Death* (New York: 1985); Christian Gizewski, 'Die Lehre des Aristoteles von der "Widerlegung der Sophismen" und die Struktur der Öffentlichkeit der Polis' [1999] *KLIO* 81, n 24.

[93] Liesbet Van Zoonen, 'A Day at the Zoo: Political Communication, Pigs and Popular Culture' [1998] *Media, Culture and Society* 183.

[94] Kevin Barnhurst, 'The Makers of Meaning: National Public Radio and the New Long Journalism' (2003) 20(1) *Political Communication* 2, covering television as well.

[95] Ido De Haan, 'From Moses to Maggie' (2000) 7 *The Public* 37.

[96] 'Meanwhile' refers to Habermas Structural Transformation of the Public Sphere', who treated other spheres merely as 'training ground' for political publicity (Jürgen Habermas, *Strukturwandel der Öffentlichkeit* (Frankfurt: 1962) 29).

[97] Frands Mortensen, 'The Bourgeois Public Sphere' in M Berg et al (eds), *Current Theories in Scandinavian Mass Communication Research* (Copenhagen: 1977) 292.

discourse. The main reason why cultural activities can be seen as part of the public forum is that the reception of life contexts as a practice of consumption leads to shared experiences which form the starting point for a proto-public sphere.[98] Therefore they can be treated as the basis of any public political expression.

The second assumption to be criticized deals with the universalistic character of both law and Pop. For a long time the global extension of Pop music has been treated almost exclusively with post-colonial approaches.[99] But in times of Bollywood and at least seven national versions of 'The Ketchup Song' (my count), there is a need to modify this a bit. I would like to differentiate between three steps. First, there is the wish to transform international Pop music into a specific cultural context, either by translating and contextualizing the lyrics[100] or even by imitating the sound in local Pop music. Second, on an intermediate level the audience wishes to receive the international productions unfiltered, and third and most interesting, Pop music becomes truly international by taking stimuli from various local contexts. Who would have thought that major Pop albums can be produced in Croatia or Morocco? The key to all this seems to be the idea of making music understandable for a wide audience.[101] Commercialism is one reason for this, but there are many more related and relevant aspects, for example those of cultural identity.

Law and politics face the danger of participating in this in the form of populism.[102] Yet, the flip side of this, the far more promising one, is to create a form of politics quite close to the ideals of republican cities.[103] Some allusions to this idea can be found in communitarian publications,[104] but the perspective seems to me to be more national than global. But some practical steps have been taken in this direction, for example the discussion about the specific approach an Islamic human rights theory could have. If we look back to Islamic enlightenment after the 9th century some theorists argue that there is enough substance for a human rights theory in Islamic law.[105] This could enlarge the number of political options immensely, because a Euro-Islam could play an important role in the process of a true European integration.[106] On the other hand the situation in Islamic countries could improve,

[98] Göran Bolin, 'Film Swapping in the Public Sphere' (2000) 7 *The Public* 60.

[99] Dianne Otto, 'Subalternity and International Law' in E Smith and P Fitzpatrick (eds), *Laws of the Postcolonial* (1999) 145.

[100] A satire on this period is Shinehead's 'Jamaican in New York' (1992).

[101] Philip Tagg, 'Analysing Popular Music—Theory, Method, and Practice' in R Middleton (ed), *Reading Pop, Approaches to Textual Analysis in Popular Music* (Oxford: 2000) 19, also about the reverse phenomenon with classical music; see also Ray Pratt, *Rhythm and Resistance: Explorations in the Political Uses of Popular Music* (New York: 1990).

[102] De Haan, n 95 above.

[103] Which was politics by everyone and for everyone: John Leonard, 'Public versus Private Claims' 12(4) *Political Theory* 491.

[104] An overview can be found at Charles Jones, *Global Justice* (Oxford: 2001) 109.

[105] Bassam Tibi, *Der Islam in Deutschland* (Stuttgart: 2000), 342; Wolfgang Loschelder, 'Der Islam und die religionsrechtliche Ordnung des Grundgesetzes' in *Essener Gespräche zum Thema Staat und Kirche* (1986) 149.

[106] Bassam Tibi, 'Les conditions d'une Euro-Islam' in R Bistolfi and F Zabbal (eds), *Islams d'Europe. Integration ou Insertation Communautaire?* (Paris: 1995) 230.

because certain legal concepts would no longer be perceived as something external. In addition a discourse about human rights that includes Islamic positions may serve as a foundation for any further development at a supranational level.

Another example is the project to form a democracy model adaptable to South-East Asian societies.[107] Global as referred to in the title of this paper therefore should be understood as a way to promote the concept of law without implanting isolated fragments into a society. Thus, the strategy can either be a careful selection of the fragments used to make a democracy concept sound, or underpinning it by a network of popular elements. More important than a decision about how to tackle this is that this process is a matter of open discourses and not of clandestine management boards.[108] The scepticism against certain aspects of globalization is rightfully concerned more about the modes of communications used to reach certain results than with the results themselves. The fact that members of the anti-globalization movement rely on the technical side of globalization, such as telecommunication and internet, has been criticized, but this is not a contradiction at all. It is precisely the fact that global communication about values and democratic institutions does not follow the same discoursive standards that are considered fair in a national context which has exclusive effects. Consequently there is a need for trans-national modes of value discourses.

Popular music is trying to stimulate cross-group communication in various circumstances. As shown above, music styles limited to a special social or ethnic group in order to become popular need to find forms of expression that have enough qualities to be attractive to non-group members as well. Rap for instance underwent many changes before it became ready for the charts. It would be too much to talk about consensus on a musical ground already. Nevertheless it would not be wrong to characterize the idea of popular music as an agreement about how to exchange different music styles. Therefore—assuming that incorporated in this music we find representation of different values—Pop music is opening the gates for political discourse.

IV. Conclusion

'It's the singer, not the song' Mick Jagger once said.[109] Law has been spinning around mechanisms to neutralize the individual such as veils of ignorance, Archimedic points etc. In terms of Pop culture this is a problematic approach. Even

[107] Daniel Bell, David Brown, Kanishka Jasuriya and David Martin Jones (eds), *Towards Illiberal Democracy in Pacific Asia* (London and New York: 1995), where the concept of civil societies is stressed (163) as well. Karl-Heinz Pohl, 'Zwischen Universalismus und Relativismus' (1999) 71 *ASIEN* 39.

[108] Commission of Global Governance (ed), *Our Global Neighbourhood—Report of the Commission on Global Governance* (Oxford: 1995) section 9; most practically this has been attempted in drafting the UNESCO declaration on the human genome and human right. David Held, *Democracy and the Global Order. From Modern State to Cosmopolitan Democracy* (Cambridge: 1995); Klaus Dingwerth, *Globale Politiknetzwerke und ihre demokratische Legitimation* (Potsdam, Berlin, Oldenburg: 2003) 20.

[109] Peter Kaden, *Des Lebens wilder Kreis* (Kassel: 1993) 205.

though the performers of Pop music are often treated as anonymous and exchangeable subjects, there is at least the wish to be authentic and unique. Individuality and a richly constructed self is nothing law should be afraid of.[110] This is why I suggest in this paper that any form of legal globalization should be started from a subject-normative point. In conclusion there is a need to look after quite personal normative attitudes, because they are linked to the identity of citizens.

The first exercise field has been civil society. I chose this concept because it has been used successfully at the state level. Whereas any claims for governmental action need to be directed to a certain etatistic entity, civil society is independent from that. This independence however is under attack by those who prefer to construct a structure in which para-governmental organizations form a modified opponent for the people. Overall a theory of a global civil society should refrain from focusing on institutions and organizations only, but centre around the autonomy of people. Facing globalization from this perspective implies that singular decisions may lead into a culture of popular normative positions.

Yet Pop culture is not intrinsically better than other cultural styles. Back in the fifties many white singers could be successful in covering black music, because they could rely on the fact that black music would never reach a wide audience.[111] But speed being one characteristic of Pop culture helped it to learn one thing quite fast: being available for as many people as possible gives power to the ideas you want to promote. Pop culture does not tell the high art story of a hermeneutic gap between recipients who are fit for full capability and those who are not. Neither should law be a commodity with limited accessibility. So far it is just that, even in states with a strong judicial review, but especially from a global perspective.

This perspective seems to demand that there should be a certain focus on procedural law/formal law concepts. Even though within a community of shared values the material approach seems to be preferable, at a multi-national level it contains more obstacles than are helpful.[112] Suitable procedural concepts might be a procedural understanding of human rights or, as discussed here, the civil society concept. I am aware of the fact that there might be some doubt as to whether civil society can be treated simply as procedural concept, but as a concept of participation in social and political affairs there is a strong procedural element in it. This dimension is extremely dependent on making items visible and audible against a parliamentary process and within a cacophony of voices. This is almost inevitably going to lead to conflicts between different interests within an extra- and intra-legal context, but in the end, the agenda is most likely quite similar to the parliamentary process, only with a more fashionable model of representation. Popular culture, and that is almost a translation of this term, cares about the ideas of normal people. That is what law should do as well. That is why law needs Pop.

[110] Pierre Schlag, 'The Problem of the Subject' in Dennis M Patterson, *Postmodernism and Law* (Dartmouth: 1994), 1643.

[111] Peter Wicke, note 1 above, 183.

[112] Bell, n 52 above 219.

PART V

CRIME AND PUNISHMENT

Badfellas: Movie Psychos, Popular Culture, and Law

Nicole Rafter

It can be useful to think of movie analysis in terms of variously-sized boxes. The smallest boxes hold individual movies. The next size up holds series, such as Dirty Harry films or all movies by Hitchcock. Big boxes hold genres, such as Westerns or courtroom films. The biggest boxes of all hold thematic groupings of related genres; one of these, for example, is the 'crime films' category, which includes the genres of cop films, courtroom films, and prison films.[1] Currently, specialists in law and popular culture are in the process of identifying the contents of another very large box: the thematic grouping of law films.[2] This article is part of that effort. I will be proposing recognition of a new film genre, 'psychopath movies', and suggesting that this genre can profitably be included in the larger grouping of law films.[3]

Now, having made these distinctions among series, genres, and thematic groupings, I also must say that what is most important is not definitional labels but rather analyzing and understanding the complex relations between film and society—the ways they reflect and influence one another. In the long run, therefore, how the boxes are labelled—including whether psychopath movies qualify as a distinct genre or genre-like category—is less important than what this exercise reveals about film, culture, law, and society. Thus we must keep the box lids loose

[1] I make the argument for this definition of 'crime films' in more detail in N Rafter, *Shots in the Mirror: Crime Films and Society* (New York: 2000).

[2] For an excellent discussion of the issues involved in defining the category 'law films', see Guy Osborn, 'Borders and Boundaries: Locating the Law in Film' in S Machura and P Robson (eds), *Law and Film* (Oxford: 2001) 164. I get around what Osborn terms 'the most fundamental question' of deciding the contents of 'the law film genre' by avoiding it entirely and instead conceptualizing 'law films' as an umbrella category that encompasses genres, including courtroom films, non-courtroom lawyer films, psycho films as defined in this paper, some cop films, and so on. However, I do agree that the process of delineating the contents of the 'law films' category is ongoing and far from easy. For an attempt to define law films in terms of 'automatic reflexivity' instead of genre, see DA Black, *Law in Film* (Urbana: 1999) esp Part 2; and for an expansion of the arguments begun in Osborn, ibid, see S Greenfield, G Osborn, and P Robson, *Film and the Law* (London: 2001).

[3] Readers who prefer more sophisticated terminology should think of my 'boxes' as 'frames'. On the concept of frames and frame analysis, and ways in which these concepts relate to media constructions of reality, see William A Gamson, David Croteau, William Hoynes, and Theodore Sasson, 'Media Images and the Social Construction of Reality' (1992) 18 *Annual Rev of Sociology* 373.

so that we can shift films around, juxtaposing and regrouping them to yield new meanings, notably meanings about law in popular culture.

Definitions, however, are obviously helpful, and careless labelling can hamstring analysis before it starts. Although several people have already written about psychopath films, their definitions tend to be slack to the point of analytical uselessness. Two of these works are picture books with alarming photos of real life serial killers and movie characters with decomposing faces. One of them, John McCarty's *Movie Psychos and Madmen*, is the second edition of a book with chapters on 'master fiends', 'female psychos', 'real-life psychos', made-for-TV films, and so on. The other, Christian Fuch's *Bad Blood: An Illustrated Guide to Psycho Cinema*, includes 47 case histories with photographs of murderers who inspired movies, followed by chapters on 'psycho killers', 'amok killers', 'Sadean killers', and so on. Both books attempt to create one of the very large thematic groupings I spoke of earlier, but they fail to frame psychopath films in a meaningful way, either as genre or larger category.[4]

Three other works deal more thoughtfully with psychopath films. Philip Simpson's *Psycho Paths: Tracking the Serial Killer Through Contemporary American Film and Fiction* (2000), relates multiple-murder films to the Gothic tradition and 'the aesthetics of apocalypse'.[4a] But, unfortunately, at least for my purposes, it does not focus on psycho films per se and covers just a handful of movies. Wayne Wilson's *The Psychopath in Film* (1999) deals more extensively with the films I will be discussing here but also with numerous others, including *2001: A Space Odyssey* (the computer HAL as psychopath), *Hud* (the lady's man as psychopath), and the *James Bond* series (Goldfinger as psychopath).[5] While its scope is, then, broad relative to Simpson's book, Wilson's study suffers from a lack of clarity about its topic. A final work, Gordon Banks's article on 'Kubrick's Psychopaths', zeroes in very precisely on its target, analyzing director Stanley Kubrick's psychopathic characters in terms of a long-term psychiatric effort to define and understand the 'antisocial personality'. But Banks confines his analysis to Kubrick's films, whereas I am interested in a broader classification.[5a]

In search of a sound basis for defining psycho movies as a genre, I turned to clinicians for an exact description of the psychopath. Psychologist Robert Hare,

[4] J. McCarthy, *Movie Psychos and Madmen: Film Psychopathy from Jekyll and Hyde to Hannibal Lecter* (New York, 1993); C. Fuchs, *Bad Blood: An Illustrated Guide to Psycho Cinema* (London, 2002).

[4a] PL Simpson, *Psycho Paths* (Carbondale, Illinois: 2000), 173.

[5] W. Wilson, *The Psychopath in Film* (Lanham, Maryland, 1999).

[5a] Wayne J Douglass, 'The Criminal Psychopath as Hollywood Hero' (1981) 8 *J of Popular Film and Television* 30, traces the emergence of psycho movies from older gangster films and makes useful observations about cop heroes as psychopaths. However, Douglass's definition of the psychopath as existential hero and as anti-hero is too dated to provide a sound foundation for discussions of psycho-protagonists in film today. Gordon Banks, 'Kubrick's Psychopaths: Society and Human Nature in the Films of Stanley Kubrick' (1990) downloaded from http://www.visual-memory.co-uk/amk/doc/0004.html, 28 June 2002.

the leading specialist in this area, defines psychopathy in terms of key symptoms, including:

- deceitfulness and manipulation;
- lack of remorse or guilt and lack of empathy (psychopaths are 'completely indifferent to the rights and suffering of family and strangers alike');
- egocentricity and grandiosity ('Psychopaths have [a] narcissistic and grossly inflated view of their own self-worth and importance . . . and see themselves as the center of the universe');
- glibness and superficiality ('Psychopaths are often voluble and verbally facile. They . . . are often very likeable and charming');
- emotional shallowness ('a kind of emotional poverty that limits the range and depth of their feelings');
- impulsivity, shortness of temper, and craving for excitement;
- irresponsibility ('Obligations and commitments mean nothing to psychopaths');
- behaviour problems dating from childhood, followed by anti-social behaviour in adulthood ('They make their own rules').[6]

Similar symptoms are used by the American Psychiatric Association to define *antisocial personality disorders*, its current term for psychopathy.[7] Neither Hare nor the APA expects every psychopath to exhibit every one of these symptoms. Rather, they apply the diagnosis to people in whom combinations of these symptoms predominate. The key traits, stressed by clinicians since the condition of psychopathy was first identified in the 18th century, are self-centredness and lack of conscience: psychopaths lack remorse for the harms they commit to gratify themselves.

As the clinical symptoms suggest, psychopaths can add an engrossing and entertaining dimension to films. Many viewers enjoy identifying with characters who cleverly evade responsibility, mow down their enemies, and defy legal authorities. Moreover, because psychopaths are so far off the normal curve, behaviourly, their characters can be amusing, gripping, or spectacular—or all three at once, as in the case of the thug in *Fargo* who stuffs his partner in a wood chipper. Thus many movies include a cameo psychopath, a minor character to up the entertainment ante. Examples extend from *Deliverance*, with its backwoods sex perverts, through *Goodfellas*, with Joe Pesci's explosive Tommy DeVito ('Funny like a clown? I amuse you?'), to *Reservoir Dogs*, in which Mr Blond performs a mating

[6] Robert D Hare, 'Predators: The Disturbing World of the Psychopaths Among Us' (1994) 27 *Psychology Today* 54 (downloaded from http://web7.infortrac.galegroup.com, 29 October 2002). Also see RD Hare, *Without Conscience* (New York: 1993) and Robert D Hare, Stephen D Hart, and Timothy J Harpur, 'Psychopathy and the *DSM-IV* Criteria for Antisocial Personality Disorder' (1991), 100 *J of Abnormal Psychology* 391.

[7] American Psychiatric Association, *Diagnostic and Statistical Manual for Mental Disorders* (4th edn, Arlington, Virginia: 2000).

dance while slicing off the cop's ear. Such cameo psychos are too minor to determine a movie's genre, but they do indicate the versatility and appeal of the psychopath as film character.

Psychopaths provide fertile material not only for film-makers and viewers but also for scholars interested in intersections of popular culture and law. Lawless by definition, psychopathic characters offer occasions for exploring what movies say about our need for law. Their narratives show how law reacts to or is rendered helpless by individuals who sneer at legal boundaries and the threat of punishment. And psycho movies present a wide range of views on the means by which disrupted legal orders are restored.

In what follows, I will ignore the cameo psychopaths, delightful though they are, to focus on movies in which a psycho plays a central role. These films either explore the psychopathic personality in depth or follow a psychopath over a period of time, tracing the trajectory of his or her career. I will not try to cover all examples of films in which the central character fits the clinical definition outlined by Robert Hare and the APA but will rather concentrate on about 20 examples.[8] My key requirement, aside from centrality, is that the character be depicted as conscienceless and innately evil; psychopathy is an ongoing condition, not a transitory affliction. This means excluding *Taxi Driver*'s Travis Bickle, partly because he has a conscience (an overactive one, in fact), partly because his evil is not innate. My definition also excludes Hitchcock's *Marnie*, even though the main character has killed a man and steals compulsively, because the film attributes Marnie's criminality to childhood trauma, and she is cured of it by her wonderful husband Sean Connery. To be included on my list, a film must feature a character whose cruelty is disproportionate to the events that trigger it; the nastiness must be to some degree inexplicable. This means omitting *Natural Born Killers*, which fully explains Mickey and Mallory's violence (and which, in any case, rehabilitates them at the end, sending them off in a camper with their children). It also means that I will not cover films like *Bonnie and Clyde* that are not seriously interested in evil. I am looking for, not the goodfellas—the ordinary criminals who cook pasta and blunder through life like the rest of us—but the badfellas, the truly wicked criminals who seem monstrous.

Psycho movies are basically concerned with control: its loss and its restoration. In the experience of viewers, the loss of control and regaining of it are equally

[8] The films themselves are listed in the next section of the text. In selecting these films, I aimed, first, at chronological coverage, thus choosing some works from the earliest days of sound movies as well as recent examples. I also tried for range in terms of the characteristics of the psychopathic figures. I excluded ho-hum Hannibal knock-offs such as *Kalifornia*, though I did include one rather dull film, *Black Widow*, because I wanted an early example of a female psycho. I tried to include films that readers would expect to find here (*Psycho*, Mitchum's *Cape Fear*, *Seven*) and some of my own favourites, such as both versions of *Kiss of Death*. (The remakes of *Cape Fear*, *Scarface*, and *The Vanishing* seems to me less successful than their originals; thus I excluded them from primary consideration, though I do refer to them in footnotes.) I readily admit that two of my examples, *Frankenstein* and *The Shining*, are as much horror films as psycho movies. I also recognize that there is no way to be sure my examples are truly representative of the universe of psycho movies.

important elements. Together they foster a delicious hypocrisy. By concentrating on a central psychopathic figure, these films encourage viewers' fantasies of violent egotism, self-indulgent predation, domination, and control. However, the films nearly always bring us back to a world of law through the capture, defeat, or death of the psychopath. That is, through psychopath movies we get to have it both ways—to identify with the lawless criminal and yet return to the lawful world of order in the end.[9] On the level of legal discourse, the theme of control plays out in demonstrations of the need for law. Psycho movies tend to proceed through three stages. First they demonstrate the necessity of law by displaying a central character who invades the ordinary world and disrupts or destroys it. Then they show the inadequacy of law to contain these characters. Most conclude with the restoration of legal order, but in many cases this control is achieved through extra-legal means. I will return to these points after surveying the most central and defining element of psycho movies: the characterizations of psychos themselves.

In what follows, I will be trying to define psycho movies as a distinct genre or genre-like category—to temporarily remove certain works from the boxes labelled 'cop films', 'horror films', 'gangster films', and 'thrillers' and put them in a new box, 'psycho movies', to see what that yields in terms of fresh analysis and discourses about law and order. A film genre is defined partly in terms of its stock figures—characters who vary from film to film but are easily recognized for what they are and remain essentially unchanged across time. A genre is also defined by plot formulas,[10] basic themes and settings, and standard tone and message.[11] The single most important element in psycho movies, in terms of definition, is the characters. These films are completely rooted in character and the meanings that the characters generate. This distinguishes psycho movies from the slashers, spatters, and serial-killer films with which they are often misgrouped. Slashers, serial-killer films, and their kin have little concern with character. Their protagonists, as Philip Jenkins points out in his excellent study *Using Murder*, are essentially flat, faceless, and almost supernatural, more closely related to the cannibals, werewolves, and vampires of earlier horror stories and

[9] Not just psycho films but crime movies generally give readers this pleasure of first identifying with the bad guys and then bringing them to heel. Psycho movies provide an especially interesting instance of this double movement, however, because in theory their protagonists are much more difficult to identify with. Another difference between other crime films and psycho movies is that the protagonists of the latter pose much more severe tests to the law than do ordinary criminals.

[10] Since I will not be analyzing the standard plots of psycho movies in the text of this paper, let me note here that there seem to be three basic formulas. One follows the career of the psycho, tracing it from an initial point of intrusion through increasingly monstrous predations to a final downfall. A second plot pattern is built around the hunt for a psychopath, a search that is often led by a legal authority. The third type combines the other two, sometimes juxtaposing the psycho's career with the avenger's hunt in alternating sequences and occasionally drawing parallels as well as contrasts between the two.

[11] Genres have histories as well. The history of the psycho movie is already being written by scholars such as Douglass, n 5 above, and P Jenkins, *Using Murder: The Social Construction of Serial Homicide*, (New York: 1994). Related historical work has been done in the area of mystery novels; see Lawrence M Friedman and Issachar Rosen-Zvi, 'Illegal Fictions: Mystery Novels and the Popular Image of Crime' (2001) 48 *U of California at Los Angeles L Rev* 1411. A thumbnail history of psycho movies appears in P Hardy (ed), *The BFI Companion to Crime* (Berkeley: 1997) 275–277.

myths than to disturbed human beings.[12] They give us devils, whereas psycho movies give us villains. Thus I will begin by analyzing characterization in psycho movies, distinguishing three broad types. Then I will return to the legal discourses of psycho films and what these tell us about the nature of law.

The Stock Characters of Psycho Movies

Most psycho movies revolve around a single character who is male. This at any rate is the conclusion suggested by the films on my list, which include Fritz Lang's *M* (1931); James Whale's *Frankenstein* (1931); the original version of *Scarface* (1932), directed by Howard Hawks; both versions of *Kiss of Death*, the first (1947) directed by Henry Hathaway, the second (1995) by Barbet Schroder; Raoul Walsh's *White Heat* (1949); Alfred Hitchcock's *Strangers on a Train* (1951) and his *Psycho* (1960); Charles Laughton's *Night of the Hunter* (1955), starring Robert Mitchum; *Cape Fear* (1962), another Mitchum film, this one directed by J Lee Thompson; two movies by director Stanley Kubrick, *Clockwork Orange* (1971) and *The Shining* (1980); the Dutch/French version of *The Vanishing* (1988), directed by George Sluizer; John Schlesinger's *Pacific Heights* (1990), starring Michael Keaton as the renter-from-hell; and David Fincher's *Seven* (1995). In three other examples on my list, there is again only one psychopath, but it is female: *Body Heat* (1981), directed by Lawrence Kasdan and starring Kathleen Turner; Bob Rafelson's *Black Widow* (1987), with Theresa Russell as the predatory husband-hunter; and Barbet Schroeder's *Single White Female* (1992), in which Jennifer Jason Leigh preys on apartment-mate Bridget Fonda. Two other examples give us a psychopathic couple: director Joseph H Lewis's *Gun Crazy* (1949) and Terrence Malick's *Badlands* (1973), starring Martin Sheen and Sissy Spacek as killers on the run. My list also includes two demographic outliers: Mervyn LeRoy's *The Bad Seed* (1956), in which the psychopath is a child; and Jonathan Demme's *Silence of the Lambs* (1991), in which there are two psychopaths, Hannibal Lecter and Buffalo Bill, but they are antagonists, not lovers.

These demographics are not surprising, since most film protagonists, regardless of genre, are male. A more revealing way to classify the protagonists of psycho movies is by the impulses that propel them to commit their evil deeds. This perspective yields three categories: predators, whackos, and aspiring Nietzsches.

Predators

The most rational of the three character types, the predators, have an excuse such as money or revenge for their psychopathic behaviour, although that behaviour is by

[12] Jenkins, n 11, above; also see CJ Clover, *Men, Women, and Chainsaws* (Princeton: 1992). The differences between the psycho movie and the serial-killer/slasher film emerge clearly from a comparison of the two versions of *The Vanishing*. The first (1988) is a pure psycho movie (maybe the purest of them all), while the second (1993), again directed by George Sluizer, is really a horror movie, with Jeff Bridges' face decomposing in a manner reminiscent of characters in *Texas Chainsaw Massacre* and with (to use Clover's felicitous term) a triumphant Final Girl.

definition an overreaction. For instance, the gangster protagonist of the first *Scarface* movie, modelled after Al Capone and played by Paul Muni, is out for money, slinky blondes, and power. But he is not an ordinary gangster. As his simian face suggests, Tony Camonte is incapable of identifying with others. Animalian in his cruelty, he is someone who lives ruthlessly by the law of tooth and claw. Similarly, Tom Udo, the psychopathic gangster of the first version of *Kiss of Death*, is after money, dames, and underworld power. But, as played by Richard Widmark in the role that made him famous, Tom Udo combines fatuous stupidity with menace. Unlike other criminals, he does not care when he is sentenced to a prison term in Sing Sing. He pushes an elderly woman in a wheelchair down a staircase, laughing uncontrollably as she tumbles to her death. Simultaneously calm and hysterical, Udo is a connoisseur of cruelty. 'You know what I do to squealers?' he asks. 'I let 'em have it in the belly, so they can roll around for a long time, thinking it over.' In the 1995 remake of *Kiss of Death*, Nicolas Cage is equally chilling as Little Junior Brown. Extraordinarily brutal and always on the edge of exploding, Junior rules his gang through terror. That he is also dim-witted, insensitive, and self-centred merely ups the level of nervous tension.[13]

Psychopathic predators are not necessarily gangsters, however. The protagonist of *Night of the Hunter* is an ersatz preacher who has killed 12 widows so far and, as he explains to God in the opening sequence, is now after another 'widow with a little wad of bills hidden away in the sugar bowl'. Sexually perverted as well, he loathes 'perfumed things with curly hair' who weaken his self-control and make him feel unclean. After ritually sacrificing widow Willa Harper but failing to locate her money, the preacher pursues her children as they flee downstream in a small boat. Eventually, just a few notes of the song the preacher sings during his relentless pursuit ('Leaning on Jesus, leaning on the everlasting arm') gives viewers, as well as the children, the creeps. Another memorable Mitchum predator is the ex-convict Max Cady of *Cape Fear*, in which Cady torments Sam Bowden, a lawyer (played by Gregory Peck) who helped send him to prison eight years earlier. Although Sam did nothing more than testify as witness to a rape, Cady's thirst for revenge is overwhelming and unstoppable. It can be slaked only by raping Sam's teenage daughter. Utterly fearless, arrogant, and crafty, Cady knows precisely what he can get away with and calibrates his taunts accordingly, to the millimetre.

Pacific Heights brings new meaning to the concept of predation with its story of a young couple who rent part of their Victorian fixer-upper to a lodger (Michael Keaton) who, as it turns out, plans to drive them mad and assume ownership of the mansion himself. To this end he destroys his quarters in the house, frightens the owners out of their wits, and tricks them into making blunders, for example by goading the landlord into assaulting him so he can play the victim when the police arrive and have the landlord evicted. *Body Heat*, too, rings changes on the theme of predation by forcing the viewer to share the viewpoint of Ned Racine (William Hurt), the poor

[13] Brian de Palma's remake of *Scarface* (1983) similarly updates the character of Tony, relocating him to a contemporary context and intensifying the violence while retaining the core notion of a psychopathic predator.

chump whom the glamorous Mattie (Kathleen Turner) persuades to kill her rich husband. Not till the end do we realize that Mattie prearranged everything, including her initial encounter with Ned. Even while Ned is off bludgeoning her husband, she is destroying his alibi so she can dump him in prison.

Predatory psychos are Machiavellis—cold, cunning, and calculating. Monomaniacal in pursuit of their goals, abnormal by dint of what they will do to achieve those goals, they are what Wayne Wilson terms 'overcontrolled psychos',[14] antisocial types who scheme and plot to satisfy their desires.

Whackos

Whacko psychopaths are far less rational. Gripped by insane desires, they are incapable of self control. While the whackos, too, are often predatory, their movies emphasize psychological deviation. One example can be found in *The Bad Seed*, the tale of blonde-haired, goody-goody little Rhoda who has, alas, inherited a homicidal gene from her maternal grandmother. Rhoda kills again and again, till she is finally struck dead by lightning.

Boris Karloff created a classic whacko in the role of the Monster. Even though *Frankenstein* is usually classified as a horror film, it seems to me a seminal psycho movie as well. Certainly its main character became a model for subsequent psychopaths. Infantile, only half human, and cursed with a criminaloid's brain, the Monster yearns for goodness and light but clumsily destroys the things he loves. Like Norman Bates, his most famous descendant, the Monster is drawn to blondes but impulsively murders them. And like Norman Bates, the Monster is not fully responsible for his criminal acts. In keeping with the psychiatry of the early 1930s, the Monster's psychopathy is explained partly in terms of mental retardation, while Norman is more of a 1950s sex psycho. But both films are visually structured around alternating bright and dark scenes that symbolize the main characters' losing struggle between childlike innocence and grownup evil.

The whacko psychopath role has generated a host of other remarkable film crazies. One is the failed novelist Jack Daniel Torrance (Jack Nicholson) of *The Shining*, who, like little Rhoda and Dr Frankenstein's Monster, is governed by homicidal impulses over which he has no control. In *Silence of the Lambs*, Buffalo Bill, too, is helpless in the face of his obsessions. (Hannibal Lecter, in contrast, is a predatory psychopath who stays on top of his madness.) The protagonist-lovers of *Gun Crazy* are fixated on guns, and one of them (interestingly, the female, played brilliantly by Peggy Cummins) finds sensual pleasure in shooting people. Alex (Malcolm McDowell), the exuberantly delinquent protagonist of *Clockwork Orange*, engages in crime because it is the most amusing activity he can think of.

[14] W Wilson, *The Psychopath in Film*, n5 above, 98. Wilson distinguishes overcontrolled psychopaths from 'undercontrolled' psychos (equivalents of my 'whackos') and 'classic' psychopaths, the latter being a residual category.

Kit and Holly, the protagonists of *Badlands*, are lost, empty souls who murder because there is nothing else to do.

The differences between predatory and whacko psychos come into focus through a comparison of *Black Widow* with *Single White Female*. Theresa Russell's predatory widow is motivated solely by greed; her film is organized around her repetitive searches for a new rich husband and by the hunt for her by federal agent Debra Winger. On the other hand, Hedy Carlton (Jennifer Jason Leigh), the psychopath of *Single White Female*, is twisted psychologically. Desperate for a friend, she tries to endear herself to her apartment-mate by dressing similarly, tossing her dog out the window, and braining her lover with a stiletto shoe heel. Whereas the Black Widow is unflappable and unchanging, Hedy ricochets among personalities and trips over her own lies. *Black Widow* stresses the cold rationality and extraordinary patience of its predator, while *Single White Female* concentrates on Hedy's frantic nuttiness.[15]

Aspiring Nietzsches

A third type of psychopathic protagonist assumes the right to toy with others and inflict pain. These characters aspire to be supermen, gods who decide the fate of others. They, too, are predatory and mentally unbalanced, but their films emphasize their Nietzschean ambition to rise above the human condition.[16]

In *White Heat*, Cody Jarrett (James Cagney) assumes powers of life and death over others by virtue of his leadership of a criminal gang. But, egged on by his ambitious, doting mother[17] (Margaret Wycherly), Cody aspires even higher, to the 'top of the world'. Taking this goal literally, Cody achieves it in the spectacular final scene, where, cornered by cops, he climbs an oil tank and blows it up, yelling 'Made it, Ma! Top of the World!' He dies in a triumph of deluded egotism.

Bruno, the psychopath of *Strangers on a Train*, explicitly articulates his sense of entitlement to decide life and death matters for others. Like Cody, Bruno (Robert Walker) is a mama's boy; like Cody, he suffers from strange spells or fits. But Bruno is much more arrogant, a spoiled rich guy, vain, insensitive, presumptuous, and greedy. During the first scene, in the lounge car of the train, Bruno presses his new acquaintance, Guy Haines (Farley Granger), to 'Ask me anything, I know the answer.' Later, Bruno responds to a remark by Guy with 'Oh, I've got a wonderful theory about that'. He explains that his absurd father wants him to get a job and:

> work my way up. . . . I want to kill him. . . . I want to do something—everything. Now, I've got a theory that you should do everything before you die. Have you ever driven a car

[15] As one might expect, some psychos combine aspects of the predator and the whacko. One example is the paedophile Hans Beckert of *M*.

[16] In the remake of *Cape Fear*, someone reports having seen psycho Max Cady in the public library reading Nietzsche's *Thus Spake Zarathustra*.

[17] As Douglass, n 5, above, 33 points out, Ma's credentials for being labelled a psycho are at least as strong as Cody's.

blindfolded, at 150 miles per hour? . . . I did. . . . And I'm going to make a reservation on the first rocket to the moon.

It turns out that Bruno is serious in suggesting that he and Guy switch victims, with Guy murdering Bruno's father and Bruno getting rid of Guy's floozy of a wife. 'What is a life or two, Guy? Some people are better off dead.'

The psychopath of *Seven*, John Doe (Kevin Spacey), plays God by turning New York City into a stage for the production of a medieval morality play. Inflamed by the city's indifference to the seven deadly sins, John Doe creates a Dantesque hell on earth as he punishes one sin at a time, spectacularly working his way through Gluttony, Greed, Sloth, Lust, and Vanity. Playing God to himself as well, John Doe arranges to be struck down for his Envy of the younger detective's normality. On another level, John Doe controls the movie's plot as well, generating this morality play for the edification of Detective Lt William Somerset (Morgan Freeman) and the movie's viewers, much as God has generated the world for the edification of Everyman.

Most Nietzschean of all psycho protagonists is Raymond Lemorne (Bernard-Pierre Donnadieu), the central figure in the Dutch/ French version of *The Vanishing*. This tightly-wrought film single-mindedly explores the motivations of Lemorne, who appears to be an innocuous man, a chemistry instructor with a wife and two daughters. Despite his bland exterior, however, Lemorne is obsessed with control, as we gather from his constant counting, measuring, and timing of things. To Rex Hofman, his second victim, Lemorne explains that at age 16 he realized that he could go beyond 'what is predestined' by forcing himself to jump from a high balcony. Although he broke an arm and lost two fingers, he has always been glad that he jumped, because it proved he can defy fate. Then Lemorne tells Rex about a family holiday during which he saved a child from drowning. When one of his daughters congratulated him, Lemorne recalls, he responded: 'Watch out for heroes. A hero is someone who is capable of excess.' His daughter's admiration, Lemorne continues, encouraged him to think of the worst thing he could imagine doing ('since there is no white without black'). Killing, he casually observes, is not the worst thing he can conceive of.

What makes *The Vanishing* devastating is not just the nature of Lemorne's 'worst thing' but the fact that Rex becomes like his killer in his own Nietzschean defiance of fate. After his girlfriend vanishes during a holiday in southern France, Rex spends three years trying to figure out what happened, in the process becoming obsessed and unhinged. Lemorne finally comes to him and starts driving Rex through the night to the spot where Saskia disappeared. At any point during the car trip, Rex could kill Lemorne, or at least break out and escape. But he remains of his own free will. Similarly, in order 'to go against what's predestined', Rex agrees to drink the drugged coffee that Lemorne offers him. Lemorne knows all along that Rex will try thus to defy fate. Like the praying mantis in the opening and closing shots, Lemorne preys on others while sitting motionless and blending in with the landscape.

Secondary Stock Figures

In addition to these stock protagonists, psycho movies often include a predictable secondary character or set of characters. Some parallel the central figure, others contrast sharply; but either way, they are designed to emphasize the psychopath's lawlessness.

Good Bad-guys

Fairly common are what we might call good bad-guys, secondary characters whose lesser moral flaws throw the psychopath's monstrosity into higher relief. When the psychopath is an arch criminal, the good bad-guy often will be a pettier offender who looks like a sweetheart in comparison. In *M* we find an entire underworld of ordinary criminals, all of them shocked to the bone by Hans Beckert's sex murders and anxious to help the authorities hunt him down. Similarly, both versions of *Kiss of Death* contrast their psycho with a criminal who is trying to go straight for the good of his family. In both versions the good bad-guy struggles with the bad bad-guy in a battle that signifies the psychological struggle within the reforming offender as well as the universal struggle of good against evil. *Night of the Hunter* compares the evil preacher with Willa's first husband, Ben Harper, an essentially decent man who, made desperate by financial woes, began robbing to feed his family. The two criminals share a prison cell together, which is where the preacher learns that Willa and her children are sitting on a pile of stolen money. But whereas Ben, the good criminal, gave money to the family, the other intends to take it away.

Playing with the convention of the good bad-guy, *Strangers on a Train* trots out goofy Babs, the bespectacled younger sister of Guy's new love. Like Bruno, Babs talks too much; she, too, is insensitive, presumptuous, snoopy, pushy, and a bit overexcited sexually. But, we are encouraged to notice, she does not kill anyone and indeed seems more of a potential victim than a villain.[18] The contrast does not flatter Bruno. Even more playfully, *Body Heat* makes the good bad-guy, Ned Racine, the unwitting accomplice of Mattie, the psycho-predator. In stark contrast to Mattie, Ned is lovable and straightforward. He is not very smart, as Mattie immediately remarks, and he is unsophisticated, an ordinary fellow with simple lusts. Mattie chooses him for these qualities, which differ so dramatically from her own.

Pure Innocents

Another common stock character in psycho movies is the pure innocent who illustrates the weakness of virtue when faced with malice, and hence the need for law. *M* opens with a mother making lunch for a little girl who (it turns out) will

[18] The character of Babs also functions as a surrogate for Bruno's actual victim, Guy's wife Miriam.

never return from school; this maternal figure, along with all the child victims, underscores Hans Beckert's destructiveness. Children again fill the role of lambs-in-danger in *Kiss of Death*, in both versions of which the psycho attempts to prevent the milder criminal from reforming by threatening the latter's offspring. *Night of the Hunter*, casting the psychopathic preacher as a stepfather and the innocent children as his prey, takes on a mythic dimension in which a Bad Father is intent on destroying childhood itself.

The figure of the innocent child matures slightly in *Cape Fear*, becoming 16-year-old Nancy, Max Cady's intended rape victim. The innocent is again a very helpless young woman in *Seven*, in which Gwyneth Paltrow's ingenue is overwhelmed by the noise, confusion, and crime of New York City and, eventually, by the psychopath who represents them. Her film husband, Detective David Mills (Brad Pitt), while less innocent, is also young and extremely naïve, traits that inspire psychopath John Doe to teach him a lesson. *Frankenstein* includes two innocents, first Little Maria, the playmate whom the monster accidently drowns, and then The Bride in full regalia, her gown and long white train contrasting vividly with the ill-fitting black worsted suit of the figure clambering through her window.

Hitchcock has fun with this pure innocent role in *Psycho*. At first, viewers think the role may be being filled by the nice young motel keeper, to whom Marion confesses her theft and who helps her decide to return the money. Later we realize that Marion herself is the innocent (as well as the good bad-guy to Norman Bates's psycho). Later still, we wonder if Norman himself might have initially been the innocent victim of a psychopathic mother—or if the police and their psychiatrist may be innocents duped by a madman. Since we the viewers cannot tell, perhaps we are innocents being victimized by a psychopathic film director.

Thanks to the women's movement, as well as to innovations like the role reversals in *Psycho*, the pure innocent increased in complexity during the 1990s. First came *Silence of the Lambs*, with Clarice Starling (Jodie Foster), the clear, birdlike naif who is nonetheless eager to learn and ends up coping heroically with two psychopaths at once. On its heels came *Pacific Heights*, which portrays Patty (Melanie Griffith), the female half of the victimized couple, as a lot smarter and tougher than her partner, Drake. Whereas Drake fights back physically, thus earning a restraining order that forbids him from coming within 500 feet of his own house, Patty combats the psychopath with cunning. She realizes that, if she is to save her house and her life, she must take the law into her own hands. During the final scene, when she and psychopath Carter Hayes stalk one another in the mansion, Carter notes that she is taking on some of his own Nietzschean qualities: 'You crossed the line, and it felt good'. He proves to be right: she enjoys killing him. A faint smile crosses her face and her eyes sparkle as she moves in for the kill.[19]

[19] Here *Pacific Heights* echoes *Gun Crazy*, in which Annie Laurie Starr's eyes similarly light up with the thrill of killing.

Equally impressive are the transformations of the pure innocent in *Single White Female*. Ally Jones (Bridget Fonda), the apartment owner who advertizes for a 'single white female' roommate, is a bit of a Barbie Doll but no ethereal maiden. Her competence, independence, and generosity contrast with Hedy's mean-spirited dependency. Whereas Ally is poised and self-confident, Hedy is mousy, dreary, and (who can blame her?) filled with self-loathing. Ally has a healthy heterosexual relationship; Hedy sneaks out to sex clubs and exhibits lesbian tendencies. Ally remains cool under pressure, Hedy falls apart. Unlike Hedy, who is consumed with guilt about having killed her twin in childhood, Ally has the fortitude to kill when necessary and get on with life. The pure innocent has become a psycho-slayer.[20]

One way or another, nearly all the stock characters in psycho movies demonstrate the need for law. The predators scheme and bully to break the law; the whackos, impelled by inner demons, blunder into law-breaking; and the Nietzsches assume right to make their own laws. Through contrasts, the good bad-guys and pure innocents highlight the barbarity of the psychos' transgressions, making a return to lawfulness seem even more imperative.

Legal Themes in Psycho Movies

Psycho movies set up their fundamental dialectic of disorder and control through not only stock characters but also discourses about law: the need for law; the inadequacy of law in extreme circumstances such as those posed by psychos; and means through which the lawful order is restored. These legal issues are often organized around the theme of *intrusion*. A psycho penetrates a previously lawful space, creates havoc, and immobilizes the law. Rendered helpless, other characters do not know how to react. They turn to traditional legal means only to find these ineffective. Gradually they conclude that they must take the law into their own hands. In *M*, the psycho intrudes on the nurturing, quotidian world in which mothers fix lunch for children who return from school; Franz Becker shatters this world with his sex slayings. *Scarface* opens with the shadow of an armed man gliding along a wall; Tony Camonte is about to intrude violently on the aftermath of a late-night party. In *Pacific Heights*, lodger Carter Hayes not only intrudes into the normal world of the young property owners; he also lures their fluffy white cat, an emblem of Patty and Drake's innocent domesticity, into his own apartment. This happens innocuously, but we know it means doom. Similarly, in *Single White Female*, Hedy makes her first entrance into Ally's apartment unannounced and unnoticed. Here as in

[20] Much ink has been spilled in discussing why Martin Scorsese's remake of *Cape Fear* is less successful than the original. The basic problem, I think, is that the characters of both the pure innocent and the psycho are diluted. Lawyer Sam Bowden (Nick Nolte in the remake) is more flawed than the original character, just as the secondary innocent, his young daughter, is less innocent. Meanwhile, Max Cady (Robert De Niro in the second version) is given a stronger motive for coming after Sam. The net result is loss of the psycho movie's stock characters and with it, loss of the stark struggle between good and evil that one expects to find in this type of film.

most psycho films, the victim is someone with simple aspirations, trying to repair an old house, fixing lunch, arguing with a lover, sobering up after a party. What the psychopath intrudes on, ultimately, is the normality of our ordinary lives. Often the psycho is discovered at the centre of a placid family or community, hidden there after the initial intrusion, working malignantly from within.

In *Frankenstein*, the key scene of intrusion comes relatively late in the film, when the Monster penetrates the Bride's bedroom. Usually, however, the most powerful images of intrusion occur near the start of a movie, where they start the plot rolling. The preacher in *Night of the Hunter* drives into the movie in an open-topped convertible, his broad-brimmed hat tilted back, on his way to Willa Harper's place; the cataclysm is about to begin. *Cape Fear* opens with a tracking shot of Mitchum, wearing that hat again, ambling across a town square to the courthouse. More than an intrusion of lawlessness into the territory of law, this is a sexual invasion as well, as the huge cigar protruding from Max Cady's mouth signifies. Cady removes the cigar for a puff, cooly checks out some women passers-by, and takes his first step into the court building. Climbing the stairs (and rudely ignoring an librarian struggling with a stack of books), Cady strolls into Sam Bowden's courtroom. Its intense, multi-layered rendering of the theme of intrusion makes this one of the most effective opening scenes in movie history.

Sometimes the psycho's intrusions are mental or symbolic. *Strangers on a Train* begins with a casual encounter between two men who have never met; Bruno invades Guy's life not physically but through psychological insinuation. *Psycho* casts the intrusion theme into metaphors of spying and peering: the cop in the sunglasses; the eye at the peephole; the shining eyes of the birds of prey, ready to pounce; the camera watching as Mr Arbogast invades the mansion and starts mounting those fatal stairs. In this movie even a glance into forbidden places incurs guilt and complicity (a lesson Norman Bates seems to have learned in childhood through spying on his mother). In *The Shining*, too, viewers accompany the characters into forbidden spaces, visually penetrating intricate, empty mazes that hold hideous secrets.

The point of these intrusions, then, is not just that the psychopath kills people and sows disorder. The psychopath *is* disorder, the destroyer of predictability in the ordinary world. We need law because the ominous-looking men under the streetlight may be Alex and his droogies from *Clockwork Orange*, preparing to beat us up and wreck our expectations of normalcy. (Underscoring the anonymous, ubiquitous nature of the psychopath, *Seven* names him John Doe and denies him even fingerprints.) The psychopath is always there, waiting to intrude, to knock innocent people off their feet and take over. What can protect us, if not law?

The Failure of Law and Restoration of Order

But even law, we find, is powerless to contain the psychopath, and in fact, it can turn a situation from bad to worse. Two films make this point with special acerbity by featuring a lawyer as the psychopath's main victim and showing that he simply cannot cope.

Ned Racine of *Body Heat* is a lawyer with little ambition, few skills, and almost no integrity. Before he met Mattie, we learn, he botched a case involving a will. He fails to guess that Mattie will use the same loophole in Florida's inheritance law to walk away with her murdered husband's entire fortune. (This same loophole is invoked in *Black Widow*, another psycho film in which law protects the lawless.) *Body Heat* concludes with a faint gesture toward the restoration of law and order when Ned, in prison, manages to get hold of a copy of Mattie's high school year book and figure out her true identity. But as hunts for the psychopath go, this one lacks promise.

Cape Fear's chief victim is not just a lawyer but Gregory Peck, an actor whose very appearance conveys moral and legal rectitude. (*Cape Fear* was released in April 1962, eight months before *To Kill a Mocking Bird*, in which Peck stars as the heroic lawyer Atticus Finch. Anyone who saw *Cape Fear* after 25 December 1962, then, might also have associated its lawyer, Sam Bowden, with Atticus.[21]) Sam turns for help to his old friend the police chief, who uses police harassment to encourage Max Cady to leave town. But Cady has been studying law in prison for eight years and outsmarts them, bringing in a sleazy lawyer to halt the chief's campaign. Sam, who of course knows his rights, then warns Cady to 'Stay off my property'. Moments later in the garden of his house, Nancy's dog starts yelping and expires, poisoned, with Bernard Herrmann's violins shrieking in the background. Evidently Cady is unimpressed by property rights and lawerly injunctions. Sam and the police chief begin wondering whether law should be able to 'prevent' crime through denial of civil liberties. 'Either we have too many laws', one of them observes, 'or not enough.' Later, after Max Cady has beaten a girlfriend to a pulp, the police beg her to press charges; but she refuses—another round for Cady in his match against the law. When Sam finds Cady leering at his daughter on a boat dock, he throws a punch, but Cady refuses to respond: 'You're not going to push me into anything, counsellor. . . . I'll make my stroke later'.

Cady has figured out how to use the law against Sam: if his daughter is raped, Sam will not ask Nancy to testify. 'It's the clinical reports and the questions and the detailed answers that she'd have to give', Sam explains to his wife. 'Cady *knows* we'd never put her through an ordeal like that.' Running out of lawful solutions, Sam has Cady beaten by thugs, but the moment they leave, Cady goes to a payphone, calls Sam's house, and announces: 'You just put the law in my hands, and I'm going to break your heart with it. I've got something planned for your wife and kid that

[21] 'The fictional Atticus Finch has become the icon of the "legendary old-fashioned country lawyer"—a person of virtue, rectitude, and decency who represents all that is good about the practice of law. . . . So common are references to Finch . . . as the ideal lawyer that lawyers or law students being recognized for their public interest work are often described as an embodiment of Finch' (Gerald J Thain, '*Cape Fear*—Two Versions and Two Visions Separated by Thirty Years' in Machura and Robson, n 2 above, 40).

they'll never forget, and neither will you, counsellor.' At this point Sam realizes that to save his family, he will have to kill Cady himself. As a lawyer, he is helpless.[22]

Non-lawyer victims fare no better when they turn to the law for help. In the first version of *Kiss of Death*, ex-con Nick Bianco (Victor Mature) decides to go straight and turn state's evidence. Encouraged by a good-hearted district attorney, he even testifies at Tom Udo's trial. Justice miscarries, however. Udo walks, and Nick's life is in danger, along with that of his new wife and kids. Realizing that the law has only gotten him into hotter water, Nick takes law into his own hands and ends up doing what the DA was unable to do: bringing Udo to justice. The second version of *Kiss of Death*, evidently hesitant to portray a good-hearted district attorney, splits this figure into two other characters, one an overly-slick DA (Stanley Tucci), the other a compassionate plainclothes cop (Samuel L Jackson). Jimmy (David Caruso), the punk who wants to go straight, wears a wire and collects evidence against not only psychopathic Junior but also the DA who cares more about his own career than justice. Order is restored, but with little help from the law. In fact, in this version of *Kiss of Death*, law is incompetent, chaotic, and deadly, incapable of protecting even its own representatives from violence.[23]

In *Pacific Heights* as in some other psycho movies, the law actually protects the wicked. Beset by Carter, their psychopathic lodger, Patty and Drake turn to a lawyer for help; she has to inform them that, unfortunately, the law ties their hands. At another point the law in the form of a restraining order prevents Drake from going back to his own house, leaving Patty stranded there with the psychopath. Carter, they learn from his executor, has 'been out of control for a long time'; law has never been able to contain him, though he has a long history of scamming landlords and bilking heiresses. At one point, Patty and Drake do manage to get an eviction order against Carter; but when the bailiff unlocks the lodger's apartment, they find a scene of total destruction—even the toilet is gone. Law fails again. Only when Patty fully realizes the powerlessness of law does she conclude that she herself must act. Rex, in *The Vanishing*, after a similar realization of law's impotence, decides to go after the psychopath himself. In *Seven*, the psychopath's lawyer sets up the final scene of the morality play, and the impetuous younger detective allows himself to be manipulated into breaking the law, thus enabling the psycho to win.

Night of the Hunter has a little more faith in law, but not much. It accuses the legal system of making Willa and the children vulnerable in the first place by hanging Ben Harper, the head of the family. In this film the failure of the law is part of a more general breakdown of the grownup world, including religion. All the adults fail the children, Pearl and John, starting with their father, who is

[22] Law is even less helpful in the second version of *Cape Fear*, where Cady beats Sam in the race to hire 'the best criminal lawyer in the state' and a judge puts a restraining order on Sam.

[23] Similarly, in Martin Scorsese's 1991 remake of *Cape Fear*, the lawyer is ambiguous morally and professionally. In this version, lawyer Sam Bowden is guilty of having withheld evidence in the background rape trial. For a comparison of the images of the lawyer in the two versions of *Cape Fear*, see Thain, n 21 above.

imprisoned and hanged; continuing with their mother (Shelley Winters) and the local ice cream shop owners who cannot see through the preacher's hypocrisy; and including John's only adult friend, an old man who lives in a houseboat and promises to help but gets too drunk to act at the crucial moment. For much of the movie, the only good parent is pint-size John, leading little Pearl to safety and helping to conceal the money.

In one early scene, a prison guard grouses about having participated in the hanging of Ben Harper. Even though Ben had killed two men, the hanging left his family defenceless. Law begins to find its feet again after Lillian Gish, the Good Mother figure who saves the children, becomes a vigilante, waiting up at night with a shotgun, wounding the preacher, and arranging for his arrest. The unhappy prison guard cheers up when law in the form of a judge sentences the preacher to execution. Although Walt and Icy Spoon, the owners of the ice cream emporium, lead a lynch mob demanding the preacher's life, their lawlessness is thwarted when legal officials hustle the preacher out of the jail. Law is redeeming itself.

Retributions and Resolutions

The legal order is restored at the end of most psycho movies. In some cases the agent of restoration is a legal authority, such as a law enforcement officer. Examples include *Frankenstein*, in which townfolks led by local bigwigs pursue the Monster to the Old Mill; *Scarface*; *White Heat*; *Black Widow*; *Silence of the Lambs*; *Seven*, in which the world-weary older detective decides to remain on the police force; and *Badlands*.[24] In *The Bad Seed*, Nature itself restores law and order. A bolt of lightning wipes out little Rhoda, and this is no doubt fitting, since Nature, in the form of a bad gene, created this monstrous tot in the first place. Nature plays a role in *The Shining*, too, where a fortuitous snow storm freezes the psycho to death and enables his family to flee the cursed hotel.[25] But most of the time, at least in the films discussed here, the psycho-slayer is either one of the psycho's victims or a victim surrogate: in *Night of the Hunter*, the elderly woman who saves the children; in *Strangers on a Train*, Guy Haines, who kills Bruno; in *Psycho*, Lila Crane, Marion's sister; in *Cape Fear*, Sam Bowden; in *Pacific Heights*, Patty Palmer, the brainier half of the landlord couple; in *Single White Female*, Ally Jones, who fittingly wipes out Hedy in the basement of her apartment building.

Psycho movies, then, begin by demonstrating that danger is ubiquitous, lurking even in apparent normality. Like death itself, a psycho may intrude upon us at the next roadside reststop, or by ringing the doorbell one evening, or by creeping

[24] However, *Badlands* lets Holly, the female partner in crime, off the hook, even while it sends Kit to the electric chair. In actuality, Caril-Ann Fugate, the real-life model for Holly, spent many years in prison.

[25] In the second version of *Cape Fear*, Nature in the form of a storm kills Max Cady, drowning him just before Sam's lethal blow hits. Whereas in the first version the lawyer is still able to vanquish the psychopath, in the remake the lawyer is denied this redemptive agency.

up while we are out bowling with the family. The very randomness of the threat intensifies the need for law. But, the movies go on to observe, law is often powerless, at least initially, against such intruders; thus psychos turn ordinarily pacific people into vigilantes, forcing even lawyers to take up arms. Eventually, the world returns to normality with the defeat and punishment of the psycho. In a few interesting exceptions, however, the psycho is not really defeated. Holly survives in *Badlands* to tell the tale. The end of *Body Heat* finds Mattie sunning herself on an exotic beach with a new hunk, almost beyond the reach of Ned in his prison cell. In *Seven*, psycho John Doe engineers his own arrest and death, even while punishing the law in the form of the younger detective. *Psycho* closes with a complicitous smile that may mean that Norman Bates has triumphed after all. More grimly, *The Vanishing* concludes with not the law but the psychopath savouring victory.

Conclusion

One of the great gifts of crime movies generally is their ability to transform us into happy hypocrites. They enable viewers to enjoy and condemn the forbidden simultaneously. Certainly this licence for hypocrisy is one of the strongest pleasures of psycho movies, many of which invite us to identify with the villain and then participate in his or her destruction, to go berserk and be restored to normalcy, to become as self-centred and imperious as a two-year-old and yet exit the movie feeling grownup and even a bit heroic.[26]

Individually and collectively, psycho movies speak of the need for law, the limitations of law, and the last-ditch usurpation of law by individuals who are forced to become vigilantes. The centrality and significance of these themes argues for defining the category 'psycho movies' with some rigour. It is particularly important, I think, not to put psycho movies in the same conceptual box as slashers and serial-killer films. The latter are concerned with gory spectacle and psycho-sexual excitement; many are close to pornography. Psycho movies, while they are not above cheap thrills, focus instead on the boundaries between order and chaos, and their bad guys are characters, not depersonalized killing machines.[27] Even though

[26] My happy-hypocrites explanation of viewers' pleasure in psycho movies meshes well with the discussions of the attractions of film violence in Clark McCauley, 'When Screen Violence Is Not Attractive' in JH Goldstein (ed), *Why We Watch: The Attractions of Violent Entertainment* (New York: 1998) 144 and in D Zillmann, 'The Psychology of the Appeal of Portrayals of Violence' in Goldstein, ibid, 179, 202 ('justified hatred and the call for punishment allows us to uninhibitedly enjoy the punitive action when it materializes. *Negative affective dispositions, then, set us free to thoroughly enjoy punitive violence*' (emphases in original). See also Jeffrey H Goldstein, 'Why We Watch' in Goldstein, ibid, 212.

[27] Jenkins, n 11 above, esp 86. The definitional problems for film scholars are likely to grow worse as the lines among psychos, serial killers, and terrorists continue to blur, as they did in Fall 2002 in the case of the Washington, DC, area sniper killings. For discussion of this category merger and some of its implications, see Jeffrey Gettleman, 'When Just One Gun Is Enough', *New York Times*, 27 October 2002, WK 3.

film categories inevitably overlap, there are benefits to recognizing psycho movies as a distinct category, with standard characters, themes, and a degree of coherence that may qualify it as a genre.

Analysis of that category reveals an extensive subtext about control and loss of control, law and lawlessness. Recognition of these themes leads, in turn, to deeper understanding of relationships between law and society and ways in which popular culture mirrors conflicting needs and desires. These include the desire to indulge ourselves in the sort of fantasies that the psychopath enacts for us, together with the need to be protected against those fantasies and the psychos who embody them. Ideally that protection comes through law, although these movies show that in the popular imagination, scepticism about and distrust of law are at least as powerful as reverence.

Reel Violence: Popular Culture and Concerns about Capital Punishment in Contemporary American Society

*Roberta M Harding**

Introduction

Recent legislative and executive activities and changes in death penalty sentencing and execution patterns arguably reflect the American public's increasing uncertainty about the appropriateness of capital punishment as a penalty for the commission of certain criminal offences. Popular culture can shape as well as reflect public sentiment. The purpose of this article is to examine how popular culture might have contributed towards this burgeoning shift in the public's attitude to this controversial subject.

Given the 'public['s] fascination with [capital punishment's] screen . . . depictions',[1] film will be the popular culture medium providing the text for this examination.[2] It is anticipated that analyzing the films *Dead Man Walking*[3] and *The Green Mile*[4] will reveal some of the capital punishment issues to which the viewers were exposed. And, since popular culture is a powerful and effective way to convey information, it is possible that the education on these issues provided by the film makers might have contributed towards the public's mounting uncertainty about the continued presence of capital punishment in American criminal jurisprudence.

* I am indebted to my research assistant Todd Osterloh for the help he provided in preparing this paper.

[1] Jean E Giles, 'Pop Culture Portrayals of Capital Punishment: A Review of *Dead Man Walking* and *Among the Lowest of the Dead*' (1995) 20 *American J of Criminal Justice* 137, 138. Giles also notes that this obsession is lucrative as 'the entertainment business . . . seeks to capitalize on public fascination with the death penalty'. ibid, 145.

[2] Professor Nicole Rafter notes that '[m]ovies have become the central vehicle for the dissemination of popular culture in the United States'. Nicole Rafter, *Shots in the Mirror: Crime Films and Society* (Oxford: 2000) vii. Furthermore, law and film is an accepted method of legal analysis whereby films are examined in order to comment on legal issues, including a society's perspective on a particular point. See John Denvir (ed), *Legal Reelism: Movies as Legal Texts* (Chicago: 1996) xii–xiii. See also Giles, n 1 above; Stefan Machura and Peter Robson (eds), *Law and Film* (Oxford: 2001); David A Black, *Law in Film: Resonance and Representation* (Chicago: 1999).

[3] *Dead Man Walking* (PolyGram, 1995).

[4] *The Green Mile* (Castle Rock, 1999).

To accomplish this task, a brief history of the death penalty in the United States will first be explored. This section is followed by a review of *Dead Man Walking* and *The Green Mile*, the two films selected for this examination. The penultimate section examines how the theme of fairness and capital punishment resonates in both films. This theme encompasses issues pertaining to status and the death penalty. Geography and socio-economic status are the two status issues that will be the focal points of this discussion.[5] Concluding comments are contained in the last section.

The Death Penalty in America: Past and Present

English colonists brought capital punishment with them when they settled in the New World in the early seventeenth century.[6] Captain George Kendall's execution in Jamestown, Virginia in 1608 for espionage was the first recorded judicially sanctioned execution in the United States.[7] Since then the death penalty has been a fixture in American society.[8]

Today, 40 United States jurisdictions (38 states, the federal government, and the United States military) have criminal laws sanctioning capital punishment as a penalty for the commission of certain criminal offences.[9] In contrast, only 13 jurisdictions (12 states and the District of Columbia) expressly prohibit the imposition of this penalty.[10]

If the situation in the state of New Hampshire is taken into account, then arguably there would be 14 abolitionist jurisdictions. In the 27 years since the

[5] Race is another status related point included in the fairness category that is addressed in both films. Both films also explore issues relating to a capital offender's culpability, an issue included in the second major thematic category of justice and the death penalty. Race and justice issues, however, are beyond the scope of this article.

[6] See Hugo Adam Bedau (ed). *The Death Penalty in America: Current Controversies* (Oxford: 1997) 3; Herbert H Haines, *Against Capital Punishment: The Anti-Death Penalty Movement in America, 1972–1994* (Oxford: 1996) 7; Nina Rivkind and Steven F Shatz, *Cases and Materials on the Death Penalty* (St Paul, Minnesota: 2001) 21 (noting that '[t]he English settlers carried the death penalty to America'); Death Penalty Information Center (hereinafter 'DPIC'), http://www.deathpenaltyinforg/history2.html (noting that 'Britain influenced America's use of the death penalty more than any other country') (last visited 21 September 2003).

[7] Bedau, n 6 above, 3; Rivkind and Shatz, n 6 above, 19; DPIC, n 6 above. There is a dispute as to the method of execution. Watt Epsy and John Smykla state that Kendall was executed by firing squad. M Watt Epsy and John Ortiz Smykla, 'Executions in the United States, 1608–1991: The Epsy File' (3rd edn, ICPSR 1994) available at http://www.icpsr.umich.edu/cgi/archive.prl?study = 8451&path = NACJD (last visited 21 September 2003) (hereinafter 'The Epsy File'), while Bedau states that Kendall was executed by hanging, Bedau, n 6 above, 3.

[8] See James R Acker, Robert M Bohm, and Charles S Lanier, *America's Experiment With Capital Punishment: Reflections on the Past, Present, and Future of the Ultimate Penal Sanction* (Durham, North Carolina: 1998) 5 (opining that '[c]apital punishment was a part of American culture long before the United States was founded').

[9] National Association for the Advancement of Colored People, 'Death Row U.S.A.' (Spring 2003) 1, available at http://www.naacpldf.org/pdfdocs/deathrow_summer03.pdf (last visited 21 September 2003) (hereinafter 'Death Row USA').

[10] ibid.

United States Supreme Court reinstated the death penalty in *Gregg v Georgia*,[11] New Hampshire has never imposed a death sentence.[12] In fact, there have been no executions in New Hampshire for more than 60 years.[13] In May of 2000, New Hampshire's legislature attempted to codify the state's *de facto* abolitionist status by passing a bill that removed the death penalty from the list of approved criminal sanctions. Governor Shaheen, however, vetoed the bill. Lawmakers decided not to seek an override of the gubernatorial veto because the slim majority in both chambers (the Senate voted 14–10 in favour of abolition) made it unlikely that the necessary two-thirds vote could be secured.[14]

Death penalty foes in New Hampshire remained undaunted and reintroduced the abolition bill during the next year's legislative session.[15] This time the measure was eight votes shy of being passed by the state's House of Representatives.[16] The close miss was partially attributed to the belief that Governor Shaheen would once again exercise her veto power.[17] This historical overview supports the conclusion that New Hampshire has implicitly rejected capital punishment.

New Hampshire is not the only retentionist state whose legislature recently has considered adopting legislation to repeal the death penalty. Several legislators in New Mexico have launched an aggressive campaign to abolish the death penalty. For three successive years—2001, 2002, and 2003—members of the New Mexican legislature have introduced bills to abolish the death penalty, but none passed.[18] During the 2001 legislative session the proposed repeal bill was one vote short of being passed by the New Mexico Senate.[19] When the measure was reintroduced at the 2002 session, it was not expected to come to a vote because the short 30 day session was supposed to be limited to handling pressing budgetary matters.[20] Nonetheless, it was during this session that the governor at that time, Republican Gary Johnson, stated that if the bill repealing the death penalty passed, it was highly probable he would sign it.[21]

[11] *Gregg v Georgia*, 428 US 153 (1976).

[12] See Death Row USA, n 10 above. See also DPIC, http://www.deathpenaltyinfo.org/article.php?scid = 9&did = 188#state (noting that no one is confined to New Hampshire's death row) (last visited 21 September 2003).

[13] 'New Hampshire Senate Votes to Abolish Death Penalty', *Maranatha Christian Journal*, 19 May 2000.

[14] ibid; Kevin Landreigan, 'Lawmakers Return to Discuss Vetoed Bills', *Nashua (NH) Telegraph*, 27 June 2000.

[15] Tom Fahey, 'Death Penalty Repeal Killed by House', *The Union Leader*, 7 April 2001, A1.

[16] The bill was rejected by a 180–188 vote. ibid.

[17] ibid.

[18] See, eg, HB 377, 46th Leg, Reg Sess (NM 2003); SB 651, 46th Leg, Reg Sess (NM 2003); SB 277, 45th Leg, Reg Sess (NM 2002); HB 239, 44th Leg, Reg Sess (NM 2001); SB 165, 44th Leg, Reg Sess (NM 2001).

[19] See SU Mahesh, 'Aragon Puts Death Penalty on Table', *Albuquerque Journal*, 24 January 2002, A8.

[20] Jim Belshaw, 'Only Governor Knows Death Penalty Stance', *Albuquerque Journal*, 20 January 2002, A2.

[21] SU Maresh, 'Governor Makes Opposition to Death Penalty Clear', *Albuquerque Journal*, 16 January 2002. Johnson's successor, Governor Bill Richardson, presently indicates that he supports the retention of the death penalty. David Miles, 'Bill Would End Death Penalty', *Albuquerque Journal*, 31 January 2003, A6.

Johnson was not the sole executive who expressed concern about the practice of capital punishment in contemporary America. For example, in January of 2000, Illinois Governor George Ryan took the momentous step of imposing a moratorium on capital punishment in that state.[22] Almost two and a half years later, Maryland's former governor Parris Glendening imposed a similar moratorium.[23] Robert Ehrlich, Glendening's successor, promised to lift the moratorium at his inauguration in January of 2003.[24] Several months later, a legislatively imposed moratorium narrowly missed being passed by the Maryland Senate.[25] At the other end of the spectrum, in January of 2003 Governor Ryan granted clemency to all inmates on Illinois' death row. One hundred and fifty-four inmates had their sentences commuted from death to life without the possibility of parole, and three death sentences were commuted to 40 years. Ten inmates waiting for new sentencing hearings after their death sentences, but not convictions, were vacated received sentences of life without the possibility of parole.[26] Ryan granted full pardons to four others.[27]

Longevity is not capital punishment's sole notable feature. It has also flourished as more than 15,000 men, women, and children have been judicially executed on American soil since Captain Kendall's execution in 1608.[28] Eight hundred and seventy-five[29] of these judicially sanctioned executions were carried out between 17 January 1977 and 21 September 2003 after the United States Supreme Court lifted the legal moratorium on executions imposed by its 1972 decision in *Furman v Georgia*.[30] Although this figure indicates there has been little hesitancy about

[22] Press Release, Governor George Ryan (31 January 2000) available at http://www.state.il.us/gov/press/00/Jan/morat.htm (last visited 21 September 2003).

[23] Governor Glendening imposed the moratorium on 9 May 2002. Dennis O'Brien and David Nitkin, 'Glendening Halts Executions', *The Baltimore Sun*, 10 May 2002, 1A.

[24] Stephanie Hanes and Sarah Koenig, 'Md. Judge Agrees to Execution of Oken', *The Baltimore Sun*, 22 January 2003, 1A.

[25] The measure missed being passed by a single vote. Stephanie Desmon, 'Death penalty Freeze Rejected; Moratorium Bill Seeking more study of disparities is defeated in the Senate', *The Baltimore Sun*, 19 March 2003, 1B.

[26] DPIC, 'Illinios Death Row Inmates Granted Commutation by Governor George Ryan on January 12, 2003', at http://www.deathpenaltyinfo.org/article.php?did=485&scid=13 (last visited 21 September 2003).

[27] 'Death Row Inmates Receive Life', *Chicago Tribune*, 12 January 2003 (listing the 156 inmates); Steve Mills and Christi Parsons, 'The System Has Failed', *Chicago Tribune*, 11 January 2003 (listing the names of the four pardoned inmates). Governor Ryan pardoned at least one other inmate named Steven Smith while in office. See DPIC, 'Cases of Innocence' at http://www.deathpenaltyinfo.org/article.php?scid=6&did=109 (last visited 21 September 2003).

[28] Starting with Kendall's execution in 1608, approximately 15,353 judicially sanctioned executions have been recorded. 14,634 of the executions occurred between 1608 and 24 April 1991, see The Epsy File, n 7 above, and 719 occurred between 25 April 1991 and 21 September 2003. See DPIC, 'List of Individuals Executed since 1976', http://www.deathpenaltyinfo.org/article.php?did=414&scid=8#1 (last visited 21 September 2003).

[29] DPIC, 'Executions by Year', at http://www.deathpenaltyinfo.org/article.php?scid = 8&did=146 (last visited 21 September 2003).

[30] The Court's opinion in *Furman* marked a momentous milestone in the history of the death penalty in the United States. In a five to four split, the Court declared the death penalty as

carrying out death sentences, recent execution practice figures indicate that this might no longer be the case because the pace of executions has undergone a noticeable decline in recent years. For example, since 1976 seven retentionist jurisdictions (Connecticut, Kansas, New Hampshire, New Jersey, New York, South Dakota and the United States military) have not executed anyone.[31] The relative infancy of the capital punishment statutes in Kansas and New York, respectively enacted in 1994 and 1995,[32] could explain why no executions have been carried out in those jurisdictions. Five other retentionist jurisdictions have executed only one person in the 27 years since the Supreme Court reinstated capital punishment. These states are Colorado, Idaho, New Mexico, Tennessee, and Wyoming.[33] Kentucky, Montana, and Oregon have had only two executions since the states were permitted to resume the practice.[34] The situations in these states suggest the imposition of *de facto* moratoria on executions.[35] The circumstances in these states and the execution implementation practices in other retentionist jurisdictions have contributed towards the continuing downward trend in the number executed annually. In 1999 98 individuals were executed.[36] This figure declined to 85 in 2000 and dipped sharply to 66 in 2001.[37] Although the number of executions

administered unconstitutional because it was arbitrarily and capriciously imposed in violation of the Eighth Amendment's prohibition against the imposition of cruel and unusual punishments. *Furman v Georgia*, 408 US 238 (1972) (per curiam). The pertinent section of the Eighth Amendment states: '[C]ruel and unusual punishment [shall not be] inflicted'. The Court's ruling effectively imposed a legal moratorium on the practice of capital punishment in the United States. The penalty was later reinstated by the Court's 1976 decision in *Gregg v Georgia* 428 US 153 (1976) (joint opinion). The first *post-Furman* execution occurred on 17 January 1977 when the state of Utah executed Gary Gilmore by firing squad. Death Row USA, n 9 above, 11. See also DPIC, http://www.deathpenaltyinfo.org/article.php?scid=8&did=146 (last visited 19 June 2003) (listing most recent figures for those executed since 1976).

[31] DPIC, n 9 above, 15. As previously noted, New Hampshire has not had an execution in more than 60 years. See n 13 above. One commentator categorizes these jurisdictions as 'inactive'. William S Lofquist, 'Putting Them There, Keeping Them There, and Killing Them: An Analysis of State-Level Variations in Death Penalty Intensity' (2002) 87 *Iowa L Rev* 1505, 1520, 1539–1540.

[32] KSA 21-4624 *et seq* (effective 1 July 1994); 1995 NY Laws ch1 section 27 (effective 1 September 1995).

[33] Death Row USA, n 9 above, 10–11; DPIC, http://www.deathpenaltyinfo.org/article.php?scid=8&did=186 (last visited 21 September 2003). The absence of executions and low execution rates also suggests that these states as well as Connecticut, New Hampshire, New Jersey, New York, and South Dakota have 'virtual *de facto* moratorium[s] on the death penalty'. Lofquist, n 31 above, 1539.

[34] DPIC, http://www.deathpenaltyinfo.org/article.php?scid=8&did=186 (last visited 21 September 2003).

[35] See Lofquist, n 31 above, 1539 (similarly concluding that the absence of executions means 'there is a virtual de facto moratorium on the death penalty').

[36] Death Row USA, n 9 above, 9; 'Capital Punishment 1999' Bureau of Justice Statistics Bulletin, United States Department of Justice (December 2000) available at http://ojp.usdoj.gov/bjs/pub/pdf/cp99.pdf (last visited 21 September 2003).

[37] Death Row USA, n 9 above, 9; 'Capital Punishment 2000' Bureau of Justice Statistics Bulletin, United States Department of Justice (December 2001) available at http://ojp.usdoj.gov/bjs/pub/pdf/cp00.pdf; 'Capital Punishment 2001' Bureau of Justice Statistics Bulletin, United States Department of Justice (December 2002) available at http://ojp.usdoj.gov/bjs/pub/pdf/cp01.pdf (last visited 21 September 2003).

carried out in 2002 slightly increased by five, the downward trend is still evident because the cumulative figure is still significantly below the execution totals for 1999 and 2000.[38]

A similar trend is evident in the rate at which capital sentences are imposed, as measured by death row populations. As of 1 July 2003, 3,517 men and women resided on death rows across the United States.[39] Of course, no one is on New Hampshire's death row.[40] Three other retentionist jurisdictions also have a paucity of condemned inmates. Wyoming's death row has only two occupants, New Mexico's has three, and Colorado's has six.[41] The death row populations in other retentionist jurisdictions also experienced a lower growth rate as a report recently released by the federal government notes that in 2001 only 155 offenders in the nation received death sentences,[42] which 'represent[s] the smallest number of admissions since 1973'.[43]

Recent sentencing data from three retentionist jurisdictions supports the conclusion that it is likely that the slowdown in the growth of death row populations will continue. 2002 marks the first time in a decade that juries in conservative Orange County, California, historically known for their willingness to impose death sentences, have not imposed a death sentence.[44] During the same year only 4 per cent of the death qualified defendants in Ohio were sentenced to death. This is the lowest percentage since the state began compiling this data.[45] Lastly, juries in 15 of the last 16 federal death penalty trials refused to impose death sentences.[46]

Cumulatively this suggests that public attitudes about capital punishment might be changing; specifically, uncertainty about retaining the death penalty as a penalty option in contemporary American society.[47] The findings from recent

[38] Death Row USA, n 9 above, 10–11. See DPIC, http://www.deathpenaltyinfo.org/article.php?scid=8&did=146 (last visited 21 September 2003).

[39] See Death Row USA, n 9 above.

[40] See n 13 above and accompanying text.

[41] See DPIC, http://www.deathpenaltyinfo.org/article.php?scid=9&did=188#state (last visited 21 September 2003).

[42] Bureau of Justice Statistics Bulletin, United States Department of Justice (December 2002), n 37 above, 1.

[43] ibid. See also Lofquist, n 31 above, 1516, n 76 (noting that '[b]etween 1973 and 1979 death row populations grew by 250% with an average of 174 new admissions . . . In the 1980s, death row populations grew by 214% with an average of 269 new admissions . . . Between 1990 and 1998, death row pupulations grew by 47% with an average of 277 admissions . . .').

[44] See Stuart Pfeifer, 'Death Penalty is a Tougher Sell', *Los Angeles Times*, 20 January 2003, B1.

[45] Bill Sloat, 'Fewer Killers Going to Ohio Death Row', *The Plain Dealer*, 21 August 2001 (Cleveland, Ohio); see also Alex Kotlowitz, 'The Unwitting Abolitionists, In the Face of Death', *The New York Times Magazine*, 6 July 2003, 36 (using a capital trial in Indiana to illustrate how 'pro-death penalty jurors are increasingly sparing lives').

[46] Adam Liptak, 'Juries Reject Death Penalty in Nearly All Federal Trials', *New York Times*, 15 June 2003, A12.

[47] The *New York Times* article noted that 'legal experts say the trend [of declining death sentences in federal death penalty cases] might have a number of explanations, like . . . some jurors' growing unease with the death penalty'. Ibid. Alan Vinegrad, a former United States attorney in Brooklyn, NY opined that the recent decline in federal death sentences 'reflects that the tide is turning in this country with regard to attitudes about the death penalty'. Ibid.

public opinion polls reinforce this conclusion. In a Gallup poll, 74 per cent responded affirmatively when asked if they were in favour of the death penalty for a person convicted of murder.[48] A poll conducted earlier in 2003 by ABC News and the *Washington Post* found a similar level of support with 64 per cent approving of capital punishment as a penalty for murder.[49] A critical caveat to both polls is that the subjects who indicated they supported retaining the death penalty were not provided with an alternative sentencing option.[50] When the respondents to both polls were presented with an alternative sentencing option, support for the death penalty declined substantially. In the latter poll when death penalty supporters were given life in prison as an alternative to death, 45 per cent of them selected the life in prison option instead of the death penalty; only 49 per cent continued to support the death penalty.[51] The Gallup poll had a comparable outcome. According to the poll's results, support for the death penalty dropped from 74 per cent to 53 per cent when life without the possibility of parole was given as an alternative penalty.[52]

With 40 jurisdictions expressly providing for capital punishment, the penalty undoubtedly formally retains its historical position. Nonetheless, the recent legislative and executive activities and the existing and potential trends regarding the pace of executions and the imposition of death sentences indicate that the collective conscience harbours some degree of apprehension about the future of this ultimate criminal penalty. But why are more and more members of American society becoming unsure about the position capital punishment should occupy in contemporary society? Popular culture in its cinematic format provides the perspective from which a response to this query will be formulated.

The Films

A number of feature films with capital punishment themes were released in the late twentieth century and the early part of this century. These include 2001's *Monster's Ball*[53] and 2003's *The Life of David Gale*.[54] *Dead Man Walking* and *The Green Mile* are two other popular films that address this subject matter. The latter two films

[48] Press Release, The Gallup Organization, 'Support for the Death Penalty Remains High' (19 May 2003), available at http://www.deathpenaltyinfo.org/article.php?scid=23&did=592 (last visited 21 September 2003).

[49] See Dalia Sussman, 'No Blanket Commutation' available at http://abcnews.go.com/sections/us/DailyNews/commutation_poll030124.html. The results of the ABCnews.com/*Washington Post* poll were released on 24 January 2003.

[50] ibid.

[51] Press Release, The Gallup Organization, n 48 above.

[52] ibid.

[53] Halle Berry, Billy Bob Thornton, and Sean Combs star in *Monster's Ball* (Lion's Gate Films, 2001). Halle Berry won the 2001 Academy Award for Best Actress for her portrayal of the executed man's ex-wife. '74th Academy Awards Nominees and Winners' at http://www.oscars.org/74academyawards/nomswins.html (last visited 21 September 2003). See also 'Death Penalty in Pop Culture, Movies and Documentaries', Criminal Justice Education Fund, at http://justice.policy.net/cjedfund (last visited September 21, 2003).

[54] *The Life of David Gale* (Universal, 2003).

have been selected to provide the cinematic texts for this analysis because of their popularity with moviegoers.[55] Their popularity means that many people were exposed to the films' subtexts that facilitate edifying the public about critical capital punishment issues.

Dead Man Walking and *The Green Mile* are both dramatic big screen adaptations of books with the same titles. *The Green Mile* is based on a novel by noted horror author Stephen King.[56] *Dead Man Walking* is based on the non-fiction memoirs of Sister Helen Prejean, a Roman Catholic nun.[57] The film adaptation of *Dead Man Walking*, however, does include a major fictional element. Tim Robbins, the film's screenplay writer and director, opted to create the fictional character Matthew Poncelet, the condemned inmate befriended by Sister Helen Prejean. Poncelet is a composite of Pat Sonnier and Robert Lee Willie, the two condemned men who are the actual subjects of her book.[58]

Interestingly, the film making styles reflect this fiction/non-fiction distinction. When viewing *The Green Mile*, the audience sees what is most accurately characterized as a film made in the big budget 'Hollywood blockbuster' tradition, which are typically fictional cinematic presentations. This film making style also facilitates attracting a broader audience base which enables more people to be informed about issues that are fuelling the present death penalty debate in America. The film making style used in *Dead Man Walking* is distinctively different. Film maker Tim Robbins opted to use understated and sometimes stark film making techniques. This gives the film a noticeable documentary style; or, at the minimum, one that resembles a docudrama. The docudrama analogy is heightened when the supernatural aspects of the story related in *The Green Mile* are considered[59] because it reinforces the fictional basis for that film, which, in turn, emphasizes the documentary qualities evident in *Dead Man Walking*. These stylistic and format differences did not hinder either movie from being successful.

Dead Man Walking was released in December of 1995[60] and enjoyed both critical and box office success. Actress Susan Sarandon garnered an Oscar for Best Actress for her portrayal of Sister Helen Prejean. Sean Penn's performance as condemned killer Matthew Poncelet earned him a nomination for an Academy

[55] Given the size of the gross box office returns for each film it can be inferred that they were viewed by a large number of people. *Dead Man Walking* grossed $136.8 million worldwide, and *The Green Mile* nearly doubled that total with $268.7 million. Worldwide Box Office Grosses, at http://www.boxofficeguru.com/intlarch2.html (last visited 21 September 2003). This figure excludes returns received from video rentals, sales, and television broadcasts, which would increase the number of people who viewed the films.

[56] Stephen King, *The Green Mile* (New York: 1997).

[57] Sister Helen Prejean, *Dead Man Walking* (New York: 1993). *Dead Man Walking* was also made into an opera that premiered in San Francisco on 8 October 2000. Joshua Kosman, 'Walking Tall Opera's "Dead Man" is a masterpiece of music, words, and emotions', *San Francisco Chronicle*, 9 October 2000, F1.

[58] Prejean, n 57 above, 4, 117.

[59] The primary supernatural aspect of the film is protagonist John Coffey's ability to perform miracles—in particular, his ability to resurrect the dead and to heal the sick.

[60] Jim Craddock (ed), *VideoHound's Golden Movie Retriever 2001* (Farmington Hills, MI: 2001) 257–258.

Award for Best Actor. Tim Robbins was nominated for an Academy Award in the Best Director category.[61]

Four years later *The Green Mile* played in movie theatres. In the film, Hollywood superstar Tom Hanks portrays Paul Edgecomb, a central protagonist who supervises the fictitious E Block, otherwise known as The Green Mile, where the condemned inmates are housed. Newcomer Michael Clarke Duncan plays death row inmate John Coffey, the movie's other central character. Like *Dead Man Walking, The Green Mile* enjoyed box office success and received critical recognition. In 1999 Michael Clarke Duncan received an Academy Award nomination for Best Supporting Actor for his performance as John Coffey and the movie was nominated for Best Picture.[62]

In addition to the similarities mentioned above, the two films also have related settings and topics. For example, geography provides what turns out to be an important similarity because both films are set in Louisiana. In accordance with the fiction/non-fiction dichotomy, the events in *The Green Mile* transpire at the fictional penitentiary at Cold Mountain. Those in *Dead Man Walking* occur at the actual Louisiana State Penitentiary at Angola. In addition, the events related in both films happen in the twentieth century; albeit at different ends of the continuum. *The Green Mile* is set in the 1930s during the depression era[63] while *Dead Man Walking* relates events that occurred in the late twentieth century.[64] Of course, the most important feature shared by the films is that capital punishment is the central theme. Accordingly, the films provide a rich and varied text for identifying and examining crucial issues underlying the present uncertainty about the future of the death penalty in America.

Dead Man Walking, The Green Mile, and Capital Punishment in Modern American Culture

Dead Man Walking and *The Green Mile* identify and explore a plethora of capital punishment issues. For example, both films expose the public to and educate it about a variety of points related to the theme of fairness and the death penalty. These issues are primarily derived from the condemned's status. Race, geography and socio-economic status are examples of status based fairness issues that both films raise. Because of the history of chattel slavery in the United States and the

[61] Academy Awards History available at http://www.oscars.org/awardsdatabase/index.html. In addition, all three received nominations in their respective categories for the Golden Globe awards in 1996, but none of them won these awards. Golden Globe Awards History at http://www.hfpa.org/GoldenGlobehistory.html (last visited September 21, 2003).

[62] Academy Awards History, n 61 above.

[63] The book states that the story is set in 1932, *The Green Mile*, n 57 above, 3, 8, but the film sets the story in 1935.

[64] The film character Matthew Poncelet is executed on 13 April 1994. The murders for which he was sentenced to death were committed six years earlier.

practice's legacy, race has received the most public exposure. Consequently, this fairness inquiry focuses on the equally important but less publicized geography and socio-economic status issues.

The Issue of Fairness: Status and Capital Punishment

Geography and the Death Penalty in the United States

As previously noted, *Dead Man Walking* and *The Green Mile* are both set in Louisiana. It is noteworthy that the films' viewers were exposed to this fact because there is a strong correlation between geography and executions.[65] In addition, with the critical events in *The Green Mile* occurring in the early twentieth century and those in *Dead Man Walking* in the late twentieth century, people who viewed both films are informed about the longevity of this correlation. In the past, a substantial number of executions occurred in Southern states, including Louisiana.[66] More disturbing is that this regionalization still exists.[67] The results from a study of recent execution rates confirms this. The study determined that 85.8 per cent of the executions carried out between 1976, the beginning of the post-*Gregg* era, and 1998 occurred in retentionist jurisdictions that permitted slavery in 1860.[68] Furthermore, 76.4 per cent of these executions were performed by former Confederate states.[69] An examination of more recent data reveals that 719 of the 875 executions, or approximately

[65] See Lofquist, n 31 above, 1514 (noting that '[p]atterns of executions . . . show substantial regional variations'); ibid, 1517 (noting that 'actual executions remain overwhelmingly regionalized').

[66] See Keith Harries and Derral Cheatwood, *The Geography of Execution: The Capital Punishment Quagmire in America* (Lanham, MD: 1997) 22–23 (noting that since the early twentieth century the South has been an 'execution region'); Charles David Phillips, 'Social Structure and Social Control: Modeling the Discriminatory Execution of Blacks in Georgia and North Carolina, 1925–35' (1986) 65 *Social Forces* 458, 458–459 (noting that in the early twentieth century the majority of the executions for murder occurred in the South). Here 'Southern states' includes all present retentionist jurisdictions that permitted slavery prior to 20 December 1860, the date South Carolina became the first state to secede from the Union. These states are: Alabama; Arkansas; Delaware; Florida; Georgia; Kentucky; Louisiana; Maryland; Mississippi; Missouri; North Carolina; South Carolina; Tennessee; Texas; and Virginia. The states of Arizona, New Mexico and Oklahoma were part of territories permitting slavery. Ira Berlin et al (eds), *Free at Last* (New York: 1992) xxvii.

[67] See Lofquist, n 31 above, 1523 (noting that it 'is commonly recognized' that a dominant feature of post-*Furman* death penalty patterns is 'the way in which high levels of death penalty intensity cluster in the South'); see also Harries and Cheatwood, n 67 above, 30 (observing that the contemporary use of the death penalty 'exhibit[s] a southern emphasis in terms of number and rate of executions and of persons convicted to die'); see also Thomas J Keil and Gennaro F Vito, 'The Effects of the *Furman* and *Gregg* Decisions on Black-White Execution Ratios in the South' (1992) 20 *J of Criminal Justice* 217, 219 (noting that 'the South consistently has had a greater number of Blacks than whites executed during the course of the twentieth century').

[68] See Lofquist, n 31 above, 1518–1519(noting that for the period studied from 1976 until 1998 the majority of executions were carried out by states that had permitted slavery in 1860); ibid, 1529–1530 and Table IV(concluding that '[d]eath penalty intensity is strongly correlated to . . . a history of slavery'); ibid, 1536.

[69] Lofquist, n 31 above, 1518 (noting that for the period studied from 1977 until 1998 the majority of executions were carried out by Southern states that had joined the Confederacy); ibid, 1529–1530 and Table IV (concluding that '[d]eath penalty intensity is strongly correlated to [having been a] Confederate state'); see also Michael Mitchell and Jim Sidanius, 'Social Hierarchy and the

82 per cent,[70] carried out between the time the death penalty was reinstated in 1976 and 21 September 2003 happened in Southern jurisdictions.[71] In fact, of the 13 states that have executed the greatest number of people during the post-*Furman* era, 11 are located in the Southern region of the United States.[72] Two of these states—Texas and Virginia—account for 56 per cent of the executions carried out since 1976.[73] Missouri and Arizona, two other former slave holding jurisdictions, are excluded from these figures. If the execution figures from Missouri and Arizona are included, then the 13 states executing the greatest number of people since 1976 are lands in which slavery was permitted in 1860.[74]

The federal government is not exempt from this bias. In 2000 the federal government released a report confirming that the same geographical bias exists in the federal death penalty system.[75] '[T]he report . . . shows that United States attorneys who have most frequently recommended seeking the death penalty are

Death Penalty: A Social Dominance Perspective' (1995) 16 *Political Psychology* 591, 603 (finding that '[s]tates in the Old Confederacy . . . showed greater use of the death penalty'). Alabama, Arkansas, Florida, Georgia, Louisiana, Mississippi, North Carolina, South Carolina, Tennessee, Texas, and Virginia formed the Confederacy. Berlin, n 66 above, xxvii.

70 See DPIC, http://www.deathpenaltyinfo.org/article.php?scid=8&did=186 (last visited 21 September 2003).

71 See Lofquist, n 31 above, 1517 (noting that 'though a majority of death row inmates are outside the South, more than 80% of executions continue to occur in the South'). Here 'the South' is limited to the following retentionist states: Alabama; Arkansas; Delaware; Florida; Georgia; Kentucky; Louisiana; Maryland; Mississippi; North Carolina; Oklahoma; South Carolina; Tennessee; Texas; and Virginia. DPIC, http://www.deathpenaltyinfo.org/article.php?scid=8&did=480 (last visited 21 September 2003).

72 The states and execution figures are: Texas (310); Virginia (89); Oklahoma (69); Florida (56); Georgia (33); Alabama (28); South Carolina (28); Louisiana (27); Arkansas (25); North Carolina (25) and Delaware (13). DPIC, http://www.deathpenaltyinfo.org/article.php?scid = 8&did = 186 (last visited 21 September 2003). In contrast, the states in the Midwest accounted for only 94 of the total executions, 59 of all executions were carried out by states in the Western region, and three occurred in the Northeastern region. Ibid.

73 ibid.

74 DPIC, http://www.deathpenaltyinfo.org/article.php?scid=8&did=186 (last visited 21 September 2003). Interestingly, since 1976 Missouri, a jurisdiction that permitted chattel slavery, carried out 60 of the 94 executions that occurred in the Midwest region. While 22 of the 59 executions carried out in the West region occurred in Arizona, another slave holding jurisdiction in 1860. Ibid. Since both states are no longer officially classified as Southern states, what has been labelled and thought of as geographic unfairness might instead be more accurately characterized as an unfairness that originates from a state's status in 1860 as a slave-holding jurisdiction. Thus, it is a jurisdiction's cultural and social affinity with states that are officially declared Southern states that becomes the critical factor. Consequently, this could transform the issue of geographical bias into one that reflects a bias created by racial and social legacies. See, eg, Lofquist, n 31 above, 1530 (observing the parallels between the geography of executions and the geography of slavery); Keil and Vito, n 67 above, 219 (noting that for the period studied, 1900–1987, 'the number of Blacks executed [in the South] exceeded the number of whites'). Nonetheless, the issue can still be properly presented in its geographical posture. In fact, the effectiveness and success of the educational process might be better served if this is done. Since executions have an easily discernable geographic pattern it should render the concept more concrete and consequently enhance public comprehension. In addition, the geographical posture presents the information in a less emotionally charged context.

75 'Federal Death Penalty System: A Statistical Survey (1988–2000)' 1 (US Department of Justice, 12 September 2000), available at http://www.usdoj.gov/dag/pubdoc/dpsurvey.html (last visited 21 September 2003) (hereinafter 'Federal Death Penalty System Report'). See Raymond Bonner and Marc Lacey, 'Pervasive Disparities Found in the Federal Death Penalty', *New York Times*,

from states with a high number of [state] executions, including Virginia, Texas and Missouri.'[76] During the pre-protocol period, United States Attorney Generals sought approval to seek the death penalty in 52 cases. Permission was granted in 47 of the cases.[77] Thirty-one, or 59.6 per cent, of the requests came from prosecutors located in the former slave holding jurisdictions.[78] The same pattern is evident with the present protocol. Between 1995 and 2000 United States Attorneys sought approval to seek the death penalty in 183 instances. One hundred and fifteen of these cases came from jurisdictions that permitted slavery in 1860. Retentionist states in the Southern region generated 96, or 52.5 per cent,[79] of these requests. The practice in New York, a Northeastern state that relatively recently joined the retentionist jurisdictions, but was not a slave holding jurisdiction in 1860, is notably different. 'The Eastern and Southern [federal] district [courts] generate a lot of death penalty eligible cases, but, in the end, the number of cases where New York prosecutors actually recommend to the [US] Attorney General to seek the death penalty are very few.'[80] Seventeen of the 20 men, or 85 per cent, presently on federal death who were condemned after the 1994 expansion of federal capital crimes had their sentences imposed in former slave holding jurisdictions.[81] Though only three federal executions have been carried out since 1988, the federal execution pattern mirrors that found in state executions. All of these executees were executed for crimes committed in Texas and Oklahoma, two states that allowed slavery in 1860.[82]

12 September 2000, A18 (noting that the report indicates the federal death penalty is geographically skewed).

The federal death penalty was reinstated in 1988. Anti-Drug Abuse Act of 1988, Public Law Number 100–690, §7001, 102 Statutes at Large 4382, 4387; codified in 21 USC § 848. The number of capital crimes was subsequently increased by legislation enacted in 1994 and further expanded in 1996. Violent Crime Control and Law Enforcement Act of 1994, Public Law Number 103–322, §§60003–60024, 108 Statutes at Large 2141; Antiterrorism and Effective Death Penalty Act of 1996, Public Law Number 104–132, §708, 110 Statutes at Large 1226. The United States Attorney for the district located in the state where the crime was committed decides whether or not to seek the death penalty. This decision has to be approved by the Review Committee and the United States Attorney General. Federal Death Penalty System Report, 2. Decisions made between 1988 and 1994, prior to the implementation of the present system, are assigned to the 'pre-protocol' era. Ibid, 3, n 4. Those made after 1994 belong to the 'death protocol' era. Male capital offenders are housed at the Special Confinement Unit at the United States Penitentiary in Terre Haute, Indiana. All federal executions are carried out there. Federal Bureau of Prisons, http://www.bop.gov (last visited 21 September 2003).

[76] ibid. As previously noted, see n 69 above, these states authorized slavery in 1860, prior to the formation of the Confederacy. Virginia and Texas participated in the formation of the Confederacy, and are presently categorized as Southern states. See n 71 above.

[77] Federal Death Penalty System Report, n 71 above, 2.

[78] ibid, T18–T21. In comparison, 25 out of the 52 prosecutorial requests to pursue the death penalty came from states forming the Confederacy, and 33 of the requests arose in 'Southern' jurisdictions, as labelled by the Due Process Information Center.

[79] ibid, T14–T17

[80] Mark Hamblett, 'Few Federal Juries In New York Asked to Impose Death Penalty, Prosecutors Subject to Death-Eligible Cases to a Three-Part Review Process', *New York Law Journal*, 23 April 2002, 7.

[81] The jurisdictions and figures are: Arkansas (2), Georgia (1), Louisiana (1), Maryland (1), Missouri (4), North Carolina (2), Texas (5), and Virginia (1).

[82] DPIC, http://www.deathpenaltyinfo.org/article.php?scid=29&did=149 (last visited 21 September 2003).

Socio-Economic Status and the Death Penalty in the United States

In addition, both films expose their audiences to the strong correlation between a lower socio-economic status and executions, another critical status based issue that questions the fairness of capital punishment. The texts of *Dead Man Walking* and *The Green Mile* provide many examples of specific variables that are typically referred to when evaluating socio-economic status.

For example, both films make good use of character development to provide the audience with a sense of who is at greater risk of being condemned and executed. One way this is accomplished is by assigning racial and ethnic attributes to their condemned characters in order to introduce the critical variable of membership in a marginalized or oppressed group. In *The Green Mile*, Arlen Bitterbuck, the first Mile resident to be executed, is Native American. Eduard Delacroix's, another Green Mile resident, roots are in Louisiana's Cajun community, a marginalized group indigenous to Louisiana. John Coffey is black, a group with a well documented history of oppression and exploitation in the United States. This point is more subtly presented in *Dead Man Walking*. In an exchange between Matthew and Sister Helen, Matthew explains that one reason why his impending execution is likely to occur is because the last few executees were black.

The lack of education is another factor often associated with a person's inclusion in a lower socio-economic status group. The following exchange that occurs between John Coffey and Paul Edgecomb, the Green Mile's supervising correctional officer, after Coffey is placed in his cell, and that refers to Coffey's illiteracy, illustrates this point:

Edgecomb: Your name is John Coffey.
Coffey: Yes, sir, boss, like the drink, only not spelled the same way.
Edgecomb: So you can spell, can you? Read and write?
Coffey: Just my name, boss.

Employment opportunities is yet another variable of the socio-economic status calculus that is presented in both films. For example, in *The Green Mile* the audience sees William 'Billy the Kid' Wharton, a late arrival to the Green Mile, employed as a day labourer, often a temporary menial job. John Coffey describes himself as a transient and his trial attorney tells Edgecomb that it was as if John Coffey simply 'fell out of the sky', which suggests he was unemployed. *Dead Man Walking* contains no evidence that Matthew Poncelet was employed. In fact, the film indicates that he spent a good deal of time getting high, drinking, shooting pool, and committing criminal offences. Occupational information included in the comprehensive Epsy File[83] confirms the validity of the films'

[83] See n 7 above for a description of the Epsy File.

respective portrayals. The Epsy File found that of the 14,634 recorded cases for which professional information could be located, 'the overwhelming majority of these individuals were unemployed or employed in lower-paying professions'.[84] The study reveals that professional diversity of the executees included apprentices in a variety of vocations, employees in the hospitality profession, such as bell hops, bell boys, maids, and bus boys, labourers, such as general labourers, farm workers and hands, factory workers, handymen, gas station workers, and custodians.[85] The largest occupation category was slavery.[86] These individuals were employed against their will to work at menial and gruelling domestic and agricultural tasks.

Lower paying jobs and the absence of employment opportunities have a direct connection to income level, another variable used to measure socio-economic status. *Dead Man Walking* uses visual images and dialogue to convey directly the link between poverty and the death penalty. For example, as Sister Helen Prejean approaches the Poncelet home to meet with Matthew's mother, the audience first sees the family's small rundown home and one of Matthew's younger brothers fixing the family's dilapidated automobile. While conversing with Mrs Poncelet Sister Helen asks whether she had heard that Matthew's execution was coming up soon. Mrs Poncelet affirmatively answered and noted that the prison had already called to notify her and to ask whether she had death insurance. With a touch of irony in her voice, Mrs Poncelet tells Sister Helen: 'What a laugh [the question about whether there was death insurance for Matthew]. I ain't even got food money.' At their first meeting, Sister Helen asks Matthew if he was 'brought up poor'. He aptly responds: 'Ain't nobody with money on death row'. In a later scene, Hilton Barber, Matthew's new attorney, commencing his presentation before the Louisiana Parole Board, in a last ditch effort to save Matthew's life, confirms the reality of Matthew's statement. Barber reminds the board members that poverty is what got them at the hearing. Barber implores the board to ' be honest. You're not going to find many rich people on death row. Matthew Poncelet's here today because he's poor.'

The contents of Barber's speech also educates the board, as well as the audience, about capital trial counsel, an important aspect of the relationship between capital punishment and socio-economic status. During his presentation Barber elaborates on the pivotal role Matthew's poverty played in securing his death sentence. He notes that because Matthew was impoverished, he 'didn't have money for representation so he had to take what the state gave him. The state gave him a tax attorney who never tried a capital case before. An amateur.' Barber argues that Matthew's capital trial counsel's ineffectiveness is beyond argument. As evidence of the utter failure of defence counsel, Barber refers to the fact that the tax attorney took four hours to select a capital jury, which is quite unusual for a capital trial, the trial's short duration (it only lasted five days), and the attorney 'raised one

[84] ibid, 18–32. [85] ibid. [86] ibid, 29.

objection the entire trial'.[87] Consequently, the film informs the public about how the quality of representation often mirrors the accused's socio-economic status.[88]

The Green Mile viewers are introduced to the same issue. After John Coffey performs one of his miracles, hence the hallowed initials 'JC', Paul Edgecomb cannot believe that the gentle man he knows, the one who cries because he is afraid of the dark, could have committed the horrendous crime for which he was condemned. His disbelief and puzzlement lead him to call in sick one morning so he can meet with Mr Hammersmith, the attorney who represented John Coffey at his capital trial. Unlike Matthew's lawyer, Coffey has had at least some experience trying death penalty cases because he tells Paul Edgecomb how two or three of his former clients had been executed at the penitentiary. Paul explains to Mr Hammersmith that he has come to chat about the John Coffey case and specifically whether Coffey could be innocent. The moment Paul makes this revelation Mr Hammersmith's attitude undergoes an appreciable change. He makes it quite clear that he does not like Coffey and thinks he is guilty. Hammersmith accomplishes this by using an analogy. Hammersmith's family once had a sweet mongrel dog. He goes on to note that the dog 'in many ways was like a nigra'. For example, mongrel dogs and 'nigras' can be kept around you, so long as you have both eyes open, and loyal but both can turn on you with no warning. One day, for apparently no reason, the mongrel dog bit Hammersmith's young son, disfiguring him. Even though it was the first time the dog had ever bitten, Hammersmith related how he jumped up, grabbed the dog by its collar, and blew its brains out. He then advises Edgecomb to not turn his back on Coffey or 'in the end he'll get bitten by him'. Equating Coffey to an animal suggests that Coffey's attorney did not consider his former client human. And, since Hammersmith's analogy seems to suggest that the best course of action would have been to take Coffey, a poor man, out back and shoot him like a dog (Hammersmith appears to be advocated lynching), it is very unlikely that Coffey received the type of zealous defence to which all capital defendants are entitled. Once again, an individual's socio-economic status dictated the quality of the legal counsel he received in a fight to save his life.

These scenes not only expose audiences to the adage 'capital punishment means them without the capital gets the punishment', but also embody the conclusions

[87] The Sixth Amendment guarantees the right to counsel. The United States Supreme Court has interpreted this to mean the right to effective assistance of counsel. See *Strickland v Washington*, 466 US 668 (1984). Though the test the Court formulated to make this evaluation has been attacked for being insufficiently rigorous. For example, in one case involving defence counsel who napped during part of his client's capital trial a three judge panel of the United States Court for the Fifth Circuit Court of Appeals used the Court's *Strickland* standard to conclude that the naps Burdine's counsel took during his capital trial constituted harmless error and consequently the panel refused to reverse his conviction and death sentence. Subsequently the Fifth Circuit granted petitioner Burdine's request for an en banc reconsideration of the panel's decision. After a rehearing en banc the Circuit Court reversed the panel's decision to vacate the federal district court's finding that Burdine had received ineffective assistance of counsel. *Burdine v Johnson*, 262 F 3d 336 (5th Cir 2001) (en banc), certiorari denied sub nom *Cockrell v Burdine*, 535 US 1120 (2002).

[88] See Stephen Bright, 'Counsel for the Poor: The Death Sentence Not for the Worst Crime but for the Worse Lawyer' (1994) 104 *Yale LJ* 1835.

reached in two separate studies examining socio-economic status and the death penalty. The researchers in the earlier of the two studies found that 'social hierarchy . . . will still be positively associated with the number of executions'.[89] Poverty played a crucial role in the study's design because class hierarchy, which 'assessed the degree of inequality of individual income distribution in the state',[90] was one of the three indicators used to determine social hierarchy.[91] The findings of the more recent study led to the same general conclusion: that there is 'a series of strong correlations between measures of social well-being and death penalty intensity'.[92] Like the earlier study, this research found 'a significant and strong correlation' between poverty and death penalty intensity.[93] The intersection between socio-economic status and geography was also presented to the viewers. As previously described, the death row residents in both films are awaiting execution by the state of Louisiana. In general, the South has been and continues to be considered an impoverished region.[94] This could create situations where social status becomes a significant variable in this region's execution practices.[95] Consequently, in some instances, this aspect of the fairness issue can also be analyzed from a geographic perspective.[96]

Conclusion

Recent legislative activity, results from public opinion polls, and capital sentencing and execution rates support the contention that the public is increasingly questioning capital punishment's place in modern American society. Since movie going is a popular American pastime, films reach a large number of people. This makes cinema an ideal tool to use to educate the public. *Dead Man Walking* and *The Green Mile* are two popular films that could have been used to edify the public about critical issues in the modern debate about capital punishment.

In particular, the vivid texts of both films instructed their respective audiences about fairness and the death penalty, an issue that strikes a chord with most people. Interestingly, both films exposed their viewers to geography and the death penalty

[89] Mitchell and Sidanius, n 69 above, 600–603. [90] ibid, 597. [91] ibid, 596.

[92] Lofquist, n 31 above, 1534–1535 (Table VI). [93] ibid.

[94] See 'Poverty in the United States: 2000', United States Department of Commerce (US Census Bureau) (September 2001), 15 available at http://ict.cas.psu.edu/resources/Census/PDF/C2K_Poverty_in_USA.pdf (citing that the South has the highest of the four geographic regions and that its 12.5% poverty rate is the historic low for that region; 'Poverty in the United States—Poverty by Region', at http://www.plu.edu/~poverty/hist/graphs.html (last visited 21 September 2003).

[95] See Harries and Cheatwood, n 66 above, 30 (noting that the South is a historically poor region prone to pathologies typical of poor societies.').

[96] This, in turn, sets the stage for exploring how the convergence of race and the legacy of slavery, geography, and socio-economic status issues impacts the administration of the death penalty. As previously noted, n 5 above, the topic of race is outside the scope of this paper. For more information on the subject, see generally Lofquist, n 31 above, 1534–1535, 1548–1549.

and socio-economic status and the death penalty, two status based issues that question the fairness of the death penalty. By having both films set in Louisiana the audience is able to witness the connection between executions (as well as death sentences) and the geographic location of the capital offender—specifically that geography is an important factor in determining who lives and who dies as the Southern region of the United States still has the highest execution rate. In order to instruct their respective audiences about the interrelationship between socio-economic status and the death penalty, both films effectively use visual images, dialogue, and character development to convey the message that 'where marginalization and deprivation are greatest, the death penalty is more likely to be used and more likely to be used aggressively'.

In sum, *Dead Man Walking* and *The Green Mile* allow moviegoers to digest valuable information relating to the current death penalty debate in the United States. Given the impact popular culture can have on altering viewpoints, it is fair to conclude that this form of popular culture, as manifested in these two films, played some role in stimulating the shift in public sentiment about the retention of capital punishment in American criminal jurisprudence, as evidenced by the changes in the modern death penalty practice.

Public and Private Eyes

Lawrence M Friedman

At the beginning of one of the countless mysteries in which Erle Stanley Gardner's lawyer-detective, Perry Mason, solves the case (*The Case of the Stepdaughter's Secret*), a rich man, Harlow Bancroft, comes to see Mason. Bancroft thinks he is the target of a blackmailer. He wants Mason to help him in this situation. In fact, it turns out, it is his daughter or her fiancé who is being blackmailed. The blackmailer is murdered, Bancroft's wife is apparently guilty—at least the police think so—and Mason, as usual, takes on the job of representing her. Naturally, she is innocent (all of Mason's clients are innocent), despite appearances (all of Mason's clients *seem* guilty). But Mason saves her, and unmasks the true criminal; and he does it in his usual way: in the middle of a dramatic trial.

The Perry Mason books are written to a formula.[1] The details vary of course. Murder is always involved; but there are all sorts of motives for murder. It is quite common for blackmail to be involved. One of the clichés of murder mysteries is the death of a blackmailer. It ranks right up there with other prominent motives—murdering the old uncle before he can change his will, for example. Mysteries, by convention, must have at least one murder. Sometimes there is a second murder. The victim in the second murder is often somebody who 'knows too much', sometimes somebody who not only knows too much, but can use this knowledge to expose the killer—or to extort money.

Mysteries are, after all, mysterious; in the classic mystery, the identity of the killer is revealed only at the very end of the book. In a well-crafted mystery, the clues to the solution are scattered throughout the text; but not too obviously. Indeed, if the solution is not a surprise, and if the average reader can guess the killer's identity, then the mystery is not really successful. Hence at the heart of the classic mystery is a secret, a well-kept secret; some person has a secret, so carefully hidden that nobody but the clever detective can (finally) uncover it, a secret that includes a motive for murder. Thus an essential aspect of the mystery is a masked identity, a person who is something other than what he or she seems.

[1] Mason has also been the subject of a popular American television series; and a number of movies. See J Dennis Bounds, *Perry Mason: The Authorship and Reproduction of a Popular Hero* (Westport, Conn. 1996).

It is an interesting historic fact, that the detective himself, the detective story, and the law against blackmail, all date from about the same time, roughly the first half of the 19th century.[2] Whether it was Edgar Allan Poe who invented the 'mystery', or someone else, the chronology is more or less the same. Poe wrote 'The Murders in the Rue Morgue' in the 1840s. In England, Wilkie Collins published *The Moonstone* in 1868, a genuine mystery, with a genuine (fictional) detective, Sergeant Cuff. Sherlock Holmes was launched in 1887. In the United States, Anna K Green published *The Leavenworth Case* in 1878, which was a fantastic best-seller. The mystery has been a non-stop success ever since.[3]

As for the detective himself, although in some ways it has an earlier pre-history, essentially the detective squad was a product of this period, too. Boston organized such a squad in 1846, New York in 1857, Philadelphia and Chicago shortly afterwards.[4] The term 'blackmail' referred to extortion; but in the 19th century it added another meaning. The money was to be extorted, not by threatening violence, but by threatening to reveal a secret.

All three phenomena respond to the same general social fact. They were the product of a mobile society—a society in which people move about, from place to place; and in which the lines between classes and strata of society are more porous and indistinct, and more permeable, than they were in earlier times. All modern societies are more mobile than traditional societies, in every sense of the word; but some were more mobile, and earlier, than others. Certainly, the United States, as an immigrant country, full of new people, strangers, rolling stones, was more mobile at least in this sense than England or France.

The social fact of spatial mobility has enormous consequences. One of them, which is relevant here, is that for the first time, *identity* becomes problematic. In a traditional society, people travel very little, marriages are arranged between families, life is lived in small villages, and everybody basically knows everybody else. Any stranger who comes into town is instantly recognized as such. But in, say, 19th century America, the growing towns and cities are full of people who have come from somewhere else. They present themselves, they parade a certain identity. But can we believe them? It has become very easy to lie. It has become very easy to invent a new self.

The detective was an expert in 'detecting', that is, in ferreting out secret, hidden crime. The role of the policeman was to keep order on the surface and in public places. He walks a beat. He is plainly visible. He wears a uniform and a badge. But in a mobile society, there were many crooks, confidence men, swindlers, who

[2] See Lawrence M Friedman and Issachar Rosen-Zvi, 'Illegal Fictions: Mystery Novels and the Popular Image of Crime', (2001) 48 *UCLA L Rev* 1411.

[3] There is, of course, a big literature on the detective story. See David R Papke, *Framing the Criminal: Crime, Cultural Work and the Loss of Critical Perspective, 1830–1900* (New York 1987); Ian Ousby, *Bloodhounds of Heaven: The Detective in English Fiction from Godwin to Doyle* (Cambridge, Mass. 1976).

[4] See David R Johnson, *Policing the Urban Underworld: The Impact of Crime on the Development of the American Police, 1800–1887* (Philadelphia 1979) 65.

masked their identities. The detective wore plain clothes; he was covert, sly, underground. He was therefore particularly useful for the newly invented crimes of the mobile society—especially the various swindles and confidence games that flourished in the 19th century.

One of these crimes was blackmail. There is a big literature today about blackmail, or what is called the puzzle or paradox of blackmail. A number of scholars, especially legal economists, have trouble understanding why blackmail should be a crime at all.[5] If you have information about someone, why can't you sell your silence? If you can buy and sell knowledge, why not buy and sell your right to keep your knowledge to yourself? Why is the deal that a blackmailer makes any different from 'an ordinary bargain'?[6] These are, in a way, interesting questions; but the issue here is not whether blackmail laws are justified, but what they were meant to accomplish, and why.

The word blackmail originally referred to extortion. Extortion is a much less problematic crime. If I threaten to blow your brains out unless you pay me, there is no puzzle as to why this should be a crime. But in the 19th century, blackmail began to be applied to something quite different—buying silence about a guilty secret. In the United States, a Georgia statute, in the early 19th century, was one of the first to suggest the more modern meaning of the term. This statute made it a crime to 'send or deliver any letter or writing, threatening to accuse another person of a crime, with intent to extort money' (Laws Ga. 1816, No 178). A statute of Illinois in 1827 (no 145) made it a crime to 'send or deliver any letter, or writing, threatening to accuse another person of a crime or misdemeanor, or of exposing and publishing any of his or her infirmities or failings, with intent to extort [money]'. Under a Massachusetts statute of 1835, the requirement of a 'letter or writing' was dropped; verbal threats would be enough to constitute blackmail. Ultimately, about half of the states had some kind of statute criminalizing blackmail, that is, the threat to expose some secret, unless money changed hands. Meanwhile, in England, the Libel Act of 1843 (s 3) made it a misdemeanour to promise 'directly or indirectly' to 'abstain from printing or publishing . . . any matter or thing touching any other person, with intent to extort any money . . . or any valuable thing'.

Whatever else their purpose, clearly the blackmail laws were meant to protect people who had guilty secrets.[7] The blackmailer is someone who rakes up the dead past. In England, even in the 18th century, it was widely believed that sexual blackmail was common—in particular, accusations of homosexual behaviour; or women who accused men of rape; though whether this was so or not is somewhat problematic.[8] The sexual element is not very pronounced in American blackmail cases.

[5] Walter Block, 'Trading Money for Silence', (1986) 8 *U of Hawaii L Rev* 57.

[6] Leo Katz, *Ill-Gotten Gains: Evasion, Blackmail, Fraud and Kindred Puzzles of the Law* (Chicago 1996). There are many attempts in the literature to answer the question: see Richard A Posner, 'Blackmail, Privacy and Freedom of Contract', (1993) 141 *U of Pennsylvania L Rev* 1817.

[7] On this point, see Lawrence M Friedman, 'Name Robbers: Privacy, Blackmail, and Assorted Matters in Legal History', (2002) 30 *Hofstra L Rev* 1093, 1110–1114.

[8] See Antony E Simpson, 'The "Blackmail Myth" and the Prosecution of Rape and its Attempt in 18th Century London: The Creation of a Legal Tradition', (1986) 77 *J of Criminal Law & Criminology* 101.

If we ask, what was the social function of blackmail, what did the law accomplish (or try to accomplish), it seems clear that the tendency was supposed to be to protect the upper class, and, in general, respectable people. They were to be protected from accusations that would ruin that reputation. No matter that the accusations were true (which was usually the case with blackmail). In England, the protection seemed to run strongly along lines of class. The blackmailer was almost always socially inferior to the victim. The blackmailers were working class men and women, and servants in general, who had damning information about their betters—usually information about sexual behaviour.

The United States had greater social and geographic mobility than England in the 19th century. It was also a more egalitarian society, at least as far as manners and behaviour were concerned. In the United States, blackmail had less class aspects than English blackmail. It concerned much more men (almost always men), who had shed one life like a dead skin, and started another. This was true of fact; and also of fiction. In the Perry Mason mystery we mentioned at the beginning, the rich client, Harlow Bancroft, was once convicted of a crime: if his fingerprint data were ever released, the whole world would know his secret, that 'Harlow Bissinger Bancroft, the great philanthropist and financier, is a criminal who served fourteen months in a penitentiary'.

Blackmail, then, presupposes a mystery, a guilty secret. It is, in other words, constructed on the same general basis as the detective story (and often is the motivating force in the detective story). And both of them reflect the mobility of the 19th century.[9] They reflect the world of the 19th century in general: the advent of the railroad, later the telephone, telegram—rapidity in travel and communication, in short, the creation of a modern world, a world much more fluid and ambiguous, with many more opportunities for disguises and for secrecy, many more lives that twist and turn.

I have no way of estimating how many 'mysteries' or 'detective novels' have been written. The number is surely vast. One guess that I have seen is that as many as a fourth of all books published in the English-speaking world could fall into this category.[10] In any event, there have been perhaps hundreds of thousands of mysteries published in the last century and a half. The English-speaking world probably produces the bulk of these. Obviously, you can find support in this huge milky way of words for almost anything you might want to say about this literary form. And you can find exceptions to every generalization you might want to make about the subject. But there are some traits that at least *most* mysteries share. The crime is almost always a murder. The identity of the murderer is unknown at first; we find out who it is, but only at the very end of the book. At least this is the pattern in the classic mystery novel. A large minority, especially today, are somewhat different, in that we know who the killer is, but the question is, how to catch him. I will come back to this point.

[9] See Lawrence M Friedman, 'Crimes of Mobility', (1991) 43 *Stanford L Rev* 637.

[10] See John McAleer, 'The Game's Afoot: Detective Fiction in the Present Day', *Kansas Quarterly*, Fall 1978, 22.

In most classic, conventional mysteries, the real criminal is unmasked in the last chapter, or near the last chapter, and (if it is a successful book), the reader is genuinely surprised. The surprise means that somebody was pretending to be something that he or she was really not. This nice young man or this gentle woman turns out to be a ruthless killer. The classic mystery, especially of the British sort, usually takes place in a closed, upper class environment. There are no poor people, no street people, drug addicts, slums, working-class people. The victims and the suspects are well-to-do—often from the nobility or the landed gentry; at the very least, 'gentlemen' and 'ladies'. The mystery is 'closed', in that there is a finite, fixed, definite group of suspects. Sometimes this is literally the case: the murder takes place in a country house, there are no signs of a break-in, and the murderer must have been one of the family, or a guest, or possibly a servant. In Agatha Christie's famous novel, '*And Then There Were None*', ten men and women are alone on an island, cut off from the rest of the world. They are murdered one by one.[11]

In all of these novels, someone is out of place, morally or otherwise, someone is wearing a mask. In many of these books, the 'detective' is a skilled amateur, not an actual working detective. The classic example, of course, is Sherlock Holmes; another well-known example is Agatha Christie's Miss Marple, a village spinster (Patricia Wentworth's Miss Silver is another 'detective' of this type). These amateurs succeed because of their skill in piercing through the masks and detecting the underlying realities. Sherlock Holmes could tell who you were by the shape and cut of your walking stick, or something about the ashes of a cigar. Miss Marple simply knows human nature, through her keen observation of life in her little village. They do what forensic science, or the professional detective, is supposed to do: they dig beneath the surface and find a hidden and disguised reality.

The classic (British) mystery takes place in a closed setting; but, in a way, it was not as closed as it seemed to be. Society was changing. Society lines, though still rigid by American standards, were becoming more fluid. The classic English mystery arose in a society which was on the road to greater mobility, in which the old order was changing. Yes, in many of the classic mysteries, some or all of the suspects were ladies and gentlemen. Contrary to legend, the butler rarely 'did it'; and other servants almost never. But one or more of these ladies and gentlemen turns out to be bankrupt, dishonest, disloyal, a victim of blackmail, or a blackmailer; and at times even murderous. Identity is not as distorted as in instances of bigamy, or the confidence game; but in a deeper sense, identity has become problematic.

Most mysteries end with the great revelation: identifying the true killer. It is more or less assumed that the murderer will be tried and convicted. Often, the murderer confesses, or gives himself away, or (sometimes) kills himself, or is killed trying to kill the detective. No critique of the legal system is either express or

[11] The trick here, of course, is that at the end (or nearly at the end) of the book, there are literally *no* suspects left. Yet one of the ten victims in fact was the killer. Instead of a group of suspects, one of whom is the killer, there are ten bodies, but among them there is one who was not really dead, and was picking off the others one by one.

implied. Once we know 'who did it', we lose interest in what happens afterwards, as if it is clear that justice will be done. In books where the 'detective' is strictly an amateur, the real police and detectives are often portrayed as stupid or clumsy, which of course they are, compared to, say, Sherlock Holmes. In other novels, the detective is the protagonist—Inspector Morse, or Richard Jury, among many others. And among the thousands and thousands of detective stories, it would be difficult to think of an occupation or type which is *not* represented. There is an English lord (Peter Wimsey) and a Catholic priest (Father Brown); also rabbis, stockbrokers, lawyers, doctors, and just about everything else one can imagine.

Many writers have emphasized what they consider the conservatism of the classic mystery. The mystery involves an interruption, a disturbance, in the placid surface of society; but by the end of the book, there is total closure. The mystery is solved, the interruption ended, the disturbance has been brought to an end; and all's right with the world. In Agatha Christie's novel, *The Body in the Library*, first published in 1942, the body of a beautiful young woman is discovered dead in the library of the country home of Colonel and Mrs Bantry. The woman was a complete stranger to them. What could be more incongruous, or out of place? The discovery sets tongues to wagging all over the village. Could it be that the woman was somehow connected, in some shameful way, to Colonel Bantry himself? This turns out not to be true; and the mystery is solved by the formidable Miss Marple. In the end, the small world gets back its balance. Evil is undone and punished. The crisis is ended, and Colonel Bantry can go back to his life as a country squire.

The conservatism is real enough; but of course, there *is* a murder, there *is* a body in the library, and it does not belong there. The balance is indeed restored in the end; but after all, there was a need to restore it. Something had disturbed the equilibrium. What sets the plot going, after all, is the worm in the bud, the canker in the heart of the social order, the confusion of identity, the masks and hidden places. The detective story flourished in Victorian England; in Victorian England there was a goodly dose of corruption and change, sex and debauchery, chicanery and hypocrisy, underneath a smooth surface of propriety, prudery, prosperity, tradition, and empire.

In *The Body in the Library*, as in many other novels, outside forces invade Miss Marple's village, and disturb its classic calm. Agatha Christie is the great classicist of the detective novel; and her work is entirely 20th century. Yet even as she wrote, another form of mystery was emerging in the United States, a country where the lines between classes were much more blurred, and where social and geographical mobility were more pronounced than in England. The American rival was the so-called hard-boiled mystery: the novels of Raymond Chandler and Dashiell Hammett; of Mickey Spillane, and countless imitators.

The American hard-boiled mystery reflects a more egalitarian (and violent) society. In these stories, the critique of regular police and detective forces is much sharper. They are not merely incompetent, they are corrupt, and often themselves are violent. The protagonist is not the amateur, certainly not a shrewd village spinster, but a 'private eye'. A 'private eye' has a sharply different character from

Miss Marple, on the one hand (or Sherlock Holmes), and the real-life detective, employed by the state, on the other hand. The 'private eye' is certainly more macho. Many of the writers of the classic mysteries were women; all the famous writers of hard-boiled mysteries were men.

There were (and are) of course private detectives, and the work of the Pinkerton agency in the United States is famous (sometimes infamous).[12] The 'private eye' can work quietly and confidentially, like the lawyer. Moreover, the very role of the private eye is an implied critique of the legal system, and the regular forces of law and order. The system is sometimes bumbling and inadequate. At other times—or most times—it is corrupt. The private eye bypasses the system; and he also can and does make use of tactics that would shock Miss Marple or Hercule Poirot. He skirts the line between legality and illegality. In some ways, this is a reflection of reality. In real life, at least in many American cities, the line between police, detective, and criminal is itself quite fuzzy.

The 'hard-boiled' detective novel supplemented the classic mystery; it did not replace it. Both forms still flourish, although the classic, upper-class mystery is probably less common than it once was, at least relatively speaking. And there are many hybrids—what some have called the 'soft-boiled' detective novel, which 'maintains the outlines of the Chandlerian novel, but with slightly more genial characters and less violence'.[13]

In recent years, a third type has become quite prominent. In these 'thrillers', the killer is insane, a psychopath, a murderer who kills randomly, or without regard for the classic motives; or out of sheer viciousness or hatred. This development surely reflects the fears of ordinary people, and the emphasis, in the media and elsewhere, on random, horrific crimes, visited on strangers, and perpetrated by the criminally insane. This type of crime is relatively uncommon, of course; but it gets heavy media coverage. And it fuels the political movement to 'get tough' on crime.

In these novels, there is much more emphasis on technology, on forensics, on the scientific search for the criminal. Less emphasis is placed on 'the little grey cells'. The immensely popular novels of Patricia Cornwell, in the United States, feature as the main character a tough and well-trained woman Medical Examiner. The villains in these books are mostly psychopaths. Kay Scarpetta, the Medical Examiner, is forever carving up bodies to find out their forensic secrets. Her work is described in grisly detail:

> The dead woman was nude and pitiful. . . . Areas of flesh excised from her shoulder were ghastly patches of darkened blood. Her skin was bright pink from cold livor mortis. . . . The

[12] On the Pinkerton agency, see Frank Morn, '*The Eye that Never Sleeps*': *A History of the Pinkerton National Detective Agency* (Bloomington, Ind. 1982). There were and are, of course, private police as well. Private police—security guards, for example—are, like the official police, visible, uniformed, and patrol the surfaces. The private eye, like the official detective, works more in secret, in plain clothes, and somewhat underground.

[13] Richard B Schwartz, *Nice and Noir: Contemporary American Crime Fiction* (Columbia, Missouri. 2002) 101. Schwartz mentions Sue Grafton as an example.

gunshot wound to her right temple was large caliber. . . . We worked in the dark for more than an hour, and she was revealed . . . inches at a time.[14]

But the clues uncovered from these autopsies will usually lead her on the dangerous path toward discovery of the identity of the psychopath, who often seems to target her as a possible victim.

Now, both in law and in literature, the stalker and the madman move to the centre of the stage, to be added to the corrupt policeman and politician, the blackmailer, the profligate nephew who murders an uncle about to change his will, and the other villains of classic and hard-boiled detective stories. The stalker usually stalks 'within the family'; or, more usually, the stalker is a former boyfriend, husband, or lover.[15] Murder, too, takes place mostly within the family, or among lovers and ex-lovers. Strangers who stalk, spy, or kill, are a distinct minority; yet, perhaps paradoxically, this is what people seem to fear most.

The image of law in these new novels, like those in the hard-boiled novels, reflects a good deal of paranoia and suspicion. It would be interesting to trace the image of law enforcement agencies in the literature and in the movies. The CIA, the FBI, the British intelligence services—these were once usually depicted as honest, heroic, battling for the good; now they are seen not so much as corrupt as amoral, sinister, and outside the rules of the due process game. This change—at least this is my impression–is particularly marked in the movies, especially spy movies (and spy novels in general). In any event, the image of the law is much sharper in modern crime fiction. It is more in the forefront. It is in many ways more powerful—more devious, but also more scientific. It now also faces cunning and intractable enemies. And the formal law—the official law—is constantly subverted, not just by criminals, but also by law-enforcement people themselves.

The 19th century was a century of mobility; but the mobility of the 20th (and 21st) centuries is vastly greater. There is constant interaction with strangers. City life is anonymous life; or at least, a life in which part of each day is spent in total anonymity. Some people are not what they seem; and in any event, most of the people we see, hear, touch, observe are completely unknowable. This is fertile ground, not only for the classic confidence man, but also for the serial killer, that most dreaded of all modern criminals.[16] He may move from place to place. He kills without motive—crimes of opportunity; and the lack of motive makes him that much harder to trace. The actual serial killer, of course, is not entirely contemporary. Jack the Ripper was a famous serial killer. In Chicago of the 1890s, there was Dr Henry Holmes, a heartless and compulsive killer.[17] These were essentially

[14] Patricia Cornwell, *From Potter's Field* (New York 1995) 52–53.

[15] On the stalker, and stalker laws, see Paul E Mullen, Michele Pathé, Rosemary Purcell, *Stalkers and Their Victims* (New York 2000); Stephen J Morewitz, *Stalking Violence: New Patterns of Trauma and Obsession* (New York 2003).

[16] See David Schmid, 'The Locus of Disruption: Serial Murder and Generic Conventions in Detective Fiction', in Warren Chernaik et al (eds), *The Art of Detective Fiction* (New York 2000) 55.

[17] On Holmes, see Erik Larson, *The Devil in the White City* (New York 2003).

motiveless murders—at least they lacked conventional motives. The American 'crime of the century', the Loeb-Leopold case, was notoriously also lacking in motive.[18] The two killers were young and wealthy men. They murdered a young boy, apparently just for the thrill of it, or to commit the perfect crime; at any rate, there was no other obvious reason. But this behaviour is the antithesis of the classic mystery, where motive was everything; and the killing was, in its way, always rational. No matter how weird and bizarre the crime, or how impossible it seems to explain, or how deep the mystery, there is always a rational explanation. This is true, for example, in 'locked door' mysteries, where nobody could have killed the victim, and yet somebody did.

In the classic mystery, the puzzle was unravelled in the end; and along with the identity of the killer, you finally discovered *why* the murder occurred. Many modern thrillers, on the other hand, lack motive entirely. The killer kills for no reason; or for reasons that defy rational explanation. Many are psychopaths or worse: beasts in human form. A prime example would be Hannibal Lecter, in *The Silence of the Lambs* and its sequels. A killer of this type, in theory, could plead the insanity defence; but in a mystery or thriller this rarely occurs, and would not be particularly satisfying. At the end of the story, quite often, the author finds a way to kill the psychopath off.

It is a short step from the irrational killer, the beast in human form, to the villain who in fact *is* a beast; or at least non-human. Oddly enough, in one of the very first mysteries, Poe's 'Murders in the Rue Morgue', the 'criminal' was literally a beast, specifically an ape. The non-human villain is more often found in science fiction, where the author is free to invent new worlds, new creatures, and alien life-forms of the most bizarre form. In the movie classic, *Invasion of the Body Snatchers* (first made in 1956), the horror lies in the fact that aliens from outer space take over human bodies, and assume human forms. They look, talk, and act just like the rest of us. You see them on the streets, or in your house, and you never know: is this my friend, or is it something strange and awful, inhabiting his body? This movie came in a period of intense paranoia: the McCarthy era. It was at the height of the cold war and the anti-Communist witch-hunt. There are various ways of interpreting the movie. One plausible reading sees it as an artefact of McCarthyism. Communists, like the body snatchers, look like ordinary people, like neighbours and friends; but they are in fact profoundly alien, and bent on subverting and destroying our society.

The creatures, the aliens in *Invasion of the Body Snatchers*, look like the rest of us. In this sense, the movie is quite unlike most of the 'slasher' and horror movies. In these movies, horrible, deformed creatures, some human, some not, are on a rampage, killing right and left (in the 'slasher' movies, the victims are usually very young and good-looking). There are also the 'alien' movies, where non-human monsters (sometimes burrowing inside peoples' bodies) destroy most of the human characters in the movie. In some movies, they breed and spread and threaten to overwhelm the human race. Our age is the first in human history that

[18] Hal Higdon, *The Crime of the Century: The Leopold and Loeb Case* (New York 1975).

is *capable* of committing total suicide. This makes it more plausible to have villains (even in such camp classics as the James Bond movies) whose ultimate aim is to control or destroy the world.

The fear of spies, moles, communists has subsided at the beginning of the 21st century; fear of terrorists has replaced these outmoded bogeymen: members of the shadowy Al Qaeda, suicide bombers and the like. What is common is that these are people burrowing from underneath. Hidden, sinister dangers haunt the public mind. Popular literature feeds and feeds on mass fears and perceptions. All this has a real and baneful effect on the criminal justice system. It leads to a demand for more draconian laws. Of course, actual crimes play a crucial rule—more important than fiction, though not perhaps more important than the way these crimes are reported in the media. In California, young Polly Klaas was kidnapped from her own home, raped and murdered in the early 1990s. This was random, motiveless crime, stranger crime. It horrified the public. The killer had to be a monster in human form. Largely in reaction to this crime, the voters of California adopted the harsh 'three-strikes' law; and similar crimes have brought about similar reactions in other states.[19]

In the United States—and to a lesser degree in other Western countries—crime rates have risen quite markedly since the 1950s. In the United States in particular, the homicide rate jumped upwards; and this, plus the (perhaps overdone) media coverage of crime, produced what has been called a culture of fear.[20] Newspapers, magazines, and television play out what is most sensational and lurid. The more horrific the crime, the more inches of space it gets in the press, the more minutes it commands on TV. This is the age of 'tabloid justice'.[21] To this can be added, today, the war against terror. The attack on the World Trade Center, in September 2001, was another striking demonstration that nobody is safe and that nowhere is there a safe haven. In the United States, this has produced a mass of anti-terror legislation, much of it no doubt foolish and unnecessary, some of which seems to chip away at constitutional safeguards; rules and regulations about immigrants and foreigners have become tight almost to the point of a chokehold; and there are elaborate security measures at airports and other places. Fiction here follows fact.

Detective fiction, in short, grew out of a particular social milieu, and its forms and manners have been bent, throughout its history, by changes in that particular social milieu. Of especial importance has been the crime rate and (even more so) public perceptions of crime. Perhaps detective fiction, in turn, has had an impact on images of law, and may even have led to changes in law. This is impossible to show. The impact of movies and television seems more likely and more palpable. The detective story, in its various incarnations, may only be a dim, silvery, pale reflection of these powerful social forces.

[19] The California law is Cal Penal Code, s 667.

[20] Tonya L Brito, 'Paranoid Parents, Phantom Menaces, and the Culture of Fear', [2000] *Wisconsin L Rev* 519; Barry Glassner, *The Culture of Fear: Why Americans are Afraid of the Wrong Things* (New York 1999).

[21] See Richard L Rox and Robert W Van Sickel, *Tabloid Justice: Criminal Justice in an Age of Media Frenzy* (Boulder, Co. 2001).

Seeing Blind Spots: Corporate Misconduct in Film and Law

Michael Robertson

Introduction

Films are designed to show you something. Most commentators on law and film are interested in what films purport to show you about law and lawyers. But in this paper I am going to look in the opposite direction. I am going to investigate what types of things films do not show you about law and the reasons for these absences. Now, one category of what is not shown is easy to identify. This category consists of aspects of legal reality that a film maker *could* show, but chooses not to because they are boring or undramatic. However, I am interested in exploring whether there is another category of absences that is the product of something deeper and more structural. In this hypothesized second category, the film maker is *unable* to represent some aspect of legal reality on film. My goal in this paper is to explore whether such structural blind spots exist, and to investigate how they limit the ability of film to reflect legal realities.

More particularly, I will be looking at the area of socially harmful corporate conduct, and considering whether some categories of such conduct cannot be represented in films. I will start by looking at the way corporate misconduct is portrayed in classical Hollywood films, and then move on to other types of films, such as documentaries. My claim, if it can be established, has both ideological and political consequences. Film is an important mass medium and a powerful tool to spur outrage and reform. If film is disabled from portraying some forms of corporate misconduct, then the publicity given to this wrongdoing is less, and the chances of remedial action are reduced.

Classical Hollywood Films and the Law

I start with classical Hollywood films because cinema has tended to be dominated by this narrative form, both in America and overseas.[1] The film historian David

[1] D Bordwell and K Thompson, *Film Art. An Introduction* (4th international edn, New York: 1993) 82.

Bordwell gives us this description of the structural requirements of the classical Hollywood film:

The classical Hollywood film presents psychologically defined individuals who struggle to solve a clear-cut problem or to attain specific goals. In the course of this struggle, the characters enter into conflict with others or with external circumstances. The story ends with a decisive victory or defeat, a resolution of the problem and a clear achievement or nonachievement of the goals. The principal causal agency is thus the character, a distinctive individual endowed with an evident, consistent batch of traits, qualities, and behaviors.[2]

Those dealing more specifically with law and film have noted the same requirements. Norman Rosenberg in his article, 'Looking for Law in all the Old Traces: the Movies of Classical Hollywood, the Law, and the Case(s) of Film Noir', writes that:

The dominant model for screenwriting has long decreed that a cinematic drama must create goal-oriented characters who confront a series of obstacles, conflicts, complications, and crises before the movie provides some kind of resolution. Although obstacles and complications—as in the famous case of Humphrey Bogart's Rick Blaine in Casablanca—can be inner, psychological ones, a screenplay must also create external ones: 'antagonists' who 'personify the protagonist's obstacles' and concrete problems that require practical solutions.[3]

What these passages bring home forcefully is that the classical Hollywood narrative is centred on individuals—their desires, decisions, relationships, conflicts, character and development—and that individuals are the prime causal agents in these films.

Many aspects of law meet these narrative requirements admirably. Charles Rosenberg notes that:

A part of what lawyers do just happens to mesh nicely with the perceived structural needs of drama. Aristotle, in the Poetics, said that drama requires conflict and resolution. Lawyers are frequently engaged in conflict, and verdicts provide a neat form of resolution. Even better, the conflicts in which lawyers engage are often direct, personal, and confined to the intimate space of a courtroom. The fact that this confrontational part of law is only a small part of what lawyers do is of little concern to the dramatist.[4]

Crimes and criminal trials can provide all of the required ingredients. 'Characters associated with the law, such as police officers or attorneys, and concrete legal problems, such as arrests and trials, have long provided filmmakers with a wide array of realistic obstacles to place in front of goal-oriented characters.'[5] Some of the most

[2] D Bordwell, 'Classical Hollywood Cinema: Narrational Principles and Procedures' in P Rosen (ed), *Narrative, Apparatus, Ideology. A Film Theory Reader* (New York: 1986) 17. See too the description in Bordwell and Thompson, n 1 above, 82–97.

[3] N Rosenberg, 'Looking for Law in all the Old Traces: the Movies of Classical Hollywood, the Law, and the Case(s) of Film Noir' (2001) 48 *UCLA L Rev* 1443, 1449 (footnotes omitted).

[4] C Rosenberg, 'An L.A. Lawyer Replies' (1989) 98 *Yale LJ* 1625, 1626.

[5] N Rosenberg, n 3 above, 1449. See too N Rafter, 'American Criminal Trial Films: An Overview of their Development, 1930–2000' (2001) 28 *J of Law and Society* 9.

famous Hollywood films about law, such as *To Kill a Mockingbird, 12 Angry Men,* and *Judgment at Nuremburg* deal with crimes and trials. The dramatic requirement for individual conflict and resolution can also be satisfied by a law film which does not involve a criminal trial. A civil action can serve just as well, as seen in films such as *A Civil Action, The Verdict,* and *Philadelphia.* It is not even necessary to have a trial of any kind, for example films dealing with divorce and child custody (*Kramer vs. Kramer*).

But the same narrative requirements that bring some aspects of legal reality to the fore in Hollywood films also condemn other aspects to oblivion. If the individual interactions do not generate the required degree of conflict or drama, if they involve only trivial or incomprehensibly technical activities, the film maker will choose not to show them.[6] As Lawrence Friedman pithily put it, '[n]o songs have been composed about the Robinson-Patman Act, no movies produced about the capital gains tax. This is not surprising, since most people do not have a clue as to what these are all about. But there are also no songs, movies, or TV programs about medicare, dog licences, zoning laws, or overtime parking, all of which most people certainly *do* know something about.'[7] Stephen Gillers, in 'Taking L.A. Law More Seriously', expands on why the trivial or technical aspects of law do not get shown:

> Not once, so far as I am aware, has the show dwelt on, or even mentioned, the usual content of much law practice and legal scholarship—issues like the parole evidence rule, collateral estoppel, riparian water rights, or ancillary jurisdiction. The simple explanation for this distortion is, of course, that to the extent the 'Law' half of L.A. Law is able to remain part of the show, it has to earn its keep. That means it has to engage a lay audience. To be engaging, it has to be difficult, morally difficult, and that means it has to be about people and their responsibilities to each other: the responsibilities of lawyers to clients, partners and associates, and others; and the responsibilities of individuals to each other and of corporations (preferably large ones) to individuals . . . Absent an extreme situation, the holder in due course doctrine is just not going to be great entertainment, not even in L.A.'[8]

Stefan Machura and Stefan Ulbrich go so far as to argue that the classical Hollywood film's need for individual drama and conflict explains why trial films set in other jurisdictions often do not show their domestic criminal procedure at work, but instead borrow from American criminal procedure:

> American [legal] procedure has provided the foundation for almost all cinematic legal procedures, even in films set in a country like Germany that has a different system. . . . American legal procedure is structurally more suitable for a film than is the so-called inquisitorial procedure found in civil law systems, such as we find on the continent . . . because it is more hospitable to scenes of intense drama, featuring classical confrontations between two antagonists and conflicts between good and evil which have to be resolved. Such conflicts

[6] Or the facts will be massaged to fit the dramatic requirements. See S Greenfield, G Osborn and P Robson, *Film and the Law* (London: 2001) Ch 3 ('Presumed Accurate? Fact, Fiction, and Cinematic Law').

[7] L Friedman, 'Law, Lawyers, and Popular Culture' (1989) 98 *Yale LJ* 1579, 1588.

[8] S Gillers, 'Taking L.A. Law More Seriously' (1989) 98 *Yale LJ* 1607, 1608.

can be made a great deal more powerful in an adversary procedure than in German criminal procedure, in which the principle of official investigation (*Amtsermittlungsgrundsatz*) requires the public prosecutor to investigate all aspects of the case including those that favour the defendant.[9]

All these examples of aspects of legal reality which are absent from classical Hollywood cinema fall within the first category mentioned in my introduction. That narrative form requires that individuals and their significant projects, contests, quandaries, relationships etc, be at the centre of the film and drive its action. Consequently it is not surprising that film makers choose not to show individuals engaged in law-related activity that is undramatic or uninteresting to non-lawyers. But while the requirements of the Hollywood film can fail to be satisfied by individual conduct which is too trivial or technical, they would also be unsatisfied by aspects of legal reality in which individuals are not important actors at all. Indeed, the absence of individuals from the stage is even more catastrophic for the Hollywood form than merely having individuals who are not doing anything dramatic. Such absences could not be depicted in a Hollywood film; they would step so far outside the narrative conventions as to be unfilmable. It is not that they would produce a boring film; rather a film maker adhering to the classical Hollywood narrative form would not be able to make the film. But are there any such instances of legal reality where individuals are unimportant? To answer this, we have to look in more detail at different types of corporate misconduct.

Corporate Misconduct

Socially harmful action by corporations and corporate employees is a very broad notion, and so we must begin by drawing lines and making some distinctions. The first distinction I want to make is between 'white collar misconduct' and 'corporate misconduct'. The first category captures activity engaged in by corporate employees for their personal benefit alone. Often the corporation which employs them is the victim of these activities, as in embezzlement or the appropriation of corporate opportunities. By contrast, corporate misconduct results when corporate employees are acting to advance the economic interests of the corporation itself.

Many of the familiar instances of corporate misconduct, as I have defined it, result from deliberate and conscious actions by corporate officers or employees. Within this category one would find intentional frauds such as stock manipulation, false or deceptive advertising, financial fraud (as seen in Enron's deceptive accounting practices), and tax evasion. Other types of corporate misconduct that involve the deliberate acts of corporate employees would be bribery, anti-competitive

[9] S Machura and S Ulbrich, 'Law in Film: Globalizing the Hollywood Courtroom Drama' (2001) 28 *J of Law and Society* 117, 123–124. I am not sure myself if this hypothesis holds up. At least on American television, programmes about coroners and crime scene investigators who seek the truth rather than act as partisan prosecutors or defenders are sufficiently dramatic to do well.

conspiracies, obstruction of justice (as seen in Enron's document shredding activities), and union-busting. Corporate misconduct need not always be the product of deliberate individual acts though. Unsafe work environments, unsafe consumer products, or unsafe pollution can sometimes be the results of negligence, as well as callous or reckless decisions.

But can significant corporate misconduct result even in the absence of willing, reckless, or negligent individuals? Can it result from impersonal organizational features or system disfunctions which are built into the corporate structure and which tend to produce bad corporate outcomes regardless of the individuals working within the organization? Christopher Stone, in *Where the Law Ends. The Social Control of Corporate Behavior*, gives a classic account of how very harmful corporate misconduct can occur without the intention, recklessness, or negligence of any 'bad' individuals within the organization. '[T]here is . . . in many corporations and industries a smaller group of law violations and law circumventions that are systematic and chronic—not the happenstance of some particular ne'er-do-well employee on the make, but products of the organizational system itself. . . .'[10]

He identifies the important elements of the organizational system which can produce such unintended misconduct. One key element is the corporation's 'information net':

> The importance of a company's information processes cannot be overstated; they are as vital to the corporation as the nervous system of a human being to the body. What information the corporation seeks from its environment, where it looks for feedback (both within and without itself), where it dispatches what it learns, what it stores in memory, and what, for all intents and purposes, it 'forgets', (or destroys)—all these features of its information system are fundamental determinants of the corporation's behavior.[11]

One problem with the corporate information net is the natural tendency for bad news not to rise, compounded by the desire of those at the top to shield themselves from potential liability by being able to claim honestly that they did not know what was going on below them.[12]

Another problem is the fragmentation and dispersal of knowledge among different functional units of the enterprise.[13] The compounding of factors such as these can lead to situations where the corporation honestly does not know that it is causing serious harm to others. Stone makes this point by describing a New Yorker cartoon:

> In the cartoon, two men, apparently public officials, have led a third, a high corporate officer, to a wall of his plant which abuts and overlooks a waterway. From this prospect, the officer can look down to see three huge pipes from which the company is dumping pollutants into the water. With a look of perfectly ingenuous surprise, he remarks, 'So *that's* where it goes! I'd like to thank you fellows for bringing this to my attention.' Some viewers of the cartoon will interpret the corporate officer's remarks cynically: Surely he must have known all along. But

[10] C Stone, *Where the Law Ends. The Social Control of Corporate Behavior* (New York: 1975) 163.
[11] ibid, 201. See too 169 and 32–33. [12] ibid, 45–46, 62–63. [13] ibid, 52.

the fact is, the intelligence-gathering operations of any organization have to be limited, and, at present, the areas in the organization's environment from which it seeks data are typically those that will inform it upon prospective sales volume, demand shifts, competitor behavior, and the like. . . . Yet, if the processes through which the corporation perceives can be identified, is it not possible that the society can structure the corporation's information net so the corporation will get feedback on the harm it is causing through pollution?[14]

Organizational complexity, and the resulting need to divide the organization into sub-groups based on factors like geography or function can also lead to corporate misconduct for which no individual or group of individuals is responsible. The different sub-groups have their own distinct targets, objectives, even values, and the people working within these groups pursue those local goals. But sometimes an intense focus on the pursuit of these local goals can produce a blindness as to the conduct of the corporation as a whole. Indeed, a narrow focus on achieving the goals of some sub-group can wind up harming the interests of the corporation as a whole. Stone describes a problem that developed at one corporation in developing a military aircraft. The unit responsible for designing the brakes had made a commitment early in the process to four discs on the brakes being sufficient. It transpired that this was inadequate, but the unit refused to accept the evidence of this. The members of the brake unit did not intend to produce a defective aircraft and expose the corporation to massive liability. They were just focusing on performing the limited task assigned to them, and once they had reported that they had achieved this, they were rendered less able to 'see' that the facts didn't support their claims. Why does Stone think that this is a system problem rather than simple negligence by individuals? In the first place, he says there was a 'defect in the system [because] the testing of the brake was entrusted to the same personnel who had designed it'.[15] As well as this 'basic system flaw' or 'organizational shortcoming', there was insufficient linkage of the sub-unit's goals with those of the larger enteprise, so that 'organizational inertia' allowed the sub-unit to drift off on a trajectory of its own.[16]

Finally, Stone notes that:

the corporation, like any modern complex organization . . . is built upon an elaborate network of institutional roles, or offices. This division of functions . . . involves specifying such matters as who is to develop and evaluate what data, what sorts of things are to be considered by whom, and who has the authority (preliminarily and finally) to make what classes of decision. . . . But it is important to remember that such vital 'procedural' matters as which threshold questions will pass into the decisional system, and how each of them will be defined—matters inseparable from how the organizational roles are established—have an obvious influence on outcome. . . .[17]

Much of his book consists of proposals to *alter* the defined roles, decision procedures, and information nets within the corporation so that more socially

[14] C Stone, *Where the Law Ends. The Social Control of Corporate Behavior* (New York: 1975) 116–117.

[15] ibid, 166. [16] ibid, 165. See too 43–44. [17] ibid, 122.

desirable outcomes result. But for my present purposes, the important point to take from Stone is the ways in which significant corporate misconduct can result just from the organizational or structural features of a corporation. Individuals, with their values, goals, relationships, and conflicts are not the primary causal agents in this situation. It is impersonal structure, rather than conscious agency, which produces the harm here.

Sadly, there have been a number of examples of such system errors leading to deaths, especially in the areas of public transport. There was the Zeebrugge ferry that capsized, killing 187; there was the Piper Alpha oil platform fire that killed 167; there was the Clapham rail crash that killed 35; there was the Paddington train crash that killed 31; there was the Kings Cross fire, and there were more deaths in the Potters Bar crash. Because these deadly disasters were not simply the results of deliberate or negligent decisions of identifiable individuals, but instead strongly implicated system problems within the organizations, no corporate manslaughter convictions were obtained.[18]

Classical Hollywood Films and Corporate Misconduct

My claim is that corporate misconduct which results from intentional, reckless, or negligent acts can be shown in classical Hollywood films without any problem, because it satisfies the requirement that individual agency be central. But conversely, corporate misconduct that results from organizational or system effects of the type that Stone described will not be able to be represented in such films because it lacks the individual agency that those films require. Now I need to test this claim against Hollywood films dealing with corporate misconduct.

In order to make this test manageable, I will confine my analysis to what I take to be the major Hollywood films dealing with corporate misconduct made and set in the last 25 years. This excludes films like John Sayles's *Matewan*, which was made within the last 25 years, but which dealt with deadly anti-union violence in the 1920s. It also excludes films made and set within the last 25 years but which deal with white collar misconduct, rather than corporate misconduct. This would rule out, for example, Oliver Stone's *Wall Street*, which dealt with insider trading. This leaves me with a list of nine Hollywood films to consider:

(1) *The China Syndrome* (1978)

(2) *Norma Rae* (1979)

(3) *The Verdict* (1982)

(4) *Silkwood* (1983)

[18] Suggestions to reform the law of corporate manslaughter in the UK have been around since the 1996 Law Commission report No 237. Recently the government has said it will publish a draft bill on corporate manslaughter and announce a timetable for legislation in the autumn. See Home Office Press release, 20 May 2003.

(5) *Class Action* (1990)
(6) *The Rainmaker* (1997)
(7) *A Civil Action* (1998)
(8) *The Insider* (1999)
(9) *Erin Brockovich* (2000)

These films fall pretty evenly into two camps: those that involve corporate misconduct only, and those that involve both corporate misconduct and subsequent legal action where the corporation resists liability for that misconduct.

Five of these films have the dual structure of both an initial act of corporate misconduct and then a later legal action: *The Verdict*, *Class Action*, *The Rainmaker*, *A Civil Action*, and *Erin Brockovich*. The crucial point for my thesis is that in none of these five films was the initial act of corporate misconduct due to an impersonal system effect of the sort Stone described. Rather in four of the five films wrongful conduct is committed knowingly and deliberately by some high corporate officer in order to safeguard the profits of the corporation. In the fifth film, the wrongful conduct is negligence by employees for which the organization is vicariously liable.

In *Class Action*, a car manufacturer deliberately declines to recall and fix a defective model which explodes in certain situations, because the company estimates that it is cheaper just to settle the law suits for death and injury as they come in. (I take it that the film is based on the infamous Ford Pinto case.) The responsibility for this decision is shown to rest ultimately with the CEO.

In *The Rainmaker*, an insurance company has a deliberate policy of initially declining all claims on policies which it has targeted at poor people, and then engaging in bureaucratic foot dragging so that the claimants become discouraged and give up. Interestingly, there is mention of a system effect in this film. Incoming claims are channelled to two departments, claims and underwriting, and since each does not know what the other is doing, the claimant is bombarded with confusing and conflicting letters. However, the film makes it very clear that those at the top, including the CEO, have deliberately structured the organization this way to aid the corporate goal of not having to pay out on policies.

In *A Civil Action*, environmental pollution results from the deliberate dumping of toxic chemicals used in the production processes of the corporate defendants. The film establishes that the top managers instructed subordinates to perform the dumping.

In *Erin Brockovich*, the pollution was due to defective construction by a utility company of settling ponds without linings. This allowed a dangerous toxin to poison the water of over 600 people. The reason for this deficiency was not explained, although cost savings are implied. But it was made clear that the top management of the corporation became aware of the defect and its consequences, and tried to minimize knowledge of it by outsiders so as to avoid bad publicity and expensive damage awards.

Only *The Verdict* does not feature an act of intentional misconduct by a corporate defendant which harms the public, but which increases the profits of the corporation. The personal injury in this film was caused by the negligence of two doctors at a hospital, and the hospital is joined in the action as vicariously liable for the acts of its employees. However, the hospital is not an avaricious, profit-seeking corporation. Rather it is a church hospital owned by the archdiocese of Boston, and the church is shown as being concerned for the victim of the negligence. The church seeks to make a settlement offer, but when it is refused, the insurance company and its lawyers take over. It turns out that the negligent doctors have altered documents and intimidated witnesses, but the church is not shown as having any knowledge of this.

In addition to this initial corporate misconduct, these five films go on to show legal proceedings in which the corporation seeks to avoid liability for this misconduct. An initial question is why the legal proceedings are added, since the remaining four films in the list manage to deal with corporate misconduct without them. One answer we have already noted: trials are excellent sources of the individual conflict and emotion that the classic Hollywood narrative requires, so it is not surprising that many films dealing with corporate misconduct have trials.[19] But questions remain. First, in three of the five films under discussion, the lawyers defending the corporate defendant do not just act diligently for their client and engage in a dramatic courtroom struggle with the plaintiff's lawyer. In addition, they actually go on to commit new acts of misconduct in the course of defending the corporation. In *The Verdict*, the insurance company's lawyers send one of their number to pose as a romantic interest so as to be able to spy on the plaintiff's lawyer. In *Class Action*, a lawyer for the car manufacturer destroys crucial evidence and lies under oath about it. In *The Rainmaker*, the lawyers for the corporate defendant plant a microphone in the offices of the plaintiff's lawyers, and seek to use what they hear to damage the plaintiff's case. These acts of misconduct by the corporation's lawyers seem contrived and implausible, so why are they there?

Michael Asimow points to an answer in his article, 'Embodiment of Evil: Law Firms in the Movies': 'The filmmaker who wants to vilify big business needs a human face to serve as the focus for the audience's hatred. It is difficult to show the corporate structure from the inside, and far easier to pick on the lawyer who is fronting for the corporation.'[20] Or, as I would say, the workings of complex organizations can be hard to show within the classical Hollywood narrative form, so as narrative insurance add on a trial where a separate lawyer bad guy can be clearly identified. Even if a corporate bad guy has been identified, as most of these movies strive to do, two sets of bad guys for the good guys to take on and defeat just makes

[19] In *Erin Brockovich*, the matter is settled prior to trial, while in the other four films, a trial results. This itself is a distortion of legal reality, where most civil actions settle prior to trial. (A number of the films showing trials remark on this themselves.)

[20] M Asimow, 'Embodiment of Evil: Law Firms in the Movies' (2001) 48 *UCLA L Rev* 1339, 1374.

the Hollywood narrative more exciting. But note again that none of these acts of misconduct in the course of defending the corporation in court undermines my thesis. They are all conscious and deliberate acts by the corporation's legal team. None of them is the result of organizational defects of the type Stone describes.

A second question about the subsequent legal component of these five films is why they are all civil actions, rather than criminal actions. This does not matter in terms of the requirements of the Hollywood narrative, since both civil and criminal trials can be equally dramatic. Anthony Chase, in 'Civil Action Cinema', looks at films about torts instead of crimes, and seeks to describe their 'master discourse'.[21] They all have a villain, which is 'basically, (crooked) corporate America', and in most cases the villain is challenged and loses, even though corporate America was achieving significant legal and political victories during the period that the films were made.[22] But whatever their 'master discourse', this use of civil actions rather than criminal actions still needs to be explained. Given the serious nature of many of the examples of corporate misconduct listed earlier, one might have expected that some of the films dealing with corporate misconduct would have been crime films. It is not that the civil actions depicted deal with minor matters, because in each case deaths or an irreversible coma were involved. I will return to this question after I have completed my analysis of the nine films.

In the remaining four films, there is only corporate misconduct, without the dramatic component of a subsequent legal action. None of these four films contradicts my thesis. In no case is the corporate misconduct depicted due to organizational or structural factors of the type which Stone described. Rather all of the misconduct, either shown or implied, is due to deliberate acts of violence, callousness, or greed by some individuals within the organization.

In *The China Syndrome*, the construction company which built a nuclear power plant deliberately did not submit the required separate radiographs of the welds in crucial metal components. (Instead they just submitted the same radiograph many times over to save money.) An employee of the power plant discovers this, and becomes convinced that a defective weld in the supports for a pump is likely to cause a rupture in the water cooling system, leading to exposure of the core of the reactor, and a 'meltdown'. His efforts to have this problem exposed and dealt with meet with violence on the part of the construction company. One person seeking to expose the problem is run off the road and injured, and a similar attempt is made on the employee. The employee's attempts to have the problem taken seriously by the separate utility corporation which owns the nuclear power plant are initially dismissed as groundless. The corporation is shown to be concerned that an extended shutdown of the plant would lose nearly half a million dollars a day, and would also potentially damage the corporation's attempts to get an operating licence for a second nuclear facility. When the employee takes drastic action to

[21] A Chase, 'Civil Action Cinema' [1999] *Law Review Michigan State University-Detroit College of Law* 945.

[22] ibid, 951–952.

bring the problem to the public's attention, the chairman of the board of the utility company is shown trying to block the news getting out. Eventually he approves a course of action which leads to the death of the employee.

In *Norma Rae*, the managers of a textile mill which pays low wages and has a low concern for the health of its employees seek to block a union organizing drive. They fire an activist employee and have her arrested. They violate labour laws by putting a racially divisive notice on the company bulletin board in an attempt to stop black and white employees joining in one union. But eventually the union is certified, and the implication is that the company will be forced to devote more money to employee health and wages.

In *Silkwood*, an employee of a plant processing material for the fuel rods of nuclear reactors brings safety deficiencies to the attention of the national office of her union. This attracts the disapproval of not only the managers of the plant, but also her fellow workers, some of whom fear losing their jobs, and one of whom has been altering radiographs of welds in the fuel rods. She becomes contaminated by nuclear material, apparently deliberately. However, it is left unclear whether this was done by management or a fellow employee. While driving to a meeting with a *New York Times* reporter to disclose her evidence, she is involved in a car accident and dies. It is left unclear whether she was deliberately run off the road.

In *The Insider*, a corporate vice-president of a tobacco company who is also the head of research and development is forced to resign when he objects to the addition of a substance to the company's cigarettes which would increase sales but which is related to a known carcinogen. He also knows that the heads of seven large tobacco companies perjured themselves before a congressional hearing by saying that they had no knowledge that cigarettes were addictive. He knows that the addictive nature of cigarettes was common knowledge inside the tobacco industry, and that this addictive effect was deliberately enhanced by the use of 'impact boosting' chemistry. A confidentiality agreement forms part of his severance package, and he initially tries to abide by this agreement. However, when a reporter for the television show '60 Minutes' contacts him on an unrelated matter, the reporter intuits that the ex-employee has a story to tell, and seeks to draw him out. This produces heavy handed warnings from his ex-employer. The ex-employee is followed, threatening e-mails are sent to him, and a bullet is left in his mailbox. His anger at these threats, and his concern for public safety, lead him to tape an interview with '60 Minutes' in which he divulges his incriminating inside information. The strategy is to get around the confidentiality agreement by having the ex-employee be compelled to testify in a suit by the state of Mississippi against the tobacco companies to recover the health care costs resulting from cigarette smoking. The deposition is taken, but immediately sealed. However, the tobacco company threatens the television company with massive damages in a civil action based on the tort of wrongful interference with contractual relations (the confidentiality agreement), and the television company backs down. Eventually the reporter who induced the ex-employee to talk leaks the story of the television company's back-down to the print media, and the subsequent embarrassment and the unsealing of the deposition in the Mississippi case finally allow the interview to be broadcast.

I conclude from my analysis of this group of nine films dealing with corporate misconduct that none of them contradicts my thesis that the narrative form of the classical Hollywood cinema has a blind spot when it comes to Stone-like system effects. The need to have individuals as key causal agents and to focus on human relationships, morality, conflicts, and struggles means that impersonal organizational defects cannot occupy centre-stage in films of this category. Of course, this does not conclusively prove that my thesis is correct. It is possible that there are Hollywood films outside the constraints of my sample which do contradict the thesis. (Even worse, there may be a film which meets the constraints of my sample and which contradicts the thesis but which I have overlooked.) Moreover, even if I am correct that a Hollywood film cannot have the impersonal system effects of corporations as its core subject, it can deal with them more indirectly. That is, a film could just focus on the *effects* at the individual level of organizational deficiencies, rather than dealing with how those effects were produced. Would such a film still hold the viewing audience?

In *The China Syndrome*, if the incorrect radiograph of the weld was due to a systematic problem with the way the data were stored, rather than deliberate deceit, and if the organization's refusal to respond to the employee's concerns was due to a malformed information net, rather than concerns with profit, I think that the film could still work. It would involve one individual seeking to get others to believe that a massive danger to public safety was looming. As time ticked away, the struggle to be believed would become more intense. This is a dramatic situation regardless of whether the public danger is due to system effects or individual wrongdoing. There would still be high emotion, an individual struggle which involved overcoming the opposition of others, etc.

But in *The China Syndrome* the device of a looming massive danger provides the drama. In the absence of this feature, taking away morally culpable agents who are responsible for some harm is more significant. What if the toxic poisoning in *A Civil Action* and *Erin Brockovich* were the results of Stone-like problems which nobody in the corporations knew about or tried to conceal? There would be no more search for a crucial eye witness who could provide the missing proof of corporate greed and deception, as occurs in both films. There would be no morally charged debate between just quietly taking the money in a settlement or exposing the bad corporation to public shame and condemnation in a trial, as occurs in both films. Instead the films would deal with the scientific problems of proving causality and the economic problems of calculating the value of the damage caused. This would more closely resemble a real law suit, but would for that very reason be much less dramatic and much less able to satisfy the narrative requirements of a Hollywood film.

So although I think it would be possible for the Hollywood film to deal with system effects in an indirect way in some cases, I also think it is significant that

I have not been able to find any instances where it has done so. Rather the films that I have found dealing with corporate misconduct all involve morally culpable individual actors, typically located at the highest levels of the corporation or its large-firm legal advisors. As far as I can tell, the blind spot is complete.

Law and Corporate Misconduct

The Hollywood film's difficulties in dealing with corporate misconduct are mirrored in the law. Both white collar misconduct and corporate misconduct tend to be less 'seen' by the law, and when they are noted, they are typically treated less seriously than the social harm caused would lead one to expect. They tend to be dealt with through civil actions rather than criminal actions, and even when they are categorized as criminal, they are often put into a less serious category of regulatory offences.

Edwin Sutherland, in his 1940 article, 'White Collar Criminality' gave a classic statement of the case that the law has trouble seeing white collar personnel as criminals.[23] He noted that theories of crime which attributed it to poverty or a bad environment failed to take account of the huge amount of white collar and corporate crime. This crime was systematically left out of the criminological theories because it was either not being dealt with by the law at all, or if it was dealt with, it was commonly categorized as not really criminal. Sutherland thought that it was the class and status of the perpetrators which produced the difficulty in categorizing them together with common street criminals.

Alan Norrie, in his more recent book *Crime, Reason, and History*, argues that the criminal law finds it hard to deal with organizational deviance because this area of law is built on the paradigm of individual human wrongdoers.[24] Organizations like corporations do not fit this paradigm well, because it seems impossible for them to have *mens rea*. He describes how one response of the criminal law was to develop strict liability offences for business organizations which did not require *mens rea*, but such offences were also seen as less serious than true crimes. They were only regulatory offences, or quasi-criminal, or *malum prohibitum* rather than *malum in se*. The other response was to push the corporation into the individualistic mould by seeking some individual within it whose *mens rea* could be identified with that of the corporation. Again, a very simple paradigm was at work here. The directors and top managers were seen as the 'head' of the body corporate, and the head commanded the 'hands' to do its will. An appreciation of the organizational complexity of corporations caused some jurisdictions to move to an approach where the fragmented knowledge or intentions of many dispersed corporate actors

[23] E Sutherland, 'White Collar Criminality' (1940) 5 *American Sociological Rev* 1–12.

[24] A Norrie, *Crime, Reason and History. A Critical Introduction to Criminal Law* (London: 1993) Ch 5.

could be 'aggregated' together. However, even where this doctrinal development was accepted, it was still only a refinement of an approach which treated the corporation the same as a human individual. The criminal law is still only feeling its way towards an approach to the corporation which finds *mens rea* not in individuals, but in organizational structure and procedures.

So law, like the Hollywood film, has difficulties dealing adequately with some aspects of the modern business corporation, and for similar reasons. Like the Hollywood film, criminal law is centred on the individual. More particularly, it is centred on the paradigm of a low status individual wrongdoer. This makes it hard for the criminal law to see both *high status* individual wrongdoers, and wrongdoers which are *organizations* rather than individuals, particularly organizations with structures which produce misconduct without any individual intending it.

Films Other than Classical Hollywood Narratives

Not all narrative films follow the Hollywood conventions. What might be called 'art house' narrative films deliberately ignore, subvert or play with the conventions of Hollywood cinema:

> In 1920s Soviet films, such as Sergei Eisenstein's *Potemkin, October*, and *Strike*, no *individual* serves as protagonist. More recently, Jacques Rivette's *L'Amour Fou* and Robert Altman's *Nashville* experiment with eliminating protagonists. In films like those of Eisenstein and Yasujiro Ozu, many events are seen as caused not by characters, but by larger forces (social dynamics in the former, an overarching Nature in the second). In narrative films such as Michelangelo Antonioni's *L'Avventura*, the protagonist is not active but passive. So the active, goal-orientated protagonist, though common, does not appear in every narrative film.[25]

Greater freedom from Hollywood narrative conventions might seem to bode well for dealing with Stone-like system effects on film. However, I do not know of any art house films which have used this freedom to deal more adequately with the full range of corporate misconduct. Indeed, to the extent that art house films move away from Hollywood narrative conventions in the direction of greater ambiguity with respect to space, time, and causality,[26] this seems to render them *less* able to depict the complex reality of corporate misconduct. Non-narrative 'avant-garde' films, such as those which focus on abstract form, or which explore the associations between images, seem even less adapted to dealing with this reality.[27]

However, documentary films hold out greater promise of dealing with subject matter which falls within the blind spots of other types of cinema. Documentary films are various, and can be categorized in many ways. One way of categorizing is

[25] Bordwell and Thompson, n 1 above, 83.
[26] ibid, Ch 10 which deals with 'narrative alternatives to classical filmmaking' in more depth.
[27] ibid, 119–139.

by subject matter, such as nature, travel, ethnographic, propaganda, etc.[28] Another way is by style, such as the direct address style, which features an authoritative voice-over directing the viewer's response, or the cinema verité style, which has no commentary and seeks to provide 'fly on the wall' access to the subject matter, or the interview style, where different witnesses relate their experiences directly to the camera, or the self-reflexive style, 'where epistemological and aesthetic assumptions become more visible'.[29] For the purposes of this paper, I think that the most useful distinction is that drawn by David Bordwell and Kristin Thompson between categorical documentary films and rhetorical documentary films. 'Categorical films, as the name suggests, divide a subject into parts, or categories. . . . [R]hetorical form . . . presents an argument and lays out evidence to support it.'[30] They give Leni Riefenstahl's film about the 1936 Olympic Games, *Olympia*, as an example of a categorical documentary, in which the main categories structuring the film are the different sports events.[31] As an example of a rhetorical documentary they give Pare Lorentz's 1937 film *The River*, which supports President Franklin Delano Roosevelt's New Deal policies to deal with the Great Depression in America. The central argument in this film it that 'the Tennessee Valley Authority (TVA) [is] the solution to problems of flooding, agricultural depletion, and electrification . . .'.[32]

Corporate misconduct could potentially be examined by documentaries employing either categorical or rhetorical form. Frederick Wiseman is a famous documentary maker who used the categorical form and a cinema verité style to investigate the inner workings of large organizations both public and private. His 35 documentaries include institutional subjects such as high schools (*High School*), department stores (*The Store*), and insane asylums (*Titicut Follies*). It would seem that there is nothing to stop his technique being applied to show how the complex inner workings of a large corporation generate results which no-one intended.

But as has often been noted, even cinema verité films do not simply present the world as it is in an unmediated fashion.[33] Such films do not show us random bits of reality. Decisions are made as to when the camera is turned on; decisions are made as to what footage is shown and what is edited out; decisions are made as to the juxtapositions of the individual pieces of footage finally included within the film. These choices are made so as to give the film a structure that is interesting to the viewer. And here Hollywood narrative structure can re-enter the picture, even though we are now dealing with a non-fiction film. Bill Nichols says of much American cinema verité that it is:

> characterized by a romantic individualism and a dramatic, fiction-like structure, but employing 'found' stories rather than the wholly invented ones of Hollywood. . . . We

[28] See eg E Barnouw, *Documentary. A History of the Non-Fiction Film* (2nd edn, New York: 1993).

[29] B Nichols, 'The Voice of Documentary' in B Nichols (ed), *Movies and Methods* (Berkeley: 1985) Vol II, 258, 260.

[30] Bordwell and Thompson, n 1 above, 102–103. For more detail see 104–105, 112–114.

[31] ibid, 105–112.

[32] ibid, 114–115. For more detail see 114–119.

[33] Nichols, n 29 above, 261: 'Many documentarists would appear to believe what fiction film-makers only feign to believe, or openly question: that film-making creates an objective representation of the way things really are. Such documentaries use the magical template of verisimilitude without

never hear the voice of the film-maker or a narrator trying to persuade us of this romantic humanism. Instead the film's structure relies heavily on classical narrative procedures. . . .[34]

Bordwell and Thompson, in their close analysis of Wiseman's *High School* describe elements which seem to reflect a partial reliance on the classical Hollywood narrative:

In one respect, the film is categorical. The main category is high-school life, and the subcategories consist of typical activities: classes, student/teacher confrontations, sports activities, a pep rally, and so on. From another angle, the film's form can be seen to depend on narrative principles as well. Many of the episodes constitute small scenes fraught with conflict . . . Wiseman has concentrated on one aspect of high-school life: how the power of the authorities demands obedience from pupils and parents.[35]

This gravitational pull of the Hollywood narrative form can also be seen at work in documentaries employing the rhetorical form. In *Roger and Me*, Michael Moore considers the effect on Flint, Michigan of the closure of the GM automobile factories there. Such closures were not illegal, but Moore makes a powerful case that they represent corporate misconduct nevertheless. His central argument is that it is wrong for a profitable corporation to close plants which are making money and which have had a long relationship with a community, just because it can make even more money by relocating the plants. The extra profit is achieved by eliminating well-paying jobs in places like Flint, and replacing them with low-paid workers in Mexico. In effect, the good wages represented a greater sharing of the profits of the company with those who made its products. The shift to less-well-paid workers was not done because the company was in financial trouble. Rather it represented a clawing back of a greater share of the profits for the managers and shareholders. The consequences for the ex-GM employees in Flint, and for the city of Flint itself are catastrophic, as his documentary shows.

But it is significant for my thesis that Moore structures his film very much on Hollywood narrative lines. The film's basic structure is a quest, in which Moore seeks to meet Roger Smith, the Chairman of the Board of GM, and invite him to come to Flint to see the devastation which his corporation has wrought there. So here we have an everyman figure representing the damaged community, and a person at the top of GM who is portrayed as personally responsible for the relocation strategy and the Flint closings. The goal of the aggrieved Moore is to meet Smith and throw down a moral challenge, and the goal of Smith is to evade Moore. Moore seeks Smith in many places, but constantly meets obstacles, usually in the form of security guards and public-relations people. He is shown turning up at a

the story teller's open resort to artifice. Very few seem prepared to admit through the very tissue and texture of their work that all film-making is a form of discourse fabricating its effects, impressions, and point of view.' See too Greenfield et al, n 6 above; Bordwell and Thompson, n 1 above, 407.

[34] Nichols, n 29 above, 262.

[35] Bordwell and Thompson, n 1 above, 407–408.

GM shareholders' meeting and coming to the microphone to speak, but Smith immediately closes the meeting, preventing the question. Finally at the end of the film Moore gets close enough to Smith to ask him to come to Flint, but Smith curtly declines. In between these efforts to meet Smith, Moore shows us the sad lives of many ordinary people in Flint, and places beside these the views of various celebrities and rich Flint citizens as to the reason for the situation and how those unfortunate people could improve their lot. (Optimism and a 'can-do' attitude are the most common suggestions.)

I think that this film has the power it does because it borrows so cleverly from Hollywood narratives. What happened to Flint is not analyzed in the abstract terms of social or economic theory. Rather the film makes its point by focusing upon particular individuals and highlighting their pain or callousness. It shows both Moore and ordinary Flint citizens striving to prevail against obstacles that prove obdurate time and time again. It accuses others of not living up to their moral obligations which long relationships of interdependence have created. Thus it can happen that documentaries are pulled towards the same focus on individuals and their motivations and duties and conflicts as the classical Hollywood film. To the extent that this happens, the documentary is deflected from exploring pure system effects where individual agency is much less important.

However, not all documentaries fall back on the individualistic focus of the classic Hollywood narrative. *Manufacturing Consent* is a documentary on Noam Chomsky's analysis of the mass media in America which I think points the way to how a documentary could deal with Stone's system effects. Like Moore, Chomsky wants to convince us that corporate conduct currently seen as normal is in fact socially harmful misconduct. In Chomsky's analysis, the corporate misconduct is not factory closings, but the limiting of popular democratic participation, both economic and political, and the stifling of most viewpoints outside a narrow band of acceptability. But unlike Moore, Chomsky's analysis is not personalized. He very rarely names individuals or even corporations. His analysis is instead 'institutional', and seeks to describe the structural features of the mass media and the market system in which they operate which will have the effect of limiting the range of viewpoints and popular democratic participation regardless of the motivations or values of the people working within those organizations. Although the film is centred on Chomsky, and he is on screen much of the time, being interviewed or lecturing or participating in panel discussions, the focus is on his ideas, not his individual attributes or agency. Unlike Michael Moore, Chomsky engages in no quests; he has no discrete project that he seeks to realize within the confines of the film. He faces some rude interlocutors, but not the thinly veiled force that Moore had to contend with. He merely lectures or replies to questions in a calm quiet voice in halls and studios around the world which all look alike.

How does a film largely about ideas, about the effects of impersonal structures—a film without a strongly defined, causally efficacious individual at its centre—manage to hold a viewer's interest for three hours? Obviously part of the answer is the inherent importance and novelty of Chomsky's ideas, but another part is the way the film makers present the ideas to us. The talking head syndrome is not allowed to develop. Whenever possible, the film cuts from Chomsky's image to images of things which make his point concrete. As one simple example, when Chomsky is talking of how a piece on East Timor in the London *Times* was picked up but altered by the *New York Times*, the visuals show a team of gowned doctors in an operating theatre using scalpels to cut out the passages in the original text. The resulting piece of paper, riddled with many oddly shaped gaps, makes the point in a visually powerful way. Elsewhere in the film Chomsky says that the mass media make most of their money from delivering customers to advertisers. This results in the concerns and values of advertisers being important factors in the decisions which filter out what is and what is not to be included in those media. The point is made visually on screen by a team of people cutting up an edition of the *New York Times* in fast action and spreading the news content and the advertising content out in separate areas. The area covered by the advertising is seen to be much larger than that covered by news. This adds visual interest and helps to make the point more powerfully than a person saying that the *New York Times* is 60 per cent advertising.

What we can see from *Manufacturing Consent* is that it is possible for documentary film makers to deal with the effects of impersonal institutional structures in a way that is visually interesting and engaging for the audience, without having to fall back on Hollywood narrative forms which emphasize the individual more. I think that the techniques employed here could equally well be turned to the task of representing cinematically the corporate system effects Stone described.

Conclusion

As we have seen in this paper, there are many forms of corporate misconduct. There are intentional, reckless and negligent acts of corporate employees which lead to crimes, regulatory offences, and civil wrongs. There are also less familiar instances of corporate misconduct. In this category are the unintended and impersonal system effects of corporate organizational structure that Stone described. Also found here is corporate conduct that is not currently categorized as a crime, or a tort, or even misconduct, but which people like Moore and Chomsky argue should be so recategorized.

How good is film at showing or telling us about this full range of misconduct? The first thing to note about Hollywood films is the relative scarcity of films dealing with *any* form of corporate misconduct. I found nine films dealing with corporate misconduct made and set in America in the last 25 years. How long would the list be of films that dealt with mafia-type crime? Perhaps Edwin Sutherland's observation in the 1940s that there is a bias against seeing high status individuals as criminals still has force.

Even when a Hollywood film does deal with corporate misconduct, it often shows only a mild form of it. The one film on my list dealing with union-busting activity by a corporation, *Norma Rae*, has the corporation firing one employee on dubious grounds, obscuring the union's notices on the bulletin board and putting up a racially divisive notice of its own. Given the violent history of unionising attempts in America, and the enduring antipathy towards unions by many businesses there, I cannot believe that this is near to the worst that this category has to offer.

Finally, Hollywood films do not show the types of corporate misconduct that Stone describes. My argument has been that this is not simply a matter of choice. It is due to the structural requirement of the Hollywood-type narrative for individual character and individual agency/causality to be at the centre of the story. This requirement will allow the representation of corporate misconduct which is due to the intentional, reckless, or negligent acts of individuals. But it will not allow impersonal system effects to be at the centre of the story, because individuals are not the prime cause of such effects.

Documentaries are a form of cinema much more able to deal with such system effects, but as we have seen, the Hollywood narrative forms tend to play an important role in the way documentaries are filmed too. Even when we find a form of documentary which can deal with such subject matter well, we face a final sobering fact: not many people watch documentaries compared to the number of people who watch Hollywood-type films.

Why is this important? Film is a powerful mass medium that has the potential to educate and activate people about corporate misbehaviour. This is true particularly of the classical Hollywood narrative film, which is the most-watched form, both in America and overseas. To the extent that it chooses not to do so, or is unable to do so, it operates ideologically. That is, it operates to deny or obscure the ways in which powerful actors in our society abuse their power.

Repressed Memory Revisited: Popular Culture's Impact on the Law—Psychotherapy Debate

Stuart Weinstein[1]

The art of remembering is the art of thinking. When we wish to fix a new thing in our own mind or a pupil's, our conscious effort should not be so much to impress and retain it as to connect it with something else already there. The connecting is the thinking; and, if we attend clearly to the connection, the connected thing will certainly be likely to remain within recall.[2]

Too much clarity and neat conclusions are the enemies of thought. I love Freud's view that there is no remembering, it is all misremembering . . . [t]hat is the yeast of life. Make it too real and it doesn't work.[3]

Introduction

Repressed memory of childhood sexual abuse figured prominently in American popular culture long before the actress Roseanne Barr's story came to the attention of the public.[4] While the 1980s saw a tide of mass child abuse cases brought by prosecutors across the country alleging sensational acts committed by nursery school, day care workers and after-school educators,[5] the 1990s has been characterized as

1 The author acknowledges the guidance and suggestions received at the Colloquium particularly from the convenor, M Freeman, and participants, M Asimow and N Rafter.

2 William James, *Talks to Teachers* (1899) Ch 12, available at http://www.emory.edu/EDUCATION/mfp/memory.html.

3 Melvyn Bragg quoted in C O'Brien, 'A Show-Off? If You Go On Television You've Got To Be', *The Times*, 16 June 2003, T2, 6.

4 'A well-known case is Roseanne Barr's claim to have recovered a memory of being abused by her mother when she was six months old. This memory was uncovered during therapy, along with memories of subsequent abuse by her parents. Her story has been told in national magazines, on television talk shows, and on newsmagazines (CBS's *60 Minutes*, 17 April 1994). 'Joining Roseanne Barr are a legion of glitterati, including a former Miss America, several popular singers, a talk show host and elected officials . . . 'quoting SJ Ceci and M Bruck, *Jeopardy in the Courtroom* (2nd edn, Washington, DC: 2002), 188.

5 A number of these cases have been the subject of extensive popular culture attention: the story of the Friedman family was examined in Andrew Jarecki's documentary *Capturing the Friedmans*; and the McMartin family has been portrayed in the film *The Indictment* and examined on the PBS *Frontline* series. Of the McMartin case, one commentator notes: 'Dubious procedures by one particular therapist and district attorney investigators combined with the effects of sensationalist wide coverage by the

the era of the repressed memory syndrome.[6] Popular psychology books such as *The Courage to Heal: A Guide for Women Survivors of Child Sexual Abuse* and *Secret Survivors: Uncovering Incest and its Aftereffects in Women* sold thousands of copies.[7] Not only did these books suggest that victims of childhood sexual abuse were to be found everywhere, they offered practical advice on how to sue as well on as how to heal.

The resulting 'hysteria' had tragic effects on many lives. Ray and Shirley Souza were sentenced to long jail terms when a judge concluded that the testimony of their grandchildren that their grandparents had 'tied them in a cage in the basement and then raped them with elbows and feet and a big machine' was credible.[8] Therefore, it was not surprising that during the same decade, a good number of civil lawsuits were brought in various US courts alleging sexual abuse many years after the events complained of occurred.[9] The debate over whether memories of childhood sexual abuse can be repressed and later recovered suffused popular culture from Oprah Winfrey to the *National Enquirer* in the 1990s. Powerful stories of incest survival and sexual abuse that long lay dormant in the dark recesses of the collective subconscious of the 'baby boomer'generation came to surface in an ugly surfeit of emotion and recrimination. These alleged instances of delayed recall of childhood sexual abuse and the traumatic impact that such claims had upon the families involved challenged very basic understandings that Americans had of themselves and how they were raised.

Greater self-awareness, unfortunately, has also led to increased anger at the role of psychotherapists in 'stirring up the hornet's nest', placing the profession on the defensive in society and in the courtroom. For instance, Ofshe and Watters write scathingly of psychotherapists that they 'pretend what they do in their offices is similar to medicine to the extent that their decisions, suggestions and techniques are the end result of knowledge gathered through careful scientific observation of the human condition. Unfortunately, for many practitioners, this pretence is an utter fraud.'[10] An examination of case law in several US jurisdictions indicates an increasing reluctance to give credence to claims of childhood sexual abuse that arise

media ensured that the principle of the innocence of those accused until proven guilty went out of the window, forever marring the lives of the children themselves and their families as well as the innocent individuals falsely accused and kept in custody for years'. A Kapardis, *Psychology and Law—A Critical Introduction* (Cambridge: 1997), 105.

[6] D Rabinowitz, *No Crueler Tyrannies: Accusation, False Witness, and Other Terrors of Our Times* (New York: 2003), 90.

[7] E Bass and L Davis, *The Courage to Heal* (New York, 1988; 2nd edn, New York, 1994), 318–320; 382; ES Blume, *Secret Survivors: Uncovering Incest and its Aftereffects in Women* (New York, 1990; New York, 1998), 280–286.

[8] *Commonwealth v Souza*, 689 NE 2d 1359 (Mass App Ct 1998) and 653 NE 2d 1127 (Mass App Ct 1995).

[9] See *Shahzade v Gregory*, 930 F Supp 673 (D Mass 1996) where the abuse alleged took place 47 years earlier.

[10] R Ofshe and E Watters, *Making Monsters: False Memories, Psychotherapy, and Sexual Hysteria* (Berkeley, 1994; paperback edition 1996), 323.

from the efforts of psychotherapists working with their patients to uncover repressed memories. From whence did this scepticism arise?

It is the thesis of this article that the reluctance of US courts to give credence to claims of childhood sexual abuse arising from repressed memory is a direct response to prevailing sentiment in the popular culture. As the general public becomes more familiar with repressed memory and how the mind processes traumatic events, they have become increasingly dubious that psychotherapists can play any useful role in unravelling suppressed memories of alleged events of childhood sexual abuse. Consequently, the law has had to adjust its views on the usefulness of psychotherapy in this area to bring itself in line with the popular culture. A failure by the US legal system to align itself with the popular sentiment towards repressed memory would, in effect, render it ineffectual in acting as the primary social arbiter of the relationship among psychotherapists, the patients they treat and those third parties affected by such treatment. In an age in which Americans devour self-help books, retain life coaches to reshape their lives and obtain mental health advice from radio call-in psychologists, it is not surprising that the courts have had to play 'catch-up' to keep up with a general public that increasingly feels itself competent to judge the professional work of psychotherapists, an area formerly left to elites such as the American Psychological Association and academicians.[11] In essence, the law has had to reach out to save psychotherapy from its own-self inflicted wounds by forcing psychotherapy to get in line with the popular culture.

When Psychotherapy Goes Pop

Before an examination of popular culture's effect on the law-psychotherapy debate can be considered, some attention ought to be paid to what we mean by *popular culture*. Margaret Thornton notes that 'popular culture' encompasses 'the panoply of beliefs, practices and wisdom of ordinary people, which is handed down from generation to generation'.[12] Thornton writes that 'popular culture is implicitly distinguished from the more intellectual, theoretical and scholarly pursuits associated with the term "high culture" ' and 'tends to crystalise most commonly in print media, popular music, film and television'.[13]

Richard Sherwin speaks of the phenomenon 'when law goes *pop*'[14] and the resulting 'erosion of the law's legitimacy'[15] in the eyes of the general public.

[11] The trend is not limited to America alone. Newspapers in the UK carried extensive coverage of the lurid details of the case of a psychiatrist brought before the General Medical Council accused of using leading questions and suggestions to help persuade a disturbed 13-year old girl that she had been sexually abused by another physician. O Wright, 'Psychiatrist "led disturbed girl into false recall sex claims" ', *The Times*, 2 September 2003, 1.

[12] M Thornton (ed), *Romancing the Tomes: Popular Culture, Law and Feminism* (London: 2002), 6.

[13] ibid.

[14] R Sherwin, *When Law Goes Pop: The Vanishing Line Between Law and Popular Culture* (Chicago: 2000), 5.

[15] ibid.

In Sherwin's view, the communication practices of law, both inside the courtroom and in the court of public opinion, are 'increasingly going the way of contemporary political discourse—law too is succumbing to the influence of public relations, mass advertising, and fabricated media events'.[16] As a consequence, the law finds itself today involved in an 'increasing conflation of truth and fiction; the image based manipulation of irrational desire, prejudice, and popular passions; and the concerted effort to deliberately construct preferred versions of (and judgments about) self and social reality'.[17]

Cannot the same be said of psychotherapy? Surely if law has gone pop, the same must be true of psychotherapy. Consider the case of Adam Phillips, the psychotherapist busy working with a group of translators on the first major new Freud translation to appear in 30 years. Philips is of the view that Freud is not a sacred text:

> I never thought psychoanalysis had anything to do with science. It has been servile in its wish to meet scientific criteria to legitimise [Freud]. I want people to read Freud as you would any great novelist. His books are not accurate accounts of people. Every psychoanalytic text, as Auden said, should begin with: 'Have you heard the one about . . . '[18]

What happens when a previously respected discipline such as psychotherapy goes pop? The repressed memory controversy is the best example of this phenomenon. No matter what ails a patient, it will be traced back to an incident of childhood sexual abuse at the hands of a relative or trusted friend. Whether such an event of abuse actually took place will be considered by the therapist to be immaterial, so long as the 'realization' leads to a cure. Celebrities will go on television accusing their parents of hideous acts of abuse that took place when they were infants. The fact that infants have no ability to recall specific events does not deter these 'true believers' in their insistence in their unfounded beliefs. Likewise, books will appear by psychotherapists diagnosing everyone in a simple reductionist fashion, offering everyone an equally reductionist solution to their psychological problems.

At the same time, clinical psychologists and their academic counterparts will attack each other and their differing opinions on the repressed memory controversy with a level of nastiness and vituperation that best should be left to *The Jerry Springer Show*.[19] Bruce Grierson writes of this phenomenon:

> It is not considered good judgment to wade into the issue of recovered memories without skin as thick as permafrost and caller ID on the phone. Rare is the academic field in which colleagues on opposite sides of a debate—people with international reputations—dismiss the very foundations of one another's work, sometimes not so privately, with common barnyard epithets; in which two of the most prominent reference books are almost

[16] ibid. [17] ibid, at 8.

[18] Adam Phillips quoted in D Merkin, 'The Literary Freud', *New York Times Magazine*, 13 July 2003, 40.

[19] See A Adler, 'The Perverse Law of Child Pornography' (2001) 101 *Columbia L Rev* 209, 221–227 for a discussion of these 'memory wars'.

Jesuitically contradictory; in which more than a decade of fairly sound research has done little to settle a debate that has raged ever since Freud popularised the term 'repression'.[20]

In short, chaos exists, a discipline discredited, people in need of help are harmed and innocent people are wrongly accused of horrific acts.

Given this dire situation, it is not surprising that the law has become dismissive of the usefulness of psychotherapy to uncover repressed memory. Can the law have a role in redeeming psychotherapy from the consequences of its going pop? Or is the law, in light of its own experience in Sherwin's view, ill equipped to pull psychotherapy back from the abyss? Before we can address these issues, however, some more clarification is needed as to what we mean by psychotherapy and the repressed memory controversy.

What is Psychotherapy?

Psychotherapy has been described as 'essentially a conversation which involves listening to and talking with those in trouble with the aim of helping them understand and resolve their predicament'.[21] Developing a relationship between patient and therapist and talking are the primary tools to treat emotional and psychiatric disorders.[22] There are two prominent schools of psychotherapy: the psychodynamic school originating with Freud's psychoanalytic approach and the behaviourial school originating with Pavlov's conditioning experiments. While recently cognitive behavioural psychotherapy has achieved a certain *vogue* with mental health practitioners, it is the dynamic approach to psychotherapy that has figured prominently in the repressed memory controversy.

Dynamic psychotherapy approaches the patient 'empathetically from the *inside* in order to help him to identify and understand what is happening in his inner works, in relation to his background, upbringing, and development'.[23] Troubled persons may seek help with problems or symptoms when they are in '*conflict* over unacceptable aspects of themselves or their relationships'.[24] These aspects may be so disturbing that they cause *anxiety* or *psychic pain* that may be consciously rejected, and become more or less *unconscious*.[25] *Defence mechanisms* may be used to 'deny, suppress or disown what is unacceptable to consciousnesses irrespective of whether such mechanisms are helpful or harmful'.[26] Unacceptable wishes, feelings or memories may arise in connection with basic *motivational* drives such as those associated with sex or aggression.[27]

An important source for how individuals manage the conflict between the various drives and their derivative causes can be found in an examination of an

[20] B Grierson, 'A Bad Trip Down Memory Lane', *The New York Times Magazine*, 27 July 2003, 36.

[21] A Bateman, D Brown and J Pedder, *Introduction to Psychotherapy: An outline of principles and practice* (London, 1979; 2nd edn, London, 2002), xiii.

[22] ibid, 1.

[23] ibid, 3.

[24] ibid, 3.

[25] ibid, 3.

[26] ibid, 3.

[27] ibid, 4.

individual's infancy and early childhood.[28] It is thought that the issues which are central to infancy and early childhood shape the way in which an individual will deal with conflict throughout his or her adult life, for example, the response of others (mother, father, siblings, etc) to our basic needs.[29] Psychotherapy seeks to heal the emotional scars that have been created during childhood.[30] Memories from childhood—traumatic as well as ordinary ones such as being chronically ignored and deprived of attention or tenderness by one's parents, abandonment or loss, or social rejection—are believed to have left their imprint on the emotional brain, creating distortions in intimate relationships later in life.[31]

The Repressed Memory Controversy

The repressed memory controversy traces its origins back to Freud. Some of Freud's early cases involved young women thought to have hysterical disorders (now, many would be considered borderline), whose symptoms were traced to dammed-up feelings associated with sexuality.[32] Through the use of hypnosis in therapy, Freud tried to uncover repressed memories and release the feelings held back by his patients because they were unacceptable to the patient's conscious view of herself.[33] Freud noticed that his hypnotised patients revealed to him sexual experiences that occurred to them in early childhood.[34] Freud believed that these early sexual experiences were not capable of being processed psychologically by the individual.[35] Consequently, these experiences were actively removed from consciousness or repressed thereby giving rise to neurotic symptoms later.[36] Later on in his life, Freud came to the conclusion that the early childhood sexual experiences described by his patients that appeared repressed may have, in fact, been imagined rather than actually experienced.[37]

Given the difficulty that Freud had in distinguishing between reality and fantasy whilst listening to his patients relating their childhood sexual experiences, it is not surprising that this problem still plagues psychotherapy a century on. Uncertainty exists as to whether abuse and other traumatic events can be forgotten completely and later return to consciousness.[38] Some experts maintain that because of the traumatic nature of some events, these events become 'blocked' or 'repressed'.[39] The term 'repressed' is used to describe the memories that are assumed to have split off from conscious awareness because of their threatening nature.[40] 'Blocking' and 'unblocking' repressed traumatic memories have found their way into the courtrooms in the form of adults' recovery of 'repressed memories' of childhood sexual

[28] ibid, 4. [29] ibid, 4.

[30] D Goleman, *Emotional Intelligence: Why it can matter more than IQ* (London, 1995; 2nd edn, London, 1996), 213. [31] ibid, 213.

[32] ibid, 96. [33] ibid. [34] ibid. [35] ibid. [36] ibid.

[37] ibid. An excellent discussion of the implication of Freud's change of mind and its impact on psychiatric thought can be found in Adler's article. See Adler, n 19 above, 221. [38] ibid.

[39] Ceci and Bruck, n 4 above, 187. [40] ibid.

abuse.[41] In the typical repressed memory case, such a 'memory' surfaces for the first time in therapy or in a support group for survivors of childhood incest.[42] After weeks or months of therapy, a client will make a startling 'discovery', namely, that someone—perhaps a neighbour, family member or even a parent—sexually abused them when they were young.[43]

Is it possible to repress something that is as personally significant as sexual abuse, and to regain access to the memory of it years or decades later?[44] Over the years, many clinicians have reported that patients recover memories during clinical sessions.[45] These clinicians believe that such 'discoveries' that surface in therapy and support groups are 'legitimate memories that reflect the mind's unburdening of its deep, dark, ego-threatening secrets'.[46] A number of techniques have been used by therapists with some success to assist survivors of childhood sexual abuse to make contact with their lost memories of abuse, for example, age regression, body memory interpretation, etc.[47] These efforts 'at therapeutic probing of dormant memories' have been supported, in part, by the recent edition of the *Diagnostic and Statistical Manual* of the American Psychiatric Association (1994) which suggests that cognitive and affective dissociations are common sequelae of sexual abuse.[48]

Most people now accept that traumatic events can be forgotten and then remembered.[49] There is now a consensus view[50] that memories may be recovered from total amnesia, and that such memories may be essentially accurate, partially accurate or wholly inaccurate. The Royal College of Psychiatrists ('RCPsych'), however, has been decidedly more sceptical. In its working report, the RCPsych suggested that there was little evidence of the possibility of recovering memories from total amnesia implying that complete loss of memory of traumatic sexual abuse was unlikely and that there was little evidence for repression (Bateman, Brown and Pedder).[51]

A second question that must be addressed is whether memories of child sexual abuse are 'actively inhibited, keeping them out of consciousness as Freud originally suggested'.[52] Some research suggests that there is evidence for the clinical hypothesis of repression and of its importance in psychological function.[53] Recent data from neurocognitive science suggests that there are inhibitory processes in both attention

41 Ceci and Bruck, n 4 above, 187. 42 ibid. 43 ibid. 44 ibid.

45 Bateman, Brown, and Pedder, n 21 above, 98. 46 Ceci and Bruck, n 4 above, 191.

47 ibid.

48 ibid; the current edition of the work referenced is the American Psychiatric Association, *Diagnostic and Statistical Manual of Mental Disorders, Fourth Edition, Text Revision* (2000).

49 Bateman, Brown and Pedder, n 21 above, 99.

50 The consensus view of the British Psychological Society's Working Party on Recovered Memories (1995) and the American Psychological Association's Working Group on Investigation of Memories of Childhood Abuse (1995).

51 Royal College of Psychiatrists, 'Reported recovered memories of child sexual abuse: recommendations for good practice and implications for training, continuing professional development and research' (1997) 17 *Psychiatric Bulletin* 695–698 cited in Bateman, Brown and Pedder, n 21 above, 99.

52 Bateman, Brown and Pedder, n 21 above, 99. 53 ibid.

and memory, especially in certain individuals.[54] Similarly, research into hypnosis has shown that people 'can temporarily block access to certain memories and that unconscious memory can influence present experience and thoughts'.[55]

Some cognitive psychologists specializing in memory are of the opinion that memories are reconstructed using bits of fact and fiction and that 'false memories' can be induced by expectation and suggestion.[56] Are the memories recovered in therapy then merely the product of inappropriate suggestion? Harvard psychologist Susan Clancy posits that 'memory's tendency to be reconstructive, combined with the desire to believe, combined with a culturally available script leads to a false memory'.[57] According to Bateman, Brown and Pedder, even if there is inappropriate suggestion, such as a readily-handy 'cultural script', this does not account for those memories that are retrieved at other times.[58] Surveys of practitioners suggest that memories are often recovered before, rather than during therapy, and are the stimulus to seek therapy.[59] The RCPsych in its practice guidelines warns against the use of certain techniques in therapy such as literal dream interpretation, body memories and memory recovery techniques, all of which are seen as being too prone towards suggestion.[60] Bateman, Brown and Pedder conclude 'that the representation of psychoanalytic therapy as an archaeological dig searching for early memories is related more to Hollywood than to actual practice'.[61] Bowman and Mertz note with irony the following about the repressed memory controversy:

> In an intriguing replay of the events of the late nineteenth-century Vienna, the modern-day psychological profession and the media have, in recent years, first uncovered, and to some degree renounced, child sexual abuse as a widespread source of adult psychological illness, particularly when the adult has recovered forgotten or repressed memories of abuse.[62]

Legal Responses

Initially, the response of many jurisdictions to the repressed memory controversy was to rethink the length and applicability of civil statutes of limitation.[63] In

[54] ibid. [55] ibid.

[56] E Loftus and K Ketcham, *The Myth of Repressed Memory*, (2nd edn, New York: 1996), 79.

[57] Grierson, n 20 above, 39. [58] Bateman, Brown and Pedder, n 21 above, 99.

[59] ibid. [60] ibid. [61] ibid.

[62] Cynthia Grant Bowman and Elizabeth Mertz, 'A Dangerous Direction: Legal Intervention in Sexual Abuse Survivor Therapy' (1996) 109 *Harvard L Rev* 549, 625.

[63] Review of the criminal law with respect to issues involving childhood sexual abuse is beyond the scope of this inquiry. However, readers should note the decision (October Term, 2002) of the United States Supreme Court in *Stogner v California*, 539 U S 633 (2003) issued on 26 June 2003. In *Stogner*, the Supreme Court struck down 1993 Cal Stats ch 390, §1(codified as amended at Cal Penal Code Ann §803(g)) and related 1996 Cal Stats ch 130, §1 (codified at Cal Penal Code Ann §803(g)(3)(A)). These statutes allowed for prosecutions of persons accused of committing sex-related child abuse crimes many years beforehand—where the original limitations period has expired—as long as such prosecution began within a year of a victim's first complaint to the police. A prosecution under this

particular, how could it be fair that statutes of limitations could 'run' before a person became conscious that they had suffered childhood sexual abuse. As a result of this quandary, some states adapted the approach found in other tort claims; namely, the statute of limitations is tolled for the period in which a person labours under a disability. In other words, the 'clock stops ticking' until such point in time at which a person becomes conscious of the fact that he or she may have been the victim of childhood sexual abuse. A qualification to the tolling is that the statute will not stop running in those situations where a person should have reasonably known that he or she may have been the victim of childhood sexual abuse. Two states worth examining for their differing approaches to the public policy concept of repose in the context of repressed memory cases are California and Colorado.

California has implemented California Civil Procedure Code (CCPC) § 340.1 setting forth applicable statutes of limitations and protocols that must be followed in civil actions for damages arising out of alleged acts of childhood sexual abuse. The statute is applicable against the alleged abuser and any organization that fails in its duty through its own negligence, recklessness or wanton conduct to protect its charges from abuse at the hands of its employees and agents. The classic *legal cause* defendant is, of course, the Catholic Church, accused many times over of turning a 'blind eye' to the problem of child sexual abuse by its clergy.

Generally, California requires that an action for damages suffered as a result of childhood sexual abuse must be commenced before the plaintiff achieves 26 years of age or within three years of the date that such plaintiff discovers or reasonably should have discovered a psychological injury or illness caused by the sexual abuse, *whichever is later*.[64] If the plaintiff is 26 years of age or older, he or she must also file with the court two certificates of merit: one to be executed by his or her attorney; and the other, to be executed by a licensed mental health practitioner.[65]

The attorney's certificate must affirm that:

(1) he or she has consulted with at least one mental health practitioner who is licensed to practise in California and currently practising in the state;

(2) in the reasonable opinion of the attorney, the mental health practitioner consulted is knowledgeable of the relevant facts and issues involved in the particular action; and

(3) reasonable and meritorious cause for the filing of the action exists based upon the attorney's review of the case and consultation with the mental health practitioner.[66]

new law was held to violate the Constitution's Ex Post Facto Clause, Art I, §10, cl 1, which forbids revival of a previously time-barred prosecution. California had tried to prosecute Mr Stogner for sex-related child abuse committed decades earlier (between 1955 and 1973), when the statute of limitations governing prosecutions at the time the crimes were allegedly committed had set forth a three-year limitations period (which had run some 22 years or more before the present prosecution).

[64] Cal Civ Proc Code § 340.1(a). [65] ibid, § 340.1(h). [66] ibid, § 340.1(h).

The mental health practitioner must affirm in his or her certificate:

(1) that he or she is licensed to practise and practises in California and is not a party to the action;
(2) that the practitioner is not treating and has not treated the plaintiff;
(3) that the practitioner has interviewed the plaintiff, is knowledgeable of the relevant facts and issues involved in the particular action; and
(4) in his or her professional opinion there is a reasonable basis to believe that the plaintiff has been subject to childhood sexual abuse.[67]

Not until the court reviews the two certificates of merit and has found, in camera, based solely on them, that there is reasonable and meritorious cause for the filing of the action against that defendant can the plaintiff's attorney serve the defendant with process.[68]

But, what relief is available to a defendant who successfully defends himself in a civil action alleging he or she sexually abused a minor? Attorneys' fees may be recoverable in the event that the plaintiff's attorney failed to file the requisite certificates of merit. Under CCPC § 340.1(q), when the litigation concludes favourably in respect of a particular defendant, that particular defendant or the court, on its own motion, may require the attorney for the plaintiff who failed to provide a certificate pursuant to CCPC § 340.1(h) to reveal to the judge in camera and in the absence of the moving party, if there was one, the names of the individuals who the attorney consulted to base the allegations of childhood sexual abuse. In the event that the court concludes that there was a failure on the part of plaintiff and/or his attorney to comply with CCPC § 340.1 et seq, the court may order a party or its attorney, or both, to pay any reasonable expenses, including attorney's fees, incurred by the defendant for whom a certificate of merit should have been filed.

Unfortunately, CCPC § 340.1(q) suggests that attorneys' fees may only be awarded where no certificates of merit were filed, not where certificates of merit have been filed on the basis of an inadequate or negligent investigation. Furthermore, the statute does not provide any statutory remedy for the wronged defendant to bring an action against the mental health practitioner who signed a certificate of merit on an erroneous basis. Other than filing a complaint with the appropriate licensing board against the mental health practitioner, it appears that the defendant's primary recourse is against the plaintiff for abuse of process and not the mental health practitioner who gave succour to the 'false memory' claims.

The Colorado statute of limitations for civil actions based on a sexual assault or a sexual offence against a child is six years either (i) after a disability has been removed for a person under disability; or (ii) after a cause of action accrues, *whichever occurs later*.[69] A 'person under disability' means any person who is a minor under 18 years of age, a mental incompetent or a person under other legal disability and who does not have a legal guardian.[70] Perhaps the most interesting

[67] ibid, § 340.1(h). [68] ibid, § 340.1(j). [69] Colo Rev Stat Ann § 13-80-103.7.
[70] ibid, § 13-80-103.7(3.5)(a)

provision of Colorado Revised Statutes Annotated § 13-80-103.7(3.5)(a) is the provision that limits the type of damages that may be recovered if a plaintiff brings a civil action 15 years or more after the plaintiff attains the age of 18. Under these circumstances, a plaintiff may only recover damages for medical and counselling treatment and expenses, plus costs and attorneys' fees. Thus, the plaintiff who waits 15 years or more after achieving the age of majority may find his or her prospects for recovery significantly reduced as he or she will be time barred from recovering punitive damages and for non-economic loss (pain and suffering). Additionally, Colorado prohibits an action under section 3.5 (above) if the defendant is deceased or is incapacitated to the extent that he or she is incapable of rendering a defence.

Between the California and Colorado statutes, it is evident that state legislatures are growing increasingly wary of claims based on repressed memory. California now requires the filing of a certificate of merit by both an attorney and a licensed mental health practitioner. The certificates of merit are meant to be a 'belt and braces' approach to preventing claims that may not be based on the soundest of evidence.[71] Moreover, they expose two different professionals—the attorney bringing the action on behalf of his client and the mental health practitioner affirming the reasonableness of the alleged childhood sexual abuse claim—to the risks of venturing a professional opinion as to whether someone's claim may in fact have legitimate grounds. Colorado now limits the type of damages an individual may recover if he or she waits too long to bring an action alleging childhood sexual abuse. A premium is now placed on resolving these issues earlier as opposed to later. If a plaintiff waits too long, he or she may be out of luck in recovery. The limitation on the types of damages an individual may recover seriously impairs the attractiveness of taking on a repressed memory case to a plaintiff's attorney who is being paid on a contingent fee arrangement. In essence, Colorado has for the most part legislated repressed memory claims 'out-of-business' by making them economically unappealing to the attorneys who might prosecute such claims. Finally, Colorado is very interested in providing repose. Thus, cases brought against decedent defendants or those who are incapacitated are not allowed. Clearly, the legislature in Colorado has 'pulled the rug out from under' the plaintiffs' bar which in the past may have been too keen on repressed memory lawsuits.

While California and Colorado focus significant legislative attention on the repressed memory controversy, other states through judicial review by their highest courts have formulated law in the same area. Wisconsin, for instance, has held that the parents of an adult child may maintain third-party professional negligence actions against their adult child's mental health care providers where the negligent therapy and psychiatric care provided resulted in the implanting and reinforcing of

[71] 'It has also become more difficult to prove abuse in the [English] civil courts, as the courts, in a well-meaning effort to protect innocent parents, have increased the standard of proof' writes Freeman on the status of civil actions in England by children accusing their parents of abuse. See M Freeman, 'The Convention: An English Perspective' in M Freeman (ed), *Children's Rights: A Comparative Perspective* (Aldershot: 1996), 99.

false memories of sexual abuse in their child.[72] In *Sawyer v Midelfort*, the Wisconsin Supreme Court considered the case of Nancy Anneatra. From a young age, Ms Anneatra suffered a variety of psychiatric problems, including anxiety, panic attacks, and severe depression, and on at least one occasion prior to meeting either of the defendants in the case, she required psychiatric hospitalization.[73]

At the time Ms Anneatra first met the defendants for treatment, it was unclear when she began having memories of being sexually abused by her father; whether she always had such memories, or whether her first memories were repressed and brought forward only a short time before the treatment.[74] Once undergoing treatment with the defendants, Ms Anneatra confronted her parents at a therapy session and accused both of them of physically abusing her during her childhood, and accused her father of sexually abusing her.[75] The parents, the Sawyers, denied any abuse occurred. After further treatment with the defendants, Ms Anneatra also indicated to the treating psychiatrist defendant that she was sexually abused by her father, paternal grandfather, uncle, brother and two priests and that an aunt and cousins were also involved as sexual perpetrators or observers of the sexual perpetration of others.[76]

In early 1995, Ms Anneatra died of cancer. Shortly thereafter her mother, Delores Sawyer, was appointed administrator of Ms Anneatra's estate and gained access to her deceased daughter's medical records. Upon examination of the records, the Sawyers concluded that the defendants failed properly to diagnose and treat their daughter's psychiatric problems. In particular, the Sawyers believed that the treating therapist and her consulting psychiatrist misdirected Ms Anneatra's therapy to recover false memories of sexual abuse through the negligent performance of hypnosis and failed to recognize the problems created by such hypnosis. Furthermore, the psychiatrist was accused of negligently handling the transference and counter-transference phenomenon existing in the therapeutic relationship thereby exacerbating matters. Finally, both the therapist and the psychiatrist were accused by the Sawyers of implanting and reinforcing false memories in Ms Anneatra, and of failing to recognize that the memories which were being created in Ms Anneatra were false.

In holding that the parents of an adult child may maintain third-party professional negligence actions against their adult child's mental health care providers, the Wisconsin Supreme Court thought that the facts in *Sawyer* were most similar to those in *Schuster v Altenberg*.[77] In *Schuster*, the same court held that a psychiatrist may be held liable to third parties for injuries that such third parties sustain as a result of the psychiatrist's negligent diagnosis and treatment of a patient.[78] The

[72] *Sawyer v Midelfort*, 595 N W 2d 423 (Wis 1999). An excellent discussion of the issue of third party claims against psychotherapists for false memory syndrome can be found in JM Berger, 'False Memory Syndrome and Therapist Liability to Third Parties for Emotional Distress Injuries Arising From Recovered Memory Therapy: A General Prohibition on Liability and a Limited Liability Exception' (2000) 73 *Temple L Rev* 795.

[73] *Sawyer*, 595 N W 2d at 427.

[74] ibid.

[75] ibid.

[76] ibid.

[77] 424 N W 2d 159 (Wis 1988).

[78] *Schuster v Altenberg*, 424 N W 2d 159 (Wis 1988).

plaintiff in *Schuster* was injured in an automobile accident while her mother, who was medicated, was driving; the daughter alleged that her mother's psychotherapist did not warn her mother of the side effects of her medication.[79]

The court extended the *Schuster* holding to the facts in *Sawyer* on the basis of public policy considerations and its belief that there would be little actual impact on the dynamic of the therapist-patient relationship generally. In applying the public policy considerations set forth in *Garret v City of New Berlin*,[80] the court concluded that the imposition of liability on the *Sawyer* defendants was reasonable because the harm the defendants may have caused was reasonably foreseeable under the circumstances. The *Garret* factors preclude the imposition of liability when:

(1) the injury is too remote from the negligence;
(2) the injury is too wholly out of proportion to the culpability of the negligent tortfeasor;
(3) in retrospect it appears too highly extraordinary that the negligence should have brought about the harm;
(4) allowance of recovery would be too likely to open the way for fraudulent claims; or
(5) allowance of recovery would enter a field that has no sensible or just stopping point.[81]

In the *Sawyer* case, the court concluded that the five factors above did not preclude the imposition of liability for public policy reasons.

More significant, from the perspective of defining the relationship between psychotherapist and patient, is the court's consideration of whether holding a therapist 'liable to third parties for their emotional health will push therapists to cease treating patients who believe they may have been sexually abused, or refrain from using new and untested forms of therapy which they believe are best suited for treating their patients'.[82] The *Sawyer* court was not convinced that therapists will be limited in their treatment choices by virtue of being subject to third-party professional negligence claims.[83] The court noted that the choice of treatment used by a therapist would not be restricted by allowing third party claims because imposing such liability would place no higher duty on a therapist than what already exists at the present time, namely, to provide a competent and carefully considered course of treatment for a patient in therapy.[84]

Not all courts agree with the conclusion of the *Sawyer* court. Some courts believe that allowing third party claims against psychotherapists would open the floodgate to all sorts of harms. This is the view of the highest courts in Illinois and Maine. The Maine Supreme Court concluded that public policy precluded imposing liability upon a health care professional for a duty of care to injured third parties because such a duty would intrude directly on the professional-patient

[79] *Schuster v Altenberg*, 424 N W 2d 159 (Wis 1988). [80] 362 N W 2d 137 (Wis 1985).
[81] See *Garret*, 362 N W 2d at 137. [82] ibid, 147. [83] ibid, 148. [84] ibid, 148.

relationship.[85] The Illinois Supreme Court also expressed the view that the spectre of liability to third parties might cause a therapist to deviate from a normal course of treatment to the ultimate detriment of their patient.[86] While the New Hampshire Supreme Court ruled in *Hungerford v Jones*,[87] along the lines of the Wisconsin Supreme Court in *Sawyer, Hungerford* limits third-party actions only to those cases where an accusation of sexual abuse has been made public.[88]

The Supreme Court of Iowa, however, as a matter of law declined to find that a duty runs from a mental health care provider to non-patient family members.[89] In its ruling in the case of a minor child who sued the defendant mental health care provider for loss of parental consortium arising out of the alleged negligent treatment of plaintiff's mother, the Iowa Supreme Court concluded for public policy reasons that the child had no viable cause of action against the defendant.[90] Despite the fact that the plaintiff's claim for loss of consortium was an independent one based on the defendant's duty to his mother, the court declined on public policy grounds to find that this independent basis gave rise to a special duty owed by defendant mental health care providers to the plaintiff separate and apart from the duty owed to the patient.[91] Nonetheless, it must be noted that the value of the decisive position taken by the Iowa Supreme Court in *JAH v Wadle & Assoc*,[92] as precedent is seriously curtailed by the fact that the court states that the holding is limited to the facts of the case before it.[93] By limiting the holding in *JAH*, the Iowa Supreme Court seems to have 'left the door open' in the future to depart from its current concurrence with the rulings of the highest courts in Maine and Illinois.

A California case, *Trear v Sills*,[94] considered the same question as *Sawyer* did, namely, whether the professional duty of the therapist extends beyond the patient to the patient's parent and concluded that it did not. In *Trears*, a father claimed he was wrongly accused of sexually abusing his daughter because his daughter's therapist implanted the idea in her mind.[95] The father sued the daughter's therapist for 'professional negligence', that is, *malpractice*, despite the fact that *he* was never the therapist's patient.[96] The court held that 'to extend the duty of a therapist to persons who have a relationship with the patient in the context of a perceived recovered memory of childhood sexual abuse is to saddle the therapist with a divided loyalty in an inherently adversarial situation'.[97] Given the inherently adversarial nature of the therapeutic problems posed by possible childhood sexual

[85] *Flanders v Cooper*, 706 A 2d 589, 591 (Me 1998).
[86] *Doe v McKay*, 700 N E 2d 1018, 1024 (Ill 1998). [87] 722 A 2d 478 (N H 1998).
[88] *Hungerford v Jones*, 722 A 2d 478, 480 (N H 1998).
[89] *JAH v Wadle & Assoc*, 589 N W 2d 256 (Iowa 1999). [90] ibid, 257. [91] ibid, 265.
[92] ibid. [93] ibid, 265.
[94] 82 Cal Rptr 2d 281 (Cal Ct App 1999). This case is not binding precedent in California because it is the opinion of the Court of Appeal of California, Fourth Appellate Division, and not that of the Supreme Court of California. Nonetheless, n 44 of the opinion indicates that the California Supreme Court declined to hear an appeal from this ruling. Thus, one may safely conclude that the Supreme Court did not find the Court of Appeal ruling contrary to sound legal principles.
[95] *Trear v Sills*, 82 Cal Rptr 2d 281, at 282. [96] ibid. [97] ibid, 283.

abuse, the court ruled that the therapist's duty could not be extended to a possible abuser.[98]

Turning the 'touchy feely' nature of psychotherapy against itself, the California court argues that the lack of a true scientific discipline in the therapeutic process mitigates against imposing a duty on therapists to safeguard third parties who may be injured as a result of the exploration of repressed memories:

> The very inexactitude of the therapeutic enterprise puts the good faith therapist in an untenable position if a duty is imposed upon him or her toward the patient's possible abuser. It would subject the therapist to inherently conflicting incentives, to the detriment of the patient. The *patient* would be denied the benefit of the nonquantifiable aspects of the therapist's diagnosis: the 'feel' that is conveyed by personal contact (as all trial lawyers who work with juries can appreciate), the gray subjective sense of the person that is part of the therapist's professional training, and the discretionary and judgment calls involved in determining whether a given patient really was abused: It would put the therapist in the position of a jury called upon to make a determination according to well-established and predetermined rules of evidence, rather than as a 'helping' professional—except that, unlike judges and juries, the therapist would face personal liability if the determination were wrong. Either way.[99]

Stating that 'there is no truth machine which allows one to determine whether the so-called recovered memory of abuse is accurate',[100] *Trear* is critical of those who are quick to find a psychotherapist negligent where a patient produces a false memory of sexual abuse which foreseeably could damage the person falsely accused of the abuse.[101] This assumes a 'level of ascertainability and verifiability on the part of the therapist which is unrealistic'.[102] *Trear*'s dispassionate analysis highlights the difficulty that psychotherapists have in diagnosing and treating victims of alleged child sexual abuse. In confirming the dilemma courts face in deciding whether to impose liability on psychotherapists for harm to third parties, *Trear* provides an excellent contrast to *Sawyer*. While both courts reach opposite conclusions, they both do so in a thoughtful and considered manner underscoring the complex issues that repressed memory presents for both psychotherapists treating patients and the courts which have to deal with the public policy implications that arise when such treatment goes woefully awry.

Beyond the issue of psychotherapist liability to third parties for negligence, another aspect of the repressed memory controversy that has recently attracted considerable scrutiny is who may be an appropriately qualified expert witness to explain to lay jurors scientific[103] data with respect to the authenticity of recovered

[98] *Trear v Sills*, 82 Cal Rptr 2d 281, at 287. [99] ibid, 289 [100] ibid, 289.

[101] ibid. [102] ibid.

[103] See DL Steele, 'Expert Testimony: Seeking an Appropriate Admissability Standard for Behaviorial Science in Child Sex Abuse Prosecutions' (1999) 48 *Duke LJ* 933, 954: 'Increasingly, however, experts trained in social science are being used in American courtrooms, and these witnesses do not uniformly rely upon the scientific methods as the basis for their testimony. A curious problem arises, then, when expert testimony is not grounded in the scientific method. The problem arises out of the fact that both the *Frye* and *Daubert* approaches to expert testimony are based upon scientific method principles, principles not always compatible with social science'.

memories. For instance, the Arizona Supreme Court in *Logerquist v Superior Court*,[104] vacated a trial court's decision to preclude expert testimony of the plaintiff's alleged repressed memory in a case where the plaintiff alleged that her paediatrician sexually abused her when she was eight to ten years old. The plaintiff claimed that she had amnesia about those events until some 20 or so years later when her memory was triggered by watching a television commercial featuring a paediatrician. *Logerquist* demonstrates the difficulty that courts have in weighing expert testimony in the fields of repressed memory and trauma's effect on memory.

The plaintiff in *Logerquist* sought to introduce evidence, through the expert testimony of Dr Bessell van der Kolk, a clinical psychiatrist who specializes in dissociative amnesia, that severe childhood trauma, including sexual abuse, can cause a repression of memory, and that in later years this memory can be recalled with accuracy.[105] Dr van der Kolk would testify, among other things, that his experience and observations over many years, together with extensive literature on the subject have led him to conclude that the phenomenon of repressed memory exists in some patients.[106] To counter Dr van der Kolk, the defendant sought to introduce the testimony of Dr Richard Kihlstrom, a research psychologist, who would testify that there were serious flaws in the many studies supporting repressed memory, citing other studies finding that trauma usually enhances memory rather than causes amnesia.[107] Dr Kihlstrom, however, did not have any personal experience treating or dealing with people claiming to suffer from repressed memory; nor had he participated in any studies on trauma's effect on memory.[108] The trial judge determined that Dr van der Kolk's theories 'were not generally accepted in the relevant scientific community of trauma memory researchers and that in later years this memory can be recalled with accuracy'.[109]

At the heart of the *Logerquist* case is how a court should interpret repressed memories in the light of two seminal cases that govern the admission of evidence in federal cases:[110] *Frye* and *Daubert*.[111] The rule of *Frye v United States*,[112] requires a hearing to determine the admissibility of evidence that is based on novel scientific theories that are not readily accepted by the medical and scientific communities. However, if a trial court determines that *Frye* is inapplicable to the scientific evidence because it is of a generally accepted nature, then the applicable test is *Daubert*. The rule of *Daubert v Merrell Dow Pharmaceuticals*,[113] rejects the *Frye* test and construes Federal Rule of Evidence 702 to create a 'gatekeeper' function for federal judges. Expert evidence based on the actual experience, observation or

[104] 1 P 3d 113 (Ariz 2000). [105] Steele n 103 above, 472. [106] ibid, 472.

[107] ibid, 472. [108] ibid, 472.

[109] Minute Entry Order, 11 June, 1998, quoted ibid, 472.

[110] The reason the federal cases are *apropos* to a case interpreting the state law of Arizona is that the statute that governs admissibility in Arizona is Arizona Rule of Evidence 702. This statute is an adaptation of Federal Rule of Evidence 702.

[111] An excellent discussion of *Frye* and *Daubert* in the context of child sex abuse prosecutions can be found in Steele, n 103 above, 950. [112] 293 F 1013 (D C Cir 1923).

[113] 509 U S 579 (1993).

study made by a qualified witness is subject only to a reliability determination applied to the expert's conclusions and methodology by the district judge hearing the case.[114] Confirming the primacy of the *Daubert* rule, the US Supreme Court in *Kumho Tire Co Ltd v Carmichael*,[115] held that *Daubert* was applicable to all opinion evidence offered under Rule 702. The rule in *Kumho* came down after the trial court conducted the *Frye* hearing in June 1998.[116]

The Arizona Supreme Court *in dicta* in *Logerquist* addressed the repressed memory controversy:

> To compare the repressed memory controversy between clinical psychiatrists and psychologists on the one hand and research psychologists on the other to a debate over astrology [as the trial court did] is, to put it tactfully, quite a stretch. Our decision, like *Kumho*, does not turn on an attempt to determine whether repressed memory is 'scientific' or 'unscientific.' Plaintiff does not claim her memories are proved true as a matter of scientific fact. *Frye* is applicable when an expert witness reaches a conclusion by deduction from the application of novel scientific principles, formulae, or procedures developed by others. It is inapplicable when a witness reaches a conclusion by inductive reasoning based on his or her own experience, observation, or research.[117]

The opinion goes on to state that *Logerquist* turns on a non-scientific issue:

> In many respects, the phenomenon of repressed memory, whatever its validity, presents a classic problem for the law and science relationship . . . It remains woefully short of being empirically verified and, indeed, heralds from a non-rigorous school of psychology in which empirical validation is not a core tenet. The theory of repressed memories has its roots in clinical therapy, a domain in which validity is not a factor of overriding concern . . . We believe the jury must decide what to do about the lack of empirical support. The [trial court's decision] would not even let this jury hear of the controversy and would, in effect, throw it and the case out of the courthouse, thus letting the judge decide the dispute if *Frye* were applied, and even if *Daubert* were applied.[118]

In sum, the court concludes that the issue of repression should be decided by a jury: 'whether or not the jury finds plaintiff's claims well founded, we are willing to indulge the presumption that the jurors will probably be right, or at least as right as the trial judge'.[119] The *Logerquist* court fully embraces the popular culture *zeitgeist* that the general public is at least as capable as any psychological expert to assess fully the veracity of a particular instance of repressed memory recovered.

Similarly, in *Commonwealth v Frangipane*,[120] the Supreme Judicial Court of Massachusetts reversed a conviction of a defendant of forcible rape of a child that was based, in part, on admitted expert opinion testimony about the loss and recovery of a traumatic memory through dissociation. The court felt that the opinion testimony, in significant respects, concerned scientific and medical matters beyond the scope of the witness's competence.[121] The witness was an expert in child abuse as

[114] *General Electric Co v Joiner*, 522 US 136 (1997). [115] 526 US 137 (1999).
[116] 197 Ariz at 475. [117] 197 Ariz at 490 (Ariz 2000).
[118] ibid. [119] ibid, 491 [120] 744 N E 2d 25 (Mass 2001). [121] ibid, 31.

she spent many years counselling children who were victims of child sexual abuse.[122] While the witness had 18 years' experience as a psychotherapist and was licensed as an independent certified social worker with degrees in social work, the court felt she was not qualified to testify about how a victim stores and retrieves, or dissociates, a traumatic memory. Those particular issues involve pronouncements concerning the physical functioning of the brain which require a qualification in neurology or medical functioning of the brain, areas beyond the expertise of the witness in the field of child abuse.[123]

Moving beyond the use of expert testimony in repressed memory cases, *Kansas v Plaskett*[124] considered whether a teenager's testimony on childhood sexual abuse was a 'repressed' memory. The Kansas Supreme Court upheld the aggravated incest conviction of William Plaskett which was based, in part, on memories of childhood sexual abuse related by his adopted daughter, AW, in psychotherapy sessions. The court concluded that the testimony of AW was not a result of false or repressed and subsequently recovered memory or hypnosis or a hypnosis-like process and was not erroneously admitted.[125] On direct examination, AW testified in some detail about the sexual abuse she suffered at the hands of the defendant.[126] AW was testifying to events which occurred when she was nine years old.[127] AW was 16 years old at the time of trial.[128] She first told others about the abuse when she was 11 years old. AW, thus, was not an 'adult' woman recalling for the first time the sexual abuse she endured as a child.[129] She was a child testifying to what occurred to her at an earlier age.[130]

AW's testimony was different from the evidence usually offered in most repressed memory cases. First, there was no claim that AW ever forgot about the abuse she was alleged to have suffered. This is different from the typical repressed memory case in which the memory of child abuse comes out just before psychotherapy starts or during psychotherapy. Second, there was no evidence whatsoever that AW ever suffered from traumatic amnesia as a result of the alleged sexual abuse. Most of the adults who recovered memories of childhood sexual abuse experienced some type of dissociative amnesia of the sought researched by Dr van der Kolk. And, third, AW's testimony was not the result of recollection refreshed by hypnosis or a hypnosis-like process. In some cases, the child-abuse memories come out only as a result of hypnosis or some other sort of 'suggestive' processes. Given that none of the typical repressed memory indicia existed in AW's case, the court concluded very simply that AW did not have a case of repressed memory. Thus, the testimony of AW was rightly heard and no expert testimony was required to explain the phenomenon of repressed memory to the jury given the circumstances of AW's testimony.

Whether or not AW was coached or given suggestions by her psychotherapist to recall the instances of childhood abuse is an issue that the Kansas Supreme Court

[122] ibid, 31. [123] ibid. [124] 27 P 3d 890 (Kan 2001).
[125] *Plaskett*, 27 P 3d 890 at 892. [126] ibid, 897. [127] ibid. [128] ibid.
[129] ibid. [130] ibid.

did not want to delve into at all. In essence, the court does 'cartwheels' to avoid finding that AW's testimony (the only way through which a conviction of the defendant could be had) had anything to do with repressed memory or false memory syndrome. Thus, we see that in the course of a mere decade, repressed memory had gone from being a *New Age concept* embraced by many jurisdictions through the amending of statutes of limitation to allow for claims to be made based on events that took place many years ago to it now being seen as an 'unwieldy distraction' that could possibly jeopardize the successful prosecution of an abuse case involving a precocious teenage witness testifying against her allegedly abusive stepfather.

The Law-Psychotherapy Debate

The repressed memory controversy burst onto the scene in 1990s America. When the storm finally died down, this popular culture fixation had transformed both psychotherapy and the law. The implications of this controversy are startling from a law and popular culture perspective. The law was reluctantly forced to address issues in psychotherapy brought to its attention as a result of a mass hysteria that developed in the last quarter of the twentieth century that child sexual abuse was to be found in just about every family in America. Perhaps the repressed memory controversy was a natural outgrowth of America's discomfort with the juxtaposition of childhood and sexuality. Nonetheless, in giving rise to a search for victims and perpetrators in the parent-child relationship, psychotherapists suffered a strong backlash in the popular culture that was reflected in developments in court. Courts are now ever so sceptical of psychotherapists and the profession, as a whole. Thus, not only has the repressed memory controversy diminished psychotherapists in the eyes of the general public but they have also been diminished in the eyes of the courts as well. For better or worse, the popular culture has transformed the law's perception of psychotherapy.

Given all the problems unleashed through the exploration of repressed memory, it might be argued that psychotherapy would have been better off letting 'sleeping dogs lie'. Nonetheless, it could not do so, nor should it have been expected to do so. After all, psychotherapy is a humanistic approach to putting the individual in order with himself, his thoughts, his emotions and his relationships to others and the world around him. In this sense, psychotherapy has much in common with its sister social science, the law. After all the law, which took up the cudgel for psychotherapy in the repressed memory controversy, seeks to do the same as psychotherapy, except on behalf of society as opposed to the individual. Some fields of law such as public international law and human rights law approach their work in the same vein as psychotherapy, seeking to place the individual at peace with the rest of society.

This viewpoint, namely, expressing the interrelatedness and similarity of law and psychotherapy as disciplines, has found a powerful voice in the new and developing field known as the philosophy of psychiatry:[131]

> It cannot escape notice that the aims of psychotherapy, achieved in different—sometimes medical and scientific—ways, have much in common with the aims of law, at least where law is part of a larger context respectful of the dignity of the person. Therapy and law seek to enhance life by enlarging the possibilities for what is finally the good in life. Both are intended to be 'liberating', where liberation includes freedom from what is otherwise destructive of life's higher purposes. Both, then, rest on certain assumptions about the goods of life—assumptions that arise from a conception of human nature as this conception has been tested and refined over the course of millennia. In these respects, the data of human history are vastly more richly and relevantly informing than anything concocted in the Orwellian simplicity of the 'psych lab'.[132]

In the decade or so since law has had to come to terms with the elusive concept of repressed memory, it has attempted to put some rational order and structure to some of the most complex concepts of psychotherapy. In doing so, law has acted to liberate psychotherapy from psychotherapy's own shortcomings as a discipline. In this process, law has imposed greater discipline on psychotherapy as a whole. Yet, at the same time, the law has learned much from psychotherapy, namely, that not all things can be understood rationally and empirically. Most particularly, the recesses of the mind, that most uncharted of all territories, may never be able to be fully assembled and disassembled as if it were a simple Rubik's cube.

Repressed memory in the context of child sexual abuse is a great challenge that psychotherapy has placed upon the law. It requires the law to go beyond the narrow confines of its own Cartesian rationality, to accept the empiricism of psychological experts who have categorized and analyzed strange phenomena in memory. In this area, psychotherapy can instruct the law. Psychotherapy can guide the law to understand better how many things in life cannot be understood in a rational manner, least of all, human consciousness. As we learn more and more about the mind's capacity to repress, there is the possibility that the whole repressed memory debate will be rendered unnecessary as fact will illuminate what was once the provenance of fiction.

A century ago, at the same time as psychotherapy was coming into its own as a discipline, legal thinkers such as Holmes were deconstructing the legal formalism of the age. Attacking the prevailing view that law was to be studied like an empirical science, Holmes took legal thought out from the process of categorizing 'distinct phenomena'.[133] Instead, Holmes saw legal reasoning as the process of 'drawing lines to create distinctions among essentially indistinguishable phenomena'.[134]

[131] See generally B Fulford, K Morris, J Sadler and G Stanghellini, *Nature and Narrative: An Introduction to the New Philosophy of Psychiatry* (Oxford: 2003).

[132] ibid, 95, 96.

[133] KJ Vandevelde, *Thinking Like A Lawyer—An Introduction to Legal Reasoning* (Westview Press: 1998), 124.

[134] ibid, 124.

Holmes famously declared in *The Common Law* that 'the life of the law has not been logic: it has been experience'.[135] Given this tradition in law, it would be unwise for lawyers and judges summarily to dismiss the work of psychotherapists exploring repressed memory as 'quackery' more in line with the *X Files* than reality. Nonetheless, a healthy scepticism with respect to repressed memory testimony and the value to be placed thereon is necessary. This view, derived from popular culture, informs the law's response to psychotherapy in America. The law-psychotherapy debate continues.

[135] R Posner (ed), *The Essential Holmes* (Chicago: 1992), xx.

What Law Cannot Give: *From the Queen to the Chief Executive*

Anne SY Cheung

Introduction

Hong Kong, as a former colony, inherited the virtues and follies of the English legal system. While the colonial master has long moved ahead in law reform to keep pace with social development, this former colony sadly lags behind. One aspect that continues to haunt the Hong Kong legal system is the sentence reserved for youngsters who committed murder under 18. They were 'to be detained at Her Majesty's pleasure', a sentence with ancient roots dating back to 1800. A group of youngsters below age 16 committed horrendous murders before 1997,[1] and their fate has since been sealed under the colonial sentence. In effect, they were sentenced to an indeterminate term. The plight of youngsters in England in a similar situation has been corrected in the case of *R v Secretary of State for the Home Department, ex p Venables*[2] and its appellant decision before the European Court of Human Rights in *V v United Kingdom*.[3] In stark contrast, Hong Kong prisoners were only granted 'a minimum sentence' ranging from 15 to 30 years after the political handover. Their stories of violence, remorse and tears were vividly depicted in the film, *From the Queen to the Chief Executive* (hereafter *From the Queen*).[4]

In the movie, the central story is about a group of juvenile prisoners fighting against their indeterminate sentence and against a rigid legal system. Their struggle is based on real life stories. Herman Yau, the director of the movie, is known for his passion in filming law related stories.[5] Hong Kong audiences have also acquired a taste for watching movies and TV series on crime-detective stories, triad-police antagonism, court room drama and lawyers' glamorous life. However, in *From the Queen*, Yau deliberately abandoned his previous style of shooting and ignored his peers' advice. Rather than adopting a sure success commercial formula by dramatizing the brutal tale of murder, he used a way descriptive of the grim realities

[1] On 1 July 1997, Hong Kong's sovereignty was handed from the British Government to the Government of the People's Republic of China.

[2] [1998] AC 407.

[3] (2000) 30 EHRR 121.

[4] The movie was shown in Hong Kong in 2001.

[5] Five out of Yau's 56 directed movies are related to law. See Herman Yau's homepage at http://www.hermanyau.com/cfilmography.htm.

to convey his message. His goal is to display through sound and vision his dissatisfaction and frustration with how Hong Kong society and its legal system have treated a minority marginalized group.[6] The story is about justice and injustice, but unlike many legal stories or movies, *From the Queen* is not about wrongful conviction, nor about miscarriage of justice. It is about a group of young offenders who have actually committed vicious terrible murders in their youthful days. The question probed by the movie is how society has treated them and should have treated them after their full hearted repentance. Yau has spun a tapestry rich in political, social and legal issues. The movie accuses both the colonial and the present Hong Kong legal systems. It questions the aim of punishment and revisits the meaning of justice.

Other than the above clear messages, I would like to introduce another perspective of *From the Queen* and argue that it is a movie about law and not about law. The prisoners, the hero and the heroine who embark on the rescue mission have invested much energy in fighting for legislative reform. The movie has also tried hard to explain the substantive legal rules in the most comprehensible way so that an audience without legal knowledge could have a basic understanding. Yet the legal struggle is fruitless because law will not and cannot forgive. What the movie has portrayed is that forgiveness is the ultimate redemption for the young offenders and for society as a whole. As the story progresses, one will notice that the dichotomies in the movie have moved from crime/sin, to law/justice and eventually to punishment/forgiveness. The heavy legal connotation in the movie is in fact a façade hiding the macro moral lesson of forgiveness. The greatest and saddest irony is that the victim families whose children had been murdered are willing to forgive the prisoners but law will not grant its pardon and will not give another chance to the murderer. Unless society is willing to face squarely the problem of juvenile delinquency as a societal problem, and has the courage and faith to forgive, legal reform and change in judicial attitude are unlikely to follow. On the other hand, even with the lofty virtues of forgiveness and understanding being acquired by individual members in society, without the liberation of law, the prisoners will still be behind bars. The most difficult question presented by *From the Queen* is whether the concept of forgiveness can ever be instilled in the criminal justice system.

To capture the dichotomies in the movie, the discussion in my paper will zigzag between the real world, the movie and the legal world. After the Introduction, I will outline the narrative scheme in the movie and the real murder case that shocked colonial Hong Kong back in 1985. The second part of this paper will examine the inevitable question of legal rules that have been referred to in the movie. The legal reasoning that has been played out in Hong Kong, English and European Courts will be covered. At the time of writing, an appeal is pending for

[6] See Herman Yau, 'Three Months After the Production of *From the Queen to the Chief Executive*' (27 January 2001), translated by Vicky Lau, at http://www.hermanyau.com/efromQtoCE.htm.

two Hong Kong prisoners who were once sentenced to be detained at Her Majesty's pleasure. To better appreciate the irony and absurdity in the movie and in reality, this second part involves orthodox legal analysis of cases and statute. Following the discussion of heavy substantive legal reasoning, the third part of the paper is about the portrayal of law in the movie. To the prisoners, law is essentially faceless, blind and cold. Most telling, the prisoners in real life expressed their woe through their painting of the Lady of Justice. This painting had been used in the actual protest in fighting for a determinate sentence in 1997. It was also shown in the movie. After discussion about law, the fourth part moves to deal with the moral theme of forgiveness as played out by the major characters in the movie. It is not forgiveness that is extended to the immediate parties affected but forgiveness that is necessary for human interaction and at every level in society.

Adding to this rich complexity, the movie, as in real life episodes, is filled with ironies. These range from the nature of the sentence, the legislative and judicial stance, the victims' attitude to the cast chosen. The movie itself is critically acclaimed but was neglected at the box office. All these issues will be gradually unfolded.

From the Queen to the Chief Executive—A Crisscross Between Fictional and Real Worlds

Herman Yau's inspiration for the movie comes from the book with the same title.[7] The book is based on several stories of young offenders who are detained at Her Majesty's pleasure. They are helped by a lawyer who has an unhappy childhood. In the movie, the role of the lawyer is discarded so, unlike many law related movies, there is no lawyer hero in *From the Queen*. One common trait between the book and the movie is that both are based on real life stories. Yau conducted his own research and stated that 90 per cent of the movie had its basis in reality.[8]

The movie is interwoven by three main stories led by Yue-ling, Leung and Ming. The fate of these three characters crosses a 12 year period from 1985 to 1997. Yue-ling is the only fictional character that has no single parallel in real life. According to Yau, she is the embodiment of the tragic fate of five females rolled into one. When the audience first meet Yue-ling, she is a high school girl newly emigrated from Mainland China in 1985. Freshly arrived in Hong Kong, she suffers from poverty, discrimination and loneliness. She is sexually abused and exploited by her uncle. Appearing in the same year and working in the same squatter area where Yue-ling resides is Leung, an idealistic young man fighting for social justice and helping factory workers to organize themselves to protest against unfair working conditions. However, the stories of Yue-ling and Leung fade in comparison with what Ming did in 1985. Ming is a 16 year old boy, who gets involved with a group

[7] Elsa Chan, *From the Queen to the Chief Executive* (1998) (in Chinese).
[8] Interview with Herman Yau in Hong Kong on 8 November 2001.

of gangsters, and commits the Braemar Hill double murder. Since then, Ming has been detained in prison at Her Majesty's pleasure.

The central line of the story is Ming who holds the narrative scheme together. By 1997, after 12 years, Ming is still in prison without a determinate sentence. Through a writing competition in Open University, Yue-ling comes to know Ming and decides to help him and the group of prisoners detained at Her Majesty's pleasure.[9] Yue-ling approaches the help of Legislative Council (Legco) members. Out of 60 members, only one replies and that is Leung.[10] The story picks up its momentum from that juncture onwards when Yue-ling and Leung commit themselves to helping Ming and other prison inmates to fight for a determinate sentence.

Throughout the movie, there are flashbacks to the lives of Yue-ling and Ming, going back to their teenage days in 1985. Though Yue-ling is the heroine and Ming is a murderer in the movie, both are victims of fate and have been continuously haunted by their own past. Adding to their personal stories, Yue-ling and Ming live in a time of great political and historical significance. 1985 was one year after the Sino-British Joint Declaration, in which Britain agreed to transfer the sovereignty of Hong Kong to China. The actual handover date was 1 July 1997. To strengthen the impact of the movie and to reinforce the message that it is not entirely fictional, *From the Queen* has used various news footage. This includes the handover ceremony, where the last Governor, Chris Patten, was shown with tear-filled eyes, where the first Chief Executive of the Hong Kong Special Administrative Region proudly swore allegiance, and where the famous democrat, Martin Lee, announced his determined comeback after the last Legco meeting at the end of the colonial era. This news footage not only reinforces a sense of reality, it also familiarizes the audience with the context of the movie. It reminds the audience that the problem of Ming and other juvenile offenders is a remnant of colonial days that has spanned a spectrum of more than a decade. The 'home-rule' after 1997 not only fails to deliver them but deepens their entrapment in their situation.

The sentence of 'to be detained at Her Majesty's Pleasure' is a feature unique to the English criminal justice system and Hong Kong's colonial past. In Ming's case, it could be seen as the ultimate revenge by the colonial master for what Ming and his gangster group had done to two English teenagers in 1985.

On a Saturday in April, 1985, Ming and his gang of five were strolling in Braemar Hill, an area largely populated by expatriates and upper middle class. They spotted an English teenage couple. Both of them were students at the International Island School. Ming's gang decided to rob them. Tragically, the robbery turned into a double-murder of the most horrific and ugly kind. Kenneth McBride, 17 at the time, suffered more than 100 abrasions and died. Nicola Myers, 18, a notable athlete in

[9] Before 1 July 1997, there were 23 offenders who were detained at Her Majesty's pleasure.

[10] In the movie, Leung Chung Kan is modelled on Legco member Leung Yiu-chung, who has fought for the young offenders. Leung Yiu-chung considered 80% of the movie to be a reflection of real life episodes. See 'Leung Yiu-chung Finally Cries', *Ming Pao Daily News*, 28 May 2001 (in Chinese), E1.

school, struggled profusely which caused her to suffer more than 500 abrasions and lacerations. Most gruesome, she was beaten, tortured, gang-raped and stripped naked to die. Their murder hit the headline news of all local newspapers. The cold-blooded nature of the attack triggered moral panic and condemnation in society. Yet, the shock of the murder was derived not only from the cruelty but also due to the identity of the victims. As Whitehead rightly puts it, '[i]t was not the brutality of this double slaying that made it such a high-profile case. It was the racial implications.'[11]

The Police Department quickly dispatched 350 officers, a rare outpouring of such massive manpower, to search the hillside for any clues and evidence. A businessman offered HK$500,000,[12] the highest reward that had ever been offered in a murder case in Hong Kong, to track down the murderers. After investigating for eight months, the gang was caught. The leader in the gang was a youngster of 24 years of age. The youngest was 15. Ming was 16 at the time of the murder. Ming confessed to taking part in the attack and sexual assault but not rape. The three who were over 18 were sentenced to death but their sentences were commuted to life imprisonment two years later in 1988. The younger two were to be detained at Her Majesty's pleasure. Sympathy was not expected at the time of trial and sentencing. Even after more than a decade, it is probably hard for most to agree to give a lenient sentence.

Before the gang was caught, some speculated whether the murder was politically motivated due to the sensitive timing of the murder and the identity of the victims. The Chinese media also criticized the extensive use of manpower for this double murder.[13] Indisputably, the gang of five did not have any political or racial agenda in their minds when they committed the crime. However, as things turn out, the younger two have since been held at the mercy of the lingering effect of a colonial criminal justice system.

Justice and Injustice in the Legal Labyrinth

With a sadistic murder, the cry for justice sounds unconvincing. Fighting for justice for criminals convicted of the most heinous crime is a weak and seemingly groundless course. With the risk of offending the above assumption, Yau introduces another aspect of the story. What 'agitates' his sense of justice and motivates him to film the movie,[14] despite the fact that he knows the movie will not be a commercial success and that he had spent two years to find a sponsor and distributor, is the very nature of the sentence—detention at Her Majesty's pleasure.

Highlighted in the movie, the unfairness and injustice in the sentence have two main aspects. First, detention at Her Majesty's pleasure is an indeterminate,

[11] Kate Whitehead, *Hong Kong Murders* (New York, 2001) 138. The information on the Braemar Hill murders is taken from Ch 12 of Whitehead's book 'Braemar Hill—Double Murder'.

[12] This is approximately equivalent to £42,000.

[13] See Whitehead, n 11 above, 141.

[14] Yau, n 6 above.

open-ended sentence. No one knows how long the prisoners will have to spend behind bars. Second, the young offenders fare worse than adult murderers. A sentence which is meant to be merciful for them turns out to be a hopeless form of waiting.

For those who are unfamiliar with the criminal justice system in this area, they may think that no matter how long the detention at Her Majesty's pleasure may be, it cannot be worse than life imprisonment. The truth is that this is the contrary. In the movie, Yue-ling and Leung show a list of statistics to confirm the above point. In actual practice, life imprisonment is never meant to be life incarceration. In most cases, after five years in prison, an adult inmate who has committed murder and who is sentenced to life imprisonment will receive a determined sentence. There has been a long tradition in both England and Hong Kong that prisoners could obtain remission of sentence for good behaviour. In most cases prisoners having served not less than two thirds of the sentence may be released under supervision.[15] There is also the possibility of parole once a third of the sentence has been served. For instance, Au Yeung, an adult murderer who committed a crime as equally horrific and cruel as the Braemar Hill murder in Hong Kong in which he killed a teenage girl, cut off her nipples, scorched her pubic region with a soldering iron and put her body in a cardboard box, was sentenced to life imprisonment in 1975. In prison, Au Yeung repented, spent his time studying and got qualified as an accountant.[16] He was released in 2002, after spending 27 years in prison.[17] In contrast, no matter how well the young offenders have been rehabilitated, there is no chance for them to have a determinate sentence, let alone to obtain remission.

Due to the concerns and limitation of a movie, it is difficult to cover the substantive legal issues in detail. For those who have watched the movie, they may ask whether the legal rules are indeed as absurd as the movie has portrayed. And for those, like me, who are agitated enough to check the law books, they will find that the logic in this area of law is entangled in ironies. What the movie has shown is only the tip of the iceberg.

Historical Development: Detention at Her Majesty's Pleasure vs Mandatory Life Imprisonment

Historically, the sentence of detention at Her Majesty's pleasure was imposed solely on criminally insane adults. It has its roots in Hadfield's attempted assassination of King George III in 1800.[18] As Hadfield was found to be mentally disabled, he was held in protective custody so that he was unable to commit further offences. As the

[15] Long Term Sentences Review Ordinance (Cap 524), ss 15 and 29.

[16] See Whitehead, n 6 above, 'The Body in the Box: A Forensic First', 127.

[17] Liu Si Wen, 'Let's Put Down our Prejudice, Give a New Chance to Prisoners' (in Chinese), *Ming Pao Daily News*, 3 October 2002, E3.

[18] For an account of the incident, see Claire McDiarmid, 'Children Who Murder: What is Her Majesty's Pleasure' [2000] Crim LR 547, 548–549.

crime was directed at King George, it was an offence directed at the King personally. Consequently, it seemed reasonable in those days to detain Hadfield at His Majesty's pleasure. The Criminal Lunatics Act was passed as a direct result of the incident in 1800,s 2 of which stated that the court could order that such an insane person 'be kept in strict custody until his Majesty's pleasure shall be known'.

It was only in 1908 that the Children Act abolished the death sentence for anyone aged 15 or under. Detention at His Majesty's pleasure has since replaced it. In 1933, the Children and Young Persons Act raised the age threshold from 15 to 18. Between 1908 and 1983, the Home Secretary had absolute discretion to decide on the length of detention and date of release. The criminal justice system during this period tended to be merciful and lenient to the offenders committing murders at a young age when they were still immature. As things turned out in both England and in Hong Kong, the pendulum of punishment has swung to the other extreme since 1983. Between 1983 and 1999, the sentence mutated from a lenient flexible sentence to a rigid and harsh form of punishment. The situation in England was finally corrected by the English House of Lords in 1997 and the European Court in 1999, but the Hong Kong legal and judicial institutions have remained stubbornly unresponsive. To appreciate the irony that youngsters detained at Her Majesty's pleasure eventually end up in a worse situation than adult murderers, one has to understand the legal development and argument in England.

In 1983, Home Secretary Leon Brittan announced that the life sentence for adult murderers would be divided into two parts.[19] The first part was the tariff, referring to the period necessary to meet the requirements for retribution and deterrence. The second part was the post-tariff period, where continued detention would be authorized if the offender constituted a risk to the public. Brittan recommended that the tariff for adult murderers should at least be 20 years in custody. After satisfying the tariff period, it would be up to the Parole Board to review individual cases and recommend release. In essence, until the tariff had expired, the Home Secretary would not exercise his discretion.

The immediate complication is the application and interpretation of the tariff for those who were sentenced to mandatory and discretionary life imprisonment. Under the English system, life imprisonment is divided into mandatory and discretionary. The former is passed on any adult convicted of murder, whereas discretionary life imprisonment is only imposed for any crime that carries the maximum penalty of life imprisonment. Common examples are robbery and rape. The issue then becomes, under the tariff regime, what exactly is the difference between one that is sentenced to mandatory life imprisonment and one sentenced to discretionary life imprisonment?

In the case of *Thynne, Wilson and Gunnell v United Kingdom*,[20] the European Court of Human Rights ruled that for prisoners under discretionary life imprisonment,

[19] *Hansard*, HC col 506 (30 November 1983), cited in *R v Secretary of State for the Home Department, ex p Venables* [1998] AC 407, at 416.

[20] (1990) 13 EHRR 666.

once the tariff had been served, the Parole Board had to review their case. Unless the prisoner is mentally unstable or would present a danger to the public, the Board must recommend release.[21]

Following the European Court's ruling, England enacted the Criminal Justice Act in 1991. Under s 34, treatment for persons sentenced to a discretionary life sentence (discretionary lifers) is judicialized. The tariff will be set by the judge at trial in an open court with the possibility of appeal. Once the tariff has expired, the applicant is entitled to apply to a court to have the lawfulness of his detention revised. The only justification for continued detention will then be whether he presents a dangerous risk to the public.

The Criminal Justice Act formalized and widened the difference between mandatory and discretionary lifers. In contrast, the fate of mandatory lifers was still in the single hand of the Home Secretary. As described by the Home Office Minister, Angela Rumbold, the assumption behind mandatory life imprisonment is entirely different from discretionary life imprisonment. The offenders have forfeited their liberty for the rest of their lives and 'the presumption is that they should remain in custody till public interest is better served'.[22]

The critical issue for young offenders detained at Her Majesty's pleasure became how the tariff should be applied to them; whether they should be considered on a par with discretionary lifers, with mandatory lifers or under a separate system. The severe blow came in 1993 when Home Secretary Michael Howard announced that the policy for mandatory life sentence prisoners applied equally to young offenders detained at Her Majesty's pleasure.[23] The flexibility that was meant to take into account the progress and rehabilitation of young offenders during detention vanished. For them, the tariff would be set by the Home Secretary, guided by the recommendation of the trial judge and advised by the Lord Chief Justice. The detainees were not entitled to have the right of appeal. They could only ask for judicial review. To satisfy the tariff was the basic requirement. Even after serving the tariff, their custody could still be substantially longer because they could not benefit from the ruling of *Thynne*. The question whether to release or not would depend on whether it was safe to release the prisoner and on whether public opinion would find this acceptable. The final decision to release was also at the discretion of the Home Secretary.

Royal Verdict vs Colonial Sentence

Parallel to the English system, the discretion to release young offenders rested with the Governor before the political handover. Prior to 1993,[24] for those who were 18

[21] (1990) 13 EHRR, 686.

[22] *Hansard*, HC cols 309–310 (16 July 1991), cited in *ex p Venables*, at 419.

[23] *Hansard*, HC cols 863–864 (27 July 1993), cited in *ex p Venables*, at 421.

[24] Death penalty was abolished in Hong Kong in 1993 under the Crimes (Amendment) Ordinance 1993.

or under and committed murder, they would be detained at Her Majesty's pleasure.[25] It was the Governor who could then commute the detention to a fixed term sentence.[26] In the interim, the Prison Parole Board would review the cases of detainees every year till they were 21. After their twenty first birthday, the Board would review their case every two years.[27] The eventual date of release was still dependent on the Board's recommendation and the Governor's decision. The political handover in 1997 intensified the anxiety and urgency of the matter. Understandably, the young offenders were desperate to ask for a determinate sentence before the handover.

The movie mentions that out of 23 prisoners, Governor Patten only dealt with six cases. Four young offenders were released and two were given determined sentences. The rest were left for the Hong Kong Special Administrative Region (HKSAR) to decide. This is a true reflection of reality. At present, there are 17 prisoners who were originally detained at Her Majesty's pleasure. Leung in the movie criticized Patten's handling of the matter as a typical political compromise. In his words, 'if you ask a politician for ten favours, he will only grant you two'. After the transition, the Chief Executive has essentially converted detention at Her Majesty's pleasure into a minimum sentence rather than a definite sentence. Hence, the unfairness or injustice as highlighted in the movie and encountered in real life is that the uncertainty about the exact period for young offenders at Her Majesty's Pleasure renders the sentence particularly punitive. Described vividly by Leung, the authorities have treated the youngsters as garbage disposal, being passed along from one collector to another, only to be swept aside.

However, what marks a difference between the English criminal system and the Hong Kong criminal justice system in this regard is the development after 1996. The English system has restored the original spirit behind the sentence of detention at Her Majesty's pleasure by instilling flexibility and leniency in its application while Hong Kong has fossilized the much criticized policy statement of the English Home Secretary into its statute. The bitter irony is that this was done in the post-colonial era.

The English Position

The development in England has taken a gradual but significant turn since 1996. An opportunity to redraw the line between detainees at Her Majesty's pleasure and adult murderers first presented itself before the European Court of Human Rights in the case of *Hussain v United Kingdom*.[28] In that case, the applicant had been sentenced to detention at Her Majesty's pleasure for causing the death of his two year old brother. The murder was committed when he was 16. After the expiry of his tariff, he brought an action before the court under article 5(4) of the European Convention on Human

[25] s 70 of the Criminal Procedure Ordinance, repealed in 1993. After 1993, all persons convicted of murder, regardless of their age, are sentenced to mandatory sentence of life imprisonment.

[26] Article XV of the Letter Patent delegated to the Governor the exercise of the royal prerogative of mercy.

[27] Rule 69A of Prison Rules, repealed in 1997.

[28] (1996) 22 EHRR 1.

Rights,[29] asserting his right to access to court and arguing that he was entitled to have the continued lawfulness of this detention determined by a court. In effect, he argued that his detention should be treated the same as an adult prisoner sentenced to a discretionary life sentence rather than one under a mandatory life sentence. The European Court accepted Hussain's argument and further held that to equate the sentence for a mandatory life prisoner with detainees at Her Majesty's pleasure is severely out of proportion. Though both sentences share a penal element, the latter sentence is primarily preventative. A better interpretation would be to assimilate detention at Her Majesty's pleasure with the discretionary life sentence. Once the tariff has expired, the applicant is entitled to challenge the lawfulness of his detention. The presumption is to release unless there is a real risk to society. Because Hussain's tariff had already been served, it was not necessary for the court to examine the tariff system or the lawfulness of detention at Her Majesty's pleasure. Nevertheless, *Hussain* marks the first significant attempt in the legal battle on behalf of young offenders detained at Her Majesty's pleasure.

The next watershed came in 1997, in *R v Secretary of State, exp Venables and Thompson*.[30] The application for judicial review arose out of a notorious murder that shocked not only the whole of England but the world. In 1993, Venables and Thompson, two ten and a half year old boys, abducted a two year old toddler in a shopping mall, tortured him to death and left his body to be run over on a railway track. They were sentenced to detention at Her Majesty's pleasure in 1994, with a tariff of 15 years set by the Home Secretary. One of the main issues before the appellant courts was whether the Home Secretary had lawful authority to exercise his discretion. More important, the applicants also challenged that detention at Her Majesty's pleasure had violated procedural fairness because it denied one's right to a fair trial and access to court. The House of Lords was, thus, forced to examine the underlying nature of detention at Her Majesty's pleasure, including the initial setting of the tariff and the ultimate decision to release.

On the first issue of whether the Home Secretary had acted unlawfully in setting the tariff, the Court quickly and easily concluded that setting of a tariff amounted to judicial sentencing because it involved the determining of an appropriate punishment. In fixing the tariff, the Home Secretary had acted contrary to the constitutional principle of separation of power. In light of the fact that treatment of prisoners under a discretionary life sentence has been judicialized, a similar procedure should also apply to prisoners under a mandatory life sentence and to young offenders.[31] In addition, because the Home Secretary in *Venables* had given much weight to public opinion and pressure in setting the tariff, the Court further held that this amounted to 'double accounting'[32] in punishment and was an improper exercise of his discretion.

[29] Article 5(4) provides that 'everyone who is deprived of his liberty by arrest or detention shall be entitled to take proceedings by which the lawfulness of his detention shall be decided speedily by a court and his release ordered if the detention is not lawful'.

[30] [1998] AC 407.

[31] ibid, 435–436.

[32] ibid, 436. The trial judge recommended eight years for tariff. The Lord Chief Justice recommended ten years but the Home Secretary, after receiving petitions from the public, raised it to 15.

The second immediate issue before the Court, which was the crux of the entire judgment, was whether the tariff for young offenders detained at Her Majesty's pleasure should be treated the same as adult murderers under a mandatory life sentence. Not only does the majority judgment conclude the contrary, the Court ruled that it was equally wrong to treat young offenders as being the same as prisoners under a discretionary life sentence.

To the Court, it is simply and obviously wrong to put adult murderers on the same footing with young offenders. As pointed out by Lord Justice Pill in the Divisional Court, whose view was endorsed by Lord Woolf:

> justification for a tariff in the case of a mandatory life prisoner is that the true and judicially imposed tariff is life and that stating a term of years by way of a tariff is a form of remission which the Secretary of State is entitled to grant. The nature of detention during Her Majesty's pleasure does not permit of such an approach. There is no judicially imposed tariff from which to remit . . . [T]he essence with respect to a child or a young person . . . is to keep the need for detention under regular review.[33]

The simple logic, as argued by Lord Hope, is that if the same theory could be applied to both child and adult murderers, there is no need to provide a separate and distinct penalty for young offenders.[34]

The Law Lords further traced the origin of the sentence to its historical root in 1908.[35] Following the development in 1908 of the Children Act, the Children and Young Persons Act 1933 had stated clearly that detention at Her Majesty's pleasure was 'in lieu of' imprisonment for life. Thus, the sentence for children or young murderers has always been intended to be a less severe and a more merciful form of sentence in view of the age of the offender at the time of the offence. Though the notion of the tariff has been formulated and has been used for both categories of adult and young prisoners, it should not follow that the symmetry in name would lead to an exact result.[36] Lord Woolf expressly lamented that by a 'side wind', the sentencing of young offenders has ironically become 'materially more punitive'[37] and has defied its original intention.

Following the same line of argument that young offenders should be treated differently from adult murderers, the *Hussain* decision to put young offenders into the same category of adult prisoners under discretionary life imprisonment would be equally unsatisfactory. In other words, a tariff should not be interpreted as a minimum sentence for young offenders and it is not adequate to treat it as the maximum sentence. For young offenders, the tariff should represent only a target date for release. The House of Lords reiterated that the core of detention at Her Majesty's pleasure is that it is a flexible sentence which ought to accommodate a range of different situations. Namely, they are exceptional progress, rehabilitation and welfare

[33] ibid, quoted by Lord Woolf, at 414.
[34] ibid, 531.
[35] ibid, see judgments *per* Lord Woolf, *per* Lord Browne-Wilkinson, *per* Lord Hope and *per* Lord Steyn.
[36] ibid, 425.
[37] ibid, 426.

of the applicants. The Court has specifically relied on the United Nations Convention on the Rights of the Child. Article 3 of the Convention stipulates that the best interests of the child should be the primary concern of state institutions, which includes the court. Article 40(1) states that when a child is an accused in court, the state should act in the interests of the desirability of promoting the child's integration into society so that the child can assume a constructive role in society. The House of Lords is careful to confirm that detention at Her Majesty's pleasure has a definite penal and retributive element in the punishment and rightly so. Prevention of risk is also a legitimate concern. But the child's welfare should also be considered.[38] The crucial point is that detention at Her Majesty's pleasure should be sufficiently flexible to reconsider the position of the applicant from time to time in light of the development and progress of the child. In fact, Lord Browne-Wilkinson and Lord Hope suggested that a scaling down of the tariff should be warranted if the progress of the child is remarkable. It is the concept of continuing review, with the prospect of rehabilitation and release from custody that marks the uniqueness of the sentence.

As the House of Lords only condemned the then existing approach to young offenders detained at Her Majesty's pleasure without fixing a sentence for the applicants, the case went to the European Court of Human Rights in *V v United Kingdom*.[39] In a comparatively modest approach, the European Court upheld the decision of the English Court. It did not go as far as the English Court to rule that a tariff could be scaled down but it confirmed the ruling that the tariff-fixing policy deprived the right of the detainee to a periodic review of detention by a judicial body. Therefore a tariff should represent the maximum period of detention and serve to satisfy the requirements of retribution and deterrence. It is only legitimate to continue detention if this appears to be necessary for the protection of the public. As a result, *V v United Kingdom* is a midway between *Hussain* and *ex p Venables*. Essentially, it modifies the reasoning in *Hussain* and adds the requirement that the tariff must be set by a judicial body at the initial stage.

As a result, both the House of Lords and the European Court ruled that the interpretation of the tariff system has violated both procedural and substantive justice. In response to the judgments, the UK Parliament enacted the Criminal Justice and Court Services Act in 2000. The procedures for reviewing tariffs are not stated in the statute but the rule that the tariff represents the maximum sentence is stipulated in the statute. The applicants in *ex p Venables* were conditionally released in June 2001 and have assumed new identities to start their new lives.

Post-Colonial Deviation

While England has finally reformed its law in this area of the criminal justice system, Hong Kong has replicated the English mistakes. Worse, it legitimizes an objectionable exercise of executive discretion in its statutory provisions.

[38] [1998] AC, 500.

[39] (2000) 30 EHRR 121.

Prima facie, the Hong Kong position has adhered to the English position. After 1997, when a judge sentences a young offender who committed murder to life imprisonment, this would be equivalent to sentencing him to a discretionary life sentence.[40] In turn, under the Criminal Procedure Ordinance of 1997, a judge must specify the minimum sentence for discretionary life imprisonment.[41] Adding these two together, young offenders who are convicted of murder will no longer be detained at Her Majesty's pleasure, nor detained at Executive discretion. The 17 prisoners who were detained at Her Majesty's pleasure before 1997 are now being detained at the Executive's discretion. Under s 67C of the Criminal Procedure Ordinance, the Chief Justice submitted his recommendation to the Chief Executive specifying the minimum term for each of them after the political handover. Before making the recommendation, the prisoners were given the opportunity to make a written representation.

The above arrangement may have appeared reasonable and sensible. What is deeply disappointing is that the 'minimum' term recommended by the Chief Justice and adopted by the Chief Executive is being taken at its literal meaning, stripped of all the legal intricacies elaborated in the English and European courts. Effectively, 'minimum term' implies that the detention could be substantially longer. The Long Term Prison Sentences Review Board is not authorized to recommend early release before any minimum term is exhausted.[42] In other words, the young offenders cannot obtain remission on the grounds of good behaviour. The movie does not deal with any case law or the statute in detail. However, on hearing the final decision from the Chief Executive that the sentence is a 'minimum sentence', the young offenders in the movie not only break down in tears but are also on the verge of mental breakdown.

In reality, the legal battle continues. Two prisoners brought an action in judicial review similar to Venables and Thompson. Regrettably, unlike their English counterparts, they only gained a partial victory in *Yau Kwong Man v Secretary for Security*.[43] The issues in *Yau* are whether it is lawful for the Chief Executive to pass a minimum sentence on the young offenders and how the punitive term should be calculated.

The HKSAR High Court did not have any trouble in ruling that the Chief Executive has exceeded his power in passing a minimum sentence despite the fact that he was essentially endorsing the recommendation of the Chief Justice regarding the terms of imprisonment. What is most disappointing is that Justice Hartman distinguished the House of Lords and the European Court decision by adopting the narrowest interpretation of law. He upheld the legitimacy of the minimum sentence. To be specific, the Court ruled that the English approach after *Venables* is inapplicable to Hong Kong.

[40] Offences Against the Persons Ordinance (Cap 212).

[41] s 67B of the Criminal Procedure Ordinance (Cap 221).

[42] s 12 of the Long Term Prison Sentences Review Ordinance (Cap 524).

[43] HCAL 1595/2001 (unreported judgment), available at http://legalref.judiciary.gov.hk.

The Hong Kong Court reads much into the term 'minimum sentence'. In Justice Hartman's opinion, had Hong Kong's criminal justice system meant to follow the English approach, the Hong Kong system would have adopted the same term 'tariff'.[44] Rather than following the House of Lords and the European Court decision, the High Court felt itself bound by a previous decision in Hong Kong which had interpreted minimum term to be the 'minimum term of years which the convicted person must actually serve before release', emphasizing the caveat that 'minimum term' does not say 'that that is the stage at which the convicted individual is to be, or even should be, released'.[45]

Though Justice Hartman acknowledged the English approach that the tariff represents the 'imperatives of retribution and deterrence' and may constitute the full sentence to be served in most cases on condition that the prisoner no longer represents a risk to society, he was equally quick to point out that the assessment of minimum term in Hong Kong is just one of a broad range of matters that must be taken into account in determining when a prisoner is ready to be integrated back into society. The concern of rehabilitation must be assessed at the end of tariff as required by s 12 of the Long Term Sentence Review Board Ordinance.[46] Justice Hartman concluded that because the English system is markedly different from the Hong Kong position and the European Court decision is about the English system, *V v United Kingdom* is therefore irrelevant to Hong Kong.

It may well be true that the Hong Kong Legco intended that minimum sentence should simply mean absolute minimum. Nevertheless, it is an oversight to disregard the English position and to dismiss the significance of the European authority.

First, the Long Term Prison Sentence Ordinance was passed in a hurry just before the handover on 23 June 1997. As depicted in the movie, the welfare of prisoners was a minor issue compared with other more pressing concerns in those days of transition. It is most likely that none of the Legco members was aware of the House of Lords judgment.[47] *Ex p Venables* was only delivered on 12 June 1997.

Second, critics have pointed out that the distinction between 'minimum term' and a 'tariff' is a most artificial form of distinction.[48] In the English decision, the Law Lords used the two terms interchangeably.[49] Lord Hope has warned that the word 'tariff' risks replacing 'the duty of review with the blanket of rigidity'.[50] His prophecy was unfortunately fulfilled in Hong Kong.

[44] HCAL 1595/2001 (unreported judgment), available at http://legalref.judiciary.gov.hk., para 30.

[45] Justice Stock's reasoning in *HKSAR v Hui Chi Wai and others*, CACC 78/1999 (unreported judgment) at http://legalref.judiciary.gov.hk/, cited in para 31 of *Yau*.

[46] See n 43 above, paras 78, 80, 96.

[47] Neither the case nor the English development was discussed in the Legco Meeting on the Long Term Prison Sentence Review Ordinance. See Hong Kong Hansard, 23 June 1997 at http://yr96–97/English/lc-sitg/general/yr9697.htm.

[48] See Amanda Whitfort, 'Determining an Indeterminate Sentence', (2003) 33 HKLJ 35, 48.

[49] For instance, see *ex p Venables*, [1998] AC 407, judgments *per* Lord Woolf at 413 and 422, *per* Lord Browne-Wilkinson at 492–493 and Lord Hope at 537.

[50] [1998] AC 407, at 536.

Third, it is most unsatisfactory to exclude the concerns of rehabilitation and welfare of young offenders during the period of the minimum term. To treat and limit these elements only at the expiry of the minimum sentence is unfair to the youngsters. Throughout the judgment, Justice Hartman emphasizes that the English approach concentrates on the potential and perception of risk to society while the Hong Kong approach is to focus on rehabilitation.[51] To him, even if a prisoner is no longer a danger to society, it does not mean that he has been rehabilitated. These two are distinct concepts and should be handled in two different stages. The simple truth and logic, however, is that unless an offender has been fully rehabilitated, he will still present a risk to society. The close affinity between these two concepts is well illustrated in the words of Chief Justice Andrew Li. In his recommendation to the Chief Executive on the case of Ming,[52] he wrote:

> These murders were brutal. Unless and until he is rehabilitated, the Prisoner would present a danger to the public.

Chief Justice Li did not draw any distinction between 'risk to society' and 'rehabilitation'. To treat 'prevention of risk' and rehabilitation as two different stages is not only artificial but it is against the spirit of flexibility and leniency built into the nature of detention at Her Majesty's pleasure, of which the House of Lords has reminded us. Because of the immaturity and youth of the offenders at the time of committing the murder, continuing review and reconsideration are necessary. A rigid policy has resulted in young offenders, no matter how well they have progressed, spending their puberty, adolescence, and young adulthood behind bars.[53]

It is also perplexing as to how the Hong Kong Court has interpreted international jurisprudence. There is selective reading of the United Nations Convention on the Rights of the Child, which was extended to Hong Kong in 1994. The Court relied on article 37(a) to support its contention that detention under an indeterminate sentence is not unlawful under international treaty provided there is a possibility of release. What is missing from the Hong Kong Court discussion are articles 3(1) and 40(1), the clauses respectively on 'best interests' of the child and welfare of the child as mentioned in *ex p Venables*.

To brush aside the European Court decision on *Venables* on the ground that the English system is not applicable to Hong Kong is missing the core of the debate. While the minimum term is written into Hong Kong statute, its legitimacy is still subject to challenge under human rights jurisprudence. Under the present statutory regime, after serving the minimum period, the young offenders cannot challenge their detention before a court. Their representation before the Long Term Sentence Review Board personally or through a representative is subject to the consent of the Board. In other words, their rights to take proceedings before a court

51 See n 43 above, paras 107 and 109.

52 Ming in the movie is Cheung Yau Hang in real life. Letter from Chief Justice Andrew Li to Tung Chee Hwa, the Chief Executive of the HKSAR on the case of Cheung Yau Hang, 15 December 1997 (letter on file with author).

53 [1998] AC 407, *per* Lord Browne-Wilkinson at 494.

to challenge the lawfulness of their detention may possibly have been violated. This ground was argued in *V v United Kingdom*. The equivalent provision of article 5(4) of the European Convention is article 5(4) of the Hong Kong Bill of Rights.

The only hint and hope suggested by Justice Hartman is to resort to habeas corpus. Consequently, another action is pending before the Hong Kong court at the time of writing.

In asking the young offenders to wait first for Her Majesty's pleasure, then wait for a minimum sentence to end before deciding further, the whole procedure is like throwing away the prison key.[54] The triple irony in legal development is that the sentence has defied its original meaning, that Hong Kong's statute has crystallized the mistakes that the English system has corrected, and the post-colonial ruler has turned out to be tougher than the colonial master.

Law? What Law?

When the movie was filmed, the Yau's application had not started. It is not to be expected that legal reasoning in cases will be ironed out in a movie. It may very well already be a difficult challenge to the audience in asking them to digest the legal argument underlying the statutes, which the director has endeavoured to do.

On top of substantive legal argument, the absurdity in the criminal justice system is reflected and revealed in the movie through the images and sounds of law.

One notable feature in the movie is that most of the time law is faceless. Of all the six specific scenes in the movie that are law related, there is only one scene where a lawyer appears briefly for about one minute. The lawyer is nameless. He explains in his professional way to Leung that there is nothing that law can do to help the young offenders. Every time a sentence is handed down in the movie, law becomes 'faceless'. There is no court room drama, no judge and no jury. The initial sentence of detention at Her Majesty's pleasure is 'announced' through a mere voice. When the chief prison officer passes on the message from the Chief Executive on the minimum sentence to Ming, the camera only shows the back of the officer. When Leung discusses the matter with the Chief Executive, the camera again only shows the back of the Chief Executive.

The only significant legal image in the movie is the statue of the Lady of Justice. Whenever the movie shows any shots of the Legco debate, she is shown standing at the top of the Hong Kong Legco Building. The featuring of the Legco Building has rich symbolic significance. The building itself is a two-storey neo-classical structure in pink-grey granite, with Greco-Victorian Ionic columns, Chinese style roofs, and a dome. The carved stone figure of the Lady of Justice is above the main portico. The colonial style building and the Lady of Justice are conventional

[54] McDiarmid, n 18 above, 559, yet McDiarmid is only referring to the English position before reform.

images often used in movies. While the concept of justice may be diffuse and ambiguous to many, they remain powerful and enduring symbols that make social communication and understanding possible. In addition, the historical significance is that between 1912 and 1985 the building was the Supreme Court of Hong Kong. As a result, the Lady of Justice has witnessed both the judicial and legislative process in Hong Kong.

In particular, the Lady of Justice is commonly invoked as a personification of justice. She is draped in flowing robes, mature but not old, widely known as Justitia, the Roman goddess of justice.[55] She wears a blindfold, carries a sword in one hand, and holds an evenly balanced pair of scales in the other. The sword represents the power of the state and the scales are for the weighing of souls in accordance with the Egyptian Book of the Dead. Together they symbolize the paramount significance of law being 'fair and equal, without corruption, avarice, prejudice or favour'.[56] Different authors, however, have revealed that the blindfolded Justitia has an initial meaning contrary to the contemporary understanding.[57] The blindfold carries a negative implication of imbalance well illustrated by a 1494 famous wood engraving of a Fool covering the eyes of Justice.[58] The engraving suggests that the Lady of Justice has been 'robbed of her ability to get things straight'.[59] It is only after 1530 that the image was transformed into a positive emblem of impartiality and equality before the law.

Thus, the covered eyes of the Lady of Justice have a double meaning. The prisoners in real life and the movie director decide to show their frustration by returning to the original satirical meaning. The young offenders painted a picture of the Lady of Justice in their fight for a determinate sentence in 1997. The same design of this picture was later used as a book cover for *From the Queen to the Chief Executive*.[60] The original picture is used in the film.

The background of the picture is the Queen of Hearts card. The Lady of Justice is holding a slanted scale, with a prisoner in tears on one side crying out 'mayday mayday', the call for rescue at sea. The sword that the Lady of Justice is holding pierces the Children and Young Persons Act of 1933, the statute that clearly stipulates that young offenders should not be sentenced to life imprisonment as adult murderers. The left foot of the Lady of Justice is stepping on the Chinese characters for 'human rights'. The pedestal that the Lady of Justice is standing on is marked with the initials HK DAHMP, referring to detention at Her Majesty's pleasure. At the right hand corner of the picture is a badge divided equally between

[55] For a brief introduction to the historical and mythical origin of the Lady of Justice, see Barbara Swatt, *Themis, Goddess of Justice* (updated 11 June 2001), at http://lib.law.washington.edu/ref/themis.html.

[56] Answer to Question about Origin of Lady of Justice, at http://www.commonlaw.com/Justice.html.

[57] Eg, Steve Greenfield et al, *Film and the Law* (2001) 32 and Martin Jay, '*Must Justice Be Blind?*' in Costas Douzinas and Lynda Nead (eds), *Law and the Image* (Chicago, 1999).

[58] 'The Fool Ties the Eyes of Justice', from Sebastian Brant, *La nef des folz du monde* (Lyon, 1497), Bibliothèque Nationale, Paris.

[59] Martin Jay, n 57 above, 20.

[60] See n 7 above.

the bauhinia emblem of the HKSAR and the Crown symbol of the Queen of England. In addition, water is coming up to the knees of the Lady of Justice, slowly climbing up a measuring stick. The message is obvious. The Lady of Justice is blind to the tilted scale and helpless with regard to the water that comes up to her knees. The fate of the young offenders is taken as lightly as a simple card game.

The representation of law through sound and images is complemented by rhetorical expression. When Yue-ling first visits Ming, she does not know Ming's personal story but is only curious to find out why Ming is so keen to study law. She says that she cannot understand Ming's passion. To her, whenever she 'hears about law', she becomes scared. During the legal battle, Leung claims that law has become 'blind to the point of being unconscionably oppressive'.[61]

In addition, the protagonists who start the rescue mission are not the lawyer-heroes that one can find in most of the movies. In fact, the movie is adapted from the book but the role of the lawyer in the book is deliberately cut out. All the law agents in the movie remain unmoved by the tales of the young offenders. While the prison social worker supports release of the young offenders as all of them are model prisoners, the prison wardens are not sympathetic. They mock the prisoners' fight. The hero and heroine who are willing to help do not possess any legal training. Their virtues are not based on legal knowledge or advocacy skills. Rather, they are based on the noble qualities of courage and compassion in helping an unpopular group of youngsters to the extent that they will incur displeasure and rejection by a large majority of society. Leung is a Legco member, representing the grassroots and labour workers. Yue-ling is an immigrant from the Mainland, forced to be on the fringe of Hong Kong society.[62] Different from many Hong Kong residents, she has the compassion to fight for the offenders though she is not related to any of them. Another irony is that the actor who is chosen to play the role of Leung is Stephen Tang, a lawyer turned actor.[63]

Together, the forms of representation of law in the movie add up to show that, to the young offenders and many of us, law is a mere voice, cold, faceless and blind.

The Macro Moral Concern of Forgiveness

Without dispute, the movie is an accusation against the criminal justice system. Indirectly, it is advocating for legal reform and is keen to push for change. But it would be an understatement and an oversimplification to limit the changes that the movie envisages to legal reform. It is a movie about a battle attempting to achieve not only legal justice but also social justice and even to gain ground in the moral field.

The upbringing of Ming is recounted in the movie. Ming is a teenage boy, brought up in an orphanage, later adopted by his own father just for the sake of

[61] In Chinese, the expression is 'ma mu bu ren'.
[62] Ai-jin was chosen to play the role of Yue-ling. Ai-jin is a rock singer in the Mainland.
[63] Stephen Tang is an acclaimed theatre actor in Hong Kong.

getting government housing accommodation but soon kicked out by his step-mother. Ming falls in with a group of gangsters, gets involved in the gruesome Braemar Hill murders and has spent his life locked behind bars since he was 16 years old. Similar stories of other offenders are also covered and explained, though to a lesser extent. All of them are based on real life episodes. Through the words of Leung, the message is clear—problematic youngsters are the products of a problematic society. The movie does not defend the murders carried out by the youngsters. Instead, the lesson is that each individual lives in relation to one another. We are locked in chains and our conduct has triggered a succession of causes and effects, affecting one another. Our present aloof attitude may affect our future generation or may even backfire on us one day. Watching society locking up young offenders behind bars for an indefinite period and doing nothing, we are not being responsible to ourselves. It only reflects an overwhelming penal and vengeful attitude on our part.

Thus, Leung in the uphill battle is fighting not only for a determinate sentence, but also leading an unpopular social course, fighting for a transformation of social attitude. He is rejected by his colleagues in Legco. His own assistants threaten to resign. His supporters express reservations in voting for him as he helps convicted murderers. Even the families of the young offenders are reluctant to be identified with the prisoners. Unless society's attitude is willing to change, the battle is unlikely to be successful.

As the story progresses, one notices that the movie is not merely about the crime of murder, it is about sin and forgiveness. The religious connotation behind the notion of forgiveness is foreshadowed at the beginning of the movie when Leung approaches the Chief Executive. Other than the reply that the Chief Executive is ignorant about his power to commute the sentence to a definite term, his response is to inquire about whether the young offenders have any religious belief. To him, this is enough as a form of liberation and solace. The tone of the movie is, thus, set at this early stage.

Ming is not the only one who has sinned by committing the crime of murder. The other two main characters have also 'sinned'.

Yue-ling comes to Hong Kong as a teenage girl, suffering from loneliness and rejection; she mistakes the sexual exploitation that her uncle inflicts upon her as a kind of love and care. Out of jealousy, she attempts to kill her aunt. She fails but her aunt is crippled and she is kicked out of the house by her mother. At one point in the movie, after Yue-ling has read the newspaper reporting on the Braemar Hill murders, she cannot accept Ming and his past. She hesitates to continue to fight for him. It is only when she realizes that she is also a 'sinner' that she musters her courage and faith to help Ming. She also comes to the realization that the only difference between herself and Ming is that she was never caught by the police.

While Leung assumes the role of the hero, righteous and proper in public, his family is falling apart. His wife asks for a divorce. His seven year old son is angry at him for Leung has never kept his promise to spend time with his family. Whenever his son makes the request, he will deliver an 'indeterminate' answer by saying 'later'.

Towards the end of the movie, the theme of forgiveness is most outstanding. Because the families of the victims of the Braemar Hill murders wrote to the Governor and asked for leniency for Ming,[64] the characters are awakened by this incident. Yue-ling goes back to the squatter area to visit her mother and reconcile with her. Leung realizes that the trust between him and his son has been badly shaken and asks for 'forgiveness' from his son. He also wins back the understanding from his wife. Before Ming attempts suicide, which he fails, he writes to the victims' families to ask for forgiveness. Through the stories of Ming, Leung and Yue-ling, the movie imparts to the audience the knowledge that in one way or another, each one of us is a perpetuator of suffering and sin and each one is also the victim.

Despite the fact that human hearts may soften, law remains coldly unresponsive in the movie, as in real life. Ming is still in prison for an unknown period of time. The hope projected in the movie, is not a definite date, but understanding and forgiveness. The last scene of the movie features Yue-ling in the long corridor of a housing estate, knocking on one of the nameless doors, looking for Ming's mother. The answer is negative but she keeps on explaining the story of Ming and the scene goes black only with the sound of the conversation going on. The wish that Ming cherishes, other than to be released, is to find his mother. the person with whom he longs to restore a loving relationship. With this fervent hope to build a relationship, Yue-ling is knocking on the door of each one of us, explaining the story of the youngsters, asking for our understanding and forgiveness.

Conclusion

To complete the motif of irony, the movie is highly acclaimed and has won international awards[65] but it is a box office disaster. It is widely discussed in the media but the prisoners are still behind bars. It is caught in a double discourse of accusing the unfairness of the criminal justice system but begging for mercy for the young offenders. In sum, the stories of the young offenders may leave many pondering on the rationality of Hong Kong's criminal justice system, cruelty in society, and the ironies of life.

The fate of the young offenders in the movie urges us to reconsider the aim of punishment and the nature of incarceration. Orthodox teaching of criminology and penology tells us that the aims of imprisonment are punishment, deterrence, protection of community and rehabilitation. The critical problem of the present criminal justice system in Hong Kong regarding the young offenders is exactly that

[64] According to Herman Yau, the victims' families wrote to the Governor but the content is unknown. It is generally believed that they asked for leniency for the murderers as the families were converted to Christianity after the tragedy. Interview with Herman Yau, n 8 above.

[65] It was the official selection of the 51st Berlin International Film Festival and was the opening film of Panorama in 2001.

it has misplaced them in the continuum of punishment and rehabilitation. Writing about the English system in this regard, critics argue that the tough law and order regime reflects a 'deeply punitive and retributive constituency'[66] within contemporary society. One treats young offenders, particularly child murderers, as demons that are difficult, if not impossible, for us to forgive.

The solution, as the movie suggests, seems to lie in virtues yet to be offered by the criminal justice system. They are human compassion and forgiveness, virtues not catered for by legal institutions and legal rules. Criminal law is mainly about order and punishment, while justice is an ambiguous concept mixed with ideology, rules and subjective interpretation. Combining the two sets of logic together has only yielded an answer that focuses on the redress of wrongs of the past and a system that is overwhelmingly vindictive. An alternative vision of justice that can accommodate wrongs and their redress, punishment and forgiveness is offered by the movie. This powerful yet humane form of justice, in turn, needs to be sustained by elements beyond law.

After watching the movie, one may be deeply interested in the criminal justice system and may even be deeply moved by the stories of the young offenders. But movies, bound by their nature, can only deal with stories of crime but not elaborate legal reasoning. Law, by its nature, can only deal with crime and punishment but not sin and its expiation.

[66] Deena and Phil Scraton, ' "Condemn a Little More, Understand a Little Less" The Political Context and Rights Implications of the Domestic and European Rulings in the Venables-Thompson Case' (2000) 27 *J of Law and Society* 416, 422.

PART VI

LAW, SEXUALITY, AND THE POPULAR CULTURE

It's about *This*: Lesbians, Prison, Desire

*Jenni Millbank**

[Helen, the Prison Wing Governor, enters a garden shed where Nikki, a prisoner, is working.]

NIKKI: Here comes the blushing bride to be—you kept that quiet didn't you.
HELEN: Sean had just asked me to marry him. Not that it's any of your business, actually.
NIKKI: Why are you telling me then?
HELEN: I really don't know, but I certainly don't need to explain myself to you.
NIKKI: Fine.
HELEN: You know . . . for some odd reason it seems to upset you that Sean and I are getting married
NIKKI: Odd reason, that's a good one!
HELEN: Nikki, what the hell is this about?
NIKKI: You really don't know?
HELEN: If I knew I won't be asking you would I?
NIKKI: You wanna know what this is about? It's about *this*.
[Nikki grabs Helen's hand and clasps it to her own breast.]
HELEN: Jesus Christ !!!!

(Bad Girls, Series 1, Episode 7)

Lesbians, as symbols, are disruptive and highly charged. They evoke active, autonomous female sexuality; women as sexual subjects and sexual objects—desirous and desirable to each other. It is therefore entirely predictable that in mainstream culture lesbians are still very often characterized—when they appear at all[1]—as violently transgressive. In film, lesbian characters have been closely associated with film noir, women-in-prison and horror genres where they often symbolize the abject, the depraved, the anti-social.[2]

* Many thanks to the organizers of the *Mediating Law* Conference 2002 and to Kirsten Anker, Didi Herman, and Mehera San Roque for their comments on an earlier draft of this paper and Tiffany Hambley for her invaluable research assistance.

1 See Renee Hoogland, *Lesbian Configurations* (New York: 1997).

2 See, eg, Andrea Weiss, *Vampires and Violets: Lesbians in the Cinema* (London: Jonathan Cape, 1992); Patricia White, 'Female Spectator, Lesbian Specter: The Haunting' in Diana Fuss (ed), *Inside/Out: Lesbian Theories, Gay Theories* (New York: 1991); Mary Wings, 'Rebecca Redux: Tears on a Lesbian Pillow' in Liz Gibbs (ed), *Daring to Dissent: Lesbian Culture from Margin to Mainstream* (London: 1994); Rhonda Berenstein, ' "I'm not the sort of person men marry": Monsters, Queers and

In earlier work I argued that the trend of portraying lesbians as violent aggressors, usually with men as their victims, worked as a 'cruel reversal' when in fact lesbians continue to suffer high levels of violence usually at the hands of heterosexual men.[3] I have argued that such portrayals do contribute to a culture of anti-lesbian discrimination and violence by normalizing it as a form of self defence or just desert.

While theorists such as Lynda Hart have thoroughly interrogated the manner in which 'the shadow of the lesbian is laminated to the representation of women's violence',[4] a number of queer theory and post-modern cultural studies works through the 90s revived pop-cultural images of transgressive lesbians in a less critical and rather more celebratory tone.[5] Several writers have even 'rehabilitated', in a cultural sense, the image of the lesbian killer. One reason for this is that, in the words of Cherry Smyth, the 'tyranny of positive images' has now:

> shifted so much that lesbians who wield ice-picks . . . can be embraced without the movement collapsing under the burden of their irresponsibility. A lesbian heroine who kills . . . is not immediately dissed as an inappropriate role model. We are now more irreverent and robust . . .[6]

Yet hegemonic imagery of insanely aggressive lesbians does produce real material effects on how lesbians are treated within the criminal justice system.[7] So, while I concur with post-modern and queer theorists in rejecting reductive readings of cultural texts as if they contained and passed on simple 'messages' about sex and sexuality, I still have grave concerns about what it means to represent lesbians in a context in which they are presumed to be inherently violent. But where does that leave us with stories of violent lesbians, or with true stories? In earlier work, I asked the question: why choose these particular lesbians, why tell these stories? I did not answer this question, afraid then as I am now, that it would lead to a 'tyranny of positive images' implication that we should overlook, or even self-censor, such stories, or worse, that lesbians would be reduced to assimilation into dominant

Hitchcock's *Rebecca*' in Corey Creekmur and Alexander Doty (eds), *Out in Culture: Gay, Lesbian and Queer Essays on Popular Culture* (Durham: Duke University Press, 1995) 236–261; Valerie Traub, 'The Ambiguities of "Lesbian" Viewing Pleasure: The (Dis)articulations of Black Widow' in Creekmur and Doty, ibid, 115–136.

[3] Jenni Millbank, 'From Butch to Butcher's Knife: Film, Crime and Lesbian Sexuality' (1996) 18 *Sydney L Rev* 451–473.

[4] Lynda Hart, *Fatal Women: Lesbian Sexuality and the Mark of Aggression* (London: 1994), x; see also Barbara Creed, *The Monstrous-Feminine: Film, Psychoanalysis, Feminism* (London: 1993); Lisa Duggan, *Sapphic Slashers: Sex, Violence and American Modernity* (Durham: 2000).

[5] eg Shameem Kabir, 'Lesbian Desire on the Screen: The Hunger' in Gibbs, n 2 above; Tanya Krzwinska, 'La Belle Dame Sans Merci?' in Paul Burston and Colin Richardson (eds), *A Queer Romance: Lesbians, Gay Men and Popular Culture* (New York: 1995).

[6] Cherry Smyth, 'The Transgressive Sexual Subject' in Burston and Richardson, n 5 above, 125.

[7] See, eg, Kathryn Farr, 'Defeminising and Dehumanising Female Murderers: Depictions of Lesbians on Death Row' (2000) 11 *Women and Criminal Justice* 49–66; Diana Fishbein, 'Sexual Preference, Crime and Punishment' (2000) 11 *Women and Criminal Justice* 67–84; Ruthann Robson, *Lesbian Outlaw: Survival Under the Rule of Law* (Ithaca: 1992) 109.

ideology, defined by it through attempting to oppose it. Opposing hetero-normative imagery of aggressive, pathologized lesbians through producing '*pro*-social' images of 'normal' feminine lesbians arguably conforms to, and reinscribes, rather than undoes dominant cultural codes of gender and sexuality.[8] In essence, I am not convinced that *Ellen* (1994–1998) or *Kissing Jessica Stein* (2002, wr: Juergensen & Westfeldt, dir: Herman-Wurmfeld) are ultimately any more non-normative than *Basic Instinct* (1992, wr: Eszterhas, dir: Verhoeven). So, to reverse my earlier question: for those of us who are committed to querying social norms on the basis of a progressive, queer or feminist politic, why *shouldn't* lesbians be anti-social?

Ruthann Robson, in her book, *Lesbian Outlaw*, developed the concept of 'domestication' to consider the ways in which lesbians have become implicated in and dependent upon, oppressive legal and social structures. Domestication, she argues, 'occurs when the views of the dominant culture are so internalised that they seem like common sense'.[9] I think that the past ten years have witnessed a dramatic domestication of lesbian and gay political struggles in the developed world, with a heavy—indeed now virtually exclusive—emphasis upon assimilation through marriage, family and capitalist relations.[10] The frame of reference for our struggles has shifted inexorably from liberation to equality to inclusion. But as Ruthann says, 'domestication also contains within it that idea of its opposite . . . there is the possibility of a feral future'.[11] In this context of domestication, and with the hope for a feral future, I think that a feminist and lesbian-centred revival of the lesbian outlaw is timely and full of possibilities. The lesbian outlaw returns our attention to both *the lesbian* and *the law* and in doing so opens space to revisit the long lost quest of *liberation* which has been elided through our focus on assimilation. So, I will argue against my earlier position and suggest that perhaps—at least these three—lesbian outlaw tales are indeed the very stories that are worth telling at this moment.

In this paper I explore three narratives of violently transgressive lesbians in a prison setting. The stories are two English novels, *Nights at the Circus* by Angela Carter (1984), *Affinity* by Sarah Waters (1999) and an English TV series, titled in an apparently tongue in cheek moment, *Bad Girls* (1999-ongoing). What links these three tales, and the reason I have chosen them, is that their portrayal of transgressive sexuality posits such transgression as not only normal, but necessary, important and desirable. All of the stories are authored or originated (in the case of the TV series[12]) by feminist women. In each the transgressive impact of lesbianism

[8] Laura Cottingham, *lesbians are so chic* (New York: 1996); Hoogland, n 1 above, 46.

[9] Robson, n 7 above, 20.

[10] See Ruthann Robson, 'To Market, To Market: Considering Class', reproduced in *Sappho Goes to Law School: Fragments in Lesbian Legal Theory* (New York: 1998); and David Skover and Kellye Testy, 'LesBiGay Identity as Commodity' (2002) 90 *California L Rev* 223–255.

[11] Robson, n 7 above, 18.

[12] The two producers, Maureen Chadwick and Eileen Gallagher, and script executive, Ann McManus, devised the series together, and also wrote some of the scripts. Although many scripts in the series are written and most directed by men, Chadwick and McManus edit all scripts and state that they have re-written many of those that do not credit them as writers; Maureen Chadwick and Ann McManus, *Q&A 2002*, online at www.badgirls.co.uk/fansite/interviews (accessed 16 August 2002). This paper focuses

is deliberately centred as a *positive* force at the heart of the narrative. As with hegemonic images of violent lesbians, the lesbian characters and their desires *are* explicitly representative of a threat to the family and the social order. However, unlike the general trend of hetero-normative imagery, the authorial voice, style of characterization, and critical context of each narrative make it clear that this is a very good thing indeed. The authors question oppressive legal and social systems, exemplified by the coercive force of the prison, and they offer implicit and explicit support for an anti-social challenge to these normative systems. Each story suggests lesbianism as a rupture that crosses, and thereby dissolves, the hierarchical lines of gaoler and prisoner—both literally and figuratively freeing the women imprisoned.

In this paper I touch on a number of disruptive and counter-hegemonic aspects that run through these stories including their portrayal of violence as a reasonable response to oppressive social conditions, a distinct problematizing of heterosexuality and the metaphor of a prison panopticon to explore the constraints imposed on all women's lives. The main focus of the paper is on the role of lesbian desire. I argue that the representation of lesbian desire in all three tales is truly radical in that it acts to dissolve unequal power dyads, although I also come to question the extent to which it is possible, even in fiction, to sustain such rupture in the face of dominant cultural imperatives to 're-capture' and 'domesticate' homo-normative images.

Three Tales

This paper posits that all three of the narratives I focus upon are *homo-normative* in that they centre and naturalize lesbian perspectives and experience. Didi Herman defines homo-normativity as a perspective that 'represents gay and lesbian identity as normal, natural, good and unremarkable in and of itself' as well as offering an 'insider common sense' way of looking that is 'rooted in lesbian and gay sub-cultures'.[13] This is in a sense all the more remarkable when they are placed at the heart of what has traditionally been one of the most exploitative and lesophobic fictional settings or genres: the women-in-prison story.[14]

Nights at the Circus, the eighth of Angela Carter's nine novels, is a burlesque, fantastical and densely inter-textual tale centring on the exploits of Fevvers, the Cockney Venus. Fevvers claims to have been born with wings, raised virginal in a whorehouse and to have worked for a time in a museum of female monstrosities

exclusively on the first three series: 1999–2001. Chadwick and McManus described themselves in a 2001 interview as 'straight-down-the-line, dyed-in-the-wool, committed, do-or-die, go-to-the-wall, in-your-face feminists' (cited in Didi Herman, 'Bad Girls Changed My Life: Homonormative Values in a Women's Prison Drama' (2003) *Critical Studies in Media Communication* 141).

[13] Herman, n 12 above.

[14] See Beverly Zalcock and Jocelyn Robinson, 'Inside Cell Block H: Hard Steel and Soft Soap' (1996) 9 *Continuum* 88–97; see also Judith Mayne, *Framed: Lesbians, Feminist and Media Culture* (Minneapolis: 2000).

before finding her vocation as an aerial artiste in a travelling circus. The story is set at the brink of the 'new' century, the 20th century, and Fevvers is the New Woman. In the midst of Fevvers' brash and bawdy tale, full of Carter's complex, surreal and satiric meditations on women's sexual and economic freedom, there is an almost entirely self-contained chapter concerning a Siberian women's prison. This private prison is the dreadful scheme of Countess P, located in the midst of a wilderness, housing entirely women who have killed their husbands. It is a penitentiary designed to prompt penitence, and the Countess sits at the centre of a panopticon watching her inmates for signs of contrition. The women are kept isolated and forbidden to speak or to look at each other or the guards; they are able to leave the prison only through death. The guards too are women, and are likewise trapped in the wilderness. An uprising eventually occurs in the prison, brought about through the clasped hands and met eyes of one woman and her guard. The women escape with their lovers, the guards, and set off to found the republic of free women. It is a self consciously utopian story told in the bald, spare style of a fairy tale, indeed it is almost a morality tale in form, in that all characters play out their roles as symbols. This section of the novel has been utterly ignored by almost all critical commentary, as readers do not seem to know what to make of it, or how it connects to the novel as a whole.

This set-piece, like the main story in the novel, is centred on a female community. In my view, it also parallels a sub-plot in the main story, the lesbian love affair between two other characters, Mignon and the Princess, who are part of the travelling circus in which Fevvers performs. Mignon is a bedraggled young woman who has been misused and abused by a series of men. The Princess of Abyssinia (actually a rough lass from Marseille) works in the circus where her act involves playing the piano to dancing tigers. When Mignon is rescued from her violent male partner, Fevvers introduces her to the Princess as a vocal accompanist for the tiger act. The Princess does not speak, and she and Mignon do not share a common language in any case, but they fall in love through their music. Later in the story, they leave the cages of the circus and form a musical community in the wilds of Siberia, where they find refuge in the house of an elderly man who was once a music professor. Tigers come from the woods and lie on the roof of the house to hear them. They, and the tigers, are freed, and like the Siberian prison escapees, they set up an idealistic and idealised, new community.

Through the measureless wilderness around them roamed the savage audience for which the women must make a music never before heard on earth although it was not the music of the spheres but of blood, of flesh, of sinew, of the heart.

This music, proclaimed Mignon, they had been born to make. Had been brought together, as women and as lovers, solely to make—music that was at the same time a taming and a not-taming; music that sealed the pact of tranquillity between humankind and their wild brethren, their wild sistern, yet left them free.[15]

[15] Angela Carter, *Nights at the Circus* (London 1984) 275.

These two lesbian storylines also arguably parallel that of the heterosexual heroine, Fevvers, in that she is constantly escaping imprisonment, whether from the Female Monsters Museum or the Grand Duke who literally wants to put her into a gilded cage.

Affinity, the second novel by Sarah Waters, centres on a women's prison in central London in the 1870s. Millbank Prison is also a panopticon, like the prison in *Nights at the Circus*, in which the prisoners are kept silent and ever under watch. Unlike Carter's fantastical form and style, *Affinity* is based on an actual prison and is darkly detailed in its historical frame of reference,[16] although it, too, contains supernatural elements. The story is told through the not quite parallel diary entries of two women, Margaret the Lady Visitor, and Selina the prisoner. Margaret's point of view is the principal one, as she becomes increasingly obsessed with Selina and struggles with her own fragile mental health and the oppression of both the brutal prison regime and her family life at home. Selina is a spiritualist and the narrative is infused with questions about her history as Margaret is afraid to, and yet wants to, believe in her powers. Margaret colludes with Selina to procure her escape, but nothing is ultimately what it seems.

Bad Girls is an ITV television series in its fifth year. Unlike the literary *Nights* and *Affinity*, it is a popular cultural product pitched somewhere between the quality drama and soap opera genres (although *Affinity* is in the process of being adapted for a three part BBC series). The show is set in a London women's prison, Larkhall, G wing. Although this narrative is contemporary, unlike the two novels which are set in the Victorian era, it has interesting Victorian resonances. Larkhall prison is visually an unmistakably Victorian era prison. The producers also stated at the outset that they chose to have a forbidden lesbian relationship at the heart of the series because they wanted to create a love story with 'an almost Victorian sense of thwarted passion'.[17] The show is an ensemble piece, with a stable of main characters, but the first two series focused heavily on the attraction and developing relationship between Nikki Wade, a lesbian serving life for murder, and the new young affianced female wing-governor, Helen Stewart. While the producers claimed high social ideals for the series,[18] it was received as 'trashy' by most critics

[16] The novel includes accurate historical detail such as the 'silent system' and 'separate system', the fabric of the dresses, punitive labour involving picking apart tar encrusted rope (coir), a 'star' class of prisoners, the 'darks' (punishment cell), 'breaking out' (violent outbursts) and fumigation in sulphur of personal property (see Lucia Zedner, *Women, Crime and Custody in Victorian England* (Oxford: 1991)). But note Aiden Day's argument that, despite the fantastic elements in *Nights at the Circus*, 'for all its flamboyant craziness, it makes sense *specifically in relation to* the historical context that is sketched in by Carter' (Aiden Day, *Angela Carter, The Rational Glass* (Manchester: 1998)).

[17] Megan Radclyffe, 'Thwarted Passions' (undated, c 2000), online at www.geocities.com/simone_lahbib_online/articles33.jpg (accessed 28 March 2003).

[18] Maureen Chadwick states that she was 'inspired' by meeting the founder of the campaigning group Women in Prison, Chris Tchaikovsky. Tchaikovsky was an adviser on the series and some incidents are based on her observations and experiences (Chadwick and McManus, n 12 above). The current official website 'Library' section is filled with fact sheets and social science data provided by prison groups Payback and The Centre for Crime and Justice Studies: see www.badgirls.co.uk/library/

and reviewers.[19] The series has had consistently high ratings in the UK, averaging 7 million viewers for the first series and between 8 and 9 million viewers thereafter. It tops its timeslot in the under 35 audience,[20] and 60 per cent of its audience are women.[21] The series also inspired a large and mostly lesbian cult following, which was responsible for developing over 100 internet sites.[22] The official website alone recorded over 300,000 hits through the course of the third series.[23]

Homicide Might be the Only Way for Her to Preserve a Shred of Dignity

In these three stories, lesbians are imprisoned for violent crimes. In *Affinity* Selina Dawes is imprisoned for fraud and assault upon a young girl, in *Nights at the Circus*, all the inmates have killed their husbands, and in *Bad Girls* Nikki Wade is convicted of murder for stabbing a police officer. The use of violence by women is not pathologized and indeed considerable steps are taken to rationalize or even justify the use of violence by women to defend their own safety. The characters respond violently to their circumstances, but the narratives frame and interrogate these circumstances, rather than simply portraying violent, irrational or out-of-control lesbians. Sexuality is implicated in each crime, but never posited as causal.

In *Nights at the Circus* it is *heterosexuality* that is the problematized site of the violence as it takes place within violent heterosexual marriages. Carter frames and expressly justifies the actions as self defence with her classic insouciance:

> There are many reasons, most of them good ones, why a woman should want to murder her husband; homicide might be the only way for her to preserve a shred of dignity at a time, in a place, where women were deemed to be chattels . . . But it turned out the court thought otherwise than she . . .[24]

And when the women rise up and escape, leaving the Countess behind, locked in her own creation, they do so as a unified 'army of lovers'. It is the Countess, not the prisoners, individually or collectively, who bears responsibility for her fate.

libindex.htm (accessed 30 November 2004). Angela Devlin quotes Ann McManus that, '[t]he drama was written because we were so shocked by what we saw in women's prisons', but Devlin goes on to suggest that the show is a 'criminal waste of meticulous research'. Angela Devlin, 'They'll be laughing in their cells', *The Independent*, 22 June 1999.

19 Tina Ogle, 'How the Bad Girls came good', *The Observer*, 10 June 2001.

20 ibid.

21 Chadwick and McManus, n 12 above; Veronica Lee, 'Come and have a go', *Independent on Sunday*, 6 February 2002.

22 Many of the sites were lesbian-orientated or lesbian-run, and a selection have built large international lesbian fan-communities through their interactive message boards—many of which have spilled over into 'real' life through a range of community events (monthly meet-ups, fund-raisers, special events to coincide with series finales, etc).

23 James Rampton, 'Locked up with the pouting lip-gloss lifers', *Express on Sunday*, 21 January 2001.

24 Carter, n 15 above, 211.

The murder in *Bad Girls* is likewise justified in that Nikki was protecting her partner from a police officer who was attempting to rape her. Again it is a heterosexual locus—in this instance men's sexualized violence specifically against lesbians—that engenders the female character's violent response. It is perhaps more remarkable that Nikki's violence is not portrayed as out of character, but rather as an integral part of her character. Her bravery borders on recklessness as she is unable to stand by while injustice occurs, and uses violence when and if necessary to challenge it. Nikki continues to be violent throughout the series: while on occasion this is retaliation when Nikki is herself attacked, her aggression is far more commonly in the service of others as she repeatedly protects other women. Nikki is not simply excused for being violent; she is frequently portrayed as heroic. Nikki is the moral and political centre of her environment, and this is no accident: the producers stated publicly that she was the 'political heart'[25] of the show and her character 'spoke for' their own values.[26]

Only in *Affinity* is there any sense of ambivalence over the heroine's crime, and that is interesting in itself as she is the least serious offender of the three. Selina is also the most apparently innocent of the offending women, and is more traditionally feminine in that she is young, sensitive and waif-like. Selina claims that the assault was committed by a naughty male spirit—her 'control' Peter Quick—and not by her. The complex unfolding of the narrative, layered in diaries, leaves this mystery open until very late in the book, but the milieu of spiritualism is explored as an environment in which a young, poor, orphaned working class woman could become a powerful and courted figure. Lynda Hart notes that it was a well-established convention of Victorian-villainess literature that the woman accused was frequently innocent or an unknowing accomplice to a male mastermind.[27] It is particularly subversive then, that the 'man' behind Selina's crime is not a man, or a spirit, but her lover and former maid. Selina *is* a fraud, but of an unexpected kind, and the story must then be read in reverse—revealing, in my view, a rather sly admiration for her ingenuity. Sarah Waters has repeatedly stated that she writes for a lesbian audience[28] and it is possibly this sense of insider knowledge that meant *Affinity* did not need to be as utopian or as 'positive' as *Nights at the Circus* or *Bad Girls*. In writing for lesbians, there is far greater latitude to write homo-normatively but also to not structure characters *in opposition to* hetero-normative constraints.

Being, Not Happening to Be

The narratives are all homo-normative in that the lesbianism of the characters is unquestioned and naturalized. There is no cause, no spectacle offered by 'coming out' and no explanation offered for how they got there. In *Bad Girls*, several

[25] Chadwick and McManus, n 12 above. [26] Cited in Herman, n 12 above.

[27] Hart, n 4 above, 30.

[28] See, eg, Kate Muir, 'What the Butler Didn't See', *The Times*, 5 October 2002.

characters are placed as out lesbians from the very outset, with no back-story of when, why, etc; they simply *are*. The series does not focus upon 'situational' lesbianism which is a staple of the 'sex starved' women-in-prison genre. Nikki, as well as two younger women, Denny and Shaz, are all dykes. Nikki, in particular, is not an apolitical lesbian; she is expressly aligned with feminist politics and this forms the basis of her initial bond with Helen.[29] Indeed, there are quite political aspects to the foregrounding of Nikki's lesbianism, as in early episodes *Bad Girls* highlights not lesbian sexuality but homophobia. Nikki is identified as lesbian in the early episodes through the homophobic taunts of fellow lifer Shell and prison officer Jim Fenner: it is *their* prejudice that is spotlighted.

In *Affinity*, in the repressed 1870s, Margaret has already had a relationship with another woman, and her desire for women is linked to her quest for personal, political and intellectual freedom. While Margaret's prison visits are initially an expression of her feminist politic, they become increasingly focused on her desire to see Selina. Like Nikki in *Bad Girls*, Margaret's lesbianism is an unquestioned given, but is not deprived of its context or political implications—it is not a love story where one just 'happens to be' a woman. Margaret's status as a 'spinster' renders her vulnerable to pressure from her family and sexual suspicion from the prison matrons. As a sexual and social subject, Margaret is belittled, surveilled and deprived of liberty. In neither home nor prison does Margaret accept her given place. Margaret's rejection of feminine family duties, her prison visits and her unacknowledged lesbianism are all intuitively connected by her mother who senses the danger of her non-conformity. 'Your place is here!' her mother snaps:

> . . . you must take up your proper duties in the house. Your place is here, your place is here. . . . She could not bear to have her friends believe me weak, or *eccentric*—she almost spat the word at me. 'You are not Mrs Browning, Margaret, as much as you would like to be. You are not, in fact, Mrs Anybody. You are only *Miss Prior*. And your place—how often must I say it?—your place is here, at your mother's side.[30]

In *Nights at the Circus* lesbianism appears only as lesbian desire, not as a separately experienced identity. Lesbianism arises through a recognition or a dawning between women, as they look at and truly see each other (or listen to, and truly hear, in the case of Mignon and the Princess). Love is a natural response to the recognition of each other's humanity. This naturalization of lesbian desire is also true, to a lesser extent, in the representation of women who are initially coded or identified as heterosexual in the texts and who become involved in a lesbian relationship. In *Nights*, all of the women were originally in heterosexual marriages, in *Bad Girls* Helen lives with a man, and identifies herself both as 'a heterosexual' and 'engaged to be married', while in *Affinity* Selina does not apparently have a relationship history or any sexuality identification (and such a blank is still typically read as a heterosexual default). Yet the characters in each story respond to their own desire for another woman, and hers for them, in a fairly matter of fact way. These things happen.

[29] See Robson, n 10 above, Ch 6.

[30] Sarah Waters, *Affinity* (London 1999) 252–253.

While coming-out stories, and particularly the love-across-the-lines love story in which a straight woman converts to lesbianism are common staples of both hetero-normative and lesbian-centred cultural texts,[31] these three tales do not replicate the journey to/realization of true lesbian self (or indeed the brief dabble and return to true heterosexual self) format. Rather, female sexuality is present as fluid and permeable rather than fixed or essential, and characters exercise a range of choices at different times about their sexuality and relationships.

Desire

Sally Munt argues that heroic lesbian images are transformative on a number of levels:

> We might also say 'desire' is that wild zone, and that 'Heroic Desire' is the engine of the machine which produces imaginative lesbian identities. This is an emancipatory journey that assumes intersections between the phantasmatic and the real and that reading therefore performs a simultaneous function of escape and transformation, throwing the reader back into a perceptibly changed world on her return. Crucially this metamorphosis takes place through a process of identification and desire—we want the hero, and we want to *be* the hero; the phallic economy of either/or is superseded.[32]

Perhaps the most potentially radical aspect of these three tales is in their depiction of lesbian desire as producing both personal transformation and structural social change. The prisoner in each tale is freed through her desire.

A common archetype of lesbian relationships is that of narcissistic mirroring—with women visually paired, or engaged in deranged mimicry, à la *Single White Female* (1992, wr: Roos, dir: Schroeder) or *Basic Instinct* (1992 wr: Eszterhas, dir: Verhoeven).[33] The phallic economy of subject/object, desiring/desired, mentioned by Sally Munt, is unable to accommodate female sexual agency or attraction between two desiring female subjects. So *wanting* a woman is collapsed into, and contained by, *wanting to be* that woman. Within such a framework lesbian desire is made sterile and de-sexualized, it circles back in on and is consumed by the self. This conflation of desire with identification has featured extensively in dominant cultural representations of lesbian attraction as well as in much feminist film theory.[34]

When lesbian desire is not contained within identification, it is frequently marked by another 'difference' in order to maintain the subject/object divide. Because representations of lesbian relationships cannot be marked by sex as difference, they are excessively laden with another marker to signify a gender or power

[31] See Robson, n 10 above.

[32] Sally Munt, *Heroic Desire: Lesbian Identity and Cultural Space* (London: 1998) 11–12.

[33] See Hart, n 4 above and Hoogland, n 1 above, Ch 2.

[34] See White, n 2 above and Teresa de Lauretis, 'Film and the Visible' in Bad Object Choices (ed), *How Do I Look?: Queer Film and Video* (Seattle: 1991) 223–264 (and discussion 264–276) and *The Practice of Love: Lesbian Sexuality and Perverse Desire* (Bloomington, 1994).

divide. Hetero-normative images of lesbian relationships routinely mark 'difference' through large age differentials, clear polarization of wealth, class or, more commonly, race of the two women.[35] Power imbalance is concomitant with 'difference' in hegemonic understandings of lesbian relationships. Mainstream imagery has produced many versions of lesbian couples as powerful/powerless and active/passive dyads: mother/daughter, sadist/masochist, vampire/victim, butch/femme, pursuer/pursued, 'really' lesbian/'really' straight.[36] In such portrayals, lesbian relationships are deeply pathologized as essentially, universally and necessarily unbalanced and abusive. Moreover such portrayals tend to *reinscribe* power abuse through the relationship in the course of the narrative—for instance with an older or butch partner maintaining or enhancing her empowered status at the expense of her victim/lover.

Estelle Freedman's history of women in US prisons is an instructive exemplar: she notes that when criminologists, psychologists and prison officials first focused on lesbian relationships in prison in 1913, it was only inter-racial romances that were targeted, and a reform committee suggested racial segregation in order to put an end to it. Freedman documents how from the 1920s through the 1940s, criminologists emphasized race as a substitute for gender, locating aggression and masculinity in black women as the essential 'cause'. White women were posited as the passive recipients, who would return to heterosexuality once they were freed. Only in the 1950s did racial difference fade as a focus, and Freedman notes that class then became the active marker: it was working class white women whose rejection of traditional gender roles marked them as the aggressive, butch, lesbian loci.[37] Although the markers on each side of the divide changed over time, the divide itself remained firmly in place, on one side power signified by masculinity, the active subject, with aggressive sexuality located in black or working class women as 'real' lesbians, and on the other side femininity, passively receiving sexual attention, 'situational' or temporary lesbians who are 'really' heterosexual signified by white women or middle class women.

Moreover, Lynda Hart argues:

> If desire inevitably confirms masculinity, so does crime. Masculinity is as much verified by active desire as it is by aggression.[38]

Thus the maintenance of masculinity through the powerful/powerless archetype of lesbian relationships is a staple, indeed a core element, of the women-in-prison genre.

All three narratives under discussion portray couples who are placed in unequal and opposed positions—prisoner/guard, prisoner/lady visitor and prisoner/governor.

[35] See, eg, Linda Nochlin, *The Politics of Vision: Essays on Nineteenth Century Art and Society* (New York: 1989); Ruby Rich in Bad Object Choices, n 34 above, 274; Hart, n 4 above and Mandy Merck, *In Your Face: 9 Sexual Studies* (New York: 2000).

[36] Judith Mayne, 'A Parallax View of Lesbian Authorship' in Fuss, n 2 above.

[37] Estelle Freedman, 'The Prison Lesbian: Race, Class, and the Construction of the Aggressive Female Homosexual, 1915–1965' (1996) 22 *Feminist Studies* 397–423.

[38] Hart, n 4 above, x.

What is so extraordinary about these stories is that although they commence with classic power dyads in a setting that is ripe for exploitation—the sadistic lesbian guard being a mainstay of the women in prison genre—the relationships transform rather than conform. The power imbalance and power structures are not reinscribed on each side of the dyad, or even simply inverted by reversing them. Rather the women occupy mixed and contradictory positions, and the power structures that surround them are melted, rather reinforced, by the rupture of transgressive lesbian desire.

Firstly, and most obviously, none of the stories commences by matching the active/passive or lesbian/straight components to their 'proper' side of the subject/object power dyad. In all of the stories the prisoner is an active subject as well as a desiring subject. Nikki in *Bad Girls* and Selina in *Affinity* are self contained, self possessed, assured and indeed charismatic characters who are personally powerful despite their powerless circumstances. Neither Nikki nor Selina accept their subordinate position in the prison system or accord any deference to the authority figures they deal with, including their lovers-to-be.

Teresa de Lauretis has argued that heterosexuality is doubly enforced on women:

> in the sense that women can and must feel sexually in relation to men, and enforced as hetero-sexuality in the sense that desire belongs to the other, originates in him. In this standard frame, amazingly simplistic and yet authoritative, and reaffirmed again and again, alas even in feminist theory, whatever women feel towards other women cannot be sexual desire, unless it be a masculinization, a usurpation, or an imitation of man's desire.[39]

These three tales offer a strong contrast to typical hetero-normative representations of lesbians as the 'masculine' desiring subject. In *Affinity* and *Nights at the Circus*, it is the prisoner, who is not lesbian-identified, who initiates the relationship and expresses the attraction. In neither story is lesbianism aligned with or reduced to an active-subject/pursuit position. Didi Herman characterizes the development of the relationship in *Bad Girls* as homo-normative in that it is Helen, the straight-identified woman, who actively and repeatedly seeks out Nikki and courts her attention. In *Bad Girls*, Nikki is not the pursuer, nor is she in any way predatory on an unknowing straight love object. The story line is that Helen is attracted to Nikki, but takes all of Series 1 to 'realize' it. Although Helen pursues Nikki, it is Nikki who forces the issue by articulating what is happening between them. It is Nikki who says, more than once, it's about *this*. In this way, Nikki, like Selina and Olga in the other two stories, causes a double rupture, both through her transgressive desire and through breaking the taboo on *speaking* it.

It is lesbian desire that enlivens and ultimately liberates each of the prisoners. Angela Carter makes this point expressly in her text:

> Desire, that electricity transmitted by the charged touch of Olga Alexandrovna and Vera Andreyevna, leapt across the great divide between the guards and the guarded. Or, it was as if a wild seed took root in the cold soil of the prison and, when it bloomed, it scattered seeds around in its turn. The stale air of the House of Corrections lifted and stirred, was moved

[39] de Lauretis, *The Practice of Love*, n 34 above, 111.

by currents of anticipation, of expectation, that blew the ripened seeds of love from cell to cell. . . . Contact was effected, first, by illicit touch and glance, and then by illicit notes, or, if either guard or inmate turned out to be illiterate, by drawings made on all manner of substances, on rags of clothing if paper was not available, in blood, both menstrual and veinous, even in excrement, for none of the juices of the bodies that had so long been denied them were alien to them, in their extremity—drawings, as it turned out, crude as graffiti, yet with the effect of clarion calls. And if the guards were all subverted to the inmates' humanity through look, caress, word, image, then so did the inmates wake up to the knowledge that, on either side of their own wedge-shaped cubes of space, lived other women just as vividly alive as themselves.[40]

In *Affinity*, desire is explored in a more complex and contradictory manner and as such it stands as a counter-point to the idealism of *Nights at the Circus*. Selina argues that she must escape to be with Margaret because that is the purpose they have both been made for—their flesh needs to leap to each other. She claims that this realization is what will give her the power to escape, that she can and will travel to Margaret on the outside because Margaret's spirit is calling hers. But the physical reality of her freedom is made possible through the Matron's set of keys. The Matron liberates Selina because of her own desire—a desire to see her dead son, as Selina has tricked her into believing that such a vision is only possible outside the prison walls. Selina steals Margaret's life, both literally and figuratively—she takes her money, clothes, passport and dream of a life in Italy with her lesbian lover—in order to give it to her own secret lover, Ruth. Ruth was Selina's maid before she was imprisoned and we discover at the conclusion of the novel that Selina has managed to dupe Margaret (and the reader) by having Ruth work as Margaret's maid known only by her surname, Vigers. (That'll teach you to know your servants' first names.) Selina's passionate love for Ruth is an unwritten background to the mystery of Selina's powers, and the story concludes with a possessive assertion that pre-dates the action of the tale: ' "Remember," Ruth is saying, "whose girl you are." '[41]

Through the reach of desire, the heavily marked borders of institutional hierarchy are transgressed. This transgression does not reinscribe the lovers as victor and vanquished. Nor, with the possible and partial exception of *Affinity*, does it maintain such roles through inverting them. Rather, the transgression of lesbian desire liberates the women from their power roles through dissolving the hierarchical bind between them.

The All Seeing Eye

Judith Mayne argues that, 'the women-in-prison film thematizes in a very pronounced way the capacity of the cinema not only to objectify the female body, but also to create dramas of surveillance and visibility'.[42] In both *Affinity* and

[40] Carter, n 15 above, 216–217.

[41] Waters, n 30 above, 352.

[42] Mayne, n 14 above, 117.

Nights at the Circus, the prison in the story is actually a panopticon. The panopticon, a circular prison in which every cell is visible from a central tower, but not to each other, was the brainchild of Jeremy Bentham. In Foucault's well-known rendition, the panopticon is the eye from which we all may, or may not, be watched. As a metaphor it is the centrepiece of a social system in which we are all disciplined, and all in a sense imprisoned.

Nights at the Circus was published in 1984, in the same year that feminist film theorists Mary Ann Doane, Patricia Mellencamp and Linda Williams published a volume of essays on film which they introduced with reference to the panopticon as a defining metaphor for the relationship between 'the gaze' and power. They argued that Foucault's conception of the panopticon perfectly describes 'the condition not only of the inmate in Bentham's prison but of women as well'.[43] The panopticon is used in both *Nights at the Circus* and *Affinity* to reveal a continuum of imprisonment. In both stories, the guards as well as the detainees are portrayed as imprisoned by their circumstances, unable to work elsewhere, to escape or to lead fulfilling lives over which they have any control. *Affinity* draws more subtle parallels between the continued surveillance of the silenced prisoners in Millbank, and the familial and medical surveillance of Margaret, who has attempted suicide after a depression. Her mother, her doctor, her friends, her servants, are all watching her, all the time, for a return of her symptoms or any sign of disorder. Likewise the matrons and the head of the wing watch Margaret increasingly closely as she spends time with Selina, for signs that she is a lesbian. These duel systems of surveillance are linked. When the Matron, Miss Haxby, tries to prevent Margaret from continuing to visit they argue and Margaret is given a telling Freudian slip as she nearly calls the matron 'Mother'.[44]

The confines of family and class expectation about appropriate feminine behaviour in combination with heavy medication weave a strait-jacket around the intellectual, lesbian-identified and feminist-inclined Margaret. Margaret's middle class prison is not privileged over Selina's very concrete one, but their experience of confinement is mirrored. As Margaret is suffocated by her mother's oppressive presence, Selina is held in a jail which Waters has stated she deliberately made 'feminine' in form, through its presentation as moist, fissured.[45] Waters also notes the resonances between 'the treatment of women prisoners and the treatment of women mediums, a fetishisation of restraint and observation and darkness and silence—and that most importantly for me, these things were completely pertinent to our sense of the place of women in general, and lesbians in particular, in Victorian society'.[46]

Judith Mayne takes issue with the argument of Doane et al and early feminist film theorists that the 'gaze' of the audience and of the panopticon is a male one. Mayne notes that the prison genre is 'predicated on the possibility that women

[43] Mary Ann Doane, Patricia Mellencamp and Linda Williams (eds), *Re-Vision: Essays in Feminist Film Criticism* (Los Angeles: 1984) 14.

[44] Waters, n 30 above, 267.

[45] Sarah Waters, Address to Sydney Writers Festival, May 2001.

[46] Arsdale, 2000.

observe other women', both in the sense of women looking at and desiring each other, and in the sense of official surveillance as women occupy positions of power in the jail hierarchy.[47] Mayne's approach reflects developments in later feminist analysis that resisted positing either a system of unified male power or a uni-focal male-centred gaze. Notably both *Nights* and *Affinity* have a woman, not a man, at the centre of the panopticon watching over her prisoners and all three narratives investigate, to differing degrees, female complicity in patriarchal power structures. Indeed, each story barely touches on the male authority figures and explores far more closely the complicity of women in systems of oppression of other women. In *Nights*, the prison is the nightmarish vision of Countess P who seeks to punish other women in order to absolve herself of her own, less justifiable, homicide. In both *Affinity* and *Bad Girls*, the wing governor is a woman, second in command to the overall prison governor who is a man—so in a sense it is not so much the rule of the father as the rule of the patriarchal *family*; mother is implicated too.

The presence of the panopticon and the deep complicity of women in perpetuating oppressive power structures sounds a warning bell about the conclusions that I have drawn in the previous section. Is it ever really possible to transcend hierarchy? To transform a genre? To liberate? As Ruthann Robson says of the lesbian outlaw, we are always both inside and outside of the law, we are ' "always already" domesticated'.[48] Is a bunch of women falling in love with each other *really* going to change anything?

Nights at the Circus is the most utopian of the three tales and the most openly symbolic in its alignment of lesbian desire with freedom and transformation. Yet the union of the escaped prisoners with their guards, and of Mignon and the Princess, is made possible *only* through their exit from family, community and society; they cannot stay within the place that has built the prison or caged the tigers, and survive intact. When the prisoners initially consider returning to their homes after their escape, this option expressly forecloses the possibility of their lesbian loves. They choose to remain together and abandon their families forever to build the republic of free women. Mignon and the Princess are always teetering on the brink of chaos with the caged tigers while they are in the circus; their position is infused with uncertainty. To truly escape the full implications of the prison and the cages the women must form new communities somewhere entirely new—in the wilderness. In a sense, then, the lesbian characters must step outside of the social, rather than actually transforming it.

In *Affinity*, despite all we are lead to believe in the course of the story, Selina's escape depends upon others' entrapment. There is liberation and lesbian love for Selina, but at a price—and that price is paid by other women. Selina escapes through Margaret's and the Matron's entrapment, and by the novel's conclusion Margaret is doomed to a yet more suffocating domestic fate as a result.

In *Bad Girls*, Nikki and Helen do not really commit to a relationship (for longer than a couple of episodes) until they have left both the prison and the series—

[47] Mayne, n 14 above, 117. [48] Robson, n 7 above, 19.

Helen resigns, Nikki wins her appeal and the lovers reunite in the closing minutes of the final episode of Series 3 in an embrace on a public street—signalling that they are both, finally, 'out'. Neither character returned in the series that followed, so the full expression of lesbian desire both fulfils and *concludes* the story. In this sense lesbianism acted as a narrative closure rather than as the fissure it at first appeared to be.

'Domestication' is also possible through audience reception. There is little available material as yet on how *Affinity* has been received, but it is notable that the dozen volumes of literary discussion and criticism of *Nights at the Circus* are almost universally silent on the panopticon chapter. Likewise when minor characters or sub-themes from the novel are discussed it is almost always the clowns and the place of carnival in the work, not the Princess-Mignon or Siberian prison storylines and how they relate to the themes of sexuality and imprisonment.[49] In *Bad Girls*, in particular, there were strong imperatives to reassert dominant hetero-normative ideologies both within the production itself and through the process of audience reception. Despite all I have said so far, it is arguable that the transgressive lesbian images *Bad Girls* created were in fact recaptured and domesticated in the course of the first three years of the series. This recapture was played out in a number of ways, including: audience readings of the story, writers and producers 'toning down' the lesbian content of the story as it progressed, the media spectacle that grew up around the series, and producers gaining control over lesbian-oriented fan internet sites.

Recaptured and Domesticated?

Didi Herman has argued that much of the Nikki and Helen relationship in *Bad Girls* reflects and speaks to, lesbian 'insider' knowledges.[50] Lesbian viewers enjoyed a sense of their own cultural competency, and a sense of being—for once—the designated audience rather than having to read against the grain or between the lines. However, just as lesbian and gay audiences have read cultural texts against the grain in order to relate to them, so too did straight audiences re-read the Nikki and Helen relationship to make it conform more closely to hegemonic understandings of lesbian sexuality. Many of the non-lesbian participants in message board discussions insisted that it was Nikki who had pursued Helen, who had behaved improperly or aggressively and had misunderstood Helen's pure intentions which were to 'help' Nikki. For instance,

[49] Exceptions to this silence are brief and partial. Paulina Palmer spares a few lines for both the panopticon chapter and the Princess and Mignon as examples of 'woman-identification and female collectivity' (extracted in Sarah Gamble, *The Fiction of Angela Carter: A Reader's Guide to Essential Criticism* (Cambridge: 2001)). See also a de-sexualized discussion of the panopticon chapter in Joanne Gass, 'Panopticonism in Nights at the Circus' (1994) 14 *Rev of Contemporary Fiction* 71–77. Aiden Day rather awkwardly refers to the Princess and Mignon as evidence that Carter's version of history will be 'large enough to accommodate sexual orientations not articulated in patriarchal history' (Day, n 16 above, 193).

[50] Herman, n 12 above.

viewers argued that Nikki 'took advantage' when she kissed Helen in the scene where Helen visited her in her cell after lock-up as a shoulder to cry on (Series 1, Episode 9).

Viewers were able to make these readings in part because Helen said and did very different things throughout the series. By listening only to her words and blocking out the flow of non-verbal cues or the context in which it is always Helen seeking Nikki out, it was possible, even easy, to see Nikki as a rather irrational pursuer of a heterosexual woman who was 'only trying to help'. Whereas Helen's touches could be 'just friendly', it is Nikki who initiates the overtly sexual physical contact between the two. Even in Series 2, when the writers finally erased any room for ambiguity about the reciprocity of the attraction, some viewers still continued to label Nikki as 'aggressive' and 'taking advantage' (a term that echoed the language used in the series to describe a male officer's (Fenner) systematic sexual abuse of inmates). Because Nikki is a lesbian and Helen is not, these 'lesbian' traits must be located in Nikki. The threat of fluid sexuality in Helen, rather than transforming hegemonic understandings of sexuality as essentialist, was displaced onto the lesbian character, who was denigrated as a trespasser. In this sense, the series was arguably 're-captured', at least temporarily, by heterosexual viewers who read against the grain to produce an aggressive, predatory and unboundaried lesbian pursuer.

The fully transgressive potential of the Nikki-Helen relationship was also significantly muted within the construction of the story itself as the later series unfolded. In Series 2 Helen persuades Nikki to try for an appeal, and also urges Nikki to 'stay out of trouble' in the meantime. In Series 3 the relationship is put on hold for almost the entire series, ostensibly because of Helen's (belatedly discovered) ethical qualms, but this shift entailed both re-heterosexualizing Helen through a relationship with a man, and a much reduced role for Nikki. As the series progressed, Nikki ceased to exist as a character in the series except in her relation to Helen, she rarely appeared in other storylines, even major ones that involved her close friends. This reinscribed a hetero-normative approach, that lesbians are *only* their lesbianism, and only signified in their romantic relations to others.[51] In part, the muting of the Nikki and Helen relationship was a function of producers wanting to stretch it out as long as possible (and the soap opera convention of get together, break up, obstacle, get together), but the decision was premised on the basis that only an implicit, not an explicit, lesbian relationship could be portrayed over a 40 episode period. Moreover, the choice of a 'taboo' relationship as the lesbian centrepiece entailed both a depletion of dramatic tension once the 'secret's out', and a displacing of silence, shame, and secrecy from lesbianism in general onto *this* lesbian relationship in particular. Lesbianism in this schema is still inflected as 'wrong'.[52]

[51] Robson, n 10 above.

[52] A more markedly homophobic subtext appeared when Nikki was pursued and became interested in another prisoner (after being dropped by Helen). This woman is ultimately revealed to be a child pornographer. Although her crime was in partnership with her boyfriend (so she is not a 'real' lesbian), it reinscribed the egregious homosexual/paedophile conflation. Likewise, the cameo character of 'Mad Tessa Spall' contained both the homophobic associations of psychotic/violent lesbian and HIV/diseased/homosexual.

The strongly homo-normative aspects of *Bad Girls* were also contradicted or undermined in many respects by media reception and by media 'performance' by those connected with the series. Initial interviews with the actors who play Helen (Simone Lahbib) and Nikki (Mandana Jones) focused on how flattered they were to have a lesbian fan base, their interest in and support of the lesbian-focused *Larkhall Insider* fan website and their sense of 'responsibility' at presenting lesbian characters and lesbian relationships in a positive light. While the actresses appeared together at lesbian events,[53] and even kissed and cuddled for the cameras on numerous occasions, in later coverage, articles go to greater and greater lengths to stress the actresses' heterosexuality, and many hint at or openly characterize lesbian fans as crazed stalkers.[54]

In numerous press articles and interviews after the second series the producers and cast members expressed 'concern' that the series was very popular with teenagers, especially young girls. The repeated nature of these references suggests that there was a conscious decision to distance the series from appearing to attract a juvenile audience. This 'concern' was frequently linked to lesbianism, or to 'lesbianism and violence' as 'issues' that children should not be exposed to.[55] In press coverage, lesbianism was repeatedly conflated with violence and drugs; as staple elements of the women-in-prison genre,[56] as 'issues' that needed to be explored[57] or as 'dark' aspects that were improper or salacious objects of spectacle.[58] Notably, the word 'lesbianism' appeared most frequently in sentences where it was immediately followed by 'and' connecting it to drug abuse or violence.[59]

Seduced and Abandoned? Click Here

Issues of recapture were played out even more strongly in relation to the web-based fan community. Hundreds of *Bad Girls* websites appeared since 1999, and this web culture reflected a refreshing homo-normativity in the sense that majority lesbian participation was assumed and lesbian perspectives naturalized. The *Larkhall Insider* was the first such site, and in 2000 during the hiatus between the first and second series, the production company responsible for *Bad Girls*, Shed Productions, asked the *Larkhall Insider* to move to the 'official' domain

[53] I am not intending to suggest that this was simply a media grab. Many cast members appeared at lesbian community events through 2000–2002, including acting as judges in the 'Miss Lesbian Beauty Contest' in 2001, and appearing at fundraisers for issues such as Lesbian Cancer and local gay and lesbian pride centres.

[54] See Christine Smith, 'How my obsessive fans have freaked me out', *Mirror Weekend Magazine*, online at www.badgirlsweb.co.uk/media/media_articles_2001.htm; Ogle, n 19 above.

[55] See, eg, Syrie Johnson, 'So, How Does it Feel to be a Lesbian Icon?', *Evening Standard*, 16 March 2001.

[56] Ogle, n 19 above.

[57] Gavin Docherty, 'Simone's out of jail and going straight', *The Express*, 16 February 2002.

[58] Alex Pell, 'Bras and Knickers: Bad Girls 2, Lesbian Convicts on the Bog', *Loaded*, 2000.

[59] See, eg, Josephine Munro, 'Violent reactions', *Sunday Times*, 30 May 1999; Ogle, n 19 above; Rampton, n 23 above.

name and act as the official website of the show. I thought, and still do think, that this was a wild development, with the producers of a new, successful, top-rating television series handing over their official imprimatur to a bunch of dyke fans.

Apart from an initial, predictable clean up of the site to remove copy-written material, and replacing of the tongue-in-cheek and in-joke filled episode summaries with 'straight' factual summaries and appropriate lists of credits, the site was not really 'straightened up' in any other way. The message board grew and flourished with a strong lesbian presence, and fanfiction written by viewers continued to be hosted on the site through 2000. Like the viewers of the show generally, the web fans were almost all women, with a high number of young women. Message board participants included a lot of teenage girls, many of whom were struggling with their sexuality and numerous discussion threads covered topics such as girls' desire to confess their love of their best friend, where they hide their *Bad Girls* gear, and how best to come out to their mothers. A number of lesbian fan events were also organized through the message board in 2000 and 2001 and Shed participated in and sponsored some of those events.

A stronger sense of control arose when the website moderator suggested that fanfiction with (lesbian) sexual content should contain warnings or be located elsewhere. Much of the fanfiction was subsequently moved onto another site, although new arrivals and updates continued to be heralded on the *Larkhall Insider*. Through Series 3, a number of fans expressed disappointment at the way the Helen and Nikki storyline developed, as well as a general sense that the quality of the series was declining. The height of fan displeasure appeared in a 'Rant at Shed' thread on the message board, although complaints about poor writing, (more than usually) unbelievable story-lines and continuity errors were common discussion points at that time. As a direct result of this participation (which apparently included some very personal attacks upon the producers), Shed closed down the message board in late 2001. Shed also hired the creator of one of the most popular lesbian-run rival sites, *Zanweb*, to redesign the official site—and this recruitment led to the shutdown of *Zanweb*. The redesign of the official site involved a re-naming, and a distinct de-emphasis on fan material and participation. The *Larkhall Insider* was dropped as a title, and a separate section of the site was designated 'the fan site' to distinguish it from the rest of the site which is presumably no longer a fan site. The 'Library' section was stocked with a lot of worthy information on prisons and criminal justice, and by 2003 contained only one link in the 'support' section of the links page, right down at the bottom, to a lesbian and gay site.[60]

The producers expressly blamed lesbian fans for their decision to shut down the fan forum, stating that a 'collective hysteria' had been 'whipped up'.

[60] The link in 2003 was to 'Rainbow Network' and was subtitled 'Everything concerning gay and lesbian lifestyles'. In my view, 'lifestyle' is a peculiar and peculiarly heterosexist word used to connote lesbian and gay lives and issues. One does not, for example, refer to heterosexual 'lifestyles', nor (running down the list on the site) alcoholic or prisoner or victim of crime lifestyles. In 2004 there were no links at all.

As a long-time 'out' and politicised lesbian myself (Chad), for whom BG is a fantastic opportunity to promote 'homo-normatization' to a mass audience, I invite all those who presumed to slag off my integrity to come out from behind the secrecy of their webnames and own up to being *more culpable than the right-wing press of anti-lesbian/feminist activities.* It is certainly thanks to them that the rest of the LI/BG fans were deprived of the message board. Ask yourselves, why would any individual or company spend £40K a year of their own money (which is what it cost us to set up and staff a site with that superior kind of MB capacity) to provide a platform for a few self-aggrandising and bitter individuals to perpetuate their poisonous mud-slinging. Most companies would have pulled the plug or censored the negative contributions immediately.[61]

While *Bad Girls* did mark a significant achievement in popular representation of lesbians, as this paper has made clear, there is a great deal that requires unpacking in the above statement. Criticizing the—significantly less homo-normative—third series is here characterized as an 'anti-lesbian/feminist' activity and lesbian fans are identified as more culpable than the right wing press. If criticizing *Bad Girls* is anti-lesbian, even though done by lesbians, and done because of poor representation of lesbians, this statement suggests that there is an official or correct lesbian position—which belongs to the production company—that has been damaged by feral fans. Moreover, the producers could, and did, destroy the message board as a result of this criticism. While the producers go on in the interview, above, to state that they deserve to be paid properly for their work, they ignore the fact that they are, in fact, the owners of capital in this exchange. They own the site, and their censorship of it is possible because of that economic power. The *Larkhall Insider* was a lesbian-run and lesbian-oriented fan site that was created elsewhere, successfully co-opted, and then ultimately shut down when it was not sufficiently tame.

Conclusion

In this paper I have explored three narratives of transgressive lesbian desire and argued that each of them offers a challenge to hetero-normative representational codes. Yet despite the rupture that each text offers, there remains the possibility that they can be re-captured or domesticated back within hegemonic cultural codes.

Teresa de Lauretis considers the paradox of how it is possible to deconstruct dominant codes of representation *through* representation when she says:

It's one thing to criticize codes of representation and another to say that lesbians don't exist or that women don't exist. We're not saying that; we're trying to construct a representation that is not simply one using the dominant codes. Though we might be speaking from within the lessons of theory, I think we are trying to develop, whether as women critics or

[61] Chadwick and McManus, n 12 above (emphasis added).

film-and-video makers, representations that are simultaneously deconstructions of dominant codes. But this can only be done through codes of representation; otherwise it would be an entirely solipsistic endeavour. In other words, what we produce has to be legible. What we are trying to explore in our work are ways in which certain presences, certain lesbian presences, are—precisely—legible, in spite of theories that say they're not.[62]

The challenge of transforming representation cannot always, or perhaps even often, be successful. The possibility of mis-reading and co-option is inescapable. The likelihood of mis-reading is perhaps enhanced when one is writing over an established genre, such as the women-in-prison genre, because the archetypes or pre-understandings of the genre are able to gleam through. But the boundaries of genre, like the boundaries of hierarchy, call attention to themselves as worthy objects of transgression precisely because of their definitional and delimiting qualities.

These three tales are doubly ambitious in their challenge to dominant imagery by attempting to present homo-normative images of lesbian desire in the midst of the traditionally homophobic women-in-prison setting. In this sense they accord with Joan Nestle's invocation that lesbians 'should be mistresses of discrepancies, knowing that resistance lies in the change of context'.[63]

This leads me back to the breast clasp where I began. For many viewers this scene deepened their conception of Nikki as a violent and sexually aggressive lesbian. It was a shocking and confronting scene, encapsulating both aggression and vulnerability. It was also open-textured. Nikki says: it's about this. But what is the *this* in this? Is *this* her heart? Is she saying: it's about love, or about the hurt you have caused me. Is *this* her breast? Is she saying: it's that I am a woman, see, feel, here I am. Or, more earthily perhaps, grab me, shag me: it's about time. Whatever interpretation one ultimately settles upon, this was a decidedly anti-social expression of lesbian desire. In doing so, it acted as a symbolic rupture not only of the silence between Nikki and Helen, but of the cultural imperative of silence around lesbian sexuality. Perhaps, after all, we can take the risk of saying: it's about *this*.

[62] Bad Object Choices, n 34 above, 281.

[63] Mayne, n 36 above, 179.

'Juliet and Juliet Would be More My Cup of Tea': Sexuality, Law, and Popular Culture[1]

Didi Herman

Introduction

The field of law and popular culture has tended to read popular culture in terms of what it says about law, lawyers, law firms, or indeed how popular culture shapes understandings about law in everyday consciousness.[2] While I will return to these concerns, in this paper I want to forefront a different approach to the field. I turn away from a preoccupation with representations of law and legal culture per se to focus instead on wider issues of regulation and governance. I specifically explore the governance of sexuality in mainstream, network television. I am interested in how popular television plays a role in constructing and reproducing regulatory norms around sexuality, and the extent to which it is possible to represent non-normative sexualities in prime-time.

My case study for this analysis is *Bad Girls* (*BG*), a women's prison drama. *BG* premiered in 1999 on ITV, the UK's main commercial broadcaster, who will broadcast the seventh series in 2005. *BG* is shown from 9–10pm, attracts over 8 million viewers each week, and has sparked the creation of numerous fan websites, special events, media cover stories, and its own book.[3] It has been the 5th most popular drama in the post-9pm slot, and, amongst the 'under 35s' (in this same time slot), *BG* has held the top position.[4] The series has been sold to markets in Finland, New Zealand, Australia, Israel, and South Africa, and 'changed format' versions to Spain, and the USA. In the UK, *BG* video sales have been at number 7 in the chart, ahead of *Friends* and *Buffy*, and just behind *Star Trek* and *The Simpsons*.[5]

[1] Parts of this paper previously appeared in D Herman, '"*Bad Girls* Changed My Life": Homonormativity in a Women's Prison Drama' (2003) 20 *Critical Studies in Media Communication* 141, reproduced by permission of *Critical Studies in Media Communication*.

[2] See, eg, J Denvir (ed), *Legal Reelism: Movies as Legal Texts* (Urbana and Chicago: 1997); S Redhead, *Unpopular Cultures: The Birth of Law and Popular Culture* (Manchester: 1995); RK Sherwin, *When Law Goes Pop: The Vanishing Line Between Law and Popular Culture* (Chicago and London: 2000); M Thornton (ed), *Romancing the Tomes: Popular Culture, Law and Feminism* (London and Sydney: 2002).

[3] J Reynolds and J McCallum, *Bad Girls: The Inside Story* (London: 2001).

[4] Figures provided by Shed Productions, 2001. Source: DGA/Barb.

[5] ibid (figures for June, 2000).

Over its four years, *BG* has followed the stories of a range of characters, inmates and officers. It focuses critically on issues such as prison healthcare, officer violence, and the institutional sexism faced by employees, while simultaneously constructing a 'camped up' environment often giving rise to outrageous dialogue and sub-plots. Woven throughout every episode are scenes representing the prison as a place of warmth, solidarity, and community for the women incarcerated there. While the show has had many strands during its run, in this paper I focus on one, predominant in the first three series: the ways in which *BG* centres, validates, and normalizes lesbian sexuality.

My analysis highlights two characters in particular—Helen Stewart and Nikki Wade. Helen is a heterosexual prison manager, trying to reform prison practice in the face of resistance from 'the old boy's network'. Nikki, a lesbian inmate, is serving a long, discretionary sentence for killing a police officer whom she found raping her girlfriend. Helen is very aware of the institutional struggles she faces, while Nikki is an outspoken activist who commands respect within the prison. The two women fall in love with each other, and a key storyline throughout the first three series charts the ups and downs of their relationship. By the end of the third series, Helen has given up her job to safeguard Nikki's appeal, Nikki is released from prison, and Helen finally acknowledges she 'wants a woman'.

Analyses of lesbian images in mainstream television are still few and far between.[6] Some writers argue that lesbians either do not exist, or that their representation is largely unsatisfactory in a range of ways.[7] Others analyze and advocate readings 'in' or 'against the grain', conjuring lesbian narrative out of what first appears to be rather thin air.[8] A third and overlapping approach is to deconstruct homophobic and spectral representations[9] in cultural products never intended to show lesbians positively nor directed at lesbian viewers as 'a knowing part of the mainstream audience'.[10]

[6] But see, B J Dow, '*Ellen*, television, and the politics of gay and lesbian visibility' (2001) 18 *Critical Studies in Media Communication* 123.

[7] See, eg, R Collis, 'Screened Out: Lesbians and television' in L Gibbs (ed), *Daring to Dissent* (London: 1994) 120; L Gross, 'Minorities, majorities and the media' in T Liebes and J Curran (eds), *Media, Ritual and Identity* (London: 1998) 87; DM Hantzis and V Lehr, 'Whose desire? Lesbian (non)sexuality and television's perpetuation of hetero-sexism' in RJ Ringer (ed), *Queer words, Queer Images: Communication and the Construction of Homosexuality* (New York and London: 1994) 107; M Moritz, 'Old Strategies for New Texts: How American Television is Creating and Treating Lesbian Characters' in J Ringer (ed), *Queer Words, Queer Images* (New York: 1994) 122; Chris Straayer, '*Personal Best*: Lesbian Feminist Audience' (1984) 29 *Jump Cut* 40.

[8] A Doty, *Making Things Perfectly Queer: Interpreting Mass Culture* (Minneapolis: 1993) Ch 3; MR Farwell, *Homosexual Plots and Lesbian Narratives* (New York: 1996); B Johnson, 'Lesbian Spectacles: Reading *Sula, Passing, Thelma and Louise*, and *The Accused*' in M Garber, J Matlock and RL Walkowitz (eds), *Media Spectacles* (New York and London: 1993) 160; Z I Nataf, 'Black Lesbian Spectatorship and Pleasure in Popular Culture' in P Burston and C Richardson (eds), *A Queer Romance: Lesbians, Gay Men, and Popular Culture* (London: 1995) 57; C Smyth, 'The Transgressive Sexual Subject' in P Burston and C Richardson, ibid, 123.

[9] T Castle, *The Apparitional Lesbian* (New York: 1995); R Collis, n 6 above; L Hart, *Fatal Women: Lesbian Sexuality and the Mark of Aggression* (Princeton: 1994); J Mayne, *Framed: Lesbians, Feminists and Media Culture* (Minneapolis: 2000) 128.

[10] P Florence, 'Portrait of a Production' in T Wilton (ed), *Immortal, Invisible* (London and New York: 1995), 144; on 'race', see also H Gray, *Watching Race: Television and the Struggle for 'Blackness'* (Minneapolis: 1995) 95.

A significant proportion of scholarship on lesbian images in popular culture explores the 'women in prison' (WIP) genre, a category *BG*, at first glance, appears to occupy neatly.[11] Most of this writing focuses on film, although it includes a small body of work analyzing the popular Australian television series *Prisoner Cell-Block H*.[12] Judith Mayne has argued that the WIP film genre contains a 'fairly simple' formula that involves a relatively innocent, heterosexual heroine being sent to prison and is subsequently abused by a range of women whom she encounters there.[13] Lesbianism is usually either marginalized, pathologized, or at best situational, and lesbian characters usually face grim futures or suffer violent deaths.[14]

In contrast, *BG* disrupts the WIP genre significantly. *BG* foregrounds lesbian heroines who have 'happy endings', and the normalization of lesbianism occurs *outside* as well as within the prison. Much, although by no means all, of the abuse inmates suffer is at the hands of male officers. Mayne has suggested that one of the most 'striking' aspects of the WIP genre 'is how marginal male figures really are'[15]—this is simply not true of *BG*, where several male characters play an important role in advancing the show's feminist agenda.

I argue that, in contrast to any other prime-time, network offering I am aware of, *BG* has embodied a non-dominant perspective on sexuality, namely a homonormative one. By calling the series homonormative, I mean that it represents lesbianism as both unremarkable and as common-sense desire, that viewers are often invited to see and know with a lesbian perspective, and that other forms of sexuality are, at times, represented as aberrant or distinctive in some way (in the way that heteronormativity usually portrays homosexuality). At the same time, the homonormativity *BG* constructs is a particular one in that it is rooted in a white, lesbian feminist perspective,[16] rather than a gay, queer, or 'of colour' one. *BG*'s hononormativity is thus inflected by particular understandings of race, gender, and sexuality, and, as I will return to later in the paper, law and justice.

I illustrate this argument by exploring several themes in the series: a lesbian heroic; the coming out story; lesbian feminist politics (including the breadth and diversity of lesbian representations, homonormative reversals around sexual agency, the forefronting of an erotic lesbian romance with a happy ending, the use of 'insider' humour and common sense, the failure to explain homosexuality, and the denigration of nuclear families); and the show's strategies of estrangement around hetero and bi sexualities. The final section of the paper turns away from the governance of sexuality to examine representations of prison, crime, and the rule of law.

[11] See Hart, n 9 above, 76; Mayne, n 9 above, Ch 7; A Morey, '"The Judge Called Me an Accessory": Women's Prison Films, 1950–1962' (1995) *J of Popular Film and Television* 80.

[12] B Zalcock and J Robinson, 'Inside Cell-Block H: Hard Steel and Soft Soap' (1996) 9 *Continuum* 88.

[13] Mayne, n 9 above, 115–116.

[14] ibid, 128, 135; also Hart, n 9 above, 76.

[15] Mayne, n 9 above, 118.

[16] *BG*'s creators and authors have described themselves as 'straight-down-the-line, dyed-in-the-wool, committed, do-or-die, go-to-the-wall, in-your-face feminists', M Chadwick and A McManus, '*Bad Girls Q & A*'. Available online at http://www.badgirls.co.uk/q&a. Accessed 6 August 2001.

Homonormative Constructions

Episode 7, Series 1:
(Helen enters library where Nikki is reading)

Helen: *Romeo and Juliet*—I'm impressed.
Nikki: Juliet and Juliet would be more my cup of tea.
Helen: . . . Have you never been interested in men?
Nikki: Not my flavour, no.
Helen: But, I thought . . .
Nikki: What?—I just hadn't met the right one? No, they do nothing for me.
Helen: How can you be sure?
Nikki: The same way as you are . . . if you are.
Helen: I'm not interested in women—not in that way.
Nikki: Well, you should give it a go sometime. Don't know what you're missing.

(Nikki hands Helen a copy of Jeanette Winterson's *Oranges are not the only fruit* and exits)

A Lesbian Heroic

Sally Munt has argued that 'outlaw status' is emblematic of a particular *lesbian* heroic.[17] In *BG*, this heroism is personified in the character of Nikki, an out inmate. Nikki's centrality to the show, her role as a moral centre in the prison, is, I would argue, an important aspect of *BG*'s homonormativity. Nikki's role in befriending and protecting vulnerable inmates exemplifies her heroism—it is a pattern repeated often—and underscores her leadership role in the prison generally. Although Nikki at times resents the position of trust and authority in which she is placed, her concern for inmates' welfare is presented in a wholly positive manner.[18]

As important as her concern for individual inmates, Nikki is also the political conscience of the show. Again, this is set up from the first episode, where Nikki challenges the prison authorities over their treatment of Carol, who has had a miscarriage during the night and been left to bleed in her cell. It is when faced with the inhumanity of 'the system' that Nikki's temper and impulsive behaviour emerge, often leading to her being sent 'down the block' (put into segregation). Other inmates clearly respect Nikki as an important advocate and activist within the prison, and she is used by the show's writers to comment critically on a range of 'women in prison' issues, including prison healthcare, the incarceration of women forced to abandon vulnerable children, and the treatment of non-English speaking inmates.

[17] S Munt, *Heroic Desire: Lesbian Identity and Cultural Space* (London: 1998) Ch 4.

[18] Eg, Nikki warns a young prisoner about an abusive prison officer, she assists another after a 'de-crutching' episode, she helps two older women come to terms with their incarceration and acts as an important catalyst for each to change in a positive way, she physically intervenes to save inmates in dangerous situations, and she even consoles and counsels a 'good' prison officer at one point.

In contrast to heteronormative genres where 'the lesbian' is often portrayed as out to get something (sex/power/etc), Nikki is presented as a thoroughly decent, caring, committed, and, in many respects, selfless person. Having said that, Nikki does not appear as some kind of saint; she is tempestuous, impulsive, and, sometimes, jealous and possessive. We learn early on that she is imprisoned for the brutal, and arguably unnecessary, killing of a police officer, whom she found raping her partner. In this sense, there is no straight-forward 'deification' of Nikki—a problem Brookey and Westerfelhaus identify with 'positive images' of lesbians and gay men.[19]

That Nikki is a *lesbian* heroine is signalled early on, initially through the device of another character's homophobia (Shell). In episode 1 of the first series, Shell calls out, as Nikki checks on Carol, 'missed your goodnight kiss?'. And later, in the same episode, when Nikki has been stripped and sent to segregation, Shell exclaims: 'not wearing your dress then?'. These remarks continue throughout the first series, for example in episode 3 when Shell passes Nikki and Monica on the stairs and says, 'Going for someone a bit more upmarket are you Wade? . . . What's she got the other girls ain't—mink instead of beaver?'. The thoroughly 'bad' prison officer, Jim Fenner, is the other key lesbian-baiter, and, arguably, his and Shell's taunts play an important role in valorizing Nikki's lesbianism for, as I discuss below, their own heterosexuality (and sexual relationship with each other) is represented as dysfunctional, abusive, and out of control. Aside from the homophobia Nikki encounters from Shell and Jim, her lesbianism is outed to viewers early in the first series when she is visited by Trish, her partner. Thus, in contrast to Hart's analysis of typical lesbian representations in popular culture, there is no 'secret' here waiting to be revealed.[20]

The other heroine in *BG*, at least for the first and third series, is Helen, the governor of the prison wing. Helen's heroism is found partly in the *Cagney and Lacey* and most assuredly not in the 'women in prison' genre—she is a feminist crusader, personally, to break the glass ceiling in the prison service, and politically to force the service to respond more effectively to inmates' needs. While Helen battles against instances of individual officer corruption, many of her most important struggles are with her own boss's condescension, patronization, and refusal to oust the 'bad apple' officers. In episode 1 of the first series, she explicitly attempts to enlist Nikki's help to fight 'the old boy's network'. Indeed, it is Helen and Nikki's feminist politics that initially creates a bond between them. As Clark has argued in a different context, the integration of the 'personal and political' is what constitutes feminist heroism in popular culture.[21]

Although Helen's sexual dithering and inconstancy were serious sources of disquiet to many lesbian *BG* viewers (expressed often on the *BG* message boards),

[19] RA Brookey and R Westerfelhaus, 'Pistols and petticoats, piety and purity: *To Wong Foo*, the Queering of the American Monomyth and the Marginalising Discourse of Deification' (2001) 18 *Critical Studies in Media Communication* 141.

[20] Hart, n 9 above, 4.

[21] D Clark, '*Cagney and Lacey*: Feminist Strategies of Detection' in ME Brown (ed), *Television and Women's Culture: The Politics of the Popular* (London: 1990) 117.

her valiant attempts to 'feminize' the prison service were heroic if, in the end, doomed to failure. She suffers a litany of discrimination and sexist abuse, including sexual assault, and continues to fight back. Arguably, Helen's institutional struggle serves to construct the prison not simply as a place of oppression, but also as a place of feminist heroics, like *Cagney and Lacey*'s police station.[22] Helen too is not a 'perfect' heroine by any means; her motivations are not always clear, and she appears to enjoy exercising power over others. Indeed, the inability of network executives to 'read' Helen (they found her incoherent and unpredictable) nearly led to her character being written out of the series,[23] and may also be an effect of *BG*'s failure to conform to a recognizable genre. However, for many women, and particularly feminist viewers, Helen is a character with whom we can empathize, and one who deserves our respect, and admiration. That she chooses to come out at the end of the third series only serves to strengthen the homonormative/ narrative—both of these key *BG* heroines choose women.

However, the lesbian heroic *BG* constructs is a white one. The only non-white lesbian character, Denny, is introduced as a nasty bully, and although she eventually becomes sympathetic and likeable, she remains slow-witted, selfish, and naïve. There are also class ideologies at play here. While the class backgrounds of Nikki and Helen are ambiguous, Helen is university-educated and Nikki soon will be. They share an interest in 'good' literature and Nikki is found often in the library. In contrast, Denny is illiterate, and while she acquires literacy in a later series, she is never shown reading in the library. To picture Nikki or Helen as Black or Asian, for example, or Denny reading novels in the library, challenges what is, in essence, the white lesbian normativity of *BG*. And yet, it is also important to complicate the meaning of 'white'. Nikki and Helen are played by actors with non-English backgrounds. These non-Anglo—and therefore 'off' white in an English national context—identities complicate any simple reading of a dominant racial narrative in *BG*.[24]

The Coming Out Story

Helen's relationship with Nikki, and her ensuing 'sexuality dilemma', which takes three years to resolve, is one of the key themes of *Bad Girls*. Judith Roof has noted that 'the quintessential lesbian narrative is the coming out story', and *BG* is no exception in deploying what Roof believes to be this inherently problematic tool.[25] She suggests the coming out story functions *conservatively* because it offers a narrative of individual identity-affirmation that does little to disturb 'heterosexual systems'.[26] I want to suggest that the coming out story in *BG* appears to confirm Roof's critique as the series unfolds, but in fact its final resolution takes quite a different turn.

[22] G Whitlock, '"Cop it Sweet": Lesbian Crime Fiction' in D Hamer and B Budge (eds), *The Good, the Bad, and the Gorgeous* (London: 1994) 161.

[23] Interview with Maureen Chadwick and Ann McManus, Shed Productions, 11 November 2001.

[24] Thanks to Jenni Millbank for highlighting this point.

[25] J Roof, *Come as You Are: Sexuality and Narrative* (New York: 1996) 104. [26] ibid, 107.

In the initial stages of their friendship in the first series, Helen is represented as not 'owning' her growing feelings for Nikki, although she openly acknowledges Nikki's sexuality, and is keen to appear non-homophobic. When Nikki tries to discuss their mutual attraction in episode 7, Helen is quick to declare not only her heterosexuality and imminent marriage, but also tells Nikki that 'everything I have done for you I have done for professional reasons'. However, Helen continues to seek Nikki out, and in episode 9 they eventually kiss. Helen is thrown into great confusion and, in the next episode, she calls Nikki into her office, ostensibly to discuss an exam Nikki is taking for her distance-learning university degree.

Helen: Take a seat. It's about your exam. I'll arrange for an invigilator to come in.
Nikki: Thought you'd given up taking an interest in me, miss.
Helen: Oh, look.
Nikki: Why've you been avoiding me then?
Helen: You know what I'm avoiding.
Nikki: Why don't you tell me?
Helen: Oh for goodness sake, Nikki. All I've been trying to do is to help you to do yourself some good. Because I don't want you to waste your potential . . . You had no right taking advantage of me.
Nikki: Well, put me down the block then, go on. Rule 47, subsection 16, being disrespectful to the wing governor—by kissing her. Or do you expect me to apologise? (Nikki goes to leave)
Helen: Nikki stop. Honestly, I'm telling you, if you carry on like this one of us is going to have to leave Larkhall. I mean it.

Although the 2000 series begins with Helen still 'in denial' about her feelings for Nikki, episode 2 ends with Helen resigning her job, acknowledging to Nikki that she can no longer fight her emotions, and kissing her, this time without any hesitation or regret. In the rest of this series (and through most of the next), however, Helen still appears to identify as straight, despite her relationship with Nikki. She also expresses a number of reservations about lesbianism, in terms of her own identity and sense of her future.

At the start of the third series, Helen ends her relationship with Nikki, saying 'we've got to let go'. It is not clear whether Helen's primary motivation for ending it comes from her professional/personal role conflict, or whether, as she puts it, their feelings are 'too strong' and she cannot handle them. Although there are several hints that she may still be in love with Nikki, Helen enters a serious relationship with Thomas, the new prison doctor, who appears to play the familiar role of the 'male intermediary' destined to thwart the women's love,[27] and confirm a heroine's heterosexuality,[28] but this is not the case.

In the 16th and final episode of this series, entitled 'Coming Out', Helen's dithering again comes to the fore. As Nikki is about to go to court for her appeal hearing, Helen tells her to 'forget about me' and says 'goodbye'. Helen goes out to

[27] C Straayer, 'The Hypothetical Lesbian Heroine in Narrative Feature Film' in CK Creekmuir and A Doty (eds), *Out in Culture* (Durham and London: 1995) 53, 55.

[28] Hart, n 9 above,75.

dinner with Thomas, who accuses her of 'not even being honest with yourself', in relation to her feelings for Nikki. The next day, Nikki's lawyers (both women) win her appeal, and we see Helen drinking alone in a bar, watching the story on the television news. Helen then arrives at Nikki's victory party, although she quickly leaves, believing Nikki to have re-united with Trish, her previous partner. Nikki follows Helen out on to the street, and invites her back in for a drink.

Helen: Thomas and I split up. I've been such an idiot.
Nikki: I know what you're saying.
Helen: No, let me say it. Thomas is gorgeous, he's everything you'd want in a man. But I want a woman.
Nikki: We'll take things slowly.
Helen: Ya, dead slow.
(they kiss)

Helen's coming out is thus completed in a scene that evokes the 'coming out' genre while at the same time disturbing it. Helen does not say 'I'm gay', or 'I want you', but says, 'I want a woman'; she makes this statement in a public street (thus also breaking the containment of lesbianism within the prison) using words very carefully chosen by the show's writers.[29] While Helen's dilemma is reminiscent of Evelyn's personal process in *Desert Hearts*, *BG* makes a stronger statement: Helen's storyline affirms a life choice, not just an instance of same-sex love. Despite the opportunity of a relationship with a 'perfect' man,[30] Helen does not want him, nor does she say she wants Nikki specifically (although this is clearly implied in the scene): what Helen 'wants' is 'a woman'.

The sexual agency of a 'wanting' Helen stands in stark contrast to the 'I'm gay' public confessional in *Ellen*,[31] or Kerry Weaver's similar revelation in *ER*. Ellen's 'I'm gay' follows the familiar pattern of the confessional identity claim. As Judith Roof has argued in a different context: 'Its subversiveness is fleeting . . . it is, in effect, already over, since its essence was the announcement of identity'.[32] Helen's 'I want' expresses desire not identity; the statement 'I want a woman' is unusual but it is this very discordance that I would suggest disrupts the conventions of heteronormativity rather than reproducing them.[33] In this sense, *BG* constructs a homonormativity that other representations of prime-time lesbians do not.

A Lesbian Feminist Perspective

BG's homonormativity is perhaps most advanced by the lens through which much of the action/dialogue is viewed. *BG* provides a space where lesbian feminist knowledge is an organizational principle, partly through having 'a lesbian character as the

29 Interview with Chadwick and McManus, n 23 above.
30 Chadwick and McManus, n 16 above.
31 Dow, n 6 above.
32 Roof, n 25 above, 111.
33 It may also disrupt the commodification of identity by avoiding identity-claiming altogether.

[show's] reference point for the normal psyche'.[34] To paraphrase Marshment and Hallam, lesbian identity is the basis of *BG*'s 'common sense'.[35] There are several specific ways in which *BG*'s lesbian lens is highlighted, and, in the following discussion, I focus on five of these: diversity of representation; sexual agency; an insider common-sense; the portrayal of an erotically-charged love story with a happy ending; and the representation of 'family'.

In terms of diversity of representation, *BG* parts company from similar genres by having several lesbian characters. Nikki, for example, is an early 30s business owner with access to economic resources. Denny, another member of the show's primary cast, is a young, working class lesbian of mixed-race heritage. Nikki and Denny have very little to do with each other in the show. While heteronormative perception might insist on these two characters 'hanging out' together by virtue of their shared lesbianism, *BG*, instead, reflects a different order—other than being lesbians, these two women, who clearly mix in different class/social circles, have virtually nothing in common.

Unlike Nikki, Denny begins the series as a nasty bully. Also in contrast to Nikki, Denny's offence is not a 'crime of passion'—she set fire to her children's home. Later, in the second series, Denny changes, becomes softer and far more likeable, and becomes involved with a new woman on the wing—Shaz. Shaz is also young, and in prison for employment-related manslaughter. While Nikki's crime is more conventionally lesbian in the 'women's prison genre' sense, in that it is sexualized, arguably out of control violence, Denny and Shaz's convictions are different. Their violence is rooted in familial and work-related despair. The lesbianism of all three is also entirely naturalized: it is taken-for-granted and unpathologized in any way. Indeed, as I discuss further below, the homophobia of 'bad' characters stands out as unnatural.

In addition to these three women, as well as background same-sex couples, there are other, minor, lesbian characters in the show. *BG*'s creators were keen to show 'bad' lesbians as well,[36] and they did this primarily through the character of 'Mad Tessa Spall', who appears in one episode in the second series and again in the third. At first glance, Tessa is a lesbian at home in the women's prison genre—she is aggressive, mentally unbalanced, dangerous, and sexually obsessive. No other lesbian character in *BG* remotely resembles Tessa. Indeed, if lesbian viewers were to watch only the episodes in which 'Mad Tessa' appears, it is possible that many would phone up the network to complain about the show's extreme homophobia. However, in the context of the series as a whole, the depiction of Tessa is rendered harmless (in homophobic terms), mainly because of the dominance of heroic Nikki, and fun, likeable, Denny and Shaz, and partly because the Tessa scenes are such high camp. While the show's creators were unhappy with aspects of how the

[34] C Patton, 'What's a Nice Lesbian Like You Doing in a Film Like This?' in T Wilton (ed), *Immortal, Invisible* (London and New York: 1995) 22.

[35] M Marshment and J Hallam, 'From String of Knots to Orange Box: Lesbians on Prime Time' in Hamer and Budge, n 22 above, 165.

[36] See n 23 above.

actor playing Tessa was directed,[37] Fiske has argued it may be just this sort of 'excess' that facilitates oppositional readings.[38] Mad Tessa's 'lesbian otherness' is even more underlined by having her attempt to bully Nikki, leading to a fight between the two, and Nikki losing prison privileges. Unsympathetic lesbians are also found in the Dedicated Search Team, a prison officer drugs squad. Again, their contrast with 'good' Nikki is highlighted by their abuse of her.

Second, the show's lesbian lens is sustained through the representation of Helen's sexual agency. Throughout the first series, Helen continually finds Nikki—in her cell, in the library, in the prison yard. In contrast to Evelyn and Cay's relationship in *Desert Hearts*,[39] for example, we rarely see Nikki waiting for Helen, or trying to contact her, and certainly not at all until much later in that series. Even Helen's fiancé, in episode 3, tells Helen that her interest in Nikki has become 'an obsession'. While a heteronormative look would render Nikki the initiator, and Helen the pursued, in *BG* the writers undertake a homonormative reversal. This is accomplished even more strongly during Helen and Nikki's sexual encounters. For example, when they spend the night together at Helen's home at the end of the second series (following Nikki's escape, disguised as a nurse), it is Helen who takes the sexual initiative, unbuttoning Nikki's uniform and beginning to undo her bra before the cut to another scene. Later, in bed, Nikki is cradled in Helen's arms, rather than the reverse. While this dynamic is more complicated than I have suggested, Nikki is hardly a passive onlooker, my point is simply that the idea of the heterosexual woman as the initial instigator of intimacy is more homo than hetero normative.

Helen and Nikki's romance constitutes the third element of *BG*'s lesbian perspective. As several commentators have noted in relation to popular culture,[40] 'images of lesbian sex are conspicuous by their absence'.[41] 'It would seem', writes Jackie Stacey, 'that the category of the *popular lesbian romance* . . . is a virtual contradiction in terms'.[42] But I would argue this is just what *BG* constructs. Although the intimate scenes between Nikki and Helen are not graphic or prolonged by any means, they are firmly located in the show's lesbian feminist perspective. These scenes are erotic, without being exploitative in the WIP sense, and when, at the end of the second series, Nikki and Helen finally have sex in Helen's home (again disrupting the conventional WIP containment of lesbianism within the prison) it is an 'amazing' experience for them both. Viewers on the *BG* message boards joked that their videotapes were worn out in these spots. While this was no doubt partly due to the almost complete absence of realistic, erotic, lesbian sex on mainstream television, I also discuss, further below, the way in which the appeal of these scenes contrasts with the mostly lurid, groping, unerotic depictions of

[37] ibid. [38] J Fiske, *Television Culture* (London and New York: 1987) 91,164,192–194.

[39] J Stacey, ' "If You Don't Play You Can't Win": *Desert Hearts* and the Lesbian Romance Film' in Wilton, n 34 above, 104. [40] Eg, Collis, n 7 above,139.

[41] J Kitzinger and C Kitzinger, ' "Doing It": Representations of Lesbian Sex' in G Griffen (ed), *Outwrite* (London: 1993) 9; see also Hantzis and Lehr, n 7 above; Moritz, n 7 above.

[42] Stacey, n 39 above, 112.

heterosexuality in the show. Nikki and Helen's happy ending at the end of the 2001 series is also another example of the show's homonormativity, standing in stark contrast to the usual forms of narrative closure for lesbian characters in popular television.[43]

A fourth aspect of *BG*'s lesbian lens is the ubiquity of a gay and lesbian insider, common-sense, or, as Evans and Gamman have argued in a different context, the appeal to lesbian 'cultural competencies'.[44] One example of this occurs in episode 1 of the third series as Helen drives Nikki back to prison following her escape in a nurse's uniform. Nikki grabs the wheel, the car swerves, and they are stopped by a woman police officer. The officer sees Nikki's uniform, and asks, 'are you nurses?'. Helen smiles and nods, the officer looks from Helen to Nikki and clearly believes she recognizes fellow lesbian travellers: 'you better get home to your bed then girls', she says, with a knowing wink. While heterosexual viewers may well read this scene as intended, it is clearly deeply embedded in a gay and lesbian 'interpretive community'.[45]

The high-camp manner in which characters express homophobia may also appear as 'insider humour' to a gay and lesbian audience. Shell's taunts to Nikki, for example in episode 7 of the 1999 series, are ludicrous and fundamentally unthreatening: 'what's this about—lesbi love poems? . . . what's up dyke, are ya scared?'. In episode 1 of the second series, Shell refers to Nikki as 'the evil lezzie bitch', and, in episode 6, warns a new inmate against getting too close to Nikki.

Shell: New girlfriend, Wade? Who goes on top, you or her?
Nikki: Shut it Dockley.
Shell: (to Barbara) You haven't got a clue what's going on, have ya?
Barbara: I'm sorry, I don't understand.
Shell: Well, if you can't work it out for yourself darling, just keep your knickers on after dark, that's all.
Barbara: What?
Shell: (lapping tongue) Lezbo, ain't she?

Shell's representation of Nikki is so untrue to the Nikki viewers know, and so patently absurd, that it is far more likely to be read as funny than offensive—including by a gay and lesbian audience. Indeed, as Straayer notes, these sorts of counter-hegemonic (within the show's normative framework), homophobic intrusions can actually serve to homoeroticize the situation further.[46]

Finally, in addition to its *Cagney and Lacey* style plot lines and anti-discrimination stories, *BG*'s lesbian narrative is also tinged with more than a little feminism. This is significantly expressed in the show's treatment of homosexuality, and, more specifically, in Helen's coming out story. In terms of the former, *BG*'s lesbian

[43] Moritz, n 7 above.

[44] C Evans and L Gamman, 'The Gaze Revisited, or Reviewing Queer Viewing' in Burston and Richardson, n 8 above, 35; see also R Lewis, 'Looking Good: The Lesbian Gaze and Fashion Imagery' (1997) 55 *Feminist Rev* 92.

[45] Lewis, ibid, 95.

[46] Straayer, n 27 above, 55.

perspective is a feminist one in the sense that, unlike other genres with gay characters, the causes or origins of inmates or officers' sexual orientation is never mentioned, much less discussed in any depth. Although we do learn about the background, and in some cases childhoods, of lesbian inmates, their own coming out stories are never told, but simply assumed and taken for granted. Viewers are never given genetic or psychological explanations for characters' lesbianism. Marshment and Hallam have argued that this silence is in itself evidence of lesbian, and I would argue feminist, authorship.[47] *BG*'s highlighting of the implicit feminist politics of Helen and Nikki also stands in contrast to mainstream, apolitical representations of so-called 'lesbian chic', or the apolitical or even anti-political approach of *Ellen* or *Will and Grace* or even *Queer as Folk*.

When considering the way in which Helen comes out, *BG*'s feminism becomes more apparent. Helen is initially drawn to Nikki's politics and interest in literature (*Sophie's World* is another novel that makes an appearance early in the first series), and, then, finds her relationship with Sean, her fiancé, *emotionally* unsatisfying. By the end of the 2001 series, Helen appears to make a *choice* to come out—'I want a woman'. Although, as I suggested earlier, this statement can be read as a challenge to essentialist identity-claiming, *BG*'s writers, who agonized over the line, intended it to reflect Helen's self-realization that she was, in fact, a lesbian.[48] Indeed, the writers chose this particular phrasing as a way of Helen acknowledging her authentic self. In this sense, it is not the intention of the show to be 'queer'; sexuality is not really fluid and 'gender bending' and transgenderisms are entirely absent. *BG*'s politics are rooted in an older lesbian feminism, one that celebrates women's solidarity and community, and this is most closely seen in its depiction of 'family'.

In *BG*, nuclear families are either invisible or dysfunctional. There is a total absence of idealized family relations in the show, and this distinguishes it from other quasi-feminist dramas that retained at least one model, nuclear unit as the comparative norm.[49] We know very little about most inmates' or officers' family backgrounds; the few times we encounter characters' parents they are either alcoholics, abusive, neglectful, or dismissed as uncaring and unsupportive. Nor does a single character in the series appear to have a satisfying relationship outside the prison. Instead, *BG* constructs an environment where relationships between women inside are paramount, and where the community of women inmates functions as a real family, providing the warmth, support, and, in some cases, mothering that the prisoners have not experienced on the outside. In more than one instance, inmates sacrifice relationships with men, and even with their own children, for each other. That this is a *lesbian* feminist construction of family is evidenced by the fact that lesbians are at the heart of this community—not outside it, opposed to it, or taking advantage of it.

[47] Marshment and Hallam, n 35 above, 163–164.

[48] Interview with Chadwick and McManus, n 23 above.

[49] J D'Acci, *Defining Women: Television and the Case of Cagney and Lacey* (Chapel Hill: 1987) 222; M Byers, 'Gender/Sexuality/Desire: Subversion of Difference and Construction of Loss in the Adolescent Drama of *My So-Called Life*' (1998) 23 *Signs* 711.

Strategies of Estrangement

I discussed above the ways in which homophobia is expressed solely by the 'bad' characters, and how this may render the remarks harmless and, perhaps, even amusing. The few instances where 'good' characters are homophobic are used as educational devices. Crystal, for example, when she first enters the prison, in episode 3 of the first series, tells Denny and Shell they will 'burn in hell' for their unnatural activities. However, Crystal soon becomes friendly with Denny, and later with Nikki, and we never again hear her make such a remark. She learns, presumably, that homophobia is uncalled for and undeserving. Barbara, another sympathetic character, initially 'freaks out' when forced to share a cell with Nikki. Within the same episode, however, Barbara regrets her reaction, realizes that her homophobia has helped to forge an unwanted alliance with a 'bad' officer, and she and Nikki quickly become fast friends. When Nikki leaves the prison at the end of the third series, Barbara is heart-broken. The estrangement of homophobia is, therefore, an important element in securing the show's homonormativity.

Another significant move in *BG*, at least to some extent, is to represent heterosexuality as a largely unappealing problematic. Although the show's creators vehemently disagree with this interpretation,[50] I would argue that a large proportion of *BG*'s representations of heterosexuality and bisexuality could be said to inhabit the violent, spectral place that Hart suggests is usually the province of lesbianism in popular culture.[51] Or, as Marshment and Hallam have written in the context of the BBC's *Oranges* adaptation, *BG* could be said to:

> . . . take for granted that which the dominant ideology would marginalize; investing the 'deviant' relationships with all the highly valued qualities that 'normal' relationships are supposed to possess, while denying them to those relationships that might technically be defined as 'normal'. It thus establishes within itself an oppositional commonsense. . . .[52]

While one straight couple have an idealized romance that is not so central to the first three series, no other heterosexual relationship is portrayed in a positive fashion. Jim Fenner's sexual relationships (with his wife and four other women) are embedded within scenes of violence, abuse, and exploitation, or, at best, deception and manipulation. Unlike the 'women in prison' genre, where, Mayne has argued, male characters tend to be marginal to storylines,[53] the centrality of the Jim Fenner character in *BG* plays a crucial role in 'othering' heterosexuality.

Similarly, Sylvia's (a 'bad' officer) marital relationship is depicted as being sexually unsatisfying, and she is represented as sexually repressed. We believe Yvonne and 'her Charlie' to have a good relationship, until it becomes clear that she has ended up in prison due to his duplicitous adultery. Yvonne then betrays him in court, and, following his acquittal, Yvonne's daughter has Charlie shot by a

[50] Email correspondence with Maureen Chadwick, on file with author. Chadwick argues that *BG* 'promotes loving relationships of all kinds'.

[51] Hart, n 9 above, x.

[52] Marshment and Hallam, n 35 above, 151.

[53] Mayne, n 9 above, 66.

contract-killer. Robin, Zandra's boyfriend, is shown to be an upper-class, weak-willed 'bastard' who takes Zandra's child away from her, leading to her attempting suicide. Other ostensibly straight inmates (ie, Monica, the two Julies, Barbara) either have no relationships with men (Monica), or (in the case of one of the Julies) have a fleeting relationship they appear to give up for a woman friend, or they have killed them (in Barbara's case, a 'mercy-killing').

Heterosexuality is also depicted as a site for out of control, dangerous, excessive behaviour. This is most acutely drawn through the characters of Shell, and Di Barker, an officer. Shell's sexuality is described explicitly, by a visiting psychologist, as being that of a 'raving nymphomaniac', and in episode 5 of the second series she begins a course of therapy to deal with it. Di Barker at times behaves like an obsessive stalker, who makes the lives of relatively good men miserable, and whose out of control desire even leads her to treat prisoners badly, a pattern that is not her normal mode of interaction. Early in the fourth series, Di falls for a psychopathic new officer who treats her with violent cruelty and contempt.

Bisexuality is similarly problematized and, to some extent, exists in what Cindy Patton has called an AIDS-era 'in between', 'netherworld'.[54] To the extent that viewers, bringing their own readings to the text, interpret Shell's character as bisexual,[55] her bisexuality may appear as evidence of her general 'sexual dysfunction'.[56] The only other bisexual inmate we encounter is revealed to be a child pornographer. Helen's bisexuality is represented as both problematic, and, in the end, an unviable life choice for this sympathetic, feminist crusader. Arguably, *BG*'s strategies of estrangement around hetero and bi sexualities are linked to its construction of a lesbian heroic that idealizes monogamy and fidelity.

Valorizations of monogamy are developed through several characters, including Nikki. Nikki shows no interest in Helen until Trish ends their relationship, and she shows no interest in anyone else until Helen does the same. Nikki over-embodies concepts of loyalty and fidelity, while *BG* invites viewers to criticize Helen's inconstancy (until the end). Faith and virtue are also glorified in the show's other idealized couple, Crystal and Josh. That they remain 'true' to each other, despite severe obstacles and temptations, is one of *BG*'s overarching themes throughout the series. Denny and Shaz, another normalized couple within the parameters of the show's discourse, also profess their exclusivity in episode 1 of the third series.

Shaz: Still fancy her, then?
Denny: Shell?
Shaz: Would you shag her if she came on to you?
Denny: Shell? What for? You're my baby now, in'it?
Shaz: Ya, I am, Den. And you're mine, right? So get back in bed then.

54 Patton, n 34 above, 21.

55 Against authorial intention, see Chadwick and McManus, n 30 above.

56 Several fans on the *BG* message board were worried that 'people out there' believed Shell to be a lesbian. The fans were concerned by this, particularly after a gruesome episode in Series 3 where Shell and Denny set someone alight, accompanied by much kissing.

This is virtually the only sexualized scene between Denny and Shaz, and at least part of the point here must be to show that Denny has pledged herself to Shaz, and is no longer one of the promiscuous characters in the series. While exclusive coupledom is no doubt a realistic scenario in terms of real inmate relationships, *BG*'s celebration of monogamous couples is heightened by the show's corresponding condemnation of infidelity and sexual excess.

In *BG*, adultery is the province of bad or weak men, Jim Fenner being the prime example. But there are other, less obvious, ones. Gina, an officer who joins the cast in the third series, suffers a miscarriage as a result of her partner's infidelity with Di Barker. Yvonne's husband is killed as a result of his extra-marital affair, as is his lover, whom Yvonne poisons. Robin, Zandra's boyfriend, becomes a thoroughly dislikeable character after ditching Zandra for another woman. The two most morally bankrupt characters in the series, Shell and Jim, are also the most sexually promiscuous. In addition to his wife, Jim has sexual relationships with many other women, while Shell is involved with Denny and Jim, and tries it on with several other men. *BG*'s 'good' men are partly distinguished by their refusal to fall for Shell's charms. However, the show's feminist inflection is apparent in the fact that we are given an explanation for Shell's 'nymphomania'—her childhood sexual abuse. At the same time, her sexuality is also explicitly medicalized (unlike characters' lesbianism) and rendered abnormal within the terms of *BG*'s sexual framework.

On the other hand, it is important to note how ideas of fidelity and exclusive commitment are embedded within the inmates' non-sexual relationships. Crystal, for example, sacrifices her freedom and happiness with Josh in order to stay on the inside with Zandra, who is dying. While the two Julies, whose deep friendship predates their incarceration, show their love for each other in a range of ways, including breaking *into* prison in order to be together. Importantly, this action, too, involves sacrificing (at least in the short term) a relationship with a man.

Thus far in this essay, I have suggested a number of ways in which *BG* is both interesting and important. I have argued that *BG* is, in a sense, genre-less: it displays elements of drama, soap, comedy, and, at times, docu-drama. This failure to conform to any particular genre facilitates the ability to convey non-dominant ideologies—in this case, a homonormativity that goes beyond the (re)production of 'positive images', or the conventional homosociality or 'situational lesbianism' of the prison context. While arguing that the show is homonormative, I have tried to flesh out just what homonormativity might mean in this context, most particularly in terms of narrative, perspective, and strategies of familiarity and estrangement. I have also suggested the importance of understanding that even 'good' lesbian representations may, at the same time, convey a set of other, more problematic ideologies. *BG* also has broader significance beyond the content of its texts, including the ways in which the lives of individuals have been 'changed' through watching the show, and through interacting on *BG* websites.[57]

[57] Herman, n 1 above.

Nevertheless, Rosemary Hennessy has argued that queer images in popular culture are rarely worth celebrating because such representations almost invariably are situated within and consolidate middle class, consumer culture.[58] The homonormative constructions of *Bad Girls* do not confirm her critique in so far as this particular cultural product focuses, with few exceptions, on the lives of working class women, many of whom come from backgrounds of extreme deprivation, and all of whom are in no position to consume much of anything. However, *BG*'s challenge to dominant gay market images, combined with its explicit feminist politics and narrative subversions, may be unsustainable under conditions of prevailing capitalist heteronormativity.[59] Yet, it may be that such challenges become more frequent, and arguably more embedded, as new spaces emerge for cultural communication.[60] In the UK, the success of one independent, feminist television company, and its product, *Bad Girls*, may be one example of this space and possibility. But I now wish to turn to the more conventional purview of 'law and popular culture': what does *BG* have to say about prison, justice, and the relationship between gender, sexuality, and law in popular cultural representations?

Prison

BG's critique of penal policy and practice with respect to women inmates is not oblique. The show highlights a range of prison practices including poor healthcare, the treatment of mothers, the inadequacy of mental health provision, and the plight of inmates who cannot speak English, to name just a few. These concerns reflect the authors' explicit intentions to use the series to comment critically on 'women in prison' issues, including the position of women governors in what Helen Stewart calls 'the old boys' club' of the prison service.

At the same time, this prison is not simply a place where women are disciplined and oppressed by power exercised from above. *BG* represents the prison as a place where inmates exercise agency, their actions have effects, and where power is more diffused and contested. This echoes, for example, recent work in criminology on resistance and agency in men's and women's prisons.[61] And, in keeping with the authors' feminist agenda, *BG* also represents the prison as a workplace where women employees do battle—against corruption, glass ceilings, and other forms of sexism. At one level, then, inmates and officers thus share considerable common ground and this was rendered explicit in a series 5 story involving the female wing governor and inmates banding together to fight a prison privatization scheme orchestrated entirely by men.

[58] R Hennessy, *Profit and Pleasure: Sexual Identities in Late Capitalism* (New York and London: 2000) Ch 4.

[59] J Millbank, 'It's About this: Lesbians, Prison, Desire' (2004) 13 *Social and Legal Studies* 155 above.

[60] M Curtin, 'Feminine Desire in the Age of Satellite Television' (1999) 49 *J of Communication* 55, 68.

[61] M Bosworth, *Engendering Resistance: Agency and Power in Women's Prisons* (Aldershot: 1999); M Bosworth and E Carrabine, 'Reassessing Resistance: Race, Gender and Sexuality in Prison' (2001) 3 *Punishment and Society* 501.

However, alongside these more radical narratives, *BG* offers a vision of prison as a place where racism has been all but vanquished and where those who complain of it are over-reacting or being manipulative. For example, in Series 3, Buki, a Black character, accuses an officer of calling her a 'nigger'. Although the officer in question is not one of the 'good ones', we have never heard her act or speak in such a racist fashion and so we must doubt the inmate's story (particularly as we already know Buki is a lying drug addict).

Perhaps most unrealistically, racism is never perpetrated by any of the prison officers. The most racist character is a thoroughly unsympathetic minor prisoner (Renee Williams), who is poisoned and dies after appearing in just two episodes. When Crystal complains about Renee's racism, the prison officers, even 'bad' Jim Fenner, are appalled and take immediate action. This stands in contrast to Fenner's constant and threatening homophobia, a juxtaposition that illustrates the extent to which *BG*'s homonormativity is a white one.

The only storyline perhaps taking racism within the prison seriously is one involving a minor character, Femi, a Nigerian 'drugs mule' who cannot speak English. Arguably, however, Femi's story is more about language than 'race' per se, and her 'foreign dress' and incomprehensible speech simply serve her up to the predominantly white audience as a Black 'spectacle'.[62] And while *BG* clearly shows how the prison system is not set up to cater for non-English speakers, we do realize wing governor Helen Stewart, our feminist heroine, always had Femi's interests at heart and was doing her best, and Femi herself is never seen again. Thus, for *BG*'s white, feminist authors, the prison system has clearly 'dealt with' racism in a way it has yet to tackle sexism and homophobia.

Law and Justice

One of *BG*'s creators has been quoted as saying that *BG* is not intended to question constructions of guilt or innocence, but rather to challenge the appropriateness of forms of punishment[63]—and this is just what *BG* conveys: women in prison are 'guilty as charged', but their punishment is ineffective and too harsh. *BG* constructs a critique of *sentencing* policy, while implicitly endorsing 'rule of law' ideology. Interestingly, the only inmate *BG* ever allows to have been 'proved innocent' is white, middle-class Monica, convicted of fraud. *BG*'s allegiance to the legitimacy of the rule of law is further advanced in other ways, for example, by story lines about peaceful protests degenerating into unjustified violence, by the fact that inmates like Monica, and even our homonormative heroine Nikki, see justice done at the end of the day.

[62] H Gray, 'Prefiguring a Black cultural formation: The New Conditions of Black Cultural Production' in D T Goldberg, M Musheno and L Bower (eds), *Between Law and Culture: Relocating Legal Studies* (Minneapolis: 2001) 74, 81.

[63] Quoted in Millbank, n 59 above.

Another illustration of the way in which *BG*'s 'take' on crime and justice is arguably a liberal one that ultimately plays into prevailing legal ideology is how the series deploys a privatizing strategy of blaming 'dysfunctional families' (particularly abuse and exploitation of girls and women) for criminal acts. Unlike the homonormative unintelligibility of the phrase 'causes of homosexuality' within the context of the show's politics, explaining, on the other hand, the causes of women's crime is an explicit goal of the series' creators/writers. And women's criminality is explained largely through the device of 'bad' or 'absent' parenting. While the show no doubt promotes empathy with women in prison, and crucially highlights gender injustices within prison practice, and these things are important, it does little to develop an analysis of how economic and social inequalities cause crime, problematize notions of what constitutes 'crime' itself, or show that crime is in fact 'normal' practice and a *requirement* of democratic capitalist law.[64] Instead, *BG* reinforces dominant ideologies about individual responsibility, violence, and lack of parenting skills in working class communities.

Further, once again dynamics of race and racism are marginalized and even trivialized. An example of the latter is the following exchange between Crystal and Nikki, in episode 7 of the first series, about Monica's appeal process:

Crystal (to Monica):	You're lucky you're a white woman, girl. You only got 5 years and now you're gonna walk.
Nikki:	Don't be daft Crystal.
Crystal:	If she'd been black she'd have got life and that's a fact.

Crystal's final comment is patently ridiculous, as we know that Monica was convicted of fraud, and only serves to represent Crystal as 'playing the race card' with no real justification. If, as the show's creators have stated, Nikki speaks for them as 'the political heart and soul of the series',[65] and viewers see things very much through Nikki's eyes, then to have Nikki call Crystal's views here 'daft' is rather telling. This interaction between Nikki and Crystal also denies a bond they could have shared—the experience of discrimination in the criminal justice system—particularly given Nikki's allusions to having suffered anti-gay discrimination in her trial and sentencing. Crystal's mistaken sense that she has been discriminated against in her sentencing is highlighted again in a conversation with Helen, where Crystal says, 'white girls don't get 12 months for what I've done', and we then discover that this is Crystal's third offence and her first incarceration.

Although I argued earlier that Hennessy's critique of queer 'commodity fetishism' did not seem borne out by *BG*'s form of homonormativity, *BG*'s valorization of the rule of law, and its marginalizing of the ways in which economic and social processes not only 'cause' crime, but construct and define it, do seem to sustain Hennessy's critique in a different way. Together with how the series deals,

[64] S Silbey, 'Mutual Engagement: Criminology *and* the Sociology of Law' (2002) 37 *Crime, Law & Social Change* 163.

[65] Chadwick and McManus, n 30 above.

or to be more precise does not deal, with racism, this implicit endorsement of democratic capitalist justice underlines the show's reinforcement of hegemonic understandings. Homonormativity, therefore, can, and in this case does, exist as one form of prime-time oppositional politics, but conveyed within a context of prevailing dominant ideologies.

PART VII
HUMAN RIGHTS

Image as Evidence and Mediation: The Experience of the Nuremberg Trials

Christian Delage

The influence of trials, like those in Nuremberg, on the first historical studies of the Second World War and of Nazism is well-known. The Nuremberg Trials appealed to young and established scholars in order to collect and inventory documentary evidence. Thus, it made it possible for historians in the postwar period to gain access to a significant volume of sources. This explains why the first histories of the Second World War followed these sources as well as the prosecution's case. However, there has been little attention given to the material and intellectual conditions surrounding the juridical administration of the evidence. And yet, the analysis of its status of truth not only refers back to the comparison of the methods of the judge and of the historian. It is more about envisioning that any trial is a location of 'historiographical experimentation' where 'one plays the sources *de vivo*, not only because they have been collected, but also because they have been confronted, submitted to cross-examination, and incited to reproduce, like in a psycho-drama, the affair of the judged'.[1]

In 1945, this 'living' dimension of the trial was particularly acute in so much as most of the people present at the Tribunal had been participants or witnesses, even at a distance, of the 'event', ie the Second World War. To that may be added, for the members of the American team charged with preparing the indictment, the knowledge acquired from the official or confidential reports written between 1939 and 1945 of the principal facts—in particular the infractions and crimes—that would permit the indictment of the Nazi leaders. The alleged criminals and their crimes were identified. The Allies agreed to the constitution of the International Military Tribunal (IMT) in order to avoid repeating the errors of the Leipzig trials held after the First World War before the Reich's High Court.[2] Thus, all of the pieces were assembled except one: it was necessary to produce the documents that would sustain the charges registered against the accused.

[1] *Diritto e ragione. Teoria del garantismo penale* (Bari: 1989) 32, cited by Carlo Ginzburg, *The judge and the historian: marginal notes on a late-twentieth-century miscarriage of justice* (trans Antony Shugaar, London and New York: Verso, 1999) 37.

[2] For a summary, see J-J Becker, 'Les Procès de Leipzig' in A Wieviorka (ed), *Les Procès de Nuremberg et de Tokyo* (Paris and Brussels: 1995), 51–60. In addition, see M Marrus, *The Nuremberg War Crimes Trial, 1945–1946. A Documentary History* (Boston and New York: 1997), 1–14.

According to Telford Taylor, the first question a prosecuting attorney asks in such a situation is: 'Where is the evidence?' The blunt fact was that, despite what 'everybody knew' about the Nazi leaders, virtually no judicially admissible evidence was at hand.[3]

I intend to show how, since the beginning, this search for evidence was widened to include filmed sources, and the manner in which the collection, presentation, and the reception of these sources posed some completely new problems to film directors, lawyers, and historians concerned with such a procedure. If there is no precise mention of an audiovisual document being retained as evidence in American criminal law, there is likewise nothing seeming to forbid it. Since the 1920s, one finds personal accident cases where the plaintiffs have had recourse to medico-legal films. Taken together, these diverse cases have led to a sort of jurisprudence founded on the general premise that film is not 'redundant proof' and that, characterized by movement, it brings forth something more than a fixed image:

> The general rule is that . . . motion pictures are admissible in evidence, within the sound discretion of the court, where such pictures are relevant to the issues, and are an accurate reproduction of persons and objects testified to in oral examination before the jury.[4]

At Nuremberg, if films had been presented as evidence (objective, physical traces), proof (demonstration of truth), and witness testimonies (affidavits attesting to the good faith of the filming or of the editing), the IMT had insisted in its statute that: 'The Tribunal shall not be bound by technical rules of evidence. It shall adopt and apply to the greatest possible extent expeditious and non-technical procedure, and shall admit any evidence which it deems to have probative value' (Article 19). This spirit of openness, although not excluding prior control of the sources ('The Tribunal may require to be informed of the nature of any evidence before it is offered so that it may rule upon the relevance thereof' Article 20), allowed, in particular, the admission of films projected onto a large screen during the hearings.

How did this experiment unfold? After all, this is how one must qualify the American initiative. Did this approach prove to be pertinent when the time came to evoke the 'Nazi atrocities'? Did these images effectively provide the proof?

The Educational Virtue of the Trials

The diffusion in the United States of the first images of the concentration and extermination camps in April 1945 contributed to Congress' increasing impatience with 'the absence of official information concerning the government's anticipated policy toward war crimes'.[5] In response to this wait, President Truman, by

[3] T Taylor, *The Anatomy of the Nuremberg Trials: A Personal Memoir* (London: 1993), 49.
[4] Quoted by P R Paradis, 'The Celluloid Witness' (1965) 37 *U of Colorado L Rev* 236.
[5] Cited by Taylor, n 3 above, 39.

a decree published 2 May 1945, designated Justice Robert H Jackson:

to act as the Representative of the United States and as its Chief of Counsel in preparing and prosecuting charges of atrocities and war crimes against such of the leaders of the European Axis powers and their principal agents and accessories as the United States may agree with any of the United Nations to bring to trial before an international military tribunal.[6]

In forming his team without delay, Jackson called upon the services of the ex-Coordination of Information, which, created in 1941, became the Office of Strategic Services (OSS) in 1942. Under the strong leadership of its director, General William J Donovan, the OSS had established the Field Photographic Branch (FPB) under the direction of John Ford. The celebrated director had already been called to active duty with the rank of commander, just weeks before Pearl Harbor, to take charge of the Navy's 11th Photographic Unit. He directed newsreels and documentaries that earned him not only recognition from the military and political authorities, but also from Hollywood. He brought into this new unit most of the esteemed film making professionals who had worked with him before the war. In the bi-monthly reports of the OSS, the rubric 'War Crimes', which appeared in 1944, regularly raised the question of the collection of evidence—written or audiovisual. Previously, in 1942, the Office of War Information had produced a training manual for the motion picture industry. Later, the OSS added an instruction dedicated to the documentation of war crimes and atrocities:[7]

In the performance of normal duties, officers and men frequently encounter evidence of war crimes and atrocities that should be preserved for future consideration. Because human memory is faulty and because objects constituting physical evidence decompose, change or are lost, it is important that a contemporary record be made of the event in such form that it will constitute an acceptable proof of occurrence, identify the participants, and afford a method of locating principals and witnesses so far as may be possible at some future time. To record such evidence in a uniform manner and in a form which will be acceptable in military tribunals or courts, it is essential that the instructions herein be followed closely. Study them and carry the manual with you in the field to serve as a guide.[8]

Jackson presented President Truman with a detailed report on 1 June 1945 which was made public on 7 June. The foundations upon which the IMT must be constituted were thus set out:

The groundwork of our case must be factually authentic and constitute a well-documented history of what we are convinced was a grand, concerted pattern to incite and commit the aggressions and barbarities which have shocked the world. We must not forget that when the Nazi plans were boldly proclaimed they were so extravagant that the world refused to

[6] Executive Order 9547 by President Truman, 2 May 1945, Washington DC.

[7] *Government Information Manual for the Motion Picture Industry*, Summer 1942 (Office of War Information).

[8] [*Instruction*], Archives of the OSS, Record Group 226, Entry 133, Box 124, Folder 1077, National Archives and Records Administration, Washington DC, hereafter cited as NARA followed by the record number.

take them seriously. Unless we write the record of this movement with clarity and precision, we cannot blame the future if in days of peace it finds incredible the accusatory generalities uttered during the war. *We must establish incredible events by credible evidence.*[9]

The 'Nazi Atrocities': Myth and Reality

In New York where the Russians presented the first newsreels showing Majdanek and Auschwitz at the time of their opening or liberation, they decided to call them *Nazi atrocities*. By using such a phrase, the Russians did exactly the same as the other countries, that is, they demonstrated an initial unwillingness to qualify as genocide what happened in the Nazi extermination camps. But, as the films came from the USSR, there was suspicion as to their credibility. The Americans had to see the images made by their own cameramen in order to believe those released by Artkino.[10] Despite this, and contrary to the indications given by polls,[11] the spectators were struck by a double sense of disbelief: firstly, the memory of the doubts about the 'atrocities' committed by the Germans during the First World War remained, particularly the stories relating to the invasion of Belgium in 1914.[12] Early on, some documented reports established that these atrocities did take place. But, at the same time, in the heart of a battle of propaganda, some myths were spread, such as the one concerning enemies crucified by the Germans.[13] In the interwar period, during which public opinion was mostly pacifist, 'German atrocities were considered, at least in the Anglo-Saxon countries', Alan Kramer reminds us, 'exemplary of the falsifications peculiar to war propaganda'.[14] The Nazis kept alive the memory of this confusion and tried to make people believe in the existence of 'exemplary camps', thereby contradicting the 'atrocity propaganda'

[9] 'Report from Mr. Justice Jackson, Chief of Counsel for the United States in the prosecution of Axis War Criminals,' NARA, RG 226, E 90, B 12, F 126, p 3. Emphasis added.

[10] See T Doherty, *Projections of War. Hollywood, American Culture, and World War II* (New York: 1993), 247–250.

[11] 'The success of the campaign to educate Americans about Nazi atrocities was demonstrated in a Gallup poll taken in early May of 1945, one that indicated progress from the poll taken in November 1944. A cross section of the American public was asked: "What do you think of the reports that the Germans have killed many in concentration camps or let them starve to death—are they true or not true?" Eighty-four percent answered "true"; 9 percent believed the statement to be "true, but exaggerated"; only 4 percent answered "doubtful, hard to believe" or "not true"; 3 percent couldn't decide,' R A Abzug, *Inside the Vicious Heart. Americans and the Liberation of Nazi Concentration Camps* (New York: 1985), 135–140.

[12] See S Audoin-Rouzeau and A Becker, *14–18, retrouver la guerre* (Paris: 2000), 61–68, 120–124.

[13] See J Horne, 'Les mains coupées, "atrocités allemandes" et opinion française en 1914' in J-J Becker, J Winter, G Krumeich, A Becker, and S Audoin-Rouzeau (eds), *Guerre et cultures, 1914–1918* (Paris: 1994), 133–146. John Horne and Alan Kramer, *German Atrocities: A History of Denial* (New Haven, 2001).

[14] A Kramer, 'Les "atrocités allemandes": Mythologie populaire, propagande et manipulations dans l'armée allemande', ibid, 147. Kramer cites the American historian Ralph H Lutz, who was saying that, in 1933, '[t]he accusations issued against the German army during the war were like fabrications conceived to demonize the German nation for propaganda purposes'.

(*Greuelpropaganda*).[15] Jackson himself stated that 'I am one who received during this war most atrocity tales with suspicion and skepticism'.[16]

The second disbelief came from the difficulty of obtaining a clear idea of the seriousness and scope of the crimes committed against the Jews. In 1938, *Kristallnacht* had looked terrifying, but its violence was looked on as that of an act of barbarity belonging to a bygone age. In 1945, in order to win the spectators' trust, Eisenhower, particularly shocked by the visit he paid with Patton to the Ohrdruf Camp on 12 April, ordered the Army to organize and film the arrival of Hollywood professionals, journalists and Congressmen. Nobody in the USA was to be left in doubt. In a letter written three days later, Eisenhower wrote:

> The things I saw beggar description. While I was touring the camp I encountered three men who had been inmates and by one ruse or another had made their escape. I interviewed them through an interpreter. The visual evidence and the verbal testimony of starvation, cruelty and bestiality were so overpowering as to leave me a bit sick. In one room, where they [there] were piled up twenty or thirty naked men, killed by starvation, George Patton would not even enter. He said he would get sick if he did so. I made the visit deliberately, in order to be in position to give *first-hand* evidence of these things if ever, in the future, there develops a tendency to charge these allegations merely to 'propaganda'.[17]

The qualification of 'atrocity' was maintained so as to underline the uncertainty with which the Allies were, Nuremberg included, to determine specifically what follows an indictment of a war crime, crime against humanity and, mainly, genocide.

In his Opening Statement, where he devotes a long section to the 'Crimes against the Jews', Justice Jackson says: 'If I should recite these horrors in words of my own, you would think me intemperate and unreliable. Fortunately, we need not take the word of any witness but the Germans themselves.'[18] Actually, he cited as evidence against the defendants a large amount of orders and official reports written by them. However, the films shown during the trial were rarely part of this procedure. Those coming from the perpetrators themselves were rare and always made outside the camps, recording without any permission some of their acts of violence, particularly in the ghettos. Most of the existing images were to be taken by the Allied forces at the moment of the Liberation of the camps:

> We will show you these concentration camps in motion pictures, just as the Allied armies found them when they arrived, and the measures General Eisenhower had to take to clean them up. Our proof will be disgusting and you will say I have robbed you of your sleep. But

[15] See K Margry, ' "Theresienstadt" (1944–1945): The Nazi Propaganda Film Depicting the Concentration Camp as Paradise' (1992) 12(2) *Historical J of Film, Radio and Television*, 145–162.

[16] 'Justice Jackson's Opening Statement,' 21 November 1945, *Trial of the Major War Criminals before the International Military Tribunal, Nuremberg, 14 November1945–1 October 1946*, 42 vols, 2:129; herein cited as IMT.

[17] 'To George Catlett Marshall,' in AD Chandler, Jr (ed), *The Papers of Dwight David Eisenhower. The War Years* (Baltimore: 1970), 2616.

[18] 'Justice Jackson's Opening Statement' (IMT, 2:122).

these are the things which have turned the stomach of the world and set every civilized hand against Nazi Germany.[19]

At first, the arrival of the Allied troops provoked a strange situation where the liberator and deportee exchanged their first glances under the gaze of a shaky, and shaken, movie camera.[20] The Soviet officer in charge of the photographic team following the progress of the Red Army describes in a poignant manner how, at their arrival in Auschwitz, they were shocked, as were the 7,000 prisoners still in the camp at that time who did not react.[21] The cameramen needed a certain amount of time before beginning to film; but this moment proved to be too long for the deportees to show what the Soviets were waiting for: their consciousness—if not the happiness—of being liberated. Sometimes, by the time they were ready to fix the cameramen's gaze, the camp inmates had already gone,[22] and were beginning their long road home. Talking in front of the Allied movie-cameras was already a difficult experience, but for some of the surviving deportees who were brought to give testimony in a pre-legal framework, it involved the risk of seeing the person 'disappear behind the few facts that were to be established'.[23]

Many gazes stare out of these first images: those of the 'liberated' deportees, of their liberators, of the cameramen, but also those, under duress, of the butchers regarding their victims or those of the people living near the camps required to go inside them in order to acknowledge their existence. Far from being unequivocal or straightforward, the camera's eye recorded the complexity of embracing the reality of the camps, which required the presence of all the protagonists. That is

[19] 'Justice Jackson's Opening Statement' (IMT, 2:122), 139.

[20] This staggering effect had already been endured by the Jews taken to the Babi Yar ravine when they realized, *in extremis*, that the pit was full of bodies following the mass executions of 29 and 30 November (altogether, more than 33,000 Jews were murdered in two days by the Sonderkommando directed by Paul Blobel). During his cross-examination, Fritz Höfer explained: 'The Jews arriving in the ravine were so scared by the horrible image (*grausige Bild*), that they were completely without any will (*vollkommen willenlos*). It even happened that they laid down in rank and file (*in Reih und Glied*) waiting to be shot.' 27 August 1959, ZStL, 2 AR-Z 21/58 (Ehrlinger Case, [BdS Kiev, Sk 1b.]), vol 6, folios 4013–4047, description of Babi-Yar, folios 4035–4045.

[21] A Vorontsov, *The Liberation of Auschwitz, 1945* (Chronos UK, VHS, 60 mins, 1994). According to Primo Levi: 'The first Soviet patrol came close to the camp around noon, 27 January 1945 . . . They did not greet us, did not give us a smile. To their pity was added a confused feeling of embarrassment which oppressed them, made them mute and chained their eyes to this gloomy sight.' See P Levi, *La Trêve* (trans E Genevois-Joly, Paris: 1997), 9–10. My translation.

The Soviet Army could hardly film the deportees because there was no electricity after the destruction caused by the fleeing Nazis: it was in the darkness that the first glimpses were exchanged and that is the reason why most of the images were taken outside the barracks.

[22] 'In the late afternoon', recalls Envir Alimbekov, sergeant in the Red Army, 'some of them kept crying and took us in their arms, then whispered some words in a language that we could not understand. They wanted to talk; they began to tell their story. But we did not have enough time. The night was falling. We had to leave.' See his interview in *Contre l'oubli*, a documentary written by William Karel, Jean-Charles Deniau and Philippe Alfonsi, directed by William Karel (Taxi Productions, VHS, 80 mins 1995).

[23] As Michael Pollak explains: 'These statements show . . . signs of the principles of the juridical way of establishing proof: limitation to the case of the trial, elimination of all elements considered as off the subject'. See M Pollak, *L'Expérience concentrationnaire* (Paris, 1990; 2nd edn, 2000), 188.

why the historical value of the newsreels shown during the trial came from their documentary as well as their testimonial evidence. In trying to give examples of the numerous methods of killing and torture, and by bringing out the characteristics, even minor, of the different liberated camps, something of the exhaustiveness of the techniques of crime was suggested, if not shown.[24] The point was not at that time to give an idea of what was to become known later as the 'Holocaust of the European Jews', neither to think of the 'unspeakable' fact of genocide. What was needed was just to stand on the doorstep of the inhumanity endured by the deportees and to show what, until then, had largely been hidden.[25] This view of the camps was suitable for educating public opinion which had been little informed of their existence between 1941 and 1945.[26]

The Filmic Evidence

The first film shown in the courtroom of Nuremberg, on 29 November 1945, was entitled *Nazi Concentration Camps (PS-2430)*.[27] It was supervised by Ray Kellogg, assistant of the famous director John Ford, who was at the head of the Film and Photographic Branch of the OSS.[28] If George Stevens is credited with the film, it is because he was, as Lt Colonel, from 1 March to 8 May 1945, on active duty with the United States Army Signal Corps. Attached to the Supreme Headquarters Allied Expeditionary Forces (SHAEF), he directed the photographing of Nazi concentration camps and prison camps as liberated by Allied forces.

Despite its title, the film did not tell the story of the Nazi camps, the 'Final Solution,' but testified to 'the most representative camps, mirroring the conditions of daily life in them,' ie those liberated or discovered by the Americans and the

[24] It may be possible that the cameramen wondered about what those responsible for atrocities had in mind, particularly when they filmed some of the perpetrators at the scene of their crimes. In his study of the violence perpetrated by the leaders of the *Einsatzgruppen*, Christian Ingrao describes the way 'they played an essential role in the emergence of the imagination of the genocide, by applying the Nazi model of racism to the experience of total war': 'Culture de guerre, imaginaire nazi, violence génocide. Le cas des cadres du SD' (2000) 47(2) *Revue d'histoire moderne et contemporaine* 287.

[25] About Ellis Island, Georges Perec wrote: 'This is what you see today, and the one thing we know is that this is not the way it was at the turn of the century, but this is what is left for us to see and we have nothing else to exhibit,' G Perec with R Bober, *Ellis Island* (trans H Mathews, New York: 1995) 47. In addition, see C Delage and V Guigueno, ' "Ce qui est donné à voir, ce que nous pouvons montrer." Georges Perec, Robert Bober et la Rue Vilin' (1997) 3 *Études photographiques* 121–140.

[26] See B Genton, ' "A Sea of Shoes . . ." La perception de la Shoah aux États-Unis (1941–1945)' (1999) 6 *Sources* 99–136.

[27] See L Douglas, 'Film as Witness: Screening *Nazi Concentration Camps* before the Nuremberg Tribunal' (1995) 105 *Yale LJ* 449–481, reprinted in L Douglas, *The Memory of Judgment: Making Law and History in the Trials of the Holocaust* (New Haven: 2001), 11–37.

[28] In a letter addressed to John Ford on 20 November 1945, Ray Kellogg explains how impatient he was, waiting for the moment of showing the film: '. . . I can hardly wait until we hit them with the Concentration Camps' film, which, by the way, has become not only the highlight of the Prosecution, but the main support of Count #4 of the Indictment—which is "Crimes Against Humanity," ' John Ford Papers, Lilly Library (Bloomington, Indiana), Manuscripts Department.

British troops:[29] Leipzig (mass graves), Penig (care provided by Americans to some young women), Ohrdruf (Eisenhower's visit), Hadamar (exhumation and post-mortem examination of bodies poisoned or badly treated; interrogation of the Nazi in charge of the so-called 'asylum'), Breendonck (reconstruction of the methods of torture used against Belgian resistants), Nordhausen (a few surviving, albeit very weak, deportees among thousands of dead), Harlan (first meal taken by the deportees in a long time), Arnstadt (exhumation of bodies), Mauthausen (account given by an imprisoned American officer), Buchenwald (compulsory visit of the camp by 1,200 people coming from Weimar; images—including those of the crematoria—linked to the report made by the American Commission in charge of the POWs and of the displaced persons), Dachau (aerial shots of the camp, giving an idea of its size; series of shots explaining the working of a gas chamber) and Bergen-Belsen.[30]

This last sequence was shot by the British Army.[31] In it, an officer explains that 'the most difficult task is to force the SS, who are about 50, to bury the bodies. We have already buried 17,000 people and there's still as many.' This scene was to be put in a film produced for the German people after 1945, but it was finally shown only in the 1980s. In 1986, it was broadcast on English TV under the title *Memory of the Camps*.[32] Sidney Bernstein, who was charged with this project, worried that

[29] A first documentary was made in a newsreel series designed for the German population: see *Welt im Film* 5 (15 June 1945) for shots of Ohrdruf, Ziegenheim, Kaunitz, Holzen, Schwarzenfeld, Göttingen, Hadamar, Arnstadt, Bergen-Belsen, Gardelegen, Tekhla, Nordhausen, Buchenwald.

[30] Even if there is a sort of established hierarchy in the importance between the first and the last of these 'camps', the distinction is not always made between their diverse functions (concentration, Kommando, institutes for medical experiments, etc). In any case, at the liberation or the opening of these camps their situation did not necessarily reflect what had happened there. This is how it was at Bergen-Belsen, just before the arrival of the Allies: 'The camp administration broke down. As tens of thousands of new inmates were dumped in the camp (in the single week of April 4–13, 1945, the number was 28,000), the food supply was shut off, roll calls were stopped, and the starving inmates were left to their own devices', Raul Hilberg, *The Destruction of European Jews* (London: 1961; 2nd edn, New York: 1985), 986. In the commentary to the film, there is only one mention of the Jews: 'Among the 4,000 victims of Ohrdruf were Poles, Czechs, Russians, Belgians, Frenchs, Jews and German political prisoners'. On the American authorities' deliberation on this policy, see DE Lipstadt, *The American Press and the Coming of the Holocaust, 1933–1945* (New York: 1986), 250–254, and A Wieviorka, *Déportation et génocide. Entre la mémoire et l'oubli* (Paris: 1992), particularly the chapter entitled 'Diversité des situations dans les camps', 190–235.

[31] Many of these images were presented 'as "principal witnesses" during the trial of the Belsen Butchers. Such a screening was the first of this kind inside a courtroom and took place in the British Tribunal established in Luneburg 20 September 1945,' says M-A Matard-Bonucci, *La Libération des camps et le retour des déportés* (Brussels and Paris: 1995), 76.

[32] We must not be mistaken about the reasons why this film was shown neither in Germany nor in England in 1946. Should the images taken by the British cameramen have been immediately released, their reception would have given some information about the reactions of the audience and the best way to show such pictures. The gathering and the editing of the footage of *F3080*, the code number given to the film we know now as *Memory of the Camps*, lasted many months; the producers could not gauge audience response. It caused real concern in official circles, where the opinion grew that it would be better to roll up one's sleeves and help Germany to rebuild, instead of overwhelming it with the burden of the crime perpetrated. See E Sussex, 'The Fate of F3080' (1984) 53 *Sight and Sound* 97. After verification at the Film Department of the Imperial War Museum, it looks as if the actual print of the film corresponds to the editing and the commentary made in 1946. There is one reel missing, the fifth

it would be considered as proof even though it was not made for the Nuremberg Trial: 'The film should be in the form of a Prosecuting Counsel stating his case', he explained on 30 April 1945. 'It is of extreme importance that German audiences see the faces of the individual directly responsible . . . Efforts should be made to secure the names and personal background of all persons thus shown, attempting to establish that they were once "ordinary people".'[33] From that perspective, he asked the advice of one of his old friends, Alfred Hitchcock, who had come back for a while to England as he wanted to create a new independent production company.

He paced up and down and talked about it and had a lot of ideas as to what should be done. . . . One of his things was that we should try to prevent people from thinking that any of this was faked. One of the big shots I recall was when we had priests from various denominations who went to one of the camps. . . . It was all shot in one shot so that you saw them coming along, going through the camp, and you saw from their point of view all that was going on. And it never cut.[34]

The sequence-shot, if continuous and large-scale, used to be considered the most respectful toward the event filmed, as there was no alteration coming from the editing. The concern for the status of truth of the image demonstrates the proximity of the British and the US politics of production in war time. On the American side, thanks to the professionalism of the reporters and the need for the soldiers to be filmed as witnesses of the atrocities, a kind of editing was made live. The length of the shots and the size of the frame were used to tell a story right away, in the manner of the Hollywood *savoir-faire* (long shots alternating with short ones, narration of a story centred on individuals, happy ending).[35] In both experiences, all was conditioned to collect evidence that could then become part of the indictment against war criminals.

After *Nazi Concentration Camps*, two other moving pictures were presented in the courtroom. On 13 December 1945, a document called *Original German 8-millimeter Film of Atrocities against Jews* (PS-3052), taken by a member of the SS and captured by the United States military forces near Augsburg, Germany was shown. The scene is the extermination of a ghetto by Gestapo agents, assisted by military units. It contains pictures of beatings and mistreatment of naked women and other atrocities, all in the presence of and with the apparent concurrence of

one, regarding Majdanek and Auschwitz. For a complete view of the content of the film, consult *Concentration Camp film Scenes as assembled on 7th May, 1946* and *Proposed line of commentary for film on the concentration camps* (Textual Record F 3080, Imperial War Museum).

[33] S Bernstein, 'Material needed for Proposed Motion Picture on German Atrocities', SHAEF. Psychological Warfare Division. Public Records Office (PRO).

[34] Interview with P Tanner, *A Painful Reminder* (Documentary, Granada TV, 1985).

[35] That is why it is always important to pay attention to the film footage of the newsreels, and to the notes written by the cameramen, in order to understand their meaning and the work done by the editors. This is made possible at the archives of the NARA and, in France, at the Etablissement Cinématographique et Photographique des Armées (ECPA, Ivry-sur-Seine).

armed German soldiers and SS men in uniform. James Donovan, who presented the film for the American prosecution, said that:

> The scene presented to the Tribunal is probably one which occurred a thousand times all over Europe under the Nazi rule of terror. The film was made on an 8-millimeter home camera. Because of this, because of the fact that part of it is burned, because of the fact that it runs for only 1 1/2 minutes, and because of the confusion on every hand shown on this film, we do not believe that the Tribunal can properly view the evidence if it is shown only once. We therefore ask the Tribunal's permission to project the film twice as we did before the Defense Counsel.[36]

The strength of that document, as it was shown, served as a counterpoint to the previous films, since it had been made by the perpetrators themselves, revealing the complacent attitude to their crimes. It was also interesting because of the location of the scene, an urban place, whose familiarity increased the gap between the ordinary life of the residents and the terror implemented.

Finally, on 19 February 1946, the Soviet prosecution presented a documentary edited by the Red Army, *The Atrocities committed by the German Fascist Invaders in the U.S.S.R.* (URSS-81),[37] showing the sad fate that awaited the Soviet prisoners of war, as well as the civilians and the deportees. The shots were very close to the bodies, so that the commentary could specify the identity and the profession of the victims, particularly for the civilians. Many of these bodies were mutilated; some of them were hung from street lamps. During the funerals, some women were mourning their son or their husband. It then became difficult to endure when raped and murdered women or children with broken skulls were shown, and, at the end, shots of crematoria and gas chambers, piles of clothes and bundles of hair in Majdanek and Auschwitz. Nevertheless, the film was ambiguous about the nature of the process that was going on from the crimes against civilians and Soviet troops to the ones committed in the extermination camps: here, the Jews appeared only in a list of nationalities deported to Auschwitz ('Poles, Russians, Jews, French, Belgians . . .'). Goering took advantage of this to call into question the sincerity of the Soviets:

> First of all, a film that *they* made is not proof, just looking at it from a legal point of view. They could just as easily have killed a few hundred German PW's and put them in Russian uniforms for the atrocity picture—you don't know the Russians the way I do. Secondly, lots of those pictures were probably taken during their own revolution like the baskets of heads. Thirdly, those fields covered with bodies.—Well, such pictures are easy to get any time in a war. I've seen thousands of bodies myself. And where did they get the fresh corpses to photograph? They couldn't have come right in ready to take pictures. They must have shot those people themselves.[38]

[36] IMT, 7:600.

[37] A copy of this picture, along with the description of its content made for the Nuremberg Trial (call number CCCLIX-1), is available at the Centre de documentation juive contemporaine (CDJC, Paris).

[38] GM Gilbert, *Nuremberg Diary* (New York: 1947), 162.

Separated from the first sequence, the images of the extermination camps of Majdanek and Auschwitz would have provoked a reaction of terror still more intense than what the defendants felt in front of the American film *Nazi Concentration Camps*. However, by including them in the continuity of the crimes committed by the Germans against the Soviets, it became thus possible for Goering, in a cynical manner, either to claim responsibility—implicitly—for them, or to try to deprive them of the specificity of their genocidal violence. By adopting this attitude, he isolated himself from the other defendants, for most of whom it was a great blow.[39]

The Hermeneutic Prerogative of the Image

In Nuremberg, the screening of films took place in a context where there was no prior judgment or historiographical tradition. This anteriority allowed the film to display fully its own specificity, which might look contradictory: mechanical recording of an event, the position nevertheless given in advance to the spectator. Because a film is always directed at somebody, and because the director knows well that he can only proceed to a reconstruction of the spectacle of life, the accuracy of the camera does not lie in any technical attribute, but in the fact of assuming that subjectivity and giving a value of truth to it. Recalling the descriptions made by Herodotus in his *Histories*, François Hartog mentions that they 'make see, and make see a knowledge: they actually have the eye as the focal point; that is the eye which organizes them (the visible), delimit the proliferation (the field of vision), and authenticate them (witness). So, that is it which makes believe that one sees and knows, it which is producing *peitho*, persuasion; I have seen, so I believe.'[40]

The radical otherness of the atrocities committed by the Nazis could have led to an effect of terror that would be harmful to the credibility of the images taken. The first eyewitnesses, the cameramen, did not mask this first shock; on the contrary, they demonstrated their presence by inscribing it during the shooting. Added together, these images made a whole, allowing an understanding of the scale of the Nazi crimes, even if there was no mention of the extermination camps. The OSS Team, in charge of the direction of the editing of *Nazi Concentration Camps*, tried to build a story, a kind of plotting of the 'Barbarity of the Nazis', making up a piece of evidence to be discussed in the courtroom. The presence of motion pictures was thus not restricted only to the visual part of them, but included what Pierre Legendre describes elsewhere as 'a structural position of a *fictional third party*, working as an hermeneutic prerogative'.[41] The qualification of *fiction* might surprise, considering

[39] Gilbert concluded his narration of the events of 19 February by quoting some of the words he heard from Fritzsche: 'I have—the feeling—I am drowning in filth—whether their or ours—it is immaterial—I am choking in it—.' Ibid, 164.

[40] F Hartog, *Le Miroir d'Hérodote. Essai sur la représentation de l'autre* (Paris: 1980; 2nd edn, 2001), 383.

[41] P Legendre, 'Lortie à la rencontre de son image. Note sur la diffusion de l'enregistrement vidéo pendant le procès,' *Leçons VIII. Le Crime du caporal Lortie. Traité sur le Père* (Paris: 1989), 102.

what is at stake in the legal system. Perhaps one should interpret this statement as a way to play down definitively the idea that the realism of film comes from the recording machine. If a film helps to understand a fact, it is because of its double ability to prove and to testify. Renaud Dulong quite rightly emphasizes the question of the modification of 'the ideal of the eyewitness' regulation':

Has not the use of these mechanical means surreptitiously encouraged the tendency to devalue the witness by comparison to the filmed representation? In denouncing the defectiveness of testimony, one is at least entitled to ask what role the impression of perfect fidelity offered by the photographic images and the magnetic tape recordings plays.[42]

By deciding to show films in the Nuremberg courtroom as proof of the guilt of the Nazi leaders on trial there, the Allies first wanted to demonstrate that the filter of the image enabled the vision of genocidal violence for the reporters faced with its consequences or its visible traces as well as for the viewers of newsreels and people participating in or attending the Nuremberg trial. They made it possible to look at what the protagonists saw and what the Nazis wanted to show to German society (the self-representation of *The Nazi Plan*, a montage composed of German news only presented on 11 December 1945) and what they wanted to hide (the genocidal violence, *Original German 8-millimeter Film of Atrocities against Jews*). This prerogative also manifested itself in the way in which the Allies, setting aside for a moment the written archives that were the basis of the indictment of the accused, testified about their own experience of the discovery of the camps (*Nazi Concentration Camps, The Atrocities of the German-Fascist Invaders in the USSR*), and the difficulties—past and present—of informing their respective public opinions.[43] The night before the showing, it occurred to the Documentary Evidence Section that, with the lights off, it would be impossible to watch the reactions of the defendants to this evidence. They decided to run a neon tube just beneath the top of the dock fence, which 'would throw a soft light onto the defendants' faces without affecting the screen'.[44] On 29 November, everybody could see simultaneously the film and the defendants. 'Suddenly', wrote Joseph Kessel, *France-Soir*'s special correspondent:

I had the feeling that the resurrection of the horror was not, at that moment, the main thing. . . . The point was not to show to the court a document which they certainly knew very well. It was about the way to put the defendants face-to-face with their enormous crimes, to throw the murderers, the butchers, right in the middle of the mass graves they created, and to surprise the reactions generated by this show, this shock.[45]

[42] R Dulong, *Le Témoin oculaire. Les conditions sociales de l'attestation personnelle* (Paris: 1998), 30.
[43] cf M Osiel, *Mass Atrocity, Collective Memory and the Law* (New Brunswick: 1997). Without making a direct reference to film as evidence, but concerning the Holocaust, Osiel writes that: 'If courts are to influence collective memory of such historical episodes to persuasive ways, they must admit a wider range of evidence and argument than are often cognizable within legal terms', ibid, 97.
[44] See S Schulberg, 'An Eyewitness Reports' (1947) 2 *Hollywood Quarterly* 413.
[45] J Kessel, *France-Soir*, 3 December 1945.

These reactions were carefully written down by the psychologist in charge of the defendants:

> Piles of dead are shown in a slave labor camp . . . von Shirach watching intently, gasps, whispers to Sauckel . . . Funk crying now . . . Goering looks sad, leaning on elbow . . . Doenitz has head bowed, no longer watching . . . Sauckel shudders at picture of Buchenwald crematorium oven . . . as human skin lampshade is shown, Streicher says, 'I don't believe that' . . . Goering coughing . . . attorneys gasping . . .[46]

The following day, the headlines in the *New York Herald Tribune* read: 'Atrocity Films In Court Upset Nazis' Aplomb . . . At the end, the courtroom was perfectly silent. The presiding judges retired without a word and the defendants walked slowly out.'[47]

Far from subjecting the audience of the trial to a complacent show, or assigning the film a simple documentary value, the point was to force the Nazi dignitaries to recognize, before a court, the crimes for which they were responsible. Against their wishes, the defendants had to show themselves, close to the images screened in the courtroom. This approach followed the one initiated in the Nazi camps by the Allies, when it was necessary to include in the same frame the mass graves and the 'official' witnesses coming from the USA or from England. In both cases, it is the filter of the image which enabled the cameramen as well as the spectators to see the violence of the genocide. Discovering these films in the United States after having worked on Nazi propaganda,[48] Siegfried Kracauer wrote that:

> they beckon the spectator to take them in and thus incorporate into his memory the real face of things too dreadful to be held in reality. In experiencing . . . the bitter of tortured bodies in the films made of the Nazi concentration camps, we redeem horror from its invisibility behind the veils of panic and imagination. And this experience is liberating in as much it removes a most powerful taboo.[49]

In 1945, the mediation by film of the responsibilities of the Nazi state contributed to elucidating what happened in the camps. Any pretension of arrogance was transformed into humility on the part of the defendants and prosecution. It has forced the evolution of historical scholarship, social knowledge, and memory of the Holocaust in western societies since 1945.

[46] Gilbert, n 38 above, 46. [47] 30 November 1945, 11.

[48] See C Delage, 'Luis Buñuel et Siegfried Kracauer au service de la propagande anti-nazie du Musée d'art moderne: de New York à Nuremberg, 1939–1945' in *Les Européens dans le cinéma américain. Émigration et exil* (Paris: 2005).

[49] S Kracauer, *Theory of Film. The Redemption of Physical Reality* (New York: 1960), 306.

Film, Culture and Accountability for Human Rights Abuses

Carolyn Patty Blum

Introduction: In a Florida Courtroom

The scene opens on a Florida courtroom. Inside, it is sweltering hot. A ceiling fan turns round and round. On one side of the courtroom sit two lawyers. Behind them, on a hard, wooden bench sit their clients, the plaintiffs in a civil lawsuit. They are the surviving brothers and sisters of four American churchwomen who were raped and murdered in El Salvador in December, 1980 by five National Guardsmen, during one of the most repressive years in El Salvador's decade-long conflict.[1]

On the other side of the courtroom sit two elderly men and their lawyer. The defendants are General Jose Guillermo Garcia, the former Salvadoran Minister of Defence and General Eugenio Vides-Casanova, the former Director of the National Guard at the time of the murders. These men are being sued under a unique US statute, the Torture Victim Protection Act, which enables US citizens who are the surviving relatives of persons extra-judicially executed to sue the murderers or their commanders for these acts.[2]

The jury—ten men and women—listen as the lawyers summarize the evidence in the month-long trial. The judge, in a kindly manner, explains the law of command responsibility. This doctrine, which has its origins in the most fundamental concepts of the laws of war and the codes of military conduct, holds commanders responsible for the acts of their subordinates when they should have known of abuses subordinates were committing and failed to stop them or to punish them for the abuses.[3]

The audience, plaintiffs, and defendants wait three days for the jury to reach a decision. The deliberating jury's questions to the judge reveal their confusion about the legal standard of command responsibility. The courtroom is gripped with anxiety as these questions are read, considered and answered by the judge.

[1] *Ford et al v Garcia et al*, No 99-8359 (SD Fla filed 14 May 1998). The trial, before Judge Hurley, occurred in October, 2000.

[2] Torture Victim Protection Act, 28 USC §1350 Note.

[3] An excellent discussion of the doctrine of command responsibility can be found in Elizabeth Van Schaack, 'Proving Command Responsibility: the Anatomy of Proof in *Romagoza v. Garcia*' (2003) 35 *U of California Davis L Rev* 1213.

The last scene in this drama finally unfolds. The jury returns to the courtroom. The bailiff intones: is General Jose Guillermo Garcia, Minister of Defence, liable for the rape and murder of Maryknoll nun Ita Ford? No. Is Eugenio Vides-Casanova liable for the rape and murder of Maryknoll nun Ita Ford? No. And so it goes, as the bailiff enumerates the rest of the claims, the names of the other nuns who were murdered, and the finding that the defendants are not liable.[4]

The audience sits incredulous. How can this be? How could this jury have listened to a month of trial testimony from a variety of witnesses, including the Ambassador from the United States to El Salvador at the time and every leading expert from Amnesty International and Human Rights Watch who documented the methods of state terror and persecution targeting church workers? This jury had been taught about the historical and political context in El Salvador, demonstrating that the generals knew about the abuses that were occurring and did nothing to stop or deter them. If the men at the pinnacle of command were not ultimately responsible for the actions of their troops, then who were? Just the men who pulled the triggers? Not the men who created a climate of impunity where a soldier could rape and kill nuns and not be concerned about the consequences? How could it be that this jury did not feel persuaded by an avalanche of evidence? How could they not feel compelled to hold these commanders responsible for the acts of their subordinates?

Those of us working for the plaintiffs sensed the enormity of our legal and cultural challenge when the lawyer for the generals made a powerful argument that resonated deeply in American culture. In the United States, he said, we are responsible only for our own wilful, volitional actions. That is where accountability begins and ends. Lt William Calley directly ordered his men to commit murder at My Lai during the war in Vietnam, and he joined in the slaughter.[5] The policemen who beat Rodney King were placed on trial for their behaviour. But mainstream American culture did not want to extend responsibility for My Lai to those who were above Calley in the chain of command nor to those who established or condoned the war norms that made My Lai predictable and a manifestation of similar atrocities, only on a larger scale. Likewise, there was no cry to investigate or charge those in the Los Angeles Police Department who supervised the police officers who beat King or who created and/or tolerated a police culture with a long history of police abuse. It seemed to us, by the end of the trial, that we were battling a deeply ingrained cultural and legal value that greatly circumscribed the nature of responsibility.

In the lexicon of law and morality, when analyzing responsibility for mass violence and human rights abuses, one distinguishes between individual/ personal

[4] The appellate decision in this case, upholding the decision below, is reported as *Ford v Garcia*, 289 F 3d 1283 (11th Cir 2002). *cert denied* 123 S Ct 863 (2003).

[5] For further discussion of this case, see James S Olson and Randy Roberts (eds), *My Lai: A Brief History with Documents* (Boston: 1998) and Michal R Belknap, *The Vietnam War on Trial: The My Lai Massacre and the Court-Martial of Lieutenant Calley* (Kansas: 2002).

responsibility, command responsibility, political and collective responsibility, and the responsibility of those on the side lines, the bystanders.[6] I will explore here how popular culture reflects broader notions of responsibility and political accountability. Further, I ask whether dominant cultural paradigms, over the past 40 years, have shifted how individual responsibility is conceptualized. In particular, I will examine the way in which popular culture examines the relationship between the individual and the broader context of his own actions.

My focus will be on Hollywood films of the past 40 years. And I want to argue that this period can be bifurcated. In the first two decades, 1960 to the early 1980s, some American films aggressively raised issues of individual and collective responsibility for human rights violations. But in the past two decades, films that touch on the venue of rights abuses have shied away from a deeper and more thoughtful analysis of responsibility. On the contrary, these more recent films reflect and reinforce a culture that assigns responsibility narrowly to those with visible blood on their hands.

Allocating Responsibility for Atrocities: The Seminal US Films

Judgment at Nuremberg

Judgment at Nuremberg[7] stands out as the seminal work of American film art that explores the theme of allocating responsibility in the wake of mass violence. Not coincidentally, it was produced at an important historical moment, 1961, during the struggle for civil rights. In an important sense, the film reminded the American people of the logical extension of racial superiority. It was also set on location in the city of Nuremberg, the locus of numerous Nazi rallies where Hitler addressed the multitudes of his supporters and whipped up sympathy for his radical, anti-Semitic ideology.

The focus of this film was not the major Nuremberg War Crimes Tribunal, but the subsidiary trials, of judges and prosecutors who enforced Nazi laws.[8] Although about individual trials, the film, at its core, is about determining collective responsibility. The questions which truly haunt Judge Haywood, portrayed by Spencer

[6] In relationship to the Holocaust, see discussions of these categories in Raul Hilberg, *Perpetrators, Victims and Bystanders: The Jewish Catastrophe 1933–1945* (New York: 1992) and David H Jones, *Moral Responsibility in the Holocaust: A Study in the Ethics of Character* (Lanham, MD: 1999).

[7] *Judgment at Nuremberg* (35 mm, 178 mins United Artists, Los Angeles, 1961). The film was nominated for 11 Academy Awards, including Best Picture, Best Director (Stanley Kramer), Best Actor (Spencer Tracy), Best Supporting Actor (Montgomery Clift), and Best Supporting Actress (Judy Garland), among others. The film won Oscars for Best Supporting Actor (Maximilian Schell) and Best Screenplay Adaptation (Abby Mann).

[8] Punishment of Persons Guilty of War Crimes, Crimes Against Peace and Against Humanity, Control Council Law No 10 (December 20, 1945) cited in Matthew Lippman, 'The Other Nuremberg: American Prosecutions of Nazi War Criminals in Occupied Germany' (1992) 3 *Indiana Intl and Comparative L Rev* 1.

Tracy as the home-spun judge from Maine and the moral compass of the film, include: How could the Holocaust have happened? Where were the German people? How could they not have known what was going on? And if they knew, why did they not do something to stop it?

These questions are developed in a number of ways, such as Judge Haywood's relationship with Madame Bertholt, the character played by Marlene Dietrich. The widow of a German military leader previously executed, she tells Haywood that she is on 'a mission to convince (you) we're not all monsters'. She takes him to beer halls where Germans longingly sing nostalgic songs. After the presentation in the courtroom of documentary footage of the concentration camps, a shortened version of the George Stevens-directed film actually used during the Nuremberg War Crimes Tribunal,[9] Madame Bertholt cries out to Judge Haywood, 'Do you think that's who we are? That we wanted to murder women and children? We didn't know!' And Judge Haywood responds, 'As far as I can tell, no one knew!'

Other scenes in the film reveal the preoccupation with collective and personal responsibility for the crimes of the Holocaust. In informal discussions among the American judges and prosecutors, the hot-shot US prosecutor, Colonel Lawson, angrily says that many people think it is time that 'we forgive and forget'. He vehemently resists the political pressure to stop the prosecutions because of new geo-political realities. It is now the beginning of the Cold War, and there is a perceived, over-riding necessity to solidify political alliances and to strengthen Germany against the Soviets. Thus, the need to mollify German dissatisfaction with the trials, it is argued, should outweigh any attempts to continue the judicial process.

Nowhere are these questions more explicitly expressed than in the defendants' central arguments during the screen trial. Defence counsel, Hans Rolfe, brilliantly created by Maximilian Schell, urges that the indictments against the defendants are not ultimately directed against them personally but are a vehicle to indict the entire German people. The defence counsel raises a protest against the screening of the documentary footage and states that it is 'unfair to show [it] in this court at this time against these defendants' since 'few knew; none of us knew'.

In the final scene of the film, Judge Haywood meets with one of the defendants, Dr Ernst Janning, in his cell. Janning tries to offer an apology and a reiteration of the position that he did not know of the Nazis' ultimate goal of the annihilation of the Jews. But Judge Haywood reminds him that the first time he signed an order for a man's execution, knowing that he was not guilty of the alleged crime, he knew that he was creating a legitimate front for the regime he was assisting.

This film confronts a complex range of questions about the allocation of responsibility. It does not try to answer all of these questions, but it is not afraid to pose them. Moreover, in using the venue of the trials of judges and prosecutors, the film examines how, under the guise of legality, heinous crimes are perpetrated for which

[9] Lawrence Douglas, 'Film as Witness: Screening *Nazi Concentration Camps* Before the Nuremberg Tribunal' (1995) 105 *Yale LJ* 449.

individuals can and must be held accountable. This was one of the most important principles to emerge from the major and subsidiary war crimes trials at the end of World War II.[10] So while grappling with questions of political and collective responsibility, the film reinforces notions of individual/personal responsibility, especially of the leaders of the legal establishment.

Missing

In the 1970s, as dictatorships ruled in Central and South America and as a coup in Chile brought General Augusto Pinochet to power, films tried to address larger questions of political culpability. One important example is *Missing*,[11]the 1982 Costa Gavras film set in the first weeks after the Chilean coup overthrowing the democratically-elected government.

The film focuses on the true story of an American.[12] Charles Horman is drawn to Chile because of the idealism, reformism and energy of the Popular Unity government of Salvador Allende. Within days of the coup, Horman is arrested and murdered by the military. The story is an apt vehicle to address questions of culpability for the coup, because the quest to understand what happened to Horman necessarily reveals layers of US involvement in Chile.

Immediately before the 1973 military coup, Horman and a companion are unable to leave the coastal town of Vina del Mar where they had ventured on a day trip. They soon come to realize that the coup has occurred and that Vina is teeming with American military personnel. Horman's hubris, in believing his American citizenship would protect him and his circle of ex-patriot friends, mirrors the hubris of the American military officers. As they arrogantly claim, they were sent to Chile 'to get a job done and now she's done'. And Horman's hubris mirrors that of the American Embassy officials and business people who applaud the Chilean military troops as they pass under the US Embassy windows where a gala event is held within days of the coup. But Horman is not protected by his citizenship, as the movie frighteningly demonstrates. Horman is relegated to the position of thousands of other Chilean victims of the brutality of regime whose bodies we see floating in the rivers or stacked in the morgues or whom we see detained by the thousands in the National Stadium.

[10] The Agreement for the Prosecution and Punishment of the Major War Criminals of the European Axis (8 August 1945), 59 Stat 1544, 82 UNTS 284 encompassed two sections, the London Agreement and the Charter of the International Military Tribunal. The sections addressing individual culpability are: London Agreement, art 1 (establishment of the tribunal for prosecution of war criminals accused 'individually or in their capacity as members of organizations or groups or in both capacities'); Charter art 7 (the official position of a defendant does not absolve him of individual responsibility).

[11] *Missing* (35 mm, 123 mins, Universal Pictures, Universal City, 1982). The film was nominated for four Academy Awards, including Best Picture, Best Actor (Jack Lemmon), and Best Actress (Sissy Spacek). It won an Oscar for Best Screenplay Adaptation (Costa-Gavras and Donald Stewart).

[12] The film is based on a book. Thomas Hauser, *The Execution of Charles Horman* (New York: 1976).

Within this story, the movie's fundamental preoccupation is with the role of the United States before, during and after the coup. This film came at a time when most of the information relevant to the US involvement was clouded by a haze of secrecy. In the film, as the Hormans, Charles' father Ed, played by Jack Lemmon, and wife Beth, played by Sissy Spacek, try to locate him, they confront the prototypical lies, obfuscations and denials that characterize the rhetoric of authoritarian regimes and their collaborators. For the Hormans, and for many other victims of the Pinochet regime and their families, this was the beginning of a 30-year quest for the truth about what happened in Chile and the American role in encouraging, supporting, and assisting the regime. This search has spread from South America to Spain to England and throughout Europe and redounded back to Chile in re-invigorated investigations there.[13]

The quest for truth about the United States' political responsibility for toppling Allende has been edified by the declassification of many crucial US government documents; yet, it is still an on-going investigation.[14]*Missing* firmly locates the individual responsibility for Charles Horman's assassination within a larger examination of political responsibility for the coup.

In short, some mainstream star-studded Hollywood films of the 1960 to early 1980s period tackled the issue of responsibility for human rights abuses in a deep way. They asserted that culpability had to extend beyond the soldier or policeman who pulled a trigger or wielded an instrument of torture. But this more soul-searching approach did not just disappear. More insidiously, it was replaced by a depiction which fairly explicitly articulates an ethic of responsibility which extends only to those who commit hands-on crime or who willingly admit their involvement.

Shirking the Issues of Responsibility: An Examination of Recent Films

Rules of Engagement

At the centre of the 2000 film, *Rules of Engagement*,[15] is a massacre of civilians by US military forces. The subsequent trial of the commanding officer explicitly raises issues of personal and command culpability for mass violence. It also poses the question of the value placed on the lives of some (the members of the crowd) versus the lives of others (the US servicemen and the Embassy officials).

[13] A summary of the legal rulings that have emanated from the arrest of Pinochet in England in 1998 can be found in Diana Woodhouse (ed), *The Pinochet Case: A Legal and Constitutional Analysis* (Oxford: 2000).

[14] Peter Kornbluh's recent book which analyzes the declassified US government documents is a rich addition to our understanding of this period. Peter Kornbluh, *The Pinochet File: A Declassified Dossier on Atrocity and Accountability* (New York: 2003).

[15] *Rules of Engagement* (35 mm, 128 mins, Paramount Pictures, Los Angeles, 2000).

Col Terry Childers, played smartly by Samuel Jackson, a career military officer who served in Vietnam, is ordered to direct an elite team of commandos to rescue the US Ambassador and his family in Yemen. A large crowd of protesters has gathered in front of the Embassy, evidently a regular occurrence. While some members of the commando team carry out the rescue, others are engaged in securing the area. In Childers' view, the demonstrators pose a deadly threat to these troops and to the Ambassador. As an audience we are left with a somewhat ambiguous portrait of what is actually occurring outside the Embassy, although, like Childers, we believe that some members of the demonstration are using deadly force against the troops. In defence of his troops, Jackson ends up ordering them to open fire on all the demonstrators, and a wholesale massacre ensues.

The action of the film turns on the court martial of Childers as he tries to defend his actions as justified, given the circumstances. He is deftly assisted in this endeavour by Col Hayes 'Hodge' Hodges, played by Tommy Lee Jones, whose life Childers saved in Vietnam. The audience, however, is in on the secret of the film—Embassy security tapes exist which exonerate Childers but which have been suppressed by the National Security Advisor so that Childers can be the 'fall guy' for what has devolved into an international incident. This fact detracts from the impact of the film as the audience can by-pass the harder questions raised by the scenario. These questions should have included: Were there alternatives that could have avoided a deadly confrontation with the demonstrators? As he initially implied, did the Ambassador have means to address the situation diplomatically that were not utilized? What level of threat is necessary to justify the use of deadly force? Does a soldier's training in violent response to confrontation necessarily colour his response? How do we calculate these trade-offs, as Jackson apparently did here, of killing some to save others?

During the course of the trial, a North Vietnamese officer, Col Binh Le Cao, is called to the witness stand. He recounts an incident that occurred during the war in Vietnam. Childers captured him and a fellow North Vietnamese soldier. Childers sought information from him about a potential Vietnamese ambush of American troops. Childers held a gun to the head of Col Binh's comrade and threatened to kill him if Col Binh did not divulge the information about where the Vietnamese were hiding. He refused, and Childers shot the other soldier, fully disarmed and out of combat, in cold blood. When asked in court about this incident, Col Binh testifies that he would have done the same thing as Childers to obtain the information.

As he did with the attack on the civilians in Yemen, Childers again was confronted with using murderous tactics to save the greater number. This profoundly moral—as well as legal—dilemma is presented in the film as having an obvious answer. When Col Binh bonds with Childers through their shared language of the necessity of deadly force born of conflict, the film drains the scene of any space to consider seriously where culpability for Childer's actions in Yemen should lie—much less, the justifiability of his earlier actions in Vietnam.

Before a jury of military officers, Childers is exonerated because the jury understands his central argument that his own soldiers had to be protected at all costs, and that this is his primary duty as their commander. By so doing, the jury never seriously considers whether the taking of so many Yemeni lives is justified, just as Childers, while in Vietnam, never considered whether his killing a disarmed soldier, to extract information, was an act of unjustified torture and murder. Thus, the film squanders an opportunity to examine more closely the line between justifiable and unjustifiable acts in situations of conflict, a concern made all the more urgent for troops stationed in a variety of hot spots throughout the world today.

High Crimes

A massacre is also at the epicentre of the 2002 film, *High Crimes*.[16] The question of individual responsibility for the massacre drives the arc of the film. At the outset, the film introduces the audience to a seemingly loving couple, Claire and Tom Kubik, actors Ashley Judd and James Caviezel. But this tranquil scenario is disrupted when Kubik is arrested and accused of committing a massacre in El Salvador in 1988 as a soldier named Ron Chapman. He is subject to a court martial for this crime. Claire Kubik decides to assume his defence herself, with the help of a once-successful military law specialist, Charlie Grimes, played expertly by Morgan Freeman. As the drama unfolds, the 'top brass' clearly do not want the full truth of what happened in El Salvador to emerge. In fact, the only person who seems to know the truth is an elusive Salvadoran, who seems to want to exact a revenge of his own. Ultimately, the court martial proceedings are terminated at the behest of the higher-ups who are afraid that the secret about the events that led to the massacre will be revealed. What the audience ultimately learns, uncovered in the most convoluted way, is that US soldiers accidentally killed three American students. To cover up this crime, or so it appears, they blamed the guerrillas and then had to massacre some Salvadorans to demonstrate the continued callousness of the guerrillas.

The film initially offers a version of what really happened that day in El Salvador that is so implausible in the context of what actually occurred in that country during its civil conflict as to make the entire film seem like a work of science fiction. But the film-makers depend on the audience's ignorance and that the conflict in El Salvador has turned into ancient history. But its strained premise that guerrillas were somehow responsible for the massacre is contrary to what is publicly known about how the guerrillas operated, the level of abuses that were carried out by the military and right-wing paramilitary forces,[17] and the role of the United States in bolstering the fortunes of the corrupt, oppressive Salvadoran military.[18] Thus, any informed observer cannot accept the basic trajectory of the film.

[16] *High Crimes* (35 mm, 115 mins, Twentieth Century Fox, Los Angeles, 2002).

[17] See the conclusions of the Report of the United Nations Truth Commission on El Salvador available at www.derechos.org/nizkor/salvador/informes/truth.html.

[18] Ray Bonner, *Weakness and Deceit: U.S. Policy and El Salvador* (New York: 1984).

In the final moments of the film, Tom Kubik/Ron Chapman confesses to his wife that he did carry out the massacre. However, he claims that he was told by his superiors that the people he killed were terrorists. He explains, appropriating early twenty-first-century jargon, that he was trained to get the terrorists so that is what he did. In his mind, his actions were wholly justified.

Crucially, the film portrays crack US forces at work in El Salvador. But, supposedly, the US role in El Salvador was a more limited one, as military advisors only. The presence of elite units was not known to the American people. Was the film, then, trying to raise a larger question about the scope of US involvement in the Salvadoran conflict? Was it metaphorically raising the question by showing American troops actually engaged in abuses, instead of the Salvadoran military surrogates whom the US shored up with billions of dollars in economic and military aid? If it was trying to address these more profound questions, it failed to bring them to a conscious level of narrative exposition or dramatic conflict.

Further, the main protagonist's own culpability, who should have known not to carry out the illegal order to kill unarmed civilians, was never fully examined. The only reason the film lets the audience find anyone responsible for this atrocity, an atrocity almost trivialized by the film, given the enormous scale of the massacres in El Salvador,[19] is because the protagonist confesses to the crime. This gimmick obscures the larger questions of responsibility for the massacre portrayed in the film, a stand-in for the many massacres that occurred in El Salvador. The course of events in El Salvador, and the particular question of US involvement which, by contrast, was so well-engaged in *Missing*, is absent from this film treatment of the subject. The film makes no use of its setting in war-ravaged 1988 El Salvador to raise the broader themes of political and command culpability for the atrocities that were a routine part of that landscape.

Black Hawk Down

The Somalia-mission true story, *Black Hawk Down*[20] is a 2001 war-action film. Embedded within it, however, are concerns about mass violence, the changing nature of conflict, and the role of the military. The film is set in October, 1993 during the US mission to open supply lines for humanitarian assistance.[21] But Somali war lords prevent the accomplishment of the mission as they routinely disrupt the equitable distribution of assistance from humanitarian organizations.

The US military mission determines that the arrest of several key members of the Somali war lord leadership would help cripple that organization. However, the

[19] Mark Danner, *The Massacre at El Mozote: A Parable of the Cold War* (New York: 1993).

[20] *Black Hawk Down* (35 mm, 144 mins, Columbia Pictures, Los Angeles, 2001). The film was nominated for four Academy Awards, including Best Director (Ridley Scott) and Best Cinematography (Slavomir Idziak). It won Oscars for Best Editing (Pietro Scalia) and Best Sound (Michael Minkler, Nyron Nettinga and Chris Munro).

[21] The film is based on a book account of the events. Mark Bowden, *Black Hawk Down: A Story of Modern War* (New York: 1999).

mission does not proceed as planned. A fierce battle ensues in the streets of Mogadishu. The ugliness and brutality of war are displayed in abundance. During the course of the operation, two US Black Hawk helicopters are shot down by the Somalis. They swarm over the helicopters; the body of one of the downed soldiers is removed from the helicopter and dragged through the streets of Mogadishu. Another soldier is captured. Others lie dead in the wreckage of the helicopters and the fighting. Ultimately, the United States pulls out of the country, and by all measures, the mission is a failure.

The film focuses on the transformation of one particular soldier, the idealistic Staff Sergeant Matt Eversmann (Josh Harnett), who came to Somalia 'to make a difference'. By the end of the film, he is convinced by SFC 'Hoot' Gibson, the cynical, battle-hardened DELTA force warrior (Eric Bana), who tells him, 'you can't control who lives and dies and why it happens. It's just war.'

Black Hawk Down has been criticized for being a racist and simplistic portrayal of Africans and a jingoistic celebration of 'our boys in uniform'. I do not want to take on these issues, which I think are more complex than the film's fans or detractors suggest. But, in terms of themes of responsibility and guilt, I think the film can be criticized.

To be fair to the movie, it is much easier to raise these issues in films like *Judgment at Nuremberg* or *Missing* which are 'talky' dramas explicitly about issues of responsibility. *Black Hawk Down* is primarily a powerful, visceral action film. And in that genre, having a few talking heads articulate a 'good' message often feels didactic and something thrown in as a salve to the conscience of the film maker or to placate liberal critics.

That caveat notwithstanding, the film still fails, even in its own genre and message terms, to deal with the responsibility issues that are organic to it. Despite its cross-cutting subplots, that engender tremendous tension, the film never strays too far from its core character and his development. And Matt Eversmann needs to believe that his military career is more than an adventure and the jeopardy and deaths of his friends have some moral significance. And the film does raise issues of responsibility at two levels. It asks how this situation in Somalia got so bad that American involvement was necessary. And it focuses on the commander of the botched mission and his responsibility for the catastrophe.

However, here the film could have dug deeper. Director Ridley Scott never offers an explanation for how the situation in Somalia arose and the complicity of Westerners in the desecration and tribalization of modern Africa. Moreover, it never explores how a humanitarian mission, that has such limited objectives and eschews dealing with the underlying political realities, can possibly succeed. Given this vacuum of understanding at the film's core, it becomes a tragedy of military hubris and a ratcheting down of military morality to have the mission simply be about watching the back of your brother soldier.

The film should be about the changing role of the military, in the post-Cold War world. It should address whether the military can accomplish humanitarian purposes. It should ask what the preconditions are for such a role. It should provide something more than the most cursory of understandings of Somalia as a country. It should ask who should bear the moral, political and legal responsibility for the failures of the military mission in Somalia. But it does not do any of these things. Instead, it focuses on the individual soldier. Its commentary on the motives and responsibilities of a soldier are summed up in one soldier's perspective, 'it's about the man next to you and that's it, that's all it is'.

The film is a missed opportunity. Its attempts to explain the political context of events in Somalia at the beginning and end of the film are just bookends to a narrative that—while showing the horrors of war in its graphic violence—ends up feeling simplistic and minimalist. The audience is left with only discomfiting feelings that war is ugly, and Africa is a mess. But the audience wants to understand who should be held responsible for the mess these boys found themselves in; the audience knows it is wrong that they should have been sacrificed. But since the audience has no comprehension of the larger political canvas on which the decision to send troops to Somalia was taken nor the underlying political trajectory and reality of Somalia as a country, the crucial questions posed by the film cannot be answered.

Tears of the Sun

The most recent addition to this group of films is *Tears of the* Sun,[22] a 2003 release. This film attempts to address the question of the responsibility of the bystander, the person who witnesses atrocities and must decide whether to act in the face of them. This film is set in Nigeria, but that country stands in as a composite for all of Africa. A coup d'etat has occurred, and a brutal rebel Army has seized power. Every type of atrocity—rape, mutilation, arming child soldiers—is found in this movie to such a degree that the audience is reviled and turns away from it.

As in *Rules of Engagement* and *Black Hawk Down*, a unit has to perform a rescue. This time, the elite Navy SEAL team must rescue the high-minded Dr Lena Kendricks, a US citizen by marriage, who is working in a rural Catholic hospital. But when the team, headed by Bruce Willis as Lt AK Waters arrives, the doctor refuses to leave unless the refugees for whom she has been providing medical care are rescued as well. Thus, Lt Waters faces a moral dilemma: should he follow orders, or will he defy his superiors and agree to help the refugees in addition to saving the doctor. He finally decides that he must help all of the people. By doing this, he also is imposing his personal, moral decision on his team who supposedly must also decide if they support his actions but who, in reality, have no choice but to support their commander.

Much of the film follows the group through numerous situations of jeopardy as they try to reach a rescue rendezvous site. This jeopardy comes primarily from the murderous rebels who kill everyone at the village outpost and then in another

[22] *Tears of the Sun* (35 mm, 121 mins, Columbia Pictures, Los Angeles, 2002).

village. They are also hunting one particular member of the group of refugees, who is the son of the overthrown leader and who could take power, if democracy is restored. In addition, the danger emanates from the US commanders who, essentially, abandon the team because they have gone far beyond the limited objectives of their mission.

Like *Black Hawk Down*, this film has the best of intentions. It is certainly responding to the new role of the military in humanitarian interventions and the particular question of how military power should respond to human suffering. This is a thorny, complex issue, but a crucial one, especially in the post-Iraq war world. The film also seeks to address the responsibility of the bystander, the witness to human suffering. Both when Lt Waters confronts the people at the village hospital and when the US soldiers witness a rebel massacre of another village, they must decide whether to relinquish their positions as observers, standing by while atrocities occur or become actively engaged—even at risk to themselves. But the film's oversimplifications—particularly, the message that white people get moral redemption by helping suffering black victims—squelches any nuanced exploration of the ambiguity of the situation that Lt Waters, and many other soldiers like him, confront.

At one point in the film, Waters' commanding officer tries to force him to abandon his mission by telling him that his actions are having a negative effect on US diplomacy, since his actions are interfering in the internal affairs of a sovereign nation. But since the state is now controlled by the murderous rebels, why should the audience care about protecting their autonomy? And it does not. The audience reaction is to want to revile the commander. The film is right to try to provoke these reactions. But the film does not explore, in any depth, how one might parse the moral obligation of the individual US soldier to protect and assist people subject to abuses and alleviate their suffering, particularly when confronted with contrary command instructions which limit the scope of the soldier's mission. Further, the movie fails to explore the nuances of the relationships with indigenous peoples in the countries where humanitarian operations occur. These themes would have resonated with the real life situations confronting soldiers in conflict zones today.

A Few Good Men

Along with *Judgment at Nuremberg*, *A Few Good Men*[23] is the most important film of the last 40 years on this topic. Its importance lies in its commercial success and the strengths and limits of its analysis.

I believe film scholars often err in discussing the significance of films by referring to their implicit and explicit messages independent of their cultural impact. It

[23] *A Few Good Men* (35 mm, 138 mins, Columbia Pictures, Los Angeles, 1992). The film was nominated for four Academy Awards, including Best Picture and Best Supporting Actor (Jack Nicholson).

might be interesting to compare the racial assumptions in *Gone with the Wind*[24] and *El Norte*,[25] but it would be foolish not to acknowledge that one had little historical impact, and the other is a cultural icon. And while I have been arguing that interesting and important values can be gleaned from the films discussed here, only *Judgment at Nuremberg* and *A Few Good Men* can be presumed to have a broader impact on American cultural conceptions of the issues raised here.

A Few Good Men is ostensibly about the scope of the defence of superior orders, another guiding principle of the Nuremberg statute[26] and one of extreme salience in the United States during the Vietnam War era.[27] The film also raises, but does not answer, two additional, crucial questions about command control and political responsibility.

The setting of the precipitating events in the film is the US Naval base at Guantanamo Bay, Cuba. There, a young private, William Santiago, dies, during the administration of a 'Code Red', by two of his fellow Marines, Louden Downey and Harold Dawson. A 'Code Red' is an 'off-the-books' punishment, given for an infraction of an unwritten Marine code of honour. In this story, Santiago had complained about the oppressive atmosphere at Guantanamo and asked for a transfer off the base. Downey and Dawson claimed that they did not intend to kill the victim but merely to scare him. They also claimed that they were ordered to administer the 'Code Red' by their superior officer, Lt Kendrick, played by Kiefer Sutherland. The action of the film centres on the courts-martial of the two soldiers and whether the defence team, JAG Corps lawyers, Lt Daniel Kaffee (Tom Cruise), Lt Cmdr JoAnne Galloway (Demi Moore) and Lt Sam Weinberg (Kevin Pollak), can successfully raise a defence of superior orders. In the final dramatic courtroom scene, Col Jessup, the commanding officer of the base, played memorably by Jack Nicholson, admits that the informal 'Code Red' punishment system exists, and that he personally ordered that the young victim be given a 'Code Red'. This scene dramatically concludes with Nicholson being arrested by military police to face his own court martial. Further, Downey and Dawson, who are punished by being dishonourably discharged from military service, acknowledge that they should have known better than to carry out an order which required them to victimize one of their own. Thus, they recognize that they cannot defend their own actions as based on those of a superior when they should have known that the orders were improper.

A Few Good Men is the creation of the liberal and gifted Aaron Sorkin. While it preaches respect for the men who serve in the armed forces, it is absolutely clear that

[24] *Gone with the Wind* (35 mm, 238 mins, Selznick International Pictures, Los Angeles, 1939). The film was nominated for 13 Academy Awards. It won eight Oscars for Best Picture, Best Director (Victor Fleming), Best Actress (Vivien Leigh), Best Supporting Actress (Hattie McDaniel), and Best Screenplay (Sidney Howard), among others.

[25] *El Norte* (35 mm, 139 mins, American Playhouse, Los Angeles, 1984).

[26] Nuremberg Charter, n 10 above, art 8.

[27] The events at My Lai generated public debate on individual, command and political responsibility for the massacre. See n 5 above. This defence is being raised by some of the lower-ranking soldiers accused in the Abu Ghraib prison scandals as well.

immoral orders should not be obeyed, and that responsibility for immoral actions applies to both the individual perpetrators and their commanding officers. At this level, *A Few Good Men* stands in the shadows of *Judgment at Nuremberg* in rejecting the 'I was only following orders' defence. And officers who command immoral orders are as culpable as those who carry them out.

But like most other liberal films, it showcases the two limits of this perspective. First, while it acknowledges responsibility for specific orders, it begs the question of command responsibility that creates an environment that fosters immoral actions and command responsibility that tolerates that environment. Essentially, the commander of the base, Col Jessup, has created an environment that encourages the use of this off-the-books disciplinary system. But until Col Jessup brazenly admits in court his use of this disciplinary system, then, and only then, can he be found culpable as a commander. But even without that admission, the murder of the young Santiago was squarely within the command responsibility of Jessup. Even had he not expressly given the order, he had a direct responsibility for that kind of behaviour by the men under his command.

The film also begs the question of responsibility of those within the military who suspected 'Code Reds', disapproved, and did nothing. There are several references in the film suggesting that higher-ups in the Navy suspected 'something fishy' was going on 'down there' and refused to investigate. The audience is left to believe that had not a soldier died, the abuses would have continued indefinitely, despite an awareness that they were probably going on.

Thus, in order for the film to deal directly with the issues it tries to raise—that of command and control and the defence of superior orders—the film needs to be less about Jessup as a crazy fanatic and more about Guantanamo as a closed system in which commanders like Jessup are powerful dictators while clothing themselves in the guise of 'protecting lives'. This otherwise smart and well-written[28] film underestimates its audiences' ability to grapple with a more textured treatment of these important issues.[29]

An Exception: Three Kings

One film that more successfully and artfully raises fundamental questions about political and moral responsibility is David Russell's 1999 film *Three Kings*.[30] This

[28] Aaron Sorkin adapted the screenplay from his stage play of the same name.

[29] On viewing the film from the perspective of 2003, one is struck by the incongruity of the fact that the United States continues to maintain an 'unfriendly' base on the sovereign territory of Cuba. Further, the current infamy of that particular location—where the United States is holding incommunicado 'enemy combatants,' not subject to the protections of the Geneva Conventions or any other legal norms—makes the film feel particularly chilling. One of the iconic speeches of the film is Col Jessup's explanation in the courtroom of his justification for his own actions. He states that, 'you want me on that wall; you need me on that wall'. He is referring to American citizens' dependence on the US military to keep us safe from our enemies on the other side of the 'wall'. Jessup's view would not be universally held, at the present time, especially in regards to the use of the base on Cuba.

[30] *Three Kings* (35 mm, 114 mins, Warner Brothers, Los Angeles, 1999).

film is set at end of the 1991 Persian Gulf War. It unflinchingly examines the price paid by Iraqi rebels who supported US intervention in the region.

In the film, four ambitious and somewhat unscrupulous American soldiers, played by George Clooney, Mark Wahlberg, Ice Cube and Spike Jonze, seek to profit personally from their presence in the region, by stealing Saddam Hussein's gold secreted in an underground vault. In their quest to locate the gold, they are confronted by Iraqi rebels who were supported and armed by the United States. The rebels have been abandoned by the US government, once the United States decides to leave the region without accomplishing the goal of overthrowing Saddam Hussein. In reality, this means these men and their families will be arrested, tortured and killed by Hussein. In a graphic scene, the mother of a young girl and wife of one of the rebels is murdered before the child's eyes. Eventually, the soldiers realize that they must assist this group to safety, even if it means risking their own profit.

The American protagonists, all very different kinds of men, are simultaneously cynical and pained. Thus, their story provides a much richer canvas to explore the profound question of the moral responsibility of the bystander. As in *Tears of the Sun* and *Judgment at Nuremberg*, one of the crucial questions that humans face, as moral actors and witnesses to continuing atrocities, genocide and massive human rights abuses is what does it mean to watch atrocities and fail to intervene? How proximate does one have to be to bear responsibility to act? What is the distinct role of the military? This film, more than any other in this more recent spate of films attempting to explore these issues, does not flinch from these questions.

Conclusion: Back to the Florida Courtroom

Finally, the drama returns to the humid courtroom in Florida. It is almost two years after the courtroom was first seen. A new trial is in progress. This time, the same judge presides but a different jury, again ten men and women, watch and listen. The same generals are the defendants, former Salvadoran Minister of Defence Jose Garcia and former Director of the National Guard, Eugenio Vides-Casanova. But we see three different plaintiffs, three survivors of torture in El Salvador. Juan Romagoza was a doctor who treated the poor in rural health clinics; Neris Gonzalez was a lay church-worker who helped peasants learn to count so they would not be cheated by the landowners; Carlos Mauricio was a professor at the National University who continued to offer classes even after the military shut down the university.

The generals are being sued again.[31] This time, the plaintiffs testify about their lives before they were tortured, about their brutal experiences after their capture by

[31] *Romagoza et al v Garcia et al*, No 99-8364 (DS Fla filed 14 May 1998). The trial, before Judge Hurley, took place in June and July, 2002. The case is currently on appeal by the defendants before the US Court of Appeals for the Eleventh Circuit. It was argued on 31 July 2003 and is awaiting decision. Further information about this case is available at www.cja.org.

official security forces, about their flights from their country and their attempts to create new lives in the United States. In this trial, an Argentine military officer explains to the jury the concept of the chain of command and the responsibility of command leaders to know about the actions of subordinates down the chain of command. A Stanford professor, a specialist in Latin American Studies, teaches the jury about the tormented history of El Salvador and the deliberate state of terror created by the men on trial and their cohorts in the military. And this time, the jury returns a finding of command responsibility for the torture of the three plaintiffs. As the verdict is read, many of the jurors weep—these ten average citizens—and the lawyers and supporters join in the weeping too.

The emotion of this case is not just rooted in its being the first time for any legal—and moral—accountability for the atrocities perpetuated in El Salvador, nor just because it is the first US case in which commanders who defended their actions in court were found liable. But the case signifies a willingness on the part of an American jury to grapple with the broader questions of the responsibility of commanders and leaders. By doing this, ten ordinary Americans were willing to enlarge the way that they conceptualize responsibility. They willingly went beyond the more constrained view portrayed in recent American films that eschews a richer, more textured understanding of how mass violence occurs and how responsibility for its perpetration should be addressed. Perhaps, American film making again will push beyond simple and easy characterizations and address the hard questions that justice and accountability in the wake of mass violence raises. It will be the richer for it and will enhance a collective understanding of these complex, but critical moral, legal, and political questions.[32]

[32] The Abu Ghraib prison scandal, in which US soldiers engaged in abuses against Iraqi prisoners, makes the need to address command and culpability all the more present and urgent. See Seymour Hersh, *Chain of Command: The Road from 9/11 to Abu Ghraib* (New York, 2004); Mark Danner, *Torture and Truth: America, Abu Ghraib and the War on Terror* (New York, 2004).

Science Fiction as a World Tribunal

Wai Chee Dimock

What exactly is a world tribunal? The designated object is by no means self-evident, and perhaps should not be referred to in the singular at all. For a range of entities in fact answer to that name, bearing the imprint of a range of globalizing forces, not all coordinated, and not coming into being at the same time. International law is both rapidly expanding and impossibly byzantine in its multiple articulations. At the present moment, there are at least four courts set up by four multilateral bodies, operating at different levels: the International Court of Justice at the Hague; the International Criminal Court, also at the Hague; the Court of Justice of the European Communities at Luxembourg; and the European Court of Human Rights at Strasbourg. This multi-loci playing field, emerging piecemeal over the course of some 60 years, is hardly a model of central planning.[1] Grey areas abound, both within particular jurisdictions and in the interstices between them, with aims and procedures not meshing at all at some points and overlapping too much at others.[2]

There is a kind of uncertainty of cross-reference in this global landscape, if for no other reason than that there are so many entities involved. The infrastructure is not all fleshed out, and any fleshing out is likely to be done not by national governments but a transnational network of activist groups, such as Amnesty International and Human Rights Watch. The global legal scene is decentralized both by necessity and on principle. Historically as well as philosophically it is guided by an idea of 'adjudication' exercised outside a strict definition of law. The Council of Europe[3] (the parent organization of the European Court of Human

[1] The International Court of Justice (ICJ) was created in 1945 under the Charter of the United Nations. See http://www.icj-cij.org/icjwww/generalinformation/ibbook/Bbookframepage.htm. The Court of Justice of the European Communities, the legal institution of the European Union, whose charge is to enforce 'community law . . . separate from, yet superior to national law', was initially created under the Treaties of Paris and Rome in 1952. See http://europa.en.int/institutions/court/index_en.htm. The European Court of Human Rights (ECHR), the judicial arm of the Council of Europe, started out as the Convention for the Protection of Human Rights and Fundamental Freedoms (1950), and became consolidated as a single, full-time court on 1 November 1998. The International Criminal Court (ICC) was established on 17 July 1998 when 120 states adopted the Statute of Rome. The Statute provides for its entry into force 60 days after 60 states have ratified it, which happened on 11 April 2002. Accordingly, the ICC came into effect on 1 July 2002.

[2] See, eg, Christopher Harding, 'The Identity of European Law: Mapping Out the European Legal Space' (2000) 6 *European LJ* 128.

[3] The Council of Europe is distinct from the European Union. All 15 nations of the European Union are members of the Council of Europe; however, the latter has a broader membership: 'Any

Rights) is explicit about this, and explicit too about its incorporation of a grass-roots democracy into its proceedings. Among its stated objectives is a 'platform for voluntary associations', making non-governmental groups an integral part of its 'programme of work in the new millennium':

> By granting consultative status to over 350 non-governmental organisations (NGOs), the Council of Europe is building a real partnership with those who represent ordinary people. Through various consultation arrangements (including discussions and colloquies) it brings NGOs into intergovernmental activities and encourages dialogue between members of parliament and associations on major social issues.[4]

The rule of law, as understood by the Council of Europe, has a sphere of operation wider than that provided by a few formal vehicles. This wider sphere, an informal network, a kind of penumbra tracking and shadowing the legal domain, makes up what we might call a 'global civil society'.[5] The vitality of law, especially of international law, rests on this penumbra, this civil society unofficially constituted, for a decentralized landscape needs the input of a new set of players, not only non-state but also non-juridical. The European Court of Human Rights (ECHR) reflects this change. Unlike the older International Court of Justice, which arbitrates only between sovereign states,[6] the ECHR has a much broader class of litigants: it has a specific provision stating that complaints can be brought before it 'against Contracting States either by other Contracting States or by individual applicants (individuals, groups of individuals, or non-governmental organisations)'.[7] Law and democracy are intersecting in new and complex ways. The traditional dividing line between the legal and the extra-legal is becoming less meaningful, and 'justice', from being a legal category, is being exercised, more and more, as a political category, perhaps even a civic category.

It is in this context that I want to think of science fiction: as part of this emerging landscape, part of the new alignment between the formal vehicles of law and the informal, non-binding, but also non-trivial adjudication of world citizens. Science fiction is an ideal genre for addressing these questions. It is a democratic genre, read all over the world, as popular in Japan and Russia as it is in the US and the UK. Not everyone agrees that it has artistic merit, but it does have a poetics of its own, and, I would argue, also a taxonomy, a classifying system loosely based on popular science, with its own nomenclature, its own rationale for grouping things

European state can become a member of the Council of Europe provided it accepts the principle of the rule of law and guarantees human rights and fundamental freedoms to everyone under its jurisdiction'. See the Council of Europe's web-site: http://www.coe.int/T/E/Communication_and_Research/Contacts.

[4] ibid.

[5] For an important theorization of this concept (though not specifically linking it to the legal domain), see Mary Kaldor, *Global Civil Society: An Answer to War* (Cambridge: 2003).

[6] The mandate of the ICJ is to decide 'in accordance with international law disputes of a legal nature submitted to it by states, while in addition certain international organs and agencies are entitled to call upon it for advising opinions'. See the ICJ's web-site, http://www.icj-cij.org.

[7] ibid.

under a common name, and its own rationale for meting out punishment and reward. We can think of science fiction, then, as a 'para' phenomenon on several fronts: para-literary, para-scientific, as well as para-legal. It is on the edges of these fields, a low-level operation, but, by the same token, it is also the meeting place for all three disciplines.

Science fiction is without question low-brow, but it does actually, and surprisingly, have something in common with what is usually called 'high culture'. Like modernist fiction, for example, it is anti-naturalistic. It has one leg in the 'real' world, the world that conforms more or less to our expectations; its other leg, though, is quite literally somewhere else, off into a space-time that is in no way an extension of the world as we know it. Because the whole point of science fiction is to depict an alien universe, one that violates, in some fundamental way, the condition we call 'normal'. Darko Suvin says that science fiction is a 'literature of cognitive estrangement'.[8] The estrangement occurs, most obviously, on the level of contents, in the shape of futuristic technologies and machines. But, once in a while, it can also extend to the entire semantic field, it can bend and shift all those coordinates that give us our bearing. When this happens, the world literally gets turned around. Adverbs such as 'here' and 'there' change sides, and pronouns such as 'we' and 'they' get reconstituted. Norms that have previously been experienced only from the inside are now seen through an inverted lens, from the outside. Seen in this way, they reveal themselves to be manmade conventions—artifacts really—normative only at their instituted locales and not generalizable beyond. They are site-specific, site-dependent, and site-limited. Science fiction is anti-naturalistic in this sense: in that it does not allow *any* version of the 'natural' to naturalize itself. Because of its perspective from space, there is an ontological switch built into its image of the world. What is internalized can always become externalized.

I find this aspect of science fiction especially important. Its cognitive estrangement, its ability to turn any phenomenon inside out, seems to me to capture at least one aspect of the dynamics of globalism, insofar as the global represents an 'outside' to the nation. This 'outside' is often no more than heuristic, it is not necessarily geographical, and certainly not fully jurisdictional. It is just a virtual space, a projected horizon that has the ability to subject familiar data to an alienating frame, to turn events that look like they are discrete and autonomous into events that are constituted by many sides and can be scrutinized from all those sides. This reversal of perspective might turn out to be the greatest challenge to the sovereignty of the nation state. The opposition of the Bush administration to the International Criminal Court shows just how threatening such a virtual horizon can be.

This virtual horizon depends, in turn, on a taxonomy, a way of classifying the world's population, that we can only call virtual at the moment. I am referring, of course, to the human species as the basis of classification. This classification is scientifically impeccable—all of us belong to the species, homo sapiens—but, in

[8] Darko Suvin, 'On the Poetics of the Science Fiction Genre' in Mark Rose (ed), *Science Fiction: A Collection of Critical Essays* (Englewood Cliffs: 1976), 57–71, 58.

practice, very few of us actually identify ourselves using this term. If I were to meet you for the first time on the street and if I were to say, 'I'm a human being', you would think I am out of my mind. On the other hand, if I were to say, 'I am Chinese', or 'I am American', you would not raise an eyebrow. It is the nation, rather than the species, that classifies us right now, that gives us a taxonomic category whose membership we find intelligible and usable. In the US this is particularly the case. Here the nation, as a taxonomic category, is so deeply ingrained that it is naturalized in quite a literal sense. It is routine for the US government and the US media to speak of the 'loss of American lives', as if 'American' were a biological rather than jurisdictional fact, as if it operated on the level of physiology rather than the level of citizenship.

This is no doubt naturalization at its most extreme. But it is fair to say that, in a less extreme form, this linguistic usage is the rule rather than the exception for all self-declared nationals, not just Americans. Certainly, the Chinese phrase merges the fact of jurisdiction and the fact of humanness in almost exactly the same way, as if the Chinese were the only real, substantial, and central species, all foreigners being 'ghosts'. It is these linguistic usages that make racism such a natural phenomenon, which is to say, unremarkable, unremarked upon, and reproduced as such across the centuries and across the globe. Elevating a subset of humanity into a self-sufficient set, a presumed unity, it further divides the world into other sets also presumed to be unified, all of which it sees as its potential enemies. Racism of this sort naturalizes divisiveness if only to naturalize its own integration. An unaccented (and also unashamed) belligerency towards the world goes hand in hand with a postulate of unity within. Even as it locks an entire population into an a priori grouping, it makes antagonism to every other group a constitutive principle. This neo-racism, a differential racism, Etienne Balibar argues, underwrites not only the sovereign form of the nation state but also the identity-based and therefore proudly segregated memories of the human past, splitting a single species 'into tendentially incompatible masses'.[9]

Will this racism endure? Will it continue to haunt the nation state that articulates it and militarizes it? The answer at the moment is yes. But it is a yes that is getting a bit tenuous, for to the extent that a global civil society is more than just a dream, there is also the contrary hope that human ties will proceed along other

[9] Etienne Balibar, 'Is There a Neo-Racism' and 'Racism and Nationalism' in Etienne Balibar and Immanuel Wallerstein, *Race, Nation, Class: Ambiguous Identities* (trans of Balibar by Chris Turner, London: 1991) 17–36, 37–67, 44. Balibar sees racism as a deeply ingrained—and therefore extremely durable, extremely versatile—cognitive principle, articulated in different forms throughout history and permeating the very category of memory itself: 'it is racism which represents one of the most insistent forms of the historical memory of modern societies. It is racism which continues to effect the imaginary "fusion" of past and present in which the collective perception of human history unfolds' (45). As historical memory, racism 'is not an "expression" of nationalism, but a *supplement of nationalism* or more precisely a *supplement internal to nationalism,* always in excess of it, but always indispensable to its constitution and yet always still insufficient to achieve its project, just as nationalism is both indispensable and always insufficient to achieve the formation of the nation or the project of a "nationalization" of society' (54).

lines, orienting itself towards the species as a planetary ideal, over and against the borders of naturalized jurisdictions. NGOs do not follow the map laid down by sovereign states and, sooner or later, they are going to weaken the classifications imposed by those states. Even though 'humankind' is not a name that grips us just yet, even though it seems to have zero membership and zero political clout, there is no reason why this should always be the case. And the more it becomes a name that is thinkable and credible, a many-sided name, reflecting the many habitats of the species, the more it can serve as a check on the unilateralism of one nation. In short, the word 'human' seems to me to have an incalculable future. Its heuristic force is measured by its mapping of a robust scientific taxonomy onto the domain of law, ethics, and politics. That mapping gives the lie to the naturalized artifact that is the nation state. It invites dwellers of this planet to reflect critically on (rather than identify automatically with) those jurisdictions where they happen to be born, or where they happen to be living.

Among fictional genres with a broad readership, none is more dedicated than science fiction to making 'human' an intelligible concept. True to its roots in science, the taxonomic basis here is the species. And, because this species is often faced with a disaster global in scope, its fate as a collectively surviving or collectively perishing unit is squarely in the foreground. Non-survival is a distinct possibility. Death, as a physiological event that is guaranteed to happen to all of us and which might happen sooner than we would like, is often the starting point for science fiction (and, as we know from Martin Rees' new book, *Our Final Century*, for many practising scientists as well).[10] It is the starting point for a globalism that embraces the sum total of the world's population as a co-dependent, co-evolving, and (just possibly) co-vanishing unit. In the rest of this paper, then, I will focus on one particular work, *Inferno*, by Larry Niven and Jerry Pournelle, to look at the image of the world that emerges when death is seen as this kind of starting point, when the unity of the species is predicated on it.

As suggested by the title, *Inferno* is about dead people, dead people in hell. This hell, though, is no ordinary one, it comes with a pedigree. From the outset, beginning with the dedication, we know that this book is 'For Dante Alighieri'. This gesture toward a canonical poet might seem odd for practitioners in this lowly genre, but there is in fact every reason to read Dante as a science fiction writer, taking a trip to alien space in the Middle Ages. This, at any rate, is how Niven and Pournelle read him. And they are literally following in his footsteps. In Canto 3, for example, Dante is in the Vestibule to Hell, where he hears shrieks of lamentation coming from a long train of people, 'so many, I had not thought death had undone so many'.[11] These are the people who, in life, had given their allegiance to nothing, and so in death they are rejected by both heaven and hell, and have to

[10] In *Our Final Century* (New York: 2003), Sir Martin Rees, Astronomer Royal of Britain, gives the human species only a 50/50 chance of surviving through the next century.

[11] These lines are, of course, from *The Waste Land*, where TS Eliot quotes Dante verbatim, from *Inferno* 3:56–57.

spend all of eternity in the Vestibule, chasing a banner they can never catch. All these details are faithfully transposed by Niven and Pournelle. Allen Carpentier, their protagonist, also finds himself in the Vestibule to Hell, confronted with a group of people chasing a banner. Then we get this conversation:

> I remembered then. 'Dante's *Inferno*?'
>
> Benito nodded, his big square jaw heaving like a broaching whale. 'You have read the *Inferno*, then. Good. That was the first clue I had to the way out of here. We must go down—'[12]

Niven's and Pournelle's *Inferno* is not the journey of a sole protagonist, because Dante's *Inferno* is not. In both cases, two companions are involved. Dante has a guide, Virgil, referred to sometimes as the *maestro*,[13] master, and sometimes as the *duca*,[14] leader. The bond between these two—the solicitude on the part of Virgil and the trust on the part of Dante—runs through the *Inferno* like a shimmering thread, a grave affirmation of something alien to hell, sturdy enough and supple enough to withstand the horror of the sinners' suffering. Niven and Pournelle are faithful to this structure as well. Allen Carpentier is not alone. He is accompanied, every step of the way, by a guide, someone called Benito.

Who is this Benito? That turns out to be the pivot of this novel, its central mystery. And bits of information are given to us along the way. We found out, just now, that he has a big square jaw jutting out. We are told that he speaks 'with an accent: Mediterranean; Spanish perhaps, or Italian' (15). He seems to know Dante's *Inferno* very well; and it also seems that, when alive, he was used to giving orders.

The secret is revealed at the end of the book, when the two companions have reached the very bottom of hell, the Bolgia of the Evil Counselors. The sinners here are those public figures who use their power of persuasion to push through evil policies, and, as punishment, they have been turned into tongues of flame that burn even as they speak:

> 'Come down!' one of the flames called to Benito. It was eerily compelling. That thrumming voice. The tip of the flame wavered, turned to me. 'Throw him down, you, if you're an American! That's Mussolini! Benito Mussolini!'
>
> Jolted, I turned to Benito. He shrugged.
>
> Mussolini?
>
> Another voice thrummed from the pit. 'You *are* American. I know your accent. Do you understand? That's Mussolini! Throw the bastard down here where he belongs!'
>
> 'Who are you?'
>
> 'Does it matter? I approved the firebombing of Dresden.' (188)

12 Larry Niven and Jerry Pournelle, *Inferno* (New York: 1976), 22. Hereafter cited by page in the text.

13 In *Inferno* 1:85, for instance, Dante addresses Virgil: 'Tu se' lo mio maestro e' l mio autore' (You are my master and my author).

14 In *Inferno* 3:94, Dante writes: 'E' l duca lui: "Caron, no ti curcciare" ' (And my leader: 'Charon, do not torment yourself').

National citizenship is suddenly dramatized at this moment. Americanness is written into Allen Carpentier's accent and, true to that accent, he knows just where he stands on World War II and how he should feel about the man who has so far been his guide and companion. A fit of patriotism surges up in him. But, we soon find out, only a fit, lasting only for about a minute, because patriotism is not, in fact, the dominant force in his emotional make-up. His personal loyalty is much stronger. It is this personal loyalty, this non-governmental bond, that makes him pull Benito out, and makes him, at the end of the book, a witness to his friend's escape from hell.

Why is Benito, or rather, Mussolini, given this second chance, this chance to be a second Virgil, and, in the end, to fare better than the ancient poet? Dante's Virgil, a virtuous pagan, born too early to be baptized, is destined to spend eternity in hell, in the painless but mournful first circle. It is his fate never to set eyes on Paradise. He can accompany Dante only part of the way, only through Purgatory but not beyond. *Purgatorio* 30, where he disappears, is one of the most traumatic moments in the *Divine Comedy*. From WS Merwin's new (2001) translation:

> I turned to the left with the confidence that
> a little child shows, running to its mother
> when something has frightened it or troubled it,
> to say to Virgil, 'Not even one drop
> of blood is left in me that is not trembling:
> I recognize the signs of the old burning.'
> But Virgil had left us, he was no longer there
> among us, Virgil, most tender father,
> Virgil to whom I gave myself to save me,[15]

The companionship of Virgil and Dante has to be cut short because, within a Christian taxonomy, those who are baptized and those who are not belong to two separate classes. They are to be separate for eternity. This is the taxonomy that reigns supreme in the *Inferno*. But, Dante being what he is—not only a Christian but also a poet—we can also be sure that this reigning taxonomy will not reign unmodified, that other idioms will intervene. Virgil is, after all, the most important poet as far as Dante is concerned. 'You are then Virgil, that fountain which pours forth so rich a stream of words?' he had said in Canto 1. 'O glory and light of

[15] Dante Alighieri, *Purgatorio. A New Verse Translation by WSMerwin* (New York, 2001), 30: 43–51. The Italian lines are as follows:

> volsimi alla sinistra col rispitto
> col quale il fantolin corre alla mamma
> quando ha paura o quando elli e afflitto,
> per dicere a Virgilio: 'Men che dramma
> di sangue m'e rimasso che non tremi:
> conosco i segni dell'antica flamma';
> ma Virgilio n'avea lasciati scemi
> di se, Virgilio dolcissimo patre,
> Virgilio a cui per mia salute die'mi;

other poets, . . . You are my master and my author.'[16] This is how a *poetic* taxonomy would classify Virgil: it is as lavish in its praise as the Christian taxonomy is severe in its damnation. This poetic taxonomy is no match for its Christian counterpart: it has no power to abolish hell, no power to assign Virgil to a different address; but it does have the power to change the nature of his sentence, to confer on him a more complex verdict.

The last words spoken by Dante to Virgil do just that. For these turn out to be a verbatim quotation from Virgil himself, an alternate 'afterlife' for the ancient poet. This afterlife—a strictly human affair, born of the longevity of words and of the memorizing that extends it—takes Virgil momentarily out of hell and restores him to the realm of the living. The quoted line is one of the most famous in the *Aeneid*, spoken by Dido, whose ancient passion, ancient flame, for Aeneas still has her in its grip: 'Adgnosco veteris vestigia flammae' (*Aeneid*, 4:23). Dante now turns this line into Italian, 'conosco i segni dell'antica flamma', and renders it back to Virgil. It is the ultimate tribute of a poetic offspring, for the very words coming out of Dante's mouth testify to his parentage. Testifying to that parentage, he is able to call Virgil by a different name. The pagan poet, inhabitant of hell, is all the same Dante's *dolcissimo patre*, sweetest father, rivalling the importance of God the Father.

Dante's *Inferno* is a struggle between two taxonomies, two ways of classifying human beings. Niven's and Pournelle's *Inferno* repeats that logic. Benito is two things at once: he is Mussolini, the enemy of all American citizens in World War II; but he is also a second Virgil, companion and guide in this difficult journey through hell. The Virgilian identity depends, of course, on some foreign help: it needs the pre-existing frame of a medieval poem, and it also needs a little Italian joke. The *duca* that was Virgil has literally morphed into the *Duce* that is Mussolini. The joke requires us to switch from English to Italian, and the switch is not just linguistic, it is also emotional, perhaps even ontological. We have to switch sides; we have to embrace an axis of vision naturally alien to us, which is to say, alien to our perspective as national citizens. Only then can we see Mussolini in an Italian context, not as a fool, a knave, a lackey of Hitler's, but as a tragic figure, someone whose disastrous end was not so much a foregone conclusion as a monstrous conjunction of events, a cruel insult to what was once a splendid beginning.

Italian historiography has portrayed Mussolini in just that light. Almost immediately after the war, Giorgio Pini and Duilio Susmel set to work to write a four-volume biography, sympathetic to the Duce.[17] But it is the monumental labour of Renzo De Felice that stands as a benchmark for all other researchers. Devoting some 40 years of his life to the papers in the *Archivio Centrale dello Stato* in Rome, De Felice produced what was eventually to become an eight-part biography of

[16] 'Or se' tu quel Virgilio e quella fonte/ che spandi di parlar si largo fiume?/ . . . / O delli altri poeti onore e lume,/ . . . / Tu se' lo mio maestro e 'l mio autore' (*Inferno* 1: 79–80, 82, 85).

[17] Giorgio Pini and Duilio Susmel, *Mussolini, l'uomo e l'opera*, 4 vols (Florence: 1953–55).

Mussolini, over 6,000 pages, published between 1965 and 1998.[18] The first volume, *Mussolini il rivoluzionario*, sets forth the central argument, one that De Felice would affirm over and over again:

> The most important influence upon Mussolini's development, all the relationships and influences of the successive years notwithstanding, was that exercised by revolutionary syndicalism. Even after Mussolini concluded his socialist phase, the influence of revolutionary syndicalism revealed itself in the characteristic manner he conceived social relations and political struggle.[19]

Fascism, as analyzed by De Felice, was born on the left, a radical movement rooted in the Italian socialist tradition. Drawn from the syndicalism of Georges Sorel—with its rejection of parliamentary politics and its reliance on trade unions as seats of direct action[20]—this early socialism was opposed to liberal democracy in ways that would later be extended and exploited in the Fascist mass rallies and dismantling of the parliamentary form. This was Mussolini's heritage. His parents had named him Benito Amilcare Andrea Mussolini in honour of three of these socialists: Benito Juarez, Amilcare Cipriani, and Andrea Costa.[21] True to these namesakes, he would go on to become, in 1912, the editor of the largest socialist daily in Italy, *Avanti!*, while founding at the same time his own theoretical journal, *Utopia*, in 1913.[22] His subsequent agricultural policy—for instance, reclaiming 150,000 acres of the Pontine Marshes in 1931 and distributing these to 75,000 peasants[23]—continued to reflect this early socialist commitment.

A radicalism on the right can grow out of a radicalism on the left. This is De Felice's argument about Italian Fascism. The German historian, Ernest Nolte, makes a parallel argument within a larger frame. Concerned with the kinship between communism and fascism, and not wishing to write the history of either as the necessary outcome of the totalitarian form,[24] Nolte emphasizes not only the interactive dynamics between these two but also the extent to which political history itself is genealogical, which is to say, conditioned by a prior matrix, a prior layer (or layers) of historical development. Fascism, on this view, was a reaction-formation,

[18] The eight volumes are: *Mussolini il rivoluzionario, 1883–1920* (Turin: 1965); *Mussolini il fascita, I: La conquista del potere, 1921–1925* (Turin: 1966); *Mussolini il fascita, II: L'organizzione dello Stato fascita, 1925–1929* (Turin: 1968); *Mussolini il duce, I: Gli anni del consenso, 1929–1936* (Turin: 1974); *Mussolini il duce, II: Lo Stato totalitario, 1936–1940* (Turin: 1996); *Mussolini l'alleato I: Italia in guerra, 1940–1943, vol.1: Dalla guerra breve alla guerra lunga* (Turin: 1996); *Mussolini l'alleato I: Italia in guerra, 1940–1943, vol.2: Crisi e agonia del regime* (Turin: 1996); *Mussolini l'alleato II: La Guerra Civile, 1943–1945* (Turin: 1998).

[19] Rezo De Felice, *Mussolini il rivoluzionario, 1883–1915* (Turin: 1965), 40, translated and quoted in A James Gregor, *Young Mussolini and the Intellectual Origins of Fascism* (Berkeley: 1979), 29.

[20] Gregor, n 19 above, 21–28.

[21] Denis Mack Smith, *Mussolini* (New York: 1982) 1.

[22] ibid, 134–135.

[23] Richard Lyttle, *Il Duce: The Rise and Fall of Benito Mussolini* (New York: 1987), 97–98.

[24] The theorists most often associated with an analysis of communism and fascism as the structural consequences of totalitarianism are Hannah Arendt and Carl Friedrich. See Carl Friedrich, *Totalitarianism* (Cambridge, MA: 1945); Carl Friedrich and Zbigniew K Brzesinski, *Totalitarian Dictatorship and Autocracy* (Cambridge, MA: 1965); Hannah Arendt, *The Origins of Totalitarianism* (Cleveland and New York: 1961).

a sequel to Bolshevism that was half-mimetic, half-antagonistic, rehearsing and inverting its challenge to liberal democracy.[25] What united the two, then, was a kind of philosophical hubris, an ambition to go beyond the modest scope of liberalism, an ambition inscribed in their revolutionary zeal, embracing every aspect of life, seeking to transform human nature itself. 'The radical Left and the radical Right', George L Mosse writes, 'were apt to demand control of the whole man, not just a political piece of him.'[26]

Fascism was a utopianism with no self-imposed limits. It was unwieldy for that reason, improvised along the way.[27] Its foreign policy, in particular, was haphazard in the extreme. Until June 1940, when the non-belligerency of Italy officially ended, its military alliance with Germany was by no means inevitable.[28] On the contrary, Mussolini was seen by many as a moderating force, a restraint on Hitler. Sigmund Freud presented him with a book inscribed 'to the Hero of Culture'; Pope Pius XI pronounced him 'a man sent to us by Providence'; Gandhi called him 'Saviour of Italy'.[29] On 'his return to Italy' from the Munich Conference in 1938, Nolte writes, 'he was welcomed by millions upon millions—some of them even on their knees—who, deeply and sincerely moved, looked on him as the savior of peace and of Europe'.[30] Charles de Gaulle—even after World War II—insisted that 'Mussolini was a great, a very great man'.[31]

Ezra Pound, living in Italy during the war and subsequently charged with treason because of his pro-fascist radio broadcasts, summed up this sense of Mussolini

[25] For Nolte, whereas Bolshevism represented 'the most unequivocal affirmation of material production and at the same time of practical transcendence', Fascism gestured toward a form of transcendence broader in scope and therefore confronting liberalism with a more complex challenge, because not limited to economics: 'Fascism has its command forces which are born of the emancipation process and then turn against their own origin. If it may be called the despair of the feudal section of bourgeois society for its traditions, and the bourgeois element's betrayal of its revolution, now it is clear what this tradition and this revolution actually are. Fascism represents the second and gravest crisis of liberal society, since it achieves power on its own soil, and in its radical form is the most complete and effective denial of that society.' See Ernst Nolte, *Three Faces of Fascism* (trans Leila Vennewitz, London, 1965) 452–453. The eminent French historian, Francois Furet, disagrees with Nolte's characterization of fascism as a sequel and a reaction. For Furet, fascism is not a *counter*-revolution, but a revolution in itself. In his published correspondence with Nolte, Furet writes: 'For me, the novelty of fascism in history consists in its emancipation of the European Right from the impasse that is inseparable from the counterrevolutionary idea. In effect, in the nineteenth century, the counterrevolutionary idea never ceased being trapped in the contradiction of having to use revolutionary means to win without being able to assign itself any goal other than the restoration of a past from which, however, the revolutionary evil arose. There is nothing like this in fascism. It is no longer defined by a re-action (reversal) against a revolution. It is itself the revolution.' See *Fascism and Communism: Francois Furet and Ernst Nolte* (trans Katherine Golsan, preface by Tzvetan Todorov, Lincoln, Nebraska: 2001), 89.

[26] George L Mosse, *The Fascist Revolution: Toward a General Theory of Fascism* (New York: 1999) 5.

[27] All the major biographies of Mussolini emphasize the extent to which he was hedging his bets. See, eg, Mack Smith, n 21 above; Lyttle, n 23 above; RJB Bosworth, *Mussolini* (New York: 2002).

[28] Galeazzo Ciano, Mussolini's son-in-law and chief foreign negotiator, was opposed to an alliance with Germany up until the last moment. See Lyttle, n 23 above, 131–142.

[29] Anthony James Joes, *Mussolini* (New York: 1982), 2.

[30] Nolte, n 25 above, 231.

[31] Joes, n 29 above, 2.

as a noble dream gone awry, someone whose squalid end was all the more heartbreaking because the beginning had not been squalid. From the *Pisan Cantos*:

> The enormous tragedy of the dream in the peasant's
> bent shoulders
> Manes! Manes was tanned and stuffed,
> Thus Ben and la Clara a Milano
> by the heels at Milano[32]

Mussolini and his companion, Clara Petacci, were killed by the Italian partisans on 27 April 1945, a few months before the end of the war; their bodies were publicly displayed in Milan, hanged by the heels. To Pound, any utopian hope died on that day, any hope that the peasants' bent shoulders might one day be unbent. There is in fact an interesting connection between the *Pisan Cantos* and the *Inferno* of Niven and Pournelle: both are updates of Dante, visions of World War II as hell. But to say that is also to say that there is a connection between a poet charged with treason against the United States and two popular science fiction writers.

That connection is especially worth pondering, given the storm whirling around a recent book, *Treason: Liberal Treachery from the Cold War to the War on Terrorism*, by Ann Coulter. Since its publication at the end of June, 2003, Coulter has already appeared on 160 television, radio, and newspaper interviews.[33] The book was No 2 on the *New York Times* Bestseller list on 20 July 2003. For Coulter, treason is a long-practised and never-acknowledged sin of the Democrats; it needs to be named, to be 'outed'. She recommends a return to McCarthyism. I find myself strangely in agreement with her on the former point. Treason, in my view, ought indeed to be 'outed', called by its unadorned and undisguised name: a name that can bear the weight of indictment (as Coulter would have it), and, by the same token, also the weight of advocacy. For if a global civil society is to serve as a check on the unilateralism of one nation, it must invite citizens of all countries to face up to 'treason' as a thinkable thought. And, to the extent that science fiction is a part of this global civil society, its virtual space is nothing less than the testing ground for this dangerous but world-minded kind of treason.

That, in any case, is the nature of the virtual space in Niven's and Pournelle's *Inferno*. World tribunal that it is, not only does it fail to side with the United States, it also fails to side with Britain, for even as Mussolini is given clemency, released from hell, another public figure, someone just as well known, is conspicuously not. He is stuck in hell for good because it was he who ordered the firebombing of Dresden.

Who could this be? And why was Dresden firebombed in the first place? One of the most horrifying events of World War II, coming at the very end—on 13, 14, and 15 February 1945—it 'aroused a revulsion', Max Hastings writes, 'which has

[32] Ezra Pound, *The Pisan Canatos* (London: 1949) Canto LXXIV.

[33] David Carr, 'Blond Lightning on the Far Right', *New York Times*, 20 July 2003, section 9, p 1, 6.

not been diminished by the passing of one generation'.[34] And there was apparently no tactical need for it, as Peter Calvocoressi, Guy Wint, and John Pritchard make clear in their magisterial *Total War*:

> The German armour, which was to defend the Hungarian oilfields, was believed to be routed through Dresden, but when Ultra revealed the division's orders this belief was found to be wrong. The mistake was pointed out to the British and American bomber headquarters concerned; the latter expressed willingness to cancel the raid if the other would do so too, but the former saw no reason to alter its plans. The presumed passage of the German armour through Dresden was only an ostensible reason for the operation. Equally dubious is the plea that the raid was executed in aid of the advancing Russians. There was no Russian request for a raid on Dresden.[35]

The magnitude of the attack and the lack of any tactical objectives created a public furor. On 16 February, the Associated Press made known to the world this 'unprecedented daylight assault on the refugee-crowded capital, with civilians fleeing from the Red tide in the East'.[36] The *Daily Mirror* editorialized in response: 'Not only does it make nonsense of all our protestations about our war aims and about our bombing policy; it gives official proof for everything that Goebbels ever said on the subject. It is wicked as well as being typically un-British.'[37] On 6 March 1945, Richard Stokes, Labour MP, spoke in the House of Commons. The massive killing of civilians in an unarmed city, he said, was a 'blot on our escutcheon'.[38] The ensuing debate was such that Churchill felt the need, on 28 March 1945, to compose this memorandum for his bomber units:

> It seems to me the moment has come when the question of bombing of German cities simply for the sake of increasing the terror, though under other pretexts, should be reviewed. Otherwise we shall come into control of an utterly ruined land. We shall not, for instance, be able to get housing materials out of Germany for our own needs because some temporary provision would have to be made for the Germans themselves.[39]

The bomber units were outraged. To them, the memorandum was a 'monstrous insinuation' on the part of the Prime Minister that they had been running a terror campaign on their own, as if 'he had never advocated or even ordered that sort of thing'.[40] Sir Charles Portal, Chief of the Air Staff, refused to accept the memo. Churchill had to retract his words.[41]

Where should the blame fall? The historian David Irving, who has done extensive archival work for his book, *Apocalypse 1945: The Destruction of Dresden*,

34 Max Hastings, *Bomber Command* (New York: 1979), 340.

35 Peter Calvocoressi, Guy Wint, and John Pritchard, *Total War: Causes and Courses of the Second World War* (2nd edn, New York: 1989), 561.

36 Quoted in Alexander McKee, *Dresden 1945: The Devil's Tinderbox* (London: 1982), 263.

37 ibid, 264.

38 David Irving, *Apocalypse 1945: The Destruction of Dresden* (1963; rpt London: 1995), 264.

39 Churchill, memorandum to Sir Charles Portal, Chief of Air Staff, quoted in Hastings, n 34 above, 343–344 and Irving, n 38 above, 267.

40 Irving, n 38 above, 268.

41 ibid, 268.

is careful not to make any point blank allegation, but he does have a tight web of circumstantial evidence. The general policy of 'area bombing' had originated not from Sir Archibald Sinclair, Secretary of State for Air, but from the Prime Minister himself, over the objection of American generals.[42] The specific choice of Dresden as a target came from a level of command higher than that of the Royal Air Force. Sir Arthur Harris, Marshal of the RAF, later wrote in his book, *Bomber Offensive*: 'the destruction of so large and splendid a city at this late stage of the war was considered unnecessary even by a good many people who admit that our earlier attacks were as fully justified as any other operation of war. Here I will only say that the attack on Dresden was at the time considered a military necessity by much more important people than myself.'[43]

This 'military necessity' apparently had to do with the Soviet Union, whose Red Army was scoring decisive victories on Germany's eastern front, putting the western allies to shame. 'The years between 1941 and 1944 saw Soviet prestige higher than ever before. From the perspective of the ordinary citizen who was no expert in military affairs, it looked as if Russia were doing all the fighting, while Britain and the United States were standing idly by. For nearly three years, the war in the east dwarfed the struggle in the west', H Stewart Hughes writes.[44] When Churchill met with Stalin in Moscow in October 1944, cruel cartoons appeared in the world press featuring 'an enormous red Stalin in giant hobnailed boots by far outweighing and hoisting high a tiny, frustrated Winston Churchill'.[45] Something had to be done before the next scheduled meeting with Stalin, at Yalta on 4 February 1945.

On the night of 25 January 1945, Churchill phoned Sir Archibald Sinclair to inquire what plans Bomber Command had for 'basting the Germans in their retreat from Breslau'.[46] As it turned out, because of weather conditions, that 'basting' could not take place until 13 February 1945, two days after the conclusion of the Yalta Conference, but the executive order was not cancelled. So the bombers went out, dropping mostly incendiaries and high-explosives. The goal was to create, in the words of Sir Arthur Harris, 'fire tornadoes',[47] whose gale-force wind would then spread the fire to the rest of the city, achieving total destruction in this way rather than through bombing. These raids were repeated three times, specifically targeting the assembled firefighters and rescue workers. The civilian casualties were estimated to be between 68,000 and 135,000.[48] The figure was higher than the total number of casualties in Britain during the entire war, estimated at 60,595 over five and a half years.[49] This was apparently a proud achievement for Churchill.

[42] Irving, n 38 above, 96–97.

[43] Sir Arthur Harris, *Bomber Offensive* (1947; rpt Novato, CA: 1990), 242.

[44] H Stuart Hughes, *Contemporary Europe: A History* (6th edn, Englewood Cliffs, NJ: 1987), 331.

[45] McKee, n 36 above, 97.

[46] Hastings, n 34 above, 341; Irving, n 38 above, 94.

[47] Sir Arthur Harris, n 43 above, 83.

[48] The estimated casualty figures varied. See Calvocoressi, Wint, and Pritchard, n 35 above, 562; Irving, n 38 above, 260.

[49] McKee, n 36 above, 12.

It was the aerial view of the completely gutted city that he would later display, in the stereoscopic apparatus in his Cabinet War Rooms.[50]

A world tribunal, looking simply at the loss of lives, and attaching no national prefix to those lives, would have to consider the war crime of the person who ordered that firebombing. Judgment of this sort is the necessary penumbra to the rule of law, what underwrites its species-wide aspirations. If this is an act of treason, science fiction stands convicted.

[50] Irving, n 38 above, viii.

PART VIII

SOME OTHER CULTURAL PHENOMENA

Neoliberalism, Shopping Malls and the End of 'Property'?

Malcolm Voyce

Introduction[1]

This chapter examines new forms of property, which I claim are emerging within neoliberal forms of economy. These forms of property, I argue, arise within a reconfigured state, based on privatization, where distinct forms of power have been developed through consumption. The forms of property which thus arise are characterized by first, new forms of citizenship, secondly, an end to localized space and thirdly the use of spatial practices which construct norms as to who may enter the new forms of quasi-public property.[2]

To establish this argument, I examine the operation of a new mall at Hornsby, to show how the owners of the mall, Westfield, *govern*, through *spatial practices*, the physical space in the mall and the shopping practices of the people who enter the mall. By these spatial practices, I argue, Westfield creates a certain ambiance in the mall, which conveys the message that the mall is an attractive and safe location, which welcomes certain customers and excludes others. This collective impression of mall atmosphere, I argue, acts as a spatial practice, which in effect governs the mall. In general the growth of shopping malls is symptomatic of how consumers are being shaped by discourses of consumption.

To develop the argument in this chapter I divide my argument up into the following sections. First, I outline how shopping malls are an example of the privatization of public space and how this has led to the exclusion of certain sections of the community. Secondly, I outline how neoliberalism as a new form of political/economic governance based on privatization, competition and deregulation, has led to the creation of a society governed by information, where law is not the dominant form of governance, but rather subjects are governed through consumption. Thirdly, I examine the idea of property as described by property lawyers as ownership, alienation and exclusion. I do this to argue that this traditional view of property, as understood through the culturally powerful view of lawyers, should

[1] My thanks to the local history librarian at Hornsby Library and George Watts who allowed me access to Hornsby Council records and planning applications. My thanks also to Gabriella Gwyther, Roger Keil, Paul Henman and Robert Baker.

[2] An earlier version of this article was published in (2003) 21(1) *Urban Policy and Research* 249.

be modified as it has been superseded by more hegemonic discourses based on consumption. Fourthly, to situate these arguments I examine the new shopping mall at Hornsby. I conclude that a wider conception of property is necessary to enable us to see property as more than a relationship between the owner of land and the physical form of the property. Neoliberalism, I argue, as a form of economic governance breaks this link between a particular piece of property and the owner, so that within neoliberalism property is governed through new forms of expertise within an economy built on consumption.

Malls and Public Space

One of the features of shopping malls is that public or civic space is replaced with 'semi-public space' owned by developers. In Sydney, as elsewhere, large tracts of property and previously owned public land (as in Hornsby) are now controlled—and policed—by private corporations. In this context the protection of private property has coalesced with the preservation of public order.[3] In Sydney shopping malls undesirable characters have been excluded and shops found in the high street such as pawnshops and second hand bookshops are not offered rentals in shopping malls. Other unwelcome folk include the homeless and groups of teenagers.

In other situations developers have entered into a private-public partnership with local authorities over what was once private property. Such examples are found in gated communities, festive market places and casinos.[4] As regards shopping malls, one of the ironies is the way planners have been authorized in architectural terms to recreate 'the street' as an organic 'civil milieu'.[5] In effect the goal has been to increase profits from real estate sales, to which end political campaigners and artists have been excluded on the basis of the strict ethics of a 'consumerist citizenship'.[6] With the development of privatized urban property, practices of social exclusion for those already marginalized and disadvantaged have developed.

The other such feature of these marketized public spaces is that they do not reflect the local histories or the democratic needs of the community, but instead inculcate the tastes and identities of global consumer culture.[7] Thus the local loses its uniqueness and there is little space for notions of locality or local public opinion. When consumers are inside such places they could be anywhere in the world, as all these types of places seem to be the same whether they be downtown

[3] K Gray and S Gray, *Elements in Land Law* (London: 2000) 166.

[4] For overseas literature especially in the United States, see M Sorkin, *Variations on a Theme Park* (New York: 1992); J Gross, 'The Magic of the Mall: An Analysis of the Form and Function and Meaning in the Contemporary Retail Built Environment' [1993] *Annals of the Association of American Geographers* 18.

[5] Gross, ibid.

[6] S Christopherson, 'The Fortress City: Privatised Spaces, Consumer Citizenship' in A Amin (ed), *Post-Fordism: A Reader* (Oxford: 1994).

[7] J Brodie, 'Imagining Democratic Urban Citizenship' in EF Isin (ed), *Democracy, Citizenship and the Global City* (London: 2000), 111, 114.

centres, airports or shopping malls. These privatized public spaces construct relationships between individualized consumers and the market, which is detached from a physical space. In this form these spaces lose their true capacity for social integration based on local history and meaning.[8]

This development has taken place alongside the recent debate in Sydney over the proper use of public property and the appropriateness of quality private acquisition of key civic sites, such as the opera house area, the privatization of public roads and foreshore developments. In some countries the courts have developed an area of law known as quasi-public land to resolve the conditions of access to those commercial zones which are neither wholly public nor private in character but where some constraints are needed to restrain the conditions of market dominance. In the United States and Canada the public in varying degrees have been granted rights to shopping malls, petrol stations, libraries, educational establishments, airports and recreational outlets.[9]

In the wider context of a debate over the role of property use some legal commentators admit that the power relationship in property is not absolute but is relative in the sense that there may be gradations of property ownership. However, the dominant legal explanation still articulates the notion of property in terms of raw exclusionary power and a landowner is seen to enjoy an unqualified prerogative—no matter how arbitrary—to selectively and capriciously determine who has access to land.[10]

Westfield has clearly utilized the dominant discourse that insulates property from full public access. There were very few objections to the private use of public or 'semi-public space' by Westfield in Hornsby. I refer here to the lack of substantial protest about Westfield's purchasing of public roadway to build the mall and the fact that its civic amenities (banks, the post office and health insurance companies) are subject to Westfield's control over access. Further there has been no court case contesting, as in the United States, the absolute rights of property owners.

Shopping centres in Sydney have developed the practice of issuing banning notices to those members of the public they wish to exclude from the mall, usually young people. While the practice varies from centre to centre the specified person is usually banned from entering the centre for from six months to two years. There has been a case of a life ban. Should a person return to the mall the police charge him or her with trespass. Shopping centres appear to have given security guards an open discretion on issuing notices. In practice, notices are often given for frivolous reasons (such as an association with adversely known peers, etc)—such youths often 'hang out' at the entry of malls to socialize rather than to shop. There have only been a few cases where youths have been prosecuted for trespass and where the judgments are available. The available cases reveal that youths have not been successful in defending a charge of trespass, since they have not been able to prove that they

[8] ibid. [9] Gray and Gray, n 3 above, 161–162.

[10] K Gray and S Gray, 'Private Property and Public Property' in J McLean (ed), *Property and the Constitution* (Oxford: 1999), 12–13.

had 'a lawful excuse' for being on the shopping mall premises.[11] In the last few months Westfield in Hornsby has started to issue banning notices.

The Importance of Neoliberalism in Governing Consumption

In the early years of the settlement of Australia, it was seen as necessary to build up a manufacturing base to assist nation building. To achieve this, local manufacturers were subsidised by the government and protected by high tariffs. From the 1970s with the worldwide recession Australia adopted neoliberal policies based on competition, deregulation and privatization. These policies saw, in the apt words of the title of Paul Kelly's book *The End of Certainty* or the end of the 'Australian Settlement' based on White Australia, industry protection, wage arbitration, state paternalism and imperial benevolence.[12] Under neoliberal policies, led by a new information elite, the market came to be seen as the dominant method for the allocation and distribution of goods. Further tariffs were dismantled and many public services such as agricultural research were privatized.

The term 'neoliberalism' denotes a form of political-economic governance based on the centrality of market relationships. This term is more widely used than similar terms known as economic rationalism, monetarism, neo-conservatism, managerialism and contractualism.[13] Larner argues that we should not merely characterize neoliberalism as a policy response to the policy exigencies of the global economy as dictated by the dominance of the 'New Right'. To do so, she argues, runs the risk of under-estimating the significance of the contemporary transformation of governance. Neoliberalism is both a policy discourse about the nature of rule *and a set of practices that facilitate the governing of individuals from a distance.*[14] In this context neoliberalism should not be seen as a prescription for state retreat based on fiscal conservatism but as a complex set of *changing technologies of power.*[15] It is not the hollowing out of the state but a reorganized state in that the functions of the state (as a centralized form) may be carried out at the periphery or by analogous institutions which have more or less power than the central or 'lean state'. With neoliberalism, it is claimed, the state has 'disappeared' and its sovereignty passed elsewhere, perhaps going sideways to the market, upwards to international regulatory bodies,[16] and downwards to the local through decentralization to the individual. In this situation the neoliberal state embraces the market *both* over the state and inside the state.

[11] A Grant, 'Banning the Banning Notice' (2000) 25(1) *Alternative LJ* 32. For case law see *O v Wedd* [2000] TASSC 74 dealing with a Northgate Shopping Centre at Glenorchy, Tasmania and *Police v Street*, Magistrate's Court Sydney, before Magistrate Gilmour. This case dealt with a trespass to the Macquarie Centre, Sydney.

[12] P Kelly, *The End of Certainty: Power, Politics and Business in Australia* (Sydney: 1992)

[13] W Larner, 'Neoliberalism Policy, Ideology, Governmentality' (2000) 63 *Studies in Political Economy* 5.

[14] ibid

[15] R Keil, 'Common Sense Liberalism' [2002] *Antipode* 582.

[16] Brodie, n 7 above, 110.

In the context of Australia, neoliberalism involves competition, deregulation and privatization. Privatization, it is argued by its advocates, gives choice and opportunity. The process of privatization is seen as the 'return' of state run entities to the legitimate owners. This type of argument was seen recently in the 'hand over' of homes to the aged. Here I am referring to the Minister for Family Services, who claimed that in deregulating the aged care sector she was providing the aged with 'their new home'. In reality all she was doing was exposing the aged to the forces of the deregulated market for private property.[17] Similar comments have been made by developers, that by building shopping malls 'for the public' they are 'returning land to the public'.

Isin argues that with the advent of neoliberalism, capitalist societies have undergone three characteristic shifts. First, there is a new relationship between expertise and politics. Isin argues that under liberalism, knowledge played a central role in government through its ability to raise claims as to truth and validity. Liberal technologies of power were verity, validity, and reliability. However under neoliberalism there has been a shift in the importance from older occupations, such as law and medicine, to the newer occupations of consultancy, the promotional professions and accountancy with their respective technologies of enumeration, calculation, monitoring and evaluation.[18] These disciplines or technologies are provided through the operation of surveillance, data storage and consumer research, all of which are fundamental in the shopping mall industry.[19] Consistent with this argument, I propose to follow an indication of Foucault,[20] which suggests that while law was a primary form of power in the premodern era, in modernity it is undermined or supplemented by widely dispersed disciplines associated with these professional knowledges based on these new informational and 'expert' technologies.

Secondly, there has been a shift in the technologies of power towards privatization and away from accountable public process. We are all familiar with the increase of new non-governmental organizations providing services once provided by former governmental agencies, for instance the contracting out of services in prisons, health and welfare. Modern city local government becomes increasingly like an empty shell whose territory once exhibited the previously meaningful boundaries of the political.[21] With the shift in the use of these new technologies (as outlined above) neither the size nor will of the government to govern declines—rather it is

[17] *Hansard*, 12 March 1997, 3192, Judy Moylan.

[18] S Brint, *In An Age of Experts: The Changing Role of Professionals in Politics and Professional Life* (Princeton: 1994).

[19] For the emerging literature on surveillance see D Lyon, *Surveillance and Society* (Buckingham: 2001) esp 122 for a discussion of geodemographic devices for the use of experts as regards the development of markets and investments.

[20] M Foucault, *History of Sexuality* (London: 1976) and 'Governmentality' in G Burchell, C Gordon and P Miller (eds), *The Foucault Effect: Studies in Governmental Rationality* (Chicago: 1991) 87.

[21] E Isin, 'Governing Toronto Without Government: Liberalism and Neoliberalism' (1998) 56 *Studies in Political Economy* 169, 176.

the form in which individuals are constituted. Subjects are now governed by the entrepreneurial professions which emphasize client and consumer control. Subjects, argues Isin, are formed as consumers who are endowed with the capacities to make free choices. In this environment there is a shift from the situation where state officials exercised authority over subjects, from 'trustee professionals' to 'expert professionals'.[22] As Brint argues, the exercise of power shifts from government as an authority to technology experts in the social body—hence providing government without government.[23]

Thirdly, under neoliberalism there is a new specification of the subjects of governance, through patterns of consumption, where subjects are defined as 'clients' and autonomous market participants who are responsible for their own success, health and well-being. In this vision of society the state is a facilitator which 'steers' from the centre and is crucially involved in developing ideas of community through such notions as personal responsibility and autonomous individuality. In this state, identity is not based on citizenship formation and nation building, as in the nineteenth century, but is focused on practices of identity formation through consumption where affluent lifestyle choices are presented as available to everybody.[24]

It is possible with privatization to trace the emergence of the consumer and 'identify the institutional conditions' where it became intelligible to generalize about the identity of the consumer across the whole of society. In this regard Larner claims market governance is not about improving economic production (as it is claimed) but as a means of governance through consumption.[25]

Scholars of consumption have noted that there are three processes connected with new forms of consumption within neoliberalism. First, there is the increasing net of commodification through the widening use of the proliferation of signs that lead to the aestheticisation of reality.[26] Secondly, with the greater number of people involved in consumer culture, with greater spending power, there has been the fragmentation of individuality and the corresponding segmentation into different groups and 'fractured selves'. Thus there has been, in the language of Giddens, the 'pluralisation of lifewords'[27] and the 'broadening and deepening of individuality'.[28] In this situation the notion of a single national citizenship is obsolete, as multiple and fluid identities render the term meaningless.[29]

The consolidation of retail marketing power away from department stores, which sold goods to a relatively homogeneous group of customers, has been

[22] E Isin, 'Governing Toronto Without Government: Liberalism and Neoliberalism' (1998) 56 *Studies in Political Economy* 169, 176.

[23] Brint, n 18 above.

[24] N Rose, 'Inventiveness in Politics' (1999) 28(3) *Economy and Society* 467.

[25] W Larner, 'The Legacy of the Social: Market Governance and the Consumer' (1997) 26(3) *Economy and Society* 373, 396.

[26] See, eg, J Baudrillard, *Simulations* (New York: 1993).

[27] A Giddens, *Modernity and Self-Identity* (Cambridge: 1991).

[28] P Glennie and NJ Thrift, 'Modernity, Urbanism, and Modern Consumption' (1992) 10 *Environment and Planning D: Society and Space* 423.

[29] G Parker and N Ravenscroft, 'Land Rights and the Gift: the Countryside and Rights of Way Act 2000 and the Negotiation of Citizenship' (2001) 41(4) *Sociologia Ruralis* 383, 388.

replaced, with this deepening form of commodification, through the marketing techniques of the retail industry to mobilize the consumer to form a distinctive self by creating complex connections between the subject's psyche and the particular characteristics of consumer goods.[30] The contribution of neoliberal forms of governance, is that in this situation, new selves become visible through the *expert* monitoring by new technologies and thus have become subject to new forms of governance.[31] In this context I utilize the notion of *governance*[32] to show that those connected with the Westfield mall are shaped by a variety of techniques and practices, which Westfield has developed as a result of its experience with other shopping centres. I therefore envisage subjects who are morally free and yet are shaped from a distance by shopping mall practices.[33]

To complement the above characterizations of neoliberalism, by Isin, I argue that neoliberalism is involved in the creation of new forms of space. By this I refer to the new spatial practices, built on new technologies which are involved in monitoring and surveillance practices which in effect create new communities to govern and new spatial practices which manage who may enter the mall area. I expand on this point when I later discuss the promotion of the mall and the way the mall is advertised.

Governmentality theorists use the term 'political rationalities' to describe how governmental knowledge operates to conceptualize and problematize particular areas where governments should assist or intervene.[34] Such areas may be in the areas of social security, health care or the treatment of the aged. I argue that those political rationalities emerge not only from the formal organizations of state but may emerge within the business sector. In the context of the operation of large privately owned shopping malls, I regard spatial practices as a form of political rationality.

Property and Neoliberalism

Having outlined neoliberalism, I now discuss the development of the notion of property, to show the change in the form of governance in the development from liberalism to neoliberalism. To do this, I must first outline how the notion of property has been deployed by the state.

[30] P Miller and N Rose, 'Mobilizing the Consumer: Assembling the Subject of Consumption' (1997) 14(1) *Theory, Culture and Society* 1.

[31] Larner, n 25 above, 377.

[32] I use the terms *govern* and *governance* interchangeably. Here I follow Hunt who, on writing on the 'sociology of governance', argues that governance is conceived of as practices and discourses directed towards the control of any social agents and institutions. A Hunt, 'The Governance of Consumption: Sumptuary Laws and the Shifting Forms of Regulation' (1996) 25(3) *Economy and Society* 412.

[33] On these issues within the governmentality literature see Foucault, 'Governmentality', n 20 above.

[34] N Rose and P Miller, 'Political Power beyond the State: Problematics of Government' (1992) 43 *British J of Sociology* 173.

Foucault argues that at the end of the Middle Ages, large nation states began to rise above their feudal form and become nation states, raising the question of 'governmentality'.[35] As sovereignty emerged in the sixteenth to eighteenth centuries there was a concern to develop governance for all forms of life. At this time there developed a series of disciplines to organize the emerging populations. New disciplines such as economics, public health and statistics all indicated a new set of tactics where the central state began to exercise subtle control over citizens.[36] There was thus a change in ideas in forms of rationalization, the schematization of human behaviour, the functional sharing out to individuals of strict and stable spaces. It meant the creation of a new form of government based on knowledge and discipline. In essence the eighteenth-century government sought a new relationship with resources, population and discipline.[37]

With the establishment of the Australian colony within the metropolitan power network, the policy of the British government at this time was to develop the colonies through free trade. This policy was seen to require the ending of mercantilism and the propagation of a bourgeois economy, based on individual ownership of land rather than a subservient peasant class.[38]

At the time Australia was settled the market in England was becoming the dominant factor in the regulation of life. Settlers who arrived in Australia bought the traditions of the older order as well as the new. Some of these settlers bought ideas of plebian culture at odds with the new commercial culture and different expectations about property rights and conditions of employment.[39] Importantly some of these people bought out ideas of the Enlightenment based on moral improvement. Enlightenment ideals enshrined the notion that subjects could be improved as a result of conspicuous planning and discipline within the confines of industry, sobriety and the advancement of prosperity.[40] Importantly, these ideals resonated with the notion that the proper allocation of land could lead to moral improvement. There were two implications. First, it allowed British investors 'long distance control' of their investments[41] and secondly, through the ownership of land, settlers were encouraged to develop their own autonomy through the idea 'of regulated freedom' in that each settler was allocated land at a sufficient distance from his neighbour but yet close enough to keep him in view.[42]

As part of the transfer of English culture to Australia, came the sciences and the disciplines[43] which underpinned the use of surveys and cartography, thus

[35] Foucault, 'Governmentality', n 20 above; M Foucault, *Power /Knowledge: Selected Writings and Other Interviews 1972–1977*, C Gordon (ed) (London 1980).

[36] ibid.

[37] U Kalpagam, 'Colonial Governmentality and the Public Sphere in India' (2000) 15(1) *J of Historical Sociology* 35.

[38] C Goodwin, *Economic Inquiry in Australia* (Durham: 1966), 618–619.

[39] S Macintyre, *Winners and Losers: the Pursuit of Social Justice in Australian History* (Sydney: 1985), 10–12.

[40] J Gascoigne, *The Enlightenment and The Origins of European Australia* (Cambridge: 2002) 12.

[41] R Connell and T Irving *Class Structure and Australian History* (Sydney: 1992), 45.

[42] M Voyce, 'The Spatial Settlement of Australia' in A Ioan (ed), *Lost in Space* (Budapest: 2003) 315–317.

[43] Here I am referring to the deployment of cartography and mapping which permitted the construction of space as a universal, measurable and divisible entity. See S Ryan, *The Cartographic Eye*

facilitating the sale of land in lots or parcels. The Torrens registration system based on public registration of title further simplified the transfer of land. Finally the transplants of English legal culture saw the introduction of trust law, company law and accountancy practices.[44] The pedigrees of these transplants were maintained through legal education and the foundational classifications of English law.[45] Australian lawyers as a specialized group of professionals built on this discourse, which organized property law as a disciplinary code, to maintain the strength of the 'absolutist property paradigm' which links conceptually the notion of property with a particular owner.

As part of this colonial legacy lawyers have considered property to represent ideas of ownership, alienation and exclusion. Property in this context is seen as a set of consolidated rights, which has one bearer who is identifiable through formal title.[46] The most common formulation was that property is a 'bundle of rights'. The metaphor's image is that property is a bundle of sticks in which each stick in the bundle represents a different right associated with property.[47] This description, formulated by professional lawyers, is seen as inadequate, for a variety of reasons.[48] These are best expanded on by Arnold who argues that the bundle of rights conception of property is confusing as first it focuses on rights rather than duties; secondly this formulation masks an essentially individualistic, commodifying, acquisitive concept of property every bit as anti-social as the Blackstonian concept; thirdly this formulation lacks any economically efficient boundaries or bundling principles; and fourthly the formulation fails to provide any coherent theory to distinguish property rights from any other rights and so reduces property as a meaningful legal category.

I argue that ideas of ownership that link the control of a particular piece of territory with a particular owner in the neoliberal economy are now seen as outmoded as new forms of power have shifted the meaning of 'property' into alignment with the rhetoric of 'social efficiency and community benefit'. In this environment the power and significance of land declines.[49]

(Cambridge: 1996). On the production of the instrumentation for this process and its link with the colonialism see R Sorrenson, 'The State's Demand for Accurate Astronomical and Navigational Instruments in 18th Century Britain' in A Bermingham and J Brewer (eds), *The Consumption of Culture 1600–1800: Image, Object, Text* (New York: 1992), 263.

44 On the colonial use of trusts see M Voyce, 'Governing from a Distance: The Significance of the Capital Income Distinction in Trusts' in S Scott-Hunt and H Lim (eds), *Feminist Views on Equity and Trusts* (London: 2001), 153. On the importance of accounting see P Miller, 'Accounting and the Construction of the Governable Person' (1987) 12(3) *Accounting, Organisations and Society* 235; D Neu, 'Discovering Indigenous Peoples: Accounting and the Machinery of Empire [1999] *Accounting Historians Journal* 53.

45 On the maintenance of English law forms see B Edgeworth, 'Tenure, Allodialism and Indigenous Rights at Common Law: English, United States and Australian Law Compared after Mabo v. Queensland (1994) *American L Rev* 397. On the influence of legal education and classical English texts see D Sugarman, 'Legal Theory, The Common Law Mind and the Making of the Textbook Tradition' in W Twining (ed), *Legal Theory and the Common Law* (Oxford: 1986), 26.

46 E Engelen, 'Corporate Governance, Property and Democracy; a Conceptual Critique of Shareholder Ideology' (2002) 31(3) *Economy and Society* 391.

47 CA Arnold, 'The Reconstruction of Property: Property as a Web of Interests' (2002) 26 *Harvard Environmental L Rev* 281.

48 ibid, 290.

49 Parker and Ravenscroft, n 29 above, 381, 391–392.

I argue therefore that it is time to examine other discourses, emanating from neoliberalism, which sit alongside these notions of property, and which emanate from sources which are unconnected to the formal sources of law (the courts, parliament). Some legal academics, in order to overcome the problems of understanding the concept of property, have looked at what we may loosely call a 'social side of property'. For instance Gray and his co-author have described property as a 'socially approved power' over a socially valued resource.[50]

I argue that it is time to separate legal notions of property from the various social ideas concerning property. I therefore propose to make a distinction between *legal notions of property* (such as ownership, alienation and exclusion) and *property in the sense of a social idea*.

Readers familiar with the work of law and society scholars (such as Merry) may question this approach as 'law and society scholars' argue that law and society are mutually defining and are therefore inseparable.[51] They argue that law is intimately involved in the *constitution of* social relations and that the law *is constituted through social relations*.[52] This article presents a different perspective, in that I argue that, what I call *propriety relationships (prescriptive* behaviour in relation to the mall) are shaped by ideas from neoliberalism and ideas concerning the centrality of the market. It is not my task to attempt to show the causal connection between 'market ideas' and 'the law', but to follow what I perceive to be the spirit of Foucault's work, to show how from a unruly shoppers' perspective there may be a divergence (or convergence) of *narrow* and *wider* ideas of property.

I call the former approach the *narrow* view of property and the latter the *wider* view of property. This approach enables me to examine more clearly the set of ideas emanating from socioeconomic ideas within neoliberalism which, I argue, shape what I call *propriety relationships* and the form of prescriptive social ideas, which govern entry to the mall.

Spatial Practices and Governance

Whenever we go shopping, how many times have we either overheard others or heard ourselves saying to our partners, kids or even ourselves, 'I'm just going to *my* butcher' or 'hey they've moved *my* newsagent'. Most of us experience this every time we shop. It is a perfect example of how the public takes ownership of privately owned and operated spaces.

In order for us to bring the shopping experience to the table of discussion of contextual renewal, we now embark on a process that aims to bring the various levels of authority and constituency into the fold as stake holders of the proposal. Why? *Because they take figurative ownership at the end of the day.*[53]

50 Gray and Gray, n 3 above, 96.

51 S Merry, 'Culture, Power and the Discourse of Law' (1992) 37 *New York U L Rev* 209.

52 ibid.

53 F Alvarez, 'Common Area' in J Barrett and C Butler-Bowden (eds), *Debating the City: an Anthology* (Sydney: 2001), 217–218.

Social ideas of property are important because the method and means of their deployment shapes a particular social environment. This study builds on the 'spatial turn' in social theory, which associates social space with relations of power.[54] I argue that the spatial areas which we are familiar with, such as our homes, streets, offices and malls, reflect and reinforce relationships of power.[55] These spatial practices assign meaning to lines and spaces in order to control the physical world. What is controlled, in effect, are the social relationships and experiences of people.[56]

I do not deny that the social spaces that appear, for instance, in shopping malls, may be different to that intended by the owners. I admit to a reciprocal relationship between the produced spaces and the expression of some local social practice.[57] While I acknowledge 'resistance' or 'agency' by customers and tenants, my stress is on the degree of *intentional* control exercised by the mall owners. It appears that Westfield have achieved their intentions to date in Hornsby, to limit the mall to only those people who wish to avail themselves of the mall's facilities as customers.

Some studies have linked the construction of a specific identity to a 'place' and have attempted to see this as a spatial practice. For instance, Mort has described how a particular locality has been utilized to create a new gay consumer market.[58] This study indicates how 'place' is not a passive backdrop but is, as Moran and Skeggs write, 'implicated with the production of security and insecurity, identity and community, which may intervene in the construction of difference'.[59]

I wish to show how the construction of a specific identity at a particular site of consumption acts as a spatial practice. Spatial practices govern social spaces in two

[54] For Foucault's approach to space see M Foucault, *Discipline and Punish* (London: 1975); *Power /Knowledge*, n 35 above; 'Of Other Spaces' (1986) *Diacritics* 22. For material that develops this approach see F Driver, 'Power, Space and the Body: a Critical Assessment of Foucault's Discipline and Punish' (1985) 3 *Environment and Planning D: Society and Space*, 425, C Philo, 'Foucault's Geography' (1992) 10 *Environment and Planning D: Society and Space* 137. For recent theoretical approaches to space see generally, EJ Soja, *Postmodern Geographies: the Reassertion of Space in Critical Social Theory* (London: 1989); N Blomley, 'The Properties of Space: History, Geography and Gentrification' (1997) 18(4) *Urban Geographer* 286 and 'Landscapes of Property' (1998) 32(3) *Law and Society Rev* 567; J Holder and C Harrison, *Law and Geography* (Oxford: 2003). The connection between planning law and social control has been made by some scholars: MC Boyer, *Dreaming the Rational City; the Myth of American City Planning* (Cambridge: 1983); C Perin, *Everything in its Place; Social Use and Land Use in America* (New Jersey: 1997). In the Australian context see K Gibson and S Watson, *Metropolis Now: Planning and the Urban in Contemporary Australia* (Sydney: 1991). For a Foucauldian approach, see H Lewi and G Wickham 'Modern Urban Geography' (1996) 14(1) *Urban Policy and Research* 51; G Kendall and G Wickham, 'Governing the Cultures of Cities: a Foucauldian Perspective' (1996) 33(2) *Southern Rev* 20.

[55] N Blomley, 'Landscapes of Property' (1998) 32(3) *Law and Society Rev* 569.

[56] D Delaney, *Race, Place and the Law 1836–1948* (Austin: 1997) 7.

[57] C Minca, 'Postmodern Temptations in Postmodern Geography' in C Minca (ed) *Postmodern Geography* (Oxford: 1997).

[58] F Mort, *Cultures of Consumption: Masculinities and Social Space in the late Twentieth Century Britain*' (London: 1996); B Forest, 'West Hollywood as a Symbol: the Significance of Place in the Construction of Gay Identity' (1995) *Environment Planning and Space D: Society and Space* 133.

[59] L Moran and S Skeggs, 'The Property of Safety' (2001) 23(4) *J of Social Welfare and Family Law* 379.

ways. First by *material practices* and secondly by *spatial representations*. I describe first what I mean by material practices by referring to the link between planning and social control.

Material practices, I argue, are inherent in basic notions of property in the sense that owners have the right physically to exclude whomever they wish from their property. At the same time owners of property may regulate their tenants as strictly as power inequalities between landlord and tenant tolerate. Furthermore mall owners' legal standing allows them the right to oppose nearby developments by others that they see as restricting their profits. Material practices also refer to the factors found in shopping malls based on the architectural space created which is a meticulously regulated, controlled and predictable environment.[60]

By 'spatial representations' I mean the way that Westfield manages and projects the image of the mall. This includes the means by which Westfield promotes the mall as a safe place for family shopping by propagating the idea that the mall is a safe and secure environment.[61] Implicit in this activity is the advertising of the mall, which projects the image of the mall as a 'destination' to connect 'Westfield' with the aspiring life styles of the affluent middle class suburban citizens in the area.

The promotional campaign of Westfield, typical of retail developments, was based on studies of the suburban catchment. The campaign drew at a deeper level on the reasons underlying the creation of the suburbs. In this context some urban theorists have seen the suburbs as a reaction to the chaos of the emerging city.[62] Fishman sees the emergence of the suburbs as a refuge from the city and also from the 'discordant elements in bourgeois society itself': in this context suburbia reflects 'the alienation of the middle classes from the urban-industrial world they themselves were creating'.[63] We may thus see 'malls as enclaves', which are hermetically sealed, which, when examined, reveal the continuum of middle class consumers and their involvement in shopping and recreation insulated from the unsavoury city streets.[64] At the same time malls are attractive places as they are destinations which replace the old 'civic' meeting places of old (such as town squares), they provide respite from the heat and cold and they provide possible places to disaffected elements of the community.

Spatial representations which govern the mall also include ideas of community, which incorporate developmental and entrepreneurial notions. To develop this argument I return to Alvarez, who considers that the 'shoppers own the mall'; the 'public takes ownership'.[65] This highlights a fundamental notion of property as a social

[60] DR Judd, 'The Rise of New Walled Cities' in H Liggett and D Perry (eds), *Spatial Practices: Critical Explorations in Social/Spatial Theory* (London: 1995), 144.

[61] Interview with Terro Blinnikka, Regional Marketing Manager, Westfield Hornsby. Recently Westfield has provided family entertainment and child minding facilities to increase its family appeal for shoppers.

[62] C Fischer, *The Urban Experience* (New York: 1976).

[63] R Fishman, 'Bourgeois Utopias: Visions of Suburbia' in S Fainstein and S Campbell (eds), *Readings in Urban Theory* (Massachusetts: 1996) 24.

[64] L Sandercock, 'From Mainstreet to Fortress: The Future of Malls as Public Spaces—or "Shut Up and Shop" ' (1997) 9 *Just Policy* 27.

[65] Alvarez, n 53 above, 217.

space, or as *propriety*, which is the particular characteristic or quality of a thing, which might be described as its nature or its essence (the proper, the respectable).[66] Property is also connected to social ideas about the use and the realization and preservation of the qualities and attributes of a thing.[67] The type of space that results is treated, as Alvarez argues, as that which should be created and accordingly preserved as it is linked to the notion of community. This connection between the quality of a thing and the preservation of its essence is an important conflation, as it links property to the personal sphere. In this connection we may be reminded that Radin's work developed the distinction between *personal* and *fungible* property. To Radin, personal property is bound up with the person. This is contrasted with fungible property, which is held instrumentally in the sense that should the property be lost it is perfectly replaceable in the market place.[68] The importance of property as a thing and the conflation with the notion of the essence of property which should be preserved in a personal sense and the communal sense is highlighted by Alvarez. The importance of this quotation is that he shows us that notions of property, the individual and the community are made collective and communal. The significance is that the public realm is made private and the private realm is made public.[69]

This type of space created by mall owners, which I may now call *community space*, links with the notion of community currently prevalent in public policy debates. This claim requires me to show how the connection between particular connotations of community is linked to different audiences in the context of the discourses of mall ownership and control.

Central to notions of community in the public arena are notions of hard work, enterprise and social cohesion. In the specific context of the Hornsby mall the concept is linked to the notion of progress and 'enterprise culture': that a particular form of culture is desirable wherein consumption is seen as a part of freedom and independence.

These values emphasize moral citizenship and the entrepreneurial self as well as the notion of user-pays which in essence fulfils the central notion of consumerism that we must choose and formulate a self.[70] As Larner has shown, these values have become what she calls the 'hegemonic political identity'.[71] These positive values are contrasted with the notion of dependency culture and the need for social exclusion for those groups that are perceived to threaten neoliberal policies.

Implicit in these ideas of community is the question of social order.[72] The essence of current neoliberal social and economic policy is the reintegration of

[66] M Davies, 'Feminist Appropriations: Law, Property and Personality' (1994) 3 *Social and Legal Studies* 365.

[67] Moran and Skeggs, n 59 above, 381.

[68] M Radin, *Reinterpreting Property* (Chicago: 1993) 37.

[69] Moran and Skeggs, n 59 above, 383.

[70] D Slater, *Consumer Culture and Modernity* (Massachusetts: 1997) 92–97.

[71] W Larner, 'The Legacy of the Social: Market Governance and the Consumer' (1997) 26(3) *Economy and Society* 398.

[72] D Adams and H Hess, 'Community in Public Policy: Fad or Foundation' (2001) 60(2) *J of Public Administration* 13.

those marginalized by economic productivity. While *in*clusion is the explicit aim of contemporary neoliberal policy, exclusion is the main ideological effect.[73] In the context of the righteous shopping community, any threat to this community must be excluded.[74]

The planning application for Westfield found sympathy in a climate based on the neoliberal reform agenda where notions of competition, deregulation and privatization have become the dominant orthodoxy. In contemporary urban policy economic development has been given priority over 'social and environmental objectives'. This climate has bred the notion of the city as a 'growth engine'[75] through the designing of a 'competitive place' as a vehicle for quality of life and urban renewal.[76] As I will later demonstrate, the linkage of ideas of Westfield property as a 'community-space' and as a 'community-resource' for development for the expanded 'rate paying community' in this growth environment, found favour with residents in Hornsby. These residents, convinced of rising house prices, encouraged by the Westfields development, believed that redevelopment would consequently provide local growth, and a safe shopping area.

The Planning Law Background to the Hornsby Development

In order to develop my argument and explain the impact of spatial practices it is essential to give the planning background to the development of the Hornsby mall. This explanation will also demonstrate the economic and political power that large corporations enjoy in Australia and their role in the planning process. We will then understand how mall owners may manipulate what I call 'semi-public space' to meet their particular marketing needs.

I therefore outline how Hornsby Council dealt with Westfield's planning application.[77] I do this to indicate why Westfield was concerned with the building of the mall in a particular way and to stress Westfield's control over the planning outcome. This is important for my argument as it shows how the mall owners wanted the physical space of the mall to fit with their vision of controlled entry. I first note that local government in Australia is undertaken by Councils, which are elected locally and are supervised at State level by State Government. Local Councils concern themselves with a variety of functions such as control of land use, sewage, parks and the administration of rates. They also supervise

[73] C Everingham, 'Reconstituting Community: Social Justice, Social Order and the Politics of Community' (2001) 36(2) *Australian J of Social Issues* 105.

[74] G MacLeod, 'From Urban Entrepreneurialism to a "Revanchist City"? On the Spatial Injustices of Glasgow's Renaissance' (2002) 34(3) *Antipode* 602.

[75] H Molotch, 'Urban America: Crushed in a Growth machine' in YH Lo and M Schwarz (eds), *Social Policy and the Conservative Agenda* (Maldon: 1976) 54–69.

[76] B Gleeson, and L Low, 'Revaluing Planning, Rolling Back Neo-Liberalism' (2002) 53 *Progress in Planning* 83.

[77] D Farrier, *Planning and Land Use in New South Wales* (Sydney: 2002).

planning control. In this regard an important role of Local Councils is that they are able to exact contributions from developers for the provision of services and amenities. Under the planning legislation there must be a nexus between the development and the services that the increased population generates by the development. In the case of Westfield at Hornsby the approval was given at a local level after several years of pressure put on the council by Westfield. In the case of the Hornsby development, Westfield contributed to road maintenance and the upgrading of the public mall area.

The first Westfield shopping mall in Australia was a small mall (by modern standards), built by Westfield in Hornsby in the 1960s. Since then Westfield has developed 29 other centres throughout Australia. Westfield is widely regarded as the leading developer of shopping malls in Australia.

By the 1990s the small Westfield centre in Hornsby needed updating. The opportunity for Westfield to buy the adjacent Northgate centre allowed Westfield the chance to redevelop their investment by linking the two developments into one complex.

In 1998 Westfield applied to the Council to build one of the largest centres in Australia. In addition to the anchor stores of Grace Brothers, David Jones and K-Mart there were to be over 200 specialty shops. The controversial part of the application proved to be the size of the project, the buying up of public land by Westfield, and the integration of the proposed development into the adjacent areas. As regards the size of the project, the outcome of the development was that Westfield would control 75 per cent of the retail space in the Hornsby Town Centre and would eventually account for 95 per cent of the turnover.[78] To help evaluate the Westfield planning application Hornsby Council employed an independent firm of planning and development consultants. Their report recommended that the Council reject the proposal.

However the proposal did go ahead with only a few modifications to the original plan. The strong recommendation of rejection from the consultants was ameliorated by the fact that, while the consultants rejected the proposal, they acknowledged rather grudgingly that it could be approved subject to a wide range of matters being attended to. These included a range of matters that later led to public objections to the scheme. The consultants considered that a 'just good enough' scheme was not acceptable, as the public interest demanded a better solution.[79] Overall, the consultants considered that the suggested plan was a 'mean proposal' and that the basis of its success depended on acquiring parts of the public domain and returning nothing to it. They considered that a smaller, less internally focused centre, could create opportunities for greater interaction between it and the balance of the town centre.[80]

Under planning law the Council was obliged to consider the economic impact of the proposal.[81] In preparing their planning application Westfield argued that

[78] Design Collaborative Economic Report, contained in Planning Application, Hornsby Council, PA 580/96 at 24.

[79] ibid.

[80] ibid, 8, 14–15.

[81] s 90 of the Environmental Protection Act; see Farrier, n 77 above, 205.

the proposed scheme would have a minimal impact on the Hornsby Town Centre and the adjacent trade area (the consultants considered the effect on the whole North Shore area). Westfield claimed that the turnover in these areas would only be reduced by 2.2 per cent.[82] The consultants noted that these figures should be treated with caution. The consultants also expressed their concern for West Hornsby, the area isolated from the centre of Hornsby because of the railway line.[83] In general the consultants concluded it was not possible to state what the impact would be in both the North Shore area of Sydney and more generally on the Hornsby Town Centre.[84]

Of particular concern to the consultants was Westfield's proposal to buy a public road so that they could integrate their shopping area into one block. (The consultants noted the obvious fact that the Council in effect held this land in trust for the public.) Concern was expressed over the appearance of the over-head link between the two properties which comprised use of public space in the town centre. The consultants noted the effect of the proposed over-head link, which, it argued, was to keep shoppers in Westfield, and to stop them straying into other areas outside of Westfield control.[85] This was exemplified, the consultants argued, 'by the applicant's insistence on the overhead link and the proposed subterranean link' underneath the two properties.

Other concerns of the consultants included the lack of interaction of the proposal with the Hornsby Town Centre. In this regard the consultants noted that the rest of the town centre consisted of 'light offices'; the consultants were concerned with how the two would integrate commercially, socially and aesthetically. The consultants concluded that the proposed developments were conceptually flawed and that the conceptual basis appeared to place private interests above the public interest.[86]

There was little opposition to the Westfield application from the public. Westfield carried out a sophisticated promotion of the mall against the background that Hornsby urgently needed to be developed. The Council, after delaying the proposal for some time, was eventually persuaded by Westfield. The Council was also due for re-election and they did not want to be seen to be holding up progress. In this light it is understandable that despite the major objections of the planning consultants the Westfield plan was approved subject only to minor concessions by Westfield.

The Governance by Westfield Over Tenants, Customers and the Owners of Adjacent Businesses Outside the Mall

I have indicated that property is usually seen by lawyers as a set of rights to exclude, alienate and transfer land. However property may be seen more as a social idea as regards a set of spatial practices as to whom may enter property. In this sense

82 Design Collaborative Economic Report, n 78 above, 4.
83 Economic Assessment report in Hornsby Planning Aplication PA 580/96 at 14.
84 ibid, 24. 85 ibid, 16. 86 ibid.

property consists of material practices or 'behaviourable data' exercisable by corporations to protect their enterprises.[87] It is therefore necessary to outline the material practices of Westfield as landlord. In view of my interest in spatial practices it is instructive to note its control of its customers as well as its attempts to control the adjacent area and its policy regarding perceived threats to its business interests.

With the growth of shopping centres, shop owners have been forced to open up in large-scale malls or to risk the decline of their customer base in street areas. This places pressure on shopkeepers 'to starve outside the mall' or to pay high rents inside the mall. Should shopkeepers open up in the mall they suffer longer trading hours, higher employment costs and higher rents. In addition, tenants in malls suffer from lack of secure tenure. Such problems include the inability to sell the business and the loss of good will. Landlords also insert 'ratchet clauses' in their leases so that as retail sales increase, the rent is raised. Landlords control this process by monitoring till outings via computerized banking controls. Tenants also have to pay shopping centres management expenses, suffer from changes in tenancy mix, and, during the term of the lease, they may suffer relocation should it suit the landlord's interests. At the same time the mall owner exerts control over shopkeepers through various clauses in leases covering shop design, logo, opening hours etc.[88] These problems are endemic in shopping centres and now exist in Hornsby.[89]

I have noted how shopping malls consist of meticulously regulated and controlled and predictable environments.[90] Malls provide a predictable, uniform and profitable venue for such chains for national franchise stores. Mall owners encourage well known franchise stores to open in malls as they have the financial backing, expertise and marketing skill to ensure success.[91]

The most significant feature of shopping malls is their totally controlled environment in which everything is pre-ordained by the developer and nothing is left to chance. As Brown argues, the size of the shopping centre, the shape, accessibility, contents, parking and the psychology of the milieu are manipulated to maximize customer spending.[92] Malls thus are represented as safe and secure places for consumption and the formation of particular life styles.

For instance, centres are designed to control the flow of pedestrians past as many outlets as possible; hence the tenant mix is a major concern with the placement of anchor stores at each end of the ground floor. This placement of anchor stores, such as Woolworths and Coles (major grocery stores) has the effect of drawing customers along a wider shopping area. The lower levels, for instance in the

[87] Gray and Gray, n 3 above, 111.

[88] Report by the House of Representatives Standing Committee on Industry, Science and Technology (Canberra: 1997) 16.

[89] This assertion is based on the interviews of several shop owners who requested to remain anonymous.

[90] Judd, n 60 above, 149.

[91] G Ritzer *The McDonaldization of Society* (Thousand Oaks: 1996).

[92] B Brown, 'Tenant Mix, Tenant Placement and Shopper Behaviour in a Planned Shopping Centre' (1992) 12(3) *The Services Industry J* 384.

Hornsby mall, create a particular sense of urgency through the confined space. The upper levels are constructed to attract leisure customers with more money to spend. At the same time there is a hybrid quality to the space created, as there is no attempt to create a *sense of a particular space*, but rather a progressive or global sense of place.[93]

Historically there has been great tension between landlord and tenant and legislation, both state and federal, has sought to regulate the relationship. Retail tenancies are regulated in Australia by State legislation. In addition, the Commonwealth Trade Practices Act regulates unfair and uncompetitive business practices. This Federal legislation may be of assistance to tenants but few tenants have been able to bring successful action under this Act. There has been a long history of complaints to various governments about the retail tenancies legislation, culminating in an inquiry by the House of Representatives called *Finding a Balance: Towards Fair Trading in Australia*.[94] The Committee considered elements of the Trade Practices Act, franchising and retail arrangements. Under the law of retail tenancies, landlords must covenant to give quiet enjoyment of premises, hold rent stable, and give tenants a right of renewal after the expiration of their term. The business conduct issues raised by the Hornsby retail tenants have included all the issues referred to above.

The Committee concluded that there was a great disparity of power between landlord and tenants in large shopping centres. The Committee noted that the idea that there is a 'war going on' between the two accurately conveys the tenor of the evidence presented to the Committee. Retail tenants who gave evidence to the Committee considered that they had lost most of the battles to date. Much of the evidence to the Committee was given *in camera* because of fears of victimization by property managers.

One expert to the Committee considered that the 'agreements' between landlords and tenants were not really leases as such but rather trading rights for the retail of goods in a particular shopping centre.[95]

Westfield claimed, through their lawyers typically, that their development would have little impact on local business.[96] However, the opposite is true, as local businesses now appear to be suffering.[97] At the same time, Westfield has pursued its policy of attempting to block other developments, as in the case of the movie cinema, which it claimed threatened its chain of cinemas.[98] At the same time Westfield has opposed, against strong public opinion, the restoration of Sunday markets in Florence Street. Finally for some time Westfield was allowed to utilize its security guards to control the Florence street mall. Public protest resulted in Hornsby Council withdrawing this permission.

[93] D Miller, P Jackson, N Thrift et al, *Shopping, Place and Identity* (London: 1998); JSP Hopkins, 'West Edmonton Mall: Landscapes of Myths and Elsewhereness' (1990) 34 *Canadian Geographer* 2.

[94] House of Representatives Standing Committee on Industry, Science and Technology (1997) *Finding a Balance: Towards Fair Trading in Australia*, AGPS, Canberra.

[95] ibid, Professor Millington at 75.

[96] Economic Assessment Report, n 83 above, 22.

[97] *Hornsby Advocate*, 2 May 2002, 14.

[98] ibid, 16 May 2002, 5 and 11 July 2002, 11.

In conclusion the evidence given on the pressure of mall owners on tenants reflects the enormous political and legal power exercised by corporate power in Australia and the power of large companies to use legal means to achieve their goals. In this context the legal system may be seen as a means to protect the power of the business elite and to enable enterprises to generate business.[99]

These comments also raise an issue concerning the extent of the law's relevance to business in Australia. Is the law only a forum for the times when matters do not go the way big business intends? A long line of research indicates that there is always a large gap between law and practice.[100] Other scholars have argued that under neoliberalism, the volume of legislation became unnecessary and burdensome, hence if there is a failure of law, this is not undesirable.[101] Finally there is the Foucault critique that argues that while law is still present as an influence in modern society, there is an increase in the shift in the influence of the disciplines (for example psychology, demography) and consequently a displacement of law as a form of regulation.

We might now ask the question, 'given the empirical evidence surrounding landlords' treatment of their tenants, does this evidence indicate that the commercial retail industry operates outside the law?' Should we follow the Foucault approach, we might see that it is not only perhaps that the law is ignored by companies but also those subjects in modernity are subjects to other discourses, such as the discourse of consumption. If this seems to be the case, what is the implication for our conceptions of property law? I come back to this issue in my conclusion.

The Promotion of the Mall

I have suggested that the social idea of property as a set of spatial practices involves both material and spatial representations. I have discussed material representations in the last section. I now wish to discuss the ability of owners to make spatial representations concerning the mall. The importance of spatial representations is that they discursively construct the class of people who may enter the mall and by implication those who may not enter.

In the Hornsby area Westfield faces severe competition from rival shopping centres. Westfield's market researchers have advised Westfield to adopt different marketing strategies for different segments of the perceived market.[102] By way of response the mall market managers have adopted classic mall-market strategies for

[99] J Caulfield and J Wanna, 'Power and Community: Theoretical Approaches' in J Cauldfield and J Wanna (eds), *Power and Politics in the City* (Melbourne: 1995).

[100] R Cotterrall, *The Sociology of Law* (London: 1992); D Nelken, 'The Gap Problem in the Sociology of Law; A Theoretical Review' (1981) *Windsor Yearbook of Access to Justice.*

[101] This argument underpins much of the new economic right's thinking. For a classic view see F Hayek, *The Constitution of Liberty* (London: 1960).

[102] Interview with Terry Blinnikka.

the development of an appropiate shopping format, market segmentation and the development of the mall as a pleasant and attractive destination.[103] In this regard, according to Blinnikka, its market researchers have deployed forms of computerized surveillance to monitor databases on personal consumption. In one sense the physical form of the building reflects the resultant data.

The Hornsby shopping centre catchment has one of the highest demographic incomes in Australia.[104] As perceived by Westfield, local people have a choice of environment and desire comfortable places where they can rest and be entertained. The greater part of the area of Hornsby thus consists of residential suburbs for middle class citizens or the 'new *petite bourgeoisie*' class. This term refers to an entrepreneurial, well-paid class, whose members define themselves through globally oriented, populist value systems and through the ownership of expensive consumer goods. This group may be characterized by its involvement in the global economy through the manipulation of signs and symbols.[105] As in other global cities, this new elite is well educated, politically empowered and is fluent at manipulating diverse symbolic systems.[106] The significance of this group has been well researched by market researchers and the consequent high market area of the mall is aimed, according to Blinnikka, at the 'high socio-economic achievers who understand quality'. The image the Marketing Manager of the Hornsby store has of the desirable up-market customers is that 'they are conservative people from the better end of town and they appreciate quality and convenience. These visible achievers appreciate through their education and travel the high quality shops and Borders bookshop'.

I conclude that the mall space at Hornsby reflects the perception of the customer base. The physical layout of the mall therefore reflects this. In essence different areas of the mall have been created to coincide with the perceived and desired market base. For instance the ground floor of the mall is designed for everyday basic shopping with its anchor food shops. The top level has been designed for the market need of people who have more money to spend. At the same time certain contained areas are created for young people who attend movies. Finally it must be emphasized that no space has been developed specifically for young people who merely wish to congregate.

Conclusion

This article has two roles. First I have been concerned with formulating a new understanding of property in a 'wider' sense by examining discourses within

[103] L Melody, A LeHew, AA Fairhurst, 'US Shopping Mall Attributes: an Exploratory Investigation of their Relationship to Retail Productivity' (2000) 28(6) *Intl J of Retail and Distribution Management* 261–279.

[104] Westfield states that the social spending of the trade area on which the Hornsby mall will draw has a retail spending capacity per capita of 8,484 dollars per person compared to the average Australian average of 7,303 dollars per person, cited in *Shopping Centre News*, 19 May 2001, 21.

[105] P Knox, and J Taylor, *World Cities in a World-System*, (Cambridge: 1995).

[106] R Reich, *The Work of Nations: Preparing Ourselves For 21st Century Capitalism* (New York: 1991).

neoliberalism other than those 'connected' with property in the form of property as ownership, alienation and exclusion. Secondly I have attempted to show how the mall is governed by spatial practices.

The first characteristic of property in the sense of ideas of ownership, alienation and exclusion (in what I called the 'narrow sense' of property) is that law's 'force' or impact is being eclipsed by other discourses associated with consumption and a desirable life style. In the context of neoliberalism 'law (ie the narrow view of property) loses its significance'.[107] I argue that neoliberal discourses associated with market ideologies and entrepreneurial professions, which emphasize accountability and control, are supplementing legal notions of property.

Secondly, property in the wider sense is constructed by discursive practices but also material practices. Here I refer to the vast array of physical and technical arrangements (such as the different forms of surveillance) that concretize or embody the discursive practices. I refer here both to the forms of surveillance which work to exclude undesirable people and also to the forms of surveillance which construct the desired form of customer base. I thus see material practices as enabling 'fidelity' or confidence of outcome to be obtained within the space of the mall through a complete integration of 'protective practices'.

Thirdly, property in the wider sense involves the notion that the mall is private property in the sense that the 'public' take ownership of the mall. Through the action of selected shoppers, the landscape (ie the mall property) is seen as belonging to the 'appropriate-shopping public'. In this context users are owners. Here I have referred to ideas of entrepreneurial discourse that the appropriate community is one which forges an identity through forms of consumption. It is this community of shoppers that paradoxically 'owns' the mall. It is clear that this form of ownership is not to be understood in terms of ownership of lands and buildings but rather in terms of a proper form of behaviour or propriety.[108]

As regards the usage of mall property I have shown that the mall is constructed to form a predictable controlled environment which acts like a 'prison in reverse: to keep deviant behavior on the outside' and to form a 'consumerist form of citizenship' inside.[109] The outcome of these practices is a form of property, which is neither public nor private. My conclusion argues that shopping malls represent a semi-privatized form of property that is developing as a result of the discourses of neoliberalism.

'Property' in this context is coterminous with safety and particular discourses on consumption. Spatial representations promote the mall property as an intrinsically safe public space for individuals and family shoppers. At the same time the mall is linked with ideas that resonate with middle-class ideals. These notions reinforce

[107] 'Governmentality', n 20 above.

[108] This form of argument relies on Moran and Skeggs, n 59 above; L Moran, B Skeggs, P Tyrer and K Corteen, 'Property, Boundary, Exclusion: Making Sense of Hetero-Violence in Safer Spaces' (2000) 2(4) *Social and Cultural Geography* 407.

[109] S Christopherson, 'The Fortress City: Privatised Spaces, Consumer Citizen' in A Amin (ed), *Post-Fordism, A Reader* (Oxford: 1994).

the notion of the 'righteous shopping community'. The righteous community by implication includes those enterprising individuals constructed as hegemonic under neoliberalism.[110] The 'community' in Westfield terms means the shopping public, which should not be interrupted. It follows that any activity detrimental to consumption must be limited. Hence all disruptive potentialities real or imagined should be removed.

While these recent exclusionary practices of Westfield may contradict promotional material which advertises the space as being the 'new village green', they nonetheless resonate with those seeking secure and safe shopping for themselves or their families.[111] Ironically such ideas of community and the intrinsic notion of security sit well with the concept of citizenship and place contained in the exclusive suburbs where most shoppers reside.

As a final conclusion I observe what some scholars have noted as regards the processes of globalization, postmodernism and the 'informational revolution'. One strand of this work is the argument that the materiality of boundaries has been derived by delineating systems of signs as much as from the concrete demarcation on the ground.[112] In terms of my examination of shopping malls, I have observed that within the political economic form of governance, known as neoliberalism, new forms of spatial governance have emerged where linkages between the land and the owner of the property have been transformed or broken. Thus mediating institutions, such as consumers as a form of political entity, construct what are property rights.

I expand on this new aspect of property by outlining first what have been seen as the key characteristics of property. I take the approach of Kevin and Susan Gray to be exemplary. These 'characteristics' include the[113] ability of a person to vindicate his sovereign control over a territorial space, a conceptualized definitional space (area) and the fact that property is a socially derived privilege granted by the state.

I argue that this approach to property must be extended as regards quasi-public land.[114] In this context property, in the context of the consumer as the hegonomic political-economic identity,[115] has become *deterritorialised*.[116] Scholte uses this concept to argue that globalization represents what she calls an 'ontological shift from a territorial reference' point to a situation where territory (or what I call property) is not linked to any one geographical space.[117] I take this line of argument to open the possibility that, through new forms of consumption, there is a break with the nexus between property and a legal entity as an owner.

[110] W Larner, 'Neoliberalism Policy, Ideology, Governmentality' (2000) 63 *Studies in Political Economy* 5.

[111] Sandercock, n 64 above.

[112] A Cameron and R Palan, 'The Imagined Economy: Mapping Transformations in the Contemporary State' in N Brenner, B Jessop, M Jones and G Macleod, *State/Space: a Reader* (Oxford: 2003), 164.

[113] Gray and Gray, n 3 above, 111–118.

[114] ibid, 161.

[115] W Larner, 'The Legacy of the Social: Market Governance and the Consumer' (1997) 26(3) *Economy and Society* 398.

[116] J Scholte quoted in J Brodie, 'Imagining Democratic Urban Citizenship' in E Isin (ed), *Democracy, Citizenship and the Global City* (London: 2000), 113.

[117] ibid.

To illustrate what I mean here I refer to two cases which illustrate how the link with property (ie a given piece of land) and the owner has been changed. The first instance concerns the new 'roaming' legislation in the United Kingdom.[118] In this case territorial control of the land is wrested from the landowner back to the state, the media and a range of mediating institutions. In this situation the power of and significance of the land itself declines as those with the right to control the land take precedence as the cultural and symbolic significance of ownership declines.[119]

The second example consists of the rural governance of uneconomic farmers in Australia. Due to a range of factors such as falling produce prices, drought and lack of subsidies, many farmers are becoming uncompetitive and their farms are thus considered 'marginal'. To govern such farmers and encourage amalgamations of larger units, governmental programmes assist such unviable farmers to exit from the industry. This has been achieved, not by policies to control specific properties (ie farms) but by the monitoring, surveillance and control by 'experts' of the 'farm problem' and the 'categorisation of subjects' rather than the land units they occupy.[120]

In both these instances the physical space of the 'property' involved is governed by social forces beyond the respective territory of such property. With the case of the Hornsby shopping mall, the reinvention of the 'community' as a form of governance and the new subject positions it implies, has resulted in new modes of governance. These modes of governance take place through a form of autonomization or individualization where subjects affirm their own political entity through consumption.[121] This has come about as new information technologies make new categorizations of subjects. Westfield's influence or connection to the physical space of the mall is transcended by the economic environment. Ironically the physical form of the mall we may say is 'owned', if we can use that word at all, in one sense, by forces beyond the state and beyond Westfield. In this context we have the death of the notion of 'absolutist property'.

[118] This legislation allows the right of public access to rural private lands in the United Kingdom. The legislation is called the Countryside and Rights of Way Act.

[119] Parker and Ravenscroft, n 29 above, 384.

[120] V Higgins, 'Governing the Boundaries of Viability: Economic Expertise and the Production of the Low-Income Farm Problem in Australia' (2001) 41(3) *Sociologia Ruralis* 358.

[121] This approach rests on N Rose, 'The Death of the Social?: Reconfiguring the Territory of Government' (1996) 25(3) *Economy and Society* 327 and Larner, n 115 above.

'Do You Want Fries With That?' The Franchise as a Cultural and Legal Phenomenon

Rex J Ahdar

The franchise is a very well established and familiar legal concept. The royal franchise and the political franchise are of some antiquity.[1] 'A franchise', wrote Joseph Chitty, 'is defined to be a royal privilege or branch of the royal prerogative subsisting in the hands of a subject, by grant from the King.'[2] It is the commercial franchise, however, that has come to dominate popular consciousness in the latter part of the twentieth century and onwards into the new millennium. Franchises are a major vehicle for commerce and feature significantly in the modern economy. So, for instance, franchising accounting for about a third of all retailing in the United States and 13.5 per cent of GDP.[3]

Popular culture is, in part, disseminated and reinforced through the legal vehicle of the franchise. Both the product or trade mark franchise (for example, Coca-Cola, Hoover, Reebok) and the business or system format franchise (McDonald's, Toys 'R Us, Weight Watchers, Blockbuster, Subway and so on) are major carriers of Western, particularly American, culture—the 'coca-colonisation' as some have called it.[4] A swift stroll down any United Kingdom high street, from Durham to Dalkeith, Chiswick to Cheltenham, testifies to the predominance of franchised outlets, whether American imports or home-grown offspring such as the British 'green' cosmetics chain, The Body Shop. The same familiar, and some might add dreary, procession of outlets is repeated in the sprawling shopping malls. Until one chances by a local landmark one could be anywhere.

[1] See A Reeve, 'Franchise and Referendum' in C Gray (ed), *The Philosophy of Law: An Encyclopaedia* (New York) Vol 1, 311–312.

[2] Joseph Chitty, *A Treatise on the Law on the Prerogatives of the Crown* (London: 1820) 119. He added (ibid): 'In its more extensive sense the term franchise signifies every description of political right which a freeman may enjoy and exercise'.

[3] F Lafontaine, 'The Role of Franchising in the U.S. Economy Now and Beyond' (July 1995) http://webuser.bus.umich.edu/departments/busecon/research/wp.lafontaine.1995.07.01.html. In New Zealand, a 2001 survey of franchising estimated that the franchise sector accounted for a total annual turnover of NZ$10.4 billion, *Franchise New Zealand* magazine, http://www.franchise.co.nz/articleview.php?param=54&AdCode=default. In Australia, a 1998 survey estimated the total annual turnover to be A$36.5 billion: *Dymocks Franchise Systems (NSW) Pty Ltd v Bilgola Enterprises Ltd* (1998) 8 TCLR 612, 628. The Franchise Council of Australia estimates some 12 per cent of Australia's GDP is attributable to franchising. http://franchise.org.au/content/.

[4] Richard Kuisel, *Seducing the French: The Dilemma of Americanization* (Berkeley: 1993).

This paper examines the growing dominance of the franchise form and its extension beyond the commonplace areas of business enterprise (food, automobiles and the like) into realms of social life such as education,[5] sport,[6] personal relationships,[7] and even medical[8] and legal practice.[9] While there are undoubtedly beneficial aspects to franchising there are also potential dangers, concerns that derive from the standardization and uniformity intrinsic to the business format franchise form, the most important kind of franchise.

After a short explanation of the legal and economic characteristics of the franchise, I shall delve briefly into some recent sociological writing which has pinpointed the franchise, and McDonald's in particular, as both a mechanism and a manifestation of intangible but important forces shaping society—what George Ritzer has dubbed the 'McDonaldization' of society.[10] Is the franchise a significant mechanism in what Max Weber described as the 'rationalization' process (what Ritzer has renamed McDonaldization)—an insidious transformation of persons, institutions and communities producing dull uniformity and systemic dehumanization and disenchantment? Under this view, the franchise model, to the extent it is used as a rigid template for more and more areas of human activity, represents a threat to creative expression and liberty. On the premise that these are more than just imaginary concerns of some paranoid social theorists I turn then to the law to consider just what its response might be. Can the courts or the legislature do anything to reform the franchise concept by, for example, importing a duty of 'good faith' dealing or by passing suitable mandatory ethical codes? Or, is the law itself swept up in the very rationalizing forces that have penetrated the rest of society?

The Nature of Franchising

A franchise is essentially a business idea and system of delivery that one licences to others, without ever relinquishing control of the intellectual property and know-how. . . . The essence of franchising is not the burger in the bun, but 'two all-beef patties' served at high speed by a smiling uniformed teenager in a sparkling environment, repeated exactly

[5] Eg, 'Technocatz', a franchise providing tuition for adults and delivered via the computer suites of schools outside normal school hours: 'Business Opportunities and Franchising,' *NZ Herald* supplement, 6 August 2002, E7.

[6] Eg, the professional sports team franchises of American baseball, football, basketball, ice hockey etc. The brand (Tigers, Lakers etc) is more important that the city or state where it is based (hence explaining the somewhat oddly named Utah Jazz basketball franchise, a business relocated from Louisiana to the homeland of the Mormon church).

[7] Eg, 'Mars Venus Coaching', a new franchise utilizing the principles expounded in Dr John Gray's best-selling book, *Men are from Mars, Women are from Venus*. Franchisees 'coach clients to reach their potential in their personal and professional relationships': 'Business Opportunities and Franchising', n 5 above, E12.

[8] Eg, 'The Doctors', a New Zealand medical centre group 'offering convenience, flexibility and value to patients through proven business systems': *Franchise New Zealand* magazine, Winter 2002, 87.

[9] A business format franchise law practice called 'Worried?' was launched in Auckland, New Zealand in June 2002: 'Business Opportunities and Franchising', n 5 above, E6.

[10] George Ritzer, *The McDonaldization of Society* (New Century edn, Thousand Oaks, CA: 2000); George Ritzer, *The McDonaldization Thesis: Explorations and Extensions* (London: 1998).

from Melbourne to Madras. Though the product is ostensibly the burger and fries (or the steam-cleaning, the accounting service, the dance classes or the bed-and-breakfast), the franchise pivots on the control of its trademark and other intellectual property, which allows instant recognition and successful duplication.[11]

'Franchises are extremely numerous and are of various kinds', noted Chitty in 1820,[12] and nothing has changed to render that assessment any less accurate. There is actually a bewildering array of commercial arrangements that are loosely labelled 'franchises', indeed, the word seems to have passed into general usage.[13] Strictly speaking there are two main types of commercial franchise.[14] The *product* or *trade name franchise* is one where the franchisee acquires rights to distribute a product and use the franchisor's trademark, such as Pepsi, Whirlpool or Matchbox. The parties remain at arm's length with little in the way of close, interdependent dealings.

It is the second kind of franchise, the *system* or *business-format franchise*, which is the concern of this paper. This concept, comprising the 'cloning' of entire business and management systems, was refined in the United States in the 1950s by the leading fast-food companies.[15] Today, it is commonly described in laudatory terms as 'revolutionary'[16] and 'the dominating force in the distribution of goods and services'.[17] The British Franchise Association define this type of franchise as:

A contractual licence granted by one person (the franchisor) to another (the franchisee) which:

(a) permits or requires the franchisee to carry on, during the period of the franchise, a particular business under or using a specific name belonging to or associated with the franchisor;

(b) entitles the franchisor to exercise continuing control during the period of the franchise over the manner in which the franchisee carries on the business which is the subject of the franchise; and

(c) obliges the franchisor to provide the franchisee with assistance in carrying on the business . . . ; and

(d) requires the franchisee periodically . . . to pay the franchisor sums of money in consideration for the franchise, or for the goods or services provided by the franchisor to the franchisee; and

(e) is not a transaction between a holding company and its subsidiary . . . [18]

[11] Veronica Taylor, 'Contracts with the Lot: Franchises, Good Faith and Contract Regulation' [1997] *New Zealand L Rev* 459, 460–461.

[12] Chitty, *Law on Prerogatives of the Crown*, n 2 above, 119.

[13] John N Adams and K V Prichard Jones, *Franchising: Practice and Precedents in Business Format Franchising* (4th edn, London: 1997), 1.

[14] See Gillian Hadfield, 'Problematic Relations: Franchising and the Law of Incomplete Contracts' (1990) 42 *Stanford L Rev* 927, 932–933; D Carlton and J Perloff, *Modern Industrial Organization* (3rd edn, Reading, Mass: 2000), 410–412.

[15] Andrew Terry, 'The E-business Challenge to Franchising' (2002) 30 *Australian Business L Rev* 227.

[16] ibid.

[17] US House of Representatives Committee on Small Business, *Franchising in the US Economy: Prospects and Problems* (Washington DC: 1990) 1: quoted in Terry, n 15 above, 228.

[18] Adams and Jones, *Franchising*, n 13 above, 21.

The franchisee operates pursuant to a format or system designed entirely by the franchisor. The latter furnishes the marketing strategy, product ideas and design, operating manuals, quality control and so on. The franchisor may or may not supply the franchise with the actual product. The key point is that 'the franchisee is under the control of the franchisor and thus is instructed how to run her business much as an employed manager would be'.[19] Thus, 'the foundation and essence of the McDonald's system is adherence by licensees to standards and policies of McDonald's . . . providing for the uniform operation of all McDonald's restaurants within the McDonald's System'.[20] The duties of the franchisee are propounded in lengthy documents in meticulous detail such that nearly every aspect of the operation is covered.[21] A McDonald's raw hamburger weighs exactly 1.6 ounces, is 3.875 inches in diameter between a bun of 3.5 inches.[22] McDonald's goal is a total service times of 90 seconds or less per customer.[23] A franchise may be owned by the franchisee but, as Naomi Klein's best-seller *No Logo* puts it, 'every detail of the outlet—from the sign out front to the precise temperature of the coffee—is controlled by a head office hundreds or even thousands of miles away'.[24] The 'first commandment of franchising' is 'You must follow the system'.[25] The following is typical language contained in a franchise agreement. Note the emphasis upon uniformity and stringent adherence by the franchisee to the terms propounded by the franchisor:

> The Franchisor and related companies have developed a unique and integrated system . . . for the design and operation of retail stores specialising in the sale of books, magazines, stationery and other associated items. . . . The Dymocks system is a comprehensive retail sales system. Its foundation and essence is the *strict adherence* by Franchisees to standards, specifications, procedures and policies of the Franchisor providing for the uniform operation and image of all Dymocks stores. . . .
>
> The most important management and control device in the regulation of our Franchise System is the Franchise Agreement. . . . *Strict adherence* by the Franchise owner to all the terms in the Agreement is absolutely essential as any deviation may have catastrophic effects on every Store in the chain. . . . *Uniformity* within our whole Franchise System is the overriding objective and the Franchise Agreement has been written to protect this vital interest. . . . Your *rigid* application of the terms of the Franchise Agreement will assist with the development of a mutually rewarding experience with Dymocks. Dymocks' role is to advise on and *control* the standards at every franchise and we will be *uncompromising* in doing so for the overall benefit of all Franchise Owners as a whole.[26]

[19] Hadfield, 'Problematic Relations', n 14 above, 934.

[20] *Far Horizons Pty Ltd v McDonald's Australia Ltd* [2000] VSC 310, para 16.

[21] The median length of a Franchise Agreement is 50 pages and that of the accompanying Operations Manual is 250 pages: Paynter, 'Sector Tops $10 billion'.

[22] Ritzer, *The McDonaldization of Society*, n 10 above, 79.

[23] D Cohen, 'Would you like better service with that Big Mac?', *Otago Daily Times*, 30 August 2003, A26.

[24] Naomi Klein, *No Logo* (London: 2001), 131–132.

[25] Taylor 'Contracts with the Lot', n 11 above, 463.

[26] The opening section of the Operations Manual of the Dymocks Bookshop franchise; reproduced in *Dymocks* (1999) 8 TCLR 612, 679, 689 (emphasis added).

The franchise is a contract of a special type, falling within the class of 'relational contracts'. These include distributorships, joint ventures, agency relationships, partnerships and some employment agreements. It has even been suggested that 'most commercial contracts are in fact relational contracts'.[27] In contrast to the classical contract conception of the contract as a discrete, one-off transaction or exchange, relational contracts are typified by continuing, highly interactive, ongoing relations requiring a high degree of mutual trust, loyalty and co-operation.[28] Thomas J explains:

> In essence, relational contracts recognise the existence of a business relationship between the parties and the need to maintain that relationship; the difficulty of reducing important terms to well-defined obligations; the impossibility of foretelling all the events which may impinge upon the contract; the need to adjust the relationship over time to provide for unforeseen factors or contingencies which cannot readily be provided for in advance; the commitment, likely to be extensive, which one party must make to the other, including significant investment.[29]

Franchise agreements, noted the Privy Council in a recent leading case, are 'not ordinary commercial contracts but contracts giving rights to long term mutual obligations in pursuance of what amount[s] in substance to a joint venture and therefore dependent upon co-ordinated action and co-operation'.[30] Despite the fact that franchise agreements typically attempt to spell out in minute detail a vast number of duties, no contract, not even a franchise one, can anticipate every future circumstance or contingency. A franchise contract 'is necessarily an incomplete one'.[31]

For franchisees—as the glossy franchising magazines trumpet—franchising is an attractive business enterprise for it offers the benefits of an established business system whilst avoiding the notorious perils of starting from scratch. The high failure rate of small businesses is well documented.[32] Franchising has been described as 'arguably the most liberating development since the Industrial Revolution' for it enables persons of limited means and experience to acquire a viable business.[33]

All is not entirely roses however. The relationship between franchisor and franchisee is usually tilted in favour of the former. The typical franchise contract is a contact of adhesion,[34] a lengthy standard form contract heavily weighted in

[27] *Bobux Marketing Ltd v Raynor Marketing Ltd* [2002] 1 NZLR 506, 515 *per* Thomas J. This view is supported by Melvin Eisenberg, 'Relational Contracts' in J Beatson and D Friedmann (eds), *Good Faith and Fault in Contract Law* (Oxford: 1995), Ch 11, 298.

[28] See *Bobux*, ibid, 517. See also *Dymocks* (1999) 8 TCLR 612, 629, for a most instructive discussion by Hammond J.

[29] *Bobux*, ibid, 516.

[30] [2002] UKPC 50 at [63]. [2004] 1 NZLR 289.

[31] Hadfield, 'Problematic Relations', n 14 above 948.

[32] See Hadfield, 'Problematic Relations', n 14 above, 938 (purported 5 per cent failure rate for franchisees compared with a 50 per cent failure rate within the first five years for small businesses generally). In New Zealand, the failure rate over a three year period is reported to be less than 6 per cent: Paynter, 'Sector Tops $10 billion'.

[33] Taylor, 'Contracts with the Lot', n 11 above 467.

[34] *Dillon Holdings Ltd v Stirling Sports Franchises Ltd*, High Court Invercargill, CP10/00, 28 March 2002, para 54, *per* William Young J Hadfield, 'Problematic Relations', n 14 above, 961, suggests that this unevenness is 'an essential component' of the typical franchise.

favour of the franchisor. Taylor suggests there is almost a feudal character to the relationship: 'as with feudal contracts, duties are owed upwards by the franchisee but there is little reciprocity'.[35]

Amongst the risks for franchisees[36] is the potential for franchisor opportunism. Specifically, given the usual heavy investment by franchisees in the venture, the franchisee will have significant specialized assets or 'sunk costs'—assets not easily realizable or recoverable should the franchisee exit. A franchisor may be able to 'hold up'[37] the franchisee—threaten to terminate the franchise unless the franchisee agrees to pay higher royalties, increased rent, increased prices for any goods supplied, greater sums towards advertising, and so on. Another concern is 'encroachment', the territorial or other business expansion by the franchisor that impinges upon the actual or perceived rights of an existing franchisor. Encroachment is described as 'one of the most sensitive pressure points in franchising today',[38] due in part to the fact that exclusive operating territories are no longer the norm, franchisors preferring to grant site-specific franchises with no geographic protection.[39]

The McDonaldization Thesis

Weber's critique of Western capitalism contains numerous important insights, but a central one was his emphasis upon bureaucracies and their pivotal role in the broader phenomenon he called the 'rationalization' process.

> For Weber, the principal experience of capitalist modernity was a process of rationalization in which the principles of ascetic discipline and scientific regulation were imposed upon the everyday world through a process of increasing bureaucratic constraint and state regulation.[40]

The confining effects of such bureaucracies upon individual liberty were likened by Weber to 'iron cages'. Weber 'anticipated a society of people locked into a series of rational structures, who could move only from one rational system to another—from rationalized educational institutions to rationalized workplaces, from rationalized recreational settings to rationalized homes'.[41] University of Maryland sociology professor, George Ritzer, updated Weber's rationalization critique in an imaginative fashion, connecting it to the exponential growth of the

[35] Taylor, 'Contracts with the Lot', n 11 above, 468.

[36] There are risks too for the franchisor, principally concerning the need to maintain quality control over the franchisees' operation: see Hadfield, 'Problematic Relations', n 14 above, 949.

[37] See Jeannie M Paterson, 'Good Faith in Commercial Contracts? A Franchising Case Study' (2001) 29 *Australian Business L Rev* 270, 282; Hadfield, 'Problematic Relations', n 14 above, 952.

[38] Terry, 'E-business Challenge to Franchising', n 15 above, 229.

[39] ibid, 230.

[40] Bryan Turner, 'McCitizens: Risk, Coolness and Irony in Contemporary Politics' in B Smart (ed), *Resisting McDonaldization* (London: 1999), Ch 6, 84.

[41] Ritzer, *The McDonaldization of Society*, n 10 above, 25.

global franchise phenomenon, McDonald's. Ritzer explains:

> The McDonaldization thesis . . . is the idea that (as Weber predicted) society and the world are growing progressively rationalized and characterized by the predominance of efficiency, calculability, predictability, and control by non-human technologies (as well as the irrationalities of rationality) . . . [42]
>
> McDonaldization . . . is the process by which the principles of the fast-food restaurant are coming to dominate more and more sectors of American society as well as the rest of the world.[43]

Although Ritzer readily concedes[44] his work is a contemporary amplification of Weber's work, Ritzer can, I suggest, be credited for at least one critical new insight. His use of the apparently mundane yet ubiquitous fast-food franchise, McDonald's, as the exemplar of the rationalization process has highlighted the important role that myriad units in the *private* enterprise sector (and not public institutions pursuant to state objectives) have played in the process.

Ritzer identifies four main dimensions of McDonaldization.

The first dimension is *efficiency*. The optimum method of completing a task is identified and adopted. There is no room for individuality. The pursuit of efficiency (Ritzer is focusing upon *operational* or *productive* efficiency here and not other economic notions of efficiency such as allocative efficiency[45]) has 'largely been a matter of streamlining various processes, simplifying products, and having customers do work formerly done by paid employees'.[46]

Next is *calculability*: outcomes are assessed according to objective, quantifiable rather than subjective, qualitative criteria. If it cannot be counted, in practice it simply does not count. Numerical standards are set for processes (the speedier the better) and end results (more is better than less). It becomes a question of quantity over quality: 'They sell the Big Mac, not the Good Mac'.[47] The downside, notes Ritzer, is that 'in a society that emphasizes quantity, goods and services tend to be mediocre'.[48]

Third is *predictability*: the production process is organized to guarantee a standardized product. Systems are designed to ensure that things are the same from one time or place to another. Surprises are an anathema. Predictability is attained through such things as 'the replication of settings, the routinization of employee behavior, the offering of uniform products and processes, and the minimization of danger and unpleasantness'.[49]

[42] Ritzer, *The McDonaldization Thesis*, n 10 above, 174. There is even a website created by Timothy Burleson, an ardent admirer of Ritzer, explaining and extending his work: see www.McDonaldization. com.

[43] Ritzer, *The McDonaldization of Society*, n 10 above, 1.

[44] ibid, 23.

[45] See eg FM Scherer, 'Antitrust, Efficiency and Progress' (1987) 62 *New York U L Rev* 998 for a description of the three main types of efficiency.

[46] Ritzer, *The McDonaldization of Society*, n 10 above, 41.

[47] From 'What is it?', a section of Burleson's website, McDonaldization.com.

[48] Ritzer, *The McDonaldization of Society*, n 10 above, 82.

[49] ibid, 102.

Fourth is *control*: the process sees, where possible, the substitution of more predictable non-human technology for human labour. Technology includes not only machines and tools but also materials, skills, knowledge, rules, regulations, procedures, and techniques: 'A human technology (a screwdriver, for example) is controlled by people, a nonhuman technology (the order window at the drive-through, for instance) controls people'.[50] Take modern banking services. When I wish to withdraw money from my bank account I need only go to the nearest ATM (automatic teller machine) at the local shopping centre. By using my touch-tone telephone I can check my bank balances or transfer funds. I can go many weeks, even months, without ever speaking face-to face with a flesh and blood employee of the bank. Indeed, the bank encourages this by making over-the-counter services more expensive than telephone or internet transactions.

There is, adds Ritzer, a fifth dimension of McDonaldization also, namely the *irrationality of rationality*. These are ironic side-effects of over-rationalized systems. The queues encountered whilst waiting for service in 'fast' food outlets and the parade of idling cars grinding their way through drive-through lanes are examples. Weber was adamant that one of the key negative by-products of rationalized society would be a widespread disenchantment: the world would gradually become stripped of magic and mystery as efficient, logical, mechanical, routinized, predictable systems gained sway. An outstanding popular music expression of this disenchantment is 'The Logical Song' by the English rock group, Supertramp:

> When I was young
> It seemed that life was so wonderful
> A miracle, oh it was beautiful, magical
> And all the birds in the trees
> Well they'd be singing so happily
> Oh joyfully, oh playfully watching me
> But then they sent me away
> To teach me how to be sensible
> Logical, oh responsible, practical
> And they showed me a world
> Where I could be so dependable
> Oh clinical, oh intellectual, cynical
> There are times when all the world's asleep
> The questions run too deep
> For such a simple man
> Won't you please, please tell me what we've learned
> I know it sounds absurd
> But please tell me who I am.[51]

For Ritzer, the fast-food restaurant rather than Weber's bureaucracy is as good, if not a better, model for advancing the rationalization process in today's world.

[50] ibid, 104.

[51] 'The Logical Song' from the album, *Breakfast in America* (A & M Records, 1979).

Just as McDonald's restaurants proliferate, McDonaldization continues to grow both in terms of its geographic spread and the range of activities it encompasses. Is this a problem? Yes, for the encompassing effects of rationalization mean 'escape' is increasingly difficult. Eventually we find ourselves an iron cage. For Ritzer:

> McDonaldized systems (though rules, regulations, scripts, and so on) do encroach upon, and ultimately threaten, the ability of those involved in them to think intelligently. It is clearly dehumanizing to find oneself mindlessly functioning like a robot or an automaton in a McDonaldized system.[52]

Is there, nonetheless, anything to be said *for* McDonaldization? Ritzer acknowledges that it does have positive features.[53] A range of goods and services may now be accessible to large numbers of people (including those in the lower end of the socio-economic scale). Small, isolated rural communities may now have convenient access to products formerly the preserve of the urban consumer. McDonaldization has stimulated the creation of a large number of new jobs. Many managers began their careers as junior employees of a Pizza Hut, Denny's or Kentucky Fried Chicken outlet. Franchises, particularly food ones, have liberated parents, especially mothers, from the drudgery of daily cooking, and provided a hygienic, safe venue for youth and elderly to socialize. The basic dimensions of McDonaldization—efficiency, predictability, calculability and substitution of non-human technology[54]—can be seen as virtues. What is praiseworthy about an inefficient, over-priced, haphazard system dependent upon wearisome human toil?

Ritzer's McDonaldization thesis has generated tremendous interest in sociological circles, drawing both praise and criticism.[55] His 'stroke of genius' was to seize upon a familiar symbol and industry 'as a way in to the labyrinth which we in the West inhabit'.[56] His original book—written for 'a general literate audience'[57] rather than academic specialists—provided a popular, digestible analysis 'of key aspects of the processes of rationalization, commodification, American economic and cultural imperialism, and globalization'.[58]

An Iron Cage?

Is talk about the business system franchise and rationalized environments being an iron cage a mite exaggerated? No one is forcing people to work in such enterprises. Entrepreneurs commence such businesses presumably for the material benefits

[52] Ritzer, *The McDonaldization Thesis*, n 10 above, 3. [53] ibid, 183–184.

[54] ibid, 174, 184.

[55] See Smart's anthology, *Resisting McDonaldization*, n 40 above, for a sample.

[56] P Beilharz, 'McFacism? Reading Ritzer, Bauman and the Holocaust' in Smart (ed), *Resisting McDonaldization*, n 40 above, 222.

[57] Ritzer, 'Assessing the Resistance' in Smart (ed), *Resisting McDonaldization*, n 40 above, 234.

[58] B Smart, 'Resisting McDonaldization: Theory, Process and Critique' in Smart (ed), *Resisting McDonaldization*, n 40 above, Ch 1, 19.

they entail; workers ply their trade for similar reasons. It may well be, of course, that the opportunities for industry and employment outside franchised systems are shrinking. But they are hardly non-existent. Palpably not everyone 'buys into' the franchise dream.

The celebrated 'Mclibel' litigation in the late 1990s[59] is, for example, testimony to the stern resistance to McDonald's itself, if not McDonaldization, in some quarters. McDonald's, it will be recalled, won something of a pyrrhic victory against Helen Steel and David Morris, two members of London Greenpeace who distributed the now infamous leaflet, 'What's wrong with McDonald's: Everything they don't want you to know.'[60] After the longest civil trial in English legal history the High Court awarded damages to McDonald's for being defamed. Bell J held that the leaflet contained a number of libellous assertions including claims that McDonald's was destroying rain forests, contributing to starvation in the third world, causing heart disease, bowel and breast cancer, exposing consumers to the risk of food poisoning and so on. Yet the damages awarded hardly matched the huge legal costs incurred nor the ongoing adverse publicity,[61] particularly the residual tarnished image which followed the findings by the court that McDonald's had, as the pamphlet claimed, contributed to cruelty to animals, engaged in advertising designed to manipulate children, provided food with little nutritional value and paid substandard wages to its English employees.

Ritzer entertains the prospect that a de-McDonaldization process may be underway.[62] Certainly, McDonald's itself seems to have passed its peak. In January 2003, the McDonald's parent company reported losses of US $343.8 million in the previous December quarter, its first losses since Ray Kroc went public with his concept in 1965. The more health conscious Subway sandwich chain assumed the top spot in terms of having the largest number of outlets in the United States.[63] Yet McDonalds (the franchise) and McDonaldization (the diffuse rationalization process) are not the same thing. The waning of the most famous franchise may be a red herring for the numbers and spread of new franchises generally increase unabated. There are signs aplenty that human creativity and diversity are as unquenchable as ever. So, for example, one sees the emergence of small, regionalized companies making idiosyncratic, high-quality products. There is also the threat of customization that addresses the market demand of those who stubbornly eschew the 'one-size-fits all' approach of McDonaldized firms. Nonetheless, even here it is possible to see counter-McDonaldizing forces quickly responding. For example, true customization can be met with a form of pseudo customization ('sneakerization' as Ritzer dubs it) where an extensive range

[59] *McDonald's v Steel*, Bell J, 1997; *Steel and Morris v McDonald's Restaurants Ltd* [1999] EWCA Civ 1144. See Marlene A Nicholson, 'McLibel: A Case Study in English Defamation Law', (2000) 18 *Wisconsin Intl L J* 1.

[60] The leaflet is reproduced in the appendix to Nicholson's article, ibid.

[61] See the comprehensive website dedicated to critiquing McDonalds: 'McSpotlight' http://www.mcspotlight.org.

[62] Ritzer, *The McDonaldization Thesis*, n 10 above, 174ff.

[63] Ruth Laugesen, 'The Tears of a Clown', *Sunday Star-Times*, 13 April 2003, C3.

and variety of mass-produced 'customized' products attempt to meet a very large number of niches in the market. As for the small high-quality local enterprises, the swift takeover of such promising upstart entrants by the large incumbent franchise operators is hardly unknown.[64] 'Market-driven globalization,' rails Klein, 'doesn't want diversity. Its enemies are national habits, local brands and distinctive regional tastes'.[65]

At the metaphorical level, some object to the image of the iron cage. The connotations of imprisonment and restriction are perhaps misplaced. A better translation of Weber's metaphor might be the shell on a snail's back—a burden in one sense, but also a home or shelter that is impossible to live without.[66] As Ritzer acknowledges, the consequences of McDonaldization are not necessarily all deleterious.[67] I mentioned the benefits earlier. One could vary the metaphor: the 'velvet' or 'rubber' cage[68] may be more apposite: those who have been reared in McDonaldized societies appreciate a world uncluttered with a bewildering kaleidoscope of unguided choices and like the predictability and cool efficiency of McDonaldized systems.[69] One scholar offers the 'plastic fun house'[70] as a better metaphor to capture the phenomenon. Perhaps this last image is not so facetious.[71] It may be, as Smart contends, that people are not so much 'trapped' as 'seduced' by the pleasure, economy and sociability of the franchise marketers.[72]

Franchising Law: The Emergence of 'Good Faith'?

A most protracted and expensive franchise dispute recently received its final resolution in the Privy Council in London. The Judicial Committee was called upon to determine a bitter battle between an Australian bookshop franchisor, Dymocks, and its largest New Zealand franchisee, Bilgola Enterprises Ltd, a company run by a Mr and Mrs Todd. Regrettably, *Dymocks Franchise Systems (NSW) Pty Ltd v Todd*[73] casts little new light on the nature of the franchise contract and franchise lawyers are frustratingly still left in limbo on a key issue that had been explored

64 Ritzer, n. 10, above, 177.

65 Klein, *No Logo*, n 24 above, 129.

66 Smart, 'Resisting McDonaldization', n 58 above, 10 (quoting Derek Sayer, *Capitalism and Modernity: An Excursus on Marx and Weber* (London: 1991), 144).

67 Ritzer, 'Assessing the Resistance', n 57 above, 248–249.

68 Douglas Kellner, 'Theorizing/Resisting McDonaldization: A Multiperspectivist Approach' in Smart (ed), *Resisting McDonaldization*, n 40 above, Ch 12, 190.

69 Ritzer, *The McDonaldization of Society*, n 10 above, 200.

70 Kellner, 'Theorizing/Resisting McDonaldization', n 68 above, 190.

71 Ritzer himself agrees that McDonaldized systems can be seen as 'monkey bars': 'a playground apparatus that can become anything the people involved with it want it to be': *The McDonaldization of Society*, n 10 above, 259. Yet, as he adds (ibid), a cage is still a cage, a structure that is often resistant to attempts to modify it.

72 Smart, 'Resisting McDonaldization', n 58 above, 12–13.

73 [2002] UKPC 50; [2004] 1 NZLR 289. For commentary, see P Sumpter, 'Relational Contracts Mark II' [2002] *New Zealand LJ* 449; G Gunasekara, 'Good Faith, Repudiation and Franchise Agreements' [2002] *New Zealand LJ* 453.

in the lower courts: do the parties to a franchise agreement owe each other an obligation of good faith in the performance of their contract?

Interestingly, the Supreme Court of Victoria, albeit in an obiter passage, had answered that question in the affirmative in 2000. Byrne J in *Far Horizons Pty Ltd v McDonald's Australia Ltd* proceeded 'on the basis that there is to be implied in a franchise agreement a term of good faith and fair dealing which obliges each party to exercise the powers conferred on it by the agreement in good faith and reasonably, and not capriciously or for some extraneous purpose'.[74] On the facts, McDonald's had not been motivated by any improper motive in opening up new McDonald's stores close to the plaintiff's outlet. The plaintiff had not been granted an exclusive territorial franchise and the agreement had been entered into in an environment where both parties were well aware that expansion was a normal part of McDonald's business modus operandi.[75]

Returning to the *Dymocks* case, the New Zealand High Court was quite prepared to recognize a duty of good faith:

> The relationship between franchisor and franchisee is not merely a simple bilateral contract. It is a relational contract in which the working, ongoing, relationship is set up for the mutual benefit of both parties. And, from an economic point of view, what is central is the joint maximization of economic benefits. Both parties are to work in good faith to that end.[76]

The Todds had secretly discussed the possibility of a joint venture with Blue Star, the major competitor of Dymocks, and disclosed to Blue Star copious information from Todd's *own* financial records concerning its turnover, margins, profitability and so on.[77] This information was not confidential information about the operation of the Dymocks franchise system and it did not, said the court, constitute a breach of an express clause in the franchise agreement that required the franchisee to protect 'trade secrets' and other confidential information disclosed 'from the franchisor to the franchisee'.[78] Nevertheless, it was not entirely innocent conduct. Hammond J continued: 'It involves no violence, or undue extension of the law, to say that as part of that overall duty of good faith a franchisee must not (inappropriately) disclose even that own franchisee's information'.[79] This untoward behaviour justified Dymock's action in summarily terminating the franchise.

On appeal, the Court of Appeal held that the Todds had not breached any of their contractual duties: Dymocks had no valid grounds for terminating the contract and, indeed, its summary cancellation itself constituted a repudiation. The Court tersely dismissed the merits of recognizing any such novel implied duty as good faith, especially where the contract already contained (in clause 5E) an express duty upon the parties to 'at all times faithfully, honestly and diligently perform their obligations' under the contract and to 'continuously exert their best efforts' to promote the business. In light of such a clause, 'there is no room for

[74] [2000] VSC 310, para 120. [75] ibid, para 130.
[76] *Dymocks Franchise Systems (NSW) Pty Ltd v Bilgola Enterprises Ltd* (1999) 8 TCLR 612, 652.
[77] ibid, 625. [78] ibid, 652. [79] ibid.

superimposing further undefined obligations of good faith'.[80] The 'significance of the need for certainty' especially where, as in the instant case, the parties to 'an arm's length commercial transaction' had meticulously propounded the details of their relationship, strongly pointed against the implication of any further terms.[81]

The Privy Council allowed Dymock's appeal and were ultimately able to decide the appeal on grounds other than the good faith issue. Their Lordships, however, were not prepared to rule out the recognition of such a duty in the future:

> These comments [of the Court of Appeal] suggest that in their view, the development of the law so as to make an obligation of good faith implicit in the relationship between franchisor and franchisee . . . is not desirable. Their Lordships propose to express no concluded view on these comments and wish to reserve their opinion on the suggestion that the implication of an obligation of good faith in the relationship between franchisor and franchisee would be an undesirable development.[82]

As it was, the franchisee had clearly repudiated the contract by breaching certain express terms. The fact that, unbeknown to Dymocks, the Todds had held discussions with the major rival of Dymocks and passed on valuable information to this firm was a matter that the Privy Council passed no final judgment on for there were more obvious grounds vindicating the franchisor's decision to terminate. There were two clear repudiations. First, the Todds had steadfastly refused to pay outstanding or future franchise fees until Dymocks changed the terms of the agreement in a fashion favourable to the franchisee. Second, the Todds had fomented disquiet and incited revolt amongst the other franchisees in New Zealand by sending a 'mutinous' fax in which the Todds indicated they would no longer participate in Dymocks group buying activities, the franchisor being a struggling enterprise that had 'no future in th[e] country'. In Lord Browne-Wilkinson's summation:

> Whether or not the agreement is such as in law to give rise to an obligation of good faith, the expressed terms of the contracts (incorporating the Operations Manual) which their Lordships have quoted imposed contractual obligations of cooperation, and contain (clause 5B) a covenant by the Todds to maintain its business in compliance with the 'DYMOCKS' Image prescribed . . . in the Confidential Operations Manual'. The manual refers to the franchisee being 'obliged to support group buys'. It also stresses 'We must be a united team, we must be seen as a team. We must act as a team and we must be the best team'. In their Lordships' view a statement by a franchisee that for the future he will not participate in group activities is a fundamental breach of the basic principles underlying the contract which, however vaguely they may be expressed, the franchisee has undertaken to comply with. On any basis the stance taken by the Todds in 1997 and 1998 was in direct conflict with the express contractual obligations by which they had undertaken to act in co-operation and as a team.[83]

The *Dymocks* litigation was not the best occasion on which to argue the case for the recognition of a novel duty of good faith dealing since the facts were far from those

[80] *Bilgola Enterprises Ltd v Dymocks Franchise Systems (NSW) Pty Ltd* [2000] 3 NZLR 169, 180.
[81] ibid. [82] [2002] UKPC 50 at [57]. [83] ibid, at [63].

that advocates of the duty usually have in mind. This was not the much-touted predicament of a small, hard-pressed franchisee being bullied by an overbearing franchisor but, rather, an instance of a powerful franchisee acting forthrightly in an attempt to change the entire franchise system to suit itself.

The Contribution of the Law

The law has a role to play in softening the worst excesses of franchise contracts. There are at least two different courses that might be adopted, one judicial, the other legislative.

First, the recognition of a duty of good faith performance in franchise contracts by the courts is one suggested measure to bring a semblance of equality back to what can often be a decidedly one-sided arrangement. A major obstacle looms however. Several common law jurisdictions, such as England, Australia and New Zealand, have been reluctant to recant from their longstanding rejection of a free-standing concept of good faith[84] and belatedly absorb it into contract law.[85] The precise character, incidents and scope of this rather nebulous and elastic concept are the principal concern: 'Good faith is more likely to produce idiosyncratic judgments . . . [it] could well work practical mischief if ruthlessly implanted in our system of law'.[86] There is also the objection that the good faith concept is otiose since existing equitable and common law remedies are perfectly adequate to meet any problems of unfairness and untoward conduct.[87] The topic has become perhaps the liveliest subject of academic debate for Commonwealth contract lawyers in recent years.[88]

In America, by contrast, the good faith concept has been entrenched in commercial law for some time—one thinks immediately of s 1-203 of the Uniform Commercial Code. Unfortunately, the experience from the United States suggests that the reservations voiced by opponents of the good faith principle are

[84] See eg *Interfoto Picture Library Ltd v Stiletto Visual Programmes Ltd* [1988] 2 WLR 615, 620–621 *per* Bingham LJ; *Bobux Marketing Ltd v Raynor Marketing Ltd* [2002] 1 NZLR 506, 514.

[85] 'Throughout the common law world it is a matter of controversy to what extent obligations of good faith are to be found in contractual relationships.' Privy Council in *Dymocks* [2002] UKPC 50 at [54].

[86] Michael Bridge, 'Does Anglo-Canadian Contract Law Need a Doctrine of Good Faith?' (1984) 9 *Canadian Business LJ* 385, 413, 426. For similar scepticism see T Carlin, 'The Rise (and Fall?) of Implied Duties of Good Faith in Contractual Performance in Australia' (2002) 25 *U of New South Wales LJ* 99.

[87] See eg Roy Goode, *Commercial Law in the Next Millennium* (London: 1998), 19.

[88] The literature is huge but for a small slice, see J Beatson and D Friedmann (eds), *Good Faith and Fault in Contract Law* (Oxford: 1995); ADM Forte (ed), *Good Faith in Contract and Property Law* (1999); and R Brownsword, N Hird and G Howells (eds), *Good Faith in Contract: Concept and Context* (Aldershot: 1999). Roger Brownsword's chapter, Ch 2 of the last named collection, entitled 'Positive, Negative, Neutral: the Reception of Good Faith in English Contract Law' is an excellent overview of the positions of the rival camps. Thomas J in *Bobux Marketing Ltd v Raynor Marketing Ltd* [2002] 1 NZLR 506, 514–515, provides a comprehensive bibliography.

not without substance. Allan Farnsworth records that the doctrine of good faith performance there 'has provided employment to many US lawyers, who have produced the tangled case law that has marked the doctrine's somewhat uncertain course'.[89] To take a recent franchise case, in *Burger King Corp v Weaver*, the United States Court of Appeals for the Eleventh Circuit commented that: 'The applicability of the implied covenant of good faith in the context of franchise encroachment disputes has generated *considerable disagreement* in the courts. . . . Indeed, consistency is hard to find even within an individual judicial district.'[90] Encroachment by the franchisor upon the franchisee's area is, as I noted earlier in this essay, one of the most important pressure points in contemporary franchising, and so it is disappointing to see the relative impotency of the good faith doctrine here.

The American courts have also stressed that the rights conferred by the implied term of good faith and fair dealing are quite limited. The party who has performed all the express contractual duties in the franchise agreement is effectively immunized from further challenge based on a supposed breach of the implied duty of good faith. The Eleventh Circuit in *Burger King* declared:

> We hold that no independent cause of action exists under Florida law for breach of the implied covenant of good faith and fair dealing. Where a party to a contract has in good faith performed the express terms of the contract, an action for breach of the implied covenant of good faith will not lie. More specifically, a cause of action for breach of the implied covenant cannot be maintained (a) in derogation of the express terms of the underlying contract or (b) in the absence of breach of an express term of the underlying contract.[91]

So in *Burger King*, an encroachment case, the franchisee's claim for breach of the implied term of good faith failed as he could point to no express provision of the agreement that had been breached. Weaver's agreement expressly did *not* grant him a right to an exclusive territory and so Burger King incurred no duty to refrain from licensing new franchises in the area. Andrew Terry, a leading Australian commentator, remains optimistic that, despite the United States experience, the good faith doctrine in Australia may have more teeth: it might, he hopes, develop into an independent cause of action with the potential to override or modify the express terms of franchise agreements rather than simply guiding the construction of express terms or clarifying ambiguous terms which remains the modest role of the good faith concept in America.[92] If the common law itself offers limited assistance there is always of course the legislature.

The second response has seen some jurisdictions pass mandatory statutory codes of franchising designed to address 'systemic'[93] problems in this relationship. Industry self-regulation as implemented by way of voluntary codes of ethics have

[89] A Farnsworth, 'Good Faith in Contract Performance' in Beatson and Friedmann (eds), *Good Faith and Fault in Contract Law*, n 88 above, Ch 6, 169.

[90] 169 F 3d 1310, 1315 (11th Cir 1999) (emphasis mine).

[91] ibid, 1317–1318.

[92] Terry, 'E-business Challenge to Franchising', n 15 above, 235.

[93] Hammond J in *Dymocks*, 631.

their place but are increasingly seen, at least in some countries, as inadequate.[94] The Australian Federal Government's *Code of Franchising Conduct* represents one example of the turn to mandatory regulation.[95] The Code, which came into effect on 1 July 1998 and applies to franchises entered into after 1 October 1998, was, in the words of Professor Allan Fels, the Chairman of the Australian Competition and Consumer Commission:

> part of a package introduced by the Commonwealth Government . . . to protect small businesses from unreasonable behaviour of large parties with whom they have commercial relationships. . . . The clear signal, simply, is that governments and the community believe that small businesses are given what we in Australia call 'a fair go'. This doesn't exclude hard bargaining negotiations, etc., but it does target exploitative behaviour. . . . The Code was introduced to address serious market failure problems, particularly in terms of information failure and the transaction costs associated with franchisees gaining information or obtaining affordable redress when things went wrong in the course of the franchise agreement. There have been some well-known cases where franchisees have lost their shirts as a result of the acts of unscrupulous franchisors. Apart from being a disaster for the franchisees in question, it reflects poorly on the franchising sector as a good place in which to invest. The previous voluntary system was perceived as inadequate to address these market failures because . . . there was less than total coverage of the franchising sector. The very people who needed to be covered were the ones who did not participate. There was also a perception that when 'push came to shove' the voluntary scheme lacked teeth.[96]

In brief, the main features of the Code are as follows.[97] The franchisor has extensive disclosure obligations and must supply the prospective franchisee with detailed information regarding supply requirements, territory and site limits, marketing duties, franchise payments, earnings data and so on within 14 days of the franchisee entering the agreement. Thereafter, the franchisee has a seven-day cooling-off period in which to change its mind. The franchisor must ensure, as evidenced by a signed statement, that the franchisee has had independent legal, business and accounting advice. There are carefully designed termination rights where, for instance, the franchisee is allowed a reasonable time to remedy any breach prior to the franchisor cancelling the agreement. Finally, there are obligatory mediation procedures to be followed before resorting to litigation.

In addition, franchises, along with other businesses, are caught by the general prohibition in s 51AC of the Trade Practices Act 1974: corporations must not

[94] As Goode notes, self-regulation 'does not work . . . because it is expecting too much of human nature in light of the overwhelming influence of competitive forces': *Commercial Law in the Next Millennium*, n 87 above, 48.

[95] Pursuant to s 51AE of the Trade Practices Act 1974 (Cth), which authorizes the prescription of mandatory industry codes, the Trade Practices (Industry Codes—Franchising) Regulations 1988 (1998 No 162), known as 'the Franchising Code of Conduct', were passed. The Code is reproduced in full in Russell V Miller, *Miller's Annotated Trade Practices Act 1974* (24th edn, Sydney: 2003) 1375.

[96] 'Administering the Franchising Code of Conduct', a speech delivered in Melbourne, 1 September 1998: http://www.accc.gov.au/docs/speeches/franspc.html.

[97] See F Zumbo, 'Reviewing the 2001 Franchising Code of Conduct Amendments' (2001) 29 *Australian Business L Rev* 435.

'engage in conduct that is, in all the circumstances, unconscionable' in business transactions involving the supply of goods or services below a stipulated monetary ceiling. A recent illustration is *Australian Competition and Consumer Commission v Simply No-Knead (Franchising) Pty Ltd*[98] where the Federal Court found the respondent franchisor had clearly contravened the section. Simply No-Knead, a business which supplied training and materials for making bread in the home, had competed with five of its franchisees, refused to supply (on at least two occasions) products for contrived reasons, omitted the franchisees' names from promotional brochures that the franchisees were nonetheless still required to pay for, refused to negotiate or discuss matters of concern to the franchisees and dealt with them in a 'hostile and pugnacious manner'. Sundberg J concluded that 'the accumulation of incidents . . . disclose[d] an overwhelming case of unreasonable, unfair, bullying and thuggish behaviour in relation to each franchisee that amount[ed] to unconscionable conduct by SNK for the purposes of s 51AC(1)'.[99]

While the most egregious aspects of the franchise relationship may be ameliorated, the law would hardly seem designed to stem the broader process of McDonaldization.

First, the law itself has been marked by the very sort of rationalization process that Ritzer identifies. Dimensions of McDonaldization such as efficiency, calculability and predictability are all regarded as virtues in the law. Regarding efficiency, a whole movement within jurisprudence—law and economics—is devoted to extolling the virtues of economic efficiency as an aspiration for the law. At a more mundane level, case management systems aim to reduce delays in bringing cases to trial and to maximize scarce judicial resources. Persons ought to be able to (broadly) calculate their potential legal liability before undertaking action. Adherence to the doctrine of precedent ensures a degree of stability and predictability. Control by non-human technologies is perhaps not such a distinctive feature of the law yet but that too may change. The irrationalities of rational law are all too dismally evident: for example, laws to protect consumers may result in the burdened providers of the goods or services withdrawing them altogether.

Harold Berman, speaking of the contrast between law and religion and the secularization of modern Western law, observes:

> The law of the modern state, it is said, is not a reflection of any sense of ultimate meaning and purpose of life; instead its tasks are finite, material, impersonal—to get things done, to make people act in certain ways. This concept of the secular character of law is closely linked with the concept of its rationality. . . . The lawmaker, in inducing people to act in certain ways, appeals to their capacity to calculate the consequences of their conduct, to measure their own and others' interests, to value rewards and punishments. Thus legal man, like his brother economic man, is conceived as one who uses his head and suppresses his dreams,

[98] [2000] FCA 1365. [99] ibid, para 51.

his convictions, his passions, his concern with ultimate purposes. At the same time, the legal system as a whole, like the economic system, is seen as a huge, complex machine—a bureaucracy (in Max Weber's definition)—in which individual units perform specific roles according to specific incentives and instructions, independently of the purposes of the whole enterprise.[100]

'The fate of our times', wrote Weber, 'is characterized by rationalization and intellectualization and, above all, by the disenchantment of the world'.[101] Anthony Kronman has chronicled this latter phenomenon in his book, *The Lost Lawyer*.[102] Kronman's account of the failing ideals and spiritual crisis afflicting the American legal profession is a chronicle writ large of the disenchanting effects of the rationalization of the profession. The growth of the mega law firm 'has changed forever the practice of lawyers in them and created a new, more openly commercial culture in which the lawyer-statesman ideal [the lawyer possessing the character-virtue of practical wisdom not just technical expertise] has only a marginal place'.[103] The courts have undergone a 'bureaucratization' whereby the 'ancient art of judging' has been 'transformed into a species of office management whose main virtue is efficiency rather than wisdom'.[104] The 'managerial judge', as Kronman dubs him, resembles a manufacturer as 'he too faces a similar challenge as the superintendent of a complex process of production in which various ingredients (including most importantly, his own time and energy) are combined to produce a particular good, namely dispute resolution. And like the manufacturer, he is above all concerned to discover the combination of ingredients that will enable him to produce the most of this good in a given period of time'.[105] Kronman here is describing the McDonaldization process. 'Justice', not the quarter-pounder, is the good ('maximand') that the judge is seeking to maximize.[106]

Secondly, the law is there to facilitate the franchise—a key vehicle for doing business and a highly important cog in the modern economy—not to hinder it. Commercial law is considered by many to function best when it recognizes prevailing business needs and commercial practices and fashions legal rules and standards to give effect to the reasonable expectations of those operating in the marketplace. 'If entrepreneurial activity', urged Roy Goode in his Hamlyn Lectures, 'is to be undertaken and to flourish, the legal system which accommodates it must be flexible and responsive to rapid change'.[107] English commercial law, argues Goode, has demonstrated this very responsiveness. It has, enthused Lord Irvine of Lairg in a similar vein, long assumed an active role as 'an engine for trade.'[108]

[100] Harold Berman, *Faith and Order: The Reconciliation of Law and Religion* (Atlanta: 1993) Ch 1, 6.

[101] Weber, 'Science as a Vocation' in Hans Gerth and C Wright Mills (eds), *Max Weber: Essays in Sociology* (New York: 1946), 155: quoted in Anthony Kronman, *The Lost Lawyer: Failing Ideals of the Legal Profession* (Cambridge, Mass: 1993), 368.

[102] Kronman, *The Lost Lawyer*, ibid.

[103] ibid, 4.

[104] ibid.

[105] ibid, 332–333.

[106] ibid, 335.

[107] Goode, *Commercial Law in the Next Millennium*, n 87 above 6.

[108] Lord Irvine, 'The Law: An Engine for Trade' (2001) 64 MLR 333.

Three features, facilitation, integration and regulation, mark the English approach. Regarding the first two:

> The law has facilitated trade by recognising the effect of commercial agreements and practices, giving effect to the intentions of contracting parties to support the free market economy. The law has integrated key mercantile customs into its structure, establishing coherent and predictable legal frameworks in a number of areas important to business, from bills of exchange to sales of goods.[109]

The third aspect, regulation, is a necessary adjunct but again sensitivity to the needs of business is crucial. There is, urges Lord Irvine, 'the principle of minimum regulation' whereby the law should 'avoid tying the hands of business with an excessive number of rules'.[110]

Conclusion

Rationalization, modernization, McDonaldization, globalization—these and other convoluted 'ization' terms are readily lumped together in what appears to be a ominous phalanx of impersonal and inexorable processes that threaten individuals and communities. One can of course contest the value judgment made by those commentators and theorists that unhesitatingly and vociferously denounce these forces as destructive. It is, however, considerably harder to dismiss the empirical charge that they are intensifying and expanding. So much of our everyday experience confirms the rationalization that Weber prophesied would occur. There are counter forces, postmodernist pockets of resistance, but they do not detract from the overall tidal surge.

The ancient legal device of the franchise has played a part in the furthering of the rationalization process. Private enterprise has found the business format franchise to be a superb vehicle for expanding trade. There are, however, certain inherent features of the system franchise, especially the emphasis on efficiency, standardization and stringent control, which mirror the suffocating effects of state run bureaucracies. To the extent that the business system franchise model expands and is used as a template for shaping relationships in more and more areas of life, the danger increases of iron cages of conformity coming into being. They may be cages voluntarily agreed to by the participants and freely availed of by the public but once in place they remain cages nonetheless.

In resisting McDonaldization and freeing oneself from iron cages the law has, I suggest, at best but a modest role to play. Judicial or legislative measures to humanize the business format franchise may smooth a few of the 'rough edges' of the relationship but the law remains firmly behind the concept. The franchise is the very sort of successful business vehicle commercial law seeks to accommodate and foster.

[109] Lord Irvine, 'The Law: An Engine for Trade' (2001) 64 MLR 348.

[110] ibid, 343.

One must look to something other than the law for full emancipation from cages of conformity engendered by suffocating rationalized environments. At the risk of being accused of lapsing into sentimentality or metaphysics there is, I believe, an ancient remedy to this modern malaise. Love transcends and love emancipates. Love is not opposed to the law but begins when the limits of logic, reason and law are reached. Love can dispel the gloom of disenchantment and heal the hurts generated from dehumanizing systems. No iron cage can contain it. Coca Cola got it wrong: love really is 'the real thing'.

PART IX

LAW, LAWYERING, AND THE POPULAR CULTURE

Legal Negotiation in Popular Culture: What Are We Bargaining For?

Carrie Menkel-Meadow[1]

Introduction: Getting to Yes or No in Negotiations in Popular Culture

Treatments of the law in popular culture seem to prefer sharp drama. The courtroom scene has been such a popular trope and formula for so long we can hardly think of a depiction of law and legal phenomena that does not 'end up in court'. There are winners and losers and bitter confrontations of witnesses and lawyers as the 'truth' emerges and the guilty are punished or a travesty of justice is perpetuated. Depictions of law in popular culture, however, may lag far behind the developments of legal processes and institutions in the real world, at the same time that they tell us much about what 'the people' want to know about the legal system. Why do we prefer a world of winners and losers, with zero-sum or even negative sum games, in which one party 'defeats' another and the truth is black or white, but hardly ever (except in the most sophisticated depictions) grey or pink?[2]

Just as legal scholars have been studying and documenting the effects of 'bargaining in the shadow of the law',[3] in legal negotiations, we can see the influence of 'bargaining in the shadow' of conventional forms of competitive drama in the

[1] Thanks for the research assistance of I Glenn Cohen of Harvard Law School and James Bond of Georgetown Law Center and to Peter Reilly, Georgetown-Hewlett Fellow in Conflict Resolution for comments and to the many colleagues who love to chat about their favorite negotiation movies. The Harvard Program on Negotiation has presented a negotiation film series for several years, focusing not only on popular culture, but on the many documentaries made about efforts to negotiate peace and conflict reduction in the many troubled spots of the world. This paper is dedicated to the thousands of brave souls who act as peace seeking negotiators in the real, and much more difficult, world than that of the depictions of negotiation in the celluloid, video-tape and pages of popular culture.

[2] Two recent depictions of law, a murder trial and the negotiations for a new bill in Congress were decidedly 'pink' in *Legally Blond* (Robert Luketic, 2001) and *Red, White and Blond (Legally Blond 2)* (Charles Herman-Wurmfeld, 2003). See Carrie Menkel-Meadow, 'West Meets East in Legally Blond', http://www.usfca.edu/pj/ blonde_menkel.htm (2001) and Carrie Menkel-Meadow, 'Ms. Wood Goes to Washington But Is She as Virtuous as Mr. Smith: Legally Blonde 2', http://www.usfca.edu/pj/blonde2-meadow.htm (2003). In general see website *Picturing Justice: The On-Line Journal of Law and Popular Culture* at http:www.usfca.edu/pj for articles and reviews about treatments of the law and legal issues in popular culture.

[3] Robert H Mnookin and Lewis Kornhauser, 'Bargaining in the Shadow of the Law: The Case of Divorce' (1979) 88 *Yale LJ* 950.

depictions of legal negotiations in most forms of popular culture, including films, television programmes and popular literature. Negotiation in popular culture is most often an arena for competition, the use of power, manipulation, cleverness and high drama in which the goal of whatever interaction is depicted is to 'defeat' or to get 'the best of' the 'other' side. This elaboration of negotiation in popular culture is often formulaic and simplistic and reinforces conventional negotiation ploys, themselves exhorted in the growing popular literature on negotiation for the general public, in such works as Herb Cohen's *Negotiate This!*[4] or *You Can Negotiate Anything!*[5] or Jim Camp's *Start With No*,[6] which encourage negotiators to think of ways to take advantage of the other side in negotiation, by manipulating information, the circumstances of the negotiation and threatening or using 'hard-ball' tactics.[7]

While competitive sports or war-like struggles are dramatic,[8] they no longer represent either the growing scholarship on effective, efficient and more just negotiation practices[9] or the evolving practice of legal negotiation in the real world.[10] If trial by ordeal was a human evolutionary development over unrestricted violence in individual or group conflicts, then trial by court or verbal conflict with a 'victor' is still seen as the end result of an evolutionary legal process that has moved away from violence without rules to a contained form of structured verbal 'violence' in conflict resolution.[11] The dominant form of adversarialism that characterizes so much of law and legal process in both real life and popular culture sadly limits how we might solve both legal and human problems and, in my view, blocks us from literally 'seeing' more advanced forms of human and legal problem solving.

I have long criticized conventional legal processes for perpetuating these limited adversarial, two party, zero-sum, binary and polarized methods for achieving legal

[4] Herb Cohen, *Negotiate This!* (New York: 2003).

[5] Herb Cohen, *You Can Negotiate Anything* (New York: 1980).

[6] Jim Camp, *Start With No* (New York: 2002).

[7] For the best (and most controversial) treatment of these competitive and manipulative tactics in legal negotiations, see Michael Meltsner and Philip Schrag, 'Negotiation Tactics' in *Public Interest Advocacy* (Boston: 1974).

[8] See Elizabeth Thornburg, 'Metaphors Matter: How Images of Battle, Sports and Sex Shape the Adversary System' (1995) 10 *Wisconsin Women's L J* 225.

[9] The classic text is Roger Fisher, William Ury and Bruce Patton, *Getting to YES: Negotiating Agreement Without Giving In* (2nd edn, New York: 1991). See also, Robert H Mnookin, Scott Peppet and Andrew Tulumello, *Beyond Winning: Negotiating to Create Value in Deals and Disputes* (Cambridge, Mass: 2000); Howard Raiffa, *Negotiation Analysis: The Science and Art of Collaborative Decision Making* (Cambridge, Mass: 2003); Richard G Shell, *Bargaining for Advantage* (New York: 1999); Max H Bazerman and Margaret Neale, *Negotiating Rationally* (1992); Deborah Kolb and Judith Williams, *Everyday Negotiations* (San Francisco: 2003); David Lax and James Sebenius, *The Manager as Negotiator* (New York: 1986); Russell Korobkin, *Negotiation Theory and Strategy* (New York: 2002) and Carrie Menkel-Meadow, 'Toward Another View of Legal Negotiation: The Structure of Problem Solving' (1984) 31 *UCLA L Rev* 754.

[10] Andrea Kupfer Schneider, 'Shattering Negotiation Myths: Empirical Evidence on the Effectiveness of Negotiation Styles' (2002) 7 *Harvard Negotiation L Rev* 143.

[11] Robert Cover, 'Violence as the Word' (1986) 95 *Yale L J* 1601. See also Edward L Rubin, 'Trial by Battle, Trial by Argument' (2003) 56 *Arkansas L Rev* 260.

results;[12] here I will suggest that popular depictions of adversarial and competitive negotiations dangerously perpetuate the notion that legal negotiations are about 'winning' or besting the other side. These images limit what consumers of popular culture can come to see as possible as human and legal problem solving must become more sophisticated, nuanced, creative and joint, not individual, gain-seeking if we are to survive. In my view, we are living in times of legal evolution, as legal processes and institutions are changing, even if only incrementally in some cases. Instead of leading with utopian or creative 'futurism' as popular culture in other genres does, depictions of legal negotiations in popular culture are sadly behind both actual legal evolution (in the development of problem-solving and interest-based negotiation) and the growing scholarship on integrative and mixed motive bargaining[13] and alternative dispute resolution mechanisms, both in legal disputes and in legal deals and transactions.[14] There are a very few glimpses of how it might be otherwise, with a scarce number of newer depictions of how legal negotiations might actually be used to solve problems, rather than only to 'defeat the other side'.

I write this paper to de-centre the trial and courtroom as the central locus of where justice and legal process is depicted in popular culture, to encourage more critical thinking among the critics of popular culture of the overused tropes, metaphors and literal depictions of negotiations in film, television and popular novels, and to encourage creators of popular culture to take a closer and more creative look at how negotiations, in both disputing and deal cultures, are evolving to solve problems, or at least expose them as more complex than just two sides with a single issue to be decided by some form of verbal jousting. While this paper serves as a preliminary filmography, bibliography and taxonomy of legal negotiations depicted in popular culture, there are, in my view, at least two more dramatic forms for the stories of legal negotiation to take. One is the macro tale of how legal culture has evolved from unmitigated conflict to attempts at human engagement through rules (court procedures and the negotiation norm equivalents[15]), and bargained for preferences, creative solutions and newer forms of legal institutions and practices (is there a mediation or ADR depiction in modern film?). The other is the many

[12] Carrie Menkel-Meadow, 'The Trouble With the Adversary System in a Post-Modern, Multi-Cultural World' (1996) 38 *William & Mary L Rev* 5; Carrie Menkel-Meadow, 'Whose Dispute Is It Anyway? A Philosophical and Democratic Defense of Settlement (in Some Cases)' (1995) 83 *Georgetown L J* 2663; see also Michael Asimow, 'Popular Culture and the Adversarial Ideology', (p 606 below) and Deborah Tannen, *The Argument Culture: Moving From Debate to Dialogue* (New York: 1998).

[13] Thomas Kochan and David B Lipsky (eds), *Negotiations and Change: From the Workplace to Society* (Ithaca and London: 2003).

[14] Carrie Menkel-Meadow, Lela Love, Andrea Kupfer Schneider and Jean Sternlight, *Alternative Dispute Resolution: Beyond the Adversarial Model* (New York: 2004); Michael Palmer and Simon Roberts, *Dispute Processes: ADR and the Primary Forms of Decision Making* (London: 1998); Michael Freeman (ed), *Alternative Dispute Resolution* (Aldershot: 1995).

[15] See, eg, Melvin Eisenberg, 'Private Ordering Through Negotiation: Dispute Settlement and Rulemaking' (1976) 89 *Harvard L Rev* 637 and PH Gulliver, *Disputes and Negotiations: A Cross Cultural Perspective* (New York and London: 1979) for descriptions of the 'norms', both substantive and processual, that negotiations have exhibited across legal and cultural variations in context.

'micro' stories of actual negotiations, in all their many varieties, to demonstrate that human engagement on problems of needing to deal with others, takes many more forms than the conventional 'offer-demand-threat-compromise or win-lose outcomes' that we so often see in popular culture. Negotiation is dramatic. Its practices are changing as we attempt to 'Get to Yes'[16] with some of our fellow human beings and as we ask 'what are we bargaining for?' Total victory? Annihilation of the Other? Of Ourselves? Unprincipled Compromise? Or some other desired end-state? Solved Problems? Justice and Peace? Co-existence? Value Creation?

In this paper I will briefly review the several genres of negotiation depicted in various forms of popular culture (illustratively, not exhaustively), to illuminate the underlying conceptions of negotiation that popular culture transmits—most often conventional conceptions of harsh bargaining, threats, force and 'total victory' or commercially cynical 'bargains' of gain or unprincipled compromises, in which 'justice' or creative human problem solving is the absent player and manipulation, strength and cleverness win the day. I will contrast these briefly with depictions of actual negotiations in popular culture forms ('true' legal stories and a few documentaries of legal and international negotiations), once again to expose the foundational conceptions or models of negotiation at play in the minds of both popular culture writers and legal actors. I will conclude with some newer and more sophisticated treatments of negotiations and dispute resolution processes and outcomes that are just beginning to suggest how the newer forms of problem solving or integrated bargaining models might appear and why it is so important that they do.

Genres of Negotiation in Popular Culture: Deals and Disputes; Civil and Criminal; Individual and Systemic

It has become quite commonplace to assert that there are major differences in the structure and processes of legal negotiations in the different legal contexts of transactional negotiations (the making of 'deals', the creation of legal entities, the buying and selling of property) and litigation (already framed disputes) including such factors as the voluntariness of the negotiation, the alternatives to a 'settled outcome' (no deal, other deals or court decisions), differences in tone or style of collaboration or competition and the varieties of outcomes that are possible (infinite variations on drafted 'deal points' versus more limited remedial solutions, 'shadowed' by the jurisdictional limits of court power and authority over litigation). In the interstices between these two larger categories lie a variety of more complicated and mixed forms of negotiations, such as bankruptcy/insolvency proceedings, intra-family disputes, collective bargaining agreements in labour relations, multi-party international and diplomatic negotiations, trade agreements,

[16] Fisher, Ury and Patton, n 9 above.

plea bargaining, hostage negotiations, intergovernmental sector negotiations, community and organizational negotiations and sadly, but truly, the modern era practices of 'negotiating with terrorists'.

Despite the legal and sociological variations of where and how negotiations occur, popular depictions of negotiations are quite 'stock', wooden and repetitive. The anthropologist PH Gulliver has attempted to describe the almost uniform regularity in movements of parties from positions of conflict to more consensual agreement seeking behaviours after some almost ritualistic behaviours of posturing, arguing and trading, and negotiations depicted in movies, television programmes and popular novels serve as virtual formula or templates for easy script writing. Most often there are two lead figures in negotiation, who assert diametrically opposed positions and attempt to persuade, coerce, cajole, manipulate or otherwise 'get the better' of the other side, by making offers or demands, asserting, arguing, or debating with each other and eventually winning, compromising in the middle[17] or coming to an impasse, with a need for another form of resolution.

In a series of scenes of 'deal' making or simple property transactions, we see the cleverness of the party who manipulates others, by hiding information, by appearing more naïve then they really are (*Local Hero*) or by craftily tricking people (*Other People's Money*), into buying or selling at higher or lower prices than they really desire or can afford. I could imagine creating (and should for my negotiation classes) an anthology tape or collage of 'price negotiations', ranging from Julia Roberts' price negotiations with Richard Gere for prostitution services in *Pretty Woman*,[17a] Richard Gere's own 'prostitution' services as a gigolo in *American Gigolo*,[18] Robert Redford's *Indecent Proposal*[19] to test the 'value' or 'price' of a faithful wife,[20] to the more topical and amusing recent negotiation by Sandra Bullock's character, Lucy Kelson, as she bargains for salary and pro bono work time as a corporate lawyer for Hugh Grant's property mogul, George Wade in *Two Weeks Notice*.[21] More conventional price negotiations for property include American oil company attempts to buy a whole Scottish town in *Local Hero*,[22] aluminum siding sales (and car accidents and general *mano a mano* competition and rivalry) in *Tin Men*,[23] and corporate 'liquidator' Lawrence Garfield (Danny DeVito) in *Other People's Money*[24] who represents the self-centred and self-interested corporate and individual greed of the 1990s. A more realistic depiction of modern venture capital and business negotiations can be seen in the documentary *Startup.com*[25] which chronicles the ups and downs of raising capital, hiring employees, running an

[17] One of the few clear 'rules' of negotiation theory is that the most common outcome of a negotiation is the mid-point between the first two offers (in a single issue, two party negotiation). Howard Raiffa, *The Art and Science of Negotiation* (Cambridge, Mass: 1982). [17a] Garry Marske (1990).

[18] Julian Kaye (1980). [19] Adrian Lyne (1993).

[20] Consider what price anyone would have to be paid to sleep with Robert Redford or Demi Moore!

[21] Marc Lawrence (2002). [22] Bill Forsyth (1983). [23] Barry Levinson (1987).

[24] Norman Jewison (1991). [25] Chris Hegedus and Jehane Noujam (2001).

innovative business (creation of the govWorks.com website to facilitate municipal government communications) and negotiating business and personal relationships (some of them overlapping) at the same time.

More extreme forms of negotiation include the depictions of criminal acts of kidnapping or hostage taking in *Ruthless People,*[26] *Speed,*[27] *Ransom*[28] and *The Negotiator,*[29] to name but a few of this ever popular genre. And who could ever forget perhaps the most classic line about negotiations in the movies, from *The Godfather,*[30] in which Marlon Brando, as the godfather in the Mob, 'makes an offer you can't refuse' (to get a part for the Frank Sinatra-like young crooner from a major director by placing a severed horse head in his bed—probably the most dramatic 'threat' in cinematic negotiation history). Though these films are often viewed as exaggerated and suspenseful thrillers, they quite accurately depict a wide variety of conventional negotiation behaviours, used both in extreme criminal negotiations, such as hostage and terrorism negotiations, as well as in calmer, but more conventional plea bargaining (more on this later as seen weekly on TV's most common genre, the cop show, in which virtually every night criminal defendants play real 'prisoner's dilemma' games as they decide whether to defect and confess, see, for example, *NYPD Blue*[30a]) and even in some forms of civil bargaining. For example, the writers and director of *The Negotiator* actually met with and trained with professional hostage negotiators from the New York City Police Department when developing such dialogue as 'Never say No' (the real negotiators say 'never say never'[31]) to a hostage taker. Learning to 'keep them talking' to calm them down, to engage the hostage takers and prevent them from taking more violent action against hostages were graphically depicted on screen, but were 'ripped from' the actual practices of New York City police negotiators who have developed not only taxonomies of hostage takers (the 'crazies, crusaders and criminals'[32]) but protocols of actions for different kinds of hostage takers and different contexts.[33] As dramatic as these fictional filmic moments are, they do present in visual and verbal forms the tropes, actions, images, strategies, phrases, words and behaviours that constitute our cultural understanding of negotiation (including demands, offers, threats, use of force, deception, trickery in bargaining behaviour and ultimately, outcomes and resolutions, whether satisfactory for the parties (and outsiders) or not).

[26] Jim Abraham and David Zucker (1986), and written by Dale Launer, based on a story by O'Henry. This is the comedic outlier in this genre. Sam Stone, a harsh businessman, cheats others who kidnap his wife to retaliate, but then they learn he really doesn't want her back—a kind of 'reverse negotiation' if there is such a thing.

[27] Jan de Bont (1994).

[28] Ron Howard (1996).

[29] F Gary Gray (1998).

[30] Francis Ford Coppola (1972).

[30a] Steve Bocho David Milch (1993-2005).

[31] Jack Cambria, Richard J De Filippo, Robert J Louden and Hugh McGowen, 'Negotiation Under Extreme Pressure: The "Mouth Marines" and the Hostage Takers' (2002) 18 (4) *Negotiation J* 331.

[32] ibid, 334.

[33] See the NYPD's own film, *Talk To Me: Hostage Negotiators of the NYPD* (New York, Hybrid Films, 2002).

Negotiations have also been depicted in international and political thriller contexts, whether in fictionalized treatments of real negotiations such as *Thirteen Days*[34] (the Cuban Missile Crisis), *Seven Days in May*,[35] *Air Force One*[36] and the whole Tom Clancy Jack Ryan oeuvre (for example, *Patriot Games*,[37] *Clear and Present Danger*,[38] *Hunt for Red October*[39]) or that classic on-board negotiated thriller, *The Caine Mutiny*.[40] While all too often this genre 'deteriorates' into the much loved actual physical violence of its *mano a mano* combat, these films do demonstrate the well known theory of negotiation that it is almost always easier to escalate then de-escalate conflict[41] and the films, if taken seriously, can actually make real the dangers of extreme escalation, which might, it is hoped, at least by this critic, argue for less destructive forms of conflict resolution. In recent years, both teledocumentaries and full length film documentaries (some discussed more fully below) have revealed the complexities of real world international and intra-nation state conflicts and negotiations. It is interesting to consider whether real-world depictions of actual negotiations will have some effect on the images presented by popular culture, though analogically speaking, the presence of real trials depicted on 'Court TV' in the United States has done little to change the verisimilitude of dramatic court scenes in the more popular genre of trial movies and television programs (like *LA Law*,[42] *The Practice*[43] or the now franchised *Law & Order* series).[44]

Perhaps most relevant for discussion in this paper are the films, television programmes and depictions in modern popular culture of explicitly legal negotiation scenes, most in fiction, but many in either slightly fictionalized (*Erin Brockovich*[45]) or close to reality (*A Civil Action*[46]) scenes of settlement negotiations of various sorts, most in the 'shadow' of an upcoming trial. Think of *The Verdict*,[47] *Kramer vs. Kramer*,[48] *War of the Roses*,[49] *Class Action*,[50] *Disclosure*,[51] or that classic (and rare) film of negotiations in the jury box, *12 Angry Men*.[52]

There are also the classic 'nibbles' of *Columbo*, the detective, as he negotiates the facts out of his suspects, the good cop-bad cop negotiations to get confessions in *NYPD Blue* and *Law and Order*, and the plea negotiations on *Law and Order*,

[34] Roger Donaldson (2000).
[35] John Frankenheimer (1964) based on novel by Fletcher Knebel and Charles W Bailey.
[36] Wolfgang Peterson (1997). [37] 1992. [38] 1994.
[39] John McTiernan (1990). [40] Edward Donytryk (1954) based on novel by Herman Wouk.
[41] Dean G Pruitt and Jeffrey Z Rubin, *Social Conflict, Escalation, Stalemate and Settlement* (New York: 1986). [42] Steven Bocho and Terry Louise Fisher (1986–92).
[43] David E Kelley, (1997-present).
[44] Dick Wolf (1990-present), now including, *Law & Order*, *Law & Order: Special Victims* (1999-present) and *Law & Order: Criminal Intent* (2001-present). [45] Steven Soderbergh (2000).
[46] Steven Zaillian (1998) based on book by Jonathan Harr. [47] Sidney Lumet (1982).
[48] Robert Benton (1979) based on a novel by Avery Corman.
[49] Danny DeVito (1989). By now, you should be wondering, as am I, why Danny DeVito is so over represented in movies about negotiations, as writer, director and actor!
[50] Michael Apted (1991). [51] Barry Levinson (1994), based on novel by Michael Crichton.
[52] Sidney Lumet (1957).

The Practice and other criminal shows. There were Arnie Becker's dramatic divorce negotiations on *LA Law* and most recently, *The Practice* has taken on a few civil cases and class actions to demonstrate the standardized negotiations in personal injury, products liability and other more ordinary civil matters. Even popular novels have begun to direct attention to legal negotiations in a few scattered legal settlement scenes and the common in real life, but rarely depicted, judicial settlement conference (see *The Street Lawyer*[53]) or even a mediation scene.[54] Labour negotiations of various kinds have been depicted in the popular *ER*[55] (including both doctors' and nurses' strikes and many scenes of negotiation with hospital management and some brief encounters with medical malpractice litigation and settlement activities).

Consider depictions of the classic legal negotiation 'scene'—the *face en face* confrontation of plaintiffs' and defence counsel as they meet across a table to discuss a case settlement offer. In *The Verdict*, down and out Frank Galvin (portrayed by Paul Newman) is a washed up alcoholic who has not won a case in years but who is offered a sizable settlement from the Archdiocese of Boston for a medical malpractice case he is handling. The 'victim', a now comatose young woman in a Catholic hospital, cannot consent to this settlement offer so Frank Galvin rejects it out of hand, in his representation of her family. Though the settlement is large and would most certainly have been accepted by the family had they been told of the offer, Frank is trying to make a legal comeback and he turns down the offer with flare and promises of his hard work and future success in the full arena of the courtroom. As any experienced American lawyer would know, Frank Galvin's behaviour is a classic violation of the Model Rules of Professional Conduct for lawyers[56] which requires lawyers to consult with their clients before accepting or rejecting settlement offers. But if Mr Galvin had accepted this offer there would have been no

[53] John Grisham (1998).

[54] In the movie version of *Disclosure*, Michael Crichton, always attempting to describe the newest technology and medical developments, sought to depict this new form of legal 'technology'—the mediation process. The scene in the film is one of the most inaccurate depictions of a mediation, treated as cross between a judicially hosted settlement conference in a private office, deposition or arbitration. There was nothing mediative about it, even given the current practice and scholarly debates about evaluative vs facilitative mediation processes, see eg Lela Love, 'The Top Ten Reasons Why Mediators Should Not Evaluate' (1997) 24 *Florida State L Rev* 937. A more realistic depiction of a divorce mediation actually appeared on the short-lived television programme, *Once and Again* (Robert Berlinger and Robert Black, 1999–2002), a series about 40 something divorcees trying to form second or 'blended' families.

[55] Michael Crichton (1994-present).

[56] The American Bar Association promulgates the Model Rules of Professional Conduct, which then must be adopted by the appropriate regulatory body in the state, which in some states is the state legislature and in others, the state Supreme Court, for these ethical rules to have the force of positive law. Every state has passed some version of the Model Rules, though California has codified its own version in the Business and Professions Code, which departs from the ABA Code more than any other state (did the Hollywood writers of this film, thus, not know the rules?). In this case Frank Galvin has violated Rule 1.2 which requires lawyers to consult with clients about offers to settle cases. There are few 'black letter' rules in American ethics rules—but this is one of them and one that could subject Mr Galvin to disciplinary proceedings, which could go as far as disbarment, especially if, unlike in the film, he turned down the settlement offer and then lost the case.

movie—the whole point of the film is that by refusing this offer with full adversarial panache and devoting himself to recovering from alcoholism and laziness, Galvin can return to the courtroom and regain his lawyering soul by mounting a successful case against the 'army' of the big Boston corporate law firm. Although this film is largely remembered for its trial scenes, with the solo practitioner eventually defeating the large law firm, Galvin violates several ethical precepts in the process (stealing mail, not sharing information) and sadly, may be instructing many would-be lawyers (and those educated before legal ethics and professional responsibility became a mandatory subject in American legal education[57]) that it is permissible for a lawyer to refuse a settlement offer without client consultation.

While the power of a bishop was not enough to force Frank Galvin to accept a settlement offer, the *mis en scene* of the power negotiation across the table remains a popular device for negotiations. Scenes from *The War of the Roses, Class Action* and *Disclosure* all feature the classic 'across the table' power play in efforts to negotiate divorce and civil law settlements, all of them unsuccessfully, so that the more commonly favoured trial scene can occur. In *The Accused*,[58] prosecutor Kathryn Murphy (Kelly McGillis) negotiates a plea bargain with the defence counsel in a rape charge (victim Sarah Tobias is portrayed by Jody Foster) across a table with video tapes and photographs to bolster her case, arguing the evidence in a more realistic setting than the courtroom. As in reality, defence counsel point out that the less than pristine past history of the victim will likely affect her credibility and a fast paced 'bargaining down' of the charges ensues with rape being left out of the final charge. (*The Accused*, like many such films, is loosely based on a real rape which occurred in a Massachusetts bar with many on-lookers and which received much media attention in 'real time'.) An embittered victim then confronts her lawyer for 'selling her out' because she wanted to get on with her middle class professional and social life, rather than doing the hard work of real representation. Negotiation in the criminal context is regarded as a weaker, selling-out sort of

[57] A course in legal ethics and professional responsibility became the only upper-class required course in the American legal curriculum following the political scandals of Watergate in 1974, in which it was revealed that a disproportionate number of lawyers had been involved in deception, cover-ups and unfair campaign tactics, used by the Republican National Committee to prevent President Nixon from losing the 1972 Presidential election. While that election appeared to have been the highpoint of electoral adversarialism (perhaps until the 2000 *Bush v Gore* election wound up in the US Supreme Court), it was thought that requiring lawyers to learn the ethical rules of the profession might decrease their inappropriate rapacity for victory. This always struck this scholar as a bit odd, since the Rules in effect in 1974, when the ABA began to require instruction in ethics, also required 'zealous advocacy' on the part of lawyers (Canon 7 of the 1969 Code of Professional Responsibility), which was most used to justify quite extreme acts of adversariness, not only in courtrooms but in the negotiations which preceded almost all trials. Rule 4.1 ('A lawyer shall not make a misrepresentation of fact or law to a third person'.) is the only rule which explicitly governs the conduct of lawyers in negotiation with each other, but it is more honoured in the breach, see JJ White, 'Machiavelli and the Bar: Ethical Limitations on Lying in Negotiation' (1980) *American Bar Foundation Research* 405. See Carrie Menkel-Meadow, 'Ethics and Professional Responsibility in Legal Negotiations' in P Bernard and B Garth (eds), *Dispute Resolution Ethics* (Washington DC: 2000) and Carrie Menkel-Meadow and Michael Wheeler (eds), *What's Fair?: Ethics for Negotiators*, (San Francisco: 2004).

[58] Jonathan Kaplan (1988).

justice, not the real thing of contested and dramatic trials[59] and not the same use of power, tricks and manipulations of depicted civil negotiations.[60]

In *A Civil Action*, based on the real case of Jan Schlictman's efforts to win justice for those sickened by contaminated water in Woburn, Massachusetts,[61] the plaintiffs' lawyers prepare a pricey breakfast meeting across the hotel table at the Ritz Carlton in Boston, thinking that to win a dollar one must demonstrate one's strength by sparing no expense and not appearing weak or underfinanced. This costly choice (a failed negotiation with a very high demand) is matched by a 'power play' of the large corporation, who is one of the defendants, when Schlictman is summoned to corporate headquarters and made to feel insignificant and out of place in the stratospherically high offices and gentlemen's clubs of 'innocent' corporate America. These depictions of negotiations as power plays across the hostile 'turfs' of law firm, hotel or corporate offices and their dark wooden conference tables have nothing to do with the merits of the cases being negotiated. They appear to be taken from the pages of the popular psychology books that urge negotiators to appear strong, 'outnumber the other side', and use one's own turf to command power and produce discomfort on the other side. (Shadows of Charlie Chaplin's famous scene in *The Great Dictator*[62] where the furniture is literally altered to manipulate size and power.)

Playing on this now common set-piece of legal negotiation in the movies (or on TV), the recent film, *Erin Brockovich*, also based on a real story, turns the tables on this scenario. As the larger number of big firm lawyers march in to take their places at the plaintiffs' counsel's conference table and 'ridiculous' settlement offers are made (and also rejected by counsel without client consultation) for horrific diseases caused by polluted and contaminated water (Erin asks one of the defence counsel how much she would value her own womb), Erin Brockovich, the heroic paralegal, quietly informs her adversaries that the water they are drinking at the negotiation conference is from their own contaminated wells. This is, perhaps, an extreme form of adversarial tactic for a negotiation session, but movie cleverness

[59] The argument that plea bargaining is a weaker form of justice (both for defence and prosecution) has long been made by social scientists and lawyers in the United States who have studied the process empirically and jurisprudentially, see eg Albert W Alschuler, 'The Changing Plea Bargaining Debate' (1981) 69 *California L Rev* 652; Stephen J Schulhofer, 'Is Plea Bargaining Inevitable? (1984) 97 *Harvard L Rev* 1037; Milton Heumann, *Plea Bargaining: The Experiences of Prosecutors, Judges and Defense Attorneys* (Chicago: 1978). Perhaps the most interesting study of comparative negotiations in criminal law, now many years old, was done by Pamela Utz, in which she noted that flexible and responsive variations in plea bargaining cultures in two different jurisdictions led to different outcomes and different recidivist rates (more tailored plea bargains with treatment in Northern California led to better outcomes and lower recidivism than more rigid and more 'determinate sentencing' in the criminal courts of Southern California). See Pamela Utz, *Settling the Facts: Discretion and Negotiation in Criminal Court* (Lexington, Mass: 1978).

[60] In reality, civil negotiations are what socio-legal scholars would call 'low intensity' events of one or two offers being suggested and accepted with little actual bargaining on the merits, or in efforts to engage in the sort of problem-solving and tailored negotiation suggested by this author, see eg Herbert Kritzer, *Let's Make a Deal: Understanding the Negotiation Process in Ordinary Litigation*, (Madison, Wisconsin: 1991); Hazel Genn, *Hard Bargaining: Out of Court Settlement in Personal Injury Actions* (Oxford: 1988).

[61] See Jonathan Harr, *A Civil Action* (New York: 1995).

[62] Charles Chaplin (1940).

aside, it at least purports to relate the negotiation tactics to the merits of the case. As a depiction of a conventional across the table negotiation encounter, this scene has already made it into the annals of classic scenes by upending the presumed power of the large firm and converting the technique of calmly presented settlement offers to 'neutralize' the opposition into an opportunity for the underdog and injured, through their paralegal (not lawyer), to gain the upper hand. Legal negotiations are not just about power suits and unlimited litigation budgets anymore. Efforts to achieve justice, obtain fair payments for injuries and demand admissions of guilt and apologies may happen at the negotiation table (not only in hard-won verdicts in court), thus moving the action, at least sometimes, to the more realistic locus of its actual occurrence. The negotiation table has become a site, not only of drama, but of justice, as the power plays and tricks of the more powerful are now being turned on them, albeit in the same spirit of adversarial victory-seeking.

John Grisham's popular novels have mostly turned on the common trial scene but in *The Street Lawyer* he provides one of the few modern glimpses into other settings of legal activities. While the opening scene of a hostage taking in a law firm by a deranged and angry homeless person plays out conventional negotiations *in extremis* (and the protagonist of the book, Michael Brock is transformed from a partnership-seeking large law firm lawyer to a legal aid lawyer for the homeless), the book concludes with what I believe is the first depicted judicial settlement conference, now the norm in all civil actions in the US[63] and more common in the UK.[64] At the settlement conference, the judge not only 'nudges' the parties to a settlement but also manages to adjudicate some ethics charges as well. (This depiction of a judge pursuing ethics charges is laudable in the attention he pays to the Professional Rules of Conduct, but is procedurally quite incorrect. Ethics issues of the sort considered here would be handled by a separate Bar Association (Law Society) disciplinary tribunal).

A new genre of legal representation, in both film, through documentaries, and in print, through 'true' stories about legal cases (called variously 'true crime', 'legal memoirs' or, as I have labelled some of them, 'bill and tell' stories[65]) have explored and depicted the stories of actual negotiations in real cases. Probably beginning with

[63] Federal Rule of Civil Procedure, Rule 16 requires a pre-trial conference which often turns into a settlement conference, either with the judge or a magistrate, see Carrie Menkel-Meadow, ' For and Against Settlement: The Uses and Abuses of the Mandatory Settlement Conference' (1985) 33 *UCLA L Rev 485*.

[64] Since reforms have been introduced to the civil justice system in the UK by Lord Woolf's report and reforms, 'managerial judging' and settlement like conferences are more common in British justice as well, see Lord Woolf, *Access to Justice: Report on the Civil Justice System of England and Wales to the Lord Chancellor* (London: 1996); see also Roger Smith (ed), *Achieving Civil Justice: Appropriate Dispute Resolution for the 1990s* (London: 1996).

[65] Carrie Menkel-Meadow, 'Telling Stories in School: Using Case Studies and Stories to Teach Legal Ethics' (2000) 69 *Fordham L Rev* 787; Carrie Menkel-Meadow, 'The Sense and Sensibilities of Lawyers: Lawyering in Literature, Narratives, Film and Television, and Ethical Choices Regarding Career and Craft' (1999) 31 *McGeorge L Rev* 1; Carrie Menkel-Meadow, 'Can They Do That? Legal Ethics in Popular Culture: Of Character and Acts' (2001) 48 *UCLA L Rev 1305*.

Gerald Stern's *The Buffalo Creek Disaster: The Story of the Survivors' Unprecedented Lawsuit*,[66] both lawyers telling their own stories and reporters telling the stories of others have chronicled a growing number of legal cases for the general public, some recounting tales of mass disaster[67] and class actions[68] and others reporting on single cases with dramatic stories of injustice,[69] personalities[70] or new legal issues. In a more sociological or autobiographical vein, some lawyers have simply tried to understand and explain their daily, often mundane work, in representing clients, both corporate and individual, both civil and criminal.[71] This genre has illuminated the more realistic aspects of legal negotiations and, in some rare cases, when they are accurately televised in documentary form for TV or film, they demonstrate both more conventional forms of adversarial or 'power negotiating', as well as more modern and creative forms of problem solving.

In *The Buffalo Creek Disaster*, for example, a large Washington DC law firm lawyer takes on the case of a community devastated by the collapse of a dam and subsequent flooding, produced by the fire and collapse of a negligently maintained coal mine in West Virginia, in one of the most celebrated cases of *pro bono publico* representation. Despite the chronicling of all the litigation manœuvres in discovery, depositions, expert witness preparation, documents, physical examinations and case preparation, the case ends, many would say, anticlimactically, in a large settlement, which even the author cannot justify in terms of 'principles', 'reasons' or the 'merits' as we would describe them, according to modern negotiation theory. Despite efforts to argue multiples of damages based on physical and psychic pain of individuals, the lawyers, like so many conventional civil bargainers, use such ploys as 'splitting the difference' (between largely arbitrary numbers of millions of dollars based on assumptions about insurance coverage limits and multipliers of pain and suffering) and arbitrarily inflated offers to account for the conventional process of 'nibbling' or 'dancing' around offers ('now that I had \$10 million I wanted to try for \$15 million. To get them to 15 from 10 I probably would have to ask for 20').[72] That case settled for \$13.5 million, at the time one of the largest multiple plaintiff disaster cases filed (without benefit of class action filing). The offer by offer description provided by Stern is one of the first reports we have of actual negotiations in such a large case, but its recitation of the reasons or rationales

[66] Gerald M Stern, *The Buffalo Creek Disaster: The Story of the Survivors' Unprecedented Lawsuit* (New York: 1976).

[67] Richard Sobel, *Bending the Law: The Story of the Dalkon Shield Bankruptcy* (Chicago: 1991).

[68] Clara Bingham and Laura Leedy Gansler, *Class Action: The Story of Lois Jenson and the Landmark Case That Changed Sexual Harassment Law* (New York: 2002).

[69] Barry Werth, *Damages: One Family's Legal Struggles in the World of Medicine* (1998).

[70] David Margolick, *Undue Influence: The Epic Battle for the Johnson & Johnson Fortune* (New York: 1993); Ken Crispin, *The Crown versus Chamberlain, 1980–1987* (Sutherland, Australia: 1987).

[71] See, eg, William R Keates, *Proceed With Caution: A Diary of the First Year at One of America's Largest, Most Prestigious Law Firms* (New York: 1997); Cameron Stracher, *Double Billing* (New York: 1998); David Heilbroner, *Rough Justice: Days and Nights of a Young DA* (New York: 1990); James S Kunen, *How Can You Defend Those Guilty People?* (New York: 1983); Paul M Barrett, *The Good Black: A True Story of Race in America* (New York: 1999).

[72] Stern, n 66 above, 295.

for particular amounts, offers, demands or client needs is a stunning counter-example to today's negotiation texts, suggesting that no 'movement' should ever be made in a negotiation without justification, principle, reason and mathematical calculations to support particular offers.[73]

Unfortunately, both the Jan Schlictman of real life and his portrayal by John Trovolta in *A Civil Action* is not much of an improvement on Gerald Stern's 'seat of the pants' negotiating. There is some effort to calculate the value of individual claims of death, serious illness and medical, social, physical and mental harm and then to aggregate such amounts, but in the end the jockeying of numbers is not much better than the bargaining for rugs or silver in a souk or exotic market.[74] Negotiations demonstrating the pursuit of clients' underlying needs and interests, searches for creative solutions or even more conventional settlements that map the merits (whether legal, monetary or emotional) of the case remain few and far between in conventional treatments of legal negotiations.

Beyond the portrayal of particular legal cases, some films (in both documentary and fictional forms) have begun to represent systems of negotiated justice, demonstrating how legal cultures develop patterns of negotiation within, outside and in the 'shadow' of formal legal institutions. Documentarists Michael Moore (*Roger and Me*)[75] and Barbara Kopple (*Harlan County*[76] and *American Dream*[77]) have presented real stories of efforts of ordinary people to negotiate for their legal rights, in Moore's case, corporate accountability from General Motors, and in Kopple's the reporting of two major labour strikes in search of justice for mineworkers and meatpackers. Americans pride themselves on self-actualizing behaviour, but these films demonstrate both courage and passivity in the face of unequal bargaining power and raise important questions about individual, group and organizational negotiations and the need for formal legal representation, alongside other forms of negotiations.

Laura Nader and other anthropologists have now spent decades recording and reporting on the many ways in which different cultures manage dispute resolution, both in handling disputes within a particular community and when disputants are from different communities.[78] In summarizing her decades of work for a more popular audience, Nader produced a documentary film (which has been shown on public television in the United States many times and which I, and other legal academics have shown to their negotiation or dispute resolution classes for many years) called *Little Injustices*[79] which contrasts the justice systems of the community

[73] See eg Menkel-Meadow, n 9 above; Fisher, Ury and Patton, n 9 above; and Marjorie Corman Aaron and David P Hoffer, 'Decision Analysis As a Method of Evaluating the Trial Alternative' in Dwight Golann, *Mediating Legal Disputes: Effective Strategies for Lawyers and Mediators* (Boston: 1996).

[74] Steven Lubet, 'Notes on the Bedouin horse trade or "why won't the market clear, daddy?"' (1996) 74 *Texas L Rev* 1039.

[75] Michael Moore (1989).

[76] Barbara Kopple (1976).

[77] Barbara Kopple (1990).

[78] Laura Nader and Harry Todd (eds), *The Disputing Process: Law in Ten Societies* (New York: 1978).

[79] Laura Nader, *Little Injustices: Laura Nader Looks at the Law* (Public Broadcasting Associates: 1980). See also Laura Nader, *Harmony Ideology: Justice and Control in a Mountain Zapotec Village* (Stanford, California: 1990).

of Talea, a Zapotec Indian village in Mexico, with efforts by American consumers to negotiate complaints about their purchased products from mass society's manufacturers in a modern industrialized and judicialized culture.

Although the American legal system formally offers more avenues of redress, depicted in the film in the various forms of individual customer complaints and negotiations, appeals to management, small claims court and self-representation, formal lawsuits with lawyers, class actions, appearances on consumer assistance television programmes, and reported exposés by both print and electronic media, modern Americans are largely unable to negotiate relief and solutions to their problems when automobiles, kitchen appliances, washing machines and even mobile homes fail to operate as warranted. *Little Injustices* portrays an indomitable spirit on the part of American citizens who seek to negotiate on their own behalf with all the vigour of the lawyers depicted in popular films, but in a mass society, even with a federal court system, offering many points of entry to the system, most efforts to negotiate replacement, repair, reparations, or damages fail.

In contrast, Nader shows us how a smaller community uses both direct negotiation between neighbours who know each other (in a dispute about damaged chillies, the mainstay of economic support) and a form of mediated negotiation when a dispute ensues with outsiders (truck drivers who damage a house while delivering goods from the outside world) to craft tailor-made solutions that both provide redress for the harm done and preserve or heal relationships between the disputants. In this form of community negotiation, not only the actual parties, but the whole community is involved in suggesting solutions and merging a form of hybrid justice that includes both penalties (criminal law) and civil redress (assistance in rebuilding the house).

Nader is not a 'mediation romanticist'. In an epilogue to the film, she suggests that as modern 'civilization' has crept into Talea's sheltered mountain space, both personal and consumerist relationships have become more complex and it is becoming more difficult to maintain more 'problem-solving' orientations to negotiated justice. In her own country, Nader has remained a strong advocate of more formal legal approaches to achieving justice,[80] despite the arguments of many that courts are unlikely to mete out precise justice. Whether injured parties are better off negotiating for themselves in a face to face society where they are 'empowered' to handle their own disputes and transactions or by having skilled and expert agents negotiate for them continues to engage the scholarly negotiation community,[81] as we watch enactments of the negotiations of both agents and principals in popular culture settings.

The film, *The Story of Qiu Ju*,[82] compellingly portrays the clash of direct and individualized negotiated justice with a strong and centralized political regime in

[80] Laura Nader, *The Life of the Law: Anthropological Projects* (Berkeley, California: 2002).

[81] Robert H Mnookin and Lawrence E Susskind (eds), *Negotiating on Behalf of Others: Advice to Lawyers, Business Executives, Sports Agents, Diplomats, Politicians, and Everybody Else* (Thousand Oaks, California and London: 1999).

[82] Zhang Yimou (1993).

Maoist China, itself struggling with both communitarian and communist forms of mediated justice and the tensions of individual empowerment and formal legal systems embedded in group and locally based traditional cultures.[83] Qiu Ju seeks to negotiate justice on behalf of her husband who has been kicked in the groin by the village chief. The injury is both personal and symbolic, as the chief has been unable to conceive a son and Qiu Ju is pregnant with what is considered likely to be a son. (This is all in the time of China's one child policy.) Qiu Ju does as her society requires, starting with a direct negotiation and confrontation with the perpetrator of the assault, as she then moves from level to level of the Chinese mediation, administrative and ultimately, 'adjudicative' system. (The film was made in the period immediately following the first law permitting individuals to sue the state—the chief is a communist party official in the village.) Though both traditional (Confucian) and political (Communist) cultures suggest she should accept the apology and small monetary payment that she is offered by the chief, she feels the apology is insincere and she wants her form of 'justice'. (In such cross-cultural travels in art and scholarship, translations of such words as 'justice' and 'apology' are highly problematic, if rich, for pointing out the failure of any language to capture fully what people really want when they negotiate with others. I have seen this film many times with fluent Chinese speakers and, as with all acts of interpretation, have heard many different versions of translations of the key words which Qiu Ju uses to express what she wants, as well as the various responses she receives from her foe, government officials, her lawyer and even her husband, her own 'client'.)

Qiu Ju's attempts to negotiate both for herself and for her husband's dignity in a legal culture that is changing from hybrid forms of traditional and politically structured institutions powerfully represents what is both 'cultural' and universally 'human' about negotiations. Negotiation is necessary whenever we need or want something from someone else and yet, we cannot negotiate without the 'default' norms and procedures of both the social and legal cultures in which we live. Qiu Ju wants a 'real' apology and she wants justice, beyond a token monetary payment, as American consumers want more than money as a proxy for measuring the injuries they have suffered when products fail or there are man-made mass disasters. Yet, both social and legal cultures determine both what someone can hope to gain from a negotiation (the 'substantive' endowments) and how what one negotiates for can be achieved (the procedural norms or customs and restraints in negotiations). Informal and formal processes are thus always already intertwined and casting shadows on each other—both ways. If law gives us certain legal endowments but we cannot hire lawyers or afford the legal system or the system itself does not conform to its own promises, more informal negotiations will be used to develop more responsive solutions. When more decentralized informal systems fail, as they did

[83] Stanley Lubman, 'Dispute Resolution in China After Deng Xiaoping: Mao and Mediation Revisited' (1997) 11 *Columbia J of Asian Law* 229.

for Qiu Ju, and as they might for the citizens of Talea, demands will be made on a more centralized system to rationalize and make more transparent an institutionalized form of justice. This tension of what negotiation gives (both more and less than the formal legal system in both tailor-made, but also unprincipled 'compromised' solutions) is best demonstrated when negotiations under different cultural endowments are juxtaposed to each other.

Some recent documentaries have begun to explore inter-cultural negotiations at the individual, group, and nation-state levels to give us a fuller, if sadder, picture of how human conflicts are handled within the full spectrum of human behaviour. Films about inter-ethnic violence in Rwanda, India-Pakistan, Northern Ireland, the Balkans and the Middle East are exploring the efforts of individual peace seekers and peacekeepers, negotiators, non-governmental organizations (such as *Search for Common Ground*)[84] and even formal diplomatic negotiations, mediations and other efforts at conflict resolution. As one illustration of this genre, the documentary *Promises*[85] explores the lives of several Jewish and Palestinian children living in different sectors of Israel and the occupied territories as they report on their diametrically opposed understandings of the conflicts between their groups. What makes this film particularly compelling is the way in which the film maker, like an activist mediator, departs from the 'neutrality' of the reportorial camera, to bring several of the children together across ethnic lines to use their love of sports to effectuate a 'negotiated' friendship between them. By demonstrating more than the 'formal' moves of diplomatic negotiation or cultural understanding projects, this film movingly and eloquently depicts the complexity of actual cross-cultural negotiations, that will be necessary for any real lasting peace to develop in such situations of high conflict. The difficulty of breaking out of conventional forms of conflict (as we are taught by our families and the larger cultures in which we are embedded) is painfully demonstrated here. This film operates at the levels of individual negotiation and understanding with more formal cultural and political institutions setting the backdrop. Other films in this genre focus more on institutional efforts to negotiate conflict resolution, peace terms and reconciliation efforts and are in contrast to community and international criminal tribunals to punish for past acts.[86] Such more 'realistic' depictions of political, ethnic and cultural conflict demonstrate the difficulty of reconciling past harms to future relationships that will clearly require more than traditional adjudicative justice.

When one expands consideration of depictions of negotiations beyond an obviously legal frame, one begins to see a glimpse of how modern negotiation theory might be represented in popular culture—in both 'high' culture and more popularized versions.

[84] See website at http://www.sfcg.org.

[85] Justine Shapiro, BZ Goldberg and Carlos Bolado (2001).

[86] Antonia Chayes and Martha Minow (eds), *Imagine Coexistence: Restoring Humanity After Violent Ethnic Conflict* (San Francisco: 2003).

Models of Negotiation: Schemas of Representation

Negotiations are 'represented' in cultural depictions most often against a template of conventional negotiation 'representation' as conducted by lawyers or other agents—adversarial and competitive contests over scarce resources (money, physical safety and bodies, criminal charges and penalties) to be distributed to an individual or nation-state maximizer.[87] When, as in the movies, most negotiations fail, the real drama, trial in civil settings, physical combat in hostage, criminal and international thriller settings, can begin. Yet, a few cultural outliers are beginning to represent a different conception of negotiation, more congruent with modern scholarship.

If most legal negotiations derive their intellectual schema from game theory[88] and the prisoner's dilemma game in particular, then at least two recent representations of game theory's concerns with human cooperation or defection[89] have allowed the literate public to view the greater complexity of human interaction when there are more than two negotiators or where value can be created, if and before it must be divided.

Though not about legal phenomena, two recent works of popular culture have demonstrated the importance of coordinating communications and preferences in 'games' and human interaction to achieve better negotiated outcomes. The film *A Beautiful Mind*,[90] based on the book of the same name,[91] chronicling the life of schizophrenic game theorist John Nash, demonstrates, perhaps a bit simplistically, how, when all try to maximize individual gain, there may be one winner and a lot of losers. In the film, John Nash has gone with fellow graduate students in mathematics to a local pub where a beautiful blonde is the desideratum of all the men. She is surrounded by less desirable brunettes. As the men all compete for the blonde's attention, John Nash points out that if all the men choose their 'second best' and pair off with brunettes, the well being of the whole group will be maximized (even if the blonde is left alone, all the others will be paired with a date). Though a highly simplified (and game theorists would say somewhat inaccurate) depiction of how utilitarian equilibria for the many may be effectuated through a form of collaboration or cooperation, rather than competition, this beautifully executed (if somewhat sexist and annoying to me as a brunette—why should I be 'second best'?) movie moment and 'game' move demonstrates that contrary to the assumptions of pure game theory, when communication is possible, negotiators may share information, assess preferences and resources and allocate resources so as to

[87] Avinash Dixit and Barry Nalebuff, *Thinking Strategically: The Competitive Edge in Business, Politics and Everyday Life* (New York: 1991).

[88] See eg, John von Neumann and Oskar Morgenstern, *The Theory of Games and Economic Behavior* (1944); William Poundstone, *Prisoner's Dilemma* (1992); Douglas Baird, *Game Theory and the Law* (1994).

[89] Robert Axelrod, *The Evolution of Cooperation* (New York: 1984).

[90] Ron Howard (2001).

[91] Silvia Nasar, *A Beautiful Mind: The Life of Nobel Laureate John Forbes Nash* (New York: 1999).

maximize gain for the many (rather than to produce one 'winner' of the blonde and a lot of unmatched pairs of men and brunettes in a competition for the few). In my view, this brief moment in a film was a brilliant execution by the screenwriter[92] to demonstrate complex ideas of human interaction, vividly, filmically and probably more effectively, for the general population, than the more accurate and formal papers of John Nash's exploration of equilibria points in games of cooperation and competition or defection, in game theoretic terms.[93] This film demonstrates the 'substantive' problem-solving possibilities of negotiations that are conducted through analysis, rational thinking, and coordination, rather than power-plays, competition and deception.

A second depiction of some of the elements of the prisoner's dilemma game occurs in the elegant first chapter of Ian McEwan's novel *Enduring Love*.[94] Joe Rose, a science writer, has planned an idyllic picnic with his wife in the countryside only to discover a large helium balloon travelling above with a body dangling from a rope. In an effort to save the young boy caught in the balloon Joe leaps up and runs, as do four other men, to catch hold of the balloon and bring it safely to ground. Instead, as a wind blows the balloon up over an escarpment, each man, but one, lets go of the balloon and chooses to 'defect' and save himself, rather than continue to hold and provide the weight to bring the balloon safely down. Tragedy ensues. It is no accident that Joe Rose is a science writer, who, in reporting his own strange tale, sees in what has just happened to him the basic human dilemma abstracted in the prisoner's dilemma—the human instinct to cooperate or to defect. He says:

> Selfishness is also written on our hearts. This is our mammalian conflict; what to give to others and what to keep for yourself. Treading that line, keeping the others in check and being kept in check by them, is what we call morality . . . our crew enacted morality's ancient, irresolvable dilemma: us or me.[95]

In this example, which Rose describes, in retrospect, as a failure of coordination and leadership, the would-be rescuers begin with an altruistic instinct to save and cooperate with each other. But, since, as in the formal prisoner's dilemma game (taken from our own world of law, in which two prisoners are locked up and prevented from communicating with each other as they choose whether to confess and 'squeal' on the other, or to remain silent and risk the defection of the other[96]), the parties are unable to communicate (the wind gusts are making communication as difficult as being locked up in separate cells), they must each individually choose whether to hang on (cooperate) or let go (defect from the group enterprise and save the self).

[92] Akiva Goldsman.

[93] See eg John Nash, 'The Bargaining Problem' (1950) 18 *Econometrica* 155; John Nash, 'Two Person Cooperative Games' (1953) 21 *Econometrica* 129.

[94] Ian McEwan, *Enduring Love* (London, 1997; New York, 1998).

[95] ibid, 14–17.

[96] This now classic formula, assumed as a hypothesis in studying strategic decision-making in game theory, is now enacted weekly in the formulaic scripts of *NYPD Blue*, as two criminal offenders are locked up in separate cells and must decide whether to bargain for a better deal for themselves, by 'ratting out' their compatriot in crime. The prisoner's dilemma is now seen weekly by millions who may be unfamiliar with its more formal properties and teachings for negotiation behaviour.

The choice of defection or cooperation marks the ultimate process choices in every negotiation and as McEwen demonstrates, left to their own devices, most humans choose self-preservation, competition and defection, a marker of human behaviour, that his science writer protagonist, Joe Rose, undoubtedly knows. I cannot do justice to McEwan's fine writing (as the recent film failed to do as well [96a]) but this book, which is more 'high culture' than popular culture to me (its best-selling numbers qualify it for treatment here in a work about popular culture), slowly builds suspense in a reader who must confront considering what he or she would do in such a situation. While McEwan's character chooses a reflection on the importance of leadership and coordination in situations of multiple actors (with obvious implications for the coordination of multi-party negotiations or mediation[97]) this scene can also be read as an exercise in problem solving, from both a process and substantive perspective. How can/should human beings coordinate their actions and decide whether to maximize group/joint or individual welfare?

The game theory that gave rise to much of competitive negotiation theory, based on the need to develop strategies to maximize individual gain (and survival) was itself derived from the need of defence strategists during the Cold War to 'out think' the other side, a presumed evil adversary.[98] To the extent that modern negotiation (and game) theory is more interested in the conditions under which it makes sense to defect and compete and in what situations it is more rational to coordinate and cooperate with others to create value, seek creative solutions or improve the lot of the many before dividing what must be allocated, this scene vividly portrays modern human survival and negotiation dilemmas. (And how timely, as we consider whether nations in the diplomatic and international contexts should 'go it alone' (as our nations have[99]) or whether joint action and coalitions or multi-lateral action are more advised.)

At the level of process, social philosopher Stuart Hampshire has recently reminded us that where we cannot achieve agreement on the substantive good, developing good processes for conflict resolution may be one of the few human universals.[100] Hampshire, unfortunately in my view, equates good process with Anglo-American 'adversary' process (*audi alteram partem*— 'hear the other side'). By modifying his principle to 'hearing *all* other sides' we may have a model for multiple party negotiations and conflict processes that takes account of needs and interests of all sides and allows communication, coordination, and rational

[96a] Roger Mitchell, 2004.

[97] See Howard Raiffa, 'Post-Settlement Settlements' (1985) 1 *Negotiation Journal* 9, reprinted in Carrie Menkel-Meadow (ed), *Mediation: Theory, Practice & Policy* (Aldershot: 2001).

[98] Thomas Schelling, *The Strategy of Conflict* (Cambridge, Mass: 1960). Compare the works of post Word War II negotiation and game theory strategy with the focus on 'constructive conflict' of Mary Parker Follett, working on labour relations and the new business management discipline in the 1920s, see eg 'Constructive Conflict' in Pauline Graham (ed), *Mary Parker Follett: Prophet of Management: A Celebration of Writings from the 1920's* (Boston, Mass: 1996).

[99] I refer here to the US-UK 'invasion' of Iraq in 2003 in the name of removal of a dictator and reduction of the 'terrorist threat' and use of 'weapons of mass destruction'.

[100] Stuart Hampshire, *Justice is Conflict* (Princeton: 2000).

negotiation, based on principles, preference-trading and emotional claims made by all parties and perhaps coordinated by a negotiation facilitator.[101]

As if to demonstrate the failures of modern and conventional adversarial legal processes, a recent movie has become what I would call the 'first Alternative Dispute Resolution' movie. In *I Am Sam*,[102] Sean Penn plays a mentally challenged (scored development of a seven year old) father, trying to retain custody of his young daughter, as the state seeks to take his child away when her own intellectual development exceeds his own. In painful and conventional scenes of the depiction of state-ordered child custody hearings, in which Sam Dawson, the father, hires a high strung competitive lawyer (played by Michele Pfeiffer), adversarial negotiations and a trial are shown. Sam's literal minded intelligence cannot learn the 'adult' ironies of witness talk—the overly prepared, orchestrated and manipulated language of the courtroom. His kindly neighbour (played by Dianne Wiest) is exposed as a psychologically harmed agoraphobic who is 'broken down' in a brutal cross-examination that serves no one's interest. As Sam's daughter is put in foster care, she begins to express her own preferences by using her feet to run away to her father, as the Beatles' soundtrack stirringly plays 'All You Need Is Love'. As the people who love the child, Lucy Diamond ('in the skies') Dawson, begin to learn, it does really 'take a village' to raise a child and a subtle (mostly off-screen) negotiated solution begins to take shape of shared custody[103] and an unusual and loving extended family. Perhaps this 1960s-raised viewer reads too much into the hopeful new recordings of Beatles' music in the background, but the music in this film suggests all the hopefulness of my generation, which imagined there would be new family forms and more creative solutions to complex legal and human problems than the conventional and traditional forms we grew up with. *I Am Sam* offers visions of both more responsive multi-party negotiation processes and more individually tailored substantive solutions to human problems. Whether the law could ever really catch up to this human evolutionary practice is left unanswered by the film, but at least this film represents the beginning of demonstrations of the greater complexity in legal negotiations, both in terms of legal process and substantive problem solving.

Why It Matters: What Depictions of Legal Negotiations in Popular Culture Tell Us About Ourselves

Negotiations between human beings are as old as Adam and Eve and are necessary whenever one person needs something from someone else. Legal negotiations are only a drop newer, beginning whenever the first 'rule' was promulgated and

[101] For my expanded argument on the three kinds of discourses necessary for good deliberative problem solving see Carrie Menkel-Meadow, 'The Lawyers' Role in Deliberative Democracy: Facilitating Consensus and Other Processes,' Nevada L Rev (forthcoming, 2005).

[102] Jessie Nelson (2001).

[103] Others have suggested to me that there are other depictions of 'shared' solutions to negotiated resource allocation in the movies, see, eg *It Could Happen To You* (Andrew Bergman, 1994) in which a police officer and a waitress share a winning lottery ticket.

someone tried to argue how it did not apply to them or a promise needed to be enforced or a dispute settled without violence. The conceptualization of negotiation as a field of human study is much more recent.[104] Depictions of legal negotiations in modern popular culture (discounting the great legal novels of the nineteenth century, like Charles Dickens' *Bleak House* or Anthony Trollope's *Orley Farm*) have tended to focus on dramatic court room and trial scenes where drama is easily created in the confrontations of the adversary system, with dramatic cross-examinations, stirring closing argument and that moment of highest drama—the verdict. To the extent that certain formulaic conceptions of drama have become the norm, much of what constitutes legal activity is actually ignored in popular culture—there are relatively few scenes of lawyer-client interviews,[105] few scenes of document drafting, deposition taking or library research[106] and surprisingly few depictions of legal transaction negotiations, even the dramatic mergers and acquisitions negotiations that are so important in the 'urban legends' lawyers tell themselves. Most legal work is considered tedious and movie scriptwriters, teleplay writers and even popular novelists have, for the most part, not developed ways of representing the less visible venues of legal representation.

To the extent that legal negotiations are depicted in popular culture, they have, for the most part, tracked the 'high drama' demands of the convention of the trial or courtroom drama. There is adversary debate, argument, demands and either one party scores points by clever trickery, manipulation or overpowering the other side, or more likely, an across the table negotiation fails so that the parties can move on to the real action—the trial. In the United States at the present time only about 2–3 per cent of all cases filed in courts (civil, criminal, family, equity or probate) actually conclude with a full trial. A vast majority of cases are settled by some form of negotiation, or increasingly other forms of dispute resolution, like mediation or private or court assisted arbitration.

To the extent that trial scenes or adversarial negotiation scenes still dominate popular culture, they are, in my view, dangerous models and representations. If the general population and potential would-be lawyers continue to eat from this limited fare they will continue to think that law is always a battleground, whether in the courtroom or at the conference table. There will be loud and stylized talk, grand arguments and debates and 'winners' and 'losers' or more often, stalemate and impasse or unprincipled compromises. This perpetuates a conception of the world as in a constant state of war or competition. Sports and war metaphors dominate talk about negotiation—'going to the mat' (wrestling), 'scoring a touchdown' (football), 'beating them at their own game' (generic). This continues a conception

[104] See Carrie Menkel-Meadow, 'Legal Negotiation: A Study of Strategies in Search of a Theory' [1983] *American Bar Foundation Research J* 905.

[105] Except for Travers' famous witness coaching scene in *Anatomy of a Murder*.

[106] The film of John Grisham's *Pelican Brief*, Alan J Pakula (1993) actually does have a scene of Julia Roberts doing legal research in what happens to be my local law library—the library of Georgetown University Library—the beautifully architected Edward Bennett Williams Library, named for one of the United States' most renowned trial lawyers.

that negotiation is about vanquishing the other side, seeking to maximize individual gain and rewards seem to go to those who are clever, deceptive, manipulative and more powerful, whether or not they are legally 'right' or 'just'. This privileging of a capitalistic hegemonic game within the rubric of claims about how much better and fairer our Anglo-American system of justice is (we have 'the rule of law' after all), compared to other systems, is troubling and problematic.

As negotiation theorists, and now practitioners, are beginning to learn, not all negotiations are about scarce resources with a limited pie to divide. In the parlance of our own vocabulary, there are ways to 'expand the pie and create value' before it must be divided (if at all). With a need stronger than ever to demonstrate that humans are capable of resolving problems creatively, creating, as well as dividing or destroying, wealth, trying to 'get along' where there are vast differences of political values, culture, religion or economics, it would seem that demonstrations of different kinds of negotiations would be both more socially valuable, and probably more accurate as increasingly lawyers are being trained to 'think outside the box'.[107]

Whether consumers of popular culture on legal topics are more concerned with 'outcomes' or results in assessing both the enjoyment of a work of 'art' or evaluating whether justice has been done, or can consider how things are actually achieved—the processes by how we get to outcomes—would be an interesting question for reader-response or film scholars to study. As both a scholar and teacher of negotiation and law and popular culture I am concerned about the heuristics we transmit with the images, representations and plot lines that are currently available to us. If we are trying to teach human beings to negotiate by exploring parties' needs and interests, by looking for both common interests, and 'tradeable' complementary interests and ways of creating value and making spaces for peaceful co-existence, it would seem to me we need some new popular culture.

So far, I have found most of my models of good negotiation outside of legal settings. Consider the success of *Bend It Like Beckham*[108] on both sides of the Atlantic, as a young girl negotiates the differences in her immigrant parents' Sikh culture (of traditional gender roles and marriage) and her own desire to play football (soccer to us Americans) and choose her own girl and boyfriends in the UK she has grown up in. If all human stories have some conflict in them for the drama that is necessary for success in popular culture, why are there not more interesting stories about conflict resolution?—both in negotiated solutions and in the process by which people get to new solutions. If it takes some creativity to make popular culture, why have not more creative processes and solutions to human and legal

[107] This now over-used phrase actually comes from a brainteaser that requires the player to connect three rows of dots with four straight lines without taking a pen off the page. The solution lies in 'thinking outside the box' (and perhaps outside the conventional legal system for lawyers), see James Adams, *Conceptual Blockbusting: A Guide to Better Ideas* (Reading, Mass: 1974). British readers might be more familiar with similar concepts developed by Edward DeBono, *Lateral Thinking: Creativity Step by Step* (London and New York: 1990). See also Carrie Menkel-Meadow, 'Aha? Is Creativity Possible in Legal Problem Solving and Teachable in Legal Education?' (2001) 6 *Harvard Negotiation L Rev 97.*

[108] Gurinder Chadha (2002).

problems been written and filmed? Are popular culture creators as stuck in their own boxes of formulaic scripts and plots as lawyers are stuck in the causes of action, behaviours and models of their own legal work? I would like to think that we are capable of demonstrating more productive and creative processes and solutions to human and legal problems. Is peace, empathy, value creation, the development of new legal entities or forms that uninteresting to us? Do we read and watch only to have what we already think confirmed, or can we learn new ways of being and solving problems? When we go to the movies, watch a TV programme about law, or read a new legal novel, we might ask, just what are we bargaining for?

Popular Culture and the American Adversarial Ideology

*Michael Asimow**

Let's begin with a thought experiment. Imagine two courtroom movies. *Both involve jury trials.* The movie can involve a civil or a criminal case, whichever you prefer. The trial is fairly lengthy and involves sharply conflicting testimony from numerous witnesses, including experts. However, the legal procedures in the two movies are quite different.

In the first movie, the lawyers control the proceedings. The lawyers pick the jury, each side using all of its peremptory challenges. Each one makes an opening statement. The lawyers decide which witnesses to call and in which order. Each side calls its own paid expert witnesses, whose opinions differ sharply. Each lawyer cross examines the other's witnesses at length. Each lawyer delivers a lengthy closing argument. The judge has little to do during the trial except to keep order, rule on evidentiary objections, and instruct the jury. The jury retires. The first movie is a gripping, suspenseful drama. We have seen hundreds of similar films and television shows.

In the second movie, the judge has much greater control of the proceedings and the lawyers play subordinate roles. Before trial, the judge has been heavily involved in the discovery process. The judge has conferred extensively with the attorneys about the issues in the case, the structure of the trial, and the potential witnesses. There are no peremptory jury challenges (only challenges for cause). The lawyers do not make opening statements. The judge decides which witnesses to call to provide oral testimony and in which order they will be called. There are no separate plaintiff (or prosecution) and defence cases. The judge, not the lawyers, retains the expert witnesses. The judge questions the witnesses (or might allow them to testify in narrative form). The lawyers are allowed to question witnesses after the judge is finished.

Toward the end of the second movie, the lawyers deliver closing arguments. The judge instructs the jury. The instructions include the judge's summation of the evidence and may indicate a preference for the story told by one side or the other, although the jury is told that the decision is up to them. The jury retires.

* I am most grateful for helpful advice received from Richard Abel, Robert Altman, Paul Bergman, David Binder, Steve Derian, Max Factor III, Arthur Gilbert, Julian Mann, Albert Moore, Roger C Park, Charles Rosenberg, Tom Rowe, Lynn Stout, and Steven Yeazell, most of whom disagree with me, and for the research assistance furnished by JinAh Lee.

The second movie is rather boring since the lawyers have relatively little to do. Many audience members have fallen asleep before the movie ends. None of them has ever seen any movies or TV shows like this before.

After seeing the two movies, the members of the audience are asked which of the two systems they have just seen in action is more likely to uncover the truth about what really happened and to produce a just and correct outcome with a minimum of unnecessary cost and delay. First year students at UCLA School of Law (surveyed on the second day of classes) favoured the first system (lawyer control) by a vote of 61 to 16 (or about 79 per cent to 21 per cent).[1] I have conducted numerous informal conversations with lawyers and non-lawyers with about the same result: most Americans believe that lawyer control is much better and that judicial control is a terrible idea.[2]

I will refer to the lawyer-control system in the first movie as the adversary model. I will also refer to an 'adversarial ideology'. I take an 'ideology' to be a worldview that determines how society is and should be organized and how power is and should be exercised.[3] I assert that adversarialism is the dominant, usually unquestioned, ideology of the US justice system. As a consequence, the US employs a more extreme version of the adversarial system *than in any other country*.[4]

The adversary ideology presupposes that the best way to attain justice is to have two attorneys fight it out, then leave the decision to a neutral fact-finder. Thus a leading proponent of adversarialism writes:

The central precept of the adversary system is that out of the sharp clash of proofs presented by adversaries in a highly structured forensic setting is most likely to come the information

[1] This survey is cited herein as *2003 UCLA Law Student Survey*. I make no claim that first year American law students represent a valid sample of the population at large. They are obviously better educated than the general population. Since they have committed themselves to a profession deeply imbued with the adversary system, it is not surprising that they believe in that system even before studying it in law school. They also may be more competitive and argumentative than the general population.

I also asked the question at the beginning of my presentation at the Law and Popular Culture Conference at University College, London. I did not count the hands, but I would estimate the response as about 20 voting for judicial control and about three voting for lawyer control! Clearly, a group of academics is an even less representative sample of the general public than law students. Still, the participants at the UCL programme were predominantly from the UK, the US, and from Commonwealth countries. Only a few came from continental Europe. The preference of these academics for the inquisitorial system over the adversarial system which is used in almost all of their countries is a striking result.

[2] However, one study indicated that small claims court litigants expected that judges would help them make their claims and were disappointed and frustrated by the adversarial procedures actually used. W O'Barr and J Conley, 'Lay Expectations of the Civil Justice System' (1988) 22 *Law & Society Rev* 137, 159–160.

[3] See L Grossberg et al, *Media Making: Mass Media in a Popular Culture* (Thousand Oaks, Calif: 1998) 177–201; S Silbey, 'Ideology, Power, & Justice' in B Garth and S Sarat (eds), *Justice and Power in Sociolegal Studies* (Evanston, Illinois: 1998), 272. I seek to avoid the pejorative or political connotations which the word 'ideology' usually bears in discussions about popular culture.

[4] W Pizzi, *Trials Without Truth* (New York: 1999), Ch 6 (comparing criminal procedure in the US, UK, Norway, and Germany). The UK and Commonwealth countries make much less use of juries than the US and accord trial judges considerably greater judicial power in jury trials than occurs in the US.

upon which a neutral and passive decisionmaker can base the resolution of a litigated dispute acceptable to both the parties and society.[5]

I will refer to the judge-control system in the second movie as the 'inquisitorial model'. That model resembles the way in which criminal and civil trials are conducted outside the US and the UK and Commonwealth countries.[6] Note that the inquisitorial model has no counterpart in the actual procedures of any country, European or otherwise,[7] because my model leaves the *ultimate decision to a jury* rather than to a judge or a judge plus lay assessors.[8]

The unquestioned dominance of the adversarial ideology in the US seems paradoxical because the general public despises and distrusts lawyers. In a recent ABA poll conducted by M/A/R/C Research, only 14 per cent of the public were extremely or very confident in lawyers and 42 per cent were slightly or not all confident. People had far more confidence in judges: 32 per cent were extremely or very confident in judges, and only 22 per cent had no or only slight confidence in judges.[9] *Why, therefore, would people want to turn over something as important as control of the trial process to lawyers in whom they utterly lack confidence rather than to judges in whom they repose much greater confidence?* This article seeks the answer to this puzzle.

People might believe in the adversarial ideology for several reasons despite their distrust of lawyers and despite the practical problems with adversarial trials that are discussed in Part I. Some of these reasons are explored in Part II. However, Part III

[5] S Landsman, *The Adversary System: A Description and Defense* (Washington, D C: 1984) 2.

[6] The inquisitorial model is nothing like the Spanish inquisition and probably should be renamed the 'inquiry system' or some other title that does not suggest torture.

[7] In fact the civil and criminal procedures employed in both common law and civil law countries vary enormously, so there is no single adversarial system or inquisitorial system. *See* A Zuckerman, *Civil Justice in Crisis* (Oxford: 1999) (summarizing systems of many countries). In addition to the presence of juries in my inquisitorial model, numerous differences exist between that model and the real inquisitorial system. For example, the model does not suggest that we delegate pretrial investigation to the judge or that we bar settlements, guilty pleas, or plea bargains (as some inquisitorial systems do). Nor does the inquisitorial model suggest that lawyers abandon zealous representation or any of the canons of ethics. The privilege against self-incrimination and the reasonable doubt rule would remain intact (in fact most inquisitorial systems respect both).

[8] I hold the presence of a jury constant in both models because the 6th and 7th amendments to the US constitution (and corresponding provisions in state constitutions) guarantee the right to a jury in most civil and virtually all criminal cases. Since I want to talk about American procedural systems and ideologies, I accept this constitutional constraint. Juries are used sparingly in some countries outside the US. In the UK, juries are employed in serious criminal cases in the Crown Court and in defamation cases. Criminal juries are also used (although infrequently) in some European countries such as Norway, Denmark, Belgium, Russia or Spain. The fact that juries are sometimes employed in these countries shows that the jury system is compatible with inquisitorial procedures.

[9] American Bar Association, *Perceptions of the U.S. Justice System* (February, 1999) [*M/A/R/C Study*] 50. Only the media (at 8% confidence) ranked below lawyers. These results are consistent with a great deal of polling data. A Gallup poll of 27 November 2000, asked for the public's view of the honesty and ethics of 32 professions. Only 17% of the public gave lawyers a high or very high rating. The only professions ranked lower were newspaper reporters, insurance salesmen, advertising practitioners, and car salesmen. See generally M Asimow, 'Bad Lawyers in the Movies' (2000) 24 *Nova L Rev* 533, 536–549 (discussing many such polls and speculating as to the reasons for the abysmal public image of lawyers).

suggests that there is another important, though usually overlooked, reason for the dominance of the adversarial ideology. Popular culture has taught us to trust adversarialism and to regard the lawyer as the champion for our personal interests, indeed for our liberty. Almost from the cradle, we have been absorbing narratives that glorify the work of lawyers in securing justice. Even more important, these narratives teach us that the adversarial system discovers the truth about what really happened. We have internalized countless versions of the first movie, a story that exalts the work of lawyers within the adversarial process, but few if any versions of the second movie.[10] By endlessly valorizing the adversary system as a method for uncovering the truth, the media may have reinforced the adversary ideology.[11]

The purpose of this article is not to argue in favour of either the adversarial or inquisitorial models. Nor is it to set forth a case for any particular reform of the adversary system, or to describe or advocate any of a multitude of possible alternatives, or to argue that the benefits of a major change would outweigh the costs of making the transition.[12] The adversarial ideology is so deeply rooted in the US, so compatible with its competitive culture, and so well protected politically, that any fundamental change is unthinkable.[13] Instead, my objective is to speculate on why the adversarial ideology is so dominant in the US despite the unpopularity of lawyers and the practical problems of the adversarial system.

I. Comparing the Adversarial and Inquisitorial Systems

Most people, I believe, think the purpose of the dispute resolution system should be to achieve substantive justice at reasonable cost. For my purposes, substantive justice means discovering the 'truth' and reaching the 'right' result. Reaching the 'right'

[10] The film *Excellent Cadavers* (1999), an HBO movie produced for television, is the rare exception: a gripping film involving a heroic investigating judge that includes an inquisitorial trial. However, the trial was extremely unusual—hundreds of Mafia thugs were put on trial simultaneously in a Sicilian courtroom. In general, the absence of films about inquisitorial trials is quite understandable. Most would be rather undramatic. John Langbein discusses the undramatic nature of German civil trials and how these differ from the tense drama of US trials as shown in films and TV. 'The German Advantage in Civil Procedure' (1985) 52 *U of Chicago L Rev* 823, 831.

[11] Here I build on an insight tossed off by Carrie Menkel-Meadow in a footnote. 'The Trouble with the Adversary System in a Postmodern, Multicultural World' (1996) 38 *William & Mary L Rev* 5, 19, n 64.

[12] *See* J Leubsdorf, 'The Myth of Civil Procedure Reform', in Zuckerman, n 7 above, Ch 2 (questioning utility of various civil procedure reforms and noting difficulty of finding out whether they solved the problems or made them worse).

[13] Scholarly questioning of the adversary system dates back to Roscoe Pound's famous 1906 address to the ABA that condemned the sporting theory of justice. 'The Causes of Popular Dissatisfaction with the Administration of Justice' (1906) 29 *American Bar Association J* 395 (1906). See P Verkuil, 'The Search for a Legal Ethic: The Adversary System, Liberalism and Beyond' (1977) 60 *Soundings* 54, 58–61. Numerous American academics have urged the adoption of inquisitorial methods, but such suggestions have gone nowhere. See M Langer, 'From Legal Transplants to Legal Translations: The Globalization of Plea Bargaining and the Americanization Thesis in Criminal Procedure' (2004) 45 *Harvard Int LJ* 1 n 127; G Van Kessel, 'Adversary Excesses in the American Criminal Trial' (1992) 67 *Notre Dame L Rev* 403.

result in civil or criminal cases has (or at least often has) at least four components: (i) ascertaining the applicable law; (ii) ascertaining physical facts concerning what actually happened (who did what or said what to whom); (iii) ascertaining states of mind; (iv) correctly and wisely applying often vague and value-laden legal standards (such as reasonableness, malice aforethought, foreseeability or materiality) to the facts. In the US, task (i) is for the judge and tasks (ii), (iii), and (iv) are normally reserved for the jury.[14]

If the judge and jury correctly perform each of these chores, the system will deliver the 'right' result and achieve substantive justice. Substantive justice also means resolving disputes consistently so that people in like circumstances are treated alike.[15] Finally, substantive justice entails an efficiency component, meaning that the process does not consume too many public or private resources and it operates with reasonable promptness.

Many American lawyers (though certainly not all of them) object to the idea that the dispute resolution system should be held accountable for discovering the truth or delivering substantive justice.[16] Because we can never know with certainty the truth about disputed past events or states of the human mind, they argue that truth-finding is a dream. Perhaps they take the postmodern tack in questioning whether 'truth' exists at all. These lawyers believe we should seek 'procedural' rather than 'substantive' justice and be satisfied with 'trial truth' instead of 'factual truth'.[17]

[14] I recognize that this account oversimplifies what really happens in a well-tried case, particularly one tried under the adversarial system. In an adversarial trial, each lawyer seeks the jury's acceptance of a complex, value-laden narrative (carefully crafted by the lawyer before the trial) that expresses some familiar and compelling human meaning *See* R Burns, *A Theory of the Trial* (Princeton: 1999). The adversary system creates a large space within which the attorneys can structure their presentations and promote their chosen narrative approaches to the case. An inquisitorial model shrinks this space by dispensing with opening statements and delegating to the judge control of the framing of issues, the choice of witnesses and the order in which they testify. It also allows the judge to conduct the initial questioning of the witnesses which substitutes in part for both direct and cross examination. Finally it allows the judge to sum up the evidence for the jury. Thus the inquisitorial approach would limit (though not eliminate) counsel's ability to craft and present to the jury a persuasive narrative account of the events that created the dispute. Since I believe that the jury is often led astray by the narrative-based tactics of skilful adversarial lawyers (particularly those drawn from pop culture sources), the inquisitorial approach may be more likely to deliver a 'correct' result, meaning one that more closely conforms to the truth. See generally R Sherwin, *When Law Goes Pop* (Chicago: 2000). Burns would disagree. *See A Theory of the Trial*, Ch 8.

[15] See C Sunstein et al, 'Predictably Incoherent Judgments' (2002) 54 *Stanford L Rev* 1153 (justice requires that outcomes in different cases must be consistent).

[16] A memorable statement of this view occurs in the film *A Civil Action* (1998). Defence lawyer Jerome Facher (Robert Duvall) says to plaintiff's lawyer Jan Schlichtmann (John Travolta) as they sit in the hallway awaiting the verdict and discussing settlement: 'If you're really looking for the truth, Jan, look for it where it is. At the bottom of a bottomless pit.' Apparently, Facher really spoke words to that effect. See C Harr, *A Civil Action* (New York: 1995) 340.

[17] See W Wendel, 'The Bilateral Ethics of Narrative: Toward a General Theory of Deception in Lawyering' (2003) (available from Social Science Research Network, http://law.wlu.edu/lawcenter/papers). Burns refers to this as 'practical truth'. He says: 'Thus the truth of trial judgments rests on the primary (or ultimacy) of "the practical". To say something useful about truth in the context of the trial is thus "to explore practice rather than theory . . . action rather than contemplation." The kinds of

If we furnish the contestants with a fair process, consisting in part of combat between attorneys, whatever emerges from that process is 'trial truth'.[18] Lawyers also tend to brush aside considerations of efficiency or consistency as immaterial; what counts is a fair process, even if it is costly and slow and produces inconsistent or unwise outcomes.

But I wonder how many ordinary people agree with the lawyers. Are they really satisfied to settle for procedural justice, for 'trial truth'? Do they not believe that systems that are *more likely* to discover factual truth and achieve wise and consistent application of legal principles are better than ones that are *less likely* to achieve these things? Do they not think that a system that is cheaper and quicker is better than one that is costlier and slower? I think most people expect their justice system to deliver truth, accuracy, wisdom, consistency and efficiency. They expect fair procedures that assure that the voices and stories of both sides will be heard and considered by an impartial decisionmaker, but not necessarily extremely adversarial procedures. Without considering the alternatives, most Americans unquestioningly endorse the adversary approach to civil and criminal litigation.

A good way to evaluate procedural systems is to balance three fundamental criteria: accuracy, acceptability to the parties, and efficiency.[19] This is a consequentialist or utilitarian approach to determining what the best procedure might be.[20] I consider some non-consequentialist arguments in Part II.

Ideally, a good system should reach accurate and consistent results, should be viewed as fair by the disputants, and should function efficiently (meaning with as little delay and with as little cost to litigants and to the public as possible). However, there are always tradeoffs between the criteria. For example, providing numerous levels of appeal to make the results more accurate or consistent could serve the goals of accuracy and acceptability but be unacceptably slow and costly. On the other hand, a process might be efficient and accurate but totally unacceptable to the disputants who are subject to it. In the following discussion, I attempt a rough balancing of these three criteria. This balancing analysis seems to cast

issues presented by the trial 'are not to be judged by limiting oneself to [or by ignoring!) questions like, "Does that assertion get it right." . . . The truth that emerges at trial is, then, analogous to that which is implicit in a traditional mimetic theory of drama. Drama does not produce a copy of reality; rather, it manifests an aspect of reality that is not visible outside the artistic representation.' Burns, n 14 above, 233, 235.

[18] Landsman, n 5 above, 37: 'Truth is not the end the courts seek. Truth is nothing more than a means of achieving the end, justice. The disclosure of material facts is not the only means of achieving justice, and to treat it as the end is to open the way to unsavory abuses.'

[19] See M Asimow, 'Toward a New California Administrative Procedure Act: Adjudication Fundamentals' (1992) 39 *UCLA L Rev* 1067, 1081; P Verkuil, 'The Emerging Concept of Administrative Procedure' (1978) 78 *Columbia L Rev* 258, 279–293.

[20] Jeremy Bentham wrote: 'A measure of government . . . may be said to be conformable to or dictated by the principle of utility, when . . . the tendency which it has to augment the happiness of the community is greater than any which it has to diminish it'. J Burns and H Hart (eds), *An Introduction to the Principles of Morals and Legislation* (London: 1983).

doubt on the utility of the adversary system.[21] If that is so, people's adherence to the adversarial ideology becomes an even more puzzling phenomenon.

A. Accuracy

A good dispute resolution system should deliver 'accurate' results.[22] As discussed above, accuracy means correctly ascertaining past facts and states of mind and wisely and consistently applying legal rules to those facts. In this article, I compare adversarial and inquisitorial models, *both* of which culminate in jury verdicts. I ask whether an inquisitorial trial might result in more accurate and fewer capricious jury verdicts than are generated by adversary trials.

This inquiry immediately runs into difficulty because there is such profound disagreement about the performance of juries in civil and criminal cases. Some scholars think juries do an excellent job in both simple and complex cases and therefore would discount the need for any significant changes in the system.[23] Others are less sanguine and believe that jury errors are common in both simple and complex cases.[24] An unpredictable or capricious verdict—even an extreme outlier—is always possible, something that trial lawyers never forget.[25]

[21] This article exaggerates the differences between the adversary system and the inquisitorial system in actual practice. Thus, in the adversary system, the vast majority of cases are settled rather than tried, often with the aid of mediators. Of the relatively few cases that are tried, a large number are tried to a judge rather than a jury. In civil jury trials, judges have numerous techniques to take the case from the jury such as summary judgment or directed verdict. Through motions in limine, judges control what evidence the jury will hear. Particularly in bench trials, judges are more active than the model would suggest. They frequently participate in questioning witnesses, for example. In addition, many important segments of the American justice system are more inquisitorial than the trial courts. For example, in both arbitration and administrative agency adjudication, decisionmakers are active in shaping the issues, protecting unrepresented or under-represented parties, questioning witnesses, and in trying to ferret out the truth.

[22] Accuracy in adjudication is important because it helps assure that legal rules will function as intended with the least amount of adverse social and economic consequences. See generally L Kaplow, 'The Value of Accuracy in Adjudication: An Economic Analysis' (1994) 23 *J of Legal Studies* 307. Of course, the legal system often consciously departs from the goal of finding accurate results because other values trump accuracy. The law of privilege, for example, sacrifices accuracy to other objectives. However, all other things being equal, an accurate result is better than an inaccurate result.

[23] See, eg, N Vidmar, 'The Performance of the American Civil Jury: An Empirical Perspective' (1998) 40 *Arizona L Rev* 849 (reporting many studies); S Diamond and J Casper, 'Blindfolding the Jury to Verdict Consequences: Damages, Experts, and the Civil Jury' (1992) 26 *Law & Society Rev* 512 (juries are active information processors in complex civil case and well able to deal with expert testimony).

[24] F Strier, *Reconstructing Justice* (Chicago: 1994) Ch 4; R Hastie and W Viscusi, 'What Juries Can't Do Well: The Jury's Performance as a Risk Manager' (1998) 40 *Arizona L Rev* 901 (judges better able to deal with risk judgments than juries); G Priest, 'Justifying the Civil Jury' in R Litan (ed), *Verdict: Assessing the Civil Jury System* (Washington, DC: 1993) 103, 129–130 ('the civil jury is an engine of uncertainty'); R Kagan, *Adversarial Legalism* (Cambridge, Mass: 2001) 114–115 (judges reduce jury damage awards 20–25% of the time).

[25] The fact that mean jury verdicts are much higher than median verdicts suggests that outlier verdicts (which raise the arithmetic average) are not uncommon. See R MacCoun, 'Inside the Black Box: What Empirical Research Tells Us About Decisionmaking by Civil Juries,' in Litan, n 24 above, 137, 147–150; P Schuck, Mapping the Debate on Jury Reform, ibid, 306, 312 (reporting research on large variability in jurors' assessments of damages).

The leading researchers on the American jury indicate that trial judges disagree with jury verdicts in about 20 per cent of both civil and criminal cases.[26]

Of course, regardless of one's assessment of the quality of jury verdicts and regardless of what system of trial is employed, some jury verdicts will necessarily be capricious (of course, hopefully fewer rulings of judges will be capricious also). There might be procedural reforms that would preserve the political and legitimating advantages of jury trials while reducing the risk of jury errors or outlier verdicts.

1. Disparities in Lawyer Skills and Resources

The adversary system presupposes a fair fight between lawyers who serve as the champions of their clients. If such a system is to deliver accurate results, there must be at least a rough equality between the two sides in their advocacy skills, their experience, and in the resources they bring to the struggle.[27]

If one side is substantially superior to the other, either in lawyer skills or experience or in resources, the likely result is a mismatch.[28] Such imbalances are, in fact, quite common.[29] Frequently, one lawyer is substantially superior in skill and experience to the other. Even more frequently, one lawyer (or more likely a team of lawyers) is backed by much greater resources than the other side and can afford to spend vastly more money in investigation, trial preparation, and trial resources. Thus the better financed team can purchase such costly inputs as jury

[26] In their seminal studies of American juries, Harry Kalven and Hans Zeisel found that judges usually agreed with juries, but there was a significant band of disagreement. In both criminal and civil cases, judges disagreed with the jury verdict about 20% of the time. See H Kalven, Jr, 'The Dignity of the Civil Jury' (1964) 50 *Virginia L Rev* 1055, 1064–1065. In the 20% band of disagreement between judge and jury, in criminal cases judges would have convicted the defendant much more often than the jury. In civil cases, when the judge and jury disagreed about liability, the differences were about equally split between plaintiff and defendant. When both agreed on a plaintiff verdict, the judge would have awarded about 20% lower damages. I regard these differences as quite significant. Diamond reports similar results in more recent studies. S Diamond, 'Convergence and Complementarity between Professional Judges and Lay Adjudicators' in P van Koppen and S Penrod (eds), *Adversarial versus Inquisitorial Justice* (New York: 2003) 325. Diamond also reports studies in which judges express strong support of the jury system. ibid, at 322–325.

Obviously we have no way to know who was 'right' when the judge and the jury disagreed. However, in my view, it is more likely that the judge was correct, given the judge's vast experiential advantage. I have reservations about the Kalven and Zeisel results. I believe that the actual rate of disagreement must be higher than 20%, because the judge was asked about agreement with a jury verdict *after* knowing what that verdict was. There is a natural tendency in a case involving a close factual or legal issue to shrug and assume the jury made a reasonable call. This is an example of the post hoc fallacy that is often noted by cognitive psychology researchers: people make very different assessments and predictions depending on whether their decision is made in hindsight or foresight.

[27] W Rubenstein, 'The Concept of Equality in Civil Procedure' (2002) 23 *Cardozo L Rev* 1873–1874; Menkel-Meadow, n 11 above, 22. Langbein refers to the 'wealth effect' which inevitably arises in an adversary system in which one side has greater resources than the other. J Langbein, *The Origins of Adversary Criminal Trial* (Oxford: 2003), 314–318, 332–333.

[28] Indeed, there is truth in the observation that a jury consists of 12 people whose job it is to decide which side had the better lawyer. M Frankel, *Partisan Justice* (New York: 1978) 34.

[29] Strier, n 24 above, 75–82 (reporting a survey of 3,800 jurors; one-third observed a difference in courtroom skills and felt it probably affected the verdict). *See also* J Frank, *Courts on Trial* (New York: 1969), 94–97; Kagan, n 24 above, 93–96.

consultants,[30] the best qualified experts, audio-visual aids, computer simulations, and the like.[31] Indeed, it is frequently true in our modern litigation system that one side cannot afford a lawyer at all and is acting pro se.[32] Pro se litigants are likely to be annihilated by the opposing lawyer. Under modern conditions, little is done to equalize resources; legal service programmes are generally underfunded or defunded entirely. Public defender systems groan under impossible caseloads and a severe shortage of resources.[33]

Obviously, not every trial involves a mismatch. Some civil cases involve pitched battles between large law firms with virtually unlimited litigation budgets. A few major tort cases pit experienced and well-financed plaintiffs' firms against equally able defence teams. Occasional criminal cases (especially involving white-collar crime) pit determined and adequately resourced prosecutors against well-financed defendants. But these are not typical situations (and when they do occur they tend to generate costly pretrial discovery and complex trials).

Where inequalities of skill or resources emerge, a basic tenet of the adversary system is that the judge should remain neutral and not intervene to rectify the imbalance.[34] If an inept attorney has overlooked a vital argument or issue or failed to object to inadmissible evidence, or made some other tactical blunder, the judge is expected to keep silent.[35] If the less skilful, or less resourced, litigant loses a winnable case, so be it.[36] As in a baseball game, the umpire should continue to call balls and strikes the same even if the score is 22–0.

[30] Because the inquisitorial model dispenses with peremptory jury challenges, the wealthier litigant's ability to hire jury consultants will be neutralized. Dispensing with peremptories would also prevent the parties from indulging their stereotypes and engaging in various sorts of discrimination in jury selection.

[31] Strier, n 24 above, 178–180. *See* M Galanter, 'Why the "Haves" Come out Ahead: Speculations on the Limits of Legal Change' (1974) 9 *Law & Society Rev* 95 (emphasizing the advantage that repeat players have over one-shot litigants).

[32] Thus, a 1990 study in the Maricopa County, Arizona, domestic relations court found that in 88% of divorce cases, at least one of the parties was unrepresented; both parties were unrepresented in 52% of the cases. American Bar Association, *Litigants Without Lawyers* (2002). See also American Bar Association, Commission on the 21st Century Judiciary, *Justice in Jeopardy* (2003) 53–54. Nolo Press, Berkeley California, publishes a successful line of books advising people how to solve their legal problems, including engaging in civil and criminal litigation, without the aid of lawyers.

[33] Kagan, n 24 above, 94 (noting that public defenders seldom visit crime scenes or make pretrial motions).

[34] Some judges will help unrepresented parties or overwhelmed attorneys in small ways such as by suggesting evidence objections or helping them put questions to witnesses in correct form. It is unclear whether this is appropriate, since it would seem to compromise the judge's impartiality. See *Litigants without Lawyers*, n 32 above, 11, 15.

[35] In administrative adjudication, an administrative law judge is expected to rectify such inequalities to make sure that the public purposes behind the regulatory statute in question are served. See, eg, *Echevarria v Secretary of Health and Human Services*, 685 F2d 751 (2d Cir 1982) (where claimant is unrepresented, administrative law judge has duty to explore for all the relevant facts). Not so in the judicial system.

[36] 'In an ideal adversary system, the less skillful antagonist is expected to lose the dispute, which under the laissez-faire notion is the proper outcome.' Marian Neef and Stuart Nagel, 'The Adversary Nature of the American Legal System from a Historical Perspective' (1974) 20 *New York Law Forum* 123, 162. See also Frankel, n 28 above, 121–125.

An inquisitorial model could be more attentive to issues of distributive justice than the adversarial model. In the inquisitorial model, differences between the lawyers become less important. The judge's control over the proceedings functions as an equalizer. The judge frames the issues, selects and questions the witnesses,[37] and sums up the evidence for the jury. The lawyers have less space in which to employ tricks and stratagems and the jury should be less likely to be affected by disparities between lawyer skills and resources.

2. The Trial Process

A trial lawyer's responsibility under the adversary model is not to assist and facilitate the jury's search for the truth, but, whenever possible within the rules, to obstruct and obfuscate that search if such favours the interests of the client. I believe this system excessively rewards the advocacy skills of the attorneys, encourages one or both attorneys to sow confusion, and makes jury errors more likely than under competing systems.[38] The inquisitorial model might lessen the number of jury errors. Although space limitations preclude an extensive discussion of the differences between trials under the inquisitorial and adversarial models, I believe that there are several ways that an inquisitorial model might improve the accuracy of jury verdicts. These include the use of neutral rather than biased expert witnesses, primary witness questioning by the judge rather than the lawyers (which might lessen the effects of witness coaching), a trial structure that is less confusing to the jury, and the judge's obligation to summarize the evidence as part of the jury instruction process.

B. Acceptability to the Parties

The prevailing wisdom in the social-scientific literature is that litigants strongly prefer a system in which they (and their counsel) control the trial.[39] The large body

[37] In inquisitorial trials, the rules of evidence are much relaxed in comparison to those in adversarial trials with the result that more relevant evidence can be considered by the trier of fact. However, because the inquisitorial model discussed in this article preserves the jury, it might be necessary to retain some rules of evidence. Doing so would complicate the question whether witnesses should be questioned by the judge. Because of space limitations, I have excluded the question whether the rules of evidence should differ as between the two models.

[38] Strier, n 24 above, Ch 3; Langbein, n 27 above, 332; Menkel-Meadow, n 11 above, 21–22; Frankel, n 28 above, 75. Frankel states that it is the rare case in which either side yearns to have the witnesses, or anyone, give *the whole truth*. 'The Search for Truth: An Umpireal View' (1975) 123 *U of Pennsylvania L Rev* 1031, 1038 (emphasis in original). According to David Luban, the two adversary attorneys 'are each under an obligation to present the facts in the manner most consistent with their client's position—to prevent the introduction of unfavorable evidence, to undermine the credibility of opposing witnesses, to set unfavorable facts in a context in which their importance is minimized, to attempt to provoke inferences in their client's favor. The assumption is that two such accounts will cancel out, leaving the truth of the matter. But there is no earthly reason to think this will happen—the facts may simply pile up the confusion.' *Lawyers and Justice* (Princeton: 1988) 69–70.

[39] See generally E Lind and T Tyler, *The Social Psychology of Procedural Justice* (New York: 1988); T Tyler, 'Justice and Power in Civil Dispute Processing' in Garth and Sarat, n 3 above, 309.

of research in support of this view is derived from the seminal experiments conducted in the early 1970s by Thibaut and Walker.[40] Thibaut-Walker staged a simulated 'trial' involving undergraduates who were found 'guilty' or 'innocent' of business plagiarism by a 'judge'. Half of the subjects experienced an 'adversarial' trial, meaning that each of the subjects chose 'lawyers' who argued on the subjects' behalf to the 'judge'. The other half experienced an 'inquisitorial' trial, meaning that the subjects did not have their own lawyers; instead, a single appointed 'lawyer' made arguments for both sides to a 'judge'.

By substantial margins, the students expressed greater satisfaction with the fairness of the adversarial procedure than with the inquisitorial procedure. This result held *regardless* of whether the subjects believed they were 'innocent' or 'guilty' of the charges against them and *regardless* of whether they were actually found 'innocent' or 'guilty' by the 'judge'.[41] Thibaut-Walker's findings are the basis for many subsequent works involving the social psychology of the dispute resolution system. They showed that the perception of litigants that they have been treated fairly is extremely important *even if they are disappointed with the substantive outcome*.[42]

I do not question the fundamental insight of Thibaut-Walker and many subsequent studies that procedural justice matters greatly independent of the outcome. People are deeply concerned that decisionmakers seem neutral, unbiased, and honest as well as fair, polite, and respectful.[43] They care greatly about the opportunity for self-expression. And litigants are sensitive to whether they (or their advocates) control the proceedings, because that affects whether they will have sufficient opportunity to tell their side of the story. However, it may be that the disputants are concerned less about the details of how control is exercised than their perception that the decisionmaker is trying to be fair, respectful of their rights, and polite.[44]

[40] J Thibaut and L Walker, *Procedural Justice: A Psychological Analysis* (Hillsdale NJ: 1975) Ch 8.

[41] Unsurprisingly, those found innocent were much happier with either process than those found guilty, but in each of the various combinations, the subjects found the adversary approach to be fairer than the inquisitorial approach.

[42] Thibaut and Walker also surveyed 'observers' who had watched the proceedings but were not themselves 'litigating'. The observers agreed that the adversarial approach was better. Thibaut and Walker wondered whether their results mirrored the fact that American students are accustomed to adversary procedures so would naturally prefer them. They found that English, French and German students had about the same preferences as the American students. This experiment involved a written questionnaire describing different trial and decisional models, not a simulated trial. J Thibaut et al, 'Procedural Justice as Fairness' (1974) 26 *Stanford L Rev* 1271.

[43] T Tyler, *Why People Obey the Law* (New Haven, Ct: 1990), Ch 11.

[44] See Lind and Tyler, n 39 above, 107–110; Tyler, in Garth and Sarat, n 3, above, 326–327. Tyler conducted an ethnographic study of Chicago residents who had actual experiences with the police and courts (as opposed to Thibaut who studied college students who had no such experience). Tyler was able to derive a ranking of the importance in the minds of respondents of the various elements of procedural justice. He found that the decisionmaker's effort to be fair ranked first and ethicality (meaning politeness and respect for the rights of the parties) ranked second. Representation (which includes the extent to which the disputants have an opportunity to present arguments, be listened to, and have their views considered) ranked third. Tyler, n 43 above, Ch 11.

I do not believe that the Thibaut-Walker findings can be easily applied to the choice between my adversarial and inquisitorial models.[45] In my inquisitorial model, each litigant chooses its own advocate, whereas this was not true in any of the Thibaut-Walker inquisitorial simulations. Under my inquisitorial model, the advocates have numerous opportunities to represent their clients. For example, they make arguments to the judge before trial concerning the framing of issues, identity of witnesses, the order in which they will testify, and the questions the judge will ask them. The lawyers may question witnesses after the judge does so and seek thereby to discredit what the witness has said. They give closing arguments to the jury setting forth their interpretation of witness testimony and fitting it into the narrative that favours their client. There is ample opportunity for the litigants to tell their story to the judge and jury and have it fully considered.

It is wholly understandable that experimental subjects in the Thibaut-Walker study would distrust a system in which they are deprived of their own champion. Naturally, they are suspicious of a system in which they must depend on the judge alone or on a single assigned 'investigator' to state their side of the dispute fairly. It is not so clear whether the subjects would equally resent an inquisitorial model like the one I propose: the litigants have a lawyer who zealously represents their interests at every stage of the proceedings. Their stories and voices are clearly and repeatedly heard even though a judge, rather than the lawyers, controls the course of the trial.

Indeed, a follow-up study reported by Thibaut and Walker suggests that parties who can choose their own advocates find little difference between an active and a passive judge.[46] Here the subjects were undergraduates in both the US and Paris. The case was a simulated trial involving an assault arising out of a fight in a bar and a possible self-defence excuse. The 'plaintiff' and 'defendant' each chose advocates to present their side of the dispute, but in half the cases the 'judge' asked the questions and in the other half the advocates presented the evidence without interference from the judge. The subjects in both the US and France were *equally satisfied with both versions.*

Assume, however, that Thibaut and Walker's findings that people prefer adversarial approaches could be generalized to my quite different models. Even so, it is not clear that the results derived from studying undergraduate students in a pristine environment would describe the opinions of real litigants in our real and heavily flawed civil and criminal justice systems. The stakes were very low; the students did not have to pay their lawyers, and the whole process wrapped up in an hour. Nor were they subjected to the problem of capricious or confused juries,[47]

[45] Obviously, Thibaut and Walker did not consider the allocation of responsibilities within the context of jury trials; they considered only the allocation of control between counsel and judge where the judge is the trier of fact.

[46] Thibaut and Walker, n 40 above, Ch 10.

[47] Thibaut and Walker conceded that an inquisitorial approach 'is more likely to produce truth' as compared to an adversarial system. They were concerned only with acceptability of the two systems. J Thibaut and L Walker, 'A Theory of Procedure' (1978) 66 *California L Rev* 541.

inconsistent results,[48] lawyer strategies that obscure the truth, or inequalities between advocates of skill, experience or resources. Confronted with some of these rather unpleasant realities of the adversarial litigation process, each of which might be ameliorated in a judge-controlled jury trial, the undergraduates might reconsider their preferences.

C. Efficiency

Most people hope that their justice system will deliver outcomes in a reasonable time and at reasonable cost to themselves and to the taxpayers. Thus in an efficient system, a unit of justice is delivered at lower cost and greater speed than in an inefficient system. Defenders of the adversary system are likely to admit that it is not a very efficient process but they say that efficiency does not matter. You should not ration justice, they say.

But efficiency does matter. Litigation has become the major profit centre for large law firms; the major business litigation and tort defence cases in which they specialize are immensely profitable. But these profits come from the pockets of the litigants and are ultimately passed on to consumers. The costs of dispute settlement are a deadweight loss to the parties and to the economy as a whole. Higher litigation costs price potential users out of the justice system (either as plaintiffs or defendants).[49] Delays in trying cases that are ready for trial are unconscionably long in many jurisdictions.[50] Many civil cases involve long and costly discovery[51] and produce lengthy and complex trials. They are very costly for the litigants[52] and for the taxpayers who pay the costs of judges and courthouses.[53] Anything that

[48] Tyler found that consistency was the major criterion on which people assessed procedural justice. Tyler, n 43 above, 120.

[49] Richard L Marcus, 'Malaise of the Litigation Superpower' in Zuckerman, n 7 above, 92–95.

[50] ibid, 88–92.

[51] The process of pretrial discovery in civil litigation consumes substantial time and resources. Some discovery is necessary to prevent trial surprises and some of it facilitates settlement by exposing the weaknesses in each side's case. Unfortunately, a good deal of pretrial discovery is intended to run up the costs of the opposition to force settlement. Some unnecessary discovery is designed to generate additional fees and some to prevent any possibility of malpractice claims. A switch from an adversarial to an inquisitorial model might transfer responsibility for pretrial fact development and case management from counsel to judges by making discovery a matter of judicial discretion rather than a matter of right. See Zuckerman, n 7 above, 16–18, which discusses recent changes in the English civil procedure rules to give judges much greater control over discovery. The objective is to save expense, place the parties on an equal footing, and ensure that the allocation of resources to a given case is proportionate to the amount involved, each party's financial position, and the complexity of the issues. Because of space limitations, I do not discuss reform of the pretrial investigatory phase in this paper.

[52] Kagan, n 24 above, 104–106, discusses the high attorneys' fees incurred in American civil cases, especially in cases involving small stakes. These fees are far higher than in comparison countries.

[53] Estimates of the cost of judicial time range between $600 and $1,750 per hour, only a small part of which is offset by litigation filing fees. Marcus, n 49 above, 95.

might speed up and simplify trials, and might decrease both the public and private costs of the justice system,[54] would be worth considering.

The costs and delays engendered in the adversary system undoubtedly induce many litigants to settle cases that they would prefer to try.[55] Only a small percentage of civil or criminal cases are actually tried (about 3 per cent of federal civil cases, between 4 per cent and 12 per cent of California civil cases).[56] Many are dismissed by the courts on pretrial motions (such as demurrer or summary judgment) and many parties default or fail to press their case (about 30 per cent on average).[57] Perhaps 60 per cent of civil cases are settled through negotiation.[58] As many as 98 per cent of criminal cases are plea bargained.

When settlements are consensual and reflect a shared appraisal of the value of the claim, such settlements are good for the justice system and plainly efficient. Settlements can be win-win affairs in which the parties come up with compromises that could not be achieved through a trial.[59] However, some settlements are dubious (though the exact number of these is unclear). Some plaintiffs must settle cheaply because they cannot pay the costs of an epic struggle in court or endure delays sometimes amounting to several years until trial and appeal are concluded.[60] In other cases, defendants enter into nuisance settlements because it is cheaper to settle than to contest a claim that they believe is without any merit. Settlement denies the party who is in the right a judicial judgment affirming the value of his claim and may provide less than complete justice, especially in complex cases, cases involving groups, continuing disputes, and cases involving important public interest concerns.[61]

In criminal cases, some plea bargains are desirable because they represent a shared appraisal of the risk of conviction and the attributes of the defendant. Many

[54] Injury victims receive only about 50% of the premiums paid by for accident insurance. Legal fees of claimants consume about 30% of the total compensation paid to plaintiffs, and defendants' legal fees range from 16% in auto cases to 28% in non-auto cases. See M Franklin and R Rabin, *Tort Law and Alternatives* (7th edn, Westbury, NY: 2001) 786–787. Kagan, n 24 above, 82, quotes Albert Alschuler: 'The American jury trial . . . has become one of the most cumbersome and expensive fact-finding mechanisms that humankind has devised'.

[55] Some lawyers bemoan the plummeting rate of cases that are actually tried. They argue that more cases should be tried to create precedents and jury verdicts that can be used as markers and to allow more people to have their day in court. See H Samborn, 'The Vanishing Trial', *American Bar Association Journal* (October 2002), 24.

[56] See Marcus, n 49 above, Ch 3, 82, 85, 114. These figures represent the percentage of civil cases tried of those that are filed. Perhaps ten disputes are settled without any litigation filings at all for every case that is actually filed. D Trubek et al, 'The Costs of Ordinary Litigation' (1983) 31 *UCLA L Rev* 72, 86–87.

[57] ibid, 82.

[58] ibid.

[59] Because of space limitations, I cannot explore alternate dispute resolution here. Negotiation, mediation, and arbitration are normally less adversarial than trials.

[60] See O Fiss, 'Against Settlement' (1984) 93 *Yale L Rev* 1073, 1076–1078 (plaintiff may need damages immediately; may be unable to finance the litigation including the various discovery costs and attorneys' fees).

[61] ibid, 1085–1087; Frank B Cross, 'In Praise of Irrational Plaintiffs' (2000) 86 *Cornell L Rev* 1 (settlement deprives plaintiff of day in court and opportunity for vindication).

plea bargains, however, are coerced by the cost of trial (particularly when the defendant is paying for his lawyer) or by the caseload. Both prosecutors and public defenders must deal somehow with an enormous caseload that precludes either trials or carefully tailored plea bargains. Such massive utilization of plea bargains can be justified only on expediency grounds.[62] Depending on relative bargaining positions and the state of the caseload, defendants may receive a sentence much more or much less severe than is merited. Often the result is inconsistent with that in similar cases. The prevalence of plea bargaining probably leads to prosecutorial overcharging (so the prosecutor will have bargaining leverage) and it may encourage legislators to make criminal penalties harsher than would otherwise be the case. Perhaps worst of all, plea bargains deny the defendant and the crime victim their day in court. A system that made trials quicker and cheaper should result in fewer civil settlements or criminal plea bargains.[63]

Finally, the taxpayers who must pay the costs of the dispute settlement system such as the salaries of judges and upkeep of the courthouse get less and less for each dollar they invest in that system. Reducing the cost and delay of trials would be a very good thing.[64]

How might the inquisitorial model save time and money? First, it would greatly speed up jury selection by abolishing most voir dire and peremptory challenges. That would put jury consultants out of business. Putting the judge in charge of the trial could also save time. At present, judges can do little to prevent the calling of redundant witnesses or to cut off unproductive lines of questioning. Under an inquisitorial approach, there would be fewer witnesses called, and the examination of each witness would take less time. Probably opening statements would be dispensed with.

On the other hand, it may be that the inquisitorial model would actually save little time or money because it preserves the right to a jury trial. Jury trials always take longer than bench trials. The judge's new responsibility to sum up the evidence would consume additional time. And it is possible that the same number of witnesses will testify for about the same amount of time as under the adversarial

[62] See, eg, A Alschuler, 'The Prosecutor's Role in Plea Bargaining' (1968) 36 *U of Chicago L Rev* 50; John Langbein, 'Land Without Plea Bargaining: How the Germans Do It' (1979) 78 *Michigan L Rev* 204; Van Kessel, n 13 above; Pizzi, n 4 above, Ch 4.

[63] See eg S Schulhofer, 'Is Plea Bargaining Inevitable?' (1984) 97 *Harvard L Rev* 1037 (discussing Philadelphia practice of conducting relatively short but contested non-jury bench trials; system allowed far higher percentage of criminal cases to be tried rather than plea bargained). Also contrast the British magistrates' courts where 98% of the cases are efficiently tried in a dignified way by lay judges who conscientiously consider defendant's individual circumstances. Kagan, n 24 above, 89–93.

[64] Even Cross, a staunch defender of the adversary system, concedes the importance of efficiency. Cross, n 61 above, 206. Samuel Gross disagrees. He argues that the high cost of litigation forces settlement (sometimes in ways that are different from results that would have been obtained in court) and leads to under-enforcement of bad laws. 'Under this view, efficiency is a troublesome measure: useful in part, irrelevant in part, and potentially stifling and destructive.' 'The American Advantage: The Value of Inefficient Litigation', (1987) 85 *Michigan L Rev* 734, 757. I disagree. Of course, efficiency is not the only criterion for designing a procedural system but it is certainly important and, all other things being equal, efficiency is better than inefficiency.

model. On the other hand, given an inquisitorial model, some litigants would probably opt for a bench trial rather than a jury trial, since they would be fearful of the judge's ability to influence the jury. Thus the number of jury trials might be reduced. Therefore, the question whether there would be significant savings cannot be answered on an a priori basis.

II. Reasons for Belief in the Adversarial Ideology

This section explores, in a brief and tentative way, some of the reasons (both instrumental and non-instrumental in nature) why people might justify their belief in the adversary ideology, even if they distrust lawyers and even if they would otherwise prefer a system more oriented to truth-seeking. Many of these reasons are closely related to one another and people are likely to believe in several of them (or even all of them).

A. Tradition and Lack of Knowledge of Alternatives

Of course, an important reason why people believe in the adversarial ideology is that it has always been done that way and they know of no alternative. People are often surprised and intrigued to learn that the US brand of adversarialism is more extreme than that which is practised anywhere else in the world, including the UK.

Thus in the 1999 ABA M/A/R/C/ survey, only 30 per cent of respondents were either extremely or very confident in the US justice system. Yet, remarkably, 80 per cent agreed or strongly agreed to the statement 'in spite of its problems, the American justice system is still the best in the world!'[65] Needless to say, few, if any, of these respondents had a clue as to what the justice systems in the rest of the world look like.

However, people may believe there are important reasons to adhere to traditional ways of resolving disputes even when they are aware of the alternatives.[66] Certainly many of the framers of the Constitution and the Bill of Rights were familiar with different models of dispute resolution. Various provisions of the founding documents seem more consistent with an adversarial than an inquisitorial approach to litigation.[67] These include the due process and self-incrimination clauses of the 5th amendment, the rights to jury trial in the 6th and 7th amendments, the right to confrontation and counsel in criminal cases in the 6th amendment, the right to bail

[65] M/A/R/C study, n 9 above, 50, 59. Of the same respondents, 78% agreed or strongly agreed that the 'jury system is the most fair way to determine the guilt or innocence or a person accused of a crime;' 69% agreed or strongly agreed that 'juries are the most important part of our judicial system'.

[66] See J Molot, 'An Old Judicial Role for a New Litigation Era' (2003) 113 *Yale L Rev* 27.

[67] Molot, n 66 above, argues that the adversarial system is more consistent with these constitutional provisions than an inquisitorial system would be. Nevertheless, I believe my inquisitorial model is consistent with these constitutional provisions.

in the 8th amendment, and the limits on suspension of habeas corpus in Article I section 9.

In addition, traditionalists point to the law of unintended consequences and argue that the devil you know is usually better than the one you don't. An ideal inquisitorial system may look better than a flawed adversarial one, but the ideal system will have its own flaws if it is ever put into practice and turned over to fallible human beings. Moreover, the substantial transitional costs of changing from one system to a radically different one may be a sufficient reason to leave well enough alone.

B. Personal Autonomy

The adversary system allows a litigant to make the major strategic decisions about his own case such as whether to settle the case and on what terms. It also allows the lawyers to make the tactical decisions about how to conduct the case, such as which jurors to challenge, what the issues are, what witnesses to call, what questions to ask, and what arguments to make to the jury.[68] Judges make none of those decisions. Thus the adversary system exalts the value of personal autonomy.

The idea that we should make our own decisions about how to conduct our own lives is deeply cherished in Anglo-American society. Our economic system is rooted in personal choice, laissez faire values. The market allows a person great freedom in making decisions to buy or sell or in choosing to take risks that may lead to success or failure. Conservative economists believe that government regulation can be justified only in cases of market failure, such as the failure to internalize externalities. Although litigation is not an exchange transaction in the market, many people would surely apply the same principles and oppose government regulation absent a strong showing that the system of individual choices is somehow damaging to the general public as opposed to the parties themselves.[69]

Philosophers extending back to John Stuart Mill insist that government should never interfere in decisions involving only an individual's personal life or welfare. In *On Liberty*, Mill wrote:

> . . . the only purpose for which power can be rightfully exercised over any member of a civilized community, against his will is to prevent harm to others. His own good, either physical or moral, is not a sufficient warrant . . . The interference of society to overrule his judgment and purposes in what only regards himself must be grounded on general presumptions; which may be altogether wrong, and even if right are as likely as not to be

[68] Granted, litigants may have little actual control over these tactical decisions and may disagree with them. Nevertheless, lawyers are generally constrained by their clients' desires in making tactical decisions with which the client disagrees. In any event, the client hired the lawyer who makes the decisions and the client can discharge the lawyer at any time.

[69] In the *2003 UCLA Law Student Survey*, n 1 above, six of the 61 students who favoured the adversarial approach said the inquisitorial approach interfered with personal autonomy.

misapplied to individual cases, by persons no better acquainted with the circumstances of such cases than those are who look at them merely from without.[70]

C. Dislike of Government Officials in General

A generalized distrust of government officials and government power is a recurrent strain in American history. The original colonists—and probably most of the millions of immigrants who followed them—sought to escape from oppressive, authoritarian governments at home. The American Revolution threw off the despised British rule. The Revolution was followed by enormous popular resistance to the centralization of federal power.[71] Ever since, Americans seem to suspect government officials and agencies of meddlesomeness, incompetence, or corruption.[72] These convictions, shared by people on both the left and right of the political spectrum, are the same whether the subject is the police, the IRS, the FBI, the Bureau of Alcohol, Tobacco and Firearms, or the local Department of Motor Vehicles. The degree to which people trust government has fluctuated throughout American history, but confidence in government has been at a low ebb for the last generation.[73] People who routinely distrust government officials will firmly oppose any proposal to give a government bureaucrat called a judge greater control over dispute-settlement functions than the judges have already.

D. Distrust of Judges in Particular

Based on numerous conversations I have conducted, I am convinced that a good many Americans, and almost all lawyers, are deeply suspicious of the competence

[70] J Mill, *Utilitarianism, On Liberty, Considerations on Representative Government* (Geraint Williams (ed), (London: 1993) 78, 144. Similarly, John Locke stressed that in leaving a state of nature and joining civil society, man gave up no more liberty than was absolutely necessary to secure the benefits of government. It should follow that, along with all other liberties, man retained the power to decide precisely how his own dispute should be presented in court. *Two Treatises of Government* (Peter Laslett (ed), Cambridge, 1967). Another libertarian philosopher, F A Hayek, makes the same point. 'It is because freedom means the renunciation of direct control of individual efforts that a free society can make use of so much more knowledge than the mind of the wisest ruler could comprehend.' *The Constitution of Liberty* (Chicago: 1960) 30. Similarly, see R Nozick, *Anarchy, State and Utopia* (New York: 1974); Verkuil, n 13 above, 56–57; Neef and Nagel, n 36 above, 161–62. Van Koppen and Penrod, n 26 above, 352–354, attribute the difference between American and Dutch criminal procedure to American individualistic traditions (which they call the John Wayne version of justice).

[71] See G Wills, *A Necessary Evil: A History of American Distrust of Government* (New York: 1999), 17, 318.

[72] 'In sum, the distinctive aspect of the American Creed is its antigovernment character. Opposition to power, and the suspicion of government as the most dangerous embodiment of power, are the central themes of American political thought.' S Huntington, *American Politics: The Promise of Disharmony* (Cambridge, MA: 1981), 33. See ibid, 34, 88, 95.

[73] See generally J Alford, 'We're All in This Together: The Decline of Trust in Government, 1958–1996' in J Hibbing and E Theiss-Morse (eds), *What Is It About Government That Americans Dislike* (Cambridge: 2001).

and impartiality of judges.[74] As a result, many people would oppose any measure that would transfer control over the trial process from lawyers to judges.[75] Every lawyer, it seems, has an anecdote about an atrociously biased or hopelessly incompetent judge.

Some people doubt the ability of many judges to do what they would be called on to do in an inquisitorial system. Judges might lack the energy, motivation, skills, or time to gain an understanding of the issues, and make intelligent choices of which witnesses to call, how to organize the trial, how to question the witnesses, and how to appraise their testimony. Instead, people might well believe that adversarial lawyers, who are paid by their clients and intensely motivated to win, will do a better job of fact investigation and presentation of their client's position than a judge ever could do.[76]

These arguments have considerable merit. As the legal realists have taught us, judges, like every other human being, have their own political and social opinions. Judges might not be able to set these opinions aside and act neutrally when called upon to make all of the discretionary determinations inherent in an inquisitorial role. Some judges are lazy and would do a poor job if the structure of the trial and examination of witnesses were left in their hands. Reasonable people could reject all inquisitorial approaches because they fear any measure that would increase unchecked judicial power.

There are fundamental differences between US and European judges. In continental Europe, judges are trained professionals. Only the best law school graduates are admitted into judicial training institutes. Judging is a career track. Judges are trained and re-educated throughout their careers, and the judges are promoted to more responsible roles depending on their performance.[77] In the UK, judging is not a separate career track; however, the appointment of judges has always been non-political, and generally the most capable barristers are selected to become judges.[78]

The manner in which American judges are selected bears no resemblance to these European models and does not contain built-in protections to assure

[74] Recall, however, that the general public has much more confidence in judges than lawyers. See text at n 9 above. However, that opinion is based on the role of judges in the adversary system where they have relatively little power vis-à-vis lawyers. The public might have much less confidence in judges if the judges were given much greater powers in the courtroom as would occur under the inquisitorial model.

[75] The *2003 UCLA Law Student Survey*, n 1 above, asked students the reasons for their choice of the adversarial or inquisitorial approach. Of the 61 respondents who favoured the adversary system, 13 mentioned their fear of biased judges. Another 14 believed that the inquisitorial system would confer too much power on judges.

[76] In the *2003 UCLA Law Student Survey*, n 1 above, of 61 students who favoured the adversarial system, 18 thought that lawyers would do a better job than judges of conducting a fair trial because of the lawyers' desire to win and because of the financial incentives for doing so.

[77] Langbein, n 10 above, 848–855. See, eg, Eva Steiner, *French Legal Method* (Oxford: 2002), Ch 6.

[78] This system of appointments is in the process of change. The Lord Chancellor was responsible for judicial appointments, but it has been proposed to abolish that office and make appointments to the bench by means of an independent judicial appointments commission. See Neil Rose, 'Lawyers Backing Revolution Despite Consultation Worry,' (June 19, 2003) *Law Society Gazette* 3.

neutrality or competence. The quality of judges is mixed, depending on the jurisdiction. A few states have merit selection systems. Most states, and the federal system, rely on political appointments. Appointments at the federal level have become increasingly politicized. Although governors generally try to appoint qualified judges—if only to avoid being blamed for later fiascoes—politics has everything to do with these appointments. In most states, a prospective judge must be an active member of the governor's political party. Indeed, a newly appointed judge may be a politico who has been defeated for election and needs a new job. Campaign contributions don't hurt. In many places, particularly big cities, the judges may be the dregs of the profession.

In states that rely on judicial elections (and the majority do), there are deeper reasons for concern about judicial quality and independence. Elected judges are sometimes reluctant to render unpopular decisions that might arouse the groups likely to organize non-retention campaigns. Increasingly, judicial elections feature the same sort of attack television advertising and corrupt fundraising practices as do elections generally.[79] Regardless of the selection method, judges are drastically underpaid relative to successful practising lawyers and often receive inadequate staff support. As a result, many able lawyers cannot afford to become or remain judges and some lawyers who cannot make a living practising law want to become judges.

All these concerns about biased, lazy, or incompetent judges have merit. But the present system of adversarial lawyer combat has problems aplenty too. At least most trial judges are experienced in finding facts, appraising witness credibility, and conducting trials, unlike jurors who do not have a clue.[80] Judges have better access to knowledge about results in other trials and so can facilitate fair and consistent applications of vague legal standards. While judges are prone to making cognitive errors, like the rest of us, some research indicates that they are less likely than juries to make such errors.[81] And at least judges are trained and socialized to act in a fair and neutral manner, regardless of their political biases.

[79] A 2002 study of over 2,400 state court judges showed that 46% of both trial judges and appellate judges believe that campaign contributions influence judicial decisions to at least some degree. Greenberg Quinlan Rosner Research, 'Justice at Stake: State Judges Frequency Questionnaire', http://faircourts.org/files/JASJudgesSurveyResults.pdf.

[80] Obviously, judges are inexperienced when first appointed. In most systems, however, they are assigned to less difficult cases (such as misdemeanours) until they get some experience. Since judges tend to remain on the bench for lengthy periods, the odds are that any given judge will have considerable experience.

[81] C Guthrie et al, 'Inside the Judicial Mind', (2001) 86 *Cornell L Rev* 777, 826–827. However, Guthrie and his co-authors believed that juries might have an advantage over judges since group decisionmaking could reduce some cognitive errors. A common cognitive error consists of 'anchoring', meaning that the choice of the correct amount of damages is heavily influenced by the numbers initially presented. Thus, it appears that the more plaintiffs ask for, the more a jury is likely to award. See G Chapman and B Bornstein, 'The More You Ask For, The More You Get' (1996) 10 *Applied Cognitive Psychology* 519; C Sunstein, 'Behavioral Law and Economics: A Progress Report', (1999) 1 *American Law & Economics Review* 115, 141–144. Judges who are accustomed to seeing exaggerated damage claims should be less susceptible to this error than juries.

E. Fuller's Hypothesis

Harvard Professor Lon Fuller famously criticized the inquisitorial system on neutrality grounds. Fuller argued that a judge who is involved in framing the issues and choosing witnesses prior to the trial would decide prematurely which side should win and downgrade the other side's evidence. In contrast, Fuller argued, the more passive judge in an adversarial trial is likely to remain neutral until all the evidence is in.[82] Fuller cited no authority for this proposition. Fuller's hypothesis is a serious criticism of the inquisitorial model, since that model calls on the judge to make pretrial decisions about the issues and witnesses, then question witnesses and sum up the evidence for the jury. An inquisitorial trial would not be fair unless the judge remains neutral until all of the evidence was in.

Fuller's insight was subsequently validated by Thibaut and Walker.[83] They constructed an experiment in which undergraduate students were asked to serve as 'judges' in an assault case involving a self-defence issue. Half of the subjects were 'biased' and half were not 'biased'. The experimenters biased the 'judges' by exposing them to a series of similar self-defence cases in which the similar conduct had been found unlawful. Half of the trials simulated an 'adversary' mode because the facts were presented by two 'lawyers' labelled 'prosecution' and 'defence'. The other half simulated an 'inquisitorial' mode, meaning that a neutral 'lawyer' presented the facts to the judge.

Thibaut and Walker concluded that the biasing information had a larger impact on the 'judge' when the case was presented in an inquisitorial mode than an adversarial mode.[84] When the judge was not 'biased', the conviction rates were the same whether an adversarial or inquisitorial trial occurred. When the judge was biased, however, the judge was more likely to convict the defendant in an inquisitorial rather than adversarial trial.

Nevertheless, Fuller's hypothesis remains open to question. The 'judges' in the Thibaut-Walker experiment were relatively unmotivated undergraduates. Could not professional judges who hear cases every day and are socialized to remain neutral do better? At least, could they not do a better job of remaining neutral than kids who may or may not be serious about what they are doing, have never done anything like this before, and are doing it in a simulated, laboratory setting?[85]

[82] L Fuller, 'The Adversary System' in Harold Berman (ed), *Talks on American Law* (2nd edn, New York: 1971), 43–44; L Fuller, 'The Forms and Limits of Adjudication' (1978) 92 *Harvard L Rev* 353, 382–384.

[83] See n 40 above, Ch 6.

[84] Thibaut and Walker also discovered that the *order* in which the case was presented made an even bigger difference, regardless of which trial mode was used and whether or not biasing information was presented. The last evidence presented was the most influential under both the inquisitorial and adversarial modes. Thus defendants did much better when the order was unlawful-lawful than when the order was lawful-unlawful.

[85] See Gross, n 65 above, 734, 740, n 22. Gross wrote 'it is pointless to use college students and first-year law students to simulate the roles of judges and lawyers in adversary and investigatory systems for litigation; even if these subjects develop the appropriate motivation for their roles, they cannot possibly have the essential training'. Indeed Gross thought an investigatory judge should be better able than a

In any event, Thibaut-Walker's experiments provided for no advocates for the contending sides. In my inquisitorial model, however, advocates are involved at every stage. This feature should significantly check the possibility that the judge will jump to conclusions as a result of involvement in pretrial decisionmaking. In any event, Fuller's hypothesis seems somewhat quaint. The citadel has long since been breached. At least in civil matters, judges now routinely engage in a host of pretrial case management activities, decide on preliminary injunctions or summary judgment motions, and become deeply involved in promoting settlement.[86] All of this exposes them to vast quantities of information about the case and could cause them to lose their neutrality.[87]

F. Relation to Sport and War

Some people think that a substantial reason for the widespread belief in the adversarial ideology is that people enjoy contests. Certainly, the media coverage of many notorious trials (most importantly the OJ Simpson case) was similar to coverage of a sports event, concentrating on gimmicks and who was ahead on a given day. Scholars trace the origins of the adversarial system back to primitive systems of trial by battle and trial by ordeal.[88] It may be that people enjoy adversarial contests for some of the same reasons they like sporting events and other contests and perhaps for the same reasons that many of them have a taste for war. Moreover, as pointed out at the beginning of this article, the adversarial system (with its potential for lawyerly strategy and gamesmanship) is vastly more entertaining for spectators and probably for the participants than the inquisitorial system (in which lawyers have relatively little to do).

G. Lawyers' Preference

One reason why we retain pure adversarialism is that lawyers like it. On this point, there is near-consensus among prosecutors and criminal defenders as well as plaintiffs' and defendants' lawyers.[89] Like all human beings, lawyers prefer a

passive one to confirm or disconfirm his initial hypotheses. Mirjan Damaska criticized the Thibaut-Walker experiment because no 'evidence' was presented, only a set of conflicting facts, and because the decisionmaker was passive under both the adversary and inquisitorial simulations. 'Presentation of Evidence and Factfinding Precision' (1975) 123 *U of Pennsylvania L Rev* 1095–1103.

[86] Marcus, n 49 above, 102–108; Judith Resnik, 'Managerial Judges' (1982) 96 *Harvard L Rev* 374.

[87] ibid, 425–431 (raising concerns about impartiality).

[88] See Neef and Nagel, n 36 above, 133–147, 153–161.

[89] At least, so I assume based on many informal conversations but no methodologically acceptable studies. First year law students prefer the adversarial model by a 79%–21% margin and it is unlikely that three years of law school will narrow the gap (in fact legal education will probably increase the gap). See *2003 UCLA Law Student Survey*, n 1 above. I have not discussed the issue with many judges. Some judges like the idea of increased power, but others would prefer to avoid the political heat that might come from exercising that power. Others have little desire for the increased work and responsibility that

system that they control (whether through trials or through settlements and plea bargains) rather than one that subordinates them to power figures like judges whom they cannot control.[90]

III. The Adversary System in Popular Culture

A. Popular Culture as a Teacher

Popular culture is a powerful and prolific producer of ideological messages.[91] According to numerous studies, we draw much of our information (or misinformation) and beliefs from movies and television. The cognitive device through which this occurs is called 'the cultivation effect'. In answering questions or forming opinions, people access information in mental 'bins' consisting of information they have stored there.[92] People internalize movie and TV stories, often forgetting to discount for the fact that these stories were fictitious.[93]

Another branch of culture theory (sometimes called the 'active audience' or 'uses and gratification' approach) focuses on the way that differently situated audiences

would come with a transition to the adversary system. A judge obligated to sum up the evidence, for example, has to pay much closer attention to trial testimony than a judge who delegates the full responsibility for fact-finding to the jury.

[90] Of course, financial considerations also come into play. Certainly, judicially unsupervised discovery and lengthy trials are good for lawyers' income if they are paid by the hour. Indeed, for big firms, litigation is the engine that drives their profits. Procedural reform in all countries is typically resisted by lawyers with vested interests in the status quo. Zuckerman, n 7 above, 44–45.

[91] Grossberg, n 3 above, 177–201. According to Richard Sherwin: 'For many, perhaps most, the mass media today are in fact the primary if not the exclusive source of the public's knowledge about law, lawyers, and the legal system as a whole . . . Put simply, [popular culture, especially visual mass media] is a source of both meaning and the meaning-making tools people use to think and speak with. [It is the source of the] common narratives that organize our experience, [that we] use to make sense of things in our everyday lives. . . . This vast electronic archive provides us with the knowledge and interpretation skills we need to make sense of ordinary reality. From these familiar sources we learn the familiar plot lines, story genres, and character types out of which meanings are made. In a sense, we 'see' reality the way we have been trained to watch film and TV. The camera is in our heads. We've internalized the media's logic.' Sherwin, n 14 above, 18–20.

[92] This is an application of the well-known 'availability' heuristic which suggests that we are heavily influenced in our behaviour or opinions by the most recent and most vivid information available to us. For example, people are most concerned by risks that have been heavily publicized, such as shark attacks or the Washington DC sniper, despite the extremely low probability of being a victim of sharks or the sniper. See, eg, C Sunstein, 'What's Available? Social Influences and Behavioral Economics' (2003) 97 *Northwestern U L Rev* 1285. The stock stories of pop culture are highly 'available' to TV or film consumers, since they are likely to be recent, repeated, and vivid.

[93] See Asimow, n 9 above, 531, 553–561, for discussion of studies supporting the existence of the cultivation effect. The *2003 UCLA Law Student Survey*, n 1 above, asked about the sources of information the students found helpful in deciding whether they preferred the adversary system or the inquisitorial system. Students could mark each source from 1 (very unhelpful) to 5 (very helpful). By far the most helpful information source was classes in school (60% marked 4 or 5). News coverage of trials came in second (22% marked 4 or 5). Popular culture—novels, movies, or television—came in a very close third (21% marked 4 or 5). Discussions with friends tied for third (also 21%). These four sources came in far ahead of friends and family who are lawyers (14%), personal experience in court (13%), and being on a jury (4%).

construct their own meanings out of materials presented to them in pop culture products. These meanings may vary or even contradict those that the producers of the product intended.[94] Space limitations do not permit a detailed discussion of either of these competing approaches, but they are complementary rather than inconsistent. Some consumers are like sponges, passively soaking up the information and messages conveyed to them through the media of pop culture. Other consumers are more active and fashion their own meanings out of the cultural raw materials available to them. Both theoretical approaches help explain how endlessly repeated tributes to adversarial behaviour in television and movies could produce and propagate the dominant adversarial ideology.[95]

This section discusses some of the powerful and persuasive pop cultural teachers of adversarial ideology.

B. Perry Mason and his Descendants

I believe that we sit at the feet of that revered teacher of trial advocacy, the greatest lawyer role model who ever lived: the immortal Perry Mason. Mason, played by Raymond Burr, starred in 271 hour-long TV shows from 1957 to 1966. These shows were commercially successful when first shown and have remained popular in syndication to this very day.[96] Thirty made-for-TV movies between 1985 and 1995 featured the return of Perry Mason (played by an aging Raymond Burr).[97] These movies were also commercially successful[98] and continue to be shown on cable. Thus a great many TV watchers have observed the great cross-examiner at work.[99]

[94] See, eg, J Fiske, *Television Culture* (London: 1987).

[95] See Kimberlianne Podlas, 'Please Adjust Your Signal: How Television's Syndicated Courtrooms Bias our Juror Citizenry' (2001) 39 *American Business LJ* 1 (documenting sharp differences concerning the appropriate role for judges as between people who frequently watch *Judge Judy* and those who rarely or never watch it). An earlier study of small claims court litigants indicated that many of them were relying on what they had learned from watching Judge Wapner on 'The People's Court'. This was the popular show that still runs on TV (presided over by Judge Wapner's successors) and which inspired *Judge Judy* and the many similar afternoon judge shows. O'Barr and Conley, n 2 above, 152, n 11. For discussion of the TV judge shows, see Michael Asimow, ' "Justice with an Attitude:" Judge Judy and the Daytime Television Bench' (Fall 1999) 38 *Judges' Journal* 24.

[96] See the Perry Mason TV Show web site, which contains synopses of all the episodes and has numerous links to other sites. http://www.oz.net~daveb/perry.htm (last visited 27 May 2003).

[97] In the last four of the made-for-TV movies, Burr was replaced by Paul Sorvino in one film and Hal Holbrook in the other three. J Bounds, *Perry Mason* (Westport, Connecticut: 1996) 191. These four post-Burr movies pulled much lower ratings than the earlier made for TV films starring Burr. ibid, 159.

[98] Bounds, n 97 above, Ch 7. Raymond Burr died in 1993.

[99] Older generations are more likely to have consumed significant numbers of *Perry Mason* episodes. The *2003 UCLA Law Student Survey*, n 1 above, indicated that none of the students watched *Perry Mason* frequently but 19% watched it rarely. This is a respectable result given that *Perry Mason* is shown only in daytime syndication on cable channels in Los Angeles. More students watched *Perry Mason* than watched *JAG* which is shown on network TV (11% watch *JAG* frequently or rarely). The *Perry Mason* result was not too far behind *Judge Judy* (26% watch it frequently or rarely), and *Judge Judy* is the highest rated show on daytime television. Thus significant numbers of young people are exposed to *Perry Mason* at least occasionally. By comparison 54% of the 1Ls watch *Law & Order* frequently or rarely, 33% watch *The Practice* frequently or rarely, and 50% watched *Ally McBeal* frequently or rarely when it was on (*Ally* was no longer running in 2003).

The Perry Mason character originated in 82 best-selling novels written by the prolific lawyer-turned-author Erle Stanley Gardner (1889–1970). All were titled *The Case of the* . . . and they had all had the same formula as the television shows.[100] Warner Brothers made six low budget[101] Perry Mason films between 1934 and 1937. Each was an adaptation of a Gardner novel, but Gardner had no creative involvement in the film making process and he hated the films. The Warner films tried, not too successfully, to emulate the wisecracking sensibility of William Powell in MGM's *The Thin Man*.[102] Especially in the first four films, in which Warren William starred, the Perry Mason character drank heavily and often cut ethical corners.

Gardner retained creative control over the radio version of *Perry Mason* and restored the character's virtue.[103] The radio show ran as a daytime serial for 15 minutes, six days per week, from 1944 to 1955—an awe-inspiring total of 3,221 episodes. On the radio, Mason functioned in a variety of legal roles, including as a compassionate counsellor and office lawyer. Unlike the Warner movies, the radio show was serious and reflected solid family values. It was sponsored by Procter & Gamble from beginning to end. Gardner also owned the production company that made the television shows for CBS, and thus he continued to retain creative control. He supervised and edited every script.

The televised Perry Mason was quite different from the other pop culture heroes of the 1950s who were mostly cowboys and detectives.[104] Cowboys and detectives were loners who achieved justice at the point of a gun and in spite of the law, which was typically portrayed as corrupt and ineffectual.[105] But Mason (aided by his trusty investigator Paul Drake and secretary Della Street) always achieved true justice through the legal process and he never relied on gunplay or vigilantism. The criminal justice system in which Mason worked was inept, but it was never corrupt.

Perry Mason on television was asexual, stolid and humorless. He was a combination detective and lawyer (and the work thus fits into both the detective story genre and the courtroom genre).[106] Mason seemed completely indifferent to collecting fees or to any aspect of human life other than representing his clients. He

[100] Bounds, n 97 above, Ch 2. See also Patricia Kane, 'Perry Mason: Modern Culture Hero' in Ray B Browne et al (eds), *Heroes of Popular Culture* (Bowling Green, Ohio: 1972).

[101] Budgets for the six films ran from $127,000 to $207,000. See Bounds, n 97 above, Ch 3 for the story of Mason in the movies.

[102] *The Thin Man* was released in 1934 and had numerous successful sequels.

[103] Bounds, n 97 above, Ch 4.

[104] N Rosenberg, 'Perry Mason' in R Jarvis and P Joseph (eds), *Prime Time Law* (Durham, North Carolina: 1998) 117–118.

[105] S Stark, 'Perry Mason Meets Sonny Crockett: The History of Lawyers and the Police as Television Heroes' (1987) 42 *U of Miami L Rev* 235–242.

[106] For discussion of the courtroom genre, see Paul Bergman and Michael Asimow, *Reel Justice* (Kansas City, Missouri: 1996); J Denvir (ed), *Legal Reelism* (Urbana, Illinois: 1996); S Greenfield, G Osborn and P Robson, *Film and the Law* (London: 2001); A Chase, *Movies on Trial* (New York: 2002); S Machura, p 148 above.

always represented innocent clients who were wrongly charged by the police and prosecuted by the DA. He *always* succeeded, by brilliant detective work plus resourceful cross examination, in disclosing the identity of the real killer who was sitting in the courtroom or who broke down on the stand. The judicial proceeding (usually a California preliminary hearing, occasionally a jury trial) provided the mechanism for revealing the true killer and thus resolving the mystery story. The formula never varied—never.[107]

Although modern viewers might view *Perry Mason* shows as campy[108] and lawyers groan at the mention of his name, I believe that the show has gone far in cementing the myth of the lawyer as truth-discoverer.[109] Television, after all, stands alone in its ability to shape the opinions of mass audiences. An extremely popular, long-running, successfully syndicated, tenaciously formulaic TV series like *Perry Mason*, starring a beloved and respected actor, surely must be among the most powerful opinion-makers and ideology-entrenchers in human history.[110]

Anyone who has learned their law from Perry Mason knows that you can never rely on the police, the prosecutor, or the judge for justice. Although these functionaries are honest and hard working, they are not too bright. They *always* go off in the wrong direction and prosecute the wrong person. It is only through the noble lawyer/detective that the legal system can achieve justice. It can do so only through adversarial fact investigation and cross examination. Most important, Mason always finds out *the truth*. His clients do not weasel out under reasonable doubt. They are proved affirmatively innocent because the real killer *always* confesses. The seductive over-simplification of the Perry Mason plot helped to sell American TV consumers a way of thinking and believing that they have never deserted.

[107] Bounds, n 97 above, Ch 2.

[108] Rosenberg, n 104 above, 115–116.

[109] Burr himself considered the show and its central character as a 'public trust' with the actor serving as 'chief executor'. Bounds, n 97 above, 1. When Burr died, *People Magazine* noted that Burr and Mason 'had become not only America's Lawyer but the world's'. ibid, 157. Asked to name a lawyer they admired, 52% of respondents to a 1993 National Law Journal poll could not name one. The few respected lawyers cited more than once included Perry Mason and Matlock along with Thurgood Marshall, Janet Reno, Abraham Lincoln, and F Lee Bailey. R Samborn, 'Who's Most Admired Lawyer?' (1993) 15 *National LJ* 1, 24.

[110] Dennis Bounds concluded his study of Perry Mason as follows: 'Mason's activities are a confirmation of the culture. Here the collective ideal of justice within the American culture, embodied in the American judicial system, is identified, examined, and vindicated with every novel, film, episode, or made-for-TV movie. Crimes are committed, but the guilty are punished. The innocent client may be charged with the heinous crime of murder, but because of the adversarial system of law in this country the defense attorney stands ready to prove the innocence of his/her client. This is done in the most idealistic, and ultimately sure, way by not only proving innocence but by catching the truly guilty. Inferred from every version of Perry Mason is the idea that though the system may seem out of control, the presence of the defense attorney celebrates justice—only when a hero such as Mason is involved . . . As a system of ritual mythmaking and of contemporary ideology, Perry Mason supports, even when it appears to appears to prove the injustice of, the American judicial system. Mason is the ultimate lawyer—a defender who never rests. From this the audience can infer that the established system of law is fundamentally just—as long as a Perry Mason takes the case.' Ibid, 163–164. Steven Stark believes that Perry Mason, and the image of the bumbling police, helped pave the way for *Miranda*. Stark, n 105 above, 229–230.

After Perry Mason, countless television shows have reinforced the idea that the way to justice lies through the work of a noble lawyer-champion.[111] *Matlock* ran from 1986 to 1995 and continues to thrive in syndication. Starring the beloved Andy Griffith, *Matlock* reinvented the Perry Mason cliché in Southern drag.[112] Many old and new television shows about law and lawyers repeat the same, stale Perry Mason message.[113] Truth and justice flow from the work of dedicated, committed, zealous lawyers, usually criminal defence lawyers. If you find yourself in trouble, you'd better have a lawyer by your side. You might hate lawyers in general, but when you need one, you'd better get the best.[114]

Some modern television shows have blessedly departed from the Perry Mason storyline. On these shows, particularly *The Practice* and *L.A. Law*, the adversary system is fallible and does not necessarily produce truth and justice. On these shows, innocent people are sometimes convicted and the guilty sometimes walk free or plea bargain serious crimes down to light sentences. The lawyers deliberately blame people they know are innocent to create reasonable doubt ('Plan B'). Their ethical practices are situational.[115] Unlike Perry Mason, the lawyers have personal and relationship problems and they are trying to earn big bucks (or at least a decent living). Perhaps, after a few more years of anti-Perry Mason TV lawyer shows, people's confidence in the adversary system will begin to falter.

That has not yet happened. I believe we have learned the lesson too well from our master, Perry Mason, and his countless television progeny. We carry his teachings down to the present day. In our bones, we know that only a system that empowers lawyers can discover the *real truth* about what actually happened when the crime was committed—who done it and why. For that reason, Americans react with horror to the idea of a judge-controlled trial because that would decentre the lawyer, particularly the criminal defence lawyer, and would thus devalue the truth-seeking function of the law.

[111] *The Defenders* ran during the *Perry Mason* era (130 episodes, spanning the years 1961–65)—indeed it followed *Perry Mason* on CBS on Saturday nights. The show won 13 Emmys (compared to four for *Perry Mason*) and consistently maintained high levels of writing, acting, and production values. Unfortunately, this superb series has never gone into syndication. *The Defenders* portrayed a very different world from *Perry Mason*. The father-son team of Lawrence and Kenneth Preston attacked a different legal or social problem every week, always from a politically liberal point of view. *The Defenders* also championed the adversary system by reinforcing the message that ordinary people could confront the legal system only with the aid of noble lawyers. See David Ray Papke, 'The Defenders,' in *Prime Time Law*, n 104 above, Ch 1.

[112] See Gail Richmond, 'Matlock,' in *Prime Time Law*, n 104 above, Ch 5. Unlike Perry Mason, Ben Matlock had a personal life. His daughters were his associate attorneys at different times, and he had an unresolved relationship with prosecutor Julie March.

[113] S Lichter, L Lichter, S Rothman, *Prime Time* (Washington, DC: 1994) 313 (Perry Mason structure used as model for numerous courtroom dramas).

[114] See R Post, 'On the Popular Image of the Lawyer: Reflections in a Dark Glass' (1987) 75 *California L Rev* 379 (arguing that lawyers are both respected and despised for their ability to perform insincere roles in the interests of clients).

[115] W Simon, 'Moral Pluck' (2001) 101 *Columbia L Rev* 421(analyzing ethics of characters on *L.A. Law*).

C. The Adversary System in the Movies

Countless movies have valorized the adversarial lawyer. Often (especially in recent films) the lawyers are personally flawed and their ethics are dubious. Despite their efforts, the adversarial system sometimes fails. Nevertheless, without lawyer-champions, there would be no hope of justice, no way to uncover the truth.[116] Needless to say, this narrative is wildly out of synch with the reality of legal practice, in which the work of lawyers (civil or criminal) has little to do with securing justice or in revealing truth and everything to do with using craft to serve the interests of clients. Here it is possible only to suggest a few examples of films that glorify lawyers, but readers of this paper could instantly identify many more.

1. Cross-examination

A staple of lawyer movies is the brilliant cross-examination that destroys a lying, deceptive or mistaken witness and reveals the truth. Although many such movies are instantly forgettable, some are exceptionally vivid. Just to name a couple, take the immortal *My Cousin Vinny*.[117] Vinny Gambini has recently passed the New York Bar exam (after numerous failures) before travelling to Alabama to defend his young cousin and a friend in a murder trial.

Vinny is clueless about Alabama culture and criminal procedure, but nevertheless turns into a brilliant trial lawyer. His cross-examinations are devastating. For example, one eye-witness claims he saw the two 'utes' enter the Sack o' Suds convenience store and exit five minutes later in a green car. He knows it was five minutes because he looked up just as he started and just as he finished cooking his morning grits. Vinny points out that in the rest of the grit-eating world, it takes 20 minutes to cook grits. The witness is destroyed. Vinny also deploys his girlfriend Mona Lisa Vitto, an unemployed hairdresser, as a reluctant expert witness on auto mechanics to devastating effect, thus effectively validating the existing system of partisan expert witnesses.

In *To Kill a Mockingbird*,[118] the saintly Atticus Finch cross-examines Mayella Ewell, the alleged rape victim. He shows clearly that his client, the defendant Tom Robinson, could not have committed the rape since Mayella was assaulted by a right handed person and Tom Robinson has no use of his right hand. Unfortunately, the all-white jury is not about to take the word of a black man over two white witnesses and convicts him of rape. We, however, know better. Brilliant cross-examination exposed the truth—even if the adversary system failed to produce a just result.

[116] Sometimes, as in . . . *And Justice for All* (1979), the lawyer must attack the adversary system itself in order to reveal the truth about his all-too-guilty client. See John Denvir's account of the film in this volume. Denvir makes the broader point that the typical lawyer film shows the 'good' lawyer wrenching justice from the 'bad' system.

[117] (1992).

[118] (1962).

2. Advocates in Civil Cases

Numerous films have involved civil litigation. These films almost invariably pit a noble plaintiff's lawyer against a vicious corporation and its unethical and ignoble big-firm defence lawyer.[119] Take, for example, *The Rainmaker*.[120] Novice lawyer Rudy Baylor finds himself locked in litigation with a major defence firm in an insurance bad faith case. It seems that Great Benefit sold medical insurance door to door. It collected premiums but never paid any claims. As a result, Donny Ray Black failed to receive a bone marrow transplant in time to save his life.

The defence firm, led by Leo Drummond, engages in all sorts of tricky and unethical behaviour. It stalls the case, hoping the plaintiff will die. It taps the phones in Baylor's office. Key witnesses are fired before he can take their depositions. Great Benefit produces its claims manual, but only after removing the part that instructed employees to deny all benefit claims. Baylor personifies grit, tenacity, and client loyalty. He wangles a $50 million punitive damage award from the jury. Unfortunately, by that time, the insiders have looted Great Benefit, which files for bankruptcy. Disillusioned, Baylor retires from the practice of law. But the message is clear: if you get sick or hurt, you have no chance without a tenacious and self-sacrificing plaintiff's lawyer to champion your cause. (Even then, because of the flawed system, you may get little or nothing). The same message is transmitted in *The Verdict*,[121] *Class Action*,[122] *A Civil Action*,[123] *Philadelphia*,[124] and *Erin Brockovich*[125] (which also features a heroic paralegal). Episodes of *L.A. Law* and *The Practice* included numerous civil cases driving home the identical message.

D. Heroic Prosecutors

Sometimes pop culture glorifies heroic and dedicated prosecutors. The phenomenally successful *Law & Order* provides a weekly seminar about the role of prosecutors in the justice system. 'These are their stories.' *Law & Order* teaches us that dedicated, selfless, and resourceful lawyers like Jack McCoy (and his numerous female sidekicks) protect us from predatory criminals. In every new (and repeatedly syndicated) show, the prosecutors unmask perjury and conspiracy in the courtroom and trounce slithery defence lawyers. Often the judges seem cynical and burned out; they have heard it all and just want to get through the calendar. The prosecutors, however, seek justice. They want the truth and they reveal it—not just a conviction or a plea

[119] Chase, n 106 above, Ch 4 (in film corporate America looks less like a public profession than a specialized branch of organized crime). Big law firms and big business are generally portrayed negatively in film. See M Asimow, 'Embodiment of Evil: Law Firms in the Movies' (2001) 48 *UCLA L Rev* 1339. An exception to the statement in the text is *The Sweet Hereafter* (1997) which features a predatory plaintiff's lawyer and does not demonize any corporate defendants or their lawyers.

[120] (1997). See Asimow, n 118 above, 1354–1355.

[121] (1982). [122] (1990). [123] (1998). [124] (1992). [125] (2000).

bargain.[126] *Law & Order* has probably done more to burnish the image of prosecutors than just about any popular culture product in history, but its message is really the familiar *Perry Mason* narrative from the prosecution's side of the table: you need dedicated lawyers, working in an adversary system, to get at the truth.

Justice-seeking prosecutors are rarer in the movies than on television, but one stands out: Kathryn Murphy in *The Accused.*[127] Sarah Tobias was gang-raped in a bar and Murphy quite rationally plea bargains the case against the rapists down to 'reckless endangerment'. Tobias thinks Murphy sold her out, so Murphy prosecutes the barflies who cheered on the rapists for 'solicitation'. Although it seems odd that the cheerleaders receive harsher sentences than the rapists, the message of the film is clear: a courageous prosecutor can buck the bureaucracy and achieve justice in the case of a vicious rape.

E. When Judges get in the Way

In most popular culture products, the trial is to a jury and judges are minor figures.[128] Once the trial begins, the judges pound their gavels, threaten to clear the courtroom if the spectators do not behave, rule on evidence objections, and otherwise try to stay awake and out of the way. Normally trial judges in fictional films or TV shows are as uninteresting and undramatic as baseball umpires.[129]

Occasionally, we find trial judges who do get into the action. When this happens, judicial intervention usually thwarts the search for justice. Thus in *The Verdict*, it is clear that Judge Hoyle is firmly in the defence's pocket. At one point, the judge takes over the questioning of the plaintiff's not very qualified expert witness and destroys him. Spluttering in rage, the plaintiff's lawyer Frank Galvin tells the judge: 'If you're gonna try my case for me, I wish you wouldn't lose it'. In *A Civil Action*, another judge, who seems to be extremely pro-defendant, makes procedural rulings requiring a bifurcated trial.[130] This puts true justice out of reach for the sick and dying victims.

[126] Most of the 300-odd *L&O* shows follow this model. In an imaginative episode called 'Absentia' (12 February 2003), the prosecutors lose a case when an eye-witness to a robbery-murder fails to turn up for a trial. The missing witness has not been rubbed out, however; he was convicted of murder in absentia 20 years before and was afraid to get involved in new legal proceedings. Overcoming various obstacles and defence stratagems, the prosecutors manage to try him again for murder. They convincingly establish what really happened 20 years before and win a conviction.

[127] (1988).

[128] When the judge has power to make a discretionary decision, they often go badly wrong as in *Losing Isaiah* (1995) or *Kramer vs. Kramer* (1979).

[129] See Greenfield et al, n 106 above, Ch 6 (referring to the 'invisible judge' in film). An exception was the genial and highly competent Judge Weaver in *Anatomy of a Murder* (1959). Interestingly, in French movies, judges are usually shown as possessing great integrity and heroism even though hindered in their pursuit of truth by the judicial hierarchy. Lawyers, in contrast, are futile and dishonorable. A Garapon, 'French Legal Culture and the Shock of Globalization' (1995) 4 *Social and Legal Studies* 492, 497.

[130] In *The Rainmaker*, the first of two judges is impatient and rude and obviously is colluding with the insurance company to settle a case for less than its value. The second judge does a good job. Some trial judges have come off well in film. One who seems to do right (for unexplained reasons) is Judge

Occasionally, pop culture judges are vicious[131] or crooked[132] and sometimes they prove to be the real criminals.[133] In *Judgment at Nuremberg*,[134] the defendants are Nazi judges who used their positions to enforce the laws of the Third Reich. The judges are responsible for various horrible misdeeds, such as falsely convicting a Jew of having sex with an Aryan (a capital offence) or requiring sterilization of retarded people.[135] On *The Practice*, a recurring character was a nymphomaniac judge who tried to have sex with everybody in the courthouse. In the ultimate anti-judge film, *The Star Chamber*,[136] we meet a group of evil judges who are fed up with freeing vicious criminals on legal technicalities. The judges investigate these cases and hire hit men to assassinate the criminals. But the judges go badly wrong in one case; the criminals whose deaths they have ordered are actually innocent of the crime. Thus the judges prove to be inept even as vigilantes, unlike the successful police vigilantes we have grudgingly admired in *Magnum Force*[137] and *Dirty Harry*[138] and their innumerable successors. In short, if you have learned your law from pop culture, you surely would not want to give any more responsibility to judges.

IV. Conclusion

Americans could have many reasons to resist proposals for making fundamental changes to the adversarial justice system. Of course, they know little or nothing of alternative systems, and they are rationally dubious about the costs and unintended consequences of replacing a familiar system with an unfamiliar and untried one. Many Americans believe strongly in individual autonomy and distrust government officials in general and judges in particular. People may believe that adversarialism, like democracy, is the worst possible system except for the alternatives.

This paper identifies a dominant ideology that legitimates the adversary system. We despise and distrust our lawyers, yet we depend on them to uncover the truth and lead us to justice, and we want them by our side when we are in legal trouble. The dominance of the American adversarial ideology owes a lot to its glorification

Simmons in *Erin Brockovich* who halts PG&E's delaying tactics. A second is Judge Roosevelt in *The Client* (1994) who restrains prosecutorial misconduct. A third is Judge Sarokin who frees the wrongly convicted Ruben Carter at the end of *Hurricane* (1999). See Greenfield et al, n 106 above, Ch 6.

[131] As in *The Paradyne Case* (1947) or *Let Him Have It* (1991).

[132] As in *Night Falls on Manhattan* (1997) (judge backdates warrant); *The Penalty Phase* (1986) (judge backdates warrant, appoints defence lawyer who will not raise the warrant issue); *Presumed Innocent* (1990) (judge involved in bribery scheme, dismisses case to avoid exposing his own past misdeeds).

[133] As in *Suspect* (1987) and . . . *And Justice for All* (1979). A second judge in . . . *And Justice for All* is a suicidal nut.

[134] (1961).

[135] Judge Haywood is the chief judge in the war crimes trial of the Nazi judges. Haywood, a washed up state court judge who was defeated for election, turns out to be a heroic character. He insists on the personal responsibility of the Nazi judges and resists calls by American authorities to go easy on them in order to avoid antagonizing the German public at the time of the Berlin blockade.

[136] (1983).

[137] (1973).

[138] (1971).

in television and film. Pop culture has taught generations of Americans that lawyer-controlled trials are the only way to uncover truth and attain substantive justice (even though lawyers deny that their function has anything to do with finding truth or attaining substantive justice). When trouble strikes, we want a lawyer committed to us and us alone and we want that lawyer to have every possible tactical advantage. The timeless story of *Perry Mason* lives on as myth and supports this dominant, deeply rooted, and usually unquestioned adversarial ideology.

The Double Meaning of Law: Does it Matter if Film Lawyers are Unethical?

Steve Greenfield and Guy Osborn

Judge Rayford:	They want you. You're a very principled ethical lawyer with no political ties.
Arthur Kirkland:	I tell ya . . . They want me . . . they want me to defend Fleming because of my moral integrity. And if I don't defend him I'll be disbarred for being unethical.

. . . *And Justice for All* (1979, Norman Jewison)

Introduction

Academic engagement with film and the law has covered a diverse range of themes and topics, ranging from the application of film theory, to single film analysis.[1] An increasingly large body of work has been devoted to one broad question that revolves around the cinematic portrayal of lawyers. At its most straightforward this has evolved into a question as to whether lawyers are shown in a negative or positive light. Whilst this may seem to be a relatively easy issue to resolve it may in fact be open to a number of alternative examinations.[2] Approaches to the question (of whether lawyers are shown as good, bad or indifferent) may vary, as may the application of the material. One such pedagogical use can revolve around the contrast between the theory and screen practice of lawyering. This in itself is part of a wider application of law film as a teaching tool for both substantive and procedural matters.[3] Examples from films may be used to demonstrate impressive or indeed

[1] For a review of work in the area see S Machura and P Robson (eds), 'Law and Film' (2001) 28 *J of Law and Society* and S Greenfield, G Osborn, P Robson, *Film and the Law* (London: 2001).

[2] See, eg the approaches of M Asimow, 'Bad Lawyers in the movies' (2000) 24 *Nova L Rev* 533 and Greenfield, Osborn, Robson, n 1 above. See also Berets' comments in 1996. 'Lawyer bashing in film continues. Although there are some halfway sympathetic portraits of attorneys in film, on the whole they are still an opportunistic, self aggrandizing lot.' R Berets, 'Lawyers in Film 1996' (1998) 22 *Legal Studies Forum* 99.

[3] See, eg, S Greenfield and G Osborn, 'The Living Law: Popular Film as Legal Text' (1995) 29 *The Law Teacher* 33 and G Osborn, 'Borders and Boundaries: locating the law in film' (2001) 28 *J of Law and Society* 164. The use of films, as a teaching tool, is not of course confined to law but covers numerous disciplines. See eg www.teachwithmovies.org where it is argued that: 'A movie provides an alternative

poor examples of advocacy or merely to show alternative approaches.[4] A narrower thread that may be drawn out, from the portrayal of legal practice, relates to the cinematic treatment of professional ethics. Again this area may be developed in a number of different ways and there is a rising body of academic work.[5] Furthermore there is then the question of the effect of cinematic lawyers' ethics on the public perception of lawyers. This is a dimension that has concerned the professions and can be crudely represented as the good lawyer/bad lawyer debate. Thus the ethical values of screen lawyers is part of a wider debate concerning the characteristics of lawyers and the effect the portrayal this has had on the wider public perception of the legal profession. Academics working in the area of law and film have spent considerable time attempting to analyze the general characteristics of screen lawyers and seemingly trying to determine both the means by which lawyers are portrayed and, to a lesser extent, the effect of the portrayal.[6]

This chapter is not concerned with the question of the legitimacy or accuracy of the portrayal of professional legal ethics, or to any great extent, the contribution this dimension within law film makes to the good lawyer/bad lawyer debate. Rather its thrust is to examine the role and function of ethical issues within legal films and why this is often so important. It considers both the ethical norms that exist, and the extent to which lawyers are prepared to depart from codes of professional conduct in order to achieve what is perceived to be 'justice', or at least to achieve the result that the lawyer subjectively requires.

Cinematic lawyers are often presented with difficult moral or ethical issues that require resolution. In a broader sense this may be part of the context to the case, or perhaps an issue that develops through the progress of the case. Examples of the former would be the racism of the community (towards the unpopular defendant) in *To Kill a Mockingbird* or *A Time to Kill*. Here the traditional view is of the superhero lawyer stepping forward to represent the 'outsider' and in doing so inflating his own ethical currency.[7] The second strand relates to case management and the extent to which the search for justice dominates and subsumes codes of ethics and

educational experience and highlights points covered by the curriculum. Each *Learning Guide* can easily be made into a lesson plan. Teachers can give students a list of films to watch at home with classmates or their families. *Teach With Movies* makes it easy to extend learning time beyond the school day and to enlist parents as active participants in their children's education.'

[4] There are numerous examples and they are generally tinged with gross subjectivity but we suggest the following. Poor advocates include Dennis Denuso in *The Castle*, and the public defender in *My Cousin Vinny*. Much finer performances can be seen from Frank Galvin in *The Verdict* and Ian McKenzie in *A Dry White Season*. There is also the impassioned judgment from Judge Sarokin in *The Hurricane*. There are examples of showmanship such as the public prosecutor in *Suspect* and of course the concluding wild ranting of Arthur Kirkland in . . . *And Justice for All.*

[5] See eg W Simon, *Moral Pluck: Legal Ethics in Popular Culture* (2000) Stanford Public law and Legal Theory Working Series, Number 17, July; D Spitz, 'Heroes or Villains? Moral struggles vs Ethical Dilemmas: An examination of dramatic portrayals of lawyers and the legal profession in popular culture' (2000) 24 *Nova L Rev* 725; T Haddad, 'Silver Tongues on the Silver Screen' (2000) 24 *Nova L Rev* 673; C Menkel-Meadow, 'Can they do that? Legal Ethics in Popular Culture: Of characters and facts' (2001) 48 *UCLA L Rev* 1305.

[6] See Greenfield, Osborn and Robson, n 1 above.

[7] ibid.

legal rules, to the extent that lawyer behaviour may transgress the ethical norms of the profession. That lawyers may be seen to have some 'immunity' when dealing with law is identified in Post's discussion of *Talk of the Town* and the scene where Ronald Colman enters the courtroom to quieten the mob who are about to lynch the town anarchist, played by Cary Grant:

> It is a wonderful moment. The man who has just forcibly kidnapped the criminal is lecturing the crowd on the virtue of the law. The paradox is not accidental, for the very thrust of the film is that Colman's willingness to break the law qualifies him for the Supreme Court. Sometimes, in other words, the lawyer must be lawless in order to uphold the law.[8]

As Post himself notes, this theme is a classic one replicated throughout a number of films on different levels (see for example *Suspect, The Verdict, In the Name of the Father, Cape Fear*), and is a bi-product of the tension between law and justice and the fact that, as Post puts it, the concept of law may be subject to different readings;

> When lawyers as a profession are negatively associated with lawlessness, the thrust of the accusation is something different. It is not that all lawyers are actual criminals, literally breaking the law, it is rather that the concept of 'law' itself has assumed a double meaning.[9]

Previous work has argued that this particular aspect can be seen in a trope of films such as *Young Mr Lincoln*. This law and justice intersection is often a key feature of the ethical dilemmas that appear. The emergence of legal procedure as a barrier to justice may lead the lawyer into a corner where difficult decisions may have to be made. This is the micro level where there is a much broader inclusion of great moral or ethical questions that are at the very heart of much legal drama. Thus ethical issues will be considered at two distinct levels. First, the contribution of wider ethical or moral issues to the creation of legal drama itself and, secondly, the function of controversial professional ethics within film itself.

Dramatic Landscapes and Legal Detail

A quite unlikely starting point is to consider whether a large number of films that are claimed as films about 'law' and 'lawyers' are appropriately classified. This is essentially a problem of genre and whether we can really identify the strand that we might call law films and then determine what characteristics contribute to the genre or sub-genre. Whilst this idea might be viewed as a notion that belongs firmly within film theory rather than law, we would argue that genre is important for two distinct reasons. First, it is important that those writing about film and the law are able to identify and classify the primary material with which they are working. Parameters need to be set to determine what is the target of our work. That said, this does not prevent attempts to stretch and adapt the idea to encompass an enormous variety of films.

[8] R Post, 'On the Popular Image of the Lawyer: Reflections in a Dark Glass' (1987) 75 *California L Rev* 382.

[9] ibid.

Indeed it is possible to find work in the area of film and the law that includes examples as diverse as *Judge Dredd* and *Cape Fear*; genre should not be seen as a restrictive strait-jacket but rather as a means of determining what we are studying. It need not be a rigid concept but rather one that is responsive to the development of the area. It ought to be remembered that whilst there is a growing body of work that addresses a multiplicity of issues in the area of film and the law, the domain is relatively new and its parameters undecided. Secondly, we need to engage with genre from an audience perspective and here there are other concepts from film theory that could be usefully applied. Genre introduces conventions that affect understanding and the reading of films. One recent attempt to tackle the issue of law films and genre suggested the following approach;

> In order to qualify as a law film the following characteristic(s) must be present in some shape or form: the geography of law, the language and dress of law, legal personnel and the authority of law. This excludes films where 'justice is enforced outside of any legal framework for example, war films, social dramas and family sagas'.[10]

Detailed analysis of the thorny question of genre is beyond the remit of this paper and there have been some attempts to tackle the problem whilst it is an area that requires further more detailed work.[11] The more limited, though overlapping, point we make here is that many films that we might claim as being about 'law' could be happily located within other categories such as 'dramas' or 'thrillers' and this is part of the genre debate. However it could be argued that many of the films that appear, on the face of it, to be obvious law films (even if we adopt a very narrow 'courtroom drama' definition) are actually about much broader issues. Law, or more specifically the courtroom, becomes the vehicle by which social issues can be dramatized. Thus we can use the adversarial system of justice to enjoin a debate on controversial issues. This is the beauty of the adversarial system; it allows the case for both sides to be presented, not by the parties themselves but rather by lawyers, whom the audience know to be acting as professional advocates. An interesting variation on this idea, that we will turn to later, is the position where the advocate becomes identified with the cause itself, when the professional mask is dislodged. The shift from dispassionate to committed brings an additional dimension that may alter our feelings about the lawyer and add a further ethical dimension as professional detachment is dissipated.

We can find many examples of the wider dramatic landscape. Is *To Kill A Mockingbird*, for example, a social commentary on racism told through a legal story, an individual rape case with a racial dimension, a rather one dimensional courtroom drama, or even all of these?[12] An important point here is that deciding

[10] Greenfield, Osborn and Robson, n 1 above, 24. [11] ibid.

[12] *To Kill a Mockingbird* is probably the film that has been subject to the broadest and deepest analysis by legal academics; see, eg, Symposium (1994) 45 *Alabama L Rev*. Interestingly the central figure, Atticus Finch, has more recently been subject to detailed criticism that has sought to knock him off his lofty perch as the lawyers' favourite film lawyer. See M Freedman, 'Atticus Finch—Right and Wrong,' (1994) 45 *Alabama L Rev* 473 and also S Lubet, 'Reply to comments on reconstructing Atticus Finch' (1999) 97 *Michigan L Rev* 1382.

what a film is about is not a simple, or more importantly, a fixed idea, how the audience 'reads' the film and reacts to the characters is dependent on a whole host of factors. Films may also tell a number of different stories. A useful illustration is provided by Kramer's *Inherit the Wind*. The film is described by Halliwell thus:

> Splendid theatrics with fine performances, marred by boring subplots but enhanced by a realistic portrayal of a sweltering Southern town.[13]

The website www.teachwithmovies.org takes the view that *Inherit the Wind* can be used;

> . . . to introduce children to the pivotal question that must be resolved in each democracy, i.e. the balance between the rights of the majority and those of individuals. In addition it will serve as a platform to discuss the debate over 'creationism,' which is still raised on occasion by some Americans, the red scares, and fundamentalist religion.[14]

A further perspective is provided by Harris;

> . . . the historical implications of the trial—the fact that the outcome resulted in the loosening of restrictive teaching practices in some states, but not Tennessee—take a back seat in both the film and the play to the histrionics of the principal players.[15]

Further to this, one industry perspective suggests that the major feature of the film is the opportunity for actors to show the prowess of their advocacy;

> Here was an attempt to jaw about Big Issues—fundamental faith versus intellectual freedom,—censorship, religion, politics, education—and it worked.[16]

Here we see a number of angles on the one film, some of which overlap and some of which illustrate neatly the plethora of perspectives, or readings that a text, or a film for our present purposes, might evince. It is perhaps unsurprising that films are subject to different interpretations, but crucially are we able to determine if any is 'right', or to evaluate which approach is the more 'important'? Interestingly, Harris quotes the director Stanley Kramer who sets *Inherit the Wind* in the context of two of his other films, *The Defiant Ones* and *On the Beach* and describes them as a trilogy of thought provoking films.[17] In a similar vein, we have *In the Name of the Father*, a film that on one level deals with the arrest and conviction of the Guildford Four. However, the film has a number of different themes and issues that run through it; one critic's view was that 'the film is very much about Northern Ireland politics and the relations between Northern Ireland and Britain',[18] whilst the director, Jim Sheridan, saw it as a film about the relationship between a father and his son, and there are also other further interpretations or angles around the

[13] J Walker (ed), *Halliwell's Film Guide* (13th edn, London: 1997), 390.
[14] See www.teachwithmovies.org/guides/inherit-the-wind.html.
[15] T Harris, *Courtroom's finest hour in American cinema* (1987), 125.
[16] Anon, 'See You in Court' (September 1989) *Empire*, 30.
[17] See Kramer's comments reproduced in Harris, n.15 above.
[18] K Domaille, *In the Name of the Father* (London: 2001), 35.

areas of justice and law more generally. Again this shows us both the macro and micro dimensions which might exist within a single film.[19] For example, other ostensible law films explore issues such as family relationships (*Cape Fear*), homophobia (*Philadelphia*), and racism (*The Hurricane*) although they can be read on a narrower level as films about the law.[20]

Personal Foibles and Professional Dilemmas

A distinction may be drawn between the imperfections of the screen lawyers themselves, as individuals, and the issues of professional ethics and their adherence to these. The line may, at times, be an artificial one and indeed we would argue that the crucial factor is the overall image that the character presents. We have identified two distinct groupings of ethical values, and we are necessarily adopting a broad definition of ethics to embrace both wider moral values as well as the narrower code of professional behaviour. These two perspectives may well be in harmony, but they can conflict as detailed, for example, in Fried's illustration of the lawyer who acts assiduously on behalf of his client (professional ethics) whilst his approach may be of questionable benefit to society as a whole (moral probity and ethical values).[21] There are other examples of these two sets of values clashing; for example we can see lawyers prepared to compromise their own professional standards in order to achieve a much broader ethical commitment to justice. Perhaps the best example is from *Cape Fear* when Sam Bowden fails to disclose the report that would have helped acquit his client. His reasoning for doing so is interesting, based as it is upon an abrogation of his duty as a lawyer, and betrayal of his client, but with the aim of serving some sort of higher ideal and protecting society generally.[22] Here Bowden is apparently concerned for the victim and the community, and is seemingly prepared to sacrifice his own career in the pursuit of a wider ethical stance. An interesting counterpoint to this can be seen in *Suspect*, where Riley (Cher) places the interests of her client above herself. She puts herself in an invidious (and unethical) position by her relationship with a juror, but again sees this act as a conduit to some higher ideal of justice that might not be found with a rigid adherence to procedural law.

Another example of this can be seen, perhaps surprisingly given his canonization in some quarters, in the figure of Atticus Finch. Finch is often held up as a paragon of legal ethics and an embodiment of all that is, or can be good about being a lawyer. Indeed, he is cited by some as one of the reasons they chose to go to Law School and become lawyers in the first place. However, whilst his taking on the unpopular client in a segregated deep south is to be applauded on many levels,

[19] ibid,37.

[20] Greenfield, Osborn and Robson, n 1 above, ch 4.

[21] C Fried, 'The Lawyer as Friend: The Moral Foundations of the Lawyer-Client Relation' (1976) 85 *Yale L J* 1060.

[22] Greenfield, Osborn and Robson, n 1 above, 38.

Finch himself is not ethically pure in his actions. At the end of the Harper Lee book and the film, Finch conspires with the sheriff to lie by saying that Ewell, killed by Boo Radley while defending Finch's children, in fact died in a tragic accident:

> There is no question that the killing was justifiable. But the sheriff convinces Finch that the local court system, which has just sent the patently innocent Tom Robinson to his death, has not proven itself so reliable that it can be trusted to vindicate Radley. So the sheriff persuades Finch to go along with the accident story. In other words, the novel concludes with Atticus Finch engaging in what today could only be called obstruction of justice.[23]

Again we see different, and perhaps contentious, readings of the film, drawing upon different aspects and perhaps focusing on issues that may not have been initially apparent, or at least overlooked on initial viewings.

Outside of this broader moral dimension to the lawyer, there are numerous examples of dubious professional legal ethics. These include Galvin in *The Verdict* and Riley in *Suspect* as outlined above, and the film *The Firm* provides myriad examples of a law firm engaging in a series of criminal activities. Interestingly, this willingness to go beyond the strictly legal in the pursuit of some higher idealized notion of what is right is often what the public feel makes a 'good lawyer', as they are prepared to risk themselves professionally, are seen as less individualistic, and have the wider good of other people or the community at large as the focus for their actions. By the same token, the lack of concern for professional ethics (in that they are compromised by broader duties or beliefs) is in many ways part of the constituents of the 'successful' cinematic lawyer. This is an integral part of the attractiveness of the characters, they are mavericks who are fixed on wider notions of justice or truth often at the expense of professional codes. Even Lincoln (in *Young Mr Lincoln*) is shown in this light, seemingly not concerned with the law, or with the legal process but far more concerned with the 'upshot'. This is beautifully captured in his riposte to the prosecuting counsel in the murder trial, when he is accused of knowing little about the law itself and the legal procedures that should be followed in court. His well known response is of course that whilst he may not be versed in the intricacies of the law, he 'knows what is right'. To the viewing public this not only earmarks him as someone who has the interests of justice and fairness at heart, but pitches his opponent as someone who is bound up in the law and who sees the law itself as more important.

The Critical Audience: It's Only a Film

A key issue for the bodies representing the professions, notably the American Bar Association (ABA), is the relationship between the image and public perception of the profession. An easy, and rather lazy, connection can be constructed along

23 Simon, n 5 above, 2.

the lines of; 'our screen image is unfair and unrealistic and this feeds and informs public opinion'. Indeed, the Model Code of Professional Responsibility puts it thus; '[b]ecause of his position in society, even minor violations of law by a lawyer tend to lessen public confidence in the legal profession'.[24] This ignores a whole host of variables that need to be examined further, and many of these are covered below. Perhaps most importantly, the evidence that has been presented on the connection between the unethical lawyer and apparently decreasing public respect needs to be examined and deconstructed,[25] for as Spitz observes: '[d]o these fictional portrayals create attitudes and perceptions about lawyers, or do they simply mirror, embellish, and reinforce attitudes and perceptions that already exist in our culture?'[26]

Furthermore, when we have a clash of ethics what is the perception that we, the audience, have of the lawyer? What image(s) do we draw from T*he Verdict*? The drunken unethical ambulance chaser or the heroic advocate (the impassioned speech to the jury is one of the hallmarks of the film) who wins the increased damages for the claimants? The desperate and downtrodden character at the beginning, or the revitalized and reinvented character at the end? Spitz's view of *The Verdict* is that his risky and unethical conduct leaves an indelible and distasteful impression in the mind of the viewer. The obvious riposte to this is to consider instead the question of 'who is the viewer'? Another take from a different perspective might be to consider the outcome (ie what actually happened, and to take a holistic view of the film) and not be tied in too much to the process (the procedural and filmic means by which this was reached). For example, we see Galvin metamorphose during the course of the case (and film), from the negative initial impression to a reformed image by the end. Outside of the personal idiosyncrasies of Galvin himself and how the viewer might see the lawyer, does the viewer necessarily view Galvin's act of not disclosing the offer negatively? A broader view, which looks not at the process and the minutiae of legal procedure, focuses more on the end product, the *outcome*. In addition to cleaning himself up personally and professionally, Galvin also succeeds in his 'David and Goliath' battle and obtains compensation far higher than both the participants in the film, and the viewers would have thought possible. Is this not a positive image, of the right result being achieved in a broader sense and a man's redemption on the other? It can be argued that this is the real view that viewers take of such law films, as opposed to the lawyer/viewer watching the law film and reading it on a procedural level.

This raises a further point about context. In particular, does a viewer familiar with previous work by the same director make different links and connections that affect the view of the immediate film, than someone who is not versed in the directorial canon? We need to have some understanding as to how the film and the characters are judged by those who, it is claimed, are influenced in their perception

[24] This is quoted in ibid, 27.

[25] In a 1964 study it was found that ethical and moral practices of lawyers had improved, so had the image of the legal profession (ABA, *A Review of Legal Education in the United States*, cited in Spitz, n 5 above).

[26] Spitz, n 5 above, 728.

of law and lawyers. Put bluntly, does the portrayal of a 'bad' lawyer (whatever that may be) create a more general impression in the minds of the audience about lawyers. In many ways this proposition can be reduced to the bad lawyer/good lawyer debate. A number of alternative interpretations have been brought to the fore to try and establish any general perspective that might exist. As noted above, essentially this debate centres upon the issue of whether cinematic lawyers are portrayed in a positive or negative light. The delineations between the two concepts are in fact more complex than might first be imagined with a number of grey areas making definitive explanations between the two difficult. One approach is to try and provide a framework by which depictions can be placed into one of the two categories. This is the approach adopted, for example, by Asimow who has argued that most recent lawyer depictions have been negative, certainly since the 1970s.[27] This view, of essentially a negative portrayal, can then feed into some understanding of the perspective that the American public has a very low opinion of lawyers.

The device adopted by Asimow was to consider the screen depiction of a lawyer on two levels in order to ascertain whether the portrayal was positive or not. His approach was to consider whether he would want this lawyer as his friend (recalling Fried's points about the lawyer-client relationship), and/or as his lawyer. If both of these could be answered in the affirmative, the character portrayal was deemed to be positive. Whilst Asimow's approach has its merits and it provides a useful intervention in the debate, it has been argued that such an approach is rather one-dimensional in that it fails to appreciate the broader context and complexity of the portrayal of lawyers.[28] For example, an unethical screen lawyer might be seen to be Frank Galvin in T*he Verdict*, as detailed above, and in particular his specific breach of his client duty. Asimow would argue that he would want Galvin neither as his lawyer (did not have the best interests on the client at heart) nor his friend (precious little evidence of attributes such as warmth and loyalty, whilst there is much evidence of his character flaws). However does this necessarily make the portrayal negative? A holistic approach taking into account the redemptive qualities of the film might be to consider the character at the end of the film, devoid of vices and 'cleaned up', rather than his initial portrayal and the journey he undertakes throughout the course of the film.

So as part of this more general debate, ethics has a central role to play. We need to identify a number of representations of ethics, both on a broader perspective of personal morality and on the more narrow professional basis, and then to consider how these representations fit in to our understanding of the characteristics of the screen lawyer. Perhaps most importantly this helps elicit what work needs to be carried out to make use of our initial excavations. Thus we may identify issues and themes, but also need to make sense of what these might mean.

Consider here the depiction of the lawyer Gareth Pierce, and the legal process, in *In the Name of the Father*. Outside of any concerns of the accuracy of portrayal

[27] Asimow, n 2 above. [28] Greenfield, Osborn and Robson, n 1 above.

and the difficulties in filming true stories,[29] what does the viewing public understand from the film in terms of its understanding of the legal system itself? The film concerns the Guildford Pub bombing of the early 1970s as part of the Irish Republican Army mainland campaign against British occupation, and the subsequent convictions and imprisonment of the four alleged bombers. Much of the film shows the British criminal justice and legal system in a very negative light; Conlon (Daniel Day Lewis) is seen having a confession beaten out of him, and all the 'bombers' are shown to have no involvement in the events. However, at the conclusion of the film it is the very same system that frees them on appeal, notwithstanding the dramatic licence taken with both the method and delivery of this in the film. So we have conflicting views of the system, the evil and rigid machine that put four innocent people in prison and the vehicle of justice that sees the wrong put right. Arguably, despite the miscarriage of justice that the film is predicated upon, *In the Name of the Father* can be seen as celebrating the potential of the law to fight injustice, and it is possible that it is this aspect of the legal system that the public focuses upon.

To take a different slant upon this, does it matter to the general public *why* lawyers breach rules? If the choice is made in the interests of the client this may not reinforce negative stereotypes; if done for the lawyer's self interest this may reinforce the stereotype of the selfish uncaring lawyer. However, as can be seen from our readings of *The Verdict, Cape Fear and In the Name of the Father* above, perhaps the chief concerns are the wider issues or upshot rather than a limited reading based on narrow issues:

> [W]hen a fictional lawyer is faced with an ethical dilemma and makes a decision based upon a moral choice, the viewer may disagree with his ethics but admire his choice. In the viewer's eyes, this increases the characters moral worth and creates a feeling of empathy. The process of judging that lawyer requires one to judge him first as a person.[30]

This taps into Simon's observations regarding what he called 'moral pluck', a phrase inspired by Bernard William's 'Moral Luck', but denoting here 'a combination of transgression and resourcefulness in the vindication of justice'.[31] Simon argues that this notion runs through all recent favourable portrayals of lawyers and cites his examples primarily via the Grisham novels and two TV series; *LA Law* and *The Practice*. He gives a number of examples of the lawyer venturing outside of the law:

> . . . the hero has to extricate himself through cleverness and initiative. His efforts invariably require violations of various enacted norms. Sometimes the violations affront professional responsibility norms: Rudy Baylor in The Rainmaker engages in bedside solicitation of a personal injury victim. Gray Grantham, a reporter in The Pelican Brief, spies to discover the identity of a telephone source after promising not to do so. Sometimes the violations are major felonies: Baylor and Mitch Deere of The Firm both commit homicides. Deere's seems to be without legal justification or excuse, and although Baylor's might be legally

[29] Ibid; S Greenfield and G Osborn, 'Pulped Fiction? Cinematic Parables of (In)justice' (1996) 30 *U of San Francisco L Rev* 1181.

[30] Spitz, n 5 above, 742.

[31] Simon, n 5 above, 3.

excusable self-defense (or defense of another), he contrives an elaborate and flagrantly lawless cover up.[32]

Simon argues that the works he considers support a hypothesis that rather than lawyer transgressions negatively affecting the public's perceptions of lawyers, in fact the audience is sophisticated enough to judge these acts contextually:

> The moral orientation of these works is neither cynical nor indifferent to principle. It just doesn't share the categorical, authoritarian premises of elite moralism. If these works are any guide, the public is less susceptible to elite influence than the elites like to think. It is less troubled by defiance of authority because it has much lower expectations of authority. And it tends not to see ethical norms and issues categorically. It is more willing to see formally enacted norms as qualified by more informal norms and more inclined to see all norms as presumptions that can be rebutted in situations where competing values of greater weight are at stake. The appeal of these works depends on the audience's ability and disposition to judge contextually rather than categorically.[33]

So, questions such as those asking whether a lawyer is good or bad, or whether he is ethical, are short sighted and loaded questions, in that the films are too complex to allow judgments to be made in this way. Additionally, we need to allow for both the sophistication of the audience, and the potentiality that films are read in different ways by different viewers. So, dogmatic/one dimensional views of lawyers, and an over zealous adherence to ethical issues in law films take us nowhere. For a start, how can we tell what the message of a film is? Whilst the director of the film might have one view of what the film means and how certain aspects of this should be read, it does not necessarily follow that the viewer will follow this as each recipient of material may decode this in a different way. This is rather akin to the tension between subjectivity and objectivity in law. Hence while we might expect conduct within the realm of the tort of negligence to be judged on the basis of objective reasonableness, this evaluation must take place via a subjective medium (the judge). It is important to delve a little deeper into the idea of reading films, and the difficulty of adopting homogeneous views of what a film means.

Conclusion

The issue of professional ethics within film, and particularly how these are treated by cinematic lawyers, is clearly important on several levels. These include the following. First, it contributes to both the plot and the narrative—the issue of (un)ethical conduct may indeed be a central focus of the film itself. Secondly, it provides a mechanism that allows the audience to engage with complex characters and helps to add a human element to the legal coda. Finally, it contributes on a basic level to the film viewing public's understanding of law and the legal system.

[32] Simon, n 5 above, 9. [33] ibid, 29.

This latter point is an extremely contentious one, and a variant of the 'media effects' debate that permeates many areas of popular culture—from the claims of the tabloid newspaper *The Sun* to have 'won it' (the General Election) for the Conservatives in 1992, through to the relationship between screen violence and copycat crimes, the influence and effects of the media is a controversial and complex issue. This chapter is not the place to attempt to review the complexities and nuances of that debate and work in the area,[34] but the legal profession has exhibited some concern on this point in terms of the effects upon the standing of the profession of what it perceives to be a negative image, and one that is exacerbated by film and television depictions:

> The interplay between television and culture has been analogized to waves on a beach, where over time, the beach clearly changes shape under the impact of the waves. Imagine the influence of television as the waves, and the beach as the image of the profession. If practitioners do not grab the bull by the horns and make a concerted effort to improve the image of attorneys, the shape of the beach may be changed forever. We may not be able to stop the waves, but we surely can transform the beach into hard soil.[35]

However, this view assumes that the image carried by the audience is the same as that perceived by the professional. As we discuss above, while on the (banal, to the general public at least) level of narrow professional ethics, a film may certainly show lawyers acting outside of these parameters and these may be a matter of some concern to the watching (real) lawyer. However, there is an alternative view, based on the fact that in cinematic terms, the lawyer who is prepared to risk his career and the wrath of his colleagues is a far more attractive character precisely because of his sacrifice. To the non-lawyer member of the general public, this attribute may be far more memorable and worthy of praise than an adherence to some arcane Code of Conduct—again the outcome outweighs the process to all but the initiated. The lawyer who is prepared to forsake all in the pursuit of justice may indeed be clothed with the mantle of the hero:

> I understood that the hero of the story, the main character, is placed in a situation where he or she confronts a series of obstacles in order to achieve that higher state of consciousness. I saw that it was not only a physical journey but a spiritual one because it takes place inside as well as outside. On this journey the hero experiences a symbolic transformation of death and resurrection as he casts off the old parts of his life in order to be reborn and emerge into the 'birth' of his new self.[36]

This idea of developing heroic status through a journey of self discovery or redemption certainly fits in with numerous screen lawyers. Sam Bowden (*Cape Fear*), Katherine Riley (*Suspect*) and most notably Frank Galvin (*The Verdict*). Often this journey is cathartic, and usually this journey adds to the subtext of the

[34] But see, eg, L Bibbings, 'The things they make you do: researching violence in television and cinema—a review of publications' (1998) *Communications Law* 103.

[35] Spitz, n 5 above, 734.

[36] S Field, *Going to the Movies* (New York: 2001).

story. The hero needs the obstacles to progress and one of the key features is the obstruction caused by the legal process that prevents the delivery of justice. To provide justice the heroic lawyer must then abandon the strict legal rules (*In the Name of the Father*) or the professional limitations (*My Cousin Vinny, Suspect*). Thus far from being a detrimental feature the willingness to break ethical norms shows exactly what the lawyer is prepared to sacrifice in order to deliver justice. This may even involve betraying a client or even the court in order that justice can be seen to be done. To the professional lawyer this may be seen as beyond the pale, but to the viewer on the outside of the legal process it makes the lawyer, and the law, appear human(e).

Adaptation: What Post-Conviction Relief Practitioners in Death Penalty Cases Might Learn From Popular Storytellers About Narrative Persuasion

Philip N Meyer[1]

MCKEE

. . . You follow? Good.

(takes a deep breath)

Anyone else?

Kaufman timidly raises his hand.

MCKEE (CONT'D)

(to Kaufman)

Yes?

KAUFMAN

Sir, what if a writer is attempting to create a story where nothing much happens? Where people don't change, they don't have any epiphanies. They struggle and are frustrated, and nothing is resolved. More a reflection of the real world.

MCKEE

The real world?

KAUFMAN

Yes, sir.

MCKEE

. . . [N]othing happens in the world? . . . Are you out of your fucking mind? People are murdered every day. There's genocide, war, corruption. Every fucking day somewhere in the world, somebody sacrifices his life to save somebody else. Every fucking day someone somewhere makes a conscious decision to destroy someone else! People find love! People lose it!

[1] Versions of this paper were presented at the Planning Conference for a Possible Persuasion Institute at New York University Clinical Law Center, 15–17 May 2003, and at the University College London Colloquium on Law and Popular Culture, 30 June–1 July 2003. My thanks to Matt Virkstis for research assistance. And thanks T, for inviting me to the party.

For Christ's sake, a child watches a mother beaten to death on the steps of a church! Someone goes hungry! Someone else betrays his best friend for a woman! If you can't find that stuff in life, then you, my friend, don't know crap about life! And why the fuck are you wasting my two precious hours with your movie? I don't have any use for it! I don't have any bloody use for it![2]

The Beginning

At a planning group to explore the possibilities of organizing a narrative persuasion institute for death penalty litigators engaged in post-conviction relief brief-writing practice,[3] Anthony Amsterdam posed this as the 'central task' for post-conviction relief counsel on behalf of a condemned inmate:

The central task of postconviction counsel for a condemned inmate is to *change* a story that has been certified as The Truth. S/he has to deconstruct the story of people and events that was told in the appellate opinion affirming the inmate's conviction and sentence, break that story down into pieces, and recombine those pieces into a new story capable of capturing the imagination and opening the minds of judges and clemency officials and media people and even state's attorneys who think they already know the whole story. Every postconviction case starts with a story that these people believe has been officially stamped closed, so that they don't have to think about it anymore. Postconviction counsel's job is to CHANGE that story, to reconstruct the world in which that story happened, to force people who think they understand the story to THINK ABOUT IT IN A NEW WAY and to see enough new facts—facts that weren't exposed before, or weren't put into focus before—so that the old facts make a new kind of sense and turn into a quite DIFFERENT STORY.[4]

There are, however, clear pragmatic, evidentiary, and aesthetic conventions operating as obvious constraints upon the narrative practices in this legally specific context. In materials prepared for the conference, Amsterdam identifies seven constraints that shape process in post-conviction death penalty work:

Constraints on Storytelling in the 21st Century Legal Postconviction Process[5]

1. The audience demands that the story be '*true*.' S/he defines his/her job as discerning the truth. Usually s/he believes truth is 'out there' in the world.
2. Certain facts are *given*—undeniable and undisputable—because it is inevitable that the audience will have them in mind and believe them to be either
    a. Factually true, or
    b. Required by legal rules to be viewed as true, whether
        i. Categorically, or
        ii. In the absence of contrary evidence you ain't got.

[2] C Kaufman and D Kaufman, *Adaptation*, (New York: 2002), 68–69.

[3] Collected Notes and Materials from the Planning Conference for a Possible Persuasion Institute, New York University Clinical Law Center, 15–17 May 2003 (on file with author).

[4] ibid.

[5] ibid.

[Sometimes the facts that are *given* are 'ultimate' facts (for example, *your client was the triggerman*); sometimes they are evidentiary facts (for example, *your client's fingerprints were in the murder weapon*)].

3. There is an *opposing storyteller*, motivated and equipped to deconstruct your story and/or persuade the audience of the truth of a counterstory.
4. You are *viewed as an interested pleader* and often you are suspected of being a trickier one, more prone to charlatanism, than the opposing storyteller.
5. You are *retelling* a story and attempting to *change* at least some parts of a story that has been previously told and officially certified to be authentic.
6. Your audience is a *judge* (not, as in many preconviction proceedings, a jury).

[A judge is a professional factfinder, with much ego invested in the belief that s/he is capable of getting at truth. S/he often views storytelling as a scam designed to derail the search for truth. S/he is rule-oriented and is often uncomfortable with uncertainties and ambiguities. S/he will resent being 'played upon' by an adroit storyteller. S/he feels overworked, hence is impatient. Also, s/he may be biased to reject your story by (a) experience (s/he's heard *this* tale before); (b) professional identification (s/he was a prosecutor before going on the bench); (c) temperament/philosophy (s/he's a passionate Federalist Society devotee); and/or (d) political expediency (reelection or advancement requires that s/he favor the prosecution).]

7. Usually, you must tell your story in *written form*, perhaps embellished with some pictorial exhibits or video clips but not (as in many pre-conviction proceedings), by presenting the oral testimony of witnesses and physical displays or other living theater. You can get the opportunity to present live witness testimony only if and after you have convinced a judge in writing that you have a case.[6]

The multifaceted and complex task becomes how to shape the written persuasive narrative, that is both factual and truthful, within the constraints of legal practice. How to adapt and shape materials, and retell a once told story anew, preserving without distortion the integrity of the original material within the constraints of a new form. The portion of this task that I address in this paper is how might the post-conviction relief practitioner incorporate popular storytelling practices from creative non-fiction to better serve the interests of a condemned inmate. How to enhance the possibilities of telling a more effective and transformative story—without manipulation or deceit—without reducing the artful narrative practice of writing the Statement of the Case, or the narrative component of argumentation in a post-conviction relief brief to paint-by-numbers formulae.

In this paper I also hope to better locate and understand the narrative dimensions of post-conviction relief brief writing within the tensions of the structure proposed by Amsterdam, and, perhaps, to begin to suggest a relationship between popular and legal storytelling in post-conviction relief practice. I provide several examples or 'illustrations' that may suggest possibilities for innovative practices for post-conviction relief practitioners. Specifically, I believe that contemporary non-fiction may provide suggestive possibilities to the practitioner designing and drafting the Statement of the Case, or developing narrative themes for translating and converting the spine

[6] ibid.

of legal argument into persuasive story. Further, these examples may reveal the structural and stylistic latitude available potentially to the post-conviction relief practitioner. That is, the models provided by creative non-fiction supplemented with recent lawyering theory and selected instructional texts may provide lessons about making strategic choices, about effective practice, and about developing creative possibilities for reconfiguring evidentiary material into transformative stories. There are, of course, dangers here as well: the danger of telling too good a story, the danger of being perceived as a narrativist trickster and manipulator, the psychological danger of stepping outside the bounds of traditional legal discourse, and, of course, the danger of telling a compelling story that does not match with the procedural limitations imposed upon even the most sympathetic judicial reader. Still, there are important lessons to be learned by the post-conviction relief practitioner, and this comparatively unharvested territory is ripe for exploration and adaptation into practice.

This essay unfolds in three movements. Initially, drawing upon popular film in a somewhat lighthearted way, especially given the gravity of the work of post-conviction relief practitioners in death-penalty cases, I discuss the narrative dimensions of the work of post-conviction relief practitioner as akin to that of the predicament of the screenwriter/protagonist Charlie Kaufman in Spike Jonze's recent film *Adaptation*. Next, I suggest one possible illustrative narrative technique (the use of a short story embedded within an argument) and some useful vocabulary (for example, John Gardner's concept of 'profluence') that might be helpful for clinicians and practitioners interested in more systematically incorporating narrative practices into persuasive writing. Third, I identify several popular cultural 'illustrations' from recent creative non-fiction (the opening pages from James Ellroy's autobiography *My Dark Places* framed in the form of a detective mystery, and a short section of Joan Didion's essay 'The White Album') that adapt non-fiction journalistic material into powerful and truthful yet completely dissimilar non-fiction narratives. I supplement these illustrations with commentary drawn from texts on the craft of writing. These illustrations may suggest stylistic techniques of story elaboration, that may, in turn, suggest differing possibilities of narrative adaptation to post-conviction relief practices, of retelling once-told stories in the context of writing briefs in post-conviction relief work on behalf of condemned inmates.

I further suggest how these two excerpts connect to a common theme, which, coincidentally, underlies Spike Jonze's comedic exploration in *Adaptation*. This 'theme' is articulated expressly by Jerome Bruner and employed in analytical argument by Michael Roemer. These examples begin to illustrate how analytical or 'paradigmatic' argument may be translated into thematic narrative in different contexts. This, I hope, in turn suggests a vast range of other thematic possibilities, and stylistic elaborations that are available to post-conviction relief practitioners attempting to successfully reconfigure and retell a once told story that has not been completely developed in previous tellings. This may be due to limitations on the part of the initial storyteller. But often, I think, it may be caused by needlessly self-imposed constraints, including rigid adherence to the conventions of traditional legal analysis or undue deference to the initial forms of telling (at the initial trial, in the text of the appellate opinion, or at subsequent proceedings).

The exploration of possibilities suggested by creative non-fiction expands upon and enhances the truth-seeking role of the post-conviction relief practitioner. That is, the limitations upon the post-conviction relief practitioner seeking to employ conventional forms of exposition in the crucial post-conviction relief brief (for example, a chronological, linear depiction of facts subservient to and neatly domesticated by analytical principles) are often based upon external constraints of time (briefing schedules and case loads). But the post-conviction relief practitioner may also be frozen by self-imposed psychological constraints (such as fearfulness of creative alternative approaches). Perhaps, most dangerous of all, there may be false presuppositions about the psychological nature of the sceptical judicial audience, and a false sense that a truthful and factually accurate 'story' is limited to and constrained by the past-tense facts depicted in the previous versions of the story (for example, the 'facts' of the crime depicted in the version of the story in the appellate opinion). Finally, the false safety of the genre conventions of legal discourse may insulate both the advocate-storyteller and the judicial decision-maker from taking responsibility for completing the final retelling of the tale by either providing closure to the story (the execution of the condemned prisoner) or allowing narrative to continue.

If some of this introduction seems obscure, I hope that my analogy to the film *Adaptation* and the illustrations from creative non-fiction may provide some concreteness and grounding for these abstract observations. The genesis of this essay develops from my long-time experience as a teacher and director of legal writing and appellate advocacy programmes, in addition to my interest in popular culture. I believe that legal education does a great deal of damage in teaching and imposing rigid and conventional constraints upon the legal imagination: while there are 'principles' of brief-writing, and the accurate and compelling use of facts must be matched to effective legal arguments, I believe that law students and practitioners are artificially limited by rigid notions of what legal arguments should be, and of what the narrative components of a brief 'should look like', and of what forms and styles of story elaboration within the argument should take to compel the attention, rather than the dismissive judgmental scrutiny, of a judicial reader. Also, there is often a stultifying professional perspective that limits notions of theme and story to mere recitations of evidentiary facts, when the potential stories and themes for the post-conviction relief practitioner may be far more expansive. Thus, for example, as Anthony Amsterdam has observed, the truthful 'story' told in a post-conviction relief brief may pertain to the legal story casting the interpretation of the statute at the core of the thematic narrative.[7] Or the story may pertain to an expansion and retelling of one aspect of the larger story, such as the misconduct of a governmental actor.[8] Or the story may pertain to a story that was omitted from trial, and omitted

[7] Collected Notes and Materials from the Planning Conference for a Possible Persuasion Institute, New York University Clinical Law Center, 15–17 May 2003 (on file with author).

[8] Perhaps one dominant story theme in post-conviction relief practice is, traditionally, the failure of the system to 'work' and provide justice. At times this failure is the product of inadvertence and

from the appellate opinion. For example, a brief challenging a sentence may include recasting the characters, expanding the time-frame, altering the point-of-view and perspective, and retelling the story of a crime as the story of the defendant and the impact of cultural forces that compelled the crime in a brief in mitigation of sentencing. Practitioners, adhering to artificial constraints based upon limited notions of legal cultural discourse, and not recognizing the narrative possibilities and dimensions of their work, may not 'see' the full range of creative options and alternatives potentially available in their brief-writing practices, particularly those possibilities necessary for retelling a once-told tale in a transformative way. Further, I believe, many practitioners may, at times, misread the nature of judicial scepticism, or misunderstand what may possibly compel the imaginative attention of a sceptical judicial reader.

There are, of course, legitimate reasons to be careful, and to stick closely to established forms. For example, by expressly incorporating a different intentionality, and relying upon alternative techniques in developing briefs, post-conviction relief practitioners may rightfully be wary of being too easily dismissed as a 'storyteller' in a pejorative sense of a deceiver or fictionalizer, manipulating and distorting the story on appeal already predetermined to be true.

Nevertheless, in this paper, I argue that on balance the post-conviction relief practitioner should approach the narrative possibilities in the post-conviction relief brief directly and systematically. Further, I suggest how creative non-fiction may be a rich source of inspiration for alternative approaches to truthful and factual narrative persuasion, and for deepening the truth-seeking function of the brief. Finally, I hope that my 'illustrations' from popular non-fiction and academic literature may encourage the exploration of other non-fiction voices, and also encourage practitioners to read much of the recent lawyering theory. I believe that these materials provide a rich range of materials to inform the work of brief-writing on behalf of condemned inmates in post-conviction relief practice.

I. Retelling a Once Told Story in Spike Jonze's *Adaptation*

Jerome Bruner, a co-convener of the Lawyering Colloquium at NYU School of Law[9] and a member of an initial planning group exploring the possibility of developing a Narrative Persuasion Institute for Death Penalty practitioners, observes that all

oversight. At other times the product of a professional failure of one or more participants (eg, an incompetent defence attorney, an overzealous prosecutor, a police investigator making wrong decisions and premature choices, a police imformant fabricating testimony), or the product of a defendant unable to protect his own interests or incapable of fully articulating his own story (eg, mental impairment, confession without counsel). At other times the outcome may be the result of intentional manipulation and conspiracy by powerful state actors. The latter theme has been particularly effective in trial stories when employed by creative and passionate advocates (Gerry Spence and Johnnie Cochran), but may be a difficult story-theme to translate and prove to a sceptical judicial reader who may, as the embodiment of power within that system, believe firmly and presumptively in the efficacy of the system.

[9] The initial convenors of the Lawyering Colloquium at NYU School of Law were Anthony Amsterdam, Jerome Bruner, and Peggy Davis. I benefited greatly from participation in the colloquium

stories are intrinsically imagined and liminal, mediations between past and future, the mind's best attempts to reconcile memory and possibility.[10] Bruner's perception confirms the observations of Stanley Clavell, a long-time film fan. Clavell conducted an informal experiment with his graduate students. He would ask his students to retell the plots of familiar popular movies. Invariably, the stories that the students told were technically 'wrong'; that is, the plots that were reconstructed by the students were not literal or accurate recitations of the sequence of scenes in the film. Rather, the retold stories were in many ways newly constituted; stories that said as much about the story teller as about the images depicted on the screen.

Here, in this context, is my version of Spike Jonze's recent film *Adaptation*: Charlie Kaufman (portrayed by Nicholas Cage) is the protagonist of the film, a screenwriter with one successful screenplay in production (*Being John Malkovich*). Charlie is talented, but self-absorbed, obsessive, self-flagellating—a deeply neurotic personality. He is 'blocked' in his professional work, and his personal growth as well. Currently, he is attempting to adapt Susan Orlean's non-fiction book *The Orchid Thief*. It is a book of observations, a delicate *New Yorker*-ish book without a strong and apparent narrative core, a book seemingly without the possibilities of dramatic transformation into a visually compelling story. Thus, the book seemingly offers little promise of commercially successful cinematic adaptation. The book opens outwards, perhaps like a flower itself, or perhaps like life itself.[11] It also offers little possibility of the narrative closure, and a transformatively powerful ending.[12] Ultimately, as Charlie Kaufman observes, it is merely a book about flowers.[13]

If there is an implicit core around which Susan Orlean develops her multiple layers of observations, it is the story of John Laroche. Orlean's Laroche is a serial obsessive

during its early years, beginning 1991–1992, and many of the ideas in this paper have been derived from, and are surely attributable to, ideas that were floated in the colloquium during that time. I am unsure, at times, where those ideas end, and my own thoughts begin, and much of this paper is attributable to the colloquium, and Amsterdam's and Bruner's book *Minding the Law*, that develops ideas initially presented by the conveners in the Colloquium.

[10] JS Bruner, *Making Stories: Law, Literature, Life* (New York: 2002), 64–65.

[11] Donald, Charlie's pragmatic screenwriting twin brother, critiques Orlean's *The Orchid Thief* in the script of *Adaptation*:

Donald pulls a copy of The Orchid Thief from his bag. He opens it and reads[:]

DONALD (CONT'D)

'Sometimes this kind of story turns out to be something more . . . some glimpse of life that expands like those Japanese paper balls you drop in water and they bloom into flowers, and the flower is so marvelous you can't believe there was a time all you saw in front of you was a paper ball and a glass of water.' Well, first of all, that's inconsistent. She, she said that she didn't care about flowers.

Kaufman and Kaufman, *Adaptation*, n 2 above, 74.

[12] Robert McKee, the screenwriting guru, offers Charlie Kaufman the following crucial advice about endings in commercial screenplays: 'I'll tell you a secret. The last act makes the film. Wow them in the end and you got a hit. You can have flaws, problems, but wow them in the end and you've got a hit. Find an ending. But don't cheat. And don't you dare bring in a deus ex machina. Your characters must change. And the change must come from them. Do that and you'll be fine.' Kaufman and Kaufman, *Adaptation*, n 2 above, 70–71.

[13] '[Charlie] Kaufman[:] "It's about flowers." ' Kaufman and Kaufman, *Adaptation*, n 2 above, 50.

and autodidact, a man who was once obsessed with orchids and flowers, one in a sequence of serial passions. Once upon a time, Laroche hatched a clever plan while working for the Seminole Indian tribe, to take orchids from the Fahkahatchee Strand swamp in Florida for cultivation and sale. He believed Seminole Indians were exempt from laws protecting exotic plants and endangered species from poachers. Susan Orlean then wrote a successful *New Yorker* profile about Laroche and his criminal prosecution. Her book *The Orchid Thief* is an adaptation of that already once told story, converting her *New Yorker* profile on Laroche into a full length book. Orlean's psychological relationship with Laroche provides the unstated subtext of the book. While Laroche is passionate about everything, Orlean-the-narrator is psychologically adrift, and passionate, so she says, about nothing. The careful picture on the book jacket, in both the paperback and hardcover versions, depicts Orlean as a frail and delicately attractive woman, an orchid-like creature herself.[14] Reading the book, akin to the character of Charlie Kaufman in the movie, I found myself tabbing the pages of delicate prose and then turning back to the visual image of Susan Orlean on the back cover before reading on. In the book the relationship between Laroche and Orlean is purely the relationship between subject Laroche, and dispassionate and objective reporter/observer Orlean. Orlean's point of view is from outside of the action, and even Orlean's own final journey into the swamp to view the elusive ghost orchid ends without consummation or completion.

The primary conflict in the movie is much different, however, and pertains to Charlie Kaufman's internal struggle to adapt the material from the book into a successful screenplay and to adapt to his own world psychologically. Given the nature of the material and its lack of what John Gardner terms 'profluence' (forward narrative momentum), especially crucial to developing successful commercial films capable of compelling the attention of a popular audience, Charlie Kaufman is blocked in his work of 'adaptation'. To complicate matters, Charlie is a romantic of a curious sort: he wants to do 'justice' to the original material and he believes in the redemptive power of narrative, if he can just retell the once told story properly he may save himself through his artistic integrity.

The plot of the film *Adaptation* is then set in motion by the 'agent'[15]—Charlie's identical brother Donald (also portrayed by Nicholas Cage). Like the other characters in the film, Donald may be an imaginative construction, a part of Charlie's own psyche. Although Donald has no track-record as a screenwriter, he is determined to follow in his brother's footsteps. His aspirations, however, are different and narrower than Charlie's. He perceives his storytelling as merely a means to an end (success, money, women). He desires to write a successful commercial screenplay,

[14] '[Charlie] Kaufman[:] "We see Susan Orlean, delicate, haunted by loneliness, fragile, beautiful." ' Kaufman and Kaufman, *Adaptation*, n 2 above, 55.

[15] The 'Agent' is one component of Kenneth Burke's 'Pentad'. In his work, *A Grammar of Motives*, discussed in Amsterdam and Bruner's *Minding the Law*, Burke 'richly (but vaguely) characterized *dramatism* as deriving from an imbalance or misalignment among his five minimally required constituents of narrative—his famous "Pentad:" Agent, Act, Purpose (or Goal), Agency (or Means), and Scene.' AG Amsterdam and J Bruner, *Minding the Law* (Cambridge, Mass: 2002), 130.

a suspense thriller. Unlike Charlie, he is a simple and untroubled fellow psychologically: he is extroverted, direct, obvious. He lacks Charlie's endless capacity for internal psychological struggle and neurotic self-flagellation.

To fulfil his dream, Donald attends a three day Est-like Story-Structure Screenwriting Workshop taught by screen writing guru Robert McKee. The tools that Donald needs for his work are provided by McKee's lectures on narrative story-structure, and his accompanying book of screen writing principles. After attending the workshop, Donald begins his untroubled work, writing his action melodrama of murder and mayhem entitled 'Three' based on McKee's 'paradigmatic' deconstruction and analysis of the genre movie thriller *Seven*. Charlie's own agent terms the script 'amazing'.[16]

Donald shares with his brother Charlie the secret of his breakthrough and productivity—the tools provided by Robert McKee the screen writing guru. Unconvinced, but with nothing left to lose and his time running out before his own deadline for submission of the completed script, the blocked Charlie attends Mckee's course while in New York. He is there to visit Susan Orlean in person, but is psychologically unable to bring himself to speak with her. Instead, Charlie sits transfixed as Robert Mckee speaks about narrative structure, screen writing, and, it seems to Charlie, the secrets of life itself. Charlie has an epiphany at the workshop. After, he follows McKee to a bar and receives a personal transmission of the wisdom that will enable him to complete his adaptation of Orlean's book.

Charlie then breaks his block, and goes on to adapt his material successfully by writing himself in as the protagonist of his story, and by simultaneously violating all of the purported well-structured principles propounded in the course, with appropriately hilarious and mocking self-referential results. Susan Orlean's *New Yorker* non-fiction of ironic observations, delicate relationships and detachment, a book without a central core story,[17] is transformed into a bawdy and visually compelling farce. Charlie even employs the double 'deus ex machina' Mckee specifically warns him against (this climax includes an alligator attack that rescues Charlie from Laroche and an equally bizarre and coincidental car crash). Likewise, the transformative 'twist in the tale',[18] that Charlie initially hopes to avoid as mechanistic and over determined, becomes the 'coda'[19] to the story when the different aspects of Charlie's psyche are reconciled, and he is finally able to express his love, internalize his projection of Donald, and move forwards psychologically.

[16] Marty continues to Donald: 'Donald's script! A smart edgy thriller. It's the best script I've read all year . . . I'm gonna sell it for a shitload . . . In fact, you know, maybe you could bring your brother on to help you with the orchid thing . . . I mean, he's really goddamned amazing at structure.' Kaufman and Kaufman, *Adaptation*, n 2 above, 65.

[17] Charlie Kaufman removes a folded newspaper clipping and reads it to his agent Marty: ' "There's not . . . nearly enough of him [Laroche] to fill a book, so Orlean . . . digresses in long passages." Blah, blah, blah. "No narrative really unites these passages." New York Times Book Review. I can't structure this. It's that sprawling New Yorker shit . . . The book has no story. There's no story!' Kaufman and Kaufman, *Adaptation*, n 2 above, 50–51.

[18] This phrase is borrowed from Anthony Amsterdam. Collected Notes and Materials, n 3 above.

[19] Amsterdam and Bruner, *Minding the Law*, n 14 above, 122.

At least, this is my version of the story. So what, if anything, does this possibly have to teach the post-conviction relief practitioner about using popular stories as illustrations in brief writing? The story serves as cinematic trope for the plight of the post-conviction relief practitioner on several levels. First, the internal conflict within Charlie, manifest as the external conflict with his twin screenwriting brother Donald, and his initial reaction against the overly-structured and mechanistic notions of storytelling proposed by Robert McKee (and his tortured and blocked frustration that leads to his revenge fantasy against his psychological projections of the real-life characters of Laroche and Orlean), cleverly captures and expresses a primary tension for the post-conviction relief practitioner attempting to adapt and craft his retelling of a once told story to a reviewing judge. That is, Charlie's predicament humorously expresses the equally frustrating predicament of the legal post conviction relief practitioner, who, attempting to be faithful in form and substance to the initial story (for example, trial and sentencing) and subsequent retellings of that story (for example, appellate opinion, state post-conviction relief proceedings) may attempt to re-tell the story in the form that adheres not only to the supposed conventions and limitations of legal cultural discourse, but also, often unconsciously, to a repetition of the form of the previous telling. Simultaneously, the material may cry out for a new story, or at least a story reconfigured in a different narrative form, that often has not been captured or articulated by these previous texts.

On the other hand, retelling a once told story in post-conviction relief practice may be, partially, as Donald perceives it, a straightforward rhetorical and narrative practice that should adhere to legalistic genre conventions ('principles'),[20] in addition to the hard rules of practice and procedure. Furthermore, just as Donald sees it, this writing practice is a means to a specific legal end (stopping or postponing the execution of the condemned inmate). And the sceptical judicial reader, like the commercial viewing audience, may be immune to or unwilling to tolerate alternative narrative practices, particularly those stylistic practices that smack of originality. Rather than drawing the reader in, these narratives in briefs may readily make the judicial reader even more sceptical and suspicious, and suggest that there is an overt attempt by the desperate practitioner to manipulate the reader, despite the fact that all advocates at all stages of proceedings (representing the State, the Government, and the defendant/petitioner) always employ narratives to serve purposeful ends.

Consequently, the post-conviction relief practitioner representing a condemned inmate may rightfully be wary or fearful of, for example: intentionally varying from the traditional linear and chronological presentation of facts, or substituting alternative forms of time for chronology, or casting different actors into the factual

[20] '[Charlie] Kaufman: There are no rules, Donald, and anybody who says there are, is just—Donald: Oh, wait. Not rules. Principles. McKee writes that a rule says you must do it this way. A principle says this works and has through all remembered time.' Kaufman and Kaufman, *Adaptation*, n 2 above, 11.

narrative, or beginning at a different place in the story, or employing visually arresting sub-headings or pictures to supplement his narrative, or altering the writing style that is purportedly 'lawyer-like' to better serve his material, etc. The practitioner representing a condemned inmate may initially be fearful that innovation in form, structure, and style may be readily dismissed and, consequently, confine his legal narrative practice to the familiarity of 'conventional' forms of legal discourse. Of course, brief writing in post-conviction relief cases on behalf of a condemned inmate is a dangerous practice, and the results of failure, the possible outcomes, are terrible. It is not a supportive laboratory for experimentation. Furthermore, the advice that is available in legal writing books[21] is, unwittingly, often merely a Robert Mckee-esque checklist of conventional principles of form and structure, of legal genre conventions, of homilies that poorly supplement explicit court rules and procedural constraints, and often inadvertently constrain what is and may be included in the brief. Where does the practitioner turn for ideas and models for what may be properly attempted in truthfully retelling a once told story? For possible examples of creative adaptation? This paper argues that the post-conviction relief practitioner might learn a great deal from a close reading of recent popular cultural non-fiction. I also urge practitioners to take the time to read recent narrative theory, and the new and emerging lawyering theory scholarship that applies this theory to the various litigation specific practices to better understand the nature of litigation practice as narrative practice.[22]

Let me conclude this introduction by observing that 'once upon a time' legal education focused primarily and, perhaps, exclusively upon the analytical or paradigmatic mode, never upon the narrative. 'Facts' existed primarily as floating factoids in law school examinations used to call up legal rules and principles, with no independent life or complexity or narrative propulsion except in relation to the service of analytical principles: as merely illustrations subservient to legal rules. In legal analysis in law school the rules come first, and the elements of the rules are applied to the facts, and the facts have no independent significance apart from the rules that give them shape and meaning. This was, and to a large degree is still true, and the teaching of legal writing practice as a discrete form, different from other types of writing, maintains this subservience of facts to law. Consequently, law schools do not systematically facilitate law students developing the narrative and rhetorical skills crucial to effective practice, and further create the misimpression that these skills are peripheral to practice, or that the exposition of truthful narratives through more sophisticated styles and forms is somehow intrinsically deceptive. Meanwhile, skilled and successful practitioners in diverse litigation practices develop narrative skills, shifting constantly from the analytic mode into the narrative mode, translating evidence and inferential argument into truthful story.

Furthermore, in our all-consuming narrative culture, legal practice (especially in litigation) is increasingly influenced by popular stories. Successful practitioners

[21] HS Shapo et al, *Writing and Analysis in the Law* (4th edn, New York: 1999).

[22] Amsterdam and Bruner, *Minding the Law*, n 14 above, 5–7.

have learned how to 'adapt' their narrative practices, akin to the delicate Darwinian adaptation of the exotic plant—ghost—orchid that survives in the Fahkahatchee Strand swamp. Recently, cutting edge theorists, such as Peter Brooks, Jerome Bruner, and Anthony Amsterdam, have begun to harvest this ghost orchid from practice. Their explorations have, likewise, enabled practitioners in litigation-specific contexts, including post-conviction relief practitioners writing briefs in death penalty cases, to better understand the topography of the Fahkahatchee Strand swamp of practice and the nature of narrative adaptation within it. This paper attempts to participate in this exploration, and provide several simple illustrations that may suggest the relevance of this work for the post-conviction relief practitioner.

II. Illustration #1—Converting Argument into Narrative

John Gardner, novelist and writing teacher, begins his chapter on 'Plotting' in *The Art of Fiction,*[23] by suggesting to the young writer that:

> When designing a profluent plot, we've said, the writer works in one of three ways, sometimes two or more at once: He borrows some traditional story or action drawn from life; he works backwards from his climax; or he works forward from an initial steady state.[24]

Gardner notes, however, that there are other forms of narrative 'profluence'.[25] Some of these forms may align themselves closely with analytical practices. Specifically, one of the forms of creating narrative structure and movement is remarkably proximate to the form of strategic 'storytelling' often employed by effective attorneys in designing persuasive arguments built upon narrative examples. Specifically, Gardner observes:

> Though causal sequence gives the best (most obvious) kind of profluence, it is not the only possible means to that necessary end. A story or novel may develop argumentatively, leading the reader point by point to some conclusion. In this case events occur not to justify later events but to dramatize logical positions; thus event *a* does not cause event *b* but stands in some logical relationship to it.[26]

Gardner warns the writer about the limitations of using this form to sustain dramatic movement in fiction, largely because this narrative form is imposed strategically to serve intellectual ends:

> Such a story or novel might be interesting, even brilliant, but it can never achieve the power of an energetic action because the control of the action is intellectual, it does not arise out of the essence of things: It discusses reality the way a lecturer does (though perhaps more vividly), it does not reveal the modality of things. It does not capture process.[27]

[23] J Gardner, *The Art of Fiction: Notes on Craft for Young Writers* (New York, 1991), 165.
[24] ibid.
[25] Gardner defines 'profluence' as '. . . our sense, as we read, that we're "getting somewhere[.]" 'Gardner, *The Art of Fiction*, n 23 above, 48.
[26] ibid, 165.
[27] ibid, 166.

It is within this format—through a form of narrative 'profluence', or narrative construction where, as Jerome Bruner observed some years ago, the analytical or scientific method attempts to 'tame' narrative[28]—that much of litigation practice occurs.

That is, in legal argument, whether the argument is in a written brief in post-conviction relief on behalf of the condemned inmate or on behalf of the state or government, or in an oral closing argument to a jury regardless whether the argument is on behalf of the defendant or the prosecution, the attorney's job is to reconfigure past events into a story to affect the perspective and control the beliefs of the reader or listener, including the sceptical judicial audience. In legal argumentation these narratives operate in relationship to, and in interplay with, logical propositions and rules of law. Narrative practice is strategic, and must fit these analytical structures. Stories-within-stories are often employed, shaped to wrap inferential arguments and analytical propositions around a thematic narrative spine. It is, therefore, unsurprising that smaller stories nested or strategically encapsulated within larger story frames are powerful strategic tools, often at the core of narrative persuasion.[29]

This concept, especially as it pertains to employing narratives in legal briefs, may seem obscure intially. So, let me explain: for example, in constructing an analytical argument I may begin by asserting an initial theoretical proposition, a general proposition, on a comparatively high level of abstraction, or a legal rule in a general form (A). I then give the proposition or rule additional analytical focus and specificity by focusing upon the discrete and problematic piece or element of the principle (A^1). Then, to confirm or prove the principle, I do not employ the scientific method of proof (the 'paradigmatic mode'[30] discussed by Bruner). Rather, I convert the proposition into narrative. That is, the principle is confirmed through a narrative illustration (or, as John Gardner observes, a carefully structured sequence of stories strategically employed to dramatize logical possibilities).[31]

[28] J Bruner, *On Knowing: Essays for the Left Hand* (1962).

[29] Anthony G Amsterdam and Randy Hertz, 'An Analysis of Closing Arguments to a Jury' (1992) 37 *New York Law School L Rev* 55–122; Philip N Meyer, ' "Desperate for Love III": Rethinking Closing Arguments as Stories' (1999) 50 *South Carolina L Rev* 715–52; Philip N Meyer, 'Making the Narrative Move: Observations Based Upon Reading Gerry Spence's Closing Argument in *The Estate of Karen Silkwood v Kerr-McGee, Inc.*' (2002) 9 *Clinical L Rev* 229–292.

[30] Jerome Bruner, in distinguishing the 'analytical' and 'narrative' modes of writing, notes: 'There are two modes of cognitive functioning, two modes of thought, each providing distinctive ways of ordering experience, of constructing reality. The two (though complementary) are irreducible to one another. Efforts to reduce one mode to the other or to ignore one at the expense of the other inevitably fail to capture the rich diversity of thought. Each of the ways of knowing, moreover, has operating principles of its own and its own criteria of well-formedness. They differ radically in their procedures for verification. A good story and a well-formed argument are different natural kinds . . . It has been claimed that the one is a refinement or an abstraction from the other. But this must be either false or true only in the most unenlightening way. They function differently, as already noted, and the structure of a well-formed logical argument differs radically from that of a well-wrought story.' J Bruner, *Actual Minds, Possible Worlds* (New York: 1986) 11.

[31] '[F]or example, the writer might impose onto the twelve labors of Hercules—or some action from real life, or some fictional action—some logical sequence that, like any other interesting argument, keeps us reading.' Gardner, *The Art of Fiction*, n 23 above, 165.

Here is an example. The initial analytical proposition is borrowed from Jerome Bruner's most recent book, *Making Stories*. I will identify the proposition and name it the principle of NARRATIVE COMPOSABILITY OF SELF OR IDENTITY

Bruner states:

I want to begin by proposing boldly that, in effect, there is no such thing as an intuitively obvious and essential self to know, one that just sits there ready to be portrayed in words. Rather, we constantly construct and reconstruct ourselves to meet the needs of the situations we encounter, and we do so with the guidance of our memories of the past and our hopes and fears for the future. Telling oneself about oneself is like making up a story about who and what we are, what's happened, and why we're doing what we're doing.[32]

Now, I take a similar proposition as it is spun in a slightly different direction into the domain of literary and narrative theory by the film maker and literary theorist Michael Roemer, as he writes about character development in popular storytelling. Roemer employs a boldface stylistic header to identify his post-modern perspective (A):

We No Longer Believe in Character[33]

He elaborates, analytically, upon the proposition giving it specificity (A-1):

In our own day, the corrupt character has become obsolete . . . In a rapidly changing context like our own, we survive by continuous adaptation, and the Greek saying: 'You are what each day makes you' is appropriate to us. In a fluid, often unpredictable world, to 'have character' in the traditional sense—to be predictable and therefore rigid—can spell trouble, if not disaster.[34]

Here, Roemer 'spins' the development of the analytical proposition towards a segue into the narrative modality; that is, he moves from the 'paradigmatic' mode into the 'narrative' mode:[35]

We have, moreover, lost all confidence that our once seemingly impregnable character can withstand real pressure. Traditionally, in both life and fiction, character or self derived from and served a stable context, though it also preserved our integrity when the context crumbled. But in an age of concentration camps, when so many have been crushed psychologically and not just physically, we have been forced to recognize that what we are and do is largely beholden to circumstance.[36]

And now—finally, and what is most interesting to me—is the translation or 'adaptation' of the principle (that is, of the fluid nature of character or the narrative composibility of self or identity as I have previously labelled it) into a truthful and factual narrative that explains the proposition and, perhaps, makes it unassailable (B).

32 Bruner, *Making Stories*, n 10 above, 64.

33 M Roemer, *Telling Stories: Postmodernism and the Invalidation of Traditional Narrative* (Lanham, Md: 1995), 16–17.

34 ibid.

35 Bruner, *Actual Minds, Possible Worlds*, n 30 above, 11.

36 Roemer, *Telling Stories*, n 33 above, 17.

Roemer's use of a non-fiction story is akin to a litigation attorney's strategic use of stories-within-stories:

This can be true even of heroes. On a construction detail at Buchenwald, two Jews whose strength was failing drew the angry attention of an SS sergeant. He pushed them into a ditch and commanded a Polish prisoner to bury them alive. When the Pole refused, the sergeant, instead of shooting him at once, pushed *him* into the ditch and ordered the Jews to bury him.

'In terror of their lives and in the hope of escaping the ghastly fate themselves, (they obeyed). When only the head of the Pole was still uncovered, the SS man called a halt and had the man dug out.'

Once again he commanded the Jews into the ditch and again ordered the Pole to bury them. This time he did.

'Slowly the ditch was filled with soil. When the work was done, the Detail Leader personally trampled down the soil over his two victims.'[37]

Similarly, it is a conventional narrative move for litigation attorneys to use embedded or 'nested' narratives, to prove crucial analytical propositions that undergird their arguments.

The final point is the source of these stories. In jury arguments, these anecdotes or analogies are drawn from folk wisdom. They are borrowed stories: cut, shaped and pasted. These small stories may even be stored and recycled in multiple closing arguments in different cases. These stories often move outside of the record. In post-conviction brief writing, however, there is a vast amount of truthful and factual material in the previous retellings of the story to draw upon, and there may be new evidentiary material as well. For example, the embedded narrative may tell a story of evidence that was not allowed to be introduced at trial, supporting a theme of procedures and specific practices systematically preventing the defendant from receiving procedural justice (for example, a story of what was omitted from trial based upon prosecutorial misconduct and judicial indifference). Or the narrative may be a story about the law itself rather than the defendant (recasting the legislation as the antagonist in the narrative). In the next section of this paper, I show how James Ellroy and Joan Didion elaborate upon Bruner's theme of the narrative composability of self in creative non-fiction that may be powerfully suggestive of alternative aesthetic possibilities that may be employed by the post-conviction relief practitioner.

III. Two Illustrations of Elaboration Upon a Common Theme #1—Accretion of Detail and Emotional Compression in the Opening of James Ellroy's Memoir *My Dark Places*

Detective stories are useful models for a kind of story telling that can do this work because the detective-story form is specialized for creating a puzzle that cries out for solution and

[37] E Kogon, *The Theory and Practice of Hell: The German Concentration Camps and the System Behind Them* (trans H Norden, New York: 1949), 91–92 in Roemer, *Telling Stories*, n 33 above, 17.

then leading the reader to believe that a belatedly emerging theory of events satisfactorily solves the puzzle—or for weaning the reader from a plausible but mistaken impression of events by leading him or her first to question that version and then to perceive and eventually accept another version as having a more satisfying ring of truth.

Anthony Amsterdam[38]

James Ellroy's autobiographical memoir *My Dark Places*[39] adapts the form of a 'quest' or 'journey' for the identity of his mother's murderer, for the identity of his mother, and, also, for his own artistic identity at the intersection of these two searches. The story assumes the structure of a genre detective story. Initially, the dominant narrative appears to be a 'who-done-it', which, as Amsterdam notes, is a form or genre that is often employed in post conviction relief litigation brief-writing practice.[40]

Stylistically, like Ellroy's fiction, his autobiography assumes its power through the authority of the voice, and in its seeming close adherence to the genre conventions of hard-boiled detective fiction. Yet, unlike detective fiction, in *My Dark Places* there are no solutions to the murder of Ellroy's mother. Instead, a more subtle narrative emerges, and the linear surface of the plot to discover the 'identity' of the murderer of Ellroy's mother is left unresolved. The story maintains a strong narrative core, however, as the reader shares with Ellroy the search for clues in the present and in the past, emerging instead with a strong sense of the 'narrative composibility' of Ellroy's identity, and the development of his artistic voice formed in relation to his mother's absence and the circumstances of her death. The ending echoes the opening: Ellroy's strong voice is still searching the surfaces for clues in a psychological process of inspection and detection that hard-boiled detective fiction attempts to replicate in its methodology and style.[41] Thematically, Ellroy presents the classic underlying theme of the literary mystery adapted in the form of non-fiction memoir; that is, '. . . that the greatest mystery of all is the human heart'.[42]

My Dark Places begins with a title: 'The Redhead', and the crime photo of Ellroy's murdered mother, face down in the brush, her dress partially undone, the ligature marks from the strangulation still upon her neck.

Before beginning, Ellroy sets context by speaking directly to his mother, a cry of anguish, as he steps outside, and simultaneously inside the frame of the story he will tell. He puts these paragraphs into italics to differentiate this voice, and this brief section, from the detective story that follows.

[38] Collected Notes and Materials, n 3 above.

[39] J Ellroy, *My Dark Places* (New York: 1997). I have also written about this book in another context: Philip N Meyer, 'Why a Jury Trial is More Like a Movie Than a Novel' (2001) 28 *J of Law and Society* 133–146.

[40] Collected Notes and Materials, n 3 above.

[41] R Chandler, 'The Simple Art of Murder' in *The Simple Art of Murder* (New York. 1950; Vintage Books edn, 1988) 1 in D Luban, 'The Art of Honesty' (2001) 101 *Columbia L Rev* 1763, 1765–1768.

[42] D Lodge, *The Art of Fiction* (London: 1992), 34.

A cheap Saturday night took you down. You died stupidly and harshly and without the means to hold your own life dear.

Your run to safety was a brief reprieve. You brought me into hiding as your good-luck charm. I failed you as a talisman—so I stand now as your witness.

Your death defines my life. I want to find the love we never had and explicate it in your name.

I want to make your secrets public. I want to burn the distance between us.

I want to give you breath.[43]

Although it is only the second page, Ellroy has made several bold stylistic moves already. Ellroy then begins his story of his search with a past-tense reconstruction of the murder scene, the classic starting point in the detective story, the moment of completion of the crime by the unidentified perpetrator. Ellroy maintains the narrative momentum although there is a great deal of detailed description. He holds the reader by keeping the sentences and paragraphs extremely short, keeping the details extremely 'hard' and specific so the scene can be readily visualized by the reader, frozen clearly in time.

Ellroy does not allow his gaze to fall off the images into introspection or move into abstraction about the meaning of the images. He makes the reader wait; and there is the confident assumption and authority of the voice that the reader will not let go of this surface either. The hard-edged visual details are piled one atop another as if a sequence of photographic snapshots:

Some kids found her.

They were Babe Ruth League players, out to hit a few shag balls. Three adult coaches were walking behind them.

The boys saw a shape in the ivy strip just off the curb. The men saw loose pearls on the pavement. A little telepathic jolt went around.

Clyde Warner and Dick Ginnold shooed the kids back a ways—to keep them from looking too close. Kendall Nungesser ran across Tyler and spotted a pay phone by the dairy stand.

He called the Temple City Sheriff's Office and told the desk sergeant he'd discovered a body. It was right there on that road beside the playing field at Arroyo High School. The sergeant said stay there and don't touch anything.

The radio call went out: 10:10 a.m., Sunday, 6/22/58. Dead body at King's Row and Tyler Avenue, El Monte.

A Sheriff's prowl car made it in under five minutes. An El Monte PD unit arrived a few seconds later.

Deputy Vic Cavallero huddled up the coaches and the kids. Officer Dave Wire checked out the body.

It was a female Caucasian. She was fair-skinned and red-headed. She was approximately 40 years of age. She was lying flat on her back—in an ivy patch a few inches from the King's Row curb line.

Her right arm was bent upward. Her right hand was resting a few inches above her head. Her left arm was bent at the elbow and draped across her midriff. Her left hand was clenched. Her legs were outstretched.

[43] Ellroy, *My Dark Places*, n 39 above, 2.

She was wearing a scoop-front, sleeveless, light and dark blue dress. A dark blue overcoat with a matching lining was spread over her lower body.

Her feet and ankles were visible. Her right foot was bare. A nylon stocking was bunched up around her left ankle.

Her dress was disheveled. Insect bites covered her arms. Her face was bruised and her tongue was protruding. Her brassiere was unfastened and hiked above her breasts. A nylon stocking and a cotton cord were lashed around her neck. Both ligatures were tightly knotted.

Dave Wire radioed the El Monte PD dispatcher. Vic Cavallero called the Temple office. The body-dump alert went out:

Get the L.A. County Coroner. Get the Sheriff's Crime Lab and the photo car. Call the Sheriff's Homicide Bureau and tell them to send a team out.

. . .

Her face had gone slightly purple. She looked like a classic late-night body dump.

The coroner's deputy showed up. The photo deputy told him he could examine the victim.

Hallinen and Lawton pushed forward to watch. The coroner's deputy lifted the coat off the victim's lower body.

She was not wearing a slip, a girdle or panties. Her dress was pushed up above her hips. No panties and no shoes. That one stocking down around her left ankle. Bruises and small lacerations on the insides of her thighs. An asphalt drag mark on her left hip.

The coroner's deputy turned the body over. The photo deputy snapped some shots of the victim's posterior. The victim's back was dew-wet and showed signs of postmortem lividity.

. . .

It was 1:20 p.m. The temperature was up in the mid-90s.

The coroner's deputy cut off samples of the victim's head and pubic hair. He trimmed the victim's fingernails and placed the cuttings in a small envelope.

He had the body stripped and positioned face-up on his gurney.

There was a small amount of dried blood on the victim's right palm. There was a small laceration near the center of the victim's forehead.

The victim's right nipple was missing. The surrounding areola was creased with white scar tissue. It appeared to be an old surgical amputation.

Hallinen removed the victim's ring. The coroner's deputy measured the body at 66 inches and guessed the weight at 135 pounds. Lawton left to call the stats in to Headquarters Dispatch and the Sheriff's Missing Persons Squad.

The coroner's deputy took a scalpel and made a deep 6-inch-long incision in the victim's abdomen. He parted the flaps with his fingers, jabbed a meat thermometer into the liver and got a reading of 90 degrees. He called the time of death as 3:00 to 5:00 a.m.

Hallinen examined the ligatures. The stocking and cotton cord were separately lashed around the victim's neck. The cord resembled a clothesline or venetian blind sash-pull.

The cord knot was tied at the back of the victim's neck. The killer tied it so tight that one of the ends broke off—fraying and the odd lengths of the knot ends proved that fact conclusively.

The stocking around the victim's neck was identical to the stocking bunched around her left ankle.

The coroner's deputy locked up his van and drove the body to the L.A. County Morgue. Jack Lawton put out a police band broadcast:

All San Gabriel Valley units be alert for suspicious males with fresh cuts and scratches.

Ward Hallinen rounded up some radio reporters. He told them to put it on the local air:

Dead white woman found. Forty/red hair/hazel eyes/5'6"/135. Direct potential informants to the El Monte PD and Temple City Sheriff's Office—.[44]

Ellroy's opening may suggest possibilities for narrative elaboration in brief writing. The options of the post conviction relief brief writer may further be facilitated by a close reading of the excerpt in conjunction with texts on creative writing. Specifically, as a starting place, I recommend two different introductory writing texts, both, coincidentally, titled *The Art of Fiction* by John Gardner[45] and by David Lodge,[46] respectively. These texts may provide a vocabulary for better understanding a range of choices that underlie Ellroy's opening, and suggest a range of potential topics for deliberate and systematic analysis in the context of non-fiction brief writing in post conviction relief work. Just as the creative journalist, the creative historian, the creative memoirist employs narrative techniques developed initially by novelists, adaptation of these techniques may be available to the attorney.

For example, in a chapter titled 'Staying on the Surface', David Lodge provides additional illustrations of writers who, like Ellroy, '. . . focus . . . obsessively on the surface . . . of things' and where '. . . dialogue is presented flatly, objectively, without . . . any variation on the simple adverbless speech tags *he/she asks/says* . . . .'.[47] Lodge suggests that the ' "depthlessness" ' of the discourse may be further emphasized by '[a] preference for the present tense'.[48] That is, the past tense '. . . implies that the story is known to and has been assessed by the narrator in its entirety'.[49]

The use of present tense is not a choice that Ellroy makes in writing his opening, but it may provide a useful tool for the legal practitioner. Also, this form of story elaboration is one that fits where '. . . the narrative discourse impassively tracks the characters as they move from moment to moment towards an unknown future'.[50] The '. . . text's refusal to comment, to give unambiguous guidance as to how the characters should be evaluated', may be 'disturbing'[51] but may simultaneously be a source of power. These are qualities compelling in Ellroy's prose, and may serve the legal practitioner as well.

Ellroy's opening stays compulsively on the surface of the details. The details have a power of emotional compression into 'hard' objects and an equally hard-edged voice expressed in the short sentences. The rhythms of street language are heightened by the absence of commentary upon the story by Ellroy, allowing the reader to decipher and better intimate the powerful meaning of the text. The images also have credence and authority, free-standing clues, to be sifted through by the reader, rather than ascribed meanings by the author.

In a chapter titled 'Showing and Telling', Lodge identifies the virtues and vices of 'showing' as compared to 'telling'. Initially he observes that '[t]he purest form of

[44] Ellroy, *My Dark Places*, n 39 above, 3–4, 5–8.
[45] Gardner, *The Art of Fiction*, n 23 above, 1.
[46] Lodge, *The Art of Fiction*, n 42 above, 1. [47] ibid, 118. [48] ibid.
[49] ibid, 119. [50] ibid. [51] ibid.

showing is the quoted speech of characters, in which language exactly mirrors the event',[52] while the '. . . purest form of telling is authorial summary, in which the conciseness and abstraction of the narrator's language effaces the particularity and individuality of the characters and their actions'.[53] These are lessons that experienced brief writers clearly know, building briefs upon verbatim excerpts of transcripts, direct quotations, and external and purportedly objective sources. But often these are lessons that the legal writer may never have had the time to make explicit, or to translate her intuitions into systematic practice. Further, Lodge admonishes the young writer as to what the experienced brief writer also surely knows as well, that overuse of authorial summary is 'unreadable'. Nevertheless, summary has its uses, and these functions can be made explicit: 'it can, for instance, accelerate the tempo of a narrative, hurrying us through events which would be uninteresting, or *too* interesting—therefore distracting, if lingered over'.[54]

There were alternative aesthetic choices Ellroy could have made. For example, the crime is not the only place where Ellroy could have begun his story. He could have begun his narrative at an earlier point before the crime, while his mother was still alive. But Ellroy's beginning is the proper one, especially given the 'genre' in which he has chosen to tell the story, the detective story, and he matches his style of narrative elaboration to the readily recognizable genre conventions of the hard-boiled detective form that fits his material as well as his stylistic predispositions. By matching his aesthetic choices coherently, Ellroy avoids making the 'risky moves', that Lodge suggests, '. . . come near to creating the effect Erving Goffman calls "breaking frame"—when some rule or convention that governs a particular type of experience is transgressed'.[55]

Lodge further suggests how novelistic choices may differ from the choices in expository writing. For example, citing the Russian critic Bahktin, Lodge observes that the language of expository prose is '. . . "monologic", striving to impose a single vision, or interpretation, on the world by means of a single unitary style'.[56] 'The novel in contrast is "dialogic", incorporating many different styles, or voices, which as it were talk to each other, and to other voices outside the text, the discourses of culture and society at large'.[57] Among Ellroy's aesthetic tasks are how to incorporate 'telling in different voices' in the context of non-fiction. He does so in his opening by use of a title ('The Redhead'), a picture, and several brief paragraphs of personal italicized narration before beginning his narrative at the beginning of the story. Later, he will alternate between third person omniscient, third person subjective, and first person voices. He will also incorporate sections of police reports, transcriptions of interviews, verbatim and without commentary, building his composition of evidence and clues. His use of narrative devices in his opening (such as the use of sub-title, picture, or speaking directly to his deceased mother) does not appear to be a gimmick or trick that disserves his narrative; there is no

[52] Lodge, *The Art of Fiction*, n 42 above, 122. [53] ibid. [54] ibid.
[55] ibid, 11. [56] ibid, 128. [57] ibid.

'frame breaking' to distract the reader, or to move the reader even momentarily outside the narrative, raising questions about the truthfulness or facticity of the story. Achieving this proper and difficult aesthetic balance, attempting to carefully cross a high-wire tightrope of language, may also be the task of the post-conviction relief practitioner attempting to incorporate novelistic techniques into narrative brief-writing practice.

#2—Confronting the Unspeakable in Joan Didion's *The White Album*[58]

In my analyses of closing arguments, I have begun to study how prosecutors' closing arguments differ from defence attorneys' closing arguments in criminal cases. Specifically, I am currently analyzing prosecutor Vincent Bugliosi's closing argument in *The State of California v Charles Manson, et al.*[59] This argument is often cited as a model of efficiency, order, clarity, and effective persuasion and storytelling by a prosecutor in a multi-defendant criminal prosecution[60] It is a hard and moralistic closing argument; the story it tells is simple, clear and one-dimensional—it is a story of a criminal mastermind who systematically plots and orders five horrific murders at the residence of Sharon Tate, and the separate murders of Leno and Rosemary LaBianca.

The argument tracks the structure of the inferential arguments taught in clinical advocacy programmes, and follows the paradigmatic analytical frame taught in doctrinal law school courses. That is, Bugliosi initially and accurately sets forth the law of murder and conspiracy—the elements of the primary offences—and then connects the evidence and testimony that structurally fulfil and satisfy each of these elements. He relies, especially, upon the lengthy and meticulous testimony of one eye-witness, Linda Kasabian, a member of the Manson 'Family' who has been granted immunity for her testimony against Manson and the other perpetrators from the family who carried out the executions. Kasabian provides the primary perspective from inside the family, and she identifies and persuasively singles out Manson as the evil culprit who directly masterminded, orchestrated, and ordered the murders. Manson did not attend or actually commit the acts himself. Kasabian further explains Manson's motive for the murders—his use and interpretation of the meaning of the songs on the Beatles album, especially the lyrics of the song 'Helter Skelter'. Manson had interpreted the text as setting forth an apocalyptic vision in which there would be a war between poor blacks rising up against white oppressors. Manson planned to precipitate this violent 'Revolution' (another song on the Beatles' *White Album*) through the initial murders, attributing the blame to

[58] J Didion, *The White Album* (New York, 1979), 1.

[59] MS Lief et al, *Ladies and Gentlemen of the Jury: Greatest Closing Arguments in Modern Law* (New York: 2000), 223–287.

[60] ibid, 232.

black perpetrators, and then to escape to a hideaway in a hole that would open beneath the desert near the Manson Family compound. The blacks would be victorious in their revolution against the whites. Manson would re-emerge after the blacks had taken over. And the blacks would choose Manson as the new leader of the world to save them from anarchy. Manson and the Family would return and, in this druggy, bizarre, and primitive fantasy, rule the world.

Relying extensively upon Kasabian's 18 days of courtroom testimony,[61] Bugliosi's closing argument tells the damningly melodramatic story of Manson, demented yet purposefully evil, employing carefully programmed minions from his family to complete these horrible crimes to precipitate 'Helter Skelter'. The closing argument is powerful and simple. The closing argument is also a call to the jury, as Amsterdam suggests,[62] to provide dramatic closure to the present-tense story of the trial, and to rectify the sins of the past. The closing argument presents a closed, self-contained and circumscribed world; it focuses exclusively upon the murder, upon the actions and motivations of the defendants. The time frame is narrow. The cast of characters is limited. The theme of the story is about an evil madman who butchers random, unsuspecting, and innocent victims. Bugliosi's call to the jury is to take the action, preserve the community and society, and eradicate the evil that is Charles Manson and his followers.

Bugliosi coherently reconfigures the material monologically; no alternative 'lens' or perspective for viewing the material seems possible. Yet, recalling those times, something is omitted from Bugliosi's version of the story. And I wondered whether there were alternative ways to reconfigure the material of the story, to elaborate upon the text—not to change the outcome or save Manson but, perhaps, merely to suggest that there might be alternative 'modes' of story elaboration for retelling the story.

I recalled my fondness for Joan Didion's essays about the late 1960s and early 1970s, and, specifically, her essay 'The White Album'. I thought that selected portions of this essay might provide a contrasting 'adaptation' to Bugliosi's approach to some of the same material. Of course, Didion's purposes and audience are much different. She is not, directly, attempting to identify a culprit, to attribute blame, or to punish a criminal wrongdoer. Her purposes are artistic and exploratory. Nevertheless, I believe a post conviction relief brief-writer might have much to learn from her style, and selected paragraphs of her essay, especially given the thematic similarities between her theme and James Ellroy's (the 'narrative composibility of self and identity').

Here is an illustrative section of 'The White Album'. It is a self-contained elliptical and numbered piece in a sequence of numbered pieces, arranged in a non-chronological and non-linear sequence. This piece is followed by several sentences from the next piece (Section 11) in the composition. I believe that these pieces or

[61] MS Lief et al, *Ladies and Gentlemen of the Jury: Greatest Closing Arguments in Modern Law* (New York: 2000), 239.

[62] Amsterdam and Hertz, n 29 above.

vignettes might suggest other possibilities for organization and ordination of images. Also, there are lessons to be learned from the strength and power of the narrative voice, that coheres the story as it powerfully pulls together Didion's cultural observations from those far different times:

10.

We put 'Lay Lady Lay' on the record player, and 'Suzanne.' We went down to Melrose Avenue to see the Flying Burritos. There was a jasmine vine grown over the verandah of the big house on Franklin Avenue, and in the evenings the smell of jasmine came in through all the open doors and windows. I made bouillabaisse for people who did not eat meat. I imagined that my own life was simple and sweet, and sometimes it was, but there were odd things going around town. There were rumors. There were stories. Everything was unmentionable but nothing was unimaginable. This mystical flirtation with the idea of 'sin'—this sense that it was possible to go 'too far,' and that many people were doing it—was very much with us in Los Angeles in 1968 and 1969. A demented and seductive vortical tension was building in the community. The jitters were setting in. I recall a time when the dogs barked every night and the moon was always full. On August 9, 1969, I was sitting in the shallow end of my sister-in-law's swimming pool in Beverly Hills when she received a telephone call from a friend who had just heard about the murders at Sharon Tate Polanski's house on Cielo Drive. The phone rang many times during the next hour. These early reports were garbled and contradictory. One caller would say hoods, the next would say chains. There were twenty dead, no, twelve, ten, eighteen. Black masses were imagined, and bad trips blamed. I remember all of the day's misinformation very clearly, and I also remember this, and wish I did not: *I remember that no one was surprised.*

11.

When I first met Linda Kasabian in the summer of 1970 she was wearing her hair parted neatly in the middle, no makeup, Elizabeth Arden 'Blue Grass' perfume, and the unpressed blue uniform issued to inmates at the Sybil Brand Institute for Women in Los Angeles.

...

In fact we never talked about 'the case,' and referred to its central events only as 'Cielo Drive,' and 'LaBianca.' We talked instead about Linda's childhood pastimes and disappointments, her high-school romances and her concern for her children. This particular juxtaposition of the spoken and the unspeakable was eerie and unsettling, and made my notebook a litany of little ironies so obvious as to be of interest only to dedicated absurdists. An example: Linda dreamed of opening a combination restaurant-boutique and pet shop.[63]

Again, the initial question is what, specifically, might the practitioner writing a post-conviction relief brief on behalf of a condemned inmate observe about Didion's opening that might be suggestive or helpful, contrasting so vividly with Ellroy's simpler intensely focused facticity? Obviously, unlike Ellroy, Didion attempts to go deep beneath the surface with language, and into the self as well. Her gaze is not so purposefully fixed on external details as Ellroy's. Her sentences and rhythms are more complex. Likewise, she does not order her story from the moment of the crime,

[63] Didion, *The White Album*, n 58 above, 41–44.

or, seemingly, work backwards from an ending. Rather, she moves the narrative not through a continuous linear chronology but through an accumulation of discrete pieces. These vignettes are carefully composed. Furthermore, unlike Ellroy, Didion is not obsessive about the accretion of evidentiary detail, not fearful about inadvertently overlooking a crucial piece of evidence. Instead, she is extremely selective and the eye-catching images she chooses seem ironic, almost inadvertent. Yet the narrative is compelling, truthful and factual, and it intentionally evokes a more complex world, and a peculiar historical moment, in a way, for example, that Bugliosi's unreflective and flat melodramatic closing argument does not.

Another 'how to' book on fiction writing may provide a vocabulary for better understanding some of Didion's compelling stylistic choices in a way that, I believe, may also be useful to post-conviction relief attorneys attempting to retell a once told story in a brief to a sceptical judicial audience. This second text, or tool, is John Gardner's *The Art of Fiction: Notes on Craft for Young Writers.*

In a chapter appropriately titled 'Interest and Truth', Gardner explores the fiction writer's relationship to truth-telling and facticity, in relationship to his story. The relationship of the brief-writer to his material, of course, differs from the novelist's verisimilitude. But many of the issues that Gardner raises, and the strategic choices that the writer must make as to style, character, point of view, plotting, are clearly relevant for the brief writer developing a Statement of the Case, or incorporating narrative themes into argument, just as for the novelist. Thus, for example, Gardner observes about style:

> The writer must of necessity write in a style that falls somewhere on the continuum running from objective to subjective; in other words, from the discursive, essayist's style, in which everything is spelled out as scientifically as possible, to the poetic style, in which nothing (or practically nothing) is explained, everything is evoked, or, to use Henry James' term, 'rendered.' The essayist's style is by nature slow-moving and laborious, more wide than deep. It tends towards abstraction and precision without much power, as we see instantly when we compare any two descriptions, one discursive, one poetic. In the essayist's style, we might write, for instance, 'The man in the doorway was large and apparently ill at ease—so large that he had to stoop a little and draw in his elbows.' The poetic style can run harder at its effects: 'He filled the doorway, awkward as a horse.' Both styles, needless to say, can be of use. One builds its world up slowly and completely, as Tolstoy does in *Anna Karenina*, where very few metaphors or similies appear; the other lights up its world by lightning flashes.[64]

Didion's style, like Ellroy's, can be better located through Gardner's novelist's eye, and teaching lens, and his commentary is equally suggestive for the stylistic choices that the brief writer must make in developing her material. Didion chooses a style that affords her room to shift from the surface of events into a type of speculation and abstraction. In Didion's artistic hands, however, the essayist's style is neither 'slow moving' nor 'laborious'. Instead, at least to this reader, it is dangerous, edgy and compelling. Didion is attempting to find deep candour and truthfulness in her observations. To do so she attempts to confront the seemingly inexplicable and

[64] Gardner, *The Art of Fiction*, n 23 above, 44–45.

unimaginable, and directly proffers possible alternative meanings for events (unlike Ellroy, for example, who is always 'concrete' in his descriptions, leaving it for the reader, exclusively, to decipher the meanings of his imagistic composition).

There is a fearlessness in Didion's voice, and a willingness to use language to look creatively over the edge of facts, or deep within the self, to articulate a truth beyond simple facticity. For example, there is her dangerous intimation that, perhaps, Manson and the family were not merely the embodiment of some purely external evil, but, instead, were the manifestation of something that was brewing deep within the culture at that time. And Manson and his Family gave articulation to this energy, a minion of external cultural forces, just like his Family minions were the ciphers for his own commands. Didion quickly tempers the implications of her observation with her shift to the irony of her observations about Linda Kasabian at the Sybil Brand Institute, with compelling and eye-catching throwaway details. Again, like Ellroy, she maintains a careful aesthetic balance on a tightrope of language. In many ways, her theme in this essay is akin to that of Ellroy's memoir, the search for identity in a dangerously shifting and unstable culture. The theme is a variant on the analytical observation by Bruner (the narrative composibility of self) as developed by Roemer in the context of literary analysis of popular storytelling practices (WE NO LONGER BELIEVE IN CHARACTER).

It is interesting to note that another version of this theme, mitigation of the sentence of the condemned prisoner based upon social history or circumstance (for example, mental retardation, horrific background circumstances, or failure of counsel at trial to develop evidence pertaining to the social history of the defendant) is commonly developed in many post-conviction relief briefs. (Other common themes include, for example: failure of procedure justice, actual innocence, systematic corruption, etc). It is my belief that the sceptical judicial reader, a professional fact-finder and critic, may readily recognize the theme, and dismiss the particulars of the story unless they are presented in an especially compelling way. It is my argument that awareness of alternative stylistic options and structural possibilities would better facilitate the effective development of these narratives, and that examples of alternative approaches, from non-fiction and from other post-conviction relief briefs, supplemented by teaching texts and theory, might provide useful and suggestive tools for the creative post conviction relief practitioner.

The Ending

I end this essay by returning to Spike Jonze's film *Adaptation*, and by reaffirming my simple premise: recent creative popular non-fiction (supplemented by lawyering theory, narrative theory, and even texts on the art of narrative) provides a rich terrain for exploration by post-conviction relief practitioners attempting, somewhat akin to Charlie Kaufman in Spike Jonze's film *Adaptation*, to successfully and truthfully retell a once-told story. These sources may suggest creative possibilities to the practitioner.

In closing, I observe that Charlie Kaufman's true 'epiphany',[65] or transformative moment in the film *Adaptation* is not Charlie's false realization at the Robert McKee Story Structure Workshop, that there is much to draw upon, structurally, in the techniques and teachings that may help him in his work (both professionally and psychologically). Nor does the climax occur in the double deus ex machina ending that McKee explicitly warns him against (including a chase through the swamp, the appearance of a hungry alligator, and a sudden car crash). Rather, this moment occurs when the creative and inspired Charlie Kaufman is reconciled with the other part of his psyche—his plodding, systematic, learn-by-following-the-rules brother Donald. This moment provides, or—pardon me— 'seeds' (afterall, it *is*, as Charlie observes, a movie about 'flowers'), the inspirational ending that McKee specifies will save the movie—where Charlie (and perhaps the viewer) is saved as well from descending into a spiral of depression and frustration and despair, and discovers the proper artistic form for his screenplay, and for his life-story as well. This ending, I believe, also works nicely as a metaphor for ending this essay, by providing symbolic affirmation of the possibilities available to the post-conviction relief brief-writing practitioner who attempts to draw systematically upon innovative non-fiction narrative practices, and lawyering and writing theory, and reconciles these practices with traditional legal and analytical practice to retell difficult, complex, and compelling stories that are both truthful and factual in these equally difficult and challenging times.

[65] David Lodge observes that, in the modern narrative, '. . . an epiphany often has the function performed by a decisive action in traditional narrative, providing a climax or resolution to a story or episode.' Lodge, *The Art of Fiction*, n 42 above, 147.

Narrative Determination and the Figure of the Judge

David A Black

The Filmic Judge, Breadth First

My purpose here is to explore the specific significance, if any, of the figure of the judge in the law-in-film landscape.

That landscape, to begin with, is replete with interconnections among the many figures and themes with which it is peopled.[1] Criminals watch victims; detectives watch criminals; viewers watch detectives. Justice is enacted in the courtroom, which in turn is embodied on the screen; critics watch movies, and attack or defend them; lawyers attack or defend; cognitive data pop in and out of the visible field and the ken of now this, now that stakeholder in the narrative economy.

To speak of the specific significance of any one figure in the law-in-film landscape, then, is not to speak of that figure in complete isolation. Rather, the process consists of putting the centre of analytical gravity on that figure—the judge, in this case—of favouring the view toward and from that figure's position over other imaginable views, and seeing what happens.

As the above sketch suggests, 'figures' in the sense that I define the judge as a 'figure' may be figures on the screen, such as the detective and the eyewitness, or figures near but not on the screen, such as the viewer and the critic. Indeed, much of what is lastingly interesting about the representation of law in film lies in the many crossings of the line between film and non-film that present themselves as one goes increasingly deeply into the topic. This is not (one hopes) a matter of confusing the line between fiction and reality. Rather, it is a question of obliqueness: many of the most intriguing lines of inquiry running through the law-in-film landscape run oblique to the line separating film from non-film, offering alternative paths which take in a bit of both. Thus, for example, detective work in a film not only provides an analogue for the cognitive 'work' of the viewer, but unfolds in a network of interdependencies with it: we see and process some subset or superset of what the detective or investigator sees and processes, and the margin of difference one way or the other can completely transform the experience of watching the film.

[1] For an extensive examination of this and a number of the underlying, overarching themes in this essay, see DA Black, *Law in Film: Resonance and Representation* (Urbana, IL: 1999).

Theatricality in the courtroom—the theatricality *of* the courtroom—takes on an irreducible, non-zero degree of reference to the theatricality of the movie theatre. The figure of the judge, too, cuts across the screen/non-screen line. The simplest way in which this transection manifests itself is in the fact that people, including casual viewers as well as professional critics, judge films. What I shall say here will involve both extending the terms of analysis beyond this simple insight, and suggesting that even this insight may not be as simple as it seems.

Doing justice to the filmic judge involves a kind of breadth-first approach. I shall escort the judge through a sequence of three potentially relevant and revealing analytical frameworks, namely *character, genre*, and *reflexivity*. Collectively, these frameworks offer a reasonably systematic way of getting at the significance of many a figure—detective, viewer, critic, eyewitness, judge, and others—in the law-in-film landscape. But even in motion among this trio of analytical concepts, all of what I shall say I intend to hang on a further, singular analytical peg, and that is the peg of *narrative determination*. As I will explain, it seems to me that the most salient and specific characteristic of the filmic judge, as opposed to other figures in the law-in-film landscape, is encapsulated by that phrase. The felicity of the fit between figure and phrase, moreover, obtains precisely because the phrase can be reasonably understood to mean two things, and two rather opposite things at that—both of which, opposite though they be, fit the figure of the judge snugly.

Narrative determination can be understood, first, as an active principle, the determining of narrative by an agent of determination. Judges in film enjoy this kind of narrative determination—they are such agents—in the sense that they have the privilege of determining the narrative, steering it, constraining it to take certain forms to the exclusion of others. In most cases, judges decide that something will or will not happen (an imprisonment, a divorce, an execution), and the thing happens, with the rest of the narrative constrained to fall into place around it.

The second, opposite connotation of the phrase 'narrative determination' is a passive one: the state of being determined by the (or a, or some) narrative. Here we meet up with the filmic judge again. For all their decision-making and narrative-steering power, judges in film tend to be, in a word, predictable—specifically, predictable on the basis of narrative likelihood, antecedent, and idiom. As magisterial as they may appear, they are there in the first place more often than not for the most banal reasons of verisimilitude, the simplest exigencies of a plot about law; and while their decisions are necessary to propel the plot forward, those decisions rarely provide any surprises.

In sum, the judge in film functions both as a determiner of narrative and a narrative determinee, both the wielder and the subject of narrative necessity. The simultaneous embodiment of both of these senses of 'narrative determination' tags the judge as an ironic, even paradoxical figure and thus goes to the heart of the specificity of the judge in the law-in-film landscape. The trajectory of analysis of the filmic judge, as I view it, leads up to, and then away from, this characterization. Accordingly, I will lead back up to it, say something further about it, and then finally look at the question of where it might take us—in the form of the passage through the concepts of character, genre, and reflexivity described above. Having charted its territory breadth-first, the essay will then turn to a case study in the analysis of the filmic judge, in the form of a discussion of the film *The Star Chamber*.

Character

To put it trivially, the judge in film is a character. To put it less trivially, the judge in film is often a trivial character.

This is by no means universal; there are films whose central characters include judges, generally judges who throw a wrench into their own and other peoples' agendas by means of corruption or crookedness. But most filmic judges are uninteresting, throwaway characters. They pronounce, and powerfully at that, but their power to affect the future course of events is often their *only* distinctive feature. Like L-shaped corner-joints in a plumbing system, they facilitate a change of direction. But that is all they do, and all they can do, and they have no choice but to do it.

Judgehood in film tends to be constrictive, not only procedurally but also architecturally. Filmic judges operate almost exclusively in the courtroom. This is not a particularly surprising state of things, but it stands in sharp contrast to other character types. Filmic cowboys, for example, have a natural narrative habitat, but also carry their central identities with them into a variety of spaces and times. The same is true of nuns, baseball players, and soldiers. All of these characters can appear outside of their original or obvious space, to comic or tragic or neutral effect, but always without loss of identity and identification with their type. The filmic judge, however, depends for his or her identity as a judge, at least largely, on actually being in the courtroom, the natural habitat.

Filmic judges can, of course, appear in non-courtroom scenes. But it is in the courtroom that they attain both their greatest power over the narrative and the highest level of predictability and banality of which they are capable. Moreover, narrative power and banality tend to vary together. The more predictable a judge is, the more he or she controls what happens. Less predictable judges—those who make unexpected decisions or perhaps operate outside the law—may be more interesting or more developed as characters (even if some of those characters, like the corrupt judge, are themselves a bit clichéd). But they are actually less likely to determine the eventual outcome of the narrative than their predictable, cardboard, courtroom-bound colleagues. After all, in most cases an interesting, psychologically developed judge in a film is also corrupt—a 'bad guy'—and does not ultimately succeed in controlling the flow of the narrative. The filmic judge's power and predictability—his or her narrative determination in the first sense and narrative determination in the second sense—vary inversely.

Genre

Character as a determining narrative force is a fairly close cousin of genre, as in, for example, the fairly close connection between the figure of the cowboy and the Western genre, or the very existence of the detective genre. One might ask, then, where things stand as between filmic judges and genre.

To begin with, the question of genre in the realm of films about law is a vexed one overall. In brief, my view tends to be that while there is no law film genre, there is at least operationally a courtroom film genre.[2] But judges have little or no causative relation to even this genre. One might refer to a Western as a cowboy film and be understood. I have never heard a film, courtroom-based or otherwise, referred to as a 'judge film'. Even the phrase 'nun film' conveys something, albeit perhaps no more than a bizarre conjunction of *Sister Act, The Sound of Music*, and *Lilies of the Field*. 'Judge film' conveys nothing or very nearly nothing. The judge is at most a necessary, never a sufficient, component of a genre.

This may have to do with the judge's banality, that banality being the price the judge has to pay for power. If judgehood decreases as one leaves the courtroom and does non-judge-like things—or if there is no such thing as a truly judge-like thing, outside of the courtroom—then the judge cannot enjoy a causative relation to a genre. On the other hand, a nun cannot sentence someone to death.

Reflexivity

The limitations of genre as a useful concept in the study of films about law need not and do not mean that there is nothing to say about such films collectively. Films about law in general gain a certain unity by virtue of the fact that they are reflexive; that is, that they may be understood as alluding to themselves and to the process of their own creation. I base this argument on the fact that films about law are, in general, films about the construction, cognition, and interpretation of narrative, the fundamental activities on which the phenomenon of narrative cinema rests in the first place.[3]

Where does the figure of the judge fit into this theory of reflexivity? What elements of narrativity and narrative creation is the filmic judge 'about'?

One rich vein of the study of reflexivity in films about law is the vein of analogy and metaphor. Examples abound: courtroom and movie theatre, detective and film viewer, viewer and eyewitness, critic and prosecutor, and so forth. The figure of the judge represents a particular busy hub of analogical and metaphorical

[2] For an extensive examination of this and a number of the underlying, overarching themes in this essay, see DA Black, *Law in Film: Resonance and Representation* (Urbana, IL: 1999), Ch 3.

[3] ibid, esp Ch 3 and 4.

connectedness. As I suggested earlier, people who see films judge them. That much is obvious; less obvious, at least in its significance vis-à-vis other examples from the world of law in film, is the fact that people are *aware* of the fact that they judge films. By way of contrast, consider the detective. It is hardly common to hear people hold forth in detail on the tenets of constructivist psychology which might link their cognitive processes to the actions of the detective in a film they have just seen. But it is not particularly unusual for people to describe themselves as 'judging' a film, or at least to perform an act which they would not blink at hearing described as 'judging'. This rather literal connection between on- and off-screen behaviours and terminology sets the figure of the judge apart.[4]

The difference between the figure of the judge and other legal figures, then, is not that the judge alone exhibits metaphorical connections with the filmic spectator, but that spectators are in many cases fully aware of these connections and recognize them as natural and non-arcane. At the same time, however, another difference operates. When people do happen to reflect on the correspondences between the detective and themselves as viewers, they really mean the detective in the film. But when people render judgment against or return 'verdicts' on films, and describe themselves as doing so, they do not appear to be mean to draw a straight line between themselves and the judge in the film. A viewer rendering such a judgment, explicitly or otherwise, is performing an action which has similarities to the actions performed by the judge in the film, but no actual connection. For example, feeling any sort of identification with Scotty in *Vertigo*, as he undergoes the process of acquiring knowledge and information, involves a kind of synonymy between character and viewer which does not manifest itself in the realm of the judge: which is to say, even if one described oneself as 'judging' or giving a 'verdict' on *Vertigo*, one would probably not identify that act with the magistrate at the inquest into the death of Madeleine.

The judge in a film, in sum, proves to be both the most easily recognizable and the most abstract model of analogy among those on offer in the law film landscape. But the judge has another analogue—and this takes us back, via reflexivity and the realm of metaphor, to narrative determination, in the first sense I have described. As active determiners of narrative, judges in film exhibit clear characteristics of *authorship*. Naturally this authorship is circumscribed by the film's real authorship; fictional judges do not actually decide anything, or make anything happen. But so circumscribed, it does operate. Just as detectives in film determine what the story

[4] Perhaps not surprisingly, films about law seem to inspire a particularly high occurrence of legally-inflected comments, some involving judging and more involving the rendering of verdicts, as well as miscellaneous procedural references. While there is probably a quickly diminishing return, in point of analytical interest, on any attempt to support this observation empirically, a convenient sample of quotations from reviews of Jonathan Lynn's *Trial and Error* can at least illustrate the idiom: 'The verdict is in, "TRIAL AND ERROR" is hysterical. . . .'; 'Verdict is in—director Jonathan Lynn ("MY COUSIN VINNY") wins again!'; 'You'll be guilty of laughing yourself silly in this wacky comedy!'; 'Jeff Daniels and Michael Richards team up for gavel-to-gavel laughter!'; 'The verdict is in . . . hilarious!' (quoted at http://www.jonathanlynn.com/films/trial_and_error/trial_and_error_quotes.htm).

actually was, judges determine (with occasional assistance from one or more lawyers) what the story will be: who will go to jail, who not, who will or will not henceforth be officially recognized as Santa Claus—the legal nicety on which the plot of *Miracle on 34th Street* hinges—and so forth. The active form of narrative determination, in this sense, harbours the power of authorship and therefore, *a fortiori*, involves a degree of reflexivity, a referential relationship to the film's own process of creation.

The passive form of narrative determination, on the other hand—the state of being determined by the narrative, or more precisely by a set of narrative conventions and traditions—entails the opposite. It means that the filmic judge is the object of authorial action: authored, rather than (or as well as) authoring. The literal authors of the judge are the scenarists and screenwriters (and/or producers, directors, and/or actors, depending on one's take on filmic 'authorship'). But in practice, those writers are themselves guided, even constrained, by a vast body of antecedent texts, conventions, idioms, and stereotypes. The limitations of the filmic judge—a character who has the power to kill people but not the power to leave the room—come from these antecedents and conventions.

To some extent the foregoing analysis relies on half truths—suggestive half truths, perhaps, but half truths nonetheless. Judges in films are not really authors; and scenarists and screenwriters are not really magically prevented from writing scenes in which judges do unexpected, unpredictable things. But the bulk of representation appears and behaves as if these things were the case. They may, indeed, be quarter or eighth truths, and their spontaneous conjunction all the less likely. Yet it is along that path, that one-sixteenth or even less combination of behaviours, that the general case appears to lie, and the general case becomes a remarkable case exactly for that.

Determination and Precedent

This breadth-first treatment of the presence of judges in film, specifically courtesy of a look at the character, genre, and reflexive aspects of such judges, takes us back to the observation of a state of things where the filmic judge, while from one point of view an author, a determiner of narrative, is nonetheless partly determined—not only as to character, but also as to the scope of possible narrative influence—by what might be called the weight of *precedent*.

To refer to narrative tradition in film by a term as saturated in legal significance as 'precedent' is, admittedly, to stack the analytical deck a little. But film and non-film do resonate rather strongly together at this juncture. Furthermore, the most interesting characteristic of this resonance is how indirect it is. It does not describe a straight line between real judges and judges in films—which is to say that however gratifying it may be to see the connection it brings into view, the phrase 'the weight of precedent' means two different things in the two cases. Of course, filmic judges can and often do get into matters of legal precedent, and plots can hinge on such matters. But to say that judges in film are constrained by (narrative) precedent does not mean, as we have seen, that those judges appear in scenes where they talk about or act on (legal) precedent. Constraint by precedent means something in the respective cases of the real-life judge and the filmic judge; but it means different things. The same is true of the other type of narrative determination, the enjoyment of authority and authorship. Real-life judges and filmic judges exhibit different forms of this power, but both do exhibit it.

'*We're* the god-damned law!': Looking at *The Star Chamber*

A pointed and sustained example of a film involving judges operating outside the courtroom, and entering into a variety of relationships with the weights of both legal and narrative precedent, is *The Star Chamber* (Peter Hyams, 1983). The story involves Judge Stephen Hardin (Michael Douglas) who, finding himself repeatedly forced to let criminals off on technicalities, accepts the overtures of his quondam Harvard mentor, Judge Benjamin Caulfield (Hal Holbrook), to join a consortium of nine judges who meet privately and pass sentence on criminals who have escaped punishment by the system—and then send a hitman to kill them.

The nine judges sit in a private house and render death sentences, following a procedure based on—grotesquely parodic of, one might say—courtroom procedure: the member of the group bringing the complaint describes the case (name of person or persons who got away with a crime; the nature of the technicality which let them off), and asks for a verdict. One by one, the rest of the judges give their verdicts (all of which are 'Guilty' in the cases shown in the film).

Hardin's willingness to participate in this group stems from his increasing frustration at his own powerlessness in the face of legal process and precedent. In particular, he finds himself forced to exclude some important evidence in a case involving a series of child murders: a shoe belonging to one of the victims is found in the van being driven by two men, but the men go free when Hardin rules that the search of the van had not followed correct procedure.

Hardin has extensive contact with Dr Harold Lewin (James B Sikking), the father of the child whose shoe was found; Lewin reproaches Hardin for releasing the suspects in the case of his son's death and blames him directly for the death of the next victim in the series of child murders. Some of this contact takes place at a prison where Lewin is held after drawing a gun and firing at the two suspects after they are set free in Hardin's court. (Lewin misses them, but wounds a police officer.) Hardin sympathizes with the father's anguish, and with his anger at the manifest separation of law and justice. But, at least at this point, he declares his loyalty to that separation, in slightly different terms. 'As a man', he tells the father, 'I would have tried to kill them too. As a judge, I can't.'

Here, constraint by legal precedent, as a plot device, and constraint by narrative precedent, as a general condition of the representation of judges in film, coincide. Hardin's decision to join the group of vigilante judges, however, represents his escape from both: he becomes a judge who can ignore legal precedent, while the film gains its interest in the first place from the circumstance of a judge escaping the traditional narrative constraints of courtroom representation.

Once inside the secret group of nine judges, Hardin votes 'Guilty' in various cases along with the rest of them. Eventually he brings his own case—namely that of the two accused child murderers. The nine vigilante judges sentence the two to death. Presently, however, it transpires that they were not guilty after all. But Hardin cannot persuade the other eight judges to call off the death sentence. He therefore undertakes his own private attempts to warn and rescue the two soon-to-be victims of the extra-judicial court.

The refusal of the judges to reverse their verdict and sentence stems from a sense of narrative constraint—a little odd, perhaps, in a group whose activities involve subverting and coercing traditional trajectories of events, but necessary for the furthering of the plot of the film. 'We cannot let this happen', says Hardin, referring to the upcoming 'executions' of the two defendants. To this, Caulfield responds, 'There is nothing we can do'. If this fatalism makes little sense in terms of the plot ('How about a phone call to the hitman?' one finds oneself asking the screen), it nonetheless illustrates rather dramatically the concept of narrative determination as an active principle binding judges. These characters see themselves as being constrained by procedure, even when they are not.

Striking about the group, at a more fundamental level, is the fact that they describe themselves as judges in the context of their, in fact, extra-judicial activities, and model their enterprise on a courtroom. This enables them to affirm, or pretend, that what they are doing is a manifestation of their judgehood, not something extraneous to it. In the scene where Caulfield explains the existence and background of the group of judges, in the course of recruiting Hardin into the group, he puts it like this:

> We're the judges, for Christ's sake, we're the law. We let it all happen. There were nine of us. We became a court, our own court of last resort. We review cases, the excruciating ones, the ones where it's all been perverted. We make judgements, we carry out sentences.

He also tells the story of the group's creation, on the occasion of which another judge summed up the absurdity of the problem facing the judges—that is, their inability to surmount the obstacles represented by legal technicalities—by asserting, '*We're* the god-damned law!'

Caulfield's recruitment speech thus effects a smooth transition between official judgeship and membership in the private 'court'. Legally, of course, a group of people sitting around plotting murder has nothing to do with judicial procedure. But referring to it as a court restores the judges to something akin to their natural habitat; here, what it means for a filmic judge to operate as a judge outside the courtroom is to carry the courtroom along, like a snail carrying its own house on its back. This binding by decree of space to character provides a solution, albeit a brittle and doomed one, to the problem of the judge lacking judgehood in the world at large.

Narrative determination in the active sense becomes something that can travel into the world with the judge, but by definition that travel, the escape from the courtroom, involves a suspension of narrative determination in the passive sense. This, in turn, comes with a cost; as we watch these nine judges meeting privately to hand out death on their own terms, we see the filmic judge completely out of equilibrium and out of control—the control of narrative tradition—to the point of monstrosity. But tradition gets a bit of its own back, inasmuch as the enterprise of the nine judges ultimately fails. If *The Star Chamber* goes against the grain of traditional or typical representations of judges by allowing judges to take their judgehood with them out of the courtroom, it does so to a large extent in the form of a cautionary tale.

Closing Argument

The phrase 'narrative determination' denotes not only a connector between two aspects of the filmic judge, but also a tunnel running underneath the level of plot and manifest action and connecting the basic situations of the filmic and real-life judge. How loose or tight this connection may be is of course subject to debate. My inclination is to see it as a tight or at least non-trivial connection. The 'narrative determination' bridge represents one of those oblique paths of inquiry I mentioned earlier: a path oblique to the dividing line between film and non-film, that is, taking in something of both, describing something which pertains simultaneously to both.

A connection like this matters, because it harbours the possibility of explanatory power. Films can illustrate the workings of the legal system in their plots, and gain explanatory power that way; but the less obvious, more oblique, more institutional connections like 'narrative determination' may tell us more, or at least tell us something different, about the workings of forces such as 'precedent' across narrative-driven regimes. Importantly, and whatever its merits, the film/non-film connection represented by narrative determination takes us out of the orbit of the question of empirical realism or plausibility. To say that real-life and filmic judges share the state of narrative determination—and in ways that go beyond the ways in which all real-life and fictional characters live in such a state—is to bypass the process of deciding whether filmic judges behave in a true-to-life way, which is a question not only of a different degree but of an entirely different kind.

The 'narrative determination' avenue is a bit subterranean and a bit asymmetrical, and I cannot predict how much explanatory power it will, in the event, actually wield or yield, as to either filmic or legal process. But it seems to me that it takes us to the right strata, when it comes to furthering the process of mining for institutional ties.

Index

. . . *And Justice for All* (film) 150, 155, 185–6, 192, 638
12 Angry Men (film) 18, 29, 387, 589
2001: A Space Odyssey (film) 340
abortion
 law and popular culture 12–15
The Accused (film) 591–2, 635
Adaptation (film) 651–2, 654, 657–60, 675–6
Adorno, T 41, 71, 75–6
Aeschylus 4–5
L'Affaire Dreyfus (film) 155
Affinity (novel) 451, 454, 455, 456, 457, 460, 461, 462–3, 464
Agamben, Giorgio 71, 239–41
 Homo Sacer 239–40
Agamemnon (Greek play) 4
Air Force One (film) 589
Allen, Woody 2
Altman, Robert 166
Alvarez, F 548–9
American Dream (documentary film) 595
American Film Institute 150
 catalogues 109–10, 161
American Gigolo (film) 587
An American Tragedy (film) 111–12
Amsterdam, Anthony 652, 655, 665–6
Ancient Greece
 law and popular culture 2–5
Andrew, Geoff 105
Ann Carver's Profession (film) 111
Anouilh, Jean 3
Antigone (plays) 3–4
Ariès, Philippe 51, 63, 68
Aristodemou, Maria 280
Armstrong, Nancy 203
Arnold, C A 545
art house films 398
artists
 courtroom sketching 180–2
As the Devil Commands (film) 112–13
Asimow, Michael 24, 27, 34–5, 36, 38, 42, 393, 646
Assault at West Point: The Court-Martial of Johnson Whittaker (film) 167–8, 169, 170, 171
The Atrocity Exhibition (fiction) 274, 281, 282, 283–90
Attorney for the Defense (film) 117–18

Baca, Jimmy Santiago 310
Bad Girls (TV series) 451, 454–5, 456–7, 460, 463–88
The Bad Seed (film) 344, 346, 355
Badlands (film) 344, 346, 355, 356
Balibar, Etienne 523
Ballard, J G
 The Atrocity Exhibition 274, 281, 282, 283–90
 Crash 212, 216–25
Banks, Gordon 340
Barr, Roseanne 404
Barrymore, Lionel 111
Barthes, Roland
 La Chambre Claire 291–300
Basic Instinct (film) 458
Bateman, A 410, 411
Bates, Norman 346, 350, 356
Baudrillard, Jean 41
Bauman, Z 233
Bayer-Barenbaum, L 227, 233
A Beautiful Mind (film) 599–600
Beck, Ulrich 233
Bellisario, Donald
 J.A.G. TV series 164–5, 167
Bend It Like Beckham (film) 604
Benjamin, Walter 76
Bennett, William 312
Bentham, Jeremy 462
Bergman, Harold 576–7
Bergman, P 24, 27, 38
Bernstein, Sidney 498–9
Bible
 jurisprudence in the Old Testament 1–2
Birmingham Centre for Contemporary Cultural Studies 41
Black, David 27–8, 33, 42, 325–6
Black Hawk Down (film) 512–14
Black Widow (film) 344, 347, 353, 355
blackmail
 in fiction 375–8
Bleak House 197
Blinnikka, Terry 556
Bloom, Harold 229
Blue's Crews (TV show) 146–7
Body Heat (film) 344, 345–6, 349, 353, 356
Bohnke, M 37, 42
Boisset, Yves 155
Bordwell, David 385–6, 399, 400
Botting, Fred 227, 228, 232, 233
Bowman, Cynthia Grant 411
Braddon, Mary Elizabeth 204–5
Breaker Morant (film) 158, 161
Brecht, Bertolt 3

Breen, Joseph 126
Brint, S 542
Britten, Benjamin 1–2
Brookey, R A 474
Brooks, Peter 226, 236
Brown, B 553
Brown, D 410, 411
Bruner, Jerome 654, 656–7, 663–4
Buckeridge, Anthony 15–16
The Buffalo Creek Disaster 594
Bugliosi, Vincent 671–2
Buker, Eloise A 199
Burke, Edmund 229, 233
Burroughs, William S 281, 282–3

Cagney and Lacey (TV series) 475
The Caine Mutiny (film) 161, 162, 163–4, 171, 589
The Caine Mutiny Court-Martial (TV drama) 166, 170
Calley, William L 161
Calvocoressi, Peter 531
Camp, Jim 584
Cape Fear (film) 40, 156, 344, 345, 350, 352, 353–4, 355, 643, 647, 649
capital punishment
  popular culture and public attitude 358–74
Carter, Angela 451, 452–4, 455, 460–1
The Case of the Howling Dog (film) 128
Cash, Johnny 308, 309–10, 315
Cathy Come Home (film) 17, 22, 131
Caudill, D 235
Cecil, Henry 16
censorship 125–9
  Crash 216–25
Chandler, Raymond 380
Chase, Anthony 23, 152, 394
Chicago 115, 128
child abuse
  repressed memory and the law-psychotherapy debate 404–24
children
  detention at Her Majesty's pleasure for murderers under 18 years in Hong Kong 425–45
children's literature
  law and 15–16, 47–70
The China Syndrome (film) 391, 394–5, 396
Chitty, Joseph 560, 562
Chomsky, Noam 401
Christie, Agatha 379, 380
Churchill, Winston 531–2
Cinader, Robert 136–7, 140
cinema *see* film
A Civil Action (film) 150, 187–8, 190, 191, 193, 392, 589, 592, 595, 635
Clancy, Susan 411
Clark, D 474
Class Action (film) 392, 393, 396, 589, 591
Clavell, Stanley 657
Clear and Present Danger (film) 589
Clockwork Orange (film) 344, 346, 352
Cobb, Humphrey 161
Cobbe, Frances Power 10
Cohen, Herb 584
Collins, Wilkie 376
  The Woman in White 9–10, 11, 199
consumers
  shopping malls and privatization of public space 537–59
contracts
  franchises and duty of good faith 570–8
Corcos, Christine Alice 260
Cornell, Drusilla 198, 235
Cornwell, Patricia 381
corporate misconduct
  film portrayal 385–403, 595
Coulter, Ann 530
Counsellor at Law (film) 122–5
country music 307–11
The Court-Martial of Billy Mitchell (film) 162
court martials
  American film and television 160–72, 515–16
courtroom
  image 173–82, 279, 603–4
  Merchant of Venice trial 5–6
  photographs 178–80
  sketch 17, 180–2
  trials 175–7, 279, 642
Crash 212, 216–25
  research study 216–17
Crime Without Passion (film) 127–8
Crimes and Misdemeanors (film) 2
criminal justice
  unfairness portrayed in *From the Queen to the Chief Executive* 425–45
Criminal Justice Act 1925 178, 179–80
Criminal Justice Act 1991 432

Daily Mail
  Crash debate 217
Daily Mirror
  mass circulation 177
Dangerous Evidence: the Lori Jackson Story (film) 161, 166, 167, 168, 169
Dawidoff, Nicholas 307, 310
De Felice, Renzo 527
de Gaulle, Charles 529
de Lauretis, Teresa 460, 468–9
Dead Man Walking (film)
  capital punishment issues 358, 364–7, 370–2, 373–4
death penalty

popular culture and public attitude 358–74
post-conviction relief practitioners and narrative persuasion 651–76
***The Defense Rests* (film)** 122
***The Defiant Ones* (film)** 642
***Deliverance* (film)** 341
Demme, Jonathan 344
Denvir, John 18, 27
Derrida, Jacques 54, 56, 65, 81, 201–2, 210, 237–8, 297
detective novels 375–84
Deutsch, Morton 158
Dickens, Charles 9, 198, 203–6
Didion, Joan 672–5
***Dirty Harry* (film)** 188–9, 636
***Disclosure* (film)** 589, 591
dispute resolution
adversarial ideology in America 606–37
Little Injustices documentary film 595–6
negotiation in popular culture 584–605
Dmytryk, Edward 163
Doane, Mary Ann 462
documentary films 398–401, 403
on negotiations 589, 593–5, 598
Doherty, Thomas 125–6, 128–9
domestic law
popular fiction critiquing 197–211
domestic violence
in novels 9–12
Donovan, James 500
Douzinas, Costas 17, 173, 235, 238, 239
Doyle, Roddy
The Woman Who Walked Into Doors 9, 11–12
Drabble, Margaret 14–15
Dulong, Renaud 502
Durkheim, Emile 61
Dylan, Bob 2
Dymocks Bookshop 563
Dymocks Franchise Systems (NSW) Pty Ltd v Todd case 570–3

Earle, Steve 310, 311
East Lynne 205, 206–11
***Eight O'Clock Walk* (film)** 155
***Ein Richter in Angst* (film)** 155, 157
Eisenhower, President 495
Elias, Norbert 49–50, 52, 61
Eliot, George 9, 10
Elliot, Jeanne B 210
Ellroy, James 665–71
***Emergency!* (TV show)**
influence on legalization of paramedic services 130–47
Eminem 320
***Enduring Love* (novel)** 600–1
Erasmus 50
***Erin Brockovich* (film)** 150, 155, 392, 396, 589, 592–3
ethics *see* legal ethics; professional ethics
***Eumenides* (Greek play)** 4–5
Euripides 3
European Convention on Human Rights 214
European Court of Human Rights 520–1
Evans, C 480
Everard, John 178
evidence
use of film at Nuremberg Trials 491–503
***The Execution of Private Slovik* (TV film)** 170, 171

fairness
law films 148–59
Fallon, William J 113–22
***Fargo* (film)** 341
Felman, S 235
***A Few Good Men* (film)** 161, 163–4, 167, 515–17
fiction *see also* novels;
domestic law critiqued through popular fiction 197–211
lawyers as authors of twentieth-century American fiction 16, 243–72, 630
Fiedler, Leslie A 330
film *see also* psychopath movies
about negotiations 587–602
accountability for human rights abuses in 504–19
adversary system in legal proceedings 633–5
American military justice 160–72
art house 398
characteristics of a law film 641
corporate misconduct, portrayal of 385–403
Crash and the moral debate 216–25
documentary 398–401, 403
evidence at Nuremberg Trials 491–503
fairness of prime importance in legal films 148–59
first talking movies 110–13, 127
influence on public attitude to capital punishment 358–74
judges in 635–6, 677–85
jurisprudence in *Red* 39, 90–108
lesbians-in-prison 449–69
Moulin Rouge as an ethical-legal discourse 323–4
old law-related movies 109–29
professional ethics of screen lawyers 636–50
silent cinema 110
film censorship
effect on law films 127–9
Hollywood 1930–1934 125–9
Williams Committee 219–20

film studies
law and 17–18, 21–46, 323–4, 325–6
what law students can learn from 183, 191–3
film technique
law films 37, 43
Finch, Atticus 125, 150, 353, 633, 643–4
Fincher, David 344
***The Firm* (film)** 644
Fishman, R 548
Fiske, J 479
Fletcher, George 1
***For the Defense* (film)** 115
Ford, John 37, 42–3, 155, 156, 162
war documentaries 493
Young Mr Lincoln 183–4
Foucault, M 541, 544
Fowler, Gene
The Great Mouthpiece 113–15
franchises
characteristics of 561–5
Dymocks Bookshop 563, 570–3
law 570–8
McDonalds 563, 566–70
shopping malls 553
***Frankenstein* (film)** 344, 346, 350, 352, 355
***A Free Soul* (film)** 111
Freedman, Estelle 459
freedom
Crash and the moral debate 216–25
freedom of speech
swing music and 322
Freud, Sigmund 408, 409–10, 529
Fried, Charles 643
Friedman, Lawrence 22, 29, 131
***From the Queen to the Chief Executive* (film)** 425–45
Fuch, Christian 340
Fugard, Athol 3–4
Fuller, Lon 56, 64, 626–7
***Für immer verloren* (film)** 149–50, 152
***The Furies* (film)** 112
Furniss, T 233
Fyfield, Frances 16

Gaete, Rolando 241–2
Gamman, L 480
Gandhi, Mahatma 529
gangsta rap 311–15
Gardner, Erle Stanley 375
lawyer and American fiction writer 253–8, 630
Gardner, John 662, 669, 674
Gavras, Costa 508
gays
Bad Girls TV series 451, 454–5, 456–7, 460, 463–88
film portrayal 449–69
Gearey, Adam 16
Geertz, Clifford 96
Gest, J 21
Giddens, A 233, 542
Gillers, Stephen 387
Gladwell, Malcolm
The Tipping Point 145–7
globalization
pop culture 326–35
***The Godfather* (film)** 588
Golden Gate Law School 29
good faith
franchise law 570–8
Goode, Roy 577
***Goodfellas* (film)** 341
Goodrich, Peter 234, 235, 236–7
Gordon, Neil 2
Gramsci, A 41
Gray, Kevin 558
Gray, Susan 558
Greek plays
law and popular culture 2–5
***The Green Mile* (film)**
capital punishment issues 358, 364–7, 370–1, 372–4
Green, Anna K 376
Greenfield, Steve 28, 35, 41, 150, 158
Greenpeace 569
Grierson, Bruce 407
Grisham, John
lawyer and American fiction writer 265–71, 593, 647
Gulliver, P H 587
***Gun Crazy* (film)** 344, 346
Gunn, David 23
Gunnarsson, Sturla 166
Gysin, Brion 283

Haggard, Merle 308–9, 310
Hallam, J 478, 481, 482
Halttunen, Karen 227
Hammett, Dashiell 380
Hampshire, Stuart 601
Hare, Robert 340–1
***Harlan County* (documentary film)** 595
Harris, Sir Arthur 532
Harris, Emmylou 307
Harris, T 642
***Hart's War* (film)** 148, 161
Hart, Herbert Lionel Adolphus 55–6, 72, 74
Hart, Lynda 450, 456, 459
Hartog, François 501
Hastings, Max 530–1
Hathaway, Henry 344
Hawkes, Howard 344
***Hecuba* (Greek play)** 3
Hegel, Georg 71, 75
Heidegger, M 293

Hemingway, Ernest 11, 13–14
Hennesy, Rosemary 485, 487
Herman, Didi 452, 460, 464
***High Crimes* (film)** 161, 511–12
Hill, Wycliff A 254
Hillis Miller, J 211
hip-hop
gangsta rap 311–15
Hitchcock, Alfred 344, 499
Hofstadter, Richard 267
Hogarth, William 9
Holmes, Sherlock 376, 379
Holocaust
legal ethics 71–84
use of film evidence at Nuremberg Trials 491–503
Honan, Park 5
Hong Kong
detention at Her Majesty's pleasure for murderers under 18 years 425–45
Horkheimer, M 41
***Hud* (film)** 340
human rights
accountability for abuses in film and popular culture 504–19
film evidence at Nuremberg Trials 491–503
military 160
science fiction 524–7
Humphreys, Anne 202
***Hunt for Red October* (film)** 589
husband and wife
popular fiction critiquing of domestic law 197–211
Hutchings, Peter 228

***I Am Sam* (film)** 602
Ice Cube 313, 314
Iglesias, Enrique 320–1
image
courtrooms 173–82, 279, 603–4
jurisprudence in J G Ballard's writing 273–90
law and justice 34–6, 41, 644–8
photograph of condemned prisoner evoking emotion 291–300
prison in popular culture 303–15
***In the Name of the Father* (film)** 642–3, 646–7, 650
incest
repressed memory and the law-psychotherapy debate 404–24
***Indecent Proposal* (film)** 587
***Inferno* (science fiction)** 524–7
***Inherit the Wind* (film)** 642
***The Insider* (film)** 392, 395–6
internet sites
censorship 213–14
***Invasion of the Body Snatchers* (film)** 383
Irving, David 531–2
Isin, E 541, 542

***J.A.G.* TV series** 164–5, 167
Jackson, Bruce 305
Jackson, Robert H 493–4, 495–6
Jarvis, Simon 74, 75–6
Jenkins, Philip 343
Jonson, Ben 9
Jonze, Spike 654, 657, 675
Joyce, James 11
judges
distrust by Americans 623–5
fictional 263
in film 635–6, 677–85
The Star Chamber 683–5
***Judgment at Nuremberg* (film)** 162, 167, 171, 387, 636
allocating responsibility for atrocities 506–8
jurisprudence
cinematic 39, 87–108
imagery of J G Ballard 273–90
Latin pop and 320–2
meaning 274–5
justice
film portrayal 35–6, 191–2

Kafka, Franz 17, 237–8
Kant, Immanuel 71, 229–31, 234–5, 241
Karloff, Boris 346
Kasdan, Lawrence 344
Kaufman, Charlie 657–60, 675–6
Kelley, Robin 313, 314
Kellogg, Ray 497
Kelly, Andrew 161
Kelly, Paul 540
Kelsen, Hans 72, 74–5
Kessel, Joseph 502
Kieslowski, Krzysztof
Red 96–108
Three Colours trilogy 93–4
***King and Country* (film)** 158, 161
King Lear 7–8
King, Rodney 279
King, Stephen 365
***Kiss of Death* (films)** 344, 345, 349, 350, 354
Kitto, H 2–3
Klein, Naomi 563
Kopple, Barbara 595
Kracauer, Siegfried 503
Kramer, Alan 494
Kramer, Stanley 161, 163, 170, 642
***Kramer vs. Kramer* (film)** 589
***Kriegsgericht* (film)** 161
Kronman, Anthony 577
Kubrick, Stanley 340, 244
Kurosawa, Akira
Rashomon 29

LA Law (TV series) 589, 590, 632, 647
landlord and tenant
  shopping malls 552–5
Lang, Fritz 344
Larner, W 540, 542, 549
Laughter in Paradise (film) 22
Laughton, Charles 344
Law and Order (TV series) 589, 634–5
law firms
  fictional 262–4, 268
  film portrayal 393–4
  law students learning from movies on choice of employers 192
law school
  critique in fiction of 258–9, 265–6
Lawrence, D H 11
Lawyer Man (film) 119–20
lawyers
  American twentieth-century fiction authors 16, 243–72, 630
  Fallonesque shyster films 115–22
  female in film 167
  fictional characters 245–8, 250–3, 255–8, 262–6, 268–71
  first talking movies 111–13, 127
  images in court-martial dramas 167–8
  in psychopath movies 353–4
  popular image in films 183, 189–90
  professional ethics in film 636–50
  professional image 183, 189–91, 644–50
  protagonists in law films 35, 40, 111–12, 150, 183–9, 633–5, 643–50
  Young Mr Lincoln 183–4
Lead Belly 306–7, 310
Ledbetter, Huddie 306–7
Lee Thompson, J 344
legal ethics
  Holocaust 71–84
  in *Where the Wild Things Are* 68, 73–84
legal negotiations
  film portrayal 589–95, 602
legal positivism 3, 72–84
  in *Where the Wild Things Are* 72–84
legal proceedings
  adversarial ideology in America 606–37
  fairness of prime importance in legal films 148–59
  film portrayal 36, 387–8, 393
  inquisitorial and adversarial systems compared 609–21
  popular culture and the adversary system 628–37
Legendre, Pierre 235, 501
Leitch, T 169
LeRoy, Mervyn 344
lesbians
  Bad Girls TV series 451, 454–5, 456–7, 460, 463–88
  film portrayal 449–69
Lesser, Wendt 181
Leventhal, Guy 151, 154
Levinas, Emmanuel 64–5, 77, 105
Lewis, Joseph H 344
life imprisonment
  compared to detention at Her Majesty's pleasure 430–40
The Life of David Gale (film) 364
Lind, E Allen 151
Linton, Eliza Lynne 203
literature *see also* **children's literature; fiction; novels**
  law and 17, 21–2
Little Injustices (documentary film) 595–6
Llewellyn, Karl 6, 18
Local Hero (film) 587
Lodge, David 669–70
Loesberg, Jonathan 210
Lomax, Alan 304, 305–6
Lomax, John 304, 305–6
Lorentz, Pare 399
Luhmann, Niklas 148
Lyotard, Jean-Françoise 71

M (film) 344, 349, 351
Macaulay, Stewart 18, 24
McCarty, John 340
McCuskey, Brian 210
McDonalds
  franchise system 563, 566–70
McEwan, Ian 600–1
Machura, Stefan 18, 28, 387
McKee, Robert 659–60, 676
MacNeil, William 227
Magnum Force (film) 636
Malick, Terence 344
Man in the Middle (film) 170, 171
Manderson, Desmond 15, 72–84
Manson, Charles 671–2
marriage
  popular fiction critiquing of domestic law 197–211
Marshment, M 478, 481, 482
Mason, Perry 128, 255–8, 375, 629–32
mass media
  documentary film by Noam Chomsky 401–2
Mayne, Judith 461, 462–3, 472
Measure for Measure 6–7
Mellencamp, Patricia 462
Menkel-Meadow, Carrie 269
Merchant of Venice 5–6
Mertz, Elizabeth 411
Meyer, P 18, 26, 39
Mighall, R 236

military justice
American film and television 160–72
Mill, John Stuart 10, 622–3
Miller, Richard 2
Mintz, Alan 162
miscarriage of justice
film portrayal 36–7, 150, 647
Missing **(film)** 508–9
Mitchum, Robert 344, 352
Monster's Ball **(film)** 364
Moore, Michael 400–1, 595
morality
Crash 216–25
Moran, L 36–7, 40, 547
Morris, David 569
Mort, F 547
Mosse, George L 529
Motion Picture Production Code 125–9
Moulin Rouge **(film)** 323–4
The Mouthpiece **(film)** 116–17
movies ***see*** **film**
Munt, Sally 458, 473
murder mysteries 375–84
music
gangsta rap 311–15
outlaw country 307–11
pop 316–36
prison songs 304–7
Mussolini, Benito 525–30
My Cousin Vinny **(film)** 633, 650
My Dark Places **(autobiography)** 665–71

Nader, Laura 595–6
Nancy, Jean-Luc 230
National League of Decency 126
Nazi atrocities
allocating responsibility for atrocities in *Judgment at Nuremberg* 506–8
use of film evidence at Nuremberg Trials 491–503
Nead, Lynda 17
negotiation
in popular culture 584–605
Little Injustices documentary film 595–6
The Story of Qiu Ju 596–8
The Negotiator **(film)** 588
Nevins, F M 154, 156
newspapers
photographs 177–80
trial reports 174–7
Nichols, Bill 399–400
Night of the Hunter **(film)** 344, 345, 349, 350, 352, 354–5
Nights at the Circus **(novel)** 451, 452–4, 455, 457, 460–1, 462–3, 464
Niven, Larry 524–7, 530
Nolte, Ernest 528, 529
Norma Rae **(film)** 391, 395, 403
Norrie, Alan 397
novels ***see also*** **fiction**
domestic law critiqued through popular fiction 197–211
domestic violence in 9–12
fictional lawyers 245–8, 250–3, 255–8, 262–6, 268–71
Gothic imagination and jurisprudence 17, 226–42
imagery in J G Ballard's writing 273–90
The Nuisance **(film)** 120–1
Nuremberg Trials
film evidence 491–503
Judgment at Nuremberg 162, 167, 171, 387, 506–8, 636
NYPD Blue **(TV series)** 588, 589

Obscene Publications Act 1959 214
Ofshe, R 405
Old Testament
jurisprudence in the story of Abraham 1–2
Oliphant, Margaret 203, 205, 209
Oliver Twist 203
On the Beach **(film)** 642
One Kill **(film)** 161
The Orchid Thief **(novel)** 657–9
Oriard, Michael 261
Orlean, Susan 657–60
Osborn, Guy 41, 150
Other People's Money **(film)** 587

Pacific Heights **(film)** 344, 345, 350, 351, 354, 355
Papke, David Ray 16
paramedic services
influence of the TV show *Emergency!* 130–47
Pateman, Carol 198
Paths of Glory **(film)** 158, 161, 168, 171
Patriot Games **(film)** 589
Patton, Cindy 483
Patton, George 495
Paulin, Tom 3
Peach-o-Reno **(film)** 111
Peck, Gregory 353
Pedder, J 410, 411
Petacci, Clara 530
Phillips, Adam 407
photographs
image of condemned prisoner evoking emotion 291–300
newspapers 177–80
Piaget, Jean 15, 60–2, 64, 66
Piesiewicz, Krzysztof 93
Pini, Giorgio 527

Pittman, Robert W 332
Podlecki, Anthony 4
Poe, Edgar Allen 376, 383
politics
  pop culture and 329–31
'pop'
  meaning of 316
pop music 316–36
popular culture
  meaning 406–7
pornography
  Crash and the moral debate 216–25
Portal, Sir Charles 531
Posner, Richard 3, 7
***Possessed* (film)** 112
Post, Melville Davisson
  lawyer and American fiction writer 243–8
Post, R 640
Pound, Ezra 529–30
Pournelle, Jerry 524–7, 530
***The Practice* (TV series)** 589, 590, 632, 636, 647
press photography 177–9
***Presumed Innocent* (fiction)** 260–1, 262, 264
***Pretty Woman* (film)** 587
prison
  Bad Girls TV series 451, 454–5, 456–7, 460, 463–9, 485–6
  country music 308–11
  films of lesbian prisoners 449–69
  gangsta rap 311–15
  image in popular culture 303–15
  life imprisonment compared to detention at Her Majesty's pleasure 430–40
prison songs 304–7
***Prisoner of Shark Island* (film)** 155
Pritchard, John 531
privacy
  pop culture and 331–3
problem solving
  negotiation in popular culture 584–605
professional ethics
  role and function within legal films 636–50
***Promises* (documentary film)** 598
property
  shopping malls and privatisation of public space 537–59
psychiatrists
  film portrayal 169–70
***Psycho* (film)** 344, 346, 350, 352, 355, 356
psychopath movies 339–57
  aspiring Nietzsches 347–9
  characters 344–51
  failure of law 352–4
  good bad-guys 349
  legal themes 351–2
  predators 344–6
  pure innocents 349–51
  retributions and resolutions 355–6
  whackos 346–7
psychotherapy
  popular culture's impact 404–24

***R v Bywaters and Thompson* case** 175–7
R v Stephane Laurent Perrin 213
Radin, Margaret 549
Rafelson, Bob 344
Rafter, Nicole 27, 34–5, 40, 155
***The Rainmaker* (film)** 155, 392, 393, 634
***Ransom* (film)** 588
rap
  gangsta rap 311–15
Rawls, John 149
***Red* (film)** 96–108
Rees, Martin 524
Reiner, Rob 163–4
Reinhardt, Gottfried 162
Reiter, Paula Jean 197
repressed memory
  popular culture's impact on the law-psychotherapy debate 404–24
***Reservoir Dogs* (film)** 341
retailers
  shopping malls and privatization of public space 537–59
Richards, Frank 15–16
Riefenstahl, Leni 399
Ritzer, George 561, 565–70
Robbins, Tim 365, 366
Robson, P 41
Robson, Ruthann 451, 463
Roddenberry, Gene 165
Rodgers, Jimmy 307
Roemer, Michael 664–5
***Roger and Me* (documentary film)** 400–1, 595
Roman Catholic church
  censorship 125–9
  child sexual abuse by clergy 412
Roof, Judith 475, 477
Rorty, Richard 94, 96
***Rosen für den Staatsanwalt* (film)** 157
Rosenberg, Charles 386
Rosenberg, Norman 37, 386
Rosenzweig, F 105
Rosiek, Jan 229
Roughley, N 300
***Rules of Engagement* (film)** 161, 162–3, 171, 172, 509–11
Russell, David 517
Russell, Margaret 27
***Ruthless People* (film)** 588

***The Sacrifice of Isaac* (novel)** 2
Sanders, Valerie 203

Sartre, Jean-Paul 293–4
***Scarface* (film)** 344–5, 351, 355
Schlesinger, John 344
Scholte, J 558
Schroder, Barbet 344
science fiction
human rights 524–7
Scott, Ridley 513
self-censorship 126
Sendak, Maurice
Where the Wild Things Are 15, 47–70, 72
***Serial Mom* (film)** 29–30
***Serjeant Rutledge* (film)** 162, 169
Sesame Street 146
***Seven* (film)** 344, 348, 350, 352, 354, 355, 356, 659
***Seven Days in May* (film)** 589
sex
Crash and the moral debate 216–25
sexual abuse
repressed memory and the law-psychotherapy debate 404–24
sexuality
films of lesbians in prison 449–69
governance in television 470–88
Seymour, David M 15
Shakespeare, William
law and popular culture 5–9
Shelter 131
Sheridan, Jim 642
Sherwin, Richard 18, 26, 39, 41, 323, 406–7
When Law Goes Pop 95, 316, 317
***The Shining* (film)** 344, 346, 352, 355
shopping malls
privatization of public space 537–59
Showalter, Elaine 210
Silbey, J 37, 43
***Silence of the Lambs* (film)** 344, 346, 350, 355, 383
***Silkwood* (film)** 391, 395
Simon, W 647–8
Simpson, O J 189, 279
Simpson, Philip 340
Sinclair, Sir Archibald 532
Singer, Isaac Bashevis 11
***Single White Female* (film)** 344, 347, 351–2, 355, 458
Skeggs, S 547
Sluizer, George 344
Smart, B 570
Smyth, Cherry 450
social change
role of film in representing legal phenomena 25–6, 131
social exclusion
shopping malls 537–40, 543, 549–59
Sontag, Susan 294
Sophocles 3
Antigone 239
Sorel, George 528
Sorkin, Aaron 516
***Speed* (film)** 588
Spilka, Mark 11
Spillane, Mickey 380
Spitz, D 645
Stacey, Jackie 479
***The Star Chamber* (film)** 150, 636, 683–5
Star Trek 165
Star Trek: The Next Generation 165, 168
***Startup.com* (film)** 587–8
***State's Attorney* (film)** 118–19
Staudte, Manfred 157
Steel, Helen 569
Steinbeck, John 11
Stevens, George 497
Stewart Hughes, H 532
Stokes, Richard 531
Stone, Christopher 389–91
***The Story of Qiu Ju* (film)** 596–8
Straayer, C 480
***Strangers on a Train* (film)** 344, 347–8, 349, 352, 355
***The Street Lawyer* (novel)** 590, 593
***The Sun Shines Bright* (film)** 156–7
Susmel, Duilio 527
***Suspect* (film)** 643, 644, 649, 650
Sutherland, Edwin 397
Suvin, Darko 522
Swomley, John 160

***Talk of the Town* (film)** 640
Taylor, Telford 492
Taylor, Veronica 565
***Tears of the Sun* (film)** 514–15
television
American military justice 164–6
Bad Girls series 451, 454–5, 456–7, 460, 463–88
depicting negotiations 589–90
governance of sexuality 470–88
influence of *Emergency!* TV series on legalization of paramedic services 130–47
Terry, Andrew 574
Thibaut, John 149, 154, 616–17, 626–7
***Thirteen Days* (film)** 589
Thompson, Kristin 399, 400
Thompson, Nicola Diane 210–11
Thornton, Margaret 406
***Three Colours* trilogy (film)** 93–4
***Three Kings* (film)** 517–18
thrillers 381
***A Time to Kill* (film)** 639
***Tin Men* (film)** 587

To Kill a Mockingbird (film) 125, 150, 152, 353, 387, 633, 639, 641
Top Gun (film) 167
Town Without Pity (film) 162, 168
Train, Arthur
lawyer and American fiction writer 248–53
treason 530
trial reports
history 174–5
Tromp, Marlene 9, 17
True Believer (film) 184–5, 192
Truman, President 492–3
Turner Classic Movies (TCM) 109
Turrow, Scott
lawyer and American fiction writer 258–65
Presumed Innocent 260–1, 262, 264
Two Weeks Notice (film) 587
Tyler, Tom 151

Ulbrich, Stefan 387
United States
adversarial ideology 606–37
death penalty 359–64, 367–9
utopian negativity 75–6

The Vanishing (film) 344, 348, 354, 356
The Verdict (film) 150, 187, 391, 392, 393, 589, 590–1, 635, 644, 645, 646, 649
Vertigo (film) 681
violence
Crash and the moral debate 216–25
films of lesbians in prison 449–69
gangsta rap lyrics 312–15
Visser, Margaret 52

Walker, Lawrens 149, 154, 616–17, 626–7
Walsh, Raoul 344
war crimes
allocating responsibility for atrocities in *Judgment at Nuremberg* 506–8
use of film evidence at Nuremberg Trials 491–503
war films
court martials in American film and television 160–72
War of the Roses (film) 589, 591
Ward, Mrs Humphrey 203
Warrington, R 235, 238, 239
Waters, Sarah 451, 454, 456, 462
Watters, E. 405
Webb, Jack 136–7, 142
Weber, Max 561, 565, 567, 577
websites
Bad Girls TV series 466–8
West, Cornell 314
Westerfelhaus, R 474
Whale, James 344
Wheeler, Bert 111
Where the Wild Things Are (children's fiction) 15, 47–70, 72
Whipple, Edwin P 205
The White Album (essay) 672–4
White Heat (film) 344, 347, 355
Wigmore, John 21, 252
Williams Committee on Obscenity and Film Censorship 219–20
Williams, Bernard 222–3, 224, 647
Williams, Hank 307
Williams, Linda 462
Williams, Melanie 280
Williams, Robbie 319–20, 322, 324
Wilson, Terry 27
Wilson, Wayne 340, 346
Wilt, Judith 12, 13, 15
Wint, Guy 531
Wiseman, Frederick 399, 400
The Woman in White 9–10, 11, 199
The Woman Who Walked Into Doors (novel) 9, 11–12
women
courtroom trials 175–7
Dickens's characters 205–6
fictional characters 205–11
lawyers in film 167
popular fiction critiquing of domestic law 197–211
The Women in His Life (film) 121–2
Wood, Ellen 204–5
East Lynne 205, 206–11
Woolsey, Robert 111
Wouk, Herman 163, 166
Wray, Fay 111
Wright, Paul 314

Yau, Herman
From the Queen to the Chief Executive 425–45
Yonge, Charlotte 203
Young, J 233
Young Mr Lincoln (film) 155, 183–4, 640, 644
young offenders
detention at Her Majesty's pleasure for murderers under 18 years in Hong Kong 425–45